Company Law

Mayson, French & Ryan on

Company Law

1998-99 Edition

Stephen W. Mayson LLB, LLM, FRSA
Barrister
Hildebrandt Professor of Legal Practice and
Director of the Centre for Law Firm Management,
Nottingham Law School, The Nottingham Trent University

Derek French BSc
and

Christopher L. Ryan LLB (Hons), LLM
Barrister and Solicitor (N.Z.)
Reader in Law and Head of the Department of Law at the City University
Formerly Chief Examiner for Regulation and Compliance, for the
Securities Industry Examination of the Stock Exchange

BLACKSTONE PRESS LIMITED

This edition published in Great Britain 1998 by Blackstone Press Limited, Aldine Place, London W12 8AA. Telephone: 0181-740 2277

© Stephen W. Mayson and Derek French 1982

ISBN: 1 85431 758 X

First edition 1982
Second edition 1985
Third edition 1986
Fourth edition 1987
Fifth edition 1988
Sixth edition 1989
Seventh edition 1990
Eighth edition 1991
Ninth edition 1992
Tenth edition 1993
Eleventh edition 1994
Twelfth edition 1995
Thirteenth edition 1996
Fourteenth edition 1997
Fifteenth edition 1998

British Library Cataloguing in Publication Data
A CIP catalogue record for this book is available from the British Library

Typeset by Style Photosetting Ltd, Mayfield, East Sussex
Printed in Great Britain by Ashford Colour Press, Gosport, Hampshire

Contents

Preface   ix

Table of Cases   xi

Table of Statutes   lxxi

Table of Statutory Instruments   xci

Table of References to Listing Rules   xcv

Table of References to the Treaty Establishing the European Community   xcvii

Table of European Directives   xcix

Introduction   1

0.1 Incorporation   0.2 Purpose of company law   0.3 Sources of company law

1   Registration   36

1.1 Introduction   1.2 Procedure   1.3 Classification of companies   1.4 Numbers of companies   1.5 Prohibition of large partnerships   1.6 Registration of companies not formed under companies legislation

2   The Memorandum of Association   59

2.1 Introduction   2.2 Registration of a memorandum   2.3 Content   2.4 Alteration of memorandum   2.5 Copies of the memorandum for members

3   The Articles of Association   88

3.1 Introduction   3.2 Registration of articles   3.3 Content   3.4 Effect of memorandum and articles   3.5 Alteration of articles   3.6 Copies of the articles for members

4   Disclosure   119

4.1 Introduction   4.2 Registry information   4.3 Notification in the *Gazette*   4.4 Company information   4.5 Business documents and places of business   4.6 Annual returns

5   Corporate Personality   133

5.1 Introduction   5.2 Separate personality   5.3 Corporate law theory   5.4 Company singular or plural?

6 Shares   170

6.1 The nature of shares   6.2 Contracts of allotment   6.3 Principles of accounting
6.4 Timing and size of the capital contribution   6.5 Form of contribution   6.6 Minimum
capital of a public company   6.7 Remedies of a wronged allottee   6.8 Shares of subscribers to the memorandum

7 Offering Shares to the Public   203

7.1 Introduction   7.2 Market-places for shares   7.3 Financial Services Act 1986
7.4 Official listing   7.5 Public offers of unlisted shares   7.6 Misleading statements and
omissions in listing particulars or prospectuses 7.7 Investment advertisements
7.8 Criminal liability   7.9 Underwriting   7.10 Inadequate response

8 Transfer of Shares   229

8.1 Introduction   8.2 Share certificates; uncertificated shares   8.3 Transfer procedures
8.4 Forged or fraudulent transfers   8.5 Transmission of shares   8.6 Share warrants
8.7 Third-party interests in shares   8.8 Takeovers   8.9 Register of substantial shareholdings   8.10 Shares bought on the basis of erroneous accounts or professional advice

9 Accounts   258

9.1 Introduction   9.2 Accounting records   9.3 Annual accounts and reports for members
9.4 Annual accounts and reports for the registrar   9.5 Abbreviated accounts and reports of
private companies   9.6 Group accounts   9.7 Contents of directors' report   9.8 Publication
of accounts   9.9 Revision of accounts   9.10 Half-yearly reports   9.11 Accounts of a
partnership composed of entities with limited liability

10 Distributions and the Maintenance of Capital   290

10.1 Controls on payments out of capital   10.2 Reduction of capital   10.3 Redeemable
shares   10.4 Capitalisations and bonus shares   10.5 Distributions   10.6 Purchase of own
shares   10.7 Employees' share schemes   10.8 Financial assistance for purchase of
own shares

11 Borrowing, Credit and Security   320

11.1 Introduction   11.2 Security for financial obligations   11.3 Registration of non-
possessory charges   11.4 Legal and equitable charges   11.5 Recourse to charged property
11.6 Floating charges   11.7 Registration of charges on company property

12 Marketable Loans   354

12.1 Introduction   12.2 Stock   12.3 Trustees   12.4 Stock certificates   12.5 Contracts for
the allotment of debt securities   12.6 Information for debenture holders   12.7 Convertibles
12.8 International bonds

13 Insider Dealing   358

13.1 Reasons for prohibiting insider dealing   13.2 Definition of the offence of insider dealing   13.3 London Stock Exchange model code   13.4 Options   13.5 Civil liability 13.6 Register of directors' interests

14 Shareholders   372

14.1 Introduction   14.2 Definition   14.3 Register   14.4 Meetings   14.5 Decision-making without meeting   14.6 Alteration of class rights   14.7 Holding and subsidiary companies

15 Directors   423

15.1 Directors in the legal structure of the company   15.2 Appointment to office 15.3 Termination of office   15.4 Publicity   15.5 The board of directors   15.6 Remuneration   15.7 Powers of management   15.8 Legal categorisation of directors   15.9 Directors are not agents of members   15.10 Directors' liability for a company's wrongs 15.11 Two-tier boards

16 Directors' Duties   483

16.1 Introduction   16.2 Duty of skill and care   16.3 Fiduciary duty   16.4 Constraints on the exercise by directors of their powers   16.5 Conflict of interest and duty   16.6 Transactions to which the company is a party   16.7 Transactions to which the company is not a party   16.8 Ratification of profiting and conflict of interest   16.9 Relief from liability

17 Corporate Officers and Promoters   536

17.1 Introduction   17.2 Managers   17.3 The secretary   17.4 Auditors   17.5 Relief from liability   17.6 Promoters

18 Remedies for Maladministration   554

18.1 Introduction   18.2 Action by the company   18.3 The rule in *Foss* v *Harbottle* 18.4 Proper plaintiff principle   18.5 Irregularity principle   18.6 Unfairly prejudicial conduct of the company's affairs   18.7 Just and equitable winding up of quasi-partnerships   18.8 Company investigations

19 Dealings with a Company   613

19.1 Introduction   19.2 Authentication and execution of documents   19.3 Company contracts   19.4 Contractual capacity   19.5 Authority   19.6 Pre-incorporation and post-dissolution contracts   19.7 Vicarious liability for torts   19.8 Identification of humans with a company   19.9 Companies in court

20 Company Insolvency and Liquidation   664

20.1 Introduction   20.2 Administrative receivership   20.3 Administration   20.4 Voluntary arrangements   20.5 Voluntary liquidation   20.6 Compulsory liquidation   20.7 Appointment of a provisional liquidator   20.8 Commencement of winding up: going into liquidation

20.9 Investigation of the affairs of a company in liquidation   20.10 Liability for fraudulent trading   20.11 Misfeasance proceedings   20.12 Wrongful trading   20.13 Order of application of assets   20.14 Dissolution

Index   721

Preface

This book is intended to be a clear, straightforward, up-to-date introduction to English company law.

Readers of the book are assumed to have had an introduction to English law, but no special knowledge of any other branch of the law is assumed.

Although it is inevitable that a book of this character will be used mainly by students, it is hoped that it can also serve as a useful, compact and up-to-date statement of the law for lawyers, accountants, bankers, insolvency practitioners and other professionals.

Our primary aim in this book is to state what the law currently is with as much technical accuracy as can be achieved in the process of writing a textbook, but we also try to present something of the context in which that law has developed, looking at its purposes and history, and introducing some of the debate about both the controversial details and the fundamental nature of company law. English company law is currently the subject of a very detailed examination by the Department of Trade and Industry and the Law Commission, and this edition notes many of the consultation documents that have been issued so as to warn readers where changes are under consideration.

The greatest challenge in the study of company law is that it is a very large subject. An introductory book like this must concentrate on providing a framework of basic principles with some detail of how those principles are worked out in practice. The practice of company law involves the use of a very large legislative code, and requires familiarity with the way the courts interpret the legislation and how they fill in missing details. It is also necessary to know how the concepts of equity are applied by judges and lawyers in the areas of company law which are not exclusively governed by statute. This book deals with the main topics of company law, saying what the legislative provisions are and giving examples of how problems have been dealt with by the courts. The number of references to primary sources (legislation, cases, articles) is very large and we would advise readers who are studying the subject for the first time to be very selective about following up those references. Quotations of significant passages from legislation and judgments are given in this book where appropriate. The text of all relevant enactments, incorporating amendments and repeals up to 29 July 1998 will be found in D. French, *Blackstone's Statutes on Company Law* (London: Blackstone Press, 1998). Further extracts from cases and articles will be found in cases and materials books such as A. Hicks and S.H. Goo, *Cases and Materials on Company Law*, 2nd ed. (London: Blackstone Press, 1997). It is hoped that this book will provide its readers with the techniques required to use the original sources successfully.

In this edition the law is stated as it was thought to be on 29 July 1998. I am very grateful to Anne Marshall, who has copy-edited many previous editions of this book and kept the tables up to date, for copy-editing and tabling this edition as well.

Derek French

Table of Cases

A1 Biscuit Co., re (ChD 1899) [1899] WN 115, 43 SJ 657   3.4.4

A. & B. C. Chewing Gum Ltd, re (ChD 1974) [1975] 1 WLR 579, [1975] 1 All ER 1017,
119 SJ 233   18.7.2

A & C Group Services Ltd, re (ChD 1993) [1993] BCLC 1297   15.2.5.6

Abbey Glen Property Corporation v Stumborg (SC of Alberta 1975) 65 DLR (3d) 235,
[1976] 2 WWR 1; affirmed by CA (1978) 85 DLR (3d) 35, [1978] 4 WWR 28, 9 AR 234,
4 BLR 113   16.7.3.5, 16.7.4

Abbey Leisure Ltd, re; see Virdi v Abbey Leisure Ltd

Abbey Malvern Wells Ltd, the v Ministry of Local Government & Planning (ChD 1951)
[1951] Ch 728, [1951] 2 All ER 154, 1 P & CR 467, [1951] 1 TLR 1050, 115 JP 389, 95
SJ 381, 49 LGR 776   5.2.2.6

Abbey National Building Society v Cann (HL 1990) [1991] 1 AC 56, [1990] 2 WLR 832,
[1990] 1 All ER 1085, 22 HLR 360, 60 P & CR 278   11.7.10.3

Abbot of Hulme's Case (1491) YB 21 Edw IV, f. 12, Mich., pl. 4   19.9

Aberdeen Railway Co. v Blaikie Brothers (HL 1854) 1 Macq 461, 9 ScRR (HL) 365,
2 Eq Rep 128, 23 LT OS 315, [1843–60] All ER Rep 249, 17 D (HL) 20, 26 Sc Jur 622
  16.5.3, 16.6.1

Acatos and Hutcheson plc v Watson [1995] 1 BCLC 218, [1995] BCC 441   5.2.1, 10.8.3

ACGE Investments Ltd v House of Fraser plc; see House of Fraser plc v ACGE
Investments Ltd

Action Waste Collections Pty Ltd, re (Victoria SC 1976) 2 ACLR 253   14.5.1

Adams v Cape Industries plc (CA 1989) [1990] Ch 433, [1990] 2 WLR 657, [1990] BCLC 479,
[1990] BCC 786   5.2.2.1, 5.2.2.4, 5.2.2.8, 5.2,2.9, 5.2.2.11

Adams v The Queen (PC 1994) [1995] 1 WLR 52, [1995] BCC 376   16.5.5.4, 18.2.2

Addis Ltd v Berkeley Supplies Ltd (ChD 1964) [1964] 1 WLR 943, [1964] 2 All ER 753,
108 SJ 481   2.3.4

Adelaide Company of Jehovah's Witnesses Incorporated v Commonwealth (Australia HC 1943)
67 CLR 116, [1943] ALR 193, 17 ALJ 134   19.8.8

Adelaide Electric Supply Co. Ltd v Prudential Assurance Co. Ltd (HL 1933) [1934] AC 122,
103 LJ Ch 85, 150 LT 281, [1933] All ER Rep 82, 50 TLR 147, 39 Com Cas 119,
77 SJ 913   14.6.2.6

ADT Ltd v BDO Binder Hamlyn (QBD 1995) [1996] BCC 808   8.10

Advance Bank of Australia Ltd v FAI Insurances Australia Ltd (CA of New South Wales (1987)
9 NSWLR 464, 12 ACLR 118, 5 ACLC 725   14.4.5.5, 16.4.10, 18.3.3.4

Adviser (188) Ltd, re; see Bishopsgate Investment Management Ltd

Agip (Africa) Ltd v Jackson (CA 1990) [1991] Ch 547, [1991] 3 WLR 116, [1992] 4 All ER 451
  17.2, 18.2.2

Agricultural Wholesale Society Ltd v Biddulph & District Agricultural Society Ltd; see
Biddulph & District Agricultural Society Ltd v Agricultural Wholesale Society Ltd

Airlines Airspares Ltd v Handley Page Ltd (ChD 1969) [1970] Ch 193, [1970] 2 WLR 163,
[1970] 1 All ER 29   20.2.7.1

Airtours plc v Shipley (QBDC 1994) 158 JP 835   19.8.6.2

Akerhielm v De Mare (PC 1959) [1959] AC 789, [1959] 3 WLR 108, [1959] 3 All ER 485,
103 SJ 527   6.5.3

Al Saudi Banque v Clark Pixley (ChD 1989) [1990] Ch 313, [1990] 2 WLR 344,
[1989] 3 All ER 361, [1990] BCLC 46, 5 BCC 822, 1989 PCC 442   8.10

Albacruz v Albazero; see The Albazero

Albazero, the (QBD 1974) [1977] AC 774, [1975] 3 WLR 491, [1974] 2 All ER 906,
[1974] 2 Lloyd's Rep 38 (sub nom. Concord Petroleum Corporation v Gosford Marine
Panama SA); affirmed by CA (1975) [1977] AC 774 at 802, [1975] 3 WLR 491 at 516,
[1975] 3 All ER 21, [1975] 2 Lloyd's Rep 295 (sub nom. Concord Petroleum Corporation
v Gosford Marine Panama SA); affirmed by HL (1976) sub nom. Albacruz v Albazero
[1977] AC 774 at 825, [1976] 3 WLR 419, [1976] 3 All ER 129,
[1976] 2 Lloyd's Rep 467   5.2.2.8
Albert Locke (1940) Ltd v Winsford Urban District Council (ChD 1973) 71 LGR 308   5.2.2.4
Alberta Gas Ethylene Co. Ltd v Minister of National Revenue (Canada FedC 1988)
24 FTR 309   5.2.2.1, 5.2.2.3
Aldermanbury Trust plc, re (ChD 1993) [1993] BCC 598   15.2.5.6
Alexander v Automatic Telephone Co. (CA 1900) [1900] 2 Ch 56, 69 LJ Ch 428,
82 LT 400, [1900–3] All ER Rep Ext 1755, 16 TLR 339, 48 WR 546, 44 SJ 407   18.4.4
Alexander v Simpson (CA 1889) 43 ChD 139, 59 LJ Ch 137, 61 LT 708, 1 Meg 457,
6 TLR 72, 38 WR 161   14.4.5.5
Alexander Ward & Co. Ltd v Samyang Navigation Co. Ltd (HL 1975) [1975] 1 WLR 673,
[1975] 2 All ER 424, [1975] 2 Lloyd's Rep 1, 1975 SC (HL) 26, 1975 SLT 126,
119 SJ 319   15.7.3, 15.7.7
ALI Finance Ltd v Havelet Leasing Ltd (ChD 1990) [1992] 1 WLR 455; sub nom. Arbuthnot
Leasing International Ltd v Havelet Leasing Ltd: [1991] 1 All ER 591, [1990] BCLC 802,
[1990] BCC 627   19.9
Allarco Group Ltd v Suncor Inc. Resources Group, Oil Sands Division (Alberta CA 1987)
[1987] 5 WWR 159, 53 Alta LR (2d) 107 (sub nom. Suncor Inc. Resources Group,
Oil Sands Division v Allarco Group Ltd)   5.2.2.1
Allen v Gold Reefs of West Africa Ltd (CA 1900) [1900] 1 Ch 656, 69 LJ Ch 266,
82 LT 210, [1900–3] All ER Rep 746, 16 TLR 213, 7 Mans 417, 48 WR 452, 44 SJ 261
    3.4.2.3, 3.5.4, 3.5.3.1, 3.5.3.3, 3.5.3.5, 14.4.9.4, 16.4.3, 18.4.9
Allen v Hyatt (PC 1914) 30 TLR 444, 17 DLR 7   13.5, 15.9
Allen, Craig & Co. (London) Ltd, re (ChD 1934) [1934] Ch 483, 103 LJ Ch 193, 151 LT 323,
50 TLR 301, 78 SJ 223   17.4.5
Allied Irish Coal Supplies Ltd v Powell Duffryn International Fuels Ltd (Republic
of Ireland HC 1996) [1997] 1 ILRM 306   5.2.2.8
Allprint Co. Ltd v Erwin (Ontario CA 1982) 136 DLR (3d) 587, 38 OR (2d) 13,
18 BLR 81   19.2.6
Alma Spinning Co., re, Bottomley's Case (MR 1880) 16 ChD 681, 50 LJ Ch 167, 43 LT 620,
29 WR 133   15.1.3
Alphacell Ltd v Woodward (HL 1972) [1972] AC 824, [1972] 2 WLR 1320,
[1972] 2 All ER 475, 70 LGR 455, [1972] Crim LR 41   19.8.4
Altim Pty Ltd, re (New South Wales SC 1968) [1968] 2 NSWR 762   15.2.5.1
Aluminium Industrie Vaassen BV v Romalpa Aluminium Ltd (CA 1976, affirming QBD 1975)
[1976] 1 WLR 676, [1976] 2 All ER 552, [1976] 1 Lloyd's Rep 443, 120 SJ 95   11.7.10.3
Aluminum Co. of Canada Ltd v Toronto (Canada SC 1944) [1944] 3 DLR 609,
[1944] SCR 267   5.2.2.1, 5.2.2.3
Amalgamated Investment and Property Co. Ltd v Texas Commerce International Bank Ltd
(CA 1981) [1982] QB 84, [1981] 3 WLR 565, [1981] 3 All ER 577,
[1982] 1 Lloyd's Rep 27   5.2.2.1
Amalgamated Pest Control Pty Ltd v McCarron (Queensland SC 1994)
[1995] 1 QdR 583   3.5.3.3
Amalgamated Society of Railway Servants v Osborne (HL 1909) [1910] AC 87, 79 LJ Ch 87,
101 LT 787, 26 TLR 177, 54 SJ 215   0.1.6
Amalgamated Syndicate, re (ChD 1897) [1897] 2 Ch 600, 66 LJ Ch 783, 77 LT 431,
4 Mans 398, [1895–9] All ER Rep 340, 46 WR 75, 42 SJ 13   2.3.5.8
Ambrose Lake Tin & Copper Mining Co. Ltd, re (CA 1880) 14 ChD 390, 49 LJ Ch 457,
42 LT 604, 28 WR 783   17.6.3.2
AMEC Properties Ltd v Planning Research & Systems plc [1992] BCLC 1149   20.2.7.1
Anderson v James Sutherland (Peterhead) Ltd (C Sess 1st Div 1941) 1941 SC 203, 1941 SN 15,
1941 SLT 235   15.5.3
Anderson v Midland Railway Co. (ChD 1901) [1902] 1 Ch 369, 71 LJ Ch 89, 85 LT 408,
18 TLR 5, 50 WR 40, 46 SJ 14   18.4.10

Anderson (W.B.) and Sons Ltd v Rhodes (Liverpool) Ltd (Assizes 1967) [1967] 2 All ER 850   19.7

Andreae v Zinc Mines of Great Britain Ltd (KBD 1918) [1918] 2 KB 454, 87 LJ KB 1019,
34 TLR 488, 24 Com Cas 49   6.4.1

Andrews v Gas Meter Co. (CA 1897) [1897] 1 Ch 361, 66 LJ Ch 246, 76 LT 732,
[1895-9] All ER Rep 1280, 13 TLR 199, 45 WR 321, 41 SJ 255   6.1.3

Anglo-American Insurance Co. Ltd, re (ChD 1991) [1991] BCLC 564,
[1991] BCC 208   1.3.2.1, 10.2.5

Anglo-Austrian Printing & Publishing Union, re, Brabourne v the Company (ChD 1895)
[1895] 2 Ch 891, 65 LJ Ch 38, 72 LT 442, 12 TLR 39, 2 Mans 614, 44 WR 186,
40 SJ 68   20.11.1

Anglo-Austrian Printing & Publishing Union, re, Isaacs's Case (CA 1892) [1892] 2 Ch 158,
61 LJ Ch 481, 66 LT 593, 40 WR 518, 8 TLR 501, 36 SJ 427   3.4.4

Anglo-Continental Corporation of Western Australia, re (ChD 1898) [1898] 1 Ch 327,
67 LJ Ch 179, 78 LT 157, 46 WR 413, 14 TLR 218, 42 SJ 270, 5 Mans 184   6.1.3, 20.13.1

Anglo-Danubian Steam Navigation & Colliery Co., re (MR 1875) LR 20 Eq 339,
44 LJ Ch 502, 33 LT 118, 23 WR 783   12.2

Anglo-Eastern (1985) Ltd v Knutz (Hong Kong CA 1987) [1988] 1 HKLR 322   18.4.3

Anglo-Overseas Agencies Ltd v Green (QBD 1960) [1961] 1 QB 1, [1960] 3 WLR 561,
[1960] 3 All ER 244   2.3.5.8

Anglo-Universal Bank v Baragnon (CA 1881) 45 LT 362   6.4.2, 16.4.13, 18.3.3.1

Ansett, re (Victoria SC 1990) 3 ACSR 357   15.2.5.1

Anthony v Wright (ChD 1994) [1995] 1 BCLC 236, [1995] BCC 768   8.10

APA Oceanic Funds Management Ltd v Smith (No. 1) (SC of New South Wales 1987)
9 NSWLR 569, 11 ACLR 879, 5 ACLC 975   4.4

Appletreewick Lead Mining Co., re (V-C 1874) LR 18 Eq 95, 43 LJ Ch 793, 30 LT 287,
22 WR 678   3.4.2.4

Applin v Race Relations Board (HL 1974) [1975] AC 259, [1974] 2 WLR 541,
[1974] 2 All ER 73, 72 LGR 479, 118 SJ 311   0.1.9

APT Group Services Pty Ltd v Ferguson (Victoria SC 1991) 6 ACSR 231,
10 ACLC 27   15.2.3.3, 15.5.1

Arab Bank Ltd v Ross (CA 1952) [1952] 2 QB 216, [1952] 1 All ER 709, [1952] 1 TLR 811   19.2.6

Arab Bank plc v Merchantile Holdings Ltd (ChD 1993) [1994] Ch 71, [1994] 2 WLR 307,
[1994] 2 All ER 74, [1994] 1 BCLC 330, [1993] BCC 816 (sub nom. Arab Bank plc v
Mercantile Holdings plc)   10.8.4

Arab Monetary Fund v Hashim (No. 3) (HL 1991) [1991] 2 AC 114, [1991] 2 WLR 729,
[1991] 1 All ER 871   0.1.6, 0.1.7

Arbitration between London County Council and London Tramways Co., re an
(QBDC 1897) 13 TLR 254   19.9

Arbuthnot Leasing International Ltd v Havelet Leasing Ltd; see ALI Finance Ltd v
Havelet Leasing Ltd

Arbuthnot Leasing International Ltd v Havelet Leasing Ltd (No. 2) (ChD 1990)
[1990] BCC 636   19.9

Arctic Engineering Ltd (No. 2), re (ChD 1985) [1986] 1 WLR 686, [1986] 2 All ER 346,
[1986] PCC 1, [1986] BCLC 253, 1 BCC 99, 563, [1986] 1 FTLR 59, 130 SJ 686,
83 LS Gaz 1895   15.2.5.3

Ardmore Studios (Ireland) Ltd v Lynch (Republic of Ireland HC 1964) [1965] IR 1   20.2.7.1

Ariadne Australia Ltd, re (Queensland SC 1990) [1991] 2 QdR 377, 2 ACSR 791,
8 ACLC 1,000   14.4.3

Armagas Ltd v Mundogas SA (HL 1986) [1986] AC 717, [1986] 2 WLR 1063,
[1986] 2 All ER 385, [1986] 2 Lloyd's Rep 109, 2 BCC 99, 197, 130 SJ 430   19.5.3, 19.5.4.2

Armagh Shoes Ltd, re (Northern Ireland ChD 1981) [1982] NI 59, [1981] 9 NIJB,
[1984] BCLC 405   11.8.5

Armour v Thyssen Edelstahlwerke AG (HL 1990) [1991] 2 AC 339, [1990] 3 All ER 481,
1990 SLT 891, [1991] BCLC 28, [1990] BCC 925   11.7.10.3

Armstrong v Jackson (KBD 1917) [1917] 2 KB 822, 86 LJ KB 1375, 117 LT 479, 33 TLR 444,
[1916–17] All ER Rep 1117   6.7.4, 17.6.3.1

Arnison v Smith (CA 1889) 41 ChD 348, 61 LT 63, 5 TLR 413, 1 Meg 388, 37 WR 739   6.5.3

Arnot v United African Lands Ltd (CA 1901) [1901] 1 Ch 518, 70 LJ Ch 306, 84 LT 309,
17 TLR 245, 49 WR 322, 8 Mans 179, 45 SJ 275   14.4.9.2

Arrows Ltd, re (No. 2) (CA 1992) [1994] 1 BCLC 355   20.9.3
Arrows Ltd, re (No. 4); see Hamilton v Naviede
Arthur Rathbone Kitchens Ltd, re (ChD 1997) [1997] 2 BCLC 280, [1998] BCC 450   14.4.1
ARV Aviation Ltd, re (ChD 1988) [1989] BCLC 664, 4 BCC 708   20.3.4
Ashburton Oil NL v Alpha Minerals NL (HC of Australia 1971) 123 CLR 614, 45 ALJR 162
                                                                      15.7.1, 16.4.10, 16.4.11
Ashbury v Watson (CA 1885) 30 ChD 376, 54 LJ Ch 985, 54 LT 27, 33 WR 882   2.4.1
Ashbury Railway Carriage and Iron Co. Ltd (the directors etc. of the) v Riche (HL 1875)
    LR 7 HL 653, 44 LJ Ex 185, 33 LT 450, 24 WR 794   0.3.2.3, 2.3.5.3, 19.4.1
Ashley's case; see Re Estates Investment Co.
Ashpurton Estates Ltd, re (CA 1982) [1983] Ch 110, [1982] 3 WLR 964, [1982] 3 All ER 665
    (sub nom. Victoria Housing Estates Ltd v Ashpurton Estates Ltd)   11.7.9
Associated Color Laboratories Ltd, re (SC of British Columbia 1970) 12 DLR (3d) 338,
    73 WWR 566, 14 CBR NS 35   14.4.1, 15.5.1
Association of Certified Public Accountants of Britain v Secretary of State for Trade
    and Industry (ChD 1997) [1998] 1 WLR 164, [1997] 2 BCLC 307, [1997] BCC 736   2.4.2
Atkin v Wardle (CA 1889) 5 TLR 734   4.5.1
Atlantic Computer Systems plc, re (CA 1990) [1992] Ch 505, [1992] 2 WLR 367,
    [1992] 1 All ER 476, [1991] BCLC 606 (sub nom Re Atlantic Computer Systems plc
    (No. 1)), [1990] BCC 859   11.6.4, 20.3.6
Atlantic Computer Systems plc, re (No. 1); see Re Atlantic Computer Systems plc
Atlantic Computers plc, re, National Australia Bank Ltd v Soden (ChD 1995)
    [1995] BCC 696   5.2.2.8
Atlantic Medical Ltd, re (ChD 1992) [1993] BCLC 386, [1992] BCC 653   11.6.4
Atlas Maritime Co. SA v Avalon Maritime Ltd (No. 1) (CA 1990) [1991] 4 All ER 769,
    [1991] 1 Lloyd's Rep 563   5.2.2.1, 5.2.2.7
Attorney-General v Equiticorp Industries Group Ltd (New Zealand CA 1995)
    [1996] 1 NZLR 528   5.2.2.10
Attorney-General v Great Eastern Railway Co. (HL 1880) 5 App Cas 473, 49 LJ Ch 545,
    42 LT 810, 28 WR 769   2.3.5.6
Attorney-General for the Dominion of Canada v Standard Trust Co. of New York
    (PC (SC of Canada) 1911) [1911] AC 498, 80 LJ PC 189, 105 LT 152   16.8
Attorney-General for Tuvalu v Philatelic Distribution Corporation Ltd (CA 1989) [1990]
    1 WLR 926, [1990] 2 All ER 216, [1990] BCLC 245, [1990] BCC 30   15.10
Attorney-General's Reference (No. 2 of 1982) (CA 1983) [1984] QB 624, [1984] 2 WLR 447,
    [1984] 2 All ER 216, 78 Cr App R 131, [1984] BCLC 60, 1 BCC 98,973,
    128 SJ 221   19.8.5, 20.11.4
Attorney-General's Reference (No. 1 of 1985) (CA 1986) [1986] QB 491, [1986] 2 WLR 733,
    [1986] 2 All ER 219, 83 Cr App R 70   16.5.5.4
Attree v Hawe (CA 1878) 9 ChD 337, 47 LJ Ch 863, 38 LT 733, [1874–80] All ER Rep 197,
    43 JP 124, 26 WR 871   11.6.3
Atwool v Merryweather (V-C 1868) LR 5 Eq 464 n, 37 LJ Ch 35   18.4.3
Aubanel & Alabaster Ltd v Aubanel (ChD 1949) 66 RPC 343   16.7.3.3
Augustus Barnett & Son Ltd, re (ChD 1985) [1986] BCLC 170, 1986 PCC 167, 2 BCC 98, 904
                                                                              20.10.2, 20.10.3
Austinsuite Furniture Ltd, re (ChD 1990) [1992] BCLC 1047   15.2.5.6
Austral Brick Co. Pty Ltd v Falgat Constructions Pty Ltd (New South Wales SC 1990)
    2 ACSR 766, 8 ACLC 1011   20.6.7
Australian Agricultural Co. v Oatmont Pty Ltd (Northern Territory CA 1992) 106 FLR 314,
    8 ACSR 255   2.3.5.1, 18.4.10
Australian Coal & Shale Employees' Federation v Smith (New South Wales CA 1937)
    38 SR (NSW) 48, 55 WN (NSW) 19   3.4.1.2, 3.4.2.8, 18.4.9
Australian Fixed Trusts Pty Ltd v Clyde Industries Ltd (SC of New South Wales 1958)
    [1959] SR (NSW) 33, 76 WN (NSW) 88   3.5.3.5
Australian Growth Resources Corporation Pty Ltd v Van Reesema (South Australia SC (FC) 1988)
    13 ACLR 261, 6 ACLC 529   16.4.6.1
Australian Pacific Technology Ltd, re (Victoria SC 1994) [1995] 1 VR 457   1.3.2.1
Australian Securities Commission v Marlborough Gold Mines Ltd (Australia HC 1993)
    177 CLR 485, 112 ALR 627   1.3.4.1

Australian Securities Commission v Multiple Sclerosis Society of Tasmania
   (Tasmania SC 1993) 10 ACSR 489   16.4.3
Automatic Bottle Makers Ltd, re (CA 1926) [1926] Ch 412, 95 LJ Ch 185, 134 LT 517,
   [1926] All ER Rep 618   11.6.1
Automatic Self-Cleansing Filter Syndicate Co. Ltd v Cuninghame (CA 1906) [1906] 2 Ch 34,
   75 LJ Ch 437, 94 LT 651, 13 Mans 156, 22 TLR 378, 50 SJ 359; affirming ChD (1906)
   [1906] 2 Ch 34, 94 LT 651   3.4.3, 15.7.2.4, 15.7.4
Aveling Barford Ltd, re (ChD 1988) [1989] 1 WLR 360, [1988] 3 All ER 1019, [1989] BCLC 122,
   1989 PCC 240, 4 BCC 548   20.9.3
Aveling Barford Ltd v Perion Ltd (ChD 1989) 5 BCC 677   2.3.5.1, 10.5.2, 10.5.10

B v B (FamD 1978) [1978] Fam 181, [1978] 3 WLR 624, [1979] 1 All ER 801   5.2.2.5
Baby Moon (UK) Ltd, re (ChD 1984) 1985 PCC 103, 1 BCC 99, 298   2.3.4
Baden v Société générale pour favoriser le développement du commerce et de l'industrie en
   France SA (ChD 1982) [1993] 1 WLR 509, [1992] 4 All ER 161, [1983] BCLC 325,
   [1983] Com LR 88; affirmed by CA (1985) [1993] 1 WLR 509 at 613, [1992] 4 All ER 279,
   [1985] BCLC 258 n   16.4.7, 18.2.2
Badgerhill Properties Ltd v Cottrell (CA 1991) [1991] BCLC 805, [1991] BCC 463,
   54 BLR 23   4.5.1, 19.2.1
Baglan Hall Colliery Co., re (LJJ 1870) LR 5 Ch App 346, 39 LJ Ch 591, 23 LT 60,
   18 WR 499   5.2.1
Bagnall v Carlton (CA 1877) 6 ChD 371, 47 LJ Ch 30, 37 LT 481, 26 WR 243   17.6.2
Bagot Pneumatic Tyre Co. v Clipper Pneumatic Tyre Co. (CA 1901) [1902] 1 Ch 146,
   71 LJ Ch 158, 85 LT 652, 18 TLR 161, 9 Mans 56, 19 RPC 69, 50 WR 177   19.6.2
Bagshaw v Eastern Union Railway Co. (V-C 1849) 7 Hare 114, 68 ER 46, 6 Ry & Can Cas 152,
   18 LJ Ch 193, 13 Jur 602; affirmed by LC (1850) 2 Mac & G 389, 42 ER 151, 2 H & Tw 201,
   47 ER 1655, 19 LJ Ch 410, 14 Jur 491, 6 Ry & Can Cas 152 at 169   18.3.4, 18.4.9, 18.4.11
Bahia & San Francisco Railway Co. Ltd, re (Court of Queen's Bench 1868) LR 3 QB 584,
   9 B & S 844, 37 LJ QB 176, 18 LT 467, 16 WR 862   8.2.2, 8.4
Bailey v Birkenhead, Lancashire & Cheshire Junction Railway Co. (MR 1850) 12 Beav 433,
   50 ER 1127, 6 Ry & Can Cas 256, 19 LJ Ch 377, 14 Jur 119   6.4.2
Bailey v New South Wales Medical Defence Union Ltd (Australia HC 1995) 184 CLR 399,
   69 ALJR 890, 132 ALR 1, 18 ACSR 521   3.4.2.5, 3.5.4
Bailey Hay & Co. Ltd, re (ChD 1971) [1971] 1 WLR 1357, [1971] 3 All ER 693,
   115 SJ 639   14.5.2
Baillie v Oriental Telephone & Electric Co. Ltd (CA 1914) [1915] 1 Ch 503, 84 LJ Ch 409,
   112 LT 569, [1914–15] All ER Rep Ext 1420, 31 TLR 643   14.4.5.5, 16.8, 18.4.9
Baily v British Equitable Assurance Co. (CA 1904) [1904] 1 Ch 374; reversed by HL (1905)
   sub nom. British Equitable Assurance Co. Ltd v Baily [1906] AC 35, 75 LJ Ch 73, 94 LT 1,
   22 TLR 152, 13 Mans 13   3.5.3.4
Bainbridge v Smith (CA 1889) 41 ChD 462, 37 WR 594   15.3.7
Baird v J. Baird & Co. (Falkirk) Ltd (C Sess OH 1949) 1949 SLT 368   14.4.9.3, 16.6.3
Baird's case; see Re Bangor & North Wales Mutual Marine Protection Association
Baku Consolidated Oilfields Ltd, re (ChD 1943) [1944] 1 All ER 24, 88 SJ 85   2.3.5.4
Baku Consolidated Oilfields Ltd, re (ChD 1993) [1994] 1 BCLC 173, [1993] BCC 653
                                                                               2.3.5.4, 8.2.1, 14.2
Balkis Consolidated Co. Ltd v Tomkinson (HL 1893) [1893] AC 396,
   63 LJ QB 134, 69 LT 598, [1891–4] All ER Rep 982, 9 TLR 597, 42 WR 204,
   37 SJ 729, 1 R 178   8.2.2, 8.4
Ball v Metal Industries Ltd (C Sess OH 1956) 1957 SC 315, 1957 SLT 124   14.4.3
Balston Ltd v Headline Filters Ltd (ChD 1988) [1990] FSR 385   16.7.2, 16.7.3.3
Baltic Real Estate Ltd, re; see Re Baltic Real Estate Ltd (No. 2)
Baltic Real Estate Ltd, re (No. 2) (ChD 1992) [1993] BCLC 503, [1992] BCC 629 at 633
   (sub nom. Re Baltic Real Estate Ltd)   18.6.3
Bamford v Bamford (CA 1969) [1970] Ch 212, [1969] 2 WLR 1107, [1969] 1 All ER 969,
   113 SJ 123   16.4.1, 16.4.14, 18.4.12, 20.11.4
Bamford Publishers Ltd, re (ChD 1977) 74 LS Gaz 711, *The Times*, 4 June 1977   18.8.3.3
Bangor & North Wales Mutual Marine Protection Association, re, Baird's Case (ChD 1899)
   [1899] 2 Ch 593, 68 LJ Ch 521, 80 LT 870, 47 WR 695, 7 Mans 160, 43 SJ 605   1.3.2.3

Bank of Credit and Commerce International SA, re (No. 2); see Re Bank of Credit and
    Commerce International SA (No. 3)
Bank of Credit and Commerce International SA, re (No. 3) (CA 1992) [1993] BCLC 1490,
    [1992] BCC 715 at 720 (sub nom. Re Bank of Credit and Commerce International SA
    (No. 2))   5.2.2.11
Bank of Credit and Commerce International SA, re (No. 4); see Re Bank of Credit and
    Commerce International SA (No. 10)
Bank of Credit and Commerce International SA, re (No. 7) (ChD 1993) [1994] 1 BCLC 455   20.9.3
Bank of Credit and Commerce International SA, re (No. 8) (HL 1997) [1998] AC 214,
    [1997] 3 WLR 909, [1997] 4 All ER 568, [1998] 1 BCLC 68, [1997] BCC 965
    (sub nom. Morris v Rayners Enterprises Inc.); (CA 1995) [1996] Ch 245,
    [1996] 2 WLR 631, [1996] 2 All ER 121, [1996] BCC 204 (sub nom. Morris v
    Agrichemicals Ltd)   11.2.1, 11.5.6, 11.7.10.1
Bank of Credit and Commerce International SA, re (No. 10) [1995] 1 BCLC 362, [1995] BCC 453
    (sub nom. Re Bank of Credit and Commerce International SA (No. 4))   5.2.2.11
Bank of Credit and Commerce International SA v Dawson (QBD 1987)
    1987 FLR 342   19.8.3, 19.8.6.1
Bank of Cyprus (London) Ltd v Gill (CA 1979) [1980] 2 Lloyd's Rep 51   11.5.1
Bank of Montreal v Canadian Westgrowth Ltd (Alberta QB 1990) 72 Alta LR (2d) 319;
    (Alberta CA 1992) 2 Alta LR (3d) 221   5.2.2.3, 5.2.2.10
Bank of Syria, re, Owen and Ashworth's Claim; Whitworth's Claim (CA 1900) [1901] 1 Ch 115,
    70 LJ Ch 82, 83 LT 547, 17 TLR 84, 8 Mans 105, 49 WR 100   15.5.1, 19.5.4.1
Bank of Tokyo Ltd v Karoon (CA 1984) [1987] AC 45 n, [1986] 3 WLR 414 n,
    [1986] 3 All ER 468 n   5.2.2.9
Banque de l'Indochine et de Suez SA v Euroseas Group Finance Co. Ltd and others (QBD 1981)
    [1981] 3 All ER 198, [1981] Com LR 77   4.5.1
Barber & Nicholls Ltd v R & G Associates (London) Ltd (CA 1981) 132 NLJ 1076   4.5.1
Barbor v Middleton (C Sess OH 1987) 1988 SLT 288, 1988 SCLR 178, 4 BCC 681   14.3.3
Barclays Bank Ltd v TOSG Trust Fund Ltd (ChD 1981) [1984] BCLC 1; reversed by CA
    (1983) and HL (1984) [1984] AC 626 (CA and HL), [1984] 2 WLR 49 (CA),
    [1984] 1 All ER 628 (CA), [1984] BCLC 27 (CA), 1 BCC 99,017 (CA),
    [1984] 2 WLR 650 (HL), [1984] 1 All ER 1060 (HL), [1984] BCLC 259 (HL),
    1 BCC 99,081 (HL)   19.5.5
Barclays Bank plc v British and Commonwealth Holdings plc; see British and Commonwealth
    Holdings plc v Barclays Bank plc
Baring-Gould v Sharpington Combined Pick & Shovel Syndicate (CA 1899) [1899] 2 Ch 80,
    68 LJ Ch 429, 80 LT 739, 15 TLR 366, 6 Mans 430, 47 WR 564, 43 SJ 494   3.4.2.1
Barings plc v Coopers and Lybrand (CA 1996) [1997] 1 BCLC 427,
    [1997] BCC 498, [1997] PNLR 179   17.4.5, 18.4.6
Barleycorn Enterprises Ltd, re (CA 1970) [1970] Ch 465, [1970] 2 WLR 898,
    [1970] 2 All ER 155, 114 SJ 187   20.2.9, 20.13.1
Barned's Banking Co., re, ex parte Contract Corporation (LJ 1867) LR 3 Ch App 105,
    37 LJ Ch 81, 17 LT 269, [1861–73] All ER Rep Ext 2068, 16 WR 193   8.8.3
Barnes v Addy (LJJ 1874) LR 9 Ch App 244, 43 LJ Ch 513, 30 LT 4, 22 WR 505   18.2.2
Barrett v Duckett (CA 1994) [1995] 1 BCLC 243, [1995] BCC 362   18.4.7
Barron v Potter (ChD 1914) [1914] 1 Ch 895, 83 LJ Ch 646, 110 LT 929, 30 TLR 401,
    21 Mans 260, 58 SJ 516   14.4.5.4, 15.7.7
Barry Artist Ltd, re (ChD 1985) [1985] 1 WLR 1305, [1985] BCLC 283, 1985 PCC 364,
    129 SJ 853, 83 LS Gaz 436   0.3.2.5, 10.2.5, 14.5.1
Barton's case; see Re National Patent Steam Fuel Co.
Bateman v Service (PC 1881) 6 App Cas 386, 50 LJ PC 41   1.2.1, 2.4.3
Bath v Standard Land Co. Ltd (CA 1911) [1911] 1 Ch 618, 80 LJ Ch 426, 104 LT 867,
    27 TLR 393, 18 Mans 258, 55 SJ 482   16.4.7
Bath Glass Ltd, re (ChD 1987) [1988] BCLC 329, 4 BCC 130   15.2.5.6
Batten v Wedgwood Coal & Iron Co. (ChD 1884) 28 ChD 317, 54 LJ Ch 686, 52 LT 212,
    33 WR 303   20.2.9, 20.13.1
Baume and Co. Ltd v A.H. Moore Ltd (CA 1958) [1958] RPC 226   2.3.3.6
Beattie v E. & F. Beattie Ltd (CA 1938) [1938] Ch 708, [1938] 3 All ER 214, 107 LJ Ch 333,
    159 LT 220, 54 TLR 964, 82 SJ 521   3.4.2.7, 3.4.2.8

Bechuanaland Exploration Co. v London Trading Bank Ltd (QBD 1898) [1898] 2 QB 658,
    67 LJ QB 986, 79 LT 270, 14 TLR 587, 3 Com Cas 285   12.4
Beckers Pty Ltd, re (New South Wales SC 1942) 59 WN (NSW) 206   14.4.4
Bede Steam Shipping Co. Ltd, re (CA 1916) [1917] 1 Ch 123, 86 LJ Ch 65, 115 LT 580,
    33 TLR 13, 61 SJ 26   8.3.4
Bell v Lever Brothers Ltd (HL 1931) [1932] AC 161, 101 LJ KB 129, 146 LT 258, 48 TLR 133,
    37 Com Cas 98, [1931] All ER Rep 1, 76 SJ 50   16.7.1
Bell Bros Ltd, re (ChD 1891) 65 LT 245, 7 TLR 689   8.3.4
Bell Houses Ltd v City Wall Properties Ltd (CA 1966) [1966] 2 QB 656, [1966] 2 WLR 1323,
    [1966] 2 All ER 674, 110 SJ 268; reversing QBD (1965) [1966] 1 QB 207   2.3.5.10
Bell Resources Ltd v Turnbridge Pty Ltd (Western Australia SC 1988) 13 ACLR 429,
    6 ACLC 842   14.4.5.5
Bellador Silk Ltd, re (ChD 1965) [1965] 1 All ER 667   18.7
Bellerby v Rowland & Marwood's Steamship Co. Ltd (CA 1902) [1902] 2 Ch 14, 71 LJ Ch 541,
    86 LT 671, [1900–3] All ER Rep Ext 1290, 18 TLR 582, 9 Mans 291, 50 WR 566,
    46 SJ 484   6.4.2
Belmont Finance Corporation Ltd v Williams Furniture Ltd (CA 1977) [1979] Ch 250,
    [1978] 3 WLR 712, [1979] 1 All ER 118, 122 SJ 743   19.8.3, 19.8.6.3, 20.11.4
Belmont Finance Corporation Ltd v Williams Furniture Ltd (No. 2) (CA 1979)
    [1980] 1 All ER 393   10.8.4, 10.8.5, 18.2.2, 18.6.4, 19.8.3
Benjamin Cope and Sons Ltd, re (ChD 1914) [1914] 1 Ch 800,
    83 LJ Ch 699, 110 LT 905, 21 Mans 254, 58 SJ 432   11.6.1, 11.6.2
Bentinck v Fenn (HL 1887) 12 App Cas 652, 57 LJ Ch 552, 57 LT 773, 36 WR 641;
    affirming CA (1885) sub nom. Re Cape Breton Co. 29 ChD 795, 54 LJ Ch 822, 53 LT 181,
    1 TLR 450, 33 WR 788   17.6.4, 20.11.1
Bentley-Stevens v Jones (ChD 1974) [1974] 1 WLR 638, [1974] 2 All ER 653,
    118 SJ 345   14.4.5.1, 18.5
Berg Sons & Co. Ltd v Adams (QBD 1992) [1993] BCLC 1045, [1992] BCC 661   8.10, 17.4.5
Berlei Hestia (NZ) Ltd v Fernyhough (SC of New Zealand 1980) [1980] 2 NZLR 150
                                                                               9.2.4, 15.7.7, 16.7.4
Bermuda Cablevision Ltd v Colica Trust Co. Ltd (PC 1997) [1998] AC 198,
    [1998] 2 WLR 82, [1998] 1 BCLC 1, [1997] BCC 982   18.6.1, 18.6.3, 18.6.4
Bernhardt v Beau Rivage Pty Ltd (New South Wales SC 1989) 15 ACLR 160,
    7 ACLC 639   2.3.5.8
Besson (A.P.) Ltd v Fulleon Ltd (ChD 1985) [1986] FSR 319   15.10
Biala Pty Ltd v Mallina Holdings Ltd; see Dempster v Mallina Holdings Ltd
Biala Pty Ltd v Mallina Holdings Ltd (No. 4); see Dempster v Mallina Holdings Ltd
Biddulph & District Agricultural Society Ltd v Agricultural Wholesale Society Ltd (HL 1926)
    [1927] AC 76, 95 LJ Ch 576, 136 LT 163, 42 TLR 761; affirming CA (1925) sub nom.
    Agricultural Wholesale Society Ltd v Biddulph & District Agricultural Society Ltd
    [1925] Ch 769, 94 LJ Ch 397, 133 LT 274, 41 TLR 470, 69 SJ 557   1.3.2.3, 3.4.2.5, 3.4.4
Biggerstaff v Rowatt's Wharf Ltd (CA 1896) [1896] 2 Ch 93, 65 LJ Ch 536, 74 LT 473,
    44 WR 536   11.6.3, 19.5.4.6
Birch v Cropper (Re Bridgewater Navigation Co. Ltd) (HL 1889) 14 App Cas 525, 59 LJ Ch 122,
    61 LT 621, [1886–90] All ER Rep 628, 5 TLR 722, 1 Meg 372, 38 WR 401   6.1.3, 6.1.5
Birch v Sullivan (ChD 1957) [1957] 1 WLR 1247, [1958] 1 All ER 56, 101 SJ 974   18.4.3
Bird & Co. (London) Ltd v Thomas Cook & Son (Bankers) Ltd (KBD 1937) [1937] 2 All ER 227,
    156 LT 415   4.5.1
Bisgood v Henderson's Transvaal Estates Ltd (CA 1908) [1908] 1 Ch 743, 98 LT 809,
    [1908–10] All ER Rep 744, 24 TLR 510, 15 Mans 163, 52 SJ 412   3.4.2.2, 18.4.9
Bishop v Bonham (CA 1988) [1988] 1 WLR 742, [1988] BCLC 656, 4 BCC 347, 1988 FLR 282
    (sub nom. Bonham v Bishop)   11.5.1
Bishopsgate Investment Management Ltd v Maxwell (CA 1992) [1993] Ch 1, [1992] 2 WLR 991,
    [1992] 2 All ER 856, [1992] BCC 222 (sub nom. Re Bishopsgate Investment Management Ltd)
                                                                                             20.9.1, 20.9.8
Bishopsgate Investment Management Ltd v Maxwell (No. 2) (CA 1993)
    [1994] 1 All ER 261   16.4.1
Bishopsgate Investment Management Ltd, re (CA 1992); see Bishopsgate Investment
    Management Ltd v Maxwell

Bishopsgate Investment Management Ltd, re (CA 1993) [1993] Ch 452 at 481,
    [1993] 3 WLR 513 at 535, [1993] 3 All ER 861 at 885, [1993] BCLC 1222 at 1247,
    [1993] BCC 492 (sub nom. Re Adviser (188) Ltd)   20.9.3
Bishopsgate Investment Management Ltd, re (No. 2) (ChD 1992) [1994] BCC 732   20.9.3
Bisset v Wilkinson (PC (Court of Appeal New Zealand) 1926) [1927] AC 177, 96 LJ PC 12,
    136 LT 97, [1926] All ER Rep 343, 42 TLR 727, (1926) NZPCC 93   6.7.3
Black White & Grey Cabs Ltd v Fox (CA of New Zealand 1969) [1969] NZLR 824   15.7.2.4
Blair v Consolidated Enfield Corp. (Canada SC 1995) 128 DLR (4th) 73   14.4.7
Blair Open Hearth Furnace Co. Ltd v Reigart (ChD 1913) 108 LT 665, 29 TLR 449   15.7.4
Blackspur Group plc, re (CA 1997) [1998] 1 WLR 422, [1998] BCC 11 (sub nom.
    Re Blackspur Group plc (No. 2))   15.2.5.6
Blakely Ordnance Co., re, Stocken's Case (LJJ 1868) LR 3 Ch App 412, 37 LJ Ch 230,
    17 LT 554, 16 WR 322, [1861–73] All ER Rep Ext 2064   6.4.2
Blaker v Herts & Essex Waterworks Co. (ChD 1889) 41 ChD 399, 58 LJ Ch 497, 60 LT 776,
    37 WR 601, 5 TLR 421, 1 Meg 217   11.5.1
Bligh v Brent (Court of Exchequer in Equity 1837) 2 Y & C Ex 268, 160 ER 397, 6 LJ Ex Eq 58
                                                                                    0.1.1, 6.1.9
Bloomenthal v Ford (liquidator of Veuve Mannier & ses Fils Ltd) (HL 1897) [1897] AC 156,
    66 LJ Ch 253, 76 LT 205, 4 Mans 156, 13 TLR 240, 45 WR 449   8.2.2
Blue Arrow plc, re (ChD 1987) [1987] BCLC 585, 1988 PCC 306, 3 BCC 618   18.6.3
Bluechel v Prefabricated Buildings Ltd (British Columbia SC 1945) [1945] 2 DLR 725,
    [1945] 2 WWR 309, 61 BCR 325   18.4.12
Blum v OCP Repartition SA (CA 1987) [1988] BCLC 170, 1988 PCC 416, 1988 FLR 229,
    4 BCC 771   4.5.1
Blyth's Case; see Re Heaton's Steel and Iron Co., Blyth's Case
BML Group Ltd, re: see Harman v BML Group Ltd
Boardman v Phipps (HL 1966) [1967] 2 AC 46, [1966] 3 WLR 1009,
    [1966] 3 All ER 721   16.5.3
Bobbie Pins Ltd v Robertson (SC of New Zealand 1949) [1950] NZLR 301   14.5.1
Bodega Co. Ltd, re (ChD 1903) [1904] 1 Ch 276, 73 LJ Ch 198, 89 LT 694, 11 Mans 95,
    52 WR 249, [1900–3] All ER Rep 770   15.3.1
Bolton, re (ChD 1930) [1930] 2 Ch 48, 99 LJ Ch 209, 143 LT 425, [1929] B & CR 141,
    [1930] All ER Rep 628   6.4.2
Bolton (H.L.) (Engineering) Co. Ltd v Graham (T.J.) & Sons Ltd (CA 1956) [1957] 1 QB 159,
    [1956] 3 WLR 804, [1956] 3 All ER 624, 168 EG 424, 100 SJ 816   19.8.6.2
Bonang Gold Mining Co. Ltd, re, Brown's Case; see Smith v Brown
Bond v Barrow Haematite Steel Co. (ChD 1902) [1902] 1 Ch 353, 71 LJ Ch 246,
    86 LT 10, 18 TLR 249, 9 Mans 69, 50 WR 295, [1900-3] All ER Rep 484, 46 SJ 280 10.5.1
Bond Worth Ltd, re (ChD 1979) [1980] Ch 228, [1979] 3 WLR 629, [1979] 3 All ER 919,
    123 SJ 216   11.7.10.1, 11.7.10.3
Bondina Ltd v Rollaway Shower Blinds Ltd (CA 1985) [1986] 1 WLR 517, [1986] 1 All ER 564,
    [1986] BCLC 177, 1986 PCC 325, 1 BCC 99, 590, 136 NLJ 116, 83 LS Gaz 36,
    130 SJ 264   19.2.6
Bonelli's Telegraph Co., re, Collie's Claim (V-C 1871) LR 12 Eq 246, 40 LJ Ch 567, 25 LT 526,
    19 WR 1022   15.5.1, 19.5.4.1
Bonham v Bishop; see Bishop v Bonham
Bonsor v Musicians' Union (CA 1954) [1954] Ch 479, [1954] 2 WLR 687, [1954] 1 All ER 822;
    reversed by HL (1955) [1956] AC 104, [1955] 3 WLR 788, [1955] 3 All ER 518   3.4.3, 5.3.1
Bonus Breaks Ltd, re (ChD 1991) [1991] BCC 546   2.3.3.8
Borden (UK) Ltd v Scottish Timber Products Ltd (CA 1979) [1981] Ch 25, [1979] 3 WLR 672,
    [1980] 1 Lloyd's Rep 160   11.7.10.3
Borland's trustee v Steel Brothers & Co. Ltd (ChD 1900) [1901] 1 Ch 279, 70 LJ Ch 51,
    17 TLR 45, 47 WR 120   3.4.2.1, 6.1.9
Boschoek Proprietary Co. Ltd v Fuke (ChD 1905) [1906] 1 Ch 148, 75 LJ Ch 261, 94 LT 398,
    54 WR 359, 22 TLR 196, 13 Mans 100, 50 SJ 170   3.5.1, 18.5
Boswell & Co. (Steels) Ltd, re (ChD 1988) 5 BCC 145   18.6.6, 18.7
Bottomley v Brougham (KBD 1908) [1908] 1 KB 584, 77 LJ KB 311, 99 LT 111, 24 TLR 262,
    52 SJ 225   20.9.5
Bottomley's case; see Re Alma Spinning Co.

Boulting v Association of Cinematograph, Television & Allied Technicians (CA 1963)
[1963] 2 QB 606, [1963] 2 WLR 529, [1963] 1 All ER 716, 107 SJ 133   16.4.16, 16.8
Bovey Hotel Ventures Ltd, re (ChD 1981) 31 July 1981 unreported   18.6.3
Bower v Marris (LC 1841) Cr & Ph 351, 41 ER 525, 10 LJ Ch 356   20.13.2
Bowling and Welby's Contract, re (CA 1895) [1895] 1 Ch 663, 64 LJ Ch 427, 72 LT 411,
2 Mans 257, 12 R 218, 43 WR 417, [1895–9] All ER Rep 920, 39 SJ 345   8.5
Bowman v Secular Society Ltd (HL 1917) [1917] AC 406, 86 LJ Ch 568, 117 LT 161,
33 TLR 376, [1916–17] All ER Rep 1, 61 SJ 478   1.2.1, 2.3.5.1
Bradford Banking Co. Ltd v Henry Briggs, Son & Co. Ltd (HL 1886) 12 App Cas 29,
56 LJ Ch 364, 56 LT 62, 35 WR 521, 3 TLR 170   3.4.1.2
Bradford Investments plc, re (ChD 1990) [1991] BCLC 224, [1990] BCC 740   14.4.7, 14.4.9.1.1
Bradford Investments plc, re (No. 2) (ChD 1991) [1991] BCLC 688,
[1991] BCC 379   0.3.1.3, 6.5.6
Brady v Brady (HL 1988) [1989] AC 755, [1988] 2 WLR 1308, [1988] 2 All ER 617,
[1988] BCLC 579, 1988 PCC 316, 4 BCC 390   0.2.2.1, 10.8.4, 10.8.5
Brant Investments Ltd v KeepRite Inc. (Ontario CA 1991) 80 DLR (4th) 161, 3 OR (3d) 289
                                                                   14.4.9.4, 16.3.1, 16.4.3
Bratton Seymour Service Co. Ltd v Oxborough (CA 1992) [1992] BCLC 693, [1992] BCC 471
                                                                           3.4.1.1, 3.4.1.3
Bray v Ford (HL 1895) [1896] AC 44, 65 LJ QB 213, 73 LT 609, 12 TLR 119,
[1895–9] All ER Rep 1009   16.5.1, 16.5.2, 16.5.5.5
Bray v Smith (ChD 1908) 124 LT Jo 293   15.5.5
Brazilian Rubber Plantations and Estates Ltd, re (ChD 1910) [1911] 1 Ch 425, 80 LJ Ch 221,
103 LT 697, 27 TLR 109, 18 Mans 177   16.2.1.2, 16.2.1.3, 16.9.1
Breay v Browne (QBDC 1897) 41 SJ 159   18.4.12
Breay v Royal British Nurses' Association (CA 1897) [1897] 2 Ch 272, 66 LJ Ch 587,
76 LT 735, 13 TLR 467, 46 WR 86   2.3.5.6
Breckland Group Holdings Ltd v London & Suffolk Properties Ltd (ChD 1988)
[1989] BCLC 100, 1989 PCC 328, 4 BCC 542   15.7.2.4, 15.7.3, 18.4.1
Brenfield Squash Racquets Club Ltd, re (ChD 1995) [1996] 2 BCLC 184   18.6.6
Brereton v Nicholls (ChD 1992) [1993] BCLC 593, [1992] BCC 538 (sub nom.
Re SEIL Trade Finance Ltd)   20.3.7.4
Brian Sheridan Cars Ltd, re (ChD 1995) [1996] 1 BCLC 327, [1995] BCC 1035   15.2.5.7
Briess v Woolley (HL 1954) [1954] AC 333, [1954] 2 WLR 832, [1954] 1 All ER 909, 98 SJ 286   15.9
Briggs, ex parte; see Re Hop & Malt Exchange & Warehouse Co.
Brightlife Ltd, re (ChD 1996) [1987] Ch 200, [1987] 2 WLR 197, [1986] 3 All ER 673,
[1986] BCLC 418, 1986 PCC 435, 2 BCC 99, 359   11.6.2, 11.6.4, 11.7.10.2
Brinks Ltd v Abu-Saleh (No. 3) (ChD 1995) *The Times*, 23 October 1995   18.2.2
Bristol Joint Stock Bank, re (ChD 1890) 44 ChD 703, 59 LJ Ch 722, 62 LT 745, 2 Meg 150,
38 WR 574   2.3.5.4
British Airways Board v Parish (CA 1979) [1979] 2 Lloyd's Rep 361, 123 SJ 319   4.5.1
British America Corporation Ltd, re (ChD 1903) 19 TLR 662   16.6.5
British America Nickel Corporation Ltd v M.J. O'Brien Ltd (PC 1927)
[1927] AC 369, 96 LJ PC 57, 136 LT 615, 43 TLR 195, [1927] 1 DLR 1121,
[1927] 1 WWR 869   14.4.9.4
British & American Trustee & Finance Corporation Ltd and reduced v Couper (HL 1894)
[1894] AC 399, 63 LJ Ch 424, 70 LT 882, [1891–4] All ER Rep 667, 10 TLR 415, Mans 256,
6 R 146, 42 WR   6.1.3, 10.2.1, 10.2.2
British & Commonwealth Holdings plc, re (No. 1) (CA 1991) [1992] Ch 342, [1992] 2 WLR 931,
[1992] 2 All ER 801, [1992] BCLC 641, [1992] BCC 165   20.9.3
British and Commonwealth Holdings plc v Barclays Bank plc (CA 1995) [1996] 1 WLR 1,
[1996] 1 All ER 381, [1996] 1 BCLC 1, [1995] BCC 1,059 (sub nom. Barclays Bank plc v
British and Commonwealth Holdings plc)   10.8.4
British & Commonwealth Holdings plc v Spicer & Oppenheim (HL 1992) [1993] AC 426,
[1992] 3 WLR 853, [1992] 4 All ER 876, [1993] BCLC 168, [1992] BCC 977   20.9.3
British Asbestos Co. Ltd v Boyd (ChD 1903) [1903] 2 Ch 439, 73 LJ Ch 31, 88 LT 763,
[1900–3] All ER Rep 323, 11 Mans 88, 51 WR 667   15.2.6
British Bank of the Middle East v Sun Life Assurance Co. of Canada (UK) Ltd (HL 1983)
[1983] BCLC 78, [1983] 2 Lloyd's Rep 9, [1983] ComLR 187, 133 NLJ 575   19.5.4.2

British Diabetic Association v Diabetic Society Ltd (ChD 1995) [1995] 4 All ER 812,
  [1996] FSR 1   2.3.3.6
British Empire Match Co. Ltd, re (ChD 1888) 59 LT 291   15.1.3, 15.2.1, 15.2.2, 15.5.1
British Equitable Assurance Co. Ltd v Baily; see Baily v British Equitable Assurance Co.
British Murac Syndicate Ltd v Alperton Rubber Co. Ltd (ChD 1915) [1915] 2 Ch 186,
  84 LJ Ch 665, 113 LT 373, 31 TLR 391, 59 SJ 494   3.5.3.4
British Racing Drivers' Club Ltd v Hextall Erskine and Co. (ChD 1996)
  [1996] 3 All ER 667, [1997] 1 BCLC 182, [1996] BCC 727   0.3.1.3, 16.6.7
British Seamless Paper Box Co., re (CA 1887) 17 ChD 467, 50 LJ Ch 497, 44 LT 498,
  29 WR 690   17.6.3.2
British Thomson-Houston Co. Ltd v Federated European Bank Ltd (CA 1932) [1932] 2 KB 176,
  101 LJ KB 690, 147 LT 345, [1932] All ER Rep 675   19.5.4.6
British Thomson-Houston Co. Ltd v Sterling Accessories Ltd (ChD 1924) [1924] 2 Ch 33,
  41 RPC 311, 93 LJ Ch 335, 131 LT 535, 40 TLR 544, 68 SJ 595   5.2.2.3
Britoil plc, re (CA 1989) [1990] BCC 70   8.8.2.3
Broadcasting Station 2GB Pty Ltd, re (SC of New South Wales 1964) [1964–5] NSWR 1648
    15.2.3.2, 16.4.15
Broderip v Salomon; see Salomon v A. Salomon & Co. Ltd
Broderip v A. Salomon & Co. Ltd; see Salomon v A. Salomon & Co. Ltd
Brook Martin & Co. (Nominees) Ltd, re (ChD 1992) [1993] BCLC 328   20.9.3
Brooke Marine Ltd, re (ChD 1987) [1988] BCLC 546   20.6.1
Brooks Transport (Purfleet) Ltd, re (ChD 1993) [1993] BCC 766   15.2.5.6
Broomhead (J.W.) (Vic) Pty Ltd v Broomhead (J.W.) Pty Ltd (Victoria SC 1985) [1985] VR 891,
  9 ACLR 593, 3 ACLC 355   19.2.2
Broughton v Broughton (LC 1855) 5 De G M & G 159, 43 ER 831, 25 LJ Ch 250, 1 Jur NS 965,
  3 WR 602   16.5.2
Brown v British Abrasive Wheel Co. Ltd (ChD 1919) [1919] 1 Ch 290, 88 LJ Ch 143,
  120 LT 529, [1918–19] All ER Rep 308, 35 TLR 268, 63 SJ 373   3.5.3.5
Brown v Cole (V-C 1845) 14 Sim 427, 60 ER 424, 14 LJ Ch 167, 9 Jur 290   11.2.2
Brown v Director of Public Prosecutions (QBDC 1998) 162 JP 333   19.8.4
Browne v La Trinidad (CA 1887) 37 ChD 1, 57 LJ Ch 292, 58 LT 137, 4 TLR 14, 36 WR 289
    3.4.2.3, 3.4.3, 14.4.5.1, 18.5, 19.6.2
Browne v Panga Pty Ltd (Western Australia SC 1995) 120 FLR 34, 14 WAR 393,
  17 ACSR 75   15.3.3, 15.3.7
Brush Aggregates Ltd, re (ChD 1983) [1983] BCLC 320, 1 BCC 98, 904   11.7.10.2
BSB Holdings Ltd, re, (No. 2) (ChD 1995) [1996] 1 BCLC 155   16.4.3, 16.4.9
BTR plc, re (ChD 1987) 4 BCC 45   6.2.10
Buchan v Secretary of State for Employment (EAT 1996) [1997] IRLR 80   15.6.1.5
Buck v Robson (V-C 1870) LR 10 Eq 629, 39 LJ Ch 821, 23 LT 391   3.4.1.2
Bugle Press Ltd, re (application of H. C. Treby) (CA 1960) [1961] Ch 270, [1960] 3 WLR 956,
  [1960] 3 All ER 791, 104 SJ 1057   5.2.2.7, 8.8.2.3
Bulawayo Market & Offices Co. Ltd, re (ChD 1907) [1907] 2 Ch 458, 76 LJ Ch 673, 97 LT 752,
  23 TLR 714, 14 Mans 312, [1904–7] All ER Rep 759   15.1.3
Bulkeley v Schutz (PC 1871) LR 3 PC 764, 8 Moore PCC NS 170, 17 ER 276   1.2.1, 1.6
Bumper Development Corporation v Commissioner of Police of the Metropolis (CA 1991)
  [1991] 1 WLR 1362, [1991] 4 All ER 638   0.1.6, 0.1.7
Burgess's case; see Re Hull & County Bank
Burgoine v London Borough of Waltham Forest (ChD 1996) [1997] 2 BCLC 612,
  [1997] BCC 347   16.9.1
Burkinshaw v Nicolls (HL 1878) 3 App Cas 1004, 48 LJ Ch 179, 39 LT 308, 26 WR 819   8.2.2
Burland v Earle (PC 1901) [1902] AC 83, 71 LJ PC 1, 85 LT 553, 9 Mans 17, 18 TLR 41,
  50 WR 241   2.3.5.6, 10.5.1, 16.6.7, 18.3.1, 18.3.2, 18.4.4, 18.5
Burn v London & South Wales Coal Co. (ChD 1890) 7 TLR 118, [1890] WN 209   9.2.4
Burnet v Francis Industries plc (CA 1987) [1987] 1 WLR 802, [1987] 2 All ER 323,
  84 LS Gaz 2194   5.2.2.7
Burnham Marketing Services Ltd, re (County Court 1992) [1993] BCC 518   15.2.5.6
Burrows v Becker (Canada SC 1968) 70 DLR (2d) 433, [1969] SCR 162   18.4.2
Bushell v Faith (HL 1969) [1970] AC 1099, [1970] 2 WLR 272, [1970] 1 All ER 53, 114 SJ 54;
  affirming CA (1969) [1969] 2 Ch 438, [1969] 2 WLR 1067, [1969] 1 All ER 1002, 113 SJ 262
    3.5.3.3, 14.4.8.2, 14.4.9.8, 15.3.3

Business Computers Ltd v Anglo-African Leasing Ltd (ChD 1977) [1977] 1 WLR 578,
[1977] 2 All ER 741, 121 SJ 201 — 20.2.8.2
Byng v London Life Association Ltd (CA 1988) [1990] Ch 170, [1989] 2 WLR 738,
[1989] 1 All ER 560, [1989] BCLC 400 — 14.4.1, 14.4.10

Caddies v Harold Holdsworth & Co. (Wakefield) Ltd; see Harold Holdsworth & Co. (Wakefield)
Ltd v Caddies
Cade (J.E.) & Son Ltd, re (ChD 1991) [1992] BCLC 213, [1991] BCC 360 — 18.6.2, 18.6.3, 18.6.6
Cairney v Back (KBD 1906) [1906] 2 KB 746, 75 LJ KB 1014, 96 LJ 111, 22 TLR 776,
14 Mans 58, 50 SJ 697 — 19.8.3
Calmex Ltd, re (ChD 1988) [1989] 1 All ER 485, [1989] BCLC 299, 1989 PCC 233,
4 BCC 761 — 4.2.2
Cambrian Peat, Fuel, & Charcoal Co. Ltd, re, De La Mott's and Turner's Case (1875) 31 LT 773,
23 WR 405 — 14.4.1, 14.4.6.1
Cameron v Glenmorangie Distillery Co. Ltd (C Sess OH 1896 affirmed by 1st Div 1896)
23 R 1092, 33 SLR 781, 4 SLT 93 — 2.3.5.6
Cameron's Coalbrook Steam Coal, & Swansea & Lougher Railway Co., re, Bennett's Case
(LJJ 1854) 5 De G M & G 284, 43 ER 879, 18 Beav 339, 52 ER 134, 24 LJ Ch 130 — 16.4.10
Campbell v Australian Mutual Provident Society (PC 1908) 77 LJ PC 117, 99 LT 3,
24 TLR 623, 15 Mans 344 — 14.4.5.5
Campbell v Kitchen & Sons Ltd (High Court of Australia 1910) 12 CLR 513; affirmed
(1910) 12 CLR 515 at 517 — 18.4.13
Campbell Coverings Ltd, re (No. 2) (ChD 1954) [1954] Ch 225, [1954] 2 WLR 204,
[1954] 1 All ER 222, 98 SJ 93 — 20.9.8
Canada Enterprises Corporation Ltd v MacNab Distilleries Ltd (CA 1976) [1987] 1 WLR 813,
[1981] Com LR 167 — 5.2.2.7
Canada National Fire Insurance Co. v Hutchings (PC (Manitoba CA) 1918) [1918] AC 451,
39 DLR 401, 87 LJ PC 106, 118 LT 484, 34 TLR 225 — 0.1.7
Canada Safeway Ltd v Thompson (SC of British Columbia 1950) [1951] 3 DLR 295 — 16.6.7, 16.7.2
Canadian Aero Service Ltd v O'Malley et al. (SC of Canada 1973) 40 DLR (3d) 371, [1974]
SCR 592, 11 CPR (2d) 206 — 16.3.1, 16.7.3.1, 16.7.3.2, 16.7.3.3, 16.7.3.5, 17.2
Canadian Dredge & Dock Co. Ltd v R (Canada SC 1985) [1985] 1 SCR 662, 19 DLR (4th) 314,
19 CCC (3d) 1, 45 CR (3d) 289, 59 NR 241 (sub nom. R v Canadian Dredge & Dock Co. Ltd),
9 OAC 321 (sub nom. R v Canadian Dredge & Dock Co. Ltd) — 19.8.6
Cane v Jones (ChD 1979) [1980] 1 WLR 1451, [1981] 1 All ER 533, 124 SJ 542 — 3.5.1
Cannon, ex parte; see Re Leicester Club & County Racecourse Co.
Cannonquest Ltd, re; see Official Receiver v Hannan
Caparo Industries plc v Dickman (HL 1990) [1990] 2 AC 605, [1990] 2 WLR 358,
[1990] 1 All ER 568, [1990] BCLC 273, [1990] BCC 164,
1 ACSR 636 — 8.10, 9.1, 9.3.1, 9.3.4, 17.4.5
Cape Breton Co., re; see Bentinck v Fenn
Caratti Holding Co. Pty Ltd v Zampatti (PC 1978) 52 ALJR 732, 23 ALR 655, 3 ACLR 950;
affirming FC of SC of Western Australia (1976) 2 ACLR 152; affirming SC (1975)
1 ACLR 87 (sub nom. Re Caratti Holding Co. Pty Ltd) — 1.3.5, 3.4.1.3, 3.4.2.2, 3.4.3, 18.6.4
Carecraft Construction Co. Ltd, re (ChD 1993) [1994] 1 WLR 172, [1993] 4 All ER 499,
[1993] BCLC 1259, [1993] BCC 336 — 15.2.5.6
Cargo Agency Ltd, re (ChD 1992) [1992] BCLC 686, [1992] BCC 388 — 15.2.5.6, 15.2.5.7
Caribbean Co., re, Crickmer's Case; see Re Carribean Co. Ltd, Crickmer's Case
Carl Zeiss Stiftung v Rayner & Keeler Ltd (No. 3) (ChD 1969) [1970] Ch 506,
[1969] 3 WLR 991, [1969] 3 All ER 897 — 2.4.3
Carlen v Drury (LC 1812) 1 Ves & B 154, 35 ER 61 — 18.3.3.1
Carlton v Halestrap (ChD 1988) 4 BCC 538 — 16.5.5.4, 16.7.3.1
Carney v Herbert (PC 1984) [1985] AC 301, [1984] 3 WLR 1303, [1985] 1 All ER 438,
[1985] BCLC 140, 128 SJ 874, 59 ALJR 41, 57 ALR 691, [1984] 3 NSWLR 85, 9 ACLR 213,
2 ACLC 798 — 10.8.5
Carribean Co. Ltd, re, Crickmer's Case (V-C 1875) 44 LJ Ch 595; affirmed by LJJ (1875)
46 LJ Ch 870, LR 10 Ch App 614 (sub nom. Re Caribbean Co., Crickmer's Case),
24 WR 219 — 3.4.2.4
Carrington Viyella plc, re (ChD 1983) 1 BCC 98, 951 — 18.6.2, 18.6.3

Carruth v Imperial Chemical Industries Ltd (HL 1937) [1937] AC 707, [1937] 2 All ER 422,
   156 LT 499, 53 TLR 524, 106 LJ Ch 129   14.4.9.3
Case v Edmonton Country Club Ltd; see Edmonton Country Club Ltd v Case
Castiglione, Erskine & Co. Ltd, re (ChD 1958) [1958] 1 WLR 688, [1958] 2 All ER 455,
   102 SJ 454   10.2.5
Castle New Homes Ltd, re (ChD 1978) [1979] 1 WLR 1075, [1979] 2 All ER 775,
   123 SJ 569   20.9.3
Catesby v Burnett (ChD 1916) [1916] 2 Ch 325, 85 LJ Ch 745, 114 LT 1022,
   32 TLR 380   15.3.7, 18.4.9
Catley v Herbert (New Zealand CA 1984) [1988] 1 NZLR 606   10.8.4
Cawley & Co., re (CA 1889) 42 ChD 209, 58 LJ Ch 633, 61 LT 601, 5 TLR 549,
   1 Meg 251, 37 WR 692   8.3.4
Cayne v Global Natural Resources plc (ChD 12 August 1982) unreported; affirmed by CA (1982)
   [1984] 1 All ER 225   16.4.10, 16.4.12
CCG International Enterprises Ltd, re (ChD 1993) [1993] BCLC 1428, [1993] BCC 580   11.6.4
Cedar Developments Ltd, re (ChD 1994) [1994] 2 BCLC 714, [1995] BCC 220   15.2.5.4
Centrafarm BV v Sterling Drug Inc. (case 15/74) (ECJ 1974) [1974] ECR 1147,
   [1974] 2 CMLR 480   5.2.2.9
Chaff & Hay Acquisition Committee v J.A. Hemphill & Sons Pty Ltd (Australia HC 1947)
   64 CLR 375, [1947] ALR 330, 21 ALJ 158   0.1.6
Chan v Zacharia (HC of Australia 1984) 154 CLR 178, 58 ALJR 353, 53 ALR 417
       16.5.2, 16.5.3, 16.5.5.2, 16.5.5.3
Channel Collieries Trust Ltd v Dover, St Margaret's & Martin Mill Light Railway Co.
   (CA 1914) [1914] 2 Ch 506, 84 LJ Ch 28, 111 LT 1051, 30 TLR 647, 21 Mans 328,
   [1914–15] All ER Rep 265   15.2.3.3, 15.2.6
Chaplin v Young (No. 1) (MR 1864) 33 Beav 330, 55 ER 395, 11 LT 10, 3 New Rep 449   11.5.3
Chapman v Smethurst (CA 1909) [1909] 1 KB 927, 78 LJ KB 654, 100 LT 465, 25 TLR 383,
   14 Com Cas 94, 16 Mans 171, 53 SJ 340   19.2.1, 19.2.6
Chapman's case; see Re General Rolling Stock Co.
Charge Card Services Ltd, re (ChD 1986) [1987] Ch 150, [1986] 3 WLR 697,
   [1986] 3 All ER 289, [1987] BCLC 17, 1987 PCC 36, 2 BCC 99,373 (sub nom.
   Re Charge Card Services Ltd (No. 2)), 1987 FLR 1; affirmed by CA (1988) [1989] Ch 497,
   [1988] 3 WLR 764, [1988] BCLC 711, 1988 PCC 390, 4 BCC 524   11.4.2, 11.7.10.1
Charles Atkins & Co. Ltd, re (South Australia SC 1929) [1929] SASR 129   16.6.3
Charles (L.H.) & Co. Ltd, re (ChD 1934) [1935] WN 15   11.7.9
Charles P. Kinnell & Co. Ltd v Harding, Wace & Co. (CA 1918) [1918] 1 KB 405, 87 LJ KB 342,
   118 LT 429, 34 TLR 217, 62 SJ 267   19.9
Charter Oil Co. Ltd v Beaumont (CA of British Columbia 1967) 65 DLR (2d) 112,
   62 WWR 617   15.7.2.4
Charterbridge Corporation Ltd v Lloyds Bank Ltd (ChD 1968) [1970] Ch 62, [1969] 3 WLR 122,
   [1969] 2 All ER 1185, [1969] 2 Lloyd's Rep 24, 113 SJ 465   16.4.3
Charterhouse Investment Trust Ltd v Tempest Diesels Ltd (ChD 1985) [1986] BCLC 1,
   1 BCC 99,544, 1985 PCC 466   10.8.4, 15.5.1
Chartmore Ltd, re (ChD 1989) [1990] BCLC 673   15.2.5.6, 15.2.5.7
Chase Manhattan Asia Ltd v Official Receiver & Liquidator of First Bangkok City
   Finance Ltd (PC 1990) [1990] 1 WLR 1181, [1990] BCC 514, [1990] 2 HKLR 215   11.7.10.2
Chase Manhattan Equities Ltd v Goodman (ChD 1990) [1991] BCLC 897, [1991] BCC 308   13.4.6
Cheah Theam Swee v Equiticorp Finance Group Ltd (PC 1991) [1992] 1 AC 472,
   [1992] 2 WLR 108, [1991] 4 All ER 989, [1992] BCLC 371, [1992] BCC 98,
   [1992] 1 NZLR 641   11.4.3
Chesterfield Catering Co. Ltd, re (ChD 1975) [1977] Ch 373, [1976] 3 WLR 879,
   [1976] 3 All ER 294, 120 SJ 817   8.8
Chez Nico (Restaurants) Ltd, re (ChD 1991) [1992] BCLC 192, [1991] BCC 736
       0.3.1.3, 7.7, 8.8.1, 8.8.2.1, 8.8.2.2, 8.8.2.3, 13.5
Chida Mines Ltd v Anderson (KBD 1905) 22 TLR 27   8.3.4
China Steam Ship Co., re, Dawes's Case (MR 1868) LR 6 Eq 232, 37 LJ Ch 901, 16 WR 995   6.4.2
China Steamship & Labuan Coal Co., re, Drummond's Case (LJJ 1869) LR 4 Ch App 772,
   21 LT 317, 18 WR 2   6.5.1
Christensen v Scott (New Zealand CA 1995) [1996] 1 NZLR 273   18.4.6

Chuter v Freeth and Pocock Ltd (KBDC 1911) [1911] 2 KB 832, 80 LJ KB 1322, 105 LT 238,
    27 TLR 467, 9 LGR 1055, 75 JP 430, 22 Cox CC 573   19.8.4
Cimex Tissues Ltd, re (ChD 1994) [1994] BCC 626   11.6.4
Citizens' Life Assurance Co. Ltd v Brown (PC 1904) [1904] AC 423, 73 LJ PC 102,
    90 LT 739, 20 TLR 497, 53 WR 176, [1904–7] All ER Rep 925   19.7
City Equitable Fire Insurance Co. Ltd, re (ChD 1924) [1925] Ch 407, 94 LJ Ch 445,
    133 LT 520, 40 TLR 664, [1925] B & CR 109; (CA 1924) [1925] Ch 407 at 500,
    94 LJ Ch 445 at 486, 133 LT 520 at 548, 40 TLR 853, [1925] B & CR 109 at 194
                                              16.2.1.1, 16.2.1.2, 16.9.1
City Investment Centres Ltd, re (ChD 1991) [1992] BCLC 956   15.2.5.6
City Property Investment Trust Corporation Ltd (C Sess 1st Div 1951) 1951 SC 570,
    1951 SLT 371   2.4.7, 14.6.2.2
Civica Investments Ltd and others, re (ChD 1982) [1983] BCLC 456, 126 SJ 446,
    79 LS Gaz 919   15.2.5.5
Civil Service Cooperative Society Ltd v Chapman (KBD 1914) 30 TLR 679, [1914] WN 369   4.5.1
Cladrose Ltd, re (ChD 1989) [1990] BCLC 204, [1990] BCC 11   15.2.5.6
Clark v Urquhart (HL 1929) [1930] AC 28, 99 LJ PC 1, 141 LT 641   7.6.6
Clark v Workman (Ireland ChD 1919) [1920] 1 IR 107   15.5.2
Clayton's case; see Devaynes v Noble
Clemens v Clemens Bros Ltd (ChD 1976) [1976] 2 All ER 268   1.3.5, 14.4.9.5, 14.4.9.7
Cleveland Trust plc, re (ChD 1990) [1991] BCLC 424, [1991] BCC 33   10.4
Clifton v Mount Morgan Ltd (New South Wales CA 1940) 40 SR (NSW) 31, 57 WN (NSW) 35   15.3.7
Clough Mill Ltd v Martin (CA 1984) [1985] 1 WLR 111, [1984] 3 All ER 982, [1985] BCLC 64,
    128 SJ 850, 81 LS Gaz 2375   11.7.10.3
Cloverbay Ltd, re (No. 2); see Cloverbay Ltd v Bank of Credit & Commerce International SA
Cloverbay Ltd v Bank of Credit & Commerce International SA (CA 1990) [1991] Ch 90,
    [1990] 3 WLR 574, [1991] 1 All ER 894, [1991] BCLC 135, [1990] BCC 414 (sub nom.
    Re Cloverbay Ltd (No. 2))   20.9.3
Club Flotilla (Pacific Palms) Ltd v Isherwood (SC of New South Wales 1987) 12 ACLR 387,
    5 ACLC 1027   15.7.3, 19.5.10
Coachcraft Ltd v SVP Fruit Co. Ltd (PC 1980) 28 ALR 319, 4 ACLR 816, (1980) ACLC 29,924
                                              14.4.9.1.3, 14.4.9.1.6
Coachman Tavern (1985) Ltd, re (New Zealand HC 1988) [1988] 2 NZLR 635   15.7.2.4
Coal Economising Gas Co., re, Gover's Case (CA 1875) 1 ChD 182, 45 LJ Ch 83, 33 LT 619,
    24 WR 125   17.6.4
Coalport China Co., re (CA 1895) [1895] 2 Ch 404, 64 LJ Ch 710, 73 LT 46, 2 Mans 532,
    12 R 462, [1895–9] All ER Rep Ext 2021   8.3.4
Cockburn v Newbridge Sanitary Steam Laundry Co. Ltd (Ireland CA 1914) [1915] 1 IR 237
                                      18.4.4, 18.4.10
Coleman v Myers (New Zealand CA 1977) [1977] 2 NZLR 225   13.5
Collie's Claim; see Re Bonelli's Telegraph Co., Collie's Claim
Collins v Associated Greyhound Racecourses Ltd (CA 1929 affirming ChD 1929)
    [1930] 1 Ch 1, 99 LJ Ch 52   6.7.2
Collins Bros Stationers Pty Ltd v Zebra Graphics Pty Ltd (New South Wales SC 1985)
    10 ACLR 267   19.9
Colman v Eastern Counties Railway Co. (MR 1846) 10 Beav 1, 50 ER 481, 16 LJ Ch 73,
    11 Jur 74   2.3.5.2
Colonial Bank v Whinney (HL 1886) 11 App Cas 426, 56 LJ Ch 43, 55 LT 362,
    [1886–90] All ER Rep 468, 2 TLR 747, 3 Morr 207, 34 WR 705   6.1.9
Commercial Management Ltd v Registrar of Companies (New Zealand CA 1987) [1987]
    1 NZLR 744, 3 NZCLC 100,221   15.1.3
Commissioner for Corporate Affairs v Bracht (Victoria SC 1988) [1989] VR 821,
    14 ACLR 728   15.2.5.2
Commissioner of Police of the Metropolis v Caldwell (HL 1981) [1982] AC 341,
    [1981] 2 WLR 509, [1981] 1 All ER 961, 73 Cr App R 13   6.7.6, 7.8.2
Commissioners of Customs & Excise v Hedon Alpha Ltd (CA 1981) [1981] QB 818,
    [1981] 2 WLR 791, [1981] 2 All ER 697, 125 SJ 273   16.9.2
Commissioners of Inland Revenue v Bew Estates Ltd (ChD 1956) [1956] Ch 407,
    [1956] 3 WLR 139, [1956] 2 All ER 210   0.1.6

Commissioners of Inland Revenue v Crossman (HL 1936) [1937] AC 26, [1936] 1 All ER 762,
  105 LJ KB 450, 154 LT 570, 52 TLR 415, 80 SJ 485   6.1.9
Commissioners of Inland Revenue v Ufitec Group Ltd (QBD 1977) [1977] 3 All ER 924,
  [1977] STC 363   19.5.4.2
Compaction Systems Pty Ltd, re (New South Wales SC 1976) [1976] 2 NSWLR 477,
  2 ACLR 135, (1977) ACLC 29, 305   14.4.5.2, 14.4.5.4, 14.5.1
Compagnie de Mayville, La, v Whitley (CA 1896) [1896] 1 Ch 788, 65 LJ Ch 729, 74 LT 441,
  12 TLR 268, 44 WR 568, 40 SJ 352   15.5.1
Compañía de Electricidad de la Provincia de Buenos Aires Ltd, re (ChD 1978) [1980] Ch 146,
  [1979] 2 WLR 316, [1978] 3 All ER 668, 122 SJ 145   3.4.2.9, 14.2, 20.13.1
Company, re a (No. 00996 of 1979) (CA 1979) [1980] Ch 138, [1980] 2 WLR 241,
  [1980] 1 All ER 284, [1979] Crim LR 650, 123 SJ 584; reversed by HL (1980) sub nom.
  Re Racal Communications Ltd [1981] AC 374, [1980] 3 WLR 181, [1980] 2 All ER 634   17.2
Company, re a (No. 002567 of 1982) (ChD 1983) [1983] 1 WLR 927, [1983] 2 All ER 854,
  [1983] BCLC 151, 1 BCC 98,930, 127 SJ 508, 80 LS Gaz 2133   18.7
Company, re a (No. 004475 of 1982) (ChD 1982) [1983] Ch 178, [1983] 2 WLR 381,
  [1983] 2 All ER 36, [1983] BCLC 126, 127 SJ 153   18.6.2, 18.6.5
Company, re a (ChD 1984) [1985] BCLC 37   20.6.3
Company, re a (No. 002612 of 1984); see Re Cumana Ltd
Company, re a (No. 007623 of 1984) (ChD 1986) [1986] BCLC 362, 2 BCC 99,191   18.6.5
Company, re a (CA 1985) [1985] BCLC 333, 1 BCC 99,421, 82 LS Gaz 2016 (sub nom.
  X Bank Ltd v G)   5.2.2.4, 5.2.2.11
Company, re a (No. 005287 of 1985) (ChD 1985) [1986] 1 WLR 281, [1986] 2 All ER 253,
  [1986] BCLC 68, 1986 PCC 290 (sub nom. Re FM Ltd), 1 BCC 99,586   18.4.2, 18.6.4
Company, re a (No. 007828 of 1985) (ChD 1985) 2 BCC 98,951   18.6.1
Company, re a (No. 008699 of 1985) (ChD 1986) [1986] BCLC 382, 1986 PCC 296,
  2 BCC 99,024   16.4.12, 18.6.4
Company, re a (No. 00477 of 1986) (ChD 1986) [1986] BCLC 376, 1986 PCC 372, 2 BCC 99,171
         1.3.5, 18.6.3, 18.6.5
Company, re a (No. 001761 of 1986) (ChD 1986) [1987] BCLC 141   18.6.4
Company, re a (No. 003160 of 1986) (ChD 1986) [1986] BCLC 391, 2 BCC 99,276,
  1987 PCC 104 (sub nom. Re Mossmain Ltd)   18.6.1
Company, re a (No. 003843 of 1986) (ChD 1987) [1987] BCLC 562, 3 BCC 624   18.6.6, 18.7
Company, re a (No. 004377 of 1986) (ChD 1986) [1987] 1 WLR 102, [1987] BCLC 94,
  1987 PCC 92 (sub nom. Re XYZ Ltd), 2 BCC 99,520 (sub nom. Re XYZ Ltd)
         18.6.3, 18.6.5, 18.6.6
Company, re a (No. 005136 of 1986) (ChD 1986) [1987] BCLC 82, 2 BCC 99,528 (sub nom.
  Re Sherborne Park Residents Co. Ltd)   16.4.12, 18.4.2.3, 18.4.12
Company, re a (No. 00370 of 1987) (ChD 1988) [1988] 1 WLR 1068, [1988] BCLC 570,
  1988 PCC 351, 4 BCC 506   16.4.2, 18.6.2, 18.7.4
Company, re a (No. 00789 of 1987) (ChD 1989) [1990] BCLC 384, 5 BCC 792   18.6.6
Company, re a (No. 003096 of 1987) (ChD 1987) 4 BCC 80   18.6.5, 18.7
Company, re a (No. 003318 of 1987); see Re Oriental Credit Ltd
Company, re a (No. 005009 of 1987) (ChD 1988) [1989] BCLC 13, 4 BCC 424; further
  proceedings (sub nom. Re MC Bacon Ltd) (ChD 1989) [1990] BCLC 372, [1990] BCC 78
         11.6.4, 15.1.6
Company, re a (No. 001363 of 1988) (ChD 1988) [1989] BCLC 579, 5 BCC 18   18.7
Company, re a (No. 001418 of 1988) (ChD 1990) [1991] BCLC 197,
  [1990] BCC 526   20.10.2, 20.10.4
Company, re a (No. 002470 of 1988); see Nicholas v Soundcraft Electronics Ltd
Company, re a (No. 004502 of 1988) (ChD 1991) [1992] BCLC 701, [1991] BCC 234   18.6.6
Company, re a (No. 006834 of 1988) (ChD 1988) [1989] BCLC 365, 5 BCC 218   18.6.5, 18.6.6
Company, re a (No. 00314 of 1989) (ChD 1989) [1991] BCLC 154, [1990] BCC 221   18.6.1
Company, re a (No. 008126 of 1989); see Re Hailey Group Ltd
Company, re a (No. 001029 of 1990) (ChD 1991) [1991] BCLC 567   19.9
Company, re a (No. 008790 of 1990) (ChD 1990) [1991] BCLC 561, [1992] BCC 11   20.6.3
Company, re a (No. 00330 of 1991) (ChD 1991) [1991] BCLC 597,
  [1991] BCC 241   18.6.1, 18.6.6
Company, re a (No. 0032314 of 1992); see Duckwari plc v Offerventure Ltd

Company, re a, ex parte Burr (ChD 1992) [1992] BCLC 724   9.7.3
Company, re a (No. 003061 of 1993) (ChD 1993) [1994] BCC 883   18.6.6
Company, re a (No. 007816 of 1994) (ChD 1995) [1995] 2 BCLC 539   18.8.3.3
Company, re a (No. 007923 of 1994) (No. 2) (ChD 1995) [1995] 1 BCLC 594,
   [1995] BCC 641   18.8.3.3
Company, re a (No. 00836 of 1995) (ChD 1996) [1996] 2 BCLC 192,
   [1996] BCC 432   18.6.1, 18.6.6
Company, re a (No. 004415 of 1996) (ChD 1997) [1997] 1 BCLC 479   18.6.4
Compaq Computer Ltd v Abercorn Group Ltd (ChD 1991) [1993] BCLC 602,
   [1991] BCC 484   11.7.10.3
Concord Petroleum Corporation v Gosford Marine Panama SA; see The Albazero
Conservative & Unionist Central Office v Burrell (CA 1981) [1982] 1 WLR 522,
   [1982] 2 All ER 1, 55 TC 671, [1982] STC 317, [1981] TR 543   3.4.1.1
Consolidated Goldfields of New Zealand Ltd, re (ChD 1953) [1953] Ch 689, [1953] 2 WLR 584,
   [1953] 1 All ER 791, 97 SJ 190   20.13.1
Consolidated Nickel Mines Ltd, re (ChD 1914) [1914] 1 Ch 883, 83 LJ Ch 760, 111 LT 243,
   30 TLR 447, 21 Mans 273, 58 SJ 556   15.2.6, 15.3.2, 15.7.3
Constitution Insurance Co. of Canada v Kosmopoulos (SC of Canada 1987) 34 DLR (4th) 208,
   [1987] ILR 1–2147 (sub nom. Kosmopoulos v Constitution Insurance Co. of Canada),
   74 NR 360 (sub nom. Kosmopoulos v Constitution Insurance Co. of Canada),
   [1980–84] LRC (Comm) 784   5.2.1
Consul Development Pty Ltd v DPC Estates Pty Ltd (HC of Australia 1975) 132 CLR 373,
   49 ALJR 74, 5 ALR 231; see also DPC Estates Pty Ltd v Grey   16.7.2, 16.7.3.3, 16.7.3.4
Consumer & Industrial Press Ltd, re (No. 2) (ChD 1987) 4 BCC 72   20.3.3
Conway v Petronius Clothing Co. Ltd (ChD 1977) [1978] 1 WLR 72, [1978] 1 All ER 185   9.2.4
Cook v Deeks (PC 1916) [1916] 1 AC 554, 85 LJ PC 161, 114 LT 636, 27 DLR 1,
   [1916–17] All ER Rep 285   16.6.7, 16.7.2, 16.7.3.1, 16.7.3.2, 16.7.3.4, 16.8, 18.4.4
Coolgardie Consolidated Gold Mines Ltd, re (CA 1897) 76 LT 269, 13 TLR 301, 41 SJ 365   2.3.5.8
Cooper v Gordon (V-C 1869) LR 8 Eq 249, 38 LJ Ch 489, 20 LT 732, 33 JP 761, 17 WR 908   18.3.3.2
Coöperatieve Rabobank 'Vecht en Plassengebied' BA v Minderhoud (case C-104/96)
   (CJEC 1997) [1998] 1 WLR 1025, [1998] 2 CMLR 270   19.5.5
Copal Varnish Co. Ltd, re (ChD 1917) [1917] 2 Ch 349, 87 LJ Ch 132, 117 LT 508   8.3.4
Cope v Butcher (Western Australia SC 1996) 20 ACSR 37   18.4.13
Copecrest Ltd, re; see Secretary of State for Trade & Industry v McTighe
Cornish Manures Ltd, re (ChD 1967) [1967] 1 WLR 807, [1967] 2 All ER 875   20.14.2.5
Cotman v Brougham (HL 1918) [1918] AC 514, 87 LJ Ch 379, 119 LT 162, 34 TLR 410, 62 SJ 534
   1.2.1, 2.3.5.1, 2.3.5.5, 2.3.5.6, 2.3.5.9, 15.8.2.2, 19.5.7
Cotronic (UK) Ltd v Dezonie (CA 1991) [1991] BCLC 721, [1991] BCC 200   2.3.3.1, 19.6.1
Cotter v National Union of Seamen (CA 1929) [1929] 2 Ch 58, 98 LJ Ch 323, 141 LT 178,
   [1929] All ER Rep 342, 45 TLR 352, 73 SJ 206   18.3.1, 18.4.8, 18.4.13
Country Farm Inns Ltd, re; see Secretary of State for Trade and Industry v Ivens
Country Traders Distributors Ltd, re (New South Wales SC 1974) [1974] 2 NSWLR 135   20.6.7
County Life Assurance Co., re (LJJ 1870) LR 5 Ch App 288, 39 LJ Ch 471, 22 LT 537,
   18 WR 390   19.5.4.2
County of Gloucester Bank v Rudry Merthyr Steam & House Coal Colliery Co. (CA 1895)
   [1895] 1 Ch 629, 64 LJ Ch 451, 72 LT 375, 2 Mans 223, 12 R 183, 43 WR 486, 39 SJ 331,
   [1895–9] All ER Rep 847   15.5.1, 19.5.4.1
Cousins v International Brick Co. Ltd (CA 1931) [1931] 2 Ch 90, 100 LJ Ch 404, 145 LT 471,
   47 TLR 217   14.4.9.1.3
Covacich v Riordan (New Zealand HC 1993) [1994] 2 NZLR 502   11.6.2
Cowan de Groot Properties Ltd v Eagle Trust plc (ChD 1991) [1992] 4 All ER 700,
   [1991] BCLC 1045   16.5.3, 16.6.2, 16.6.5, 18.2.2
Cox v Dublin City Distillery (No. 2) (Ireland CA 1915) [1915] 1 IR 345   16.6.3
Craig v Iona Hotels Ltd (Scotland Sheriff Court 1987) 1988 SCLR 130   20.6.3
Craven-Ellis v Canons Ltd (CA 1936) [1936] 2 KB 403, [1936] 2 All ER 1066, 105 LJ KB 767,
   155 LT 376, 52 TLR 657, 80 SJ 652   15.6.1.5, 17.2
Creasey v Breachwood Motors Ltd (QBD 1992) [1993] BCLC 480,
   [1992] BCC 638   5.2.2.11
Credit Development Pte Ltd v IMO Pte Ltd (Singapore HC 1993) [1993] 2 SLR 370   14.4.5.7, 15.7.24

Crestjoy Products Ltd, re (ChD 1989) [1990] BCLC 677, [1990] BCC 23   15.2.5.4
Cretanor Maritime Co. Ltd v Irish Marine Management Ltd (CA 1978) [1978] 1 WLR 966,
   [1978] 3 All ER 164, [1978] 1 Lloyd's Rep 425, 122 SJ 298   20.2.5, 20.2.8.1
Crickmer's case; see Re The Carribean Co. Ltd
Cristina v Seear (CA 1985) [1985] 2 EGLR 128   5.2.1, 19.8.1
Croftbell Ltd, re (ChD 1990) [1990] BCLC 844, [1990] BCC 781   20.2.2, 20.3.2
Crompton & Co. Ltd, re (ChD 1914) [1914] 1 Ch 954, 83 LJ Ch 666, 110 LT 759,
   21 Mans 200, 58 SJ 433   11.6.2
Crookston v Lindsay, Crookston & Co. Ltd (Bill Chamber of Scotland 1921) 1922 SLT 62   3.5.3.5
Cross v Aurora Group Ltd (New Zealand HC 1988) 4 NZCLC 64,909   2.4.2, 19.6.1
Crown Bank, re (ChD 1890) 44 ChD 634, 59 LJ Ch 739, 62 LT 823, 38 WR 666   2.3.5.10
C S Holidays Ltd, re; see Secretary of State for Trade and Industry v Taylor
CSTC Ltd, re (ChD 1994) [1995] BCC 173   15.2.5.6
Cuckmere Brick Co. Ltd v Mutual Finance Ltd (CA 1971) [1971] Ch 949, [1971] 2 WLR 1207,
   [1971] 2 All ER 633, 22 P & CR 624, 115 SJ 288   11.5.1, 20.2.10
Cumana Ltd, re (CA 1986) [1986] BCLC 430, 2 BCC 99,485 (sub nom. Re a Company
   (No. 002612 of 1984); earlier proceedings (ChD 1984) sub nom. Re a Company
   (No. 002612 of 1984) [1985] BCLC 80, 1 BCC 99, 262   18.6.2, 18.6.4, 18.6.6
Cumberland Holdings Ltd v Washington H. Soul Pattinson & Co. Ltd (PC 1977) 13 ALR 561,
   2 ACLR 307   18.7
Cumbrian Newspapers Group Ltd v Cumberland and Westmorland Herald Newspaper and
   Printing Co. Ltd (ChD 1986) [1987] Ch 1, [1986] 3 WLR 26, [1986] 2 All ER 816,
   [1986] BCLC 286, 1987 PCC 12, 2 BCC 99,227, 130 SJ 446   3.4.2.6, 3.5.3.4, 14.6.1
Cunliffe Engineering Ltd v English Industrial Estates Corp. (ChD 1994) [1994] BCC 972
   11.4.1, 11.6.2
Currie v Cowdenbeath Football Club Ltd (Scotland CSess OH 1991) 1992 SLT 407   15.3.7
Curtain Dream plc, re (ChD 1990) [1990] BCLC 925, [1990] BCC 341 (sub nom. Curtain
   Dream plc v Churchill Merchanting Ltd)   11.7.10.3
Customs & Excise Commissioners; see Commissioners of Customs & Excise
Cyclists' Touring Club v Hopkinson (ChD 1909) [1910] 1 Ch 179, 79 LJ Ch 82, 101 LT 848,
   26 TLR 117, 17 Mans 11, 54 SJ 134   2.3.5.6

D (J), re (Court of Protection 1981) [1982] Ch 237, [1982] 2 WLR 373, [1982] 2 All ER 37,
   126 SJ 85   20.14.2.2
Dafen Tinplate Co. Ltd v Llanelly Steel Co. (1907) Ltd (ChD 1920) [1920] 2 Ch 124,
   89 LJ Ch 346, 123 LT 225, 36 TLR 428, 64 SJ 446   3.5.3.5
Daimler Co. Ltd v Continental Tyre & Rubber Co. (Great Britain) Ltd (HL 1916)
   [1916] 2 AC 307, 85 LJ KB 1333, 114 LT 1049, [1916–17] All ER Rep 191, 32 TLR 624,
   22 Com Cas 32, 60 SJ 602   0.1.1, 15.7.3, 19.5.10, 19.8.2
Dale & Plant Ltd, re (ChD 1889) 61 LT 206, 5 TLR 585, 1 Meg 338,
   [1886–90] All ER Rep Ext 1325   19.6.3
   further proceedings (1889) 43 ChD 255, 62 LT 215, 59 LJ Ch 180, 6 TLR 123, 2 Meg 25,
   38 WR 409, [1886–901 All ER Rep Ext 1328   3.4.4
Dallas v Dallas (British Columbia CA 1960) 24 DLR (2d) 746   5.2.2.5
Daniels v Daniels (ChD 1977) [1978] Ch 406, [1978] 2 WLR 73, [1978] 2 All ER 89,
   121 SJ 605   16.2.2, 16.8, 18.4.4
Daniels v Fielder (Ontario HC 1988) 52 DLR (4th) 424   14.4.9.2
Danish Mercantile Co. Ltd v Beaumont (CA 1951) [1951] Ch 680, [1951] 1 All ER 925,
   95 SJ 300   19.5.8
D'Arcy v Tamar, Kit Hill, & Callington Railway Co. (Court of Exchequer 1867) LR 2 Ex 158,
   4 H & C 463, 36 LJ Ex 37, 14 LT 626, 30 JP 792, 12 Jur NS 548, 14 WR 968   15.5.1
Darvall v North Sydney Brick & Tile Co. Ltd (New South Wales CA 1989) 16 NSWLR 260,
   15 ACLR 230   16.4, 16.4.12, 18.3.1
Data Express Ltd, re (ChD 1987) *Independent,* 13 April 1987   14.3.3
Davey & Co. v Williamson & Sons Ltd (QBDC 1898) [1898] 2 QB 194, 67 LJ QB 699,
   78 LT 755, 46 WR 571, 42 SJ 525   11.6.3
David Payne & Co. Ltd, re (CA 1904) [1904] 2 Ch 608, 73 LJ Ch 849, 91 LT 777, 20 TLR 590,
   11 Mans 437, 48 SJ 572   19.5.7, 19.8.3
Davidson v Smith (Western Australia SC 1989) 15 ACLR 732   16.4.16

Davidson v Tulloch (HL 1860) 3 Macq 783 — 18.3.4

Davidson and Begg Antiques Ltd v Davidson (Scotland CSess OH 1996)
[1997] BCC 77, 1997 SLT 301 — 15.5.1

Davies v Elsby Brothers Ltd (CA 1960) [1961] 1 WLR 170, [1961] 1 All ER 672, 105 SJ 107 — 4.5.1

Dawes's case; see Re China Steam Ship Co.

Dawson, re (CA 1915) [1915] 1 Ch 626, 84 LJ Ch 476, 113 LT 19, 31 TLR 277 — 11.6.3

Dawson v African Consolidated Land & Trading Co. (CA 1897) [1898] 1 Ch 6, 67 LJ Ch 47,
77 LT 392, 14 TLR 30, 4 Mans 372, 46 WR 132, 42 SJ 45 — 15.2.6

Dawson International plc v Coats Patons plc (C Sess OH 1988) 1988 SLT 854, 1988 SCLR 371,
[1989] BCLC 233, 1988 PCC 362, 4 BCC 305; affirmed by 1st Div (1989) 1989 SLT 655,
1989 SCLR 452, [1990] BCLC 560, 1989 PCC 361, 5 BCC 405 — 14.4.5.5, 16.4.12

De Courcy v Clement (ChD 1970) [1971] Ch 693, [1971] 2 WLR 210, [1971] 1 All ER 681,
115 SJ 93 — 20.5.3

De La Mott's and Turner's Case; see Re Cambrian Peat, Fuel, & Charcoal Co. Ltd

Deans, re (New Zealand HC 1986) [1986] 2 NZLR 271, 3 NZCLC 99,620 — 8.8.2.3

Deffell v White (Common Pleas 1866) LR 2 CP 144, 36 LJ CP 25, 15 LT 211, 12 Jur NS 902,
15 WR 68 — 19.2.2

Della Rocella, re the estate of the Marchesa (ChD of Ireland 1892) 29 LR Ir 464 — 20.2.5

Demite Ltd v Protec Health Ltd (ChD 1998) *The Times*, 25 July 1998 — 16.6.7

Dempster v Mallina Holdings Ltd (Western Australia SC FC 1994) 13 WAR 124, 15 ACSR 1;
(Western Australia SC 1993) 13 WAR 11 (sub nom. Biala Pty Ltd v Mallina Holdings Ltd
(No. 4)), 11 ACSR 785 (sub nom. Biala Pty Ltd v Mallina Holdings Ltd) — 18.4.2, 18.4.13

Dermatine Co. Ltd v Ashworth (KBD 1905) 21 TLR 510 — 4.5.1

Derry v Peek (HL 1889) 14 App Cas 337, 58 LJ Ch 864, 61 LT 265, 1 Meg 292, 5 TLR 625,
38 WR 33, 54 JP 148 — 6.7.1, 6.7.5, 6.7.7, 18.4.4

Deuchar v Gas Light & Coke Co. (HL 1925) [1925] AC 691, 94 LJ Ch 382, 133 LT 565,
41 TLR 563, 89 JP 177, 23 LGR 525, [1925] All ER Rep 720 — 2.3.5.6

Deutsche Genossenschaftsbank v Burnhope (HL 1995) [1995] 1 WLR 1580,
[1995] 4 All ER 717, [1996] 1 Lloyd's Rep 113, [1996] BCC 180 — 0.1.9, 19.8.4

Devala Provident Gold Mining Co., re (ChD 1883) 22 ChD 593, 52 LJ Ch 434, 48 LT 259,
31 WR 425, [1881–5] All ER Rep Ext 1568 — 14.4.1

Devaynes v Noble, Clayton's Case (Rolls Court 1816) 1 Mer 572, 35 ER 781,
[1814–23] All ER Rep 1 — 11.6.5.1

Deverges v Sandeman Clark & Co. (CA 1902) [1902] 1 Ch 579, 71 LJ Ch 328, 86 LT 269,
[1900–3] All ER Rep 648, 18 TLR 375, 50 WR 404 — 11.5.1

Devlin v Slough Estates Ltd (ChD 1982) [1983] BCLC 497, 126 SJ 623 — 9.9

Dexine Patent Packing & Rubber Co., re (ChD 1903) 88 LT 791, [1903] WN 82 — 3.3.3, 3.5.1

Dey v Pullinger Engineering Co. (KBDC 1920) [1921] 1 KB 77, 89 LJ KB 1229, 124 LT 534,
37 TLR 10, [1920] All ER Rep 591 — 19.5.4.6

DHN Food Distributors Ltd v Tower Hamlets London Borough Council (CA 1976)
[1976] 1 WLR 852, [1976] 3 All ER 462, 32 P & CR 240, 74 LGR 506, [1976] JPL 363,
120 SJ 215 — 5.2.2.1, 5.2.2.8, 5.2.2.9

Diamond v Oreamuno (New York CA 1969) 248 NE 2d 910, 301 NYS 2d 78 — 13.5

Diamond Fuel Co., re (CA 1879) 13 ChD 400, 49 LJ Ch 301, 41 LT 573, 28 WR 309 — 20.6.7

Dibble v Wilts & Somerset Farmers Ltd (ChD 1923) [1923] 1 Ch 342, 92 LJ Ch 168,
128 LT 643, 39 TLR 174, 67 SJ 297 — 1.3.2.3

Diligenti v RWMD Operations Kelowna Ltd (SC of British Columbia 1976)
1 BCLR 36 — 1.3.5

Dimbleby & Sons Ltd v National Union of Journalists (HL 1984) [1984] ICR 386,
[1984] 1 WLR 427, [1984] 1 All ER 751, [1984] IRLR 161, 128 SJ 189 — 5.2.2.2

Dimbula Valley (Ceylon) Tea Co. Ltd v Laurie (ChD 1961) [1961] Ch 353, [1961] 2 WLR 253,
[1961] 1 All ER 769, 105 SJ 129 — 14.6.2.6

Direct Line Group Ltd v Direct Line Estate Agency Ltd (ChD 1996) [1997] FSR 374 — 2.3.3.6

Director General of Fair Trading v Pioneer Concrete (UK) Ltd (HL 1994) [1995] 1 AC 456,
[1994] 3 WLR 1249, [1995] ICR 25, [1995] 1 All ER 135 (sub nom. Re Supply of
Ready Mixed Concrete (No. 2)), [1995] 1 BCLC 613 (sub nom. Re Supply of
Ready Mixed Concrete (No. 2)), [1995] IRLR 94 — 19.8.6.1

Director of Public Prosecutions v Gomez (HL 1992) [1993] AC 442, [1992] 3 WLR 1067,
[1993] 1 All ER 1 — 19.8.5

Director of Public Prosecutions v Kent & Sussex Contractors Ltd (KBDC 1943) [1944] KB 146,
  [1944] 1 All ER 119, 113 LJ KB 88, 170 LT 41, 60 TLR 175, 42 LGR 10, 108 JP 1,
  88 SJ 59   19.8.4
Discoverers Finance Corporation Ltd, re, Lindlar's Case (CA 1910) [1910] 1 Ch 312,
  79 LJ Ch 193, 102 LT 150, 26 TLR 291, 17 Mans 46, 54 SJ 287   8.1
D'Jan of London Ltd, re (ChD 1993) [1994] 1 BCLC 561, [1993] BCC 646
     16.2.1.2, 16.2.2, 20.11.1, 20.11.4
DKG Contractors Ltd, re (ChD 1990) [1990] BCC 903   16.8, 20.11.4, 20.12
Doherty v Allman (HL (CA in Ireland) 1878) 3 App Cas 709, 39 LT 129, 26 WR 513   20.2.7.1
Donrob Enterprises Pty Ltd v Queensland Petroleum Management Ltd; see Re Queensland
  Petroleum Management Ltd
Dorchester Finance Co. Ltd v Stabbing (ChD 1977) [1989] BCLC 498   16.2.1.1
Double S Printers Ltd, re (ChD 1998) *The Times*, 2 June 1998   11.6.4
Dovey v Cory [1901] AC 477, 70 LJ Ch 753, 85 LT 257, 17 TLR 732, 8 Mans 346, 50 WR 65,
  [1895–9] All ER Rep 715 at 724   10.5.10, 16.2.1.4
Downes v Grazebrook and Chamberlayne (Rolls Court 1817) 3 Mer 200, 36 ER 77   11.5.1
Downsview Nominees Ltd v First City Corporation Ltd (PC 1992) [1993] AC 295, [1993] 2 WLR 86,
  [1993] 3 All ER 626, [1994] 1 BCLC 49, [1993] BCC 46, [1993] 1 NZLR 513   20.2.10
Dowse v Marks (SC of New South Wales 1913) 13 SR (NSW) 332, 30 WN (NSW) 85   15.7.2.4
DPC Estates Pty Ltd v Grey (CA of New South Wales 1973) [1974] 1 NSWLR 443; for the appeal
  by the second defendant, see Consul Development Pty Ltd v DPC Estates Pty Ltd
     16.3.1, 16.7.3.1, 16.7.3.2, 16.7.3.3, 17.2
Dreyfus v Commissioners of Inland Revenue (CA 1929) 14 TC 560   0.1.6
Driver v Broad (CA 1893) [1893] 1 QB 744, 63 LJ QB 12, 69 LT 169, 9 TLR 440,
  4 R 411, 41 WR 483   11.6.3
Drummond's Case; see Re China Steamship & Labuan Coal Co., Drummond's Case
Duck v Tower Galvanizing Co. Ltd (KBDC 1901) [1901] 2 KB 314, 70 LJ KB 625,
  84 LT 847   19.5.4.2
Duckett v Gover (MR 1877) 6 ChD 82, 46 LJ Ch 407; further proceedings (MR 1877)
  25 WR 554   15.7.3
Duckwari plc, re (CA 1998) *The Times*, 18 May 1998   16.6.7
Duckwari plc v Offerventure Ltd, Re a Company (No. 0032314 of 1992) (CA 1994)
  [1995] BCC 89, [1997] 2 BCLC 713 (sub nom. Re Duckwari plc (No. 1))   16.6.7
Duke v GEC Reliance Ltd (HL 1988) [1988] AC 618, [1988] 2 WLR 359, [1988] ICR 339,
  [1988] 1 All ER 626, [1988] IRLR 118, [1988] 1 CMLR 719   0.3.3.1
Duke's Case; see Re New Buxton Lime Co., Duke's Case
Duncan Gilmour & Co. Ltd, re (ChD 1952) [1952] 2 All ER 871, [1952] 2 TLR 951,
  [1952] WN 550   2.3.1
Dunderland Iron Ore Co. Ltd, re (ChD 1909) [1909] 1 Ch 446, 78 LJ Ch 237, 100 LT 224,
  16 Mans 67   12.3
Dunn v Banknock Coal Co. Ltd (C Sess OH 1901) 9 SLT 51   18.4.12
Dunston v Imperial Gas Light & Coke Co. (KB 1832) 3 B & Ad 125, 110 ER 47   15.6.1.1, 15.6.1.5
Duomatic Ltd, re (ChD 1968) [1969] 2 Ch 365, [1969] 2 WLR 114, [1969] 1 All ER 161,
  112 SJ 922   14.5.1, 15.6.1.2, 15.6.2.1, 16.9.2
Durham Fancy Goods Ltd v Michael Jackson (Fancy Goods) Ltd (QBD 1968)
  [1968] 2 QB 839, [1968] 3 WLR 225, [1968] 2 All ER 987, [1968] 2 Lloyd's Rep 98,
  112 SJ 582   4.5.1
Dutton v Gorton (Australia HC 1917) 23 CLR 362, 23 ALR 341   3.4.3

Eagle Trust plc v SBC Securities Ltd; see Eagle Trust plc v SBC Securities Ltd (No. 2)
Eagle Trust plc v SBC Securities Ltd (No. 2) (ChD 1994) [1996] 1 BCLC 121,
  [1995] BCC 231 (sub nom. Eagle Trust plc v SBC Securities Ltd)   18.2.2
Earle (G. & T.) Ltd v Hemsworth Rural District Council (KBD 1928) 44 TLR 605;
  affirmed by CA (1928) 140 LT 69, [1928] All ER Rep 602, 44 TLR 758   11.7.5
East v Bennett Brothers Ltd (ChD 1910) [1911] 1 Ch 163, 80 LJ Ch 123, 103 LT 826,
  27 TLR 103, 18 Mans 145, 55 SJ 92   14.4.11, 14.5.1, 14.5.4
East Anglian Railways Co. v Eastern Counties Railway Co. (Court of Common Pleas 1851)
  11 CB 775, 138 ER 680, 21 LJ CP 23, 18 LT OS 138, 16 Jur 249, 7 Ry & Can Cas 150   19.4.1
East Midlands Electricity Board v Grantham (County Court 1980) [1980] CLY 271   4.5.1

Eaton v Robert Eaton Ltd (EAT 1987) [1988] ICR 302, [1988] IRLR 83 15.6.1.5

EB Tractors Ltd, re (Lombard & Ulster Ltd v Edgar) (Northern Ireland ChD 1986) [1986] NI 165,
1987 PCC 313, [1986] 3 NIJB 1 20.10.2

Ebbw Vale Urban District Council v South Wales Traffic Area Licensing Authority (CA 1951)
[1951] 2 KB 366, [1951] 1 All ER 806, [1951] 1 TLR 742, 95 SJ 334,
49 LGR 515 5.2.2.3

Ebeed v Soplex Wholesale Supplies Ltd (CA 1984) [1985] BCLC 404 19.5.4.1, 19.5.4.2

EBM Co. Ltd v Dominion Bank (PC (Ontario CA) 1937) [1937] 3 All ER 555, 81 SJ 814 5.2.2.1

Ebrahimi v Westbourne Galleries Ltd (HL 1972) [1973] AC 360, [1972] 2 WLR 1289,
[1972] 2 All ER 492, 116 SJ 412 1.3.5, 14.4.9.5, 18.6.3, 18.7, 18.7.2, 18.7.3, 18.7.4

Ebsworth & Tidy's Contract, re (CA 1889) 42 ChD 23 20.6.7

EDC v United Kingdom (application No. 24433/94) (European Commission of
Human Rights 1997) [1998] BCC 370 15.2.5.4, 15.2.5.6

Eddystone Marine Insurance Co., re (CA 1893) [1893] 3 Ch 9, 62 LJ Ch 742, 69 LT 363,
9 TLR 501, 41 WR 642 6.4.1

Edgington v Fitzmaurice (CA 1885) 29 ChD 459, 65 LJ Ch 650, 53 LT 369,
[1881–5] All ER Rep 856, 1 TLR 326, 50 JP 52, 33 WR 911 6.7.3

Edinburgh Workmen's Houses Improvement Co. Ltd (C Sess 1st Div 1934) 1935 SC 56,
1934 SN 85, 1934 SLT 513 14.4.4

Edman v Ross (SC of New South Wales 1922) 22 SR (NSW) 351, 39 WN (NSW) 86 9.2.4

Edmonton Country Club Ltd v Case (Canada SC 1974) [1975] 1 SCR 534, 44 DLR (3d) 554,
[1974] 4 WWR 626, 1 NR 563 (sub nom. Case v Edmonton Country Club Ltd) 1.3.2.3

Edward Collins & Sons Ltd v Commissioners of Inland Revenue (C Sess 1st Div 1924)
1925 SC 151, 12 TR 773 9.3.8

Edwards v Halliwell (CA 1950) [1950] 2 All ER 1064, [1950] WN 537, 94 SJ 803
18.3.1, 18.3.2, 18.3.4, 18.4.3, 18.4.9, 18.4.11, 18.4.13

Edwards Books & Art Ltd v R (Canada SC 1986) [1986] 2 SCR 713, 35 DLR (4th) 1,
30 CCC (3d) 385, 55 CR (3d) 193, 87 CLLC 14,001, 71 NR 161 (sub nom. R v Videoflicks Ltd),
19 OAC 239, 28 CRR 1 19.8.7

Ehrmann Brothers Ltd, re (CA 1906) [1906] 2 Ch 697, 75 LJ Ch 817, 95 LT 664,
22 TLR 734, 13 Mans 368 11.7.3, 11.7.9

Einhorn v Westmount Investments Ltd (CA of Saskatchewan 1970) 11 DLR (3d) 509,
73 WWR 161 20.2.7.1

Eisenberg v Bank of Nova Scotia; see Walton v Bank of Nova Scotia

El Sombrero Ltd, re (ChD 1958) [1958] Ch 900, [1958] 3 WLR 349, [1958] 3 All ER 1,
102 SJ 601 14.4.4

Electrical, Electronic, Telecommunication & Plumbing Union v Times Newspapers Ltd
(QBD 1979) [1980] QB 585, [1980] 3 WLR 98, [1980] 1 All ER 1097 0.1.6

Electrical Equipment of Aust. Ltd v Peters (New South Wales SC (FC) 1956)
[1957] SR (NSW) 361, 74 WN (NSW) 243 19.2.6

Eley v Positive Government Security Life Assurance Co. Ltd (CA 1876) 1 ExD 88, 45 LJ QB 451,
34 LT 190, 24 WR 338 3.4.2.3, 3.4.2.7, 3.4.3, 19.6.2

Elgindata Ltd, re (ChD 1991) [1991] BCLC 959 16.2.1.1, 18.6.1, 18.6.3, 18.6.4, 18.6.6

Ellenborough, re (Towry Law v Burne) (ChD 1903) [1903] 1 Ch 697, 72 LJ Ch 218, 87 LT 714,
[1900–3] All ER Rep Ext 1171, 51 WR 315, 47 SJ 255 11.2.1

Elliott v Pierson (ChD 1948) [1948] Ch 452, [1948] 1 All ER 939, [1948] LJR 1452,
92 SJ 271 5.2.2.5

Elliott v Wheeldon (CA 1992) [1993] BCLC 53, [1992] BCC 489 1.3.5, 16.3.1

Ellis v McQueen (HC of Ontario 1967) 63 DLR (2d) 678, [1967] 2 OR 399 18.4.13

ELS Ltd, re (ChD 1994) [1995] Ch 11, [1994] 3 WLR 656, [1994] 2 All ER 833, [1994] 1 BCLC 743,
[1994] BCC 449 11.4.1, 11.6.2

Eltham Co-operative Dairy Factory Co. Ltd v Johnson (New Zealand CA 1930) [1931] NZLR 216,
[1931] GLR 81 3.4.2.5

Emmadart Ltd, re (ChD 1978) [1979] Ch 540, [1979] 2 WLR 868, [1979] 1 All ER 599 15.7.2.2

Empress Engineering Co., re (CA 1880) 16 ChD 125, 43 LT 742, 29 WR 342 19.6.2

English v Dedham Vale Properties Ltd (ChD 1977) [1978] 1 WLR 93, [1978] 1 All ER 382,
35 P & CR 148, [1978] JPL 315, 245 EG 747, 839 16.3.1

Environment Protection Authority v Caltex Refining Co. Pty Ltd (Australia HC 1993)
118 ALR 392 19.9

Equiticorp International plc, re (ChD 1989) [19891 1 WLR 1010, [1989] BCLC 597, 5 BCC 599
    15.7.2.2, 20.3.2

Erlanger v New Sombrero Phosphate Co. (HL 1878) 3 App Cas 1218, 39 LT 269,
    [1874–80] All ER Rep 271, 27 WR 65   17.6.3.1, 17.6.3.2

Ernest v Nicholls (HL 1857) 6 HL Cas 401, 6 WR 24, 10 ER 1351   2.2, 3.2, 15.1.1, 19.1

Ert Stefanie, The (QBD 1987) [1987] 2 Lloyd's Rep 371   19.8.1

Esal (Commodities) Ltd, re (CA 1988) [1989] BCLC 59, 1988 PCC 443, 4 BCC 475   20.9.3

Esberger & Son Ltd v Capital & Counties Bank (ChD 1913) [1913] 2 Ch 366, 82 LJ Ch 576,
    109 LT 140, 20 Mans 252   11.2.1

Esparto Trading Co., re (ChD 1879) 12 ChD 191, 48 LJ Ch 573, 28 WR 146   6.4.2

Esplanade Developments Ltd v Dinive Holdings Pty Ltd (Western Australia SC 1980)
    [1980] WAR 151, 4 ACLR 826, [1980] ACLC 34,232   16.3.1

Esso Standard (Inter-America) Inc. v JW Enterprises Inc. (Canada SC 1963) 37 DLR (2d) 598,
    [1963] SCR 144   5.2.2.7, 8.8.2.3

Estates Investment Co., re, Ashley's Case (MR 1870) LR 9 Eq 263, 39 LJ Ch 354, 22 LT 83,
    18 WR 395   6.7.4

Estates Investment Co., re, Pawle's Case (CA in Chancery 1869) LR 4 Ch App 497, 38 LJ Ch 412,
    20 LT 589, 17 WR 599   6.7.4

Estmanco (Kilner House) Ltd v Greater London Council (Vacation Court 1981) [1982] 1 WLR 2,
    [1982] 1 All ER 437   14.4.9.5, 18.4.2, 18.4.4, 18.4.13

Etic Ltd, re (ChD 1928) [1928] Ch 861, 97 LJ Ch 460, 140 LT 219, [1928] B & CR 81   20.11.1

European Assurance Society Arbitration, Manisty's Case (1873) 17 SJ 745   6.4.2

European Home Products plc, re (ChD 1988) [1998] BCLC 690, 4 BCC 779   10.2.2

Eurostem Maritime Ltd, re (ChD 1986) 1987 PCC 190   15.2.5.6

Evans v Brunner, Mond and Co. Ltd (ChD 1920) [1921] 1 Ch 359, 90 LJ Ch 294,
    124 LT 469   2.3.5.6

Evans v Chapman (ChD 1902) 86 LT 381, 18 TLR 506, [1902] WN 79   3.4.1.3

Evans v Rival Granite Quarries Ltd (CA 1910) [1910] 2 KB 979, 79 LJ KB 970, 26 TLR 509,
    54 SJ 580, 18 Mans 64   11.6.3

Evans (C.) & Sons Ltd v Spritebrand Ltd (CA 1984) [1985] 1 WLR 317, [1985] 2 All ER 415,
    [1985] BCLC 105, [1985] FSR 267, 1 BCC 99, 316, 129 SJ 189   15.10

Evans's case; see Re London, Hamburgh & Continental Exchange Bank

Evling v Israel & Oppenheimer Ltd (ChD 1917) [1918] 1 Ch 101, 87 LJ Ch 341, 118 LT 99,
    34 TLR 109   18.4.9

Evpo Agnic, The (CA 1988) [1988] 1 WLR 1090, [1988] 3 All ER 810;
    [1988] 2 Lloyd's Rep 411   5.2.2.10

Ewart v Fryer (ChD 1900) [1901] 1 Ch 499, 82 LT 415, 48 WR 443; affirmed by CA (1900)
    [1901] 1 Ch 499, 70 LJ Ch 138, 83 LT 551, 17 TLR 145, 49 WR 145, 45 SJ 115; affirmed
    by HL (1902 sub nom. Fryer v Ewart) [1902] AC 187, 71 LJ Ch 433, 86 LT 242, 18 TLR 426,
    9 Mans 281   4.3

Exchange Banking Co., re, Flitcroft's Case (CA 1882) 21 ChD 519, 52 LJ Ch 217, 48 LT 86,
    31 WR 174   2.3.5.11, 5.2.1, 10.5.2, 10.5.10, 15.8, 20.11.2

Exco Corporation Ltd v Nova Scotia Savings & Loan Co. (SC of Nova Scotia 1987)
    78 NSR (2d) 91   16.4.2

Exeter & Crediton Railway Co. v Buller (V-C 1847) 16 LJ Ch 449, 5 Ry & Can Cas 211,
    11 Jur 532, 9 LT OS 194; affirmed by LC (1847) 16 LJ Ch 449 at 450, 5 Ry & Can Cas 211
    at 216, 11 Jur 527; further proceedings (V-C 1847) 16 LJ Ch 449 at 453, 5 Ry & Can Cas 211
    at 219, 11 Jur 532 at 535, 9 LT OS 263   15.7.2.4, 15.7.3

Exeter Trust Ltd v Screenways Ltd (CA 1991) [1991] BCLC 888, [1991] BCC 477   11.7.9

Expanded Plugs Ltd, re (ChD 1966) [1966] 1 WLR 514, [1966] 1 All ER 877   18.7

Express Engineering Works Ltd, re (CA 1920) [1920] 1 Ch 466, 89 LJ Ch 379, 122 LT 790,
    36 TLR 275   14.4.9.3, 14.5.1, 16.6.3, 16.8

Exxon Corporation v Exxon Insurance Consultants International Ltd (ChD 1981)
    [1982] Ch 119, [1981] 1 WLR 624, [1981] 2 All ER 495, 125 SJ 342; (CA 1981)
    [1982] Ch 119, [1981] 3 WLR 541, [1981] 3 All ER 241, 125 SJ 527   2.3.3.6

Fairline Shipping Corporation v Adamson (QBD 1973) [1975] QB 180, [1974] 2 WLR 824,
    [1974] 2 All ER 967, [1974] 1 Lloyd's Rep 133, 118 SJ 406   15.10

Fairway Magazines Ltd, re (ChD 1992) [1993] BCLC 643, [1992] BCC 924   11.6.5.1

Fargro Ltd v Godfroy (ChD 1986) [1986] 1 WLR 1134, [1986] 3 All ER 279, [1986] BCLC 370, 1986 PCC 476, 2 BCC 99,167   18.4.2, 18.4.3

Farrar v Farrars Ltd (CA 1888) 40 ChD 395, 58 LJ Ch 185, 60 LT 121, 37 WR 196, 5 TLR 164   5.2.1

Farrer (T.N.) Ltd, re (ChD 1937) [1937] Ch 352, [1937] 2 All ER 505, 106 LJ Ch 305, 157 LT 431, 53 TLR 581   3.4.4

Farrow v Registrar of Building Societies (Victoria SC 1990) [1991] 2 VR 589   18.3.1, 18.4.3, 18.4.4, 18.4.7

Farrow's Bank Ltd, re (CA 1921) [1921] 2 Ch 164, 90 LJ Ch 465, 125 LT 699, 37 TLR 847, 65 SJ 679, [1921] All ER Rep 511   20.6.7

Faure Electric Accumulator Co. Ltd v Phillipart (QBD 1888) 58 LT 525, 4 TLR 365   15.5.1

Fayed v United Kingdom (European Court of Human Rights 1994) 18 EHRR 393   18.8.2, 18.8.3.1

Federal Business Development Bank v Prince Albert Fashion Bin Ltd (CA of Saskatchewan 1983) [1983] 3 WWR 464, 22 SaskR 111, 47 CBR (NS) 1; affirming Saskatchewan QB (1981) [1981] 5 WWR 543, 12 Sask R 412   11.6.2

Fell v Derby Leather Co. Ltd (ChD 1931) [1931] 2 Ch 252, 100 LJ Ch 311, 145 LT 356, [1931] All ER Rep 636   3.3.5

Fenner plc, re (ChD 11 June 1990) unreported   14.4.8.3

Fenning v Fenning Environmental Products Ltd (ChD 1981) 79 LS Gaz 803   14.4.5.6

Ferguson v Wallbridge (PC (Court of Appeal for British Columbia) 1935) [1935] 3 DLR 66, [1935] 1 WWR 673   18.4.2

Ferguson v Wilson (LJJ 1866) LR 2 Ch App 77, 36 LJ Ch 67, 15 LT 230, 30 JP 788, 12 Jur NS 912, 15 WR 80   15.1.1, 19.5.6

Fine Industrial Commodities Ltd, re (ChD 1955) [1956] Ch 256, [1955] 3 WLR 940, [1955] 3 All ER 707, 99 SJ 889   20.13.2

Finger's Will Trusts, re (ChD 1971) [1972] Ch 286, [1971] 3 WLR 775, [1971] 3 All ER 1050 20.14.1

Firedart Ltd, re (ChD 1994) [1994] 2 BCLC 340   15.2.5.6

Fire Nymph Products Ltd v Heating Centre Pty Ltd (New South Wales CA 1992) 7 ACSR 365   11.6.2

Firestone Tyre & Rubber Co. Ltd v Lewellin (HL 1957) [1957] 1 WLR 464, [1957] 1 All ER 561, [1957] TR 19, 37 TC 111, 36 ATC 17, 101 SJ 228   5.2.2.3

Firmstone's case; see Re Malaga Lead Co.

First City Capital Ltd v 105383 BC Ltd (British Columbia CA 1985) 28 BLR 274   19.5.4.4

First Energy (UK) Ltd v Hungarian International Bank Ltd (CA 1993) [1993] BCLC 1409, [1993] BCC 533   19.5.4.1

Floating Dock Co. of St Thomas Ltd, re (ChD 1895) [1895] 1 Ch 691, 64 LJ Ch 361, 43 WR 344, 39 SJ 284, 13 R 491   10.2.4

FM Ltd, re; see Re a Company (No. 005287 of 1985)

Fomento (Sterling Area) Ltd v Selsdon Fountain Pen Co. Ltd (HL 1957) [1958] 1 WLR 45, [1958] 1 All ER 11, [1958] RPC 8, 102 SJ 51   17.4.5

Forster v Nixon's Navigation Co. Ltd (KBD 1906) 23 TLR 138   20.2.7.1

Forth Wines Ltd (C Sess IH 1991) [1991] BCC 638   10.2.1

Foss v Harbottle (V-C 1843) 2 Hare 461, 67 ER 189   15.7.4.2, 16.4.10, 17.6.3.1, 18.3.1, 18.3.4, 18.3.3.2, 18.3.3.4, 18.3.4, 18.4.1, 18.4.2, 18.4.3, 18.4.4, 18.4.5, 18.4.8, 18.4.9, 18.4.11, 18.4.13, 18.5.2.3, 18.5.2.4, 18.5.2.5

Foster v Foster (ChD 1916) [1916] 1 Ch 532, 85 LT Ch 305, 114 LT 405, [1916–17] All ER Rep 856   15.5.3, 15.7.2.3, 15.7.7

Foster v Greenwich Ferry Co. Ltd (ChD 1888) 5 TLR 16   15.3.7

Fountaine v Carmarthen Railway Co. (V-C 1868) LR 5 Eq 316, 37 LJ Ch 429, 16 WR 476   19.5.4,1

Four-Maids Ltd v Dudley Marshall (Properties) Ltd (ChD 1957) [1957] Ch 317, [1957] 2 WLR 931, [1957] 2 All ER 35, 101 SJ 408   11.5.3

Fraser v Whalley (V-C 1864) 2 Hem & M 10, 71 ER 361, 11 LT 175, [1861–73] All ER Rep Ext 1456   16.4.11, 18.4.9, 18.4.12

Free Fishermen of Faversham, re Company or Fraternity of (CA 1887) 36 ChD 329, 57 LJ Ch 187, 57 LT 577, 3 TLR 797   0.1.2.6

Freeman & Lockyer v Buckhurst Park Properties (Mangal) Ltd (CA 1964) [1964] 2 QB 480, [1964] 2 WLR 618, [1964] 1 All ER 630, 108 SJ 96   15.5.3, 19.5.2.1, 19.5.4.1, 19.5.4.2, 19.5.4.6

Freevale Ltd v Metrostore (Holdings) Ltd (ChD 1983) [1984] Ch 199, [1984] 2 WLR 496, [1984] 1 All ER 495, [1984] BCLC 215, 128 SJ 116   20.2.7.1

French Protestant Hospital, re the (ChD 1951) [1951] Ch 567, [1951] 1 All ER 938,
    [1951] 1 TLR 785, 95 SJ 285   16.4.7
Freudiana Music Co. Ltd, re (ChD March 1993) unreported   18.6.1
Frinton & Walton Urban District Council v Walton & District Sand & Mineral Co. Ltd
    (ChD 1938) [1938] 1 All ER 649   19.9
Fryer v Ewart; see Ewart v Fryer
Fulham Football Club Ltd v Cabra Estates plc (CA 1992) [1994] 1 BCLC 363, [1992] BCC 863,
    65 P & CR 284   16.4.16
Fulloon v Radley (Queensland SC 1991) [1992] 2 QdR 290   18.4.2, 18.4.9, 18.4.10
Furs Ltd v Tomkies (HC of Australia 1936) 54 CLR 583, 9 ALJ 419   16.6.7, 16.7.3.4, 16.8

Gaiman v National Association for Mental Health (ChD 1970) [1971] Ch 317,
    [1970] 3 WLR 42, [1970] 2 All ER 362, 114 SJ 416   2.3.2, 3.3.2, 16.4.1, 16.4.3
Galloway v Hallé Concerts Society (ChD 1915) [1915] 2 Ch 233, 84 LJ Ch 723, 113 LT 811,
    [1914–15] All ER Rep 543, [1915] HBR 170, 31 TLR 469, 59 SJ 613   1.3.2.3
Galoo Ltd v Bright Grahame Murray (CA 1993) [1994] 1 WLR 1360, [1995] 1 All ER 16,
    [1994] 2 BLC 492, [1994] BCC 319   17.4.5
Galway & Salthill Tramways Co., re (MR of Ireland 1917) [1918] 1 IR 62   15.7.2.2
Gambotto v WCP Ltd (Australia HC 1995) 182 CLR 432, 127 ALR 417, 69 ALJR 266,
    16 ACSR 1   3.5.3.5
Garage Door Associates Ltd, re (ChD 1983) [1984] 1 WLR 35, [1983] BCLC 164,
    [1984] 1 All ER 434, 1 BCC 98, 966   18.6.1
Garnac Grain Co. Inc. v H.M.F. Faure & Fairclough Ltd (HL 1967) [1968] AC 1130,
    [1967] 3 WLR 143, [1967] 2 All ER 353, [1967] 1 Lloyd's Rep 495, 111 SJ 434   5.2.2.3
Garvie v Axmith (Ontario HC 1961) 31 DLR (2d) 65, [1962] OR 65   14.4.5.5
Gaskell v Gosling; see Gosling v Gaskell & Grocott
Gas Lighting Improvement Co. Ltd v Commissioners of Inland Revenue (HL 1923) [1923] AC 723,
    92 LJ KB 665, 129 LT 48, 39 TLR 504, 12 TC 503   5.2.1, 5.2.2.3, 5.3.1
Gasque v Commissioners of Inland Revenue (KBD 1940) [1940] 2 KB 80, 23 TC 210,
    109 LJ KB 769, 56 TLR 683, 84 SJ 478   2.4.3
Gee & Co. (Woolwich) Ltd, re (ChD 1973) [1975] Ch 52, [1974] 2 WLR 515,
    [1974] 1 All ER 1149, 118 SJ 65   14.5.1
Geers Gross plc, re (CA 1987) [1987] 1 WLR 1649, [1988] 1 All ER 224, [1988] BCLC 140,
    1988 PCC 126, 3 BCC 528   8.9.7
Geisse v Taylor & Hartland (KB DC 1905) [1905] 2 KB 658, 74 LJ KB 912, 93 LT 534,
    12 Mans 400, 54 WR 215   20.2.8.3
General Auction Estate & Monetary Co. v Smith (ChD 1891) [1891] 3 Ch 432, 60 LJ Ch 723,
    65 LT 188, 7 TLR 636, 40 WR 106   2.3.5.6
General Horticultural Co. Ltd, re (ChD 1885) 53 LT 699   11.7.12
George Barker (Transport) Ltd v Eynon (CA 1973) [1974] 1 WLR 462, [1974] 1 All ER 900,
    [1974] 1 Lloyd's Rep 65, 118 SJ 240   11.6.2, 20.2.7.1
George Fischer (Great Britain) Ltd v Multi Construction Ltd (CA 1994) [1995] 1 BCLC 260,
    [1995] BCC 310   18.4.6
George Newman & Co., re (CA 1895) [1895] 1 Ch 674, 64 LJ Ch 407, 72 LT 697,
    11 TLR 292, 2 Mans 267, 12 R 228, 43 WR 483, [1895–9] All ER Rep Ext 2160
                                         10.1, 14.5.1, 15.6.1.1
George Whitechurch Ltd v Cavanagh (HL 1901) [1902] AC 117, 71 LJ KB 400, 85 LT 349,
    17 TLR 746, 9 Mans 351, 50 WR 218, [1900–13] All ER Rep Ext 1488   8.3.2
Gerald Cooper Chemicals Ltd (in liquidation), re (ChD 1977) [1978] Ch 262,
    [1978] 2 WLR 866, [1978] 2 All ER 49, 121 SJ 848   20.10.1
German Date Coffee Co., re (CA 1882) 20 ChD 169, 51 LJ Ch 564, 46 LT 327,
    [1881–5] All ER Rep 372, 30 WR 717   2.3.5.8
Gething v Kilner (ChD 1971) [1972] 1 WLR 337, [1972] 1 All ER 1164   14.4.5.5
Ghyll Beck Driving Range Ltd, re (ChD 1992) [1993] BCLC 1126   18.6.5
Gibson Davies Ltd, re (ChD 1994) [1995] BCC 11   15.2.5.7
GIGA Investments Pty Ltd, re (Australia FedC 1995) 17 ACSR 472   14.4.1
Gilbert's case; see Re National Provincial Marine Insurance Co.
Gilford Motor Co. Ltd v Horne (CA 1933) [1933] Ch 935   5.2.2.4

Gill & Duffus (Liverpool) Ltd v Scruttons Ltd (Liverpool Assizes 1953) [1953] 2 All ER 977,
    [1953] 1 WLR 1407, [1953] 2 Lloyd's Rep 545, 97 SJ 814   11.7.10.3
Glass v Atkin (Ontario HC 1967) 65 DLR (2d) 501, [1968] 1 OR 90   18.4.3, 18.4.13
Glavanics v Brunninghausen (New South Wales SC 1996) 19 ACSR 204   13.5, 16.7.4
Glaxo plc v Glaxowellcome Ltd (ChD 1995) [1996] FSR 388   2.3.3.6
Glossop v Glossop (ChD 1907) [1907] 2 Ch 370, 76 LJ Ch 610, 97 LT 372, 14 Mans 246,
    51 SJ 606   15.3.5
Gluckstein v Barnes (HL 1900) [1900] AC 240, 69 LJ Ch 385, 52 LT 393, 16 TLR 321,
    7 Mans 321; affirming CA (1898) sub nom. Re Olympia Ltd [1898] 2 Ch 153, 67 LJ Ch 433,
    78 LT 629, 14 TLR 451, 42 SJ 290, 5 Mans 139   17.6.3.1, 17.6.3.2
Glyncorrwg Colliery Co. Ltd, re (ChD 1926) [1926] Ch 951, [1926] All ER Rep 318,
    96 LJ Ch 43, 136 LT 159, 70 SJ 857   20.2.9
Godfrey Phillips Ltd v Investment Trust Corporation Ltd (ChD 1952) [1953] Ch 449,
    [1953] 1 WLR 41, [1953] 1 All ER 7, [1952] TR 507, 31 ATC 548, 46 R & IT 81   18.4.9
Godwin Warren Control Systems plc, re (ChD 1992) [1993] BCLC 80, [1992] BCC 557   15.2.5.6
Goh Kim Hai Edward v Pacific Can Investment Holdings Ltd (Singapore HC 1996)
    [1996] 2 SLR 109   16.4.2
Golden Chemical Products Ltd, re (ChD 1976) [1976] Ch 300, [1976] 3 WLR 1,
    [1976] 2 All ER 543   18.8.3.3
Goldex Mines Ltd v Revill (CA of Ontario 1974) 54 DLR (3d) 672, 7 OR (2d) 216   14.4.5.5
Goldsmith v Bhoyrul (QBD 1997), [1998] QB 459, [1998] 2 WLR 435, [1997] 4 All ER 268   5.2.1
Goldsmith (F.) (Sicklesmere) Ltd v Baxter (ChD 1969) [1970] Ch 85, [1969] 3 WLR 522,
    [1969] 3 All ER 733, 20 P & CR 787, 212 EG 33   4.5.1
Gomba Holdings UK Ltd v Homan (ChD 1986) [1986] 1 WLR 1301, [1986] 3 All ER 94,
    [1986] BCLC 331, 1986 PCC 449, 2 BCC 99, 102   19.6, 20.2.3
Goodwin v Brewster (CA 1951) 32 TC 80, [1951] TR 1, 44 R & IT 253, 30 ATC 1,
    [1951] WN 126, 95 SJ 236   15.6.1.5
Gordon Grant & Co. Ltd v Boos (PC (West Indian CA) 1926) [1926] AC 781, 95 LJ PC 167,
    137 LT 740, 42 TLR 694   11.5.6
Gore Bros v Newbury Dairy Co. Ltd (New Zealand SC 1919) [1919] NZLR 205,
    [1919] GLR 119   3.4.2.5
Gosling v Gaskell & Grocott (HL 1897) [1897] AC 575, 66 LJ QB 848, 77 LT 314, 13 TLR 544,
    [1895–9] All ER Rep 300, 46 WR 208; reversing (sub nom. Gaskell v Gosling)
    CA (1896) [1896] 1 QB 669, 65 LJ QB 435, 74 LT 674, 12 TLR 335   11.5.3, 20.2.5
Goulton v London Architectural Brick & Tile Co. (V-C 1877) [1877] WN 141   6.4.2
Governments Stock & Other Securities Investment Co. Ltd v Christopher (ChD 1955)
    [1956] 1 WLR 237, [1956] 1 All ER 490, 100 SJ 186   6.5.3
Governments Stock and Other Securities Investment Co. Ltd v Manila Railway Co. Ltd
    (HL 1896) [1897] AC 81, 66 LJ Ch 102, 75 LT 553, 45 WR 353   11.6.1
Gramophone & Typewriter Ltd v Stanley (CA 1908) [1908] 2 KB 89, 77 LJ KB 834, 99 LT 39,
    24 TLR 480, 15 Mans 251, 5 TC 358   5.2.2.3, 15.1.6, 15.7.2.4, 15.9
Grant v United Kingdom Switchback Railways Co. (CA 1888) 40 ChD 135, 58 LJ Ch 211,
    60 LT 525, 1 Meg 117, 37 WR 312   16.8, 19.5.8
Gray v Lewis (LJJ 1873) LR 8 Ch App 1035, 43 LJ Ch 281, 29 LT 12, 21 WR 923 18.3.3.3, 18.4.10
Gray v New Augarita Porcupine Mines Ltd (PC (CA of Ontario) 1952) [1952] 3 DLR 1
    16.5.5.2, 16.6.2, 16.6.4
Gray v TCB Ltd; see TCB Ltd v Gray
Gray Eisdell Timms Pty Ltd v Combined Auctions Pty Ltd (New South Wales SC 1995)
    122 FLR 253, 17 ACSR 303   16.4.14
Grayan Building Services Ltd, re (CA 1994) [1995] Ch 241, [1995] 3 WLR 1, [1995] 1 BCLC 276
    (sub nom. Secretary of State for Trade & Industry v Gray), [1995] BCC 554   15.2.5.6
Great Cobar Ltd, re (Beesen v the company) (ChD 1915) [1915] 1 Ch 682, 84 LJ Ch 468,
    113 LT 226   20.2.7.1
Great Luxembourg Railway Co. v Magnay (No. 2) (MR 1858) 25 Beav 586, 53 ER 761   16.6.7
Great Western Railway Co. v Rushout (V-C 1852) 5 De G & Sm 290, 64 ER 1121,
    7 Ry & Can Cas 991, 16 Jur 238   15.5.5
Great Wheal Polgooth Co., re the (ChD 1883) 53 LJ Ch 42, 49 LT 20, 47 JP 710,
    32 WR 107   17.6.2

Greater London Properties Ltd's lease, re (ChD 1959) [1959] 1 WLR 503, [1959] 1 All ER 728,
   103 SJ 351   5.2.2.6
Green v Bestobell Industries Pty Ltd (SC of Western Australia FC 1981) [1982] WAR 1   17.2
Greene, re (Greene v Greene) (ChD 1948) [1949] Ch 333, [1949] 1 All ER 167,
   93 SJ 27   3.3.2, 8.3.1
Greenhalgh v Arderne Cinemas Ltd (CA 1946) [1946] 1 All ER 512, 90 SJ 248
                                                                                         3.5.3.5, 14.4.9.5, 14.6.2.6
Greenhalgh v Arderne Cinemas Ltd (CA 1950) [1951] Ch 286, [1950] 2 All ER 1120,
   94 SJ 855   3.5.3.5
Greenhalgh v Mallard (CA 1943) [1943] 2 All ER 234   8.3.4, 14.4.9.5, 14.4.9.8
Greenwell v Porter (ChD 1902) [1902] 1 Ch 530, 71 LJ Ch 243, 86 LT 220,
   9 Mans 85   14.4.9.8, 15.3.3
Greenwood v Leather Shod Wheel Co, (CA 1899) [1900] 1 Ch 421, 69 LJ Ch 131, 81 LT 595,
   16 TLR 117, 44 SJ 156, 7 Mans 210   6.7.3
Greenwood's case; see Re The Sea Fire & Life Assurance Co. (Greenwood's case)
Gresham Life Assurance Society, re, ex parte Penney (LJJ 1872) LR 8 Ch App 466,
   42 LJ Ch 183, 28 LT 150, 21 WR 186, [1861–73] All ER Rep 903   8.3.4
Greymouth Point Elizabeth Railway & Coat Co. Ltd, re (ChD 1903) [1904] 1 Ch 32,
   73 LJ Ch 92, 11 Mans 85   15.5.1, 16.6.3
Greys Brewery Co., re (ChD 1883) 25 ChD 400, 53 LJ Ch 262, 50 LT 14,
   32 WR 381, 28 SJ 104   20.9.3
Grierson, Oldham & Adams Ltd, re (ChD 1966) [1968] Ch 17, [1967] 1 WLR 385,
   [1967] 1 All ER 192   8.8.2.3
Griffin Hotel Co. Ltd, re (Joshua Tetley & Son Ltd v the company) (ChD 1940) [1941] Ch 129,
   [1940] 4 All ER 324, 110 LJ Ch 51, 165 LT 57, 57 TLR 123, [1940–41] B & CR 38,
   84 SJ 695   11.6.2
Griffiths v Secretary of State for Social Services (QBD 1973) [1974] QB 468,
   [1973] 3 WLR 831, [1973] 3 All ER 1184, 117 SJ 873   20.2.7.2
Griffiths v Yorkshire Bank plc (ChD 1993) [1994] 1 WLR 1427   11.6.1, 11.6.2, 20.2.8.1
Grosvenor Press plc, re (ChD 1985) [1985] 1 WLR 980, [1985] BCLC 286, 1985 PCC 260,
   1 BCC 99,412   10.2.2
Grove v Flavel (South Australia SC (FC) 1986) 43 SASR 410, 11 ACLR 161, 4 ACLC 654   16.4.6.1
Grundt v Great Boulder Proprietary Mines Ltd (CA 1947) [1948] Ch 145, [1948] 1 All ER 21,
   [1948] LJR 1100   15.7.1
GSAR Realisations Ltd, re (ChD 1992) [1993] BCLC 409   15.2.5.6
Guimaraens (M.P.) and Son v Fonseca and Vasconcellos Ltd (ChD 1921) 38 RPC 388   2.3.3.6
Guinness v Land Corporation of Ireland (CA 1882) 22 ChD 349, 52 LJ Ch 177, 47 LT 517,
   31 WR 341   2.3.1, 3.3.2, 10.1
Guinness plc v Saunders (HL 1990) [1990] 2 AC 663, [1990] 2 WLR 324, [1990] 1 All ER 652,
   [1990] BCLC 402, [1990] BCC 205, [1990] LRC (Comm) 537
                                                                    3.4.4, 15.6.1.1, 15.6.1.2, 15.6.1.5, 16.6.5

H, re (Restraint Order: Realisable Property) (CA 1996) [1996] 2 All ER 391   5.2.2.4, 5.2.2.11
H and K (Medway) Ltd, re (ChD 1997) [1997] 2 All ER 321, [1997] 1 BCLC 545,
   [1997] BCC 853   20.2.8.1
Haas Timber & Trading Co. Pty Ltd v Wade (Australia HC 1954) 94 CLR 593   6.7.4
Hackney Pavilion Ltd, re (ChD 1923) [1924] 1 Ch 276, 93 LJ Ch 193, 130 LT 658,
   [1923] All ER Rep 524   8.3.4
Hailey Group Ltd, re (ChD 1992) [1993] BCLC 459, [1992] BCC 542 (sub nom. Re a Company
   (No. 008126 of 1989))   18.6.6
Halcyon Heights Estates Ltd, re (Barbados SC 1981) [1980–84] LRC (Comm) 583,
   16 Barb LR 30   14.4.9.2
Halket v Merchant Traders' Ship Loan & Insurance Association (QB 1849) 13 QB 960,
   116 ER 1530, 19 LJ QB 59, 4 Ex 529 n, 154 ER 1323 n, 14 Jur 222   1.3.2.5
Hallett v Dowdall (Exchequer Chamber 1852) 18 QB 2, 118 ER 1, 21 LJ QB 98, 19 LT OS 300,
   16 Jur 462   1.3.2.5
Halt Garage (1964) Ltd, re (ChD 1978) [1982] 3 All ER 1016   10.1, 14.4.9.4, 16.4.6.1, 20.11.4
Hamilton v Naviede (HL 1994) [1995] 2 AC 75, [1994] 3 WLR 656, [1994] 3 All ER 814,
   [1994] BCC 641, [1995] 1 Cr App R 95 (sub nom. Re Arrows Ltd (No. 4))   20.9.3

Hamilton v Whitehead (Australia HC 1988) 166 CLR 121, 63 ALJR 80, 82 ALR 626,
    14 ACLR 493   19.8.4
Hamlet International plc, re (ChD 1998) *The Times*, 13 March 1998   11.7.10.1
Hammond v Prentice Brothers Ltd (ChD 1919) [1920] 1 Ch 201, 89 LJ Ch 91, 122 LT 307,
    84 JP 25, 36 TLR 98, 18 LGR 73, 64 SJ 131   1.6
Hampshire Land Co., re (ChD 1896) [1896] 2 Ch 743, 65 LJ Ch 860, 75 LT 181, 12 TLR 517,
    3 Mans 269, 45 WR 136   19.8.3
Hampson v Price's Patent Candle Co. (MR 1876) 45 LJ Ch 437, 34 LT 711,
    24 WR 754   2.3.5.6, 2.4.2.9
Hampstead Garden Suburb Trust Ltd, re (ChD 1962) [1962] Ch 806, [1962] 3 WLR 474,
    [1962] 2 All ER 879, 106 SJ 451   2.4.4
Hannes v MJH Pty Ltd (New South Wales CA 1992) 7 ACSR 8   16.4.14
Hannibal (E.) & Co. Ltd v Frost (CA 1987) 4 BCC 3   15.7.2
Hansraj Gupta v Asthana (PC 1932) LR 60 Ind App 1   1.3.2.1
Harben v Phillips (CA 1882) 23 ChD 14 at 30, 48 LT 334 at 339, 31 WR 173;
    further proceedings (CA 1883) 23 ChD 14 at 37, 48 LT 741   14.4.9.1.3, 15.3.7, 15.7.3
Hardwick, re (ex parte Hubbard) (CA 1886) 17 QBD 690, 55 LJ QB 490, 59 LT 172n,
    35 WR 2, 2 TLR 904, 3 Morr 246   11.5.1
Harman v BML Group Ltd (CA 1994) [1994] 1 WLR 893, [1994] 2 BCLC 674, [1994] BCC 502
    (sub nom. Re BML Group Ltd)   14.4.4
Harman v Energy Research Group Australia Ltd (SC of Western Australia 1985)
    [1986] WAR 123, 9 ACLR 897, 3 ACLC 536   15.2.1
Harmer (H.R.) Ltd, re (CA 1958) [1959] 1 WLR 62, [1958] 3 All ER 689, 103 SJ 73
    14.4.9.4, 15.2.3.2, 15.3.7, 15.5.1, 18.4.12, 18.6.4
Harold Holdsworth & Co. (Wakefield) Ltd v Caddies (HL (C Sess 1st Div) 1955)
    [1955] 1 WLR 352, [1955] 1 All ER 725, 1951 SC (HL) 27, 1955 SLT 133,
    99 SJ 234   15.5.3
Harpur's Cycle Fittings Co., re (ChD 1900) [1900] 2 Ch 731, 69 LJ Ch 841, 83 LT 407,
    8 Mans 90   11.6.2
Harris v A. Harris Ltd (C Sess 2nd Div 1935) 1936 SC 183   14.4.9.4
Harris Simons Construction Ltd, re (ChD 1988) [1989] 1 WLR 368, [1989] BCLC 202,
    1989 PCC 229, 5 BCC 11   20.3.2
Harrods Ltd v Harrods (Buenos Aires) Ltd (ChD 1997) [1997] FSR 420   2.3.3.6
Hartley's Case; see Re Poole Firebrick & Blue Clay Co.
Haslam & Hier-Evans, re (CA 1902) [1902] 1 Ch 765, 71 LJ Ch 374, 86 LJ 663, 50 WR 444,
    18 TLR 461, 46 SJ 381   16.5.1
Hassell v Merchant Traders' Ship Loan & Insurance Association (Exchequer 1849) 4 Ex 525,
    154 ER 1322, 19 LJ Ex 183   1.3.2.5
Hawkesbury Development Co. Ltd v Landmark Finance Pty Ltd and others (SC of New South
    Wales 1969) 92 WN (NSW) 199, [1969] 2 NSWR 782   18.3.1, 18.4.1, 18.4.10, 18.4.13, 20.2.3
Haycraft Gold Reduction & Mining Co., re (ChD 1900) [1900] 2 Ch 230, 69 LJ Ch 497,
    83 LT 166, 16 TLR 350, 7 Mans 243   14.4.5.1, 15.5.1, 18.5
Hayes v Bristol Plant Hire Ltd (ChD 1957) [1957] 1 WLR 499, [1957] 1 All ER 685,
    101 SJ 266   15.3.7
Heald v O'Connor (QBD 1970) [1971] 1 WLR 497, [1971] 2 All ER 1105   10.8.4, 10.8.5
Hearts of Oak Assurance Co. Ltd v James Flower and Sons (ChD 1935) [1936] Ch 76,
    105 LJ Ch 25, 154 LT 156, 52 TLR 5, 79 SJ 839   14.4.11
Heather v P-E Consulting Group Ltd (CA 1972) [1973] Ch 189 at 212, [1972] 3 WLR 833,
    [1973] 1 All ER 8, 48 TC 293, [1972] TR 237, 116 SJ 824   9.3.8
Heaton's Steel and Iron Co., re, Blyth's Case (CA 1876) 4 ChD 140, 36 LT 124, 25 WR 200   6.1.11
Hedley Byrne & Co. Ltd v Heller & Partners Ltd (H L 1963) [1964] AC 465, [19631 3 WLR 101,
    [1963] 2 All ER 575, [1963] 1 Lloyd's Rep 485, 107 SJ 454   8.10
Heinhuis v Blacksheep Charters Ltd (CA of British Columbia 1987) 46 DLR (4th) 67,
    [1988] 2 WWR 444, 19 BCLR (2d) 239   19.6.2
Heiton v Waverley Hydropathic Co. Ltd (C Sess 1st Div 1877) 4 R 830, 14 SLR 532   19.5.6
Hellenic & General Trust Ltd, re (ChD 1975) [1976] 1 WLR 123, [1975] 3 All ER 382,
    119 SJ 845   8.8.3
Hely-Hutchinson v Brayhead Ltd (CA 1967) [1968] 1 QB 549, [1967] 3 WLR 1408,
    [1967] 3 All ER 98, 111 SJ 830   15.5.3, 15.8.2.4, 16.5.5.1, 16.6.4, 16.6.5, 19.5.4.1, 19.5.4.3

Hemmerling v IMTC Systems (British Columbia CA 1993) 109 DLR (4th) 582   14.3.1
Henderson v Bank of Australasia (ChD 1888) 40 ChD 170, 58 LJ Ch 197, 59 LT 856, 4 TLR 734,
   37 WR 332   2.3.5.6, 2.5.3.7
Henderson v Bank of Australasia (CA 1890) 45 ChD 330, 59 LJ Ch 794, 63 LT 597, 6 TLR 424,
   2 Meg 301, [1886-90] All FR Rep 1190   18.5
Henderson v James Loutitt and Co. Ltd (Scotland C Sess 1st Div 1894) 21 R 674   14.4.6.1
Henderson v Merrett Syndicates Ltd (HL 1994) [1995] 2 AC 145, [1994] 3 WLR 761,
   [1994] 3 All ER 506, [1994] 2 Lloyd's Rep 468   16.2.1.1
Hendon v Adelman (QBD 1973) 117 SJ 631   4.5.1
Hendriks v Montagu (CA 1881) 17 ChD 638, 50 LJ Ch 257, 44 LT 879, 30 WR 168,
   [1881–5] All ER Rep Ext 1819   2.3.3.6
Hendy Lennox (Industrial Engines) Ltd v Grahame Puttick Ltd (QBD 1983)
   [1984] 1 WLR 485, [1984] 2 All ER 152, [1984] 2 Lloyd's Rep 422, [1984] BCLC 285,
   128 SJ 220   11.7.10.3
Henry v Great Northern Railway Co. (LJJ 1857) 1 De G & J 606, 44 ER 858, 27 LJ Ch 1,
   3 Jur (NS) 1133, 6 WR 87   10.5.1
Henry Head & Co. Ltd v Ropner Holdings Ltd (ChD 1951) [1952] Ch 124, [1951] 2 All ER 994,
   [1951] 2 Lloyd's Rep 348, [1951] 2 TLR 1027, 95 SJ 789   6.5.2
Hercules Insurance Co., re, Pugh and Sharman's Case (V-C 1872) LR 13 Eq 566, 41 LJ Ch 580,
   26 LT 274   14.2
Hereford & South Wales Waggon & Engineering Co., re (CA 1876) 2 ChD 621, 45 LJ Ch 461,
   35 LT 40, 24 WR 953   19.6.2
Heron v Port Huon Fruitgrowers' Cooperative Association Ltd (Australia HC 1922) 30 CLR 315,
   28 ALR 203   3.4.2.5
Heron International Ltd v Lord Grade (CA 1982) [1983] BCLC 244, [1982] Com LR 108
   8.3.4, 16.4.12
Herrman v Simon (New South Wales CA 1990) 4 ACSR 81   14.5.1
Heymann v European Central Railway Co. (MR 1868) LR 7 Eq 154   6.7.4
Heyting v Dupont (CA 1964) [1964] 1 WLR 843, [1964] 2 All ER 273, 108 SJ 277   18.4.13
Hichens v Congreve (LC 1828) 4 Russ 562, 38 ER 917, 6 LJ OS Ch 167; further
   proceedings (V-C 1828) 1 Russ & M 150, 39 ER 58; further proceedings (V-C 1831) 4 Sim 420,
   58 ER 157   17.6.3.1
Hickman v Kent or Romney Marsh Sheep-Breeders' Association (ChD 1915) [1915] 1 Ch 881,
   84 LJ Ch 688, 113 LT 159, [1914–15] All ER Rep 900, 59 SJ 478   3.4.2.1, 3.4.2.3, 3.4.3.2
Hickman v Kent or Romney Marsh Sheep-Breeders' Association (CA 1920)
   37 TLR 163   3.4.2.1
Higgins v Nicol (Australia Commonwealth Industrial Court 1971) 18 FLR 343,
   137 CAR 1032   14.4.1
Highfield Commodities Ltd, re (ChD 1984) [1985] 1 WLR 149, [1984] 3 All ER 884,
   [1984] BCLC 623, 1985 PCC 191, 1 BCC 99,277, 81 LS Gaz 3589, 128 SJ 870   20.6.1,
Hill v Permanent Trustee Co. of New South Wales Ltd (PC 1930) [1930] AC 720,
   [1930] All ER Rep 87, 99 LJ PC 191, 144 LT 65   10.1
Hill Samuel & Co. Ltd v Laing (C Sess OH 1987) 1988 SLT 452, 4 BCC 9   20.2.7.3
Hilton v Plustitle Ltd (CA 1988) [1989] 1 WLR 149, [1988] 3 All ER 1051   5.2.2.4
Hilton International Ltd v Hilton (New Zealand HC 1988) [1989] 1 NZLR 442   10.5.10
Hindle v John Cotton Ltd (HL 1919) 56 SLR 625   16.4.10
Hirschs v Sims (PC (SC of Cape of Good Hope) 1894) [1894] AC 654, 64 LJ PC 1, 71 LT 357,
   10 TLR 616, 11 R 303   16.4.10
Hitco 2000 Ltd, re (ChD 1994) [1995] 2 BCLC 63, [1995] BCC 161   15.2.5.6
Ho Tung v Man On Insurance Co. Ltd (PC (SC of Hong Kong) 1901) [1902] AC 232, 71 LJ PC 46,
   85 LT 617, 9 Mans 171, 18 TLR 118   14.5.1
Hoare & Co. Ltd, re (ChD 1933) 150 LT 374, [1933] All ER Rep 105   8.8.2.3
Hockerill Athletic Club Ltd, re (ChD 1990) [1990] BCLC 921   14.4.1
Hogg v Cramphorn Ltd (ChD 1963) [1967] Ch 254, [1966] 3 WLR 995, [1966] 3 All ER 420,
   110 SJ 887   16.4.2, 16.4.11, 16.4.14, 18.4.11
Holders Investment Trust Ltd, re (ChD 1970) [1971] 1 WLR 583, [1971] 2 All ER 289,
   115 SJ 202   14.4.9.4, 14.6.2.4
Hole v Garnsey (HL 1930) [1930] AC 472, 99 LJ Ch 243, 143 LT 153, 46 TLR 312, 74 SJ 214,
   [1930] All ER Rep 568   1.3.2.3, 3.5.3.3

Holmes v Keyes (CA 1958) [1959] Ch 199, [1958] 2 WLR 772, [1958] 2 All ER 129, 102 SJ 329
3.3.5, 14.4.9.2, 15.2.3.2
Home Treat Ltd, re (ChD 1991) [1991] BCLC 705, [1991] BCC 165
14.5.1, 17.5
Homes Assured Corporation plc, re (ChD 1996) [1996] BCC 297
15.2.5.6
Hong Kong & China Gas Co. Ltd v Glen (ChD 1914) [1914] 1 Ch 527, 83 LJ Ch 561,
110 LT 859, 30 TLR 339, 21 Mans 242, 58 SJ 380, [1914–15] All ER Rep 1002
6.5.4
Hood Sailmakers Ltd v Axford (QBD 1996) [1997] 1 WLR 625, [1996] 4 All ER 830,
[1997] 1 BCLC 721, [1997] BCC 263
15.5.1
Hooker Investments Pty Ltd v Email Ltd (New South Wales SC 1986)
10 ACLR 443
18.4.2
Hop & Malt Exchange & Warehouse Co., re, ex parte Briggs (MR 1866) LR 1 Eq 483,
35 LJ Ch 320, 14 LT 39, 12 Jur NS 322, 35 Beav 273
6.7.4
Hope v International Financial Society (CA 1876) 4 ChD 327, 46 LJ Ch 200, 35 LT 924,
25 WR 203
18.4.9, 18.4.10
Horbury Bridge Coal, Iron & Waggon Co., re (CA 1879) 11 ChD 109, 48 LJ Ch 341, 40 LT 353,
27 WR 433
14.4.9.1.1, 14.4.9.2
Horn v Henry Faulder & Co. Ltd (ChD 1908) 99 LT 524
15.7.2.4
Horsley & Weight Ltd, re (CA 1980) [1982] Ch 442, [1982] 3 WLR 431, [1982] 3 All ER 1045,
79 LS Gaz 919, 126 SJ 492
2.3.5.6, 2.3.5.7, 2.3.5.9, 19.5.8, 20.11.4
Hospital Products Ltd v United States Surgical Corporation (HC of Australia 1984) 156 CLR 41,
55 ALR 417, 58 ALJR 587
16.3.1, 16.7.3.4
Hotel Terrigal Pty Ltd v Latec Investments Ltd (No. 2) (New South Wales SC 1963)
[1969] 1 NSWR 676; affirmed in part by HC of Australia (1965) sub nom. Latec
Investments Ltd v Hotel Teirigal Pty Ltd 113 CLR 265
5.2.1, 5.2.2.3
Houghton (J.C.) & Co. v Nothard Lowe & Wills Ltd (CA 1926) [1927] 1 KB 246, 96 LJ KB 25,
136 LT 140 [1927] All ER Rep 97; affirmed by HL (1927) [1928] AC 1, 97 LJ QB 76,
138 LT 210, 44 TLR 76
19.5.4.6
Houldsworth v City of Glasgow Bank and liquidators (HL (C Sess 1st Div) 1880) 5 App Cas 317,
42 LT 194, 28 WR 677, 7 R (HL) 53, 17 SLR 510
6.7.5
House of Fraser plc v ACGE Investments Ltd (HL 1987) [1987] AC 387, [1987] 2 WLR 1083,
1987 SLT 421, 1987 SCLR 637, [1987] BCLC 478, 1987 PCC 364 (sub nom. ACGE
Investments Ltd v House of Fraser plc), 3 BCC 201
10.2.4, 14.6.2.6
Household Fire & Carriage Accident Insurance Co. Ltd v Grant (CA 1879) 4 ExD 216,
48 LJ QB 577, 41 LT 298, 44 JP 152, 27 WR 858
6.2.2
Household Products Co. Ltd and Federal Business Development Bank, re (Ontario HC 1981)
33 OR (2d) 334, 38 CBR(NS) 164, 124 DLR (3d) 325
11.6.2, 20.2.8.1
Howard v Patent Ivory Manufacturing Co.; see Re Patent Ivory Manufacturing Co.
Howard Smith Ltd v Ampol Petroleum Ltd (PC 1974) [1974] AC 821, [1974] 2 WLR 689,
[1974] 1 All ER 1126, [1974] 1 NSWLR 68, 48 ALJR 5, 3 ALR 448, 118 SJ 330
15.7.1, 16.4.2, 16.4.10, 16.4.11, 16.4.12
Howling's Trustees v Smith (C Sess 2nd Div 1905) 7 F 390
14.4.1
Hull & County Bank, re, Burgess's Case (MR 1880) 15 ChD 507, 49 LJ Ch 541, 43 LT 54,
28 WR 792
6.7.4
Humber Ironworks & Shipbuilding Co., re, Warrant Finance Co.'s Case (CA in Chancery 1869)
LR 4 Ch App 643, 38 LJ Ch 712, 20 LT 859, 17 WR 780
20.13.2
Humes Ltd v Unity APA Ltd (No. 1) (Victoria SC 1987) [1987] VR 467, 11 ACLR 641
(sub nom. Humes Ltd v Unity APA Ltd), 5 ACLC 15
14.4.3
Hurley v BGH Nominees Pty Ltd (SC (in banco) of South Australia 1982) 31 SASR 250,
6 ACLR 791, 1 ACLC 387
18.3.1
further proceedings (1984) 37 SASR 499, 10 ACLR 197
16.4.7
Hutt Valley Energy Board v Hayman (New Zealand HC 1988) 4 NZCLC 64,244
4.5.1
Hutton v Scarborough Cliff Hotel Co. Ltd (LC 1865) 4 De G J & S 672, 46 ER 1079,
34 LJ Ch 643
3.5.1
Hutton v West Cork Railway Co. (CA 1883) 23 ChD 654, 52 LJ Ch 689, 49 LT 420,
31 WR 827
2.3.5.6, 2.3.5.7, 14.4.9.4, 15.6.1.1, 15.6.1.5
Hydrodam (Corby) Ltd, re (ChD 1993) [1994] 2 BCLC 180, [1994] BCC 161 (sub nom.
Re Hydrodan (Corby) Ltd)
15.1.6, 20.12

Ian Chisholm Textiles Ltd v Griffiths (ChD 1993) [1994] 2 BCLC 291, [1994] BCC 96
11.7.5, 11.7.10.3

Iceland Sulphur & Copper Co. Ltd, re the (ChD 1886) 2 TLR 509   3.4.4
Illingworth v Houldsworth (HL 1904) [1904] AC 355, 73 LJ Ch 739, 91 LT 602,
   20 TLR 633, 53 WR 113, 12 Mans 141; (CA 1903) (sub nom. Re Yorkshire
   Woolcombers Association Ltd) [1903] 2 Ch 284, 72 LJ Ch 635, 88 LT 811   11.6.1, 11.6.4
Imperial Chemical Industries Ltd v Commission (case 48/69) (ECJ 1972)
   [1972] ECR 619, [1972] CMLR 557   5.2.2.9
Imperial Hydropathic Hotel Co., Blackpool v Hampson (CA 1882) 23 ChD 1, 49 LT 150,
   31 WR 330   3.4.2.3, 3.5.1, 15.7.1, 15.7.2.4, 15.8
Imperial Mercantile Credit Association, the liquidators of the v Coleman and Knight
   (HL 1873) LR 6 HL 189, 42 LJ Ch 644, 29 LT 1, 21 WR 696   16.3.1, 16.6.2
Imperial Motors (UK) Ltd, re (ChD 1988) [1990] BCLC 29, 5 BCC 214   20.3.2
Incorporated Glasgow Dental Hospital v Lord Advocate (C Sess 2nd Div 1927) 1927 SC 400,
   1927 SLT 270   2.4.4
Independent Automatic Sales Ltd v Knowles & Foster (ChD 1962) [1962] 1 WLR 974,
   [1962] 3 All ER 27, 106 SJ 720   11.7.10.2
Inderwick v Snell (LC 1850) 2 Mac & G 216, 42 ER 83, 2 H & Tw 412, 47 ER 1744,
   19 LJ Ch 542, 14 Jur 727   18.3.3.1
Indian Zoedone Co., re (CA 1884) 26 ChD 70, 53 LJ Ch 468, 50 LT 547, 32 WR 481   14.4.7
Indo-China Steam Navigation Co., re (ChD 1917) [1917] 2 Ch 100, 86 LJ Ch 723, 117 LT 212,
   [1916–17] All ER Rep 793   8.3.4
Industrial Development Consultants Ltd v Cooley (Birmingham Assizes 1971) [1972] 1 WLR 443,
   [1972] 2 All ER 162, 116 SJ 255   16.7.3.1, 16.7.3.2, 16.7.3.3, 16.7.3.5
Industrial Equity Ltd v Blackburn (Australia HC 1977) 137 CLR 567, 52 ALJR 89, 17 ALR 575,
   3 ACLR 89, (1977) ACLC 29,635   5.2.2.9
Ingre v Maxwell (British Columbia SC 1964) 44 DLR (2d) 764   18.4.3
Inland Revenue v Liquidators of Purvis Industries Ltd; see Lord Advocate v Liquidators
   of Purvis Industries Ltd
Inland Revenue Commissioners; see Commissioners of Inland Revenue
Inquiry under the Company Securities (Insider Dealing) Act 1985, re an (HL 1987) [1988] AC 660,
   [1988] 2 WLR 33, [1988] 1 All ER 203, [1988] BCLC 153, 1988 PCC 134, 4 BCC 35   18.8.2.6
Instrumentation Electrical Services Ltd, re (ChD 1988) [1988] BCLC 550, 1989 PCC 101,
   4 BCC 301   15.7.2.2, 20.3.2
International Credit and Investment Co. (Overseas) Ltd v Adham (ChD 1996)
   [1998] BCC 134   5.2.2.4
International Sales & Agencies Ltd v Marcus (QBD 1981) [1982] 3 All ER 551,
   [1982] 2 CMLR 46   18.2.2, 19.5.5
International Securities Corporation Ltd, re (CA 1908) 25 TLR 31   19.9
Introductions Ltd, re (CA 1969) [1970] Ch 199, [1969] 2 WLR 791, [1969] 1 All ER 887,
   [1969] 1 Lloyd's Rep 229, 113 SJ 122; affirming ChD (1968) [1968] 2 All ER 1221
     2.3.5.9, 19.5.7
Invention Finance Pty Ltd v Flavel (South Australia SC 1988) 13 ACLR 99, 6 ACLC 408   4.5.1
Irvine v Union Bank of Australia (PC (Court of the Recorder of Rangoon) 1877)
   2 App Cas 366, 46 LJ PC 87, 37 LT 176, 25 WR 682   19.5.8
Isaacs's case; see Re Anglo-Austrian Printing & Publishing Union
Island Export Finance Ltd v Umunna (QBD 1985) [1986] BCLC 460   16.7.3.3, 16.7.3.5
Isle of Thanet Electricity Supply Co. Ltd, re (CA 1949) [1950] Ch 161, [1949] 2 All ER 1060   6.1.5
Isle of Wight Railway Co. v Tahourdin (CA 1883) 25 ChD 320, 53 LJ Ch 353, 50 LT 132,
   32 WR 297   14.4.3, 15.7.2.4

Jaber v Science & Information Technology Ltd (ChD 1992) [1992] BCLC 864   18.6.2
Jackson v Hamlyn (ChD 1953) [1953] Ch 577, [1953] 2 WLR 709, [1953] 1 All ER 887,
   97 SJ 248   14.4.10
Jackson & Bassford Ltd, re (ChD 1906) [1906] 2 Ch 467, 75 LJ Ch 697, 95 LT 292,
   13 Mans 306, 22 TLR 708   11.7.10.1
Jacobus Marter Estates Ltd v Marler (HL 1913) 85 LJ PC 167 n, 114 LT 640 n,
   [1916–17] All ER Rep 291 n   17.6.4
James v Buena Ventura Nitrate Grounds Syndicate Ltd (CA 1896) [1896] 1 Ch 456,
   65 LJ Ch 284, 74 LT 1, 44 WR 372, 12 TLR 176, 40 SJ 238   8.5

James McNaughton Paper Group Ltd v Hicks Anderson & Co. (CA 1990) [1991] 2 QB 113;
    [1991] 2 WLR 641, [1991] 1 All ER 134 (sub nom. James McNaughton Papers Group Ltd v
    Hicks Anderson & Co.), [1991] BCLC 163 (sub nom. James McNaughton Papers Group
    Ltd v Hicks Anderson & Co.), [1990] BCC 891   8.10
James Prain & Sons Ltd (C Sess 1st Div 1947) 1947 SC 325, 1947 SLT 289   14.4.6.2
Jaybird Group Ltd v Greenwood (ChD 1981) [1986] BCLC 319   18.4.7
JEB Fasteners Ltd v Marks, Bloom & Co. (CA 1982) [1983] 1 All ER 583,
    [1982] Com LR 226   6.7.7, 8.10
Jeffries (Chas) & Sons Pty Ltd, re (Victoria SC 1948) [1949] VLR 190, [1949] ALR 810   3.4.3
Jenice Ltd v Dan (QBD 1992) [1993] BCLC 1349, [1994] BCC 43   4.5.1
Jennings v Hammond (QBDC 1882) 9 QBD 225, 51 LJ QB 493, 31 WR 40   1.5
John v Rees (ChD 1968) [1970] Ch 345, [1969] 2 WLR 1294, [1969] 2 All ER 274,
    113 SJ 487   14.4.10
John Crowther Group plc v Carpets International plc (ChD 1985) [1990] BCLC 460   14.4.5.5
John Henshall (Quarries) Ltd v Harvey (QBDC 1965) [1965] 2 QB 233, [1965] 2 WLR 758,
    [1965] 1 All ER 725, 129 JP 224   19.8.6.2
John Shaw & Sons (Salford) Ltd v Shaw and Shaw (CA 1935) [1935] 2 KB 113, 104 LJ KB 549,
    153 LT 245, [1935] All ER Rep 456   15.5.1, 15.7.2.4, 15.7.3
John Smith's Tadcaster Brewery Co. Ltd, re (CA 1953) [1953] Ch 308, [1953] 2 WLR 516,
    [1952] 1 All ER 518, 97 SJ 150   14.6.2.6
John Wilkes (Footwear) Ltd v Lee International (Footwear) Ltd (CA 1985) [1985] BCLC 444,
    1 BCC 99, 452   4.5.1
Johns v Balfour (ChD 1889) 5 TLR 389, 1 Meg 181   2.3.5.6
Johnson v Lyttle's Iron Agency (CA 1877) 5 ChD 687, 46 LJ Ch 786, 36 LT 528,
    25 WR 548   3.4.2.1, 6.4.2
Johnson (B.) & Co. (Builders) Ltd, re (CA 1955) [1955] Ch 634, [1955] 3 WLR 269,
    [1955] 2 All ER 775, 99 SJ 490   20.2.7.1
Johnson (I.C.) & Co. Ltd, re (CA 1902) [1902] 2 Ch 101, 71 LJ Ch 576, 86 LT 791,
    50 WR 482, 9 Mans 307, 46 SJ 498, [1900–3] All ER Rep Ext 1331   11.7.9
Joint Stock Discount Co. v Brown (VC 1866) LR 3 Eq 139, 15 LT 174, 12 Jur NS 899   8.8.3
Jonathan Alexander Ltd v Proctor (CA 1995) [1996] 1 WLR 518, [1996] 2 BCLC 91   19.9
Jones v Hellard (QBDC 1998) *The Times*, 23 March 1998   19.8.4
Jones v Lipman (ChD 1961) [1962] 1 WLR 832, [1962] 1 All ER 442, 106 SJ 531   5.2.2.4, 5.2.2.5
Joshua Shaw & Sons Ltd, re (ChD 1988) [1989] BCLC 362, 5 BCC 188   16.4.6.1
Jubilee Cotton Mills Ltd v Lewis (HL 1924) [1924] AC 958, 93 LJ Ch 414, 131 LT 579,
    40 TLR 621, [1925] B & CR 16   1.2.1
Jupiter House Investments (Cambridge) Ltd, re (ChD 1984) [1985] 1 WLR 975,
    [1985] BCLC 222, 1 BCC 99,457   10.2.2

Kajubi v Kayanja (Uganda HC 1967) [1967] EA 301   19.8.9
Karak Rubber Co. Ltd v Burden (ChD 1971) [1971] 1 WLR 1784, [1971] 3 All ER 1118,
    115 SJ 887   18.8.3.7
Karella v Greek Minister of Industry, Energy and Technology (cases C-19/90 and C-20/90)
    (ECJ 1991) [1991] ECR I-2691, [1993] 2 CMLR 865, [1993] 2 CEC 56, [1994] 1 BCLC 774,
    [1993] BCC 677   0.3.3.1
Kaye v Croydon Tramways Co. (CA 1898) [1898] 1 Ch 358, 67 LJ Ch 222, 78 LT 237,
    14 TLR 244, 46 WR 405, 42 SJ 307   14.4.5.5, 16.8
Kaye v Massbetter Ltd (CA 1990) 62 P & CR 558, [1991] 2 EGLR 97   5.2.2.4
Kean v McGivan (CA 1981) [1982] FSR 119   2.3.3.6
Keech v Sandford (LC 1726) Sel Cas t King 61, 25 ER 223, 2 Eq Cas Abr 741, 22 ER 629   16.5.1
Keith Spicer Ltd v Mansell (CA 1969) [1970] 1 WLR 333, [1970] 1 All ER 462, 114 SJ 30   19.6.1
Kelner v Baxter (Court of Common Pleas 1866) LR 2 CP 174, 36 LJ CP 94, 15 LT 213,
    15 WR 278, [1861–73] All ER Rep Ext 2009   19.6.1, 19.6.2
Kemp v R; see R v Kemp
Kent v Freehold Land and Brick-making Co. (LC 1868) LR 3 Ch App 493, 37 LJ Ch 653,
    32 JP 742, 16 WR 990   6.7.4
Kent v Jackson (MR 1851) 14 Beav 367, 51 ER 328; affirmed by LJJ (1852) 2 De G M & G 49,
    42 ER 789   18.4.3

Kent & Sussex Sawmills Ltd, re (ChD 1946) [1947] Ch 177, [1946] 2 All ER 638,
    [1947] LJR 534, 176 LT 167, 62 TLR 747, 91 SJ 12   11.7.10.1
Kenyon Swansea Ltd, re (ChD 1987) [1987] BCLC 514, 1987 PCC 333, 3 BCC 259   18.6.4, 18.6.6
Kepic v Tecumseh Road Builders (SC of Ontario 1985) 29 BLR 85   20.2.7.1
Kernohan Estates Ltd v Boyd (Northern Ireland ChD 1965) [1967] NI 27   20.2.7.1
Kerr v John Mottram Ltd (ChD 1940) [1940] Ch 657, [1940] 2 All ER 629, 109 LJ Ch 243,
    163 LT 227, 56 TLR 711, 84 SJ 358   3.4.2.1, 3.4.4
Kerry v Maori Dream Gold Mines Ltd (CA 1898) 14 TLR 402   18.4.4
Keypak Homecare Ltd, re (ChD 1989) [1990] BCLC 440, [1990] BCC 117 (sub nom.
    Re Keypak Homecare Ltd (No. 2))   15.2.5.6
Keypak Homecare Ltd, re (No. 2); see Re Keypak Homecare Ltd
Khan v Miah (CA 1997) [1998] 1 WLR 477   0.1.4
Kingsgate Rare Metals Pty Ltd, re (Queensland SC 1940) [1940] QWN 42   15.2.5.1
Kingston Cotton Mill Co., re (No. 2) (CA 1896) [1896] 2 Ch 279, 65 LJ Ch 673, 74 LT 568   17.4.5
Kinnaird v Trollope (ChD 1888) 39 ChD 636, 58 LJ Ch 556, 60 LT 892, 5 TLR 513   11.5.6
Kinookimaw Beach Association, re (Saskatchewan CA 1979) 102 DLR (3d) 333,
    [1979] 6 WWR 84   5.2.2.1, 19.8.9
Kinsela v Russell Kinsela Pty Ltd (CA of New South Wales 1986) 4 NSWLR 722, 10 ACLR 395,
    4 ACLC 215; affirming SC (1983) sub nom. Russell Kinsela Pty Ltd v Kinsela
    [1983] 2 NSWLR 452, 8 ACLR 384, 1 ACLC 1215   16.4.2, 16.4.6.1, 16.4.14, 20.11.4
Kleinwort Benson Ltd v Malaysia Mining Corporation Bhd (CA 1989) [1989] 1 WLR 379,
    [1989] 1 All ER 785, [1989] 1 Lloyd's Rep 556, 5 BCC 337   5.2.2.8
Kleinwort Sons & Co. v Associated Automatic Machine Corporation Ltd (HL 1934) 151 LT 1,
    50 TLR 244, 39 Com Cas 189, [1934] WN 65   8.3.2
Knight & Searle v Dove (QBD 1964) [1964] 2 QB 631, [1964] 3 WLR 50,
    [1964] 2 All ER 307   0.1.6, 5.3.1
Knight's case; see Re North Hallenbeagle Mining Co.
Knightsbridge Estates Trust Ltd v Byrne (HL 1940) [1940] AC 613, [1940] 2 All ER 401,
    109 LJ Ch 200, 162 LT 388, 56 TLR 652, 84 SJ 488   11.2.2
Koffyfontein Mines Ltd v Mosely (HL 1911) [1911] AC 409, 80 LJ Ch 668, 105 LT 115,
    27 TLR 501, 18 Mans 365, 55 SJ 551   6.1.11
Kolotex Hosiery (Australia) Pty Ltd v Federal Commissioner of Taxation (Australia HC 1975)
    132 CLR 535, 49 ALJR 35, 5 ALR 89, 5 ATR 206, 75 ATC 4028   14.4.9.1.8
Kong Thai Sawmill (Miri) Sdn Bhd (PC (Federal Court of Malaysia) 1978) [1978]
    2 MLJ 227   18.3.3.2
Kosmopoulos v Constitution Insurance Co. of Canada; see Constitution Insurance Co. of
    Canada v Kosmopoulos
Kounis v Kounis (SC of Western Australia FC 1987) 11 ACLR 854   1.3.5, 3.4.1.3, 14.4.9.5
Kraus v J.G. Lloyd Pty Ltd (Victoria SC 1963) [1965] VR 232   18.4.9
Kreditbank Cassel GmbH v Schenkers Ltd (CA 1927) [1927] 1 KB 826, 96 LJ KB 501,
    136 LT 716, 43 TLR 237, 32 Com Cas 197, 71 SJ 141   19.5.4.1, 19.5.4.2, 19.5.4.6
Kreglinger (G. & C.) v New Patagonia Meat & Cold Storage Co. Ltd (HL 1913) [1914] AC 25,
    83 LJ Ch 79, 109 LT 802, 30 TLR 114, [1911–13] All ER Rep 970, 58 SJ 97   11.2.2
Kris Cruisers Ltd, re (ChD 1948) [1949] Ch 138, [1948] 2 All ER 1105, [1949] LJR 202,
    65 TLR 52, 92 SJ 706   11.7.9
Kuenigl v Donnersmarck (QBD 1954) [1955] 1 QB 515, [1955] 2 WLR 82,
    [1955] 1 All ER 46   19.8.2
Kuwait Asia Bank EC v National Mutual Life Nominees Ltd (PC (from New Zealand CA) 1990)
    [1991] 1 AC 187, [1990] 3 WLR 297, [1990] 3 All ER 404, [1990] 2 Lloyd's Rep 95,
    [1990] BCLC 868, [1990] BCC 567, [1990] 3 NZLR 513   0.1.1, 15.1.6, 15.9, 16.4.6.1, 16.4.15
Kyshe v Alturas Gold Ltd (ChD 1888) 4 TLR 331, 36 WR 496   15.3.7, 15.5.5

Ladies' Dress Association Ltd v Pulbrook (CA 1900) [1900] 2 QB 376, 69 LJ QB 705, 49 WR 6,
    7 Mans 465   6.4.2
Lady Forrest (Murchison) Gold Mine Ltd, re (ChD 1901) [1901] 1 Ch 582, 70 LJ Ch 275,
    84 LT 559, 17 TLR 198, 8 Mans 438   17.6.4
Lady Gwendolen, The (CA 1965) [1965] P 294, [1965] 3 WLR 91, [1965] 2 All ER 283,
    [1965] 1 Lloyd's Rep 335, 109 SJ 336   19.8.1

Ladywell Mining Co. v Brookes (CA 1887) 35 ChD 400, 56 LJ Ch 684, 56 LT 677, 35 WR 785,
3 TLR 546   17.6.4
Lagunas Nitrate Co. v Lagunas Syndicate (CA 1899) [1899] 2 Ch 392, 68 LJ Ch 699, 81 LT 334,
15 TLR 436, 7 Mans 165, 48 WR 74, 43 SJ 622   4.4.1, 17.6.2, 17.6.3.2
Land and Property Trust Co. plc, re (No. 2); see Re Land and Property Trust Co. plc (No. 4)
Land and Property Trust Co. plc, re (No. 4) (CA 1993) [1994] 1 BCLC 232, [1993] BCC 462
(sub nom Re Land and Property Trust Co. plc (No. 2))   19.9
Land Mortgage Bank of Victoria Ltd v Reid (Victoria SC 1909) [1909] VLR 284, 31 ALT 9,
15 ALR 234   6.4.2
Lander v Premier Pict Petroleum Ltd (Scotland CSess OH 1997) [1998] BCC 248,
1997 SLT 1361   15.6.2.2
Lands Allotment Co., re (CA 1894) [1894] 1 Ch 616, 63 LJ Ch 291, 70 LT 286, 10 TLR 234,
1 Mans 107, 7 R 115, 42 WR 404, 38 SJ 235, [1891–4] All ER Rep 1032   2.3.5.2, 18.2.2
Latchford Premier Cinema Ltd v Ennion (ChD 1931) [1931] 2 Ch 409, 100 LJ Ch 397,
145 LT 672, 47 TLR 595   15.3.5, 15.3.7, 18.4.9
Latec Investments Ltd v Hotel Terrigal Pty Ltd; see Hotel Terrigal Pty Ltd v Latec
Investments Ltd (No. 2)
Latimer (W.D.) Co. v Dijon Investments Ltd (Ontario Court 1992)
12 OR (3d) 415   5.2.2.1, 5.2.2.4
Lawrence v West Somerset Mineral Railway Co. (ChD 1918) [1918] 2 Ch 250, 87 LJ Ch 513,
119 LT 509, 62 SJ 652   10.5.2
Laxon & Co., re (No. 2) (ChD 1892) [1892] 3 Ch 555, 67 LT 85, 40 WR 621, 8 TLR 666,
36 SJ 609   1.2.1
Lazard Brothers & Co. v Midland Bank Ltd (HL 1932) [1933] AC 289, 102 LJ KB 191,
148 LT 242, [1932] All ER Rep 571, 49 TLR 94, 76 SJ 888   0.1.6
Lazarus Estates Ltd v Beasley (CA 1956) [1956] 1 QB 702, [1956] 2 WLR 502,
[1956] 1 All ER 341, 100 SJ 131   19.2.1
Lee v Chou Wen Hsien (PC (CA of Hong Kong) 1984) [1984] 1 WLR 1202, [1985] BCLC 45,
[1985] LRC (Comm) 825, 1 BCC 99,291, 128 SJ 737   15.3.3, 16.3.1, 16.4.1
Lee v Lee's Air Farming Ltd (PC (CA of New Zealand) 1960) [1961] AC 12, [1960] 3 WLR 758,
[1960] 3 All ER 420, [1961] NZLR 325, 104 SJ 869   5.2.1
Lee v Neuchatel Asphalte Co. (CA 1889) 41 ChD 1, 58 LJ Ch 408, 61 LT 11, 1 Meg 140,
[1886–90] All ER Rep 947, 37 WR 321   6.3.3
Lee Behrens & Co. Ltd, re (ChD 1932) [1932] 2 Ch 46, 101 LJ Ch 183, 147 LT 348,
48 TLR 248, [1931] B & CR 160   2.3.5.7, 15.6.1.1, 16.4.1
Lee Panavision Ltd v Lee Lighting Ltd (CA 1991) [1992] BCLC 22, [1991] BCC 620 at 629;
affirming ChD (1991) [1991] BCLC 575, [1991] BCC 620   16.4.13
Leeds Estate Building & Investment Co. v Shepherd (ChD 1887) 36 ChD 787   10.5.10
Leeds United Holdings plc, re (ChD 1996) [1996] 2 BCLC 545, [1997] BCC 131   16.4.12, 18.6.4
Leicester Club & County Racecourse Co., re, ex parte Cannon (ChD 1885) 30 ChD 629,
55 LJ Ch 206, 53 LT 340, 1 TLR 658, 34 WR 14   3.4.4
Lemon v Austin Friars Investment Trust Ltd (CA 1925) [1926] Ch 1, 95 LJ Ch 97, 133 LT 790,
[1925] All ER Rep 255, 41 TLR 629, 69 SJ 762   11.1
Lennard's Carrying Co. Ltd v Asiatic Petroleum Co. Ltd (HL 1915) [1915] AC 705,
84 LJ KB 1281, 113 LT 195, 13 Asp MLC 81, 31 TLR 294, 20 Com Cas 283,
[1914–15] All ER Rep 280, 59 SJ 411   19.8.1, 19.8.6.1
Leon Needham Ltd, re (ChD 1966) 110 SJ 652   14.3.3
Levin v Clark (New South Wales SC 1960) [1962] NSWR 686, 80 WN (NSW) 485   15.2.6
Lewis Merthyr Consolidated Collieries Ltd, re (Lloyds Bank Ltd v the company) (CA 1928)
[1929] 1 Ch 498, 98 LJ Ch 353, 140 LT 321, 22 BWCC 20, 73 SJ 27   11.6.4, 20.2.8.1, 20.2.9
Lewis Trusts v Bambers Stores Ltd (CA 1983) [1983] FSR 453   5.2.2.8
Lewis's will trusts, re (ChD 1984) [1985] 1 WLR 102, [1984] 3 All ER 930, 128 SJ 385   5.2.1
Leyland DAF Ltd, re (ChD 1994) [1995] 2 WLR 312, [1994] 4 All ER 300, [1994] 2 BCLC 760
(sub nom. Re Leyland DAF Ltd (No. 2)), [1994] BCC 658; for appeal see
Powdrill v Watson   20.2.7.2
Leyland DAF Ltd, re (No. 2); see Re Leyland DAF Ltd
Lifecare International plc, re (ChD 1989) [1990] BCLC 222, 5 BCC 755   8.8.2.3
Liggett (B.) (Liverpool) Ltd v Barclays Bank Ltd (KBD 1927) [1928] 1 KB 48, 97 LJ KB 1,
137 LT 443, 43 TLR 449   19.5.4.5

Lightning Electrical Contractors Ltd, re (ChD 1996) [1996] 2 BCLC 302   2.3.3.8
Lindgren v L & P Estates Ltd (CA 1967) [1968] Ch 572, [1968] 2 WLR 562,
    [1968] 1 All ER 917   16.3.1
Lindholst & Co. A/S v Fowler (CA 1987) [1988] BCLC 166, 4 BCC 776   4.5.1
Lindlar's Case; see Re Discoverers Finance Corporation Ltd, Lindlar's Case
Lines Bros Ltd, re (No. 2) (ChD 1984) [1984] Ch 438, [1984] 2 WLR 905, [1984] BCLC 227,
    128 SJ 261   20.13.2
Linvale Ltd, re (ChD 1992) [1993] BCLC 654   15.2.5.6
Lion Breweries Ltd v Scarrott (New Zealand HC 1986) 3 NZCLC 100,042   16.4.7
Lion Mutual Marine Insurance Association Ltd v Tucker (CA 1883) 12 QBD 176,
    53 LJ QB 185, 49 LT 674, 32 WR 546   1.3.2.3, 1.3.5
Lipkin Gorman v Karpnale Ltd (CA 1989) [1989] 1 WLR 1340, [1992] 4 All ER 409,
    [1989] BCLC 756, 1989 FLR 137   18.2.2
Litster v Forth Dry Dock and Engineering Co. Ltd (HL 1989) [1990] 1 AC 546,
    [1989] 2 WLR 634, [1989] ICR 341, [1989] 1 All ER 1134, [1989] IRLR 161   0.3.3.1
Little v Australian Securities Commission (Australia Administrative Appeals Tribunal
    1996) 22 ACSR 226   2.3.3.3
Little Olympian Each-ways Ltd, re (ChD 1994) [1994] 2 BCLC 420, [1994] BCC 947
    (sub nom. Supreme Travels Ltd v Little Olympian Each-ways Ltd)   18.6.6
Little Olympian Each-Ways Ltd, re (No. 3) (ChD 1994) [1995] 1 BCLC 636   18.6.4, 19.8.3
Littlewoods Mail Order Stores Ltd v Commissioners of Inland Revenue (CA 1969)
    [1969] 1 WLR 1241, [1969] 3 All ER 855 (sub nom. Littlewoods Mail Order Stores Ltd v
    McGregor), 45 TC 519 (sub nom. Littlewoods Mail Order Stores Ltd v McGregor),
    [1969] TR 215, 113 SJ 488   5.2.2.1, 5.2.2.3, 5.2.2.5, 5.2.2.9
Llewellyn v Kasintoe Rubber Estates Ltd (CA 1914) [1914] 2 Ch 670, 84 LJ Ch 70,
    112 LT 676, 30 TLR 683, 21 Mans 349, 58 SJ 808   8.5
Lloyd v David Syme & Co. Ltd (PC (New South Wales CA) 1985) [1986] AC 350,
    [1986] 2 WLR 69, 60 ALJR 10, 63 ALR 83, 3 NSWLR 728   19.8.8
Lloyd Cheyham & Co. Ltd v Littlejohn & Co. (QBD 1985) [1987] BCLC 303,
    1986 PCC 389   8.10, 17.4.5
Lloyd (F.H.) Holdings plc, re (ChD 1985) [1985] BCLC 293, 1985 PCC 268,
    1 BCC 99, 402   8.9.5, 8.9.7
Lloyds & Scottish Trust Ltd v Britten (ChD 1982) 44 P & CR 249, 79 LS Gaz 1291   11.5.6
Lo-Line Electric Motors Ltd, re (ChD 1988) [1988] Ch 477, [1988] 3 WLR 26,
    [1988] 2 All ER 692, [1988] BCLC 698, 1988 PCC 236, 4 BCC 415   15.2.5.6
Loch v John Blackwood Ltd (PC 1924) [1924] AC 783, 93 LJ PC 257, 131 LT 719,
    [1924] All ER Rep 200, [1924] B & CR 209, 40 TLR 732, [1924] 3 WWR 216, 68 SJ 735   18.7.1
Logicrose Ltd v Southend United Football Club Ltd (ChD 1988) [1988] 1 WLR 1256   16.5.5.1
London & Cheshire Insurance Co. Ltd v Laplagrene Property Co. Ltd (ChD 1970) [1971] Ch 499,
    [1971] 2 WLR 257, [1971] 1 All ER 766, 22 P & CR 108, 114 SJ 912   11.7.10.4
London & General Bank, re (No. 2) (CA 1895) [1895] 2 Ch 673, 64 LJ Ch 866, 73 LT 304,
    11 TLR 573, 2 Mans 555, 12 R 502, 39 SJ 706, [1895–9] All ER Rep 953   9.3.8, 10.5.10
London & Mashonaland Exploration Co. Ltd v New Mashonaland Exploration Co. Ltd
    (ChD 1891) [1891] WN 165   16.7.4
London and Northern Bank, re, ex parte Jones (ChD 1899) [1900] 1 Ch 220, 69 LJ Ch 24,
    81 LT 512, 7 Mans 60   6.2.2
London Flats Ltd, re (ChD 1969) [1969] 1 WLR 711, [1969] 2 All ER 744, 113 SJ 304   14.4.6.2
London, Hamburgh & Continental Exchange Bank, re, Evans's Case (LJJ 1867) LR 2 Ch App 427,
    36 LJ Ch 501, 16 LT 252, 15 WR 543   6.8
London Housing Society Ltd's Trust Deeds, re (ChD 1940) [1940] Ch 777, [1940] 3 All ER 665,
    109 LJ Ch 278, 163 LT 86, 56 TLR 773, 84 SJ 416   1.6
London Pressed Hinge Co. Ltd, re (ChD 1905) [1905] 1 Ch 576, 74 LJ Ch 321, 92 LT 409,
    12 Mans 219, 21 TLR 322, 53 WR 407   11.5.3, 11.6.3
London Sack & Bag Co. Ltd v Dixon & Lugton Ltd (CA 1943) [1943] 2 All ER 763,
    170 LT 70   3.4.4
London School of Electronics Ltd, re (ChD 1985) [1986] Ch 211, [1985] 3 WLR 474,
    [1985] BCLC 273, 1985 PCC 248, 1 BCC 99,394, 129 SJ 573   18.6.4
London United Investments plc, re (CA 1991) [1992] Ch 578, [1992] 2 WLR 850,
    [1992] 2 All ER 842, [1992] BCLC 285, [1992] BCC 202   18.8.2.6

Longman v Viscount Chelsea (CA 1989) 58 P & CR 189, [1989] 2 EGLR 242   19.2.5
Lonrho Ltd v Shell Petroleum Co. Ltd (HL 1980) [1980] 1 WLR 627,
  124 SJ 412   5.2.2.5, 9.2.4, 16.4.6.1
Lonrho plc, re (ChD 1987) [1988] BCLC 53, 1987 PCC 355, 3 BCC 265   8.9.7
Lonrho plc, re (No. 2) [1989] BCLC 309, 5 BCC 68 (sub nom. Lonrho plc v Edelman)   8.9.5
Lonrho plc v Edelman; see Re Lonrho plc (No. 2)
Lonrho plc v Fayed (QBD 1988) [1990] 1 QB 490, [1989] 2 WLR 356, [1988] 3 All ER 464,
  [1989] BCLC 75, 1989 PCC 173, 4 BCC 688; (CA 1989) [1990] 2 QB 479, [1989] 3 WLR 631,
  [1989] 2 All ER 65, [1989] BCLC 485, 5 BCC 411; (HL 1991) [1992] 1 AC 448,
  [1991] 3 WLR 188, [1991] 3 All ER 303, [1991] BCLC 779, [1991] BCC 641   8.10
Lonrho plc v Secretary of State for Trade & Industry; see R v Secretary of State for Trade
  & Industry, ex parte Lonrho plc
Looe Fish Ltd, re (ChD 1993) [1993] BCLC 1160, [1993] BCC 348   15.2.5.6, 16.4.11
Lord v Governor and Co. of Copper Miners (LC 1848) 2 Ph 740, 41 ER 1129, 1 H & Tw 85,
  47 ER 1337, 18 LJ Ch 65   18.3.3.1
Lord Corporation Pty Ltd v Green (New South Wales SC 1991) 22 NSWLR 532   20.6.7
Louis K. Liggett Co. v Lee (USA SC 1933) 288 US 517, 77 L ed 929, 53 SCt 481, 85 ALR 699   0.3.3.3
Lowe v Fahey (ChD 1995) [1996] 1 BCLC 262   18.4.2
Lowe (R.) Lippmann Figdor & Franck v AGC (Advances) Ltd (Victoria SC Appeal Division 1992)
  [1992] 2 VR 671, 8 ACSR 380   8.10
Lubin, Rosen & Associates Ltd, re (ChD 1974) [1975] 1 WLR 122, [1975] 1 All ER 577,
  119 SJ 63   18.8.3.3
Lundie Brothers Ltd, re (ChD 1965) [1965] 1 WLR 1051, [1965] 2 All ER 692, 109 SJ 470   18.7.2
Lundy Granite Co. Ltd, re, Harvey Lewis's Case (CA in Ch 1872) 26 LT 673, 20 WR 519   10.1
Lurgan's (Lord) case; see Re Metal Constituents Ltd
Lyford v Commonwealth Bank of Australia (Australia FedC 1995) 130 ALR 267,
  17 ACSR 211   11.6.3
Lynde v Anglo-Italian Hemp Spinning Co. (ChD 1895) [1896] 1 Ch 178, 65 LJ Ch 96,
  12 TLR 61, 73 LT 502, 44 WR 359   6.7.2
Lysaght, re (CA 1897) [1898] 1 Ch 115, 67 LJ Ch 65, 77 LT 637   4.6

M'Arthur (W & A) Ltd, liquidator of v Gulf Line Ltd (C Sess 2nd Div 1909) 1909 SC 732,
  46 SLR 497, 1909 1 SLT 279   8.3.4
Macaura v Northern Assurance Co. Ltd (HL 1925) [1925] AC 619, 94 LJ PC 154, 133 LT 152,
  [1925] All ER Rep 51, 41 TLR 447, 31 Com Cas 10, 69 SJ 777   5.2.1
McAusland v Deputy Commissioner of Taxation (Australia Federal Court 1993)
  118 ALR 577   20.6.7
McClurg v Canada (Canada SC 1990) 76 DLR (4th) 217   10.5.1
M'Cusker v M'Rae (C Sess 2nd Div 1966) 1966 SC 253   9.2.4
McDonald v John Twiname Ltd (CA 1953) [1953] 2 QB 304, [1953] 3 WLR 347,
  [1953] 2 All ER 589   19.2.1
MacDonald v Normanby Cooperative Dairy Factory Co. Ltd (New Zealand SC (FC) 1922)
  [1923] NZLR 122, [1922] GLR 491   3.5.3.3
MacDougall v Gardiner (CA 1875) 1 ChD 13, 45 LJ Ch 27, 33 LT 521, [1874–80] All ER Rep
  Ext 2248, 24 WR 118   3.4.3, 14.4.9.5, 18.3.3.3, 18.4.7, 18.4.8, 18.4.12, 18.5
MacDougall v Gardiner (LJJ 1875) LR 10 Ch App 606, 32 LT 653, 23 WR 846   14.4.4
Mace Builders (Glasgow) Ltd v Lunn (CA 1986) [1987] Ch 191, [1986] 3 WLR 921,
  [1987] BCLC 55, 1986 PCC 470, 2 BCC 99, 532   11.6.5.1
McEllistrim v Ballymacelligott Co-operative Agricultural & Dairy Society Ltd (HL 1919)
  [1919] AC 548, 88 LJ PC 59, 120 LT 613, 35 TLR 354   3.4.2.5
McEuen v West London Wharves and Warehouses Co. (LJJ 1871) LR 6 Ch App 655,
  40 LJ Ch 471, 25 LT 143, 19 WR 837   6.1.11
McGrattan v McGrattan (Northern Ireland CA 1984) [1985] NI 28, [1985] 2 NIJB   14.4.9.1.6
McGuiness v Black (C Sess OH 1989) 1990 SC 21, 1990 SLT 156   18.6.2
Macintyre v Connell (V-C 1851) 1 Sim NS 225, 61 ER 87, 20 LJ Ch 284, 15 Jur 529   0.1.2.4
McIsaac (Scotland CSess OH 1994) [1994] BCC 410   20.9.3
MacKay & Hughes (1973) Ltd v Martin Potatoes Inc. (CA of Ontario 1984) 9 DLR (4th) 439,
  46 OR (2d) 304, 51 CBR (NS) 1, 4 PPSAC 107, 4 OAC 1   20.2.8.3

Mackenzie & Co. Ltd, re (ChD 1916) [1916] 2 Ch 450, 85 LJ Ch 804, 115 LT 440, 61 SJ 29
  14.4.5.2, 14.6.2.6
McKeown v Boudard-Peveril Gear Co. Ltd (CA 1896) 65 LJ Ch 735, 74 LT 712, 40 SJ 565,
  45 WR 152 6.7.3
Mackley's Case; see Re Tal y Drws Slate Co.
Maclaine Watson & Co. Ltd v Department of Trade & Industry; see J.H. Rayner (Mincing
  Lane) Ltd v Department of Trade & Industry
McMillan v Guest (HL 1942) [1942] AC 561, [1942] 1 All ER 606, 111 LJ KB 398, 167 LT 329,
  24 TC 190, 21 ATC 73 15.6.1.5
McMillan v Le Roi Mining Co. Ltd (ChD 1905) [1906] 1 Ch 331, 75 LJ Ch 174, 94 LT 160,
  13 Mans 65, 22 TLR 186, 54 WR 281 14.4.9.2
Macmillan Inc. v Bishopsgate Investment Trust plc (No. 2) (ChD 1993) [1993] ICR 385 19.9
McQuillan, re (Northern Ireland ChD 1988) [1988] 7 NIJB 1, 5 BCC 137 15.2.5.1
Macrae (P & J) Ltd, re (CA 1960) [1961] 1 WLR 229, [1961] 1 All ER 302, 105 SJ 108 20.6.1
Macro (Ipswich) Ltd, re (ChD 1994) [1994] 2 BCLC 354, [1994] BCC 781 at 788 18.6.4
Macson Development Co. Ltd v Gordon (Nova Scotia SC 1959) 19 DLR (2d) 465
  15.2.3.3, 15.5.1, 15.7.2.4
Madrid Bank Ltd v Bayley (Court of Queen's Bench 1866) LR 2 QB 37, 8 B & S 29, 36 LJ QB 15,
  15 LT 292, 15 WR 159 20.6.7
Magnacrete Ltd v Douglas-Hill (South Australia SC 1988) 48 SASR 567, 15 ACLR 325
  14.4.1, 19.2.2
Mahony v the liquidator of the East Holyford Mining Co. (Ltd) (HL (Exchequer Chamber of
  Ireland) 1875) LR 7 HL 869, 33 LT 383, [1874–80] All ER Rep 427 2.2, 3.2, 19.1, 19.5.4.1
Maidstone Buildings Provisions Ltd, re (ChD 1971) [1971] 1 WLR 1085, [1971] 3 All ER 363,
  115 SJ 464 17.3.3, 20.10.3
Majestic Recording Studios Ltd, re (ChD 1988) [1989] BCLC 1, 4 BCC 519 15.2.5.7
Malaga Lead Co., re, Firmstone's Case (MR 1875) LR 20 Eq 524, 44 LJ Ch 617, 23 WR 867 3.4.2.4
Malayan Banking Ltd v Raffles Hotel Ltd (Singapore Federal Court 1965) [1966] 1 MLJ 206 3.4.2.3
Mancetter Developments Ltd v Garmanson Ltd (CA 1985) [1986] QB 1212, [1986] 2 WLR 871,
  [1986] 1 All ER 449, [1986] BCLC 196, 2 BCC 98,924 15.10
Manisty's case; see European Assurance Society Arbitration
Manley Inc. v Fallis (Ontario CA 1977) 38 CPR (2d) 74, 2 BLR 277 5.2.2.9, 17.2
Manlon Trading Ltd, re (ChD 1988) 4 BCC 455 20.3.6
Manlon Trading Ltd, re (CA 1995) [1996] Ch 136, [1995] 3 WLR 839, [1995] 4 All ER 14,
  [1995] 1 BCLC 578, [1995] BCC 579 15.2.5.4
Mann and another v Goldstein (ChD 1967) [1968] 1 WLR 1091, [1968] 2 All ER 769,
  112 SJ 439 20.6.2
Mannix (G.J.) Ltd, re (New Zealand CA 1984) [1984] 1 NZLR 309, 2 NZCLC 99,095 19.9
Manurewa Transport Ltd, re (SC of New Zealand 1971) [1971] NZLR 909 11.6.2
Marco (Croydon) Ltd v Metropolitan Police (QBDC 1983) [1984] RTR 24, [1983] Crim LR 395 4.5.1
Margart Pty Ltd, re (Hamilton v Westpac Banking Corp) (SC of New South Wales 1984)
  79 FLR 330, 9 ACLR 269, [1985] BCLC 314, 2 ACLC 709 11.6.3
Maritime Trader, the (QBD 1980) [1981] 2 Lloyd's Rep 153 5.2.1
Market Wizard Systems (UK) Ltd, re (ChD 1998) *The Times*, 31 July 1998 18.8.3.3
Marks v Financial News Ltd (ChD 1919) 35 TLR 681, [1919] WN 237, 64 SJ 69 18.5
Marleasing SA v La Comercial Internacional de Alimentación SA (case C-106/89) (ECJ 1990)
  [1990] ECR I-4135, [1992] 1 CMLR 305, [1993] 1 CEC 124, [1993] BCC 421 0.3.3.1, 20.14.2.2
Marra Developments Ltd, re (SC of New South Wales 1976) 1 ACLR 470 14.4.5.5
Marseilles Extension Railway Co., re, ex parte Crédit Foncier & Mobilier of England
  (LJJ 1871) LR 7 Ch App 161, 41 LJ Ch 345, 25 LT 858, 20 WR 254 19.5.6
Marshall v Southampton & South West Hampshire Area Health Authority (Teaching)
  (case 152/84) (ECJ 1986) [1986] QB 401, [1986] 2 WLR 780, [1986] ICR 335,
  [1986] 2 All ER 584, [1986] IRLR 140, [1986] ECR 723, [1986] 1 CMLR 688 0.3.3.1
Marshall's Valve Gear Co. Ltd v Manning Wardle & Co. Ltd (ChD 1908) [1909] 1 Ch 267,
  78 LJ Ch 46, 100 LT 65, 15 Mans 379, 25 TLR 69 15.7.2.4, 15.7.3
Mason v Harris (CA 1879) 11 ChD 97, 48 LJ Ch 589, 40 LT 644, 27 WR 699 15.7.3
Mawcon Ltd, re (ChD 1968) [1969] 1 WLR 78, [1969] 1 All ER 188, 112 SJ 1004 4.3
Maxform SpA v Mariani (QBD 1979) [1979] 2 Lloyd's Rep 385; (CA 1980)
  [1981] 2 Lloyd's Rep 54 4.5.1

Maxwell v Department of Trade & Industry (CA 1974) [1974] QB 523,
   [1974] 2 WLR 338, [1974] 2 All ER 122, 118 SJ 203   18.8.2
Maxwell Communications Corporation plc, re (ChD 1993) [1993] 1 WLR 1402,
   [1994] 1 All ER 737 (sub nom. Re Maxwell Communications Corporation plc (No. 2)),
   [1994] 1 BCLC 1 (sub nom. Re Maxwell Communications Corporation plc (No. 2)),
   [1993] BCC 369 (sub nom. Re Maxwell Communications Corporation plc (No. 3))   20.13.1
Maxwell Communications Corporation plc, re (No. 2); see Re Maxwell Communications
   Corporation plc
Maxwell Communications Corporation plc, re (No. 3); see Re Maxwell Communications
   Corporation plc
MB Group plc, re (ChD 1989) [1989] BCLC 672, 5 BCC 684   10.2.5
MC Bacon Ltd, re; see Re a Company (No. 005009 of 1987)
Measures Brothers Ltd v Measures (CA 1910) [1910] 2 Ch 248, 79 LJ Ch 707, 102 LT 794,
   26 TLR 488, 18 Mans 40, [1908–10] All ER Rep Ext 1188, 54 SJ 521   20.6.7
Mechanisations (Eaglescliffe) Ltd, re (ChD 1964) [1966] Ch 20, [1965] 2 WLR 702,
   [1964] 3 All ER 840, 109 SJ 230   11.7.6
Medefield Pty Ltd, re (New South Wales SC 1977) 2 ACLR 406, (1977) ACLC 29,390
                   1.3.5, 3.4.1.3, 14.4.9.2, 14.4.9.5
Melcast (Wolverhampton) Ltd, re (ChD 1990) [1991] BCLC 288   15.2.5.6
Melhado v Pôrto Alegre, New Hamburgh, & Brazilian Railway Co. (Court of Common Pleas 1874)
   LR 9 CP 503, 43 LJ CP 253, 31 LT 57, 23 WR 57, [1874–80] All ER Rep Ext 2005   19.6.2
Melias Ltd v Manchester Corporation (Lands Tribunal 1972) 23 P & CR 380   5.2.2.8
Menier v Hooper's Telegraph Works (CA in Chancery 1874) LR 9 Ch App 350, 43 LJ Ch 330,
   30 LT 209, 22 WR 396   14.4.9.5, 18.4.4
Merchandise Transport Ltd v British Transport Commission (CA 1961) [1962] 2 QB 173,
   [1961] 3 All ER 495, 60 LGR 1, 32 Traff Cas 19, 105 SJ 1104   5.2.2.7
Meridian Global Funds Management Asia Ltd v Securities Commission (PC 1995)
   [1995] 2 AC 500, [1995] 3 WLR 413, [1995] 3 All ER 918, [1995] 2 BCLC 116,
   [1995] BCC 942, [1995] 3 NZLR 7   19.1, 19.8.4, 19.8.6.1, 19.8.6.2, 19.8.6.3
Mesenberg v Cord Industrial Recruiters Pty Ltd (New South Wales SC 1996)
   39 NSWLR 128, 19 ACSR 483   18.4.13
Metal Constituents Ltd, re, Lord Lurgan's Case (ChD 1902) [1902] 1 Ch 707, 71 LJ Ch 323,
   86 LT 291, 9 Mans 196, 50 WR 492   6.7.2
Metropolitan Coal Consumers' Association v Scrimgeour (CA 1895) [1895] 2 QB 604,
   65 LJ QB 22, 73 LT 137, 11 TLR 526, 2 Mans 579, 14 R 729, 39 SJ 654, 44 WR 35   6.4.1
Metropolitan Saloon Omnibus Co. Ltd v Hawkins (Court of Exchequer 1859) 4 H & N 87,
   157 ER 769, 28 LJ Ex 201, 5 Jur NS 226, 7 WR 265   0.1.6, 5.2.1
Meux's Brewery Co. Ltd, re (ChD 1918) [1919] 1 Ch 28, 88 LJ Ch 14, 119 LT 759,
   [1918–19] All ER Rep 1192, 35 TLR 13, 63 SJ 40   10.2.3
Meyer v Scottish Textile & Manufacturing Co. Ltd; see Scottish Cooperative Wholesale
   Society Ltd v Meyer
Michaels v Harley House (Marylebone) Ltd (ChD 1997) [1997] 1 WLR 967,
   [1997] 3 All ER 446, [1997] 2 BCLC 166   14.7
Mid East Trading Ltd, re (CA 1997) [1998] 1 All ER 577   20.9.3
MIG Trust Ltd, re (CA 1933) [1933] Ch 542, 102 LJ Ch 179, 149 LT 56, 49 TLR 299,
   [1933] B & CR 91; (HL 1934 sub nom. Peat v Gresham Trust Ltd) [1934] AC 252,
   103 LJ Ch 173, 151 LT 63, 50 TLR 345, [1934] B & CR 33, [1934] All ER Rep 82   11.7.9
Migotti's Case; see Re South Blackpool Hotel Co., Migotti's Case
Milgate Developments Ltd, re (ChD 1990) [1993] BCLC 291, [1991] BCC 24   18.6.6
Mills v Mills (High Court of Australia 1938) 60 CLR 150, 11 ALJ 527   16.4.10
Mills v Northern Railway of Buenos Ayres Co. (LC 1870) LR 5 Ch App 621, 23 LT 719,
   19 WR 171   10.5.2
Mitchell and Hobbs (UK) Ltd v Mill (QBD 1995) [1996] 2 BCLC 102   15.7.3, 19.5.6
Modelboard Ltd v Outer Box Ltd (ChD 1992) [1993] BCLC 623, [1992] BCC 945   11.7.10.3
Moffatt v Farquhar (V-C 1878) 7 ChD 591, 47 LJ Ch 355, 38 LT 18, 26 WR 522   8.3.4
Monolithic Building Co., re (CA 1915) [1915] 1 Ch 643, 84 LJ Ch 441, 112 LT 619,
   [1914–15] All ER Rep 249, 21 Mans 380, 59 SJ 332   11.7.3, 11.7.9
Montagu's Settlement Trusts, re (ChD 1985) [1987] Ch 264, [1987] 2 WLR 1192,
   [1992] 4 All ER 308   18.2.2

Moodie v W. & J. Shepherd (Bookbinders) Ltd (HL 1949) [1949] 2 All ER 1044   8.3.4, 15.5.2
Moonbeam Cards Ltd, re (ChD 1992) [1993] BCLC 1099   15.2.5.6
Moore v I. Bresler Ltd (KBDC 1944) [1944] 2 All ER 515   19.8.6.1, 19.8.6.2, 19.8.6.3
Moorgate Mercantile Holdings Ltd, re (ChD 1979) [1980] 1 WLR 227, [1980] 1 All ER 40,
    123 SJ 557   14.4.5.5, 14.4.8.3
Moorgate Metals Ltd, re (ChD 1994) [1995] 1 BCLC 503, [1995] BCC 143   15.2.5.6
Mordecai v Mordecai (New South Wales CA 1988) 12 NSWLR 58, 12 ACLR 751,
    6 ACLC 370   16.7.3.3
Moreland Metal Co. Ltd v Cowlishaw (New South Wales CA 1919)
    19 SR (NSW) 231   4.5.1
Morgan v 45 Flers Avenue Pty Ltd (SC of New South Wales 1986) 10 ACLR 692,
    5 ACLC 222   18.7
Morgan v Gray (ChD 1952) [1953] Ch 83, [1953] 2 WLR 140, [1953] 1 All ER 213,
    97 SJ 48   14.4.9.1.5
Morgan v Morgan Insurance Brokers Ltd (ChD 1992) [1993] BCC 145   19.9
Morgan Crucible Co. plc v Hill Samuel & Co. Ltd (CA 1990) [1991] Ch 295, [1991] 2 WLR 655,
    [1991] 1 All ER 148 (sub nom. Morgan Crucible Co. plc v Hill Samuel Bank Ltd),
    [1991] BCLC 178 (sub nom. Morgan Crucible Co. plc v Hill Samuel Bank Ltd),
    [1991] BCC 82   8.10
Morris v Agrichemicals Ltd (CA 1995); see Re Bank of Credit and Commerce International SA (No. 8)
Morris v Director of Serious Fraud Office (ChD 1992) [1993] Ch 372, [1993] 3 WLR 1,
    [1993] 1 All ER 788, [1993] BCLC 580, [1992] BCC 934   20.9.3
Morris v Kanssen (HL 1946) [1946] AC 459, [1946] 1 All ER 586, 115 LJ Ch 177,
    174 LT 353, 62 TLR 306   15.2.6, 19.5.4.5
Morris v Rayners Enterprises Inc.; see Re Bank of Credit and Commerce
    International SA (No. 8)
Mosely v Koffyfontein Mines Ltd (CA 1904) [1904] 2 Ch 108, 73 LJ Ch 569, 91 LT 266,
    11 Mans 294, 20 TLR 556, 53 WR 140, 48 SJ 507   6.2.4, 12.7
Mossmain Ltd, re; see Re a company (No. 003160 of 1986)
Motherwell v Schoof (Alberta SC 1949) [1949] 4 DLR 812   16.4.16
Mousell Bros v London & North-Western Railway Co. (KBDC 1917) [1917] 2 KB 836,
    87 LJ KB 82, 118 LT 25, [1916–17] All ER Rep 1101, 81 JP 305, 15 LGR 706   19.8.4
Movitex Ltd v Bulfield (ChD 1986) [1988] BCLC 104, 2 BCC 99,403
                              16.5.1, 16.5.2, 16.5.3, 16.5.5.1, 16.6.2, 16.6.4, 16.8, 16.9.1
Moxham v Grant (CA 1899) [1900] 1 QB 88, 69 LJ QB 97, 81 LT 431, 16 TLR 34, 48 WR 130 10.5.10
Mozley v Alston (LC 1847) 1 Ph 790, 41 ER 833, 4 Ry & Can Cas 636, 16 LJ Ch 217,
    9 LT OS 97, 11 Jur 315   18.4.1
Mulcon Pty Ltd v MYT Engineering Pty Ltd (New South Wales SC 1996)
    20 ACSR 606   15.5.1
Multinational Gas & Petrochemical Co. v Multinational Gas & Petrochemical Services Ltd
    (CA 1983) [1983] Ch 258, [1983] 3 WLR 492, [1983] BCLC 461, [1983] 2 All ER 563,
    127 SJ 562   14.5.1, 16.2.2, 16.3.1, 16.4.3, 16.4.6.1, 16.4.12, 18.4.4, 20.11.4
Munster v Cammell Co. (ChD 1882) 21 ChD 183, 51 LJ Ch 731, 47 LT 44, 30 WR 812
                                                                           15.2.3.3, 15.3.3, 15.3.7
Munton Brothers Ltd v Secretary of State (Northern Ireland CA 1983) [1983] NI 369   5.2.2.8
Murphy v Brentwood District Council (HL 1990) [1991] 1 AC 398, [1990] 3 WLR 414,
    [1990] 2 All ER 908, [1990] 2 Lloyd's Rep 467, 89 LGR 24   8.10
Murray's Judicial Factor v Thomas Murray & Sons (Ice Merchants) Ltd (CSess 2nd Div 1992)
    [1993] BCLC 1437, [1992] BCC 596 (sub nom. Murray's Judicial Factor), 1992 SLT 824   9.2.4
Musselwhite v C. H. Musselwhite & Son Ltd (ChD 1961) [1962] Ch 964, [1962] 2 WLR 374,
    [1962] 1 All ER 201, 106 SJ 37   14.4.5.4, 14.4.9.1.2
Mutter v Eastern and Midlands Railway Co. (CA 1888) 38 ChD 92, 57 LJ Ch 615,
    59 LT 117, 4 TLR 377, 36 WR 401   4.4.1, 4.4.2
Mutual Life Insurance Co. of New York v Rank Organisation Ltd (ChD 1981) [1985] BCLC 11
                                                                                       8.8.2.1, 16.4.2
Mutual Reinsurance Co. Ltd v Peat Marwick Mitchell and Co. (CA 1996) [1997] 1 BCLC 1,
    [1996] BCC 1010, [1997] PNLR 75   17.4.6

Nankivell v Benjamin (SC of Victoria 1892) 18 VLR 543, 13 ALT 282   18.4.10

Nassau Phosphate Co., re (ChD 1876) 2 ChD 610, 45 LJ Ch 584, 24 WR 692   1.2.1
Nassau Steam Press v Tyler (QBDC 1894) 70 LT 376, 10 R 582, 1 Mans 459, 38 SJ 363   4.5.1
Natal Land & Colonization Co. Ltd v Pauline Colliery & Development Syndicate Ltd
    (PC (Supreme Court of Natal) 1903) [1904] AC 120, 73 LJ PC 22, 89 LT 678, 11 Mans 29   19.6.2
National Australia Bank Ltd v Composite Buyers Ltd (New South Wales SC 1991)
    6 ACSR 94   11.6.2
National Australia Bank Ltd v Soden; see Re Atlantic Computers plc,
    National Australia Bank Ltd v Soden
National Bank Ltd, re (ChD 1966) [1966] 1 WLR 819, [1966] 1 All ER 1006, 110 SJ 226   8.8.3
National Dwellings Society v Sykes (ChD 1894) [1894] 3 Ch 159, 63 LJ Ch 906, 10 TLR 563,
    1 Mans 457, 8 R 758, 42 WR 696, 38 SJ 601   14.4.7
National Funds Assurance Co., re (MR 1878) 10 ChD 118, 48 LJ Ch 163, 39 LT 420, 27 WR 302
    10.5.10, 15.8, 20.11.2
National Patent Steam Fuel Co., re, Barton's Case (LJJ 1859) 4 De G & J 46, 45 ER 19   6.4.2
National Provincial & Union Bank of England v Charnley (CA 1923) [1924] 1 KB 431,
    93 LJ KB 241, 130 LT 465, [1924] B & CR 37, 68 SJ 480   11.7.6
National Provincial Marine Insurance Co., re, Gilbert's Case (LJJ 1870) LR 5 Ch App 559,
    39 LJ Ch 837, 23 LT 341, 18 WR 938   6.4.2
National Rivers Authority v Alfred McAlpine Homes East Ltd (QBDC 1994)
    [1994] 4 All ER 286, [1994] Env LR 198   19.8.4
National Roads & Motorists' Association v Parker (SC of New South Wales 1986) 6 NSWLR 517,
    11 ACLR 1 (sub nom. NRMA v Parker), 4 ACLC 609   14.4.3, 15.7.2.4
National Westminster Bank Ltd v Halesowen Presswork and Assemblies Ltd (HL 1972)
    [1972] AC 785, [1972] 2 WLR 455, [1972] 1 All ER 641, [1972] 1 Lloyd's Rep 101   20.13.1
National Westminster Bank plc v Inland Revenue Commissioners (HL 1994) [1995] 1 AC 119,
    [1994] 3 WLR 159, [1994] 3 All ER 1, [1994] 2 BCLC 239, [1994] STC 580   6.1.11
Nedco Ltd v Clark (Saskatchewan CA 1973) 43 DLR (3d) 714, [1973] 6 WWR 425,
    73 CLLC 14,192   5.2.2.1
Neil M'Leod & Sons Ltd (C Sess 1st Div 1966) 1967 SC 16, 1967 SLT 46   14.4.6.2
Neilson v Stewart (HL 1991) 1991 SC (HL) 22, 1991 SLT 523, [1991] BCC 713   10.8.5
Nelson v Anglo-American Land Mortgage Agency Co. (ChD 1896) [1897] 1 Ch 130,
    66 LJ Ch 112, 75 LT 482, 13 TLR 77, 45 WR 170   4.4.1, 4.4.2
Neptune (Vehicle Washing Equipment) Ltd v Fitzgerald (ChD 1995) [1996] Ch 274,
    [1995] 3 WLR 108, [1995] 3 All ER 811, [1995] 1 BCLC 352, [1995] BCC 474   0.3.2.3, 16.6.5
Neptune (Vehicle Washing Equipment) Ltd v Fitzgerald (No. 2) (ChD 1995) [1995] BCC 1000
    16.4.13, 16.6.2, 16.6.4, 16.6.5
New Balkis Eersteling Ltd v Randt Gold Mining Co. (HL 1904) [1904] AC 165, 73 LJ KB 384,
    90 LT 494, 52 WR 551, 20 TLR 396; affirming CA (1903) [1903] 1 KB 461, 72 LJ KB 143,
    88 LT 189, 10 Mans 289, 51 WR 391   6.4.2
New British Iron Co., re, ex parte Beckwith (ChD 1898) [1898] 1 Ch 324, 67 LJ Ch 164,
    78 LT 155, 14 TLR 196, 5 Mans 168, 46 WR 376, 42 SJ 234   3.4.3, 3.4.4
New Bullas Trading Ltd, re (CA 1993) [1994] 1 BCLC 485, [1994] BCC 36   11.6.3, 11.6.4
New Buxton Lime Co., re, Duke's Case (MR 1876) 1 ChD 620, 45 LJ Ch 389, 33 LT 776,
    34 LT 713, 24 WR 341   6.8
New Cedos Engineering Co. Ltd, re (ChD 1975) [1994] 1 BCLC 797, 120 SJ 146   8.3.4, 14.5.1
New Chile Gold Mining Co., re (ChD 1889) 45 ChD 598, 60 LJ Ch 90, 63 LT 344, 6 TLR 462,
    2 Meg 355, 39 WR 59   6.4.2
New Generation Engineers Ltd, re (ChD 1992) [1993] BCLC 435   15.2.5.6
New South Wales v The Commonwealth, The Incorporation Case (Australia HC 1990)
    169 CLR 482, 64 ALJR 157, 90 ALR 355, 1 ACSR 137, 8 ACLC 120   0.3.3.3
New World Alliance Pty Ltd, re (Australia FedC 1994) 122 ALR 531, 51 FCR 425
    (sub nom. Re New World Alliance Pty Ltd (No. 2)), 13 ACSR 766
    (sub nom. Sycotex Pty Ltd v Baseler)   14.5.1
New Zealand Gold Extraction Co. (Newbery-Vautin Process) Ltd v Peacock (CA 1893)
    [1894] 1 QB 622, 63 LJ QB 227, 70 LT 110, 9 R 669, [1891–4] All ER Rep 1000   8.5
New Zealand Netherlands Society 'Oranje' Incorporated v Kuys (PC 1973) [1973] 1 WLR 1126,
    [1973] 2 All ER 1222, [1974] RPC 272, [1973] 2 NZLR 163, 117 SJ 565   16.7.3.4, 16.8
Newborne v Sensolid (Great Britain) Ltd (CA 1953) [1954] 1 QB 45, [1953] 2 WLR 596,
    [1953] 1 All ER 708, 97 SJ 209   19.6.1

Newdigate Colliery Ltd, re (CA 1912) [1912] 1 Ch 468,
    81 LJ Ch 235, 106 LT 133, 28 TLR 207, 19 Mans 155   20.2.7.1
Newhart Developments Ltd v Co-operative Commercial Bank Ltd (CA 1977) [1978] QB 814,
    [1978] 2 WLR 636, [1978] 2 All ER 896, 121 SJ 847   20.2.3
Newman (T.C.) (Qld) Pty Ltd v DHA Rural (Qld) Pty Ltd (SC of Queensland 1987)
    [1988] 1 QdR 308, 12 ACLR 257, 5 ACLC 922   16.4.13
Newspaper Proprietary Syndicate Ltd, re (ChD 1900) [1900] 2 Ch 349, 69 LJ Ch 578,
    83 LT 341, 16 TLR 452, 8 Mans 65   15.5.3
Newstead v Frost (HL 1980) 53 TC 525, [1980] 1 WLR 135, [1980] 1 All ER 363,
    [1980] STC 123, [1980] TR 1, 124 SJ 116; affirming CA (1978) [1978] 1 WLR 1441,
    [1979] 2 All ER 129, [1979] STC 45, [1978] TR 221, 122 SJ 813; affirming ChD (1977)
    [1978] 1 WLR 511, [1978] 2 All ER 241, [1978] STC 239, [1977] TR 301, 122 SJ 33   2.3.5.10
Newtherapeutics Ltd v Katz (ChD 1990) [1991] Ch 226, [1990] 3 WLR 1183,
    [1991] 2 All ER 151, [1990] BCLC 700, [1990] BCC 362   15.6.1.5
Ngurli Ltd v McCann (HC of Australia 1953) 90 CLR 425, 27 ALJ 349
                                  14.4.9.4, 16.4.11, 16.4.14, 18.4.12
Nicholas v Soundcraft Electronics Ltd (CA 1992) [1993] BCLC 360, [1992] BCC 895 (sub nom.
    Re a Company (No. 002470 of 1988))   18.6.4
Nicholson, ex parte; see Re Staffordshire Gas and Coke Co. Ltd, ex parte Nicholson
Nicholson v Permakraft (NZ) Ltd (CA of New Zealand 1985)
    [1985] 1 NZLR 242   16.4.6.1, 20.11.3
Nicoll v Cutts (CA 1985) [1985] BCLC 322, 1985 PCC 311, 1 BCC 99, 427   20.2.7.2
Nidditch v Calico Printers' Association Ltd (C Sess 1st Div 1961) 1961 SLT 282   8.8.2.3
Niemann v Smedley (Victoria SC (FC) 1972) [1973] VR 769   1.3.2.1
Niltan Carson Ltd, joint receivers & managers of, v Hawthorne (QBD 1987) [1988] BCLC 298,
    3 BCC 454   16.6.4, 16.6.7, 16.7.3.4
Nisbet v Shepherd (CA 1993) [1994] 1 BCLC 300, [1994] BCC 91   1.3.2.6, 8.3.1, 8.3.3
NL Electrical Ltd, re (ChD 1992) [1994] 1 BCLC 22   4.2.1, 10.8.7
NM Superannuation Pty Ltd v Baker (New South Wales SC 1992) 7 ACSR 105   19.5.4.1
Noble (R.A.) & Sons (Clothing) Ltd, re (ChD 1983) [1983] BCLC 273   18.6.3, 18.7.4
Noble Trees Ltd, re (ChD 1993) [1993] BCLC 1185, [1993] BCC 318   15.2.5.4
Noel Tedman Holdings Pty Ltd, re (SC of Queensland 1967) [1967] QdR 561   5.2.1
Nordberg (J.A.) Ltd, re (ChD 1915) [1915] 2 Ch 439, 84 LJ Ch 830, 113 LT 988   2.4.7, 14.6.2.2
Norglen Ltd v Reeds Rains Prudential Ltd (HL 1997) [1997] 3 WLR 1177,
    [1998] 1 All ER 218, [1998] 1 BCLC 176, [1998] BCC 44   19. 9
Norman v Norman (New South Wales SC 1990) 19 NSWLR 314   6.1.3
Norman v Theodore Goddard (ChD 1991) [1991] BCLC 1028, [1992] BCC 14   16.2.1.2, 16.2.1.4
North Eastern Insurance Co. Ltd, re (ChD 1918) [1919] 1 Ch 198, 88 LJ Ch 121, 120 LT 223,
    63 SJ 117   15.5.1, 16.6.3
North Hallenbeagle Mining Co., re, Knight's Case (LJJ 1867) LR 2 Ch App 321, 36 LJ Ch 317,
    15 LT 546, 15 WR 294   15.5.1
North-West Transportation Co. Ltd v Beatty (PC 1887) 12 App Cas 589, 56 LJ PC 102,
    57 LT 426, 3 TLR 789, 36 WR 647   3.5.4.1, 14.4.9.3, 16.6.7, 16.8, 18.4.4
Northern Bank Ltd v Ross (Northern Ireland CA) [1990] BCC 883   11.7.10.2
Northern Counties Securities Ltd v Jackson & Steeple Ltd (ChD 1974) [1974] 1 WLR 1133,
    [1974] 2 All ER 625   14.4.1, 14.4.5.5
Northern Engineering Industries plc, re (CA 1994) [1994] 2 BCLC 709,
    [1994] BCC 618   10.2.1, 10.2.4
Northern Ireland Electricity Service's Application, re (Northern Ireland QBD 1987)
    [1987] NI 271, [1987] 12 NIJB 24, 368 IRLIB 12   19.8.8
Northland Bank v GIC Industries Ltd (Alberta Queen's Bench 1985) 36 Alta LR (2d) 200,
    29 BLR 173   11.6.2
Northside Developments Pty Ltd v Registrar-General (Australia HC 1990) 170 CLR 146,
    64 ALJR 427,93 ALR 385, 2 ACSR 161, 8 ACLC 611   19.5.4.4
Northumberland Avenue Hotel Co., re (CA 1886) 33 ChD 16, 2 TLR 636, 54 LT 777,
    [1886–90] All ER Rep Ext 1746   19.6.2
Northwest/Prince Rupert Assessor, Area No. 25 v N. & V. Johnson Services Ltd
    (British Columbia CA 1990) [1991] 1 WWR 527   19.8.9

Norwest Holst Ltd v Secretary of State for Trade and others (CA 1978) [1978] Ch 201,
    [1978] 3 WLR 73, [1978] 3 All ER 280, 122 SJ 109   18.8.1, 18.8.2.1
Norwich Equitable Fire Insurance Co., re (CA 1884) 27 ChD 515, 54 LJ Ch 254, 51 LT 404,
    32 WR 964   20.9.3
Norwich Provident Insurance Society, re, Bath's Case (CA 1878) 8 ChD 334, 47 LJ Ch 601,
    38 LT 267, 26 WR 441   2.3.5.6
NP Engineering and Security Products Ltd, re (ChD 1995) [1995] 2 BCLC 586,
    [1995] BCC 1052   15.2.5.4
NRMA v Parker; see National Roads & Motorists' Association v Parker
Nuneaton Borough Association Football Club Ltd, re [1989] BCLC 454, 5 BCC 377   14.2
Nurcombe v Nurcombe (CA 1984) [1985] 1 WLR 370, [1985] 1 All ER 65, [1984] BCLC 557,
    1985 PCC 12, 1 BCC 99, 269, 128 SJ 766, 81 LS Gaz 2929   18.4.7
Nye (C.L.) Ltd, re (CA 1970) [1971] Ch 442, [1970] 3 WLR 158, [1970] 3 All ER 1061,
    114 SJ 413   11.7.6

Oakbank Oil Co. v Crum (HL (C Sess 1st Div) 1882) 8 App Cas 65, 48 LT 537,
    10 R (HL) 11   3.4.1.1, 6.1.3
Oakes v Turquand and Harding (HL 1867) LR 2 HL 325, [1861–73] All ER Rep 738,
    36 LJ Ch 949, 16 LT 808, 15 WR 1201   1.3.2, 6.7.4
Oceanic Steam Navigation Co. Ltd, re (ChD 1938) [1939] Ch 41, [1938] 3 All ER 740,
    108 LJ Ch 74, 159 LT 457, 54 TLR 1100, 82 SJ 646   2.3.5.7
Odeon Associated Theatres Ltd v Jones (ChD 1970) [1971] 1 WLR 442, [1971] 2 All ER 407,
    [1970] TR 299, 49 ATC 315; affirmed by CA (1971) [1973] Ch 288, [1972] 2 WLR 331,
    48 TC 257, [1971] TR 373, [1972] 1 All ER 681, 115 SJ 850   9.3.8
Odessa Tramways Co. v Mendel (CA 1878) 8 ChD 235, 47 LJ Ch 505, 38 LT 731, 26 WR 887
                 6.4.2, 6.4.3, 18.3.3.1
Official Custodian for Charities v Parway Estates Developments Ltd (CA 1984) [1985] Ch 151,
    [1984] 3 WLR 525, [1984] 3 All ER 679, [1984] BCLC 309, 1985 PCC 133, 1 BCC 99,
    253, 128 SJ 549   4.3
Official Receiver v B Ltd (ChD 1993) [1994] 2 BCLC 1   15.2.5.4
Official Receiver v Hannan (CA 1997) [1997] 2 BCLC 473, [1997] BCC 644
    (sub nom. Re Cannonquest Ltd)   15.2.5.2
Official Receiver v Moore (ChD 1994) [1995] BCC 293   15.2.5.3, 20.12
Old Silkstone Collieries Ltd, re (CA 1953) [1954] Ch 169, [1954] 2 WLR 77,
    [1954] 1 All ER 68   10.2.2
Oliver v Dalgleish (ChD 1963) [1963] 1 WLR 1274, [1963] 3 All ER 330   15.3.7, 18.4.9
Olson v Phoenix Industrial Supply Ltd (CA of Manitoba 1984) 9 DLR (4th) 451,
    [1984] 4 WWR 498, 27 Man R (2d) 205, 26 BLR 183; leave to appeal refused
    [1985] 1 WWR lviii   16.4.2, 16.4.10
Olympia Ltd, re; see Gluckstein v Barnes
Omnium Electric Palaces Ltd v Baines (CA 1913) [1914] 1 Ch 332, 83 LJ Ch 372, 109 LT 964,
    30 TLR 213, 58 SJ 218, 21 Mans 94   17.6.4
O'Neill v Ryan (Republic of Ireland SC 1993) [1993] ILRM 557   18.4.6
Ooregum Gold Mining Co. of India Ltd v Roper (HL 1892) [1892] AC 125, 61 LJ Ch 337,
    66 LT 427, 41 WR 90, 8 TLR 436, 36 SJ 344   0.3.1.1, 0.3.2.3, 1.3.2.1, 6.4.1
Opera Ltd, re (CA 1891) [1891] 3 Ch 260, 60 LJ Ch 839, 65 LT 371, 39 WR 705,
    7 TLR 655   11.6.3, 20.2.8.3
Opera Photographic Ltd, re (ChD 1989) [1989] 1 WLR 634, [1989] BCLC 763, 1989 PCC 337,
    5 BCC 601   14.4.4
Ord v Belhaven Pubs Ltd (CA 1998) *The Times*, 7 April 1998   5.2.2.4, 5.2.2.11
Oregon Mortgage Co. Ltd (C Sess 2nd Div 1910) 1910 SC 964, 47 SLR 702, 1910, 2 SLT 27   3.5.1
Oriental Credit Ltd, re (ChD 1987) [1988] Ch 204, [1988] 2 WLR 172, [1988] 1 All ER 892,
    1988 PCC 9 (sub nom. Re a Company (No. 003318 of 1987)), 3 BCC 564 (sub nom. Re a
    Company (No. 003318 of 1987))   20.9.3
Orion Finance Ltd v Crown Financial Management Ltd (CA 1995)
    [1996] 2 BCLC 78, [1996] BCC 621   11.7.10
Orion Finance Ltd v Crown Financial Management Ltd (No. 2) (CA 1996)
    [1996] 2 BCLC 382, [1996] BCC 621 at 631   11.7.10

Orr v Glasgow, Airdrie & Monklands Junction Railway Co. (HL (C Sess Scotland) 1860)
3 Macq 799   18.3.3.3
Orton v Cleveland Fire Brick & Pottery Co. Ltd (Court of Exchequer 1865) 3 H & C 868,
159 ER 776, 11 Jur NS 531, 13 WR 869   3.4.4
Oshkosh B'Gosh Inc. v Dan Marbel Inc. Ltd (CA 1988) [1989] BCLC 507, 1989 PCC 320,
4 BCC 795   2.4.2, 19.6.1
Ossory Estates plc, re (ChD 1987) [1988] BCLC 213, 4 BCC 460   6.5.7
Othery Construction Ltd, re (ChD 1965) [1966] 1 WLR 69, [1966] 1 All ER 145, 110 SJ 32   8.8
Oxted Motor Co. Ltd, re (KBDC 1921) [1921] 3 KB 32, 90 LJ KB 1145, 126 LT 56, 37 TLR 737,
[1921] B & CR 155, [1921] All ER Rep 646   14.4.5.4

Pacific Coast Coal Mines Ltd v Arbuthnot (PC (British Columbia CA) 1917) [1917] AC 607,
36 DLR 564, 86 LJ PC 172, 117 LT 613   14.4.5.5
Paine & Layton, ex parte; see Re South Essex Estuary & Reclamation Co., ex parte Paine & Layton
Paintin & Nottingham Ltd v Miller Gale & Winter (New Zealand CA 1970)
[1971] NZLR 164   11.7.10.3
Palace Hotel Ltd, re (ChD 1912) [1912] 2 Ch 438, 81 LJ Ch 695, 107 LT 521, 19 Mans 295,
56 SJ 649   2.4.7, 14.6.2.2
Panama, New Zealand & Australian Royal Mail Co., re (CA in Chancery 1870) LR 5 Ch App 318,
39 LJ Ch 482, 22 LT 424, 18 WR 441   11.6.1, 11.6.2
Panorama Developments (Guildford) Ltd v Fidelis Furnishing Fabrics Ltd (CA 1971)
[1971] 2 QB 711, [1971] 3 WLR 440, [1971] 3 All ER 16, 115 SJ 483   19.5.4.4, 19.5.10
Pappaioannoy v The Greek Orthodox Community of Melbourne (Victoria SC 1978) 3 ACLR 801,
(1978) ACLC 32,209   18.4.9, 18.5
Paradise Motor Co. Ltd, re (CA 1968) [1968] 1 WLR 1125, [1968] 2 All ER 625, 112 SJ 271   8.3.1
Paramount Acceptance Co. Ltd v Souster (CA of New Zealand 1981) [1981] 2 NZLR 38,
1 NZCLC 95–021   20.2.3
Paramount Communications Inc. v Time Inc. (Delaware SC 1990) 571 A 2d 1140   16.4.3
Parke v Daily News Ltd (ChD 1962) [1962] Ch 927, [1962] 3 WLR 566, [1962] 2 All ER 929,
106 SJ 704   2.3.5.7, 14.4.9.4
Parker v McKenna (LJJ 1874) LR 10 Ch App 96, 44 LJ Ch 425, 31 LT 739, 23 WR 271   16.5.5.2
Parker & Cooper Ltd v Reading (ChD 1926) [1926] Ch 975, 96 LJ Ch 23, 136 LT 117,
[1926] All ER Rep 323   14.5.1
Parker-Knoll Ltd v Knoll International Ltd (CA 1962) [1962] RPC 243   2.3.3.6
Parkes Garage (Swadlincote) Ltd, re (CHDC 1928) [1929] 1 Ch 139, 98 LJ Ch 9,
140 LT 174, 45 TLR 11, [1928] B & CR 144   11.6.5.1
Parsons v Albert J. Parsons & Sons Ltd (CA 1978) [1979] ICR 271, [1979] IRLR 117,
[1979] FSR 254   15.6.1.5
Parsons v Sovereign Bank of Canada (PC (CA of Ontario) 1912) [1913] AC 160,
82 LJ PC 60, 107 LT 572, 29 TLR 38, 20 Mans 94, 9 DLR 476   20.2.7.1
Patent File Co., re (CA in Chancery 1870) LR 6 Ch App 83, 40 LJ Ch 190,
19 WR 193   2.3.5.6, 11.2.1
Patent Invert Sugar Co., re (CA 1885) 31 ChD 166, 55 LJ Ch 924, 53 LT 737, 2 TLR 196,
34 WR 169   3.5.1
Patent Ivory Manufacturing Co., re (ChD 1888) 38 ChD 156, 57 LJ Ch 878, 58 LT 395,
36 WR 801   19.5.4.5, 19.6.2
Patrick & Lyon Ltd, re (ChD 1933) [1933] Ch 786, 102 LJ Ch 300, 149 LT 231,
[1933] All ER Rep 590, 49 TLR 372, [1933] B & CR 151, 77 SJ 250   20.10.2
Paul & Frank Ltd v Discount Bank (Overseas) Ltd (ChD 1966) [1967] Ch 348,
[1966] 3 WLR 490, [1966] 2 All ER 922, 110 SJ 423   11.7.10.2
Paul (H.R.) & Son Ltd, re (ChD 1973) 118 SJ 166   14.4.4
Pavlides v Jensen (ChD 1956) [1956] Ch 565, [1956] 3 WLR 224, [1956] 2 All ER 518,
100 SJ 452   16.2, 18.4.4, 18.4.5
Pawle's case; see Re Estates Investment Co.
Peach Publishing Ltd v Slater and Co. (ChD 1995) [1996] BCC 751;
(CA 1997) [1998] BCC 139   8.10
Peachdart Ltd, re (ChD 1983) [1984] Ch 131, [1983] 3 WLR 878, [1983] 3 All ER 204,
[1983] BCLC 225, 1 BCC 98, 920, 127 SJ 839   11.7.10.3
Peak (R.W.) (Kings Lynn) Ltd, re (ChD 1997) [1998] 1 BCLC 193   0.3.1.3. 10.6.3. 14.5.1

Pearce Duff & Co. Ltd, re (ChD 1960) [1960] 1 WLR 1014, [1960] 3 All ER 222, 104 SJ 764
    14.4.5.3, 14.4.5.4, 14.5.2
Pearks, Gunston and Tee Ltd v Thompson, Talmey and Co. (ChD 1901) 18 RPC 185,
    17 TLR 354   4.5.1
Pearks, Gunston & Tee Ltd v Ward (KBDC 1902) [1902] 2 KB 1, 71 LJ KB 656, 87 LT 51,
    66 JP 774, 20 Cox CC 279, [1900–3] All ER Rep 228   19.8.4
Peat v Gresham Trust Ltd; see Re MIG Trust Ltd
Pedlar v Road Block Gold Mines of India Ltd (ChD 1905) [1905] 2 Ch 427, 74 LJ Ch 753,
    93 LT 665, 12 Mans 422, 54 WR 44   2.3.5.8
Pedley v Inland Waterways Association Ltd (ChD 1976) [1977] 1 All ER 209, 120 SJ 569   14.4.5.6
Peek v Gurney (HL 1873) LR 6 HL 377, [1861–73] All ER Rep 116, 43 LJ Ch 19,
    22 WR 29   7.6.6
Peel v London & North Western Railway Co. (CA 1907) [1907] 1 Ch 5, 76 LJ Ch 152, 95 LT 897,
    14 Mans 30, 23 TLR 85   14.4.5.5
Pellatt's case; see Re Richmond Hill Hotel Co.
Pender v Lushington (ChD 1877) 6 ChD 70, 46 LJ Ch 317   14.4.9.3, 15.7.3, 18.4.9, 18.4.12, 18.5
Peninsular & Oriental Steam Navigation Co. v Johnson (HC of Australia 1938) 60 CLR 189,
    11 ALJ 570   16.6.7
Peninsular Co. Ltd v Fleming (Court of Common Pleas 1872) 27 LT 93   1.3.2.3, 3.4.2.9
Penn-Texas Corporation v Murat Anstalt (CA 1962) [1964] 1 QB 40, [1963] 2 WLR 111,
    [1963] 1 All ER 258   19.9
Penn-Texas Corporation v Murat Anstalt (No. 2) (CA 1964) [1964] 2 QB 647, [1964] 3 WLR 131,
    [1964] 2 All ER 594   19.9
Penney, ex parte; see Re Gresham Life Assurance Society, ex parte Penney
Penrose v Martyr (QB 1858) E B & E 499, 120 ER 595, 28 LJ QB 28, 5 Jur NS 362   4.5.1
Penrose v Secretary of State for Trade and Industry (ChD 1995) [1996] 1 WLR 482,
    [1996] 2 All ER 96, [1996] 1 BCLC 389, [1996] BCC 311   2.3.3.8
People v Awa (California SC 1865) 27 Cal 638   19.8.9
People's Pleasure Park Co. Inc. v Rohleder (Virginia Supreme Court of Appeals 1908)
    61 SE 794, 109 Va 439; affirmed (1909) 63 SE 981, 109 Va 439   19.8.9
Percival v Wright (ChD 1902) [1902] 2 Ch 421, 72 LJ Ch 846, 9 Mans 443, 18 TLR 697   13.5
Pergamon Press Ltd, re (CA 1970) [1971] Ch 388, [1970] 3 WLR 792, [1970] 3 All ER 535,
    114 SJ 569   18.8.2
Pergamon Press Ltd v Maxwell (ChD 1970) [1970] 1 WLR 1167, [1970] 2 All ER 809,
    114 SJ 453   14.4.3, 16.4.13
Permanent Houses (Holdings) Ltd, re (ChD 1988) [1988] BCLC 563, 1989 PCC 350,
    5 BCC 151   11.6.2, 11.7.10.2
Permanent Trustee Co. of New South Wales Ltd v Palmer (Australia HC 1929) 42 CLR 277,
    35 ALR 153, 2 ALJ 401   14.2
Perseus Mining NL v Landbrokers (Perth) Pty Ltd (Western Australia SC 1971)
    [1972] WAR 12   14.5.1, 15.2.2
Peruvian Guano Co., re, ex parte Kemp (ChD 1894) [1894] 3 Ch 690, 63 LJ Ch 818,
    71 LT 611, 43 WR 170, 10 TLR 585, 1 Mans 423, 8 R 544   3.4.4
Peruvian Railways Co. v Thames & Mersey Marine Insurance Co. (LJJ 1867) LR 2 Ch App 617,
    36 LJ Ch 864, 16 LT 644, 15 WR 1002   2.3.5.6
Peso Silver Mines Ltd (NPL) v Cropper (SC of Canada 1966) 58 DLR (2d) 1, [1966] SCR 673,
    56 WWR 641   16.7.3.4, 16.7.3.5
Peters' American Delicacy Co. Ltd v Heath (HC of Australia 1939) 61 CLR 457   3.5.3.5, 14.4.9.3
Peveril Gold Mines Ltd, re (CA 1897) [1898] 1 Ch 122, 67 LJ Ch 77, 77 LT 505, 4 Mans 398,
    14 TLR 86, 46 WR 198   3.3.2, 3.4.2.1
Pfeiffer (E.) Weinkellerei-Weineinkauf GmbH & Co. v Arbuthnot Factors Ltd (QBD 1987)
    [1988] 1 WLR 150, [1987] BCLC 522, 3 BCC 608   11.7.10.3
PFTZM Ltd, re (ChD 1994) [1995] 2 BCLC 354, [1995] BCC 280   15.1.6
Phillips v Manufacturers' Securities Ltd (CA 1917) 86 LJ Ch 305, 116 LT 290   14.4.9.4
Phonogram Ltd v Lane (CA 1981) [1982] QB 938, [1981] 3 WLR 736, [1981] 3 All ER 182,
    125 SJ 527   19.6.1, 19.6.2
Phosphate of Lime Co. Ltd, the v Green (Court of Common Pleas 1871) LR 7 CP 43,
    25 LT 636   14.5.2
Pickering v Stephenson (V-C 1872) LR 14 Eq 322, 41 LJ Ch 493, 26 LT 608, 20 WR 654   2.3.5.7

Piercy v S. Mills & Co. Ltd (ChD 1919) [1920] 1 Ch 77, 88 LJ Ch 509, 122 LT 20,
    [1918–19] All ER Rep 313, 35 TLR 703, 34 SJ 35   16.4.11
Pioneer Concrete Services Ltd v Yelnah Pty Ltd (New South Wales SC 1986) 5 NSWLR 254,
    11 ACLR 108, 5 ACLC 467   5.2.2.1, 5.2.2.8
Pioneer Laundry and Dry Cleaners Ltd v Minister of National Revenue (PC 1939)
    [1940] AC 127, [1939] 4 All ER 254, [1939] 4 DLR 481, [1938–39] CTC 411   5.2.2.1, 5.2.2.7
Plumstead, Woolwich and Charlton Consumers Pure Water Co., re (LJJ 1860) 2 De G F & J 20,
    45 ER 528   1.6
Poliwka v Heven Holdings Pty Ltd (Western Australia SC FC 1992) 8 ACSR 747   14.5.1
Polly Peck International plc, re (ChD 1993) [1994] BCC 15   20.9.3
Polly Peck International plc, re (ChD 1995); see Re Polly Peck International plc (No. 3)
Polly Peck International plc, re (No. 2) (ChD 1993) [1994] 1 BCLC 574, [1993] BCC 890
        15.1.7, 15.2.5.4, 15.2.5.6
Polly Peck International plc, re (No. 3) (ChD 1995) [1996] 1 BCLC 428, [1996] BCC 486
    (sub nom. Re Polly Peck International plc)   5.2.2.11
Pool Shipping Co. Ltd, re (ChD 1919) [1920] 1 Ch 251, 89 LJ Ch 111, 122 LT 338,
    36 TLR 53   8.3.4
Poole v National Bank of China Ltd (HL 1907) [1907] AC 229, 76 LJ Ch 458, 96 LT 889,
    [1904–7] All ER Rep 138, 23 TLR 567, 14 Mans 218   10.2.2
Poole Firebrick & Blue Clay Co., re, Hartley's Case (LJJ 1875) LR 10 Ch App 157,
    44 LJ Ch 240, 32 LT 106, 23 WR 203   3.4.2.4
Popely v Planarrive Ltd (ChD 1996) [1997] 1 BCLC 8   8.3.4
Poppleton, ex parte; see Re Thomas, ex parte Poppleton
Portbase Clothing Ltd, re (ChD 1992) [1993] Ch 388, [1993] 3 WLR 14, [1993] 3 All ER 829,
    [1993] BCLC 796, [1993] BCC 96   20.2.9, 20.13.1
Portuguese Consolidated Copper Mines Ltd, re (CA 1889) 42 ChD 160, 58 LJ Ch 813,
    1 Meg 246   14.4.5.4
Posgate & Denby (Agencies) Ltd, re (ChD 1986) [1987] BCLC 8, 1987 PCC 1,
    2 BCC 99,352   18.6.3
Possfund Custodian Trustee Ltd v Diamond (ChD 1996) [1996] 1 WLR 1351,
    [1996] 2 All ER 774, [1996] 2 BCLC 665   0.3.1.4, 7.6.6
POW Services Ltd v Clare (ChD 1994) [1995] 2 BCLC 435   14.3.1, 14.4.11, 15.3.5, 15.4.2
Powdrill v Watson (HL 1995) [1995] 2 AC 394, [1995] 2 WLR 312, [1995] 2 All ER 65,
    [1995] 1 BCLC 386, [1995] BCC 319   20.2.7.1, 20.2.7.2
Powell v Kempton Park Racecourse Co. Ltd (HL 1899) [1899] AC 143, 68 LJ QB 392,
    80 LT 538, 15 TLR 266, 63 JP 260, 19 Cox CC 265, 47 WR 585, 43 SJ 329   18.4.10
Powell Duffryn plc v Petereit (case C-214/89) (ECJ 1992) [1992] ECR I-1745,
    [1994] 1 CEC 293   3.4.1.1
Power v Sharp Investments Ltd (CA 1993) [1994] 1 BCLC 111, [1993] BCC 609
    (sub nom. Re Shoe Lace Ltd)   11.6.5.1
Practice Note (ChD 1930) [1930] WN 78, 69 LJ 252, 169 LT Jo 283   10.2.3
Practice Note (ChD 1995) [1996] 1 All ER 442   15.2.5.6
Pramatha Nath Mullick v Pradyumna Kumar Mullick (PC 1925) LR 52 Ind App 245   0.1.7
Precision Dippings Ltd v Precision Dippings Marketing Ltd (CA 1985) [1986] Ch 447,
    [1985] 3 WLR 812, [1985] BCLC 385, 1986 PCC 105, 1 BCC 99,539, 82 LS Gaz 3446,
    129 SJ 683   10.5.9, 10.5.10, 20.11.4
Preeco (B.G.) I (Pacific Coast) Ltd v Bon Street Holdings Ltd (British Columbia CA 1989)
    60 DLR (4th) 30   5.2.2.4
Press Caps Ltd, re (CA 1949) [1949] Ch 434 [1949] 1 All ER 1013, [1949] LJR 1460   8.8.2.3
Preston v Grand Collier Dock Co. (V-C 1840) 11 Sim 327, 59 ER 900   6.4.2
Princess of Reuss v Bos (HL 1871) LR 5 HL 176, 40 LJ Ch 655, 24 LT 641   1.2.1, 5.2.2.1
Prior v Sovereign Chicken Ltd (CA 1984) [1984] 1 WLR 921, [1984] 2 All ER 289, 83 LGR 14,
    270 EG 221, 24 RA 73   5.4
Pritchard's case; see Re Tavarone Mining Co.
Probe Data Systems Ltd, re (ChD 1989) [1989] BCLC 561, 5 BCC 384   15.2.5.4
Probe Data Systems Ltd, re (No. 3) (CA 1991) [1992] BCLC 405, [1992] BCC 110   15.2.5.4
Produce Marketing Consortium Ltd, re (ChD 1989) [1989] 1 WLR 745, [1989] 3 All ER 1,
    [1989] BCLC 513, 1989 PCC 457, 5 BCC 399 (sub nom. Re Produce Marketing Consortium
    Ltd (Halls v David)); see also Re Produce Marketing Consortium Ltd (No. 2)   20.12

Produce Marketing Consortium Ltd, re (Halls v David); see Re Produce Marketing
  Consortium Ltd and Re Produce Marketing Consortium Ltd (No. 2)
Produce Marketing Consortium Ltd, re (No. 2) (ChD 1989) [1989] BCLC 520, 1989 PCC 290
  (sub nom. Re Produce Marketing Consortium Ltd (Halls v David), 5 BCC 569 (sub nom.
  Re Produce Marketing Consortium Ltd)   20.12
Provident International Corporation v International Leasing Corporation Ltd (SC of New
  South Wales 1969) 89 WN (Pt 1) (NSW) 370, [1969] 1 NSWR 424   16.4.14
Prudential Assurance Co. Ltd v Chatterley-Whitfield Collieries Ltd (HL 1949)
  [1949] AC 512, [1949] 1 All ER 1094   10.2.4
Prudential Assurance Co. Ltd v Newman Industries Ltd (No. 2) (CA 1981) [1982] Ch 204,
  [1982] 2 WLR 31, [1982] 1 All ER 354, [1981] Com LR 265, 126 SJ 32; reversing in part
  ChD (1980) [1981] Ch 257, [1980] 3 WLR 543, [1980] 2 All ER 841   18.3.1, 18.3.2, 18.4.1,
    18.4.2, 18.4.3, 18.4.4, 18.4.5, 18.4.6, 18.4.7, 18.4.9, 18.4.13
Puddephatt v Leith (ChD 1915) [1916] 1 Ch 200, 85 LJ Ch 185, 114 LT 454, [1916–17] All
  ER Rep 624, 32 TLR 228, 60 SJ 210   14.4.9.8
Pugh and Sharman's Case; see Re Hercules Insurance Co., Pugh and Sharman's Case
Pulbrook v Richmond Consolidated Mining Co. (MR 1878) 9 ChD 610, 48 LJ Ch 65,
  27 WR 377   15.3.7, 15.5.1
Punt v Symons & Co. Ltd (ChD 1903) [1903] 2 Ch 506, 72 LJ Ch 768, 89 LT 525, 10 Mans 415,
  47 SJ 619, 52 WR 41   3.5.3.4, 16.4.11, 18.4.9, 18.4.12
Purpoint Ltd, re (ChD 1990) [1991] BCLC 491, [1991] BCC 121   20.12
Purssell, ex parte; see Re New City Constitutional Club Co., ex parte Purssell
Pyramid Building Society, re; see State of Victoria v Hodgson

Qintex Ltd, re (No. 2) (Tasmania SC 1990) 2 ACSR 479   19.5.4.1, 19.5.4.3
Queensland Mines Ltd v Hudson (PC 1978) 52 ALJR 399, 18 ALR 1, 3 ACLR 176
    13.7.1.1.3, 16.5.3, 16.7.3.4, 16.8
Queensland Petroleum Management Ltd, re (Queensland SC 1988) [1989] 1 QdR 549,
  14 ACLR 307 (sub nom. Donrob Enterprises Pty Ltd v Queensland Petroleum Management
  Ltd)   14.4.6.1
Queensland Press Ltd v Academy Instruments No. 3 Pty Ltd (SC of Queensland 1987)
  [1988] 2 QdR 575, 11 ACLR 419, 5 ACLC 175   14.4.3, 15.7.2.4
Quickdome Ltd, re (ChD 1988) [1988] BCLC 370, 1989 PCC 406, 4 BCC 296   18.6.1
Quin & Axtens Ltd v Salmon; see Salmon v Quin & Axtens Ltd

R v Allsop (CA 1977) 64 Cr App R 29   20.10.2
R v Austen (CA 1985) 1 BCC 99,528, 7 Cr App R (S) 214, 82 LS Gaz 2499   15.2.5.3
R v Bennett (New Zealand CA 1985) 2 NZCLC 99,279   9.2.1
R v Birmingham & Gloucester Railway Co. (Queen's Bench 1842) 3 QB 223, 114 ER 492,
  2 Gal & Dav 236, 3 Ry & Can Cas 148, 11 LJ MC 134, 6 Jur 804   19.8.4
R v Boal (CA 1992) [1992] QB 591, [1992] 2 WLR 890, [1992] ICR 495, [1992] 3 All ER 177,
  95 Cr App R 272, 156 JP 617, [1992] BCLC 872   17.2, 19.8.4
R v Board of Trade, ex parte St Martins Preserving Co. Ltd (QBDC 1964) [1965] 1 QB 603,
  [1964] 3 WLR 262, [1964] 2 All ER 561, 108 SJ 602   20.2.5, 20.2.7.1
R v British Steel plc (CA 1994) [1995] 1 WLR 1356, [1995] ICR 586   19.8.4
R v Brockley (CA 1993) [1994] 1 BCLC 606, [1994] BCC 131, 99 Cr App R 385   15.2.5.1
R v Campbell (CA 1983) 78 Cr App R 95, [1984] BCLC 83   15.2.5.2
R v Canadian Dredge & Dock Co. Ltd; see Canadian Dredge & Dock Co. Ltd v R
R v Clowes (Crown Court 1991) [1992] 3 All ER 440, 95 Cr App R 440,
  [1992] BCLC 1158   20.9.3
R v Cole (CA 1997) [1998] BCC 87   2.3.3.8, 15.2.5.2, 15.2.5.3
R v Cox (CA 1982) 75 Cr App R 291, [1983] BCLC 169, [1983] Crim LR 167   20.10.2
R v Cunningham (CCA 1957) [1957] 2 QB 396, [1957] 3 WLR 76, [1957] 2 All ER 412,
  41 Cr App R 155, 121 JP 451, 101 SJ 503   7.8.2
R v Deslauriers (Manitoba CA 1992) [1993] 2 WWR 401, 83 Man R (2d) 7, 36 WAC 7,
  77 CCC (3d) 329, 12 CRR (2d) 147   19.8.4
R v D'Oyly (Court of Queen's Bench 1840) 12 Ad & El 139, 113 ER 763, 4 Per & Dav 52,
  4 Jur 1056, 4 JP 532, 9 LJ MC 113 (sub nom. R v Rector & Churchwardens of St Mary
  Lambeth)   18.4.8

R v Fane Robinson Ltd (Alberta SC Appellate Division) [1941] 3 DLR 409, [1941] 2 WWR 235,
   76 CCC 196   19.8.4
R v Gateway Foodmarkets Ltd (CA 1996) [1997] 3 All ER 78, [1997] 2 Cr App R 40   19.8.4
R v Georgiou (CA 1988) 87 Cr App R 207, 10 Cr App R (S) 207, 4 BCC 322,
   [1988] Crim LR 472   15.2.5.3
R v Goodman (CA 1992) [1993] 2 All ER 789, [1994] 1 BCLC 349, [1992] BCC 625,
   97 Cr App R 210, 14 Cr App R (S) 147, [1992] Crim LR 676   15.2.5.3
R v Grantham (CA 1984) [1984] QB 675, [1984] 2 WLR 815, [1984] 3 All ER 166,
   79 Cr App R 86, [1984] BCLC 270, 1985 PCC 1, 1 BCC 99,075, 128 SJ 331,
   81 LS Gaz 1437   20.10.2
R v Great North of England Railway Co, (QB 1846) 9 QB 315, 115 ER 1294,
   2 Cox CC 70, 16 LJ MC 16, 10 Jur 750   19.8.4
R v Holmes (CA 1991) 13 Cr App R (S) 29, [1991] BCC 394, [1991] Crim LR 790   15.2.5.3
R v Home Secretary, ex parte Atlantic Commercial Ltd (QBD 1997) [1997] BCC 692   0.1.9
R v ICR Haulage Ltd (CCA 1944) [1944] KB 551, [1994] 1 All ER 691, 30 Cr App R 31,
   113 LJ KB 492, 171 LT 180, 108 JP 181, 60 TLR 399, 42 LGR 226   19.8.4
R v International Stock Exchange of the United Kingdom and the Republic of Ireland Ltd,
   ex parte Else (1982) Ltd (CA 1992) [1993] QB 534, [1993] 2 WLR 70, [1993] 1 All ER 420,
   [1993] BCLC 834, [1993] BCC 11   7.4.4
R v Kansal (CA 1992) [1993] QB 244, [1992] 3 WLR 494, [1992] 3 All ER 844,
   95 Cr App R 348, [1992] BCLC 1009, [1992] BCC 615   20.9.3
R v Kemp (CA 1988) [1988] QB 645, [1988] 2 WLR 975, 87 Cr App R 95, [1988] BCLC 217,
   1988 PCC 405 (sub nom. Kemp v R), 4 BCC 203   20.10.1
R v Kite (CA 1996) [1996] 2 Cr App R (S) 295   19.8.4
R v Lockwood (CA 1985) 2 BCC 99,333, [1986] Crim LR 244   20.10.2
R v McDonnell (Bristol Assizes 1965) [1966] 1 QB 233, [1965] 3 WLR 1138,
   [1966] 1 All ER 193   19.8.5
R v MerBan Capital Corporation Ltd (Canada FedC 1984) [1985] 1 CTC 1   5.2.2.1, 5.2.2.5
R v Merchant Tailors' Co. (KB 1831) 2 B & Ad 115, 109 ER 1086, 9 LJ OS KB 146   9.2.4
R v Miles (CA 1992) [1992] Crim LR 657   20.10.3
R v Millard (CA 1993) 15 Cr App R (S) 445, [1994] Crim LR 146   15.2.5.5
R v Morrissey (CA 1997) *The Times*, 1 May 1997   18.8.2.6
R v Murray Wright Ltd (CA of New Zealand 1969) [1970] NZLR 476   19.8.5
R v P & O European Ferries (Dover) Ltd (Central Criminal Court 1990) 93 Cr App R 72,
   [1991] Crim LR 695   19.8.5
R v Panel on Take-overs & Mergers, ex parte Datafin plc (CA 1986) [1987] QB 815,
   [1987] 2 WLR 699, [1987] 1 All ER 564, [1987] BCLC 104, 1987 PCC 120, 3 BCC 10,
   131 SJ 23   8.8.1, 20.14.2.2
R v Panel on Takeovers & Mergers, ex parte Guinness plc (CA 1988) [1990] 1 QB 146,
   [1989] 2 WLR 863, [1989] 1 All ER 509, 4 BCC 714   8.8.1
R v Paterson (N.M.) & Sons Ltd (Canada SC 1980) 117 DLR (3d) 517, [1980] 2 SCR 679,
   [1981] 2 WWR 103, 19 CR (3d) 164, 7 Man R 2d) 382, 55 CCC (2d) 289, 34 NR 597   19.29
R v Philippou (CA 1989) 89 Cr App R 290, 5 BCC 665,
   [1989] Crim LR 585   19.8.5, 20.10.1
R v Registrar of Companies, ex parte Attorney-General (QBDC 1980) [1991] BCLC 476
                                                                  1.2.1, 2.3.5.1, 20.14.2.2
R v Registrar of Companies, ex parte Bowen (KBDC 1914) [1914] 3 KB 1161, 84 LJ KB 229,
   112 LT 38, 30 TLR 707   1.2.1, 2.3.3.3, 2.3.3.5
R v Registrar of Companies, ex parte Central Bank of India (CA 1985) [1986] QB 1114,
   [1986] 2 WLR 177, [1986] 1 All ER 105, [1985] BCLC 465, 1986 PCC 235, 1 BCC 99,496,
   129 SJ 755, 82 LS Gaz 3353   1.2.1, 11.7.6
R v Registrar of Joint Stock Companies, ex parte Johnston (CA 1891) [1891] 2 QB 598,
   61 LJ QB 3, 65 LT 392, 39 WR 708, 7 TLR 720   1.6
R v Registrar of Joint Stock Companies, ex parte More (CA 1931) [1931] 2 KB 197,
   100 LJ KB 638, 145 LT 522, [1931] All ER Rep Ext 864, 47 TLR 383, 29 LGR 452,
   95 JP 137   1.2.1
R v Reid (HL 1992) [1992] 1 WLR 793, [1992] 3 All ER 673, 95 Cr App R 391,
   [1992] RTR 341   6.7.6

R v Roffel (Court of Criminal Appeal of Victoria 1984) [1985] VR 511, 9 ACLR 433,
  14 A Crim R 134   19.8.5
R v Rozeik (CA 1995) [1996] 1 WLR 159, [1996] 1 BCLC 380, [1996] BCC 271,
  [1996] 1 Cr App R 260   19.8.6.1, 19.8.6.2
R v St Mary, Lambeth (rector & churchwardens of); see R v D'Oyly
R v St Pancras, Middlesex (vestrymen & churchwardens of) (KB 1839) 11 Ad & El 15,
  113 ER 317, 4 Per & Dav 66   18.4.8
R v Saunders (CA 1995) [1996] 1 Cr App R 463   18.8.2.6
R v Secretary of State for the Home Department, ex parte Fire Brigades Union (HL 1995)
  [1995] 2 AC 513, [1995] 2 WLR 464, [1995] 2 All ER 244   0.3.1.4
R v Secretary of State for Trade, ex parte Perestrello (QBD 1979) [1981] QB 19,
  [1980] 3 WLR 1, [1980] 3 All ER 28, 124 SJ 63   18.8.1
R v Secretary of State for Trade & Industry, ex parte Lonrho plc (HL 1989) [1989] 1 WLR 525,
  [1989] 2 All ER 609 (sub nom. Lonrho plc v Secretary of State for Trade & Industry),
  5 BCC 633   18.7.3
R v Secretary of State for Trade and Industry, ex parte Lonrho plc (QBDC 1991)
  [1992] BCC 325   15.2.5.4, 18.8.3.1
R v Secretary of State for Trade and Industry, ex parte McCormick (CA 1998)
  [1998] BCC 379   15.2.5.6, 18.8.2.6
R v Secretary of State for Transport, ex parte Factortame Ltd (case C-221/89) (ECJ 1991)
  [1991] ECR I-3905, [1992] QB 680 (sub nom. R v Secretary of State for Transport,
  ex parte Factortame Ltd (No. 3)), [1992] 3 WLR 288 (sub nom. R v Secretary of State
  for Transport, ex parte Factortame Ltd (No. 3)), [1991] 3 All ER 769, [1991] 2 Lloyd's Rep 648
  (sub nom. R v Secretary of State for Transport, ex parte Factortame Ltd (No. 3)),
  [1991] 3 CMLR 589 (sub nom. R v Secretary of State for Transport, ex parte
  Factortame Ltd (No. 2))   6.1.15
R v Seelig (CA 1991) [1992] 1 WLR 148, [1991] 4 All ER 429, 94 Cr App R 17,
  [1991] BCLC 869, [1991] BCC 569   18.8.2.6
R v Shacter (CCA 1959) [1960] 2 QB 252, [1960] 2 WLR 258, [1960] 1 All ER 61,
  44 Cr App R 42, 124 JP 108, 104 SJ 90   17.4.5, 17.4.6
R v Smith (CA 1995) [1996] 2 Cr App R 1, [1996] 2 BCLC 109   20.10.1
R v Spens (CA 1991) [19911 1 WLR 624, [1991] 4 All ER 421, 93 Cr App R 194,
  [1991] BCC 140   5.5.1
R v Stanley (Central Criminal Court, 10 December 1990) unreported   19.8.4
R v Theivendran (CA 1992) 13 Cr App R (S) 601   15.2.5.1
R v Videoflicks Ltd; see Edwards Books & Art Ltd v R
R v Warwickshire County Council, ex parte Johnson (HL 1992) [1993] AC 583, [1993] 2 WLR 1,
  [1993] 1 All ER 299 (sub nom. Warwickshire County Council v Johnson), 91 LGR 130,
  157 JP 249, 12 TrLR 1   19.8.6.2
R v Wimbledon Local Board (CA 1882) 8 QBD 459, 51 LJ QB 219, 46 LT 47, 46 JP 292,
  30 WR 400   14.4.9.2
R v Young (CA 1990) 12 Cr App R (S) 262, [1990] BCC 549, [1990] Crim LR 818   15.2.5.3
R in Right of British Columbia v Federal Business Development Bank (British Columbia
  CA 1987) [1988] 1 WWR 1   11.6.3, 11.6.4
Racal Communications Ltd, re; see Re a Company (No. 00996 of 1979)
Rackham v Peek Foods Ltd (ChD 1977) [1990] BCLC 895   14.4.5.5
Radford v Freeway Classics Ltd (CA 1993) [1994] 1 BCLC 445, [1993] BCC 870
  (sub nom. Radford v Samuel)   19.9
Rafsanjan Pistachio Producers Cooperative v Reiss (QBD 1989) [1990] BCLC 352,
  [1990] BCC 730   4.5.1
Ram Kissendas Dhanuka v Satya Charan Law (PC 1949) LR 77 Ind App 128   3.4.2.7, 3.4.2.8
Ramsgate Victoria Hotel Co. Ltd v Montefiore (Court of Exchequer 1866) LR 1 Ex 109,
  4 H & C 164, 35 LJ Ex 90, 13 LT 715, 12 Jur NS 455, 14 WR 335   6.2.2
Randall (H.E.) Ltd v British and American Shoe Co. (ChD 1902) [1902] 2 Ch 354,
  71 LJ Ch 683, 87 LT 442, 18 TLR 611, 19 RPC 393, 10 Mans 109, 50 WR 697   4.5.1
Randt Gold Mining Co., re (ChD 1904) [1904] 2 Ch 468, 73 LJ Ch 598, 91 LT 174,
  53 WR 90, 20 TLR 619, 20 Mans 93   6.4.2
Ratners Group plc, re (ChD 1988) [1988] BCLC 685, 4 BCC 293   10.2.1

Rayfield v Hands and others (ChD 1958) [1960] Ch 1, [1958] 2 WLR 851, [1958] 2 All ER 194,
    102 SJ 348   3.3.5, 3.4.2.2, 3.4.3
Rayner (J.H.) (Mincing Lane) Ltd v Department of Trade & Industry (CA 1988) [1989] Ch 72,
    [1988] 3 WLR 1033, [1988] 3 All ER 257 (sub nom. Maclaine Watson & Co. Ltd v Department
    of Trade & Industry), [1988] BCLC 404, 1989 PCC 1, 4 BCC 559; affirmed by HL (1989)
    [1990] 2 AC 418, [1989] 3 WLR 969, [1989] 3 All ER 523 (sub nom. Maclaine Watson &
    Co. Ltd v Department of Trade & Industry), [1990] BCLC 102 (sub nom. Maclaine Watson &
    Co Ltd v Department of Trade & Industry), 5 BCC 872   0.1.1, 0.1.6, 5.2.2.3
Read v Astoria Garage (Streatham) Ltd (CA 1952) [1952] Ch 637, [1952] 2 TLR 130,
    [1952] 2 All ER 292   15.3.3
Real Meat Co. Ltd, re (ChD 1995) [1996] BCC 254   11.6.2
Redgrave v Hurd (CA 1881) 20 ChD 1, 51 LJ Ch 113, 45 LT 485   6.7.1
Reed v Nova Securities Ltd (HL 1985) [1985] 1 WLR 193, [1985] 1 All ER 686, 59 TC 516,
    [1985] STC 124, 1985 PCC 209, 129 SJ 116   5.2.2.8
Reese River Silver Mining Co. Ltd v Smith (HL 1869) LR 4 HL 64, 39 LJ Ch 849,
    17 WR 1042   6.7.4
Reference re Stony Plain Indian Reserve No. 135 (Alberta CA 1981) 130 DLR (3d) 636   19.8.9
Regal (Hastings) Ltd v Gulliver (HL 1942) [1967] 2 AC 134 n, [1942] 1 All ER 378
                                    15.8, 16.3.1, 16.5.2, 16.5.5.2, 16.7.1, 16.7.2, 16.7.3.3, 16.7.3.4, 18.4.5
Regent Insulation Co. Ltd, re (ChD 1981) *The Times*, 5 November 1981   15.7.2.2
Reid v Explosives Co. Ltd (CA 1887) 19 QBD 264, 56 LJ QB 388, 57 LT 439,
    [1886–90] All ER Rep 712   20.2.7.2
Reprographic Exports (Euromat) Ltd, re (ChD 1978) 122 SJ 400   20.2.3
Residues Treatment & Trading Co. Ltd v Southern Resources Ltd (South Australia SC
    (FC) 1988) 14 ACLR 375   14.4.5.5
Residues Treatment & Trading Co. Ltd v Southern Resources Ltd (South Australia SC
    (FC) 1988) 51 SASR 177, 14 ACLR 569 (sub nom. Residues Treatment & Trading Co. Ltd
    v Southern Resources Ltd (No. 4)); for further proceedings, see Southern Resources Ltd
    v Residues Treatment & Trading Co. Ltd   18.4.9, 18.4.11, 18.4.12
Resinoid & Mica Products Ltd, re (CA 1967) [1983] Ch 132, [1982] 3 WLR 979,
    [1982] 3 All ER 677   11.7.9
Revlon Inc. v Cripps and Lee Ltd (CA 1979) [1980] FSR 85   5.2.2.5
Rex Williams Leisure plc, re (CA 1994) [1994] Ch 350, [1994] 3 WLR 745, [1994] 4 All ER 27,
    [1994] 2 BCLC 555, [1994] BCC 551   15.2.5.4
Rhodesian Properties Ltd, re (ChD 1901) [1901] WN 130, 45 SJ 580   3.4.2.7
Rhodian River Shipping Co. SA v Halla Maritime Corporation (QBD 1983) [1984]
    1 Lloyd's Rep 373, [1984] BCLC 139   4.5.1
Rica Gold Washing Co., re (CA 1879) 11 ChD 36, 40 LT 531, 27 WR 715   8.8
Ricardo Group plc, re (ChD 1989) [1989] BCLC 566, 5 BCC 388   8.9.7
Richard Brady Franks Ltd v Price (HC of Australia 1937) 58 CLR 112, 11 ALJ 202,
    [1937] ALR 470   16.4.3, 16.4.10
Richmond Gate Property Co. Ltd, re (ChD 1964) [1965] 1 WLR 335, [1964] 3 All ER 936
                                                                                                                         3.4.3, 3.4.4, 15.6.1.2
Richmond Hill Hotel Co., re, Pellatt's Case (LJJ 1867) LR 2 Ch App 527, 36 LJ Ch 613,
    16 LT 442, 15 WR 726   6.5.5
Richmond London Borough Council v Pinn & Wheeler Ltd (QBDC 1989) [1989] RTR 354,
    [1989] Crim LR 510, 133 SJ 389   0.1.1, 19.8.4
Rights and Issues Investment Trust Ltd v Stylo Shoes Ltd (ChD 1964) [1965] Ch 250,
    [1964] 3 WLR 1077, [1964] 3 All ER 628   3.5.3.5
River Tone, in the County of Somerset, Conservators of the, v Ash (KB 1829) 10 B & C 349,
    109 ER 479, 8 LJ OS KB 226   0.1.2
Rivers v Bondi Junction-Waverley RSL Sub-Branch Ltd (CA of New South Wales 1986)
    5 NSWLR 362, 10 ACLR 482   18.5
Robbie (N.W.) & Co. Ltd v Witney Warehouse Co. Ltd (CA 1963) [1963] 1 WLR 1324,
    [1963] 3 All ER 613, 1076 SJ 1038   20.2.8.2
Robert Stephen Holdings Ltd, re (ChD 1967) [1968] 1 WLR 522, [1968] 1 All ER 195 n,
    112 SJ 67   10.2.1
Robinson's Executor's Case; see Re Royal Bank of Australia

Robson v Smith (ChD 1895) [1895] 2 Ch 118, 64 LJ Ch 457, 72 LT 559, 2 Mans 422, 13 R 529,
43 WR 632 20.2.8.3
Roith (W. & M.) Ltd, re (ChD 1966) [1967] 1 WLR 432, [1967] 1 All ER 427,
110 SJ 963 2.3.5.7
Rolled Steel Products (Holdings) Ltd v British Steel Corporation (CA 1984) [1986] Ch 246,
[1985] 2 WLR 908, [1985] 3 All ER 52, [1984] BCLC 466, 1 BCC 99, 158, 128 SJ 629,
81 LS Gaz 2537   2.3.5.6, 2.3.5.7, 2.3.5.9, 16.4.1, 16.4.13, 18.2.2, 19.4.1, 19.5.2.2, 19.5.7, 20.11.4
Rolloswin Investments Ltd v Chromolit Portugal Cutelarias e Produtos Metálicos SARL
(QBD 1970) [1970] 1 WLR 912, [1970] 2 All ER 673, 114 SJ 147 19.8.8
Rolls-Royce Ltd, re (ChD 1974) [1974] 1 WLR 1584, [1974] 3 All ER 646, 118 SJ 848 20.13.2
Roper v Murdoch (SC of British Columbia 1987) 39 DLR (4th) 684, 14 BCLR (2d) 385 16.7.3.1
Rosemary Simmons Memorial Housing Association Ltd v United Dominions Trust Ltd
(ChD 1986) [1986] 1 WLR 1440, [1987] 1 All ER 281, 3 BCC 65 19.4.2
Ross v Telford (CA 1997) *The Times*, 4 July 1997 14.4.4
Rother Iron Works Ltd v Canterbury Precision Engineers Ltd (CA 1972) [1974] QB 1,
[1973] 2 WLR 281, [1973] 1 All ER 394, 117 SJ 122 20.2.7.1
Rourke v Robinson (ChD 1911) [1911] 1 Ch 480, 80 LJ Ch 295, 103 LT 895 11.2.2
Rover International Ltd v Cannon Film Sales Ltd (ChD 1987) [1987] BCLC 540, 3 BCC 369;
(CA 1988) [1989] 1 WLR 912, [1989] 3 All ER 423 (sub nom. Rover International Ltd v
Cannon Film Sales Ltd (No. 3)), [1988] BCLC 710 19.6.1
Rover International Ltd v Cannon Film Sales Ltd (No. 3); see Rover International Ltd v
Cannon Film Sales Ltd
Royal Bank of Australia, re, Robinson's Executor's Case (LJJ 1856) 6 De G M & G 572,
43 ER 1356 3.4.1.2
Royal Bank of Canada v MacManus; see MacManus v Royal Bank of Canada
Royal Bank of Canada v Mohawk Moving & Storage Ltd (HC of Ontario 1985) 16 DLR (4th) 434,
54 CBR (NS) 259, 49 OR (2d) 734 20.2.8.3
Royal Bank of Canada v Starr (Ontario District Court 1985) 31 BLR 124 19.6.1
Royal Bank of Scotland plc v Sandstone Properties Ltd (QBD 1998) *The Times*,
12 March 1998 8.4
Royal British Bank v Turquand (Exchequer Chamber 1856) 6 El & Bl 327, 119 ER 886,
25 LJ QB 317, [1843–60] All ER Rep 435 19.5.4.1
Royal Brunei Airlines Sdn Bhd v Tan (PC 1995) [1995] 2 AC 378, [1995] 3 WLR 64,
[1995] 3 All ER 97, [1995] BCC 899 18.2.2
Royal Mutual Benefit Building Society v Sharman (ChD 1963) [1963] 1 WLR 581,
[1963] 2 All ER 242 14.4.5.2
Ruben v Great Fingall Consolidated (HL 1906) [1906] AC 439, 75 LJ KB 843; 95 LT 214,
[1904–7] All ER Rep 460, 22 TLR 712, 13 Mans 248 8.2.2, 19.5.4.4
Runciman v Walter Runciman plc (QBD 1992) [1992] BCLC 1084, [1993] BCC 223
15.5.1, 16.5.5.5, 16.6.2, 16.6.5
Ruralcorp Consulting Pty Ltd v Pynery Pty Ltd (Victoria SC 1996) 134 FLR 188,
21 ACSR 161, 14 ACLC 1565 18.4.2, 18.4.13
Russell v Northern Bank Development Corporation Ltd (HL 1992) [1992] 1 WLR 588,
[1992] 3 All ER 161, [1992] BCLC 1016, [1992] BCC 578
2.4.8.3, 3.4.1.3, 3.5.3.3, 3.5.3.4, 6.1.13, 10.2.1
Russell v Wakefield Waterworks Co. (MR 1875) LR 20 Eq 474, 44 LJ Ch 496, 32 LT 685,
23 WR 887 18.4.2, 18.4.10
Russell Kinsela Pty Ltd v Kinsela; see Kinsela v Russell Kinsela Pty Ltd
Russian (Vyksounsky) Ironworks Co., re, Taite's Case (V-C 1867) LR 3 Eq 795, 36 LJ Ch 475,
16 LT 343, 15 WR 891 6.7.4
Rutherford (Scotland CSess OH 1994) [1994] BCC 876 18.6.6
Ryan v South Sydney Junior Rugby League Club Ltd (SC of New South Wales 1974) 3 ACLR 486
18.4.9, 18.5

Said v Butt (KBD 1920) [1920] 3 KB 497, 90 LJ KB 239, 124 LT 413, [1920] All ER Rep 232,
36 TLR 762 20.2.7.1
St Ives Windings Ltd, re (ChD 1987) 3 BCC 634 20.3.3
St Johnstone Football Club Ltd v Scottish Football Association Ltd
(Scotland CSess OH 1964) 1965 SLT 171 18.4.9

Salmon v Quin & Axtens Ltd (ChD 1908) 25 TLR 64; reversed by CA (1908) [1909] 1 Ch 311,
  78 LJ Ch 367, 100 LT 161, 25 TLR 164, 16 Mans 127, 53 SJ 150; affirmed by HL (1909)
  sub nom. Quin & Axtens Ltd v Salmon [1909] AC 442, 78 LJ Ch 506, 100 LT 820,
  25 TLR 590, 16 Mans 230, 53 SJ 575
                              3.4.1.1, 3.4.2.7, 3.4.2.8, 3.4.3, 14.4.9.8, 15.7.2.3, 15.7.2.4, 15.7.7, 18.4.9
Salomon v A. Salomon & Co. Ltd (HL 1896) [1897] AC 22, 66 LJ Ch 35, 75 LT 426,
  [1895–9] All ER Rep 33, 13 TLR 46, 4 Mans 89, 45 WR 193; (CA 1895) [1895] 2 Ch 323
  at 333 (sub nom. Broderip v Salomon), 64 LJ Ch 689, 72 LT 755, 11 TLR 439, 2 Mans 449,
  43 WR 612; (ChD 1895) [1895] 2 Ch 323, 72 LT 261, 11 TLR 238 (all reports of the case
  in the ChD and CA except [1895] 2 Ch 323 are sub nom. Broderip v A. Salomon & Co. Ltd)
                   0.1.1, 1.3.3.2, 5.2.1, 5.2.2.1, 5.2.2.2, 5.2.2.3, 5.2.2.10, 5.2.2.11, 14.5.1, 17.6.3.2
Salomons v Laing (MR 1850) 12 Beav 377, 50 ER 1105, 19 LJ Ch 291, 6 Ry & Can Cas 303,
  14 Jur 471   18.4.10
Saltdean Estate Co. Ltd, re (ChD 1968) [1968] 1 WLR 1844, [1968] 3 All ER 829,
  112 SJ 798   10.2.4
Salton v New Beeston Cycle Co. (ChD 1899) [1899] 1 Ch 775, 69 LJ Ch 20, 81 LT 437,
  16 TLR 25, 7 Mans 74, 48 WR 92   3.4.4
Sam Weller & Sons Ltd, re (ChD 1989) [1990] Ch 682, [1989] 3 WLR 923, [1990] BCLC 80,
  1989 PCC 466, 5 BCC 810   18.6.2
Samuel Sherman plc, re (ChD 1991) [1991] 1 WLR 1070, [1991] BCC 699   2.3.5.2, 15.2.5.6
Sandys v House of Fraser plc (C Sess OH 1983) 1985 SLT 200   18.3.3.1
Sanitary Carbon Co., re (ChD 1877) [1877] WN 223   14.4.6.2
Sarflax Ltd, re (ChD 1978) [1979] Ch 592, [1979] 2 WLR 202, [1979] 1 All ER 529,
  123 SJ 97   20.10.2
Saul D. Harrison & Sons plc, re (CA 1994) [1995] 1 BCLC 14, [1994] BCC 475   18.6.3
Saunders v United Kingdom (European Court of Human Rights 1996) 23 EHRR 313,
  [1998] 1 BCLC 362, [1997] BCC 872   18.8.2.6
Saunders (G.L.) Ltd, re (ChD 1985) [1986] 1 WLR 215, [1986] BCLC 40, 130 SJ 166,
  83 LS Gaz 779   20.2.9
Saunders (T. H.) & Co. Ltd, re (ChD 1908) [1908] 1 Ch 415, 77 LJ Ch 289, 98 LT 533,
  24 TLR 263, 15 Mans 142, 52 SJ 225   8.7.1, 14.4.9.1.2
Savoy Corporation Ltd v Development Underwriting Ltd (SC of New South Wales 1961)
  80 WN (NSW) 1021, [1963] NSWR 138   16.4.13
Savoy Hotel Ltd, re (ChD 1981) [1981] Ch 351, [1981] 3 WLR 441, [1981] 3 All ER 646,
  125 SJ 585   8.8.3
Scandinavian Bank Group plc, re (ChD 1986) [1988] Ch 87, [1987] 2 WLR 752,
  [1987] 2 All ER 70, [1987] BCLC 220, 1987 PCC 193, 131 SJ 325   1.3.2.1, 6.1.3
Scarel Pty Ltd v City of Loan & Credit Corporation Pty Ltd (Federal Court of Australia 1988)
  79 ALR 483, 17 FCR 344, 12 ACLR 730   18.4.13
Schering Pty Ltd v Forrest Pharmaceutical Co. Pty Ltd (New South Wales SC 1982)
  [1982] 1 NSWLR 286   20.2.7.1
Schiowitz v IOS Ltd (CA of New Brunswick 1971) 23 DLR (3d) 102, 4 NBR (2d) 30   18.4.2, 18.4.9
Scholey v Central Railway Co. of Venezuela (LC 1868) LR 9 Eq 266 n   6.7.4
Schwabacher, re (ChD 1907) 98 LT 127   8.1
Scientific Poultry Breeders' Association Ltd, re (CA 1932) [1933] Ch 227, 110 LJ Ch 423,
  148 LT 68, 49 TLR 4, 76 SJ 798   2.4.4
SCL Building Services Ltd, re (ChD 1989) [1990] BCLC 98, 5 BCC 746   20.3.2
Scott v Frank F. Scott (London) Ltd (CA 1940) [1940] Ch 794, [1940] 3 All ER 508   2.4.1, 3.4.1.3
Scott v Scholey (Court of King's Bench 1807) 8 East 467, 103 ER 423   20.2.8.3
Scott v Scott (ChD 1942) [1943] 1 All ER 582   15.7.2.4
Scott Group Ltd v McFarlane (New Zealand CA 1977) [1978] 1 NZLR 553   8.10
Scottish & Newcastle Breweries Ltd v Blair (C Sess (OH) 1966) 1967 SLT 72   4.5.1
Scottish Cooperative Wholesale Society Ltd v Meyer (HL 1958) [1959] AC 324,
  [1958] 3 WLR 404, [1958] 3 All ER 66, 1958 SC (HL) 40, 102 SJ 617, 1958 SLT 241
  (sub nom. Meyer v Scottish Textile & Manufacturing Co. Ltd)   16.4.15, 18.6.4
Scottish Insurance Corporation Ltd v Wilsons & Clyde Coal Co. Ltd (HL 1949) [1949] AC 462,
  [1949] 1 All ER 1068, 1949 SC (HL) 90, 1949 SLT 230, [1949] LJR 1190, 65 TLR 354,
  93 SJ 423   6.1.5, 10.2.2, 10.2.4

Scottish Petroleum Co., re (CA 1883) 23 ChD 413, 49 LT 348, [1881–5] All ER Rep Ext 1536,
    31 WR 846   6.7.4, 15.1.3, 15.5.1
Scottish Special Housing Association Ltd (C Sess 1st Div 1946) 1947 SC 17, 1946 SN 52,
    1946 SLT 313   2.4.4
Scriven v Jescott (Leeds) Ltd (KBD 1908) 53 SJ 101   19.9
Scullion v Family Planning Association of Queensland (Queensland SC 1985) 10 ACLR 249   18.5
Sea Fire & Life Assurance Co., re, Greenwood's Case (LJJ 1854) 3 De G M & G 459, 43 ER 180,
    23 LJ Ch 966, 18 Jur 387, 2 WR 322   1.3.2.5
Seaboard Offshore Ltd v Secretary of State for Transport (HL 1994) [1994] 1 WLR 541,
    [1994] 2 All ER 99, [1994] 1 Lloyd's Rep 589   19.8.4
Seagull Manufacturing Co. Ltd, re (CA 1993) [1993] Ch 345, [1993] 2 WLR 872,
    [1993] 2 All ER 980, [1993] BCLC 1139, [1993] BCC 241   20.9.8
Seagull Manufacturing Co. Ltd, re (No. 2) (ChD 1993) [1994] Ch 91, [1994] 2 WLR 453,
    [1994] 2 All ER 767, [1994] 1 BCLC 273, [1993] BCC 833   15.2.5.6
Seaton v Grant (LJJ 1867) LR 2 Ch App 459, 36 LJ Ch 638, 16 LT 758, 15 WR 602   18.4.7
Second Consolidated Trust Ltd v Ceylon Amalgamated Tea & Rubber Estates Ltd (ChD 1943)
    [1943] 2 All ER 567, 169 LT 324, 87 SJ 299   14.4.9.2
Secretary of State for Trade and Industry v Bottrill (EAT 1998), [1998] ICR 564,
    [1998] IRLR 120   5.2.1, 15.6.1.5
Secretary of State for Trade and Industry v Cleland (ChD 1996) [1997] 1 BCLC 437,
    [1997] BCC 473   15.2.5.6
Secretary of State for Trade and Industry v Davies (No. 2); see Re Blackspur Group plc
Secretary of State for Trade & Industry v Ettinger (CA 1993) [1993] BCLC 896,
    [1993] BCC 312 (sub nom. Re Swift 736 Ltd)   9.1
Secretary of State for Trade and Industry v Gash; see Secretary of State for Trade
    and Industry v Taylor
Secretary of State for Trade & Industry v Gray; see Re Grayan Building Services Ltd
Secretary of State for Trade and Industry v Hasta International Ltd
    (Scotland CSess OH 1996) 1998 SLT 73   18.8.3.3
Secretary of State for Trade and Industry v Ivens (CA 1997) [1997] 2 BCLC 334,
    [1997] BCC 801 (sub nom. Re Country Farm Inns Ltd)   15.2.5.6
Secretary of State for Trade & Industry v Langridge (CA 1991) [1991] Ch 402,
    [1991] 2 WLR 1343, [1991] 3 All ER 591, [1991] BCLC 543   15.2.5.4
Secretary of State for Trade & Industry v McTighe (CA 1993) [1994] 2 BCLC 284,
    [1993] BCC 844 (sub nom. Re Copecrest Ltd); see also Secretary of State for Trade
    and Industry v McTighe (No. 2)   15.2.5.4
Secretary of State for Trade and Industry v McTighe (No. 2) (CA 1996)
    [1996] 2 BCLC 477, [1997] BCC 224 (sub nom. Secretary of State for
    Trade and Industry v McTighe)   15.2.5.5, 15.2.5.6
Secretary of State for Trade & Industry v Palfreman (Scotland CSess OH 1994)
    [1995] 2 BCLC 301, [1995] BCC 193, 1995 SCLR 172   15.2.5.7
Secretary of State for Trade & Industry v Palmer (Scotland CSess Ex Div 1994)
    [1994] BCC 990, 1994 SC 707, 1995 SCLR 30   15.2.5.3
Secretary of State for Trade and Industry v Taylor (ChD 1996) [1997] 1 WLR 407,
    [1997] 1 BCLC 341 (sub nom. Secretary of State for Trade and Industry v Gash),
    [1997] BCC 172 (sub nom. Re C S Holidays Ltd)   15.2.5.6, 20.12
Secretary of State for Trade and Industry v Tjolle (ChD 1997) [1998] 1 BCLC 333,
    [1998] BCC 282   15.2.5.4, 15.2.5.6
Secretary of State for Trade and Industry v Van Hengel (ChD 1994) [1995] 1 BCLC 545   15.6.1.4
Secure and Provide plc, re (ChD 1992) [1992] BCC 405   18.8.3.3
Securitibank Ltd, re (No. 2) (New Zealand CA 1978) [1978] 2 NZLR 136   5.2.2.1
Securitibank Ltd, re (No. 40) (New Zealand HC 1986) 3 NZCLC 100,020   15.2.5.3
Segenhoe Ltd v Akins (New South Wales SC 1990) 29 NSWLR 569, 1 ACSR 691, 8 ACLC 263,
    [1990] Aust Torts Reports 67,922   10.5.10
SEIL Trade Finance Ltd, re; see Brereton v Nicholls   20.3.7.4
Senator Hanseatische Verwaltungsgesellschaft mbH, re (ChD 1996) [1996] 2 BCLC 562;
    (CA 1996) [1996] 2 BCLC 562 at 597, [1997] BCC 112
    (sub nom. Re SHV Senator Hanseatische Verwaltungs Gesellschaft)   18.8.3.3

Sentinel Securities plc, re (ChD 1995) [1996] 1 WLR 316   18.8.3.3
Servers of the Blind League, re (ChD 1960) [1960] 1 WLR 564, [1960] 2 All ER 298,
   104 SJ 408   20.14.1
Sevenoaks Stationers (Retail) Ltd, re (CA 1990) [1991] Ch 164, [1990] 3 WLR 1165,
   [1991] 3 All ER 578, [1991] BCLC 325, [1990] BCC 765   15.2.5.5, 15.2.5.6
Severn & Wye & Severn Bridge Railway Co., re (ChD 1896) [1896] 1 Ch 559, 65 LJ Ch 400,
   74 LT 219, 12 TLR 262, 3 Mans 90, 44 WR 347, 40 SJ 337   10.5.1
Shalfoon v Cheddar Valley Cooperative Dairy Co. Ltd (New Zealand CA 1923)
   [1924] NZLR 561, [1924] GLR 121   1.3.2.3, 3.4.2.5
Shanks v Central Regional Council (C Sess OH 1986) 1987 SLT 410; affirmed by Ex Div
   (1987) 1988 SLT 212   20.2.3
Shanley (M.J.) Contracting Ltd, re (ChD 1979) 124 SJ 239   14.4.6.2, 14.4.8.3, 14.4.11, 14.5.1
Sharp v Dawes (CA 1876) 2 QBD 26, 46 LJ QB 104, 36 LT 188, 25 WR 66   14.4.6.2
Sharpley v Louth & East Coast Railway Co. (CA 1876) 2 ChD 663, 46 LJ Ch 259, 35 LT 71   6.7.4
Sharrment Pty Ltd v Official Trustee in Bankruptcy (Australia Federal Court 1988) 18 FCR 449,
   82 ALR 530   5.2.2.1, 5.2.2.9
Shaw, re; see Re Diamond Rock Boring Co. Ltd, ex parte Shaw
Shaw v Tati Concessions Ltd (ChD 1913) [1913] 1 Ch 292, 82 LJ Ch 159, 108 LT 487,
   29 TLR 261, 20 Mans 104, [1911–13] All ER Rep 694, 57 SJ 322   14.4.9.2, 18.5
Shearer v Bercain Ltd (ChD 1980) [1980] 3 All ER 295, [1980] STC 359, 124 SJ 292   6.5.2
Shears v Phosphate Co-operative Co. of Australia Ltd (Victoria SC (FC) 1988)
   14 ACLR 747   14.4.9.1.8
Sheffield & South Yorkshire Permanent Building Society, re (QBDC 1889) 22 QBD 470,
   58 LJ QB 265, 60 LT 186, 53 JP 375, 5 TLR 192   0.1.4, 1.3.2
Sheffield Corporation v Barclay (HL 1905) [1905] AC 392, 74 LJ KB 747, 93 LT 83,
   [1904–7] All ER Rep 747, 69 JP 385, 12 Mans 248, 3 LGR 992, 21 TLR 642, 10 Com Cas 287,
   54 WR 49, 49 SJ 617   8.4
Sheppard and Cooper Ltd v TSB Bank plc (ChD 1996) [1996] 2 All ER 654   20.2.2
Sherborne Associates Ltd, re (QBD 1994) [1995] BCC 40   20.12
Sherborne Park Residents Co. Ltd, re; see Re a Company (No. 005136 of 1986)
Shield Development Co. Ltd v Snyder (SC of British Columbia 1975) [1976]
   3 WWR 44   14.4.3
Shindler v Northern Raincoat Co. Ltd (Manchester Assizes 1960) [1960] 1 WLR 1038,
   [1960] 2 All ER 239   15.3.3, 15.5.3
Shoe Lace Ltd, re; see Power v Sharp Investments Ltd
Shrewsbury & Birmingham Railway Co. v North-Western Railway Co. (HL 1857) 6 HL Cas 113,
   10 ER 1237, 26 LJ Ch 482, 3 Jur NS 775   19.4.1
Shuttleworth v Cox Brothers & Co. (Maidenhead) Ltd (CA 1926) [1927] 2 KB 9, 96 LJ KB 104,
   136 LT 337, [1926] All ER Rep 498, 43 TLR 83   3.5.4, 3.5.3.5, 15.3.3, 18.3.3.1
SHV Senator Hanseatische Verwaltungs Gesellschaft, re;
   see Re Senator Hanseatische Verwaltungsgesellschaft mbH
Sidebottom v Kershaw, Leese & Co. Ltd (CA 1919) [1920] 1 Ch 154, 89 LJ Ch 113, 122 LT 325,
   36 TLR 45, 64 SJ 114   3.5.3.5
Siebe Gorman & Co. Ltd v Barclays Bank Ltd (ChD 1978) [1979] 2 Lloyd's Rep 142
                                                                                11.6.4, 11.7.10.1
Siemens Brothers & Co. Ltd v Burns (CA 1918) [1918] 2 Ch 324, 87 LJ Ch 572, 119 LT 352
                                                                                  14.4.9.2, 18.5
Simm v Anglo-American Telegraph Co. (CA 1879) 5 QBD 188, 49 LJ QB 392, 42 LT 37,
   44 JP 280, 28 WR 290   8.4
Simmonds v Heffer (ChD 1983) [1983] BCLC 298   2.3.5.6, 18.4.10
Simpson v Westminster Palace Hotel Co. (HL 1860) 8 HL Cas 712, 11 ER 608, 2 LT 707,
   6 Jur NS 985   2.3.5.2, 18.4.9, 18.4.10
Sindesmos Melon tis Eleftheras Evangelikis Ekklisias v Greece (case C-381/89)
   (ECJ 1992) [1992] ECR I-2111, [1994] 2 CMLR 348, [1994] 1 CEC 470   0.3.3.1
Singh v Atombrook Ltd (CA 1988) [1989] 1 WLR 810, [1989] 1 All ER 385   4.5.1
Skaw Prince, the (Singapore HC 1994) [1994] 3 SLR 379   5.2.2.10
Skelton's case; see Re Snyder Dynamite Projectile Co. Ltd
Skinner v Lambert (Court of Common Pleas 1842) 4 Man & G 477, 134 ER 196,
   5 Scott NR 197, 2 Dowl NS 132, 11 LJ CP 237   3.4.1.2

Sly, Spink & Co., re (ChD 1911) [1911] 2 Ch 430, 81 LJ Ch 55, 105 LT 364, 19 Mans 65
    15.1.3, 15.2.2
Smallman Construction Ltd, re (ChD 1988) [1989] BCLC 420, 1989 PCC 433,
    4 BCC 784   20.3.3
Smith v Brown (PC (SC of New South Wales) 1896) [1896] AC 614, 65 LJ PC 89, 75 LT 213,
    12 TLR 596, 45 WR 132; sub nom. Re Bonang Gold Mining Co. Ltd (Brown's case)
    7 BC (NSW) 6, 17 LR (NSW) (Eq) 220   3.4.2.4
Smith v Chadwick and others (HL 1884) 9 App Cas 187, 53 LJ Ch 873, 50 LT 697, 48 JP 644,
    32 WR 687, [1881–5] All ER Rep 242; affirming CA (1882) 20 ChD 27, 51 LJ Ch 597,
    46 LT 702   6.7.3
Smith v Croft (ChD 1986) [1986] 1 WLR 580, [1986] 2 All ER 551, 1986 PCC 412, 2 BCC 99,010;
    see also Smith v Croft (No. 2)   18.4.7
Smith v Croft (No. 2) (ChD 1986) [1988] Ch 114, [1987] 3 WLR 405, [1987] 3 All ER 909,
    [1987] BCLC 206, 1987 PCC 209, 3 BCC 207, [1988] LRC (Comm) 621 (sub nom.
    Smith v Croft); further proceedings (ChD 1986) [1988] Ch 114 at 139,
    [1987] 3 WLR 405 at 422, [1987] 3 All ER 909 at 922, [1987] BCLC 355 (sub nom.
    Smith v Croft), 3 BCC 218 (sub nom. Smith v Croft (No. 3)), [1988] LRC (Comm) 621 at 636
    (sub nom. Smith v Croft)   14.4.9.4, 18.3.2, 18.4.2, 18.4.3, 18.4.4, 18.4.5, 18.4.10, 18.4.13
Smith v Croft (No. 3); see Smith v Croft (No. 2)
Smith v Goldsworthy (QB 1843) 4 QB 430, 114 ER 960, 3 Gal & Dav 448, 12 LJ QB 192,
    7 Jur 389   3.4.1.2
Smith v Hancock (CA 1894) [1894] 2 Ch 377, 63 LJ Ch 477, 70 LT 578, 58 JP 638, 10 TLR 433,
    7 R 200, 42 WR 465, 38 SJ 416   5.2.2.4
Smith v Land & House Property Corporation (CA 1884) 28 ChD 7, 51 LT 718, 49 JP 182   6.7.3
Smith v Paringa Mines Ltd (ChD 1906) [1906] 2 Ch 193, 75 LJ Ch 702, 94 LT 571,
    13 Mans 316   14.4.5.5
Smith & Fawcett Ltd, re (CA 1942) [1942] Ch 304, [1942] 1 All ER 542, 111 LJ Ch 265,
    166 LT 279, 86 SJ 147   8.3.4, 16.4.1, 16.4.2, 16.4.13
Smith Knight & Co., re, Weston's Case (CA in Chancery 1868) LR 4 Ch App 20, 38 LJ Ch 49,
    19 LT 337, 17 WR 62   8.1
Smith (G.E.) Ltd v Smith (SC of New Zealand 1952) [1952] NZLR 470   16.7.3.1
Smith (M.H.) (Plant Hire) Ltd v Mainwaring t/a Inshore (CA 1986) [1986] BCLC 342,
    2 BCC 99,262   20.14.1
Smith New Court Securities Ltd v Citibank NA (HL 1996) [1997] AC 254, [1996] 3 WLR 1051,
    [1996] 4 All ER 769   0.3.5
Smith Stone & Knight Ltd v Birmingham Corporation (KBD 1939) [1939] 4 All ER 116,
    161 LT 371, 104 JP 31, 83 SJ 961, 37 LGR 665   5.2.2.3, 5.2.2.8
Smiths Ltd v Middleton (ChD 1978) [1979] 3 All ER 842   20.2.3
Snook v London & West Riding Investments Ltd (CA 1967) [1967] 2 QB 786,
    [1967] 2 WLR 1020, [1967] 2 All ER 518, 111 SJ 71   5.2.2.4
Snyder Dynamite Projectile Co. Ltd, re, Skelton's Case (ChD 1893) 68 LT 210   6.7.4
Sociedade Nacional de Combustiveis de Angola UEE v Lundqvist (CA 1990) [1991] 2 QB 310,
    [1991] 2 WLR 280, [1990] 3 All ER 283   5.2.1, 19.9
Société Anonyme des Anciens Établissements Panhard et Levassor, La, v Panhard Levassor
    Motor Co. Ltd (ChD 1901) [1901] 2 Ch 513, 70 LJ Ch 738, 85 LT 20, 17 TLR 680,
    18 RPC 405, 50 WR 74   2.3.3.6
Société Générale de Paris v Walker (HL 1885) 11 App Cas 20, 55 LJ QB 169, 54 LT 389,
    2 TLR 200, 34 WR 662; affirming CA (sub nom. Société Générale de Paris v Tramways
    Union Co. Ltd) (1884) 14 QBD 424, 54 LJ QB 177, 52 LT 912   8.7.1
Soden v British and Commonwealth Holdings plc (HL 1997), [1998] AC 298,
    [1997] 3 WLR 840, [1997] 4 All ER 353, [1997] BCC 952   8.10
Soden v Burns (ChD 1996) [1996] 1 WLR 1512, [1996] 3 All ER 967, [1996] 2 BCLC 636,
    [1997] BCC 308   20.9.3
South African Territories Ltd v Wallington (HL 1898) [1898] AC 309, 67 LJ QB 470,
    78 LT 426, 14 TLR 298, 46 WR 545   12.5
South Blackpool Hotel Co., re, Migotti's Case (MR 1867) LR 4 Eq 238, 36 LJ Ch 531,
    16 LT 271, 15 WR 731   6.8
South Durham Iron Co., re, Smith's Case (CA 1879) 11 ChD 579, 48 LJ Ch 480, 40 LT 572,
    27 WR 845   11.7.12

South Essex Estuary & Reclamation Co., re, ex parte Paine & Layton (LC 1869)
  LR 4 Ch App 215, 38 LJ Ch 305   20.9.3
South Hetton Coal Co. Ltd v North-Eastern News Association Ltd (CA 1893) [1894] 1 QB 133,
  63 LJ QB 293, 69 LT 844, 58 JP 196, 42 WR 322, 10 TLR 110, 9 R 240,
  [1891–4] All ER Rep 548   0.1.6, 5.2.1
South London Greyhound Racecourses Ltd v Wake (ChD 1930) [1931] 1 Ch 496,
  100 LJ Ch 169, 144 LT 607, [1930] All ER Rep 496, 74 SJ 820   8.2.2, 8.3.4, 19.5.4.4
South Rhondda Colliery Co. (1898) Ltd, re (ChD 1928) [1928] WN 126, 72 SJ 453   11.6.2
Southard & Co. Ltd, re (CA 1979) [1979] 1 WLR 1198, 3 All ER 556   5.2.2.8
Southern Counties Deposit Bank Ltd v Rider (CA 1895) 73 LT 374, 11 TLR 563   14.4.5.1, 18.5
Southern Foundries (1926) Ltd v Shirlaw (HL 1940) [1940] AC 701, [1940] 2 All ER 445,
  109 LJ KB 461, 164 LT 251, 56 TLR 637, 84 SJ 464   3.5.3.4, 3.5.4, 15.3.3, 15.5.3
Southern Resources Ltd v Residues Treatment & Trading Co. Ltd (South Australia SC (FC)
  1990) 56 SASR 455, 3 ACSR 207; for previous proceedings, see Residues Treatment & Trading
  Co. Ltd v Southern Resources Ltd   18.4.11
Spackman v Evans (HL 1868) LR 3 HL 171, 37 LJ Ch 752, 19 LT 151   6.4.2, 16.4.1
Specialised Mouldings Ltd, re (ChD 13 February 1987 unreported)   20.2.7.2
Spence v Crawford (HL 1939) [1939] 3 All ER 271, 1939 SC (HL) 52,
  1939 SLT 305   4.4.1
Spencer v Kennedy (ChD 1925) [1926] 1 Ch 125, 95 LJ Ch 240, 134 LT 591,
  [1925] All ER Rep 135   15.3.7, 18.4.9
Spicer (A.M.) & Son Pty Ltd v Spicer (Australia HC 1931) 47 CLR 151, 5 ALJ 211,
  37 ALR 357   16.6.3
Spokes v Grosvenor & West End Railway Terminus Hotel Co. Ltd (CA 1897)
  [1897] 2 QB 124, 66 LJ QB 572, 76 LT 679, 13 TLR 431, 45 WR 546,
  [1895–9] All ER Rep Ext 1779   18.4.2
Sri Lanka Omnibus Co. Ltd v Perera (PC (SC of Ceylon) 1951) [1952] AC 76,
  [1951] 2 TLR 1184   6.2.10
Standard Bank of Australia Ltd, re (SC of Victoria 1898) 24 VLR 304, 4 ALR 287   15.7.2.2
Standard Chartered Bank v Walker (ChD 1991) [1992] 1 WLR 561, [1992] BCLC 603   14.4.9.6
Standard Chartered Bank Ltd v Walker (CA 1982) [1982] 1 WLR 1410, [1982] 3 All ER 938,
  264 EG 345, [1982] Com LR 233, 126 SJ 479, 79 LS Gaz 1137   20.2.5, 20.2.10
Standard Manufacturing Co., re (CA 1891) [1891] 1 Ch 627, [1891–4] All ER Rep 1242,
  60 LJ Ch 292, 64 LT 487, 2 Meg 418, 39 WR 369   11.3
Standard Rotary Machine Co. Ltd, re (ChD 1906) 95 LT 829, 51 SJ 48   11.7.5
Stanley W. Johnson Pty Ltd, re (Victoria SC 1935) [1936] VLR 59, [1936] ALR 124   14.4.5.4
Staples v Eastman Photographic Materials Co. (CA 1896) [1896] 2 Ch 303, 65 LJ Ch 682,
  74 LT 479, 12 TLR 403, 40 SJ 513   6.1.5, 18.4.9
State of Wyoming Syndicate, re (ChD 1901) [1901] 2 Ch 431, 70 LJ Ch 727, 84 LT 868,
  17 TLR 631, 8 Mans 311, 49 WR 650, 45 SJ 656   14.4.5.1, 18.5
Stein v Blake (CA 1997) [1998] 1 All ER 724, [1998] BCC 316   18.4.6
Stein v Saywell (HC of Australia 1969) 121 CLR 529, 43 ALJR 183, [1969] ALR 481   11.6.2
Stephens v Mysore Reefs (Kangundy) Mining Co. Ltd (ChD 1902) [1902] 1 Ch 745,
  71 LJ Ch 295, 86 LT 221, 18 TLR 327, 9 Mans 199, 50 WR 509   2.3.5.2, 2.3.5.8
Stewarts Supermarkets Ltd v Secretary of State (Northern Ireland QBD 1982)
  [1982] NI 286   5.2.2.8
Sticky Fingers Restaurant Ltd, re (ChD 1991) [1992] BCLC 84, [1991] BCC 754   14.4.4, 18.6.6
Stocken's case; see Re Blakely Ordnance Co.
Street v Mountford (HL 1985) [1985] AC 809, [1985] 2 WLR 877, [1985] 2 All ER 289,
  50 P & CR 258, [1985] 1 EGLR 128, 274 EG 821, 17 HLR 402, 135 NLJ 460,
  82 LS Gaz 2087, 129 SJ 348   11.6.4
Stroud v Royal Aquarium & Summer & Winter Garden Society Ltd (1903) 89 LT 243,
  19 TLR 656   2.3.5.7
Stroud Architectural Systems Ltd v John Laing Construction Ltd (Official Referee 1993)
  [1994] 2 BCLC 276, [1994] BCC 18   11.7.10.3
Stylo Shoes Ltd v Prices Tailors Ltd (ChD 1959) [1960] Ch 396, [19601 2 WLR 8,
  [1959] 3 All ER 901   20.6.3
Suburban Hotel Co., re (CA in Chancery 1867) LR 2 Ch App 737, 36 LJ Ch 710, 17 LT 22,
  15 WR 1096   2.3.5.4

Sugar Properties (Derisley Wood) Ltd, re (ChD 1986) [1988] BCLC 146, 3 BCC 88   11.7.10.2

Sun Insurance Office v Clark (HL 1912) [1912] AC 443, 6 TC 59, 81 LJ KB 488, 106 LT 438,
  28 TLR 303, [1911–13] All ER Rep 495, 56 SJ 378   9.3.8

Sun Tai Cheung Credits Ltd v Attorney-General of Hong Kong (PC (CA of Hong Kong) 1987)
  [1987] 1 WLR 948, 3 BCC 357, [1987] HKLR 1010, [1988] LRC (Comm) 752   4.2.1

Suncor Inc. Resources Group, Oil Sands Division v Allarco Group Ltd; see Allarco Group Ltd
  v Suncor Inc. Resources Group, Oil Sands Division

Supply of Ready Mixed Concrete, re (No. 2); see Director General of
  Fair Trading v Pioneer Concrete (UK) Ltd

Supreme Travels Ltd v Little Olympian Each-ways Ltd; see Re Little Olympian Each-ways Ltd

Sussex Brick Co., re (CA 1904) [1904] 1 Ch 598, 73 LJ Ch 308, 90 LT 426,
  [1904–7] All ER Rep 673, 11 Mans 66, 52 WR 371   14.3.3

Sussex Brick Co. Ltd, re (ChD 1959) [1961] Ch 289 n, [1960] 2 WLR 665 n,
  [1960] 1 All ER 772 n, 104 SJ 329   8.8.2.3

Sutherland v Wills (Exchequer 1850) 5 Ex 715, 155 ER 313   3.4.1.2

Sutton's Hospital, case of (Exchequer Chamber 1612) 10 Co Rep 1, 77 ER 937, Jenk 270,
  145 ER 194, [1558–1774] All ER Rep 11   0.1.2

Svanstrom v Jonasson (Cayman Islands CA, 4 April 1997, unreported)   18.4.2

Swabey v Port Darwin Gold Mining Co. (CA 1889) 1 Meg 385   3.4.4

Swain (J.D.) Ltd, re (CA 1965) [1965] 1 WLR 909, [1965] 2 All ER 761, 109 SJ 320   20.6.1

Swaledale Cleaners Ltd, re (CA 1968) [1968] 1 WLR 1710, [1968] 3 All ER 619,
  112 SJ 781   8.3.4

Sweny v Smith (MR 1869) LR 7 Eq 324, 38 LJ Ch 446   6.4.2, 18.4.9

Swift 736 Ltd, re; see Secretary of State for Trade & Industry v Ettinger

Swindon Town Football Co. Ltd, re (ChD 1989) [1990] BCLC 467   6.1.13

Sycotex Pty Ltd v Baseler: see Re New World Alliance Pty Ltd

Synthetic Technology Ltd, re (ChD 1993) [1993] BCC 549   15.2.5.6

System Controls plc v Munro Corporate plc (ChD 1990) [1990] BCLC 659,
  [1990] BCC 386   6.5.4, 8.3.4

T & D Services (Timber Preservation & Damp Proofing Contractors) Ltd, re (ChD 1990)
  [1990] BCC 592   15.2.5.6

Taff Vale Railway Co. v Amalgamated Society of Railway Servants (HL 1901) [1901] AC 426,
  70 LJ KB 905, 83 LT 474, 50 WR 44, 44 SJ 714   0.1.6

Taiwa Land Investment Co. Ltd, re (Hong Kong HC 1981) [1981] HKLR 297   18.6.2

Tal y Drws Slate Co., (Mackley's case) (V-C 1875) 1 ChD 247, 45 LJ Ch 158, 33 LT 460,
  24 WR 92   6.8

Tam Wing Chuen v Bank of Credit and Commerce Hong Kong Ltd (PC 1996)
  [1996] 2 BCLC 69, [1996] BCC 388   11.5.6

Tansoft Ltd, re (ChD 1990) [1991] BCLC 339   15.2.5.6

Tasbian Ltd, re (No. 1) (CA 1990) [1991] BCLC 54, [1990] BCC 318
  (sub nom. Re Tasbian Ltd)   15.2.5.4

Tate Access Floors Inc. v Boswell (ChD 1990) [1991] Ch 512, [1991] 2 WLR 304,
  [1990] 3 All ER 303   5.2.1

Tatung (UK) Ltd v Galex Telesure Ltd (QBD 1988) 5 BCC 325   11.7.10.3, 11.7.10.4

Taunton v Sheriff of Warwickshire (CA 1895) [1895] 2 Ch 319, 64 LJ Ch 497,
  72 LT 712   11.6.3, 20.2.8.3

Taupo Totara Timber Co. Ltd v Rowe (PC (CA of New Zealand) 1977) [1978] AC 537,
  [1977] 3 WLR 466, [1977] 3 All ER 123, [1977] 2 NZLR 453, 121 SJ 692   15.6.2.2

Tavarone Mining Co., re, Pritchard's Case (LJJ 1873) LR 8 Ch App 956, 42 LJ Ch 768,
  29 LT 363, 21 WR 829   3.4.1.1, 3.4.2.4, 3.4.3

Taylor (C Sess 2nd Div 1992) 1993 SLT 375, [1992] BCC 440   5.2.2.11

Taylor v National Union of Mineworkers (Derbyshire Area) (ChD 1984) [1985] IRLR 99,
  [1985] BCLC 237   14.4.9.4, 18.2.1, 18.4.2, 18.4.5, 18.4.10

Taylor v Pace Developments Ltd (CA 1991) [1991] BCC 406   19.9

Taylor v Pilsen Joel & General Electric Light Co. (ChD 1884) 27 ChD 268, 53 LJ Ch 856,
  50 LT 480, 33 WR 134   3.5.1

Taylor's Industrial Flooring Ltd, re; see Taylors Industrial Flooring Ltd v M & H Plant Hire
  (Manchester) Ltd

Taylors Industrial Flooring Ltd v M & H Plant Hire (Manchester) Ltd (CA 1989)
  [1990] BCLC 216, [1990] BCC 44 (sub nom. Re Taylor's Industrial Flooring Ltd)   20.6.3
Tayside Floorcloth Co. Ltd (C Sess 1st Div 1923) 1923 SC 590, 1923 SLT 324, 60 SLR 361   2.4.3
TCB Ltd v Gray (ChD 1985) [1986] Ch 621, [1986] 2 WLR 517, [1986] 1 All ER 587,
  [1986] BCLC 113, 2 BCC 99, 044, 136 NLJ 93, 83 LS Gaz 520; affirmed by CA (1987)
  [1988] 1 All ER 108, 1988 FLR 116 (sub nom. Gray v TCB Ltd), 3 BCC 503, [1987] Ch 458 n,
  [1987] 3 WLR 1149 n, [1988] BCLC 281 n   19.5.5
Teck Corporation Ltd v Millar et al. (SC of British Columbia 1972) 33 DLR (3d) 288,
  [1973] 2 WWR 385   15.7.1, 16.4.1, 16.4.2
Tecnion Investments Ltd, re (CA 1985) [1985] BCLC 434   5.2.2.5
Teede & Bishop Ltd, re (ChD 1901) 70 LJ Ch 409, 84 LT 561, 17 TLR 282, 8 Mans 217,
  45 SJ 343   14.4.5.5
Telemetrix plc v Modern Engineers of Bristol (Holdings) plc (ChD 1985) [1985] BCLC 213,
  1 BCC 99,417, 82 LS Gaz 1561   20.2.7.1
Tennant v Trenchard (LC 1869) LR 4 Ch App 537, 38 LJ Ch 169, 661, 20 LT 856   11.5.3
Tesco Stores Ltd v Brent London Borough Council (QBDC 1993) [1993] 1 WLR 1037,
  [1993] 2 All ER 718, 13 Tr LR 87   19.8.4
Tesco Supermarkets Ltd v Nattrass (HL 1971) [1972] AC 153, [1971] 2 WLR 1166,
  [1971] 2 All ER 127, 135 JP 289, 69 LGR 403, 115 SJ 285   19.8.4, 19.8.6.2
Tett v Phoenix Property & Investment Co. Ltd (CA 1985) [1986] BCLC 149, 1986 PCC 210,
  2 BCC 99, 140, 83 LS Gaz 116, 129 SJ 869; reversing ChD (1984) [1984] BCLC 599,
  1 BCC 99, 327   8.3.4
Theseus Exploration NL v Mining & Associated Industries Ltd (Queensland SC 1972)
  [1973] QdR 81, (1972) ACLC 27,377   15.2.3.2
Thomas, re, ex parte Poppleton (QBD 1884) 14 QBD 379, 54 LJ QB 336, 51 LT 602,
  33 WR 583   1.5
Thomas Gerrard & Son Ltd, re (ChD 1967) [1968] Ch 455, [1967] 3 WLR 84,
  [1967] 2 All ER 525, 111 SJ 329   10.5.10, 20.11.2
Thomas Logan Ltd v Davis (ChD 1911) 104 LT 914; affirmed by CA (1911) 105 LT 419
   15.5.3, 15.7.2.4, 15.7.4
Thorby v Goldberg (Australia HC 1964) 112 CLR 597   16.4.16
Thorn EMI plc, re (ChD 1988) [1989] BCLC 612, 4 BCC 698   10.2.1, 10.2.2
Thorne v Silverleaf (CA 1993) [1994] 1 BCLC 637, [1994] BCC 109   2.3.3.8
Tiessen v Henderson (ChD 1899) [1899] 1 Ch 861, 68 LJ Ch 353, 80 LT 483, 6 Mans 340,
  47 WR 459   14.4.5.5, 16.8
TIP-Europe Ltd, re (ChD 1987) [1988] BCLC 231, 1988 PCC 28, 3 BCC 647   10.2.5
Tito v Waddell (No. 2) (ChD 1977) [1977] Ch 106, [1977] 2 WLR 496,
  [1977] 3 All ER 129   16.5.1
TNT Australia Pty Ltd v Poseidon Ltd (South Australia SC 1989) 52 SASR 379   14.4.5.5
TO Supplies (London) Ltd v Jerry Creighton Ltd (KBD 1951) [1952] 1 KB 42,
  [1951] 2 All ER 992, [1951] 2 TLR 993, 93 SJ 730   2.3.4
Tolltreck Systems Ltd, re (No. 2) (New South Wales SC 1991) 4 ACSR 804, 9 ACLC 788   10.2.3
Tomkinson v South-Eastern Railway Co. (ChD 1887) 35 ChD 675, 56 LJ Ch 932, 56 LT 812   2.3.5.6
Toms v Cinema Trust Co. Ltd (KBD 1914) [1915] WN 29   16.6.5
Toronto Stock Exchange v Regional Assessment Commissioner, Region No. 9
  (Ontario CA 1996) 136 DLR (4th) 362   5.2.2.6
Tottenham Hotspur plc, re (ChD 1993) [1994] 1 BCLC 655   18.6.3
Totterdell v Fareham Blue Brick & Tile Co. Ltd (Court of Common Pleas 1866) LR 1 CP 674,
  35 LJ CP 278, 12 Jur NS 901, 14 WR 919   19.5.3, 19.5.4.2
Towers v African Tug Co. (CA 1904) [1904] 1 Ch 558, 73 LJ Ch 395, 90 LT 298, 20 TLR 292,
  11 Mans 198, 52 WR 532   18.4.7
TR Technology Investment Trust plc, re (ChD 1988) [1988] BCLC 256, 1988 PCC 462,
  4 BCC 244   8.9.5, 8.9.7
Transamerica Life Insurance Co. of Canada v Canada Life Assurance Co.
  (Ontario Court 1996) 28 OR (3d) 423   5.2.2.1
Transatlantic Life Assurance Co. Ltd, re (ChD 1979) [1980] 1 WLR 79, [1979] 3 All ER 352,
  123 SJ 859   10.2.1, 14.3.3
Transfesa Terminals Ltd, re (ChD 1987) 3 BCC 647   10.2.5

Transvaal Lands Co. v New Belgium (Transvaal) Land & Development Co. (CA 1914)
[1914] 2 Ch 488, 84 LJ Ch 94, 112 LT 965, 31 TLR 1, 21 Mans 364, [1914–15] All ER Rep 987,
59 SJ 27   16.5.1, 16.5.3
Trebanog Working Men's Club & Institute Ltd v Macdonald (KBDC 1940) [1940] 1 KB 576,
[1940] 1 All ER 454, 109 LJ KB 288, 162 LT 305, 104 JP 171, 56 TLR 404, 38 LGR 160,
31 Cox CC 372, 84 SJ 357   1.3.5, 5.2.2.6
Trench Tubeless Tyre Co., re (Bethell v the company) (CA 1900) [1900] 1 Ch 408,
69 LJ Ch 213, 82 LT 247, 16 TLR 207, 48 WR 310   20.5.4
Trevor v Whitworth (HL 1887) 12 App Cas 409, 57 LJ Ch 28, 57 LT 457,
[1886–90] All ER Rep 46, 3 TLR 745, 36 WR 145, 32 SJ 201   0.3.2.3, 10.1, 10.2.1, 10.8.2
Tricontinental Corporation Ltd v Federal Commissioner of Taxation (SC of Queensland FC 1987)
73 ALR 433, [1988] 1 QdR 474, 18 ATR 827, 12 ACLR 421   11.6.3
Triplex Safety Glass Co. Ltd v Lancegaye Safety Glass (1934) Ltd (CA 1939) [1939] 2 KB 395,
[1939] 2 All ER 613, 108 LJ KB 762, 160 LT 595, 55 TLR 726   19.9
Tritonia Ltd v Equity & Law Life Assurance Society (HL (from C Sess 2nd Div) 1943)
[1943] AC 584, [1943] 2 All ER 401, 112 LJ PC 33, 169 LT 306, 60 TLR 3, 87 SJ 129   19.9
Trounce v NCF Kaiapoi Ltd (New Zealand HC 1985) 2 NZCLC 99,422   15.5.5
Trustees of Dartmouth College v Woodward (United States SC 1819) 17 US
(4 Wheat) 518   0.2.3, 5.3.1
Tse Kwong Lam v Wong Chit Sen (PC 1983) [1983] 1 WLR 1349, [1983] 3 All ER 54,
[1983] BCLC 88, 133 New LJ 829, 127 SJ 632, 80 LS Gaz 2368   5.2.1, 11.5.1
Tucker, ex parte; see Re Tucker
Tucker, re, ex parte Tucker (CA 1987) [1990] Ch 148, [1988] 2 WLR 748, [1988] 1 All ER 603 20.9.3
Tucker v Wilson; see Wilson v Tooker
Tudor Grange Holdings Ltd v Citibank NA (ChD 1991) [1992] Ch 53, [1991] 3 WLR 750,
[1991] 4 All ER 1, [1991] BCLC 1009   20.2.3
Tunbridge (G.E.) Ltd, re (ChD 1994) [1995] 1 BCLC 34, [1994] BCC 563   11.6.4
Turner v Berner (New South Wales SC 1978) [1978] 1 NSWLR 66, 3 ACLR 272,
(1978) ACLC 30,007   14.4.3
Turner v Canadian Pacific Ltd (Ontario HC 1979) 107 DLR (3d) 142, 27 OR (2d) 549   18.4.12
Tussaud v Tussaud (ChD 1890) 44 ChD 678, 59 LJ Ch 631, 62 LT 633, 6 TLR 272,
2 Meg 120, 38 WR 503   2.3.3.6
Twomax Ltd v Dickson, McFarlane & Robinson (C Sess OH 1982) 1982 SC 113, 1983 SLT 98;
(C Sess 1st Div 1984) 1984 SLT 424 n   8.10
Twycross v Grant (CA 1877) 2 CPD 469, 46 LJ QB 636, 36 LT 812, 25 WR 701   17.6.2
Tyne Mutual Steamship Insurance Association v Brown (QBD 1896) 74 LT 283,
1 Com Cas 345   15.2.6

UBAF Ltd v European American Banking Corporation (CA 1983) [1984] QB 713,
[1984] 2 WLR 508, [1984] 2 All ER 226, [1984] BCLC 112, 128 SJ 243, 81 LS Gaz 429
                                                                          19.2.1, 19.2.2, 19.8.1
Ultramares Corporation v Touche (New York CA 1931) 174 NE 441, 255 NY 170,
74 ALR 1139   8.10
Underwood (A.L.) Ltd v Bank of Liverpool and Martins (CA 1924) [1924] 1 KB 775,
93 LJ KB 690, 131 LT 271, 40 TLR 302, 29 Com Cas 182, [1924] All ER Rep 230   19.5.4.5
Unisoft Group Ltd, re (No. 2); see Re Unisoft Group Ltd (No. 3)
Unisoft Group Ltd, re (No. 3) (ChD 1993) [1994] 1 BCLC 609, [1994] BCC 766 (sub nom.
Re Unisoft Group Ltd (No. 2)   15.1.6, 18.6.1, 18.6.2, 18.6.3
United States v O'Hagan (USA SC 1997) 138 L Ed 2d 724, 117 SCt 2199   13.1
United States Trust Co. of New York v Australia and New Zealand Banking Group Ltd
(New South Wales CA 1995) 37 NSWLR 131   20.13.1
Uruguay Central & Hygueritas Railway Co. of Monte Video, re (MR 1879) 11 ChD 372,
48 LJ Ch 540, 27 WR 571   12.3

Vacuum Oil Co. v Ellis (CA 1913) [1914] 1 KB 693, 83 LJ KB 479, 110 LT 181   11.5.3
Van Sandau v Moore (LC 1826) 1 Russ 441, 38 ER 171, 4 LJ OS Ch 177   0.1.2.4
Vane v Yiannopoullos (HL 1964) [1965] AC 486, [1964] 3 WLR 1218, [1964] 3 All ER 820,
63 LGR 91   19.8.4

Vedelago, re (Queensland SC 1992) 8 ACSR 135, 10 ACLC 1403   1.3.2.1
Vehicle Buildings & Insulations Ltd, re (HC of Republic of Ireland 1985) [1986] ILRM 239   18.7
Verderame v Commercial Union Assurance Co. plc (CA 1992) [1992] BCLC 793   5.2.1, 18.4.6
VGM Holdings Ltd, re (CA 1942) [1942] Ch 235, 111 LJ Ch 145, 58 TLR 131, 86 SJ 63,
   [1942] 1 All ER 224   6.5.3, 10.6.1, 20.11.2, 20.11.4
Victor Battery Co. Ltd v Curry's Ltd (ChD 1946) [1946] Ch 242, [1946] 1 All ER 519,
   115 LJ Ch 148, 174 LT 326   10.8.5
Victoria Housing Estates Ltd v Ashpurton Estates Ltd; see Re Ashpurton Estates Ltd
Victors Ltd v Lingard (ChD 1926) [1927] 1 Ch 323, 96 LJ Ch 132, 136 LT 476, 70 SJ 1197   16.6.3
Viho Europe BV v Commission (case C-73/95 P) (ECJ 1996) [1996] ECR I-5457,
   [1997] ICR 130, [1997] All ER (EC) 163, 16 TrLR 59   5.2.2.9
Vincent v Premo Enterprises (Voucher Sales) Ltd (CA 1969) [1969] 2 QB 609,
   [1969] 2 WLR 1256, [1969] 2 All ER 941   19.2.5
Ving v Robertson & Woodcock Ltd (ChD 1912) 56 SJ 412   6.2.6
Virdi v Abbey Leisure Ltd (CA 1989) [1990] BCLC 342, [1990] BCC 60 (sub nom. Re Abbey
   Leisure Ltd)   2.3.5.8, 18.7
Vujnovich v Vujnovich (PC 1989) [1990] BCLC 227, [1989] 3 NZLR 513,
   5 BCC 740   18.7

Wairau Energy Centre Ltd v First Fishing Co. Ltd (New Zealand CA 1991)
   5 NZCLC 67,379   14.5.1
Waite's Auto Transfer Ltd v Waite (Manitoba KB 1928) [1928] 3 WWR 649   16.7.4
Walker v Jones (PC 1866) LR 1 PC 50, 3 Moo PC NS 397,
   35 LJ PC 30, 14 LT 686, 12 Jur NS 381, 14 WR 484   11.2.2
Walker v London Tramways Co. (ChD 1879) 12 ChD 705, 49 LJ Ch 23, 28 WR 163   3.5.3.3
Walker v Standard Chartered Bank plc (CA 1991) [1992] BCLC 535   15.5.3
Walker v Wimborne (HC of Australia 1976) 137 CLR 1, 50 ALJR 446, (1976) ACLC 28,534
   16.4.6.1, 20.11.3
Wallace v Evershed (ChD 1899) [1899] 1 Ch 891, 68 LJ Ch 415, 80 LT 523, 15 TLR 335,
   6 Mans 351   11.6.3
Wallace v Universal Automatic Machines Co. (CA 1894) [1894] 2 Ch 547, 62 LJ Ch 598,
   70 LT 852, [1891–4] All ER Rep 1156, 1 Mans 315, 7 R 316   11.6.2
Wallersteiner v Moir (CA 1974) [1974] 1 WLR 991, [1974] 3 All ER 217,
   118 SJ 464   5.2.2.1, 5.2.2.3, 5.2.2.10
Wallersteiner v Moir (No. 2) (CA 1975) [1975] QB 373, [1975] 2 WLR 389,
   [1975] 1 All ER 849, 119 SJ 97   18.4.2, 18.4.7, 19.9
Walter L. Jacob & Co. Ltd, re (CA 1988) [1989] BCLC 345, 1989 PCC 477, 5 BCC 244   18.8.3.3
Walter L. Jacob & Co. Ltd, re (ChD 1991) [1993] BCC 512   20.8
Walton v Bank of Nova Scotia (Canada SC 1965) 52 DLR (2d) 506, [1965] SCR 681
   (sub nom. Eisenberg v Bank of Nova Scotia), 7 CBR NS 264   14.5.1
Warman International Ltd v Dwyer (Australia HC 1995) 182 CLR 544, 69 ALJR 362   16.7.3.3
Warwickshire County Council v Johnson; see R v Warwickshire County Council,
   ex parte Johnson
Waters v Taylor (LC 1808) 15 Ves Jr 10, 33 ER 658   18.3.3.1
Watson v Duff Morgan & Vermont (Holdings) Ltd (ChD 1973) [1974] 1 WLR 450,
   [1974] 1 All ER 794, 117 SJ 910   11.7.3, 11.7.9
Watson v Imperial Financial Services Ltd (British Columbia CA 1994) 111 DLR (4th) 643   18.3.1
Watt v Commonwealth Petroleum Ltd (Alberta SC 1938) [1938] 4 DLR 701,
   [1938] 3 WWR 696   18.4.9
Watts v Midland Bank plc (ChD 1985) [1986] BCLC 15, 2 BCC 98, 961   20.2.3
Webb v Earle (MR 1875) LR 20 Eq 556, 44 LJ Ch 608, 24 WR 46   6.1.5, 18.4.9
Webb, Hale & Co. v Alexandria Water Co. Ltd (KBDC 1905) 21 TLR 572, 93 LT 339   8.6
Webb Distributors (Aust.) Pty Ltd v State of Victoria (Australia HC 1993) 179 CLR 15,
   67 ALJR 961, 117 ALR 321, 11 ACSR 731, 11 ACLC 1178   6.7.5
Welch v Bowmaker (Ireland) Ltd (SC of Republic of Ireland 1979) [1980] IR 251   11.7.5
Weldtech Equipment Ltd, re (ChD 1990) [1991] BCLC 393, [1991] BCC 16   11.7.10.3
Welfab Engineers Ltd, re (ChD 1990) [1990] BCLC 833, [1990] BCC 600   16.4.1, 16.4.9
Welham v DPP (HL 1960) [1961] AC 103, [1960] 2 WLR 669, [1960] 1 All ER 805,
   44 Cr App R 124, 124 JP 280, 104 SJ 308   20.10.2

Welsbach Incandescent Gas Lighting Co. v New Sunlight Incandescent Co. (CA 1900)
[1900] 2 Ch 1, 69 LJ Ch 546, 83 LT 58, 48 WR 595   19.9
Welsh Development Agency v Export Finance Co. Ltd (CA 1991) [1992] BCLC 148,
[1992] BCC 270   11.7.10.1, 20.2.7.1, 20.2.8.5
Welton v Saffery (HL 1897) [1897] AC 299, 66 LJ Ch 362, 76 LT 505, 13 TLR 340,
4 Mans 269, 45 WR 508   0.3.1.1, 3.3.2, 3.4.3, 3.5.3.3, 5.3.1
Wenlock (Elizabeth Dowager Baroness) v River Dee Co. (HL 1885) 10 App Cas 354,
[1881–5] All ER Rep Ext 1244, 54 LJ QB 577, 53 LT 62, 49 JP 773, 1 TLR 477;
affirming CA (1883) 36 ChD 675 n, 57 LT 402 n   14.5.1
West Canadian Collieries Ltd, re (ChD 1961) [1962] Ch 370, [1961] 3 WLR 1416,
[1962] 1 All ER 26, 105 SJ 1126   14.4.5.4
West India & Pacific Steamship Co., re (V-C 1868) LR 9 Ch App 11 n   3.5.1, 10.2.5
West Mercia Safetywear Ltd, Liquidator of v Dodd (CA 1987) [1988] BCLC 250,
1988 PCC 212, 4 BCC 30   16.4.6.1, 16.4.14, 20.11.3, 20.11.4
Westburn Sugar Refineries Ltd, ex parte (HL (C Sess 1st Div,) 1951) [1951] AC 625,
[1951] 1 All ER 881, 1951 SC (HL) 57, 1951 SLT 261, [1951] 1 TLR 728,
95 SJ 317   10.2.1, 10.2.2
Western Bank Ltd v Schindler (CA 1976) [1977] Ch 1, [1976] 3 WLR 341, [1976] 2 All ER 393,
32 P & CR 352, 120 SJ 301   11.5.3
Western Finance Co. Ltd v Tasker Enterprises Ltd (Manitoba CA 1979) 106 DLR (3d) 81   16.3.1
Western Mines Ltd, re (SC of British Columbia 1975) 65 DLR (3d) 307, [1976] 2 WWR 300
(sub nom. Western Mines Ltd v Shield Development Co. Ltd)   14.4.9.4
Westmid Packing Services Ltd, re (CA 1997) [1998] 2 All ER 124   15.2.5.5, 15.2.5.6
Westminster Corporation v Haste (ChD 1950) [1950] Ch 442, [1950] 2 All ER 65,
66 TLR (Pt 1) 1083, 114 JP 340, 49 LGR 67   20.2.9
Westpac Securities Ltd v Kensington (New Zealand CA 1993) [1994] 2 NZLR 555   14.5.1
Whaley Bridge Calico Printing Co. v Green and Smith (QBD 1879) 5 QBD 109, 49 LJ QB 326,
41 LT 674, 28 WR 351   17.6.2
Wheatley v Silkstone and Haigh Moor Coal Co. (ChD 1885) 29 ChD 715, 54 LJ Ch 778,
52 LT 798, 33 WR 797   11.6.1
Whitchurch Insurance Consultants Ltd, re (ChD 1992) [1993] BCLC 1359, [1994] BCC 51   14.4.4
White, re (ChD 1912) [1913] 1 Ch 231, 82 LJ Ch 149, 108 LT 319, 57 SJ 212   4.6
White v Bristol Aeroplane Co. Ltd (CA 1952) [1953] Ch 65, [1953] 2 WLR 144,
[1953] 1 All ER 40, 97 SJ 64   10.4, 14.6.2.6
White & Osmond (Parkstone) Ltd, re (ChD 1960) Unreported, 30 June 1960   20.10.2
Whitehouse v Carlton Hotel Pty Ltd (HC of Australia 1987) 162 CLR 285,
70 ALR 251, 11 ACLR 715, 61 ALJR 216, 5 ACLC 421, [1988] LRC (Comm) 725
  15.1.3, 16.4.10, 16.4.11
Whitley Partners Ltd, re (CA 1886) 32 ChD 337, 55 LJ Ch 540, 54 LT 912, 2 TLR 541,
34 WR 505   2.3.1, 3.4.1.3
Whitney v Commissioners of Inland Revenue (HL 1925) [1926] AC 37, 95 LJ KB 165,
134 LT 98, 42 TLR 58, 10 TC 88   0.1.9
Whitwam v Watkin (ChD 1898) 78 LT 188, 14 TLR 288   18.4.7
Whyte (C Sess IH Extra Div 1983) 1984 SLT 330, 1 BCC 99,044   18.4.2, 18.6.4
Whyte (G.T.) & Co. Ltd, re (ChD 1982) [1983] BCLC 311   11.6.5.1
Wilde v Australian Trade Equipment Pty Ltd (Australia HC 1981) 145 CLR 590, 55 ALJR 280,
5 ACLR 404, (1981) ACLC 33,113   11.7.9
Will v United Lankat Plantations Co. Ltd (HL 1913) [1914] AC 11, 83 LJ Ch 195, 109 LT 754,
[1911–13] All ER Rep 165, 30 TLR 37, 21 Mans 24, 58 SJ 29   6.1.5
Willaire Systems plc, re (CA 1986) [1987] BCLC 67, 2 BCC 99,311   10.2.5
William C. Leitch Brothers Ltd, re (ChD 1932) [1932] 2 Ch 71, 101 LJ Ch 380, 148 LT 106,
[1932] All ER Rep 892   20.10.4
William Cory & Son Ltd v Dorman Long & Co. Ltd (CA 1936) [1936] 2 All ER 386,
155 LT 53, 41 Com Cas 224, 55 Ll L Rep 1, 80 SJ 509   5.2.2.3
William Gaskell Group Ltd v Highley (ChD 1992) [1994] 1 BCLC 197,
[1993] BCC 200   11.6.2, 11.6.4
Williams v Burlington Investments Ltd (HL 1977) 121 SJ 424   11.7.10.1
Williams v Harding (HL 1866) LR 1 HL 9, 35 LJ Bcy 25, 14 LT 139, 12 Jur NS 457,
14 WR 503   3.4.1.2

Williams v Natural Life Health Foods Ltd (HL 1998) [1998] 1 WLR 830,
[1998] 2 All ER 577, [1998] BCC 428   15.10
Williams & Glyn's Bank Ltd v Barnes (QBD 1980) [1981] Com LR 205   11.2.3
Willis v Association of Universities of the British Commonwealth (CA 1964) [1965] 1 QB 140,
[1964] 2 WLR 946, [1964] 2 All ER 39   5.3.1
Willmott v London Road Car Co. Ltd (CA 1910) [1910] 2 Ch 525, 80 LJ Ch 1, 103 LT 447,
27 TLR 4, 54 SJ 873, [1908–10] All ER Rep 908   0.1.9
Wilson v Kelland (ChD 1910) [1910] 2 Ch 306, 79 LJ Ch 580, 103 LT 17, 26 TLR 485,
17 Mans 233, 54 SJ 542   11.7.5
Wilson v Tooker (HL 1714) 5 Bro Parl Cas 193, 2 ER 622; sub nom. Tucker v Wilson
1 P Wms 261, 24 ER 379   11.5.1
Wily v St George Partnership Banking Ltd (Australia FedC 1997) 150 ALR 329   11.6.3
Wimbledon Village Restaurant Ltd, re (ChD 1994) [1994] BCC 753   15.2.5.6
Windsor v National Mutual Life Association of Australasia (Australia Federal Court FC 1992)
106 ALR 282, 34 FCR 580, 7 ACSR 210   1.3.4.1, 14.4.3
Winkworth v Edward Baron Development Co. Ltd (HL 1986) [1986] 1 WLR 1512,
[1987] 1 All ER 114, [1987] BCLC 193, 3 BCC 4   16.4.6.1
Winthrop Investments Ltd v Winns Ltd (SC of New South Wales 1975) 1 ACLR 219;
subsequent proceedings (CA of New South Wales 1975) [1975] 2 NSWLR 666;
subsequent proceedings (SC of New South Wales 1979) 4 ACLR 1   15.7.2.4, 16.4.1, 16.4.14
Wise v Lansdell (ChD 1920) [1921] 1 Ch 420, 90 LJ Ch 178, 124 LT 502, 37 TLR 167,
[1920] B & CR 145   14.4.9.1.5
With v O'Flanagan (CA 1936) [1936] Ch 575, [1936] 1 All ER 727, 154 LT 634   6.7.3
Wombles Ltd v Wombles Skips Ltd (ChD 1975) [1977] RPC 99, [1975] FSR 488   2.3.3.6
Womersley v Merritt (V-C 1867) LR 4 Eq 695, 37 LJ Ch 19, 17 LT 43, 15 WR 1165   0.1.2.4
Wood v Dean (W. & G.) Pty Ltd (Australia HC 1929) 43 CLR 77, 36 ALR 24, 3 ALJ 356,
[1930] VLR 293   3.4.3, 8.5
Wood v Odessa Waterworks Co. (ChD 1889) 42 ChD 636, 58 LJ Ch 628, 5 TLR 596,
1 Meg 265, 37 WR 733   3.4.1.1, 3.4.3, 10.5.1, 18.4.9
Woodlands Ltd v Logan (New Zealand SC 1946) [1948] NZLR 230   3.4.2.3
Woodroffes (Musical Instruments) Ltd, re (ChD 1985) [1986] Ch 366,
[1985] 3 WLR 543, [1985] 2 All ER 908, [1985] BCLC 227, 1985 PCC 311, 129 SJ 589,
82 LS Gaz 3170   11.6.2, 11.6.3
Wood's application, re (ChD 1940) [1941] Ch 112, [1940] 4 All ER 306, 110 LJ Ch 73,
57 TLR 115, 84 SJ 718   11.6.1
Woods v Winskill (ChD 1913) [1913] 2 Ch 303, 82 LJ Ch 447, 109 LT 399, 6 BWCC 934,
20 Mans 261, 57 SJ 740   20.2.9
Woolf v East Nigel Gold Mining Co. Ltd (KBD 1905) 21 TLR 660   15.2.1, 15.6.1.5
Woolfson v Strathclyde Regional Council (HL 1978) 1978 SC (HL) 90, 38 P & CR 521,
1978 SLT 159, 248 EG 777, [1979] JPL 169   5.2.2.1, 5.2.2.8
Woolworths Ltd v Kelly (New South Wales CA 1991) 22 NSWLR 189, 4 ACSR 431,
9 ACLC 539   16.6.5
Woolworths Ltd v Luff (Australian Capital Territory SC FC 1988) 77 ACTR 1, 88 FLR 224,
33 ACrim R 144   19.8.4
Worcester Corsetry Ltd v Witting (CA 1932) [1936] Ch 640, 105 LJ Ch 385   15.3.7, 18.4.9
Wragg Ltd, re (CA 1897) [1897] 1 Ch 796, 66 LJ Ch 419, 76 LT 397, 45 WR 557,
[1895–9] All ER Rep 398   6.5.4
Wright v Horton (HL 1887) 12 App Cas 371, 56 LJ Ch 873, 56 LT 782, 52 JP 179,
36 WR 17   11.7.1, 11.7.12
Wurzel v Houghton Main Home Delivery Service Ltd (KBDC 1936) [1937] 1 KB 380,
[1936] 3 All ER 311, 106 LJ KB 197, 155 LT 575, 100 JP 503, 53 TLR 81, 34 LGR 587,
25 Ry & Can Tr Cas 59, 80 SJ 895   5.2.1

X Bank Ltd v G; see Re a Company (CA 1985) [1985] BCLC 333
XYZ Ltd, re; see Re a Company (No. 004377 of 1986)

Yenidje Tobacco Co. Ltd, re (CA 1916) [1916] 2 Ch 426, 86 LJ Ch 1, 115 LT 530, 32 TLR 709,
60 SJ 674   18.7.1

Yeovil Glove Co. Ltd, re (CA 1964) [1965] Ch 148, [1964] 3 WLR 406, [1964] 2 All ER 849,
    108 SJ 499   11.6.5.1
Yeung v Hong Kong & Shanghai Banking Corporation (PC 1980) [1981] AC 787,
    [1980] 3 WLR 950, [1980] 2 All ER 599, [1980] HKLR 195, 124 SJ 591   8.4
Yorkshire Woolcombers Association Ltd, re (Houldsworth v the company) (CA 1903); see
    Illingworth v Houldsworth
Young v Ladies' Imperial Club Ltd (CA 1920) [1920] 2 KB 523, 89 LJ KB 563, 123 LT 191,
    36 TLR 392, 64 SJ 374   14.4.5.4
Young v South African & Australian Exploration & Development Syndicate (ChD 1896)
    [1896] 2 Ch 268, 65 LJ Ch 638, 74 LT 527, 44 WR 509   14.4.5.5, 18.4.9
Yuen Kun Yeu v Attorney-General of Hong Kong (PC 1987) [1988] AC 175,
    [1987] 3 WLR 776, [1987] 2 All ER 705, 1987 FLR 291, [1987] HKLR 1154   17.4.4
Yukong Line Ltd v Rendsburg Investments Corporation (No. 2) (QBD 1997)
    [1998] 1 WLR 294   5.2.2.1, 5.2.2.3, 5.2.2.4, 16.4.6.1

Zimmers Ltd v Zimmer (KBD 1951) [1951] WN 600, 95 SJ 803   15.2.3.3
Zinotty Properties Ltd, re (ChD 1984) [1984] 1 WLR 1249, [1984] BCLC 375,
    [1984] 3 All ER 754, 1985 PCC 285, 1 BCC 99, 139, 128 SJ 783   8.3.4, 19.5.10
Zwicker v Stanbury (SC of Canada 1953) [1954] 1 DLR 257, [1953] 2 SCR 438   16.7.2

Table of Statutes

Administration of Justice Act
   1970 (c 31)
   s 44 20.13.2
'Anzac' (Restriction on Trade
   Use of Word) Act 1916 (6
   & 7 Geo 5 c 51)
   s 1 2.3.3.3
Apportionment Act 1870 (33 &
   34 Vict c 35)
   s 5 4.6
Arbitration Act 1996 (c 23)
   s 5 3.4.2.1
   s 6 3.4.2.1
   s 9 3.4.2.1
Architects Registration Act
   1938 (1 & 2 Geo 6
   c 54) 19.8.4
   ss 1 and 3 19.8.4
Banking Act 1987 (c 22)
   9.3.7.1, 9.5.2
   s 67 2.3.3.3
   s 68(4) 2.3.3.3
Bills of Exchange Act 1882
   (45 & 46 Vict c 61)
   s 3(1) 19.2.3, 19.2.6
   s 17(2) 19.2.6
   s 23 19.2.6
   s 26 19.2.1, 19.2.6
   s 26(2) 4.5.1
   s 29 19.8.6.1
   · s 32(1) 19.2.6
   s 73 19.2.6
   s 83(1) 19.2.3, 19.2.6
   s 91(2) 19.2.6
   s 97(3) 19.2.6
Bills of Sale Act 1878 (41 & 42
   Vict c 31) 11.3, 11.6.4
   s 4 11.7.12
Bills of Sale Act (1878)
   Amendment Act 1882
   (45 & 46 Vict c 43)
   11.3, 11.6.4
   s 17 11.3
British Olivetti Ltd Act 1980
   (c xxiii) 2.4.3
Building Societies Act 1986
   (c 53) 0.1.2.4

Building Societies Act 1986 –
   continued
   s 107 2.3.3.3
Business Names Act 1985
   (c 7) 0.3.1.2, 2.3.3.7
   s 1(1)(a) 2.3.3.7
   s 1(2)(c) 2.3.3.7
   s 2(1) 2.3.3.7
   s 2(4) 2.3.3.7
   s 3(2) 2.3.3.7
   s 4(1)(a) 2.3.3.7
   s 4(1)(b) 2.3.3.7
   s 4(2) 2.3.3.7
   s 4(6) 2.3.3.7
   s 5 2.3.3.7, 4.5.1
   s 7 2.3.3.7
   s 7(2) 5.4.5.1
   s 7(4) 2.3.3.7
Charging Orders Act 1979
   (c 53)
   s 1(1) 8.7.2
   s 5(2)(a) and (b) 8.7.2
Charities Act 1993 (c 10)
   0.1.2.4
   s 64(2) 2.4.4
   s 65 19.4.2, 19.5.11
   s 65(4) 19.5.11
   s 68(1) 4.5.5
   s 68(2) 4.5.5
Chartered Associations
   (Protection of Names and
   Uniforms) Act 1926 (16 &
   17 Geo 5 c 26)
   s 1 2.3.3.3
Chartered Companies Act 1837
   (7 Will 4 & 1 Vict c 73)
   1.5, 6.5.4
Clergy (Ordination and
   Miscellaneous Provisions)
   Measure 1964 (No. 6)
   s 11 15.2.5.10
Companies Act 1862 (25 & 26
   Vict c 89) 0.3.2.3, 1.2.3,
   1.3.2.5, 1.3.3.2, 1.6,
   2.4. 1, 6.1.10, 9.3.4, 9.3.8,
   11.7.1
   s 16 3.4.1.2

Companies Act 1862 –
   continued
   s 30 8.7.1
   s 75 3.4.1.2
   Schedule 1, Table A 3.2,
   9.3.4, 9.3.8
Companies Act 1867 (30 & 31
   Vict c 131)
   s 25 3.4.2.4
Companies Act 1900 (63 & 64
   Vict c 48) 5.2.1
   s 21 9.3.4
   s 22 9.3.4
   s 23 9.3.4, 9.3.8
Companies Act 1907 (7 Edw 7
   c 50) 1.3.3.2, 5.2.1
Companies Act 1928 (18 & 19
   Geo 5 c 45) 20.8
   s 25 14.4.8.3
   s 28 15.1.1
   s 78 16.5.1
Companies Act 1929 (19 & 20
   Geo 5 c 23) 1.2.3, 2.4.3
Companies Act 1947 (10 & 11
   Geo 6 c 47)
   s 26(1) 15.1.1
Companies Act 1948 (11 & 12
   Geo 6 c 38) 0.3.1.2,
   1.2.3, 1.3.3, 2.3.4, 10.3.4,
   20.4.5
   s 19 2.3.3.2
   s 20 3.4.1.1
   s 28 1.3.3.2
   s 56(2) 10.3.4
   s 58 10.3.4
   s 58(1) 10.3.4
   s 149(1) 9.3.8
   Table A 3.2.1, 6.4.2, 15.7.2,
   15.6.1.1
   art 80 15.7.2.4
Companies Act 1980
   (c 22) 1.3.3.2, 6.2.6,
   10.1.1, 10.5.2
   s 33(5) 6.1.4
   s 48 16.6.7
   ss 68 to 73 13.1
   s 74(1) 2.3.5.7

Companies Act 1980 –
  continued
  s 87(2) 6.1.11
  Schedule 3 para 5 2.3.3.2
Companies Act 1981 (c 62)
  0.3.1.4, 10.8.2
  Schedule 4 2.3.3.2, 10.3.4
Companies Act 1985 (c 6)
  0.1.2.4, 0.2.1, 0.2.2, 0.2.3,
  0.2.4, 0.3, 0.3.1.2, 0.3.2.2,
  0.3.3.3, 1.2, 1.3.4.1, 1.6,
  2.3.3.4, 2.4.2.2, 3.3.3,
  4.2.1, 6.1.14, 6.5.3, 9.3.8,
  9.6.9.1, 9.6.9.2, 10.1,
  14.4.1, 14.4.9.1.8, 15.1,
  15.1.1, 15.2.5, 15.5.1,
  18.8.3.1, 18.8.3.2
  ss 1 to 13 1.6
  s 1 1.2, 1.3.2, 5.3.2.1
  s 1(1) 0.1.1, 0.1.2.4, 1.2.1,
    1.3.2, 1.3.2.1, 1.3.2.6,
    2.3.1, 2.3.6, 5.2.2.1
  s 1(2)(a) 1.3.2, 1.3.2.1
  s 1(2)(b) 1.3.2.2
  s 1(3) 1.3.3.1, 1.3.3.2,
    15.1.3
  s 1(3)(a) 2.3.1
  s 1(3A) 0.1.1,0.1.2.4, 1.2.1,
    1.3.2.1, 2.3.1, 5.2.2.1
  s 1(4) 1.3.2.4, 1.3.4.4,
    1.3.4.6
  s 2 1.2, 2.3.1
  s 2(1) to (5) 2.4.1
  s 2(1)(b) 2.3.4, 2.4.3
  s 2(1)(c) 2.3.5.1, 2.3.5.10
  s 2(2) 2.3.4, 2.4.3
  s 2(3) 1.3.2, 1.3.2.1, 2.3.6
  s 2(4) 1.3.2, 1.3.2.2, 1.3.5
  s 2(5) 1.3.2.1
  s 2(5)(a) 1.3.2.1, 2.3.7,
    6.1.1, 6.1.2
  s 2(5)(b) 1.3.2.1, 6.8,
    17.4.1.7
  s 2(5)(c) 1.3.2.1, 6.8,
    17.4.1.7
  s 2(6) 2.3.1,
  s 2(7) 2.3.1, 2.4.1, 2.4.7,
    6.1.13, 10.2.1, 14.6.2.2
  s 3 2.3.2
  s 3(1) 2.3.2
  s 3(1)(a) 2.3.1
  s 3A 2.3.5.10
  ss 4 to 8 2.3.6
  s 4 2.4.4, 2.4.9.1, 14.4.8.3,
    15.7.5, 19.4.1
  s 4(2) 2.4.4
  s 5 2.4.4, 14.4.1
  s 5(3) 2.4.4

Companies Act 1980 –
  continued
  s 5(4) 2.4.4
  s 5(5) 2.4.4, 2.4.6, 10.8.1
  s 5(6) 2.4.8.2
  s 5(7) 2.4.7
  s 6(1)(a) 2.4.9.1
  s 6(1)(b)(i) 2.4.9.1
  s 6(1)(b)(ii) 2.4.9.1, 3.5.2.1
  s 6(3) 2.4.9.1, 3.5.2.1
  s 6(4) 2.4.4
  s 7 1.2.1, 3.2, 3.3.1
  s 7(1) 3.2
  s 7(2) 3.2
  s 7(3) 3.2
  s 7(3)(b) 3.2
  s 7(4) 3.2
  s 8 3.2, 6.6.4
  s 8(1), (2) and (3) 3.2,
    3.3.1, 3.3.2
  s 8(2) 3.3.1, 3.3.2
  s 8(3) 3.3.2
  s 8A 1.3.6
  s 8A(1) 1.3.6, 3.2, 3.3.1
  s 8A(2) 3.2
  s 8A(3) 3.3.1
  s 8A(4) 3.2
  s 9 3.4.2.1, 3.5.2, 3.5.3.3,
    3.5.3.4.1, 6.1.13, 10.2.1,
    18.4.1
  s 9(1) 3.4.1.3, 3.5.1,
    14.4.8.3, 15.7.2.4, 15.7.5
  s 9(2) 3.5.1
  s 10(1) 2.2, 2.4.3
  s 10(1)(a) 2.3.4
  s 10(2) 1.2.1, 15.2.2,
    15.2.4, 15.4.2, 17.3.2
  s 10(2)(a) 15.2.2
  s 10(2)(b) 17.3.1
  s 10(3) 1.2.1, 15.2.1, 17.3.1
  s 10(5) 15.2.2, 17.3.1
  s 10(6) 1.2.1, 2.3.4
  s 11 1.3.2.1, 1.3.3.1
  s 12(1) 1.2.1, 2.2
  s 12(2) 1.2.1, 2.2
  s 12(3) 1.2.1, 2.3.3.5
  s 13 5.2.2.1
  s 13(1) 0.1.1, 1.2.1, 1.3.4.1,
    2.2, 5.1
  s 13(3) 0.1.1, 1.2.1, 5.1
  s 13(4) 1.3.2, 5.2.2.1
  s 13(5) 15.2.2, 17.3.1
  s 13(6) 1.2.1, 1.3.3.1,
    1.3.4.1
  s 13(7) 1.2.1, 1.3.3, 2.3.4,
    2.3.5.1
  s 13(7)(a) 5.1
  s 13(7)(b) 1.3.3.1

Companies Act 1980 –
  continued
  s 14 2.5, 3.4.1, 3.4.2.1,
    3.4.2.2, 3.4.2.3, 3.4.2.5,
    3.4.3, 6.1.4
  s 14(1) 3.4.1.1, 3.4.2.9,
    3.4.4, 14.5.3.2.1
  s 14(2) 3.4.2, 3.4.2.9, 6.4.2,
    16.4.1
  s 16 2.4.8.1, 3.5.3.3, 10.4
  s 16(2) 2.4.8.1
  s 17 2.4.1, 2.4.7, 2.4.8.3,
    14.4.1
  s 17(1) 2.4.7, 2.4.8,
    14.4.8.3, 15.7.5
  s 17(2)(b) 2.4.7, 2.4.8,
    3.5.3.3, 14.6.2.3,
    14.6.2.5, 14.6.2.6
  s 17(3) 2.4.6, 2.4.7, 2.4.8.2,
    2.4.9.1, 3.5.2.1
  s 18(2) 2.4.9.1, 3.5.2.1,
    6.1.13
  s 18(3) 2.4.9.1, 3.5.2.1
  s 19 2.5
  s 19(1) and (2) 2.5
  s 20(1) and (2) 2.5
  s 22 3.4.2.3, 14.2
  s 22(1) 1.2.1, 13.2.1, 14.2,
    15.2.2
  s 23(1) 10.8.3
  s 23(2) 10.8.3
  s 23(3) 10.8.3
  s 23(3A) 10.8.3
  s 23(4) 10.8.3
  s 23(5) 10.8.3
  s 23(6) 10.8.3
  s 23(7) 10.8.3
  s 24 1.3.2, 1.3.2.6, 5.2.2.5,
    15.2.5.2
  s 25 2.3.3.1, 3.4.2.4,
    14.4.8.3
  s 25(1) 1.3.3.1, 2.3.3.1
  s 26(1) 2.3.3.1
  s 26(1)(c) 2.3.3.4
  s 26(1)(d) 2.3.3.3
  s 26(1)(e) 2.3.3.3
  s 26(2) 2.3.3.1, 2.3.3.5
  s 26(2)(b) 2.3.3.5
  s 26(3) 2.3.3.4
  s 27 1.3.3.1, 2.3.3.1
  s 27(2) 4.3.1
  s 28 2.4.2
  s 28(1) to (5) 2.4.2
  s 28(1) 2.5.2, 14.4.8.3,
    15.7.5
  s 28(2) 2.3.3.4
  s 28(6) 2.4.2
  s 28(7) 2.4.2

Companies Act 1980 –
continued
s 29(1)(b) 2.3.3.5
s 29(2) 2.3.3.5
s 29(3) 2.3.3.5
s 29(4) 2.3.3.5, 4.2.2
s 30 2.3.3.2, 4.6
s 30(3) 2.3.3.2, 2.4.2,
2.4.8.1
s 30(4) and (5) 2.3.3.2
s 31(1) 2.4.4, 2.4.8.1
s 31(2) 2.4.2, 14.4.11
s 31(4) 2.4.2
s 31(5) 2.4.4, 2.4.8.1
s 32 2.4.2
s 32(1) to (6) 2.4.2
s 33 2.3.3.1
s 33(5) 6.1.5
s 34 2.3.3.1
s 35 19.4.2, 19.5.4.1,
19.5.5, 19.5.11
s 35(1) 19.4.1, 19.5.8
s 35(2) 2.3.5.2
s 35(3) 2.3.5.2, 14.4.8.3,
15.7.5, 18.4.11, 19.5.2.3,
19.5.9, 19.5.11
s 35A 19.5.2.2, 19.5.4.1,
19.5.5, 19.5.7, 19.5.9,
19.5.11
s 35A(1) 19.5.4.1, 19.5.5,
19.5.6, 19.5.9
s 35A(2) 19.5.5
s 35A(2)(a) 19.5.5
s 35A(2)(b) 19.5.5, 19.5.7
s 35A(3) 19.5.6
s 35B 19.5.4.1, 19.5.4.5,
19.5.5, 19.5.7, 19.5.11
s 36 19.2.2, 19.2.3, 19.3
s 36(a) 19.3
s 36(b) 19.3, 19.5.1
s 36A 19.2.5
s 36A(1) 19.2.5
s 36A(2) 19.2.2, 19.2.4,
19.2.5
s 36A(3) 19.2.2, 19.2.4,
19.2.5, 19.3
s 36A(4) 19.2.4, 19.2.5,
19.3
s 36A(5) 19.2.5
s 36A(6) 19.2.4, 19.2.5
s 36C 19.6.1, 19.6.2
s 36C(1) 19.6.1, 19.6.2
s 36C(2) 19.6.1
s 37 19.2.6
s 40 8.2.1, 8.2.2
s 41 19.2.1
s 42 2.5.3, 2.4.9.2, 3.5.2.2,
4.3, 15.4.2, 20.5.1,
20.6.7

Companies Act 1980 –
continued
s. 42(1) 4.3
ss 43 to 48 1.3.4.6
s 43 1.3.4.2, 1.3.4.3,
1.3.4.5, 2.5.5
s 43(1) 1.3.4.3, 1.3.4.4,
2.4.2, 6.2.2
s 43(1)(a) 14.4.8.3, 15.7.5
s 43(2)(a) 6.2.2
s 43(2)(b) 2.4.7
s 43(2)(c) 3.5.1
s 43(3)(a) to (d) 1.3.4.3
s 43(3)(a) 2.4.9.1, 3.5.2.1
s 43(3)(b) and (c) 6.6.2
s 43(3)(e) 1.3.4.3, 6.6.2
s 43(4) 6.6.2
s 43(5) 2.4.2
s 44 6.6.2
s 45(2)(b) 6.6.2
s 45(3) and (4) 6.6.2
s 47(1) and (2) 1.3.4.3
s 47(5) 1.3.4.3
s 48(2)(a) 1.3.4.6
s 49 1.3.4.2, 1.3.4.3,
1.3.4.4, 1.3.4.5
s 49(2) 1.3.4.6
s 49(3) 1.3.4.2
s 49(5) 2.4.7
s 49(6) 3.5.1
s 49(8) 15.7.5
s 49(8)(c) 2.4.9.1
s 49(8)(d) 3.5.2. 1
s 51 1.3.4.6
s 51(1) 14.4.8.3, 15.7.5
s 51(2) 1.3.4.3, 1.3.4.4
s 51(3) 2.4.7, 3.5.1
s 51(5)(a) 2.4.9.1
s 51(5)(b) 3.5.2.1
s 52 1.3.4.6
s 53 1.3.4.2, 10.2.5
s 53(1) 17.4.2.3
s 53(1)(a) 14.4.8.3, 15.7.5
s 53(1)(b) 2.4.9. 1, 3.5.2.1
s 53(2) 2.4.7, 3.5.1
s 53(3) 1.3.4.2, 1.3.4.3
s 54 1.3.4.2
s 54(1) and (2) 1.3.4.2
s 54(3) 1.3.4.2, 10.8.7
s 54(4) 2.4.9.1, 10.8.7
s 54(5) 1.3.4.2, 2.4.7,
10.8.7
s 54(6) 1.3.4.2, 2.4.6, 2.4.7,
10.8.1, 10.8.7
s 54(7) 2.4.9.1, 3.5.2.1
s 54(8) 2.4.8.2
s 54(9) 2.4.7
s 54(10) 2.4.9.1, 3.5.2.1
s 55(1) to (3) 1.3.4.2

Companies Act 1980 –
continued
s 59 7.5.6
s 60 7.5.6
s 60(1) 7.5.6
s 60(4) 7.5.6
s 60(5) 7.5.6
s 60(6) 7.5.6
s 60(7) 7.5.6
s 80 3.5.1, 6.2.5, 6.2.6
s 80(1) 6.2.5, 15.7.4.1
s 80(2)(b) 12.7
s 80(3) 6.2.5
s 80(4) 6.2.5, 6.2.6
s 80(5) 6.2.5
s 80(6) 6.2.5
s 80(7) 6.2.5
s 80(8) 3.5.1, 6.2.5, 14.4.11
s 80(9) 6.2.5
s 80A 6.2.5, 14.4.8.4
s 80A(2) to (7) 6.2.5
s 81 7.5.6
s 81(3) 7.5.6
s 82(1) 7.5.7
s 82(2) 7.5.7
s 82(3) 7.5.7
s 82(4) 7.5.7
s 82(5) 7.5.7
s 82(7) 7.5.7
s 83 7.5.8, 7.10
s 83(5) 7.5.8
s 83(6) 7.5.8
s 84 7.10, 12.5
s 85(1) 7.5.8
s 85(2) 7.5.8
s 85(3) 7.5.8
s 86 7.5.9
s 86(4) 7.5.9
s 86(6) 7.5.9
s 86(7) 7.5.9
s 88 6.2.7
s 88(2)(b) 6.5.4
s 89 6.2.6
s 89(1) 6.2.6
s 90 6.2.6
s 91 6.2.6, 14.4.8.3
s 94(2) 6.2.6, 12.7
s 95 6.2.6
s 95(1) and (2) 6.2.6,
14.4.8.3
s 95(3) 6.2.6
s 95(5) 6.2.6, 14.4.5.5
s 95(6) 6.2.6
s 97 6.4.1
s 97(1) 7.9.2
s 97(2) 7.9.2, 7.9.3
s 98 12.5
s 98(3) 6.4.1
s 99(2) and (3) 6.5.5

Companies Act 1980 –
  continued
  s 100   6.1.1, 6.2.4, 7.9.2,
    12.7
  s 100(1)   6.4.1
  s 100(2)   6.4.1
  s 101(1)   1.3.3.1, 6.4.2,
    6.4.4, 6.6.1
  s 101(2)   1.3.3.1, 6.4.2,
    6.4.4, 6.6.1
  s 101(3) and (4)   6.4.2, 6.4.4
  s 102(1)   6.5.5
  s 102(2)   6.5.5
  s 103   0.3.1.3
  s 103(1)   6.5.4
  s 103(1)(a)   6.5.4
  s 103(1)(b) and (c)   6.5.4
  s 103(2)   10.4
  s 103(3) and (4)   6.5.4
  s 103(6) and (7)   6.5.4
  s 103(7)(b)   6.5.4
  s 104   17.6.3.3
  s 104(4)(a)   17.6.3.3
  s 104(4)(c)   15.7.5, 17.6.3.3
  s 105(1) and (2)   17.6.3.3
  s 107   6.4 1, 6.4.2, 6.4.4,
    6.5.5
  s 108(6)(d)   6.5.4
  s 109(2)(d)   17.6.3.3
  s 111(1)   4.5.5
  s 111(2)   14.4.11, 17.6.3.3
  s 111(4)   17.6.3.3
  s 111A   6.7.5, 18.4.9
  s 113   6.5.6
  s 113(5)(a)   6.5.6
  s 114   6.4.2, 6.4.4, 6.5.4,
    6.5.5
  s 115(1)   6.5.4, 6.5.5
  s 117   1.3.3.1, 5.2.2.2, 6.6.1,
    19.5.8, 20.6.3
  s 117(2)   1.3.3, 6.6.1.1
  s 117(3)   6.6.1
  s 117(3)(c) and (d)   6.6.1
  s 117(4)   1.3.3.1, 6.6.1
  s 117(5) and (6)   6.6.1
  s 117(7)   6.6.1, 11.1
  s 117(8)   5.2.2.2, 6.6.1,
    19.5.8
  s 118   1.3.2.1, 1.3.3.1
  s 118(1)   6.6.1, 6.6.2, 10.2.5
  s 119(a)   6.4.2
  s 120   6.4.2, 14.4.8.3, 15.7.5
  s 121   6.1.13, 15.7.4.1,
    15.7.5
  s 121(1)   6.1.13
  s 121(1)(c)   10.2.1
  s 121(2)   6.1.13
  s 121(2)(a) and (b)   6.1.13
  s 121(2)(c)   6.1.14

Companies Act 1980 –
  continued
  s 121(2)(d)   6.1.13
  s 121(2)(e)   6.1.13
  s 121(3)   6.1.13
  s 121(4)   6.1.1.3, 6.1.13,
    14.4.1, 14.4.8.5,
    15.7.4.1, 15.7.5
  s 121(5)   10.2.1
  s 122   6.1.13, 10.3.6
  s 123   6.1.13
  s 123(1)   6.1.2
  s 123(2)   4.2.1
  s 123(3)   14.4.1 1
  s 124(1)   14.4.8.3
  ss 125 to 127   2.4.8
  s 125   14.4.9.2, 14.6.2.1,
    14.6.2.2, 14.6.2.4,
    14.6.2.5, 15.2.8
  s 125(1)   14.6.2.1
  s 125(2)   14.4.8.3, 14.6.2.3
  s 125(3)   6.2.5, 10.2.4,
    14.4.8.2, 14.6.2.2,
    14.6.2.3
  s 125(4)   14.6.2.2, 14.6.2.3
  s 125(5)   2.4.7, 14.6.2.2
  s 125(6)   14.6.2.4
  s 125(6)(a)   14.4.10
  s 125(6)(b)   14.4.9.2
  s 125(7)   14.6.2.6
  s 125(8)   6.2.5, 14.6.2.6
  s 127   10.2.1, 14.4.1,
    14.6.2.5, 14.6.2.7
  s 127(1) to (4)   14.6.2.5
  s 127(5)   14.6.2.7
  s 127(6)   14.6.2.6
  s 128   6.1.4, 14.6.2.7
  s 128(3)   14.6.2.7
  s 128(4)   14.6.2.7
  s 130(2)   6.4.4, 10.4, 12.2
  s 130(2)(b)   7.9.4
  s 130(3)   10.2.1
  s 131   6.5.2
  s 131(1)   6.7.5
  s 133(1)   6.5.2
  s 135   0.3.2.5, 3.5.1, 6.4.2,
    8.8.3, 10.2.1, 10.2.4
  ss 135 to 141   0.3.2.2
  s 135(1)   10.2.5, 14.4.1,
    14.4.8.3, 15.7.5
  s 135(2)   10.2.1
  s 136   10.2.3
  s 136(2)   10.2.3
  s 136(2) to (6)   10.2.3
  s 136(5)   10.2.3
  s 136(6)   10.2.3
  s 137   10.2.5
  s 137(1)   10.2.3
  s 138   10.2.5

Companies Act 1980 –
  continued
  s 139   1.3.4.2
  s 139(1)   10.2.5
  s 139(2)   10.2.5
  s 139(3)   2.4.7, 3.5.1, 10.2.5
  s 139(4)   2.4.9.1, 3.5.2.1
  s 139(5)   10.2.5
  s 140   10.2.5
  s 141   10.2.3
  s 142   10.2.6, 14.4.3
  s 142(1)   15.7.4.1
  s 142(2)   10.2.6
  s 143   6.4.2, 10.2.1, 10.8.2
  s 143(1)   10.3.1, 10.6.1
  s 143(2)   10.8.2
  s 143(3)   6.4.2, 10.8.2
  s 143(3)(b)   10.2.1
  s 143(3)(d)   6.4.2
  s 144(1)   10.8.6
  s 144(2)   16.5.2
  s 144(3)   16.5.1, 16.5.2
  s 144(4)   16.5.1
  s 145(2)(a)   10.8.6
  s 146   2.4.7
  s 146(1)(a)   6.4.2
  s 146(1)(b)   10.8.2
  s 146(1)(d)   10.8.6
  s 146(2)   6.4.2, 10.8.2
  s 146(2)(a)   10.8.2, 10.8.6
  s 146(2)(b)   6.4.2
  s 146(3)   6.4.2
  s 146(3)(a)   10.8.2
  s 146(3)(b)   10.8.6
  s 146(4)   10.8.2, 10.8.6
  s 147   2.4.7, 6.4.2
  s 147(2)   14.4.11
  s 147(3)   2.4.9.1
  s 148(4)   6.4.2, 10.5.7,
    10.8.6
  s 150(1) and (2)   6.4.2,
    10.8.4
  s 151   7.9.2, 10.8.4
  s 151(1)   10.8.4
  s 151(2)   10.8.4
  s 151(3)   10.8.5
  s 152(1)(a)   10.8.4
  s 152(1)(a)(ii)   10.8.4
  s 153(1)   10.8.4
  s 153(2)   10.8.4
  s 153(3)(a)   10.8.4
  s 153(4)(a)   10.8.4
  s 153(4)(b)   10.7
  s 153(5)   14.7
  s 154   10.7, 10.8.4
  s 155(1) and (2)   10.8.4
  s 155(3)   10.8.8
  s 155(4)   10.8.7, 10.8.8,
    14.4.8.3, 15.7.5

Companies Act 1980 –
continued
s 155(5)   10.8.8, 14.4.8.3,
   15.7.5
s 155(6)   4.2.1, 10.8.7,
   10.8.8
s 155(6)(b)   10.8.8
s 156   10.8.7
s 156(1)   4.2.1, 10.8.8
s 156(2)   10.8.8
s 156(4)   10.8.7
s 156(5)(a)   10.8.7
s 156(5)(b)   10.8.8
s 156(7)   10.8.7
s 157   14.4.1
s 157(1) and (2)   10.8.7
s 157(3)   2.4.6, 2.4.7,
   2.4.8.2, 2.4.9.1, 3.5.2.1,
   10.8.1, 10.8.7
s 157(4)(a)   4.4.3, 10.8.7
s 158(2)   10.8.7
s 158(4)   10.8.7, 10.8.8
s 159(1)   10.3.1
s 159(2)   10.3.2
s 159(3)   10.3.5, 10.6.1
s 160(1)   10.3.1, 10.6.5
s 160(1)(a)   10.3.1
s 160(1)(b)   10.6.5
s 160(2)   10.6.5
s 160(3)   10.3.2
s 160(4)   10.3.1, 10.3.5,
   10.6.5
s 162(1)   10.6.1
s 162(2)   10.6.1, 10.6.5
s 162(3)   10.6.1
s 163   10.6.1
s 164   10.6.3, 14.5.1
s 164(1)   10.6.1, 10.6.3
s 164(2)   10.6.3, 14.4.8.3,
   15.7.5
s 164(3)   10.6.3, 14.4.8.3,
   15.7.5
s 164(4)   10.6.1, 10.6.3
s 164(5)   10.6.3, 14.4.8.5,
   14.4.9.2, 14.4.9.3, 14.5.1
s 164(6)   4.4.3, 10.6.3,
   14.5.1
s 164(7)   10.6.3, 14.4.8.3,
   15.7.5
s 165   10.6.3
s 165(2)   14.4.8.3, 14.4.9.2,
   14.4.9.3, 15.7.5
s 166   10.6.2
s 166(1)   10.6.1, 15.7.4.1,
   15.7.5
s 166(4)   10.6.1
s 166(6)(b)   10.6.2
s 166(7)   10.6.2, 14.4.11
s 167(2)   14.4.8.3, 15.7.5

Companies Act 1980 –
continued
s 169(1) and (2)   10.6.4
s 169(4)   4.4.1, 4.4.3, 10.6.4
s 169(5)   4.4.1, 4.4.3, 10.6.4
s 170(1) and (2)   10.3.1,
   10.6.5
s 170(4)   10.2.1, 10.3.1,
   10.4
s 171(1)   10.3.1, 10.3.5,
   10.6.5
s 171(3)   10.3.5
s 171(4)   10.3.5
s 171(5)   10.3.3
s 171(6)   10.3.5
s 172(2) to (6)   10.3.5
s 173(1)   10.3.5
s 173(2)   10.3.5, 14.4.8.3,
   15.7.5
s 173(3)   10.3.5
s 173(5) and (6)   4.2.1,
   10.3.5
s 174(1)   10.3.5
s 174(2)   14.4.8.5,14.4.9.3
s 174(3)   10.3.5, 14.4.9.2
s 174(4)   4.4.3, 10.3.5
s 174(5)   10.3.5, 14.4.9.2
s 175(1)   4.3, 10.3.5
s 175(2)   10.3.5
s 175(4)   10.3.5
s 175(5)   10.3.5
s 175(6)   10.3.5
s 175(6)(a) and (b)   4.4.2
s 176   10.3.5, 14.4.1
s 176(3)(b)   2.4.9.1, 3.5.2.1
s 176(4)   2.4.9.1, 3.5.2.1
s 177   2.4.7
s 177(3)   2.4.6, 10.8.1
s 177(4)   2.4.8.2
s 177(5)   2.4.7
s 179   0.3.1.4
s 180   10.3.4
s 180(1)   10.3.4
s 182(1)(a)   6.1.9
s 182(1)(b)   8.1
s 182(2)   6.1.14, 8.2.2
s 183(1)   3.3.2, 8.3.1
s 183(5)   8.3.4
s 184(1)   8.4
s 184(2)   8.3.2, 8.4
s 184(3)(b)   8.3.2
s 185   8.2.1
s 185(1)   6.2.9, 8.3.4, 8.3.5
s 185(5)   8.3.4
s 185(6)   6.2.9, 8.3.4
s 185(7)   6.2.9
s 186   8.2.2
s 188   8.6
s 188(2)   8.6

Companies Act 1980 –
continued
s 190(1) to (3)   4.4.1
s 190(5)   4.4.1
s 191(1)   4.4.1
s 191(2)   4.4.1
s 191(3)   12.3
s 193   11.2.2
s 195   12.5
ss 198 to 220   8.9.2
s 198(2)   8.9.2
s 199(2)(a)   8.9.2
s 199(2)(b)   8.9.2
s 199(2A)   8.9.2
s 199(4)   8.9.2
s 199(5)(a)   8.9.2
s 199(5)(b)   8.9.2
s 200(1)   8.9.2
s 200(2)   8.9.2
s 202(1)   8.9.3
s 202(2)(a)   8.9.3
s 202(2A)   8.9.3
s 202(2B)   8.9.3
s 202(3) and (4)   8.9.3
s 205   2.3.6
s 205(4)   8.9.3
s 206   8.9.2
s 208   8.9.2
s 208(1)   8.9.2
s 208(2)   8.9.2
s 208(3)   8.9.2
s 208(4)(a)   8.9.2
s 208(4)(b)   8.9.2
s 208(5)   8.9.2, 8.9.3
s 208(7)   8.9.2
s 208(8)   8.9.2
s 209   8.9.2, 8.9.5
s 209(1)(a)   8.9.2, 8.9.5
s 209(1)(b)   8.9.2
s 209(1)(c)   8.9.2
s 209(1)(g)   8.9.2
s 209(1)(h)   8.9.2
s 209(5)   8.9.2
s 209(6)   8.9.2
s 209(8)   8.9.2
s 209(9)   8.9.2
s 209(12)   8.9.2, 8.9.5
s 210   8.9.7, 18.6.4
s 210(2) and (3)   8.9.3
s 210(5)   8.9.7
s 210A   0.3.1.4
s 210(5A)   8.9.7
s 211   8.9.2, 8.9.4
s 211(8)(a)   4.4.1
s 212   8.9.5, 8.9.6, 8.9.7
s 212(1)   8.9.5
s 212(2)(b)   8.9.5
s 212(3)   8.9.5
s 212(5)   8.9.5

Companies Act 1980 –
continued
s 212(6) 8.9.5
s 213 8.9.5
s 214 8.9.6
s 214(2) 8.9.6
s 214(5) 8.9
s 215(1) 8.9.6
s 215(5) 8.9.6
s 215(7) 4.4.1, 8.9.6
s 216(1) 8.9.7
s 216(3) to (5) 8.9.5
s 216(1)(b) 8.9.7
s 217(2) and (3) 8.9.5
s 217(5) 8.9.5
s 219(1) and (2) 4.4.1
ss 221 to 262A 0.3.1.4, 9.1
s 221 17.4.1.7, 19.2.1
s 221(1)(b) 9.3.7.1
s 221(2) 9.2.3
s 221(5) 9.2.1, 9.3.7.1
s 221(6) 9.2.1, 9.3.7.1
s 222 9.2.2, 9.2.4
s 222(1) 4.4.4, 9.2.4
s 222(2) 9.2.4
s 222(3) 9.2.4
s 222(4) 9.2.4
s 222(5) 9.2.2
s 222(6) 9.2.2
s 223 9.3.2
s 223(5) 9.3.2
s 224(A) 9.3.2
s 224(5) 9.3.2
s 225 9.3.2
s 226 9.3.1
s 226(2) 9.3.7.1
s 226(3) 9.3.7.1
s 226(4) 9.3.7.1
s 226(5) 9.3.7.1
s 226(6) 9.3.7.1
s 227 9.3.1
s 227(1) 9.3.1, 9.6.1
s 227(2) 9.6.1
s 227(3) 9.3.7.1
s 227(4) 9.6.7.1
s 227(5) 9.3.7.1
s 227(6) 9.3.7.1
s 228 9.3.1, 9.6.1, 9.6.4,
        15.4.1
s 228(1) 9.6.4
s 228(1)(b) 9.6.4
s 228(2)(a) 9.6.4
s 228(2)(b) 9.6.4
s 228(2)(c) 9.6.4
s 228(2)(d) 9.6.4
s 228(2)(e) 9.6.4
s 228(3) 9.6.4
s 228(7) 9.6.1
s 229 9.6.6

Companies Act 1980 –
continued
s 229(1) 9.6.6
s 229(2) 9.6.6
s 229(3)(a) 9.6.6
s 229(3)(b) 9.6.6
s 229(3)(c) 9.6.6
s 229(4) 9.6.6
s 229(5) 9.3.1, 9.6.1, 9.6.6
s 230(3) 9.6.3
s 231 9.6.7
s 232(1) 9.3.7.1, 15.6.3.1,
         15.6.3.2, 15.6.3.3,
         15.6.3.4, 16.6.8.8,
         16.6.8
s 232(3) 15.6.3.5
s 233 9.3.1
s 233(1) 9.3.1, 9.3.6.1,
         9.3.6.2, 9.6.3, 9.8
s 233(2) 9.3.1
s 233(3) 9.3.6.1, 9.3.6.2,
         9.4.1, 9.8
s 233(5) 9.3.7.1, 9.3.8.4
s 233(6) 9.3.1, 9.3.6.1,
         9.3.6.2, 9.4.1, 9.8
s 234 9.3.3, 9.7.1
s 234(1) 9.3.3, 9.7.2,
         10.5.1
s 234(2) 9.7.2, 9.7.4
s 234A(1) 9.3.3, 9.3.6.1,
         9.3.6.2, 9.7.1, 9.8
s 234A(2) 9.3.6.1, 9.3.6.2,
         9.8
s 234A(3) 9.4.1
s 234A(4) 9.3.6.1, 9.3.6.2,
         9.4.1, 9.8
s 235 10.5.9
s 235(1) 9.3.4
s 235(2) 17.4.5
s 235(3) 17.4.5
s 236(1) 9.3.4, 17.4.5
s 236(2) 9.3.6.1, 9.3.6.2,
         9.8
s 236(3) 9.4.1
s 236(4) 9.3.6.1, 9.3.6.2,
         9.4.1, 9.8
s 237(1) 17.4.5
s 237(2) 9.2.1, 17.4.5
s 237(3) 9.2.4, 17.4.5
s 237(4) 15.6.3.5, 17.4.5
s 238 9.3.4, 9.3.6.1, 9.3.6.3,
         9.3.6.4, 9.9, 10.5.9,
         17.4.3
s 238(1) 9.3.1, 9.3.3,
         9.3.6.2, 12.6, 17.4.1.7
s 238(2) 9.3.5
s 238(2)(a) 12.6
s 238(4) 9.3.6.2
s 238(5) 9.3.6.2

Companies Act 1980 –
continued
s 239 5.2.2.3.1, 9.3.6.3,
         9.3.6.4, 12.6
s 239(1) 9.3.6.3
s 239(2) 9.3.6.3
s 239(3) 9.3.6.3
s 240 9.8
s 240(1) 9.8
s 240(2) 9.8
s 240(3) 9.8
s 240(4) 9.8
s 240(5) 9.8
s 241 9.3.1, 9.3.3, 9.3.5,
         9.3.6.1
s 241(2) 9.3.3, 9.3.6.1
s 241(3) 9.3.6.1
s 241(4) 9.3.6.1
s 242 4.2.1
s 242(1) 9.3.5, 9.4.1
s 242(2) 9.4.1
s 242(3) 9.4.1
s 242(4) 9.4.1
s 242(5) 9.4.1
s 242A 9.4.1
s 242B(1) and (3) 9.3.1
s 243 9.6.6
s 244 9.3.5
s 244(1) 9.3.5
s 244(3) 9.3.5
s 244(5) 9.3.5
s 244(6) 9.3.5
s 245 9.9
s 245(1) 9.9
s 245A 9.9
s 245A(1) 9.9
s 245A(2) 9.9
s 245A(3) 9.9
s 245B 0.3.2.2, 9.9
s 245B(1) 9.9
s 245B(3) 9.9
s 245B(4) 9.9
s 245B(5) 9.9
s 245C 9.9
s 246 9.3.8
s 246(2) 9.3.7.4
s 246(3) 9.6.7, 15.6.3.1,
         15.6.3.2
s 246(4) 9.6.5, 9.7.1, 9.7.2,
         9.7.3, 9.7.4, 9.7.9, 10.5.1
s 246(5) 9.5.3
s 246(6) 9.5.3, 15.6.3.1,
         15.6.3.2, 15.6.3.3,
         15.6.3.4
s 246(7) 9.5.3
s 246(8) 9.3.7.4, 9.5.3,
         9.7.1
s 246(9) 9.3.7.4, 9.5.3,
         9.7.1

Companies Act 1980 –
continued
s 246(A)   9.5.3
s 246A(2)   9.3.8
s 246A(3)   9.5.3
s 246A(4)   9.5.3
s 247(1)(a)   9.5.2
s 247(1)(b)   9.5.2
s 247(2)   9.5.2
s 247(3)   9.5.2
s 247(4)   9.5.2
s 247(5)   6.3.2
s 247A(1)(a)(i)   9.5.2
s 247A(1)(a)(ii)   9.5.2
s 247A(1)(a)(iii)   9.5.2
s 247A(1)(b)   9.5.2
s 247A(2)   9.5.2
s 247A(3)   9.5.2
s 247B   9.5.3
s 247B(3)(a)   9.5.3
s 247B(3)(b)   9.5.3
s 247B(4)   9.8
s 247B(5)   9.8
s 248   9.3.1, 9.6.1,
   9.6.5
s 248(1)   9.6.5
s 248(2)   9.6.5
s 248(2)(a)   9.6.5
s 248A   9.3.7.4
s 248A(5)   9.3.7.4
s 249   9.6.5
s 249(3)   9.6.5
s 249(4)   9.6.5
s 249A   9.3.4, 17.4.1.3,
   17.4.1.6
s 249A(6)   9.3.4
s 249B(1)(b) to (d)   9.3.4
s 249B(1)(f)   9.3.4
s 249B(2) to (5)   9.3.4
s 249B(1B)   9.3.4
s 249B(1C)   9.3.4
s 249C   9.3.4
s 249E(1)(a)   9.3.6.2
s 249E(1)(b)   9.3.6.1
s 249E(1)(c)   10.5.9
s 250   14.4.8.3, 17.4.1.1,
   17.4.1.7
s 250(1)(a)   17.4.1.7
s 250(1)(b)   17.4.1.7
s 250(2)   17.4.1.7
s 250(3)   17.4.1.7
s 250(4)   9.3.6.1, 9.3.6.2,
   9.4.1
s 250(4)(d)   9.5.2
s 250(5)   17.4.1.7
s 251(1)   9.3.6.4
s 251(3)   9.3.6.4
s 251(4)(b)   9.3.6.4
s 251(4)(c)   9.3.6.4

Companies Act 1980 –
continued
s 252   4.6, 9.3.1, 9.3.3,
   9.3.4, 9.3.5, 9.3.6.1,
   9.3.6.5, 14.4.8.4,
   17.4.1.5
s 252(3)   9.3.4, 10.5.9
s 253   14.4.3
s 253(1)   9.3.6.2, 9.3.6.5
s 253(2)   9.3.6.5, 14.4.5.1
s 253(3)   9.3.6.5, 14.4.5.1
s 253(4)   14.4.5.1
s 253(5)   9.3.6.5
s 253(6)   9.3.6.5
s 254(1)   9.4.2
s 254(2)   9.4.2
s 254(3)   9.4.2
s 255   9.9
s 255(1)   9.3.7.1
s 255(2)   9.3.7.1
s 255A(1)   9.3.7.1
s 255A(2)   9.3.7.1
s 255A(4)   9.3.7.1
s 255A(5)   9.3.7.1
s 255A(5A)   9.3.7.1
s 256(1)   9.3.8
s 256(2)   9.3.8
s 257   3.1.4.1
s 258   9.6.2
s 258(2)(a)   9.6.2
s 258(2)(b)   9.6.2
s 258(2)(c)   9.6.2
s 258(2)(d)   9.6.2
s 258(4)   9.6.2
s 258(5)   9.6.2
s 259(1)   9.6.1
s 259(2)   9.6.2
s 259(3)   9.6.2
s 259(5)   9.6.2
s 260   9.6.2
s 260(1)   9.6.2
s 260(2)   9.6.2
s 260(4)   9.6.2
s 260(5)   9.6.2
s 262(1)   9.3.1, 9.3.7.1,
   9.5.2
s 262(2)   9.3.1
s 262(3)   10.5.4
s 263   10.5.9
s 263(2)   10.5.2
s 263(3)   10.5.3
s 263(4)   10.4
s 264   10.5.7, 10.5.9
s 264(2)   6.3.2
s 265   10.5.8, 10.5.9
s 266   4.5.4
s 266(2)   10.5.8
s 269   10.5.5
s 269(2)   10.5.5

Companies Act 1980 –
continued
s 270(3)   10.5.9
s 270(4)   10.5.9
s 271   10.5.9
s 271(2)   10.5.9
s 271(3)   10.5.9
s 271(4)   10.5.9
s 271(5)   10.5.9
s 273   10.5.9
s 275(1)   6.3.3, 10.5.4,
   10.5.5
s 275(2)   10.5.4
s 275(4) to (6)   10.5.5
s 276   10.5.4
s 277   10.5.10
s 277(1)   10.5.10
s 277(2)   10.5.10
s 280(2)   10.4
s 282   15.1.3,
   15.2.3.3, 15.2.5.6,
   15.5.1
s 283   15.2.5.6, 15.2.5.9,
   17.3.1
s 283(4)(a)   17.3.1
s 284   17.3.1
s 285   15.2.6, 17.2
s 286(1)   17.3.1
s 287(2)   2.3.4, 2.4.3
s 287(3)   2.3.4
s 287(4)   2.3.4
s 288(1)   4.4.1, 15.4.1,
   17.3.2
s 288(2)   15.4.2
s 288(3)   4.4.1, 15.4.1
s 288(4) and (5)   15.4.1
s 289(1)(a)   15.2.4, 15.4.1
s 289(1)(b)   15.4.1
s 289(2) and (3)   15.4.1
s 289(2)(b)   15.4.1
s 289(3)(a)   15.4.1
s 289(4)   15.4.1
s 290(1) and (2)   17.3.2
s 290(1)(a)   17.3.2
s 290(1)(b)   17.3.2
s 290(3)   17.3.2
s 291(1) to (5)   15.2.9
s 292(1)   15.2.3.2
s 292(2)   15.2.3.2, 15.2.4
s 293(2)   15.2.4, 15.2.6
s 293(3)   15.2.4, 15.2.6,
   15.3.2, 15.3.6
s 293(4)   15.2.3.2, 15.2.4,
   15.3.6
s 293(5)   14.4.5.6, 15.2.4
s 293(6)   15.3.2
s 293(7)   15.2.4, 15.3.6
s 294(1)   15.2.4
s 294(2)   15.2.4

Companies Act 1980 –
continued
s 294(3)   15.2.4
s 294(4)   15.2.4
s 294(5)   15.2.4
s 303   0.2.4, 1.3.5, 3.4.2.3,
   14.4.4, 14.4.5.6, 14.5.1,
   14.5.3, 14.5.4, 15.3.3,
   15.3.7, 15.5.3, 15.7.1,
   15.7.5
s 303(1)   15.3.3
s 303(2)   14.4.5.6,
   15.3.3
s 303(4) and (5)   15.3.3
s 304(1)   14.4.8.5, 15.3.3
s 304(2)   14.4.5.5, 15.3.3
s 304(3)   15.3.3
s 305   4.5.2, 15.4.3
s 305(4)(a)   4.5.2
s 306(1)   2.3.6
s 307   2.4.5
s 307(1)   14.4.8.3, 15.7.5
s 308   14.4.8.3, 15.3.4,
   15.7.5
s 309   0.2.4, 16.4.5
s 309(3)   16.4.5
s 310   16.2.1.1, 16.9.1
s 310(2)   3.3.2
s 310(3)   16.9.1
s 311   15.6.1.5
ss 312 to 315   15.6.2.2
s 312   14.5.1, 15.2.8, 15.6.2,
   15.6.2.2, 15.7.4.1,
   15.7.5, 16.9.2
s 313   15.2.8
s 313(1)   15.6.2.1, 15.7.4.1,
   15.7.5
s 313(2)   15.6.2.1
s 314   15.2.8, 15.6.2.1
s 314(1)   15.6.2.1
s 315   15.2.8
s 315(1)   15.6.2.1, 15.7.4.1,
   15.7.5
s 316(3)   15.6.2.2
s 317   16.6.1, 16.6.2, 16.6.5,
   16.8
s 317(1)   0.3.2.3
s 317(1) to (4)   16.6.5
s 317(6)   16.6.5
s 317(7)   16.6.5
s 317(8) and (9)   16.6.5
s 318   15.6.4
s 318(1) to (3)   4.4.3
s 318(4)   4.4.3
s 318(5)   4.4.3
s 318(6)   4.4.3, 15.6.4
s 318(7)   4.4.3
s 318(11)   4.4.3
s 319   15.3.3

Companies Act 1980 –
continued
s 319(1)   15.6.4
s 319(3)   15.6.4, 15.7.5,
   15.7.4.1
s 319(5)   4.4.3, 15.6.4
s 319(6)   15.6.4
s 319(7)   15.6.4
s 319(7)(a)   15.6.1.2, 15.6.4
s 319(7)(b)   14.7
s 320   0.3.1.3, 16.6.7
s 320(1)   15.7.5, 16.6.7
s 320(2)   16.6.7
s 320(3)   16.6.7
s 321(2)(a)   16.6.7
s 321(4)   16.6.7
s 322   16.6.7
s 322(1) to (3)   16.6.7
s 322(5) and (6)   16.6.7
s 322A   19.5.7, 19.5.9,
   19.5.11
s 322A(3)   19.5.9
s 322A(5)   19.5.9
s 322A(7)   19.5.9
s 322A(8)   19.5.9
s 322B   19.5.9
s 322B(4)   19.5.9
s 322B(6)   19.5.9
s 323   13.4, 18.8.2.3
s 323(2)   13.4
s 323(5)   13.4
ss 324 to 328   9.7.4
s 324   13.6.2, 18.10.2.3
s 324(1)   13.6.2
s 324(2)   13.6.2
s 324(3)(b)   13.6.2
s 324(5)   13.6.2
s 324(6)   13.6.2
s 324(7)   13.6.2
s 324(7)(a)   13.6.2
s 324(8)   13.6.2
ss 325 to 329   13.6.1
s 325(1)   4.4.1, 13.6.3
s 325(2)   13.6.3
s 325(4)   13.6.4
s 325(5)   13.6.3, 13.6.4
s 325(6)   13.6.3
s 326   13.6.3
s 326(5)   13.6.3
s 326(6)   13.6.3
s 328   13.6.4
s 328(3) to (5)   18.8.2.3
s 329   13.6.3
s 329(1)   13.6.3
s 329(3)   13.6.3
s 330   16.4.4.3, 16.6.8,
   16.6.8.7, 16.6.8.8, 18.7
s 330(2)(a) and (b)   16.6.8.1
s 330(3)(a) to (c)   16.6.8.3

Companies Act 1980 –
continued
s 330(4)(a) and (b)
   16.6.8.3
s 330(5)   16.6.8.1
s 330(6) and (7)   16.6.8.1,
   16.6.8.5, 16.6.8.9
s 331(2)   16.6.8.1
s 331(3)   16.6.8.3
s 331(6) to (8)   16.6.8.3
s 332   16.6.8.3
s 333   16.6.8.3
s 334   16.6.8.1
s 335(1) and (2)   16.6.8.3
s 336(a)   16.6.8.2
s 337   15.7.5, 16.6.8.2,
   16.6.8.4
s 337(4)   16.6.8.2
s 338(1) to (4)   16.6.8.2,
   16.6.8.4
s 338(5)   16.6.8.4
s 338(6)   16.6.8.2
s 339   16.6.8.1, 16.6.8.3,
   16.6.8.4
s 339(1)   16.6.8.2
s 339(2)(b)   16.6.8.1
s 340   16.6.6
s 341(1)   16.6.8.1, 16.6.8.7
s 341(1)   16.6.8.7
s 341(2)   16.6.8.7
s 341(4) and (5)   16.6.8.1
s 342   16.6.8.2
s 342(1) to (5)   16.6.8.6
s 346   16.6.5, 16.6.8.10
s 346(5)   16.6.8.10
s 346(5)(a)   16.6.8.10
s 348   2.3.3.7, 4.5.1
s 348(1) and (2)   4.5.1
s 349   2.3.3.7, 4.5.1
s 349(1) to (3)   4.5.1
s 349(1)(c)   4.5.1
s 349(4)   5.2.2.5, 4.5.1,
   19.2.6
s 350   4.5.1
s 350(1)   4.5.1, 19.2.2
s 351(1)   4.5.4
s 351(1)(c)   10.5.8
s 351(2)   4.5.4, 6.1.2
s 351(5)   4.5.4
s 352   4.4.1, 6.1.1, 14.3.1
s 352(1)   4.4.1
s 352(2)(b)   14.3.1
s 352(6)   14.3.1
s 352A   14.3.1
s 353   14.3.1
s 353(1)   4.4.1, 14.3.1
s 353(2)   4.4.1, 14.3.1
s 353(3)   4.4.1, 14.3.1
s 353(4)(b)   5.4.4.1

Companies Act 1980 –
continued
s 354   14.3.1
s 355(2)   8.6
s 355(5)   15.2.3
s 356(1)   4.4.1
s 356(3)   4.4.1
s 358   4.4.1
s 359   14.3.3
s 359(3)   14.3.3
s 359(4)   14.3.3
s 360   8.7.1, 8.9.1,
   14.4.9.1.6
s 361   14.3.3
s 363(1) to (4)   4.6
s 363(7)   4.6
s 364(1)   4.6
s 364(1)(a)   4.6
s 364(1)(b)   4.6
s 364(1)(c)   4.6
s 364(1)(d)   4.6
s 364(1)(e)   4.6
s 364(1)(f)   4.6
s 364(1)(g)   4.6
s 364(1)(h)   4.6
s 364(1)(i)   4.6
s 364(2) and (3)   4.6
s 364A(1)   4.6
s 364A(2)   4.6
s 364A(3)   4.6
s 364A(4)   4.6
s 364A(5)(a)   4.6
s 364A(5)(b)   4.6
s 364A(6)   4.6
s 365(1)   4.6
s 365(2)   4.6
s 365(3)   4.6
s 366   14.4.2
s 366(2)   4.6
s 366A   4.6, 9.3.6.5, 14.4.2,
   14.4.8.4
s 366A(2)   14.4.2
s 366A(3)   14.4.2
s 367   14.4.2, 14.4.5.1
s 367(2)   14.4.6.2
s 367(5)   14.4.11
s 368   14.4.3, 14.4.4,
   14.4.5.1, 14.4.5.4,
   15.7.5
s 368(2)   14.4.3
s 368(3)   14.4.3
s 368(4)   14.4.3, 14.4.4,
   14.4.5.1
s 368(5)   14.4.4, 14.4.5.1
s 368(6)   14.4.3
s 368(7)   14.4.3
s 368(8)   14.4.3
s 369   14.6.2.4
s 369(1)   3.3.2, 14.4.5.3

Companies Act 1980 –
continued
s 369(1)(a)   9.3.6.2
s 369(2)   14.4.5.3
s 369(3)(a)   9.3.6.2, 14.4.5.3
s 369(3)(b)   14.4.5.3
s 369(4)   14.4.5.3, 14.4.8.4
s 370   14.4.6.1, 14.4.7,
   14.6.2.4
s 370(1)   3.3.2, 14.4.6.1
s 370(2)   3.3.2
s 370(4)   14.4.6.1
s 370(5)   14.4.7, 14.4.9.1
s 370A   14.4.6.1, 14.4.6.2,
   14.5.4
s 371   14.4.4
s 371(1)   14.4.4
s 371(2)   14.4.4, 14.4.6.2
s 372(1)   14.4.9.1.3,
   14.4.9.1.8, 14.4.9.2
s 372(2)(a)   14.4.6.1
s 372(2)(b)   14.4.9.1.3
s 372(2)(c)   14.4.9.1.3,
   14.4.9.2, 14.4.9.2.2
s 372(3)   14.4.5.5,
   14.4.9.1.3
s 372(5)   3.3.2, 14.4.9.1.3,
   14.4.10
s 372(6) and (7)   14.4.9.1.3
s 373   14.4.9.1.3, 14.4.9.2
s 373(1)   3.3.2, 14.4.9.2
s 373(2)   14.4.9.2
s 374   14.4.9.2
s 375   14.4.9.1.4
s 376   14.4.2.1, 14.4.5.6,
   14.4.5.7, 14.6.2.4, 15.7.5
s 376(1)   14.4.5.5, 14.4.5.7
s 376(1)(a)   14.4.5.7
s 376(2)   14.4.5.7
s 376(5) to (6)   14.4.5.7
s 376(7)   14.4.5.7
s 377   14.6.2.4
s 377(1)(a) and (b)   14.4.5.7
s 377(2)   14.4.5.7
s 378   14.4.9.1.8
s 378(1)   14.4.5.5, 14.4.8.2,
   14.4.8.3
s 378(2)   14.4.5.3, 14.4.5.4,
   14.4.5.5, 14.4.8.3
s 378(3)   14.4.5.3, 14.4.8.4
s 378(5)   14.4.9.2
s 379(1) to (3)   14.4.5.6
s 379A   6.2.5, 9.3.6.5,
   14.4.2, 14.4.5.3, 17.4.1.4
s 379A(1)   14.4.8.4
s 379A(2)(a)   14.4.8.4
s 379A(2)(b)   14.4.8.4
s 379(2A)   14.4.8.4
s 379A(3)   14.4.8.4

Companies Act 1980 –
continued
s 379A(4)   14.4.8.4
s 380   3.5.2.1, 6.1.4, 6.2.5,
   6.2.6, 10.3.5, 10.6.2,
   10.8.7, 14.6.2.7,
   15.5.3.2.5
s 380(1)   2.4.9.1, 14.4.11
s 380(2)   10.6.2, 14.4.11
s 380(4)(a)   2.4.9.1, 14.4.11
s 380(4)(b)   2.4.9.1, 14.4.11
s 380(4)(bb)   14.4.11
s 380(4)(c)   2.4.9.1, 14.4.11,
   14.4.8.3, 14.5.1
s 380(4)(d)   14.4.11
s 380(4)(e)   2.4.9.1, 14.4.11
s 380(4)(f)   14.4.11
s 380(4)(g)   14.4.11
s 380(4)(h)   14.4.11
s 380(4)(j)   14.4.11
s 380(4)(k)   14.4.11
s 380(4)(l)   14.4.11
s 380(4)(m)   14.4.11
s 380(5)   2.4.9.1, 3.5.2.1
s 381   14.4.10, 20.8
ss 381A to 381C   10.2.5
s 381A   4.4.3, 6.1.13, 6.2.6,
   10.3.2, 10.6.3, 10.8.7,
   14.4.8.3, 14.4.8.4,
   14.4.11, 14.5.3, 14.5.4,
   15.3.3, 15.6.4, 16.6.8.2,
   17.4.3
s 381A(1)   14.5.3
s 381A(2)   14.5.3
s 381A(3)   14.5.3
s 381A(4)   14.5.3
s 381A(6)   14.4.8.3,
   14.4.8.4, 14.5.3
s 381A(7)   14.5.3, 15.3.3,
   17.4.3
s 381B   14.5.3
s 381B(4)   14.5.3
s 381C(1)   14.5.3
s 381C(2)   14.5.3
s 382   15.2.6, 15.5.1
s 382(1)   14.4.11, 15.5.1
s 382(2)   14.4.11
s 382(4)   14.4.11, 15.2.6
s 382(5)   14.4.11
s 382A   14.4.11
s 382A(1)   14.4.11
s 382A(2)   14.4.11
s 382A(3)   4.4.3, 14.4.11
s 382B   14.4.11, 14.5.4
s 383(1)   4.4.3, 14.4.11
s 383(3)   4.4.3, 14.4.11
s 383(4)   14.4.11
s 384(1)   17.4.1.1
s 384(2)   17.4.1.3

Companies Act 1980 –
continued
s 384(4) 17.4.1.3
s 385(1) 17.4.1.2, 17.4.1.3
s 385(2) 17.4.1.2, 17.4.6
s 385(3) 17.4.1.2, 17.4.6
s 385(4) 17.4.1.2
s 385A 17.4.1.3, 17.4.1.5
s 385A(2) 17.4.6
s 385A(3) 17.4.6
s 386 14.4.8.4, 17.4.1.3,
    17.4.1.4, 17.4.3
s 386(2) 17.4.1.4
s 387 17.4.1.2
s 388(1) 17.4.3
s 388(2) 17.4.3
s 388(3) 14.4.5.6, 17.4.3
s 388(4) 17.4.3
s 388A(1) 17.4.1.1,
    17.4.1.6, 17.4.1.7
s 388A(2) to (5) 17.4.1.6,
    17.4.1.7
s 389A(1) 9.2.4, 17.4.5
s 389A(2) 17.4.5
s 389A(3) 17.4.5
s 389A(4) 17.4.5
s 390(1) 9.3.6.2, 14.4.5.2,
    17.4.3
s 390A(1) 17.4.4
s 390A(2) 17.4.4
s 390A(3) 17.4.4
s 390A(4) 17.4.4
s 390A(5) 17.4.4
s 391 14.5.3, 14.5.4
s 391(1) 17.4.3
s 391(2) 17.4.3
s 391(4) 14.4.5.2
s 391A 14.5.1, 17.4.3
s 391A(1) 14.4.5.6,
    17.4.1.2, 17.4.3
s 391A(2) 17.4.3
s 391A(3) 14.4.5.5, 17.4.3
s 391A(4) 14.4.5.5, 17.4.3
s 391A(5) 17.4.3
s 392A 14.4.3
s 392(1) 17.4.3
s 393 14.4.3, 14.4.5.1,
    17.4.3
s 393(1) 17.4.3
s 393(2) 17.4.3
s 393(4) 14.4.5.1, 17.4.3
s 393(5) 14.4.5.1
s 393(6) 17.4.3
s 394(1) 17.4.3
s 394(2) 17.4.3
s 394(3) to (7) 17.4.3
s 394(3) 14.4.5.5, 17.4.3
s 394A(1) to (3) 17.4.3
s 394A(4) 17.4.3

Companies Act 1980 –
continued
ss 395 to 424 11.7.1
s 395 11.3, 11.7.2, 11.7.4,
    11.7.12
s 395(1) 11.7.3, 11.7.4
s 395(2) 11.7.3
s 396(1) 11.7.2, 11.7.10,
    11.7.10.2
s 396(1)(a) 12.3
s 396(1)(c) 11.7.12
s 396(1)(e) 11.7.10.2
s 396(2)(f) 11.7.10.2
s 396(3A) 11.7.2
s 396(4) 11.2.1
s 398(1) 11.7.4
s 398(2) 11.7.2
s 398(4) 11.7.4
s 399(1) 11.7.2
s 399(3) 11.7.3
s 400 11.7.2
s 400(2) 11.7.4
s 400(4) 11.7.3
s 401 11.7.2.5
s 401(2) 11.7.6
s 401(2)(b) 11.7.6
s 401(3) 11.7.8
s 403 11.7.7
s 404 11.7.7, 11.7.9
s 406 4.4.2, 11.7.4, 11.7.12
s 407 4.4.1
s 407(1) 11.7.12
s 407(3) 11.7.12
s 408 4.4.1
s 408(1) 4.4.1, 4.4.2, 11.7.4
s 408(2) 4.4.1
ss 425 to 427 10.2.1,
    19.14.1.3, 20.3.3
ss 425 to 430 1.3.4.1
s 425 2.4.7, 8.8.3, 14.6.2.2,
    20.3.2, 20.14.2.3
s 425(1) 14.4.4
s 426 14.4.5.5
s 427 8.8.3, 20.14.2.3
s 427(5) 20.14.2.3
Part XIIIA (ss 428 to
    430F) 8.8.1, 8.8.2,
    8.8.2.1, 8.8.2.2, 8.8.2.5,
    8.8.2.6, 8.8.2.7, 8.8.2.8
s 428(1) 8.8.2.1
s 428(4) 8.8.2.1
s 428(5) 8.8.2.1
s 428(7) 8.8.2.2
s 429 8.8.2.4, 8.8.3
s 429(1) 8.8.2.2
s 429(2) 8.8.2.2, 8.8.2.3
s 429(3) 8.8.2.2, 8.8.2.3
s 429(4) 8.8.2.3
s 429(8) 8.8.2.2

Companies Act 1980 –
continued
s 430(2) 8.8.2.3
s 430(3) 8.8.2.3
s 430(4) 8.8.2.3
s 430(5) to (7) 8.8.2.3
s 430(9) to (11) 8.8.2.3
s 430(15) 8.8.2.3
s 430A 8.8.2.4
s 430A(1) 8.8.2.4
s 430A(3) to (7) 8.8.2.4
s 430B(2) 8.8.2.4
s 430B(3) and (4) 8.8.2.5
s 430C 8.8.2.3
s 430C(3) 8.8.2.4
s 430C(4) 8.8.2.3
s 430C(5) 8.8.2.2
s 430D 8.8.2.6
s 430E(1) 8.8.2.1, 8.8.2.2
s 430E(2) 8.8.2.2
s 430E(4) to (8) 8.8.2.8
s 430E(4)(b) 8.8.2.3
s 430F(1) and (2) 8.8.2.7
s 431 15.7.5, 18.8.2.4,
    18.8.2.6, 18.8.3.7,
    20.9.7
s 431(1) 18.8.2.1
s 431(2) 18.8.2.1
s 431(3) and (4) 18.8.2.1
s 432 18.8.2.1, 18.8.2.6,
    20.9.3, 20.9.7
s 432(1) 18.8.2.1, 18.8.3.1
s 432(2) 18.8.2.1
s 432(2A) 18.8.3.1
s 432(3) 18.8.2.1
s 432(4) 18.8.2.1
s 433 18.8.2.6
s 433(1) 18.8.2.2, 18.8.2.4,
    18.8.2.6
s 434 18.8.2.2, 18.8.2.3
s 434(1) 18.8.2.6
s 434(2) 18.8.2.6
s 434(3) 18.8.2.6
s 434(5) 18.8.2.6
s 435 18.8.2.3
s 436 18.8.2.3, 18.8.2.6
s 436(2) 18.8.2.6
s 437 15.2.5.3, 18.8.2.2,
    18.8.2.3, 18.8.3.1,
    18.8.3.6, 20.9.10.3
s 437(1) 18.8.3.1
s 437(1A) 18.8.3.2
s 437(1B) 18.8.2.7
s 437(2) 18.8.3.1
s 437(3) 18.8.3.1
s 438 18.4.2, 18.8.3.4
s 438(2) 18.8.3.4
s 439(1) to (5) 18.8.3.7
s 439(5) 18.8.2.1, 18.8.2.2

Companies Act 1980 –
continued
s 440   18.8.3.7
s 441(1)   18.8.3.3
s 442   8.9.7, 18.8.2.2,
   18.8.2.4, 18.8.2.6
s 442(1) to (3)   18.8.2.2
s 442(3)   8.9.6, 18.8.3.7
s 442(3A)   18.8.2.2
s 442(3B)   18.8.2.2
s 442(3C)   18.8.2.2
s 443(1)   18.8.2.4, 18.8.2.6,
   18.8.2.7, 18.8.3.1,
   18.8.3.2
s 443(2)   18.8.2.2,
   18.8.2.6
s 444   8.9.7, 18.8.2.2
s 444(2)   18.8.2.2
s 444(3)   18.8.2.2
s 445   8.9.7, 18.8.2.2
s 445(1)   8.9.7
s 445(1A)   8.9.7
s 446   18.8.2.4, 18.8.2.6
s 446(1)   13.4, 18.8.2.3
s 446(3)   18.8.2.3, 18.8.2.4,
   18.8.2.6, 18.8.2.7,
   18.8.3.1, 18.8.3.2
s 446(4)   18.8.2.3, 18.8.2.6
s 447   15.2.5.3, 15.2.5.6,
   18.8.1, 18.8.3.2,
   18.8.3.5, 18.8.3.6,
   20.9.10.3
s 447(1) to (5)   18.8.1
s 447(5)   18.8.1
s 447(5)(a)   18.8.1
s 447(5)(b)   18.8.1
s 447(6)   18.8.1
s 447(7)   18.8.1
s 447(9)   18.8.1
s 448   15.2.5.3, 18.8.1,
   18.8.3.5, 18.8.3.6,
   20.9.10.3
s 448(7)   18.8.1
s 449   18.8.3.2
s 449(1) and (2)   18.8.3.2
s 449(1)(a)   18.8.3.2
s 449(1)(ba)   18.8.3.2
s 449(1)(c) and
   (cc)   18.8.3.2
s 449(1)(d)   18.8.3.2
s 450(1)   18.8.1
s 450(2)   18.8.1
s 451   18.8.1
s 451A   18.8.3.2
s 451A(3)   18.8.3.2
s 452(1)(a)   18.8.2.6
s 452(1A)   18.8.2.6
s 452(1B)   18.8.2.6
s 452(2) and (3)   18.8.1

Companies Act 1980 –
continued
Part XV (ss 454 to
   457)   8.7.4, 8.9.7
s 454   8.9.7
s 456(1)   8.9.7
s 456(3)   8.9.7
s 456(3)(b)   8.9.7
s 456(4)   8.9.7
s 456(1A)   8.9.7
s 458   15.2.5.3, 20.10.1,
   20.10.2
ss 459 to 461   0.3.2.2,
   15.7.5, 18.6.1, 18.7.4
s 459   0.2.4, 14.4.4, 15.7.2,
   16.4.3, 16.4.12, 18.3.3,
   18.4.2, 18.6.2, 18.6.3,
   18.6.4, 18.6.5, 18.6.6,
   18.7.1, 18.8.3.5
s 459(1)   1.3.5, 18.6.1,
   18.6.2
s 459(2)   18.6.1
s 460   18.8.3.5
s 461   2.4.7, 2.4.8, 2.4.9.1,
   3.5.2.1
s 461(1)   2.4.6, 2.4.7, 18.6.6
s 461(2)   18.6.6
s 461(2)(c)   18.4.2
s 461(2)(d)   2.4.6, 2.4.7,
   10.8, 18.6.6
s 461(3)   2.4.8.2
s 461(4)   2.4.7
s 461(5)   2.4.9.1, 3.5.2.1
s 652   4.2.1, 5.2.1, 20.14.2.4
s 652(4)   20.14.2.4
s 652(5)   20.14.2.4
s 652A   20.14.2.4
s 652A(3)   20.14.2.4
s 652A(4)   20.14.2.4
s 652A(5)   20.14.2.4
s 652A(6)   20.14.2.4
s 652B   20.14.2.4
s 652(6)(a)   20.14.2.4
s 654   20.14.1
s 675   1.2.3
ss 680 to 690   1.6
s 680(1)   1.6
s 680(1)(a)   1.6
s 680(2)   1.6
s 688   1.6
s 688(1)   1.6
s 698(2)(b)   9.7.2
s 705   1.2.1
ss 706 and 707   4.2.1
s 706(3) and (4)   4.2.1
s 707(2)   4.2.1
s 707(5) and (6)   4.2.1
s 707A(2) and (3)   4.2.2
s 708   4.2.2

Companies Act 1980 –
continued
s 709(1) and (2)   4.2.2
s 710B(1) and (2)   4.2.1
s 710B(3)(a)   9.4.1
s 710B(3)(b)   4.2.1
s 710B(4)   4.2.1, 9.4.1
s 710B(6)   9.4.1
s 710B(7)   9.4.1
s 711   4.3
s 711(1)   4.3
s 711(1)(a)   1.2.1, 1.3.4.2,
   1.3.4.3, 2.4.2, 2.4.9.2,
   5.1
s 711(1)(b)   2.4.9.2, 3.5.2.2,
   6.1.13
s 711(1)(c)   15.4.2
s 711(1)(d)   6.2.5
s 711(1)(e)   6.2.6
s 711(1)(f)   6.5.4, 17.6.3.3
s 711(1)(g)   6.6.1
s 711(1)(h)   10.3.6
s 711(1)(j)   6.1.4
s 711(1)(k)   9.4.1
s 711(1)(l)   6.1.4, 14.6.2.7
s 711(1)(m)   6.2.7
s 711(1)(n)   2.3.4
s 711(1)(r)   20.14.2.5
s 711(2)   4.3
s 711A   2.2, 3.2, 19.4.1
s 713   4.2.1
s 713(3)   4.2.1
s 714   2.3.3.4
s 716   1.5
s 718   2.3.3.4
s 719   2.3.5.7, 14.4.9.4,
   20.13.2
s 719(1)   2.3.5.7
s 719(2)   2.3.5.7, 14.4.9.4
s 721   17.2
s 723   13.6.3
s 723(3)   4.4
s 723A   4.4
s 723A(6)   4.4
s 725(1)   2.3.4, 20.6.3
s 726   19.9
s 727   16.9.1, 16.9.2, 20.12
s 727(1)   17.5
s 730(5)   2.4.9.1, 3.5.2.1,
   6.4.2, 6.4.4, 6.5.4, 6.5.5,
   6.6.1, 7.5.7, 8.9.6, 9.2.1,
   9.2.4, 9.3.7.1, 9.3.6.2,
   9.3.6.3, 10.8.2, 10.8.5,
   11.7.3, 13.6.3, 14.4.11,
   19.5.9
s 732(1)   13.6.2, 13.6.3
s 732(2)(a)   13.6.2, 13.6.3
s 733(2)   19.8.4
s 735(1)(b)   1.2.3

Companies Act 1980 –
continued
s 735(3)   1.6
s 735A(2)   4.2.2
s 735B   4.2.2
s 736   9.6.2, 14.7
s 736(1)   14.7
s 736(1)(a)   14.7
s 736(1)(b)   14.7
s 736(1)(c)   14.7
s 736(2) and (3)   14.7
s 736A   14.7, 9.6.2
s 736A(2) to (12)   14.7
s 737(1)   6.1.2
s 738(1)   6.1.11
s 738(2)   6.5.4, 6.5.5
s 738(4)   6.5.4
s 739(1)   16.6.7
s 740   0.1.1, 0.1.6, 18.8.2.4
s 741(1)   15.1.4
s 741(2)   4.5.2, 15.1.6
s 741(3)   15.1.6, 15.6.4,
   16.4.5, 16.6.7, 19.5.9
s 743   10.7
s 744   0.3.1.2, 0.3.2.2, 2.3.4,
   4.3, 6.1.8, 6.1.14,
   9.3.7.1, 12.4, 17.1, 17.2,
   17.4, 17.4.6
Schedule 1   1.2.1, 17.3.2
   para 1(a)   15.2.4
Schedule 2   10.8.3
Schedule 3
   para 2   7.5.8
Schedule 4   6.3.2, 7.9.4,
   9.3.7.1, 9.3.7.2, 9.3.7.4,
   9.3.8, 10.5.4
   para 1   9.3.7.2
   para 1(2)   9.3.7.2
   para 2   9.3.7.2
   para 3(2)(b)   7.9.4
   para 3(3) and (4)   9.3.7.2
   para 4   9.3.7.2
Part I Section B   9.3.7.2
   para 9   9.3.7.3
   paras 10 to 14   9.3.7.3
   para 13   10.5.4
   para 15   9.3.7.3
   para 36A   9.3.8
   para 17   6.3.3
   para 17(1)   9.5.3
   para 17(3)   9.5.3
   para 18   6.3.3
   para 19(2)   6.3.3
   para 20   10.5.5
   para 31(2)   6.3.3
   para 32(1) and (2)   6.3.3
   para 32(3)   6.3.3, 10.5.4
   para 34   6.3.3
Part III   7.6.1, 9.3.8.1

Companies Act 1980 –
continued
paras 35 to 58   9.3.7.1
para 36A   9.3.9
para 39   6.2.8
para 43   6.3.3
para 77   6.3.3
para 89   6.3.2, 10.5.5
Schedule 4A   9.3.7.1
   para 20   9.6.7
   para 20(2)   9.6.7
Schedule 5
   para 1(2)   9.6.7
   para 1(3)   9.6.7
   para 1(4)   9.6.6
   para 1(5)   9.6.6
   para 2   9.6.7
   para 3   9.6.5, 9.6.6, 9.6.7
   para 4   9.6.7
   para 6   10.8.3
   para 7   9.6.7
   para 8   9.6.7
   para 9   9.6.7
   para 11   9.6.7
   para 12   9.6.7
   para 15(2)   9.6.7
   para 15(3)   9.6.7
   para 15(4)   9.6.6
   para 15(5)   9.6.2
   para 16   9.6.2, 9.6.7
   para 17   9.6.7
   para 20   9.6.7, 10.8.3
   para 21   9.6.7
   para 22   9.6.7
   para 30   9.6.7
   para 31   9.6.7
Schedule 6   9.3.7.1, 9.3.9.1,
   17.4.5
   para 1   15.6.3.1
   para 1(1)   15.6.3.1
   para 1(1)(a)   15.6.3.1
   para 1(1)(b)   15.6.3.1
   para 1(1)(c)   15.6.3.1
   para 1(1)(d)   15.6.3.1
   para 1(1)(e)   15.6.3.1
   para 1(2)   15.6.3.1
   para 1(3)   15.6.3.1
   para 1(4)   15.6.3.1
   para 1(5)   15.6.3.1
   para 1(7)   15.6.3.1
   para 2   15.6.3.1
   para 2(2)   15.6.3.1
   para 2(3)   15.6.3.1
   para 2(4)   15.6.3.1
   para 7   15.6.3.2
   para 9   15.6.3.4
   para 9(1)   15.6.3.4
   para 9(3)   15.6.3.4
   para 10(4)   15.6.3.1

Companies Act 1980 –
continued
para 11(1)   15.6.3.1,
   15.6.3.2
para 13(2)(a)   15.6.3.1
para 14   15.6.3.5
para 15(a) and (b)
   16.6.8.8
para 15(c)   16.6.6
para 16(a)   16.6.8.8
para 16(c)   16.6.6
para 17(1) and (2)
   16.6.6
para 18(a) and (b)
   16.6.6
para 19(a)   16.6.8.8
para 19(b)   16.6.6
para 19(c)   16.6.8.8
para 20   16.6.6
paras 21 and 22   16.6.6,
   16.6.8.8
paras 23 and 24
   16.6.8.8
para 25   16.6.6
paras 28 and 29   16.6.8.9
para 29(2)   16.6.8.9
para 30   16.6.8.9
Schedule 7   7.9.1, 9.7.1
   para 1(2)   9.7.3
   para 2   9.7.4
   para 2(1)   9.7.4
   para 3   2.3.5.6, 9.7.7
   para 6   9.7.2, 9.7.6
   para 6(a)   9.7.2
   para 6(b)   9.7.2
   para 6(c)   9.7.6
   para 6(d)   9.7.2
   para 7(a)   6.4.2, 10.3.6,
      10.6.4, 10.8.1
   para 7(c)   6.4.2
   para 8(a)   10.6.4
   para 8(b)   6.4.2
   para 8(c)   6.4.2
   para 8(d)   6.4.2, 10.3.6,
      10.8.1
   para 8(e)   6.4.2, 10.3.6,
      10.6.4, 10.8.1
   para 8(f)   6.4.2
   para 8(g)   6.4.2
   para 9   9.7.8
   para 11   9.7.9
   para 12   9.7.10
   para 12(1)(b)   9.7.10
Schedule 8   9.3.7.4, 9.3.8
Schedule 8A   9.5.3
Part II   9.5.3
Schedule 9   6.2.9, 9.3.7.1,
   9.3.7.2, 17.4.6
Part I   9.3.7.1

Companies Act 1980 –
continued
Part II 9.3.7.1
Schedule 9A 9.3.7.1
Part I 9.3.7.1
Part II 9.3.7.1
Schedule 10A
  para 4 9.6.2
  para 4(1) 9.6.2
  para 4(2) 9.6.2
  para 4(3) 9.6.2
Schedule 13
  para 1(1) 13.6.4
  para 2 13.6.4
  para 3(1)(a) and
    (b) 13.6.4
  para 3(3) 13.6.4
  paras 4 and 5 13.6.4
  paras 7 to 9 13.6.4
  para 11 13.6.4
  para 14 13.6.2
  para 16 13.6.2
  para 21 13.6.3
  para 22 13.6.3
  para 25 4.4.1, 13.6.3
  para 26 4.4.1, 13.6.3
  para 27 4.4.1, 13.6.3
  para 28 13.6.3
  para 29 13.6.3
Schedule 15A 14.5.3
  para 1 14.5.3
  para 1(a) 15.5.3
  para 1(b) 17.4.3
  para 3 6.2.6
  para 4 10.8.7
  para 5 10.6.3
  para 6 10.3.2
  para 7 15.6.4
  para 8 16.6.8.2
Schedule 24 2.4.9.1,
  3.5.2.1, 4.5.1, 6.2.5,
  6.2.6, 6.4.2, 6.4.4, 6.5.4,
  6.6.1, 7.5.7, 7.5.9, 8.3.4,
  8.8.2.4, 8.9.3, 8.9.5,
  8.9.6, 9.2.1, 9.2.4,
  9.3.6.2, 9.3.6.3, 9.3.7.1,
  10.2.3, 10.2.6, 10.8.2,
  10.8.5, 10.8.7, 11.7.3,
  13.4, 13.6.2, 13.6.3,
  14.3.1, 14.4.5.3,
  14.4.5.7, 14.4.11, 15.2.4,
  15.4.1, 15.6.3.5, 16.6.5,
  16.6.8.6, 17.4.3, 17.4.5,
  19.5.9, 20.10.1,
  20.14.2.3
Companies Act 1989 (c 40)
  0.3.1.2, 2.3.5.3, 9.3.8, 9.9,
  18.8.3.2, 19.4.1, 19.5.5
s 24(2) 17.4.1.1

Companies Act 1989 –
continued
s 25(1) 17.4.2.2
s 26(2) 0.1.7, 17.4.1.1
s 27(1) 15.2.5.9, 17.4.2.4
s 27(2) 17.4.2.4
s 27(3) 17.4.2.4
s 28(1) 17.4.2.5
s 28(2) 17.4.3
s 28(3) 17.4.2.5, 17.4.3
s 28(5) 17.4.2.5, 17.4.3
s 29 17.4.2.5
s 30(2) 17.4.2.2
s 31(1)(a) 17.4.2.3
s 31(1)(b) 17.4.2.3
s 31(4) 17.4.2.3
s 32 17.4.2.3
s 33 17.4.2.3
s 34 17.4.2.3
s 35 17.4.2.3
s 41(2) 17.4.2.3
s 41(5) 17.4.2.3
s 41(6) 17.4.2.3
ss 82 to 91 18.8.2.8
s 82(1) 18.8.2.8
s 82(2) 18.8.2.8
s 83 18.8.3.3
s 83(1) 18.8.2.8
s 83(2) 18.8.2.8
s 83(5) 18.8.2.8
s 84(4) 18.8.2.8
Part IV (ss 92 to 107)
  0.3.1.4, 11.7.1
s 108 19.1, 19.5.5
s 110(2) 2.4.4
ss 113 to 117 0.3.1.3,
  0.3.1.4
s 128 1.3.6
s 133 10.3.2
s 142 2.2, 3.2, 19.1,
  19.5.4.1, 19.5.5
s 144(2) 14.7
Schedule 11 17.4.2.2
Schedule 12 17.4.2.3
Companies Clauses
  Consolidation Act 1845
  (8 & 9 Vict c 16) 3.2
s 1 3.2
s 73 15.7.1.3
s 90 15.7.2.2, 15.7.2.4,
  15.7.3
Companies (Consolidation) Act
  1908 (8 Edw 7 c 69)
  0.3.3.3, 1.2.3
s 113(2) 9.3.8
Companies Consolidation
  (Consequential Provisions)
  Act 1985 (c 9) 0.3.1.2,
  20.6.3

Companies Consolidation
  (Consequential Provisions)
  Act 1985 – *continued*
s 1(1) 1.3.3.2
s 2(3) 14.4.11
Companies (Memorandum of
  Association) Act 1890
  (53 & 54 Vict c 62) 2.4.4
Company Directors
  Disqualification Act
  1986
  (c 46) 0.3.1.2, 0.3.2.2,
  1.5, 4.2.1, 4.2.2, 18.8.3.2,
  20.1.3, 20.9.10.1
s 1(1) 15.2.5.1, 15.2.5.7
s 2 15.2.5.3, 15.2.5.4,
  15.2.5.6, 20.10.1
s 2(2)(a) to (c) 15.2.5.4
s 2(3)(a) and (b) 15.2.5.5
s 3 4.2.1, 15.2.5, 15.2.5.3,
  15.2.5.4, 15.2.5.5,
  15.2.5.6
s 3(5) 20.9.10.5
s 4 15.2.5, 15.2.5.4,
  15.2.5.6
s 4(1)(a) 20.10.1
s 4(2) 15.2.5
s 4(3) 15.2.5
s 5 4.2.1, 15.2.5, 15.2.5.3,
  15.2.5.4, 15.2.5.6
s 5(5) 15.2.5.4
s 6 15.2.5.3, 15.2.5.4,
  15.2.5.5, 15.2.5.6
s 6(1)(a) 15.2.5.6
s 6(1)(b) 15.2.5.3, 15.2.5.6,
  20.2.3
s 6(2) 15.2.5.3, 15.2.5.4,
  20.2.3
s 6(3) 15.2.5.4
s 6(3)(d) 20.2.3
s 6(4) 15.2.5.5
s 7(1) 15.2.5.4, 20.2.3
s 7(2) 15.2.5.4
s 7(3) 15.2.5.4, 20.2.3
s 7(4) 20.2.3, 20.9.3
s 8 15.2.5.3, 15.2.5.4,
  15.2.5.6, 18.8.3.6
s 8(1) 15.2.5.4
s 8(4) 15.2.5.5
s 9 4.6, 9.2.1, 9.2.2, 9.2.4,
  9.3.1, 14.3.1, 15.2.5,
  15.2.5.6
s 10 15.2.5, 15.2.5.4,
  15.2.5.6, 15.4.1, 20.10.1,
  20.12
s 10(2) 15.2.5.5
s 11 15.2.5.1
s 12 15.2.5.1
s 15 15.2.5.1

Company Directors
  Disqualification Act
  1986 – *continued*
s 15(1)(a)   15.2.5.1
s 15(2)   15.2.5.2
s 15(3)(a) and (b)   15.2.5.2
s 15(4)   15.2.5.2
s 16(1)   5.2.5.4
s 16(2)   15.2.5.4
s 17(1)   15.2.5, 15.2.5.7
s 17(2)   15.2.5.7
s 18   15.2.5.9
s 22(4)   15.1.4, 15.2.5.1,
         15.2.5.3
s 22(5)   15.1.6
s 22(9)   14.7
s 25   20.1.3
Schedule 1   15.2.5.3
  para 1   15.2.5.6
  para 2   15.2.5.6
  paras 4 and 5   15.2.5.6
  para 4(a)   9.2.1
  para 4(b)   9.2.2, 9.2.4
  para 4(d)   14.3.1
  para 4(e)   14.3.1, 15.4.1
  para 4(f)   4.6
  para 5   9.3.1
  para 6   15.2.5.6
  para 7   15.2.5.6
Schedule 2   15.2.5
Company Securities (Insider
  Dealing) Act 1985 (c 8)
  0.3.1.2, 13.1, 18.8.2.6
Consumer Credit Act 1974
  (c 39)
  ss 116 to 121   11.5.1
Consumer Protection Act 1987
  (c 43) part III
  ss 20 to 26   19.8.6.2
s 39   19.8.6.2
Contempt of Court Act 1981
  (c 49)
s 10   18.8.2.6
County Courts Act 1984 (c 28)
s 38   20.2.2
Credit Unions Act 1979 (c 34)
s 3   2.3.3.3
Criminal Justice Act 1987
  (c 38)
s 2   15.2.5.3
s 2(2)   20.9.3
s 2(8)   20.9.3
Criminal Justice Act 1988
  (c 33)
s 62   20.3.2
s 62(2)   20.6.2
Criminal Justice Act 1993
  (c 36)

Criminal Justice Act 1993 –
  continued
  Part V   0.3.1.2, 13.1, 13.2.7,
         13.2.8, 18.8.2.5
s 52   13.2.1, 13.2.3
s 52(1)   13.2.4.1
s 52(2)(a)   13.4.2.4, 13.2.4.3
s 52(2)(b)   13.2.4.3
s 52(3)   13.2.4.1, 13.2.4.2
s 53(1)(a)   13.2.4.4
s 53(1)(b)   13.2.4.4
s 53(1)(c)   13.2.4.4
s 53(2)(a)   13.2.4.4
s 53(2)(b)   13.2.4.4
s 53(2)(c)   13.2.4.4
s 53(3)(a)   13.2.4.3
s 53(3)(b)   13.2.4.4
s 53(4)   13.2.4.5, 13.2.4.6
s 53(6)   13.2.4.4
s 55   13.2.4.1
s 55(1)   13.2.4.1
s 56   13.2.2
s 56(1)   13.2.2
s 56(2)   13.2.2, 13.2.4.1,
         13.2.4.4
s 56(3)   13.2.2, 13.2.4.4
s 57(1)   13.2.3
s 57(2)   13.2.3
s 58   13.2.2
s 58(1)   13.2.2
s 58(2)   13.2.2
s 58(3)   13.2.2
s 59(1)   13.2.4.1
s 59(2)   13.2.4.1
s 59(3)   13.2.4.1
s 60(1)   13.2.2
s 60(4)   13.2.2
s 61(1)   13.2.7
s 61(2)   13.2.7
s 62(1)(a)   13.2.4.1
s 62(1)(b)   13.2.4.1
s 62(1)(c)   13.2.4.1
s 62(2)(a)   13.2.4.2, 13.2.4.3
s 62(2)(b)   13.2.4.2, 13.2.4.3
s 63(2)   13.2.7
Schedule 1
  para 1   13.2.4.5
  para 2(1)   13.2.5
  para 2(2)   13.2.5
  para 3   13.2.5
  para 4   13.2.5
  para 5   13.2.4.6
Criminal Justice (Scotland) Act
  1987 (c 41)
s 52   20.6.5
Criminal Law Act 1977 (c 45)
s 32(1)   0.3.2.2
Dentists Act 1984 (c 24)
s 42   1.2.1

Deregulation and Contracting
  Out Act 1994 (c 40)
  Sch 5   20.14.2.4
Directors Liability Act 1890
  (53 & 54 Vict c 64)
  6.7.5, 7.6.6
Employment Act 1980 (c 42)
s 17   5.2.2.2
s 17(3) and (4)   5.2.2.2
European Communities Act
  1972 (c 68)
s 9(1)   19.5.5
s 9(2)   19.6.1
Factors Act 1889 (52 & 53 Vict
  c 45)
s 9   11.7.10.3
Finance Act 1963 (c 25)
s 55(1A)   8.3.3
s 59   8.6
Finance Act 1982 (c 39)
s 129   8.3.3
Finance Act 1983 (c 28)
s 46   8.3.3
Finance Act 1986 (c 41)
s 64   8.3.3
s 79   12.1
s 79(2)   12.4
s 79(5)   12.7
Part IV   8.3.6
s 87   8.3.6
s 87(6)   8.3.6
s 88A   8.3.6
s 91   8.3.6
s 92   8.3.6
Finance Act 1990 (c 29)
s 107   8.6
s 108   8.3.3
s 110   8.3.6
Schedule 19
  Part VI   12.7
Finance Act 1998 (c 36)
s 31   5.2.2.3.1
Financial Services Act 1986
  (c 60)   0.3.1.2, 1.5,
  4.2.1, 4.2.2, 6.7.6, 7.3,
  7.3.1, 7.3.5, 7.4.5.1,
  7.4.5.6, 7.4.6, 7.6.4.8,
  7.8.1, 7.8.2, 7.8.4, 7.8.5,
  9.5.2, 15.2.5, 17.4.1.7,
  18.8.2.6, 18.8.3.1, 18.8.3.2
s 3   7.3, 7.3.2, 7.3.3
s 4   7.8.5
s 7   7.8.3
s 9   13.4.5
s 15   7.3.3
s 22   7.3.3
s 23   7.3.3
s 24   7.3.3
s 25   7.3.3

Financial Services Act 1986 –
continued
s 31   7.3.3
s 31(4)   7.3.3
s 35   7.3.5
s 36(1)   7.3.5
s 37   7.3.4, 13.4.5
s 38   7.3.4
s 39   13.4.5
s 42   7.3.5
s 43   7.3.5
s 44   7.3.5
s 44(9)   6.7.6, 7.3.2, 7.7
s 45   7.3.5
s 47   6.7.6, 7.8.5
s 47(1)   6.7.6, 7.8.5
s 47(2)   7.8.5
s 47(5)   7.8.5
s 48   7.3.3, 13.4.4
s 57   7.7, 8.8.1
s 57(1)   7.8.4
s 57(2)   7.5.2.2, 7.7
s 57(3)   7.5.2.2, 7.7, 7.8.4
s 57(4)   7.8.4
s 57(5)   7.5.2.2, 7.7
s 57(9)   7.5.2.2, 7.7
s 58(1)(d)   7.7
s 58(3)   7.7
s 94   15.2.5.3
s 105   15.2.5.3
Part IV   7.4.1, 7.4.2,
      7.4.3.1
s 142(6)   7.2.3.2, 7.4.1,
      7.4.2
s 142(7A)   7.4.5.1
s 142(8)   7.4.2
s 143(1)   7.4.3.1
s 143(2)   7.4.3.1
s 143(3)   1.3.3.1, 7.4.3.1
s 144(2)(a)   7.4.5.1,
      7.4.5.2
s 144(2)(b)   7.4.5.1
s 144(2A)(a)   7.4.5.1,
      7.4.5.2
s 144(2A)(b)   7.4.5.1
s 144(3)   7.4.3.1
s 144(4)   7.4.3.1
s 144(5)   7.4.3.1
s 144(6)   7.4.3.1
s 145(1)   7.4.4
s 145(2)   7.4.4
s 145(3)   7.4.4
s 146   7.5.3, 7.6.2
s 146(1)   7.4.5.2
s 146(2)   7.4.5.2
s 146(3)   7.4.5.2
s 147   7.6.2, 7.6.5
s 147(1)   7.4.5.4
s 147(2)   7.4.5.4

Financial Services Act 1986 –
continued
s 147(3)   7.4.5.4, 7.6.5
s 148   7.6.2
s 148(1)   7.4.5.4
s 148(1)(a)   7.4.5.3
s 148(1)(b)   7.4.5.3
s 148(2)   7.4.5.3
s 148(3)   7.4.5.3
s 149(1)   7.4.5.1
s 149(3)   7.4.5.1
s 150   7.6.1
s 150(1)   7.6.2, 7.6.6
s 150(2)   7.6.2
s 150(3)   7.6.5, 7.6.6
s 150(4)   7.6.1
s 150(5)   7.6.5
s 150(6)   7.6.2
s 151   7.6.1, 7.6.4.3
s 151(1)   7.6.4.1
s 151(2)   7.6.4.2
s 151(3)   7.6.4.3
s 151(4)   7.6.4.4
s 151(5)   7.6.4.5, 7.6.5
s 151(6)   7.6.5
s 151(7)   7.6.4.2
s 152   7.6.1, 7.6.3
s 152(1)(a)   7.6.3
s 152(1)(b)   7.6.3
s 152(1)(c)   7.6.3
s 152(1)(d)   7.6.3
s 152(1)(e)   7.6.3
s 152(2)   7.6.3
s 152(3)   7.6.3
s 152(5)   7.6.3
s 152(8)   7.6.3
s 153   7.4.3.3
s 153(1)   7.4.3.3
s 153(2)   7.4.3.3
s 154(1)   7.4.6.1, 7.8.4
s 154(2)   7.4.6.1
s 154(3)   7.4.6.1, 7.8.4
s 154(4)   7.4.6.1, 7.8.4
s 154(5)   7.4.6.1
s 154A   7.4.5.2, 7.4.5.4,
      7.6.1
s 155   7.4.3.1
s 156(1)   7.4.5.1
s 156(2)   7.4.5.1
s 156(3)   7.4.2
s 156(4)   7.4.2
s 156(5)   7.4.2
s 156(6)   7.4.2
s 156A   7.5.5
s 156B   7.4.5.1
Part V   0.3.1.4
s 166(1)   7.6.6
s 166(3)   7.6.6
s 172   8.8.2

Financial Services Act 1986 –
continued
s 177   18.8.2.5, 18.8.3.2,
      18.8.3.3, 18.8.3.6,
      20.9.10.3
s 177(1)   13.2.8
s 177(3)   18.8.2.6
s 177(4)   18.8.2.6
s 177(5)   18.8.3.1
s 177(5A)   18.8.2.7
s 177(8)   18.8.2.6
s 178(1)   18.8.2.6
s 178(2)   18.8.2.6
s 178(2)(a)   18.8.2.6
s 179   18.8.3.2
s 192(1) and (2)   7.4.1
s 199   18.8.2.5
s 199(6)   18.8.2.5
s 200   7.8.2
s 200(1) and (5)   18.8.2.5
s 202   6.7.6, 7.4.6.1, 7.8.1
s 207(1)   7.3.4, 7.7, 15.1.4,
      15.1.6
s 207(2)   7.4.6.2
s 207(3)   7.4.6.2
s 207(5)   7.8.1
s 207(8)   14.7
Schedule 1
Part I   7.3
   para 1   7.3.1
   para 2   7.3.1
   para 3   7.3.1
   para 4   7.3.1
   para 5   7.3.1
   para 6   7.3.1
   para 7   7.3.1
   para 8   7.3.1
   para 9   7.3.1
   para 10   7.3.1
   para 11   7.3.1
Part II   7.3.2, 7.7
   para 12   7.3.2, 7.7
   para 14   7.3.2
   para 15   7.3.2
   para 16   7.3.2
Part III   7.7
   para 17(1)(a)   7.3.2
   para 17(3)   7.3.2
   para 21   7.3.2, 7.7
   para 25   7.3.2
   para 25A   7.3.2
   para 25B   7.3.5
Part IV   7.7
   para 28(1)(d)   7.3.2
   para 28(2)(b)   7.3.2
   paras 28(3) and (4)   7.3.2
Schedule 4   7.3.4
   para 2(2)(a)   7.3.4
   para 2(2)(b)   7.3.4, 13.5

Financial Services Act 1986 –
    continued
    Schedule 11A   7.4.5.1
    Schedule 12   8.8.2 .
Foreign Corporations Act 1991
    (c 44)   0.1.6
Friendly Societies Act 1992
    (c 40)   0.1.2.4
Geneva Convention Act 1957
    (5 & 6 Eliz 2 c 52)
    s 6   2.3.3.3
Health and Safety at Work etc.
    Act 1974 (c 37)
    s 2(1)   19.8.4
    s 3(1)   19.8.4
    s 33(1)   19.8.4
Hospitals for the Poor Act 1597
    (39 Eliz I c 5)   0.1.2.4
Housing Act 1988 (c 50)
    s 62   0.1.2.5
Income and Corporation Taxes
    Act 1988 (c 1)
    s 14   5.2.2.3.1
    s 20(1)   5.2.2.3.1
    s 160   10.7
    s 164   15.6.1.6
    s 231   5.2.2.3.1
    s 577   9.3.8
Industrial and Provident
    Societies Act 1965 (c 12)
    0.1.2.4, 2.3.3.3, 2.4.2.7
    s 14(1)   3.4.1.2
Insolvency Act 1985 (c 65)
    0.3.1.2, 20.1.3
Insolvency Act 1986 (c 45)
    0.3.1.2, 1.8, 4.2.1, 4.2.2,
    11.2.1, 11.8.3, 14.7, 15.7.2,
    18.8.3.2, 19.1, 19.13.1.3,
    20.3.1, 20.6.5
    ss 1 to 7   20.1.3, 20.3.2,
        20.3.3, 20.4.1
    s 1(1)   20.4.2
    s 1(3)   20.4.2
    s 2   20.2.7.2
    s 2(1) to (3)   20.4.2
    s 2(4)   20.2.7.2
    s 3(1)   20.4.2
    s 3(2)   20.4.2
    s 3(3)   20.4.2
    s 4(1)   20.4.3
    s 4(3) and (4)   20.4.3
    s 4(6)   20.4.3
    s 5(1) to (4)   20.4.3
    s 6   20.4.3, 21.2.3
    s 6(4)   20.4.3
    s 6(7)   20.4.3
    s 7(4)(b)   20.3.2, 20.6.2
    ss 8 to 27   0.3.2.2, 20.3.1
    s 8(1)(a)   20.3.2

Insolvency Act 1986 –
    continued
    s 8(2)   20.3.2
    s 8(3)   20.3.2, 20.4.2
    s 8(4)   30.3.2
    s 9(1)   15.7.2.2, 15.7.4.2,
        20.3.2
    s 9(2)(a)   20.3.2
    s 9(3)   20.3.2
    s 9(3)(b)(ii)   11.6.5.2
    s 10   20.3.6
    s 10(2)(b) and (c)   20.3.2
    s 10(3)   20.3.6
    s 11   20.3.6
    s 11(1)(a)   20.3.6
    s 11(1)(b)   20.3.2
    s 11(3)(b)   20.3.2
    s 12   4.5.3
    s 13   20.3.2
    s 14(1)   20.3.4, 20.6.2
    s 14(2)(a)   20.3.5
    s 14(2)(b)   20.3.4
    s 14(3)   20.3.3
    s 14(4)   20.3.5
    s 14(5)   20.3.4, 20.6.2
    s 14(6)   20.3.4
    s 15   20.3.4
    s 15(1) to (5)   20.3.4
    s 15(9)   20.3.4
    s 17(2)(b)   20.3.3
    s 18   20.3.3
    s 19(3) to (10)   20.3.4
    s 22   20.3.7.1
    s 23(1)   20.3.3
    s 23(2) and (3)   20.3.3
    s 24(1) and (2)   20.3.3
    s 24(4)   20.3.3
    s 24(5)   20.3.3
    s 25   20.3.3
    s 25(1)(b)   20.3.3
    s 26   20.3.3
    s 26(2)   20.3.3
    s 27   20.3.3
    s 29(1)(b)   20.2.2
    s 29(2)   11.6.2, 20.2.2
    s 32   20.2.2
    s 35(1)   20.2.2
    s 39   4.5.3
    s 40   11.6.4, 20.2.8.1, 20.2.9
    s 40(3)   20.2.9
    s 42(1)   20.2.4, 20.6.2
    s 42(2)   20.6.2
    s 42(3)   20.2.4
    s 43   20.2.8.1, 20.3.4
    s 43(1)   20.2.8.1
    s 43(3)   20.2.8.1
    s 43(5)   20.2.8.1
    s 43(6)   20.2.8.1
    s 44(1)   20.6.2

Insolvency Act 1986 –
    continued
    s 44(1)(a)   20.2.5
    s 44(1)(b)   20.2.7.2, 20.2.7.3
    s 44(1)(c)   20.2.7.2, 20.2.7.3
    s 44(2A)   20.2.7.2
    s 44(2B) to (2D)   20.2.7.2
    s 46(3)   20.9.6
    s 47   20.2.6.1.1, 20.3.7.1,
        20.9.6
    s 47(2)   20.2.6.1
    s 47(4) to (6)   20.2.6.1.1
    s 48   20.2.6.2
    s 48(1)   20.2.6.2
    s 48(2)   20.2.6.2, 20.2.6.3
    s 48(3)   20.2.6.3
    s 48(3)(b)   20.2.6.3
    s 48(4)   20.2.6.2, 20.2.6.3
    s 48(5) and (6)   20.2.6.2
    s 49   20.2.6.3
    s 49(2)   20.2.6.3
    s 74   5.2.2.1, 6.7.5, 10.1
    s 74(1)   1.3.2
    s 74(2)(d)   1.3.2, 1.3.2.1,
        10.1
    s 74(2)(f)   3.4.4, 8.10,
        20.13.1
    s 74(3)   1.3.2, 1.3.2.2
    s 76   10.3.5
    s 79(2)   20.10.4, 20.12
    s 80   3.4.1.2
    s 84(1)   15.7.5, 20.5.2
    s 84(1)(a)   14.4.11, 20.5.2
    s 84(1)(b)   14.4.8.3
    s 84(1)(c)   14.4.8.3, 20.5.2
    s 84(3)   14.4.11
    s 86   20.8
    s 89   20.5.3
    s 89(1)   15.1.3, 20.5.3
    s 89(2)(a) and (b)   20.5.3
    s 89(3)   20.5.3
    s 89(4) to (6)   20.5.3
    s 90   20.5.3, 20.5.5
    s 90(2)   20.5.4
    s 91(1)   20.5.4
    s 94(3)   20.14.2.5
    s 94(4)   20.14.2.5
    s 94(5)   20.14.2.58
    s 99   20.9.6
    s 100   20.5.5
    s 101   20.5.6
    s 103   20.5.6
    s 104   20.4.7
    s 106(3)   20.14.2.5
    s 106(4)   20.14.2.5
    s 106(5)   20.14.2.5
    s 107   20.13.1
    s 109   4.3
    s 110   20.5.6

Insolvency Act 1986 –
continued
s 110(2)   14.4.8.3, 15.7.5
s 110(3)   14.4.8.3, 15.7.5
s 110(4)   14.4.8.3, 15.7.5
s 111(2)   3.4.2.1
s 111(3)   14.4.8.3, 15.7.5
s 112   18.4.2, 20.13.2
s 112(1)   20.9.8
s 113(3)   15.7.2
s 114   20.5.4
s 114(3)   20.5.4
s 115   20.13.1
s 117(1)   0.3.2.2, 2.3.4
s 117(2)   0.3.2.2
s 117(4)   0.3.2.2
s 122   0.3.2.2
s 122(1)   11.6.2, 18.8.3.3,
      20.6.3
s 122(1)(a)   14.4.8.3, 15.7.5
s 122(1)(b)   1.3.3.1, 6.6.1
s 122(1)(f)   20.6.3
s 122(1)(g)   1.3.5, 2.3.5.4,
      15.7.5, 18.7, 18.7.1,
      18.8.3.3
s 123   11.6.5.1, 20.3.2
s 123(1)   20.6.3
s 123(1)(a)   0.3.2.5, 20.6.3
s 123(1)(b)   20.6.3
s 123(1)(c)   20.6.3
s 123(1)(d)   20.6.3
s 123(2)   20.6.3
s 124   20.6.1
s 124(1)   3.4.2.1, 15.7.2.2,
      15.7.4.2, 20.6.1, 20.6.2
s 124(4)   20.6.2
s 124(4)(b)   18.8.3.3
s 124(5)   20.6.2
s 124A   18.8.3.3
s 124A(1)   18.8.3.3
s 124A(2)   18.8.3.3
s 125(1)   20.6.1
s 125(2)   18.7.1
s 127   20.7.3
s 128(1)   11.6.2
s 129(1)   20.6.1, 20.8
s 129(2)   20.6.1, 20.8
s 131   20.9.6
s 132(1) and (2)   20.9.5
s 133   20.9.8
s 133(1) and (2)   20.9.8
s 133(4)   20.9.8
s 135   3.5.1
s 136(1) and (2)   20.6.4
s 136(5)   20.6.5
s 136(5)(a) and (b)   20.6.5
s 136(5)(c)   20.6.5
s 136(6)   20.6.5
s 137   20.6.5, 20.8.4

Insolvency Act 1986 –
continued
s 137(3)   20.6.5, 20.6.6
s 137(4) and (5)   20.6.6
s 139(2) and (3)   20.6.5
s 139(4)   20.6.5
s 140   20.6.4
s 140(1)   20.6.6
s 140(2)   20.6.4
s 141(1) and (2)   20.6.6
s 141(4)   20.6.6
s 143   20.8.5
s 143(1)   20.6.7, 20.13.1
s 144(1)   20.6.7
s 146   20.14.2.7
s 148(1)   20.13.1
s 149(3)   20.13.1
s 154   20.13.1
s 160(2)   20.6.6
s 163   20.4.4
s 165(2)(a)   14.4.8.3, 15.7.5
s 165(2)(b)   20.5.6
s 165(3)   18.4.2
s 165(6)   20.5.6
s 166   20.5.5
s 167(1)(a)   18.4.2, 20.1,
      20.6.6, 20.6.7
s 167(1)(b)   20.6.7
s 167(2)   20.6.6
s 167(3)   18.4.2
s 172(1)   20.6.4
s 172(2)   20.6.4
s 172(3)   20.6.4
s 172(8)   20.14.2.7
s 175   20.13.1
s 175(2)(a)   20.13.1
s 175(2)(b)   11.6.2, 20.2.9,
      20.11.1
ss 178 to 182   20.10.14
s 178(6)   20.13.1
s 187   20.13.3
s 187(1)   20.13.3
s 187(4)   20.13.3
s 188   4.5.3
s 189   20.13.1, 20.13.2
s 189(1) and (2)   20.13.2
s 189(3)   20.13.1
s 201(2) and (3)   20.14.2.5
s 201(4)   20.14.2.5
s 202   20.14.2.6
s 202(1)   20.6.5
s 202(2)   20.6.5, 20.14.2.6
s 202(3) and (4)   20.6.5,
      20.14.2.6
s 202(5)   20.14.2.6
s 203   20.14.2.6
s 205(1)   20.14.2.7
s 205(2)   20.14.2.7
s 205(3) and (4)   20.14.2.7

Insolvency Act 1986 –
continued
s 205(6)   20.14.2.7
s 205(7)   20.14.2.7
s 207(1)   15.1.3
s 208(1)(a) to (c)   20.9.1
s 208(3)   20.9.1
s 208(4)(a)   20.9.1
s 210   20.9.6
s 210(4)   20.9.6
s 212   15.8, 20.5.4, 20.11.1
s 212(1)   20.11.1
s 212(2)   20.11.1
s 213   5.2.2.2, 15.2.5.3,
      20.9.10.3, 20.10.1,
      20.10.2, 20.10.4, 20.13.1
s 213(2)   20.10.4
s 214   1.3.2.5, 5.2.2.2,
      15.2.5.3, 16.4.6.2,
      20.9.10.3, 20.12,
      20.13.1
s 214(1)   20.12
s 214(2)(a)   20.12
s 214(3)   20.12
s 214(4)   16.2.1.2
s 214(4) and (5)   20.12
s 214(6) and (7)   20.12
s 215(2)   20.10.4, 20.12
s 215(4)   20.10.4, 20.12,
      20.13.1
s 216   2.3.3.8
s 216(1), (2), (3), (4), (5), (6)
      and (7)   2.3.3.8
s 217   1.3.2.5, 2.3.3.8
s 217(1)(a)   2.3.3.8
s 217(1)(b)   2.3.3.8
s 217(2)   2.3.3.8
s 217(3)(a)   2.3.3.8
s 217(3)(b)   2.3.3.8
s 217(5)   2.3.3.8
s 218(1) to (6)   20.9.7
s 219(2) to (4)   20.9.7
s 230(3)   20.6.4
s 230(5)   20.6.4
s 234(1)   20.2.6.4, 20.2.8.4,
      20.2.8.5, 20.3.7.4,
      20.9.1, 20.9.2
s 234(1)(d)   20.9.1, 20.9.3
s 234(2)   20.2.6.4, 20.2.8.4,
      20.3.7.4, 20.9.2
s 234(3) and (4)   20.2.8.5
s 235   20.2.6.4, 20.3.7.2,
      20.9.1
s 235(1)   20.9.1
s 235(3) and (4)   20.9.1
s 235(5)   20.2.6.4, 20.9.1
s 236   20.2.6.4, 20.2.8.4,
      20.3.7.3, 20.9.3
s 236(1)   20.9.3, 20.9.5

Insolvency Act 1986 –
  continued
  s 236(2)   20.9.3
  s 236(3)   20.9.3
  s 236(5)   20.9.3
  s 237   20.2.8.4
  s 237(4)   20.9.3
  ss 238 to 240   19.5, 20.3.2
  s 238   10.1.1
  s 238(1)(a)   11.6.5.2
  s 238(1)(b)   11.6.5.1
  s 245   11.6.5.1, 11.6.5.2,
    20.3.2, 20.10.1
  s 245(1)   11.6.5.1, 11.6.5.2
  s 245(4)   11.6.5.1
  s 245(6)   11.6.5.1
  s 246   20.3.7.4, 20.9.3,
    20.9.4
  s 247(2)   20.8
  s 248   11.2.1
  s 249   11.6.5.1
  s 251   11.7.10.3, 14.7,
    15.1.4, 15.1.6
  s 306   8.5
  s 386   20.2.9, 20.13.1
  s 387   20.13.1
  s 387(2)   20.4.3
  s 388(1)(a)   20.6.4
  s 388(5)   20.6.4
  s 389   20.6.4
  s 411   20.1.3
  s 413   20.1.3
  s 433   20.2.6.1.2, 20.9.3
  s 435   11.6.5.1
  s 435(4)   11.6.5.1
  s 443   20.1.3
  Schedule 1   20.2.4, 20.3.4
    para 5   18.4.2
    para 21   20.6.2
  Schedule 4
    paras 1 to 3   20.5.6
    para 4   18.4.2
  Schedule 6   20.2.9, 20.13.1
  Schedule 10   2.3.3.8, 4.5.3,
    20.2.6.1.1, 20.2.6.4,
    20.5.3, 20.9.1, 20.9.6,
    20.14.2.5, 20.14.2.7
Insolvency Act 1994 (c 7)
  20.2.7.2
  s 1(4)   20.3.4
Insurance Companies Act 1982
  (c 50)   9.3.8.1, 9.5.2,
  18.8.3.2
Interpretation Act 1978 (c 30)
  s 5   0.1.9
  s 23(1)   3.3.5
  Schedule 1   0.1.9
  Schedule 2
    para 4(1)   0.1.9

Interpretation Act 1978 –
  continued
  para 4(5)   0.1.9
  para 5(a)   2.3.4
Joint Stock Banking Companies
  Act 1857 (20 & 21 Vict
  (c 49)   0.2.1.3, 1.2.2
Joint Stock Banks Act 1844
  (7 & 8 Vict c. 113)   1.2.3
Joint Stock Companies Act
  1844 (7 & 8 Vict c 110)
  0.1.2.4, 0.1.7, 0.3.1.2,
  1.2.3, 1.3.2.5, 2.2, 3.2,
  19.1
  s 7   3.4.1.2
  s 35   9.3.8
Joint Stock Companies Act
  1856 (19 & 20 Vict c 47)
  0.1.2.4, 0.3.1.2, 1.2.3,
  1.3.2.5, 1.3.3.2, 1.6, 2.2,
  2.4.1, 3.2, 3.4.1.2, 9.3.8
  s 2   1.2.3
  s 19   8.7. 1
  s 27   2.5
  s 110   1.2.3
  Table B   3.2.1
Joint Stock Companies Act
  1857 (20 & 21 Vict c 14)
  ss 25 to 27   1.2.3
Judgments Act 1838 (1 & 2
  Vict c 110)
  s 17   20.13.2
Land Charges Act 1972 (c 61)
  11.3
  s 2(1)   11.7.10
  s 2(4)(iii)   11.7.10
  s 3(7)   11.7.10
  s 3(8)   11.7.11
Land Registration Act 1925
  (15 & 16 Geo 5 c 20)
  11.3
Landlord and Tenant Act 1954
  (2 & 3 Eliz 2 c 56)   5.2.1
  s 30(1)(g)   19.8.6.1
Larceny Act 1861 (24 & 25
  Vict c 96)   7.8.3
Law of Property Act 1925
  (15 & 16 Geo 5 c 20)
  11.2.1
  s 52(1)   19.2.3
  s 53(1)(c)   19.2.3
  s 61   0.1.9, 19.8.4
  s 73   15.7.1.3
  s 74   19.2.5
  s 74(1)   19.2.5
  s 74(2)   19.2.4
  s 85(1)   11.4.1
  s 86(1)   11.4.1
  s 91(2)   11.5.5

Law of Property Act 1925 –
  continued
  s 101   11.5.1, 11.5.4, 11.6.1,
    20.2.2
  s 101(3)   11.5.2
  s 103   11.5.2
  s 105   11.5.1
  s 109(1)   11.5.4
  s 109(2)   11.5.4
  s 205(1)(xvi)   11.2.1
  s 205(1)(xxi)   19.2.5
Law of Property (Miscellaneous
  Provisions) Act 1989
  (c 34)
  s 1   19.2.5
  s 1(1)(b)   19.2.5
  s 1(2)   19.2.5
  s 1(3)   19.2.5
Legal Aid Act 1988 (c 34)
  s 2(10)   19.9
Limitation Act 1980 (c 58)
  10.5.1
  s 5   3.4.2.9, 3.4.4
  s 8   3.4.2.9, 6.4.2
Limited Liability Act 1855
  (18 & 19 Vict c 133)
  1.3.2.5
Limited Partnerships Act 1907
  (7 Edw 7 c 24)   2.3.3.4,
  2.3.6
  s 4(2)   0.1.4
  s 5   0.1.4
  s 6(1)   0.1.4
  s 15   0.1.4
Litigants in Person (Costs and
  Expenses) Act 1975 (c 47)
  19.9
Lloyds Bank Act 1981 (c viii)
  20.14.2.1
  s 12(2)   20.14.2.1
Lotteries and Amusements Act
  1976 (c 32)
  s 2   1.2.1
Magistrates' Courts Act 1980
  (c 43)
  s 87A   20.3.2
Mercantile Law Amendment
  Act 1856 (19 & 20 Vict
  c 97)
  s 3   11.2.1
Merchant Shipping Act 1894
  (57 & 58 Vict c 60)
  s 31   11.3
  s 502   19.8.1
  s 503   19.8.1
Merchant Shipping Act 1988
  (c 21)
  s 3   19.8.4
  s 14   6.1.15

Merchant Shipping Act 1995
(c 21)
s 100   19.8.4
Schedule 1
para 7   11.3
Misrepresentation Act 1967
(c 7)   6.7.5, 7.6.1
s 1   4.4.1
s 2(2)   6.7.1
National Heritage Act 1983
(c 47)
s 32   0.1.2.3
Schedule 3
para 1   0.1.2.3
Parliamentary Corporate Bodies
Act 1992 (c 27)
s 1(1) and (2)   0.1.2.1
Partnership Act 1890 (53 & 54
Vict c 39)
s 1   0.1.4
s 1(1)   5.2.2.8
s 1(2)   0.1.4
s 4(1)   0.1.4
s 4(2)   0.1.7, 5.3.1
s 5   0.1.4, 15.1.1
s 9   0.1.4
Patents Act 1977 (c 37)
s 32   11.3
Pluralities Act 1838 (1 & 2 Vict
c 106)
s 29   15.2.5.10
s 30   15.2.5.8
Police and Criminal Evidence
Act 1984 (c 60)
s 67(9)   18.8.2.6
s 76   18.8.2.6
s 76(2)   18.8.2.6
s 78   18.8.2.6, 20.9.3
Powers of Criminal Courts Act
1973 (c 62)
s 35   13.5
Public Trustee Act 1906 (6 Edw
7 c 55)
s 1(2)   0.1.2.1
Registered Designs Act 1949
(12, 13 & 14 Geo 6 c 88)
s 19   11.3
Rent Act 1977 (c 42)   5.2.2.4

Restrictive Trade Practices Act
1976 (c 34)
s 35(3) and (4)   19.8.6.1
Rivers (Prevention of Pollution)
Act 1951 (14 & 15 Geo 6
c 64)
s 2   19.8.4
Sale of Goods Act 1979 (c 54)
s 19(1)   11.7.10.3
s 25   11.7.10.3
s 61   11.7.10.3
Sexual Offences Act 1956
(4 & 5 Eliz 2 c 69)
s 1(1)   19.8.4
Sexual Offences (Amendment)
Act 1976 (c 82)
s 4   19.8.4
Stamp Act 1891 (54 & 55 Vict
c 39)
s 1   8.5
s 17   8.3.3
Schedule 1   8.6
Statute of Frauds 1677 (29 Cha
2 c 3)
s 4   11.2.1
Statutory Water Companies Act
1991 (c 58)
s 11(2)   1.6
Stock Transfer Act 1963
(c 18)   3.3.2
s 1(1)   8.3.1
s 1(4)(a)   8.3.1
s 2(1)   8.3.1
Schedule 1   8.3.1
Sunday Observance Act 1677
(29 Cha 2 c 7)   19.8.8
Supply of Goods and Services
Act 1982 (c 29)
s 13   16.2.1.1
s 15   15.6.1.5
s 16(1)   15.6.1.5
Supreme Court Act 1981 (c 54)
s 37(1)   20.2.2
s 49(1)   11.4.1
Schedule 1
para 1   0.3.2.2

Taxes Management Act 1970
(c 9)
s 79   5.2.2.3
Theft Act 1968 (c 60)
s 1(1)   19.8.5
s 2(1)(b)   19.8.5
s 15   6.7.6
s 15(2)   6.7.6
s 15(4)   6.7.6
s 18   6.7.6
Trade Descriptions Act 1968
(c 29)
s 11   19.8.6.2
s 24(1)   19.8.6.2
Trade Marks Act 1938 (1 & 2
Geo 6 c 22)
s 4(3)   5.2.2.5
Trade Marks Act 1994 (c 26)
s 25   11.3
Trade Union Act 1871 (34 & 35
Vict c 31)   0.1.6
Trade Union Act 1913 (2 & 3
Geo 5 c 30)   0.1.6
Trade Union and Labour
Relations (Consolidation)
Act 1992 (c 52)
s 10   0.1.6, 5.3.1
s 10(3)   1.2.1, 20.14.2.2
Trading with the Enemy Act
1939 (2 & 3 Geo 6 c 89)
s 2(1)   19.8.2
Video Recordings Act 1984
(c 39)
s 11   19.8.4
s 11(2)(b)   19.8.4
Wales and Berwick Act 1746
(20 Geo 2 c 42)
s 3   2.3.4
Water Resources Act 1991
(c 57)
s. 85   19.8.4
Welsh Language Act 1967
(c 66)
s 4   2.3.4
Welsh Language Act 1993
(c 38)
s 30(6)   4.2.1

Table of Statutory Instruments

1922 no 184   0.4
1972 no 1268   11.3
  art 2(2)   11.7.11
  art 4(1)   11.7.11
1974 no 1214   8.3.1
1979 no 277   8.3.1, 8.3.5
1981 no 1685   2.3.3.5,
  2.3.3.7
1982 no 1653   2.3.3.5
1982 no 1771   16.2.1.1
1983 no 713
  art 9   0.3.2.2
  Schedule 3   0.3.2.2
1985 no 437   20.13.2
1985 no 622   8.9.5
1985 no 724
  reg 2(3)(a)   4.4
  reg 3   4.4
  reg 3(1)   13.6.3
  reg 3(2)(c)   13.6.3
  reg 3(4)   4.6
  reg 5(3)   4.6
  Schedule 1   13.6.3
1985 no 802
  reg 2(a)   13.6.4
  reg 3(1)(a)   13.6.4
  reg 3(1)(b)   13.6.4
1985 no 805   2.3.2, 2.3.5.3,
  2.4.2.5, 3.2
  Table A   3.4.4, 6.1.14, 7.9.3,
    14.4.5.8, 14.4.9.1.4,
    15.3.2, 16.6.7
  art 1   14.4.5.3
  art 2   6.1.3, 6.2.5
  art 3   10.3.2
  art 4   7.9.2
  art 5   8.7.1, 14.4.9.1.6
  art 6   8.2.1, 8.3.5
  art 7   8.2.2
  arts 8 to 22   6.4.2
  art 8   3.2
  art 12   6.4.4
  art 16   6.4.3
  art 21   6.4.2
  art 23   8.3.1
  art 24   8.3.4, 8.5
  art 27   8.3.4, 8.3.5

1985 no 805 – *continued*
  art 30   5.2.1, 8.5
  art 31   8.5, 14.4.5.2,
    14.4.9.1.5
  art 32   6.1.13
  art 34   6.4.2, 10.2.5
  art 35   10.3.1, 10.3.5,
    10.6.1, 10.6.5
  art 36   14.4.3
  art 37   14.4.3, 14.4.5.1,
    15.5.1
  art 38   14.4.5.3, 14.4.5.4,
    14.4.5.5, 14.4.9.1.5,
    15.2.3.2
  art 39   14.4.5.2
  art 40   14.4.6.1
  art 41   14.4.6.1, 14.4.10
  art 42   14.4.7, 15.5.2
  art 43   14.4.7, 14.4.9.1.1
  art 45   14.4.10
  art 46   14.4.9.2
  art 47   14.4.9.2
  art 48   14.4.9.2
  art 49   14.4.9.2
  art 50   14.4.9.2, 14.4.9.5,
    15.5.2
  art 51   14.4.9.2, 14.4.10,
    18.4.4, 18.5.1
  art 52   14.4.9.2
  art 53   14.5.1
  art 54   6.1.3, 14.4.9.2
  art 57   14.4.9.1.2
  art 58   14.4.9.1.1
  art 59   14.4.9.1.3,
    14.4.9.2,
    14.4.9.2.2
  art 60   14.4.9.1.3
  art 61   14.4.9.1.3
  art 62   14.4.9.1.3,
    14.4.9.2, 14.4.10
  art 63   14.4.9.1.3,
    14.4.9.2
  art 64   15.1.3, 15.2.1,
    15.2.2
  art 65   15.2.7
  art 67   15.2.7
  art 69   15.2.7

1985 no 805 – *continued*
  art 70   10.2, 3.4.3.1,
    6.2.5, 15.1.1, 15.7.1,
    15.7.2.1, 15.7.2.2,
    15.7.2.3, 15.7.2.4,
    15.7.3, 15.7.4, 15.7.4.1,
    15.7.4.2, 15.7.5, 18.2.2,
    18.4.1, 19.1, 19.5.6
  art 71   19.5.4.2
  art 72   15.1.3, 15.2.2.1,
    15.5.3, 15.5.4, 15.5.5,
    19.5.4.2, 19.5.6
  art 73   15.2.2, 15.2.3.2,
    15.3.2
  art 74   15.3.2
  art 75   15.2.3.2, 15.2.3.3,
    15.2.4, 15.3.6, 15.7.2.3
  art 76   15.2.3.2, 15.2.3.3
  art 77   15.2.3.2, 14.4.5.5
  art 78   15.2.1, 15.2.2,
    15.2.3.2, 15.2.4, 15.3.2,
    15.3.3, 15.7.4
  art 79   15.2.1, 15.2.2,
    15.2.3.3, 15.2.4, 15.3.2,
    15.3.3, 15.7.4
  art 80   15.2.2, 15.2.3.2,
    15.7.2.3
  art 81   15.3.1
  art 82   14.5.1, 15.6.1.2,
    15.7.2.3
  art 83   15.6.1.3
  art 84   15.3.2, 15.3.3,
    15.5.3, 15.5.4, 15.6.1.4,
    15.6.1.5, 15.7.4, 16.6.5
  art 85   16.5.4, 16.6.2,
    16.6.4, 16.7.4
  art 86   16.6.2
  art 86(a)   16.5.4, 16.6.2,
    16.6.5
  art 86(b)   16.6.2
  art 86A   15.7.3
  art 87   15.7.3
  art 88   15.5.1, 15.5.2
  art 89   15.5.1, 16.6.3
  art 90   14.4.4, 15.1.3,
    15.2.3.3, 15.5.1

1985 no 805 – *continued*
   art 91   14.4.7, 15.5.2,
     15.7.4
   art 92   15.2.6, 15.3.2
   art 93   15.5.1, 16.6.3
   art 94   14.5.1, 16.5.4,
     16.6.3, 16.6.4
   art 95   15.5.1, 16.6.3
   art 96   15.7.4, 16.6.4
   art 97   15.7.4
   art 99   17.3.1
   art 100   15.5.1
   art 100(a)   15.5.2, 15.5.3
   art 100(b)   15.5.5
   art 101   15.7.1, 15.7.3,
     15.7.4, 19.2.2
   art 102   6.1.3, 10.5.1,
     14.4.1, 14.4.2.1
   art 104   6.1.3
   art 105   10.5.1
   art 110   10.4
   art 110(d)   10.4
   arts 111 to 113   14.4.5.4
   art 112   14.4.5.3
   art 114   14.4.5.8
   art 116   14.4.5.2
   art 117   14.4.8.3, 20.1.2
   art 118   16.9.1
   Table B   2.3.2, 2.3.5.6
   Table C   3.2
   Table F   2.3.2, 2.3.5.6
1985 no 806   8.3.5
1985 no 854   6.6.1, 10.3.5,
     10.8.7, 11.9.3
   reg 4(1)   4.2.1
   reg 4(2)   4.2.1, 11.7.4
   Schedule 3   4.2.1
   Schedule 4 Part I   14.2.1
   Schedule 4 Part II   4.2.1
1985 no 1052   3.2
1986 no 1924
   art 2   20.1.3
   art 3   20.1.3
1986 no 1925   4.2.1, 20.1.3
   r 1.6   20.4.2
   r 1.24(4)   20.4.3
   r 2.12(6)   20.3.71
   r 2.13   5.4.2.2, 20.3.7.1
   r 2.16(d)   20.3.71
   r 2.22(4)   20.3.3
   r 2.24   20.3.3
   r 2.28(1)   20.3.3
   r 3.5   5.4.2.2, 20.2.6.1.2
   r 3.8(3) and(4)   20.2.6.1.2
   r 4.33(6)   20.9.6
   r 4.35   20.9.6
   r 4.38(4)   20.5.6
   r 4.61(4)   20.13.1
   r 4.62(4)   20.5.6

1986 no 1925 – *continued*
   r 4.91   20.13.2
   r 4.127   20.5.6, 20.6.6
   r 4.155   20.5.6, 20.6.6
   r 4.168   20.5.6, 20.6.6
   r 4.170   20.5.6, 20.6.6
   r 4.179   20.13.1
   r 4.181   20.13.1
   r 4.183   20.5.6, 20.6.6
   r 7.34(2)   20.5.6, 20.6.6
   r 9.4(5)   20.9.3
   r 9.4(6)   20.9.3
   r 9.4(7)   20.9.3
   r 9.5   20.9.3
   r 9.5(4)   20.9.3
   r 12.8(2)   20.5.6, 20.6.6
1986 no 1994
   reg 9(2)   20.6.6
   reg 27(2)   20.5.6
1986 no 2067   15.2.5.7
1987 no 516   8.3.3
1987 no 752   8.8.2.4
   reg 4   8.8.2.3
   reg 5   4.2.1
1987 no 925   7.3, 13.4.5
1987 no 942   7.3
1987 no 2023   15.2.5.4
1988 no 738   7.3
1988 no 1359
   reg 2   4.2.1
1989 no 339   19.9
1989 no 638   0.1.2.4
   Schedule 4   2.3.3.4
1990 no 18   8.3.1
1990 no 98   0.3.1.2
1990 no 142   0.3.1.2
1990 no 354   0.3.1.2
1990 no 355   0.3.1.2
1990 no 572
   reg 3   4.2.1
   reg 5   9.4.1
1990 no 713   0.3.1.2
1990 no 1392   0.3.1.2
1990 no 1393   16.6.7, 16.6.8.3,
     16.6.8.4
1990 no 1667   9.3.8
1990 no 1707   0.3.1.2
1990 no 1766
   reg 3(1)   4.2.1
   reg 4   4.2.1
   reg 5   4.6
   Schedule   3.4.6
1990 no 2569   0.3.1.2
1990 no 2570   9.9
1991 no 13   9.9
1991 no 488   0.3.1.2
1991 no 878   0.3.1.2
1991 no 879
   reg 2   4.2.1

1991 no 1206   0.1.2.4, 1.2.1,
     2.4.2, 4.2.2, 4.6
1991 no 1259
   reg 3   4.2.1
1991 no 1452   0.3.1.2
1991 no 1566   17.4.2.3
1991 no 1646
   reg 3   8.9.7
   reg 4(a)   8.9.7
   reg 5(a)   8.9.7
   reg 8(a)   8.9.7
1991 no 1996   0.3.1.2
1991 no 1998
   reg 3(2)(a)   4.4
   reg 3(2)(b)   4.4
   reg 3(3)   4.4
   reg 4   4.4.1
   reg 5   4.4
   Schedule 2
     para 1   4.4
     paras 2 and 3   4.4
1991 no 2000
   reg 3(1)(b)   7.4.1
   reg 3(1)(d)   7.4.2
1991 no 2173   0.3.1.2
1991 no 2705   0.3.1.4, 9.3.7.1
   reg 3   9.3.7.1
   Schedule 2
     para 4   9.3.8.1
   Schedule 9 Part II   9.3.8
1991 no 2945   0.3.1.2
1992 no 1196   2.3.3.5, 2.3.3.7
1992 no 1315
   art 2(1)(b)   7.3.3
1992 no 1699   0.1.1, 0.1.2.4,
     1.2.1, 1.3.2.5, 1.3.2.6,
     1.3.3.2, 5.2.2.1, 5.2.2.2,
     14.3.1, 14.4.6. 1.14.4.11,
     19.5.9, 20.6.3
   reg 2   14.4.6.2
1992 no 2452   0.3.1.4
   reg 3   9.3.1
   reg 4(3)   17.4.5
   reg 5(3)   9.5.2
   reg 5(4)   9.5.2
   reg 6(3)   9.6.5
   reg 6(4)   9.6.5
1992 no 3003   0.3.1.4
1992 no 3006
   reg 4(1)   4.2.1
1992 no 3178   0.3.1.4
   reg 3   9.7.2
   reg 5   9.3.7.1
   reg 7   9.3.7.1
1992 no 3179
   Schedule 2
     para 13   9.7.2
1993 no 1819   0.3.1.4, 8.9.2
   reg 8   8.9.2

1993 no 1820   0.3.1.4, 9.1,
        9.6.7, 9.11
  reg 2(1)   9.11
  reg 3(1)   9.11
  reg 4   9.11
  reg 5   9.11
  reg 5(2)   9.11
  reg 7   9.11
  reg 7(3)   9.11
  reg 9(1)   9.4.2
  reg 9(2)   9.4.2, 9.11
  reg 10   9.4.2
  reg 11   9.6.7
1993 no 2689   0.3.1.4, 8.9.2
1993 no 3246   0.3.1.4, 9.3.7.1
  reg 3(2)   9.3.7.1
  Schedule 1   9.3.7.1
  reg 6   9.3.8.1
  Schedule 2, para 2   9.4.2
1994 no 117
  reg 4   9.4.1
  reg 5   4.2.1
1994 no 187   13.2.2, 13.2.4.1
1994 no 188   13.2.6
  reg 3(1)   13.2.6
  reg 3(2)   13.2.6
1994 no 233   0.3.1.4
1994 no 242   13.1
1994 no 1935   0.3.1.4, 9.3.4
  Schedule 1
     para 1(2)   9.8
     para 1(3)   9.8
1994 no 2217   0.1.2.4, 1.2.1
1994 no 2879   0.3.1.4
1995 no 589   0.3.1.4
1995 no 734   4.2.1
  reg 4   4.2.1
1995 no 736   1.3.3.2
  reg 3   4.2.1
  reg 5   4.2.1
1995 no 1352   0.3.1.2
1995 no 1536   8.8.1
  art 5   7.7
  art 8   7.7
  Schedule 4   7.7
1995 no 1537   7.4.5.1, 7.5.1
  reg 4   7.5.1
  reg 5   7.4.5.1, 7.5.2
  reg 6   7.4.5.1, 7.5.2
  reg 7   7.4.5.1
  reg 7(2)   7.5.2
  reg 7(2)(a)   7.5.2
  reg 7(2)(b)   7.5.2
  reg 7(2)(c)   7.5.2
  reg 7(2)(d)   7.5.2
  reg 7(2)(f)   7.5.2
  reg 7(2)(h)   7.5.2
  reg 7(2)(i)   7.5.2
  reg 7(2)(j)   7.5.2

1995 no 1537 – *continued*
  reg 7(2)(k)   7.5.2
  reg 7(2)(l)   7.5.2
  reg 7(2)(m)   7.5.2
  reg 7(2)(u)   7.5.2
  reg 7(6)   7.5.2
  reg 7(8)   7.5.2
  reg 7(9)   7.5.2
  reg 7(10)   7.5.2
  reg 7(11)   7.5.2
  reg 8   7.5.4
  reg 8(1)   7.5.3
  reg 8(2)   7.5.3
  reg 8(3)   7.5.3
  reg 9   7.5.3, 7.5.4, 7.6.2
  reg 9(3)   7.5.3
  reg 10   7.5.4, 7.6.2, 7.6.5
  reg 10(4)   7.6.5
  reg 12   7.5.1
  reg 11   7.5.4
  reg 11(1)   7.5.3
  reg 11(2)   7.5.3
  reg 13   7.6.3
  reg 13(1)(a)   7.6.3
  reg 13(1)(b)   7.6.3
  reg 13(1)(c)   7.6.3
  reg 13(1)(d)   7.6.3
  reg 13(1)(e)   7.6.3
  reg 13(1)(f)   7.6.3
  reg 13(1)(g)   7.6.3
  reg 13(2)   7.6.3
  reg 13(3)   7.6.3
  reg 13(4)   7.6.3
  reg 14(1)   7.6.2, 7.6.6
  reg 14(2)   7.6.2
  reg 14(3)   7.6.5, 7.6.6
  reg 14(4)   7.6.1
  reg 14(5)   7.6.6
  reg 15(1)   7.6.4.1
  reg 15(2)   7.6.4.2
  reg 15(3)   7.6.4.3
  reg 15(4)   7.6.4.4
  reg 15(5)   7.6.4.5, 7.6.5
  reg 15(6)   7.6.5
  reg 15(7)   7.6.4.2
  Schedule 1   7.5.3, 7.6.2
1995 no 1479
  reg 2   4.2.1
1995 no 1480   4.2.1
  reg 2   4.2.1
1995 no 1508   4.2.1
  reg 2   4.2.1
1995 no 1591   0.3.1.2
1995 no 2092   9.3.6.4
  reg 3   9.3.6.4
  reg 4   9.3.6.4
  reg 4(4)   9.3.6.4
  reg 4(4)(a)   9.3.6.4
  reg 4(4)(b)   9.3.6.4

1995 no 2092 – *continued*
  reg 5   9.3.6.4
  reg 6   9.3.6.4
  reg 7(2)   9.3.6.4
  reg 7(3)   9.3.6.4
  reg 7(4)   9.3.6.4
1995 no 3022   2.3.3.5, 2.3.3.7
1995 no 3272
  reg 15   8.2.1
  reg 16   8.2.1
  reg 16(6)   8.2.1
  reg 19(1)   14.3.1
  reg 20(1)   14.3.3
  reg 30   8.4
  reg 30(4)(a)   8.4
  reg 32(2)   6.2.9, 8.2.1, 8.3.1,
        8.3.5
  reg 34(1)   14.4.5.8
  reg 34(2)   14.4.5.8
  reg 34(3)   14.4.5.8
  reg 34(4)   14.4.5.8
  reg 35   8.8.2.3
  reg 40(2)   8.3.1
  reg 40(3)   14.4.11
1996 no 189   0.3.1.4, 9.3.2
  reg 14(4)   9.7.1
  reg 14(5)   9.7.1
  Schedule 1
     para 5   6.2.8
  Schedule 3   9.6.7
1996 no 1105   4.6
1996 no 1444   2.4.2, 4.2.2, 4.6
1996 no 1471
  art 2   14.4.8.4
  art 3   14.5.3
  art 4   14.5.3
1996 no 1560   0.3.1.4
1996 no 1561   13.2.2
1996 no 1571   8.3.1
1996 no 1586
  art 3(1)   7.7
  art 6   7.7
  art 7   7.7
  art 11   7.7
1996 no 2827   0.1.2.4
1996 no 3080   0.3.1.4
1997 no 220   0.3.1.4
  reg 2   9.3.7.4
  reg 2(1)   9.5.3, 9.7.1, 9.7.2,
        9.7.3, 9.7.4, 9.7.9, 10.5.1
  reg 3   9.5.3
  reg 4   9.5.2
  reg 5   9.5.3
  reg 6   9.3.7.34
  Schedule 1   9.3.7.4
1997 no 570   0.3.1.4, 15.6.3.1
  reg 6.1   9.6.7
1997 no 571   0.3.1.4, 9.7.1,
        9.7.10

1997 no 936   0.3.1.4, 9.3.4
1997 no 2704   0.3.1.4
1998 no 1747   0.3.1.2

Rules of Court
County Court Rules 1981
  ord 31
    r 2(3)   8.7.2
  ord 32   20.2.2

Rules of the Supreme Court
    1965
  ord 5
    r 6(3)   19.9
  ord 10
    r 1(7)   2.3.4
  ord 12
    r 1(2)   19.9
  ord 15
    r 12A   18.4.7

Rules of the Supreme Court
    1965 – *continued*
    r 12A(3)   18.4.7
    r 12A(12)   18.4.7
    r 12A(13)   18.4.7
  ord 50
    r 5   8.7.2
    r 12   8.7.2
    r 15   8.7.3
  ord 53
    r 4(1)   1.2.1

Table of References to Listing Rules

References are to the September 1997 edition as amended up to July 1998.

para. 1.19   13.2.6
para. 3.3(a)   17.6.1
para. 3.6   17.6.1
para. 3.8   16.2.1.1
para. 3.9   16.5.4
para. 3.15   8.3.5
para. 3.23   6.2.4
para. 4.12   7.4.3.2
para. 4.13   7.4.3.2
para. 4.30(a)   7.4.3.2
ch. 5   7.4.5.2
para. 5.1(a)   7.4.5.1
para. 5.1(b)   7.4.5.1
para. 5.1(c)   7.4.5.1
para. 5.12   7.4.5.1
para. 5.18   7.4.5.3
para. 5.23   7.4.5.1
para. 5.23A(a)   7.4.5.1
para. 5.23A(b)   7.4.5.1
para. 5.23A(c)   7.4.5.1
para. 5.27   7.4.5.1
ch. 6   7.4.5.2
para. 6.B.15(h) and (i)   7.9.6
para. 6.C.16   8.9.4
para. 6.C.21   17.6.3.2
para. 8.1   7.4.5.1
para. 8.4   7.4.5.1
para. 8.7   7.4.6.1
para. 8.10   7.4.6.1
para. 8.11   7.4.6.1
para. 8.23   7.4.6.1
para. 8.24   7.4.6.1
ch. 9   7.2.3.2, 7.4.3.3
para. 9.1   13.2.6
para. 9.2   13.2.6
para. 9.10(a)   13.2.6
para. 9.11   8.9.4, 13.2.6
para. 9.12   8.9.4, 13.2.6
para. 9.29   14.4.5.2
para. 10.4   15.7.6

para. 10.5   15.7.6
para. 10.37   15.7.6
para. 10.39   15.7.6
para. 12.42(e)   9.3.5
para. 12.43   9.7.1
para. 12.43(b)   9.7.2
para. 12.43(d)   9.7.4
para. 12.43(i)   15.1.7
para. 12.43(j)   15.1.2
para. 12.43(k)   9.7.4
para. 12.43(l)   8.9.4
para. 12.43(x)   15.6.3.1
para. 12.43A   15.1.2
para. 12.43A(c)   15.6.3.1
para. 12.45   9.3.6.4
paras 12.46 to 12.59   9.10
para. 12.48   9.10
para. 12.49   9.10
para. 12.50   9.10
para. 12.52   9.10
para. 12.54   9.10
para. 12.56(a)   9.10
para. 12.56(b)   9.10
para. 12.56(c)   9.10
para. 12.56(d)   9.10
para. 13.13   10.7
para. 13.20(e)   8.2.1
para. 13.28(a)   14.4.9.1.3
para. 13.28(b)   14.4.9.1.3
para. 13.28(c)   14.4.9.1.3
ch. 13, app. 1   3.3.4
ch. 13, app. 1, para. 5   8.3.5
ch. 13, app. 1, para. 10   8.2.2, 8.3.5
ch. 13, app. 1, para. 19   14.4.5.2
ch. 13, app. 1, para. 20   16.6.3
ch. 13, app. 1, para. 21   15.2.3.3
ch. 13, app. 1, para. 22   15.2.3.2

para. 14.1   14.4.5.5
para. 14.17   14.4.5.5
ch. 15   10.6.1
para. 15.9   10.6.4
para. 16.9   15.6.4
para. 16.13   13.2.6
para. 16.18   13.3
ch. 16, app.   13.3
ch. 16, app., para. 2   13.3
ch. 16, app., para. 3   13.3
ch. 16, app., para. 6   13.3
ch. 16, app., para. 8   13.3
Rules for approval of
  prospectuses where no
  application for listing is
  made   7.5.5
Combined Code 15.1.2
  para. A.1.4 17.3.1
  para. A.2 15.5.3
  para. A.2.1 15.5.3
  para. A.3 15.1.7
  para. A.3.1 15.1.7
  para. A.3.2 15.1.7
  para. A.5 15.2.3.2
  para. A.5.1 15.2.3.2, 15.5.5
  para. A.6 15.2.3.2, 15.3.2
  para. A.6.2 15.2.3.2
  para. B.1.7 15.3.2, 15.6.4
  para. B.2 15.6.1.4
  para. B.2.1 15.5.5,
    15.6.1.4
  para. B.2.2 15.5.5,
    15.6.1.4
  para. B.2.3 15.6.1.4
  para. B.2.4 15.6.1.4
  para. B.2.5 15.6.1.4
  para. B.3 15.6.1.4
  para. D.3.1 15.5.5, 17.4.7
  para. D.3.2 15.5.5, 17.4.7
  para. E.1 15.1.2
  para. E.2 15.1.2
Charges for listing   7.4.3

Table of References to the Treaty Establishing the European Community

The number in square brackets is the number the article will have after the Treaty of Amsterdam comes into force.

art 52 [43] 0.3.3.1
art 53 [repealed] 0.3.3.1
art 54 [44] 0.3.3.1
art 54(3)(g) [44(2)(g)] 0.3.3.1,
 0.3.3.3

art 58 [48] 0.3.3.1
art 85(1) [81(1)] 5.2.2.9
art 169 [226] 0.3.3.1

art 171 [228] 0.3.3.1
art 189 [249] 0.3.3.1
art 221 [294] 6.1.15

Table of European Directives

68/151/EEC First Company
    Law Directive 19.5.5
    art 3, para 4 4.3
    art 7 19.6.1
    art 9(2) 19.5.3.4
    art 11, para 1 20.14.2.2
    art 11, para 2 20.14.2.2
    art 12, paras 2 and 3
    20.14.2.2
77/91/EEC Second Company
    Law Directive 0.3.3.1,
    1.3.3, 6.1.16
78/660/EEC Fourth Company
    Law Directive 1.3.3,
    9.3.7.1, 10.5.4
    art 2(2) 9.3.8
    art 3, para 4 4.3
    art 7 19.6.1
    art 11 9.5.1, 9.5.2
    art 27 9.5.1, 9.5.2
    art 31, para 1 9.3.7.3
    art 31, para 12 9.3.7.3
    art 31, para 13 9.3.7.3
    art 31, para 14 9.3.7.3
    art 53(2) 9.5.2

79/279/EEC Admissions
    Directive 7.4.1, 7.4.3.1
    art 5 7.4.2
    art 9 7.4.1
80/390/EEC Listing Particulars
    Directive 7.4.1, 7.4.5.1
    art 3 7.4.5.1
    art 5, para 1 7.4.2
    art 6 7.4.5.1
    art 6(1) 7.4.5.1
    art 7 7.4.5.3
    art 18 7.4.1
    art 18(2) 7.4.5.1
82/121/EEC Interim Reports
    Directive 7.4.1, 7.4.3.1,
    9.10
    art 3 7.4.2, 9.10
    art 9 7.4.1, 9.10
84/253/EEC Eighth Company
    Law Directive 17.4.1,
    17.4.2.1
86/635/EEC Bank Accounts
    Directive 9.3.7.1
88/627/EEC 8.9.2

89/298/EEC 7.4.5.1, 7.5.1
    art 4 7.4.5.1
    art 6 7.4.5.1
    art 7 7.4.5.1
    art 8 7.5.5
    art 11(2) 7.5.3
    art 12 7.5.5
89/592/EEC 13.1
89/666/EEC 11th Company
    Law Directive 9.7.2
89/667/EEC 12th Company
    Law Directive 1.3.2.5,
    1.3.3.2
    art 3 14.3.1
    art 4 14.4.11, 14.5.4
    art 5 19.5.9
90/605/EEC 9.1, 9.11
91/674/EEC 9.3.7.1
94/8/EC 9.5.2

Introduction

In a modern capitalist economy, companies are a familiar part of everyday life. Companies own the supermarkets from which people buy their food; companies supply the water, gas, electricity and petroleum products we depend on; companies publish the newspapers we read. We deal with companies so often as purchasers and users of their products and services that the image which the word 'company' brings to mind is usually of an organisation concerned with marketing and collecting payment for products which the company has made (or bought in) or services it has provided. It is necessary to go behind this image to get to the company which is the subject of company law.

The company with which lawyers are concerned is the legal entity which owns the business which the organisation has been created to carry on and which employs the people who work in that organisation. The remarkable thing about this entity is that it is created by process of law and exists only by virtue of the law.

The legal concept that underlies company law is the idea of a corporation — an entity established by process of law in order to be a nominal, artificial party to legal relationships. (In the USA, the subject of this book would be called 'corporation law'. In Canada, and recently in Australia, too, 'corporation' has replaced 'company', but in the British Isles and in European Community documents in English, the term 'company' is always used.) This introduction to the book begins with a short discussion of the nature of corporations in general, and limited companies as a particular type of corporation, and then considers the sources of English company law.

0.1 INCORPORATION

0.1.1 The nature of incorporation and legal personality

The companies with which this book is concerned are called 'registered companies' because they are brought into existence by registration of documents (of which the most important is called a 'memorandum of association') with a public official (a registrar of companies). The most important legal characteristic of a registered company is that it is 'incorporated' and so has what is known as 'legal personality'. The Companies Act (CA) 1985, s. 1(1), provides: 'Any two or more persons associated for a lawful purpose may, by subscribing their names to a memorandum of association and otherwise complying with the requirements of this Act in respect of registration, form an incorporated company' and s. 1(3A) (inserted by SI 1992 No. 1699) provides that one person may, by subscribing a memorandum of association and otherwise complying with the Act, incorporate a private limited company for a lawful purpose (the distinction between private and public companies and between limited and unlimited companies will be explained fully in 1.3). By s. 13(1): 'On the registration of a company's memorandum, the registrar of companies shall give a certificate that the company is incorporated'.

The law is concerned with relationships, such as contracts, ownership of property and duties of care, which are entered into by 'persons', who have the duties and rights attached to the relationships they enter into. The types of relationship studied in law are based on the transactions and activities of human beings, who are described as 'natural' or 'real' persons. But legal principles are concerned with the nature of a legal relationship, such as contract or the ownership of property, and can be applied not only when a human being enters into the relationship but also when any other entity does. So the law can recognise that entities other than human beings can enter into at least some legal relationships. For the purposes of the relationships in which their participation is recognised, entities other than human beings are said to have 'legal' personality (sometimes called 'juristic' or 'juridical' personality).

'Incorporation' is a legal process by which an artificial entity (or *'persona ficta'* or *'persona iuridica'*) is created with legal personality. The legal capacity of an incorporated entity (or 'corporation' or 'body corporate') is described as 'full' legal capacity because it is limited only by two factors:

(a)   The fact that the entity is not human. For example, a corporation cannot marry, or drive a lorry (*Richmond London Borough Council* v *Pinn & Wheeler Ltd* [1989] RTR 354).

(b)   Any limitation imposed by the process of incorporation. Following recent reforms only charitable companies suffer any limitations on capacity by being incorporated as registered companies (see 19.4).

English common law recognises two basic types of corporation: the corporation aggregate and the corporation sole. However, very little of the law relating to corporations aggregate is applicable to common law corporations sole, and when CA 1985 refers to a 'corporation' or a 'body corporate' it does not refer to a corporation sole (s. 740). A registered company is said by s. 13(3) of CA 1985 to be a body corporate and so, by s. 740, must be a corporation aggregate. The characteristic feature of a corporation aggregate is that it is regarded as an incorporated association of persons (natural or legal) who are called the 'members' or 'corporators' of the corporation. (In nearly all registered companies, the members are shareholders and so the terms 'member' and 'shareholder' are virtually synonymous.) The idea of a registered company as an association is why subsections (1) and (3A) of CA 1985, s. 1, require the subscription of a 'memorandum of association' and s. 13(3) provides that: 'From the date of incorporation mentioned in the certificate [given by the registrar under s. 13(1)], the subscribers of the memorandum, together with such other persons as may from time to time become members of the company, shall be a body corporate'.

Probably the most important legal feature of a body corporate is its dual nature as both an association of its members and a person separate from its members.

Artificial entities with full legal personality are very useful (as is shown by the fact that at the end of March 1997 there were 1,091,900 registered companies in Great Britain):

(a)   Where legal relationships have to be entered into for a particular purpose those relationships can be ascribed to a separate legal person so as not to be confused with other affairs. For example, where business is conducted in the name of a registered company, the affairs of the business are kept separate from the personal affairs of the human beings who conduct it, and separate from the affairs of any other business they may conduct in the name of another registered company.

(b)   An artificial entity may continue in existence indefinitely.

(c)   Not only does an entity with full legal personality have all the legal rights, obligations, duties and liabilities arising from the legal relationships it is put into, but no other person shares any of those rights, obligations, duties or liabilities unless the entity is found to be acting as agent for some other person (*J.H. Rayner (Mincing Lane) Ltd* v *Department of Trade & Industry* [1990] 2 AC 418 per Lord Templeman at pp. 479–80, Lord Oliver of Aylmerton at p. 511). Furthermore, the facts that the members of a corporation exercise control over it, or that the sole objective of the corporation's legal relationships is to benefit the members, are not in themselves sufficient to constitute the corporation an agent of its members (*Salomon* v *A. Salomon & Co. Ltd* [1897] AC 22; *J.H. Rayner (Mincing Lane) Ltd* v *Department of Trade & Industry* [1989] Ch 72, CA, at pp. 188–9; [1990] 2 AC 418, HL, at p. 515). This is the principle of 'separate personality'. As Alderson B said in *Bligh* v *Brent* (1837) 2 Y & C Ex 268: 'The individual members of a corporation are quite as distinct from the metaphysical body called "the corporation", as any others of his Majesty's subjects are'. This principle confers on the members of a corporation the benefit of not being responsible for the corporation's debts except to the extent that they are made responsible by statute or by the corporation's constitution. Lord Parker of Waddington summarised the law as follows in *Daimler Co. Ltd* v *Continental Tyre & Rubber Co. (Great Britain) Ltd* [1916] 2 AC 307 at p. 338:

> No one can question that a corporation is a legal person distinct from its corporators; that the relation of a shareholder to a company . . . is not in itself the relation of principal and agent or the reverse; that the assets of the company belong to it and the acts of its servants and agents are its acts, while its shareholders, as such, have no property in the assets and no personal liability for those acts.

It follows that the members of a corporation cannot owe any duty of care in respect of the corporation's acts, that is, they cannot be liable in tort for the corporation's acts (*Kuwait Asia Bank EC* v *National Mutual Life Nominees Ltd* [1991] 1 AC 187).

0.1.2   Types of corporation

In the law of England and Wales, a corporation aggregate may be:

(a)   Incorporated by the Crown by the grant of a royal charter.

(b)   Incorporated by Parliament by passing an Act.

(c)   Incorporated by registration with a public official who has authority to incorporate delegated by Parliament.

(d)   Incorporated by act of a person exercising authority delegated by Parliament.

(e)   Found to be incorporated by prescription.

(In his report of *The Case of Sutton's Hospital* (1612) 10 Co Rep 1, Sir Edward Coke said, at f. 29b, that lawful authority of incorporation might be by four means: by the common law (i.e., as a corporation sole), by authority of Parliament, by the King's charter, and by prescription. See also per Littledale J in *Conservators of the River Tone* v *Ash* (1829) 10 B & C 349 at pp. 383–4.)

0.1.2.1   *Corporations sole*

English common law adopted a theory that certain public and ecclesiastical offices (such as the Crown, a bishop or a parson of the Church of England) had a separate legal personality, originally to provide a legal framework for the ownership of church land. As only one person could hold such an office at any one time, the incorporated offices are known as corporations 'sole'. Occasionally, Parliament creates a corporation sole; for example, the public trustee (Public Trustee Act 1906, s. 1(2)) and the Corporate Officer of the House of Lords and the Corporate Officer of the House of Commons (Parliamentary Corporate Bodies Act 1992, ss. 1(1) and 2(1)). Scots law does not recognise corporations sole.

0.1.2.2 Royal charter

The English theory of corporations was developed in relation to the powers of self-government possessed by certain communities (known as municipal corporations) which were stated in royal charters. The legal theory of the corporation developed slowly, and explicit statements in charters that they were creating corporations did not occur until after the legal theory had gained acceptance, which seems to have been after about 1440. See M. Weinbaum, *The Incorporation of Boroughs* (Manchester: Manchester UP, 1937).

From the 16th century onwards royal charters were granted to trading companies, especially for the purposes of overseas trading, exploration and colonisation. See C.T. Carr, *Select Charters of Trading Companies 1530–1707* (Selden Society, vol. 28) (London, 1913); M. Schmitthoff, 'The origin of the joint-stock company' (1939) 3 UTLJ 74. In the 17th and 18th centuries, and in the early 19th century, many domestic trading companies were incorporated by royal charter. Such companies are known as 'chartered companies'. The characteristic structure of the later chartered companies was that the members contributed capital to form the company's 'joint stock' which was then managed by 'governors' or 'directors' appointed by the members. They have been extensively studied by W.R. Scott, *The Constitution and Finance of English, Scottish and Irish Joint-Stock Companies to 1720* (Cambridge: CUP, 1910–12) and Armand DuBois, *The English Business Company after the Bubble Act 1720–1800* (New York: The Commonwealth Fund; London: Oxford University Press, 1938).

Since the mid 19th century, with a few exceptions, corporations have been created by the Crown only for non-profit-making, charitable and educational purposes, for example, the Law Society, the Institute of Chartered Accountants in England and Wales, the Chartered Institute of Management Accountants.

0.1.2.3 Act of Parliament

Parliament may create a body corporate by an enactment referring specifically to that body. Corporations established for public purposes (e.g., the Historic Buildings and Monuments Commission for England incorporated by the National Heritage Act 1983, s. 32 and sch. 3, para. 1) are incorporated by public general Act. Parliament may be petitioned to pass a private Act to establish a corporation for the petitioners' commercial purposes, especially where powers are required to compulsorily purchase land for public utilities: corporations formed in this way are called 'statutory companies'.

0.1.2.4 Registration with a public official

The main problem with incorporation by royal charter or by private Act of Parliament is that the Crown and Parliament have been suspicious of lending their dignity and the benefits of separate personality to commercial organisations and have therefore imposed procedural and cost deterrents. In the early 19th century, legal advisers of business people were well aware that incorporation is a convenient method of conducting the affairs of a business but were usually unable to obtain a charter or an Act of Parliament. Most joint-stock companies had therefore to be organised as unincorporated associations. This was often very inconvenient. Without separate personality a joint-stock company could not own property, make contracts or be a party to legal proceedings: everything had to be done in the joint names of the shareholders of whom there might be several thousand. Legal proceedings, in particular, could collapse under the weight of paper, as in *Van Sandau* v *Moore* (1826) 1 Russ 441, in which there were 250 defendants. Parliament did become willing to allow selected unincorporated joint-stock companies to overcome the difficulties of taking part in legal proceedings. In the early part of the 19th century it became quite common for the members of an unincorporated joint-stock company to obtain a private Act of Parliament entitling the secretary or a director of their company to take part in legal proceedings on behalf of the company. However, Parliament would pass such an Act only for an established company, and it required, as a condition, that the company had to file a list of its members in the Court of Chancery and keep the list up to date. A company which made public disclosure of its list of members in this way was known in the early 19th century as a 'public company' (see *Macintyre* v *Connell* (1851) 1 Sim NS 225). For the use of the term 'public company' in this old sense, see 4.6. In company law, the term is nowadays used in the sense discussed in 1.3.3.

Eventually Parliament conceded that it had been unnecessarily difficult and inconvenient for business people to obtain the benefits of incorporation. It passed the Joint Stock Companies Act 1844 which established the office of the Registrar of Joint Stock Companies and empowered the registrar to incorporate any company whose documents were duly registered with him. Under the 1844 Act, registration was a two-stage process: provisional registration (costing £5), which did not confer corporate status (*Womersley* v *Merritt* (1867) LR 4 Eq 695), followed by complete registration (a further £5) which did. The whole system was revised by the Joint Stock Companies Act 1856, which introduced the present system of single-stage registration (which now costs £20: SI 1991 No. 1206; SI 1994 No. 2217). The present statute governing registration of companies is CA 1985.

Incorporation by registration is in fact an old idea: a statute of 1597, 39 Eliz 1, c. 5 (Hospitals for the Poor), enabled individuals to incorporate hospitals by registration of a deed in the Court of Chancery. At present there are, essentially, seven provisions under which incorporation may be achieved by registering documents with a public official or body. They are (in alphabetical order) the Building Societies Act 1986, the Charities Act 1993, the Companies Act 1985, the European Economic Interest Grouping Regulations 1989 (SI 1989 No. 638), the Friendly Societies Act 1992, the Industrial and Provident Societies Act 1965, and the Open-Ended Investment Companies (Investment Companies with Variable Capital) Regulations 1996 (SI 1996 No. 2827). Of these, CA 1985 is by far the most important. The other provisions apply only to limited classes of association but, by s. 1(1) of CA 1985, 'Any two or more persons associated for a lawful purpose may . . . form an incorporated company' by registration under the Act and s. 1(3A) (inserted by SI 1992 No. 1699) provides that one person may incorporate a private limited company for a lawful purpose by registration under the Act.

0.1.2.5 *Incorporation by ministerial act*

The Housing Act 1988, s. 62, is an example of a statutory provision enabling incorporation by ministerial act. It empowers the Secretary of State to create bodies corporate called housing action trusts by order made by statutory instrument. However, a draft of the order must be approved by a resolution of each House of Parliament.

Ministers have powers to create corporations only insofar as they have been given such powers by Parliament.

0.1.2.6   Prescription

The essence of the doctrine of incorporation by prescription is that a body may be found by a court to be incorporated by a royal charter that has been lost if, for a sufficiently long time, it has been treated as though it were incorporated. Claims to incorporation by prescription have been quite common, particularly among municipal corporations, but have rarely been litigated. See *Re Company or Fraternity of Free Fishermen of Faversham* (1887) 36 ChD 329.

0.1.3   Dissolution

The existence of a corporation is ended by the dissolution of the corporation. Just as a corporation may only be brought into existence in manner recognised by law so it may only be dissolved by a recognised process.

Before a company is dissolved it is often necessary to wind it up — that is, to end all the legal relationships it has entered into, satisfy (or attempt to satisfy) its creditors, and distribute any surplus assets to its members.

0.1.4   Partnership

Persons (natural or legal) carrying on a business or profession in common with a view of profit, without being incorporated, are said to be in 'partnership' (Partnership Act 1890, s. 1) and their association is known as a partnership 'firm' (s. 4(1)). The law of partnership in Britain has been codified in the Partnership Act 1890. The members of a corporation aggregate are not in partnership (s. 1(2)).

Partnership is created by agreement between the partners without any action by the State. But it is not the agreement alone which creates a partnership. It is carrying on business in a particular way which creates a partnership, and a partnership comes into existence only when the partners begin to carry on business in accordance with their agreement (*Khan* v *Miah* [1998] 1 WLR 477). This may be contrasted with a registered company, which comes into existence as soon as it is registered, regardless of whether it transacts any business.

The fundamental difference between carrying on business in partnership and being a member of an incorporated company is that being a member of a partnership imposes liability for all debts and obligations of the firm incurred during membership (Partnership Act 1890, s. 9) regardless of any agreement to the contrary between the partners, whereas a member of a body corporate is not liable for the debts of the corporation unless liability is imposed on members by the constitution of the corporation or by statute. As Cave J said in *Re Sheffield & South Yorkshire Permanent Building Society* (1889) 22 QBD 470, DC, at p. 476:

> [Counsel] argued that persons who unite together for trading or making profits in any way are, at common law, liable for all debts which are incurred during the time they are members of the association, and that, if the association has ultimately to be wound up, past members must pay their shares of the debts. As a general rule — apart from legislation — that is perfectly true with respect to partners, and with respect to associations in the nature of partnership where there is no incorporation, but with respect to corporations the case is entirely different where the legislature has not thought fit to intervene, or where the charter under which the body is incorporated does not provide otherwise. A corporation is a legal persona just as much as an individual; and, if a man trusts a corporation, he trusts that legal persona, and must look to its assets for payment:

he can only call upon the individual members to contribute in case the Act or charter has so provided.

Linked to this is the further important difference that every partner in a firm may act for the purposes of the firm's business, and the acts of any one member of a partnership bind all the partners (Partnership Act 1890, s. 5); whereas in an incorporated company a board of directors must be appointed to act for the company in matters of business and no member of the company has, as a member, any authority to bind the company (see 15.1.1).

The general rule of partnership is that there is no limit on a partner's liability for his firm's debts and obligations. It is possible, however, under the Limited Partnerships Act 1907 to form a limited partnership consisting of one or more persons called 'general partners', who are liable for all debts and obligations of the firm, and one or more persons called 'limited partners', who contribute capital to the firm on entering into the partnership but are not liable to pay anything more to meet its debts and obligations (s. 4(2)). A limited partner does not have power to bind the firm (s. 6(1)). A limited partnership must be registered with the registrar of companies, otherwise the limited partner will be deemed to be a general partner with unlimited liability (ss. 5 and 15). The limited partnership form has not been popular: only 5,478 were registered at 31 March 1997. As limited partners do not take part in the management of the firm and, at one time, could not have their names included in the firm name (so as to avoid suggesting they would be liable for the firm's debts), they are sometimes called 'anonymous' partners. The idea survives in some European languages in which a public company whose members have limited liability is called an 'anonymous company' (for example, société anonyme in French, sociedad anónima in Spanish).

Sometimes partnership firms are described as 'companies'. Often the name of a firm consists of the name of one or more principal or founding partners followed by the words 'and Company' to represent the other partners.

0.1.5 Unincorporated associations

The term 'unincorporated association' is usually used to refer to any association of persons (natural or legal) which has not been incorporated but which is not a partnership firm (because the members of the association are not carrying on a business or profession in common with a view of profit).

0.1.6 Quasi-corporations

An entity may have one or more characteristics of a corporation without being incorporated, and may then be called a 'quasi-corporation'. For example, an unincorporated body of persons may, for some purposes at least, be regarded as an entity separate from its members. See, for example, *Amalgamated Society of Railway Servants* v *Osborne* [1910] AC 87, in which Lord Atkinson, at p. 102, described trade unions registered under the Trade Union Act 1871 as 'quasi-corporations, resembling much more closely railway companies incorporated by statute than voluntary associations of individuals merely bound together by contract or agreement, express or implied'. Accordingly, although it is lawful for persons to associate together to collect and administer a fund for political purposes, a registered trade union could not have such a fund because this was not one of the purposes for which Parliament permitted a trade union to be registered. Subsequently, by the Trade Union Act 1913, Parliament declared that trade unions could have any lawful objectives. See also *Commissioners of Inland Revenue* v *Bew Estates Ltd* [1956] Ch 407, in which it was held that a body, established by statute, called the War Damage Commission was a 'public office', in the sense in which that term was in the past used in income tax legislation.

An unincorporated entity may have the capacity to sue and be sued in its own name (*Taff Vale Railway Co.* v *Amalgamated Society of Railway Servants* [1901] AC 426, which concerned a trade union registered under the Trade Unions Act 1871; *Knight & Searle* v *Dove* [1964] 2 QB 631, which concerned an institution called the London Trustee Savings Bank). The Trade Union and Labour Relations (Consolidation) Act 1992, s. 10, now provides that any trade union may sue and be sued in its own name but shall not be, or be treated as if it were, a body corporate.

The fact that an entity has one attribute of corporations does not necessarily mean it has others. For example, though the London Trustee Savings Bank could be sued in its own name, it was not a person separate from its members for the simple reason that it had no members. (Whether or not the War Damage Commission, as a person separate from its members, could sue or be sued in its own name was not an issue in *Commissioners of Inland Revenue* v *Bew Estates Ltd.*) Under the Trade Union and Labour Relations (Consolidation) Act 1992, although a trade union can sue in its own name, it cannot sue for libel because it does not have sufficient personality to be libelled (*Electrical, Electronic, Telecommunication & Plumbing Union* v *Times Newspapers Ltd* [1980] QB 585) whereas a registered company does (*Metropolitan Saloon Omnibus Co. Ltd* v *Hawkins* (1859) 4 H & N 87; *South Hetton Coal Co. Ltd* v *North-Eastern News Association Ltd* [1894] 1 QB 133, CA). Accordingly, the term 'quasi-corporation' does not have a fixed meaning. In *Metropolitan Saloon Omnibus Co. Ltd* v *Hawkins,* registered companies were called 'quasi-corporations' to distinguish them from chartered corporations when it was argued that a registered company could not sue one of its own members whereas a chartered corporation could. The court held that a registered company can sue one of its own members.

See further, K.W. Wedderburn, 'Corporate personality and social policy: the problem of the quasi-corporation' (1965) 28 MLR 62 (which suggested that the courts were finding attributes of corporate personality too readily and that the matter should be clarified by legislation).

By the comity of nations, a court in one jurisdiction recognises the status of an entity established under another jurisdiction (*Dreyfus* v *Commissioners of Inland Revenue* (1929) 14 TC 560, in which it was held that the separate personality of a French *société en nom collectif* had to be recognised in England so that its income could not be said to have been earned by its *associés* as partners and so liable to be taxed as such; *Chaff & Hay Acquisition Committee* v *J.A. Hemphill & Sons Pty Ltd* (1947) 64 CLR 375, in which the unincorporated committee was held liable to be sued in its own name because it had the characteristics of a legal entity distinct from the individual committee members). An entity which has legal personality in a foreign legal system but which could not have any personality in English law is nevertheless entitled to sue in an English court if there is no conflict with English public policy (*Bumper Development Corporation* v *Commissioner of Police of the Metropolis* [1991] 1 WLR 1362, in which a Hindu temple situated in Tamil Nadu which could sue in the courts of that State was held to have standing to sue in England).

In *Lazard Brothers & Co.* v *Midland Bank Ltd* [1933] AC 289, Lord Wright said, at p. 297:

> English courts have long since recognised as juristic persons, corporations established by foreign law in virtue of the fact of their creation and continuance under and by that law.

When CA 1985 refers to a 'corporation' or 'body corporate' it includes a company incorporated elsewhere than in Great Britain (s. 740). Whether or not an entity has legal personality under foreign law for any purpose must be determined by reference to that foreign law, which is a question of fact which must be proved by evidence (*Bumper Development Corporation* v *Commissioner of Police of the Metropolis*). The question may be considered in a UK court even if the applicable foreign law is that of a State which is not recognised by Her Majesty's government (Foreign Corporations Act 1991).

Full legal personality is accorded to an international organisation if it has been given the legal capacities of a body corporate by Act of Parliament or order in council (*J.H. Rayner (Mincing Lane) Ltd* v *Department of Trade & Industry* [1990] 2 AC 418, HL) or by a foreign legal system (*Arab Monetary Fund* v *Hashim (No. 3)* [1991] 2 AC 114). English law does not, however, recognise that international law can create legal personality (*J.H. Rayner (Mincing Lane) Ltd* v *Department of Trade & Industry* per Lord Oliver of Aylmerton at p. 510; *Arab Monetary Fund* v *Hashim (No. 3)* per Lord Templeman at p. 165).

0.1.7 The concession theory

The theory of English law, as set out in 0.1.2, is that (ignoring corporations sole) an entity can be incorporated with separate personality in England and Wales only by or on the authority of the Crown or Parliament. A group of people associated to pursue a business cannot effectively declare their association to have separate personality. The principle that corporations with separate personality can be created only by act of State is known as the 'concession theory'. It is true that, in contrast to the great reluctance of Crown or Parliament to grant the privileges of incorporation before 1844 (see 0.1.2.4), the system of registration introduced by the Joint Stock Companies Act 1844 and now governed by CA 1985 offers virtually automatic incorporation. It has been said that UK companies 'are formed by contract . . . under memorandum and articles of association to which the Registrar of Joint-Stock Companies necessarily assents if the documents are regular in form' (per Sir Walter Phillimore in *Canada National Fire Insurance Co.* v *Hutchings* [1918] AC 451, PC, at p. 456). Nevertheless, the issue of the registrar's certificate of incorporation is an essential step in the incorporation of a registered company, and the ease with which it can be obtained does not negate the concession theory. The registrar may refuse to register a company formed for an unlawful purpose, see 1.2.1. As Lord Templeman said in *Arab Monetary Fund* v *Hashim (No. 3)* [1991] 2 AC 114 at p. 160:

> When the promoters of a company enter into an agreement to incorporate a company and the agreement takes the form of a memorandum and articles of association of the company, that agreement does not create a corporation. When the memorandum and articles are registered under the Companies Act 1985, that registration does not recognise a corporation but creates a corporation.

Different legal systems may confer full legal personality on different entities. For example, in Scots law, unlike the law of England and Wales, a partnership firm has legal personality (Partnership Act 1890, s. 4(2)), that is, its personality arises by virtue of the private contract between the partners and not by any act of State. (Though every partner in a partnership is directly responsible for the firm's debts in both English and Scots law.) In Hindu law, a family idol has legal personality (*Pramatha Nath Mullick* v *Pradyumna Kumar Mullick* (1925) LR 52 Ind App 245, PC; see P. W. Duff, 'The personality of an idol' (1927) 3 CLJ 42). In *Bumper Development Corporation* v *Commissioner of Police of the Metropolis* [1991] 1 WLR 1362, expert evidence was accepted that a Hindu temple has legal personality in Tamil Nadu. For a proposal that natural environmental features should be given legal personality so that they can bring proceedings to prevent, or obtain compensation for, damage, see C.D. Stone, 'Should trees have standing? — Toward legal rights for natural objects' (1972) 45 S Cal L Rev 450 and ' "Should trees have standing?" revisited: how far will law and morals reach? A pluralist perspective' (1985) 59 S Cal L Rev 1.

Within a legal system, entities may be regarded as having partial legal personality, in the sense that they may be regarded as having a capacity to enter into some but not all legal relationships. For example, English rules of court procedure permit an English partnership firm to be a party to legal proceedings, and CA 1989, s. 26(2), empowers a company to appoint an English partnership firm as its auditor.

There has been a great deal of political debate about the concession theory. In various countries at various times, there have been fears that it may be used by governments as a means of curbing freedom to associate for political purposes. In Britain, the deliberate withholding of corporate personality from trade unions so that it would be difficult if not impossible to sue them for damage caused by industrial action has been a serious political and legal issue for most of the 20th century. In the USA, controversy over the concession theory of incorporation is associated with controversy over State regulation of business activity.

0.1.8   Sole proprietorship

An individual who carries on a business or profession personally without partners is said to be the 'sole proprietor' of the business or profession. A professional person is usually described as a 'sole practitioner' whereas a sole proprietor of a business is usually described as a 'sole trader'.

In sole proprietorship there is no legal separation between the business and personal affairs of the proprietor, and he or she is directly responsible for all the debts incurred in carrying on the business or profession

0.1.9   A note on terminology

The use in this book of the terms 'natural person' and 'legal person' corresponds to the way they are used in European Community documents, and is the way in which 'legal person' was used when it was introduced into the language by the University of London's first professor of jurisprudence, John Austin (1790–1859). In French, what is here called a legal person is usually called a '*personne morale*', the adjective '*morale*' indicating that it is not a physical person but the product of human thought. In the past, this was sometimes rather inappropriately translated into English as 'moral person', but this usage seems to have died out and 'moral person' is nowadays used to refer to a person capable of moral responsibility and accountability — whether a corporation can be a moral person in this sense is an interesting philosophical and legal question: see the discussion of corporate criminal liability in 19.8.

Some writers on jurisprudence adopt a more abstract analysis. They describe any entity that has legal rights and duties as a 'legal person' and say that the rules of a legal system determine whether any particular human being or non-human entity has a legal personality. This analysis has the advantage that it allows for an entity to have more than one legal personality.

Section 5 of and sch. 1 to the Interpretation Act 1978 prescribe that in Acts of Parliament and subordinate legislation, unless the contrary intention appears, ' "Person" includes a body of persons corporate or unincorporate'. This applies to Acts passed after 1889 (Interpretation Act 1978, sch. 2, para. 4(1)) though 'person' is deemed to include a body corporate in any provision of an Act, whenever passed, relating to an offence, unless the contrary intention appears (sch. 2, para. 4(5)). For example, in *R* v *Home Secretary, ex parte Atlantic Commercial Ltd* [1997] BCC 692 it was held that in the Criminal Justice Act 1988, s. 133 (which provides for the payment of compensation to 'a person' who has been wrongfully convicted of an offence), 'person' does not include a corporation. In all deeds, contracts, wills, orders and other instruments, unless the context otherwise requires, 'person' includes a corporation (Law of Property Act 1925, s. 61; see *Deutsche Genossenschaftsbank* v *Burnhope* [1995] 1 WLR 1580 discussed in 19.8.4). The term 'individual' is used when it is intended to exclude corporations (per Viscount Cave LC in *Whitney* v *Commissioners of Inland Revenue* [1926] AC 37 at p. 43). It is usual in drafting legislation to use the pronouns 'he' and 'him' for a 'person', and use of those pronouns does not show an intention to refer only to individuals (per Lord Simon of Glaisdale in *Applin* v *Race Relations Board* [1975] AC 259 at p. 290).

0.2 PURPOSE OF COMPANY LAW

0.2.1 Service to business

Incorporation of companies has been made readily available by Parliament as a service to those who wish to take advantage of artificial entities with separate legal personality which they can control and put into legal relationships without being directly responsible for them.

Legislation providing for the incorporation of companies by registration is often described as 'enabling' or 'facilitative' legislation: it enables people to use the corporate form.

Most companies are incorporated for business purposes, which Parliament has wished to encourage. Business is risky: a venture may succeed and return profits to the providers of capital, and this is an incentive for investment. There is, however, always a risk that a venture may fail. The common law principle is that those who provide the capital for a business on the basis of taking or sharing in its profits, as sole proprietors or partners, are liable for all the debts incurred in the course of the business. Parliament has considered that people are more likely to venture their capital in business if they know that their potential loss from failure of the business is limited to loss of the amount of capital they have ventured without any further liability to pay the business's outstanding debts. CA 1985 permits the incorporation of companies with limited liability. As will be explained in more detail in 1.3.2, persons who contribute capital to a limited company, as members of the company, in return for a share in the profits made in the company's business are not liable, if the business should fail, to lose anything more than the amount of capital they have undertaken to contribute.

If business people are to be encouraged to create new businesses for which they require new companies then the creation of companies ought to be made as cheap and straightforward as possible. So one important aspect of company law which must be examined is how new companies are created (see chapters 1 to 3). Once created, the continuing operation of a company is governed by the law, and the other important aspect of company law is the operation of existing companies, which takes up most of this book. The law on existing companies is also significant for the creation of new businesses because people might be discouraged from creating new companies if they felt that the law on operating them was unsatisfactory.

0.2.2 Is company law suited to all users?

One reason for the popularity of registered companies is that CA 1985 permits a wide measure of choice in the constitution of a company, and the company format can be adapted to many different uses. Registered companies range in size and nature from huge industrial and commercial concerns like British Telecommunications plc to associations of people following a common hobby. Many companies exist only to hold one asset such as a building or a ship. Many individuals and companies divide up their business interests into scores or even hundreds of separate companies. The separate personality which incorporation of a company provides is widely exploited in tax-saving schemes. Many companies are bound by their constitutions to follow only charitable objectives. Nevertheless there have been complaints that the registered company is unsuitable in some circumstances, for example, J. Warburton, 'Charity corporations: the framework for the future?' [1990] Conv 95 argues that the company is not a suitable form for charities and that they require a special legal form. The most persistent complaint has been that the company is an unsuitable form for small businesses. According to the Inland Revenue, at the end of March 1992 there were 2.8 million sole traders and 0.6 million partnerships compared to just over 1 million companies. This was just before incorporation of single-member private companies was first permitted. It has been argued that what is believed to be a 'simpler' legal form than a company could be used by presently unincorporated businesses and by small businesses which are presently companies but for which the company form is unsuitable. A proposal in *A New Form of Incorporation for Small Firms: a Consultative Document* (Cmnd 8171) (London: HMSO, 1981) received little support. Discussion continued. J. Freedman, 'Small businesses and the corporate form: burden or privilege?' (1994) 57 MLR 555 reports empirical research on what business people actually want. As might be expected they are in practice indifferent about legal forms which they leave to their professional advisers (apart from some who are aware of positive or negative effects of incorporation on the image of their business). What business people are concerned about is financial matters such as the cost of complying with the accounting requirements of CA 1985 (since the survey, companies with small turnovers have been exempted from compulsory auditing of their accounts) and the tax effects of incorporation. Freedman also points out that small businesses have widely differing ownership structures from single individuals through small or extended families to business associates with or without investors who do not participate in management. It would not be easy to decide which particular group to design a new legal form for and it is not obvious what features would make a new design attractive. In April 1994 the Department of Trade and Industry asked the Law Commission to undertake a preliminary investigation of the problem. The Commission's report is printed in Department of Trade and Industry, *Company Law Review: the Law Applicable to Private Companies* (URN 94/529) (London: DTI, 1994). The Commission noted the difficulty of defining what a small business is and that business people do not put company law high on their list of problems. It was sympathetic to the view that creating a new legal form for small businesses would merely complicate the law and, by confining businesses to a small form, would discourage growth. It concluded that there was no need for a new legal form for small businesses. Further empirical research reported by A. Hicks, R. Drury and J. Smallcombe, *Alternative Company Structures for the Small Business* (London: Certified Accountants Educational Trust, 1995) confirms the general picture found by Freedman but makes the interesting point that most small businesses are incorporated on the advice of accountants rather than lawyers. Accountants may well emphasise the taxation effects of incorporating. Hicks et al. do support a special simple form of legal organisation for small businesses. They believe that limited liability is the cause of much of the complexity and compliance costs of the company form and their proposed 'business corporation' would have separate personality but unlimited liability and would be based on partnership concepts.

The DTI's review of company law (see 0.3.1.6) is expected to consider this question further.

0.2.3 Mandatory and enabling rules

Those who register a company under the Companies Act 1985 gain the advantages of incorporating a company with artificial separate personality. In return, Parliament requires the observance of mandatory rules on the operation of the company. These include both the legislated rules and the judge-made rules of case law described in 0.3.2. Requiring the observance of rules in return for granting the privilege of incorporation has sometimes led to incorporation being described as a contract between Parliament and corporators. For an early example of the characterisation of incorporation as a contract see the United States Supreme Court case of *Trustees of Dartmouth College* v *Woodward* (1819) 17 US (4 Wheat) 518, in which it was held that the state legislature of New Hampshire could not enact laws altering Dartmouth College's charter of incorporation (which was granted by the British Crown before the independence of the USA) without the College's agreement, because the charter was a contract between the Crown and the corporators protected by the United States Constitution, art. 1, s. 10, cl. 1 (the contracts clause), which prohibits states passing laws 'impairing the obligation of contracts'.

Because the separate personality of a company is artificial, it can be put into legal relationships only by the actions of human beings who will not, however, be directly responsible for those relationships. The persons who can put a company into legal relationships are its directors and persons they have authorised. Mandatory rules of company law regulate this situation for the protection of (a) the members of companies, (b) persons who deal with companies, especially those who become creditors of companies, (c) the public interest. A related area of law is concerned with public trading in company shares on the stock market.

Some people believe that the law should never interfere with the freedom of business people to make any contracts they choose. People with these beliefs disapprove of mandatory rules of company law. Often they deny the concession theory of incorporation and say that incorporation should be recognised as arising from private contract only. However, they usually allow that it is useful to have a model set of rules which will apply in default of other rules being chosen and will save people the costs of drafting their own rules. This has been the traditional British attitude to the regulations, known as the articles of association, governing a company's internal affairs and management (sometimes called the 'governance' of the company). Legislation provides a model set of articles (Table A), which apply in default of other rules being chosen for a particular company, but any company is almost entirely free to choose any alternative regulations (see chapter 3). However, in other areas British company law has a large mandatory content, particularly with regard to disclosure of information (see chapter 4), preparation and disclosure of accounts (see chapter 9) and the fiduciary duties of directors (see chapter 16). People who object to mandatory rules in company law usually believe that the rules which companies will have to adopt in order not to fail in a competitive market will be rules which will be of greatest benefit to the economy in which they operate. Market economists sometimes use their economic theories to work out what these theoretically wealth-maximising rules would be and propose them for adoption either as default rules or as mandatory rules. These issues were debated (in the context of United States law) in a symposium issue of the *Columbia Law Review* (vol. 89, No. 7, November 1989). For the argument that there must be mandatory rules in certain areas of company law, see M.A. Eisenberg, 'The structure of corporation law' (1989) 89 Colum L Rev 1461 (reprinted in S. Wheeler, *A Reader on the Law of Business Enterprise* (Oxford University Press, 1994)). For the contrary view, see F. S. McChesney, 'Economics, law, and science in the corporate field: a critique of

Eisenberg' (1989) 89 Colum L Rev 1530. The professors continued their debate in M.A. Eisenberg, 'Contractarianism without contracts: a response to Professor McChesney' (1990) 90 Colum L Rev 1321 and F. S. McChesney, 'Contractarianism without contracts? Yet another critique of Eisenberg' (1990) 90 Colum L Rev 1332. For a parting shot, see M.A. Eisenberg, 'Bad arguments in corporate law' (1990) 78 Geo LJ 1551.

0.2.4   The company's position in society

In 0.2.3 it was said that the mandatory rules of company law are there for the protection of (a) the members of companies, (b) persons who deal with companies, especially creditors, and (c) the public interest. It is sometimes suggested that mandatory rules of company law should protect other interest groups (or constituencies), such as employees of the company, consumers of its products, or the community in which it is located. These concerns are examined at length in a special issue of the *University of Toronto Law Journal*, vol. 43, No. 3 (Summer 1993). British company law has traditionally paid little or no attention to other constituencies. They are affected by the activities of companies but not, it is said, specially affected by the particular legal form of the registered company, so that their concerns are not a matter for company law: the dealings between employer and employee, for example, are the same whether the employer is a company, an individual or a partnership, and should be dealt with in employment law. Furthermore, company law is by no means just the law of companies that own large business organisations. Incorporation of companies under the Companies Act 1985 is allowed for any lawful purpose. Companies are not required to own large business organisations and have publicly traded shares — they are not required to have any business purpose at all. British company law has to be adaptable to a wide variety of uses. Companies will always be a focus for any debate on the control of business activities because most business activity is conducted by companies. If, however, companies are singled out for regulation then incorporated businesses will be at a disadvantage compared with partnerships and sole proprietors.

   What is special about a company is that decisions about its activities are taken by its directors. Sole proprietors and partners can, if they wish, operate their businesses in the interests of any objectives they choose, and so can be persuaded to act as good citizens and operate their businesses for the public good, but directors of a company are actually forbidden from considering any interests other than those expressly allowed by company law (see 16.4), which does not, at present, allow consideration of the public good. Traditionally the only interests which the law permitted the directors of a company to work for were the interests of the company, and for a business company this probably means only the financial interests of the company's shareholders (see 16.4.3). Statute now requires directors to have regard to the interests of the company's employees in general (CA 1985, s. 309; see 16.4.5) and, when the company is insolvent or near to insolvency, the interests of creditors (see 16.4.6.2). But neither employees nor creditors can take legal proceedings to force directors to have regard to their interests whereas members with a simple majority of votes have a statutory right to dismiss directors (CA 1985, s. 303; see 15.3.3) and even a minority of members may petition the court for relief if the conduct of the company's affairs is unfairly prejudicial to their interests (CA 1985, s. 459; see 18.6). Company law is often described as 'shareholder-centred' or based on a principle of shareholder primacy.

   Shareholder primacy is the subject of considerable political debate. On one side it is claimed that incorporation is made available to encourage business for the good of society generally and not simply for the private profit of shareholders:

. . . business is permitted and encouraged by the law primarily because it is of service to the community rather than because it is a source of profit to its owners. (E.M. Dodd Jr, 'For whom are corporate managers trustees?' (1932) 45 Harv L Rev 1145 at p. 1149)

One must remember that the corporation is a legal fiction — a creature of the law — and the benefits of participation in enterprise with limited liability are provided for the benefit of society, not of the shareholders themselves. (T.S. Norwitz, '''The metaphysics of *Time*'': a radical corporate vision' (1991) 46 Bus Law 377 at p. 387)

It is pointed out that requiring people working for companies to restrict the purpose of their working lives to maximising shareholder wealth is unhealthy, demeaning and morally corrupting (L.E. Mitchell, 'Groundwork of the metaphysics of corporate law' (1993) 50 Wash & Lee L Rev 1477; A. Wolfe, 'The modern corporation: private agent or public actor?' (1993) 50 Wash & Lee L Rev 1673; L.E. Mitchell, 'Cooperation and constraint in the modern corporation: an inquiry into the causes of corporate immorality' (1995) 73 Tex L Rev 477).

On the other side, it is claimed that restricting company management to the single objective of maximising shareholder wealth is the most efficient means of using companies to increase the wealth of society as a whole:

. . . maximising profits for equity investors assists the other 'constituencies' automatically. The participants in the venture play complementary rather than antagonistic roles. In a market economy each party to a transaction is better off. A successful firm provides jobs for workers and goods and services for consumers. The more appealing the goods to consumers, the more profits (and jobs). Prosperity for stockholders, workers, and communities goes hand in glove with better products for consumers. . . .

Frequently the harmony of interest between profit maximisation and other objectives escapes attention. (F.H. Easterbrook and D.R. Fischel, *The Economic Structure of Corporate Law* (Harvard University Press, 1991), p. 38)

For another expression of this view see M.E. DeBow and D.R. Lee, 'Shareholders, nonshareholders and corporate law: communitarianism and resource allocation' (1993) 18 Del J Corp L 393. Easterbrook and Fischel believe that if difficult moral and social questions were priced and expressed as costs to the company, they could be taken into account in corporate decision-making:

Far better to alter incentives by establishing rules that attach prices to acts (such as pollution and layoffs) while leaving managers free to maximise the wealth of the residual claimants [i.e., the shareholders — see 15.1.2] subject to the social constraints. (Op. cit., loc. cit.)

Treating corporate managers as capable only of profit-making but incapable of taking moral and social decisions is regarded by Mitchell as unnatural and objectionable. Requiring managers to take moral and social factors into account is characterised by followers of Easterbrook and Fischel as unnatural and objectionable 'social engineering' (DeBow and Lee, op. cit., at p. 404).

These issues are explored at length and in detail in J.E. Parkinson, *Corporate Power and Responsibility* (Oxford: Clarendon Press, 1993), which argues in favour of the thesis that '. . . every large corporation should be thought of as a social enterprise; that is, as an entity whose existence and decisions can be justified only in so far as they serve public or social purposes' (p. 23, quoting R.A. Dahl, 'A prelude to corporate reform' in R.L. Heilbroner and P. London (eds), *Corporate Social Policy* (Reading Mass: Addison-Wesley, 1975), pp. 18–24 at p. 18). For the opposing point of view see A. Alcock, 'Corporate governance: a defence of the status quo' (1995) 58 MLR 898. The description of large American corporations as more nearly social institutions than private enterprise was made by A.A. Berle Jr and G.C. Means in *The Modern Corporation and Private Property* (New York, 1932), p. 46.

The political debate in Britain was encapsulated by John Kay in his column in *The Daily Telegraph*, 11 September 1995 (reprinted in *The Business of Economics* (Oxford University Press, 1996), p. 86):

Is the purpose of a large public company to maximize its profits? Or to develop its business, in the interests of customers, employees, suppliers, investors, and the wider community? Like most people, I think the right answer is the second, but when I said so a few weeks ago institutions like the Institute of Directors denounced the prescription as wet, woolly, and vacuous.

Recognition by a company of the other interests listed by Kay is often seen as an element of the political idea of the stakeholding society (see J. Plender, *A Stake in the Future: The Stakeholding Solution* (London: Nicholas Brealey, 1997); P. Goldenberg, 'IALS Company Law Lecture — shareholders v stakeholders: the bogus argument' (1998) 19 Co Law 34). For a discussion of arguments for and against the stakeholder analysis of companies, see T.L. Beauchamp and N.E. Bowie (eds), *Ethical Theory and Business*, 5th ed. (Upper Saddle River NJ: Prentice Hall, 1997), ch. 2.

The shareholder-centred vision of the company is not universally held among advanced economies. In Germany companies are seen as serving both shareholders and employees, and in German company law this is reflected in the 'co-determination' principle that both shareholders and workers should take part in the governance of large companies. The conflict between the German and British views of the company has caused significant difficulties in the harmonisation of EC company law. In Japan a company is seen as a long-term coalition of investors, employees and trading partners, who are all concerned with the company's continuing prosperity. Japan's company law is modelled on Germany's, and the concern in both countries with the position of the company in society has been heavily influenced by the thinking of the German industrialist and statesman, Walther Rathenau (1867–1922), whose writings are cited by and clearly influenced Berle and Means. See M. Yoshimori, 'Whose company is it? The concept of the corporation in Japan and the West' (1995) 28 (4) Long Range Planning 33; J. Groenewegen, 'Institutions of capitalisms: American, European, and Japanese systems compared' (1997) 31 J Economic Issues 333. The German and Japanese experience has influenced the development of the idea of the stakeholding society. For recent discussions of differing forms of capitalism in different national cultures see Groenewegen, op. cit.; C. Crouch and W. Streeck (eds), *Political Economy of Modern Capitalism* (London: Sage, 1997).

Because most economic activity is conducted by companies, company law has a large potential impact on people's lives. People are naturally concerned by the power that companies have to affect their lives and wish to be assured that corporate power is legitimate and is properly controlled, just as they wish to see proper controls on the power of other institutions, such as national and local government, trade unions and educational institutions. People naturally look to the law to provide the framework for legitimation and control of power. For some people, the power of a company will be legitimate only if it is exercised in the interest of all those whom it affects. They want the law to require companies to give due consideration to all relevant interests. Other people believe that corporate power is legitimised by the contribution that companies make to the economy and that the market provides adequate control of economic activity so that legal controls are either superfluous or produce damaging distortions of the market.

0.3 SOURCES OF COMPANY LAW

0.3.1 Legislation

0.3.1.1 Importance of legislation
Because of the English concession theory of incorporation, a registered company, as an artificial person separate from its members, exists only by virtue of the Companies Act under which it was incorporated. In *Welton* v *Saffery* [1897] AC 299 Lord Macnaghten said, at p. 324, 'These companies are the creature of statute', and in *Ooregum Gold Mining Co. of India Ltd* v *Roper* [1892] AC 125 Lord Halsbury LC said, at p. 133: '. . . the whole structure of a limited company owes its existence to the Act of Parliament, and it is to the Act of Parliament one must refer to see what are its powers, and within what limits it is free to act'. The legislation on companies is therefore the primary source of company law.

0.3.1.2 History and current legislation
Incorporation of companies by registration was first legislated for in the Joint Stock Companies Act 1844. The Joint Stock Companies Act 1856 created a wholly revised system which is the basis of present-day company law. Since the 1856 Act numerous amendments have been enacted. Every now and again, Parliament consolidates the law on companies — that is, it repeals the existing statutes and re-enacts all their provisions, for convenience of reference, in a single Act. The Companies Act 1985 (CA 1985), which came into force on 1 July 1985, is the latest consolidation, and is the current principal Act governing companies. CA 1985 replaced the Companies Acts 1948 to 1983, though some provisions of those Acts were re-enacted separately in:

(a) the Companies Consolidation (Consequential Provisions) Act 1985 — known (by CA 1985, s. 744) as 'the Consequential Provisions Act' — which contains formal and transitional provisions,
(b) the Company Securities (Insider Dealing) Act 1985, which has in turn been replaced by part V of the Criminal Justice Act 1993 — known as 'the insider dealing legislation' (CA 1985, s. 744) — which is considered in chapter 13, and
(c) the Business Names Act 1985.

By CA 1985, s. 744, the phrase 'the Companies Acts' now means CA 1985 together with the Consequential Provisions Act and the insider dealing legislation.

The provisions of CA 1985 relating to the winding up of companies and to the disqualification of company directors were extensively amended by the Insolvency Act 1985. The amended provisions have now themselves been consolidated in the Insolvency Act 1986 (IA 1986) and the Company Directors Disqualification Act 1986 (CDDA 1986). (The Insolvency Act 1986 also deals with the insolvency of individuals, known as bankruptcy.)

CA 1985 has been extensively amended by CA 1989, most of which has been brought into force by 17 commencement orders (SI 1990 Nos. 98, 142, 354, 355, 713, 1392, 1707 and 2569; SI 1991 Nos. 488, 878, 1452, 1996, 2173 and 2945; SI 1995 Nos. 1352, and 1591; SI 1998 No. 1747).

The legislation on the control of public markets in company shares is contained in the Financial Services Act 1986 (FSA 1986).

In this book, a reference to a provision of legislation is a reference to that provision as amended, unless the words 'as originally enacted' are used. The text of the Companies Acts as amended may be found in one of the published collections of companies legislation, such as D. French, *Blackstone's Statutes on Company Law*, 2nd ed. (London: Blackstone Press, 1998).

0.3.1.3 Complexity

The legislation on companies forms a very large and detailed code of rules. A company as an artificial separate person exists only in writing, and there is a need for precise instructions on how this artificial entity is to be used, especially to ensure uniformity of treatment of the very large number of companies now registered in Britain. Another factor contributing to the size of the code is the detailed style of drafting customarily used in British legislation.

There is no doubt that the legislation on companies has become very much more complex during the 1980s and 90s. The most recent consolidation, the Companies Act 1985, had 747 sections and 25 schedules occupying 600 pages in the Queen's Printer's copy. The previous consolidation, the Companies Act 1948, covered the same ground in 462 sections and 18 schedules taking up 363 pages. For reviews of the changes in this period, see Lord Templeman, 'Forty years on' (1990) 11 Co Law 10; D. Milman, '1967–1987: a transformation in company law?' (1988) 17 Anglo-Am L Rev 108; D. Milman, 'Company law in transition' (1990) 24 Law Teach 3.

With a code of this length and complexity there is a great danger that people will act in ignorance of some vital legislative provision. See, for example, *Re Bradford Investments plc (No. 2)* [1991] BCLC 688, in which four people transferred their business to a public company in return for shares in the company not knowing that CA 1985, s. 103, required the preparation of an independent report on the value of the business (see 6.5.4). Because the statute was not complied with, they became liable to pay more than £1 million plus interest. They had relied on advice by solicitors, accountants in public practice, and the company's accountant. In *British Racing Drivers' Club Ltd v Hextall Erskine and Co.* [1996] 3 All ER 667, a solicitor, described as 'a senior commercial partner with extensive experience of the Companies Acts', wrongly advised that it was not necessary for a company to obtain the approval of its members for a substantial property transaction with one of its directors as required by CA 1985, s. 320 (see 16.6.7). Damages of more than £2.8 million were awarded for this negligent advice. In *Re R.W. Peak (Kings Lynn) Ltd* [1998] 1 BCLC 193 the members of a company, having consulted solicitors and the company's auditors, adopted a completely wrong procedure for selling shares back to the company (see 10.6.3), thereby probably committing a criminal offence and creating enormous problems of the validity of subsequent share issues and appointments of directors. For another example, see *Re Chez Nico (Restaurants) Ltd* [1992] BCLC 192 discussed by C. Mercer, 'Compulsory acquisition of minorities' (1992) 13 Co Law 139. See also *Brady v Brady* [1989] AC 755, in which the lawyers did not discover which statutory provision was relevant to the case until it reached the House of Lords. All the cases mentioned in this paragraph were concerned with changes introduced into the law during the 1980s, showing that particular problems have been caused by the extent of change in recent years.

Beside the spectacular cases which reach the courts, there can be no doubt that in most companies, many administrative rules, relating, for example, to meetings of members and directors, are either not followed exactly or are mostly ignored. A review by the Department of Trade and Industry during the 1980s intended to reduce burdens on business resulted in five sections of the Companies Act 1989 (ss. 113 to 117), which were headed 'De-regulation of private companies'. These do make some valuable simplifications but at the expense of introducing yet more detailed provisions covering exceptions and special cases. Moreover they are only five out of 216 sections in yet another long and complex Companies Act.

0.3.1.4 Legislative process

The length and complexity of companies legislation pose problems for the legislative process. In the debate on the third reading of the Bill that became the Companies Act 1981 (which amended the 1948 Act and is now consolidated in the 1985 Act) Mr Stanley Clinton Davies (a practising solicitor) said (Parliamentary Debates (Hansard), Commons, 6th ser., vol. 10 (1980–81), col. 68):

> Few honourable members who have served in committee on Companies Bills regard them as great examples of the efficiency of Parliamentary procedures. We are bogged down with an enormous welter of technical detail. Few of us, including myself, understand much of that detail when it is before the committee . . .
>
> The bodies with a professional interest in such matters have a great deal to contribute — more, I fear, than honourable members when dealing with highly technical, non-contentious matters.

Companies Bills are invariably government Bills. The legislators in Parliament are required to consider Bills prepared by the civil service dealing with topics chosen by the civil service. Non-government amendments are hardly ever accepted, though the minister in charge of the Bill usually undertakes to have any criticism considered and to bring forward a government amendment at a later stage if possible. Legislators are particularly annoyed that Companies Bills are usually incomplete when presented for second reading. Committee debates are usually swamped with government amendments introducing new provisions. Often, important provisions are presented as amendments at a late stage in a Bill's passage through Parliament so that they are not properly discussed. The civil service undertakes a great deal of public consultation before drafting legislation. The Companies Division of the Department of Trade and Industry 'is committed to undertaking public consultation on the development of company law' (Department of Trade and Industry, *Companies in 1992–93* (London: HMSO, 1993), p. 2) but consultation consists merely of receiving views, not arguing over them as in Parliamentary debate. Obviously it is to be welcomed that proposals for changing the law are the product of careful consideration but it often seems that the system prevents Parliament fulfilling properly its representative function in arguing the causes of different groups and its role in protecting the public interest.

In what seems like an admission of defeat Parliament has, when enacting a new provision in a Companies Act, often accompanied it with the grant of a power to the Secretary of State to amend the provisions by regulations. The amending power which has been used most often is CA 1985, s. 257, which permits the Secretary of State to modify the provisions of part VII (ss. 221 to 262A) of the Act concerning accounts and audit. This power has been exercised in SI 1991 No. 2705, SI 1992 Nos. 2452, 3003 and 3178, SI 1993 Nos. 1820 and 3246, SI 1994 Nos. 233, 1935 and 2879, SI 1995 No. 589, SI 1996 Nos. 189 and 3080, and SI 1997 Nos. 220, 570, 571, 936 and 2704. For other examples of the Secretary of State's power to amend the primary legislation, see CA 1985, s. 179 (power not yet exercised), CA 1985, s. 210A (exercised in SI 1993 Nos. 1819 and 2689, and SI 1996 No. 1560), CA 1989, s. 117 (power not yet exercised), and CA 1989, s. 135 (exercised in SI 1991 No. 1646).

More questions about the relationship between the legislature and the executive are raised by the significant number of occasions on which legislation relating to companies has not been brought into force. One example which has caused much confusion is part IV of CA 1989, which would have revised the system for registering charges on company property, but which apparently is not going to be brought into force because it is thought to be faulty (see 11.7.1). Even longer on the statute book but never brought into force was part V of the Financial Services Act 1986, which enacted a new system of controls on advertising company shares for investment when they are not listed on the London Stock Exchange. In 1995 it was repealed and replaced by regulations implementing a European Directive on the subject (see 7.5.1). These examples raise the constitutional question whether Parliament is losing control over companies legislation. Many people (and not just textbook writers) may be justifiably annoyed at having prepared for the implementation of legislation which is not in fact brought into force. It seems to us that the plaintiffs in *Possfund Custodian Trustee Ltd* v *Diamond* [1996] 1 WLR 1351 would have had a statutory remedy if part V of the Financial Services Act 1986 had been in force when their claim arose in 1992. Instead they will have to persuade the court to alter the common law to provide them with a remedy. In 7.6.6 we argue that Lightman J's *obiter* ruling that the Act would not have applied to them is wrong. In *R* v *Secretary of State for the Home Department, ex parte Fire Brigades Union* [1995] 2 AC 513 (in which people had suffered pecuniary loss when a statutory scheme for compensating victims of crime was ignored and replaced by a cheaper scheme devised by the Home Secretary), Lord Browne-Wilkinson said that when Parliament delegates to the executive the power to bring a statutory provision into force it does not mean that the executive can decide at will whether or not to bring it into force: the intent is that the power will be exercised when appropriate and unless circumstances change so as to make it inappropriate, and the executive could not change the circumstances itself by, for example, making its own regulations which are inconsistent with the Act.

0.3.1.5   Criticism
In *The Reform of Company Law* (Law Society Memorandum No. 255) (London: Law Society, 1991), the Law Society's Company Law Committee criticised the present system. The committee said that 'company law in the United Kingdom is not of a high enough standard' (at p. 1). The legislation often fails to meet its stated aims, and there is a systemic failure to take a long-term view of company law in order to set the right aims in the first place. The committee suggested the establishment of an independent company law commission to draft companies legislation. For discussion of the memorandum, see 'Can the Law Society get company law reform on the agenda?' (1991) 12 Co Law 162. There is further criticism of the complexity of the legislation in three articles in the *Gazette*, 8 December 1993. L. Sealy, 'Small company legislation' 90 (45) Gazette 16, suggests that many provisions of the all-purpose Companies Act are not appropriate for small companies; A. Hutchinson, 'Looking for direct results' 90 (45) Gazette 19, argues for fewer mandatory rules; P. Holland, 'Unclogging the wheels' 90 (45) Gazette 23, attacks particularly the way in which European Directives are incorporated into UK law as additional layers of law instead of being carefully integrated.

0.3.1.6   Review
Since November 1992 the Department of Trade and Industry has been undertaking a wide-ranging review of companies legislation. For each topic of review a working group has been established including representatives of many interested groups. The new government has decided that this review process, which has been going on for more than five years,

has merely revealed the need for an even more extensive review, which was launched in March 1998, and which is expected to take another three years. New legislation is not expected until the next Parliament, whose first session is expected to be in 2002–3. In a consultation document, *Modern Company Law for a Competitive Economy* (London: DTI, 1998), the Department says, at p. 2:

> Given that major reviews of this sort are — for good reason — infrequent events, it is right to take the time to do it properly, and to ensure that the resulting arrangements will stand the test of time.

According to the consultative document the main problems are that the legislation has become excessively complex and that it contains unnecessary provisions. The document describes the review's task in an engineering metaphor as 'The stripping out of obsolescent and over-complex provisions and the repair of defective ones' (p. 11), but says that this 'will not be easy or straightforward' (even after eight years' reviewing!). Specific areas are singled out for comment in the document and the comments will be noted when those areas are discussed in this book. The proposed terms of reference for the review are (consultative document, pp. 14–15):

(i)   To consider how core company law can be modernised in order to provide a simple, efficient and cost-effective framework for carrying out business activity which:

(a)   permits the maximum amount of freedom and flexibility to those organising and directing the enterprise;

(b)   at the same time protects, through regulation where necessary, the interests of those involved with the enterprise, including shareholders, creditors and employees; and

(c)   is drafted in clear, concise and unambiguous language which can be readily understood by those involved in business enterprise.

(ii)   To consider whether company law, partnership law, and other legislation which establishes a legal form of business activity together provide an adequate choice of legal vehicle for business at all levels.

(iii)   To consider the proper relationship between company law and non-statutory standards of corporate behaviour.

(iv)   To review the extent to which foreign companies operating in Great Britain should be regulated under British company law.

(v)   To make recommendations accordingly.

The consultative document says that one of the first subjects for review will be 'the structure and style of new legislation and how it might be made more accessible to non-specialists' (p. 19). In particular it notes two suggestions, which have often been made, (a) that the law on private and public companies should be in separate Acts (pp. 7 and 15) and (b) that provisions should be transferred to secondary legislation, which can be revised more easily (pp. 11 and 16), leaving a shorter principal statute which would be more readable.

0.3.1.7   Studying legislation

It is not the purpose of this book to set out for our readers every legislative provision relating to companies. We have selected for discussion what we believe to be the most important provisions relating to the creation, financing and management of companies, and their insolvency and winding up. We want to show the legislative framework of company law.

We believe that having this framework in mind is the best preparation for reading the legislation itself and the large commentaries on it written for practitioners (see 0.3.4), which will provide the fine detail. See further 1.3.4.1.

0.3.2 Case law

0.3.2.1 *Types of case law studied in company law*

Legal principles taken from judgments in court cases — known as case law, common law, or, simply, law, as opposed to legislation — are of great significance in company law. Three types of case law may be distinguished:

(a) The courts are given a remarkably extensive supervisory role by the legislation relating to companies (see 0.3.2.2) and a company's affairs must be conducted in the knowledge that they may be reviewed in court proceedings.

(b) As in any area of statute law the courts have an important role in determining the meaning and application of the legislation and filling gaps in the legislative code (see 0.3.2.3).

(c) There are certain types of dispute which regularly arise in relation to companies which it is appropriate to consider in a book on company law even though the principles of law involved come from other areas of law such as contract (for example, rescission of contracts of allotment of shares, see 6.7) or tort (for example, the liability of auditors for negligence, see 8.10).

0.3.2.2 *Judicial supervision of companies*

Parliament has relied heavily on court proceedings to control and supervise the operation of companies. But courts do not themselves seek out wrongdoing for investigation and punishment: their powers have to be invoked in proceedings brought by persons with the requisite standing.

The ultimate judicial sanction that may be invoked is the power to order a company to be wound up (Insolvency Act 1986, s. 122). The High Court has jurisdiction to order any company registered in England and Wales to be wound up (s. 117(1)). If the amount of a registered company's share capital paid up or credited as paid up does not exceed £120,000 then the county court of the district in which the company's registered office is situated has concurrent jurisdiction with the High Court to wind up the company (s. 117(2)). Under s. 117(4) and the Civil Courts Order 1983 (SI 1983 No. 713), art. 9 and sch. 3, about half of the county courts do not have winding-up jurisdiction: the districts of those courts are attached to other county courts or, in the London area, to the High Court for the purposes of winding-up jurisdiction.

The legislation relating to companies gives many other supervisory functions to 'the court' (which means, in relation to any particular company, the court having jurisdiction to wind up the company: CA 1985, s. 744). For example:

(a) The court has an important general power to make 'such order as it thinks fit' to give relief in respect of conduct of a company's affairs which is unfairly prejudicial to the interests of some or all of its members (CA 1985, ss. 459 to 461; see 18.6).

(b) The court has a significant control power to disqualify a former director of a company from being a director of, or taking part in the management of, companies for a fixed period of up to 15 years (Company Directors Disqualification Act 1986; see 15.2.5).

(c) If a company is, or is likely to become, unable to pay its debts, the court may make an administration order directing that its affairs, business and property shall be managed by an administrator appointed by the court (Insolvency Act 1986, ss. 8 to 27; see 20.3).

(d)   A company's authorised share capital cannot be reduced (except following cancellation of unissued shares) unless the reduction is confirmed by the court (CA 1985, ss. 135 to 141; see 10.2).

(e)   The court may declare that a company's annual accounts do not comply with statutory requirements and order its directors to prepare revised accounts (CA 1985, s. 245B; see 9.9).

(f)   On a number of matters a dissentient minority of members of a company may apply to the court to have a resolution adopted by the majority set aside (for a list of the matters see 14.4.1).

The success of this wide supervisory jurisdiction depends on judges and barristers who specialise in company law. The fact that for companies with registered offices in the London area there is no alternative to using the High Court has been particularly significant in making that court and the barristers who practise there a centre of expertise in company law. All matters involving the exercise of the High Court's jurisdiction under the enactments relating to companies are assigned to the Chancery Division by the Supreme Court Act 1981, sch. 1, para. 1. The Chancery Division in London has a separate registry for company cases, which are heard by specially designated judges, with routine applications being heard by the registrar. This is an administrative arrangement which has come to be known as the Companies Court.

The main reasons why it was appropriate for Chancery lawyers to add company law to their practice when the topic developed in the 19th century were: (a) that they had always handled partnership and insolvency matters, and (b) the Chancery court was able to deal with matters which involved continuing management, such as winding up the affairs of deceased and insolvent persons, and had available remedies such as injunction and taking accounts, which are particularly suited to dealing with long-term disputes concerning business relationships.

Because of the role of Chancery lawyers, equity has always been an important component of company law and with its emphasis on conscience and fairness has provided an extra-statutory source for judicial supervision of company affairs. This is particularly noticeable in the application to company directors of the equitable concept of fiduciary duty (see chapter 16).

There are doubts about whether the amount of court time that has to be devoted to company matters is an effective use of resources. There has been repeated criticism of the length and cost of proceedings under CA 1985, ss. 459 to 461, for relief of unfairly prejudicial conduct, and the Law Commission has made recommendations for improving the situation (*Shareholder Remedies* (Law Com. No. 246, Cm 3769) (London: Stationery Office, 1997)). The need for judicial hearings to disqualify directors has been questioned both by judges and by former directors who have to defend such proceedings (see 15.2.5.6). In the consultation document introducing its review of company law (see 0.3.1.6) the DTI has singled out the court procedure for approving reductions of capital as a matter in need of reform (*Modern Company Law for a Competitive Economy* (London: DTI, 1998), p. 7).

Another aspect of Parliament's reliance on the courts in company law is the vast number of criminal offences (over 100) created by the companies, insolvency and financial services legislation. Most of these, in particular those under CA 1985, consist in failing to supply information to the registrar of companies and such offences are normally triable only summarily (i.e., by a magistrates' court) and the only penalty that may be imposed is a fine with a limit specified in the legislation creating the offence (though, of course, it is possible to be imprisoned for failing to pay a fine). Other offences created by the legislation may be trivial or serious depending on the surrounding circumstances and are triable either way, that is in a magistrates' court or in the Crown Court, depending on, among other things, the gravity of the particular allegation involved. Generally the Acts provide that a prison sentence may be imposed (if the court thinks it appropriate), instead of or in addition to a fine, for an offence triable either way, and the maximum term of imprisonment is usually set at two years. For a few serious offences (such as being a party to fraudulent trading) the maximum sentence may be seven years. There is no limit to the size of a fine that the Crown Court may impose (Criminal Law Act 1977, s. 32(1)).

As well as the possibility of a fine or imprisonment for contravening provisions of the companies and insolvency legislation, a person may be disqualified from acting as a director of a company (see 15.2.5).

In the consultation document introducing its review of company law (see 0.3.1.6) the DTI says: 'One issue for the review will be the balance between civil and criminal sanctions: it is commonly suggested that the existing Companies Act too readily invokes criminal penalties, when civil remedies would be more appropriate' (*Modern Company Law for a Competitive Economy* (London: DTI, 1998), p. 17).

0.3.2.3   *Interpretation and gap-filling*
The legislative code governing companies is very extensive and detailed and the justification for this is that it sets out in advance the rights and duties of persons who have dealings with companies and the formalities that must be observed so that all parties know what the position is and can act accordingly. However, (a) the natural limitations of language mean that questions may arise on the interpretation and application of the provisions of a legislative code; (b) real life is complex and unpredictable and a legislative code cannot be complete, in the sense of deciding all possible questions within its scope.

The courts are often required to expound the meaning of a statutory provision by, for example, deciding whether or not it applies to a particular set of facts. For example, in *Neptune (Vehicle Washing Equipment) Ltd* v *Fitzgerald* [1996] Ch 274 it was held that the Companies Act 1985, s. 317(1), which requires a director of a company who is interested in a contract with the company to declare the nature of the interest at a meeting of the company's directors, applies when the director in question is the only director of the company.

In the late 19th century the courts were called upon to fill some rather substantial gaps in the legislation as it then existed (in the CA 1862). The House of Lords decided great cases, like *Ashbury Railway Carriage and Iron Co. Ltd* v *Riche* (1875) LR 7 HL 653, *Trevor* v *Whitworth* (1887) 12 App Cas 409 and *Ooregum Gold Mining Co. of India Ltd* v *Roper* [1892] AC 125. The law established in all those three cases has now been replaced by fresh legislation. The legislation has reversed the effect of the *Ashbury Railway Carriage* case (see 19.4.1), but the other two have been confirmed, though important exceptions have been created (see chapter 10). In some areas, though, case law still attempts to fill notable gaps in the legislation, often very cautiously. Two notable examples are the question whether a company's constitution forms a contract between the company and its members (see 3.4) and the liability of companies for crimes (see 19.8.4 to 19.8.7).

For a review of judicial interpretation of companies legislation see D. Milman, 'The courts and the Companies Acts: the judicial contribution to company law' [1990] LMCLQ 401.

0.3.2.4   *Reports of cases*
Reports of company law cases are found mainly in the Chancery section of the *Law Reports*, that is, Ch in the current series, ChD in the second series (1875 to 1890), and LR Eq and

LR Ch App in the first series (1865 to 1874). From 1865 to about 1910, an enormous number of company law cases were reported, but as law reporters became generally more selective about what cases they published, the number of new company law cases reported annually dwindled until, during the 1960s and 70s, there seemed to be a danger that only a few specialist barristers who were aware of the unreported cases could be capable of giving advice on company matters. The situation improved greatly in the 1980s with the establishment of two specialist series of reports, *Butterworths Company Law Cases* (BCLC) and *British Company Cases* (BCC), the first five volumes of which were called *British Company Law Cases* — though the market was unable to sustain a third series, *Palmer's Company Cases* (PCC), which was published only from 1985 to 1989.

0.3.2.5 *Criticism of judicial approaches*
A legal system is a set of principles on which courts base reasoned judgments. Company law appears to be a particularly intricate system of both legislative and common law principles. This leads to two criticisms:

(a)   Decisions of great practical importance to business people are made to depend on insignificant legal details. Business people may, for example, wonder why the agreement of all the members of a company to a decision to reduce its capital is not considered a good enough agreement for the court to approve under CA 1985, s. 135, if the members did not hold a meeting to come to the decision, whereas a decision come to at a meeting by a three-quarters majority is good enough even if only a quorum of members (typically two) attended the meeting. This rule was arrived at in *Re Barry Artist Ltd* [1985] 1 WLR 1305 purely by construction of the legislation. Many business people would think it ridiculous that learned judges interpreting the Insolvency Act 1986, s. 123(1)(a), disagree over whether a statutory demand for a debt (which can be the first stage in a creditor's proceeding to have a company compulsorily wound up by the court) may or may not be sent by post (see 20.6.3).

(b)   When application of a legal rule produces an unwelcome result one reaction is to assert that judges should be free to disapply the rule whenever they like (usually expressed as 'whenever justice and equity require') and insistence on applying rules whatever the consequences is described as 'formalism', which is thought to be inherently wrong. The prime example of this in company law is the long-running controversy over the circumstances in which the separate personality of a company may be ignored (see 5.2.2). But settled legal rules with predictable outcomes are also valued, especially when business arrangements are made relying on those rules. In the consultation document introducing its review of company law (see 0.3.1.6) the DTI says, 'The new arrangements should be based on principles of consistency, predictability and transparency' (*Modern Company Law for a Competitive Economy* (London: DTI, 1998), p. 6). The way in which a legal system should deal with a case in which the application of a rule would be unwelcome is to analyse what distinguishes the case from those in which the rule can be applied successfully and use that analysis to formulate an additional principle providing an exception to the rule. That new principle can then be followed in future cases and can be taken into account by people when planning their business transactions. See Lord Steyn, 'Does legal formalism hold sway in England?', *Current Legal Problems 1996*, part 2, pp. 43–58.

0.3.2.6 *Studying case law*
The number of reported cases on company law is huge. The cases up to 1990 occupy two volumes (each in two parts) of *The Digest*, taking up 1,987 pages. As with its treatment of

legislation (see 0.3.1.7), this book presents only a selection of the relevant reported cases. As with our treatment of the legislation, our aim is to provide a framework, which you can, if and when necessary, fill in with more detailed research of your own.

One of the most important skills of a lawyer is in interpreting reports of cases which he or she has never read before and determining how they apply to a problem on which advice is sought. Teaching lawyers necessarily involves teaching how to do this. Common law subjects are sometimes taught by asking students to read leading cases and derive for themselves the principles of the law from those cases. This teaches how to interpret cases as well as teaching the principles of the subject. This book adopts the approach of setting out the authors' statement of what the principles of law are, giving references to the cases from which we have derived those principles. This enables us to cite, and derive principles from, vastly more cases than could possibly be read during, for example, an undergraduate course on company law. It leaves it up to you to decide which cases you want to read for yourself, depending on your personal learning objectives and, if you are following a course at an educational institution, the requirements of that course.

0.3.3   European law

0.3.3.1   Harmonisation Directives

In order to establish a common market for goods and services throughout the European Union it is necessary to ensure that the laws governing the establishment of businesses are not significantly different in different parts of the Union, making business more favourable in one part than in others. The Treaty Establishing the European Community (Rome 1957) therefore authorises the Council and the Commission to coordinate 'to the necessary extent the safeguards which, for the protection of the interests of members and others, are required of companies or firms . . . with a view to making such safeguards equivalent throughout the Community' (art. 54(3)(g)). The process of coordination required by art. 54(3)(g) is usually referred to as 'harmonisation' of company law. A country may adopt laws restricting business within its territory conducted by companies incorporated in other jurisdictions. EU countries cannot discriminate against one another in this way because art. 52 of the EC Treaty requires the abolition of restrictions on the freedom of establishment of nationals of one member State in the territory of another member State (and art. 53 forbids member States from introducing any new restrictions), and art. 58 requires companies or firms formed in accordance with the law of a member State, and having their registered office, central administration or principal place of business within the Union, to be accorded the same rights of freedom of establishment as natural persons who are nationals of member States. See I.G.F. Cath, 'Freedom of establishment of companies: a new step towards completion of the internal market' 6 YEL 1986 247. The programme of company law harmonisation is undertaken to promote freedom of establishment (see the opening words of art. 54 and F.G. Jacobs. 'The basic freedoms of the EEC Treaty and company law' (1992) 13 Co Law 4).

This harmonisation of company law is carried out by Directives issued under art. 189 of the Treaty. The harmonisation Directives are referred to as the 'First', 'Second' etc. Directives in the order in which they were proposed by the Commission. Of the 13 proposals so far, the fifth, ninth, tenth and thirteenth have not yet been adopted. A Directive directs member States to enact laws that will have a prescribed effect, though it leaves the precise wording of the laws to the national legislative authorities. There is always a time limit within which the national laws must be enacted. If a member State fails to fulfil its obligations under a Directive then the Commission may bring the matter before the Court of Justice under art. 169 of the EC Treaty. A State must take the necessary measures to comply with the Court's judgment (art. 171). If a member State has failed to implement a Directive when the time limit expires then the terms of the Directive may be relied on, as against the State, in the State's courts, provided the terms of the Directive are unconditional and sufficiently precise, but the terms of an unimplemented Directive cannot be relied on against persons other than States (*Marshall* v *Southampton & South West Hampshire Area Health Authority (Teaching)* [1986] QB 401, ECJ; *Duke* v *GEC Reliance Ltd* [1988] AC 618, HL). In *Karella* v *Greek Minister of Industry, Energy and Technology* (cases C-19/90 and C-20/90) [1991] ECR I-2691 and *Sindesmos Melon tis Eleftheras Evangelikis Ekklisias* v *Greece* (case C-381/89) [1992] ECR I-2111 provisions of the Second Company Law Directive (77/91/EEC) were held to be sufficiently precise to be directly applicable. Because a national court is a State authority it must interpret its national law as far as possible in the light of the wording and purpose of relevant Directives (*Marleasing SA* v *La Comercial Internacional de Alimentación SA* (case C-106/89) [1990] ECR I-4135). In the UK it has been acknowledged that legislation enacted in order to implement a Directive must be construed so as to give full effect to the Directive, taking into account any relevant decisions of the European Court of Justice (*Litster* v *Forth Dry Dock and Engineering Co. Ltd* [1990] 1 AC 546). However, it has been said that legislation which was not intended to implement a Directive will not be construed so as to give effect to that Directive if to do so would distort the meaning of the legislation (*Duke* v *GEC Reliance Ltd*).

There is a very long process of consultation in the formulation of a Directive. In Britain, the Company Law Directorate of the Department of Trade and Industry monitors the development of European law on companies and collects comments on proposed Directives. The Department is also responsible for drafting legislation to implement adopted Directives.

0.3.3.2 Societas europea

It has been proposed that it should be possible to register, in any European Union country, a 'societas europea' (SE), or European public limited company, which would be governed primarily by law set out in a Council Regulation. For the text of the proposal, see OJ No. C 176, 8 July 1991, p. 1. For comment, see A. Burnside. 'The European company re-proposed' (1991) 12 Co Law 216; T.L. Blackburn, 'The societas europea: the evolving European corporation statute' (1993) 61 Fordham L Rev 695. The Department of Trade and Industry has issued a consultative document, *The European Company Statute* (URN 97/786) (London: DTI, 1997).

0.3.3.3 Jurisdictional competition or cooperation?

The problems of different jurisdictions in a market having different company laws have been faced in several parts of the world. There is little doubt that most business people incorporate their businesses in the jurisdictions in which they are based. This saves having to hire foreign lawyers to deal with compliance with the law of the jurisdiction of incorporation, and saves having to file documents both in the place of incorporation and the place of business. There must also be some suspicion by those dealing with a business which has deliberately been placed outside the jurisdiction in which it is dealing. Business people, like other people, have a natural affinity for their place of domicile. Nevertheless, where a choice is available some people will seek to evaluate the alternatives and choose the one that seems best.

The United Kingdom Parliament has always enacted what is essentially a single company law code for England and Wales and for Scotland: the Companies Act 1985 applies in both jurisdictions though some of its provisions have alternative formulations adapted to the different legal systems of the two jurisdictions. There are separate registrars of companies for England and Wales and for Scotland. Up to and including the Companies (Consolidation) Act 1908, the United Kingdom Companies Acts formed part of the law of Ireland. A Companies Registration Office was established under the UK Acts in Dublin. After partition, any company registered in Ireland in existence on 1 January 1922 with a registered office located in Northern Ireland was deemed to be registered in Northern Ireland where a separate registration office was established (SR & O 1922 No. 184). The 1908 Act continued to apply in both parts of Ireland but the parliaments of the two parts were empowered to legislate in relation to companies: the Northern Ireland Parliament created a separate Northern Ireland code in the Companies Act (Northern Ireland) 1932. In the South, the 1908 Act was not replaced until after the formation of the Republic of Ireland, when the Companies Act 1963 was passed. Legislation in both the Republic of Ireland and Northern Ireland must now comply with EC Directives. Companies can be registered under separate codes in Guernsey, Jersey and the Isle of Man.

In Australia, the Federal Parliament does not have power to legislate for the incorporation of companies (*New South Wales* v *The Commonwealth, The Incorporation Case* (1990) 169 CLR 482), but, since 1961, the States have agreed to adopt a uniform companies code (now called the Corporations Law). Among the reasons for preferring uniformity appear to be the convenience of professional advisers who have to learn only one code for application throughout the country (an obvious advantage given the length and complexity of modern companies legislation), and frustration under the old system of different laws in different States that when one State improved its legislation, other States could not benefit from those improvements until their own legislatures could find time to enact them (see R. McQueen, 'Why High Court judges make poor historians: the Corporations Act case and early attempts to establish a national system of company regulation in Australia' (1990) 19 Fed Law Rev 245).

In the USA, corporations are incorporated (or 'chartered', as it is said there) under State laws and there is no system of Federal chartering. In the 19th century there was great popular suspicion of monopolistic big business, and all States imposed upper limits on the amount of capital a corporation could have. At the end of the 19th century, States one by one abandoned those limits and other restrictions as they competed with each other for the fees they could obtain from new incorporations. The history was described by Brandeis J in *Louis K. Liggett Co.* v *Lee* (1933) 288 US 517 who talked of 'the traffic in charters' (at p. 557) and of a 'race' between States which 'was one not of diligence but of laxity' (at p. 559). The process has since become known as the 'race to the bottom'. It has been claimed that States have continued the race to the bottom, adopting corporation laws that would attract incorporations and the fees that they generate by favouring the interests of the people who decide where to incorporate, typically those who are to be, or will control the appointment of, the directors. Delaware — the second smallest of the States — is the acknowledged winner of the race: in some years corporate fees have made up one-quarter of Delaware's State revenues. Over 40 per cent of corporations listed on the New York Stock Exchange in 1987 were incorporated in Delaware. This leadership means that Delaware lawyers benefit from the fees generated by corporate litigation. W.L. Cary, 'Federalism and corporate law: reflections upon Delaware' (1974) 83 Yale LJ 663 is a famous attack on the system. Others, however, defend Delaware's system of corporate law: see C. Alva, 'Delaware and the market for corporate charters: history and agency' (1990) 15 Del J Corp L 885, which reveals that Delaware's statutes on corporate law are drafted by the Delaware Bar Association and automatically adopted by the legislature, which has no members with any expertise in the subject. For further criticism and a detailed description of Delaware's legislation procedures see 'Law for sale: a study of the Delaware Corporation Law of 1967' (1969) 117 U Pa L Rev 861.

The American system is commonly defended on the ground that competition is a good thing and in a market for incorporation where State laws are a 'product', competition must result in better product. Fears that the most successful laws are those that favour a particular interest group are countered by saying that if other interest groups really felt disadvantaged they would stop dealing with companies incorporated under the disadvantageous laws, and those laws would cease to be the most successful. In particular, it is argued that if different State laws had different effects on shareholders then this would be reflected in share prices but in fact there seems to be no evidence that moving to Delaware, for example, affects a company's share price. It may be that shareholders and directors in the USA pay less attention to State corporation laws than lawyers do. The real reason for Delaware's success at attracting corporations may just be that it has become a centre of expertise in corporate law and that the lawyers advising business people tell them to incorporate in Delaware because the lawyers' future work will be made easier if they are in a legal environment with which they are familiar and can trust (see W.W. Bratton, 'Corporate law's race to nowhere in particular' (1994) 44 UTLJ 401, which is a valuable review of the debate in this area; D.G. Kaouris, 'Is Delaware still a haven for incorporation?' (1995) 20 Del J Corp L 965).

The idea of legislation as a product which is periodically redesigned to make it more attractive to consumers who may choose whether or not to adopt it is a challenge to the traditional concept of legislation as expressing inescapable basic standards for public life enacted in the public interest by the people's representatives in the legislature. It raises the question whether the public interest does require any minimum standards in company law. In Europe there is some minimum standard setting by Directives which harmonise, in the words of art. 54(3)(g) of the EC Treaty, 'the safeguards which, for the protection of the interests of members *and others*, are required of companies' (emphasis added). If there is no element of public interest in company law then it can be made by legally expert product designers and, as in Delaware, the legislators can adopt it without worrying about its effect on the people they represent. As companies are of such pervasive influence in everyday life it is unlikely that there can be no public interest in their activities or that voters would want to give up political control over them. What is in the public interest is a political question which must be determined by political institutions in which, often, conflicting interests must be reconciled. Comparing EC and US company law, W.J. Carney, 'The political economy of competition for corporate charters' (1997) 26 J Legal Stud 303 says that EC company law Directives (and hence British company law) have far more mandatory provisions than equivalent US law. He attributes this to the lack of competition among European jurisdictions allowing interest groups to obtain legislation in their favour which he claims would be removed by market forces in the competitive USA. But another way of looking at it is that European company law is produced by democratic political institutions representing a wide range of interests, whereas Delaware corporate law is not.

In both Australia and the USA, people from one interest group have feared that central government legislation could unduly favour another group and that they would be unable to escape from laws unfavourable to them as they could when different States had different laws.

At present there are no plans for a uniform company law in Europe as there is in Australia. Article 54(3)(g) of the EC Treaty requires laws to be made 'equivalent', not 'uniform'. Even the proposed Regulation on the European company will not provide a complete code: the original idea of central registration has been abandoned and, under the latest draft, European companies would be registered in national companies registries and subject to national legislation, details of which can vary from country to country. So far the Community policy has been to create a system of minimum standards for company law which must be observed throughout the Community. According to I. G. F. Cath, 'Freedom of establishment of companies: a new step towards completion of the internal market' 6 YEL 1986 247 at p. 255:

> Though often limited in scope and having a 'compromising' character, reflecting the different schools of thought which had to be reconciled, these Directives have brought some alignment of company law and have generally raised the existing standards to a common Community level.

EC Directives have made some startling administrative changes to UK company law — for example, introducing uniform formats for the publicly available accounts of companies, introducing a new system for recognition of the qualifications of auditors and introducing single-member private limited companies. Substantive changes, altering the balance between various interest groups, are far fewer. The most significant example is the rules on security of transactions, which improve the position of persons dealing with companies and which are discussed in chapter 19, especially 19.5 and 19.6. These rules were made in the First Directive which was adopted before the UK joined the Community, and it has been very difficult to amend British company law to comply with the rules.

There is little evidence that any EU country is bidding to become the Delaware of Europe. Incorporation fees would not be a sufficiently significant contribution to any national Treasury to influence government policy. However, there are significant differences between national laws. For example, Germany insists on employee participation in any company with more than 500 employees; in Britain there is no minimum capital requirement for a private company whereas there is in Germany. American commentators, reflecting experience in their own country, suggest that these differences will increasingly influence the choice of jurisdiction of incorporation (see A.F. Conard, 'The European alternative to uniformity in corporation laws' (1991) 89 Mich L Rev 2150; C.D. Stith, 'Federalism and company law: a ''race to the bottom'' in the European Community' (1991) 79 Geo LJ 1581). But the Commission has said that the prospect of companies moving within the EU to countries with less stringent company laws 'would be unacceptable to member States' (*Commission Consultation Paper on Company Law* (1997), p. 3).

It had been thought that greater uniformity of company law would be almost inevitable as the Single Market developed, and the Commission has long argued that companies in different European States need to unite to form companies which are large enough to compete in world markets, and this requires a uniform European company law. One aspect of this hoped-for uniform law for large companies is the proposal for the societas europea, another is the Commission's proposed Fifth Directive (on the structure of public limited companies) (OJ C240, 9 September 1983, p. 2; OJ C321, 12 December 1991, p. 9). Both proposals have been unable to proceed because the biggest obstacle to greater uniformity is that different countries in the Union have established their systems of company law with very different approaches in some areas, and are now unwilling to abandon their own traditions in favour of another State's for the sake of uniformity. The most contentious problem has been the different approaches to employee involvement in management. Compulsory employee involvement in the management of large companies (known as 'co-determination') has long been central to German society and has been adopted in a modified form in the Netherlands, but relations between employees and management have traditionally been arranged very differently elsewhere in the Union. In particular the former

Conservative government in the United Kingdom was implacably opposed to any form of compulsory employee involvement. See T.E. Abeltshauser, 'Towards a European constitution of the firm: problems and perspectives' (1990) 11 Mich J Int'l L 1235; W. Kolvenbach, 'EEC company law harmonisation and worker participation' (1990) 11 U Pa J Int'l Bus L 709; J. Dine, 'Why not employee participation in the European Community context?' (1995) 16 Co Law 44.

See generally, R. Drury, 'A review of the European Community's company law harmonisation programme' (1992) 24 Bracton Law J 45; M. Andenas, 'The future of EC law harmonisation' (1994) 15 Co Law 121. For an attempt to analyse why some company law rules should be set centrally in the EU and others left to local jurisdictions see D. Charny, 'Competition among jurisdictions in formulating corporate law rules: an American perspective on the "race to the bottom" in the European Communities' (1991) 32 Harv Int'l LJ 423 (reprinted in S. Wheeler, *A Reader on the Law of Business Enterprise* (Oxford University Press, 1994)).

0.3.4 Practitioners' books and other literature

There are three practitioners' works which deal with company law at length and in detail. *Buckley on the Companies Acts* (Butterworths) first appeared in 1873 when its author, Henry Burton Buckley, was a barrister of only four years' standing. He became Buckley J in 1900 and Buckley LJ in 1906 until he retired and became the 1st Baron Wrenbury: many of his judgments are quoted in this book as are those of his son, Sir Denys Buckley. *Palmer's Company Law* (Sweet & Maxwell) first appeared in 1898. Its author, Francis Beaufort Palmer (1845–1917), was a barrister and legal author, and his work has probably been more popular than Buckley's, partly because it is arranged as a continuous narrative whereas Buckley's is a commentary on the text of the legislation. The work now known as *Gore-Brown on Companies* (Jordans) was originally written by Richard Jordan and first published in 1867 by Jordan & Sons Ltd, company registration agents. It was later edited by a barrister, Francis Gore-Brown (1860–1922).

Gower's Principles of Modern Company Law (Sweet & Maxwell) is a university textbook rather than a comprehensive practitioners' work and can therefore be rather more argumentative and controversial. Since its first edition in 1954 it has been frequently cited and discussed in academic articles and in court.

Many academic lawyers specialise in company law. Scholarly articles and case notes will be found in the general legal journals, especially the *Cambridge Law Journal* (CLJ), the *Law Quarterly Review* (LQR) and the *Modern Law Review* (MLR). There is always much that is relevant to company law in the *Journal of Business Law* (JBL). However, probably the most important forum for academic discussion of company law is the *Company Lawyer* (Co Law), which was established in 1980. There is a similar journal published in Australia, *Company and Securities Law Journal* (C & SLJ).

Articles of a more practical nature will be found in the *Solicitors' Journal* (SJ) and the *Gazette*, and in the specialist publication *PLC: Practical Law for Companies*. All are primarily intended for solicitors.

0.3.5 Morality, economics, democracy and company law

The principal object of this book is to provide an introductory description of the current rules of English company law. Those rules are intended to support and serve the country's economic system, and different views are possible on how law should do this. Some of these differences of opinion reflect differences about the function of law generally.

Law influences human behaviour (a) by prescribing the limits of acceptable behaviour (for example, insider dealing is an offence — see 13.2; using one's position as a company director to make a profit that is not permitted by the company is a breach of fiduciary duty — see 16.5) and (b) by providing for sanctions to punish or deter unacceptable behaviour (a court may fine or imprison an insider dealer; may require a profit made in breach of fiduciary duty to be handed over to the company). Human behaviour is also influenced by moral judgment (which may, for example, limit actions by a human that harm other humans, the actor, or other animals). It is natural to regard moral judgment as a precursor of law. So a Law Lord can say that: 'The law and morality are inextricably interwoven. To a large extent the law is simply formulated and declared morality' (Lord Steyn in *Smith New Court Securities Ltd* v *Citibank NA* [1997] AC 254 at p. 280). Certainly laws command greatest respect when they reflect moral judgments held almost universally and without substantial objection (for example, laws punishing murder). But laws are often controversial in areas where a variety of moral views exist, and where the variety continues despite extensive public discussion, for example, on the subjects of abortion, drug use, euthanasia, sexual activity and the uses humans make of other animals. The relationship of morality to law has been particularly illuminated by the work of the legal philosopher H.L.A. Hart, who argued for the autonomy of law and that there are some moral judgments which it is not appropriate to translate into laws. See N. MacCormick, *H.L.A. Hart* (London: Edward Arnold, 1981). In the United Kingdom the theory of Parliamentary sovereignty over law means that we look to the political forum to decide what laws to make in the knowledge of conflicting moral views.

Some legal philosophers have hoped to find a natural law, which would be a law that is a universal requirement of human societal life and which might be found by examining that life and, for some, by revelation from a deity.

Other jurists claim to have found a different underlying principle for law in the neoclassical economics of the Chicago school (so-called because its leading exponents, including Milton Friedman, George Stigler and Ronald Coase, taught at the University of Chicago). Jurists taking that view are usually known as the Chicago law and economics movement. A detailed and sympathetic account of the history of this movement, which nevertheless gives room to the criticism that has been made of it, is in N. Duxbury, *Patterns of American Jurisprudence* (Oxford: Clarendon Press, 1995), ch. 5. The best-known presentation of the movement's views is R.A. Posner, *Economic Analysis of Law*, 5th ed. (Aspen Publishers, 1998).

Chicago neoclassical economics is founded on the assumption that those who undertake economic activity do so for the sole purpose of maximising their wealth and they have both complete knowledge of what has to be done to achieve that and unfettered ability to do it – they are described as rational economic actors. If they undertake their economic activity by freely contracting in a market whose other participants also have the same knowledge and ability (known as a perfect market), it is predicted that productive resources will be acquired by those who use them to produce the greatest wealth, and so the overall wealth of the economy is maximised. It is assumed that freely contracting in markets is the best way of conducting economic activity. To the extent that law and other forms of State regulation are found to distort free contracting in a perfect market (which it is assumed they will do), they are wrong. As Milton Friedman put it in 1974 (quoted in Duxbury, op. cit., p. 366):

In discussions of economic policy, 'Chicago' stands for belief in the efficacy of the free market as a means of organising resources, for scepticism about government intervention into economic affairs, and for emphasis on the quantity of money as a key factor in producing inflation.

The fact that real people do not have the knowledge and ability assumed in the theory (they have what is called bounded rationality) is not thought to affect the value of the theory. It is assumed that real people will want to become more and more like rational economic actors in perfect markets so that they can maximise their wealth. Many who disagree with the law and economics movement are content not to be rational economic actors in perfect markets, which is a profound difference in world views that may explain why supporters and opponents of the theory often do not take each other seriously (D. Millon, 'Communitarians, contractarians and the crisis in corporate law' (1993) 50 Wash & Lee L Rev 1373 at p. 1382). As Posner points out (*Economic Analysis of Law*, 3rd ed., at p. 22), 'The most frequent criticism is that the normative underpinnings of the economic approach are so repulsive that it is inconceivable that the legal system would (let alone should) embrace them'.

Promotion of collective wealth maximisation is proposed in Chicago law and economics apparently despite individual casualties. This is counter to the view of the law as the upholder of each subject's individual rights (see G.J. Stigler, 'Law or economics?' (1992) 35 J Law & Econ 455). For example, neoclassical economists assert that laws to prevent wage discrimination between workers of different gender or ethnicity prevent wealth maximisation (H. Demsetz, 'Minorities in the market place', in *Ownership, Control and the Firm*, vol. 1 (Oxford: Blackwell, 1988), pp. 82–103; R.A. Posner, 'An economic analysis of sex discrimination laws' (1989) 56 U Chi L Rev 1311), and that the economy's wealth would be increased if women could sell their babies (E.M. Landes and R.A. Posner, 'The economics of the baby shortage' (1978) 7 J Legal Stud 323). A theory that leads to these results may look like the antithesis of law rather than a basis for it. Discrimination and baby-selling are illegal because they are disapproved of morally, not because of the effects they are predicted to have by a theory of economics. Proposing that they should be made legal because of a theory of economics supposes that the theory is superior to national moral judgment. Choosing whether to base a nation's laws on moral judgment or economic theory is a political choice.

Part of the problem is that, like much of economics, neoclassical theory is about static equilibrium states, not dynamic changing states: it predicts the ideal final state, but is not much concerned with getting there, or who might get hurt on the way (a point made by, among others, Guido Calabresi in, for example, 'The pointlessness of Pareto: carrying Coase further' (1991) 100 Yale LJ 1211). The most common criticism of the theory is that it maximises the wealth of an economy only for a given distribution of wealth within that economy, which it is not concerned to change. But in reality the present distribution of wealth gives some persons — particularly large companies — overwhelming power over others, so that there is no possibility of free contracting between them, and it is the underprivileged in this situation who require the protection of the law. For discussion of wealth maximisation as a guiding principle of public life see R.M. Dworkin, 'Is wealth a value?' (1980) 9 J Legal Stud 191, J.L. Coleman, 'Efficiency, utility and wealth maximisation' (1980) 8 Hofstra L Rev 509 and R.A. Posner, 'The value of wealth: a comment on Dworkin and Kronman' (1980) 9 J Legal Stud 243.

Supporters of the law and economics movement meet the controversy over its conclusions by claiming that they are arrived at scientifically. They say that their arguments are derived from scientific economics and they claim to have demonstrated the truth of their theory because it correctly predicts rules of common law arrived at before the theory was invented.

The congruence of law and economics with common law is a central thesis of Posner. It has been elaborated in the company law context by B.S. Black, 'Is corporate law trivial? A political and economic analysis' (1990) 84 Nw U L Rev 542 and in relation to equity, which is of great significance to company law, by A.J. Duggan, 'Is equity efficient?' (1997) 113 LQR 601. However, in reality there seems to be only a coincidental overlap of common law and Chicago law and economics. There are common law doctrines of which Chicago law and economics disapproves and much of the law desired by Chicago law and economics does not exist. That the overlap is fortuitous is hardly surprising: both the common law and Chicago law and economics arrive at their results by systematic reasoning, but from different premises. Whether the common law should adopt the same premises as Chicago law and economics, and so produce exactly the same results, is an essentially political question. For more on the scientific status of law and economics see G.S. Crespi, 'The mid-life crisis of the law and economics movement: confronting the problems of nonfalsifiability and normative bias' (1991) 67 Notre Dame L Rev 231 (which, incidentally, suggests that law and economics is best characterised as a literary genre); R.C. Downs, 'Law and economics: nexus of science and belief' (1995) 27 Pac LJ 1 (which, incidentally, notes the quasi-religious tone of much of law and economics: a tone that is particularly apparent in the more fundamentalist writings on American corporate law and which is discussed in M.A. Eisenberg, 'New modes of discourse in the corporate law literature' (1984) 52 Geo Wash L Rev 582); G. De Geest, 'The debate on the scientific status of law and economics' (1996) 40 European Economic Review 999 (which responds that law and economics is scientific if it is judged by weaker criteria than other sciences).

The fact that some predictions of Chicago law and economics are so obviously controversial shows that the theory cannot be relied on to produce laws to which there will be almost universal agreement and no substantial opposition. There are undoubtedly people who believe in it as a source of law, but equally there are many who do not. In a democratic society the law that will be made in the light of these conflicts of opinion will be the result of a political solution of the conflicts.

Many in the American law and economics movement extend their scepticism of government to scepticism about the political process of legislation, which they see as merely favouring interest groups whose aims they disapprove, rather than achieving political solutions to the conflict between their aims and those of others. For example, Delaware's success in attracting incorporations is attributed by one author to the fact that its tiny legislature accepts the proposals of the Delaware Bar Association: 'Many of the legislative pressures, which could disrupt the development of corporate law, from environmental groups, unions, and local communities, are not present in Delaware' (D.G. Kaouris, 'Is Delaware still a haven for incorporation?' (1995) 20 Del J Corp L 965 at p. 1005).

As companies are so important in economic life the Chicago law and economics movement has paid much attention to company law. The leading text in America is F.H. Easterbrook and D.R. Fischel, *The Economic Structure of Corporate Law* (Harvard University Press, 1991). This is by two convinced believers in the neoclassical economics of Chicago (where Fischel teaches). As they say in their Preface: '. . . we take a few economic principles and preach to legislatures and judges about what the law ought to be if it is to promote social welfare' (p. viii). The theory is applied in the context of English company law in B.R. Cheffins, *Company Law: Theory, Structure and Operation* (Oxford: Clarendon Press, 1997). Critics who argue that corporate law should not be captured by Easterbrook and Fischel include L. Johnson, 'Individual and collective sovereignty in the corporate enterprise' (1992) 92 Colum L Rev 2215 at p. 2217 and L.E. Mitchell, 'The cult of efficiency' (1992) 71 Tex L Rev 217 at p. 219.

In the USA many of the legal scholars who apply Chicago law and economics to company law have adopted from economists the description of a company as a 'nexus of contracts' (see 5.3.2), and such scholars are often called 'contractarians'. The following quotation from H.N. Butler, 'The contractual theory of the corporation' (1989) 11 Geo Mason U L Rev 99 at p. 100, explains the contractarian position that corporations should be regarded as created by private contract with which the State must not interfere:

> The contractual theory of the corporation is in stark contrast to the legal concept of the corporation as an entity created by the State. The entity theory of the corporation supports State intervention — in the form of either direct regulation or the facilitation of shareholder litigation — in the corporation on the ground that the State created the corporation by granting it a charter. The contractual theory views the corporation as founded in private contract, where the role of the State is limited to enforcing contracts. In this regard, a State charter merely recognises the existence of a 'nexus of contracts' called a corporation. Each contract in the 'nexus of contracts' warrants the same legal and constitutional protections as other legally enforceable contracts. Moreover freedom of contract requires that parties to the 'nexus of contracts' must be allowed to structure their relations as they please.

As explained in 0.1 our view is that the most significant legal feature of incorporation is the creation of an artificial separate personality, and, in English law, this can only be done by grant from the State.

People who have disagreed with the conclusions of the Chicago law and economics analysis of company law have, in the USA, been called 'communitarians' (M.E. DeBow and D.R. Lee, 'Shareholders, nonshareholders and corporate law: communitarianism and resource allocation' (1993) 18 Del J Corp L 393). This has been accepted by a leading critic of that analysis (D. Millon, 'Communitarians, contractarians and the crisis in corporate law' (1993) 50 Wash & Lee L Rev 1373 at p. 1378), but it implies (and was perhaps intended to imply) that the only people who disagree with the analysis are those who adopt the political philosophy of communitarianism, which is not the case. Two articles which place arguments over the economic approach to company law into the context of a very long history of opposed political values are F.R. Kaen, A. Kaufman and L. Zacharias, 'American political values and agency theory: a perspective' (1988) 7 J Bus Ethics 805; P.N. Cox 'The public, the private and the corporation' (1997) 80 Marq L Rev 391.

We now leave the political arena and return to the principal purpose of this book, which is to describe the law as it is now.

1 Registration

1.1 INTRODUCTION

The Companies Act 1985 provides for the incorporation of companies by a simple process of registration which is described in this chapter. The companies thus incorporated are known as 'registered companies'. Registration under the Companies Act 1985 makes readily available the benefits of separate corporate personality which were described in 0.1.1. However, it does not confer on the members of a registered company the benefit of not being liable for the company's debts. Instead the Act offers the choice of unlimited liability (adopted by very few companies) or limited liability (adopted by nearly all companies) — see 1.3.2.

1.2 PROCEDURE

1.2.1 Formation and registration under the Companies Act 1985

To create a new registered company it is necessary to prepare and sign a set of documents and deliver them to a registrar of companies. If a new company is to be governed by the law of England and Wales then the documents must be delivered to the registrar of companies in England and Wales, whose office is at Crown Way, Cardiff CF4 3UZ. The registrar is chief executive of a government agency called Companies House. The documents for a new company which is to be governed by the law of Scotland must be delivered to the registrar of companies for Scotland, whose office is at 102 George Street, Edinburgh EH2 3DJ.

As will be explained in 1.3, several different types of company can be registered. The contents of the documents that have to be delivered for registration depend on the type of company being registered. The two most important types are the public company limited by shares (the plc) and the private company limited by shares. (The public can be invited to invest in the shares of a public company but not in the shares of a private company.)

The documents which are required to be filed in order to register a new company provide the following basic information:

(a) The company's name and the location of a place (called the registered office) where documents can be served on the company.

(b) The type of company (public or private, limited or unlimited, with or without a share capital — see 1.3).

(c) The objects which the company is formed to pursue.

(d) The company's constitution.

(e) The names of the company's first member(s), director(s) and secretary.

(f) The proposed capital of the company (no capital need be contributed at the time of registration).

The required documents are:

(a) The company's constitution contained in two documents called the memorandum of association and the articles of association. When registering a private or public company limited by shares, articles of association need not be registered if the company is to use the standard set of articles known as Table A which has been promulgated by the Secretary of State — see 3.2 — but in practice it is usual to register articles drawn up specifically for the company.

(b) A statement naming, and giving other details of, the company's first director (or directors) and secretary, and giving the address of its registered office.

(c) A statement that all requirements of the CA 1985 in respect of registration have been complied with.

The memorandum of association states what the company's name will be (it may be necessary to check before registering that there will be no objection to the name: see 2.3.3.5), states the objects which the company has been formed to pursue, names the company's first member or members, and gives some other basic details depending on the type of company being registered. The contents of the memorandum will be considered in depth in chapter 2. For the purposes of registration the most significant point about a company's memorandum is that it must be signed by one or more persons who are called 'subscribers'. If the company is to be a private company limited by shares (or a private company limited by guarantee, a comparatively little used type of company which will be described in 1.3) then only one subscriber is required. The memorandum of a public company limited by shares or any other type of company must have at least two subscribers. There is no upper limit to the number of subscribers.

The subscribers of a company's memorandum will be the company's first members when it is registered (CA 1985, s. 22(1)). They are the persons who wish to be associated in the company, which is why the document they sign is called a memorandum of association, though this terminology has become less apt since 15 July 1992 when it became possible to register a private limited company with only one subscriber.

The fundamental principle that a company can be created by registration of a memorandum of association is enshrined in the first section of the CA 1985 as amended by SI 1992 No. 1699:

(1) Any two or more persons associated for a lawful purpose may, by subscribing their names to a memorandum of association and otherwise complying with the requirements of this Act in respect of registration, form an incorporated company, with or without limited liability. . . .

(3A) Notwithstanding subsection (1), one person may, for a lawful purpose, by subscribing his name to a memorandum of association and otherwise complying with the requirements of this Act in respect of registration, form an incorporated company being a private company limited by shares or by guarantee.

It is usual to deliver with the memorandum, under s. 7, articles of association setting out the internal regulations of the company (see chapter 3).

By s. 10(2) and (6) and sch. 1, the registrar of companies must be given a statement naming the company's first directors, and giving their addresses and other details about them (see 15.4.2), naming, and giving the address of, the company's first secretary (see 17.3.2), and stating the intended situation of the company's registered office (see 2.3.4). This statement must be signed by or on behalf of the subscribers and must contain a consent to act by each of the persons named as director or secretary (s. 10(3)).

The registrar must be given a statutory declaration by a solicitor engaged in the formation of the company or by a person named as a director or secretary in the statement delivered in accordance with s. 10(2) that all the requirements of CA 1985 in respect of registration have been complied with (s. 12(3)).

The registrar must retain and register the memorandum and articles, if any, if satisfied that 'all the requirements of [CA 1985] in respect of registration and of matters precedent and incidental to it have been complied with' (s. 12(1) and (2)), though the registrar is entitled to rely on the statutory declaration that all these requirements have been met (s. 12(3)).

On registering a company's memorandum, the registrar must allocate to the company a number, called its 'registered number' (s. 705), and must give a certificate that the company is incorporated (s. 13(1)). Such a certificate of incorporation is conclusive evidence that all the requirements of registration have been complied with, and that the company is duly registered (s. 13(7)). The registrar will publish in the *Gazette* a notice of the issue of a certificate of incorporation (s. 711(1)(a)). The registrar puts on the certificate the company's date of incorporation and the company is a body corporate from that date (s. 13(3)), which means from the first moment of that day (*Jubilee Cotton Mills Ltd* v *Lewis* [1924] AC 958). A registered company exists as from the date of its incorporation as recorded on its certificate of incorporation without any further formalities and regardless of whether it undertakes any business. In particular there is no need for a meeting of members or directors to ratify its incorporation.

A fee of £20 is payable for the registration of a company (SI 1991 No. 1206; SI 1994 No. 2217). For £100, registration will be completed on the same day if documents are presented before 3 p.m. and there is no problem with the company's name.

The subscribers of a memorandum of association may be foreigners: there is no requirement that the subscribers be domiciled in the part of Great Britain in which the company is to be registered (*Princess of Reuss* v *Bos* (1871) LR 5 HL 176). But an association which is already completely constituted as a partnership or a corporation under another legal system cannot be registered as a company under CA 1985 (*Bulkeley* v *Schutz* (1871) LR 3 PC 764). In particular, a company registered in Scotland cannot register in England and Wales or vice versa (see *Bateman* v *Service* (1881) 6 App Cas 386 on the inability of a company registered in one state of Australia to register in another).

Signature of a memorandum by a minor is valid unless the minor has repudiated the signature before registration (*Re Nassau Phosphate Co.* (1876) 2 ChD 610; *Re Laxon & Co. (No. 2)* [1892] 3 Ch 555).

CA 1985 only provides for the registration of companies formed 'for a lawful purpose' (s. 1(1) and (3A)) so the registrar is entitled to refuse to register a company formed for a purpose that is not lawful. In addition, a trade union must not be registered as a company (Trade Union and Labour Relations (Consolidation) Act 1992, s. 10(3), repeating provisions made in earlier trade union legislation). The latter provision has caused problems: see M.A. Hickling, 'Trade unions in disguise' (1964) 27 MLR 625; R.R. Drury, 'Nullity of companies in English law' (1985) 48 MLR 644.

A refusal by the registrar to register a company is subject to judicial review. For example, in *R* v *Registrar of Joint Stock Companies, ex parte More* [1931] 2 KB 197 the registrar refused to register a company because its main object was stated to be to sell in Great Britain tickets in a lottery (popularly known as the Irish Sweep) run in what was then the Irish Free State. The promoters of the company sought judicial review of this decision. The Court of Appeal held that selling such tickets in England would have been an offence under statutes then in force (it would now be an offence under the Lotteries and Amusements Act 1976, s. 2) so that the registrar was right to refuse to register the company, which was not formed 'for a lawful purpose'. (The Irish Sweep has been discontinued.)

In *R* v *Registrar of Companies, ex parte Bowen* [1914] 3 KB 1161 the court held that the registrar's refusal to register a company had been wrong: the registrar had doubted that the company's name, 'The United Dental Service Ltd', was legal because of statutory restrictions on advertising oneself as a qualified dental practitioner; however, the court held that the name was legal. There is now a procedure for vetting some company names before registration and if Mr Bowen were registering The United Dental Service Ltd today he would have to go through that procedure — see 2.3.3.5. Since 1914, further controls on dentistry have been enacted. Mr Bowen formed his company to carry on the business of dentistry. It would not now be lawful to form a company for that purpose because of the Dentists Act 1984, s. 42.

A positive decision by the registrar to register a company is less amenable to judicial review because the applicant in the review proceedings would have to present evidence to the court that the provisions of CA 1985 in respect of registration had not been complied with whereas the registrar's certificate of incorporation is conclusive evidence that they have been complied with (CA 1985, s. 13(7)). Accordingly the court cannot hear any application for review of a decision by the registrar to register a company unless the applicant is the Attorney-General, whose evidence the court must hear because the provision in s. 13(7) does not bind the Crown (per Lord Parker of Waddington in *Bowman* v *Secular Society Ltd* [1917] AC 406 at pp. 438–40 and in *Cotman* v *Brougham* [1918] AC 514 at p. 519; *R* v *Registrar of Companies, ex parte Central Bank of India* [1986] QB 1114, CA). It is important for persons who deal with a company to be confident that the company's existence cannot easily be challenged.

The Attorney-General's power to ask for reversal of a decision to register a company was used in *R* v *Registrar of Companies, ex parte Attorney-General* [1991] BCLC 476, DC, in which the court found that the registrar had wrongly decided to register a company, Lindi St Clair (Personal Services) Ltd, whose object was to 'carry on the business of prostitution'. This was held not to be a lawful purpose. Ackner LJ said, at pp. 478–9:

> It is well settled that a contract made upon a sexually immoral consideration or for a sexually immoral purpose is against public policy and is illegal and unenforceable. . . . Here . . . the association is for the purpose of carrying on a trade which involves illegal contracts.

Provided the fact of its incorporation is not questioned, the legality of the objects of a company may be questioned in legal proceedings and its certificate of incorporation is not conclusive that they are legal (*Bowman* v *Secular Society Ltd*).

1.2.2 Companies off the shelf

The preparation of documents for the registration of a new company requires careful consideration and specialist knowledge of company law and procedures. Enterprises exist which specialise in company formation. They register a large number of companies and then hold them ready for sale to anyone who wants a new company. This kind of company is called an 'off-the-shelf' or a 'shelf' or a 'ready-made' company. A shelf company is registered with persons associated with the company-formation enterprise as its subscribers (i.e., first members), its first director and first secretary. The subscribers take one share each. The company can then be sold to a customer of the enterprise by transferring its two shares to two persons nominated by the customer, at which point the first director and secretary resign and report their resignations to the registrar.

British shelf companies are remarkably cheap (as low as £45) and buying one is a very simple and quick process. According to A. Hicks, R. Drury and J. Smallcombe, *Alternative Company Structures for the Small Business* (London: Certified Accountants Educational Trust, 1995), in other European countries shelf companies are not available and persons wishing to incorporate have to employ legal advisers at about 10 times the cost of a British company. An important disadvantage of a shelf company is that its constitution will not be specially designed for the needs of its purchasers who will be unlikely to care about the deficiencies until it is too late. This is a shame because one of the great advantages of the company form is that members can have whatever constitution suits them best, if they are willing to spend time (and money) finding out what they need. Hicks et al. also think that cheap shelf companies make limited liability too freely available.

1.2.3 Companies formed and registered under the former Companies Acts

Before 1 July 1985, companies were registered under the Companies Act 1948, which came into force on 1 July 1948.

From 1 November 1929 to 30 June 1948, companies could be registered under the Companies Act 1929.

From 1 April 1909 to 31 October 1929, companies could be registered under the Companies (Consolidation) Act 1908.

From 2 November 1862 to 31 March 1909, companies could be registered under the Companies Act 1862.

From 14 July 1856 to 1 November 1862, companies could be registered under the Joint Stock Companies Act 1856, though, by virtue of s. 2 of the 1856 Act, banking companies could not register until the Joint Stock Banking Companies Act 1857 came into force, and insurance companies never could register under the 1856 Act (they were allowed to register under the Companies Act 1862 and subsequent Acts). Insurance companies were excluded from the 1856 Act so as to prevent them being registered with limited liability (see 1.3.2.5).

The Acts from 1856 to 1948 are referred to in CA 1985 as 'the former Companies Acts'. A company formed and registered in England and Wales or Scotland under any of these earlier Acts, and not since dissolved, is called an 'existing company' and is governed by CA 1985 as if registered under that Act (CA 1985, s. 675). However, companies registered in Ireland under the 1908 Act or any of its predecessors are not 'existing companies' for the purposes of CA 1985 and so are not governed by it (CA 1985, s. 735(1)(b); similarly CA 1929 and CA 1948 did not apply to Irish companies).

The first Act enabling incorporation of companies by registration was the Joint Stock Companies Act 1844, which permitted registration as from 1 November 1844 (though it did not apply in Scotland). The system under the 1844 Act was very different from that under the 1856 Act and its successors. Accordingly, all companies registered under the 1844 Act were required to re-register under the 1856 Act on or before 3 November 1856 (Joint Stock Companies Act 1856, s. 110), though this was later extended to 2 November 1857 by the Joint Stock Companies Act 1857, ss. 25 to 27. Insurance companies registered under the 1844 Act were excluded from re-registering under the 1856 Act but were required to re-register under the 1862 Act. Banking companies were not allowed to register under the 1844 Act, and the Joint Stock Banks Act 1844 prevented any association of more than six persons setting up a banking business without obtaining a royal charter of incorporation under the Act.

1.3 CLASSIFICATION OF COMPANIES

1.3.1 Introduction

CA 1985 provides for the registration of five different types of company. The wording of the documents which have to be delivered to the registrar on the registration of a company depends on which type of company it is and so it is necessary to choose which type a company is to be before registering it. There are provisions for re-registration so that a company can be changed from one type to another, though there are certain changes that are not possible by re-registration — see 1.3.4.

There are three characteristics of a company which determine which type it is:

(a) Whether the members have limited or unlimited liability.

(b) Whether the company is public or private. The classification of companies into public and private was altered on 22 December 1980. Unlimited companies must now be private companies.

(c) Whether the company does or does not have a share capital. A company without a share capital must be a private company.

This means that the following kinds of new company may now be registered:

(a) Public limited company with share capital.

(b) Private limited company with share capital (by far the most numerous type).

(c) Private limited company without share capital (called a 'company limited by guarantee' or 'guarantee company').

(d) Private unlimited company with share capital.

(e) Private unlimited company without share capital.

The features which have proved most popular have been limited liability and the capacity to have a share capital — see 1.3.2. Both features are particularly attractive to business enterprises. The share capital of a company is capital contributed by members (shareholders) for use in the company's operations. The distinction between public and private companies is that a public company may invite the public generally to contribute to its share capital whereas a private company cannot.

Guarantee and unlimited companies have been found appropriate for some specialised uses but the limited company with share capital is by far the most common form of company and this book will hardly mention other kinds of company.

1.3.2 Limited or unlimited companies and share capital

The opening provision of the CA 1985 (s. 1(1)) allows incorporation 'with or without limited liability'. Almost all registered companies are incorporated with limited liability. A registered company with limited liability is called a 'limited company' and a registered company without limited liability is called an 'unlimited company'.

The principle of separate personality of a body corporate such as a registered company means that its members are not responsible for its debts unless they are made responsible by statute or by the constitution of the corporation (*Re Sheffield & South Yorkshire Permanent Building Society* (1889) 22 QBD 470 per Cave J at p. 476).

Liability for the debts of a registered company is imposed on its members by statute. However, except in the rare circumstances in which CA 1985, s. 24, applies (see 1.3.2.6), the statutory provisions do not make the members directly responsible for the company's debts, that is, a creditor cannot sue the members personally: as Lord Cranworth said in *Oakes* v *Turquand and Harding* (1867) LR 2 HL 325 at p. 357:

There is no doubt that the direct remedy of a creditor is solely against the incorporated company. He has no dealing with any individual shareholder, and if he is driven to bring any action to enforce any right he may have acquired, he must sue the company, and not any of the members of whom it is composed.

Instead of being made directly liable to creditors of the company, the members are made liable by statute if, but only if, the company is wound up (CA 1985, s. 13(4)), and their liability then is *to the company as a separate person*, and is a liability to contribute money for the payment of the company's debts and liabilities, and the expenses of the winding up, and for the adjustment of the rights of the contributories among themselves (Insolvency Act 1986, s. 74(1)). In an unlimited company, the liability of members at this point is unlimited. Only a very small proportion of registered companies are unlimited companies and they will be almost completely ignored in this book. In a limited company the members' liability when the company is wound up is limited to a fixed amount agreed with the company when they became members: the fixed amount being either an amount payable on shares or an amount payable by guarantee (Insolvency Act 1986, s. 74(2)(d) and (3)). When drawing up the memorandum of association of a limited company for registration, a choice must be made between making the members liable on shares (CA 1985, s. 1(2)(a); Insolvency Act 1986, s. 74(2)(d)) or by guarantee (CA 1985, s. 1(2)(b); Insolvency Act 1986, s. 74(3)). Almost all limited companies are limited by shares.

The memorandum of a company limited by shares or by guarantee must state that the liability of its members is limited (CA 1985, s. 2(3)).

The difference between limitation by guarantee and limitation by shares is that in a guarantee company, the limited amount that the members are liable to pay is payable only on the winding up of the company (s. 2(4)) whereas in a company limited by shares it is expected that part at least of the payment will be made while the company is a going concern and will form the contributed capital of the company (known as its 'share capital'). In practice, nowadays, in a company limited by shares, the whole amount that the members are liable to pay is paid as contributed capital while the company is a going concern so that the members have no further liability on winding up. The creditors of a company limited by shares have to bear the risk that its capital contributed while it is a going concern may be lost in trading before it is wound up.

The position is, then, that in the statute permitting incorporation of companies by registration, Parliament has insisted that members of a registered company must be liable to contribute to its assets, but it permits that liability to be limited.

In relation to companies the terms 'limited' and 'unlimited' refer to the liability of the companies' members, not the liability of the companies as separate persons. Saying that a person has liability for an obligation does not mean that the person will actually meet the obligation in practice: a person who has run out of money cannot meet any liabilities.

A limited company as a separate person has unlimited liability to pay all its debts and can be forced to pay them until it runs out of money: but if it is wound up, its members have only limited liability to contribute further money for the payment of those debts — they cannot be required to pay more than the limit on their liability.

1.3.2.1 Companies limited by shares

The liability of members of a company limited by shares is based on the company having a 'share capital' and the members taking 'shares' issued to them by the company. Each share is assigned a 'nominal value' or 'par value' and is described in CA 1985, s. 2(5)(a), as a share 'of a fixed amount'. The nominal value of a share in a company is a sum of money that must be paid on it to the company (though, when a share is issued, the company and the person to whom it is issued may agree that an additional amount, called a 'share premium', is to be paid).

The memorandum of a company limited by shares must state a total nominal value for the shares it may issue: this is described as 'the amount of the share capital with which the company proposes to be registered' (s. 2(5)(a)) and so is known as the 'registered capital' (it is also known as the 'authorised share capital' or the 'nominal capital'). The memorandum must also state the number of shares and, therefore, the nominal value of each share.

The Insolvency Act 1986, s. 74(2)(d), provides that 'in the case of a company limited by shares, no contribution is required [when the company is wound up] from any member exceeding the amount (if any) unpaid on the shares in respect of which he is liable'. This means the amount of the *nominal value* of the shares that has not been paid (*Ooregum Gold Mining Co. of India Ltd* v *Roper* [1892] AC 125 per Lord Watson at p. 136), and a limited company cannot agree with its members that they may pay less than the nominal value of their shares (*Ooregum Gold Mining Co. of India Ltd* v *Roper*; CA 1985, s. 100). The liability of a member under the Insolvency Act 1986, s. 74(2)(d), to pay whatever is unpaid of the nominal value of shares is a statutory liability (*Hansraj Gupta* v *Asthana* (1932) LR 60 Ind App 1, PC) but it does not extend to share premium, which is a matter for contract between the member and the company (*Niemann* v *Smedley* [1973] VR 769; *Re Vedelago* (1992) 8 ACSR 135).

CA 1985, s. 1(2)(a), describes a company limited by shares as being 'a company having the liability of its members limited by the memorandum to the amount, if any, unpaid on the shares respectively held by them'. In practice it is unnecessary for the memorandum to make this statement explicitly (see the prescribed forms of memorandum discussed in 2.3.2). It is sufficient that the memorandum contains both the statement that the liability of members is limited, which is required by s. 2(3), and the statement of the registered capital required by s. 2(5). The limitation is achieved by the operation of the Insolvency Act 1986, s. 74(2)(d).

Each subscriber of the memorandum of a company limited by shares must take at least one share (s. 2(5)(b)) and the number of shares to be taken by each subscriber must be stated in the memorandum (s. 2(5)(c)). There must be at least one subscriber (s. 1(1) and (3A)), who is deemed to be a member of the company on its registration (s. 22(1)). These rules ensure that in any company limited by shares there is at least one share on which a payment must be made to the company by a member.

A person holding shares in a company limited by shares knows that liability to contribute to the assets of the company in respect of the shares is limited to a certain amount which the member has agreed with the company. Parliament has not put any restrictions on what that amount must be, apart from a rule that in a *public limited company* the *total liability of all the members* must be at least the 'authorised minimum' (s. 11), which is currently

£50,000 (s. 118). In private limited companies, it is common for the total liability of members to be a trivial amount, typically £1.

Nominal values of shares and authorised share capitals have to be stated in monetary terms but not necessarily in sterling (*Re Scandinavian Bank Group plc* [1988] Ch 87; *Re Anglo-American Insurance Co. Ltd* [1991] BCLC 564). The nominal value of a share may be an amount such as $\frac{1}{2}$p which cannot be paid in legal tender (*Re Scandinavian Bank Group plc* at pp. 99–100; *Re Australian Pacific Technology Ltd* [1995] 1 VR 457, in which the court approved the issue of shares with a nominal value of 0.01 cent each).

Almost all registered companies are companies limited by shares and in the rest of this book the term 'company' without further qualification will be used to mean a registered company limited by shares.

1.3.2.2   Companies limited by guarantee
The liability of a member of a company limited by guarantee is based on an undertaking stated in the memorandum (CA 1985, s. 2(4)) to contribute, on the winding up of the company, an amount not exceeding a sum specified in the memorandum. The contribution is to be made for the payment of the debts and liabilities of the company, and of the costs, charges and expenses of winding up and for the adjustment of the rights of the contributories among themselves. The Insolvency Act 1986, s. 74(3), confirms that in the case of a guarantee company, 'no contribution is required [when the company is wound up] from any member exceeding the amount undertaken to be contributed by him to the company's assets in the event of its being wound up'. CA 1985, s. 1(2)(b), describes a company limited by guarantee as being 'a company having the liability of its members limited by the memorandum to such amount as the members may respectively thereby undertake to contribute to the assets of the company in the event of its being wound up'. This statement has to be made explicitly in a 'guarantee clause' in the company's memorandum (s. 2(4)).

The limit on the liability of a member of a company limited by guarantee is the amount specified in the guarantee clause of the memorandum.

The total amount that members of a guarantee company are liable to contribute under its guarantee clause is sometimes called the company's 'guarantee fund'. A guarantee company does not have any contributed capital while it is a going concern — the guarantee fund comes into existence only when the company is wound up — and this is usually considered inappropriate for a business enterprise. Accordingly, guarantee companies are usually formed only to undertake charitable objects or to carry on some non-commercial undertaking. Only a very small proportion of registered companies are guarantee companies and so, like unlimited companies, they will hardly ever be mentioned again in this book.

A member of a company limited by guarantee knows that liability to contribute to the assets of the company under the guarantee is limited to a certain amount which the member has agreed with the company. Parliament has not put any restrictions on what that amount must be, and in practice it is usually nominal — typically it is £1.

1.3.2.3   Collateral liability
Parliament has insisted that every limited company must require each of its members to pay up to a fixed amount to the company on shares or under guarantee, but there must be a certain maximum amount — a company may be able to obtain a share premium when a member joins (see 1.3.2.1) but it cannot make the amount payable on its shares or under guarantee variable at its option: this is the essence of limited liability. For example, in *Edmonton Country Club Ltd* v *Case* (1974) 44 DLR (3d) 554, the Supreme Court of Canada ruled that the company could not require some of its shareholders to pay an annual

contribution. Dickson J referred, at p. 562, to 'the basic jural principle which has given limited liability companies their vitality, that a shareholder who has paid for his shares is thereafter free of pecuniary obligation in respect of those shares'.

However, it is permissible for the memorandum or articles of association of a limited company to impose on its members a collateral liability to pay money to the company otherwise than on shares held or under guarantee, as in, for example, *Peninsular Co. Ltd v Fleming* (1872) 27 LT 93, in which the collateral liability was to lend money to the company; and *Lion Mutual Marine Insurance Association Ltd v Tucker* (1883) 12 QBD 176 and *Re Bangor & North Wales Mutual Marine Protection Association, Baird's Case* [1899] 2 Ch 593, in both of which the collateral liability was to contribute to a fund for insuring the marine losses of members of the company. In *Galloway v Hallé Concerts Society* [1915] 2 Ch 233, each member had a collateral liability to contribute to the society (which was a guarantee company) such sum as the committee (equivalent to a board of directors) might determine, not exceeding in the aggregate £100: it was held that the directors could not call for different contributions from different members because of a general rule of law that members of a company must be treated equally. If a collateral liability is imposed on a member of a company by its memorandum or articles, they cannot be altered so as to increase the liability without that member's express written consent (CA 1985, s. 16; see 2.4.8.1).

Some judges have asserted that even a collateral liability offends against the principle of limited liability and so cannot be imposed (for example, Salmond J in *Shalfoon v Cheddar Valley Cooperative Dairy Co. Ltd* [1924] NZLR 561 at p. 577). In England, the question has been debated in the somewhat obscure context of societies incorporated by registration under the industrial and provident societies legislation. Members of such societies have limited liability (limited by shares) in the same form as members of limited registered companies. In *Dibble v Wilts & Somerset Farmers Ltd* [1923] 1 Ch 342, P.O. Lawrence J held that such a society could not impose a collateral liability (and Salmond J in *Shalfoon v Cheddar Valley Cooperative Dairy Co. Ltd* cited that case in support of his view). However, in *Agricultural Wholesale Society Ltd v Biddulph & District Agricultural Society Ltd* [1925] Ch 769, the Court of Appeal held that P.O. Lawrence J had been wrong, and the Court of Appeal's view was confirmed by the House of Lords in *Hole v Garnsey* [1930] AC 472; see especially the speech of Viscount Dunedin.

1.3.2.4 Hybrid companies
It was possible before 22 December 1980 to register a company limited by guarantee with a share capital (known as a 'hybrid' company). Hybrid companies in existence on that date continue in existence as hybrids but no new hybrid company may be registered (CA 1985, s. 1(4)).

1.3.2.5 The history of limited liability
When incorporation of companies by registration was first introduced by the Joint Stock Companies Act 1844, the most significant political dispute was about limited liability, which many saw as contrary to the established business ethic that a trader should be personally responsible, to the full extent of his or her fortune, for debts incurred in trading: unlimited liability was thought to be the best way of ensuring the standards of behaviour in business sought by the community.

Accordingly the Joint Stock Companies Act 1844 imposed on the members of a company a form of direct and unlimited liability for its debts: a judgment creditor of a company registered under the Act was permitted to levy execution on individual members of the company if the judgment debt was not paid by the company itself (see *Re Sea Fire & Life Assurance Co., Greenwood's Case* (1854) 3 De G M & G 459).

The argument in favour of limited liability in joint-stock companies was that normally members were only investors who did not take part in the management of the company and so should not be held responsible for it. It was for the good of the community that capital in the hands of private investors should be made available to set up new businesses; such investment would be encouraged by removing the possibility of complete disaster if the business invested in should fail.

This argument was eventually won when the Limited Liability Act 1855 allowed any registered company (other than an insurance company) with at least 25 members to limit the liability of its members to the amounts unpaid on their shares, provided it put 'limited' as the last word of its name. Shortly afterwards, the Joint Stock Companies Act 1856 reduced the minimum number of members to seven (it is now one).

Insurance companies were not permitted to register with limited liability until CA 1862 came into force. In practice, though, a company incorporated under the Joint Stock Companies Act 1844 carrying on insurance business would include in every policy a provision precluding the levying of execution against the members of the company personally for any money payable under the policy — an insurance company's deed of settlement (equivalent to a present-day company's memorandum and articles, see 2.2) would usually forbid its directors from issuing policies without such a provision, and this was the basis on which members took shares in the company. The effectiveness of such a policy provision as a method of contracting out of the personal liability imposed by the 1844 Act was confirmed in *Halket* v *Merchant Traders' Ship Loan & Insurance Association* (1849) 13 QB 960 and *Hassell* v *Merchant Traders' Ship Loan & Insurance Association* (1849) 4 Ex 525. The device was also effective when used by unincorporated insurance companies (*Hallett* v *Dowdall* (1852) 18 QB 2).

Under the 1855 Act, the liability of members was still direct to creditors but the 1856 Act introduced the principle that the liability of members of a registered company should be to the company only and should be enforced for the benefit of creditors on the winding up of the company. Guarantee companies were first allowed for in CA 1862. For more detail of the history up to 1862 see H.A. Shannon, 'The coming of general limited liability' in E.M. Carus-Wilson (ed.), *Essays in Economic History*, vol. 1 (London: Edward Arnold, 1954), pp. 358–79 (reprinted from *Economic History*, vol. 2 (1931), pp. 267–91); J. Saville, 'Sleeping partnership and limited liability, 1850–1856', *Economic History Review*, 2nd ser., vol. 8 (1956), pp. 418–33; C.E. Amsler, R.L. Bartlett and C.J. Bolton, 'Thoughts of some British economists on early limited liability and corporate legislation', *History of Political Economy*, vol. 13 (1981), pp. 774–93. Saville's article reveals the wide variety of arguments for and against wider availability of limited liability that were advanced by various interest groups.

During the second half of the 19th century, believers in the moral superiority of unlimited liability who nevertheless recognised that it was not appropriate to make mere investors in an enterprise liable for its debts to an unlimited extent promoted the compromise of limited liability for investors but unlimited liability for the directors or managers who actually conducted the enterprise's business. Their model was the French partnership *en commandite*. A business may be conducted on these lines in two ways: as a limited partnership (introduced in 1907; see 0.1.4) or as a limited company with directors or managers who have unlimited liability (introduced in 1867; see 2.3.6). See M. Lobban, 'Corporate identity and limited liability in France and England 1825–67' (1996) 25 Anglo-Am L Rev 397.

As will be explained in 1.3.3.2, in the late 19th century it was realised that although limited liability encouraged capitalists to invest money in companies which they did not manage, nothing in the law required a limited liability company to have members who did not take part in management. It became increasingly popular for small businesses to be carried on by companies whose only members were the people who operated the business. Thus business people could obtain limited liability for their own trading.

Limited liability became the dominant business ethic in the European Community when the Council adopted its 12th Company Law Directive in 1989. This required member States to provide a legal form for *individuals* to trade with limited liability, finally abandoning the view that limited liability is only appropriate for people who merely invest in a business without taking part in its management. In Britain the 12th Directive was implemented by SI 1992 No. 1699, permitting the registration of single-member private limited companies.

The justification for making limited liability freely available is that it encourages people to set up in business by making it less risky. However, making it easier to carry on businesses that become insolvent makes economic activity more risky for the community generally if it becomes more likely that money will be lost dealing with insolvent limited liability companies. Any creditor of a small company in a strong enough negotiating position (such as a bank or a landlord) usually requires personal guarantees from the individuals controlling the company and this makes limited liability meaningless for them. In the recent long economic recession, ordinary trade creditors and customers who cannot negotiate special protection for themselves have become increasingly discontented with limited liability and this has led to suggestions that it is necessary to return to the concept that limited liability should be available only for non-managing investors. See, for example, A. Hicks, R. Drury and J. Smallcombe, *Alternative Company Structures for the Small Business* (London: Certified Accountants Educational Trust, 1995).

Merely imposing unlimited liability on a company's shareholders does not make dealing with the company free of risk for creditors. They still have the risk that their debts will exceed the shareholders' assets.

So far the main legislative response to discontent with freely available limited liability has been that business people need to be made responsible for their dishonest business practices not their economic misfortunes. Accordingly, in contrast to the limited liability of members of companies, statute has increasingly exposed directors to liability if they fail to meet publicly required standards of behaviour in business — see the Insolvency Act 1986, s. 214 (wrongful trading) discussed in 20.12, and s. 217 discussed in 2.3.3.8 and the provisions on disqualification of directors discussed in 15.2.5.

For a discussion of many issues related to limited liability, see Tony Orhnial (ed.) *Limited Liability and the Corporation* (London: Croom Helm, 1982). There have been some discussions in terms of economic theory of the possible advantages of limited liability. See, for example, R.E. Meiners, J.S. Mofsky and R.D. Tollison, 'Piercing the veil of limited liability' (1979) 4 Delaware J Corp L 351; P. Halpern, M. Trebilcock and S. Turnbull, 'An economic analysis of limited liability in corporation law' (1980) 30 UTLJ 117; and F.H. Easterbrook and D.R. Fischel, 'Limited liability and the corporation' (1985) 52 U Chi L Rev 89.

Halpern et al. suggest that, as far as public companies are concerned, if they could not offer members limited liability then the market for their shares would be hampered. Shareholding would be concentrated in a few wealthy investors who were able to monitor closely the companies they invested in. Small investors would refuse to buy shares that could lead to catastrophic liability unless they could buy insurance against losses. (Insurers would depend on the effectiveness of the close monitoring by the large shareholders.) The poor experience of the English stock market with partly paid shares of high nominal value (which impose a liability that is practically unlimited), described in 6.1.1, shows that this analysis is probably correct, at least in times of economic uncertainty. If, however, investors are confident that a company is sound and the risk of catastrophe is negligible then they will buy and trade in unlimited liability shares as though they had limited liability, as they did with the American Express Company in the 1950s (P.Z. Grossman, 'The market for shares of companies with unlimited liability: the case of American Express' (1995) 24 J Legal Stud 63).

In relation to private companies, Halpern et al. support the criticism that if limited liability is too readily available then it encourages the setting up of too many businesses that will fail.

If a company's members have unlimited liability, or a high liability on partly paid shares, the company's creditors will want to check the wealth of its members, which is why it has always been considered important that a list of a company's members should be available for public inspection. If a company's members have limited liability, its creditors must turn to monitoring the company's own financial health, which is why accounting and auditing requirements are such an important feature of company law, and why limited, but not unlimited, companies must file their annual accounts with the registrar.

In the USA it has been suggested that although limited liability for contract debts may be an acceptable price for the business community, as creditors, to pay for giving enterprises the ability to raise capital easily, it is not acceptable that shareholders should have limited liability for tort when the activities of companies can do massive harm to the environment (for example, oil spills, explosions at chemical plants) and can cause serious personal injury to large numbers of consumers (for example, product negligence in vehicle and pharmaceutical manufacture, use of harmful materials such as asbestos). Clearly there is a qualitative difference between hardship caused because trading debts are not paid and hardship caused by personal injury or environmental damage. See H. Hansmann and R. Kraakman, 'Toward unlimited shareholder liability for corporate torts' (1991) 100 Yale LJ 1879. J.A. Grundfest, 'The limited future of unlimited liability: a capital markets perspective' (1992) 102 Yale LJ 387 suggests that the financial markets could invent ways of avoiding the imposition of unlimited liability but see the response by Hansmann and Kraakman (1992) 102 Yale LJ 427 and the article by Grossman cited above.

1.3.2.6 Reduction in members

A member of a registered company which has separate personality is not directly liable to the company's creditors for its debts. A member is only liable to the company, and that liability may be limited or unlimited, depending on the type of company. Apart from private companies limited by shares or guarantee, the benefit of incorporation under CA 1985 is allowed only to *two or more persons* who associate for a lawful purpose (s. 1(1)). Accordingly, s. 24 as amended by SI 1992 No. 1699 provides:

> If a company, other than a private company limited by shares or by guarantee, carries on business without having at least two members and does so for more than six months, a person who, for the whole or any part of the period that it so carries on business after those six months—
>> (a) is a member of the company, and
>> (b) knows that it is carrying on business with only one member,
> shall be liable (jointly and severally with the company) for the payment of the company's debts contracted during the period or, as the case may be, that part of it.

It will be observed that liability under s. 24 is imposed only on the remaining member (and the company) and not on the member whose departure from the company leads to the application of the section. Indeed where no members remain in the company only the company itself is liable. The section can be easily avoided by having one share registered in the name of a person who holds it only as nominee and accordingly it may be thought to be a useless provision which only traps unlucky persons who do not know about it (see per Hoffmann LJ in *Nisbet* v *Shepherd* [1994] 1 BCLC 300 at p. 305).

1.3.2.7 No liability companies
In Britain, the constitution of a registered company must impose liability on at least some of its members to contribute capital, either unlimited liability or liability limited by shares or by guarantee. In Australia, it is possible to register a no liability (NL) company, in which there is no obligation to pay calls on shares, but a company can be registered with no liability only if its objects are confined to mining. In a no liability mining company, shareholders pay an initial small part of the nominal value of their shares to pay for investigation of a new mine, and further instalments to fund development and eventually operation of the mine if it appears to be worth going further. At any stage, shareholders can refuse to pay anything more on their shares, which will then be forfeited.

1.3.3 Public or private companies

1.3.3.1 Definitions
A limited company with a share capital is a public company if its memorandum states that it is to be a public company and it was registered or re-registered as a public company under CA 1985, or under CA 1948 as amended by CA 1980, on or after 22 December 1980 (CA 1985, s. 1(3)). (Re-registration is dealt with in 1.3.4.) In addition the name of a public company must end with the words 'public limited company' or the abbreviation 'plc' (ss. 25(1) and 27) or, if its memorandum requires its registered office to be in Wales, the equivalent in Welsh (ss. 25(1) and 27). Where the registrar registers a memorandum which states that the company is to be a public company, the certificate of incorporation must say so (s. 13(6)) and is conclusive evidence of that fact (s. 13(7)(b)).

The class of public companies includes hybrid companies (see 1.3.2.4) which were in existence on 22 December 1980 and which have re-registered as public companies.

A company that is not a public company is called a 'private' company (s 1(3)).

The shares of a private company cannot be listed on the London Stock Exchange (Financial Services Act 1986, s. 143(3)). A public company's shares can be listed and the principal practical difference between public and private companies is that a public company can, if it is large enough and satisfies the conditions for listing, obtain large amounts of low-cost capital through public issues of shares on the London Stock Exchange.

A public company must have at least two members whereas a private company (other than an unlimited company or a hybrid company) may have only one member.

A further difference between a public company and a private company is that whereas a private company may have only a trivial amount of contributed capital (such as £1), the legislation sets a comparatively substantial minimum requirement for the contributed capital of a public company, and several tediously detailed provisions of CA 1985 are devoted to ensuring that no public company goes into the world without its minimum contributed capital. The requirement that a public company must have a minimum contributed capital is imposed throughout the European Union by the Second Company Law Directive which sets the minimum at 25,000 ecu. In Britain the minimum is expressed in terms of the 'authorised minimum', which is £50,000 or such other sum as the Secretary of State may by order prescribe (CA 1985, s. 118). However, a public company is not actually required to have contributed capital of £50,000. The requirement is that a public company must allot to its members shares with a nominal value of at least £50,000 but it is permissible for the members to pay up only one-quarter of the nominal value of each share allotted. Thus the amount of contributed capital of a public company may be as little as £12,500 with a right to call on members for a further £37,500. In the memorandum of a company that is to be registered as a public company its authorised share capital must not be less than £50,000 (CA 1985, s. 11).

If a company is registered as a public company when it is first incorporated then CA 1985 ensures that it satisfies the minimum capital requirements by forbidding the company from doing any business or borrowing any money until it has received from the registrar a certificate to commence business issued under s. 117. Failure of the company to obtain a certificate within a year of registration is a ground for petitioning the court to wind it up (Insolvency Act 1986, s. 122(1)(b)). The main condition for the issue of a certificate is the allotment by the company of shares with a nominal value of at least £50,000 (CA 1985, s. 117(2)), for each of which the company must have received at least one-quarter of the nominal value (ss. 101(1) and (2) and 117(4)). For further details, see 6.6.1.

1.3.3.2   History of the distinction between public and private companies

When incorporation of companies by registration was first introduced in 1844, it was assumed that the typical registered company would have a large membership of investors who would entrust the management of the company's affairs to its directors. It was also presumed that there would be public dealings in the shares of registered companies.

The Joint Stock Companies Act 1856 reduced the minimum number of members of a registered company to seven. Within 20 years or so it was realised that it was unnecessary for a company to have a large membership. The practice grew of incorporating what were informally known as 'private' companies, as described in Francis Palmer's book, *Private Companies; or, How To Convert Your Business into a Private Company, and the Benefit of So Doing*, first published in 1877. An individual in business on his or her own (a 'sole trader') would find six nominees to make up the required minimum of seven subscribers and incorporate a company to take over the business, thus achieving a separation of business and private affairs and, most importantly, limited liability. In *Salomon* v *A. Salomon & Co. Ltd* [1897] AC 22, the House of Lords confirmed that this was permitted by CA 1862 and that the members of such a company had limited liability. The popularity of the 'private' company was recognised by Parliament, which in CA 1907 created a statutory category of 'private companies' for which the minimum membership was two. From 1908, it was possible to register a company as a private company but such a company was forbidden to offer its shares to the public and was required to restrict the right to transfer its shares and limit its membership to 50 persons (excluding employees). This definition of 'private company' was last re-enacted in CA 1948, s. 28. (In some Commonwealth countries in which similar legislation was introduced, private companies were called 'proprietary' companies, and their names included the abbreviation 'Pty'.) By 1979 nearly 98 per cent of British registered companies were private companies. See further P. W. Ireland, 'The rise of the limited liability company' (1984) 12 Int J Sociol Law 239.

The system was changed by CA 1980 so that now every registered company is defined to be a private company *unless* it is registered or re-registered as a public company (CA 1985, s. 1(3)). CA 1980 removed the requirement that a private company must limit the number of its members and reduced the minimum number of members of a public company from seven to two.

A limited company with a share capital existing on 22 December 1980 which was not a private company as that term was defined by CA 1948, s. 28, is called an 'old public company' (Companies Consolidation (Consequential Provisions) Act 1985, s. 1(1)). This term is also used for a limited company with a share capital in respect of which an application for registration was pending at 22 December 1980 if the application was not for registration as a private company as defined by the 1948 Act (ibid.). Old public companies could be either companies limited by shares or hybrid companies.

All old public companies were required to apply for re-registration as private companies or as public companies (plcs) by 21 March 1982. Many old public companies opted to become private companies and at the end of March 1997, 98.9 per cent of companies were private companies.

In 1992, the minimum number of members of a private limited company (other than a hybrid company) was reduced to one by SI 1992 No. 1699, implementing the EC 12th Company Law Directive.

British company law traditionally regards private and public companies as two variants of the same basic form of legal organisation, unlike legal systems in Continental Europe which tend to treat them as different forms of organisation. Since joining the European Community, British law has made more differences between public and private companies. Before 1980 people dealing with companies did not usually know, or care, whether they were public or private. Now, the use of the two different terminations to names — plc for a public company, Ltd for a private company — makes it obvious. This is in accord with Continental practice, for example, in France the name of a public company (*société anonyme*) ends SA while that of a private company (*société à responsabilité limitée*) ends Sàrl.

Law and economics analysts, who are much concerned with companies as the subject of stock-market trading, draw a sharp distinction between companies whose shares are publicly traded and those which are not — see, for example, H.G. Manne, 'Our two corporation systems: law and economics' (1967) 53 Va L Rev 259.

1.3.4 Re-registration to change the classification of a company

1.3.4.1 Introduction

CA 1985 provides procedures for a company to change its classification by re-registering. When a company changes classification from public to private or vice versa, or from limited to unlimited, or vice versa, a new certificate of registration must be issued because the certificate is required to state if a company is limited (s. 13(1)) and if it is a public company (s. 13(6)). Curiously, although a new certificate must be issued when a company changes its name (see 2.4.2), the procedure for changing a company's name is not referred to as 're-registration'.

The re-registration provisions are a very good example of the way in which the British companies legislation attempts to prescribe every detail of a procedure, even if the procedure (like that for re-registering an unlimited company as a limited one) is hardly ever used. We will spend about three pages outlining the re-registration procedures in what we believe is enough detail for an introductory textbook like this. The legislation itself, with all its detailed provisions, in the same type size and book format, occupies over seven pages — plus nine A4 pages of prescribed forms in SI 1995 No. 736.

The specific procedures set out in CA 1985 do not cover all the possible changes of status though some changes for which there is no direct procedure can be achieved by two successive re-registrations. For example, a public company can be re-registered as an unlimited company by two re-registrations (see 1.3.4.2) but there is no procedure at all by which a guarantee company can be re-registered as a company limited by shares (see 1.3.4.4). In Australia there has been controversy over whether a court-sanctioned arrangement with members (the British provisions for which are in ss. 425 to 430 of CA 1985) can be used to effect a change of status for which there is no specific statutory procedure. In *Windsor* v *National Mutual Life Association of Australasia* (1992) 106 ALR 282 a full court of the Federal Court said that the specific procedures are the only ways of changing status; in *Australian Securities Commission* v *Marlborough Gold Mines Ltd* (1993) 177 CLR 485, the High Court of Australia would not go that far but held that there was a legislative intention that the particular change of status desired by the company — from limited to no liability — should not be carried out at all.

1.3.4.2   Change from being a public company

A public company (including a hybrid public company) may re-register as a private limited company under CA 1985, s. 53. This is a common form of re-registration. It is used, for example, when a public company is taken over by, and becomes a subsidiary of, another company. The section can be used to re-register a public company only as a private company limited by shares or limited by guarantee (s. 53(3)). There is no provision for re-registration as a private hybrid company. In order for a public company to be re-registered as a private company, the members must adopt a special resolution (which requires a majority of three-quarters of those voting, see 14.4.8.3) that it should be so re-registered (s. 53(1)).

A change from public to private status may be very unwelcome to a minority who object to the change if their shares lose their marketability. Provision is therefore made for accommodating a dissentient minority who object to re-registration as a private company.

The holders of 5 per cent or more of the nominal value of a public company's issued share capital or of any class thereof, or 50 or more of its members, may apply to the court for the cancellation of a special resolution to request re-registration as a private company, provided that the applicants did not consent to or vote in favour of the resolution (s. 54(1) and (2)). The application must be made within 28 days of the passing of the resolution (s. 54(3)). On the hearing of a s. 54 application the court may either cancel or confirm the resolution, and in any event may make its order on such terms and conditions as it thinks fit, adjourn the proceedings to enable an arrangement to be made which it finds satisfactory for the purchase of the applicants' interests in the company, and give any directions or orders which are expedient for facilitating or carrying the arrangement into effect (s. 54(5)). The court's order may provide for the purchase by the company of the shares of any members (s. 54(6)).

Once satisfied that the company is entitled to be re-registered as a private company the registrar must issue a new certificate of incorporation appropriate to a private company (s. 55(1)). The company becomes a private company on the issue of the certificate (s. 55(2)) and the certificate is conclusive evidence that the re-registration requirements have been complied with and that the company is a private company (s. 55(3)). The registrar notifies issue of the certificate in the *Gazette* (s. 711(1)(a)).

A public company cannot be directly re-registered as an unlimited company (s. 49(3)): it must first re-register as private under s. 53 and then re-register as unlimited under s. 49 (see 1.3.4.3).

A public company limited by guarantee with a share capital (a public hybrid company) may be re-registered as a private company either limited by shares or limited by guarantee (without a share capital) under s. 53. However, there is no express provision for a public hybrid company to alter its memorandum so as to become a public company limited by shares (in principle this could be achieved by first re-registering as a private company limited by shares and then re-registering again as a public company under s. 43 (see 1.3.4.3), but this is unlikely to be a practical possibility because shareholders would lose the marketability of their shares in the interval between re-registrations without being certain that a special resolution for the second re-registration would be adopted).

1.3.4.3 Change from being a private company limited by shares

A private company limited by shares or a hybrid private company may be re-registered as a public company under CA 1985, s. 43. This is a common form of re-registration. It may be used, for example, when a private company decides to 'go public' in order to obtain more capital for growth by inviting the public to subscribe for its shares.

In order for a private company to be re-registered as a public company, the members must adopt a special resolution (which requires a majority of three-quarters of those voting, see 14.4.8.3) that it should be so re-registered (s. 43(1)). An application by a private company to re-register as public must be delivered to the registrar (s. 43(1)) and be accompanied by a statutory declaration by a director or secretary of the company that the requisite special resolution has been passed and that various requirements relating to minimum capital are satisfied (s. 43(3)(e)). The registrar may accept this as sufficient evidence that the conditions for re-registration have been satisfied (s. 47(2)). Other documents which must accompany the application are specified in s. 43(a) to (d). The registrar will issue the company with a certificate of incorporation stating that it is a public company (s. 47(1)), which is conclusive evidence that the requirements of the Act relating to re-registration have been complied with and that the company is a public company (s. 47(5)). The registrar notifies issue of the certificate in the *Gazette* (s. 711(1)(a)). A company re-registered as a public company does not need a certificate to commence business.

Subject to various conditions and restrictions which will not be discussed here, a private limited company may, with the consent of all its members, lodge an application with the registrar for re-registration as an unlimited company (either with or without a share capital): see CA 1985, s. 49. Having changed from limited to unlimited, a company cannot change back again (s. 43(1) (forbidding a second re-registration as a public company) and s. 51(2) (forbidding a second re-registration as a private limited company, whether limited by shares or by guarantee)).

Although a public company limited by shares may be re-registered as a company limited by guarantee (though it must be as a guarantee company without a share capital: s. 53(3)), there is no express provision under which a private company limited by shares can alter its memorandum so as to become a company limited by guarantee: however, it seems that this change can be achieved by first re-registering the private company as a public company under s. 43 (see 1.3.4.2) and then re-registering again as a private company limited by guarantee.

1.3.4.4 Change from being a private company limited by guarantee

A private guarantee company may be re-registered as an unlimited company under CA 1985, s. 49 (see 1.3.4.3).

There is no express provision for a guarantee company without a share capital to alter its memorandum so as to become a company limited by shares. It cannot alter its memorandum to provide that it shall have a share capital and so become a hybrid company (s. 1(4)) and it is forbidden from re-registering as a public company (s. 43(1)). It could re-register as an unlimited company but could not then re-register again as a limited company (ss. 43(1) and 51(2)).

1.3.4.5 Change from being a hybrid private company

A private hybrid company can be re-registered as a public company under CA 1985, s. 43 or as an unlimited company under s. 49 (see 1.3.4.3) but there is no express provision for a private hybrid company to alter its memorandum so as to become a private company limited by shares (though this could be achieved by first re-registering as public and then re-registering again as a private company limited by shares). A private hybrid company could become a pure guarantee company by reducing its share capital to zero under the procedure described in 10.2.

1.3.4.6 Change from being an unlimited company

An unlimited company with a share capital may, if its members adopt a special resolution (which requires a majority of three-quarters of those voting, see 14.4.8.3), re-register as a public limited company under CA 1985, ss. 43 to 48 (this must be a company limited by shares: s. 48(2)(a)). An unlimited company, with or without a share capital, may, following a special resolution, re-register as a private limited company (either limited by shares or by guarantee) under ss. 51 and 52. Having changed from unlimited to limited, a company cannot change back again (s. 49(2)). An unlimited company cannot be re-registered as a hybrid company (s. 1(4)).

1.3.5 Quasi-partnership companies

The Companies Act classifications of companies do not necessarily reflect the varieties of relationships between members and especially between members and directors. The roles assigned by the law to members and directors are that members are investors who do not wish to be involved in day-to-day management, which is the province of the directors. Members are expected to see each other only at annual general meetings. In the case of a plc members are expected to have taken their shares as a result of a public advertisement. (Before 1908 this was expected of the members of any company.) Nevertheless it is common for members to be directors, and soon after incorporation of companies by registration was first allowed it was found that, contrary to expectation, many companies were formed with very small numbers of members. This trend increased when the statutory minimum number of members was reduced from seven to two in 1908.

The courts have paid particular attention to companies formed on the basis of a personal relationship between members involving mutual confidence and the understanding that certain members will be directors. Such companies are known as 'quasi-partnership' companies and the courts are willing to take into consideration the mutual understandings between members of quasi-partnership companies even if they have not been stated in the company's memorandum and articles or in separate contracts between the members.

The leading case on this topic is *Ebrahimi v Westbourne Galleries Ltd* [1973] AC 360, HL, in which a member of a quasi-partnership company sought to invoke a provision which is now IA 1986, s. 122(1)(g), under which the court can order a company to be wound up if it is 'just and equitable' to do so.

Mr Ebrahimi and Mr Nazar had carried on business in partnership dealing in Persian and other carpets. They shared equally in management and profits. In 1958 they formed a private company carrying on the same business and were appointed its first directors. Shortly after the company's incorporation, Mr Nazar's son, George, became a director. Mr Nazar and his son between them held the majority of votes exercisable at general meetings. The company made good profits which were all distributed as directors' remuneration; no dividends were ever paid. In 1969, Mr Ebrahimi was removed from his office as director by a resolution at a general meeting under what is now CA 1985, s. 303, and a provision of the company's articles (see 15.3.3). Mr Ebrahimi asked the court to find that it was just and equitable to order the winding up of the company. The House of Lords upheld Plowman J's decision to make a winding-up order because of Mr Ebrahimi's inability after his dismissal to participate in the company's management and, because profits were paid as directors' remuneration, in the company's profits. The importance of this decision justifies the following lengthy quotation from the opinion of Lord Wilberforce who, when discussing the scope of the phrase 'just and equitable', said:

> The words are a recognition of the fact that a limited company is more than a mere legal entity, with a personality in law of its own: that there is room in company law for recognition of the fact that behind it, or amongst it, there are individuals, with rights, expectations and obligations *inter se* which are not necessarily submerged in the company structure. That structure is defined by the Companies Act and by the articles of association by which shareholders agree to be bound. In most companies and in most contexts, this definition is sufficient and exhaustive, equally so whether the company is large or small. The 'just and equitable' provision does not, as the respondents suggest, entitle one party to disregard the obligation he assumes by entering a company, nor the court to dispense him from it. It does, as equity always does, enable the court to subject the exercise of legal rights to equitable considerations; considerations, that is, of a personal character arising between one individual and another, which may make it unjust, or inequitable, to insist on legal rights, or to exercise them in a particular way.
>
> It would be impossible, and wholly undesirable, to define the circumstances in which these considerations may arise. Certainly the fact that a company is a small one, or a private company, is not enough. There are very many of these where the association is a purely commercial one, of which it can safely be said that the basis of association is adequately and exhaustively laid down in the articles. The superimposition of equitable considerations requires something more, which typically may include one, or probably more, of the following elements: (i) an association formed or continued on the basis of a personal relationship, involving mutual confidence — this element will often be found where a pre-existing partnership has been converted into a limited company; (ii) an agreement or understanding, that all, or some (for there may be 'sleeping' members), of the shareholders shall participate in the conduct of the business; (iii) restriction on the transfer of the members' interest in the company — so that if confidence is lost, or one member is removed from management, he cannot take out his stake and go elsewhere.
>
> It is these, and analogous, factors which may bring into play the just and equitable clause, and they do so directly, through the force of the words themselves. To refer, as so many of the cases do, to 'quasi-partnerships' or 'in substance partnerships' may be convenient but may also be confusing. It may be convenient because it is the law of partnership which has developed the conceptions of probity, good faith and mutual confidence, and the remedies where these are absent, which become relevant once such factors as I have mentioned are found to exist: the words 'just and equitable' sum these up in the law of partnership itself. And in many, but not necessarily all, cases there has been a pre-existing partnership the obligations of which it is reasonable to suppose continue to underlie the new company structure. But the expressions may be confusing if they obscure, or deny, the fact that the parties (possibly former partners) are now co-members in a company, who have accepted, in law, new obligations. A company, however small, however domestic, is a company not a partnership or even a quasi-partnership and it is through the just and equitable clause that obligations, common to partnership relations, may come in.

By asking the court to find that it is 'just and equitable' for a company to be wound up, IA 1986, s. 122(1)(g), is expressly inviting the court to 'subject the exercise of legal rights to equitable considerations' (in the words of Lord Wilberforce quoted above). Similarly, when CA 1985, s. 459(1), asks the court to provide relief when a company's affairs have been conducted in a manner that is 'unfairly prejudicial' to a member's interests (see 18.6) the court may give relief on finding that legal rights have been exercised by some members contrary to the legitimate expectations of others (*Re a Company (No. 00477 of 1986)* [1986] BCLC 376) because 'what is unjust and inequitable is obviously also unfairly prejudicial' (per Fulton J in *Diligenti* v *RWMD Operations Kelowna Ltd* (1976) 1 BCLR 36 at p. 46). See also *Caratti Holding Co. Pty Ltd* v *Zampatti* (1978) 52 ALJR 732, PC, discussed in 3.4.3.

Clemens v *Clemens Bros Ltd* [1976] 2 All ER 268, *Re Medefield Pty Ltd* (1977) 2 ACLR 406, New South Wales, and *Kounis* v *Kounis* (1987) 11 ACLR 854, Western Australia, discussed in 14.4.9.5 may be regarded as cases in which the courts intervened to prevent a member exercising a legal right (to vote) in a way that was contrary to understandings with other members, and in these cases the courts were not acting under an express statutory authorisation.

Just as many people would think that a company is not truly a 'public company' unless it is listed on the Stock Exchange, but not all companies registered as plcs are listed, so the concept of the quasi-partnership company, with its emphasis on personal rather than financial association, may be thought to contain the essence of the truly 'private' company. See C.M. Schmitthoff, 'How the English discovered the private company', in *Quo vadis ius societatum*, ed. P. Zonderland (Deventer: Kluwer, 1972), pp. 183–93.

That company law may not exhaustively define the relationship between members of a company has been recognised in other contexts. For example, in *Lion Mutual Marine Insurance Association Ltd* v *Tucker* (1883) 12 QBD 176, the relationship between the members of a guarantee company was that of a mutual marine insurance association and the Court of Appeal held that the company law limitation on liability of members under CA 1985, s. 2(4), did not apply to their liability among themselves to insure each other's marine losses. For other examples, see *Trebanog Working Men's Club & Institute Ltd* v *Macdonald* [1940] 1 KB 576 discussed in 5.2.2.6 and *Elliott* v *Wheeldon* [1993] BCLC 53 discussed in 16.3.1.

1.3.6 Partnership companies

A partnership company is a company limited by shares whose shares are intended to be held to a substantial extent by or on behalf of its employees (CA 1985, s. 8A(1)). For a discussion of such companies, see J. Nelson-Jones and G. Nuttall, *Employee Ownership: Legal and Tax Aspects* (London: Fourmat Publishing, 1987), especially chapters 5 and 6. CA 1985, s. 8A, which will be inserted into CA 1985 when CA 1989, s. 128, is brought into force, will empower the Secretary of State to prescribe a model set of articles of association for partnership companies.

1.4 NUMBERS OF COMPANIES

According to the Department of Trade and Industry's report, *Companies in 1996–97* (London: HMSO, 1997), at the end of March 1997 there were 1,091,900 companies registered in Great Britain, of which 1,030,100 were registered in England and Wales (figures are to the nearest 100 and exclude companies in the course of liquidation). Of the total number of companies in Great Britain, 1.1 per cent are public companies.

These figures give a slightly misleading impression because many companies are members of groups controlled by holding companies. The Business Statistics Office estimates that the number of independent companies and groups in Britain is about 30 per cent of the number of registered companies (*Business Monitor MA 3*, 17th issue, figures for 1982) — which would mean that there were about 327,600 independent companies and groups in Great Britain in 1997.

1.5 PROHIBITION OF LARGE PARTNERSHIPS

By CA 1985, s. 716, an association of more than 20 persons must not be formed for the purpose of carrying on any business that has for its object the acquisition of gain by the association or its members unless it is incorporated or has received letters patent under the Chartered Companies Act 1837. (Letters patent companies are not incorporated.) However, people following certain professions (including accountants and solicitors) may form partnerships with more than 20 members if all the partners belong to appropriate professional institutions or are otherwise qualified (s. 716 and regulations made under it).

An association that had fewer than 20 members when it was formed will contravene s. 716 when its membership exceeds 20 (*Re Thomas, ex parte Poppleton* (1884) 14 QBD 379).

If an association of more than 20 persons carries on business in contravention of s. 716 then all contracts made for the purpose of carrying on the association's business are illegal and will not be enforced by the courts (*Jennings* v *Hammond* (1882) 9 QBD 225).

1.6 REGISTRATION OF COMPANIES NOT FORMED UNDER COMPANIES LEGISLATION

Sections 680 to 690 of CA 1985 provide procedures for existing companies not formed under companies legislation to be registered with the registrar of companies. Whether or not it is already incorporated, a company which registers under these provisions is incorporated by virtue of the registration (s. 688(1)). For many existing companies the primary attraction of registering is that a company can adopt the procedure for voluntary winding up which is available to registered companies under part IV of the Insolvency Act 1986, and registration for the purpose of winding up is specifically sanctioned by s. 680(1). A company incorporated by registration under the Joint Stock Companies Act 1856 is permitted to re-register under these provisions (CA 1985, ss. 680(1)(a) and 735(3)) but companies registered under later Companies Acts are not (s. 680(2)).

In order to be capable of being registered, an unregistered company must have at least two members and must either (a) have been in existence on 2 November 1862 (when CA 1862 came into force) or (b) have been formed in pursuance of an Act of Parliament (other than the Companies Acts) or letters patent or 'otherwise duly constituted according to law' (s. 680(1)). The latter phrase means that companies formed after 2 November 1862 by mere agreement between members and for the purpose of being registered under the provisions of ss. 680 to 690 do not qualify to be registered under those provisions because persons who wish to form an incorporated company under CA 1985 must do so under ss. 1 to 13 of the Act (*R* v *Registrar of Joint Stock Companies, ex parte Johnston* [1891] 2 QB 598, CA). By this decision the Court of Appeal put an end to the prevailing practice of registering under these provisions a company formed to acquire an existing business so as to avoid paying stamp duty on the transfer of the business to the company. However, the courts will not entertain claims that companies which were registered before the decision in *ex parte Johnston* were not entitled to be registered and so are not incorporated: the certificate of incorporation of such a company given by the registrar under s. 688 is conclusive that it was entitled to be incorporated (*Hammond* v *Prentice Brothers Ltd* [1920] 1 Ch 201).

Only a company formed in England and Wales can register in England and Wales under ss. 680 to 690, and only a company formed in Scotland can register in Scotland (*Bulkeley v Schutz* (1871) LR 3 PC 764).

It is submitted that when a body corporate registers under ss. 680 to 690, the registration does not create a new and different body corporate but continues the existence of the old one under a new guise. This is expressly provided in relation to statutory water companies which register (Statutory Water Companies Act 1991, s. 11(2)) and would explain the case of *Re London Housing Society Ltd's Trust Deeds* [1940] Ch 777, in which an incorporated society gave money to trustees to hold for the benefit of its employees; after the society registered as a company it was held that the trustees held the money on trust for the employees of the company. See also *Re Plumstead, Woolwich and Charlton Consumers Pure Water Co.* (1860) 2 De G F & J 20.

2 The Memorandum of Association

2.1 INTRODUCTION

In order to register a company, one or more persons must sign (or, in company lawyers' jargon, 'subscribe') and deliver to the registrar a memorandum of association stating the intention of the subscriber or subscribers to form a company with a particular name, stating whether its registered office is to be in England and Wales, Wales, or Scotland, and stating the objects the company is formed to pursue. The memorandum must state that the company is to be a limited company if that is so, and must state that it is to be a public company if that is so. This chapter considers in detail the wording of the memorandum of a company limited by shares and how it may be altered after registration.

2.2 REGISTRATION OF A MEMORANDUM

A company's certificate of incorporation is given on the registration of its memorandum (CA 1985, s. 13(1)). The memorandum must be delivered to the registrar (s. 10(1)), who must retain and register it (s. 12(2)) if satisfied that all the requirements of CA 1985 in respect of registration and of matters precedent and incidental to it have been complied with (s. 12(1)).

The requirement for registered companies to have a memorandum and articles of association in two separate documents was introduced in the Joint Stock Companies Act 1856. For a company registered under the Joint Stock Companies Act 1844, the matters contained in these two documents were required to be stated in a single document called the 'deed of settlement' of the company. The separation into two documents emphasised that the matters in the memorandum were fundamental and, under the 1856 Act, unalterable whereas the articles could be altered by the company (see 3.5). It is now possible to alter almost all the provisions of a company's memorandum, though specific procedures are prescribed for each type of alteration: see 2.4.

A person who deals with a company has constructive notice of the contents of the company's memorandum and articles of association because they are publicly registered and available for inspection (per Lord Wensleydale in *Ernest* v *Nicholls* (1857) 6 HL Cas 401 at p. 419; per Lord Hatherley in *Mahony* v *East Holyford Mining Co. Ltd* (1875) LR 7 HL 869 at p. 893). Parliament has enacted CA 1989, s. 142, inserting a new s. 711A into CA 1985 which would abolish the doctrine of deemed notice of the memorandum and articles, but this provision had not been brought into force when this edition went to press.

2.3 CONTENT

2.3.1 General

By CA 1985, s. 2, the memorandum of a company limited by shares must state the following:

(a)   the name of the company;

(b)   whether the company's registered office is to be situated in England and Wales, Wales or Scotland;

(c)   the company's objects;

(d)   that the liability of its members is limited;

(e)   the amount of share capital with which the company proposes to be registered and the division thereof into shares of a fixed amount.

The memorandum of a public company must state that it is to be a public company (s. 1(3)(a)). A subscriber to a memorandum must take at least one share in the company, and the number of shares taken by a subscriber must be shown against the subscriber's name (s. 2(5)). The memorandum must be signed by each subscriber (or an agent: *Re Whitley Partners Ltd* (1886) 32 ChD 337) in the presence of at least one witness, who must attest the signature (s. 2(6)).

Only one subscriber is required if the company is to be a private limited company (s. 1(3A)) but the memorandum of a public company or an unlimited company must have at least two subscribers (s. 1(1)).

A company's articles of association cannot modify any of the statements in its memorandum (*Guinness* v *Land Corporation of Ireland* (1882) 22 ChD 349), and provisions of a company's memorandum have to be construed without reference to its articles (*Re Duncan Gilmour & Co. Ltd* [1952] 2 All ER 871). Otherwise provisions of the memorandum could be altered by altering the articles but CA 1985, s. 2(7) (see 2.4.1), prohibits this.

A company's memorandum may contain other provisions in addition to the ones required to be made by law.

2.3.2   Form of memorandum

CA 1985, s. 3, empowers the Secretary of State to specify in a statutory instrument the form of the memoranda of companies. Thus, the memorandum of a private company must be in accordance with the form set out in SI 1985 No. 805, Table B, or as near to that form as circumstances admit and the memorandum of a public company must be in the form set out in SI 1985 No. 805, Table F, or as near to that form as circumstances admit (CA 1985, s. 3(1)). There is a great similarity between the two forms. The specified form of the memorandum of a public company (Table F) is:

1.   The company's name is 'Western Electronics Public Limited Company.

2.   The company is to be a public company.

3.   The company's registered office is to be situated in England and Wales.

4.   The company's objects are the manufacture and development of such descriptions of electronic equipment, instruments and appliances as the company may from time to time determine, and the doing of all such things as are incidental or conducive to the attainment of that object.

5.   The liability of the members is limited.

6.   The company's share capital is £5,000,000 divided into 5,000,000 shares of £1 each.

We, the subscribers to this memorandum of association, wish to be formed into a company pursuant to this memorandum; and we agree to take the number of shares shown opposite our respective names.

Names and Addresses of Subscribers	Number of shares taken by each Subscriber
1. James White, 12 Broadmead, Birmingham.	1
2. Patrick Smith, 145A Huntley House, London Wall, London EC2.	1
Total shares taken	2

Dated   19

Witness to the above signatures,
Anne Brown, 13 Hute Street, London WC2.'

The only significant differences between this memorandum and that set out for private companies in Table B are that in paragraph 1 the company's name must end with the word 'limited' rather than 'public limited company' (or their Welsh equivalents), and that paragraph 2 is not included.

In practice memoranda are never registered in the short form envisaged by the legislation, but contain much expanded objects clauses (see 2.3.5.6 and 2.3.5.9). In *Gaiman* v *National Association for Mental Health* [1971] Ch 317, Megarry J said that the prescribed memorandum was a model of form not content and doubted whether it had to be followed in anything except the use of numbered paragraphs.

2.3.3   Name

Since a company is an artificial person, it can be identified only by its name, which is thus of considerable importance. The statutory provisions which attempt to ensure that a company's name is known to those who do business with it are set out in 2.3.3.7 and 4.5.1. There are several considerations to be borne in mind when choosing a name for a company.

2.3.3.1   Indication of limited liability

If a company limited by shares is to be a private company, the last word of its name must be 'limited' (CA 1985, s. 25(2)), and if it is to be a public company, the name must end with the words 'public limited company' (s. 25(1)). These words may, however, be abbreviated respectively to 'Ltd' and 'plc' (s. 27). Where a company's memorandum states that its registered office is to be situated in Wales, the company may use the Welsh equivalents of these words and abbreviations (ss. 25 and 27). The expressions 'limited', 'unlimited', 'public limited company', and their Welsh equivalents and abbreviations can appear only at the end of a company's name (s. 26(1)).

It is an offence to carry on a trade or business using any name incorporating the word 'limited' or the words 'public limited company' or an abbreviation or Welsh equivalent thereof which the user is not entitled to use (ss. 33 and 34) but this does not invalidate contracts made in the course of such a trade or business (*Cotronic (UK) Ltd* v *Dezonie* [1991] BCLC 721).

2.3.3.2   Omission of 'limited' from the name of a limited company

Under CA 1948, s. 19 (repealed by CA 1981, sch. 4), a limited company could obtain a licence from the Secretary of State to be registered with a name not including the word 'limited' if it was a non-profit-making company engaged in work for charity or the public good. As from 22 December 1980 such licences could be granted only to private companies (CA 1980, sch. 3, para. 5).

The licensing system ended on 25 February 1982 but, under CA 1985, s. 30, companies in possession of a licence on that day may continue to omit the word 'limited' from their names if they comply with the requirements of CA 1985, s. 30(3). These are that the company's objects must be the promotion of commerce (e.g., as a chamber of commerce), art, science, education, religion, charity or any profession. There must also be provisions in its memorandum or articles which:

(a)   Require its profits, if any, or other income to be applied in promoting its objects.

(b)   Prohibit distribution to its members either in profit dividends or on winding up: if the company is wound up its assets must be transferred to another body with charitable objects.

Since 25 February 1982 it has not been possible to register a new company limited by shares with a name that does not include the word 'limited' or its Welsh equivalent. However, a newly formed guarantee company may, by CA 1985, s. 30, be registered with a name that does not include the word 'limited' or its Welsh equivalent if it complies with the requirements of s. 30(3). The registrar must be provided with a statutory declaration of compliance with the requirements (s. 30(4) and (5)).

2.3.3.3   Illegal use of words in a name

By CA 1985, s. 26(1)(d), a company shall not be registered by a name if, in the opinion of the Secretary of State, the use of the name by the company would be a criminal offence.

Statute has prohibited the use of certain words that have an association with recognised charitable organisations. For example, a company's name may not include the words 'Red Cross' or 'Geneva Cross' without the authority of the Army Council (Geneva Convention Act 1957, s. 6), nor the word 'Anzac' without the authority of the Secretary of State for Foreign and Commonwealth Affairs ('Anzac' (Restriction on Trade Use of Word) Act 1916, s. 1). Under the Chartered Associations (Protection of Names and Uniforms) Act 1926, s. 1, it is unlawful to use or imitate the names of the Boy Scouts and Girl Guides Associations, the Order of St John of Jerusalem, the Royal Life Saving Society, and the National Society for the Prevention of Cruelty to Children.

Under the Banking Act 1987, s. 67, a company carrying on business in the UK must not use any name which indicates, or may reasonably be understood to indicate — whether in English or any other language — that it is a bank or is carrying on a banking business, unless it has been authorised by the Bank of England under the Act and has a paid-up share capital and/or undistributable reserves of £5 million or more. However, the holding company of an authorised institution may include the institution's name in its own name, to indicate the connection, as may a subsidiary of an authorised institution (Banking Act 1987, s. 68(4)).

It is an offence to use a name including the words 'credit union' or any cognate term or derivative of those words without being registered, under the Industrial and Provident Societies Act 1965, as a credit union (Credit Unions Act 1979, s. 3).

It is an offence to represent oneself as being a building society without being registered as one (Building Societies Act 1986, s. 107).

In *R* v *Registrar of Companies, ex parte Bowen* [1914] 3 KB 1161, DC, it was held that the registrar has no authority to refuse to register a company with a name which the registrar considers to be misleading, but Lord Reading CJ said, at p. 1167, that the registrar could refuse registration if a company's name contained scandalous or obscene words. Now CA 1985, s. 26(1)(e), prohibits registration of a company with a name which 'in the opinion of the Secretary of State is offensive'. This would appear to mean offensive to people generally rather than offensive to a particular section of the public. In Australia, a name cannot be used if it is likely to be offensive to members of any section of the public, and in *Little* v *Australian Securities Commission* (1996) 22 ACSR 226 it was held that the name 'Virgin Mary's Pty Ltd' could not be used because it was likely to offend a section of the public. (The company operated a nightclub: the objectors were represented at the hearing by J. Santamaria QC.)

2.3.3.4 *Existing corporations and limited partnerships*
The registrars of companies for England and Wales and for Scotland are required by CA 1985, s. 714, to keep an index of the names of:

(a)   All existing corporations that are incorporated by registration as companies under the laws of England and Wales, Northern Ireland and Scotland.

(b)   All existing corporations that are incorporated by registration as industrial and provident societies under the laws of England and Wales, Northern Ireland and Scotland.

(c)   Certain chartered, statutory and letters patent companies specified in s. 718 (letters patent companies are not corporations).

(d)   Limited partnerships (which are not corporations) registered under the Limited Partnerships Act 1907 (which applies in all parts of the UK).

(e)   Corporations incorporated outside Great Britain that have established a place of business in Great Britain and delivered details of themselves to either registrar, and corporations incorporated outside Northern Ireland that have established places of business in Northern Ireland and delivered details to the Northern Ireland registrar.

(f)   European economic interest groupings or their establishments registered in Great Britain or Northern Ireland (SI 1989 No. 638, sch. 4).

The index is published on microfiche. By CA 1985, s. 26(1)(c) and (3), a company shall not be registered with a name that is the same as one appearing in this index, or where the only difference is:

(a)   The occurrence of the definite article at the beginning of the name.

(b)   The occurrence of the words 'company', or 'limited', or 'unlimited', or 'public limited company', or any abbreviated or Welsh forms of those words at the end of the name.

(c)   The typography, word division, accenting or punctuation of the name.

Section 28(2) deals with erroneous registration of a company with a name too like that of an existing company, either because of the registrar's failure to appreciate the similarity or because the existing company was omitted from the index. In those circumstances the Secretary of State can, within 12 months of the erroneous registration, direct the company to change its name (see 2.4.2).

2.3.3.5 *Words requiring permission*
By CA 1985, s. 26(2)(a), the permission of the Secretary of State is necessary in order to register a company with a name likely to give the impression that the company is connected

in any way with the government or any local authority. In addition the Company and Business Names Regulations 1981 (SI 1981 No. 1685), as amended by SI 1982 No. 1653, SI 1992 No. 1196 and SI 1995 No. 3022, give a long list of words and expressions that may only be used in company names with the permission of the Secretary of State under s. 26(2)(b). For example, permission from the Secretary of State is required in order to use the words 'England', 'Ireland', 'Scotland', 'Wales', or 'Great Britain'. The list includes several common words, such as 'association', 'chartered', 'council', 'foundation', 'group', 'holding', 'registered' and 'society'.

In relation to some of the words and expressions listed in the Company and Business Names Regulations, it is necessary to write to a Department of State or public authority specified in the regulations to enquire whether (and if so why) it has any objections to the proposed use of the word in the company's name (CA 1985, s. 29(1)(b) and (2)). For example, the Privy Council must be asked whether it has any objection to the use of the word 'university' in a company's name. The General Dental Council must be asked whether it has any objection to the use of the word 'dental', the word which had caused a problem in *R* v *Registrar of Companies, ex parte Bowen* [1914] 3 KB 1161 — see 1.2.1. The person who makes the statutory declaration that all the requirements of the Companies Act have been complied with on the application for registration (CA 1985, s. 12(3); see 1.2.1) is responsible for applying to the appropriate authority, and a copy of the application and of any response to it must accompany that statutory declaration (s. 29(3)). This correspondence is not made available for public inspection (s. 29(4)).

2.3.3.6 *Passing off*

Using a name for one's business which is deceptively similar to the name of another business so that actual damage has been, or is likely to be, caused to the goodwill and reputation of that other business is a form of the tort of passing off which may be restrained by injunction. Thus in *Hendriks* v *Montagu* (1881) 17 ChD 638, the Universal Life Assurance Society (which was not incorporated) obtained an injunction to prevent Montagu and his associates registering a company with the name Universe Life Assurance Association Ltd. It is not necessary to prove that the deception was intended (*British Diabetic Association* v *Diabetic Society Ltd* [1995] 4 All ER 812).

To counter passing off by a company that has already been registered, an injunction may be obtained requiring the company's controllers not to allow the company to continue to be registered with a deceptive name (specifying words which must not be used), so that they must either change the company's name (see 2.4.2) or dissolve it (*La Société Anonyme des Anciens Établissements Panhard et Levassor* v *Panhard Levassor Motor Co. Ltd* [1901] 2 Ch 513; *Exxon Corporation* v *Exxon Insurance Consultants International Ltd* [1982] Ch 119).

The court will not restrain an individual from trading under his or her own surname, provided the individual is acting honestly. However, a company is not entitled to the same immunity in respect of using the name of one of its members: a company does not have a right to trade under the name of one of its shareholders if to do so would damage another business (*M.P. Guimaraens and Son* v *Fonseca and Vasconcellos Ltd* (1921) 38 RPC 388, in which the defendant company was prohibited from trading in port wine under its name, which included the surname of one of its shareholders and directors, R.A. da Fonseca, because to do so would cause confusion with the plaintiff firm's old-established trade in 'Fonseca's port'). This emphasises that the business of a company is owned by the company as a separate person, not by its members. See also *Tussaud* v *Tussaud* (1890) 44 ChD 678, in which the company that owned Madame Tussaud's waxworks was granted an injunction to prevent a member of the Tussaud family from registering a company called Louis Tussaud Ltd to carry on a similar waxworks show.

It is only *business* reputation and goodwill that can be protected by an action for passing off, not, for example, the reputation of a political party (*Kean v McGivan* [1982] FSR 119). Also the business must be carried on within the jurisdiction of the court in which proceedings are taken (*Harrods Ltd v Harrods (Buenos Aires) Ltd* [1997] FSR 420). A further limitation on the passing-off action in relation to trading names is that if traders A and B have similar business names but no common field of activity then there is no passing off (*Wombles Ltd v Wombles Skips Ltd* [1977] RPC 99).

Use of the name of a person, whether an individual or a company, to mark goods so that people may believe they are the goods of another trader is another form of passing off, and is regarded particularly seriously by the courts — it is no defence that all that has been done is honestly to put on the goods the name of their maker (*Baume and Co. Ltd v A.H. Moore Ltd* [1958] RPC 226, in which the defendant company was prohibited from continuing to import watches made by a Swiss company, Baume & Mercier SA, marked 'Baume & Mercier', which the public might confuse with the 'Baume' watches which the plaintiff company had sold for about 80 years; *Parker-Knoll Ltd v Knoll International Ltd* [1962] RPC 243).

A recent development is the use of the law of passing off to counter people who register companies with names which existing traders or famous people might want to use as trading names in the future and who are then asked to pay large sums to buy the companies. This has been described as an abuse of the registration process and a mandatory injunction will be issued in such a case to require the company to change its name (*Glaxo plc v Glaxowellcome Ltd* [1996] FSR 388; *Direct Line Group Ltd v Direct Line Estate Agency Ltd* [1997] FSR 374). Unfortunately the defendants in these cases have represented themselves and have lost by being their own worst enemies. It is questionable whether passing off has been correctly applied in these cases where plaintiff and defendant did not have a common business activity and there was no proof of any damage to the plaintiffs' goodwill and reputation.

2.3.3.7 Use of a business name other than the corporate name

A company may conduct its business under a name which is not its corporate name (i.e., the name under which it is registered at Companies House and which appears on its certificate of incorporation). Carrying on a business under a name which is not the true name of the person who is carrying on the business is controlled by the Business Names Act 1985, which has two main aims:

(a) to enable people who wish to take legal proceedings against persons carrying on a business to discover those persons' true names;

(b) to control the use of undesirable names.

A company which carries on business in Great Britain is regarded as carrying it on in its true name if its business name is its corporate name. If anything is added to the corporate name then the business will not be regarded as being carried on in the company's true name (Business Names Act 1985, s. 1(1)(c)). The only exception is that a company may add to its corporate name an indication that it is carrying on a business as successor to a former owner of that business (Business Names Act 1985, s. 1(2)(c)).

If a business is carried on in Great Britain by a company under a name that is not its true name then:

(a)   The corporate name of the company carrying on the business, plus an address, within Great Britain, at which service of any document relating to the business will be effective, must be stated, in legible characters, on all business letters, written orders for goods or services to be supplied to the business, invoices and receipts issued in the course of the business and written demands for payment of debts arising in the course of the business (Business Names Act 1985, s. 4(1)(a)).

(b)   The corporate name and address of the company carrying on the business must be displayed in a prominent position, so that they can be easily read, in any premises where the business is carried on and to which the customers of the business or suppliers of any goods or services to the business have access (Business Names Act 1985, s. 4(1)(b)).

(c)   The corporate name and address of the company carrying on the business must be supplied immediately in writing to any person who asks for them and with whom anything is done or discussed in the course of the business (Business Names Act 1985, s. 4(2)).

Contravention of these rules by a company is an offence triable only summarily (Business Names Act 1985, s. 7). If an offence committed by a company is proved to have been committed with the consent or connivance of, or to be attributable to any neglect on the part of, any director, manager, secretary or other similar officer of the company, or any person who was purporting to act in any such capacity, he or she as well as the company is guilty of the offence and liable to be proceeded against and punished accordingly (Business Names Act 1985, s. 7(4)). It is a defence to show that there was a reasonable excuse for the contravention (Business Names Act 1985, s. 4(6)).

These provisions overlap with requirements of CA 1985, ss. 348 and 349, which are discussed in 4.5.1.

Apart from the possibility of a small fine for contravening the Business Names Act 1985 there is a provision in s. 5 which is a weak attempt to make the contracts of a defaulting company unenforceable. If a company takes legal proceedings to enforce a right arising from a contract made in the course of its business and the other party shows that, because of the default in disclosing the true name and address of the company, he has either suffered financial loss in connection with the contract or has been unable to pursue a claim arising out of the contract, then the proceedings taken by the company shall be dismissed unless the court is satisfied that it is just and equitable to allow them to proceed.

Under the Business Names Act 1985, s. 2(1) and (4), if a company carries on a business under a name that is not its true name then it is an offence for it to use, without the written approval of the Secretary of State, a name which:

(a)   would be likely to give the impression that the business is connected with Her Majesty's Government or with any local authority; or

(b)   includes any word or expression for the time being specified in regulations.

Words and expressions requiring permission have been listed in the Company and Business Names Regulations 1981 (SI 1981 No. 1685), as amended by SI 1982 No. 1653, SI 1992 No. 1196 and SI 1995 No. 3022, which are discussed in 2.3.3.5. In relation to some of the words and expressions listed in these regulations, it is necessary to write to a Department of State or public authority specified in the regulations to enquire whether (and if so why) it has any objection to the proposed use of the word in the business name (Business Names Act 1985, s. 3(2)). A statement that such a request has been made and a copy of any response received must be submitted to the Secretary of State when seeking his approval for the business name (s. 3(2)(b)).

2.3.3.8   Use of an insolvent company's name

When choosing a name for a company it is necessary to consider the persons who are to be its directors or take part in its management. Any such person who was a director or shadow director of a company that went into insolvent liquidation less than five years previously is in danger of committing an offence under IA 1986, s. 216, if the new company uses a name suggesting an association with the insolvent company.

The controllers of a company that has become insolvent are usually able to set up a new company, known as a 'phoenix company', immediately to carry on the same business. IA 1986, s. 216, tries to prevent a phoenix company using the insolvent company's business name in a way that misleads people who deal with it. The section applies to any person who has been a director or shadow director of a company that has gone into insolvent liquidation and who occupied that position at any time within the period of 12 months ending with the day before it went into liquidation (IA 1986, s. 216(1)). Any name which was used by the company during those 12 months, either its own name or a trading name, is a 'prohibited name', as is any name which is so similar to a name it used as to suggest an association with the company (IA 1986, s. 216(2) and (6)). A company goes into insolvent liquidation if it goes into liquidation (see 20.8) at a time when its assets are insufficient for the payment of its debts and other liabilities and the expenses of the winding up (IA 1986, s. 216(7); cf. CDDA 1986, s. 6(2), discussed in 15.2.5.3). During the period of five years beginning with the day on which the company went into insolvent liquidation, the ex director or shadow director shall not, without the leave of a court having jurisdiction to wind up companies (IA 1986, s. 216(3) and (5)):

(a)   be a director of any other company that is known by a prohibited name (i.e., has a prohibited name as its own name or uses it as a business name: s. 216(6)); or

(b)   in any way, whether directly or indirectly, be concerned or take part in the promotion, formation or management of any such company; or

(c)   in any way, whether directly or indirectly, be concerned or take part in the carrying on of a business carried on (otherwise than by a company) under a prohibited name.

For examples of applications for leave (which was granted), see *Re Bonus Breaks Ltd* [1991] BCC 546 and *Re Lightning Electrical Contractors Ltd* [1996] 2 BCLC 302. It is not right to refuse leave as a substitute for making a disqualification order where the facts of the case would not justify disqualification (*Penrose* v *Secretary of State for Trade and Industry* [1996] 1 WLR 482). The fact that the amount paid by the new company for the old company's business was determined by independent valuation will favour granting leave but the court should not require undertakings concerning adequate capitalisation of the new company or the appointment of independent directors as a condition for granting leave (ibid.). The most important consideration is whether there is any risk to creditors beyond that which is inherent in dealing with limited companies (ibid.). For detailed discussion see G. Wilson, 'Delinquent directors and company names: the role of judicial policy-making in the business environment' (1996) 47 NILQ 345.

Acting in contravention of s. 216(3) is an offence triable either way (s. 216(4) and sch. 10). The offence is one of strict liability, that is, the prosecution only have to prove that the accused did the prohibited act and do not have to prove an intention to offend (*R* v *Cole* [1998] BCC 87).

In addition to the possibility of a criminal penalty, a potentially severe civil penalty for contravention of s. 216 is imposed by s. 217. A person who is involved in the management of a company in contravention of s. 216 is personally responsible for all debts and other liabilities of the company incurred while involved in its management (s. 217(1)(a) and (3)(a)). Furthermore, any person who is 'involved in the management of' a company and acts, or is willing to act, on instructions given by a person whom he or she knows to be contravening s. 216 is also personally responsible for debts and other liabilities of the company incurred while he or she was so acting or willing to act (s. 217(1)(b) and (3)(b)). For the purposes of s. 217, a person who is a director of a company, or is concerned, whether directly or indirectly, or takes part, in the management of the company is 'involved in the management of' the company (s. 217(5)). A person liable under s. 217 is jointly and severally liable with the company and with anyone else liable under the section (s. 217(2)). For an example of the operation of s. 217 see *Thorne* v *Silverleaf* [1994] 1 BCLC 637.

2.3.4 Registered office

The memorandum of a company registered with the registrar of companies in England and Wales must state either that its registered office is to be situated in England and Wales or that it is to be situated in Wales (CA 1985, ss. 2(1)(b) and (2) and 10(1)(a)). The memorandum of a company registered with the registrar of companies in Scotland must state that its registered office is to be in Scotland. When a company is registered, a statement of the address of the company's first registered office must be delivered to the registrar (s. 10(6)) and that will be the situation of the company's registered office on incorporation (s. 287(2)).

CA 1948 and earlier companies legislation required the memorandum of a company registered with the registrar of companies in England and Wales to state that its registered office was to be in 'England', which term, by virtue of the Wales and Berwick Act 1746, s. 3, included Wales. The relevant provision of the Wales and Berwick Act 1746 does not apply to Acts passed after 27 July 1967 (Welsh Language Act 1967, s. 4; see now Interpretation Act 1978, sch. 2, para. 5(a)) so CA 1985, s. 2(1)(b), now refers to 'England and Wales'. Since 18 April 1977, it has been possible for a company's memorandum to state that its registered office is to be in Wales.

In *Re Baby Moon (UK) Ltd* 1985 PCC 103, the registrar of companies in England and Wales had registered in 1981 a company whose memorandum stated its registered office was to be in England but the statement delivered under what is now CA 1985, s. 10(6), said that its first registered office would be in Livingston, which is in Scotland. When a petition for the compulsory winding up of the company was presented to the High Court in London the court held that, by virtue of CA 1985, s. 13(7), the company's certificate of incorporation was conclusive evidence that the company was registered in England and Wales so that the High Court had jurisdiction to wind it up under what is now Insolvency Act 1986, s. 117(1). Leave was given for the petition to be served on the company outside the court's jurisdiction at the company's registered office in Scotland.

The situation of a company's registered office is of great importance to persons dealing with the company because by CA 1985, s. 725(1): 'A document may be served on a company by leaving it at, or sending it by post to, the company's registered office'. By s. 744, 'document' includes a summons, notice, order, and other legal process. Accordingly, a High Court writ may be served on a company by posting it to the company's registered office (Rules of the Supreme Court 1965, ord. 10, r. 1(7); *Addis Ltd* v *Berkeley Supplies Ltd* [1964] 1 WLR 943). 'Post' in s. 725(1) includes registered post (*TO Supplies (London) Ltd* v *Jerry Creighton Ltd* [1952] 1 KB 42).

In order for a company to change the situation of its registered office (within the territory specified in its memorandum), the company must give notice in the prescribed form to the registrar (CA 1985, s. 287(3)). Receipt of notice of a change of registered office must be notified by the registrar in the *Gazette* (s. 711(1)(n)). The change takes effect when the notice is registered by the registrar, but until the end of the period of 14 days beginning with the date on which it is registered, a person may validly serve any document on the company at its previous registered office (s. 287(4)).

2.3.5 Objects

2.3.5.1 Statutory requirement
The memorandum of a company must state the objects of the company (CA 1985, s. 2(1)(c)). The registrar may not register a company whose objects are unlawful (*R v Registrar of Companies, ex parte Attorney-General* [1991] BCLC 476, DC). By CA 1985, s. 13(7), a company's certificate of incorporation is conclusive evidence that its memorandum states its objects as required by s. 2(1)(c) (*Cotman v Brougham* [1918] AC 514, HL) but it is not conclusive evidence that those objects are lawful (*Bowman v Secular Society Ltd* [1917] AC 406). See 1.2.1.

2.3.5.2 Ultra vires *transactions beyond a company's objects*
Parliament has insisted that the memorandum of a registered company must state the objects for which it is incorporated, and the company is accordingly incorporated only for the purpose of pursuing those objects. Pursuing any other object is said to be *ultra vires* (beyond the powers of) the company. (Conversely, a transaction for a purpose that is an object of the company is described as *intra vires* — within the powers.)

Any director of a company who is responsible for it entering into a transaction outside its objects is liable to replace the money the company expended on the transaction (*Re Lands Allotment Co.* [1894] 1 Ch 616, CA) unless the members of the company relieve the director of liability, which generally requires a special resolution (three-quarters majority) (CA 1985, s. 35(3); see 19.5.8). In *Re Samuel Sherman plc* [1991] 1 WLR 1070, a director of a company who invested its money in loss-making activities outside its objects was disqualified from being a director for five years.

On the application of any member of a company, the court may order the company not to enter into a proposed transaction beyond the company's objects (*Simpson v Westminster Palace Hotel Co.* (1860) 8 HL Cas 712; CA 1985, s. 35(2)). However, the court cannot restrain the company from doing what it has already bound itself to do (s. 35(2)). If a proposed transaction is found to be beyond the company's objects, the members can alter the objects to accommodate it — see 2.4.4.

The rule that a member of a *registered* company can prevent it entering into a transaction beyond its objects follows the rule that a member of a *statutory* company is entitled to prevent it entering into a transaction for a purpose that is not one of the objects of the company set out in its incorporating Act of Parliament. For example, in *Colman v Eastern Counties Railway Co.* (1846) 10 Beav 1, the plaintiff succeeded in stopping the company (which operated the railway from London to Harwich) from giving financial support to a company it was promoting to operate a shipping service from Harwich to Rotterdam and other northern European ports — the plaintiff was probably acting for rival shipping interests.

In *Simpson v Westminster Palace Hotel Co.*, the company had been incorporated to build and operate what for that time was an unusually large hotel. The directors decided that for the first three years they would lease part of the hotel to the civil service so as to provide a guaranteed income. A member of the company sought an injunction to prevent this but the House of Lords refused the injunction, finding that the proposed lease did not take the company outside the business of running a hotel.

In *Stephens* v *Mysore Reefs (Kangundy) Mining Co. Ltd* [1902] 1 Ch 745, a company formed to acquire a gold mine in India was restrained from acquiring an interest in a gold mining property in West Africa.

2.3.5.3   Repudiation of transactions
It is possible, in some circumstances, for a company to repudiate a transaction entered into on its behalf outside its objects. It can do this on the ground that the person who acted on its behalf could not have actual authority to act on its behalf outside its objects. However, the circumstances in which this can be done have been increasingly limited by statute in recent years so as to protect people who deal with companies from having their transactions repudiated — see 19.5.5.

In the 19th century the courts established a rule (known as the '*ultra vires* rule') that a company did not have capacity to enter into a transaction which was not capable of being within its objects, so that such a transaction was void and did not bind the company (*Ashbury Railway Carriage and Iron Co. Ltd* v *Riche* (1857) LR 7 HL 653), but this rule has been abolished by CA 1989 (see 19.4.1).

2.3.5.4   Substratum
Members of a company take shares in it and contribute capital to it on the basis that it will use its money to pursue the objects stated in its memorandum. Accordingly it is just and equitable for the court to order the winding up of a company (under the Insolvency Act 1986, s. 122(1)(g)) if 'that which the company was formed to do can no longer be done' (per Kekewich J in *Re Bristol Joint Stock Bank* (1890) 44 ChD 703 at p. 712) so that anything it might do would be outside its objects. It is usually said in such a case that the company's 'substratum' has gone, using terminology apparently coined by Lord Cairns LJ in *Re Suburban Hotel Co.* (1867) LR 2 Ch App 737 at p. 750. For example, in *Re Baku Consolidated Oilfields Ltd* [1944] 1 All ER 24, the company was formed to purchase the undertakings of four companies whose undertakings were expropriated without compensation in 1920 shortly after the company was formed. Compulsory winding up was ordered. In 1990, compensation was finally agreed (see *Re Baku Consolidated Oilfields Ltd* [1994] 1 BCLC 173).

2.3.5.5   An action may be ultra vires for some purposes but not for others
According to Lord Parker of Waddington in *Cotman* v *Brougham* [1918] AC 514 at p. 520, a court may take a different view of what is within or outside a company's objects depending on whether the question before it is:

(a)   one of equity between the company and its members (for example, when deciding, at the instance of a member of a company, whether to restrain a proposed action of the company — see 2.3.5.2 and 2.3.5.6 — or whether to wind up the company for loss of substratum — see 2.3.5.4) or

(b)   one of law between the company and another person (for example, whether the company is bound by a particular contract — see 2.3.5.3).

When deciding whether a transaction between a company and an outsider can be repudiated, a court is likely to take a wide view of what is within the company's objects, and consequently a narrow view of what is *ultra vires*.

When deciding what is equitable between a company and its members, a court is likely to take a narrower view of what is within the company's objects, and consequently a wider view of what is *ultra vires*. In particular, when deciding a question of equity between a company and its members, a court may consider an action to be within the company's objects only if it is within what the court considers to be the company's 'main object' (see 2.3.5.8).

The idea of wider and narrower views of *ultra vires* has a special meaning in relation to ratification of transactions entered into for a purpose outside a company's objects. See 19.5.8.

2.3.5.6 Implied powers for incidental purposes

In *Attorney-General* v *Great Eastern Railway Co.* (1880) 5 App Cas 473, Lord Selborne LC made the important statement, at p. 478, that the *ultra vires* rule:

ought to be reasonably, and not unreasonably, understood and applied [to statutory companies], and that whatever may fairly be regarded as incidental to, or consequential upon, those things which the legislature has authorised, ought not (unless expressly prohibited) to be held, by judicial construction, to be *ultra vires*.

Accordingly, in *Deuchar* v *Gas Light & Coke Co.* [1925] AC 691, it was held that the Gas Light & Coke Co. (a statutory company formed to make gas from coal) could itself manufacture caustic soda (sodium hydroxide) for use in converting one of the by-products of its gas-making process into a substance that could be sold to dyestuff manufacturers. Mr Deuchar had acquired shares in the company to challenge the *vires* of this activity: he was the secretary of a company that made caustic soda.

The same rule is applied to registered companies. 'Any such company is treated as having implied powers to do any act which is reasonably incidental to the attainment or pursuit of any of its express objects, unless such act is expressly prohibited by the memorandum' (per Slade LJ in *Rolled Steel Products (Holdings) Ltd* v *British Steel Corporation* [1986] Ch 246 at p. 287, re-expressing a statement of Buckley LJ in *Re Horsley & Weight Ltd* [1982] Ch 442 at p. 448).

In *Johns* v *Balfour* (1889) 5 TLR 389, a company's object was to conduct mining operations in Russia and it did so on the estate of a landowner as tenant of the landowner. When the landowner died it was proposed to buy the whole estate of 17,000 hectares so as to secure the company's right to mine the land. A shareholder objected that a purchase on such a scale would make the company a landowning company, which would be outside its objects, but the court held that the land purchase was merely in furtherance of the company's stated objects and so was *intra vires*.

A trading company must have an implied power to borrow money (*General Auction Estate & Monetary Co.* v *Smith* [1891] 3 Ch 432), and a company that has power to borrow money must have an implied power to give security for its repayment (*Re Patent File Co.* (1870) LR 6 Ch App 83). A company has an implied power to invest its surplus funds (*Burland* v *Earle* [1902] AC 83). There is an implied power to pay gratuities to employees while a company is a going concern (*Hampson* v *Price's Patent Candle Co.* (1876) 45 LJ Ch 437 (which concerned a statutory company); *Cameron* v *Glenmorangie Distillery Co. Ltd* (1896) 23 R 1092; *Cyclists' Touring Club* v *Hopkinson* [1910] 1 Ch 179). Any company has an implied power to compromise claims against itself (*Re Norwich Provident Insurance Society, Bath's Case* (1878) 8 ChD 334, CA).

If an action is brought alleging that an individual committed a tort in the course of employment by a company then the company has an implied power to pay for the individual's defence (*Breay* v *Royal British Nurses' Association* [1897] 2 Ch 272 (which concerned a chartered corporation)).

On the other hand, a company does not necessarily have a power to issue negotiable instruments (for example, to accept bills of exchange) (*Peruvian Railways Co.* v *Thames & Mersey Marine Insurance Co.* (1867) LR 2 Ch App 617). In the 19th century there was considerable uncertainty over whether the courts would accept that a company had an incidental power to engage in even the simplest commercial transaction such as issuing a bill of exchange, and it became the practice to include in the objects clause of every company's memorandum of association a statement that the company's objects included engaging in a long list of classes of transaction. In *Cotman* v *Brougham* [1918] AC 514 at pp. 522–3, Lord Wrenbury protested against this:

> The objects of the company and the powers of the company to be exercised in effecting the objects are different things. Powers are not required to be, and ought not to be, specified in the memorandum. The Act [i.e., CA 1862] intended that the company, if it be a trading company, should by its memorandum define the trade, not that it should specify the various acts which it should be within the power of the company to do in carrying on the trade. . . .
>
> There has grown up a pernicious practice of registering memoranda of association which, under the clause relating to objects, contain paragraph after paragraph not specifying or delimiting the proposed trade or purpose, but confusing power with purpose and indicating every class of act which the corporation is to have power to do. The practice is not one of recent growth. It was in active operation when I was a junior at the Bar. After a vain struggle I had to yield to it, contrary to my own convictions.

Lord Wrenbury's protest went unheeded, and long objects clauses have since become normal in practice.

Although there is a legal rule that a company has implied powers to do any act reasonably incidental to the attainment or pursuit of its express objects, the objects clauses in the model forms of memoranda in Tables B and F of SI 1985 No. 805, after stating substantive objects, finish with the words 'and the doing of all such other things as are incidental or conducive to the attainment of that object'. Such an 'incidental or conducive' provision is normally included in the memoranda of companies. In *Evans* v *Brunner, Mond and Co. Ltd* [1921] 1 Ch 359, Eve J accepted the evidence of the company's directors that donating £100,000 to universities or scientific institutions for the furtherance of scientific education and research would be 'conducive to, and indeed necessary for, [the company's] continued progress as chemical manufacturers', and refused to restrain such donations at the instance of a shareholder, finding that they would be within the 'incidental or conducive' provision of the objects clause in the company's memorandum. But in *Simmonds* v *Heffer* [1983] BCLC 298, Mervyn Davies J emphasised that doing something outside the main objects of a company cannot be incidental or conducive to those main objects: accordingly contributing to a fund for the election of a Labour government was not within the objects of the League against Cruel Sports despite a Labour Party commitment to promote legislation which would achieve many of the League's aims. It is probably impossible to explain the different results in *Evans* v *Brunner, Mond and Co. Ltd* and *Simmonds* v *Heffer* except on the basis of the judges' personal choices.

In *Tomkinson* v *South-Eastern Railway Co.* (1887) 35 ChD 675 (which concerned a statutory company), it was held that donating money to exhibitions, sporting events and so on was not within the objects of the railway company, and would be restrained. The company had argued that encouraging such events was incidental to its railway business because people would want to travel to them by railway so that encouraging the events would increase the railway's traffic. However, Kay J said, at p. 680: 'To say . . . that any expenditure which may indirectly conduce to the benefit of the company is *intra vires*, seems to me extravagant'.

Potential benefit to the company, then, is not enough: a proposed act of a company may be restrained, at the instance of a dissentient member, as being outside the company's objects even if it is thought by the majority of members to be beneficial to the company. In *Evans v Brunner, Mond and Co. Ltd* [1921] 1 Ch 359, Eve J said, at pp. 368–9:

> When an act of the company is challenged on the ground that it is beyond the powers of the company the challenge is not disposed of by proving that the act is beneficial to the company, it must be established that it is an act the doing of which is authorised by the company's constitution.

Similarly, the fact that something is done in good faith does not bring it within the objects of a company (per North J in *Henderson v Bank of Australasia* (1888) 40 ChD 170 at p. 173). As Bowen LJ said in *Hutton v West Cork Railway Co.* (1883) 23 ChD 654 (which concerned a statutory company) at p. 671:

> Bona fides cannot be the sole test, otherwise you might have a lunatic conducting the affairs of the company, and paying away its money with both hands in a manner perfectly bona fide yet perfectly irrational. The test must be what is reasonably incidental to, and within the reasonable scope of carrying on, the business of the company.

Cases such as *Tomkinson v South-Eastern Railway Co.* and *Evans v Brunner, Mond and Co. Ltd* show that unless a power to make charitable and political donations is expressly provided in a company's memorandum it is always questionable whether they are within the company's objects. It has been suggested that as charitable giving is a good thing which deserves encouragement, companies should be given a statutory power to make charitable donations (P. Graham, 'Removing the Scrooge principle from company law' (1998) 19 Co Law 54). The amount a company has contributed for charitable or political purposes in a financial year, if more than £200, must be revealed in the directors' report for the year (CA 1985, sch. 7, para. 3).

2.3.5.7 Acts that are not for the company's benefit

In considering a company's objects, a court will not *imply* a power to do something that is not for the benefit of the company (*Hutton v West Cork Railway Co.* (1883) 23 ChD 654; *Stroud v Royal Aquarium & Summer & Winter Garden Society Ltd* (1903) 89 LT 243; *Parke v Daily News Ltd* [1962] Ch 927). In each of these cases a company had ceased to carry on all, or a major part, of its business and it was proposed to make severance payments to former directors or employees which the company was not contractually obliged to make and which could not be regarded as payment for past services. The courts decided that these payments could not possibly benefit the companies, unlike gratuities paid to employees by a company continuing in business which would benefit from improved relations with the employees or an enhanced reputation as an employer which would attract higher-quality employees in future. CA 1985, s. 719(1) (which was first enacted as CA 1980, s. 74(1)), now provides that the powers of a company include (if they would not otherwise do so apart from s. 719) power to provide for employees or former employees on cessation or transfer of the whole or part of the company's undertaking. Section 719(2) expressly provides that this power is exercisable notwithstanding that its exercise is not in the best interests of the company.

In *Re Lee Behrens & Co. Ltd* [1932] 2 Ch 46 the directors of the company had covenanted on behalf of the company to pay a pension to the widow of a former managing director. The matter was never considered by the members in general meeting. The company had no express power in its memorandum to enter into such a contract but it had been established by *Henderson* v *Bank of Australasia* (1888) 40 ChD 170 that a trading company continuing in business had an implied power to make such a gift to the family of a deceased former official. Eve J said ([1932] 2 Ch at p. 51) that the 'validity' of the pension had to be tested 'by the answers to three pertinent questions: (i) Is the transaction reasonably incidental to the carrying on of the company's business? (ii) Is it a bona fide transaction? and (iii) Is it done for the benefit and to promote the prosperity of the company?' Eve J found that there was no evidence that the directors of Lee Behrens & Co. Ltd had considered whether the pension was for the benefit of the company, and the matter had not been considered by the members in general meeting. Accordingly, his lordship held that the company could repudiate the obligation to pay the pension, apparently because it had not had capacity to incur the obligation under the old *ultra vires* rule.

Eve J seemed to think that even acts within a company's objects as expressed in its memorandum were invalid unless they satisfied the three tests he stated. However, it was subsequently pointed out on several occasions that the three tests could not be used to determine the capacity of a company to enter into transactions within its express objects: if an act was within the express objects of a company then it could not be said to be beyond the company's capacity on any grounds (see per Buckley LJ in *Re Horsley & Weight Ltd* [1982] Ch 442 at p. 452 and per Slade LJ in *Rolled Steel Products (Holdings) Ltd* v *British Steel Corporation* [1986] Ch 246 at p. 288). It was wrong for the court in *Re W. & M. Roith Ltd* [1967] 1 WLR 432 to apply the three tests to a transaction apparently within the express objects of a company (per Buckley LJ in *Re Horsley & Weight Ltd* at pp. 451–2).

The only possible basis for an objection to a transaction that is within a company's objects but not for its benefit is the rule that the company's directors must act bona fide in the interests of the company (see 16.4).

It is possible for a company's memorandum to be worded in such a way that making gifts of the company's property is within its objects. As Buckley LJ said in *Re Horsley & Weight Ltd* at p. 450:

> The objects of a company do not need to be commercial: they can be charitable or philanthropic. . . . Nor is there any reason why a company should not part with its funds gratuitously or for non-commercial reasons if to do so is within its declared objects.

No company has an implied power to sell or dispose of its whole undertaking: such a sale or disposal could not be incidental to the attainment or pursuit of the object of carrying on the undertaking (*Re Oceanic Steam Navigation Co. Ltd* [1939] Ch 41). In practice it is usual to state in a company's memorandum an express power to sell or dispose of its whole undertaking.

It is *ultra vires* for a company to pay the costs of legal proceedings arising out of a dispute between its members (*Pickering* v *Stephenson* (1872) LR 14 Eq 322; see 18.7.6).

2.3.5.8 Main objects

When deciding a question of equity between a company and its members, a court may consider an action to be within the company's objects only if it is within what it considers to be the company's 'main object'. This is particularly apparent in cases in which members have petitioned the court for their company to be wound up compulsorily because its substratum has gone. The court may accept in such a case that because the 'main object' of the company has failed, whatever else the company might do is sufficiently outside its objects to justify compulsory winding up.

For example, in *Re German Date Coffee Co.* (1882) 20 ChD 169, the first paragraph of the company's objects clause stated that the company was formed to 'acquire and purchase, and to use, exercise, and vend certain inventions for manufacturing from dates a substitute for coffee, for which a patent has or will be granted by the Empire of Germany to Thomas Frederick Henley. . .'. The second paragraph stated that the company was to 'make and use the said inventions . . '. In fact the Empire of Germany refused to grant a patent to Mr Henley for his method of manufacturing date coffee but the company nevertheless acquired a factory in Hamburg and made date coffee there without patent protection. Two shareholders petitioned for the compulsory winding up of the company on the ground that its substratum had failed. The company opposed the petition, saying that using Mr Henley's *invention* was within its objects even if the invention was not protected by a patent. A winding-up order was made, and was affirmed by the Court of Appeal, where Jessel MR explained that the company's business was not 'to make a substitute for coffee from dates, but to work a particular patent, and as that particular patent does not exist, and cannot now exist, [the petitioners] are entitled to say the company ought to be wound up'. There was some discussion of whether the company's activities were within para. 8 of its objects clause which referred to it being formed 'to import all descriptions of produce for the purposes of food, and the exporting of the same, and the selling and disposing thereof respectively. . .'. Lindley LJ said (at p. 188):

> General words construed literally may mean anything; but they must be taken in connection with what are shown by the context to be the dominant or main objects. It will not do under general words to turn a company for manufacturing one thing into a company for importing something else, however general the words are.

Similarly, in deciding whether to restrain a proposed action of a company it may be sufficient that the action is outside what the court finds to be the company's main object (*Stephens* v *Mysore Reefs (Kangundy) Mining Co. Ltd* [1902] 1 Ch 745, in which an injunction was granted; *Pedlar* v *Road Block Gold Mines of India Ltd* [1905] 2 Ch 427, in which an injunction was refused).

For further discussion of the identification of a company's main objects, see *Re Coolgardie Consolidated Gold Mines Ltd* (1897) 76 LT 269 and *Re Amalgamated Syndicate* [1897] 2 Ch 600.

There is sometimes said to be a 'main objects rule', which was described by Salmon J in *Anglo-Overseas Agencies Ltd* v *Green* [1961] 1 QB 1 at p. 8 as follows:

> . . . where a memorandum of association expresses the objects of the company in a series of paragraphs, and one paragraph, or the first two or three paragraphs, appear to embody the 'main object' of the company, all the other paragraphs are treated as merely ancillary to this 'main object', and as limited or controlled thereby.

In the case of a quasi-partnership company the court may go beyond the memorandum and articles to determine the members' general intention and common understanding (*Virdi* v *Abbey Leisure Ltd* [1990] BCLC 342; *Bernhardt* v *Beau Rivage Pty Ltd* (1989) 15 ACLR

160). Thus if it was originally the common understanding of the members of a quasi-partnership company that the company should undertake one project only but, on completion of that project, a member who wants the company to be wound up cannot get a special resolution for voluntary winding up adopted because some members wish to go on to another project then it may be just and equitable to order the compulsory liquidation of the company on the petition of the member who does not want to go on, even if continuing with other projects would be within the objects of the company set out in its memorandum.

2.3.5.9 Separate-objects provisions and express powers

To counter the main objects rule, it is usual to list a wide variety of objects in different paragraphs of the objects clause and conclude with a statement to the effect that 'each and every one of the above paragraphs states a separate and independent object of the company'. Such provisions were discussed in *Cotman v Brougham* [1918] AC 514 (which concerned a question between a company and a third party) and have become known as '*Cotman v Brougham*', or 'separate-objects', provisions.

The cautious drafter of a memorandum will usually include dozens of 'separate objects' and the courts have doubted whether these can be taken at face value. In *Re Horsley & Weight Ltd* [1982] Ch 442, CA, Buckley LJ said, at p. 448:

> It has now long been a common practice to set out in memoranda of association a great number and variety of 'objects', so called, some of which (for example, to borrow money, to promote the company's interests by advertising its products or services, or to do acts or things conducive or incidental to the company's objects) are by their very nature incapable of standing as independent objects which can be pursued in isolation as the sole activity of the company. Such 'objects' must, by reason of their very nature, be interpreted merely as powers incidental to the true objects of the company and must be so treated notwithstanding the presence of a separate-objects clause.

Statements in the objects clause of a company's memorandum which are regarded as not stating objects of the company are said to state 'express powers'.

In *Rolled Steel Products (Holdings) Ltd v British Steel Corporation* [1986] Ch 246 the Court of Appeal considered how the objects clause of a company's memorandum should be interpreted for the purpose of deciding whether or not a transaction is within the company's objects in order to determine whether the company is bound by the transaction. Slade LJ said, at pp. 288–9, that full force must be given, so far as possible, to a separate-objects provision. Each paragraph of an objects clause with a separate-objects provision must be treated as containing a substantive object unless either:

(a)   the subject-matter of the paragraph is by its nature incapable of constituting a separate object, or

(b)   the wording of the memorandum shows expressly or by implication that the paragraph was intended merely to constitute an ancillary power.

In *Re Introductions Ltd* [1970] Ch 199 the first exception was applied to the company's express power to borrow money. Despite a separate-objects provision it was held that borrowing money could not be a substantive object but that money could be borrowed only for the purposes of the company's true objects. At the time of the borrowing in question, the company's only business was one that was not covered by the objects clause of its memorandum and so the borrowing was not for the purpose of, or reasonably incidental to, attaining or pursuing the company's objects. It was therefore outside the scope of the directors' actual authority. The construction of the objects clause in *Re Introductions Ltd* seems to be somewhat arbitrary: it may be contrasted with the decision in *Re Horsley & Weight Ltd* that granting pensions to past and present employees and directors and their dependants and promoting charitable purposes was a substantive object of the company in the case. See further K.W. Wedderburn, 'Unreformed company law' (1969) 32 MLR 563 at pp. 565–6 and '*Ultra vires* in modern company law' (1983) 46 MLR 204 at pp. 207–8.

In *Rolled Steel Products (Holdings) Ltd v British Steel Corporation,* the second exception applied. The provision of the objects clause of Rolled Steel Products (Holdings) Ltd (RSP) that it could give guarantees or become security for 'such persons, firms or companies . . . as may seem expedient' was merely a power ancillary to its true objects, despite the presence of a separate-objects provision. The words 'as may seem expedient' could only mean 'as may seem expedient for the furtherance of the objects of the company'. RSP had given a guarantee of a debt (which had already been incurred) owed by another company to the British Steel Corporation. The other company was owned by RSP's managing director and majority shareholder who had himself already guaranteed the debt but was unable to honour his guarantee (he was subsequently adjudicated bankrupt). RSP's guarantee was secured by a floating charge on its entire property. It was held that the guarantee and charge were not for the purpose of, or reasonably incidental to, attaining or pursuing RSP's objects so that giving them was beyond the actual authority of its directors.

2.3.5.10 *Unrestricted objects: general commercial companies*
A company could avoid all problems of its activities being *ultra vires* if its memorandum set no limits on the objects it could pursue. Finding wording that will achieve this is difficult because it is strongly arguable that a simple statement in an objects clause that a company's object is to do anything does not in fact state an object as required by CA 1985, s. 2(1)(c). Parliament has now authorised the use of a very general objects clause. CA 1985, s. 3A, now permits a company's memorandum to state that 'the object of the company is to carry on business as a general commercial company'. This means, according to s. 3A, that:

(a) the object of the company is to carry on any trade or business whatsoever, and

(b) the company has power to do all such things as are incidental to the carrying on of any trade or business by it.

Like the 'incidental or conducive' provisions discussed in 2.3.5.6, para. (b) of s. 3A does not remove the need to include express powers in the objects clause, for example, a power to sell or dispose of the company's whole undertaking. Section 3A merely provides a statutory interpretation of the words 'the object of the company is to carry on business as a general commercial company' and authorises their use despite any doubts that they may not satisfy s. 2(1)(c). Logically, no other objects can be stated in an objects clause which begins with those words (because they refer to 'the object' in the singular) so that express powers cannot be included (see S. de Gay, 'Problems surrounding use of the new single objects clause' (1993) 137 SJ 146). It would seem that the best way of drafting a wide-ranging objects clause for a commercial company is to utilise the words in s. 3A's definition. Thus an objects clause could begin, 'The objects of the company are to carry on any trade or business whatsoever and to do all such things as are incidental to the carrying on of any trade or business by it' and then go on to state express powers. In the consultation document introducing its review of company law (see 0.3.1.6) the DTI acknowledges that s. 3A has not worked (*Modern Company Law for a Competitive Economy* (London: DTI, 1998), p. 8).

In *Newstead* v *Frost*, Browne-Wilkinson J at first instance ([1978] 1 WLR 511) and Viscount Dilhorne in the House of Lords ([1980] 1 WLR 135) were prepared to construe a memorandum of a company which authorised it to engage in 'all kinds ... of other operations' to mean exactly that, which would imply its objects were unlimited, though Viscount Dilhorne (and Buckley LJ in the Court of Appeal [1978] 1 WLR 1441) also thought it possible to validate the particular activities in question by construing 'other operations' as limited to operations related to the 'business as bankers, capitalists, financiers, concessionaires and merchants' which appeared to be the principal object stated in the memorandum.

One way of achieving unlimited objects could be to use so-called 'subjective' clauses which leave the choice of objects to the members or directors. In *Bell Houses Ltd* v *City Wall Properties Ltd* [1966] 2 QB 656, the plaintiff company's objects clause gave it a subjective ancillary object. The clause began by stating two main objects (building houses and acquiring land) and then said:

> to carry on any other trade or business whatsoever which can, in the opinion of the board of directors, be advantageously carried on by the company in connection with or as ancillary to any of the above businesses or the general business of the company.

Salmon LJ said, at p. 690:

> As a matter of pure construction, the meaning of these words seems to me to be obvious. An object of the plaintiff company is to carry on any business which the directors genuinely believe can be carried on advantageously in connection with or as ancillary to the general business of the company. It may be that the directors take the wrong view and in fact the business in question cannot be carried on as the directors believe. But it matters not how mistaken the directors may be. Providing they form their view honestly, the business is within the plaintiff company's objects and powers.

Danckwerts LJ pointed out that this form of memorandum only allows the company to carry out a business of the directors' choice as ancillary to the main objects: it does not authorise the directors to abandon the company's main objects and set up in some other business. In *Re Crown Bank* (1890) 44 ChD 634, North J said, *obiter*, that he thought that a company's objects clause which provided a subjective main object, 'to carry on any business whatever which the company might think would be profitable to the shareholders', would not satisfy s. 2(1)(c). Now a company does not need to use a subjective main objects clause because it can use the 'general commercial company' object, which Parliament has authorised for use in CA 1985, s. 3A, and which has practically the same effect as a subjective main objects clause. See further B.G. Pettet, 'Unlimited objects clauses?' (1981) 97 LQR 15; K.W. Wedderburn, 'Unreformed company law' (1969) 32 MLR 563 at pp. 565–6 and '*Ultra vires* in modern company law' (1983) 46 MLR 204 at pp. 207–8.

2.3.5.11 'Ultra vires' *illegal acts*

A company transaction in contravention of the general law or of the Companies Acts is usually described as '*ultra vires*'. A distinctive feature of an illegal *ultra vires* act is that it remains illegal even if all the members of the company have assented to it (see, for example, *Re Exchange Banking Co., Flitcroft's Case* (1882) 21 ChD 519 per Jessel MR at p. 533 on illegal payments of dividend out of capital; see 10.5): illegality is a matter of the public law of companies which members of companies cannot privately contract out of. Similarly, the fact that an illegal transaction of a company is formally within the express powers stated in its memorandum does not cure its illegality (*Aveling Barford Ltd* v *Perion Ltd* (1989) 5 BCC 677, in which the court rejected an argument that an illegal payment of dividend out of capital by selling a major asset at an undervalue was valid because the company's memorandum permitted it to sell its assets).

In *Australian Agricultural Co.* v *Oatmont Pty Ltd* (1992) 106 FLR 314, Mildren J in the Northern Territory Court of Appeal drew a distinction between acts contrary to the law under which a company is constituted (such as an illegal payment of dividend out of capital) — such acts could be called *ultra vires* — and acts contrary to other laws (such as, in the case before the court, holding too much land contrary to a statute which applies to any person natural or legal), which acts should not be called *ultra vires* because they are not beyond the capacity or authority of the company.

2.3.6 Limited liability

The Companies Act permits the registration of companies with or without limited liability (CA 1985, s. 1(1): see 1.3.2). If liability is to be limited, therefore, the company's constitution must make this clear (s. 2(3)). Section 306(1) provides:

> In the case of a limited company the liability of the directors or managers, or of the managing director, may, if so provided by the memorandum, be unlimited.

This provision was introduced by CA 1867, ss. 4 to 8, in imitation of the form of business organisation called the *commandite* then widely used in France. Essentially it enables a partnership operating with unlimited liability to obtain contributed capital from persons who retain limited liability. In practice the provision is now hardly ever used. Another attempt to emulate the *commandite* was made in the Limited Partnerships Act 1907 though this too has been little used. In France the *commandite* rapidly declined in popularity when it became possible to incorporate companies with limited liability by registration — as in Britain.

2.3.7 Share capital

The Companies Act 1985 envisages the formation of companies with or without share capital (see 1.3.2). If a company does have a share capital, the memorandum must give its amount and state how it is to be divided (CA 1985, s. 2(5)(a)). The nature and division of share capital are considered in chapter 6.

2.3.8 Contractual effect of a memorandum

See 3.4.

2.4 ALTERATION OF MEMORANDUM

2.4.1 Power to alter

The Joint Stock Companies Act 1856, which introduced the memorandum of association into company law, made no provision for the alteration of a memorandum. CA 1862 permitted a company to change its name and its nominal capital, but forbade any other alteration. Subsequent Acts have extended the range of alterations that may be made.

Now, CA 1985, s. 2(7), provides:

> A company may not alter the conditions contained in its memorandum except in the cases, in the mode and to the extent, for which express provision is made by this Act.

When this provision was first introduced in CA 1862 it was thought that 'conditions' referred to the items which are required to be in the memorandum of association by what is now CA 1985, s. 2(1) to (5). (The express provisions for altering these items are considered in 2.4.2 to 2.4.6.) However, it was held in *Ashbury* v *Watson* (1885) 30 ChD 376 that 'conditions' referred to all the provisions of a company's memorandum of association whether required by statute to be in it or not. Accordingly what is now CA 1985, s. 17, was enacted providing a procedure for the alteration of any condition contained in a company's memorandum which could lawfully have been contained in articles of association instead of in the memorandum. (See 2.4.7.)

If, inadvertently, the memorandum of a company does not correctly express the wishes of its subscribers the court does not have power to rectify the mistake after the company has been registered (*Scott* v *Frank F. Scott (London) Ltd* [1940] Ch 794, CA).

2.4.2   Change of name

A company may by special resolution (which requires a majority of three-quarters of those voting, see 14.4.8.3) change its name (CA 1985, s. 28(1)), though the same restrictions apply to the choice of a new name as to the choice of the original name (see 2.3.3). On a change of name, the registrar of companies enters the new name on the register in the place of the old name, and issues an altered certificate of incorporation (s. 28(6)). The change of name takes effect on the date of the issue of the altered certificate (s. 28(6)), and the issue of the certificate must be notified by the registrar in the *Gazette* (s. 711(1)(a)). The registrar charges £10 for issuing the new certificate of incorporation (SI 1991 No. 1206; SI 1996 No. 1444).

Where a company has been registered by a name which is the same as or, in the opinion of the Secretary of State, too like a name which did appear or should have appeared in the registrar's index of names at the time of registration, the Secretary of State may direct, within 12 months of the registration, that the company change its name within such period, or extended period, as he may specify (s. 28(2)). Further, where it appears to the Secretary of State that a company provided misleading information for the purposes of its registration by a particular name or gave undertakings or assurances for that purpose which have not been fulfilled, he may require, within five years of the registration, the company to change its name within such a period, or extended period, as he may specify (s. 28(3) and (4)). A company and any defaulting officer failing to comply with directions under s. 28(2) or (3) is liable on conviction to be fined (s. 28(5)).

In addition, if a company is, in the opinion of the Secretary of State, registered by a name which 'gives so misleading an indication of the nature of its activities as to be likely to cause harm to the public', the Secretary of State may direct the company to change its name (s. 32(1)). The company must comply with the direction within six weeks or such longer period as is allowed by the Secretary of State, though the company may, within three weeks, apply to the court which may set the direction aside or confirm it and specify a period for compliance (s. 32(2) and (3)). A fine may be imposed for non-compliance with a direction (s. 32(4)). Where a company changes its name as a result of a direction under s. 32, the registrar must enter the new name on the register and issue an altered certificate of incorporation (s. 32(5)), and give notice of the issue of the altered certificate in the *Gazette* (s. 711(1)(a)). In *Association of Certified Public Accountants of Britain* v *Secretary of State for Trade and Industry* [1998] 1 WLR 164 the court confirmed a direction to the Association to change its name. The form of harm to the public which was identified in the case was that people would be likely to pay more for the services of members of the Association because of the word 'Certified' in its name, which was said to give a misleading impression of the level of qualification required of members.

A change of name by a company under ss. 28 or 32 does not affect the company's rights or obligations or render defective any legal proceedings by or against the company (which may be continued or commenced against it by its new name) (ss. 28(7) and 32(6)). The company with the altered name and altered certificate of incorporation is still the company it was under its previous name; the company is not 'formed' with the new name at the time of issuing the new certificate; it was formed when it was first registered (*Oshkosh B'Gosh Inc.* v *Dan Marbel Inc. Ltd* [1989] BCLC 507, CA). Similarly, although the document issued by the registrar on registering a company's change of name is called a 'certificate of incorporation', it only records the change of name: the company is not incorporated anew — it was incorporated when it was first registered (*Cross* v *Aurora Group Ltd* (1988) 4 NZCLC 64,909).

If it appears to the Secretary of State that a company that omits the word 'limited' from its name is pursuing or applying its funds to objects other than those specified in s. 30(3), or is paying dividends to its members then he may direct the company to change its name by resolution of its directors so that its name ends with 'limited' or the Welsh equivalent or an abbreviation (s. 31(2) and (4); disobedience is an offence, s. 31(6)).

By s. 43(5), if a private company applies to be re-registered as a public company, the resolution required by s. 43(1) (see 1.3.4.3) may change the company's name by deleting the word 'Company' or the words 'and Company' or any abbreviation or Welsh equivalent thereof.

2.4.3 Change of jurisdiction

A company's memorandum is required by CA 1985, s. 2(1)(b) and (2), to state whether its registered office is to be located in England and Wales, Wales or Scotland. If the memorandum states that the registered office is to be in England and Wales or in Wales then the company must be registered with the registrar of companies in England and Wales (s. 10(1)) and the company will be subject to the law of England and Wales. The provision of a company's memorandum stating where its registered office is to be located is unalterable except that s. 2(2) allows a company whose registered office is in fact situated in Wales, but whose memorandum provides that the registered office is to be in England and Wales, to alter the memorandum so as to provide that the registered office is to be situated in Wales.

The legal system under which a company is incorporated is its domicile in private international law (*Gasque* v *Commissioners of Inland Revenue* [1940] 2 KB 80).

A company incorporated by registration with the registrar of companies in England and Wales or Scotland has no power under the Companies Acts or the general law to have itself incorporated in any other jurisdiction (*Tayside Floorcloth Co. Ltd* 1923 SC 590; see *Bateman* v *Service* (1881) 6 App Cas 386 on the inability of a company registered in one State of Australia to register in another). To put it another way, a company cannot, of its own volition, abandon one domicile and adopt another, as a natural person can (*Carl Zeiss Stiftung* v *Rayner & Keeler Ltd (No. 3)* [1970] Ch 506 per Buckley J at p. 544). A company exists as a person separate from its members only by virtue of the law under which it was incorporated, and the company itself cannot alter that law.

If the members of a company wish to move it from one jurisdiction to another then they must promote a private Act of Parliament for the purpose. The British Olivetti Limited Act 1980, for example, transferred the company (which had been registered under CA 1929) from Scotland to England. Other recent Acts have moved companies to Commonwealth countries.

See further, P. StJ. Smart, 'Corporate domicile and multiple incorporation in English private international law' [1990] JBL 126; D. Lewis, 'Corporate redomicile' (1995) 16 Co Law 295.

2.4.4 Change of objects

By CA 1985, s. 4, the members of a company may, by special resolution (which requires a majority of three-quarters of those voting, see 14.4.8.3), alter its memorandum with respect to the statement of the company's objects. If the members of a company adopt a resolution to alter its objects then members who did not vote in favour of or consent to the resolution may submit their objection to the court under s. 5, provided they hold at least 15 per cent in nominal value of the company's issued share capital or any class of it. If such an application is made then the alteration resolved upon does not have effect except insofar as it is confirmed by the court (s. 4(2)). An application has to be made within 21 days of the adoption of the resolution being objected to (s. 5(3)). The applicants may appoint one or more of their number in writing to make the application to the court (s. 5(3)). The court has the power to reject the alteration or to confirm it either in whole or in part and on such conditions as it thinks fit and may, in particular, adjourn the proceedings to allow an arrangement to be made which is to its satisfaction for the purchase of the applicants' interests in the company and make any order which facilitates or carries into effect any such arrangement (s. 5(4)). Further, the court can require the company itself to buy the shares of any shareholder and accordingly reduce the company's capital, altering the company's memorandum and articles as appropriate (s. 5(5)).

If proceedings are not taken under s. 5 or otherwise within 21 days of the passing of the special resolution, the validity of the alteration of the objects may not be questioned on the ground that it was not authorised by s. 4 (s. 6(4)). The requirement that proceedings be taken 'under section 5 or otherwise' does not allow a shareholder who does not hold 15 per cent of the company's share capital to apply under s. 5 (*Re Hampstead Garden Suburb Trust Ltd* [1962] Ch 806).

Before the law was amended by CA 1989, s. 110(2), a company had power to alter its memorandum 'with respect to the objects of the company' rather than, as now, with respect to *the statement of* its objects. The old law was held to empower a company to alter a provision in its memorandum which related to the company's objects but was not in the objects clause, that is, not in the statement of the company's objects (*Incorporated Glasgow Dental Hospital* v *Lord Advocate* 1927 SC 400; *Re Scientific Poultry Breeders' Association Ltd* [1933] Ch 227; *Scottish Special Housing Association Ltd* 1947 SC 17). It remains to be seen whether the new law can be given such a wide interpretation.

A company that omits the word 'limited' from its name, by virtue of an old licence commits an offence if it alters its objects to include any object that is not the promotion of commerce, art, science, education, religion, charity or a profession or anything incidental or conducive to promotion of those matters (CA 1985, s. 31(1) and (5)). An alteration of a charitable company's objects clause is ineffective without the prior written consent of the Charity Commissioners (Charities Act 1993, s. 64(2)).

Alteration of the objects clause was not permitted by the companies legislation until the Companies (Memorandum of Association) Act 1890.

2.4.5 Limited liability

Power is given to a limited company by CA 1985, s. 307, to alter its memorandum by special resolution (which requires a majority of three-quarters of those voting, see 14.4.8.3) so as to render the liability of its managing director, directors or managers unlimited if so authorised by its articles (see 2.3.6).

For re-registration of a limited company as unlimited and vice versa, and change from limitation by shares to limitation by guarantee and vice versa, see 1.3.4.

2.4.6 Changes in share capital

The various ways in which a company's share capital can be altered will not be discussed here (see 6.1.13 and 10.2) except to note that, when dealing with an application by a dissentient minority of a company (see 2.4.7) the court may order the company to buy the shares of the minority and the court's order may effect any consequential alteration in the clauses of the company's memorandum relating to share capital (CA 1985, ss. 5(5) (see 2.4.4.), 17(3) (see 2.4.7), 54(6), 157(3), 177(3) and 461(1) and (2)(d)).

2.4.7 General powers to alter

If a company's memorandum contains a condition which could lawfully have been contained in articles of association then the condition may be altered by the company by special resolution (which requires a majority of three quarters of those voting, see 14.4.8.3) under CA 1985, s. 17. However, the section does not apply if the memorandum itself contains a prohibition against alteration (s. 17(2)(b)). If an alteration is made under s. 17 then an application may be made to the court for the alteration to be cancelled, and then the alteration does not have effect except insofar as it is confirmed by the court (s. 17(1)). Applications to the court are governed by the same rules as control applications in respect of changes of objects (s. 17(3); see 2.4.4).

Section 17 cannot be used to vary or abrogate the special rights of any class of members (s. 17(2)(b)). If the share capital of a company is divided into shares of different classes and its memorandum attaches rights to any particular class, and neither the memorandum nor the articles provide for the variation of those rights then they may be varied if all the members of the company agree to the variation (s. 125(5)). Alternatively, class rights specified in a memorandum with no provision for variation in the memorandum or articles may be varied by a court-sanctioned arrangement under s. 425 (*Re Palace Hotel Ltd* [1912] 2 Ch 438; *Re J.A. Nordberg Ltd* [1915] 2 Ch 439; *City Property Investment Trust Corporation Ltd* 1951 SC 570).

Section 17 is drafted on the assumption that it is possible for a company to have a memorandum, containing a condition that could lawfully have been contained in articles of association, with an effective provision in the memorandum itself for the alteration of that condition, and s. 17(2)(b) provides that the section does not apply to such a memorandum. In other words, the members can proceed to alter the condition under the provision in the memorandum without reference to s. 17 and, in particular, a dissentient minority cannot apply to the court under s. 17(1). Section 2(7) prohibits the alteration of a company's memorandum in any mode for which express provision is not made by CA 1985. It seems that the express allowance in s. 17(2)(b) for a memorandum which provides for its own alteration can be regarded as an express provision such as is required by s. 2(7) to make such a mode of alteration possible.

The members of a company applying for re-registration as a company of another type (see 1.3.4) are given a general power to alter its memorandum by special resolution so far as is necessary to bring it into conformity with the requirements of CA 1985 concerning memoranda of companies of that type (CA 1985, ss. 43(2)(b) (private to public), 49(5) (limited to unlimited, for which the unanimous assent of members is required), 51(3) (unlimited to limited) and 53(2) (public to private)).

Under various provisions, a dissentient minority of members (or, in some circumstances, creditors) of a company may apply to the court for review of the company's affairs. In dealing with such applications the court is given very wide powers, including the power to make an order effecting an alteration in the company's memorandum and articles (CA 1985, ss. 5(4), (5) and (7) (minority objecting to change of company's objects, see 2.4.4), 17(3) (minority objecting to change in provisions of memorandum that could have been in articles), 54(5), (6) and (9) (minority objecting to public company re-registering as private, see 1.3.4.2), 157(3) (minority objecting to private company providing financial assistance for the purchase of its own shares, see 10.8.7), 177 (creditor or member of a private company objecting to payment out of capital for purchase or redemption of its shares, see 10.3.5), 461(1), (2)(d) and (4) (member unfairly prejudiced by manner of conduct of company's affairs, see 18.6.6)).

Any alteration of the memorandum or articles effected by the court under its statutory powers 'is of the same effect as if duly made by resolution' and the provisions of CA 1985 apply to the memorandum or articles as so altered (CA 1985, ss. 5(7), 17(3), 54(9), 157(3), 177(5) and 461(4)).

The court is empowered to order changes in a public company's memorandum in order to convert it into a private company after confirming a reduction of the company's capital to below £50,000 (CA 1985, s. 139(3); see 10.2.5).

The directors of a public company are empowered to alter its memorandum so as to convert the company into a private company if they have to do so because the cancellation of shares in certain circumstances has reduced the nominal value of the company's allotted shares to less than £50,000 (CA 1985, ss. 146 and 147; see 6.4.2).

2.4.8   Restrictions on a company's powers to alter its memorandum

2.4.8.1   Statutory restrictions
CA 1985, s. 16, provides that a member of a company is not bound by an alteration made in the company's memorandum or articles since becoming a member which requires the member to take or subscribe for more shares or in any way increases the member's liability to contribute to the company's share capital or otherwise to pay money to the company, unless (by s. 16(2)) the member gives express written agreement to be bound. This provision cannot be excluded by the memorandum or the articles themselves (s. 16(2)).

Any alteration of a company's memorandum which varies shareholders' class rights is subject to the provisions of CA 1985, ss. 125 to 127 (see 14.6.2), and CA 1985, s. 17(1) (see 2.4.7), does not authorise any variation or abrogation of class rights (s. 17(2)(b)).

By s. 31(1) and (5), a company which omits the word 'limited' from its name by virtue of an old licence (see 2.3.3.2) commits an offence if it alters its memorandum or articles in such a way that they no longer conform with the requirements of s. 30(3).

2.4.8.2 Restrictions imposed by the court

Where the court has made any order on an application by dissentient members or creditors of a company (see 2.4.7) and the order requires the company not to make any, or any specified, alteration in its memorandum or articles, then, notwithstanding anything in CA 1985, the company does not have power to make any alteration in breach of that requirement without the court's leave (CA 1985, s. 5(6) (objection to change of objects, see 2.4.4), s. 17(3) (objection to change in provisions of memorandum that could have been in articles, see 2.4.7), s. 54(8) (objection to public company re-registering as private, see 1.3.4.2), s. 157(3) (objection to private company providing financial assistance for the purchase of its own shares, see 10.8.7), s. 177(4) (objection to a payment out of capital for the redemption or purchase of a private company's shares, see 10.3.5), s. 461(3) (member unfairly prejudiced by manner of conduct of company's affairs, see 18.6.6)).

2.4.8.3 Restrictions imposed by the company itself or its members

A power to alter the memorandum of a company which has been conferred by statute cannot be restricted by the company unless the statute provides for restriction. A provision in a company's memorandum or articles, or in a contract made by the company, restricting the exercise of a statutory power to alter the company's memorandum is of no effect (*Russell v Northern Bank Development Corporation Ltd* [1992] 1 WLR 588). Only the power conferred by CA 1985, s. 17, can be restricted by a company and then only by a provision in its memorandum.

Existing members of a company may make an enforceable contract between themselves that they will not adopt a resolution to exercise one or more of the statutory powers to alter the company's memorandum unless certain conditions are satisfied (for example, that they have all given their written consent) but such a contract will not bind future members unless they expressly agree to it, and the company itself cannot be a party to the contract (*Russell v Northern Bank Development Corporation Ltd*). The validity of contracts of this kind between members was recognised in *Russell v Northern Bank Development Corporation Ltd* but is strongly attacked by J. Savirimuthu, 'Thoughts on *Russell* — killing private companies with kindness?' (1993) 14 Co Law 137 who thinks that the members of a company should not be allowed to override the statutory framework provided by Parliament for their company. However, the House of Lords proceeded on the basis that the statutory framework is for the company as a person separate from its members, leaving the members to decide for themselves what they want to do with their company. It is clear from the commonness of unanimous shareholders' agreements that they are commercially necessary, for example, to protect the interests of minority participants in private companies. There is no evidence that contracts of this kind are imposed in unequal bargaining and there seems to be no reason to stop business people arranging their affairs to suit themselves. It may be that the doctrine that a company as a separate person cannot fetter its statutory right to alter its constitution is not commercially realistic. B.J. Davenport, 'What did *Russell v Northern Bank Development Corporation Ltd* decide?' (1993) 109 LQR 553 says that it is routine for a company to agree with a bank or other lender not to alter its constitution in a way which the lender fears would prejudice its interests. Davenport argues that the doctrine of voidness of fetters on the statutory right of alteration has not been established by any judicial decision that is a binding precedent but even if this is so there can be little doubt that the doctrine is correct and that the bankers' problems, if they are as great as Davenport claims, can be dealt with only by legislation empowering companies to restrict their rights to alter their constitutions.

2.4.9 Notification of alteration

2.4.9.1 Notification to the registrar

If a company adopts a resolution altering its memorandum then a copy of the resolution must be sent to the registrar within 15 days of adoption (CA 1985, s. 380(1) and (4)(a), (c) and (e)).

Whenever a company sends to the registrar a copy of any resolution altering its memorandum, other than a resolution to alter objects under s. 4, it must also send a copy of the complete memorandum in its altered form (s. 18(2)).

If a company makes an application for re-registration then it must, as part of the application, supply the registrar with a copy of its memorandum as altered in accordance with its proposed new status (ss. 43(3)(a) (private to public), 49(8)(c) (limited to unlimited), 51(5)(a) (unlimited to limited), 53(1)(b) (public to private), 139(4) (public to private by court order) and 147(3) (public to private by directors' resolution)).

If there is an application to the court by objectors to a resolution altering a company's memorandum then notice of the application must be given forthwith by the company to the registrar (ss. 6(1)(b)(i) (alteration of objects), 17(3) (alteration of provisions that could lawfully have been in the articles) and 54(4) (re-registration of public company as private)).

If no application is made to the court by any objector to a change of objects of a company then the company's complete memorandum in its altered form must be sent to the registrar within 15 days from the end of the 21-day period during which such an application may be made (s. 6(1)(a)).

If the court makes an order on an application by dissentient members or creditors of a company (see 2.4.7) then the company must, within 15 days of the date of the order (14 days in the case of a s. 461 order), supply the registrar with an office copy of the order and if this order alters the company's memorandum or confirms a proposal by the company to atter its objects or alter a provision in the memorandum that could lawfully have been in the articles then the registrar must also be sent a copy of the complete memorandum as altered (ss. 6(1)(b)(ii) (alteration of objects), 17(3) (alteration of provision that could have been in articles), 54(7) (re-registration as private), 157(3) (objection to financial assistance), 176(3)(b) (payment out of capital for redemption or purchase of own shares) and 461(5) (allegation of prejudicial conduct of company's affairs), together with s. 18(2)). The court may grant an extension to the time-limit.

Failure of a company to supply copies of resolutions, orders and its complete memorandum, or failure to notify impending court proceedings, when required by CA 1985 (except in connection with re-registration) is a summary offence for which the company, and any officer of the company who knowingly and wilfully authorised or permitted the default, may be fined (ss. 6(3), 17(3), 18(3), 54(10), 157(3), 176(4), 380(5), 461(5) and 730(5) and sch. 24). If a company fails to submit complete sets of documents with an application to re-register then the registrar will refuse the application.

2.4.9.2 Notification in the Gazette

On receiving any document making or evidencing an alteration in a company's memorandum, the registrar publishes notice of receiving it in the *Gazette* (CA 1985, s. 711(1)(b)). In addition, under s. 711(1)(a), the registrar notifies in the *Gazette* the issue of an altered certificate of incorporation consequent on a change of name (see 2.4.2). The consequence of this requirement for 'official notification' in the *Gazette* is that the company may not rely on any alteration of its memorandum against any other person until official notification, unless the company can show that the alteration was known to the person concerned.

Additionally, the company may not rely on an alteration within 15 days *after* official notification if it is shown that the person concerned was 'unavoidably prevented' from knowing of the alteration within that period (s. 42).

2.5 COPIES OF THE MEMORANDUM FOR MEMBERS

Although a member of a company is bound by the provisions of its memorandum as if the member's signature and seal had been put on the document (CA 1985, s. 14) a person who becomes a member of a company is not automatically supplied with a copy of its memorandum. However, a company must 'send to' any member who requires one, a copy of its memorandum and articles, charging no more than 5p for doing so (s. 19(1); the maximum fee has not been changed since it was introduced in the Joint Stock Companies Act 1856, s. 27). Presumably the copy must be delivered to the member's address. The copy of the memorandum supplied under s. 19 must incorporate any change made before the time of supply (CA 1985, s. 20(1)). As mentioned in 2.4.9.1, a new version of the memorandum must be prepared for delivery to the registrar whenever there is a change. Failure to comply with either s. 19(1) or s. 20(1) is a summary offence for which the company and its officers may be fined (ss. 19(2) and 20(2)).

3 The Articles of Association

3.1 INTRODUCTION

Every company must have a memorandum of association which is required to state certain basic features of the company's constitution and which can be altered only in accordance with the detailed provisions outlined in 2.4. Every company must also have articles of association which are to regulate its internal affairs and management, and which may be altered by special resolution or unanimous agreement. It is common for the members for the time being of a private company to make among themselves a separate contract, called a unanimous shareholders' agreement (USA), which supplements the articles and binds the members to operate the articles in a particular way.

3.2 REGISTRATION OF ARTICLES

Articles of association prescribe regulations for a company. They form the rule book of the association of members and therefore ought to deal with many situations which might arise but which incorporators of a new company probably would not think of. Accordingly, CA 1985, s. 8, provides for the use of a model set of articles of association for a company limited by shares, called 'Table A', which the Secretary of State is empowered to prescribe by statutory instrument. The form of Table A in use on and after 1 July 1985 is prescribed in SI 1985 No. 805. Three amendments are made by SI 1985 No. 1052, which came into force on 1 August 1985. This form of Table A was drafted in consultation with the Law Society and other professionals and is the result of more than a century's experience of the operation of companies. In the consultation document introducing its review of company law (see 0.3.1.6) the DTI notes that 'Table A is written in technical legalistic language and would be of more practical use if it was rewritten in plain English' (*Modern Company Law for a Competitive Economy* (London: DTI, 1998), p. 6). Even before the grand review of company law announced in 1998 the DTI had already started a review of Table A in collaboration with a Law Society working group (*Companies in 1996–97* (London: Stationery Office, 1997), p. 4).

If the incorporators of a company limited by shares do not wish to have Table A in its entirety as their articles of association then when they register their memorandum of association, they may also register their own articles of association (s. 7). These must be printed, divided into paragraphs numbered consecutively, and signed by each subscriber of the memorandum in the presence of at least one witness who must attest the signature (s. 7(3)). If articles are not registered under s. 7 then s. 8(2) provides that Table A will be the company's articles.

Unless it modifies the articles, there is no need to register a unanimous shareholders' agreement, so that it could be used to set out matters which the members would prefer not to be in the publicly inspectable articles (see A. Marsden, 'Does a shareholders' agreement require filing with the Registrar of Companies?' (1994) 15 Co Law 19).

Section 8(1) permits a company to 'adopt the whole or any part of' Table A 'for its articles'. This is taken to authorise the registration as articles for a company, under s. 7, of a document which states that the articles of the company are to consist of all or part of Table A together with the additional regulations set out in the document.

Table A also, in effect, prescribes what topics must be dealt with in any alternative set of articles registered under s. 7. This is because, insofar as any articles registered under s. 7 do not exclude or modify Table A, that Table, so far as applicable, will constitute the company's articles 'in the same manner and to the same extent as if articles in the form of the Table had been duly registered' (s. 8(2)). A statement in articles registered under s. 7 that only part of Table A is being adopted would, it seems, mean that the articles excluded that part of Table A not adopted.

The form of Table A that a company has for its articles either in whole because no alternative articles were registered under s. 7 or in part insofar as alternative articles did not exclude or modify Table A, is the form that was prescribed for use at the date of the company's registration (s. 8(2)), notwithstanding any subsequent changes made by the Secretary of State in the prescribed form (s. 8(3)).

Alternatively, a company limited by shares intended to be a partnership company (see 1.3.6) may, by CA 1985, s. 8A(2), adopt all or part of another model set of articles called Table G, which is a set of articles appropriate for a partnership company, which the Secretary of State is empowered by s. 8A(1) to prescribe by statutory instrument (s. 8A(4)). The Secretary of State has not yet prescribed Table G, though in March 1995, the Department of Trade and Industry issued a consultative document discussing what might be included in Table G (*Model Articles of Association for Partnership Companies (Table G)* (URN 95/609) (London: DTI, 1995); S. Sheikh, 'Partnership companies: furthering employees' participation by Table G (1998) 19 Co Law 130). The document also asked whether there should be a Table G at all but it seems that this was answered affirmatively because the Department has decided to go ahead with drafting regulations, though not until its current review of Table A is completed.

If a company is to be registered as a guarantee or unlimited company then articles of association must be registered with its memorandum (s. 7(1)). The articles of association of a guarantee company must be in accordance with Table C in SI 1985 No. 805, or as near to that form as circumstances admit (s. 7(4)), and the articles of an unlimited company with a share capital must be in accordance with or near to Table E (s. 7(4)) and must state the amount of share capital with which the company proposes to be registered (its authorised share capital) (s. 7(2)).

The principle that a company registered as a company limited by shares on its initial incorporation will have prescribed articles unless it modifies or excludes them has been in every consolidated Companies Act from the Joint Stock Companies Act 1856 onwards (see 1.2.3). In the 1856 Act the prescribed set of articles was called Table B but from CA 1862 onwards it has been called Table A. The prescribed articles have been considerably revised from time to time: the 1985 version, which is the version considered in this book, is noticeably different from its predecessors.

A company will not have provisions of some version of Table A in its articles if:

(a)   It was incorporated before 1856 and did not adopt Table A on re-registration under a Companies Act.

(b)   It was initially incorporated as an unlimited company or a guarantee company.

(c)   It has modified Table A (that is, made an alternative provision) or excluded Table A and made no alternative provision.

The idea of prescribing a standard set of regulations for registered companies was adopted from the practice in relation to statutory companies. The Companies Clauses Consolidation Act 1845 provides a standard set of regulations for statutory companies like Table A and was deemed to be part of the special Act incorporating any statutory company after 8 May 1845 unless otherwise provided (Companies Clauses Consolidation Act 1845, s. 1).

The requirement for registered companies to have a memorandum and articles of association in two separate documents was introduced in the Joint Stock Companies Act 1856. For a company registered under the Joint Stock Companies Act 1844, the matters contained in these two documents were required to be stated in a single document called the 'deed of settlement' of the company. At first, the significant difference between the memorandum and the articles was in the company's power to alter the documents. A company has a general power to alter any provision in its articles by special resolution (see 3.5). However, the 1856 Act made no provision for altering the memorandum, and the 1862 Act, though allowing alteration of the name and capital clauses, prohibited any other alteration. Subsequent legislation has increased the range of alterations that may be made to the memorandum of a company but there is still no general power of alteration like the power to alter the articles, and powers to alter the memorandum are subject to more elaborate procedural requirements: see 2.4.

A person who deals with a company has constructive notice of the contents of the company's memorandum and articles of association because they are publicly registered and available for inspection (per Lord Wensleydale in *Ernest* v *Nicholls* (1857) 6 HL Cas 401 at p. 419; per Lord Hatherley in *Mahony* v *East Holyford Mining Co. Ltd* (1875) LR 7 HL 869 at p. 893). Parliament has enacted CA 1989, s. 142, inserting a new s. 711A into CA 1985 which would abolish the doctrine of deemed notice of the memorandum and articles, but this provision had not been brought into force when this edition went to press.

Articles of association must be 'divided into paragraphs numbered consecutively' (CA 1985, s. 7(3)(b)). In this book, we follow a common convention of calling each numbered paragraph an 'article' (abbreviation, 'art.'). Some people prefer to call each numbered paragraph a 'regulation' (abbreviation, 'reg.'), and this is the terminology used in Table A, for example, in reg. (or art.) 8, which refers to exemption 'from the provisions of this regulation'.

3.3   CONTENT

3.3.1   Tables A and G

By CA 1985, s. 8(2), on the registration of a company limited by shares, it has Table A (as in force at the date of the company's registration) as its articles of association unless it registers alternative articles under s. 7 (see 3.2). Alternative articles may adopt all or part of Table A or Table G (ss. 8(1) and 8A(1)). If the Secretary of State alters Table A (using the power conferred by s. 8(1)) or Table G (using the power conferred by s. 8A(1)) then the alteration does not affect a company registered before the alteration takes effect, or repeal, as respects that company, any portion of the Table (ss. 8(3) and 8A(3)).

The 1985 version of Table A is basically divided as follows:

arts. 2–35   shares and share capital

36–63   general meetings
64–101   directors and secretary
102–10   dividends, accounts and capitalisation of profits
111–16   notices of meetings.

Table A is not concerned with the organisation of the company's commercial affairs or the making of its products, except to say that the company's business is to be managed by the directors (art. 70).

3.3.2 Alternative articles

If alternative articles are registered for a company limited by shares then, insofar as they do not exclude or modify Table A, that Table (so far as applicable, and as in force at the date of the company's registration) constitutes the company's articles (s. 8(2)). However, if the Secretary of State prescribes an alteration to Table A (using the power conferred by s. 8(1)) then the alteration does not affect a company registered before the alteration takes effect, or repeal, as respects that company, any portion of the Table (s. 8(3)).

Exceptionally, insofar as alternative articles do not make other provision for the service of notice of members' meetings, the relevant regulations in Table A for the time being in force apply (s. 370(1) and (2)).

Apart from the possibility that provisions of Table A will be deemed by s. 8(2) or s. 370(1) and (2) to be incorporated in alternative articles, Table A may be regarded as a model of form not content: alternative articles for a company may include any provisions thought to be appropriate to the company (*Gaiman* v *National Association for Mental Health* [1971] Ch 317 per Megarry J at p. 328) subject to the following:

(a) Any provision in a company's articles which is inconsistent with the general law or the company's memorandum is void (*Welton* v *Saffery* [1897] AC 299, per Lord Davey at p. 329). The articles cannot modify any of the statements in the memorandum (see 2.3.1) (*Guinness* v *Land Corporation of Ireland* (1882) 22 ChD 349).

(b) Any provision in a company's articles which is inconsistent with the legislation governing companies is void (*Re Peveril Gold Mines Ltd* [1898] 1 Ch 122, CA, in which the articles purported to limit the circumstances in which the company could be wound up by the court; *Re Greene* [1949] Ch 333, in which the articles purported to make a transfer of shares without a proper instrument of transfer as required by what is now CA 1985, s. 183(1)).

(c) CA 1985 limits the provision that may be made by articles on certain matters and expressly enacts that inconsistent provisions in a company's articles are void. Those matters are:
(i)   relief of directors from liability (CA 1985, s. 310(2), see 16.9.1),
(ii)   length of notice of members' meetings (s. 369(1), see 14.4.5.3),
(iii)   time for delivery of proxy appointments (s. 372(5), see 14.4.9.1.3), and
(iv)   right to demand a poll (s. 373, see 14.4.9.1.3 and 14.4.9.2).
(d) It may be a waste of time including provisions not relating to membership because the members will not be contractually bound to observe such provisions (see 3.4.2.2).
(e) Under the Stock Transfer Act 1963 (see 8.3.1) members can ignore provisions in articles requiring them to use forms other than those specified in the Act to transfer their fully paid shares.

3.3.3 Authority for otherwise prohibited acts

Various provisions of CA 1985 permit a company to do things, which are otherwise prohibited by law, for example, to alter its share capital (see 6.1.13), reduce its share capital (see 10.2), issue redeemable shares (see 10.3) or purchase its own shares (see 10.6), if there is authority to do them in the company's articles. An authority in the memorandum is of no effect for the purposes of these provisions (*Re Dexine Patent Packing & Rubber Co.* (1903) 88 LT 791).

3.3.4 Listed companies

The Stock Exchange stipulates that certain provisions must be included in the articles of all listed companies (Listing Rules, ch. 13, app. 1). These provisions will be noted at appropriate points in this book.

3.3.5 Construction

In *Rayfield* v *Hands* [1960] Ch 1, Vaisey J thought that 'the proper way to construe the articles of association of a company is as a commercial or business document to which the maxim "validate if possible" applies'. In *Holmes* v *Keyes* [1959] Ch 199, CA, Jenkins LJ said, at p. 215, 'I think that the articles of association of the company should be regarded as a business document and should be construed so as to give them reasonable business efficacy'. See also 3.4.1.3.

Because it is prescribed in a piece of subordinate legislation (regulations made by the Secretary of State by statutory instrument), Table A must be interpreted in accordance with the Interpretation Act 1978 (by s. 23(1) of that Act). If alternative articles adopt all or part of Table A then the provisions that are added to or substituted for provisions of Table A must also be interpreted in accordance with the Interpretation Act 1978, unless there is a statement to the contrary (*Fell* v *Derby Leather Co. Ltd* [1931] 2 Ch 252).

3.4 EFFECT OF MEMORANDUM AND ARTICLES

3.4.1 Contractual analysis of companies

3.4.1.1 Companies Act 1985, section 14
The normal legal analysis of the nature of an association of persons is in terms of a contract between the members of the association. As Lawton LJ said in *Conservative & Unionist Central Office* v *Burrell* [1982] 1 WLR 522 at p. 525: 'The bond of union between the members of an unincorporated association has to be contractual'. There are numerous dicta treating the articles of association of a company incorporated by registration as a contract between the members of the company. In *Re Tavarone Mining Co., Pritchard's Case* (1873) LR 8 Ch App 956, Mellish LJ said, at p. 960:

> . . . the articles of association are simply a contract as between the shareholders *inter se* in respect of their rights as shareholders. They are the deed of partnership by which the shareholders agree *inter se*.

A registered company, because it is a body corporate, has a dual aspect as both an association of its members and a person separate from its members. It would seem appropriate to introduce the company as a separate person into the contractual analysis by saying that the members also have a contract with the company as a separate person. Lawyers have, however, been unwilling to rely solely on their analysis of the legal nature of companies to justify a conclusion that a contract exists between a company and its members. They have always sought to derive that contract from the Companies Acts and, in particular, from what is now CA 1985, s. 14(1):

> Subject to the provisions of this Act, the memorandum and articles, when registered, bind the company and its members to the same extent as if they respectively had been signed and sealed by each member, and contained covenants on the part of each member to observe all the provisions of the memorandum and of the articles.

In *Salmon* v *Quin & Axtens Ltd* [1909] 1 Ch 311, Farwell LJ said, at p. 318:

> The articles . . . are made equivalent to a deed of covenant signed by all the shareholders. The Act does not say with whom that covenant is entered into, and there have no doubt been varying statements by learned judges, some of them saying it is with the company, some of them saying it is both with the company and with the shareholders.

His lordship adopted as accurate the following statement by Stirling J in *Wood* v *Odessa Waterworks Co.* (1889) 42 ChD 636 at p. 642:

> The articles of association constitute a contract not merely between the shareholders and the company, but between each individual shareholder and every other.

The doctrine that the articles of a company form a contract between the members and the company as a separate person and between the members themselves is generally thought to have been arrived at by judicial construction of what is now CA 1985, s. 14. In *Oakbank Oil Co.* v *Crum* (1882) 8 App Cas 65, HL, Lord Selborne LC referred, at p. 71, to 'the contract founded upon the law which enables such companies to be constituted'. In *Bratton Seymour Service Co. Ltd* v *Oxborough* [1992] BCLC 693, Steyn LJ said, at p. 698, that the contract between a company and its members formed by the company's articles 'derives its binding force not from a bargain struck between the parties but from the terms of the statute'. The contract is therefore commonly referred to as the 'section 14 contract' (or in earlier discussions referring to CA 1948, the 'section 20 contract' — CA 1985, s. 14, is a re-enactment of CA 1948, s. 20). However, it seems that the idea for this interpretation of the statutory provision was supplied by legal theory rather than the statutory wording. As Farwell LJ made clear in the passage from *Salmon* v *Quin & Axtens Ltd* quoted above, s. 14 does not in fact form any bilateral or multilateral contract: it merely deems that each member is subject to a unilateral covenant. In contrast with English lawyers' struggles to derive a contractual analysis of companies' articles of association from legislation, the European Court of Justice has found it easy to regard as a consequence of the nature of a company that its articles of association (known to European lawyers as its 'statutes') form a contract between the members and the company as a separate person and between the members themselves (*Powell Duffryn plc* v *Petereit* (case C-214/89) [1992] ECR I-1745).

The opening words of s. 14(1), 'Subject to the provisions of this Act', make it clear that any provision of the memorandum or articles which is inconsistent with CA 1985 will not bind the company and its members.

3.4.1.2 *History of the statutory provision*

Before incorporation of companies by registration was introduced in 1844, it was usual for the partnership agreement of an unincorporated joint-stock company (known as its 'deed of settlement') to be in the form of a deed in which the members of the company covenanted with certain individuals, who were chosen by the members for the purpose and were usually referred to as 'trustees' for the company (though sometimes simply as 'covenantees'), to pay calls on shares and observe other conditions of membership. The company, being unincorporated, did not have separate personality and so could not sue for calls, but the 'trustees' could. It was later held that if an unincorporated joint-stock company with a deed of settlement in this form obtained an Act of Parliament entitling one of its officers to sue on its behalf — see 0.1.2.4 — then an action for calls could be brought by that officer instead of by the company's trustees, even though the members' covenant to pay the calls was with the trustees and not with the officer taking the action (*Skinner* v *Lambert* (1842) 4 Man & G 477; *Smith* v *Goldsworthy* (1843) 4 QB 430; *Sutherland* v *Wills* (1850) 5 Ex 715).

The Joint Stock Companies Act 1844, s. 7, required each company registered under the Act to have a deed of settlement (equivalent to the memorandum and articles of a company registered under CA 1985). Every member was required to execute the deed of settlement (or a deed referring to it) and it was required by s. 7 to contain a covenant 'with a trustee on the part of the company' to pay calls on shares and otherwise perform the engagements required of shareholders in the deed. It seems that this trustee was necessary while the company was only provisionally registered and so still unincorporated, that is, without separate personality and unable to contract with or sue its members (see 0.1.2.4). On complete registration, the company became incorporated, and s. 55 of the Act expressly provided for the company to sue for calls even though the covenant to pay them was not with the company but with the trustee.

The Joint Stock Companies Act 1856 abandoned provisional registration so there was no longer any need for trustees. The 1856 Act also abandoned the 1844 Act's requirement that each member actually had to sign, seal and deliver as his own act the company's deed of settlement, or a deed referring to the deed of settlement, and substituted the present provision that each member was *deemed* to have signed and sealed the memorandum and articles of association. However, because there are no longer trustees, there is no mention in the 1856 Act or subsequent Acts of *any* person with whom the deemed covenant is entered into (though Lord Blackburn in *Bradford Banking Co. Ltd* v *Henry Briggs, Son & Co. Ltd* (1886) 12 App Cas 29 said, at p. 33, that the effect of what is now CA 1985, s. 14, was as if a shareholder had executed a covenant 'to the company'). It is interesting that when New Zealand companies legislation (which was originally based on the British legislation) was revised in 1903, it was expressly stated that the members' deemed covenant was to be with the company.

In *Australian Coal & Shale Employees' Federation* v *Smith* (1937) 38 SR (NSW) 48, Jordan CJ discussed a provision of the New South Wales Companies Act of the time which was in the same terms as CA 1985, s. 14. His honour said, at p. 55:

> The section does not say that the memorandum and articles are to operate as if they had been executed by, and had contained a similar covenant on the part of the company; but it does say that they are to bind the company, and this should perhaps be regarded as a statutory application of the principle that a party who takes the benefit of a deed is bound by it though he does not execute it.

It may be doubted whether CA 1985, s. 14, deriving as it does from the wording of the partnership agreements of the old unincorporated joint-stock companies, is appropriately worded for a body corporate. However, exactly the same wording was adopted in the Industrial and Provident Societies Act 1862, s. 14 (now Industrial and Provident Societies Act 1965, s. 14(1)), to define the effect of the rules of a society incorporated by registration under the Act. When Australian companies legislation (which used to have the same wording as the British legislation) was revised in 1985, a provision was inserted explicitly stating that the memorandum and articles have effect as a contract between the company and each member, and between each member and each other member. It is to be regretted that in its report, *Shareholder Remedies* (Law Com. No. 246, Cm 3769) (London: Stationery Office, 1997), the Law Commission has decided that it is unnecessary to make a similar reform in British company law. So British lawyers still have to consider a large quantity of case law on a matter which should be settled by a simple statutory provision.

Some commentators have been misled about the reason for the original enactment of CA 1985, s. 14, by a report in the *Law Reports* that Bacon V-C said, during argument in *Buck v Robson* (1870) LR 10 Eq 629 at p. 631, that CA 1862, s. 16 (the equivalent at that time of CA 1985, s. 14), was enacted in order to get over a difficulty which appeared in *Re Royal Bank of Australia, Robinson's Executor's Case* (1856) 6 De G M & G 572. However, the reference to CA 1862, s. 16, in that report is clearly an error: it was CA 1862, s. 75 (now IA 1986, s. 80), which was enacted to deal with *Robinson's Executor's Case:* see per Lord Kingsdown in *Williams v Harding* (1866) LR 1 HL 9 at p. 29.

3.4.1.3 Unusual features of the contract formed by the articles

The contract formed by the articles of association is not like, for example, a contract of sale of goods or a contract for the construction of a building: it does not provide for each party to perform a specified list of obligations after which the contract ends. The articles of association of a company are part of the company's constitution, which provides the rules governing decision-making in the company. It is the framework within which the company operates. The constitution provides a mechanism for deciding on questions that will arise in the future concerning the company — questions about the day-to-day management of the company's business are to be determined by the directors while more fundamental matters are to be decided by the members (see 15.7), in either case in accordance with the procedures, voting rights, etc. set out in the articles.

The contract formed by articles of association is of a type sometimes called a 'relational contract', which is characterised by longevity and 'incompleteness', that is, the contract does not specify what is to happen in every possible circumstance. The articles of a company are not intended to be a complete statement of what is to happen in the relationship between the company and its members and between the members themselves. Instead the articles provide the procedure for deciding on each question that arises in those relationships as and when it arises.

The long-term, dynamic nature of the relationship between a company and its members, and between the members themselves, means that even the articles of association of the company may need alteration. CA 1985, s. 9(1), provides that the articles may be altered from time to time by a three-quarters majority of the members (see 3.5.1). Thus the contract formed by the articles is very unusual in that its provisions may be altered by a majority of the contracting parties against the wishes of the minority.

A minority member of a company who wishes to ensure that there will be no adverse alteration of the articles may be able to include a provision in a unanimous shareholders' agreement that no alteration will be made without that member's consent. A shareholders' agreement may aim to provide a more comprehensive contractual coverage of a company's affairs than articles of association would but it binds only the members who are parties to it — whenever a new member joins, the contract must be renegotiated with that new member (whereas the articles themselves automatically bind any new member) and the company itself cannot be a party to a contract which restricts its statutory power to alter its articles (*Russell* v *Northern Bank Development Corporation Ltd* [1992] 1 WLR 588).

Generally, if the written contract between two parties does not reflect accurately what the contracting parties have agreed upon, the court will rectify the document to give effect to the true agreement and the rectified document can then be sued upon in the event of a breach. In the case of the contract formed by the articles, however, it has been held that the articles cannot be rectified even if they do not accord with the parties' true intentions (*Evans* v *Chapman* (1902) 86 LT 381; *Scott* v *Frank F. Scott (London) Ltd* [1940] Ch 794, CA): any alteration to the articles must be made under the provisions of the Companies Act (see 3.5). However, in a quasi-partnership company, if the articles do not reflect the members' true intentions, the court may prevent them being acted on contrary to those intentions — see, e.g., *Caratti Holding Co. Pty Ltd* v *Zampatti* (1978) 52 ALJR 732, PC, discussed in 3.4.3; *Kounis* v *Kounis* (1987) 11 ACLR 854, Western Australia; and *Re Medefield Pty Ltd* (1977) 2 ACLR 406, New South Wales, discussed in 14.4.9.5.

Although the articles of association of a company should be construed so as to give them reasonable business efficacy (see 3.3.5), the court is limited to the words of the articles when implying terms into the contract between the company and its members: the court cannot look at the surrounding circumstances as it might do when considering any other type of contract (*Bratton Seymour Service Co. Ltd* v *Oxborough* [1992] BCLC 693).

For certain purposes the memorandum and articles have the effect of deeds but they are not deeds and do not have to be executed as deeds (*Re Whitley Partners Ltd* (1886) 32 ChD 337).

3.4.2   Articles as a contract between the company and its members

3.4.2.1   Nature of contract
In *Hickman* v *Kent or Romney Marsh Sheep-Breeders' Association* [1915] 1 Ch 881, Astbury J said, at p. 897:

> The wording of [CA 1985, s. 14] is difficult to construe or understand. A company cannot in the ordinary course be bound otherwise than by statute or contract and it is in this section that its obligation must be found. As far as the members are concerned, the section does not say with whom they are deemed to have covenanted, but the section cannot mean that the company is not to be bound when it says it is to be bound, as if, etc., nor can the section mean that the members are to be under no obligation to the company under the articles in which their rights and duties as corporators are to be found. Much of the difficulty is removed if the company be regarded, as the framers of the section may very well have so regarded it, as being treated in law as a party to its own memorandum and articles.

In *Hickman* v *Kent or Romney Marsh Sheep-Breeders'Association,* the association (which was a registered company) maintained a register of the flocks of the particular breed of sheep with which it was concerned. Sheep which were registered were more valuable than unregistered sheep. Mr Hickman was a member of the association but the association's officials alleged he had infringed its rules and proposed to remove his sheep from the register and expel him from the association. The association's articles required disputes between the association and any member to be referred to arbitration but Mr Hickman commenced proceedings in the High Court for an injunction to prevent the association expelling him, among other things. Under the statute law relating to arbitration, if one person commences a legal action against another in respect of a difference between them which is covered by an agreement in writing to submit present or future disputes to arbitration then the court will order a stay of the proceedings, thus forcing arbitration of the matter (see now Arbitration Act 1996, ss. 5, 6 and 9). Astbury J held that the provision in the articles requiring arbitration did constitute a written agreement so that the association was entitled to an order staying proceedings on the writ.

Astbury J held that what is now CA 1985, s. 14, means that the memorandum and articles of a company take effect as a contract between the company and its members. In doing so, his lordship was following the views earlier expressed by Stirling J and Farwell LJ quoted in 3.4.1.1 and by other judges, for example, James LJ in *Johnson* v *Lyttle's Iron Agency* (1877) 5 ChD 687, who referred, at pp. 693–4, to 'the contract between the company and the shareholders which is contained in the regulations of Table A', and Lord Herschell in the passage from *Welton* v *Saffery* [1897] AC 299, quoted in 3.4.3. See further, D.G. Rice, 'The legal nature of a share' (1957) 21 Conv NS 433 at pp. 438–42. Whether Astbury J was merely interpreting the statutory provision or whether he was supplementing it is an open question.

Mr Hickman was subsequently expelled from the association, lost actions for libel he brought against the secretary and president of the association and had to pay £75 damages for his own libel of the secretary (*Hickman* v *Kent or Romney Marsh Sheep-Breeders'Association* (1920) 37 TLR 163).

A provision in the articles of a company cannot limit a right given to the members by statute, that is, the members of a company cannot agree with the company to contract out of the statute (*Re Peveril Gold Mines Ltd* [1898] 1 Ch 122, in which the articles purported to limit members' rights to petition under what is now the Insolvency Act 1986, s. 124(1), for the company to be wound up; *Baring-Gould* v *Sharpington Combined Pick and Shovel Syndicate* [1899] 2 Ch 80, in which the articles purported to limit members' rights under what is now the Insolvency Act 1986, s. 111(2), to have the value of their shares determined by arbitration in the event of a reconstruction of the company by liquidation agreement). R. Gregory, 'The section 20 contract' (1981) 44 MLR 526 claims (at p. 534) that in *Baring-Gould* v *Sharpington Combined Pick and Shovel Syndicate* the Court of Appeal decided that the company is not a party to the contract created by the articles of association, but this seems to exaggerate the scope of the decision, which was concerned only with the content of the alleged agreement.

In *Borland's trustee* v *Steel Brothers & Co. Ltd* [1901] 1 Ch 279, the company's articles provided that the company could give notice to any member who was not a senior employee of the company initiating a procedure under which the company was required to find a senior employee who would buy the member's shares at a price determined by a formula set out in the articles. When Borland, who was a member but not a senior employee, became bankrupt, the company issued a notice but Borland's trustee in bankruptcy sought an injunction restraining the company from acting on the notice because he thought the price determined by the articles was too low. Farwell J refused to grant the injunction. In *Kerr* v *John Mottram Ltd* [1940] Ch 657, Mr Kerr sought specific performance of a contract he claimed the company had made with him for the sale to him of certain of its shares (the company was exercising a right of sale under a lien on the shares — see 6.4.2). He wished to prove that the sale had been agreed at an extraordinary general meeting of the company.

However, the minutes of that meeting, signed by the chairman, showed that no sale to Mr Kerr had been agreed. The company's articles provided that the minutes of a meeting, signed by the chairman, were to be conclusive evidence of the facts they stated. Simonds J accordingly held that Mr Kerr could not lead evidence to contradict the minutes and so his claim failed. In both these cases the judges talked of the articles only in terms of a contract between members, but it is submitted that as both cases were actions by a member against a company the articles could have been decisive of the issue only insofar as they were a contract between the company and the member — the parties to the action in both cases.

3.4.2.2   *Only provisions relating to membership are contractual by virtue of section 14*
In *Bisgood* v *Henderson's Transvaal Estates Ltd* [1908] 1 Ch 743, CA, Buckley LJ said, at p. 759:

> The purpose of the memorandum and articles is to define the position of the shareholder as shareholder, not to bind him in his capacity as an individual.

The effect of CA 1985, s. 14, in making the articles of association of a company contractual is limited to provisions of the articles concerned with the membership and constitution of the company. As Greene MR put it in *Beattie* v *E. & F. Beattie Ltd* [1938] Ch 708 at p. 721:

> . . . the contractual force given to the articles of association by the section is limited to such provisions of the articles as apply to the relationship of the members in their capacity as members.

The articles of E. & F. Beattie Ltd provided for any dispute between the company and a member to be referred to arbitration. A director of the company, who was also a member, sought a stay of legal proceedings brought against him by the company concerning his conduct as a director (for more about arbitration provisions in articles see *Hickman* v *Kent or Romney Marsh Sheep-Breeders' Association* [1915] 1 Ch 881 discussed in 3.4.2.1). The Court of Appeal held that the arbitration article was not a written agreement to submit to arbitration a difference between the company and one of its members concerning the member's activities as a director because the articles were an enforceable contract only in relation to membership matters.

More recently, it has been said that in a quasi-partnership company, which is formed on the basis that certain members shall be directors, provisions in the articles referring to 'directors' can be interpreted as referring to the class of members who are directors and therefore can be regarded as being concerned with membership rights: see *Rayfield* v *Hands* [1960] Ch 1 and *Caratti Holding Co. Pty Ltd* v *Zampatti* (1978) 52 ALJR 732, PC, discussed in 3.4.3.

Provisions of the articles of a company that are not made contractual by s. 14 may nevertheless be incorporated in a separate contract (often called a 'special contract') by express agreement. A party who wishes to rely on such a special contract must establish it in the usual way by proving offer, acceptance and consideration.

3.4.2.3   *'Outsider rights'*
As only the provisions in the articles of association of a company relating to membership are made contractual by CA 1985, s. 14, any provision purporting to confer a right on a non-member (an 'outsider') cannot be contractual by virtue of that section. Such a provision must be regarded merely as a direction or authorisation to the company to enter into a

separate contract with the non-member to confer that right. The fact that the outsider becomes a member of the company does not show that such a separate contract has been formed.

In *Browne* v *La Trinidad* (1887) 37 ChD 1, CA, Mr Browne had agreed with the promoters of a company called La Trinidad Ltd that when the company was incorporated, he would sell a mine in Mexico to it in return for fully paid shares and that he should become a director of the company for a period of four years at least. The company was registered with articles which provided that this agreement was 'incorporated with and shall be construed as part of' the articles. Mr Browne was not a subscriber of the memorandum and articles and so was not deemed by what is now CA 1985, s. 22, to have become a member of the company on its incorporation. He was appointed a director of the company, but, before the end of the four-year period mentioned in his agreement with the promoters, the company's members adopted an extraordinary resolution dismissing Mr Browne from his directorship. (The company's articles provided that any director could be removed by extraordinary resolution: the statutory provision that members can remove directors by ordinary resolution — now CA 1985, s. 303; see 15.3.3 — had not been enacted at that time.) Mr Browne sought an injunction to restrain the other directors from excluding him from board meetings and otherwise preventing him acting as a director; he claimed that the company could not dismiss him from his directorship until the agreed four-year period had ended. The Court of Appeal refused the injunction. Lindley LJ said, at pp. 14–15:

> Having regard to the terms of [CA 1985, s. 14], there would be some force, or at all events some plausibility, in the argument that, being a member, the contract which is referred to in the articles has become binding between the company and him. Of course that argument is open to this difficulty that there could be no contract between him and the company until the shares were allotted to him, and it would be remarkable that, upon the shares being allotted to him, a contract between him and the company, as to a matter not connected with the holding of shares, should arise. There are difficulties in the construction of [CA 1985, s. 14], but those difficulties have been removed by the authorities, which show that Browne has no contract with the company which he can enforce either at law or in equity.

Browne v *La Trinidad* may be contrasted with *Imperial Hydropathic Hotel Co., Blackpool* v *Hampson* (1882) 23 ChD 1, CA, in which the company claimed to have dismissed Mr Hampson from his directorship and sought an injunction to prevent him acting as a director. The injunction was refused on the ground that the company had not dismissed Mr Hampson because there was no power in its articles to dismiss any of its directors. However, this was not because there was any special restriction in the articles agreed between the directors and the company or its promoters (as there was claimed to be in *Browne* v *La Trinidad*), it was merely that the members had failed to include the necessary power in their articles — had they gone through the correct procedure of passing a special resolution to alter the articles, they could have inserted the necessary power and then dismissed Mr Hampson properly.

In *Eley* v *Positive Government Security Life Assurance Co. Ltd* (1876) 1 ExD 88, the company's articles provided that Mr Eley should be the company's solicitor and should not be removed from office except for misconduct. Mr Eley had drafted the articles but he was not a subscriber of the memorandum and articles. Mr Eley became a member of the company about a year after its incorporation. The directors of the company stopped employing Mr Eley as solicitor and used other solicitors instead, so Mr Eley sued the company for damages for breach of the contract which he alleged existed between himself and the company that only he should be employed as the company's solicitor. His action failed as the articles could not prove that such a contract had ever been made and he did not produce any other evidence that the contract existed.

Similarly, if a company's articles provide that a specific person shall be a director at a specified remuneration but that person is never appointed then that person cannot sue for breach of contract, even if a member of the company (per Jenkins LJ in *Read v Astoria Garage (Streatham) Ltd* [1952] Ch 637, CA, at p. 641).

In *Hickman v Kent or Romney Marsh Sheep-Breeders' Association* [1915] 1 Ch 881, Astbury J summarised the law as follows (at p. 897):

> An outsider to whom rights purport to be given by the articles in his capacity as such outsider, whether he is or subsequently becomes a member, cannot sue on those articles treating them as contracts between himself and the company to enforce those rights. Those rights are not part of the general regulations of the company applicable alike to all shareholders and can only exist by virtue of some contract between such person and the company, and the subsequent allotment of shares to an outsider in whose favour such an article is inserted does not enable him to sue the company on such an article.

Does a declaration of an outsider right in the articles of association of a company have any effect at all? In *Woodlands Ltd v Logan* [1948] NZLR 230, the company's articles provided that in certain circumstances, the personal representatives of the company's founder could appoint its managing director, and another provision defined the powers of a managing director. It was held that when the personal representatives exercised the outsider right to appoint a managing director he was validly appointed and had all the powers of a managing director conferred by the articles. But the opposite view was taken in Singapore in *Malayan Banking Ltd v Raffles Hotel Ltd* [1966] 1 MLJ 206, in which the landlord of a company was given by the company's articles a right to appoint a director: when the landlord exercised that right it was held that the appointment was invalid and of no legal effect. It seems that *Woodlands Ltd v Logan* was not cited to the Singapore court.

3.4.2.4   Contract of allotment of shares

A declaration in the articles of a company of the terms on which shares of the company will be allotted to a particular person is normally construed merely as an authorisation for the making of a contract of allotment on those terms — the provision in the articles is not in itself a contract. This used to be very important when CA 1867, s. 25, was in force (it was repealed by CA 1900). This section provided that if a company allotted shares to a member wholly or partly for a non-cash consideration then the non-cash part of the consideration would be deemed not to have been paid (leaving the member still liable to pay up to the full nominal value of the shares in cash) unless a written contract of allotment was filed with the registrar on or before allotment. The contract could be a pre-incorporation contract with a promoter (*Re Poole Firebrick & Blue Clay Co.* (1875) as reported in 44 LJ Ch 240; *Smith v Brown* [1896] AC 614). However, a statement in the articles of a company (which are filed on registration of the company) that the company shall make a contract to allot shares to a person for a non-cash consideration was held to be not in itself a contract made with that person, and merely filing such articles was not sufficient to comply with s. 25 (*Re Tavarone Mining Co., Pritchard's Case* (1873) LR 8 Ch App 956; *Re Malaga Lead Co., Firmstone's Case* (1875) LR 20 Eq 524; *Re Carribean* [sic] *Co. Ltd, Crickmer's Case* (1875) 46 LJ Ch 870). The statement in the articles was merely an authorisation for the making of a contract with an outsider.

In *Re Appletreewick Lead Mining Co.* (1874) LR 18 Eq 95, the articles provided that all the company's shares were to be allotted to the subscribers of the memorandum and articles. Malins V-C held that filing those articles was sufficient to comply with CA 1867, s. 25, but in *Crickmer's Case* at first instance (1875) 44 LJ Ch 595, he said that *Re Appletreewick Lead Mining Co.* was a 'peculiar' case and that his decision depended on its unusual facts.

The law under which the cases on contracts of allotment were decided was repealed long ago and it is difficult now to appreciate the context in which they were decided. Nevertheless they are still relied on by judges and academic commentators as sources of the law on the contractual effect of the memorandum and articles, which is why they have been discussed here.

3.4.2.5   Producers' cooperatives

The question of whether a provision in the articles of a company relates to membership or not has been particularly difficult to answer in relation to companies formed on the basis that members will trade with the company as a separate person, as in agricultural producers' cooperatives. If provisions of the articles of such a company prescribe the terms on which members are to trade with the company, are those provisions contractually enforceable by virtue of CA 1985, s. 14, because they concern membership or are they the terms of a separate 'special contract' made by express agreement between the company and each member when the member joins? If they are membership provisions then they can be altered by special resolution and the alteration will be binding on any member whether that member has agreed to the alteration or not. If the provisions are the terms of a separate contract then it is a question of construction of that contract whether it is altered when the articles are altered.

In *Gore Bros v Newbury Dairy Co. Ltd* [1919] NZLR 205, Chapman J thought that a provision in the articles of a producers' cooperative company concerning trading with the company was 'intimately connected with the very purpose of the incorporation of the company' and so was a membership provision. But in *Heron v Port Huon Fruitgrowers' Co-operative Association Ltd* (1922) 30 CLR 315, Isaacs J in the High Court of Australia doubted whether such a provision could be regarded as relating to membership: it was thought to be unnecessary to decide the question finally because the court held that the provision in question was in any case void as an unreasonable restraint of trade. The similar House of Lords case of *McEllistrim v Ballymacelligott Co-operative Agricultural & Dairy Society Ltd* [1919] AC 548 concerned a producers' cooperative incorporated by registration under the industrial and provident societies legislation. The provisions of the society's rules concerning trading with members were held to be void as an unreasonable restraint on trade but their lordships assumed that those provisions were otherwise part of the contract formed by the rules, which Lord Atkinson pointed out, at p. 575, are analogous to the articles of a registered company (see 3.4.1.2).

Isaacs J in *Heron v Port Huon Fruitgrowers' Co-operative Association Ltd* and Salmond J in *Shalfoon v Cheddar Valley Co-operative Dairy Co. Ltd* [1924] NZLR 561, at p. 581, doubted whether the law lords in *McEllistrim v Ballymacelligott Co-operative Agricultural & Dairy Society Ltd* considered whether the provisions concerning trading with members were part of the contract formed by the rules, but in *Agricultural Wholesale Society Ltd v Biddulph & District Agricultural Society Ltd* [1925] Ch 769, CA, Warrington LJ said, at pp. 785–6, that he was quite sure that it was deliberately assumed that the provisions were contractually enforceable.

In *Eltham Co-operative Dairy Factory Co. Ltd v Johnson* [1931] NZLR 216, the articles purported to prescribe the terms on which 'suppliers' could contract with the company, but the point was taken that a supplier did not have to be a member and a member did not have to be a supplier, even though in practice there must have been a substantial identity between the two categories. Accordingly the provisions relating to 'suppliers' were held to be not part of the contract formed by the articles.

See also *Bailey* v *New South Wales Medical Defence Union Ltd* (1995) 184 CLR 399 discussed in 3.5.4.

These cases show that it is dangerous to try to make the articles of association of a company do work which should be done by express contracts entered into between the company and its members.

3.4.2.6   Category 3 rights

In *Cumbrian Newspapers Group Ltd* v *Cumberland and Westmorland Herald Newspaper and Printing Co. Ltd* [1987] Ch 1, Scott J analysed provisions in articles conferring or purporting to confer rights or benefits on persons into three categories:

(a)   Rights or benefits which are annexed to particular shares ('category 1 rights'). These are enjoyed by any person who holds the shares and are membership insider rights. Classic examples are dividend rights and rights to participate in surplus assets on a winding up.

(b)   Rights or benefits which are purportedly conferred on a person whether or not he is a member ('category 2 rights'). These are clearly outsider rights.

(c)   Rights or benefits conferred on a person for so tong as he is a member ('category 3 rights'). Scott J held that these rights defined a class of membership — consisting of the person on whom the rights were conferred while he is a member. This would seem to make such rights membership rights.

3.4.2.7   Enforcing the provisions of the articles

In *Salmon* v *Quin & Axtens Ltd* [1909] 1 Ch 311, CA (affirmed by the House of Lords sub nom. *Quin & Axtens Ltd* v *Salmon* [1909] AC 442), the bulk of the shares in Quin & Axtens Ltd were held by William Raymond Axtens and Joseph Salmon. The articles appointed them and one other person directors of the company and also appointed Axtens and Salmon 'managing directors'. There was a provision in the articles that either of 'the managing directors, the said William Raymond Axtens and Joseph Salmon' could veto any board decision on a wide range of matters. Salmon did issue such a veto but the other directors went ahead with their decision and got the members of the company to approve it by ordinary resolution (see further 15.7.2.3). Salmon sued for an injunction to restrain the company and the other directors from acting on the decision and the Court of Appeal granted the injunction: the company was trying to bypass rules on decision-making contained in its constitution without following the procedure for altering the constitution — 'in truth this is an attempt to alter the terms of the contract between the parties by a simple resolution instead of by a special resolution' (per Farwell LJ at p. 319). The court would prevent the company acting on a decision taken unconstitutionally. Indirectly, Salmon enforced his outsider right as a managing director to veto certain board decisions by suing as a member for the enforcement of the relevant articles.

In *Beattie* v *E. & F. Beattie Ltd* [1938] Ch 708 (see 3.4.2.2), Greene MR said, at p. 722, that every member of the company (including Mr Beattie) might have had a membership right to require the company to submit the dispute with Mr Beattie to arbitration but this would have to be asserted in proceedings for an injunction, not in the application for a stay under the Arbitration Act which was before the court. In *Eley* v *Positive Government Security Life Assurance Co. Ltd* (1876) 1 ExD 88 (see 3.4.2.3), Lord Cairns LC said, at

p. 90, that the article requiring the company to employ Mr Eley as its solicitor was 'a matter between the directors and shareholders, and not between them and the plaintiff' which might suggest that every member of the company (including Mr Eley) had a membership right to prevent the directors appointing anyone else as solicitor (though his lordship, at p. 89, suggested that such a requirement was in any case against public policy; cf. *Re Rhodesian Properties Ltd* [1901] WN 130). Mr Beattie and Mr Eley failed because they confined themselves to relying on contracts that turned out not to exist.

On the other hand, in *Salmon* v *Quin & Axtens Ltd*, Mr Salmon succeeded because he sued, as a member of the company, to prevent the company acting on a decision which had been taken unconstitutionally. Similarly, in *Ram Kissendas Dhanuka* v *Satya Charan Law* (1949) LR 77 Ind App 128, PC, the articles of Lothian Jute Mills Ltd provided for the general management of the affairs of the company to be entrusted to managing agents, and provided that Andrew Yule & Co. Ltd were to be the managing agents until removed by extraordinary resolution (three-quarters majority). The members of Lothian Jute Mills Ltd passed an ordinary resolution (simple majority) removing Andrew Yule & Co. Ltd from the position of managing agents and the Privy Council granted a dissentient member, Dr Law, a declaration that this resolution was invalid. Again, a member of a company succeeded in preventing it acting on a decision which had been taken unconstitutionally. (This Privy Council case escaped the notice of academic commentators until it was rediscovered by P.StJ. Smart, 'The enforcement of outsider rights: Lord Greene and the Privy Council' [1989] JBL 143.)

3.4.2.8 Explanations by academics

Legal action by a member of a company to enforce the provisions of the company's articles is taken in the shadow of the 'internal management principle' that the company is the proper plaintiff in a matter concerning its internal management (see 18.4.8). It is difficult to explain why, despite the internal management principle, a member of a company can succeed in a case like *Salmon* v *Quin & Axtens Ltd* [1909] 1 Ch 311 or *Ram Kissendas Dhanuka* v *Satya Charan Law* (1949) LR 77 Ind App 128, both of which seemed to be about the internal affairs of companies so that the principle would require the companies to be the plaintiffs. In 18.4.12 we will suggest that the common feature of the cases in which members are allowed to bring legal proceedings in respect of their companies' internal affairs, as an exception to the internal management principle, is that they are proceedings about decisions taken unlawfully.

The thesis advanced by K.W. Wedderburn, 'Shareholders' rights and the rule in *Foss* v *Harbottle*' [1957] CLJ 194 is that in *Salmon* v *Quin & Axtens Ltd*, Mr Salmon enforced a *contractual* right which Jordan CJ in *Australian Coal & Shale Employees' Federation* v *Smith* (1937) 38 SR (NSW) 48 at p. 55 identified as 'the shareholder's right to have the articles observed by the company'. Wedderburn concluded ([1957] CLJ at pp. 212–13) that:

> . . . a member can compel the company not to depart from the contract with him under the articles, even if that means indirectly the enforcement of 'outsider' rights vested either in third parties or himself, so long as, but only so long as, he sues qua member and not qua 'outsider'.

A member sues 'qua member' if 'seeking to enforce a right which is common to himself and all other members' (in the words of Greene MR in *Beattie* v *E. & F. Beattie Ltd* [1938] Ch 708 at p. 722).

Wedderburn also states ([1957] CLJ 194 at pp. 214–15) that a member can enforce '*every* [his emphasis] provision of the contract found in the articles . . . subject only to those matters of "internal management" on which the courts have seen fit to displace his contractual rights in favour of majority rule' (this is a reference to the internal management principle discussed in 18.4.8). This aspect of Wedderburn's thesis has been controversial. It is supported by R. Gregory, 'The section 20 contract' (1981) 44 MLR 526 in a radical reappraisal of the cases. Gregory's analysis asserts that all provisions of the articles are contractual, not just those relating to membership.

G.N. Prentice, 'The enforcement of "outsider rights" ' (1980) 1 Co Law 179 asserts that not every provision of the articles is contractual but only the provisions 'definitive of the power of the company to function'. G. D. Goldberg, 'The enforcement of outsider rights under section 20(1) of the Companies Act 1948' (1972) 35 MLR 362 and 'The controversy on the section 20 contract revisited' (1985) 48 MLR 158 asserts that the crucial point is the remedy sought by the member, saying that:

> A member of a company has . . . a contractual right to have any of the affairs of the company conducted by the particular organ of the company specified in the Act or the company's memorandum or articles.

For a review of the controversy, see R.R. Drury,'The relative nature of a shareholder's right to enforce the company contract' [1986] CLJ 219.

The fact that Gregory, Prentice and Goldberg can produce three different descriptions of the contractual effect of the articles shows that contract concepts are not easily applied to the articles of association. The articles of a company are part of its constitution and what members require is that the company's affairs should be conducted constitutionally. Unfortunately, English law does not have a developed concept of enforcement of a constitution for an organisation, perhaps because the British constitution is largely unwritten. The only available legal concept is contract law, but it may be that it is not very appropriate. It is notable that in *Ram Kissendas Dhanuka* v *Satya Charan Law* the Privy Council did not refer to contractual concepts at all.

3.4.2.9   *Debts under the contract formed by the articles*
CA 1985, s. 14(2), provides that money payable by a member of a company to the company under its memorandum or articles is a debt due from the member to the company, and is of the nature of a specialty debt (that is, a debt due by virtue of a promise made in a deed), which means that the limitation period for such a debt will be 12 years (Limitation Act 1980, s. 8). This complements the provision in s. 14(1) that members are bound by the memorandum and articles as if they had signed *and sealed* them. Section 14(2) applies to collateral liabilities (see 1.3.2.3) (*Peninsular Co. Ltd* v *Fleming* (1872) 27 LT 93). However, the company is not deemed to have executed the memorandum and articles as a deed so the limitation period for any debt owed by the company to a member (such as a dividend) is only six years (Limitation Act 1980, s. 5; *Re Compañía de Electricidad de la Provincia de Buenos Aires Ltd* [1980] Ch 146).

3.4.3   Articles as a contract between the company's members

In *Eley* v *Positive Government Security Life Assurance Co. Ltd* (1876) 2 ExD 88, Lord Cairns LC said, at pp. 89–90:

> Articles of association . . . state the arrangement between the members. They are an agreement *inter socios* [that is, between business partners].

In *Welton* v *Saffery* [1897] AC 299, Lord Macnaghten (at p. 321) and Lord Davey (at p. 329) used the phrase 'social contract' as a literal translation of 'contract *inter socios*' but they were obviously not implying that any of the theory of the social contract of government, found in the writings of Locke, Hobbes and Rousseau, should be imported into company law, intriguing though that possibility is. It seems that Isaacs J was also using 'social contract' and 'social compact' merely as equivalents of 'partnership agreement' in *Dutton* v *Gorton* (1917) 23 CLR 362, especially at p. 395, and *Wood* v *W. & G. Dean Pty Ltd* (1929) 43 CLR 77. The much-quoted remark by Fullagar J in *Re Chas Jeffries & Sons Pty Ltd* [1949] VLR 190 at p. 194 that he took 'social contract' as used by Isaacs J in *Wood* v *W. & G. Dean Pty Ltd:* 'to be a Rousseau-esque synonym for the articles of association' is probably no more than a jest (his honour was counsel in *Wood* v *W. & G. Dean Pty Ltd*).

In *Re Tavarone Mining Co., Pritchard's Case* (1873) LR 8 Ch App 956, Mellish LJ, at p. 960, said — without mentioning what is now CA 1985, s. 14 — that:

> . . . the articles of association are simply a contract as between the shareholders *inter se* in respect of their rights as shareholders. They are the deed of partnership by which the shareholders agree *inter se*.

In *Wood* v *Odessa Waterworks Co.* (1889) 42 ChD 636, Stirling J — after citing what is now CA 1985, s. 14 — made the remark quoted in 3.4.1 that 'The articles of association constitute a contract not merely between the shareholders and the company, but between each individual shareholder and every other'. In *Automatic Self-Cleansing Filter Syndicate Co. Ltd* v *Cuninghame* [1906] 2 Ch 34, Cozens-Hardy LJ said, at p. 44:

> It has been decided that the articles of association are a contract between the members of the company *inter se*. That was settled finally by the case of *Browne* v *La Trinidad*, if it was not settled before.

(In fact it is very difficult to see that the question was settled by *Browne* v *La Trinidad* because it was not in issue in that case.)

Section 14 has been interpreted as making the articles of a company a contract between the company and its members only in relation to membership matters (see 3.4.2.2), and the same restriction has been put on the contractual effect of the articles between the members. In *London Sack & Bag Co. Ltd* v *Dixon & Lugton Ltd* [1943] 2 All ER 763, Scott LJ, in the Court of Appeal, said, at p. 765:

> It may well be, . . . as between . . . members of a company, . . . that [s. 14] adjusts their legal relations *inter se* in the same way as a contract in a single document would if signed by all; and yet the statutory result may not be to constitute a contract between them about rights of action created entirely outside the company relationship, such as trading transactions between members.

However, the courts have been reluctant to provide members of companies with contractual remedies in disputes between members. In *Welton* v *Saffery* [1897] AC 299, Lord Herschell said, at p. 315:

> It is quite true that the articles constitute a contract between each member and the company, and that there is no contract in terms between the individual members of the company; but the articles do not any the less, in my opinion, regulate their rights *inter*

se. Such rights can only be enforced by or against a member through the company, or through the liquidator representing the company; but I think that no member has, as between himself and another member, any right beyond that which the contract with the company gives.

The idea that rights can be enforced only 'through the company' derives from the proper plaintiff aspect of the internal management principle enunciated in *MacDougall* v *Gardiner* (1875) 1 ChD 13 and discussed in 18.4.8.

In *Salmon* v *Quin & Axtens Ltd* [1909] 1 Ch 311, Farwell LJ, at p. 318, after citing with approval the dictum of Stirling J quoted above, said: '. . . it may well be that the court would not enforce the covenant as between individual shareholders in most cases'.

The only directly relevant case is *Rayfield* v *Hands* [1960] Ch 1, which will be more intelligible if read in conjunction with the two casenotes by L.C.B. Gower, 'The contractual effect of articles of association' (1958) 21 MLR 401 and '*Rayfield* v *Hands* — a postscript and a drop of Scotch' (1958) 21 MLR 657. Mr Rayfield was a member of a company whose articles of association provided that a member who intended to transfer his shares had to inform the directors of the company who would take the shares equally between them at a fair value. Mr Rayfield wanted to transfer his 725 shares but Mr Hands and his fellow directors refused to take them. Vaisey J interpreted the reference to the directors in the article as a reference to the class of members who were directors and so held that the article concerned membership and had contractual force. He granted Mr Rayfield an order requiring the directors to take the shares but said, at p. 9:

> The conclusion to which I have come may not be of so general application as to extend to the articles of association of every company, for it is, I think, material to remember that this private company is one of that class of companies which bears a close analogy to a partnership.

In *Caratti Holding Co. Pty Ltd* v *Zampatti* (1978) 52 ALJR 732, PC, Mr Caratti and Mr Zampatti had carried on business in partnership, with each partner entitled to a stated proportion of assets and profits. Zampatti's share was 10%. The assets of the partnership were sold to a new company, the holding company, and leased back to the partnership. Caratti and Zampatti held shares in the company in the same proportions as their interests in the partnership. However, the articles of association of the company included art. 32, which entitled Caratti 'whilst he is the registered holder of the life governor's share' to compulsorily purchase any other member's share on payment of the amount paid up on it. Caratti attempted to invoke this article so as to purchase Zampatti's shares, then worth at least A$400,000, for A$3,000. At first instance ((1975) 1 ACLR 87, Western Australia), Burt J held that this provision had contractual force ('life governor' defining a class of shareholder) and there was no appeal on this point. (Clearly it was a quasi-partnership company but his honour did not say that this was crucial to his finding that the article was contractually enforceable.) His honour held that Caratti's attempted exercise of the powers given him by the articles was conduct of the company's affairs in a manner oppressive to Zampatti (see 18.6), and ordered Caratti to buy the shares at a price to be determined by the court. The Privy Council upheld the order. Lord Scarman said:

> The interest offered to and accepted by Mr Zampatti was a 10% share of 'the business'. Questions as to the legal structure of the business or as to the legal entities created to hold its assets were, so far as Mr Caratti and Mr Zampatti gave any thought to them,

matters for the accountant: they did not touch upon the basic agreement of the business, however matters were arranged, Mr Zampatti's interest was 10% of the profits earned and capital employed in the business. It would be contrary to the whole basis of such agreement for Mr Caratti to invoke art. 32, since to do so would be to seek to deprive Mr Zampatti of that which it had been agreed he should have, a 10% share in the profits and capital of the business. . . .

Though at first sight strange, there is nothing incredible or unique in two self-made businessmen getting on with the job of running the business on an agreed basis as to their respective shares in its profits and capital, while leaving its legal structure or pattern to a trusted accountant.

Article 32 was neither understood nor accepted by Mr Caratti and Mr Zampatti as having any reference to the business agreement between them: and the use of its provisions against Mr Zampatti is inconsistent with that agreement.

3.4.4 Appointment of a director upon the terms of the articles

A large number of provisions in the articles of association of a company relate to the company's directors (see, for example, arts 64 to 101 of Table A). The directors of a company are bound by such provisions in the company's articles even if they are not members of the company (Table A does not require a director of the company to be a member of it — that is, it does not impose a share qualification for directors).

In *Guinness plc* v *Saunders* [1990] 2 AC 663, HL, Lord Templeman said, at p. 692:

A director accepts office subject to and with the benefit of the provisions of the articles relating to directors.

In *Re Anglo-Austrian Printing & Publishing Union, Isaacs's Case* [1892] 2 Ch 158, CA, Sir Henry Isaacs had been one of the first directors of the company. The articles of the company provided that a first director had to acquire 100 of the company's £10 shares within one month of being appointed, and if he did not do so, he would 'be deemed to have agreed to take the said shares from the company, and the same shall be forthwith allotted to him accordingly'. The company was ordered to be wound up 18 months after it was incorporated. No shares had ever been allotted to Sir Henry but the liquidator sought to hold him liable as if he were the holder of 100 shares. The Court of Appeal confirmed that he was liable. Bowen LJ said, at pp. 167–8:

[These articles] amount to an offer put forward by the company to persons intending to become directors of the terms on which the directors are to act. It is perfectly true that the offer is contained in articles, which are not drawn up between the company and the directors, but nevertheless the company puts forward the terms of the articles as the terms by which it will be bound; and the director by becoming and acting as director of the company accepts that position.

Earlier Lord Esher MR had said in *Swabey* v *Port Darwin Gold Mining Co.* (1889) 1 Meg 385, CA, at p. 387: 'The articles do not themselves form a contract, but from them you get the terms upon which the directors are serving'. See also *Salton* v *New Beeston Cycle Co.* [1899] 1 Ch 775.

This analysis of the relationship between a director of a company and the company itself has been adopted in cases in which a company had gone into insolvent liquidation owing fees to directors who were also members of the company and the amount payable was fixed by the company's articles. It is crucial in such a case to determine whether the fees are owed to the directors in their character as members, for if so then they cannot be paid until all other creditors have been paid (Insolvency Act 1986, s. 74(2)(f)), whereas if the fees are not owed to them in their character as members then they will be paid along with other unsecured creditors. It has been held that if a member of a company is appointed one of its directors and the articles specify directors' remuneration then that remuneration is *not* payable to the director qua member even if the articles require a director to be a member (*Re Dale & Plant Ltd* (1889) 43 ChD 255; *Re New British Iron Co., ex parte Beckwith* [1898] 1 Ch 324; *Re A1 Biscuit Co.* [1899] WN 115). This confirms that the remuneration is payable by virtue of the terms of the director's appointment which come into operation on acceptance of that appointment, the terms being the relevant provisions from the articles (*Re New British Iron Co., ex parte Beckwith*).

The earlier analysis in *Orton* v *Cleveland Fire Brick & Pottery Co. Ltd* (1865) 3 H & C 868 that such a payment was made under a contractually enforceable term of the articles to the director qua member (see also *Re Leicester Club & County Racecourse Co.* (1885) 30 ChD 629 and *Re Iceland Sulphur & Copper Co. Ltd* (1886) 2 TLR 509) was described as 'no longer law' by Wright J during argument in *Re Peruvian Guano Co., ex parte Kemp* [1894] 3 Ch 690 at p. 701.

In *Re New British Iron Co. ex parte Beckwith* [1898] 1 Ch 324, the company's articles fixed the remuneration of the directors at a total figure of £1,000, which was to be divided between the directors as they thought fit. Certain shareholders acted as directors and without any express agreement between the company and the directors as to remuneration. Wright J in upholding the directors' claim to £1,000, said, at pp. 326–7:

> In this case there is a provision in the articles of association which . . . fixes the remuneration of the directors at the annual sum of £1,000. That article is not in itself a contract between the company and the directors; it is only part of the contract constituted by the articles of association between the members of the company *inter se*. But where on the footing of that article the directors are employed by the company and accept office the terms of [the article] are embodied in and form part of the contract between the company and the directors. Under the article as thus embodied the directors obtain a contractual right to an annual sum of £1,000 as remuneration. . . . the remuneration is not due to the directors in their character as members. It is not due to them by their being members of the company, but under a distinct contract with the company.

In *Re T.N. Farrer Ltd* [1937] Ch 352, Mr Jell had incorporated the company to operate a business he owned (which traded as T.N. Farrer) and the articles of the company appointed him governing director for life. Simonds J said, at p. 358:

> . . . what was the contractual relation between Mr Jell and the company? I have no doubt that Mr Jell, having signed the memorandum and articles, and having assumed the office of governing director and held it for some 16 years, must, in the absence of any evidence to the contrary, be regarded as holding office on the terms of the articles. It is from them alone that the terms of his contract of service can be ascertained.

His lordship described this in the ambiguous phrase 'the contract constituted by the articles' (at p. 359). However, counsel in the case had emphasised that the articles did not in themselves constitute a contract between the company and the governing director but only provided evidence of a contract (at pp. 354–5).

In *Guinness plc* v *Saunders* [1990] 2 AC 663, HL, Mr Ward was a director of Guinness plc. The articles of the company provided that special remuneration to directors for services outside the scope of the ordinary duties of a director had to be fixed by the board as a whole. Mr Ward had been given special remuneration by a committee of the board, an act which the committee had no authority to perform. Accordingly Mr Ward had to return that remuneration. If one person provides a service to another and the two have not agreed on the payment for that service then the court may order payment of an amount known as a *quantum meruit* (as much as he deserved). Mr Ward claimed a *quantum meruit* for the special services he had provided. However, a court will not award a *quantum meruit* if the parties have themselves agreed how remuneration is to be determined, even if they have not implemented that agreement. Mr Ward's appointment as a director of Guinness plc was upon the terms of the articles that remuneration was to be determined by the board. Accordingly the court would not grant a *quantum meruit*. If Mr Ward wanted special remuneration he had to ask the board for it. *Guinness plc* v *Saunders* is analysed in great detail in G. McCormack. 'The Guinness saga: in Tom we trust' (1991) 12 Co Law 90.

It is notable that the Law Lords in *Guinness plc* v *Saunders* paid no attention at all to whether or not Mr Ward was a *member* of Guinness plc. This shows that it was not the contract between the members of Guinness plc and the company as a separate person formed by the company's memorandum and articles which prevented Mr Ward being awarded a *quantum meruit*. It was the appointment, upon the terms of the articles, of Mr Ward as a director of the company which precluded a *quantum meruit* award.

In *Re Richmond Gate Property Co. Ltd* [1965] 1 WLR 335, Mr Walker, one of the subscribers of the memorandum of the company, was appointed by art. 9 of its articles joint managing director for life. However, after seven months, the company was wound up and he applied for payment for his services as joint managing director. The articles provided that 'A managing director shall receive such remuneration . . . as the directors may determine'. The directors had never determined Mr Walker's remuneration. Plowman J refused to award Mr Walker a *quantum meruit* because the way in which Mr Walker's remuneration was to be determined had already been fixed by contract. Plowman J's judgment in the case can be interpreted as holding that the contract which precluded the award of a *quantum meruit* was the contract formed between the members of the company and the company as a separate person by the company's memorandum and articles (see the casenote by K.W. Wedderburn, 'Contractual rights under articles of association — an overlooked principle illustrated' (1965) 28 MLR 347). As has been said in previous editions of this work, this would be an unnecessary departure from the analysis of the relationship between director and company as an appointment upon the terms of the articles which was established by the Court of Appeal in *Swabey* v *Port Darwin Gold Mining Co.* and *Re Anglo-Austrian Printing & Publishing Union, Isaacs's Case*. It is submitted that it would be more consistent with the other cases to say that it was Mr Walker's appointment as managing director, upon the terms of the articles, which prevented Mr Walker, as managing director, being awarded a *quantum meruit*. This would be consistent with the analysis adopted by the Law Lords in *Guinness plc* v *Saunders*.

It is submitted that the opposite error of classification occurred in *Biddulph & District Agricultural Society Ltd* v *Agricultural Wholesale Society Ltd* [1927] AC 76, HL, in which Viscount Cave LC, at p. 85, grouped the cases on collateral liability discussed in 1.3.2.3 with *Isaacs's Case*, giving the impression that the collateral liabilities in those cases arose under separate contracts with the members and not under the contract formed by the memorandum and articles. It is submitted, with respect, that such an interpretation of the collateral liabilities cases would be wrong; collateral liabilities arise under the contract formed by the memorandum and articles.

3.5 ALTERATION OF ARTICLES

3.5.1 Power to alter

The articles of association are concerned with the internal administration of a company. Such matters cannot remain static for all time and so alterations must be possible. The general power of alteration is contained in CA 1985, s. 9(1):

> Subject to the provisions of this Act and to the conditions contained in its memorandum, a company may by special resolution alter its articles.

A special resolution requires a majority of three quarters of those voting, see 14.4.8.3. This provision allows *some* of the shareholders to alter the articles. If *all* the shareholders agree to an alteration (whether or not they attend a meeting or pass a resolution) this will be effective as a valid alteration of the articles (*Cane* v *Jones* [1980] 1 WLR 1451; see 14.4.8.4).

Alterations to the articles effected under s. 9 will be, by s. 9(2), 'as valid as if originally contained in them, and are subject in like manner to alteration by special resolution'.

Certain other, but more specific, statutory provisions must be noted in this context.

The members of a company applying for re-registration as a company of another type are given a general power to alter its articles by special resolution so as to enable the company to be conducted as a company of the new type (CA 1985, ss. 43(2)(c) (private to public), 49(6) (limited to unlimited, for which the unanimous assent of members is required), 51(3) (unlimited to limited) and 53(2) (public to private)). When the court is dealing with applications by dissentient members or creditors it may make an order effecting a change in the company's articles in the same way as it may change the company's memorandum, see 2.4.7. The court is empowered to order changes in a public company's articles in order to convert it into a private company after confirming a reduction of the company's capital to below £50,000 (CA 1985, s. 139(3); see 10.2.5).

A company in general meeting may, under CA 1985, s. 80, give its directors authority to allot shares, grant options to subscribe for shares or issue securities convertible into shares (see 6.2.5). Such authority may be given, varied, renewed or revoked by ordinary resolution notwithstanding that the resolution alters the company's articles (s. 80(8)).

If a thing cannot be done by a company without an authorisation contained in its articles, and there is no such authorisation, then a special resolution to do that thing will not be interpreted as impliedly altering the articles to provide the necessary power (*Hutton* v *Scarborough Cliff Hotel Co. Ltd* (1865) 4 De G J & S 672). Thus, in several cases the court has refused to confirm resolutions to reduce capital because the articles did not, at the time the resolutions were adopted, authorise the company to reduce capital as required by CA 1985, s. 135 (*Re West India & Pacific Steamship Co.* (1868) LR 9 Ch App 11 n; *Re Patent Invert Sugar Co.* (1885) 31 ChD 166, CA; *Re Dexine Patent Packing & Rubber Co.* (1903) 88 LT 791; *Oregon Mortgage Co. Ltd* 1910 SC 964 — the second and fourth of these cases were concerned with the old requirement that a special resolution had to be confirmed at a subsequent meeting: see 14.4.8.3). See also *Imperial Hydropathic Hotel Co., Blackpool* v *Hampson* (1882) 23 ChD 1 discussed in 3.4.2.2 and *Boschoek Proprietary Co. Ltd* v *Fuke* [1906] 1 Ch 148 (another case involving confirmation of a special resolution).

On the other hand, if the articles prevent a thing being done then a special resolution to do that thing 'notwithstanding anything contained in the articles' will be effective (*Taylor* v *Pilsen Joel & General Electric Light Co.* (1884) 27 ChD 268).

3.5.2 Notification of alteration

3.5.2.1 Notification to the registrar

Any alteration of the articles achieved by unanimous consent or by special resolution pursuant to CA 1985, s. 9, or by ordinary resolution pursuant to s. 80 must be notified to the registrar of companies within 15 days of the alteration (CA 1985, ss. 380 and 80(8)).

Whenever a company sends to the registrar a copy of any resolution altering its articles, it must also send a copy of the complete articles in their altered form (CA 1985, s. 18(2)).

If a company makes an application for re-registration then it must, as part of the application, supply the registrar with a copy of its articles as altered to provide for its proposed new status (CA 1985, ss. 43(3)(a) (private to public), 49(8)(d) (limited to unlimited), 51(5)(b) (unlimited to limited), 53(1)(b) (public to private) and 139(4) (public to private by court order)).

If the court makes an order on an application by dissentient members or creditors of a company (see 3.5.1 and 2.4.7) and the order effects a change in the company's articles then the company must, within 15 days of the date of the order (14 days in the case of a s. 461 order), supply the registrar with an office copy of the order and a copy of the complete articles as altered (CA 1985, ss. 6(1)(b)(ii) (alteration of objects), 17(3) (alteration of provision of memorandum that could have been in articles), 54(7) (re-registration as private), 157(3) (objection to financial assistance), 176(3)(b) (payment out of capital for redemption or purchase of own shares) and 461(5) (allegation of prejudicial conduct of company's affairs), together with s. 18(2)). The court may grant an extension to the time-limit.

Failure of a company to supply copies of resolutions, orders and complete sets of articles when required by CA 1985 (except in connection with re-registration) is a summary offence for which the company, and any officer of the company who knowingly and wilfully authorised or permitted the default, may be fined (CA 1985, ss. 6(3), 17(3), 18(3), 54(10), 157(3), 176(4), 380(5), 461(5) and 730(5) and sch. 24). If a company fails to submit complete sets of documents with an application to re-register then the registrar will refuse the application.

3.5.2.2 Notification in the Gazette

Filing at Companies House of any document making or evidencing an alteration in a company's articles must be notified by the registrar in the *Gazette* (CA 1985, s. 711(1)(b)). The consequence of this requirement for 'official notification' in the *Gazette* is that the company may not rely on any alteration in its articles against any other person until official notification, unless the company can show that the alteration was known to the person concerned. Additionally, the company may not rely on an alteration within 15 days *after* official notification if it is shown that the person concerned was 'unavoidably prevented' from knowing of the alteration within that period (CA 1985, s. 42).

3.5.3 Restrictions on a company's powers to alter its articles

3.5.3.1 Statutory restrictions

A company's power to alter its articles is limited by the provisions of CA 1985 (per Lindley MR in *Allen* v *Gold Reefs of West Africa Ltd* [1900] 1 Ch 656 at p. 671). The statutory restrictions on a company's power to alter its articles are the same as the restrictions on its power to alter its memorandum (see 2.4.8.1).

3.5.3.2   Restrictions imposed by the court

The court may impose restrictions on a company's power to alter its memorandum or articles (see 2.4.8.2).

3.5.3.3   Restrictions imposed by the company itself or its members

CA 1985, s. 16, provides that notwithstanding any provision in the memorandum or articles, no shareholder can be bound by an alteration to the articles made after he became a member insofar as the alteration 'requires him to take or subscribe for more shares than the number held by him at the date on which the alteration is made, or in any way increases his liability as at that date to contribute to the company's share capital or otherwise to pay money to the company'. This section is obviously designed to protect members from having their financial obligations to the company forcibly increased, and it is therefore subject to a proviso which allows any member to agree in writing, either before or after the alteration is made, to be bound by the alteration. However, it may be doubted whether a company has, in any case, power to alter its articles so as to impose on members an increase in their liability to pay money to the company. In New Zealand, it was held that a company did not have such a power in *Macdonald* v *Normanby Co-operative Dairy Factory Co. Ltd* [1923] NZLR 122. In England, the year after what is now CA 1985, s. 16, was first enacted, the House of Lords decided in *Hole* v *Garnsey* [1930] AC 472 that an industrial society does not have such a power, and although Lord Tomlin in that case pointed out differences between registered companies and industrial societies it does not seem that those differences would make the decision in *Hole* v *Garnsey* inapplicable to registered companies. It would seem that if a company afters its articles to impose an additional liability on existing members and an existing member agrees to the alteration then he is bound not by the contract constituted by the articles (because the company did not have power to insert that provision in the articles) but by virtue of a separate contract made by him with the company on agreeing to the new provision.

A company's power to alter its articles is limited by the provisions of its memorandum (per Lindley MR in *Allen* v *Gold Reefs of West Africa Ltd* [1900] 1 Ch 656 at p. 671). Any provision in the company's articles which conflicts with the memorandum will be invalid (*Welton* v *Saffery* [1897] AC 299, HL, per Lord Davey at p. 329). If, when registering a company, it is desired to make unalterable a provision which would normally be in the articles then the provision may be put instead into the memorandum and expressed to be unalterable so that CA 1985, s. 17(2)(b) (see 2.4.7), will prevent it being altered.

Articles cannot effectively provide that they may not be altered because the company always has the statutory power provided by CA 1985, s. 9 (*Walker* v *London Tramways Co.* (1879) 12 ChD 705; *Allen* v *Gold Reefs of West Africa Ltd* [1900] 1 Ch 656 per Lindley MR at p. 671 and per Vaughan Williams LJ at p. 676). However, any member who controls sufficient votes to prevent a special resolution (three-quarters majority) being adopted can always prevent any alteration to the articles. The articles may provide for votes to be specially weighted so as to provide members with a power to block special resolutions out of proportion to their shareholding. In *Bushell* v *Faith* [1970] AC 1099, the company's articles weighted a shareholder's voting rights on a certain issue (for which see 15.3.3) and had the effect of preventing a resolution on that issue being passed. The Court of Appeal ([1969] 2 Ch 438) and the House of Lords upheld the weighted voting rights given by the articles. In the Court of Appeal, Russell LJ considered the problem of such weighted rights preventing the company from altering its articles. He said (at pp. 447–8):

[Counsel for the plaintiff] argued by reference to [CA 1985, s. 9], and the well-known proposition that a company cannot by its articles or otherwise deprive itself of the power by special resolution to alter its articles or any of them. But the point is the same one. An article purporting to do this is ineffective. But a provision as to voting rights which has the effect of making a special resolution incapable of being passed, if a particular shareholder or group of shareholders exercises his or their voting rights against a proposed alteration, is not such a provision. An article in terms providing that no alteration shall be made without the consent of X is contrary to [CA 1985, s. 9] and ineffective. But the provision as to voting rights that I have mentioned is wholly different, and it does not serve to say that it can have the same result.

Following this, in *Amalgamated Pest Control Pty Ltd* v *McCarron* [1995] 1 QdR 583, the court found nothing invalid about a provision in a company's articles giving a particular member 26 per cent of the votes on any special resolution.

It follows from *Russell* v *Northern Bank Development Corporation Ltd* [1992] 1 WLR 588 (which concerned alteration of a memorandum) that members of a company may make an enforceable contract between themselves not to alter some or all of the company's articles, but such a contract would bind only the members who agreed to it (see 2.4.8.3).

3.5.3.4   Restrictions imposed by contract

A contract made by a company that it will not exercise its statutory power to alter its articles is unenforceable (*Russell* v *Northern Bank Development Corporation Ltd* [1992] 1 WLR 588, see 2.4.8.3). Alteration of a company's articles may put it in breach of contract or make it impossible for the company to carry out its obligations under a contract. In two early cases, injunctions were granted to prevent companies altering their articles in a way that would breach contracts (*Baily* v *British Equitable Assurance Co.* [1904] 1 Ch 374, CA (though the House of Lords [1906] AC 35 subsequently held that the proposed alteration would not be in breach of contract); *British Murac Syndicate Ltd* v *Alperton Rubber Co. Ltd* [1915] 2 Ch 186). However, it is now accepted that the statutory right of a company to alter its articles cannot be taken away by injunction (this was originally held in *Punt* v *Symons & Co. Ltd* [1903] 2 Ch 506; see per Lord Porter in *Southern Foundries (1926) Ltd* v *Shirlaw* [1940] AC 701 at pp. 740–1; per Scott J in *Cumbrian Newspapers Group Ltd* v *Cumberland and Westmorland Herald Newspaper and Printing Co. Ltd* [1987] Ch 1 at p. 24).

3.5.3.5   Bona fide for the benefit of the company as a whole

The members of a company must not exercise the company's power to alter its articles otherwise than bona fide for the benefit of the company as a whole. The classic statement of this restriction placed on majority shareholders to vote as they please is to be found in the judgment of Lindley MR in *Allen* v *Gold Reefs of West Africa Ltd* [1900] 1 Ch 656 at pp. 671–2:

> The power thus conferred on companies to alter the regulations contained in their articles is limited only by the provisions contained in the statute and the conditions contained in the company's memorandum of association. Wide, however, as the language of [CA 1985 s. 9] is, the power conferred by it must, like all other powers, be exercised subject to those general principles of law and equity which are applicable to all powers conferred on majorities and enabling them to bind minorities. It must be exercised, not only in the manner required by law, but also bona fide for the benefit of the company as a whole, and it must not be exceeded. These conditions are always implied, and are seldom, if ever, expressed. But if they are complied with I can discover no ground for judicially

putting any other restrictions on the power conferred by the section than those contained in it.

The phrase 'bona fide for the benefit of the company as a whole' is a single criterion only. If the court accepts that the majority members' subjective bona fide view was that the alteration was for the benefit of the company then it cannot overrule the decision on the ground that in the court's view it was not for the benefit of the company — it is not the court's task to take business decisions (*Shuttleworth* v *Cox Brothers & Co. (Maidenhead) Ltd* [1927] 2 KB 9, CA). Nevertheless, there is an objective minimum standard below which the members' subjective view will not be accepted. In *Shuttleworth's* case, Bankes LJ said, at pp. 18–19:

> The alteration may be so oppressive as to cast suspicion on the honesty of the persons responsible for it, or so extravagant that no reasonable men could really consider it for the benefit of the company. In such cases the court is, I think, entitled to treat the conduct of shareholders as it does the verdict of a jury, and to say that the alteration of a company's articles shall not stand if it is such that no reasonable men could consider it for the benefit of the company. Or, if the facts should raise the question, the court may be able to apply another test — namely, whether or not the action of the shareholders is capable of being considered for the benefit of the company.

In the same case, Scrutton LJ said, at p. 23:

> Now when persons, honestly endeavouring to decide what will be for the benefit of the company and to act accordingly, decide upon a particular course, then, provided there are grounds on which reasonable men could come to the same decision, it does not matter whether the court would or would not come to the same decision or a different decision. It is not the business of the court to manage the affairs of the company. That is for the shareholders and directors. The absence of any reasonable ground for deciding that a certain course of action is conducive to the benefit of the company may be a ground for finding lack of good faith or for finding that the shareholders, with the best motives, have not considered the matters which they ought to have considered. On either of these findings their decision might be set aside.

A company has a dual aspect as an association of its members and as a person separate from its members. The phrase 'the benefit of the company as a whole' might refer to either (or both) of these aspects. A feature of a number of leading English cases in which the court upheld the validity of an alteration of articles is that the alteration was made primarily for the benefit of the company as a corporate entity separate from its members.

In *Allen* v *Gold Reefs of West Africa Ltd* [1900] 1 Ch 656, CA, the object of the change was to obtain payment to the company of calls due from the estate of a deceased member.

In *Sidebottom* v *Kershaw, Leese & Co. Ltd* [1920] 1 Ch 154, CA, the object of the alteration was to give the directors power to expel any member who carried on a business in direct competition with the company's business.

In *Shuttleworth* v *Cox Brothers & Co. (Maidenhead) Ltd* [1927] 2 KB 9, CA, the object of the alteration was to provide that a director should resign if requested in writing to do so by all his co-directors.

In all these cases, in assessing whether the majority have acted 'bona fide for the benefit of the company as a whole', it is the company as a separate person whose benefit is to be considered. However, as Latham CJ said in *Peters' American Delicacy Co. Ltd* v *Heath* (1939) 61 CLR 457 at p. 481:

> The benefit of the company as a corporation cannot be adopted as a criterion which is capable of solving all the problems in this branch of the law. . . . In cases where the question which arises is simply a question as to the relative rights of different classes of shareholders the problem cannot be solved by regarding merely the benefit of the corporation.

In *Greenhalgh* v *Arderne Cinemas Ltd* [1951] Ch 286, CA, a provision in the articles of Arderne Cinemas Ltd which gave existing members a preemption right to buy any shares that a member wanted to sell was altered by adding a provision that, notwithstanding the pre-emption rights, any member could transfer shares if the transfer was approved by an ordinary resolution of the members. The managing director, Mr Mallard, controlled a majority of votes and intended to sell his controlling interest to an outsider, apparently to spite Mr Greenhalgh, a minority shareholder. Mr Mallard and his supporters had already successfully defended at least four actions brought by Mr Greenhalgh which had been taken to the Court of Appeal. In voting for the change in articles, Mr Mallard and his supporters did not claim to have acted in the company's interest because they did not allege that the company as a separate person had any interest in who its shareholders were. They apparently acted in Mr Mallard's interest, though it seems that he was interested in emotional rather than financial gratification. How then could the court decide whether the majority had abused their power? Evershed MR said, at p. 291:

> . . . the phrase, 'the company as a whole', does not (at any rate in such a case as the present) mean the company as a commercial entity, distinct from the corporators: it means the corporators as a general body. That is to say, the case may be taken of an individual hypothetical member and it may be asked whether what is proposed is, in the honest opinion of those who voted in its favour, for that person's benefit.
>
> I think that the matter can, in practice, be more accurately and precisely stated by looking at the converse and by saying that a special resolution of this kind would be liable to be impeached if the effect of it were to discriminate between the majority shareholders and the minority shareholders, so as to give the former an advantage of which the latter were deprived.

The court unanimously affirmed Roxburgh J's decision that the alteration of the articles of Arderne Cinemas Ltd was valid. The alteration took away from the minority the right to acquire other members' shares if those other members could secure an ordinary resolution approving a transfer to an outsider. But in Evershed MR's view (at p. 292): 'I do not think that it can be said that that is such a discrimination as falls within the scope of the principle which I have stated'. It is difficult to follow the court's application of the discrimination principle in this case, though it may be that Mr Mallard's malevolent self-interest was an unusual factor. (For an earlier case in the Arderne Cinemas affair — *Greenhalgh* v *Arderne Cinemas Ltd* [1946] 1 All ER 512 — see 14.4.9.5.)

Evershed MR claimed that the discrimination test would explain two English cases in which alterations of articles were held to be invalid: *Brown* v *British Abrasive Wheel Co. Ltd* [1919] 1 Ch 290 and *Dafen Tinplate Co. Ltd* v *Llanelly Steel Co. (1907) Ltd* [1920] 2 Ch 124 (the latter case was criticised in *Shuttleworth's* case as a wrong application of the interest of the company test). The discrimination test would also apparently explain the Scottish case of *Crookston* v *Lindsay, Crookston & Co. Ltd* 1922 SLT 62.

In *Rights and Issues Investment Trust Ltd* v *Stylo Shoes Ltd* [1965] Ch 250, the company had two classes of shares, ordinary shares and management shares. It was proposed to issue new ordinary shares but also to double the number of votes attached to each management share so that the holders of the management shares would retain control of the company. The proposal was adopted by a very large majority at a general meeting — the holders of the management shares did not vote. Pennycuick J said (at p. 255) that he was 'not persuaded that there has been here any discrimination against or oppression of the holders of the ordinary shares'.

In *Australian Fixed Trusts Pty Ltd* v *Clyde Industries Ltd* [1959] SR (NSW) 33, the directors of Clyde Industries Ltd proposed to alter its articles so as to make it virtually impossible for votes to be cast in relation to shares held on behalf of unit trusts (as 14.6% of its shares were). The court was unable to discern any 'company purpose' for the alteration and so relied on the discrimination test. It was held that the proposed alteration would be invalid because it discriminated by reducing the voting power of specific shareholders and thereby increasing the voting power of the other shareholders.

Commentators often ignore the second paragraph in the passage from Evershed MR's judgment quoted above and suggest that the test to be applied is the hypothetical member test. But it is very difficult to understand how this test could be applied in practice. Is a hypothetical member different from a real member, and, if so, in what way? What is the hypothesis? As Evershed MR said, the discrimination test 'more accurately and precisely' tests whether an alteration of articles is valid, and that is the test which has in practice been used by subsequent courts. Commentators also ignore the words 'at any rate in such a case as the present' and assume that Evershed MR intended his test to be applied in all future cases. The true position is that the discrimination test is only necessary in cases where it is inappropriate to apply the test of benefit to the company as a whole.

In *Gambotto* v *WCP Ltd* (1995) 182 CLR 432, the High Court of Australia suggested that it was time to replace the 'benefit of the company as a whole' test entirely. The majority of the court said, at p. 444, that the test of whether an alteration of a company's articles is valid should be whether the alteration is 'beyond any purpose contemplated by the articles or oppressive as that expression is understood in the law relating to corporations'. The court refused to allow a company to alter its articles so as to give the holder of 99.7 per cent of its shares a right to purchase the remainder compulsorily so as to make the company a wholly owned subsidiary and so obtain tax advantages and administrative savings. The majority of the court said that alteration of the articles of a company so as to give the majority in the company power to expropriate the minority is a special case in which the test should be that the alteration is valid only if (a) the power could be exercised 'for a proper purpose' and (b) exercising the power would not be oppressive to the minority. The majority of the court also held that the onus was on those proposing the alteration to show that it satisfies the test. In *Gambotto* v *WCP Ltd* achieving tax and administrative savings was not a proper purpose and so the alteration was invalid. Although *Gambotto* v *WCP Ltd* now governs the law on this subject in Australia it is not a precedent in England. It seems, with respect, to have introduced yet another vague test which does not clarify the law in this difficult area where the courts are trying to protect minorities without giving them disproportionate power.

This topic has been reviewed in detail by F.G. Rixon, 'Competing interests and conflicting principles: an examination of the power of alteration of articles of association' (1986) 49 MLR 446, who concludes by observing that, in future, minority shareholders who dispute a change in articles will petition for relief of unfairly prejudicial conduct (see 18.6) rather than attempting to prove that the alteration was invalid under either the interest of the company test or the discrimination test. Nevertheless this area of company law is still important because *directors* of companies are required to use their powers 'bona fide in the interests of the company' and the courts approach the exercise of directors' powers in much the same way as they have approached members' exercise of their power to alter articles — see 16.4.3. The topic of alteration of the articles is also dealt with by P.G. Xuereb, 'The limitation on the exercise of majority power' (1985) 6 Co Law 199 and H.H. Mason, 'Fraud on the minority. The problem of a single formulation of the principle' (1972) 46 ALJ 67. See also the general discussion in 14.4.9.3 to 14.4.9.6 of reasons for invalidating decisions of members.

3.5.4 Alteration of articles which are terms of another contract

The contract between a company and its members which is formed by the membership provisions of the articles may be altered by special resolution and all members will be bound by the alteration. But if provisions of a company's articles are also terms of a separate contract which the company has made with a person (whether a member or not), then it is a question of construction of that separate contract whether or not it is altered by an alteration of the articles (*Allen* v *Gold Reefs of West Africa Ltd* [1900] 1 Ch 656, CA, per Lindley MR at pp. 673–4).

In *Shuttleworth* v *Cox Brothers & Co. (Maidenhead) Ltd* [1927] 2 KB 9, CA, the company's articles provided for five people to be its directors for life unless disqualified in any of six specified ways. The articles were subsequently altered by adding a seventh disqualifying circumstance and one of the directors was asked to resign when this seventh circumstance occurred. The director concerned sued for a declaration that he was still a director of the company but the Court of Appeal held that the company did have a power to dismiss him. Atkin LJ, at pp. 25–6, said:

> . . . the proper inference appears to be that there was a contract that the plaintiff should be a permanent director, but a contract contained in articles which could be altered by a special resolution of the company in accordance with the provisions of the Companies Act; and inasmuch as the contract contemplated the permanent office being vacated in one of six contingencies, it is not inconsistent with the contract that the article should be altered so as to add a seventh contingency. In other words, it is a contract made upon the terms of an alterable article, and therefore neither of the contracting parties can complain if the article is altered.

In *Southern Foundries (1926) Ltd* v *Shirlaw* [1940] AC 701, Mr Shirlaw was a director of Southern Foundries and had been appointed its managing director for a fixed term of 10 years. The articles of Southern Foundries were altered so as to provide that any of its directors could be removed from office by written notice signed by officers of its new parent company. When Mr Shirlaw was dismissed from his directorship of Southern Foundries using this provision it meant that he could not continue to be managing director, because both the old and the new articles specified that the office of managing director could be held only by a director of the company and that a managing director would cease to hold office on ceasing to be a director (this is the same as Table A, art. 84, see 15.5.3). Mr Shirlaw's 10-year contract was only in its fourth year when he was dismissed. A majority of the House of Lords (including Lord Atkin, as Atkin LJ had then become) held that by making it impossible for Mr Shirlaw to continue as managing director, the company had breached its 10-year contract with him and had to pay damages. Even though the dismissal was actually effected by the parent company, in the view of the majority of the House, Southern Foundries was responsible for the breach of contract because it had granted the parent company the right of dismissal. (The minority held that Southern Foundries was not responsible for the dismissal.) In Mr Shirlaw's case, as in Mr Shuttleworth's case, using altered articles to dismiss a director was not in itself wrong but in Mr Shirlaw's case it caused a separate contract (the one relating to his office as managing director) to be breached, for which damages had to be paid.

In *Bailey* v *New South Wales Medical Defence Union Ltd* (1995) 184 CLR 399, the union provided professional negligence insurance to its medical-practitioner members on terms set out in its articles of association. The High Court of Australia held that the provisions of the articles relating to insurance were not membership provisions: it was possible for people to be members but not insured, and members had to pay annual subscriptions which were fixed by the union's council and depended on the extent of insurance cover required. The union altered its articles to give it the right to discontinue assistance to any member at the sole and absolute discretion of its council. A member, who had joined before the articles were altered, had been sued for damages for his professional negligence, which was alleged to have occurred before the articles were altered. The union claimed to relieve itself of liability by acting under the altered article. It was held that it was not a term of the insurance contract that the union could alter it retrospectively by altering its articles, so the member was still insured by the union.

3.6 COPIES OF THE ARTICLES FOR MEMBERS

The rules on the supply of copies of the articles of a company to its members are the same as for the supply of copies of its memorandum, see 2.6.

4 Disclosure

4.1 INTRODUCTION

The benefits of separate corporate personality and limited liability can only be obtained in return for a certain loss of privacy. Disclosure and publicity have been a feature of company law since 1844, though their nature and extent have varied considerably since then. Disclosure is now secured in one or more of four ways: by delivery of information to the registrar of companies; by publication in the *Gazette;* by registers and information available at the company's registered office; and by publication in business documents. These four methods of disclosure will be examined in turn. In addition, one must never overlook disclosure of information by the financial press — sometimes of information which the company would rather not disclose to the public, and it should also be remembered that the Stock Exchange may impose its own additional requirements of disclosure on listed companies.

4.2 REGISTRY INFORMATION

4.2.1 Registration

The Companies Act 1985, the Insolvency Act 1986, the Company Directors Disqualification Act 1986, the Financial Services Act 1986, the Insolvency Rules 1986 and associated statutory instruments require a vast quantity of information to be delivered by a company to the registrar of companies. Requirements to deliver information are noted in this book when the events giving rise to the requirements are discussed. Two of the most important documents that have to be delivered to the registrar are the annual return (see 4.6) and the annual accounts (see 9.4).

In many of the provisions requiring information to be delivered to the registrar it is stated that the information must be 'in the prescribed form'. All the forms set out in sch. 3 to the Companies (Forms) Regulations 1985 (SI 1985 No. 854), apart from the forms listed in part 1 of sch. 4 to the regulations, are prescribed forms for the purposes of CA 1985. (For other forms prescribed for the purposes of that Act, see SI 1987 No. 752, reg. 5; SI 1988 No. 1359, reg. 2; SI 1990 No. 572, reg. 3; SI 1990 No. 1766, regs 3(1) and 4; SI 1991 No. 879, reg. 2; SI 1991 No. 1259, reg. 3; SI 1992 No. 3006, reg. 4(1); SI 1995 No. 734, reg. 4; SI 1995 No. 736, regs 3 and 5; SI 1995 No. 1479, reg. 2; SI 1995 No. 1480, reg. 2; SI 1995 No. 1508, reg. 2.)

In other provisions requiring information to be delivered to the registrar, the Secretary of State is empowered to prescribe what particulars are to be delivered (see, for example, CA 1985, s 123(2), which requires a notice of increase in authorised share capital to include 'such particulars as may be prescribed'). The Secretary of State has set out (also in sch. 3

to SI 1985 No. 854) forms for use in these circumstances and the particulars required to be entered in those forms are the prescribed particulars (SI 1985 No. 854, reg. 4(2)). However, except in three cases (see CA 1985, ss. 155(6), 156(1) and 173(5); SI 1985 No. 854, sch. 4, part 11), these forms are not 'prescribed forms' (see SI 1985 No. 854, reg. 4(1)).

A prescribed form is to be used 'with such variations as circumstances require' (SI 1985 No. 854, reg. 4(1)), and it seems that the onus is on the person filling in the form to work out how to vary it to accommodate any special circumstances in which it is being completed (*Sun Tai Cheung Credits Ltd* v *Attorney-General of Hong Kong* [1987] 1 WLR 948, PC). This causes a difficulty in the three cases in which the primary legislation requires the submission of prescribed particulars and the subordinate legislation prescribes what particulars have to be given by saying that they are the particulars required to be entered in a prescribed form (see CA 1985, ss. 155(6), 156(1) and 173(5) and SI 1985 No. 854, sch. 4, part II). As the prescribed form has to be adapted, by the person filling it in, to accommodate any special circumstances, it seems that in these three cases the onus is also on that person to adapt the particulars given to suit the circumstances, and a person who fails to make the correct adaptation will suffer the consequences of not delivering information to the registrar as required (*Sun Tai Cheung Credits Ltd* v *Attorney-General of Hong Kong*; but see the dissenting judgment of Lord Goff of Chievely).

In *Re NL Electrical Ltd* [1994] 1 BCLC 22, Harman J held that when a statutory provision requires information to be delivered 'in' a prescribed form this does not mean that it has to be delivered 'on' the prescribed form. Accordingly it is not necessary to present information using the layout and typography of the prescribed form, or even its heading: it is sufficient to provide whatever information the prescribed form asks for. This somewhat surprising decision means that there is in effect no difference between a requirement to give prescribed particulars and a requirement to give information in prescribed form.

The information that has to be provided to the registrar is recorded and kept at Companies House for inspection by the public. CA 1985, ss. 706 and 707, therefore entitle the registrar to insist that information is delivered in a form that is convenient for processing. The registrar is empowered to receive information in non-legible form (s. 707(2)). A person who has delivered information to the registrar in an unsatisfactory form may be served with a notice indicating what is wrong with it, and then has 14 days to redeliver the information in a satisfactory form, or the original document will be deemed not to have been delivered (ss. 706(3) and (4) and 707(5) and (6)).

If the memorandum of a company states that its registered office is to be in Wales then any document delivered to the registrar under the CA 1985 or the Insolvency Act 1986 may be in Welsh but must be accompanied by a certified translation into English (CA 1985, s. 710B(1) and (2) inserted by the Welsh Language Act 1993, s. 30(6)). The certification requirements are prescribed in SI 1994 No. 117, reg. 5. For 12 commonly used forms (including the annual return), Welsh-language versions have been prescribed in SI 1995 No. 734, SI 1995 No. 1480 and SI 1995 No. 1508, and a company using them need not provide an English translation (CA 1985, s. 710B(3)(b)) though the registrar must have them translated (s. 710B(4)).

If a company is in default of any of the provisions requiring information to be delivered to the registrar and fails to comply with a notice requiring the failure to be made good within 14 days, the registrar or any member or creditor of the company may apply to the court for an order requiring the company and any of its officers to make good the default (CA 1985, s. 713). This remedy is in addition to the many provisions for penalties contained in the statutory provisions requiring information (s. 713(3)). A similar power is contained in s. 242, relating to the presentation of accounts. In addition, a failure to provide information to

Companies House may give the registrar reasonable cause to believe that a company is not carrying on business or is not in operation, which may lead to the company being struck off the register under s. 652 (see 20.14.2.4). A director disqualification order may be made against a person who is persistently in default in delivering information to the registrar (CDDA 1986, ss. 3 and 5; see 15.2.5.2).

4.2.2 Inspection of registry information

The information that has to be provided to the registrar is recorded and kept at Companies House for inspection by the public. Any person may inspect any records kept by the registrar for the purposes of the Companies Acts, Insolvency Act 1986, Company Directors Disqualification Act 1986 and FSA 1986 (CA 1985, ss. 709(1), 735A(2) and 735B). Any person may require a copy of any information contained in those records, or a certified copy of, or extract from, any such record (s. 709(1)). However, there is no right to inspect an original document unless the record that the registrar has of the contents of the document is illegible or unavailable (s. 709(2)) and the registrar is not required to keep original documents for more than 10 years (s. 707A(2)). Records relating to dissolved companies may be sent to the Public Record Office two years after the dissolution (s. 707A(3)). Fees are payable to the registrar for inspection and copies (CA 1985, s. 708; SI 1991 No. 1206; SI 1996 No. 1444).

The right to inspect under s. 709(1) is subject to two limitations: first, correspondence concerning permission to use certain words and phrases in a company's name is not available for inspection or copying (CA 1985, s. 29(4); see 2.3.3.5); secondly, if a company is under administration or in administrative receivership it is possible to obtain a court order of limited disclosure of the company's statement of affairs (Insolvency Rules 1986, rr. 2.13 and 3.5).

The presence on the registrar's files of information that should not be there and which is detrimental to the company may be rectified in proceedings for judicial review of the registrar's decision to file the information (*Re Calmex Ltd* [1989] 1 All ER 485).

4.3 NOTIFICATION IN THE *GAZETTE*

The legislation governing companies requires many events affecting individual companies to be notified in the *Gazette,* which means, in relation to companies registered in England and Wales, the *London Gazette* and, in relation to companies registered in Scotland, the *Edinburgh Gazette* (CA 1985, s. 744). For example, a notice that a liquidator has been appointed in the voluntary winding up of a company must be published by the liquidator in the *Gazette* as well as being sent to the registrar (Insolvency Act 1986, s. 109), and a company is required to publish a notice in the *Gazette* if it approves a payment out of capital for the purpose of acquiring its own shares by redemption or purchase (CA 1985, s. 175(1)). Most of the notifications in the *Gazette* are made under CA 1985, s. 711, which requires the registrar to publish notice that a certificate of incorporation has been issued or that a document in any of 23 classes listed in s. 711(1) has been received at Companies House. The source of this requirement is art. 3, para. 4, of the First Company Law Directive (68/151/EEC).

Certain events affecting companies have profound effects on how other persons deal with them. Persons who deal with companies are given some protection by CA 1985, s. 42. This provides that a company cannot rely, against another person, on the happening of any event listed in s. 42(1) if, at the material time, the event had not been officially notified (which means, by s. 711(2), notified by publication of a notice in the *Gazette* under s. 711(1) or under the Insolvency Act 1986, s. 109), unless the company can prove that the other person knew of the event. In addition, if the material time was on or before the 15th day after official notification (or the next business day if the 15th day is not a business day), the company will not be able to rely on it if it is shown that the other person was unavoidably prevented from knowing of the event at that time. The events specified in s. 42(1) are:

(a)   the making of a winding-up order in respect of the company, or the appointment of a liquidator in a voluntary winding up of the company, or
(b)   any alteration of the company's memorandum or articles, or
(c)   any change among the company's directors, or
(d)   (as regards service of any document on the company) any change in the situation of the company's registered office.

Notifications by the registrar under CA 1985, s. 711(1), are published in special supplements to the *Gazette* issued only on microfiche, but other notices of company information (including those made under the Insolvency Act 1986, s. 109) appear in the conventionally printed issues of the *Gazette*.

Section 42 is primarily intended to protect persons dealing with companies rather than to protect companies themselves, and so a company cannot rely on official notification of any event specified in s. 42 as being constructive notice to other persons that the event has occurred (*Official Custodian for Charities* v *Parway Estates Developments Ltd* [1985] Ch 151, CA).

In addition, people are not deemed to have constructive notice of any information published in the *Gazette* but not covered by CA 1985, s. 42 (*Ewart* v *Fryer* [1901] 1 Ch 499 — reported on this point only in 82 LT 415 at pp. 416–17; see also the same case in the House of Lords [1902] AC 187 per Lord Macnaghten at p. 193 and Lord Lindley at p. 194). In *Re Mawcon Ltd* [1969] 1 WLR 78, Pennycuick J said that the notice in the *Gazette* that a provisional liquidator had been appointed (required at that time by SI 1949 No. 330, r. 42(1)(a) and (c)) was notice to all of the appointment; but *Ewart* v *Fryer* was not cited to his lordship and it is submitted that his decision on this point is wrong.

4.4   COMPANY INFORMATION

A company is required to maintain registers and information relating to its affairs (usually at its registered office) for inspection by various people. Some of this information may duplicate information recorded and available for inspection at the registry (see 4.2.1).

The legislation makes provision for:

(a)   Who may inspect. The following list of registers, records and documents is classified according to who is entitled to inspect them.

(b)   Where inspection may be made. If registers or records are kept in legible form then the legislation specifies where they must be kept; if they are in non-legible form then SI 1985 No. 724, reg. 2(3)(a), permits them to be kept anywhere but the rest of SI 1985 No. 724 requires that it must be possible to inspect the registers or records in legible form at one of the places where they would have to be kept if they were in legible form. Usually the place for inspection is the registered office but if any other place is allowed then notification of its location must usually be made to the registrar (or notification of the place where non-legible registers are to be inspected: SI 1985 No. 724, regs 3 and 5).

(c)   Whether a fee may be charged for inspection. Where a fee can be charged, the prescribed fee is £2.50 for each hour or part thereof during which the right of inspection is exercised (SI 1991 No. 1998, reg. 5 and sch. 2, para. 1), but a company may charge a lesser fee or no fee at all (CA 1985, s. 723A(6)).

(d)   Whether a person making an inspection may, on payment of a fee, require the company to supply a copy of the register or document. If a register is in non-legible form then a provision requiring the company to furnish a copy of it requires the company to make a copy in legible form (s. 723(3)): the company cannot be required, e.g., to supply a duplicate disk for a computer (cf. *APA Oceanic Funds Management Ltd* v *Smith (No. 1)* (1987) 9 NSWLR 569). The prescribed fees for supplying copies are set out in SI 1991 No. 1998, reg. 5 and sch. 2, paras 2 and 3, but a company may charge a lesser fee or no fee at all (CA 1985, s. 723A(6)). A company must, in addition, permit a person inspecting to copy any information made available for inspection by means of the taking of notes or the transcription of the information (SI 1991 No. 1998, reg. 3(2)(b)). This does not mean that the company is obliged to provide any facilities additional to those provided for the purposes of facilitating inspection (reg. 3(3)).

(e)   The periods during which inspection must be allowed. SI 1991 No. 1998, reg. 3(2)(a), prescribes that registers, indices and documents must be available for inspection for not less than two hours during the period betwen 9 a.m. and 5 p.m. on each business day. Every day is a business day except Saturdays, Sundays, Christmas Day, Good Friday and any day which is a bank holiday in the part of Great Britain where the company is registered, but a company may afford more extensive facilities for inspection (CA 1985, s. 723A(6)).

4.4.1   Registers and documents that may be inspected by any person

Any person may inspect:

(a)   A copy of every contract (or memorandum of the terms of an unwritten contract) made by a public company to purchase its own shares (either absolutely or contingently). A copy or memorandum of a contract must be kept at the company's registered office from the time it is concluded until 10 years after the date on which the transfer under the contract was completed or the contract otherwise determined (CA 1985, s. 169(4) and (5)). No fee for inspection (s. 169(5)).

(b)   Any register of holders of debentures (in practice, debenture stock or loan stock) — keeping such a register is not compulsory, see 12.4. Such a register must be kept at the registered office or the office of the company where the work of making it up is performed or at the office of a firm of registrars who make up the register for the company (s. 190(3)) but it must not be kept in Scotland if the company is registered in England and Wales (s. 190(1)) nor in England and Wales if the company is registered in Scotland (s. 190(2)). The registrar must be notified of where the register is kept unless it has always been kept at the registered office (s. 190(5)) and the address must also be stated in the annual return (s. 364(1)(h)).

No fee for inspection may be charged to a registered holder of the debentures to which the register refers or to a holder of shares in the company but any other person may be charged (s. 191(1)).

Copies from the company on payment (s. 191(2)).

Regulation 4 of SI 1991 No. 1998 states that a company is not obliged to provide information from a register of debenture holders classified, for the benefit of the enquirer, by the debenture holders' geographical location, nationality or size of holding, or by whether or not a debenture holder is a natural person or is of a particular gender.

(c)   The register of interests in shares which must be kept by a public company (but not a private company). It must be kept where the register of directors' interests is kept (s. 211(8)(a)). No fee for inspection (s. 219(1)). Copies from the company on payment (s. 219(2)).

(d)   Any report on an investigation made by a public company into interests in its shares. Such a report must be kept at the company's registered office for six years (s. 215(7)). No fee for inspection (s. 219(1)). Copies from the company on payment (s. 219(2)).

(e)   The register of directors and secretaries which every company must keep. It must be kept at the registered office (s. 288(1)). No fee for inspection may be charged to a member but any other person may be charged (s. 288(3)).

(f)   The register of directors' interests which every company must keep (s. 325(1)). If the company's register of members is kept at its registered office then the register of directors' interests must also be kept there; if not then the register of directors' interests may be kept either at the registered office or at the place where the register of members is kept (sch. 13, para. 25). The registrar must be notified of where the register is kept unless it has always been kept at the registered office (sch. 13, para. 27). No fee for inspection may be charged to a member but any other person may be charged (sch. 13, para. 25). Copies from the company on payment (sch. 13, para 26).

(g)   The register of members (s. 356(1)) which every company must keep (s. 352(1)). It must be kept at the registered office or the office of the company where the work of making it up is performed or at the office of a firm of registrars who make up the register for the company, but it must not be kept outside England and Wales if the company is registered in England and Wales or outside Scotland if the company is registered there (s. 353(1)). The registrar must be notified of where the register is kept unless it has always been kept at the registered office (s. 353(2) and (3)) and the address must also be stated in the annual return (s. 364(1)(g)).

No fee may be charged to a member for inspection but any other person may be charged (s. 356(1)). Copies from the company on payment (s. 356(3)). Regulation 4 of SI 1991 No. 1998 states that a company is not obliged to provide information from the register of members classified, for the benefit of the enquirer, by the members' geographical location, nationality or size of holding, or by whether or not a member is a natural person or is of a particular gender.

In the days before computers were used for keeping the registers of public companies it was necessary to 'close' the register of members — that is, to refuse to register any transfers — for several days at a time in order to make up a definitive list of members for payment of dividend, and so on. CA 1985, s. 358, allows a company to close its register of members for a total of 30 days a year, provided that notice of the closure is first given by advertisement in a newspaper circulating in the district in which the company's registered office is situated: such a notice would seem inadequate if the register is kept, not at the registered office, but at some other place where it is made up. The duty to permit inspection is suspended while the register is duly closed (s. 356(1)).

(h)   The register of charges which every company must keep at its registered office (ss. 407 and 408 as originally enacted). No fee may be charged to a member or creditor for inspection but any other person may be charged up to 5p per inspection (s. 408(1) and (2) as originally enacted). At common law, a statutory right to inspect a document or register includes a right to copy it (*Mutter* v *Eastern and Midlands Railway Co.* (1888) 38 ChD 92; *Nelson* v *Anglo-American Land Mortgage Agency Co.* [1897] 1 Ch 130).

4.4.2 Documents that may be inspected by members and creditors only

Any member or creditor may inspect:

(a)   The directors' statutory declaration and auditors' report required in connection with a payment out of capital by a company for the redemption or purchase of its own shares (CA 1985, s. 175(6)(b)). These documents must be kept at the registered office for a period of five weeks after adopting the resolution to make the payment (s. 175(6)(a)). No fee for inspection (s. 175(6)(b)).

(b)   Under s. 408(1) as originally enacted, a copy of every instrument creating a charge which requires registration under part XII (see 11.7). Such copies must be kept at the registered office (s. 406 as originally enacted). No fee may be charged for inspection (s. 408(1)). At common law, a statutory right to inspect a document includes a right to copy it (*Mutter* v *Eastern and Midlands Railway Co.* (1888) 38 ChD 92; *Nelson* v *Anglo-American Land Mortgage Agency Co.* [1897] 1 Ch 130).

4.4.3 Inspection by members only

Members of a company are entitled to inspect the following documents:

(a)   A copy of every contract (or memorandum of the terms of an unwritten contract) made by a private company to purchase its own shares (either absolutely or contingently). A copy or memorandum of a contract must be kept at the registered office from the time it is concluded until 10 years after the date on which the transfer under the contract was completed or the contract otherwise determined (s. 169(4) and (5)). No fee for inspection (s. 169(5)).

(b)   A copy of every contract of service that a director or shadow director has with the company or any of its subsidiaries, or, if such a contract is not in writing, a written memorandum of its terms (CA 1985, s. 318(1), (6) and (7)). If a contract requires the director to work wholly or mainly outside the United Kingdom then it is only necessary to keep a memorandum of the terms of the contract relating to the duration of the contract, though this memorandum must name the director concerned and if the contract is with a subsidiary, state the country in which it is incorporated (s. 318(5)). A contract that expires within the next 12 months, or which may be terminated by the company, without paying compensation, within the next 12 months, is excluded (s. 318(11)). All contracts and memoranda must be kept in the same place (s. 318(2) and (5)), which may be the company's registered office or the place where its register of members is kept or its principal place of business (provided that is in the part of Britain in which the company is registered) (s. 318(3)). Notice must be given to the registrar of the place where they are kept and any changes unless they have always been kept at the registered office (s. 318(4)). No fee for inspection (s. 318(7)).

(c)   The minutes of proceedings of any general meeting of the company held on or after 1 November 1929. These must be kept at the registered office (CA 1985, s. 383(1)). No fee for inspection. Copies from the company on payment (s. 383(3)).

(d)   In the case of a private company, the record of written resolutions agreed to under s. 381A as if they were resolutions of the company in general meeting (CA 1985, s. 382A(3)). The record must be kept at the registered office (s. 383(1) applied by s. 382A(3)). No fee for inspection. Copies from the company on payment (s. 383(3) applied by s. 382A(3)).

There are also provisions under which resolutions on certain matters will be ineffective unless documents relating to those matters are available for inspection by members when they consider the resolution. See s. 157(4)(a) (resolution of private company approving financial assistance for purchase of company's own shares or those of holding company, discussed in 10.8.7), s. 164(6) (resolutions relating to off-market purchases of the company's own shares and contingent purchase contracts, discussed in 10.6.3), s. 174(4) (approval of payment out of capital for redemption or purchase of company's own shares, discussed in 10.3.5) and s. 319(5) (approval of director's service contract, discussed in 15.6.4).

4.4.4 Records that may be inspected by officers only

A company must keep accounting records at its registered office or at such other place as the directors may determine, and these records must be open to inspection at all times by the officers of the company (CA 1985, s. 222(1); see further 9.2.4).

4.5 BUSINESS DOCUMENTS AND PLACES OF BUSINESS

There are several statutory provisions requiring a company to disclose information about itself on its business documents and at its places of business.

4.5.1 Name

Since a company, as an artificial entity, can be identified only by its name, it is only to be expected that the Companies Act should impose stringent requirements concerning disclosure of the corporate name. Thus, by CA 1985, s. 348(1):

> Every company shall paint or affix, and keep painted or affixed, its name on the outside of every office or place in which its business is carried on, in a conspicuous position and in letters easily legible.

A fine may be imposed for failure to comply with this requirement (s. 348(2) and sch. 24). In South Australia, the fact that officers of the Corporate Affairs Commission attempting on five separate occasions to serve documents on 11 companies at their registered office did not see their names (which were said to be displayed in a window above a door) was sufficient to secure conviction for failure to observe the Australian equivalent of s. 348(1) (*Invention Finance Pty Ltd* v *Flavel* (1988) 13 ACLR 99).

Section 349(1) provides:

> Every company shall have its name mentioned in legible characters—
> (a)   in all business letters of the company,
> (b)   in all its notices and other official publications,
> (c)   in all bills of exchange, promissory notes, endorsements, cheques and orders
> for money or goods purporting to be signed by or on behalf of the company, and
> (d)   in all its bills of parcels, invoices, receipts and letters of credit.

And s. 350(1) provides that a company which has a common seal must have its name engraved in legible characters on the seal.

Fines may be imposed for breaches of ss. 349(1) and 350(1) (ss. 349(2), (3) and (4), 350 and sch. 24). It is not a breach of the provisions to abbreviate 'Limited' to 'Ltd' or 'public limited company' to 'plc' (s. 27(2)), nor to abbreviate 'company' to 'Co.' (*Banque de l'Indochine et de Suez SA* v *Euroseas Group Finance Co. Ltd* [1981] 3 All ER 198). However, omitting the word 'limited' completely is a breach (*Penrose* v *Martyr* (1858) E B & E 499; *Atkin* v *Wardle* (1889) 5 TLR 734; *British Airways Board* v *Parish* [1979] 2 Lloyd's Rep 361, CA; *Blum* v *OCP Repartition SA* [1988] BCLC 170, CA). It is a breach to abbreviate a proper name to an initial (*Durham Fancy Goods Ltd* v *Michael Jackson (Fancy Goods) Ltd* [1968] 2 QB 839, where 'Michael Jackson' was abbreviated to 'M. Jackson'), because the abbreviation does not convey the full word unambiguously (as 'Ltd' and 'Co.' do). (Quaere whether the abbreviation of 'George' to 'Geo' or 'William' to 'Wm' would be acceptable on the basis that these abbreviations do convey the full word.) Although most of the reported cases have concerned omission of part of a name, adding words to the company's name may also cause a breach of s. 349(1) or s. 350(1) (*Nassau Steam Press* v *Tyler* (1894) 70 LT 376, in which The Bastille Syndicate Ltd was misnamed 'Old Paris and Bastille Syndicate Ltd').

In addition to fines for a breach, the officer of the company or any person acting on its behalf who has signed or authorised to be signed a bill of exchange, promissory note, cheque or order for money or goods which does not comply with s. 349(1)(c) is personally liable to the holder of the document for the amount of it unless the company honours its obligation (s. 349(4)). The 'holder' of an order for goods is the person to whom the order was addressed (*Civil Service Cooperative Society Ltd* v *Chapman* (1914) 30 TLR 679). This provision does not make the person who signed a guarantor of the company's obligation so as to enable him to take advantage of the defences available under the law on guarantees (*British Airways Board* v *Parish*).

In order to make an officer liable under s. 349(4) for authorising another person to sign a document it is necessary to prove that the officer specifically authorised its being in a form that did not mention the company's name, not merely that the officer gave a general authorisation to someone to sign cheques, or issue orders etc. (*John Wilkes (Footwear) Ltd* v *Lee International (Footwear) Ltd* [1985] BCLC 444, CA). Someone may be personally liable for a company's order for money or goods under s. 349(4) but not for an order for services. In *East Midlands Electricity Board* v *Grantham* [1980] CLY 271, it was held that s. 349(4) does not apply to an order for the supply of electricity but in *Hutt Valley Energy Board* v *Hayman* (1988) 4 NZCLC 64,244, the defendant conceded that the equivalent New Zealand provision applied to an order for the supply of gas.

A bank normally tries to ensure that a customer draws all cheques on printed forms supplied by the bank. Cheque forms supplied to a customer are normally overprinted with the title of the customer's account above the place where a signature would normally be written.

In *Hendon* v *Adelman* (1973) 117 SJ 631, the overprinted account title on a cheque drawn by three directors of L & R Agencies Ltd omitted the '&': the directors were held to be personally liable on the cheque. In *Barber & Nicholls Ltd* v *R & G Associates (London) Ltd* (1981) 132 NLJ 1076 the overprinted account title on a cheque drawn by a director of R & G Associates (London) Ltd omitted the parenthesised word '(London)' and the director was held to be personally liable on the cheque.

In *Blum* v *OCP Repartition SA* [1988] BCLC 170, CA, the overprinted account title on a cheque drawn by a director of Bomore Medical Supplies Ltd omitted 'Ltd' and the director was held to be personally liable. (The director sued the bank for negligence but the outcome of that action has not yet been reported.)

When a company is drawee of a bill of exchange its name may appear twice on the bill, first on the face of the bill where the drawee is named (this is normally inserted by the drawer) and secondly in words of acceptance signed by a company officer. If the company's name is given correctly as drawee then this is sufficient to comply with s. 349(1)(c) and it does not matter that it is given incorrectly in the acceptance (*Dermatine Co. Ltd* v *Ashworth* (1905) 21 TLR 510). In *Atkin* v *Wardle* (1889) 5 TLR 734, CA, the name of the company was given incorrectly both as drawee and as acceptor, but the company's correct name could have been formed by taking words from both incorrect names: it was held that this was not sufficient to comply with s. 349(1)(c). An individual accepting a bill on behalf of a company has a duty to check that the company's name appears correctly in the bill — if the drawer has made a mistake when naming the drawee then the acceptor should either correct it or mention the company's name correctly in the acceptance (*Scottish & Newcastle Breweries Ltd* v *Blair* 1967 SLT 72; *Lindholst & Co. A/S* v *Fowler* [1988] BCLC 166, CA). Exceptionally, in *Durham Fancy Goods Ltd* v *Michael Jackson (Fancy Goods) Ltd* [1968] 2 QB 839 the drawer misnamed the intended drawee company both when naming the drawee and when putting on the bill words of acceptance which it implied had only to be signed to make the bill regularly accepted. Donaldson J (as he then was) held that the drawer was estopped from denying that the bill was regularly accepted — this seems to have been a generous ruling.

In *Barber & Nicholls Ltd* v *R & G Associates (London) Ltd* (1981) 132 NLJ 1076, CA, the defendants, whose cheque form was wrongly overprinted 'R & G Associates Ltd', attempted to claim that since the company was often referred to, even by the plaintiffs, by the wrong name, the plaintiffs were estopped from claiming that it did not comply with s. 349(1)(c), but this argument failed, of course, because the statement that was claimed to estop the plaintiffs was the name on the cheque and that was a statement made by the defendants.

If a company is drawee of a bill of exchange and an agent of the company puts his or her signature on the bill without naming the company correctly then the signature will normally be construed as an acceptance by the company because that is the construction most favourable to the validity of the bill (Bills of Exchange Act 1882, s. 26(2); *Penrose* v *Martyr*; *Maxform SpA* v *Mariani* [1981] 2 Lloyd's Rep 54, CA): that construction will bring s. 349(4) into operation because it will show that the person signed 'on behalf of the company'.

In many cases the fact that a company's name is given slightly wrongly on a cheque or other financial document is accidental, and the consequential right of the creditor to proceed against the signer personally is a windfall. Nevertheless the courts have repeatedly emphasised that the statutory provision must be applied strictly. It is not open to the signer to seek rectification of the document to correct the erroneous naming of the company (*Blum* v *OCP Repartition SA*) or insert an omitted name (*Rafsanjan Pistachio Producers Cooperative* v *Reiss* [1990] BCLC 352). In *Jenice Ltd* v *Dan* [1993] BCLC 1349, R. Titheridge QC (sitting as a deputy High Court judge) tried to limit the harshness of the law by holding that a company's name is sufficiently 'mentioned' on a document even if it is misspelt. Accordingly a director of Primekeen Ltd who signed cheques on cheque forms overprinted 'Primkeen Ltd' was not personally liable. But all the previous cases on s. 349(1) could have been decided in the defendants' favour if the law was as stated by Mr Titheridge and so it must be submitted, with great respect, that *Jenice Ltd* v *Dan* was wrongly decided.

Putting a trade or business name, and not putting the registered corporate name, of a company on any of the documents covered by CA 1985, s. 349(1), is a breach of that provision (*Maxform SpA* v *Mariani* [1979] 2 Lloyd's Rep 385, point not considered on appeal).

The only sanctions for not stating a company's registered name as required by ss. 348–50 are those set out in CA 1985: failure to mention a company's name correctly in one of its transactions does not make the transaction void. For example, the fact that all documentation relating to a contract with a company is in the company's trading name without mentioning its registered name does not in itself make the contract illegal and unenforceable (*Moreland Metal Co. Ltd* v *Cowlishaw* (1919) 19 SR (NSW) 231). Similarly, the fact that a company has illegally used a business name without mentioning its corporate name does not mean that the company is precluded from bringing an action for passing off against a rival who has used a similar business name (*Pearks, Gunston and Tee Ltd* v *Thompson, Talmey and Co.* (1901) 18 RPC 185; *H.E. Randall Ltd* v *British and American Shoe Co.* [1902] 2 Ch 354). However, it is possible that refusing to disclose the true name of a company in connection with a transaction will lead to proceedings to enforce the transaction being dismissed under the Business Names Act 1985, s. 5 (see 2.3.3.7).

The fact that a company is misnamed in a document does not make the document ineffective provided it is clear that it was intended to name that company (*Bird & Co. (London) Ltd* v *Thomas Cook & Son (Bankers) Ltd* [1937] 2 All ER 227; *F. Goldsmith (Sicklesmere) Ltd* v *Baxter* [1970] Ch 85; *Badgerhill Properties Ltd* v *Cottrell* [1991] BCLC 805). If, however, it is not clear that it was intended to name the company then the document will not be effective (*Davies* v *Elsby Brothers Ltd* [1961] 1 WLR 170). In *Rhodian River Shipping Co. SA* v *Halla Maritime Corporation* [1984] 1 Lloyd's Rep 373, the court ordered rectification of a charterparty in which the wrong company had been named as owner of the ship. In *Singh* v *Atombrook Ltd* [1989] 1 WLR 810, the plaintiff had issued a writ against 'Sterling Travel', which was the trading name of Atombrook Ltd, and had obtained judgment in default of defence. The court allowed an amendment of the writ substituting as the name of the defendant, 'Atombrook Ltd, trading as Sterling Travel', because it was never doubted by anyone on behalf of Atombrook Ltd that it was the intended defendant. By contrast, in *Marco (Croydon) Ltd* v *Metropolitan Police* [1984] RTR 24, a magistrates' court summons was issued for the offence of not lighting a builder's skip bearing the name A & J Bull. The summons named the defendant as 'A J Bull Ltd'. When it was heard, counsel appeared for a company called A & J Bull Ltd but he informed the prosecutor that the skip was owned by another company in the same group, Marco (Croydon) Ltd. The magistrates allowed the name on the summons to be changed to Marco (Croydon) Ltd and found that company guilty but the Divisional Court took the view that the error in the summons had caused the wrong company to appear by counsel and so the amendment to the summons should not have been allowed. By then the time-limit for charging the right company had expired.

4.5.2 Directors

A company may not state in any form the name of any of its directors (otherwise than in the text or as a signatory) on any business letter on which the company's name appears unless it states on the letter in legible characters the name of every director of the company (CA 1985, s. 305). This provision does not require publication of the directors' names but merely requires voluntary publication thereof to be in a certain form. For the purposes of this section, a person in accordance with whose directions or instructions the directors are accustomed to act is treated as a director (CA 1985, s. 305(4)(a)), unless that person is giving advice in a professional capacity (CA 1995, s. 741(2)).

4.5.3 Insolvency

If an administration order has been made in relation to a company, or if a receiver or manager of any of its property (including an administrative receiver) has been appointed, or if the company is in liquidation, then the fact must be stated on all invoices, orders for goods and business letters in which the company's name is mentioned issued by or on behalf of the company or its administrator, receiver, manager or liquidator (IA 1986, ss. 12 (administration), 39 (receivership in England and Wales) and 188 (liquidation)). In the case of administration, the administrator's name must also be stated. Failure to state the appropriate facts is a summary offence (IA 1986, sch. 10).

4.5.4   Miscellaneous

By CA 1985, s. 351(1):

> Every company shall have the following particulars mentioned in legible characters in all business letters and order forms of the company, that is to say—
> (a)   the company's place of registration and the number with which it is registered,
> (b)   the address of its registered office,
> (c)   in the case of an investment company (as defined in section 266), the fact that it is such a company, and
> (d)   in the case of a limited company exempt from the obligation to use the word 'limited' as part of its name, the fact that it is a limited company.

If the amount of a company's share capital is mentioned on its business stationery or order forms, the reference must be to paid-up share capital (s. 351(2)).

Under s. 351(5) fines may be imposed for a failure to comply with s. 351.

4.5.5   Charitable companies

By the Charities Act 1993, s. 68(1), if a company is a charity and its name does not include the word 'charity' or the word 'charitable' then the fact that the company is a charity must be stated in English in legible characters:

(a)   in all business letters of the company,
(b)   in all its notices and other official publications,
(c)   in all bills of exchange, promissory notes, endorsements, cheques and orders for money or goods purporting to be signed by or on behalf of the company,
(d)   in all conveyances purporting to be executed by the company, and
(e)   in all its bills of parcels, invoices, receipts and letters of credit.

In this provision, 'conveyance' means any instrument creating, transferring, varying or extinguishing an interest in land (s. 68(2)).

It is important for persons dealing with a charitable company to appreciate that it is a charitable company because, unlike other companies, a charitable company's contractual capacity is limited (see 19.4.2).

4.6   ANNUAL RETURNS

Once a year every company must deliver a return to the registrar (CA 1985, s. 363(1)) containing information about prescribed features of the company's affairs. The return for a year must state what the prescribed features were on a particular date in the year, which is known as the company's 'return date'. If a company has not yet made an annual return then its return date is the anniversary of its incorporation, otherwise it is the anniversary of the date to which the company's last annual return was made up (s. 363(1)). A company commits an offence if it fails to deliver an annual return within 28 days after a return date (s. 363(3)) and every director or secretary of the company is also guilty unless he shows that he took all reasonable steps to avoid commission of the offence (s. 363(4)). The extent of a person's responsibility for any failure of a company to comply with its duty to make annual returns is a matter to which the court must have regard in deciding whether his conduct as a director or shadow director of that company makes him unfit to be concerned in the management of a company (Company Directors Disqualification Act 1986, s. 9 and sch. 1, para. 4(f)). A return must be in the prescribed form and must be signed by a director or the secretary of the company (s. 363(2)).

A company's annual return must state the date to which it is made up (s. 364(1)), and must contain the following information as at that date:

(a)   the address of the company's registered office (s. 364(1)(a));

(b)   the type of company it is (public or private; limited by shares or by guarantee or unlimited; whether exempt under CA 1985, s. 30, from requirements relating to the use of 'limited') and its principal business activities (according to the Standard Industrial Classification of Economic Activities 1992) (s. 364(1)(b), (2) and (3); SI 1990 No. 1766, reg. 5 and sch. 3; SI 1996 No. 1105);

(c)   the name and address of the company secretary (s. 364(1)(c));

(d)   the name and address of every director and shadow director of the company (ss. 364(1)(d) and 365(3));

(e)   in the case of each individual director or shadow director (ss. 364(1)(e) and 365(3)):

(i)   his or her nationality, date of birth and business occupation, and

(ii)   such particulars of other directorships and former names as are required to be contained in the company's register of directors (see 15.4.1);

(f)   in the case of a corporate director or shadow director, such particulars of other directorships as would be required to be contained in that register in the case of an individual (ss. 364(1)(f) and 365(3));

(g)   if the register of members is not kept at the company's registered office, the address of the place where it is kept (s. 364(1)(g));

(h)   if any register of debenture holders (or a duplicate of any such register or a part of it) is not kept at the company's registered office, the address of the place where it is kept (s. 364(1)(h));

(i)   a statement that the company has made an election under s. 252 (dispensing with laying accounts and reports before the company in general meeting) or s. 366A (dispensing with the holding of annual general meetings) if that is the case (s. 364(1)(i));

(j)   the total number and nominal value of the company's issued shares (s. 364A(2));

(k)   with respect to each class of shares, the nature of the class and the total number and nominal value of the issued shares of that class (s. 364A(3));

(l)   the name and address of every member (with an index if the names are not in alphabetical order) (s. 364A(4)) and the number of shares of each class held by him (s. 364A(5)(a)) — it is permissible to give this information in full only in every third annual return, with the intermediate returns merely giving changes since the previous return (s. 364A(6));

(m)   the name and address of every person who has ceased to be a member since the date to which the previous return was made up (or, in the case of the first annual return, since the company was incorporated) (s. 364A(4)), the number of shares of each class which the member has transferred since that date, and the dates of registration of the transfers (s. 364A(5)(b)).

To save form-filling, the registrar operates a 'shuttle' system. Shortly before a company's return date, the registrar sends it a return form partially completed with the information from the previous annual return and it is only necessary for the company to specify changes in the information.

The obligation to give a list of members in an annual return does not apply to a company without a share capital (s. 364A(1)). A company without a share capital must be either a guarantee company or an unlimited company (see 1.3.1).

As explained in 0.1.2.4, in the early 19th century, any company which was under a statutory duty to supply a list of its members to a public office was regarded as being a 'public company'. Accordingly, any registered company with a share capital is a 'public company' for the purposes of legislation in which that term is used without further definition, for example, the Apportionment Act 1870, s. 5 (*Re Lysaght* [1898] 1 Ch 115). This is so even if the company is a 'private company' for the purposes of the companies legislation (*Re White* [1913] 1 Ch 231).

The information contained in an annual return and the annual accounts (see 9.4) make them potentially the most useful documents which a company has to prepare and make available for registration and inspection. Until 1977 annual returns and annual accounts were filed together but the two have since been subject to separate rules.

The registrar charges a fee of £15 for registering an annual return (SI 1991 No. 1206; SI 1996 No. 1444).

5 Corporate Personality

5.1 INTRODUCTION

The single most important consequence of incorporation is the separate legal personality which the company acquires. By CA 1985, s. 13(1), on the registration of the memorandum of a company, the registrar of companies is to certify that the company is incorporated, and CA 1985, s. 711(1)(a), requires the registrar to give notice of the issue of a certificate of incorporation in the *Gazette*. A certificate of incorporation given under s. 13(1) is conclusive evidence that 'the requirements of this Act in respect of registration and of matters precedent and incidental to it have been complied with' and that the company is authorised to be, and is duly registered under the Act (CA 1985, s. 13(7)(a)). Thus, the company is born and comes into being complete with its own birth certificate (see 1.2.1).

More important for present purposes is CA 1985, s. 13(3):

From the date of incorporation mentioned in the certificate, the subscribers of the memorandum, together with such other persons as may from time to time become members of the company, shall be a body corporate by the name contained in the memorandum.

It is by this provision that a separate legal entity — the body corporate — is created.

5.2 SEPARATE PERSONALITY

5.2.1 Recognition of corporate personality

A company has a dual nature as both an association of its members and a person separate from its members. A company's property is owned by the company as a separate person, not by the members; the company's business is conducted by the company as a separate person, not by the members; it is the company as a separate person that enters into contracts in relation to the company's business and property.

The case that has long been taken to show the fundamental importance of the separate personality of a company is *Salomon* v *A. Salomon & Co. Ltd* [1897] AC 22.

As explained in 1.3.3.2, it was common in the late 19th century for businesses previously conducted by sole proprietors or partnerships to be 'incorporated': the business would be sold to a company whose only members were its previous owner or owners and sufficient nominees to make up the then minimum number of seven members (the minimum number of members of a company is now one). Mr Salomon had conducted his bootmaking business as a sole trader, and he sold it to a company incorporated for the purpose called A. Salomon & Co. Ltd whose only members were himself, his wife, a daughter and four sons. These seven individuals were the subscribers of the company's memorandum and took one £1 share each. The business was sold to the company for over £39,000. Part of the purchase price was used by Mr Salomon to subscribe for a further 20,000 £1 shares in the company, but £10,000 of the purchase price was not paid by the company, which instead issued Mr Salomon with a series of debentures (written acknowledgements of indebtedness) for £10,000 and gave him a floating charge on its assets as security for the debt (floating charges are explained in 11.6). Unfortunately the company's business failed and the company went into liquidation. As will be explained in 11.6, the holder of a floating charge on a company's assets is entitled, on the liquidation of the company, to have the assets covered by the charge applied to the payment of the debt secured by the charge. If Mr Salomon had been able to enforce his floating charge, the company's other creditors would have got nothing. The company's liquidator took a stand on behalf of the other creditors, resisted Mr Salomon's claim and suggested that, rather than take money from his company, Mr Salomon should be made responsible for paying all its debts, just as he would have if he had continued to conduct the business as a sole trader. The liquidator wanted somehow to ignore the fact that Salomon had sold his business to a separate person, A. Salomon & Co. Ltd, and that Mr Salomon now had only limited liability to that company instead of the unlimited liability he had had when he conducted the business as a sole trader.

At first instance (sub nom. *Broderip* v *Salomon* [1895] 2 Ch 323), it was held that the company had conducted the business as agent for Mr Salomon, so that he was responsible for all debts incurred in the course of the agency for him. The House of Lords rejected this approach. Lord Herschell said, at p. 43:

> In a popular sense, a company may in every case be said to carry on business for and on behalf of its shareholders; but this certainly does not in point of law constitute the relation of principal and agent between them or render the shareholders liable to indemnify the company against the debts which it incurs.

In the Court of Appeal (sub nom. *Broderip* v *Salomon* [1895] 2 Ch 323 at p. 333), it was held that Mr Salomon had incorporated the company contrary to the true intent and meaning of CA 1862, and that, because of Mr Salomon's fraud, a constructive trust should be imposed under which the company should be deemed to have operated the business as trustee for Mr Salomon who should therefore indemnify the company for all debts incurred in carrying out the trust. The House of Lords also rejected this argument. There was nothing at all in the Act to show that what Mr Salomon had done was prohibited. Indeed, Lord Macnaghten pointed out ([1897] AC 22 at p. 52) that in an earlier case (*Re Baglan Hall Colliery Co.* (1870) LR 5 Ch App 346), Giffard LJ had said (at p. 356) that it was 'the policy of the Companies Act' to enable business people to incorporate their businesses and so avoid incurring further personal liability. Lord Macnaghten said ([1897] AC 22 at p. 51):

> When the memorandum is duly signed and registered . . . the subscribers are a body corporate 'capable forthwith', to use the words of the enactment, 'of exercising all the functions of an incorporated company'. Those are strong words. The company attains maturity on its birth. There is no period of minority — no interval of incapacity. I cannot understand how a body corporate thus made 'capable' by statute can lose its individuality by issuing the bulk of its capital to one person, whether he be a subscriber to the memorandum or not. The company is at law a different person altogether from the subscribers to the memorandum; and, though it may be that after incorporation the business is precisely the same as it was before, and the same persons are managers, and

the same hands receive the profits, the company is not in law the agent of the subscribers or trustee for them. Nor are the subscribers as members liable, in any shape or form, except to the extent and in the manner provided by the Act. That is, I think, the declared intention of the enactment.

Lord Halsbury LC said, at pp. 30–1 :

> . . . it seems to me impossible to dispute that once the company is legally incorporated it must be treated like any other independent person with its rights and liabilities appropriate to itself, and that the motives of those who took part in the promotion of the company are absolutely irrelevant in discussing what those rights and liabilities are.

For the background to *Salomon* v *A. Salomon & Co. Ltd,* which is probably the most famous case in company law, see G.R. Rubin, 'Aron Salomon and his circle', in *Essays for Clive Schmitthoff,* ed. John Adams (Abingdon: Professional Books, 1983), pp. 99–120. Following the case, Parliament enacted provisions in the Companies Act 1900 requiring the public registration of charges on company property (see 11.7) and in the Companies Act 1907 enabling liquidators to avoid floating charges given to secure pre-existing debts (see 11.6.5). L.S. Sealy, 'Modern insolvency laws and Mr Salomon' (1998) 16 C & SLJ 176 discusses various statutory provisions which might have applied if *Salomon's* case had occurred a century later than it did, but concludes that it is unlikely Mr Salomon could be made liable under them.

The House of Lords in *Salomon* v *A. Salomon & Co. Ltd* recognised that a company's business is conducted by the company as a separate person (see also per Lord Sumner in *Gas Lighting Improvement Co. Ltd* v *Commissioners of Inland Revenue* [1923] AC 723 quoted in 5.3.1). It is the company as a separate person that owns the company's property and enters into contracts and incurs debts. This has been affirmed in many different contexts.

It is the company as a separate person that conducts the company's business and so any defamatory statement made about that business defames the company as a separate person, which may sue for libel or slander (*Metropolitan Saloon Omnibus Co. Ltd* v *Hawkins* (1859) 4 H & N 87; *South Hetton Coal Co. Ltd* v *North-Eastern News Association Ltd* [1894] 1 QB 133, CA). A company, as a person separate from its members, may even sue one of its own members for libel (*Metropolitan Saloon Omnibus Co. Ltd* v *Hawkins*). But if a company is a political party, it cannot sue for defamation, because of an overriding public interest in freedom to criticise political institutions (*Goldsmith* v *Bhoyrul* [1998] QB 459, which concerned the Referendum Party), though individual party members, even candidates for election, who believe themselves to be defamed can sue (per Buckley J in *Goldsmith* v *Bhoyrul* at p. 438).

In *Cristina* v *Seear* [1985] 2 EGLR 128, Mr and Mrs Cristina claimed the protection of part II of the Landlord and Tenant Act 1954, which gives security of tenure when leased land is occupied for the purposes of a business carried on by the tenant. The Cristinas were the tenants of premises on which a business was conducted but the business was carried on by a company whose shares were all owned by the Cristinas, so the business was not carried on by the tenants of the premises and the tenancy was not covered by the Act.

There is a danger that the principle that a company's business is conducted by the company rather than its members or directors could lead to people who are responsible for making a company commit criminal offences being excused because the company committed the crime, not them. As will be explained in 19.8.4, statutes creating criminal offences for the regulation of economic activity usually provide that a director or other officer of a company who consented to or connived at the company's commission of an offence may be prosecuted along with the company.

The company's property is the property of the company as a separate person not the members. This is illustrated by *Macaura* v *Northern Assurance Co. Ltd* [1925] AC 619. The owner of a timber estate sold all the timber to a company in which he owned almost all the shares. He was also the company's largest creditor. He insured the timber against fire by policies taken out in his own name. The timber was destroyed by fire and he sued the insurance company. The House of Lords held that in order to have an insurable interest in property a person must have a legal or equitable interest in the property and not merely a moral certainty of profiting or losing from the property (the so-called 'factual expectancy test'). Accordingly Macaura's claim failed because, as Lord Wrenbury said, at p. 633:

> My Lords, this appeal may be disposed of by saying that the corporator even if he holds all the shares is not the corporation, and that neither he nor any creditor of the company has any property legal or equitable in the assets of the corporation.

(In *Constitution Insurance Co. of Canada* v *Kosmopoulos* (1987) 34 DLR (4th) 208 the Supreme Court of Canada held that in Canada insurable interest was to be determined by the factual expectancy test so that the member of a single-member company incorporated in Ontario did have an insurable interest in its property.)

See also *Acatos and Hutcheson plc* v *Watson* [1995] 1 BCLC 218 discussed in 10.8.3 and *Verderame* v *Commercial Union Assurance Co. plc* [1992] BCLC 793 discussed in 18.4.6.

Generally, a member of a company cannot claim compensation for damage done to the company's property or business. So a member of a company cannot bring legal proceedings to obtain redress for injury done to the company — see 18.3 and 18.4.6.

A company does not hold its property on trust for its members and so they cannot be described as the 'beneficial owners' of its property (*The Maritime Trader* [1981] 2 Lloyd's Rep 153).

Because a company is a person separate from its members, a company can enter into transactions with its members. In particular, money which the members of a company pay to the company for their shares belongs to the company as a separate person (see chapter 10 on restrictions on the return of capital to members), and when a company has paid a dividend to its members the money paid no longer belongs to the company as a separate person (see per Cotton LJ in *Re Exchange Banking Co., Flitcroft's Case* (1882) 21 ChD 519 at p. 536 where his lordship summarised the position by saying that: 'The corporation is not a mere aggregate of shareholders'). In *Wurzel* v *Houghton Main Home Delivery Service Ltd* [1937] 1 KB 380 a vehicle owned by the defendant company was used to deliver coal to its members. The members paid delivery charges to the company. It was held that the vehicle was used for the carriage of goods for hire or reward, which went beyond the use allowed for the vehicle under the statutory scheme then in force for licensing road haulage.

Similarly, a company can employ one of its members under a contract of service. In *Lee* v *Lee's Air Farming Ltd* [1961] AC 12, PC, the company employed Mr Lee who owned 2,999 of the company's 3,000 shares, was its only director and had been appointed 'governing director' for life. Mr Lee was killed in the course of his work for the company. The company's insurers alleged that there was no contract of service so that no claim could be made under legislation which made employers liable to pay compensation for accidental personal injury suffered by their employees at work. The insurers said that it was impossible for Mr Lee, as the director of the company, to make, on its behalf, a contract with himself. But Lord Morris of Borth-y-Gest said, at p. 26:

In their lordships' view it is a logical consequence of the decision in *Salomon's* case that one person may function in dual capacities. There is no reason, therefore, to deny the possibility of a contractual relationship being created as between the deceased and the company.

The Privy Council also rejected the insurers' argument that Mr Lee as governing director could not give orders to himself as employee. Lord Morris said, at p. 30:

There appears to be no greater difficulty in holding that a man acting in one capacity can give orders to himself in another capacity than there is in holding that a man acting in one capacity can make a contract with himself in another capacity.

See also *Secretary of State for Trade and Industry* v *Bottrill* [1998] ICR 564.

In *Farrar* v *Farrars Ltd* (1888) 40 ChD 395, CA, three individuals were joint mortgagees of a stone quarry. When the interest on the mortgage debt was not paid they decided to exercise their power of sale. They sold the quarry to Farrars Ltd, a company in which two of them held shares. The mortgagors asked for the sale to be rescinded but the court refused. Lindley LJ explained, at pp. 409–10:

It is perfectly well settled that a mortgagee with a power of sale cannot sell to himself either alone or with others, nor to a trustee for himself. . . . A sale by a person to himself is no sale at all. . . .

A sale by a person to a corporation of which he is a member is not, either in form or in substance, a sale by a person to himself. To hold that it is, would be to ignore the principle which lies at the root of the legal idea of a corporate body, and that idea is that the corporate body is distinct from the persons composing it.

(A mortgagee exercising a power of sale does have a duty to take reasonable precautions to obtain the best price reasonably obtainable at the time of sale: the mortgagees in *Farrar* v *Farrars Ltd* had complied with this duty, but in the similar case of *Tse Kwong Lam* v *Wong Chit Sen* [1983] 1 WLR 1349, PC, the mortgagee failed to prove he had discharged the duty, and damages were awarded to the mortgagor. The principle of *Farrar* v *Farrars Ltd* does not apply if the purchasing company is found to be in fact the agent of the mortgagee: *Hotel Terrigal Pty Ltd* v *Latec Investments Ltd (No. 2)* [1969] 1 NSWR 676, affirmed on this point sub nom. *Latec Investments Ltd* v *Hotel Terrigal Pty Ltd* (1965) 113 CLR 265.)

In *Re Lewis's will trusts* [1985] 1 WLR 102, Mr Tudor Rhys Lewis had made a will dated 11 August 1964 by which he gave 'my freehold farm and premises, known as Talygarn, Pontyclun . . . to my son'. However, since January 1961 the farm had actually been owned by G.R. Lewis (Talygarn) Ltd in which Mr Lewis had a majority shareholding. On his death in 1978, Mr Lewis owned 750 of the 1,000 shares in the company; the remainder were owned by the son to whom the will gave the farm and the son's wife. As Mr Lewis did not own the farm at his death it was not given by his will and it was held that the statement in the will could not be taken as referring to Mr Lewis's shares in the company. Those shares were therefore to be divided between Mr Lewis's son and daughter under the rules on intestate succession.

The Australian case of *Re Noel Tedman Holdings Pty Ltd* [1967] QdR 561 is a striking illustration of the consequences of separate personality. Noel Tedman and his wife were the sole shareholders and directors of two companies. They were both killed as a result of a road traffic accident. However, their deaths did not cause the termination of their companies' legal existence. The companies continued as owners of property and parties to uncompleted contracts. The personal representatives of the deceased shareholders sought the court's assistance to enable them to appoint new directors of the companies so as to realise their property for the benefit of the deceaseds' estates. (The problem in the case and the solution found by the court depended on the special wording of the articles of the companies and will not be of general application.)

Of course, if a company whose entire membership has died has no assets worth bothering about, or there are no personal representatives to take the necessary action, then the company may itself become defunct and will eventually be dissolved by the registrar striking it off the register under CA 1985, s. 652 (see 20.14.2.4).

Persons are entitled to incorporate companies for the purpose of separating their business affairs from their personal affairs or for the purpose of separating the affairs of one part of a business from another part. In doing so they are relying on the separate personalities of the companies they incorporate and this separate personality is respected by the courts, even if it is to the detriment of the incorporators. For example, in *Sociedade Nacional de Combustiveis de Angola UEE* v *Lundqvist* [1991] 2 QB 310, the plaintiffs in an action against Mr Lundqvist had obtained a court order requiring a Liberian company, which was controlled by and was the employer of Mr Lundqvist, to give details of Mr Lundqvist's assets so that the plaintiffs could check that he complied with a *Mareva* injunction they had obtained against him. The order requiring this information nominated Mr Lundqvist to give it on behalf of his company, but Mr Lundqvist claimed that the information would incriminate him, and that he should be excused from giving it. The Court of Appeal, however, observed that the order should be amended by nominating someone else to give the information on behalf of the company. In the similar case of *Tate Access Floors Inc.* v *Boswell* [1991] Ch 512, Browne-Wilkinson V-C said, at p. 531:

> If people choose to conduct their affairs through the medium of corporations, they are taking advantage of the fact that in law those corporations are separate legal entities, whose property and actions are in law not the property or actions of their incorporators or controlling shareholders. In my judgment controlling shareholders cannot, for all purposes beneficial to them, insist on the separate identity of such corporations but then be heard to say the contrary when discovery is sought against such corporations.

5.2.2   Ignoring corporate personality

5.2.2.1   Introduction

Salomon v *A. Salomon & Co. Ltd* [1897] AC 22 is a cornerstone of English company law. Lord Templeman, speaking extra-curially, has described it as an 'unyielding rock' ('Forty years on' (1990) 11 Co Law 10). It shows that the most important characteristic of a registered company is that it is both an association of its members and a person separate from its members. As explained in 0.1.1 this separate personality is a consequence of the fact that, by CA 1985, s. 13, a registered company is defined to be a body corporate. A registered company acquires its separate personality on incorporation by registration under the Companies Act and all that is necessary to achieve this is to comply with the *formal* requirements of the Act. The motives of the persons who incorporate the company are irrelevant (see the passage in the judgment of Lord Halsbury LC in *Salomon's* case quoted in 5.2.1; see also *Princess of Reuss* v *Bos* (1871) LR 5 HL 176). It may be that when Parliament first provided for incorporation of companies by registration in 1844 it intended the procedure to be used only by entrepreneurs inviting numerous investors to join them in enterprise to increase the prosperity of the nation (see 1.3.3.2). But there is no provision to that effect in the Companies Act 1985. Accordingly, as a matter of statutory construction, it is literally true that *any* person — natural or legal — may, for a lawful purpose, register a limited company (CA 1985, s. 1(3A) inserted by SI 1992 No. 1699) which, on registration, will be incorporated (s. 13) and so have a separate legal personality. Moreover, the members of the company have limited liability (s. 13(4) and IA 1986, s. 74, discussed in 1.3.2). *Salomon's* case showed that incorporation, separate personality and limited liability are available to all, for any legal purpose. Ingenious people have discovered that companies can be used as vehicles for an enormous variety of transactions and schemes.

Some people have misgivings about this situation. They might agree with a famous description of *Salomon's* case as a 'calamitous decision' (O. Kahn-Freund, 'Some reflections on company law reform' (1944) 7 MLR 54).

The enormous practical advantage of the existence of the separate personality of a company is that the company as a separate person can be put into legal relationships, for example, as a party to contracts or as the owner of property, and it is the company as a separate person, not the members, that has the rights and obligations involved in the legal relationships to which it is a party. A company as a person separate from its members requires human agents to decide what voluntary legal relationships it is to enter into and to perform any physical acts necessary to enter into those relationships, but it is the company as a separate person that has the rights and duties of those relationships, not the humans who established them.

People sometimes dislike the results of confining the rights and especially the obligations of a company's legal relationships to the company as a separate person, and they want the rights or obligations to be transferred to the members, or perhaps to directors or other persons connected with the company. In effect they want to ignore the artificial separate personality of a company, at least in certain circumstances. There are legal principles which can be used to transfer a natural person's rights and obligations to another person in appropriate circumstances, and these can be applied to companies, recognising, not ignoring their separate personality. For example, a company could be treated as having entered into a legal relationship as an agent for another person so that the other person is liable as principal under the usual rules of agency law (see 5.2.2.3). A court may recognise that a relationship in which a company is a party is a sham for which the court may substitute what it finds to be the true relationship (see 5.2.2.4). These common law doctrines are not specific to companies but may be applied to them. Parliament may be persuaded to enact a statute transferring the rights or liabilities of a company to some other person in circumstances defined in the statute (see 5.2.2.2).

The interesting question is whether there is a common law doctrine specific to companies which would enable companies' rights or liabilities to be transferred to other persons. In other words, are there special characteristics of companies which require transfer of their rights or obligations and which do not arise in relation to natural persons? Some cases suggest that there is such a special doctrine, notably *DHN Food Distributors Ltd* v *Tower Hamlets London Borough Council* [1976] 1 WLR 852, in which land owned by a company was treated as owned by its parent company and which is discussed in 5.2.2.8. Yet when the Court of Appeal was asked in *Adams* v *Cape Industries plc* [1990] Ch 433 to rule that an English company was present in the jurisdiction of a Texas court because one of its subsidiaries had been present (so that the English company would be liable for a judgment given against the subsidiary), the Court of Appeal refused, saying, at p. 536:

> . . . save in cases which turn on the wording of particular statutes or contracts, the court is not free to disregard the principle of *Salomon* v *A. Salomon & Co. Ltd* merely because it considers that justice so requires.

Whether or not there is a doctrine which enables a company's rights or liabilities to be taken away from it, there is a common law doctrine of company law which attributes to a company the knowledge or state of mind of individuals identified with it. This overcomes the deficiency in the separate personality of a company that it does not have thought. The identification doctrine is discussed in 19.8.

People who propose more freedom for the courts to ignore corporate separate personality claim that the way the law treats separate personality already amounts to an unacknowledged practice of ignoring it. They argue that ascribing a company's rights and/or liabilities to another person is just one example of disregarding what they call the 'veil' of incorporation, and that this veil is disregarded in many other ways, which points to the existence of a specific company-law doctrine which could be used in particular to justify ascribing a company's rights and/or liabilities to another person. This approach is particularly associated with Professor Gower (see *Gower's Principles of Modern Company Law,* 6th ed., ch. 8) and with Lord Denning. See also A. Samuels, 'Lifting the veil' [1964] JBL 107 and S. Ottolenghi, 'From peeping behind the corporate veil, to ignoring it completely' (1990) 53 MLR 338. But an argument along these lines was rejected in the Ontario Court in *Transamerica Life Insurance Co. of Canada* v *Canada Life Assurance Co.* (1996) 28 OR (3d) 423, in which Sharpe J said, at p. 433:

> The cases and authorities already cited indicate that it will be difficult to define precisely when the corporate veil is to be lifted, but that lack of a precise test does not mean that a court is free to act as it pleases on some loosely defined 'just and equitable' standard.

See further C.M. Schmitthoff, *'Salomon* in the shadow' [1976] JBL 305; M.A. Pickering, 'The company as a separate entity' (1968) 31 MLR 481.

The use of the vague metaphor of the 'veil' makes it difficult to discover what the true issues are, and the subject is further complicated by the various imprecise terms used, such as 'piercing', 'lifting' or 'going behind' the veil. Some clarification was attempted by Staughton LJ in *Atlas Maritime Co. SA* v *Avalon Maritime Ltd (No. 1)* [1991] 4 All ER 769, saying, at p. 779:

> To *pierce* the corporate veil is an expression that I would reserve for treating the rights or liabilities or activities of a company as the rights or liabilities or activities of its shareholders. To *lift* the corporate veil or *look behind* it, on the other hand, should mean to have regard to the shareholding in a company for some legal purpose.

Treating the rights or liabilities or activities of a company as those of its shareholders (or of anyone else) — 'piercing the veil' in Staughton LJ's terminology — certainly ignores corporate separate personality and Lord Russell of Killowen had this to say about it in *EBM Co. Ltd* v *Dominion Bank* [1937] 3 All ER 555, PC, at pp. 564–5 :

> Their lordships [of the Privy Council] believe it to be of supreme importance that the distinction should be clearly marked, observed and maintained between an incorporated company's legal entity and its actions, assets, rights and liabilities on the one hand, and the individual shareholders and their actions, assets, rights and liabilities on the other hand.

Taking account of a company's membership when deciding its rights and liabilities — what Staughton LJ called 'lifting' or 'looking behind' the corporate veil — is not uncommon. Some of the cases are discussed in 5.2.2.5, 5.2.2.6 and 5.2.2.7. It is submitted that taking account of a company's membership has never been forbidden by company law and does not amount to ignoring corporate separate personality in the sense of treating a company's rights or liabilities as belonging to others, and the cases are not precedents for such treatment.

Canadian courts, at least, have taken the view that the examples of ignoring a company's corporate veil never involve treating the incorporation of the company as a nullity: the veil is ignored only for a specific purpose. As the Saskatchewan Court of Appeal said in *Nedco Ltd* v *Clark* (1973) 43 DLR (3d) 714 at p. 721: '. . . the fact that the court does lift the corporate veil for a specific purpose in no way destroys the recognition of the corporation as an independent and autonomous entity for all other purposes'. See also per Rand J in *Aluminum Co. of Canada Ltd* v *Toronto* [1944] 3 DLR 609 at p. 614; per Reed J in *Alberta Gas Ethylene Co. Ltd* v *Minister of National Revenue* (1988) 24 FTR 309 at p. 314.

Arguments over 'disregarding the veil' have raged throughout the common law world for the whole of the 20th century. It would be impossible to reconcile the hundreds of cases thought to be relevant to the argument or the dozens of academic opinions. Cases are decided by judges who adopt different attitudes to the question and rarely, if ever, state what their general theory of corporate personality is.

The different judicial approaches may be illustrated by two quotations from the presidents (both now retired) of the appeal courts in England and New Zealand. In *Littlewoods Mail Order Stores Ltd* v *Commissioners of Inland Revenue* [1969] 1 WLR 1241, CA, Lord Denning MR said, at p. 1254, that, 'The doctrine laid down in *Salomon* v *A. Salomon & Co. Ltd* has to be watched very carefully'. In *Re Securitibank Ltd (No. 2)* [1978] 2 NZLR 136, Richmond P responded, at p. 159: 'For myself, and with all respect, I would rather approach the question the other way round, that is to say on the basis that any suggested departure from the doctrine laid down in *Salomon* v *A. Salomon & Co. Ltd* should be watched very carefully'.

Sometimes, a court, on being invited to disregard the separate personality of a company, enumerates circumstances in which it says this may be done and then decides that the case before it does not fall within those circumstances (see, e.g., *Pioneer Laundry and Dry Cleaners Ltd* v *Minister of National Revenue* [1940] AC 127, PC; *Re Kinookimaw Beach Association* (1979) 102 DLR (3d) 333, Saskatchewan CA; *Pioneer Concrete Services Ltd* v *Yelnah Pty Ltd* (1986) 5 NSWLR 254; *Allarco Group Ltd* v *Suncor Inc. Resources Group, Oil Sands Division* [1987] 5 WWR 159, Alberta CA; *Sharrment Pty Ltd* v *Official Trustee in Bankruptcy* (1988) 82 ALR 530, Federal Court of Australia). Unfortunately the lists of circumstances provided by courts vary considerably (probably reflecting differences of view on what constitutes disregarding separate personality) and, of course, a court arguing in this way is primarily concerned with circumstances relevant to the case before it and not with producing a general theory.

In *Woolfson* v *Strathclyde Regional Council* 1978 SC (HL) 90, at p. 96, Lord Keith of Kinkel referred to 'the principle that it is appropriate to pierce the corporate veil only where special circumstances exist indicating that is a mere façade concealing the true facts'. Although this dictum is of undeniably high authority, his lordship did not explain what he meant by piercing the corporate veil or consider many previous cases, so the scope of the principle enunciated by his lordship is not clear.

In *Adams* v *Cape Industries plc* [1990] Ch 433, the Court of Appeal said, at p. 543:

From the authorities cited to us we are left with rather sparse guidance as to the principles which should guide the court in determining whether or not the arrangements of a corporate group involve a façade within the meaning of that word as used by the House of Lords in *Woolfson* v *Strathclyde Regional Council*. We will not attempt a comprehensive definition of those principles.

The practical problem for a lawyer is to discover whether what he or she wants the court to do would be regarded by the court as inconsistent with the principle of separate personality and so an attempt to disregard the corporate veil. If the court will regard it as disregarding the veil, the lawyer must then discover the conditions on which the court will disregard the veil and try to establish that his or her case satisfies those conditions. The wider the court's view of the effect of separate personality and of the occurrence of disregarding the veil, the more likely it is to accept that disregarding the veil is normal practice. A court taking a narrow view will think that disregarding the veil hardly ever occurs and so is hardly ever justified.

In both *Littlewoods Mail Order Stores Ltd* v *Commissioners of Inland Revenue* and *Wallersteiner* v *Moir* [1974] 1 WLR 991, Lord Denning MR thought that disregarding the veil was required to deal with those cases. However, it is not clear exactly what his lordship's veil disregarding was actually going to do, and in both cases the other members of the Court of Appeal said that veil disregarding was not required. It is a mark of the change in judicial attitudes in England that in 1989, in *Adams* v *Cape Industries plc* [1990] Ch 433, the Court of Appeal, at p. 543, said that Lord Denning's dicta in *Littlewoods Mail Order Stores Ltd* v *Commissioners of Inland Revenue* and *Wallersteiner* v *Moir* could provide little support for a plaintiff's claim to have the veil disregarded. In *Amalgamated Investment and Property Co. Ltd* v *Texas Commerce International Bank Ltd* [1982] QB 84, Lord Denning MR was again alone among the members of the Court of Appeal in believing that the case before them could be solved by treating money owed to one company as being owed to its parent company, which would be regarded by anyone as ignoring corporate personality.

In cases such as the *Littlewoods* case, which is discussed in 5.2.2.5, Lord Denning adopted the attractively simple approach of ignoring inconvenient corporate separate personality whereas the other members of the court found ways round it.

Lord Denning's view was that the separate personality of a company could be ignored if it was the 'puppet' of another person (*Littlewoods Mail Order Stores Ltd* v *Commissioners of Inland Revenue* [1969] 1 WLR 1241 at p. 1254; *Wallersteiner* v *Moir* [1974] 1 WLR 991 at p. 1013). Earlier, Rand J in the Supreme Court of Canada in *Aluminum Co. of Canada Ltd* v *Toronto* [1944] 3 DLR 609 at p. 614 had announced that the condition for treating the business of a subsidiary as the business of its parent company when taxing the parent company's business income was that the subsidiary was the puppet of the holding company (which in the case then before the court it was not). 'Puppet' seems to mean no more than that the company is under the other person's control. Other epithets used are that the company is the controller's 'clone' (*R* v *MerBan Capital Corporation Ltd* [1985] 1 CTC 1 at p. 4) or that the controller is the company's 'alter ego' (*Yukong Line Ltd* v *Rendsburg Investments Corporation (No. 2)* [1998] 1 WLR 294 at p. 299). The rejection of Lord Denning's view by the Court of Appeal in *Adams* v *Cape Industries plc* signals that it cannot now be argued that a company's separate personality should be ignored simply because it is controlled by another person (*W.D. Latimer Co.* v *Dijon Investments Ltd* (1992) 12 OR (3d) 415). The fact that a company is controlled by another person is also not enough to make it that other person's agent (see 5.2.2.3).

For an interesting recent discussion by a retired senior New Zealand judge see Lord Cooke of Thorndon's lecture, 'A real thing' in *Turning Points of the Common Law* (London: Sweet & Maxwell, 1997) and its sequel 'Corporate identity' (1998) 16 C & SLJ 160.

5.2.2.2   Statutory provisions
In *Dimbleby & Sons Ltd* v *National Union of Journalists* [1984] 1 WLR 427, HL, Lord Diplock said, at p. 435:

> The 'corporate veil' in the case of companies incorporated under the Companies Act is drawn by statute and it can be pierced by some other statute if such other statute so provides; but, in view of its *raison d'être* and its consistent recognition by the courts since *Salomon* v *A. Salomon & Co. Ltd* [1897] AC 22, one would expect that any parliamentary intention to pierce the corporate veil would be expressed in clear and unequivocal language. I do not wholly exclude the possibility that even in the absence of express words stating that in specified circumstances one company, although separately incorporated, is to be treated as sharing the same legal personality of another, a purposive construction of the statute may nevertheless lead inexorably to the conclusion that such must have been the intention of Parliament.

In *Dimbleby & Sons Ltd* v *National Union of Journalists* the House of Lords refused to disregard the separate personality of two wholly owned subsidiaries of a holding company. Both subsidiaries had the same directors and the same management. One subsidiary was an employer that was party to a trade dispute with the National Union of Journalists. The House of Lords held that the other subsidiary was not a party to the trade dispute for the purposes of the Employment Act 1980, s. 17(3), so that in the circumstances the union could not have immunity from an action for damages in tort in respect of industrial action taken against that other subsidiary. Lord Diplock, with whom the other Law Lords agreed, observed that the next subsection of the Act, s. 17(4), specifically dealt with a situation in which action was taken against a company in the same group as a party to a dispute so that Parliament must be presumed to have definitely excluded such a situation from s. 17(3). (The law on immunity from suit in relation to industrial action has since been changed and the Employment Act 1980, s. 17, has been repealed.)

Since the separate legal personality of a company arises only when the formal requirements of the Companies Act are complied with, it is not perhaps surprising that the legislature should wish to impose sanctions, including personal liability, on persons in breach of certain fundamental requirements. For example, under CA 1985, s. 24 as amended by SI 1992 No. 1699, if a company other than a private company limited by shares or by guarantee carries on business for more than six months without having at least two members, the member who knowingly carried on business in these circumstances becomes jointly and severally liable with the company for the payment of the company's debts contracted at any time after the six-month period. This can hardly be regarded as a denial of a corporate personality when the company itself remains liable for its debts (see 1.3.2.6). It is suggested that the same is true of IA 1986, s. 213, which imposes personal liability on any person (not just a member) who knowingly carries on a company's business with intent to defraud creditors or for any other fraudulent purpose (see 20.10). The legislature is here not allowing the fiction created by the Companies Act to be used as a vehicle of fraud, but it is significant that the liability is to make a payment *to the company,* which is hardly a denial of the company's separate personality. The same applies to IA 1986, s. 214 (liability of directors for wrongful trading).

One of the consequences of a separate legal personality is that the company can only identify itself to the outside world by its name. Parliament therefore imposes stringent requirements relating to the use of the company's name. If an officer of the company or any other person enters into a transaction and does not adequately identify the company in any bill of exchange, promissory note, cheque or order for money or goods, that officer or person is personally liable *unless it is duly paid by the company* (CA 1985, s. 349(4); see 4.5.1). Again, it is submitted that this cannot amount to a denial of or encroachment on corporate personality.

A public company may not do business or exercise any borrowing powers unless it has complied with the requirements as to share capital (see CA 1985, s. 117, discussed in 6.1.1). Since the power to trade or borrow in this situation is denied and is regarded by Parliament as a fundamental requirement of company law, it is not surprising that personal liability should be imposed on the directors for any loss or damage suffered by a third party who has entered into a transaction with a company which is in contravention of the provision (CA 1985, s. 117(8)). This liability is only imposed, however, if the company itself fails to comply with its obligations under the transaction, and it is difficult to see how this provision affects the principle of corporate personality.

It is submitted that the provisions just discussed, whilst undoubtedly imposing personal liability on shareholders, directors and others who are responsible for breach of the formal requirements consequent upon incorporation, do not represent a desire on the part of the legislature to disregard the company's separate personality, but merely impose *additional* liability on those responsible for *the expression of* the corporate personality in these circumstances.

5.2.2.3 Agency

If the legal relationship of agency exists between two persons, called the principal and the agent, then the principal is responsible for whatever the agent does within the scope of the agency. Whether one person is an agent of another is a question of fact, and agency can be inferred from the surrounding circumstances, though it can only be established by the consent of the principal and the agent (*Garnac Grain Co. Inc.* v *H.M.F. Faure & Fairclough Ltd* [1968] AC 1130). *Salomon* v *A. Salomon & Co. Ltd* [1897] AC 22 established that the circumstance that a person is a member of a company does not in itself make the company an agent of that person (and see per Viscount Cave LC in *Gas Lighting Improvement Co. Ltd* v *Commissioners of Inland Revenue* [1923] AC 723 at p. 732). Agency cannot be inferred from the control exercisable by the members over the company — either by virtue of their votes in general meeting or because they are also directors — or from the fact that the sole objective of the company is to benefit the members (per Tomlin J in *British Thomson-Houston Co. Ltd* v *Sterling Accessories Ltd* [1924] 2 Ch 33 at p. 38; Kerr LJ in *J.H. Rayner (Mincing Lane) Ltd* v *Department of Trade & Industry* [1989] Ch 72, CA, at pp. 188–9; [1990] 2 AC 418, HL, per Lord Oliver of Aylmerton at p. 515). Usually the fact that the members of a company do not intend that it is to be their agent is sufficient to show that no agency relationship exists, because there was no consent to one being created (*Yukong Line Ltd* v *Rendsburg Investments Corporation (No. 2)* [1998] 1 WLR 294 at p. 304). In practice it is very unlikely that a company will be found to be the agent of its members, see *Yukong Line Ltd* v *Rendsburg Investments Corporation (No. 2)* and *Bank of Montreal* v *Canadian Westgrowth Ltd* (1990) 72 Alta LR (2d) 319, which is discussed in 5.2.2.10.

The characteristic feature of agency is that the agent has authority or capacity to create legal relations between the principal and third parties. In order to find that a company is the agent of one or more of its members, this authority or capacity must be present. In practice, though, the whole object of creating a company to carry on a business is so that the business will be the company's business and not the members' business. It will be very rare to find that members have set up a company to run a business which they have retained ownership of, but this was what happened in *Smith, Stone & Knight Ltd* v *Birmingham Corporation* [1939] 4 All ER 116. Smith, Stone & Knight Ltd carried on a business manufacturing paper.

It acquired from a partnership a business of dealing in waste paper. It incorporated a wholly owned subsidiary company called Birmingham Waste Co. Ltd, which nominally operated the waste-paper business, but it never actually transferred ownership of the waste-paper business to that subsidiary, and it retained ownership of the land on which the waste-paper business was operated. Atkinson J found that the waste-paper business was still the business of the parent company and that it was operated by the subsidiary as agent of the parent company. Accordingly, on the compulsory purchase of the land on which the waste-paper business was operated, the parent company was entitled to compensation both for the value of the land and for disturbance of the business because it owned both the land and the business. Smith, Stone & Knight Ltd owned 497 of the 502 issued shares of Birmingham Waste Co. Ltd. The other five were held by nominees of Smith, Stone & Knight Ltd. So, unlike the position in *Salomon* v *A. Salomon & Co. Ltd,* Birmingham Waste Co. Ltd was found to be carrying on business as agent of its principal member. The crucial difference is that the business of A. Salomon & Co. Ltd was formally transferred to it by its principal member, Mr Salomon, and so had become the business of the company, whereas the business which Birmingham Waste Co. Ltd operated was never transferred to it and remained the property of its principal member.

For another case in which a wholly owned subsidiary was found to be acting as agent for its parent company, see *Hotel Terrigal Pty Ltd* v *Latec Investments Ltd (No. 2)* [1969] 1 NSWR 676, affirmed on this point sub nom. *Latec Investments Ltd* v *Hotel Terrigal Pty Ltd* (1965) 113 CLR 265.

Because of the surrounding circumstances, a company may be found to be an agent of some person who is not a member of the company. For example, in *William Cory & Son Ltd* v *Dorman Long & Co. Ltd* [1936] 2 All ER 386, a holding company was found to be carrying on a business as agent of its wholly owned subsidiary: the situation was the reverse of that in *Smith, Stone & Knight Ltd's* case in that instead of the company being the agent of its principal member, the principal member was agent of the company.

Deciding who owns a business can be important for tax purposes. Normally, for tax purposes, the business of a company is not the business of its members (*Gramophone & Typewriter Ltd* v *Stanley* [1908] 2 KB 89, CA) or of any person other than the company itself. Therefore, it is the company, not its members or any other person, which is liable to pay tax on the profits of its business (see 5.2.2.3.1). In *Firestone Tyre & Rubber Co. Ltd* v *Lewellin* [1957] 1 WLR 464, the appellant company was the wholly owned subsidiary of a United States company. The appellant company manufactured tyres for sale to distributors in Europe. Its parent company had arranged special contracts with these distributors, and with the appellant company, which were claimed to have the effect that the business of selling tyres to European distributors was not carried on in the United Kingdom and so not subject to United Kingdom tax. It was held, however, that the true effect of the arrangements was that the business was the business of the parent company carried on in the United Kingdom through the appellant company acting as its parent company's agent. Tax on the profits or gains arising through or from the agency was therefore properly assessable and chargeable in the name of the agent (the appellant company) under what is now the Taxes Management Act 1970, s. 79. The agency in this case resulted from the trading arrangements set up by the parent company. Those arrangements would have successfully avoided United Kingdom tax had it not been found, as a fact, that the business was carried on in the United Kingdom.

For a detailed discussion of the taxation of a business run by one person on behalf of another, see R. Flannigan, 'Corporations controlled by shareholders: principals, agents or servants?' (1986–7) 51 Sask L Rev 23.

The problem of treating one company as another's agent frequently arises with parent and subsidiary companies. In *Ebbw Vale Urban District Council* v *South Wales Traffic Area Licensing Authority* [1951] 2 KB 366, Cohen LJ in the Court of Appeal said at p. 370:

> Under the ordinary rules of law, a parent company and a subsidiary company, even a 100 per cent subsidiary company, are distinct legal entities, and in the absence of an agency contract between the two companies one cannot be said to be the agent of the other. That seems to me to be clearly established by *Salomon* v *A. Salomon & Co. Ltd* and by the observations of Tomlin J in *British Thomson-Houston Co. Ltd* v *Sterling Accessories Ltd.*

The reference to 'an agency contract' is unfortunate if by this Cohen LJ intended to say that only an express agency is possible between parent and subsidiary companies, though perhaps this is also implicit in the earlier statement of Atkinson J in *Smith, Stone & Knight Ltd* v *Birmingham Corporation* [1939] 4 All ER 116 at p. 120:

> It is well settled that the mere fact that a man holds all the shares in a company does not make the business carried on by that company his business, nor does it make the company his agents for the carrying on of the business. That proposition is just as true if the shareholder is itself a limited company. It is also well settled that there may be such an arrangement between the shareholders and a company as will constitute the company the shareholders' agent for the purpose of carrying on the business and make the business the business of the shareholders.

Again the word 'arrangement' may suggest an express agency though in fact his lordship found that agency existed in the case without any express agreement. Atkinson J went on to list six points which he saw as relevant to determining whether the business of a subsidiary company was being carried on by the subsidiary or its parent company. In *Yukong Line Ltd* v *Rendsburg Investments Corporation (No. 2)* [1998] 1 WLR 294 Toulson J rejected the submission that these points should determine whether a company is carrying on business as another person's agent. In *Alberta Gas Ethylene Co. Ltd* v *Minister of National Revenue* (1988) 24 FTR 309 Reed J rejected the submission that whenever the six criteria are met the company's separate personality can be ignored.

It is submitted that treating a company as the agent of its controllers is a complete affirmation of the corporate entity principle since the agency relationship demands two legally recognisable parties.

5.2.2.3.1 Note on company taxation   Shareholders complain that if a company pays tax on its profits and the shareholders pay tax when those profits are distributed to them then the profits have been taxed twice and that this is unfair. One way of dealing with shareholders' complaints on this score is to 'impute' (i.e., credit) the tax paid by a company on its profits to the company's shareholders. It would be very difficult to achieve this precisely in practice: a company is required to pay tax on all its profits for a year but does not necessarily distribute them all to its shareholders in that year; companies and their shareholders are taxed in respect of different accounting periods and pay their taxes at different times — it would be very difficult to keep track of the amounts involved so as to attribute exactly to its shareholders the tax paid by a company.

The compromise imputation system in UK taxation is that when a company pays a dividend to a shareholder, the shareholder is deemed for taxation purposes to receive a tax credit with a value linked to the value of the dividend (Income and Corporation Taxes Act

1988, s. 231). This tax credit can be offset against the shareholder's tax bill. The company is, by the Income and Corporation Taxes Act 1988, s. 14, made responsible for paying to the Inland Revenue a sum (known as 'advance corporation tax') equal to the amount of the tax credits on its dividends (though it may set off any tax credits it has itself obtained from dividends paid to it by other companies), and this sum is treated as a prepayment of the company's own tax bill for the accounting period in which the distribution was made (s. 239). In this system the amount of tax credited to the shareholders is not actually determined by the tax payable by the company on the profits out of which the dividend is paid. However, it is normally desirable for a company's taxable profits for an accounting period to be such that its tax bill is at least equal to the advance corporation tax it has already paid for that period. A tax credit received by a shareholder counts as part of the shareholder's income for tax purposes (Income and Corporation Taxes Act 1988, s. 20(1)): the amount of the tax credit is calculated so that it is equal to the lower-rate income tax payable on the sum of the tax credit plus the dividend actually paid. The Finance Act 1998, s. 31, abolishes advance corporation tax, which will not be payable on distributions made on or after 6 April 1999.

5.2.2.4 Sham or pretence; evading enforcement of existing rights

In a number of cases a person subject to a legal obligation has employed a company to evade that obligation and the court has ordered both the person and the company to comply with the obligation, describing the company as a 'sham' (usually in conjunction with other terms such as 'cloak' or 'mask'). The 'sham' epithet comes from the words of Lindley LJ in a case not involving a company, *Smith v Hancock* [1894] 2 Ch 377. In that case Mr Thomas Prosperous Hancock had sold his grocery shop, trading as 'T.P. Hancock', to Mr Smith and had promised not to carry on another grocery business within five miles of the shop for the next 10 years. Seven years later his wife and her nephew opened a grocery shop 200 yards away under the style 'Mrs T.P. Hancock' and using the goodwill attached to Hancock's name. The Court of Appeal by a majority found that this was not a breach of the covenant but Lindley LJ said, at p. 385:

> If the evidence admitted of the conclusion that what was being done was a mere cloak or sham, and that in truth the business was being carried on by the wife and [the nephew] for [Mr Hancock], or by [Mr Hancock] through his wife for [the nephew], I certainly should not hesitate to draw that conclusion, and to grant the plaintiff relief accordingly.

This was applied in *Gilford Motor Co. Ltd v Horne* [1933] Ch 935, in which the defendant, Mr E.B. Horne, attempted to evade a covenant not to compete with the plaintiff company by getting his wife, J.M. Horne, to form a company, J.M. Horne & Co. Ltd, which carried on business in competition with the plaintiff. Lord Hanworth MR said, at p. 956:

> I am quite satisfied that this company was formed as a device, a strategem, in order to mask the effective carrying on of a business of Mr E.B. Horne. The purpose of it was to try to enable him, under what is a cloak or a sham, to engage in business which, on consideration of the agreement which had been sent to him just about seven days before the company was incorporated, was a business in respect of which he had a fear that the plaintiffs might intervene and object.

The court restrained both Mr Horne and the company from enticing away the plaintiff's customers.

In *Jones* v *Lipman* [1962] 1 WLR 832, Lipman sold land to Jones, but before completion of the contract for sale sold the land to a company of which he and a nominee were the sole shareholders and directors. Russell J ordered specific performance of the contract for sale against Lipman and the company. It was accepted that an order for specific performance could be made against Lipman because he was in effective control of the property (see 5.2.2.5) but Russell J went on to say, perhaps with unneccessary mysticism, that:

> The defendant company is the creature of the first defendant, a device and a sham, a mask which he holds before his face in an attempt to avoid recognition by the eye of equity.

For another example see *Albert Locke (1940) Ltd* v *Winsford Urban District Council* (1973) 71 LGR 308.

It is clearly irrelevant that the entities used to evade the obligations in these cases were companies. In *Gilford Motor Co. Ltd* v *Horne*, for example, the court would have come to exactly the same conclusion if the competing business had been in the name of Mrs Horne personally rather than in the name of J.M. Horne & Co. Ltd. So these cases do not represent a special doctrine of company law. In both *Gilford Motor Co. Ltd* v *Horne* and *Jones* v *Lipman* the court made orders against both the individual defendant and the company, thus recognising rather than ignoring the company's separate personality.

In other cases the courts have used the term 'sham' (without accompanying 'cloak', 'mask', etc.) to describe an arrangement made by persons which the court decides to ignore and for which it substitutes what it considers to be the true arrangement. If this concept of sham were not controlled, it could be used by a court to label any arrangement of which it disapproved so that it could substitute one which it did like. In the context of company law it could be used to disregard corporate separate personality whenever the court wanted to do so. But the concept of sham (which is used in many legal contexts other than company law) has been controlled by the generally accepted definition given by Diplock LJ in *Snook* v *London & West Riding Investments Ltd* [1967] 2 QB 786 at p. 802:

> . . . it means acts done or documents executed by the parties to the 'sham' which are intended by them to give to third parties or to the court the appearance of creating between the parties legal rights and obligations different from the actual legal rights and obligations (if any) which the parties intend to create. . . . for acts or documents to be a 'sham', . . . all the parties thereto must have a common intention that the acts or documents are not to create the legal rights and obligations which they give the appearance of creating.

The definition stresses that there must be deliberate dissemblance which causes the court to ignore what would otherwise be an effective transaction. This is different from cases in which a court finds that parties to a transaction have given it the wrong label, for example, calling a lease a licence so as to deny a party statutory rights available to lessors but not licensees, or calling a floating charge a fixed charge so as to avoid responsibility for preferential debts. Although mislabelling may well involve deception the court does not have to make a moral judgment but can simply declare that the transaction was not legally capable of doing what the parties claimed it did. In a sham case the court is faced with a legally effective arrangement and must find impropriety to justify ignoring it. N. Lee, 'The concept of sham: a fiction or reality' (1996) 47 NILQ 377 thinks that Diplock LJ's definition is too restrictive and suggests that courts ought to be freer to find that transactions of which they disapprove are shams.

In *Hilton* v *Plustitle Ltd* [1989] 1 WLR 149 Miss Rose wanted a flat to live in. Mr Hilton owned a flat but would only let it to a company because a company would not be entitled to protection under the Rent Act 1977. Miss Rose acquired a shelf company, Plustitle Ltd, which rented the flat from Mr Hilton under an agreement which gave Plustitle Ltd the right to nominate the occupiers of the property. Miss Rose contended that this was a sham and that the lease was truly between her and Mr Hilton. The court concluded that, on the evidence, both parties' clear intention, with all knowledge of what it involved, was that the flat should be let to a company and not Miss Rose personally. There was no reason why public policy should override the transaction which was deliberately intended to avoid, but not evade, the Rent Act. In *Kaye* v *Massbetter Ltd* (1990) 62 P & CR 558, Lord Donaldson of Lymington MR compared the use of company lets to avoid the Rent Act with the 19th-century invention of hire-purchase to avoid statutory controls on moneylending.

Professor Schmitthoff, '*Salomon* in the shadow' [1976] JBL 305, has said that the 'sham' cases discussed in this section are characterised by 'abuse of the corporate form'. The fact that a company has been formed or used primarily to evade an existing liability or defeat the application of the law to existing rights justifies calling the company a sham and ignoring its separate personality. Schmitthoff said, at p. 311:

> In practice, it is easier to escape from the strict interpretation of the rule in *Salomon* by the agency route than by relying on abuse of the corporate form. The latter argument always implies a degree of impropriety, though not necessarily fraud, while the former argument does not imply opprobrious conduct. The former argument is thus more readily available than the latter. Only in exceptional cases the argument based on abuse of the corporate form will succeed.

In *Adams* v *Cape Industries plc* [1990] Ch 433, counsel for the plaintiffs submitted:

> that the court will lift the corporate veil where a defendant by the device of a corporate structure attempts to evade (i) limitations imposed on his conduct by law; (ii) such rights of relief against him as third parties already possess.

The Court of Appeal was prepared to assume that this was correct (though neither applied in the instant case). It is unfortunate that the statement uses the vague veil metaphor instead of explaining what the court can actually do when a defendant uses a company in the way specified. Nevertheless the summary in this statement of the circumstances in which the court will act appears to be easier to apply than the concept of sham.

The second part of the principle set out in *Adams* v *Cape Industries plc* is shown in operation in cases concerning *Mareva* injunctions. (A *Mareva* injunction prohibits a defendant in legal proceedings from disposing of assets which could be used to meet any award of damages in the proceedings.) To prevent a defendant avoiding the effect of a *Mareva* injunction by putting assets into the ownership of companies, the court will extend the injunction to cover assets owned by companies controlled by the defendant, and will similarly extend the scope of supporting orders for the defendant to disclose information (*Re a Company* [1985] BCLC 333) and for the appointment of a receiver (*International Credit and Investment Co. (Overseas) Ltd* v *Adham* [1998] BCC 134). *Re H (Restraint Order: Realisable Property)* [1996] 2 All ER 391 is a similar case involving seizure of the proceeds of alleged criminal activity.

This principle applies where a plaintiff has a right of action against a defendant, who uses a company to evade the action. Where the plaintiff's right of action is against a company in the first place, the principle cannot be applied to bring into the proceedings a person who controlled the company but is not otherwise liable to the plaintiff. For example, if a company is sued for damages for a wrong it has committed and the plaintiff alleges that the company's controller has deliberately ensured that the company has no money to pay any damages which may be awarded, the court will not make the controller liable for the damages: the wrong was done by the company and only the company can be sued for it (*B.G. Preeco 1 (Pacific Coast) Ltd* v *Bon Street Holdings Ltd* (1989) 60 DLR (4th) 30; *Yukong Line Ltd* v *Rendsburg Investments Corporation (No. 2)* [1998] 1 WLR 294). See also *Ord* v *Belhaven Pubs Ltd* (1998) *The Times*, 7 April 1998, which is discussed in 5.2.2.11. In *W.D. Latimer Co.* v *Dijon Investments Ltd* (1992) 12 OR (3d) 415 the plaintiff stockbrokers sued two companies for the price of shares they had bought in an Ontario public company called Pronto Explorations Ltd. It was alleged that an individual who controlled both defendant companies had effected the purchases in their names in order to evade a duty to report his purchases to the Ontario Securities Commission which arose because he already had a substantial holding of Pronto shares (the British requirements for reporting substantial shareholdings are described in 8.9). It was claimed that because of this the individual should be made liable for the loss which the stockbrokers had incurred. It was held that the individual had not caused the loss and so could not be sued for it.

5.2.2.5   *Control of the company's property*

In some circumstances a court may require a person to deal with property over which that person has control even though that person does not have legal title to it. The fact that the person controls a company which owns the property may be enough to put the property within the person's control.

For example, a person who is a party to legal proceedings may be ordered to produce a relevant document for inspection by another party (an order for 'discovery' of the document) if the person has control over the document despite not having legal title to it. The court may recognise that the requisite degree of control exists where the document belongs to a company controlled by the person against whom discovery is sought: the court may recognise that a company cannot prevent a person who controls it dealing with its documents (*Dallas* v *Dallas* (1960) 24 DLR (2d) 746, British Columbia; *B* v *B* [1978] Fam 181; see further *Lonrho Ltd* v *Shell Petroleum Co. Ltd* [1980] 1 WLR 627, HL, and *Re Tecnion Investments Ltd* [1985] BCLC 434, CA, in which it was found that the requisite degree of control was not present).

Another example is where a court orders specific performance of a contract of sale of property which is controlled by but not owned by the defendant. Again the requisite degree of control may be found where the property is owned by a company controlled by the defendant (*Elliott* v *Pierson* [1948] Ch 452; *Jones* v *Lipman* [1962] 1 WLR 832).

In *Littlewoods Mail Order Stores Ltd* v *Commissioners of Inland Revenue* [1969] 1 WLR 1241 Littlewoods had spent money acquiring a fixed asset (the freehold of its headquarters building) for a wholly owned subsidiary. It claimed that this was a revenue expenditure for the use of property owned by another (and so deductible from income when computing taxable profits) rather than capital to be employed in its trade (which was not deductible), but the Court of Appeal rejected the claim. Sachs LJ said, at p. 1256:

> [The money] was clearly expended for the purpose of acquiring a capital asset which happened to have been put into the ownership of [the subsidiary]. It is thus in truth expenditure of a capital nature to secure the advantage of an enduring benefit.

Karminski LJ said, at p. 1256:

It is necessary . . . to ask . . . who really benefited from getting hold of the freehold. To that in my view there can be only one answer, that it is Littlewoods and not [the subsidiary].

Both judges clearly assumed that the parent company would use its control over the subsidiary to ensure that the freehold was held for its benefit. Lord Denning MR said, at p. 1254, that he declined to treat the subsidiary as 'a separate and independent entity' and held that Littlewoods had acquired the freehold. The majority of the court, though, showed that it was unnecessary to take the drastic step of depriving the subsidiary of its property and giving that property to its parent: it was sufficient to accept that buying a capital asset for another to be held for one's own benefit amounted to non-deductible capital expenditure. Similarly in *R v MerBan Capital Corporation Ltd* [1985] 1 CTC 1 a company paid interest on a loan to its wholly owned subsidiary which was made so that the subsidiary could acquire assets and it was held that the interest could be deducted from the parent company's taxable income because it was paid for the holding company's business purposes. The fact that the revenue authorities ended up gaining tax in *Littlewoods Mail Order Stores Ltd* v *Commissioners of Inland Revenue* and losing it in *R v MerBan Capital Corporation Ltd* illustrates that the distinction between income and capital is of crucial importance for the purposes of income tax, which taxes one but not the other.

In *Revlon Inc. v Cripps and Lee Ltd* [1980] FSR 85, Revlon Inc. was the American parent of an international group of companies. Trade marks used by the companies had been assigned to Revlon Suisse SA, which was the wholly owned subsidiary of a wholly owned subsidiary of Revlon Inc. Under United Kingdom trade marks legislation Revlon Suisse was registered in the UK as the 'proprietor' of a trade mark and claimed that the defendant had infringed it by bringing into the UK goods to which that mark had been applied by Revlon Inc. in the USA. Buckley LJ, at p. 107, said that Revlon Suisse held the trade marks for the purposes of the trade carried on by companies in the group and so had impliedly consented to Revlon Inc.'s use of the mark on its goods, which was a use 'in relation to goods connected in the course of trade with the proprietor', which was deemed by the Trade Marks Act 1938, s. 4(3), not to be an infringement. (The law on trade marks has since been changed and there is now no provision equivalent to s. 4(3) of the 1938 Act.) His lordship said, at p. 105:

Since, however, all the relevant companies are wholly owned subsidiaries of [Revlon Inc.], it is undoubted that the mark is, albeit remotely, an asset of Revlon and its exploitation is for the ultimate benefit of no one but Revlon. It therefore seems to me to be realistic and wholly justifiable to regard [Revlon Suisse] as holding the mark at the disposal of Revlon and for Revlon's benefit. . . . This view does not, in my opinion, constitute what is sometimes called 'piercing the corporate veil'; it recognises the legal and factual position resulting from the mutual relationship of the various companies.

5.2.2.6 Characterisation of a company's status or acts

In a large number of cases, a court determines the character of a company's status or legal relationships by reference to persons connected with the company. Someone adopting a narrow view of the effect of separate personality would not regard these cases as lifting the veil but someone with a wider view of the effect of separate personality would.

Whilst the courts in this situation are undeniably looking at the actions and intentions of persons other than the company, it is submitted that this is not a denial of corporate personality, but a recognition of it. The courts are trying to discover the true expression of that personality and, being conscious of the necessary limitations attaching to an artificial entity, are looking to the company's controllers to determine how the company expresses its independent personality.

By far the most important example of using information about persons connected with a company to determine the character of the company's acts is when a human being is identified with the company and the human's knowledge, actions, criminal intent or other physical or mental attributes are taken to be those of the company. This is considered in 19.8.

The following three cases are further examples of information about persons connected with a company being used to characterise the company's status or legal relationships.

In *Trebanog Working Men's Club & Institute Ltd* v *Macdonald* [1940] 1 KB 567, DC, the fact that the members of a company, by their membership, constituted themselves a members' club determined that when members paid for their drinks in the club it was not a sale by retail by the company such as to require a licence under the statutory scheme for licensing the sale of intoxicating liquor.

In *The Abbey Malvern Wells Ltd* v *Ministry of Local Government & Planning* [1951] Ch 728, the fact that, by virtue of provisions of its articles, the only persons who could be directors of the company were the trustees of a deed which required them to operate the company for charitable purposes, determined that land held by the company was held for charitable purposes and so exempt from a now-abolished land tax.

Information about a subsidiary company's holding company and the way it finances its subsidiary may be taken into account in determining whether the subsidiary is a 'responsible' person to take an assignment of a lease (*Re Greater London Properties Ltd's lease* [1959] 1 WLR 503).

It is not always appropriate to consider a company's members when determining its legal status. In Canada the amount of local tax payable on the occupation of land depends on whether the occupier is using it for the purposes of a business. The key characteristic of a business, for the purposes of this tax, is that its preponderant purpose is the making of a profit. There has been difficulty in determining the correct rate of tax when land is occupied by a non-profit-making company providing its members with facilities for the purposes of their own businesses, for example, where market premises are owned by a non-profit company whose members are the firms which trade on the premises. It has now been held by the Ontario Court of Appeal, disagreeing with an earlier view by a lower Ontario court, that if the predominant purpose of a company which occupies land is not to make profits for itself but to enable its members to make profits then the company is not itself carrying on a business on the land and should not be assessed at the business rate (*Toronto Stock Exchange* v *Regional Assessment Commissioner, Region No. 9* (1996) 136 DLR (4th) 362).

5.2.2.7   Exercise of judicial discretion

If a court has a discretion whether to make an order in relation to a company then it has a duty to consider all relevant matters. One of the matters which the court may take into consideration is information about persons connected with the company. Someone adopting a narrow view of the effect of separate personality would not regard this as lifting the veil, but someone with a wider view of the effect of separate personality would.

In *Merchandise Transport Ltd* v *British Transport Commission* [1962] 2 QB 173, CA, Merchandise Transport Ltd had applied, under the statutory system then in force for licensing road haulage, for a licence to operate over 100 vehicles as a public carrier. The statute gave the 'licensing authority' (in fact, one man) discretion whether to grant a licence or not. In deciding to refuse the licence, the licensing authority took into account the fact that Merchandise Transport Ltd was the wholly owned subsidiary of a large company manufacturing furniture, Harris Lebus Ltd, and the vehicles were at the time owned by the manufacturing company and used to deliver its products. The holding company could not obtain a licence to use these vehicles for public carrier business on return journeys after delivering its goods because it could afford to charge lower rates for such journeys than full-time public carriers whom the licensing system was intended to protect. It was clear that after being transferred to the subsidiary the vehicles would continue to be used to deliver the holding company's products and would only be available for public carrier business on return journeys for which low charges would be made. Devlin LJ said, at pp. 201–2:

> The reasoning of the licensing authority is said to conflict with [the proposition that a company is a legal entity distinct from its shareholders]. I cannot see that it does. If he had refused a licence to Merchandise Transport on the ground that it had no legal existence apart from Harris Lebus Ltd and that the latter ought to have applied themselves, that would be wrong. . . .
>
> But the fact that two persons are separate in law does not mean that one may not be under the control of the other to such an extent that they constitute one commercial unit. . . . Whenever a licensing authority is satisfied that that sort of relationship exists, and that the dominant party is using it to obtain contrary to the intent of the Act an advantage which he would not otherwise get, he is entitled, if not bound, to exercise his discretion so as to ensure that the scheme of the Act is complied with in the spirit as well as in the letter.

For other examples of the exercise of judicial discretion, see *Re Bugle Press Ltd* [1961] Ch 270, CA, and *Esso Standard (Inter-America) Inc.* v *JW Enterprises Inc.* (1963) 37 DLR (2d) 598, Supreme Court of Canada, discussed in 8.8.2.3. Another example is *Burnet* v *Francis Industries plc* [1987] 1 WLR 802, CA, in which the court exercised its discretion to stay execution of a judgment obtained against a company pending determination of a separate claim against the judgment creditor made by the company's parent company. (See also *Canada Enterprises Corporation Ltd* v *MacNab Distilleries Ltd* [1987] 1 WLR 813, CA.) In *Atlas Maritime Co. SA* v *Avalon Maritime Ltd (No. 1)* [1991] 4 All ER 769, one company had used a wholly owned subsidiary to conduct a particular business operation which became the subject of legal proceedings against the subsidiary. In those proceedings the subsidiary's assets were made subject to a *Mareva* injunction, and the court refused to allow the subsidiary to repay to the parent company the money which it had provided as working capital for the venture. Neill and Staughton LJJ both said that this was not 'piercing' the corporate veil (though Stocker LJ did use that phrase). Staughton LJ said (at p. 780) that the relationship of holding and subsidiary company was a factor to be taken into account in exercising the court's discretion and preferred to describe this as 'lifting' the corporate veil. It was held that the subsidiary was not an agent of the parent company.

It is not always proper to take into account the membership of a company when exercising a discretion in relation to that company. *Pioneer Laundry and Dry Cleaners Ltd* v *Minister of National Revenue* [1940] AC 127 concerned a Canadian tax statute which gave the Minister discretion to decide how much a taxpayer could deduct from income for depreciation of fixed assets when computing taxable profit. The Minister decided that Pioneer Laundry and Dry Cleaners Ltd could not deduct any depreciation for some of its assets because they had previously been owned by another company with the same shareholders and that company had already been allowed 100 per cent depreciation on them.

The Privy Council held that this was wrong, saying (per Lord Thankerton), 'The taxpayer is the company, and not its shareholders'. Lord Thankerton said that the Minister was wrong 'to disregard the separate legal existence of the appellant company and to inquire as to who its shareholders were and its relation to its predecessors'. It is submitted that taking into account the company's membership in exercising the discretion did not disregard the company's separate personality. But the Minister's erroneous reason for taking the membership into account, that the members were the taxpayers rather than the company, did ignore the company's separate personality.

5.2.2.8 *Groups of companies*

There is currently controversy over whether the separate personalities of companies in a group of companies may be ignored. On one side is the formalistic approach that each company in a group is a separate entity exemplified by the Court of Appeal's judgment in *The Albazero* [1977] AC 774. *The Albazero* concerned a cargo of crude oil which Concord Petroleum Corporation, a wholly owned subsidiary of Occidental Petroleum Corporation, had consigned on a ship for shipment from Venezuela to Europe. During the voyage, the consigning company, Concord, transferred ownership of the cargo to another wholly owned subsidiary of Occidental Petroleum Corporation. After the transfer of ownership the ship and cargo were totally lost. Concord sued the shipowner for the loss. The shipowner argued that the true loser of the cargo was the company to which ownership had been transferred and only that company could sue for the loss. (Proceedings could not be restarted with that company as plaintiff because the limitation period had expired.) At first instance, Concord submitted that it and the company to which the cargo had been sold should be treated as one because they were both wholly owned subsidiaries of the same company. This argument was rejected. In the Court of Appeal, Roskill LJ said, at p. 807, that it was a fundamental principle of English law:

> long established and now unchallengeable by judicial decision . . . that each company in a group of companies . . . is a separate legal entity possessed of separate legal rights and liabilities so that the rights of one company in a group cannot be exercised by another company in that group even though the ultimate benefit of the exercise of those rights would enure beneficially to the same person or corporate body irrespective of the person or body in whom those rights were vested in law.

The argument was not pursued in the House of Lords where Concord succeeded (as it had at first instance and in the Court of Appeal) on the alternative argument that it was an established rule of maritime law that the consignor of cargo could sue for its loss regardless of who owned the cargo.

However, a year after the Court of Appeal gave judgment in *The Albazero,* a differently constituted Court of Appeal took an entirely different approach in *DHN Food Distributors Ltd* v *Tower Hamlets London Borough Council* [1976] 1 WLR 852. This case concerned the long-standing problem of compensation on the compulsory purchase of land where the land has been owned by one company in a group but the business conducted on the land has been the business of another company in the group which thus occupied the land as tenant or licensee. Unfortunately companies in this situation do not usually draw up formal long-term leases and so until the *DHN* case it was thought that the operating company would not be entitled to compensation for disturbance of its business because it could have been evicted from the property at short notice anyway (*Melias Ltd* v *Manchester Corporation* (1972) 23 P & CR 380). *Smith, Stone & Knight Ltd* v *Birmingham Corporation* [1939] 4

All ER 116 (see 5.2.2.3) was an exceptional case in which it was found that the business carried on by a subsidiary of the land-owning company was actually the business of the land-owning company, which could therefore be compensated for its disturbance.

In the *DHN* case, DHN Food Distributors Ltd was the holding company in a group of three companies. One wholly owned subsidiary, Bronze Investments Ltd, owned freehold land which was used in the business of the holding company but Bronze did not itself carry on business. The other subsidiary owned the vehicles used in the holding company's business. On the compulsory purchase of the land, the holding company claimed compensation for disturbance of its business. The Court of Appeal upheld the claim. Lord Denning MR said, at p. 860:

> We all know that in many respects a group of companies are treated together for the purpose of general accounts, balance sheet, and profit and loss account. They are treated as one concern. Professor Gower in *Principles of Modern Company Law*, 3rd ed. (1969), p. 216 says: 'there is evidence of a general tendency to ignore the separate legal entities of various companies within a group, and to look instead at the economic entity of the whole group'. This is especially the case when a parent company owns all the shares of the subsidiaries — so much so that it can control every movement of the subsidiaries. These subsidiaries are bound hand and foot to the parent company and must do just what the parent company says. . . . This group is virtually the same as a partnership in which all the three companies are partners. They should not be treated separately so as to be defeated on a technical point. They should not be deprived of the compensation which should justly be payable for disturbance. The three companies should, for present purposes, be treated as one, and the parent company, DHN, should be treated as that one. So DHN are entitled to claim compensation accordingly.

It is remarkable that in a single paragraph of his judgment, Lord Denning could describe the subsidiaries both as 'bound hand and foot to the parent company' and as 'partners' of the parent company. In Australia the case has been interpreted as meaning that the separate personalities of companies in a group may be ignored only if 'there is in fact or in law a partnership between' them (Young J in *Pioneer Concrete Services Ltd* v *Yelnah Pty Ltd* (1986) 5 NSWLR 254 at p. 267). Partnership is the relation which subsists between persons carrying on a business in common with a view of profit (Partnership Act 1890, s. 1(1)). Usually different companies in a group carry on different businesses and thus would not be in partnership. In the DHN group there was only one business and two of the three companies in the group did nothing but own the business's fixed assets. As Goff LJ said in the *DHN* case, at p. 861:

> . . . this is a case in which one is entitled to look at the realities of the situation and to pierce the corporate veil. I wish to safeguard myself by saying that so far as this ground is concerned, I am relying on the facts of this particular case. I would not at this juncture accept that in every case where one has a group of companies one is entitled to pierce the veil, but in this case the two subsidiaries were both wholly owned; further, they had no separate business operations whatsoever.

On the other hand, in *Woolfson* v *Strathclyde Regional Council* 1978 SC (HL) 90, the House of Lords said that the crucial factor in the *DHN* case was that the company operating the business had complete control over the land-owning company (which was its wholly owned subsidiary and had the same directors). In *Woolfson's* case, Mr Woolfson owned compulsorily purchased premises on which a business was carried on by M. & L. Campbell

(Glasgow) Ltd. Mr Woolfson owned 999 shares in the company, the other one share was owned by his wife but not as nominee for him. The company also carried on business on adjacent premises which were compulsorily purchased from Solfred Holdings Ltd, whose shares were also owned by Mr and Mrs Woolfson. Lord Keith of Kinkel said, at p. 96: 'Here, on the other hand, the company that carried on the business, Campbell, has no sort of control whatsoever over the owners of the land, Solfred and Woolfson'. This was held to distinguish the case from the *DHN* case so that Woolfson and Solfred were not entitled to compensation for business disturbance.

The fact that a company and its wholly owned subsidiary both carried on businesses and had separate boards of directors with only one director in common was sufficient to distinguish the situation in *Stewarts Supermarkets Ltd* v *Secretary of State* [1982] NI 286 from the *DHN* case.

Lord Keith in *Woolfson* v *Strathclyde Regional Council* also said that he had 'some doubts' about whether the Court of Appeal in the *DHN* case 'properly applied the principle that it is appropriate to pierce the corporate veil only where special circumstances exist indicating that is a mere façade concealing the true facts'. It is, of course, highly unlikely that Lord Denning MR had in mind any such principle as limiting the circumstances in which he could pierce the corporate veil. Lord Keith's 'principle' also seems to depend on his (unstated) view of what constitutes piercing the veil. His lordship's remark would make sense only if cases in which the court has found an agency relationship are taken to be cases in which the corporate veil is a façade concealing the true facts.

It seems that the *DHN* case has not been enthusiastically received and developed by the courts and this leaves undesirable uncertainty about which cases it will be applied to in the future. It has been applied in a case of criminal injury compensation in Northern Ireland (*Munton Brothers Ltd* v *Secretary of State* [1983] NI 369, see G. Dee, 'Lifting the veil in Ulster' (1986) 7 Co Law 248) but its application is apparently not limited to piercing the veil in order to award compensation. In *Lewis Trusts* v *Bambers Stores Ltd* [1983] FSR 453, CA, May and Dillon LJJ said they would have lifted the corporate veil so as to make a parent company liable for its subsidiary's infringement of copyright: however, it was unnecessary to do so in the case before them.

The most interesting point about the reception of the *DHN* case is that it has not been applied in the most obvious way, that is, to make one company in a group liable for the debts of another company in the group: a parent company is not responsible for the debts of its subsidiary (*Re Southard & Co. Ltd* [1979] 1 WLR 1198 per Templeman LJ at p. 1208) even if it has in the past expressed in a comfort letter a policy of supporting the subsidiary (*Kleinwort Benson Ltd* v *Malaysia Mining Corporation Bhd* [1989] 1 WLR 379, CA; *Re Atlantic Computers plc, National Australia Bank Ltd* v *Soden* [1995] BCC 696). In *Reed* v *Nova Securities Ltd* [1985] 1 WLR 193, Lord Templeman said, at p. 201: '. . . the theoretical independent existence of every corporation enables a group of companies to escape liability at common law for the losses of an individual member of the group'. A request to apply the *DHN* case to make a parent company liable for its subsidiary's debts was rejected in *Allied Irish Coal Supplies Ltd* v *Powell Duffryn International Fuels Ltd* [1997] 1 ILRM 306 because such liability is 'fundamentally at variance with the principle of separate corporate legal personality'.

The importance of the DHN case has been considerably reduced by the latest comment on it by the Court of Appeal in *Adams* v *Cape Industries plc* [1990] Ch 433. At p. 536 the court said:

The relevant parts of the judgments in the *DHN* case must, we think, . . . be regarded as decisions on the relevant statutory provisions for compensation, even though these parts were somewhat broadly expressed, and the correctness of the decision was doubted by the House of Lords in *Woolfson* v *Strathclyde Regional Council.*

See also 5.2.2.10.

5.2.2.9 *Enterprise entity*

Another approach to lifting the veil in groups is the idea that the law should have regard to the business enterprise rather than the individual company as an entity. This idea is particularly associated with A.A. Berle Jr, 'The theory of enterprise entity' (1947) 47 Colum L Rev 343. See also C.M. Schmitthoff, 'The wholly owned and the controlled subsidiary' [1978] JBL 218 and N.C. Sargent, 'Corporate groups and the corporate veil in Canada' (1988) 17 Man LJ 155. The idea was taken up by the Ontario Court of Appeal in *Manley Inc.* v *Fallis* (1977) 38 CPR (2d) 74, in which the defendant had set up in business in competition with the plaintiff company. This would have been a breach of duty if the defendant had been a senior employee of the plaintiff company but in fact he was a senior employee of a wholly owned subsidiary of the plaintiff and the business he had started was not in competition with that subsidiary's business. The court said, at p. 76:

> In our view, it would undermine the requirement of fidelity to allow an employee to successfully argue that, while his activities may have injured the parent company of his employer, they did not in fact injure his employer.
>
> This is a case where the court is not precluded from lifting the corporate veil, and, in effect, regarding the closely related respondent companies as essentially one trading enterprise, in the interests of the affiliated companies, in a circumstance where the refusal to do so would allow the appellant to escape the consequences of his breach of a fiduciary trust.

In both *Littlewoods Mail Order Stores Ltd* v *Commissioners of Inland Revenue* [1969] 1 WLR 1241 and *DHN Food Distributors Ltd* v *Tower Hamlets London Borough Council* [1976] 1 WLR 852, Lord Denning MR said that the legislative requirement that holding companies must prepare group accounts was an example of the law dealing with the enterprise entity. However, Mason J in the High Court of Australia, in *Industrial Equity Ltd* v *Blackburn* (1977) 137 CLR 567, at pp. 577–8, has said:

> . . . it can scarcely be contended that the provisions of the [legislation] operate to deny the separate legal personality of each company in a group. . . .
>
> Group accounts are an additional requirement; the holding company is still obliged to lay before its shareholders in general meeting its profit and loss account and balance sheets [showing its separate financial position].

See further F.G. Rixon, 'Lifting the veil between holding and subsidiary companies' (1986) 102 LQR 415 and *Sharrment Pty Ltd* v *Official Trustee in Bankruptcy* (1988) 82 ALR 530 at pp. 552–3.

Since the *DHN* case, further attempts to rely on the enterprise entity theory in England have been unsuccessful. In *Bank of Tokyo Ltd* v *Karoon* [1987] AC 45, Bank of Tokyo Ltd carried on a banking business in London, and its wholly owned subsidiary Bank of Tokyo Trust Co. (BTTC) carried on a banking business in New York. Mr Karoon was a customer of both banks. He complained that details of his account with BTTC had been disclosed by BTTC to its parent company without his permission in breach of a bank's duty of confidence, and sued BTTC in the New York courts for damages. The disclosure was made for the purposes of legal proceedings in the High Court in London to which Mr Karoon and the parent company were parties. The parent company sought an order restraining the action against its subsidiary. Robert Goff LJ said, at p. 64:

> [Counsel for the Bank of Tokyo Ltd] suggested beguilingly that it would be technical for us to distinguish between parent and subsidiary company in this context; economically, he said, they were one. But we are concerned not with economics but with law. The distinction between the two is, in law, fundamental and cannot here be bridged.

The same approach was taken by the Court of Appeal in *Adams* v *Cape Industries plc* [1990] Ch 433 at pp. 532–9.

EC competition law does treat a parent company and its subsidiaries as a single economic unit if the subsidiaries do not enjoy real autonomy in determining their course of action in the market, but carry out the instructions of the parent company which controls them. Arrangements made between companies in such a group for the allocation of activities among them cannot be anti-competitive agreements contrary to art. 85(1) of the EC Treaty (*Centrafarm BV* v *Sterling Drug Inc.* (case 15/74) [1974] ECR 1147; *Viho Europe BV* v *Commission* (case C-73/95 P) [1996] ECR I-5457). In *Imperial Chemical Industries Ltd* v *Commission* (case 48/69) [1972] ECR 619 it was held that anti-competitive behaviour of a subsidiary company within the Community, acting on the instructions of its parent company outside the Community, could be attributed to the parent company so as to bring the parent company within the jurisdiction of the Commission and allow the Commission to fine it: taking extraterritorial jurisdiction in this way was seen by the European Court of Justice as necessary for the effective enforcement of competition law. This decision in EC competition law may be contrasted with *Adams* v *Cape Industries plc* discussed in 5.2.2.1.

5.2.2.10   *Challenging arrangements of affairs*
Usually, the whole point of using a company to conduct transactions is to separate those transactions from other affairs of the company's owners so that liabilities incurred in the course of those transactions are the liabilities of the company rather than of its owners, who have such limited liability for the company's affairs as legislation permits. Parliament has made limited companies available for this purpose because it believes that it will encourage economic activity. Many demands for the separate personality of companies to be ignored are simply attempts to challenge advantageous uses of companies to limit liability. Since *Salomon* v *A. Salomon & Co. Ltd* [1897] AC 22, the courts consistently reject such challenges. In *Adams* v *Cape Industries plc* [1990] Ch 433 the Court of Appeal said:

> . . . we do not accept as a matter of law that the court is entitled to lift the corporate veil as against a defendant company which is the member of a corporate group merely because the corporate structure has been used so as to ensure that the legal liability (if any) in respect of particular future activities of the group (and correspondingly the risk of enforcement of that liability) will fall on another member of the group rather than the defendant company. Whether or not this is desirable, the right to use a corporate structure in this manner is inherent in our corporate law.

It is a feature of company law that it permits a group of companies to be arranged so as to separate liabilities for the various activities of the group. The unlikelihood of a court ever overriding such an arrangement and transferring liability from a company which incurred it to a company more able to meet it is demonstrated by the Canadian case of *Bank of Montreal* v *Canadian Westgrowth Ltd* (1990) 72 Alta LR (2d) 319. The plaintiff sought to make a parent company liable on a contract entered into by its wholly owned subsidiary, because: (a) the officers and directors of the two companies were identical and meetings of their two boards were held concurrently; (b) the subsidiary was funded entirely by the parent and its assets were purchased with money loaned by the parent interest free and with no terms for repayment; (c) the audits for both companies were performed by the same auditor and they had identical financial years; (d) most of the dealings and correspondence concerning the contract were with the parent's personnel and correspondence was on the parent's headed paper; (e) the parent provided management services to the subsidiary without cost. Brennan J said, at p. 327:

> In the present case there was no express contract of agency between [parent and subsidiary], and I am not prepared to find an implied contract of agency from the facts before me. . . .
> In my view the facts relied upon by the plaintiff to support its argument for a piercing of the corporate veil do not justify a finding that [parent and subsidiary] were one and the same and that [the parent] was the *de facto* contracting party, being the alter ego of [the subsidiary].
> With respect to both grounds argued by the plaintiff it is my view that the facts relied upon by the plaintiff in support thereof are nothing more than one would expect to find in the operation of two associated companies, and in particular where, as here, [the parent] provided management services for [the subsidiary].

On appeal ((1992) 2 Alta LR (3d) 221) Fraser CJA said, at p. 223:

> In this case we have a written contract which clearly says it is with one party, [the subsidiary]. In order to find that (in some way by agency or otherwise) it is not really with [the subsidiary], it is really with [the parent], one would need pretty clear — possibly overwhelming — evidence of agency or something else. The evidence which has been pointed out to us is not of that nature.

It is common for a contract of sale to provide that the purchaser can nominate a company to take legal title to the property on completion of the sale. This in itself does not constitute the nominated company an agent, trustee or partner of the nominator or otherwise justify ignoring the nominated company's separate personality, even where the purchaser and the nominated company are in the same group of companies (*Attorney-General* v *Equiticorp Industries Group Ltd* [1996] 1 NZLR 528).

It is common for each vessel in a merchant shipping fleet to be in the registered ownership of a separate company — known as a 'one-ship company' — so as to limit the liability of the fleet owner in respect of each vessel. The court will not ignore the separate personality of a one-ship company so as to transfer its liabilities to the fleet owner just because this corporate structure has been used (*The Evpo Agnic* [1988] 1 WLR 1090; *The Skaw Prince* [1994] 3 SLR 379).

5.2.2.11 *Justice and practicality*
The wide divergence of views on the question of disregarding separate corporate personality reveals a fundamental uncertainty about its nature and effect. It is highly unlikely that a theory can be found which will reveal that all past cases are consistent. A general

incorporation statute like CA 1985 allows people to create separate legal persons very easily. It has always been feared that this would have unforeseen disadvantages. It has been thought useful to retain the possibility of denying separate personality in order to overcome these disadvantages. Judges like Lord Denning have favoured the idea that the court should always be free to ignore separate personality. They have been confident that this freedom will always be used in the interests of justice. Others feel that this leads to undesirable uncertainty and encourages unnecessary litigation because it will not be known whether separate personality will be ignored in any particular case until the matter has been through the courts. The difference of opinion can be seen in two statements of the Court of Appeal only four years apart. In *Re a Company* [1985] BCLC 333 it said, at pp. 337–8 , that 'the court will use its powers to pierce the corporate veil if it is necessary to achieve justice'. In *Adams* v *Cape Industries plc* [1990] Ch 433, the court said at p. 536:

> . . . save in cases which turn on the wording of particular statutes or contracts, the court is not free to disregard the principle of *Salomon* v *A. Salomon & Co. Ltd* [1897] AC 22 merely because it considers that justice so requires.

In *Re Polly Peck International plc (No. 3)* [1996] 1 BCLC 428, Robert Walker J held that this second statement is a principle of law which is binding on first-instance judges.

In *Creasey* v *Breachwood Motors Ltd* [1993] BCLC 480 Richard Southwell QC (sitting as a deputy High Court judge) substituted one company for another as defendant to a legal action, holding that the second company was responsible for the first's liabilities. Mr Creasey had sued his former employer, Breachwood (Welwyn) Ltd, for breach of his contract of employment and had obtained judgment in default of appearance for over £60,000. Unknown to Mr Creasey, the directors of Breachwood (Welwyn) Ltd had already transferred all its business and assets to another company, Breachwood Motors Ltd, of which they were also directors and shareholders, and Breachwood (Welwyn) Ltd had been struck off the register of companies. The liabilities of Breachwood (Welwyn) Ltd, even apart from Mr Creasey's claim, exceeded its assets. Breachwood Motors Ltd paid all the trade debts of Breachwood (Welwyn) Ltd so as not to lose creditworthiness but there was nothing left to pay Mr Creasey's claim. The learned deputy judge allowed Mr Creasey to substitute Breachwood Motors Ltd as the defendant in his action (though the judge said that he would also set aside the judgment and permit the action to be defended if a suitable amount were to be paid into court). In the similar case of *Ord* v *Belhaven Pubs Ltd* (1998) *The Times*, 7 April 1998, the Court of Appeal overruled *Creasey* v *Breachwood Motors Ltd*. Hobhouse LJ said that 'It represented a wrong adoption of the principle of piercing the corporate veil and a misuse of the power granted by the rules [of court] to substitute one party for the other following death or succession'.

One effect of corporate separate personality of which courts are acutely aware is that it can increase the costs of legal proceedings. Sometimes courts have been willing to ignore separate personality so as to save costs. For example, in *Taylor* 1993 SLT 375, it was claimed that Mr George Morris and his wife had conducted the affairs of the two companies they owned in a way that did not enable the business transactions of the different companies and of Mr Morris himself to be distinguished and separated: there was only one bank account, no annual accounts had been prepared for the companies, and the accounting records were incomplete. The companies were in liquidation and Mr Morris's estate had been sequestrated (the Scottish equivalent of an adjudication of bankruptcy). It was held that the liquidator of the companies and the trustee of Mr Morris's estate could enter into a compromise with creditors under which the assets and liabilities of all the entities would be pooled. Similarly, in *Re Bank of Credit and Commerce International SA (No. 3)* [1993] BCLC 1490 and *(No. 10)* [1995] 1 BCLC 362 the court approved a compromise under which the assets and liabilities of several companies in liquidation would be pooled because their affairs were so hopelessly intertwined that it would make no sense to spend vast sums of money and much time in trying to disentangle them. In *Re H (Restraint Order: Realisable Property)* [1996] 2 All ER 391 three individuals had been charged with evasion of more than £100 million of excise duty. It was alleged that property obtained as a result of or in connection with the offence was held by two companies controlled by the accused, and the prosecutor had obtained the appointment of a receiver of that property. On appeal the Court of Appeal ruled that if the separate personality of the companies were observed then there would be no jurisdiction to seize their property as they had not been charged. However, the court accepted that charging the companies would have made the criminal proceedings needlessly complex and it affirmed the appointment of the receiver. The court disregarded the companies' separate personality and treated the companies' property as being the accused's property.

5.3 CORPORATE LAW THEORY

Probably the most important legal feature of a body corporate is its dual nature as both an association of its members and a person separate from its members. Separate personality is a powerful but perplexing legal concept and has attracted a great deal of argument. This section offers a very brief introduction to the main themes of this argument.

5.3.1 Criticism of artificial separate personality

This book adopts what is often called the 'artificial-entity' theory of corporate personality, which is that incorporation creates an artificial separate person. That separate person, though artificial (that is, produced by human artifice rather than occurring naturally), is treated by the law as being, as far as possible, a person with the same capacity to engage in legal relationships as a human person. It is an important feature of the legal systems of the United Kingdom and many other jurisdictions that they treat artificial persons in this way.

The description of corporate personality as artificial has been adopted by some judges. In *Trustees of Dartmouth College* v *Woodward* (1819) 17 US (4 Wheat) 518 Marshall CJ said, at p. 636:

A corporation is an artificial being, invisible, intangible, and existing only in contemplation of law. Being the mere creature of law, it possesses only those properties which the charter of its creation confers upon it, either expressly or as incidental to its very existence. . . . Among the most important are immortality, and, if the expression be allowed, individuality; properties by which a perpetual succession of many persons are considered as the same, and may act as a single individual.

In *Welton* v *Saffery* [1897] AC 299 Lord Halsbury LC described a registered company as an 'artificial creature', which must be dealt with 'as an artificial creation' (at p. 305).

There has been considerable criticism of what is called the 'fiction' that the process of incorporation creates a separate, artificial person.

One group of critics belongs to a long tradition of holding what may be called an 'individualistic' view, that only human beings can claim legal rights and obligations and have rights and duties arising from legal relationships. As Max Radin put it, in 'The endless problem of corporate personality' (1932) 32 Colum L Rev 643 at p. 665:

There is always a danger of indirection and confusion when, for any purpose and even for a moment, lawyers or publicists lose sight of the fact that their fundamental units are human beings, nearly all human beings but nothing but human beings. These are persons in the proper sense of the term. Law exists for them to express their relations and subserve their needs. One of these needs is to speak of collectivities as though they too were persons. But an equal need is not to forget that they are not.

Jurists adopting this view suggest that a corporation should be regarded merely as a collective name for its members. This is sometimes known as the 'symbolist' or 'bracket' theory of corporate personality because a corporation is seen as merely a symbol for, or brackets around, the names of its members. It is also known as the 'aggregate theory' of corporate personality because it regards a corporation as merely an aggregate of its members. Writers on jurisprudence who asserted this view include the German Rudolf von Jhering (1818–92) and the American Wesley N. Hohfeld (1879–1918). For references to original German sources, see M. Wolff, 'On the nature of legal persons' (1938) 54 LQR 494 at p. 497, nn. 9 and 10. (Wolff's article generally gives more detail on this and other criticisms of artificial separate personality.) Hohfeld's views are discussed in the article by Radin cited above.

In recent times, there has been important individualist criticism of economics, social sciences and political theory, associated especially with the economist Friedrich von Hayek. This criticism seeks to require society to be studied in terms of individual human beings and not as an entity in itself. This has been called 'methodological individualism'. See S. Lukes, *Individualism* (Oxford: Basil Blackwell, 1973), especially ch. 17.

The individualistic view cannot be regarded as an accurate description of the common law theory of the corporation. It ignores the fact that the corporation is a useful legal concept precisely because it is regarded by common law both as a separate person and an association of its members. As Lord Sumner said in *Gas Lighting Improvement Co. Ltd* v *Commissioners of Inland Revenue* [1923] AC 723 at p. 741:

> Between the investor, who participates as a shareholder, and the undertaking carried on, the law interposes another person, real though artificial, the company itself, and the business carried on is the business of that company, and the capital employed is its capital and not in either case the business or the capital of the shareholders. . . . the idea that [the company] is mere machinery for effecting the purposes of the shareholders is a layman's fallacy. It is a figure of speech, which cannot alter the legal aspect.

The relationship between the members of a company and the company as a separate person is the subject of a great deal of law. The individualistic view does, however, serve as a reminder that the common law principle of legal personality is not without problems, which are manifested in the controversy over lifting or piercing the veil (that is, ignoring the separate personality of a company), discussed in 5.2.2. Other problems are the extent to which a company, as a separate person, can be said to have interests (see 3.5.3.5, 16.4.3) or should have criminal liability (see 19.8), and the extent to which companies should be accorded human rights such as freedom of speech (see, for example, E.L. Richards, 'The jurisprudential sin of treating differents alike: emergence of full First Amendment protection for corporate speakers' (1987) 17 Mem St U L Rev 173; C.J. Mayer, 'Personalising the impersonal: corporations and the Bill of Rights' (1990) 41 Hastings LJ 577), freedom of religion (see 19.8.8) or the right not to give evidence incriminating oneself (see 19.9).

Another group of critics assert that an association of persons has a real personality which is merely recognised, and not created, by the process of incorporation. This assertion is called the 'realist' theory or 'natural-entity' theory and is particularly associated with the German legal historian Otto von Gierke (1841–1921). The realist theory of corporate personality is associated with opposition to the concession theory of incorporation. Supporters of the realist theory refer to the artificial-entity theory, rather scornfully, as the 'fiction theory', because they see it mainly as a denial of the reality of corporate personality.

The best known exposition in English of Gierke's work is by the legal historian Frederick Maitland (1850–1906); see F. W. Maitland, 'Introduction', in O. Gierke, *Political Theories of the Middle Age,* transl. F. W. Maitland (Cambridge: CUP, 1900), pp. vii–xlv. Like many writers on corporate law theory, Gierke was interested in both legal theory and political theory. He was interested in the position of the corporation in the polity and also in the links between theories of corporations and theories of the State. For a detailed, if at times overheated, discussion of theories of the corporation and theories of the State, see F. Hallis, *Corporate Personality* (Oxford University Press, 1930). The development of these ideas in the Middle Ages is considered with a brilliant cascade of medievalistic scholarship in E.H. Kantorowicz, *The King's Two Bodies* (Princeton University Press, 1957).

The great difficulty for realists is to describe the personality which they ascribe to a corporation. Is corporate personality comparable to human personality? Sometimes a body corporate is described in terms of a human body (see 19.8.6). Some commentators have seen the real personality of a group of persons in terms of a group psyche — a mind and will created by the group. Maitland (op. cit., pp. xxv–xxvi) said that Gierke's theory:

> . . . seems to say . . . our German Fellowship is no fiction, no symbol, no piece of the State's machinery, no collective name for individuals, but a living organism and a real person, with body and members and a will of its own. Itself can will, itself can act; it wills and acts by the men who are its organs as a man wills and acts by brain, mouth and hand. It is not a fictitious person; . . . it is a group-person, and its will is a group-will.

W.M. Geldart, 'Legal personality' (1911) 27 LQR 90 quoted the above passage, without the cautionary first three words, and said (at p. 93) that it stated the 'essence' of the realist theory and talked (at p. 94) of 'the reality of a group-personality' which was to be investigated by political science, ethics, psychology and metaphysics. J.A. Mack, 'Group personality — a footnote to Maitland' (1952) 2 Philos Q 249, suggested that Maitland did not believe the theory of the group-person and the group-will, and that what Gierke meant by it 'is not altogether clear' (p. 250, n. 6). Between Geldart's expression of support for Gierke and Mack's attempt to separate Maitland from Gierke, it had been said that Gierke's views were used in Fascist political theory to justify the dictatorial Fascist State as an organism superior to the individuals of whom it is composed (see E. Barker, 'Introduction', in O. Gierke, *Natural Law and the Theory of Society 1550 to 1800,* transl. E. Barker (Cambridge University Press, 1934) at pp. lxxxiv–lxxxvii; J.D. Lewis, *The Genossenschaft-Theory of Otto von Gierke* (University of Wisconsin Studies in the Social Sciences and History, No. 25) (Madison Wis: University of Wisconsin, 1935)).

As in the passage from Maitland quoted above, realists sometimes assert that a distinction should be drawn between a company acting by an agent and a company acting by an organ, and it is only with a realist conception of the corporation that it can be said to act by an organ (which is why the realist theory is sometimes called the 'organic' theory). English law does not, however, seem to make this distinction (see 14.4.1, 19.5.6 and 19.8.1).

The idea of a company as an entity with its own personality and will has recently emerged again through applying the political philosophy of communitarianism to companies (see D.J. Morrissey, 'Toward a new/old theory of corporate social responsibility' (1989) 40 Syracuse L Rev 1005 especially at pp. 1033–6).

A more recent approach is to say that an entity's real personality derives from the mere fact of its being referred to as a unit. This is known as the 'autopoietic' ('self-creating') theory (see G. Teubner, 'Enterprise corporatism: new industrial policy and the "essence" of the legal person' (1988) 36 Am J Comp Law 130 (reprinted in S. Wheeler, *A Reader on the Law of Business Enterprise* (Oxford University Press, 1994)). This approach can also be seen in the statement by F. W. Maitland, '. . . if *n* men unite themselves in an organised body, jurisprudence, unless it wishes to pulverise the group, must see *n* + 1 persons' ('Moral personality and legal personality', in *Collected Papers,* ed. H.A.L. Fisher, vol. 3 (Cambridge University Press, 1911), pp. 304–20, at p. 316). Maitland, giving the 1903 Sidgwick Lecture, was discussing a statement in the previous year's lecture by Dicey, 'When a body of 20 or 2,000 or 200,000 men bind themselves together to act in a particular way for some common purpose, they create a body which, by no fiction of law but from the very nature of things, differs from the individuals of whom it is constituted' (A.V. Dicey, 'The combination laws as illustrating the relation between law and public opinion in England during the 19th century' (1904) 16 Harv L Rev 511 at p. 513). Dicey was discussing the personality of trade unions. In *Bonsor v Musicians' Union* [1954] Ch 479, Denning LJ quoted Dicey to support his view that a trade union did have legal personality (the Trade Union and Labour Relations (Consolidation) Act 1992, s. 10, now provides that it does not), and in *Willis v Association of Universities of the British Commonwealth* [1965] 1 QB 140, his lordship held (again quoting Dicey) that a department of a company was 'a separate entity' (but then proceeded to find that this did not affect the case before him), claiming that his view in *Bonsor v Musicians' Union* had been upheld by the House of Lords on appeal [1956] AC 104. In fact, as Mocatta J pointed out in *Knight & Searle v Dove* [1964] 2 QB 631 at p. 635, the law lords in *Bonsor v Musicians' Union* were divided on the question. For a full discussion of these cases, see K.W. Wedderburn, 'Corporate personality and social policy: the problem of the quasi-corporation' (1965) 28 MLR 62.

Realist critics would generally admit that the common law does not give full legal personality to entities that they think should have full legal personality, for example, partnerships and most unincorporated associations (though Scots law does confer full legal personality on partnerships: Partnership Act 1890, s. 4(2)). It is also difficult to accept that such entities as wholly owned subsidiaries, shelf companies waiting to be bought, dormant companies and single-member companies have 'real' personality. Realist critics would say that this is the fault of the legal system, which ought to change its rules for conferring legal personality. They say that it is wrong for the legal system to confer personality on entities that do not have a 'real' personality while denying legal personality to entities that do have a real personality (see, for example, H.J. Laski, 'The personality of associations' (1916) 29 Harv L Rev 404). The counter-argument of the artificial-entity theory is that it is better not to seek some characteristic of entities (such as being a group-person with a group-will) which justifies them being granted legal personality but to leave it to the legal system to decide which entities are to have legal personality (see J. Dewey, 'The historic background of legal personality' (1926) 35 Yale LJ 655; M. Wolff, 'On the nature of legal persons' (1938) 54 LQR 494). H.L.A. Hart, 'Definition and theory in jurisprudence' (1954) 70 LQR 37 took this counter-argument further and suggested that it is misguided to search for the meaning of the legal concept of 'corporation' in terms of what it is that the word by itself refers to, because, like many legal concepts, it is a product of human thought rather than a description of some pre-existing entity. One should instead seek the meaning of the concept in the way in which it is used (this idea is also mentioned by Dewey, op. cit. at pp. 660–1). It seems that Hart was making an essentially philosophical point about the nature of definition. For a more abstract analysis on the same lines, see J. Wróblewski, 'Legal person:

legal language and reality' (1982–83) 11/12 Quaderni Fiorentini per la Storia del Pensiero Giuridico Moderno 1035.

The natural-entity (realist) and artificial-entity (fiction) theories produce two different policies. In a realist legal system, all entities with 'real personality' would have legal personality, and entities without 'real personality' would not have legal personality. A fictionist legal system grants legal personality simply on the basis of whether it is beneficial to do so. It is clear that the English legal system is not realist. It does not grant legal personality to trade unions (Trade Union and Labour Relations (Consolidation) Act 1992, s. 10) because trade unionists do not want it, though realists argued that trade unions do have real personality. It grants separate legal personality to wholly owned subsidiaries because of the commercial benefits of allowing them separate legal personality, though realists would argue that they do not have real personality. It grants separate legal personality to single-member companies so as to enable individuals to trade with limited liability though realists would argue that a single-member company does not have a real personality separate from that of its member.

The realist–fictionist argument may be seen (especially in Maitland's presentation) as a manifestation of the clash of world-views which pervaded much of 19th-century thought: the traditional view of cultured Europeans based on an admiring vision of Classical Greece and Rome against the newer, more nationalistic view based on a vision of a glorious medieval past. The realist critics asserted that the fiction theory was a theory of Roman law but the realist theory represented medieval German and English jurisprudence. The discussion of realism and fictionism in the late 19th and early 20th centuries was accompanied by vast amounts of history, but subsequent commentators have pointed out that there has been a search for a coherent theory of corporate personality only in modern times, and that there is no evidence of what theory ancient or medieval lawyers held because they never considered the issue (see P.W. Duff, *Personality in Roman Private Law* (Cambridge University Press, 1938), ch. 9; H. Lubasz, 'The corporate borough in the late Year-Book period' (1964) 80 LQR 228).

Some critics see the concept of the separate personality of a company as alienating people from their real conditions of existence by reifying social relationships. The view of A.A. Berle Jr and G.C. Means in *The Modern Corporation and Private Property* (New York, 1932), at pp. 66–7, was that:

The spiritual values that formerly went with ownership have been separated from it. Physical property capable of being shaped by its owner could bring to him direct satisfaction apart from the income it yielded in more concrete form. It represented an extension of his own personality. With the corporate revolution, this quality has been lost to the property owner much as it has been lost to the worker through the industrial revolution.

Later, at p. 352, they quoted Walter Rathenau, *In Days to Come*, transl. E. and C. Paul (London, 1921), pp. 120–1, writing of public companies:

No one is a permanent owner. The composition of the thousandfold complex which functions as lord of the undertaking is in a state of flux. . . . This condition of things signifies that ownership has been depersonalised. . . . The depersonalisation of ownership simultaneously implies the objectification of the thing owned. The claims to ownership are subdivided in such a fashion, and are so mobile, that the enterprise assumes an independent life, as if it belonged to no one.

Critical studies of company law, enlarging on the points just made, may be found in K.A. Lahey and S.W. Salter, 'Corporate law in legal theory and legal scholarship: from classicism to feminism' (1985) 23 Osgoode Hall LJ 543; P. Ireland, I. Grigg-Spall and D. Kelly, 'The conceptual foundations of modern company law' (1987) 14 J Law & Soc 149; and C. Stanley, 'Corporate personality and capitalist relations: a critical analysis of the artifice of company law' (1988) 19 Cambrian Law Review 98.

5.3.2 Economists and contractarians

Whether or not it is accepted that the law deals adequately with the separate personality and the membership as two aspects of the company, it is said by some critics of the common law theory of corporate personality that it pays insufficient attention to the business or other activity that the company pursues. These critics suggest that the law should have regard to the business enterprise rather than the individual company as a legal entity. This theory of enterprise entity (see 5.2.2.9) seems to involve abandoning the concession theory of incorporation in favour of requiring courts to analyse in each case the economic structures they are asked to deal with and deciding for each of them where to allocate personality. This would seem to be unworkable in practice.

Economists are usually interested in companies only in so far as they engage in economic activity. Economists are not usually interested in dormant companies or shelf companies waiting to be bought. Economists are interested in economic actors regardless of their legal form. However, they are interested in the organisation of economic actors, especially where they are organised with systems of long-term relationships between factors of production — where, for example, investors put in permanent contributed capital, or the contracts of employment of employees last for longer than the production of a single item of output. These long-term relationships surprise economists who believe that factors of production would be more efficiently allocated in a continuous market-place. R.H. Coase, 'The nature of the firm' (1937) 4 Economica NS 386 observed that not going to the market-place for each and every particle of input saves on transaction costs. A.A. Alchian and H. Demsetz, 'Production, information costs, and economic organization' (1972) 62 Am Econ Rev 777 focus on the necessity for teams of inputs (a multitude of investors to provide large amounts of capital; a team of employees to collaborate in making products) and deduce that the characteristic feature of an organised firm is not so much long-term contracting but the management coordination of teams of contractors. (O. Hart, 'An economist's perspective on the theory of the firm' (1989) 89 Colum L Rev 1757 reviews these and other contributions and suggests that economists' theories of the firm have not yet got very far.) Economists who have concentrated on analysing organised firms as alternatives to markets have described a firm as a 'nexus of contracts', a catchphrase which seems to have originated with M.C. Jensen and W.H. Meckling, 'Theory of the firm: managerial behavior, agency costs and ownership structure' (1976) 3 J Fin Econ 305, who talk, at pp. 310–11, of 'a nexus of contracting relationships'. The phrase has been adopted by many in the law and economics movement. If, as many in that movement believe, the law should not interfere with freedom of contract, the law should have little to do with a company which is only a 'nexus of contracts'. As a public service, the State may promulgate a standard-form contract to save people the expense of working out their own contracts (for example, the Table A form of articles of association) but mandatory rules of company law are likely to be either superfluous or distortions of the free market. For expositions of the nexus of contracts view see F.H. Easterbrook and D.R. Fischel, 'The corporate contract' (1989) 89 Colum L Rev 1416 and H.N. Butler, 'The contractual theory of the corporation' (1989) 11 Geo Mason U

L Rev 99. Writers adopting the nexus of contracts view are often called 'contractarians'. They scarcely mention corporate personality, which is largely irrelevant to their policy programme. Easterbrook and Fischel, for example, in the article just cited, seem to regard a company as merely a symbol for the names of its members (see p. 1426) as in the aggregate theory discussed at the beginning of 5.3.1. But in an earlier article, 'Limited liability and the corporation' (1985) 52 U Chi L Rev 89, they regard a company as a 'set of contracts among managers, workers, and contributors of capital', a view also taken in the economics literature by E.F. Fama, 'Agency problems and the theory of the firm' (1980) 88 J Polit Econ 288 at p. 289. Many adherents of the nexus of contracts view see no need for the State to be involved in creating corporate personality and disapprove of the concession theory.

The metaphor of the nexus of contracts neatly encapsulates the law and economics approach to company law, but it is the application of economic theory to law which is the distinctive feature of that approach not the application of contract law. As explained in 3.4, lawyers have long recognised a contractual analysis of companies but the practical application of contract law to company law has always been fraught with difficulty, partly because of contract law's unfamiliarity with the process of renegotiation to adjust to changes of circumstances and partly because contract law is inappropriate for handling constitutional questions (again because they involve adjustments in long-term arrangements). One problem with the nexus of contracts metaphor is that a lawyer's concept of contract is much narrower than an economist's and it is sometimes difficult to know whether people using the metaphor are talking only of legally enforceable contracts or of economically significant dealings generally.

Economists are interested in the contracts made with suppliers to a firm of goods, labour, energy and services, and in the contracts made with customers of the firm. Contractarian analysts of company law, though, generally do not want anyone other than shareholders to be regarded as having a stake in a company and tend to ignore contracts with persons other than shareholders except as aspects of markets in which the company operates, though they do devote considerable time to analysing the relationship between shareholders and directors.

An important difficulty with applying the legal concept of a contract to the constitution of a company is, as pointed out in 3.4.1.3, that a constitution is only a framework of procedures for making decisions as and when decisions are required whereas a contract is traditionally thought of as a schedule of things to be done by the parties. Members of a company do not make a contract detailing what they and their company are to do: they enter into a relationship in which they expect to benefit from whatever it is their company does do, as settled from time to time by themselves and the directors, and they agree on the form of that relationship as set out in the company's constitution. For a discussion of these problems see C.A. Riley, 'Contracting out of company law: section 459 of the Companies Act 1985 and the role of the courts' (1992) 55 MLR 782.

The idea that a company is a nexus of contracts has been useful to the law and economics movement and has been useful for promoting the application of the idea of freedom of contract to company law but it is an inadequate description of the company unless the concept of contract is expanded to take in the constitutional relationships between a company and its members and between the members themselves.

For a large-scale review, with copious references, see the pair of articles by W.W. Bratton Jr, 'The new economic theory of the firm: critical perspectives from history' (1989) 41 Stan L Rev 1471 (reprinted in S. Wheeler, *A Reader on the Law of Business Enterprise* (Oxford University Press, 1994)) and 'The ''nexus of contracts'' corporation: a critical appraisal'

(1989) 74 Cornell L Rev 407. R. Flannigan, 'The economic structure of the firm' (1995) 33 Osgoode Hall LJ 105 observes that the primary purpose of a firm is not to make contracts but to produce goods or services and that concentrating attention on the contracts a firm makes may not help in the analysis of its internal structure. Flannigan's article includes a valuable review of economic theories of the firm. There is another very helpful review of theories in S. Douma and H. Schreuder, *Economic Approaches to Organizations* (Hemel Hempstead: Prentice Hall, 1991).

5.3.3   What influence does theory have?

We have never come across an instance of a judge or legislator saying that a case was being decided in a particular way, or an enactment was worded in a particular way, so as to be in accordance with one theory of corporate personality rather than another. None of the theories can be regarded by a court as a source of law, since none has been stated legislatively or pronounced in a court judgment. The theories themselves are in fact very malleable and can rarely decide a point one way or another. This is perhaps to be expected since the theories have come after company law itself and have all had to be capable of explaining existing company law in order to be taken seriously. However, as we have suggested in our comments, the theories are never complete explanations: none of them provides a base from which company law can be deduced. The philosopher John Dewey (whose philosophy was founded on suspicion about the practical value of abstract theories) suggested that apparently conflicting theories of corporate personality had been used to serve the same ends, while one theory alone could be used to serve opposing ends ('The historic background of corporate legal personality' (1926) 35 Yale LJ 655 at p. 669). Nevertheless the theories have always provoked great interest and are widely discussed. Some scholars have discerned the influence of one theory or another in cases or legislation but this is more a matter of identifying a sympathy for a theory than finding a logical consequence of it. In an article dedicated to Gierke, F. Pollock, 'Has the common law received the fiction theory of corporations?', in *Essays in the Law* (London: Macmillan, 1922), pp. 151–79, concluded that the fiction theory was not part of the common law. D.H. Bonham and D.A. Soberman, 'The nature of corporate personality', in *Studies in Canadian Company Law*, ed. J.S. Ziegel (Toronto: Butterworths, 1967), pp. 3–32, found some evidence that courts in England and Canada have sometimes adopted a line of reasoning which coincides with one or other of the realist or fictionist standpoints. D. Millon, 'Theories of the corporation' 1990 Duke LJ 201 examines the history of corporate law in the USA. There is a very detailed examination of the influence of realist theory in England and the USA at the end of the nineteenth and beginning of the twentieth centuries in M.M. Hager, 'Bodies politic: the progressive history of organizational "real entity" theory' (1989) 50 U Pitt L Rev 575; see also M.J. Horwitz, '*Santa Clara* revisited: the development of corporate theory' (1985) 88 W Va L Rev 173. Both Hager and Horwitz claim to demonstrate that realist theory had a consistent influence, but their articles seem better to support the view of John Dewey that different corporate theories could support similar arguments and the same theory could be used both for and against an argument. The articles by Hager and Horwitz do, however, show the inaccuracy of the crude association of corporate law theories with political views given by J.C. Coates IV, 'State takeover statutes and corporate theory: the revival of an old debate' (1989) 64 NYU L Rev 806 at p. 809, n. 18 (artificial-entity theory, liberal or leftist; natural-entity theory, traditional conservative; aggregate theory, neo-conservative): the natural-entity theory was once the favourite of both the left and the right.

5.4   COMPANY SINGULAR OR PLURAL?

The idea of treating an incorporated company as a person separate from its members rather than as an aggregate of its members is a simple legal device that has very considerable consequences, as shown in this chapter. One consequence is linguistic: 'company' is always construed as a singular noun-at least by writers on company law nowadays. Anyone reading cases decided before the First World War will notice that judges in those days always construed 'company' as a plural noun: the company was 'they' rather than 'it' — linguistically the judges seemed to have been thinking of a company as an aggregate of its members. The point is illustrated by *Prior v Sovereign Chicken Ltd* [1984] 1 WLR 921, CA, in which a building would have been entitled to exclusion from rating if it had been occupied by 'persons'. It was occupied by a company so it was only occupied by one person, and in the circumstances the court held that in this instance the plural did not include the singular.

The linguistics of talking about companies, and the implications for jurisprudential theories of company law, are discussed in S.A. Schane, 'The corporation is a person: the language of a legal fiction' (1987) 61 Tul L Rev 563.

6 Shares

6.1 THE NATURE OF SHARES

6.1.1 Introduction

Membership of a company limited by shares is based on an undertaking to contribute capital to the company. The amount of capital to be contributed is a matter for agreement between each member and the company, but once the agreed amount has been contributed, neither the company nor its creditors may demand a further contribution.

The contributed capital of a company is used by it to make profits which may be shared among its members. If the company is wound up when it is solvent then the contributed capital may be returned to members; but if it has to be wound up when it is insolvent then all the assets acquired with the members' contributed capital will have to be used to pay the company's debts, and nothing will be returned to the members.

As well as sharing in profits the members of a company normally jointly control it by appointing directors to manage the company's affairs. (In many private companies, of course, the members are also the directors.)

A member of a company who contributes more capital than another will want a proportionally greater share in distributions of the company's profits and also a greater influence on the company's affairs (i.e., more votes at members' meetings). The extent of a member's undertaking to contribute capital, and of entitlement to share in distributions and vote at meetings, are all related to the number and class of shares of the company that the member holds. A description of each member's shareholding must be entered against the member's name in the company's register of members (CA 1985, s. 352).

A share is essentially a unit of account for measuring a member's interest in a company. Each share is required to have a sum of money assigned to it as its nominal value (CA 1985, s. 2(5)(a)) and this is the size of the unit of account. The nominal value of a share is the minimum value that a company must demand to receive as contributed capital in exchange for the share. So if Textbook Examples Co. Ltd has only one class of members and the nominal value of each of its shares is 50p, and I undertake to contribute £5,000 worth of capital to the company then I cannot expect to be allotted more than 10,000 of its shares. Moreover the company must not offer to allot me more than 10,000 of its 50p shares as an incentive to me to contribute only £5,000 worth of capital, because to do so would distort the way in which the shares allotted to me measure my interest in the company (CA 1985, s. 100). It is, however, permissible for a shareholder to undertake to contribute more for shares than their nominal value — the excess is called share premium. Capital contributed in exchange for shares, apart from share premium, is called share capital.

Having undertaken to contribute capital to a limited company and thereby become a member, a person may transfer that membership to someone else either by gift or sale. In most private companies, however, the members give the directors power to control admission to membership and an attempted transfer by an existing member may fail because the directors refuse to accept the transferee as a new member.

An advantage of measuring a member's interest by the number of shares held is that it is easy to transfer part of that interest. For example, a member who has been allotted two shares in a company can transfer half of that interest in the company to someone else: there will then be two members with one share each.

It is usual nowadays for an undertaking to contribute capital for shares to be fulfilled at the time when the shares are allotted. When all the capital represented by a share has been contributed the share is said to be fully paid. In the 19th century it was common for only part of the nominal value of a share to be contributed on allotment, leaving the company with the right to make a call for the remainder when it required more capital. Shares for which some of the capital has not been contributed are said to be partly paid.

For the first 20 years after registration of companies was introduced in 1844, it was thought to be essential to a company's creditworthiness that its shares should be partly paid. Shareholders were usually wealthy individuals who were known in the commercial world. The list of members of a company is available for public inspection and the presence on the list of well-known individuals of substantial means who still had a large liability to contribute to the assets of the company was thought to be a good way of encouraging traders to grant it credit. Accordingly companies typically had shares with nominal values of £10 to £100 on which only a small amount was paid up, leaving a potentially huge liability for some shareholders. More than 30 companies in this period had shares of £1,000 or more.

The disadvantage for companies of partly paid shares was that there were very few investors wealthy enough to be able to meet the liabilities on their shares and they would only invest in companies if they knew the directors personally and could keep a close watch on the companies they were liable for.

Investors became alarmed at the large amounts they had to pay up during the financial crisis of 1866–7 and the depression years of 1873–86. They realised that, in effect, they were not benefiting from limited liability. Equally, companies realised that there were many middle-class, small-scale investors who would be willing to invest if they could have effective limited liability. Accordingly, during the 1880s it became normal for company shares to be fully paid £1 shares. For a more detailed history see J.B. Jefferys, 'The denomination and character of shares, 1855–1885', in *Essays in Economic History,* ed. E.M. Carus-Wilson (London: Edward Arnold, 1954), pp. 344–57.

6.1.2 Ways of measuring share capital

If a company is limited by shares, its memorandum must state the total nominal value of the shares it may allot to members (CA 1985, s. 2(5)(a)). This figure is called the *authorised share capital* or 'nominal capital' or (in s. 123(1)) 'registered capital'.

The *paid-up share capital* of a company is the amount actually contributed to its share capital (i.e., not including share premium). If a company states the amount of its capital on its stationery used for business letters then the amount stated must be the paid-up share capital (CA 1985, s. 351(2)).

The *called-up share capital* of a company is the amount actually contributed to its share capital plus amounts presently due to be contributed by members — such amounts may arise either because the company has called for further contributions from holders of partly paid shares, or because members agreed to pay for their shares in instalments and the instalments are due on fixed dates (CA 1985, s. 737(1)).

6.1.3   Classes of shares

A company may have different classes of members with differing rights of membership if there is a provision to that effect in its articles of association (*Andrews* v *Gas Meter Co.* [1897] 1 Ch 361, CA). Table A, art. 2, provides that any shares may be issued with such rights and restrictions as the company may by ordinary resolution determine. Shares in different classes may have different nominal values.

Nominal values of different shares may be in different currencies: the authorised share capital will then be stated as a sum of amounts in different currencies (*Re Scandinavian Bank Group plc* [1988] Ch 87).

In principle, a limited company could have a class of members (perhaps called honorary members) who are not required to contribute any capital, and who each have one vote, and then no shares would be needed to measure the interests of any particular member of that class. In some companies a special class (usually with only one member) is created which can vote to veto any changes in the company's constitution. Apart from these unusual special situations, the terms 'member' and 'shareholder' are synonymous.

The nominal value of the shares held by a member of a company measures the member's liability to contribute capital to the company. In return for this liability membership confers benefits, of which the main ones are:

(a)   The right to influence the way the company's affairs are conducted, by voting at meetings of members.

(b)   The right to a return of contributed capital when the company is wound up (provided there is any property left after paying the company's creditors). Sometimes a company returns part of its contributed capital though continuing in business, but this is subject to rules of procedure which attempt to ensure that creditors are not jeopardised.

(c)   The right to participate when the company makes a distribution of its property to its members. If on winding up a company there is a surplus after paying all its creditors and repaying its contributed capital then the surplus is divided among the members. While a company is in existence it may anticipate an ultimate share-out of surplus by an annual (or more frequent) distribution of profits. A distribution of surplus or annual profits is called a dividend (i.e. amount to be divided).

In the absence of any special consideration each member of a company would have an equal right to vote and to share in surplus and profits ('Equality is equity'). However, it is usual for members to agree, by provisions in their articles, that benefits are to be proportional to the capital each has undertaken to contribute. If all the shares of a company have the same nominal value then this will mean that rights are proportional to the number of shares held. As Lord Macnaghten said in *British & American Trustee & Finance Corporation* v *Couper* [1894] AC 399, HL, at p. 417:

It seems to me that if the sum of the interests of persons concerned in a joint adventure is divided into shares of equal amount distinguished by numbers for the purpose of identification, but with no other distinction between them, express or implied, it follows as a self-evident proposition that the interests of the shareholders in respect of their shares as regards dividend and everything else must be equal.

Table A is drafted for a company with only one class of members and all shares in the company have the same nominal value. Article 54 deals with voting. In a meeting the general rule is that a vote must first be taken by show of hands, with each member entitled to exercise one vote. It is not possible to take into account different members having different voting strengths unless a written record is made stating how each member voted and how many votes he cast: a vote taken in this way is called a 'poll'. So art. 54 gives a member one vote on a show of hands but on a poll 'one vote for every share of which he is the holder'. For the rules about demanding that a poll be taken, see 14.4.9.2.

If there are shares with different nominal values, or different amounts have actually been contributed for shares, then in principle entitlements are proportional to the nominal values of shares held (*Oakbank Oil Co.* v *Crum* (1882) 8 App Cas 65, HL; *Birch* v *Cropper* (1889) 14 App Cas 525, HL; *Re Anglo-Continental Corporation of Western Australia* [1898] 1 Ch 327). However, in Table A, art. 104 says: 'all dividends shall be declared and paid according to the amounts paid up on the shares on which the dividend is paid'. So under Table A dividends are proportional to capital contributed rather than capital that it has been undertaken to contribute.

The usual rights of a member are:

(a) A dividend of profit which, while the company continues in business, may be of any size that is recommended by the directors and approved by the members (Table A, art. 102) (though the company's financial position at the time will limit the amount of dividend that may legally be paid: see 10.5). The amount of dividend distributed to each member is proportional to the nominal value of the shares he holds, or the amount paid up if they are partly paid (Table A, art. 104).

(b) The amount of surplus assets to be distributed to a member on winding up is proportional to the nominal value of the shares the member holds (*Birch* v *Cropper* (1889) 14 App Cas 525, HL; *Re Anglo-Continental Corporation of Western Australia* [1898] 1 Ch 327).

(c) On a poll each member has one vote for each share held (Table A, art. 54).

Members with these 'typical' rights are called ordinary members and their shares are called ordinary shares. The term 'ordinary share' is not used in the Companies Acts and has no statutory definition. On a question of the construction of the articles of association of a company, it was held in *Norman* v *Norman* (1990) 19 NSWLR 314 that the term meant a share other than a preference share.

6.1.4 Specification of membership rights

The rights of a member that depend on the size and class of the member's shareholding may be specified in the contract for the allotment of the shares made between the company and the member. If a company is incorporated with only one class of members then it is likely that their rights will be specified in the articles (as they are in Table A). If such a company later creates a second class of membership then the rights of those members may be specified in the contracts for the allotment of their shares; alternatively the rights of the new class may be added, by special resolution, as new provisions of the articles.

If a company is incorporated with two classes of members then the founders may put the rights of at least one of the classes into the memorandum. Alternatively the rights of both classes may be stated in their articles.

If membership rights are stated in the articles or memorandum then a new member is automatically bound to them on taking up membership (CA 1985, s. 14), though the new member may join with the other members in altering the rights where that is possible (see 3.5 and 14.6).

Before CA 1980, the rights of shareholders were not available for public inspection at Companies House unless they were contained in the memorandum or articles, or were conferred by a resolution which had to be filed with the registrar under what is now CA 1985, s. 380. However, CA 1980, s. 33(5), required every company to file with the registrar, before 22 March 1981, details of all shareholders' rights not contained in documents already filed. CA 1985, s. 128, provides that whenever new shares are allotted by a company with rights different from its existing shares then a statement of the rights must be filed with the registrar within one month of the allotment unless they are in a document required to be filed under s. 380. Filing at Companies House under s. 128 of any information relating to a public company must be notified by the registrar in the *Gazette* (s. 711(1)(j)). The registrar must also notify in the *Gazette* any filing under s. 380 of a copy of a resolution which (a) states the rights attached to any shares in a public company (other than shares which are uniform with previously allotted shares) or (b) assigns a name or other designation to any class of shares in a public company (s. 711(1)(l)). For notification of variations of class rights see 14.6.2.7.

6.1.5 Preference shares

A company may create a second class of membership with rights that seem more advantageous in order to attract contributions of capital. Such a class of members is said to hold 'preference shares' and the usual advantage is that a preference shareholder is entitled to an annual dividend, of a fixed amount per share (usually expressed as a percentage of the nominal value of the share), paid in priority to any dividend payments to other members.

Unless otherwise stated, the right to receive a preference dividend is 'cumulative', that is, if the dividend is not paid for one period then double payment is due the next period, and so on (*Webb* v *Earle* (1875) LR 20 Eq 556). It is usual to make this clear by entitling the shares 'cumulative preference shares'. For an example of non-cumulative preference shares see *Staples* v *Eastman Photographic Materials Co.* [1896] 2 Ch 303, CA.

In the absence of any express provision in the agreement between a company and its members of a particular class concerning their class rights, all members must be treated equally (*Birch* v *Cropper* (1889) 14 App Cas 525, HL). If, however, provision is made in the agreement concerning a particular matter then it is presumed to be exhaustive. For example, shares which carry a right to a fixed preference dividend cannot also receive the dividend paid on ordinary shares (*Will* v *United Lankat Plantations Co. Ltd* [1914] AC 11). (Sometimes, preference shares are issued on the basis that they will carry the right to receive all or part of the ordinary shareholders' dividend and they are known as 'participating' preference shares.) Accordingly, if, as is usual, it is provided that when the company is wound up, any surplus after paying debts is to be devoted first to repaying the capital contributed for preference shares then the preference shareholders will not be entitled to any further share in the surplus (*Scottish Insurance Corporation Ltd* v *Wilsons & Clyde Coal Co. Ltd* [1949] AC 462; *Re Isle of Thanet Electricity Supply Co. Ltd* [1950] Ch 161). In practice it has been very difficult to define unambiguously the rights of preference shareholders and there is a large volume of litigation on the meaning of articles of association from the days when preference shares were more common than they are now — see M.A. Pickering, 'The problem of the preference share' (1963) 26 MLR 499.

Although preference shares are used to provide finance in some special situations their importance as a method of financing generally has declined in recent years, partly because of changes in taxation rules. At the end of March 1988, preference shares represented only three per cent of the market value of shares listed on the Stock Exchange.

6.1.6 Deferred shares

A deferred share is a share bearing the restriction that no dividend can be paid to the shareholder for a financial year unless ordinary shareholders are paid a certain amount for that year. Companies that have issued deferred shares have often called them 'founders' shares' and issued them to the founders of a business that the company has been formed to purchase. Often the holders of founders' shares are entitled to a large proportion (e.g., one-third or one-quarter) of all profits remaining after the ordinary shareholders have received their minimum dividend.

6.1.7 Non-voting ordinary shares

Some companies have a class of members whose rights to dividend and to share in surplus assets are like those of ordinary members but who have no right to vote at members' meetings. In such a company there is usually a small class of members who hold ordinary shares with a right to vote, and entry to this class is carefully controlled. 'Non-voting ordinary' shares are strongly disapproved of by the Stock Exchange and the financial press.

6.1.8 Equity shares

A member who holds shares in a company is called an equity shareholder if there is no prior limitation to the amount which that member may receive in a distribution, either as an annual dividend of profits or as a distribution of surplus assets on winding up (CA 1985, s. 744).

6.1.9 Shares as things in action

The size of the shareholding of a company member is used to describe the relative importance of the member's interest in the company. It is also natural to think of shares as things in themselves, which are created, bought and sold. Instead of saying that a member of a company has transferred membership to someone else it is usual to say that the member has transferred shares in the company; instead of saying that the extent of a member's interest has changed it is usual to say that the member has acquired or disposed of some shares.

If a company owns real property, is a share in the company real or personal property? This was a difficult problem in the early history of company law — see C. Stebbings, 'The legal nature of shares in landowning joint stock companies in the 19th century' (1987) 8 J Legal Hist 25. The solution depended on deciding that the members of a company are not the joint owners of its property, because the company is a separate person in law and property held in the name of the company belongs to the company and no one else (*Bligh v Brent* (1837) 2 Y & C Ex 268). So, whether a company share is real or personal property does not depend on the nature of the company's property. The matter is settled by CA 1985, s. 182(1)(a), which declares that the shares or other interest of any member in a company shall be personal estate and shall not be of the nature of real estate.

Regarded as an item of property in itself, a company share comes into the class of personal property known as choses in action (or things in action) (*Colonial Bank v Whinney* (1886) 11 App Cas 426, HL). This is because holding a company share confers an entitlement to certain benefits and privileges (which may be enforced by action in the courts if they are denied to a shareholder) but does not give possession of any tangible physical object. (A shareholder is entitled to a share certificate but that is merely a memorandum: membership is not lost by being without a share certificate.)

It is perhaps better not to regard shares as items of property in themselves but to regard membership of a company as an item of property of which the size is determined by the number of shares held. One can, perhaps, discern this view in the much quoted remark of Farwell J in *Borland's trustee* v *Steel Brothers & Co. Ltd* [1901] 1 Ch 279:

> A share is the interest of a shareholder in the company measured by a sum of money, for the purpose of liability in the first place, and of interest in the second. . . . A share is not a sum of money . . . but is an interest measured by a sum of money and made up of various rights.

It is also worth noting the (dissenting) judgment of Lord Russell of Killowen in *Commissioners of Inland Revenue* v *Crossman* [1937] AC 26 at p. 66:

> A share in a limited company is a property the nature of which has been accurately expounded by Farwell J in *Borland's trustee* v *Steel Brothers & Co. Ltd.* It is the interest of a person in the company, that interest being composed of rights and obligations which are defined by the Companies Act and by the memorandum and articles of association of the company. A sale of a share is a sale of the interest so defined, and the subject-matter of the sale is effectively vested in the purchaser by the entry of his name in the register of members.

In CA 1985, though, shares are regarded as things in themselves. They are assumed to be created when the company is registered or when the company increases its authorised share capital but are then, metaphorically, kept on the shelf until 'issued' to their first holders.

For a detailed historical discussion see Robert Pennington, 'Can shares in companies be defined?' (1989) 10 Co Law 140.

6.1.10 Ways of becoming a shareholder

A person may become a shareholder of a company with a share capital:

    (a) by taking shares from the company in exchange for a contribution of capital;

    (b) through an employees' share scheme (see 10.7);

    (c) by taking a transfer of shares (on sale or gift or as a trustee) from an existing member (see chapter 8);

    (d) by operation of law under which the shares of an existing member devolve on, or are vested in, the person. (This happens, for example, when the shares of a deceased member devolve on personal representatives, or the shares of a bankrupt member are vested in a trustee in bankruptcy. Devolution or vesting of shares by operation of law is usually called *transmission* of shares.)

This chapter concentrates on the first method of becoming a shareholder.

6.1.11 Issue and allotment

The total number of shares that can be held in a company is stated in the authorised-capital clause in its memorandum. Adopting the viewpoint that shares are things in themselves it may be said that on incorporation the shares are created but none of them is held and they are said to be *unissued*. The process by which members take shares from a company is called *issuing* the shares. Similarly when a company increases its authorised share capital new shares are created but issuing them is a separate process (*Koffyfontein Mines Ltd v Mosely* [1911] AC 409, HL). A previously unissued share is said to be *allotted* when a person acquires the unconditional right to be entered in the register of members in respect of that share (CA 1985, s. 738(1)). The person who has that right is called the *allottee* of the share. Until the statutory definition of 'allotment' was introduced by CA 1980, s. 87(2), the term was usually used to refer to a decision by directors to allot shares to particular applicants. Such a decision would not necessarily give the applicants an unconditional right to be registered. For example, it might be conditional on the applicant paying a certain amount for the shares (*McEuen v West London Wharves and Warehouses Co.* (1871) LR 6 Ch App 655). Under the statutory definition, the shares would not be regarded as allotted until such conditions were fulfilled.

The subscribers of a memorandum have an unconditional right to be entered in the register of members, in respect of the shares they have subscribed for in the memorandum, as from the date of the company's certificate of incorporation.

Otherwise the time at which a person becomes an allottee of shares depends on the terms of the agreement under which he has taken the shares, i.e., the contract for the allotment of the shares.

In *National Westminster Bank plc v Inland Revenue Commissioners* [1995] 1 AC 119, a tax advantage would have been obtained if certain shares of a company had been 'issued' before 16 March 1993. The shares had been allotted before that date but the shareholders had not been entered in the company's register of members until 2 April. A majority of the House of Lords held that the shares had not been issued before 16 March. On the other hand, shares will be regarded as issued if the holder's name has been entered in the register of members even if no share certificates have been issued (*Re Heaton's Steel and Iron Co., Blyth's Case* (1876) 4 ChD 140), so it seems that registration is the final stage in the 'issue' of shares.

6.1.12 Cancellation

It is possible for a company to purchase its own shares but they must be *cancelled* on purchase. After cancellation of a share no one holds it and it is equivalent to an unissued share, so it may be *reissued*. The amount of share capital represented by a cancelled share must be deducted from the called-up share capital account in the company's accounting records.

For cancellation of unissued shares see 6.1.13.

6.1.13 Alteration of authorised share capital

By CA 1985, s. 2(7), no alteration of the memorandum of a company may be made except in the mode and to the extent for which express provision is made by CA 1985. Six types of alteration of the capital clause of a company's memorandum are permitted by CA 1985, s. 121, but only if the company's articles authorise such alterations (s. 121(1)). The six types of alteration which a company is permitted to make if authorised by its articles are listed in s. 121(2):

(a) Increase of authorised share capital by new shares of such amount as the company thinks expedient (s. 121(2)(a)).

(b)   Consolidation of all or any of the share capital and division into shares of larger amount than the company's existing shares (s. 121(2)(b)).

(c)   Conversion of all or any of the company's paid-up shares into stock (see 6.1.14 (s. 121(2)(c)).

(d)   Reconversion of stock into paid-up shares of any denomination (s. 121(2)(c)).

(e)   Subdivision of the company's shares, or any of them, into shares of smaller amount than is fixed by the memorandum (s. 121(2)(d)). If partly paid shares are subdivided then the ratio of amount paid up to amount unpaid must not be changed (s. 121(3)).

(f)   Cancellation of shares which, at the date of the passing of the resolution to cancel them, have not been taken or agreed to be taken by any person, and diminution of the company's authorised share capital by the amount of the shares so cancelled (s. 121(2)(e)). Shares cannot be cancelled under this paragraph if a person has agreed to take them, but a mere unilateral expression of willingness to take shares if they were offered is not enough to render shares uncancellable (*Re Swindon Town Football Co. Ltd* [1990] BCLC 467).

Table A makes provision in art. 32 for all these types of alteration except (c) and (d), which, as explained in 6.1.14, are now obsolete.

CA 1985, s. 121(4), provides that the powers conferred by s. 121 'must be exercised by the company in general meeting'. Table A, art. 32, provides that the alterations to the capital clause of the company's memorandum authorised by that article may be made by ordinary resolution of the members. The members of a *private company* may, by virtue of CA 1985, s. 381A, exercise s. 121 powers by unanimous written resolution without meeting — see 14.5.3.

If a company has, by a provision in its articles, adopted the s. 121 power to alter the capital clause of its memorandum then no provision of its articles or memorandum or of any contract made by the company can restrict its exercise of that power (*Russell v Northern Bank Development Corporation Ltd* [1992] 1 WLR 588, see 2.4.8.3). Existing members of a company may make an enforceable contract between themselves that they will not adopt a resolution to exercise the power unless certain conditions are satisfied (for example, that they have all given their written consent) but such a contract will not bind future members unless they expressly agree to it, and the company cannot be a party to the contract (ibid.). A company whose articles authorise it to exercise the s. 121 power can renounce that statutory power by altering its articles (under s. 9) to delete the authorisation.

Within 15 days of adopting a resolution increasing authorised capital, a copy of the resolution must, under penalty, be sent to the registrar, together with a notice giving prescribed particulars (CA 1985, s. 123), Within one month of exercising any of the other powers conferred by s. 121, the registrar must, under penalty, be given notice using a prescribed form (s. 122). As exercise by a company of any of the powers conferred by s. 121 alters the company's memorandum, the notice sent to the registrar must be accompanied by a copy of the memorandum as altered (s. 18(2)) and the registrar must notify receipt of it in the *Gazette* (s. 711(1)(b)).

The Department of Trade and Industry has published a consultative document on the problems of redesignating existing shares in euros if and when sterling is replaced by the single European currency: *The Euro: Redenomination of Share Capital* (URN 98/520) (London: DTI, 1998).

6.1.14   Stock

A company may decide to treat its paid-up share capital as a 'stock' held by the members and having a value equal to the total nominal value of those paid-up shares. Each member is regarded as being the holder of an amount of stock of a certain nominal value, rather than of a number of shares with that nominal value. In principle, a member may transfer any amount of stock he wishes though in practice it is usual to specify a 'stock unit' and require the nominal value of the amount transferred to be a multiple of the stock unit.

Rights of members who hold stock are reckoned by the nominal value of the stock held. For example, a member may be entitled to one vote for each £1 of stock held.

In the past the advantage of stock over shares was that shares had to be numbered and this caused a great deal of extra work in public companies when registering transfers. Now, however, distinguishing numbers are not required if all the issued shares of a class are fully paid up and rank equally for all purposes (CA 1985, s. 182(2)). It is unlikely, therefore, that companies nowadays would want to take advantage of the permission conferred by CA 1985, s. 121(2)(c), to incorporate in their articles a power to convert all or any of their paid-up shares into stock and reconvert stock into shares, and Table A does not contain such a provision.

In CA 1985, the term 'share' is to be interpreted as including stock except where a distinction between shares and stock is express or implied (s. 744).

6.1.15 Nationality of shareholders

There is no general requirement that any shares in a British company must be held by a person domiciled in Great Britain (or in the part of Britain in which the company is registered). A law that prevented shares being held by nationals of another EU State would contravene art. 221 of the Treaty Establishing the European Community, which requires member States to 'accord nationals of the other member States the same treatment as their own nationals as regards participation in the capital of companies'. For example, the Merchant Shipping Act 1988, s. 14, which prevented a boat being registered as a British fishing vessel if it was owned by a company in which less than 75 per cent of the shares were owned by British citizens, contravened art. 221 (*R* v *Secretary of State for Transport, ex parte Factortame Ltd* (case C-221/89) [1991] ECR I-3905).

6.1.16 No par value shares

In practice it is usual nowadays for a person who is issued shares in a limited company to contribute their entire nominal value at the time when they are issued, and the nominal value of shares is redundant as a measure of such a shareholder's liability. From time to time it is proposed that it should be possible for companies to recognise this by issuing shares without any nominal value, known as shares of 'no par value'. Although shares of no par value are common in the USA the idea has never been popular in Britain or other EU countries. In 1954 a committee reported in favour of introducing no par value shares in Britain but revealed strong opposition from trade unions, who regarded it as a device to disguise from workers the size of dividends being paid to shareholders (Board of Trade, *Report of the Committee on Shares of No Par Value* (Cmd 9112) (London HMSO, 1954)). In Belgium the par value of a share need not be stated on the share certificate, but an 'accounting value' must be assigned to each share for the purposes of the company's accounts, and this is the only system of no par value shares permitted to public companies in the EU under the Second Company Law Directive (77/91/EEC). The 1954 committee said that the Belgian system could not be recommended for use in Britain. The Department of Trade and Industry has shown new interest in the topic of no par value shares recently. There is a lengthy discussion in the Department's consultative document, *The Euro:*

Redenomination of Share Capital (URN 98/520) (London: DTI, 1998), and it is one of the topics to be considered in the new review of company law (see 0.3.1.6).

6.2   CONTRACTS OF ALLOTMENT

6.2.1   Description

An exchange of contributed capital for shares under which a person becomes a shareholder is always the result of a contract, called a contract for the allotment of shares, between the person and the company. The important details of this contract which the two parties must agree are:

(a)   The amount of capital to be contributed.

(b)   The time at which the capital is to be contributed.

(c)   The form in which the capital is to be contributed — money, goods, services, land or some other form.

(d)   The time at which the potential shareholder is to have the unconditional right to the shares.

(e)   The membership rights attached to each share.

6.2.2   Offer and acceptance

A contract for the allotment of shares, like any contract, is formed after acceptance by one party of an offer made by the other. There are two possibilities:

(a)   The offer is made by the potential shareholder. In many issues of shares by public companies, prospective shareholders make offers on the basis of an invitation to treat (called a 'prospectus') issued by the company, which sets out standard terms and conditions on which the company will accept offers, and there is no negotiation of any of the terms. In other issues an individual investor and a company may conduct lengthy negotiations to establish the terms on which the investor will put money into the company.

(b)   The offer is made by the company. This is usually done by means of a provisional allotment letter, which is a letter stating that the company has provisionally allotted certain shares to the addressee pending acceptance of the offer and specifying a date when the offer will lapse if not accepted. Usually offers of this kind are made only to existing members of a company.

If an offeror authorises acceptance of the offer by post (as is the case with most public issues of shares) then the contract is formed when a properly addressed acceptance is put into the control of the Post Office (*Household Fire & Carriage Accident Insurance Co. Ltd v Grant* (1879) 4 ExD 216, CA; *Re London and Northern Bank, ex parte Jones* [1900] 1 Ch 220). Unless a time limit is specified, an offer lapses if it is not accepted after a reasonable time. In *Ramsgate Victoria Hotel Co. Ltd v Montefiore* (1866) LR 1 Ex 109, Mr Montefiore offered on 8 June 1864 to subscribe for shares in the company. On 23 November, the company decided to accept the offer but the court held that it had lapsed and so Mr Montefiore was not liable to pay for the shares, and the company had to return his deposit.

6.2.3   Renunciation of allotment

A contract between a company and a person for the allotment of shares to the person may provide that for a period after the contract is made (typically for six to eight weeks) the allottee's right to be entered on the register of members may be transferred by the allottee to another person. Such a transfer is called renunciation in favour of another person.

Renunciation is normally allowed for in public issues of shares.

6.2.4 Options and convertibles

A company may make a conditional contract for the allotment of shares to a person (called an option holder) under which the option holder is given an option to require the allotment of shares at a time specified in the contract. An option may be transferred from one holder to another. Sometimes public companies sell large numbers of options, embodied in documents called 'option warrants' or 'warrants to subscribe for shares' which are then traded on an investment exchange until they are converted or expire. Options have also been given by some companies to staff as part of remuneration.

Unsecured loan stock, or sometimes secured debenture stock, may carry a right to require an allotment of shares in exchange for the stock at some date in the future. Convertible securities like this are considered in 12.7.

Preference shares may carry a right for the holder to convert them into ordinary shares.

The terms of an option or convertible security must not result in the company receiving less than the nominal value of the shares issued (*Mosely* v *Koffyfontein Mines Ltd* [1904] 2 Ch 108, CA; CA 1985, s. 100).

When warrants to subscribe for shares are converted the company's share capital increases. The London Stock Exchange requires that the possible increase in the equity share capital of a listed company arising from the exercise of option warrants must be limited to 20 per cent of the equity capital at the time the warrants are issued (Listing Rules, para. 3.23).

6.2.5 Authorisation of allotment

The Companies Act 1985 does not prescribe how a company is to decide on the terms and conditions of a contract of allotment. The members of each company must settle that by a provision in their articles. Table A, art. 70, assigns to the directors all powers of management of the company not specifically reserved to the members. Table A, art. 2, reserves to the members a decision on the membership rights to be attached to new shares but Table A does not mention any other terms of contracts of allotment, so the other terms are the responsibility of the directors.

However, CA 1985, s. 80, provides that directors may not allot any shares (except to the subscribers of the memorandum in fulfilment of their promise to take shares, or to an employees' share scheme), or grant options to subscribe for shares or issue securities convertible into shares without authority given either by a provision in the company's articles of association or by ordinary resolution (simple majority) of the members (s. 80(1) and (8)). A public company cannot give its directors authority for more than five years at a time. A *private company* may elect, under s. 80A, to have the freedom to give authority for longer terms — such an election must be made by elective resolution (unanimous approval) under s. 379A (see 14.4.8.4). An authority to allot shares:

(a)   Must specify the maximum number of shares that may be allotted (or in the case of an authority to grant subscription or conversion rights, the maximum number of shares that may be allotted as a result of the exercise of those rights) (s. 80(4) and (6); s. 80A(2) and (6)).

(b)   Must, unless the company has made an election under s. 80A, expire after at most five years and must state the date on which it is to expire. If the company has made an election under s. 80A then the authority may be for an indefinite period, or for a fixed period of any duration provided the expiry date is stated in the authority (s. 80A(2)).

(c)   May in any case be revoked or varied by ordinary resolution of the members (even if the revocation or variation alters the articles, which would normally require a special resolution) (s. 80(4) and (8); s. 80A(3)).

Authority may be given either for a particular allotment (or grant of subscription or conversion rights) or generally (s. 80(3)). Authority may be renewed or further renewed by ordinary resolution of the members (s. 80(5) and (8); s. 80A(4)) but, unless the company has made an election under s. 80A, never for more than five years at a time (s. 80(5)). Each renewal resolution must state (or restate) the number of shares that may be allotted (or the number remaining to be allotted) (s. 80(5); s. 80A(5)). Unless, having made an election under s. 80A, the company is renewing authority for an indefinite period, a renewal resolution must state the date on which the renewed authority will expire (s. 80(5); s. 80A(5)).

If the authority allows the company to make an offer or agreement which will or may require shares to be allotted after the authority has expired then the directors may carry out such an offer or agreement after the authority has expired (s. 80(7)).

If, after a private company has made an election under s. 80A and has given authority for a fixed period of more than five years or for an indefinite period, its election ceases to have effect, s. 80A(7) prescribes what will happen to any authority then in force: an authority given more than five years before the election ceases to have effect will expire forthwith; any other authority will be treated as if it had been given for a fixed period of five years.

A copy of any resolution giving, varying, revoking or renewing authority to allot must be sent to the registrar within 15 days of being adopted and, while in force, must be attached to every copy of its memorandum and articles issued by the company (CA 1985, s. 380 applied by s. 80(8)). If such a resolution relates to a public company then the registrar will notify receipt of it in the *Gazette* (CA 1985, s. 711(1)(d)).

If a company has a share capital divided into shares of different classes and it is desired to alter the rights attached to a particular class, in connection with the giving, variation, revocation or renewal of an authority for allotment, using a provision for the variation of class rights contained in the company's memorandum or articles then s. 125(3) requires that the variation must be approved by a three-quarters majority of that class. Class approval may be given either at a class meeting by extraordinary resolution (three-quarters majority of those voting, see 14.4.8.3) or in writing by the holders of three quarters in nominal value of the issued shares of the class. The requirement for a three-quarters majority is in addition to any other procedure specified in the memorandum or articles for variation of class rights. 'Variation' of rights in this context includes abrogation of rights (s. 125(8)). There are special rules for the conduct of a class meeting to sanction a variation in class rights — see 14.6.2.4. If a majority agree to a variation then a dissentient minority may apply to the court to cancel it — see 14.6.2.5.

An allotment of shares by directors without a proper authorisation is not invalid but the directors who made the allotment will have committed an offence triable either way (CA 1985, s. 80(9) and sch. 24).

Directors can use their power of allotment of shares to determine the composition of the membership of their company: in particular they can ensure that the majority of members support them and will keep them in office. A number of important cases concern directors' alleged misuse of powers of allotment and they are considered in the context of directors' duties generally in 16.4.11.

6.2.6 Pre-emption rights

In order to ensure that existing shareholders' rights are not diluted by the issue of new shares, CA 1985, s. 89, requires that before any *equity* shares are allotted for a wholly cash capital contribution they must first be offered to existing shareholders. Each shareholder must be offered a number of shares which will (as far as practicable) maintain that shareholder's proportionate holding in the company. Such an offer is called a 'rights issue'. The shareholders are said to have 'pre-emption rights' (rights of first refusal).

Section 89 also applies to the granting of options to subscribe for equity shares and the issue of securities convertible into equity shares (s. 94(2)).

Section 90 prescribes the manner in which a rights offer must be made. Its provisions may be excluded by the memorandum or articles of a *private company* (s. 91).

Section 95 allows the members of a company, under certain conditions, to disapply their pre-emption rights, either generally (s. 95(1)) or in relation to a particular allotment (s. 95(2)).

A general disapplication (under s. 95(1)) may be made only if the directors of the company have a general authority to allot shares under s. 80 (see 6.2.5). Pre-emption rights may be generally disapplied by giving the directors a power to allot equity shares either as if s. 89(1) did not apply or as if that subsection applied with such modifications as the directors may determine. Such a power may be given either by the articles or by a special resolution of the members. It automatically ceases to have effect when the general authority to allot expires or is revoked (s. 95(3)). (A general power to allot may be revoked by *ordinary* resolution: s. 80(4).) However, it may be renewed by special resolution if the general authority to allot is renewed (s. 80(3)).

In relation to a particular allotment, provided the directors of the company are authorised under s. 80 to make the allotment, the members may, by special resolution, resolve either that s. 89(1) is not to apply to the allotment or that it is to apply with such modifications as are specified in the resolution (s. 95(2)). Such a special resolution automatically ceases to have effect when the directors' authority to make the allotment expires or is revoked but it may be renewed by special resolution if the authority to allot is renewed (s. 95(3)). However, a special resolution under s. 95(2) (or a special resolution to renew such a resolution) must not be proposed unless it is recommended by the directors (s. 95(5)). If the resolution is to be proposed at a general meeting then the directors must circulate, with the notice of the meeting, a written statement setting out:

(a) their reasons for making the recommendation;
(b) the amount to be paid to the company in respect of the shares to be allotted;
(c) the directors' justification of that amount.

It is an offence triable either way knowingly or recklessly to authorise or permit the inclusion in such a statement of any matter which is misleading, false or deceptive in a material particular (s. 95(6) and sch. 24). If a particular disapplication resolution is to be adopted by a private company as a written resolution under s. 381A (see 14.5.3) then the statement must be supplied to each member at or before the time at which the resolution is supplied to that member for signature (sch. 15A, para. 3).

As with any special resolution, a copy of a resolution under s. 95(1), (2) or (3) must be sent to the registrar within 15 days (s. 380). If such a resolution relates to a *public company* then the registrar will notify receipt of it in the *Gazette* (s. 711(1)(e)).

An allotment in contravention of s. 89 is not invalid but the responsible directors are liable to compensate the shareholders to whom the new shares should have been offered.

The provisions on pre-emption rights do not apply to shares to be allotted to an employees' share scheme.

A *private company* may have a provision in its articles, or even in its memorandum, that any issue of shares (or any issue of a particular description) may be made without first offering them to existing members (s. 91).

The provisions on shareholders' pre-emption rights were first enacted in CA 1980. Before then, shareholders did not have such rights under the general law (*Ving v Robertson & Woodcock Ltd* (1912) 56 SJ 412) though a company's constitution might give such rights.

6.2.7 Return of allotment

Within one month of making an allotment of its shares a limited company must make a return of allotment to the registrar (CA 1985, s. 88). This states the names and addresses of the allottees and the number of shares allotted to each of them.

The registrar must notify receipt of a return of allotment from a public company in the *Gazette* (CA 1985, s. 711(1)(m)).

6.2.8 Disclosure of allotment in accounts

If a company has allotted any of its shares during a financial year then its balance sheet for that year must state:

(a) the classes of shares allotted;
(b) for each class of shares, the number allotted, their total nominal value, and the capital contributed.

This disclosure is required by CA 1985, sch. 4, para. 39 as amended by SI 1996 No. 189, sch. 1, para. 5.

6.2.9 Share certificates

Within two months after the allotment of a company's shares the company must, under penalty, complete, and have ready for delivery, share certificates for all the shares allotted, unless the conditions of issue of the shares provide otherwise (CA 1985, s. 185(1)). This does not apply if the shares are allotted in uncertificated form through CREST (SI 1995 No. 3272, reg. 32(2)).

An allottee who does not receive a share certificate as required by s. 185(1) may serve a notice on the company requiring the company to make good the default. If the company fails to do so within 10 days then the allottee may obtain a court order directing the company or any officer to issue the certificate (CA 1985, s. 185(6) and (7)). Failure to obey such an order would be contempt of court.

For more on share certificates see 8.2.

6.2.10 Failure to carry out a contract of allotment

If a company fails to carry out a contract of allotment of shares then the person to whom the shares should have been allotted may obtain an order for specific performance of the contract if damages would not be an adequate remedy (e.g., *Sri Lanka Omnibus Co. Ltd* v *Perera* [1952] AC 76, PC). However, damages are normally adequate if the company's shares are readily available in the market (*Re BTR plc* (1987) 4 BCC 45).

6.3   PRINCIPLES OF ACCOUNTING

6.3.1   Introduction

In order to appreciate the remainder of this chapter it is necessary to know some of the terminology of financial accounting, and so a very brief statement of principles is given here. Readers who have studied, or are studying, accountancy may safely pass on to 6.4.

6.3.2   Balance sheets

A balance sheet of a company is a statement of its financial position on a particular day, called the balance sheet date. As will be explained in Chapter 9, the directors of a company are required to draw up a balance sheet for their company once a year, and the annual balance sheet must conform with the requirements of CA 1985, sch. 4. In practice, balance sheets are nowadays usually presented in the way shown as balance sheet format 1 in CA 1985, sch. 4.

Items A to D of a balance sheet of a company in format 1 summarise the value of the assets that the company had on the balance sheet date. Apart from called-up share capital not paid (item A), the company would have acquired its assets by using its contributed capital, money that it has borrowed, and profits it has made from its operations. Some of the assets, such as stock in trade, are intended to be held for only a short time for the purposes of the company's business; others, such as debts owed to the company, arise as a result of the company's operations. The total value of assets shown in a balance sheet is called the balance sheet total (see CA 1985, s. 247(5)).

Items E and H of a company's balance sheet in format 1 summarise the value of the company's liabilities at the balance sheet date. These include the liabilities the company has to repay loans and to pay for goods that have been supplied on credit. The value of goods supplied on credit, and the value of assets acquired with loaned money, are included in the assets section of the balance sheet.

It is also prudent to show *provisions* in the balance sheet (item I in format 1). These are estimates of payments that the company is likely to be liable for though their size and/or timing is not yet certain (CA 1985, sch. 4, para. 89).

Net assets is defined by CA 1985, s. 264(2), as the total value of assets minus the total value of provisions and liabilities. In principle, this is the amount which would be left for the members of the company if it ceased trading on the balance sheet date, and its assets were then sold and its debts paid. The value of net assets is often called the *owners' equity* — that is, the part of the value of their company which, in equity, belongs to the owners. Investment analysts often refer to net assets as the *net worth* of the company.

A final section of a balance sheet (item K in format 1) shows the value of its capital and reserves. Two items in this section have already been referred to — called-up share capital and share premium account. Another important item in this section is called profit and loss account: it records the amount of profit that the company has retained instead of distributing to members.

If the accounts have been prepared correctly, the sum of the liabilities and provisions section and the capital and reserves section will equal the total of the assets section. (This relationship is known as the 'accounting equation' or 'balance sheet equation'.)

6.3.3   Depreciation and revaluation

The net assets of a company may not be correctly represented by its balance sheet if the assets section does not correctly state the value of the company's assets. Two accounting devices used to adjust the values of fixed assets are revaluation and depreciation.

The fixed assets of a company are its assets that are intended for use on a continuing basis in its activities; all other assets of a company are current assets (CA 1985, sch. 4, para. 77).

If any fixed asset of a company has a limited useful economic life then, for each year of that life, some of the company's income must be set aside as a provision (called a provision for depreciation) which may be regarded as providing for the future loss in value of the company's assets when the fixed asset is finally abandoned or disposed of. A provision for depreciation of a fixed asset may also be regarded as reflecting the consumption of the value of the asset by the company.

CA 1985, sch. 4, paras. 17 and 18, require systematic provision for depreciation to be made for every fixed asset with a limited useful economic life. The provision should be calculated so that over the estimated life of the asset the amount provided will add up to the difference between the purchase price or production cost of the asset (called the 'historical cost' of the asset) and its estimated residual (or scrap) value at the end of that life. A provision for depreciation is, it should be emphasised, a matter of accounting, not a physical setting aside of a sum of money. In the accounts the provision is shown as an amount to be deducted from the historical cost of the asset. The amount to be deducted from the assets section of the balance sheet must be matched by a corresponding debit to profit and loss account, which reduces the profit available for distribution to members: a provision for depreciation is deemed to be a realised loss (CA 1985, s. 275(1); see 10.5.4 and 10.5.5).

In addition it is sometimes necessary to recognise that a fixed asset has permanently lost value. If that occurs then a separate provision must be made for the amount of the loss in value and, in the assets section of the balance sheet, the value recorded for the asset must be altered to the lower amount that is now recognised as its value (CA 1985, sch. 4, para. 19(2)). A provision for diminution in value may have to be made for any fixed asset whether or not it has a limited useful economic life. However, if a provision for diminution in value is made for an asset with a limited useful economic life then the depreciation provision for that asset continues to be made on the basis of its historical cost.

The requirement, which was introduced by CA 1981, that fixed assets must be depreciated in accounts overturns the decision in *Lee* v *Neuchatel Asphalte Co.* (1889) 41 ChD 1, CA, that a company is not legally bound to allow in its accounts for depreciation.

As an example of a common method of depreciation, called the straight-line method, suppose a fixed asset is purchased for £12,500. It is expected that after five years it will be no longer useful to the company but will have a resale value of £2,500. The depreciation charge for each of those five years is then £2,000. At the end of the first year its value will be stated as £10,500; at the end of the second year as £8,500; and so on until the end of the fifth year when its value will be stated as £2,500 which is its expected sales value.

As an alternative to historical cost and depreciation, CA 1985, sch. 4, para. 31(2), permits a balance sheet to state the market value of a company's fixed asset, as determined by valuation. The year in which the valuation was carried out must be stated, and if it is the year on which the accounts are reporting then the name or qualification of the valuer must be stated together with the basis of valuation (CA 1985, sch. 4, para. 43). An allowance for depreciation must be deducted from the valuation value (assuming the valuation was made before the balance sheet date).

When the value of a fixed asset to be shown in the accounts is altered by revaluation, the increase (or decrease) must be balanced by an equal change in the capital and reserves section of the balance sheet. This is achieved by crediting (or debiting) a separate item in that section called the revaluation reserve (CA 1985, sch. 4, para. 34). In respect of a fixed asset that has been revalued the depreciation provision must be calculated on the basis of the new value (sch. 4, para. 32(1)) and is called the 'adjusted amount' (para. 32(2)). However, the depreciation deducted from profit and loss account for a particular financial year may be calculated on the historical cost basis despite revaluation (CA 1985, sch. 4, para. 32(3)). The difference between the adjusted amount and the historical cost amount must be charged to revaluation reserve.

6.3.4 Profit and loss account

A balance sheet of a company is normally supplemented by a profit and loss account which summarises the revenues and expenditures of the company during the period between the previous balance sheet date and the present one. The difference between revenues and expenditures for the period is a profit or loss of the period. It is added to (or subtracted from) the figure for profit and loss account in the balance sheet for the beginning of the period, to produce the figure for that item in the balance sheet for the end of the period.

6.4 TIMING AND SIZE OF THE CAPITAL CONTRIBUTION

6.4.1 Discounts, commission and brokerage

Parliament has insisted that members of a registered company must be liable to contribute to its assets, but a holder of shares in a company limited by shares has only a limited liability, which is to contribute the nominal value of the shares held. In the 19th century some companies tried to make membership more attractive by devising ways in which members did not have to be liable for the full nominal value of their shares. The courts slowly ruled each attempt to be unlawful. In one of the most important cases, *Ooregum Gold Mining Co. of India Ltd* v *Roper* [1892] AC 125, Lord Halsbury LC said, at p. 134:

> What is the nature of an agreement to take a share in a limited company? . . . it is an agreement to become liable to pay to the company the amount for which the share has been created. That agreement is one which the company itself has no authority to alter or qualify.

The Ooregum Gold Mining Co. of India Ltd had run into temporary difficulties and the market value of its £1 shares was only $12\frac{1}{2}$p. Its members adopted a special resolution that it should issue further £1 shares, which would be treated as having had 75p paid up on them, though the company had not in fact received that 75p. This is called 'issuing shares at a discount'. Although the Ooregum discounted shares were issued for 5p each the company's register of members recorded that they had been issued at 80p each. Holders of the discounted Ooregum shares thought they were liable to contribute only a further 20p each for them. The company was successful but a holder of ordinary shares on which the full £1 had been paid took proceedings to have the company's register of members rectified to show that only 5p had been paid on the discounted shares instead of 80p. The House of Lords, affirming the decisions of the courts below, ordered the rectification asked for. Lord Halsbury LC said, at p. 134, that 'the company were prohibited by law . . . from doing that which is compendiously described as issuing shares at a discount'. It follows that a company cannot give away its shares, treating shares as fully paid up though it has not received anything for them (*Re Eddystone Marine Insurance Co.* [1893] 3 Ch 9).

The decisions of the courts have been superseded by statutory provisions. CA 1985, s. 100(1), prohibits the allotment of shares at a discount. If a share is allotted at a discount then the allottee is liable to pay the company the amount of the discount plus interest at five per cent per year (ss. 100(2) and 107).

However, a company may pay underwriting commission on the conditions laid down in CA 1985, s. 97. Underwriting is discussed in 7.9.

A company is permitted to pay brokerage — that is, a fee paid to a person who acts as an intermediary to introduce a company to potential shareholders (*Metropolitan Coal Consumers' Association* v *Scrimgeour* [1895] 2 QB 604, CA; CA 1985, s. 98(3)). Apparently, though, brokerage may be paid only to a person carrying on business as a broker (*Andreas* v *Zinc Mines of Great Britain Ltd* [1918] 2 KB 454).

6.4.2 Partly paid shares

If a share is allotted to a member who does not contribute its whole nominal value, the share is said to be partly paid. Each partly paid share must have a distinguishing number, which is recorded against the holder's name in the register of members.

As explained in 6.1.1 it is now unusual to issue partly paid shares, but the law relating to them throws light on the nature of shareholding, and so a brief summary of it is given here.

A company that has allotted a share partly paid has the right to make a call for any or all of the remainder of the agreed capital contribution at any time, except where its members, by special resolution, determine that a portion shall not be called up otherwise than on the winding up of the company (CA 1985, s. 120). A resolution under s. 120 creates what is known as a 'reserve liability', which is very like the guarantee fund of a company limited by guarantee. In practice companies have rarely, if ever, adopted resolutions under s. 120.

The articles of a company normally assign to its directors the power to make calls, but usually set out rules of procedure, as in arts. 12 to 22 of Table A. In *Odessa Tramways Co.* v *Mendel* (1878) 8 ChD 235 and in *Anglo-Universal Bank* v *Baragnon* (1881) 45 LT 362, the Court of Appeal said that it could not review the amount called up by directors of a company on partly paid shares because it would not question their judgment on what financial resources were required by the company. The decision to make a call could only be challenged on the legal ground that it was not made bona fide in the interests of the company or was made for an improper purpose (see 16.4.1). Mr Mendel did not claim that the decision of his directors was not bona fide in the interests of the company. Mr Baragnon did make such a claim but the court rejected it. (*Bailey* v *Birkenhead, Lancashire & Cheshire Junction Railway Co.* (1850) 12 Beav 433 was a similar case concerning a statutory company.) These cases are examples of the court refusing to investigate questions of business judgment (see 18.3.3.1).

It has been held that directors' power to make calls is limited by a rule of the general law that members must be treated equally: accordingly directors cannot make different calls on different shares (*Preston* v *Grand Collier Dock Co.* (1840) 11 Sim 327). However, CA 1985, s. 119(a), permits contracts for the allotment of shares in a company to provide for different calls to be made on different shares, if there is an authorisation to that effect in the company's articles. Such an authorisation is given in Table A, art. 17.

A call is deemed to be a specialty debt due to the company (CA 1985, s. 14(2)) and so may be sued for up to 12 years from the date of the call (Limitation Act 1980, s. 8).

As an alternative to the right to sue for payment of a call, articles commonly give a company a charge on partly paid shares as a security for the payment of calls. The charge is traditionally called a 'lien'. In Table A, arts. 8 to 11 deal with lien and provide that the company may realise its security by selling the charged shares 14 days after giving notice to the shareholder demanding payment of a call. In the case of a public company, a lien for an amount payable on partly paid shares is an exception to the general rule that any charge created in favour of a public company over its own shares is void (CA 1985, s. 150(1) and (2)).

As a further alternative, articles may give the company a right to forfeit shares if a demand for payment of a call is not met (CA 1985, s. 143(3)(d)). In Table A, arts. 18 to 22 deal with forfeiture. A company does not have an inherent right to forfeit shares: the power must be provided in the articles (*Re National Patent Steam Fuel Co., Barton's Case* (1859) 4 De G & J 46). A company is permitted to accept a surrender of shares in lieu of forfeiture if this is provided for in its articles (CA 1985, s. 143(3)(d)). Table A does not contain such a provision.

The courts have always interpreted any provision for the forfeiture of property strictly. The articles specify the procedure for forfeiture and it must be followed or the forfeiture will be invalid (*Johnson* v *Little's Iron Agency* (1877) 5 ChD 687, CA — wrong amount of interest demanded in demand for call (Table A, art. 18) so that forfeiture could not be grounded on failure to meet demand; *Goulton* v *London Architectural Brick & Tile Co.* [1877] WN 141). In *Sweny* v *Smith* (1869) LR 7 Eq 324 a forfeiture was invalid because the company had wrongly refused a tender of the amount demanded.

Under Table A, art. 19, the directors have the power to forfeit shares and the exercise of this power is subject to the directors' fiduciary duty (see 16.4) to act for a proper purpose and in what they bona fide believe to be the company's interests (*Spackman v Evans* (1868) LR 3 HL 171). In *European Assurance Society Arbitration, Manisty's Case* (1873) 17 SJ 745, the main board directors had forfeited the qualification shares of a solvent branch board director who did not wish to be liable to further substantial calls in the company's impending insolvency. The forfeiture was held to be invalid so that he was still a member and liable to contribute the amount unpaid on his shares. For other cases in which forfeitures were declared ineffective because they were carried out for the improper purpose of relieving members of liability, see *Re National Provincial Marine Insurance Co., Gilbert's Case* (1870) LR 5 Ch App 559; *Re Esparto Trading Co.* (1879) 12 ChD 191.

A member whose shares have been forfeited or surrendered loses whatever capital was contributed for those shares. However, in principle the member would also be relieved of liability to pay the amounts unpaid on the shares (*Re Blakely Ordnance Co., Stocken's Case* (1868) LR 3 Ch App 412 per Lord Cairns LJ at p. 415). But this would amount to an acquisition by the company of its own shares for valuable consideration — namely, the forgiving of a debt due to the company (*Bellerby* v *Rowland & Marwoods Steamship Co.* [1902] 2 Ch 14, CA). By CA 1985, s. 143(3), forfeiture, or surrender in lieu of forfeiture, of shares is outside the general prohibition on acquisition of own shares for valuable consideration imposed by s. 143. Table A, art. 21, provides that a person whose shares have been forfeited 'shall remain liable to the company for all moneys which at the date of forfeiture were presently payable by him to the company in respect of those shares'. The same provision would normally be made in articles which allowed for surrender in lieu of forfeiture. A person who has forfeited shares in a company ceases to be a member in respect of those shares (*Re China Steam Ship Co., Dawes's Case* (1868) LR 6 Eq 232) so that the money owed by such a person to the company under art. 21 is owed as a debtor to the company not as a member of it (*Ladies' Dress Association Ltd* v *Pulbrook* [1900] 2 QB 376, CA). (Similarly, damages due from the company to a person for wrongful forfeiture of his shares are not owed to the person qua member (*Re New Chile Gold Mining Co.* (1889) 45 ChD 598).) Liability under art. 21 arises at the time of forfeiture and the debt is owed by virtue of the articles of association (*Re Blakely Ordnance Co., Stocken's Case* per Lord Cairns LJ at p. 416). However, the liability does not arise under the contract formed between the company and its members by the company's memorandum and articles; it arises because the contract of allotment of the forfeited shares was upon the terms of the articles. Therefore CA 1985, s. 14(2), does not apply to the liability, which is a simple contract debt for which the limitation period is six years (*Land Mortgage Bank of Victoria Ltd* v *Reid* [1909] VLR 284).

The company becomes the holder of shares that are forfeited or surrendered in lieu of forfeiture and must attempt to sell them to a new holder who will become liable for the whole amount unpaid on the shares including amounts left unpaid by the previous holder (*New Balkis Eersteling Ltd* v *Randt Gold Mining Co.* [1904] AC 165, HL). However, the new holder's liability is reduced by the amount of any money recovered from the previous holder under art. 21 (*Re Randt Gold Mining Co.* [1904] 2 Ch 468). Similarly, liability under art. 21 is reduced by the amount the company receives from the new holder (*Re Bolton* [1930] 2 Ch 48).

If a company holds any of its own shares on a balance sheet date then they must be shown as investments in the assets section of the balance sheet. And if the company is a public company then it must transfer an amount equal to the value of the shares from profit and loss account to an account called 'reserve for own shares' in the capital and reserves section of the balance sheet. A reserve for own shares may not be distributed to the company's members except in the liquidation of the company or in a duly authorised reduction of capital (CA 1985, s. 148(4)).

A public company must not exercise any voting rights in respect of shares it holds by forfeiture or surrender in lieu of forfeiture (CA 1985, s. 146(1)(a) and (4)). If it fails to sell such shares within three years of forfeiture or surrender then it must cancel the shares and reduce its share capital account accordingly (s. 146(2) and (3)). If this reduces the nominal value of the company's allotted share capital to less than £50,000 then the company must re-register as a private company (s. 146(2)(b)) and the directors are empowered to apply for re-registration and to make the necessary changes in the company's memorandum without consulting the members (s. 147).

The directors' report for a financial year of a company must give details of shares forfeited, surrendered or made subject to a lien during the year, as required by CA 1985, sch. 7, paras 7(a) and (c) and 8(b) to (g).

Under CA 1985, s. 135, which is discussed in 10.2, the members of a company may, by special resolution (which requires a three-quarters majority of those voting), cancel or reduce liability to pay any part of the nominal value of the company's shares that has not been called, provided authorisation is given in the company's articles (Table A, art. 34 provides such authorisation). A resolution for the reduction of liability is of no effect until confirmed by the court.

If a *public company* issues shares partly paid then at least one-quarter of the nominal value must be paid on or before allotment (CA 1985, s. 101(1)) unless the shares are being allotted to an employees' share scheme (s. 101(2)).

If a share is allotted in contravention of s. 101(1) then it must be treated as though the minimum amount had been paid up, and the allottee is liable to pay the deficiency plus interest at five per cent per annum (ss. 101(3) and (4) and 107). Further, the company and any officer of the company who knowingly and wilfully authorised or permitted the contravention will have committed an offence triable either way (CA 1985, ss. 114 and 730(5) and sch. 24).

6.4.3 Payment in instalments

A contract for the allotment of shares may provide for part payments to be made on definite dates. Sometimes one payment is made, as a deposit, on application for shares and the balance is payable on allotment, and allotment is agreed to be conditional on payment of the final instalment. Table A, art. 16, provides that part payments due on definite dates (or on allotment) are deemed to be calls so that all the company's remedies of lien and forfeiture can be employed against defaulters.

If a company does not have such a provision in its articles then it will be granted an order for specific performance of a contract to take shares (e.g., *Odessa Tramways Co.* v *Mendel* (1878) 8 ChD 235, CA).

6.4.4 Share premium

A contract for the allotment of shares may provide that the value of assets to be contributed in exchange for the shares is to be greater than their nominal value: the difference is called share premium.

Share premium is treated separately from nominal value and is recorded under a separate subheading in a balance sheet. It may be paid before the whole of the nominal value is paid but if this is done then it cannot be treated by the company as payment of part of the nominal value. A premium may be payable on or before allotment, or at a time specified in the contract of allotment, or when called by the company (art. 12 of Table A refers to calls 'in respect of nominal value or premium'). However, a premium payable to a *public company* must be paid on or before allotment (CA 1985, s. 101(1)) unless the share is being allotted to an employees' share scheme (s. 101(2)). If a share is allotted in contravention of this provision then it must be treated as though the premium had been paid up, and the allottee is liable to pay the deficiency plus interest at 5 per cent a year (ss. 101(3) and (4) and 107). In addition, the company and any officer who knowingly and wilfully authorised or permitted the contravention will have committed an offence triable either way (ss. 114 and 730(5) and sch. 24).

Share premium received by a company may be used by it to pay its preliminary expenses — that is, the legal costs and fees paid in connection with incorporation — or to pay for the expenses of making any issue of the company's shares (s. 130(2)).

Share premium may also be utilised by the company in connection with marketable loans to the company (debentures): if the amount repayable at the end of the loan period is greater than the amount initially received by the company (i.e., if there is a redemption premium) then share premium may be used to pay the difference (s. 130(2)).

There are special provisions for the use of share premium received on the allotment of redeemable shares (see 10.3.3).

The amount of share premium used for these purposes may be written off the share premium account in the 'capital and reserves' section of the company's balance sheet.

6.5 FORM OF CONTRIBUTION

6.5.1 Common forms of capital contribution

In *Re China Steamship & Labuan Coal Co., Drummond's Case* (1869) LR 4 Ch App 772, Giffard LJ said, at p. 779:

. . . if a man contracts to take shares he must pay for them, to use a homely phrase, 'in meal or in malt'; he must either pay in money or in money's worth. If he pays in one or the other, that will be a satisfaction.

The two commonest forms of capital contribution are:

(a)   money;
(b)   an existing business (including shares in an existing company) or other fixed assets.

It is also possible to count services (e.g., as managing director) or an agreement to forgive a debt as contributed capital.

6.5.2   Vendor consideration issues

An issue of shares to purchase a business or other assets is called a vendor consideration issue. Such an issue is made when the owners of a business conducted by a sole trader or partnership incorporate a company which buys the business from them and then carries it on. An issue of shares may also be made to purchase the shares of an existing company in a takeover.

If the value of non-cash assets is higher than the nominal value of the shares issued for the assets then the excess value is share premium (*Henry Head & Co. Ltd* v *Ropner Holdings Ltd* [1952] Ch 124; *Shearer* v *Bercain Ltd* [1980] 3 All ER 295). However, in a takeover, if the consideration for the issue of equity shares by a company is 90 per cent or more of the issued equity shares of another company then the difference between the nominal value of the shares issued and the value of the shares received for them is not to be regarded as share premium (CA 1985, s. 131). Also the difference in value may be ignored when recording the value of the shares received in the assets section of the company's balance sheet (s. 133(1)). These provisions permit the use of 'merger accounting' for business combinations (see FRS 6).

6.5.3   Meaning of 'subscription'

Arnison v *Smith* (1889) 41 ChD 348, CA, and *Akerhielm* v *De Mare* [1959] AC 789, PC, both concerned companies which, when negotiating new finance, said that their shares had been 'subscribed for'. In fact they had both issued their shares in exchange for non-cash assets. In each case the new suppliers of finance lost their money and claimed that they had not been told the truth about earlier issues of shares. In *Arnison* v *Smith* the court agreed and held that saying a person 'subscribed for' shares meant that he had undertaken to pay for them in cash. This was followed in *Governments Stock & Other Securities Investment Co. Ltd* v *Christopher* [1956] 1 WLR 237.

In *Akerhielm* v *De Mare,* though, the Privy Council said that there was no effective difference between, on the one hand, issuing shares for cash and using that cash to purchase other assets, and on the other hand, buying assets directly by issuing shares for them. Therefore it was legitimate in either circumstance to say that the shares had been subscribed for.

However, a supplier of finance may take a very different view about a company that has previously persuaded people to part with cash for its shares and one that has been persuaded to issue its shares in exchange for a contribution of assets whose true value is unknown. In the first case the shareholders have parted with their money to people whom they believe can use it wisely, and any purchases of assets by the company can be assumed to have been made wisely. In the second case nobody has put up any money and the whole transaction may be artificial.

A *public company* can only allot its shares for non-cash assets if those assets are independently valued, and this provision is discussed in 6.5.4.

Acquiring shares by subscribing for them and being their original allottee is not 'purchasing'the shares for the purposes of CA 1985: a purchase of shares is an acquisition from an existing holder (*Re VGM Holdings Ltd* [1942] Ch 235, CA).

6.5.4 Valuation of non-cash assets

If a company issues its shares in return for non-cash assets, crediting the shares as paid up to the extent of the value of the assets, then it is possible that the assets have been overvalued raising the possibility that further money should be paid on the shares. However, the court is generally very reluctant to decide the value of assets and will normally accept the valuation made at the time of allotment, unless it is shown to have been made dishonestly or colourably (that is, falsely for the sake of appearance), or the contract of allotment is itself set aside for fraud (*Re Wragg Ltd* [1897] 1 Ch 796, CA).

Where, however, there is an express agreement to credit shares as paid up with more than the value of the contributed assets then the shares are issued at a discount. *In Hong Kong & China Gas Co. Ltd* v *Glen* [1914] 1 Ch 527, the company had acquired from Mr Glen the right to supply gas in the city of Victoria, Hong Kong, in return for issuing 400 of its £10 shares paid up in full and had further promised that whenever it increased its capital it would allot to him 20 per cent of the newly created shares credited as fully paid up. It was held that although the allotment of 400 shares at the time of acquiring the concession was valid, the promise to treat shares allotted in the future as fully paid up was void and unenforceable.

These rules still apply to *private companies*. However, a *public company* may not accept, as part or all of the contribution made for issuing shares, any non-cash asset unless the asset has been independently valued as being worth at least as much as the amount to be credited as paid up by it on the shares to be allotted (CA 1985, ss. 103(1)(a) and 108(6)(d)).

CA 1985, s. 103(1), does not apply to a takeover by a public company in which it issues its own shares to buy the shares of an existing company, provided that the offer to exchange shares is made to all shareholders (or all of a particular class) of the other company (s. 103(3) and (4)). This exception applies to a takeover bid for any kind of body corporate (whether British or foreign) and even a bid for a company given letters patent under the Chartered Companies Act 1837 (s. 103(7)(b)).

The valuation must be by a person qualified to act as auditor of the company (see 17.4.2) or by someone appointed by a person qualified to act as auditor. (In practice, of course, the company's own auditors would arrange for the valuation.) The report must have been commissioned not earlier than six months before the date of the allotments (s. 103(1)(b)) and must state that the value of the asset is at least the amount to be credited as paid up for it on the shares to be allotted (s. 108(6)(d)). (Note that the report does not have to state the value.) A copy of the report must be sent to the allottee (s. 103(1)(c)).

If a person is allotted shares in a public company in return for non-cash assets but has not received any valuation report, or if he knows (or ought to know) that some other provision of ss. 103 or 108 has been contravened then he will be liable to pay the company in cash the amount treated as paid up by the alleged value of the assets plus interest at 5 per cent a year (ss. 103(6) and 107). In addition, the company and any officer of the

company who knowingly and wilfully authorised or permitted the contravention will have
committed an offence triable either way (ss. 114 and 730(5) and sch. 24) but any promise
by the allottee to the company is nevertheless enforceable by the company (s. 115(1)). The
knowledge that will make a person liable under these provisions is knowledge of the facts
constituting the contravention: it is irrelevant that the person does not know the legal
consequences of those facts (*System Controls plc* v *Munro Corporate plc* [1990] BCLC
659).

'Cash' in the context of these provisions means coins and banknotes, any cheque received
by the company, in good faith, which the directors of the company have no reason for
suspecting will not be paid, a release of a liability of the company for a liquidated sum or
an undertaking to pay cash to the company at a future date, and may be in sterling or a
foreign currency (s. 738(2) and (4)). It does not include an assignment of a debt (*System
Controls plc* v *Munro Corporate plc* [1990] BCLC 659).

Within one month of allotting shares otherwise than for cash, any company (public or
private) must send to the registrar a copy of the contract of allotment (s. 88(2)(b)). If the
contract was not in writing then form 88(3) must be completed to give details of the contract
— and form 88(3) will then constitute a document on which stamp duty for a conveyance
of property may be payable. A public company must also send a copy of the relevant
valuation report (s. 111(1)) and the registrar will notify receipt of the report in the *Gazette*
(s. 711(1)(f)).

6.5.5 Promises to perform services and future undertakings

A *public company* may not accept, as part or all of the contribution in exchange for issuing
shares, a promise to do work or perform services for the company or for any other person
(CA 1985, s. 99(2)). If a share is allotted in contravention of this provision then the allottee
is liable to pay in cash the amount unlawfully credited as paid on his share, plus interest at
5 per cent per annum (ss. 99(3) and 107); the company and any officer of the company who
knowingly and wilfully authorised or permitted the allotment will have committed an
offence triable either way (ss. 114 and 730(5) and sch. 24) but the allottee's promise is
nevertheless enforceable by the company (s. 115(1)). Note that past services may be paid
for in shares, provided the amount to be paid for the services is a liquidated debt of the
company (and so counts as a cash contribution) or an independent valuation report can be
made on the services (see 6.5.4).

A promise to pay cash in the future is not a non-cash asset (s. 738(2)) and so does not
have to be valued for a public company (see 6.5.4).

A *public company* may not accept, as part or all of the contribution in exchange for
issuing shares, an undertaking to provide a non-cash asset which is to be, or may be,
performed more than five years after the allotment of the shares (s. 102(1)). If a share is
allotted in contravention of this provision then the allottee is liable to pay in cash the amount
unlawfully credited as paid on his share, plus interest at five per cent per annum (ss. 102(2)
and 107); the company and any officer of the company who knowingly and wilfully
authorised or permitted the allotment will have committed an offence triable either way
(ss. 114 and 730(5) and sch. 24) but the allottee's promise is nevertheless enforceable by
the company (s. 115(1)).

In fact it is doubtful whether any company, public or private, can treat any undertaking
to provide goods or perform services in the future as payment for shares (*Re Richmond Hill
Hotel Co., Pellatt's Case* (1867) LR 2 Ch App 527).

6.5.6 Exemption from liability to company

A person who has a liability to a company by virtue of a contravention of any of the provisions discussed in 6.5.4 and 6.5.5 may apply to the court to be exempted from that liability under CA 1985, s. 113. The court may grant exemption if it appears just and equitable to do so but must have regard to the overriding principle that (s. 113(5)(a)):

> a company which has allotted shares should receive money or money's worth at least equal in value to the aggregate of the nominal value of those shares and the whole of any premium or, if the case so requires, so much of that aggregate as is treated as paid up.

For the operation of this provision, see *Re Ossory Estates plc* [1988] BCLC 213, in which exemption was granted, and *Re Bradford Investments plc (No. 2)* [1991] BCLC 688, in which it was not.

6.6 MINIMUM CAPITAL OF A PUBLIC COMPANY

6.6.1 Company initially registered as public

A company registered as a public company on its original incorporation (as opposed to a private company which re-registers as public) may not do business or exercise any power to borrow money unless the registrar has issued it with a certificate to commence business (also called a 'trading certificate') under CA 1985, s. 117. A certificate to commence business can only be issued after the company has allotted shares with a nominal value at least equal to the authorised minimum (£50,000) (ss. 117(2) and 118(1)). The assets contributed for those shares must satisfy the restrictions applicable to public companies (see 6.4.2, 6.4.4, 6.5.4 and 6.5.5). In addition, the nominal value of a share allotted to an employees' share scheme will not count towards the £50,000 limit unless (s. 117(4)) one-quarter of its nominal value and the whole of any share premium have been paid up (which is not normally compulsory: s. 101(1) and (2)).

In order to obtain a certificate for a public company to commence business, a director or secretary of the company must make a statutory declaration on form 117, stating that the nominal value of the company's allotted share capital is £50,000 or more and specifying how much has been paid up on the company's allotted shares (ss. 117(2) and (3) and 118(1): SI 1985 No. 854). It is not necessary to declare that the assets received for the shares are of the type permitted for a public company (see 6.5.4 and 6.5.5). The declaration must also state the amount (or an estimate) of the company's preliminary expenses and who is paying them, and must state any amount or benefit paid, or intended to be paid or given, to any promoter of the company and what consideration the company receives in return (s. 117(3)(c) and (d)). The registrar must issue a certificate to commence business on receipt of form 117 if he is satisfied that the nominal value of the company's allotted share capital is £50,000 or more but he may accept the declaration on form 117 as sufficient evidence of that fact (ss. 117(2) and (5) and 118(1); SI 1985 No. 854). The registrar must notify in the *Gazette* receipt of form 117 (s. 711(1)(g)). The certificate is conclusive evidence that the company is entitled to do business and exercise borrowing powers (s. 117(6)). There is no fee for the issue of a certificate to commence business.

If a company is registered as a public company on original incorporation but fails to obtain a certificate to commence business within one year then an application may be made to the court to wind it up compulsorily (Insolvency Act 1986, s. 122(1)(b); see 20.6.3).

If a public company, registered as such on its original incorporation, transacts any business or makes any borrowing before the issue of its certificate to commence business then the company and any officer of it who knowingly and wilfully authorised or permitted the transaction of the business will have committed an offence triable either way (CA 1985, ss. 117(7) and 730(5) and sch. 24). The transactions themselves are not invalid but if the company fails to honour its obligations under them within 21 days of being called upon to do so then its directors become jointly and severally liable to indemnify the other parties to the transactions for their losses caused by the company's failure to honour its obligations (s. 117(8)).

6.6.2   Private company re-registered as public

In order for a private company to re-register as a public company its members must adopt a special resolution (CA 1985, s. 43(1)) and, on the day that resolution is adopted the company must have allotted shares with a nominal value at least equal to the authorised minimum (£50,000) (ss. 45(1) and (2)(a) and 118(1)). The capital contributed for the company's allotted shares must, in effect, satisfy the restrictions applicable to forms of contribution that may be accepted by public companies. Thus at least a quarter of the nominal value of each share plus the whole of any share premium must be paid up (s. 45(2)(b); cf. 6.4.2 and 6.4.4). If the private company accepted, as part or all of the contribution in exchange for issuing shares, a promise to do work or perform services for the company or any other person, that promise must have been carried out (s. 45(3); cf. 6.5.5). If the private company accepted any other form of future undertaking to contribute non-cash assets, the undertaking must either have been performed or there must be an enforceable obligation to perform it within five years from the date of adopting the special resolution to re-register (s. 45(4); cf. 6.5.5).

In order to deal with the valuation of non-cash assets that may have been contributed for a private company's shares (cf. 6.5.4), s. 43(3)(c) requires that an application to re-register a private company as public must be accompanied by a balance sheet of the company, for a date no more than seven months before the date of the application (s. 43(4)), and an unqualified auditors' report on that balance sheet. The application must also be accompanied by a written statement by the auditors that in their opinion the balance sheet shows that the company's net assets (see 6.3.2) were, at the balance sheet date, not less than the sum of its called-up share capital and its undistributable reserves (see 10.5.7) (s. 43(3)(b)).

If, between that balance sheet date and the date of adopting the resolution to re-register, the company allotted shares for non-cash assets then it must have those assets valued in accordance with the procedure described in 6.5.4 (s. 44).

An application to re-register must be accompanied by a statutory declaration made by a director or secretary of the company that all the conditions relating to capital have been complied with and that, since the balance sheet date the company's net assets have not fallen below the sum of its called-up share capital and undistributable reserves (s. 43(3)(e)).

A private company re-registered as public does not need a certificate to commence business.

6.7   REMEDIES OF A WRONGED ALLOTTEE

This section describes the remedies available to a person who has been induced by a misrepresentation to subscribe for shares in a company. The law described here applies to misrepresentations made in any way. In 7.4 and 7.5 it will be explained that when shares are first offered to the public a prospectus must be published and when an application is made for listing on the Stock Exchange either a prospectus or listing particulars must be published. There are special rules about liability for errors and omissions in those documents which are described in 7.6. The law described in this section is most useful when an allotment has been made for which a prospectus or listing particulars was not required.

6.7.1 Rescission for misrepresentation

If one party to a contract was induced to make the contract by statements of fact made by the other party and any of those statements was untrue then there has been misrepresentation, and the misled party is entitled to repudiate the contract.

The misled party may also ask a court for an order rescinding the contract — that is, declaring that the contract never created any rights or obligations so that each party must return to the other what was received under the contract. Though it finds rescission justifiable, the court may, at its discretion, reconstitute a repudiated contract, or refuse to order rescission, and award damages in lieu of rescission (Misrepresentation Act 1967, s. 2(2)).

Rescission of a contract of allotment of shares in a company means that the company must return whatever capital the shareholder has contributed for the shares; the shareholder will cease to have any liability to pay calls if the shares were partly paid; and the company must cancel the shares.

The right to rescission for misrepresentation does not depend on the motive or reason for making the misrepresentation. Rescission may be grounded on a wholly innocent mistake (per Lord Herschell in *Derry* v *Peek* (1889) 14 App Cas 337 at p. 359).

A party who makes a misstatement is not permitted to say that the misled party could have checked it and discovered it was wrong (*Redgrave* v *Hurd* (1881) 20 ChD 1, CA).

6.7.2 Attribution of misrepresentations to a company

An allottee of shares who wants to rescind the contract for the allotment of the shares must show that a misrepresentation was made by the other party to that contract, namely the company. In practice it is unlikely that a misrepresentation would be made in a notice given by the company, except in the listing particulars or prospectus for a public issue (see chapter 7). In private negotiations between an investor and a company it is more likely that misrepresentations will be made by individuals negotiating on the company's side. How far should misstatements of fact by individuals be attributed to a company so as to make them misrepresentations made by the company? A comprehensive answer was given by Romer J in *Lynde* v *Anglo-Italian Hemp Spinning Co.* [1896] 1 Ch 178, and slightly modified by Luxmoore J in *Collins* v *Associated Greyhound Racecourses Ltd* [1930] 1 Ch 1. The combined effect of the two judgments is that a company will be liable:

(a)   where the misrepresentations are made by the directors or other general agents of the company entitled to act, and acting, on its behalf;

(b)   where the misrepresentations are made by a special agent of the company while acting within the scope of his authority;

(c)   where the company can be held affected, before the contract is made, with knowledge that the contract was induced by misrepresentations — for example, if the directors, when making an allotment, know that it was induced by misrepresentations, whether made with their authority or not;

(d)   where, to the knowledge of the company or its agents, the contract is made on the basis of particular representations that later turn out to be untrue.

In *Re Metal Constituents Ltd, Lord Lurgan's Case* [1902] 1 Ch 707, Lord Lurgan was a subscriber of the company's memorandum and in that memorandum subscription had undertaken to take 250 of the company's shares. He wished to be relieved of this obligation on the ground that he had been induced to give the undertaking by a misrepresentation made by one of the company's promoters. His claim failed because the company did not exist until its memorandum was registered, which was after Lord Lurgan had signed it and given his undertaking. Any misrepresentation inducing Lord Lurgan to sign could not be attributed to the company because at the time of the alleged misrepresentation, the company was not in existence.

6.7.3   Limitations on the statements on which rescission may be grounded

Only a misstatement of fact by the other party is a misrepresentation entitling a party to rescind.

A statement of an opinion that is wrong is not a misstatement of fact (*Bisset* v *Wilkinson* [1927] AC 177, PC) though it may be difficult to distinguish between opinion and fact (*Smith* v *Land & House Property Corporation* (1884) 28 ChD 7, CA).

A statement of an intention that is not carried out is not a misstatement of fact, but a statement of an intention that the maker of the statement actually does not have is a misstatement of fact. In *Edgington* v *Fitzmaurice* (1885) 29 ChD 459, CA, directors of a company invited people to lend it money saying that the money would be used to finance the extension of the company's buildings and plant. In fact the company was in difficulties and most of the money lent was used to pay pressing liabilities. Soon afterwards the company failed. It was held, on the evidence, that the directors had never intended to use the money in the way that they had stated, and Bowen LJ made his famous remark: 'the state of a man's mind is as much a fact as the state of his digestion'.

A statement may be a misrepresentation because it is incomplete or ambiguous. Lord Halsbury LC said in *Aaron's Reefs Ltd* v *Twiss* [1896] AC 273, HL, at p. 281:

> It is said there is no specific allegation of fact which is proved to be false. Again I protest, as I have said, against that being the true test. I should say, taking the whole thing together, was there false representation? I do not care by what means it is conveyed — by what trick or device or ambiguous language: all those are expedients by which fraudulent people seem to think they can escape from the real substance of the transaction.

In *Greenwood* v *Leather Shod Wheel Co.* [1900] 1 Ch 421, CA, the company issued a prospectus inviting the public to subscribe for its shares. The company had been formed to exploit a new method of making wheels with leather tyres. One paragraph of the prospectus correctly listed important potential purchasers who had agreed to try sets of the new wheels. The following paragraph said that various other bodies 'have already given orders'. In fact the bodies mentioned in the second paragraph had also only agreed to try the new product. The court agreed with Greenwood's contention that the prospectus gave the impression that the company had numerous orders and so would be successful but this was a misstatement because it actually had no orders.

A misstatement does not justify rescission if it is not material. For example, in *Smith* v *Chadwick* (1882) 20 ChD 27, CA, affirmed by HL (1884) 9 App Cas 187, Chadwick and partners had promoted a company and in the prospectus had stated that Mr J.J. Grieves MP would be a director. Smith took shares in the company. In fact, Grieves had withdrawn from the project the day before the prospectus was issued. On the other hand, Mr Smith admitted that he had never heard of Mr Grieves, and so it was held that the misstatement was not material to him.

The fact that a company has totally failed to mention a material fact does not justify rescission of a contract for the allotment of shares unless the omission makes what is said a misstatement (*McKeown* v *Boudard-Peveril Gear Co. Ltd* (1896) 65 LJ Ch 735, CA). There is an absolute duty to disclose all material facts in listing particulars or a prospectus when making a public offer of shares (see 7.4.5.2 and 7.5.3). However, these duties do not apply, for example, to private negotiations leading to a contract of allotment between a private company and an individual investor. In such negotiations it is for the investor to specify the matters on which information is required.

If a material statement of fact is made to induce the making of a contract but, before the contract is made circumstances change so that the statement is no longer true, then the maker of the statement has a duty to correct it, and failure to do so entitles the misled party to rescission (*With* v *O'Flanagan* [1936] Ch 575, CA).

No person can be liable for omitting a statement that he would not have had to make in listing particulars (Financial Services Act 1986, s. 150(6)) — though listing particulars must disclose all material facts.

6.7.4 Loss of the remedy of rescission

A court will not rescind a contract for misrepresentation if:

(a) It is no longer possible for the parties to return to each other substantially what they transferred under the contract. (Complete return to the previous position is usually described as '*restitutio in integrum*'.) With a contract for the allotment of shares in a company, return to the pre-contract position will not be possible after commencement of winding up of the company (*Oakes* v *Turquand* (1867) LR 2 HL 325; *Kent* v *Freehold Land and Brick-making Co.* (1868) LR 3 Ch App 493) because the allottee will not be able to return what was received under the contract (a share in a going concern): the allottee will be able to return only a contributory's interest in a company in liquidation (*Re Hull & County Bank, Burgess's Case* (1880) 15 ChD 507). The fact that the company has gone into liquidation will not be a bar to rescission of an allotment if the allottee started proceedings for rescission before the commencement of the liquidation (*Reese River Silver Mining Co. Ltd* v *Smith* (1869) LR 4 HL 64). An allottee will not be able to return shares which have been sold.

The mere fact that the market value of the shares has declined will not prevent rescission (*Armstrong* v *Jackson* [1917] 2 KB 822).

(b) After learning of the misrepresentation, the misled party acted as if the contract had nevertheless created rights and duties. With a contract of allotment the right to rescind will be lost if the allottee tries to sell the shares (*Re Hop & Malt Exchange & Warehouse Co.* (1866) LR 1 Eq 483), or votes at a meeting of members (*Sharpley* v *Louth & East Coast Railway Co.* (1876) 2 ChD 663, CA) or pays calls on partly paid shares and accepts payment of dividends (*Scholey* v *Central Railway Co. of Venezuela* (1868) LR 9 Eq 266 n).

(c) After learning of the misrepresentation, the misled party failed to act promptly to repudiate or rescind. This rule is enforced very strictly in relation to contracts for the allotment of shares. In *Re Estates Investment Co., Ashley's Case* (1870) LR 9 Eq 263, Lord Romilly MR said, at pp. 268–9:

whenever a misrepresentation is made of which any one of the shareholders has notice, and can take advantage to avoid his contract with the company, it is his duty to determine at once whether he will depart from the company, or whether he will remain a member.

Ashley had been present at a meeting of members at which allegations of misrepresentation were made. Some members formed a committee to take action against the company but Ashley did not join them, saying that he would await the outcome of their case. The case was finally decided in the shareholders' favour (though not until after the company commenced winding up) but it was held that Ashley had lost his right to rescind. On the other hand, all the allottees who did join the committee were entitled to rescind even though only one representative member actually took legal proceedings (*Re Estates Investment Co., Pawle's Case* (1869) LR 4 Ch App 497).

It has been suggested that a delay of two weeks between learning of a misrepresentation and repudiation of the contract of allotment would be too long (*Re Scottish Petroleum Co.* (1883) 23 ChD 413, CA, per Baggallay LJ at 434). In *Re Russian (Vyksounsky) Ironworks Co., Taite's Case* (1867) LR 3 Eq 795, a delay of one month in commencing proceedings after the company had refused to refund application money was held to be too long. In *Heymann* v *European Central Railway Co.* (1868) LR 7 Eq 154, a delay of three months in commencing proceedings after discovering grounds for rescission was held to be too long. In *Re Snyder Dynamite Projectile Co. Ltd, Skelton's Case* (1893) 68 LT 210, Stirling J said (at p. 212) that in every case all the circumstances must be taken into account. In the past, when most shares were partly paid, it was thought that creditors of a company relied on its list of members as indicating that there were substantial persons able to contribute further capital if calls were to be made. The court's insistence that repudiation of membership had to be done quickly if at all minimised the risk of creditors being misled. Similarly it minimises the risk of persons being misled into taking shares in a company on the strength of the list of others who have apparently thought the company a good investment. These considerations have less force in relation to a private company in which the shares are fully paid (*Haas Timber & Trading Co. Pty Ltd* v *Wade* (1954) 94 CLR 593 at p. 604).

(d) Too long a time has elapsed since the misled party acted in reliance on the misrepresentation. This does not apply if it can be shown that the misrepresentation was fraudulent (*Armstrong* v *Jackson* [1917] 2 KB 822).

6.7.5 Damages

A wronged allottee of shares may want damages instead of or in addition to rescission if rescission is no longer possible (see 6.7.4) or if compensation is required for consequential loss. Under the common law, rescission of a contract induced by a misrepresentation is available whether the misrepresentation was fraudulent, negligent or wholly innocent. However, damages could be awarded in addition to or instead of rescission only where there was a fraudulent misrepresentation, in which case damages could be awarded for the tort of deceit (per Lord Bramwell in *Derry* v *Peek* (1889) 14 App Cas 337 at p. 347). Subsequently it has been recognised that damages can be awarded in tort for negligent misstatements (see 8.10) but as the cases on negligent misstatement have not so far involved subscriptions for new issues of shares the discussion here will concentrate on the tort of deceit and the statutory liability for damages for misrepresentation introduced by the Misrepresentation Act 1967.

An action for the tort of deceit is available to a plaintiff who has suffered harm in consequence of acting in reliance on a false statement which the defendant made with intent that persons should act in reliance on it. It is essential to prove that the statement was made fraudulently. In practice this is difficult because it involves proving that the defendant knew the statement was untrue (or did not believe that it was true) or made the statement recklessly, without caring whether it was true or false. In *Derry* v *Peek*, it was held that it is not fraudulent to make a statement, which is in fact false, in the honest belief that it is true, even if one did not have a reasonable ground for that belief. *Derry* v *Peek* concerned an untrue statement in a prospectus for a public offer of shares in a statutory company, and the directors were held not liable for the losses of people who took shares on the strength of the prospectus because it was accepted that the directors honestly believed the statement was true.

The availability of damages for misrepresentation was extended by the Misrepresentation Act 1967, s. 2(1), which has created a statutory liability for damages for misrepresentation unless the misrepresentor can prove that 'he had reasonable ground to believe and did believe up to the time the contract was made that the facts represented were true'. Section 2(1) applies only where the misrepresentor is a party to the contract. Accordingly it applies to a contract for the allotment of shares in a company only if the misrepresentation which induced the shareholder to take the shares was made by, or can be attributed to, the company. If the misrepresentation can be attributed to the company then it is unnecessary to resort to the torts of negligence or deceit because the statutory remedy will be more convenient.

Formerly, there was a rule that damages for misrepresentation inducing a person to subscribe for shares could not be awarded unless the person rescinded the contract of allotment (*Houldsworth* v *City of Glasgow Bank* (1880) 5 App Cas 317). As rescission is not permitted if the allottee's action is begun after the company has commenced winding up, an allottee who was not able to begin proceedings before commencement of winding up was deprived of any remedy. Now, CA 1985, s. 111A, provides that a person is not debarred from obtaining damages or other compensation from a company by reason only of holding shares in the company. There had long been argument over why the rule had ever been adopted and what purpose it served (see J.A. Hornby, '*Houldsworth* v *City of Glasgow Bank*' (1956) 19 MLR 54, 185, and the discussion in *Webb Distributors (Aust.) Pty Ltd* v *State of Victoria* (1993) 179 CLR 15). The rule was peculiar to contracts of allotment: no other kind of contract had to be rescinded before suing for damages for misrepresentation. One of the problems in *Houldsworth* v *City of Glasgow Bank* was that it concerned an unlimited company which had gone into liquidation (so that the allottee of shares had lost the remedy of rescission). One of the reasons for rejecting the claim for damages was that the shareholder would himself have had to pay calls in order to pay his own damages, and the damages would then include the amount of the calls he had to pay, requiring an infinite series of calls. Although there is a mathematical solution to the problem of summing an infinite series, the House of Lords doubted whether it was allowed by the law on winding up companies.

6.7.6 Criminal liability

The Financial Services Act 1986, s. 47, provides that it is an offence for a person to make a statement, promise or forecast which he knows to be misleading, false or deceptive, or to dishonestly conceal any material facts, or to recklessly make (dishonestly or otherwise) a statement, promise or forecast which is misleading, false or deceptive if it is for the purpose of inducing another to enter into any investment agreement (s. 47(1)). The definition of 'investment agreement' in s. 44(9) includes an agreement under which a person subscribes for shares (see 7.3.2).

When used in statutory provisions defining crimes, the term 'recklessly' does not have any special legal meaning but is used in its ordinary everyday sense (*Commissioner of Police of the Metropolis* v *Caldwell* [1982] AC 341) though this may be modified by the context (*R* v *Reid* [1992] 1 WLR 793 per Lord Ackner at p. 805). If the definition of 'reckless' given by Lord Diplock in *Caldwell* at p. 354 (and affirmed by the House of Lords in *R* v *Reid*) is applied to the Financial Services Act 1986, s. 47, it means that a person who has made a misleading, false or deceptive statement will have made it recklessly if there was an obvious risk that it might be misleading, false or deceptive but the person either failed to give any thought to that risk or made the statement despite having recognised the risk.

The Financial Services Act 1986 creates offences in relation to the listing of shares and other securities on the Stock Exchange and the issuing of advertisements offering unlisted securities (see 7.8).

The Theft Act 1968, s. 15, makes it an offence (triable on indictment only) dishonestly to obtain by deception property belonging to another with the intention of permanently depriving the other of it. By s. 15(4), 'deception' means any deception (whether deliberate or reckless) by words or conduct as to fact or as to law, including a deception as to the present intentions of the person using the deception or any other person.

In relation to a fraudulently induced contract for the allotment of a company's shares, an offence may be committed, under either of these enactments, by the company itself or by an individual who induced the making of the contract or caused the allottee to be deprived of the consideration given for the shares. ('Obtain' in the Theft Act 1968, s. 15, includes obtaining for another or enabling another to obtain, by s. 15(2).) If an offence is committed by a company and is proved to have been committed with the consent or connivance of any director, manager, secretary or other officer of the company, then that officer as well as the company shall be guilty of an offence and liable to be proceeded against (Theft Act 1968, s. 18; Financial Services Act 1986, s. 202).

6.8   SHARES OF SUBSCRIBERS TO THE MEMORANDUM

Each subscriber of the memorandum of a company limited by shares must take at least one share (CA 1985, s. 2(5)(b)), and the number of shares to be taken by each subscriber must be stated in the memorandum (s. 2(5)(c)). These shares must be taken directly from the company: it is not enough to accept a transfer of shares allotted to another person (*Re South Blackpool Hotel Co., Migotti's Case* (1867) LR 4 Eq 238). A subscriber of the memorandum of a company who has not taken the shares committed for in the memorandum will be liable in the winding up of the company as if those shares had been allotted (*Re London, Hamburgh & Continental Exchange Bank, Evans's Case* (1867) LR 2 Ch App 427) unless all the company's shares have in fact been allotted to other persons (*Re Tal y Drws Slate Co., Mackley's Case* (1875) 1 ChD 247).

If a company has more than one class of shares, s. 2(5)(c) does not require the subscribers of its memorandum to state which class of shares they will take, and if they do make such a statement they will not be bound by it (*Re New Buxton Lime Co., Duke's Case* (1876) 1 ChD 620).

7 Offering Shares to the Public

7.1 INTRODUCTION

In a company with a small number of members it is usually the case that all the members are closely concerned with the company and take part in its management, and an important aspect of their control is that they control the admission of new members. Sometimes, though, it is decided to open up membership of a company to anyone who wants to come in. The usual reason for opening membership of a company is that it needs contributed capital and is willing to accept money from anyone. Sometimes a founder, or the heir of a founder, of a successful company wishes to sell all or part of his or her stake in the company and offers it to the public: the company may first have to subdivide the shares or make a capitalisation issue in order to represent the stake by a sufficient number of shares to be able to sell it to a large number of buyers.

When a company's shares are widely held, individual shareholders tend to be personally uninterested in participating in management: they are simply investors who, depending on their tax position, look for good dividend income or for a capital profit on selling shares.

7.2 MARKET-PLACES FOR SHARES

7.2.1 Intermediaries

In order to make a company's shares more attractive to investors it is necessary to assure them that they will be able to sell shares easily in order to realise capital profits, or liquidate the investment or switch to a different investment. Accordingly, enterprises have developed which specialise in acting as intermediaries to assist investors to sell (or, on the other hand, buy) company shares (or stocks) and associated investments such as subscription warrants and company marketable loans (see chapter 12) which are collectively known as 'company securities'. (The 'security' provided by shares and similar investments was the certainty of title provided by share, stock or debenture certificates, but now evidence of ownership of most publicly traded shares is by computer record. The term 'security' is also used with a completely different meaning in connection with borrowing — see chapter 11.)

The basic activity of securities intermediaries is 'broking' — that is, acting as an agent for a client to sell or buy securities for the client, making a profit from a commission on each deal. A broker can assist the marketability of a particular security by being willing to attempt to buy or sell that security whenever asked to do so. This is known as acting as a 'matching broker'. A security will be even more marketable if there is a 'market maker' who is willing actually to buy or sell that security whenever asked to do so. If a security has market makers who are always willing to buy and sell then it will be particularly attractive to investors but, conversely, market makers will only hold themselves out as willing to deal in the most actively traded securities since they must be assured of being able to sell, at a profit, what they are asked to buy and of being able to buy what they are asked to sell. The prices at which a market maker offers to buy and sell are called 'quotations' and if a security has a market maker it is described as 'quoted'. A security will be even more attractive to investors when there are two or more market makers competing with each other to offer the best quotations. (Market makers used to be known as 'jobbers'. Sometimes, matching brokers are considered to be a type of market maker.)

7.2.2   Investment exchanges

Historically it has been usual for securities intermediaries in a particular town to form an association to provide premises where they could transact business and establish rules for the conduct of business. Such associations have also been formed by intermediaries specialising in other forms of investment and they are generally known as 'investment exchanges'. An investment exchange whose members specialise in government stocks and company securities is often called a 'stock exchange'. An investor wishing to buy or sell securities may contact a member of a suitable exchange: the investor may deal directly with a member who is a market maker in the particular security but where there are several competing market makers with rapidly changing quotations, the investor may prefer to employ a member of the exchange as a broker to find the best quotation.

7.2.3   The London Stock Exchange

7.2.3.1   Organisation and history
The London Stock Exchange is an investment exchange for buying and selling government stocks, securities of British and foreign companies and options to buy and/or sell company securities.

Securities trading has been carried on in London since the 17th century, and the first traders' association was formed in 1762: it eventually became the London Stock Exchange, which, in March 1973, amalgamated with other exchanges in the UK and Ireland. At that time, trading on stock exchanges was conducted face to face in various premises known as 'trading floors'. Now all dealings are conducted by telephone, relying on information about prices supplied by computer. On 8 December 1995 the Irish Exchange once again became a separate entity. Member firms of the London Stock Exchange are members of a private limited company called the London Stock Exchange Ltd.

Member firms conduct investment business as market makers, matching brokers or brokers. A member firm may act in any or all of these capacities. However, in order to act as a market maker in a particular security, a member firm must be registered in respect of that security and registration imposes obligations to provide quotations of buying and selling prices. Some highly specialised securities, and securities of moribund companies, have no registered market makers.

An investor who wishes to buy or sell securities may deal directly with a market maker in those securities or may put all business through one member firm which will carry it out as a broker or as a market maker if it happens to be registered in respect of the security concerned. In order to attract permanent clients, member firms offer extensive advisory and management services.

Only securities designated by the Exchange may be traded on the Exchange.

7.2.3.2   Listed market
Listing (known formally as 'official listing') confers the highest degree of marketability on shares. It is only available for the shares of large public companies. The expected market

value of a class of shares for which listing is sought must normally be at least £700,000 and the company must normally have been trading for at least three years. A company whose shares are listed and whose business is well-conducted will normally find it easy to raise fresh capital by issuing new shares.

Over 2,000 UK-registered companies have securities listed on the London Stock Exchange. Although this number provides an investor with a remarkably wide choice it is important to remember that there are just over 1,000,000 English and Scottish registered companies. In other words, over 99.8 per cent of companies are not listed on the Exchange.

The securities of a company can only become listed in accordance with the Listing Rules made by the board of directors of the London Stock Exchange under the Financial Services Act 1986, s. 142(6) — see 7.4.2. An application for admission to listing must be made to the Exchange and must normally be accompanied by a document called 'listing particulars' containing a great deal of information about the company (see 7.4.5). In addition, after admission, an issuing company is subject to continuing obligations set out in ch. 9 of the Listing Rules to disclose all information necessary to protect investors and maintain an orderly market (see 7.4.3.3).

7.2.3.3 *Alternative Investment Market*
The London Stock Exchange opened the Alternative Investment Market (AIM) on 19 June 1995 to replace the Unlisted Securities Market (USM), which had been running since 1980. AIM is intended to provide a market-place for shares of companies that are smaller or less mature than listed companies and will also allow trading where only a small proportion of a company's shares is in public hands. There are no requirements concerning minimum value of the class of shares or minimum length of trading record or minimum percentage of shares in the hands of persons not associated with the company's directors and major shareholders.

7.2.4 Going public

There are several main reasons or advantages for seeking to have a company's shares quoted and traded publicly:

(a) It facilitates raising new finance for the company.

(b) Existing shareholders can readily realise all or part of their investment.

(c) It facilitates expansion of the company by way of takeovers in that its fully marketable securities may be used as consideration for such acquisition.

(d) It provides a higher public profile and thus may provide prestige and an enhanced trading status for the company.

Of course there are also disadvantages which include:

(a) The burden of meeting additional disclosure requirements which involves more expense for the company.

(b) The infliction on the company's management of increased scrutiny by investors, the press and the public.

(c) The company's shares may suddenly become higher in value for taxation purposes and, in particular, inheritance tax which may be very disadvantageous — especially for family and individual shareholders whose tax affairs were not considered carefully prior to the decision to go public.

(d)   The likelihood of a predator company making a takeover bid is enhanced, especially when a large portion of the company's equity is spread amongst the general public.

(e)   The company's management is likely to be put under more pressure than before to take a short rather than a long-term view and to pay out a dividend or a higher dividend.

(f)   There is an increased likelihood of a disgruntled minority opposition within the increased body of shareholders with power to initiate investigative, unfairly prejudicial and winding-up actions.

7.3   FINANCIAL SERVICES ACT 1986

Company securities are bought by people as investments. The industry that has grown up in the UK to persuade people to put their money into investments and which provides facilities for doing so is subject to the Financial Services Act (FSA) 1986.

The philosophy of FSA 1986 is that investor protection should be achieved by disclosure and by self-regulation of the industry. For a discussion of the significance of disclosure in English company law, see L.S. Sealy, 'The 'disclosure' philosophy and company law reform' (1981) 2 Co Law 51. See also R.B. Ferguson and A.C. Page, 'The development of investor protection in Britain' (1984) 12 Int J Sociol Law 287 and Page, 'Self-regulation: the constitutional dimension' (1986) 49 MLR 141. The Secretary of State has transferred many of his functions under the Act to the Financial Services Authority, which was formerly known as the Securities and Investments Board — see SI 1987 Nos. 925 and 942 and SI 1988 No. 738.

Schedule 1 to the Act defines 'investments' and 'investment business'. The fundamental principle of the Act is that no person may carry on 'investment business' in the UK unless he is an authorised person (s. 3) (though certain persons, insofar as their activities constitute investment business, are exempt from requiring authorisation; see 7.3.5), and authorised persons are subject to conduct of business rules (see 7.3.3).

7.3.1   Definition of investments

The Financial Services Act 1986 controls investment business but only in relation to certain kinds of investments specified in sch. 1, pt I. For the purposes of this book it is sufficient to note that all forms of company security are covered because sch. 1 defines the following to be investments for the purposes of the Act:

(a)   Shares and stock in the share capital of a company (para. 1).

(b)   Debentures, including debenture stock, loan stock and bonds — see chapter 12 (para. 2).

(c)   Warrants or other instruments entitling the holder to subscribe for investments falling within para. 1 or 2 (para. 4).

(d)   Certificates representing securities falling within para. 1, 2 or 4 (para. 5). (This primarily refers to depositary receipts.)

Also defined as investments for the purposes of the Act are government and local authority stocks (para. 3), units in unit trusts (para. 6), options to buy or sell anything that is an investment for the purposes of the Act, or currency, gold, silver, palladium or platinum (para. 7 and SI 1988 No. 496), futures contracts (para. 8), contracts for differences (para. 9), long-term insurance contracts (para. 10) and rights to and interests in anything which is an investment for the purposes of the Act (excluding interests under the trusts of an occupational pension scheme) (para. 11).

7.3.2 Definition of investment business

The Financial Services Act 1986, s. 3, prohibits any person from carrying on, or purporting to carry on, investment business in the UK unless he is an authorised person (see 7.3.3) or an exempted person (see 7.3.5). The definition of investment business in sch. 1, pt II, is long and complicated because it is expressed initially in very general terms with provision for a large number of exceptions. For full details, a specialised work such as the *Encyclopedia of Financial Services Law* (London: Sweet & Maxwell, looseleaf) should be consulted. For the purposes of this book it is sufficient to note that investment business includes buying, selling, subscribing for or underwriting investments as an agent (i.e., broking) (para. 12), market making in company securities (or government or local authority stocks or units in unit trusts) (paras 12, 17(1)(a) and (3)), managing other persons' assets if those assets include investments (as defined for the purposes of the Act) (para. 14), giving investment advice (except in a newspaper or periodical not principally concerned with investment or in a sound, television or cable broadcast) (paras 15, 25 and 25A) and establishing, operating or winding up a unit trust or other collective investment scheme (para. 16).

There is an exemption in para. 21 (amended by SI 1988 No. 318) for arranging a transfer of control of a company whereby the transferee obtains 75 per cent or more of the voting rights in the company, provided the transferee is a single individual, body corporate or partnership, or a group of persons who are to be directors or managers of the company and their close relatives, and provided the shares are being transferred by a single individual, body corporate or partnership or a group of directors or managers and their close relatives.

In most cases, only one party to a transaction will be conducting investment business. The issue by a company of its own securities is not investment business as far as the company is concerned (paras 12, 28(1)(d), (2)(b), (3) and (4)). Thus a company can issue its securities despite not being an authorised person. However, subscribing for an issue of securities may be investment business as far as the subscriber is concerned.

7.3.3 Authorised persons and conduct of business rules

Only an authorised person or an exempted person (see 7.3.5) may carry on investment business in the UK (FSA 1986, s. 3). The principal methods of authorisation are:

(a) By being a member of a self-regulating organisation (SRO) which has been recognised by the Financial Services Authority (s. 7). Most full-time securities intermediaries are authorised by being members of the Securities and Futures Authority (SFA), the Personal Investment Authority (PIA) or the Investment Management Regulatory Organisation (IMRO), all of which are recognised by the Financial Services Authority. Members of the SFA conduct business as members either of the London Stock Exchange or of the Association of International Bond Dealers (AIBD) (which facilitates and regulates trading in international bonds — see 12.8). Members of the PIA and IMRO do not, in general, operate as members of investment exchanges but as investment advisers and investment managers respectively.

The SFA provides regulatory cover for firms conducting business in UK and foreign company securities, UK and Irish government securities, international bonds, investment management and advice, corporate finance, financial futures and related products.

The PIA is the principal SRO for the retail sector of the financial services industry.

(b) By holding a certificate from a professional body that has been recognised by the Financial Services Authority (s. 15). This enables professionals such as accountants and solicitors to carry out investment business incidental to their main activities.

(c)   By being directly authorised by the Financial Services Authority (s. 25).

(d)   By being authorised to conduct investment business in another country in the European Union which provides equivalent protection for investors (s. 31). The Treasury are empowered to certify which countries do provide such protection (s. 31(4); SI 1992 No. 1315, art. 2(1)(b)).

In addition, insurance companies, friendly societies and collective investment schemes authorised under the regulatory schemes for those industries are authorised to carry on investment business for the purposes of their main business (ss. 22, 23 and 24).

The Financial Services Authority is empowered by s. 48 to make conduct of business rules dealing with: limitations on the kind or scale of business to be conducted, market making, advertising, disclosure of charges, Chinese walls (arrangements whereby information known to persons involved in one part of a business is not made available to persons involved in another part and decisions are taken in each separate part uninfluenced by conflicting interests of persons elsewhere in the business), stabilisation of the prices of new issues, dispute procedures, record keeping and capital adequacy.

7.3.4   Recognised investment exchanges

An investment exchange becomes a recognised investment exchange (RIE) following an application under FSA 1986, s. 37, to the Financial Services Authority if its head office is in the UK or an application to the Treasury if its head office is outside the UK. An RIE with headquarters outside the UK is called an overseas investment exchange (s. 207(1)). Recognition will be granted if the exchange has adequate financial resources and provides a fair and efficient market (sch. 4). In particular, the exchange must limit dealings on the exchange to specific investments, which must be investments in which there is a proper market (sch. 4, para. 2(2)(a)), and must, where relevant, impose continuing obligations on the issuers of traded investments to provide information for determining the proper value of the investments (sch. 4, para. 2(2)(b)).

The London Stock Exchange is an RIE for UK and foreign company shares, government stocks and traded options.

7.3.5   Exempted persons

In so far as their activities constitute investment business, the following are exempt from requiring authorisation under FSA 1986: the Bank of England (s. 35); recognised investment exchanges and clearing houses (s. 36(1)); the Society of Lloyd's and persons permitted by the Council of Lloyd's to act as underwriting agents at Lloyd's (s. 42); intermediaries in the wholesale markets for sterling, foreign exchange and bullion who have been listed by the Financial Services Authority (s. 43); 'appointed representatives' who act as agents for authorised persons who have accepted responsibility for them in writing (s. 44); various public officials including official receivers (s. 45) and approved international securities SROs (sch. 1, para. 25B). In addition, orders made under s. 46 have exempted organisations ranging from the International Monetary Fund to the Westminster Roman Catholic Diocese Trustee either generally or in relation to specified activities.

7.4   OFFICIAL LISTING

7.4.1   The legal framework

The 'Official List' of the London Stock Exchange is the list of securities dealt in on its Listed Market. Official listing on stock exchanges in the European Union is subject to minimum standards set by three Directives: the Admission Directive (No. 79/279/EEC, OJ No. L66, 16 March 1979, p. 21), the Interim Reports Directive (No. 82/121/EEC, OJ No. L48, 20 February 1982, p. 26) and the Listing Particulars Directive (No. 80/390/EEC, OJ No. L100, 17 April 1980, p. 1). These Directives are implemented in UK law by FSA 1986, part IV.

Article 9 of the Admission Directive requires each member State to designate a national authority competent to decide on the admission of securities to official listing on stock exchanges in its territory. The Interim Reports Directive, art. 9, and the Listing Particulars Directive, art. 18, require competent authorities to be appointed for the purposes of those Directives. The UK government has nominated the London Stock Exchange as the competent authority for the purpose of all three Directives (FSA 1986, s. 142(6); SI 1991 No. 2000, reg. 3(1)(b)).

The exercise by the London Stock Exchange of its functions under FSA 1986, part IV, is subject to the reserve power of the Secretary of State to direct it to comply with either the requirements of the Directives or any other international obligations (FSA 1986, s. 192(1) and (2)).

7.4.2 Listing rules

The board of directors of the London Stock Exchange is authorised to make rules, called 'listing rules', for the purposes of the provisions in FSA 1986, part IV, and thereby for the implementation of the Directives (FSA 1986, s. 142(6) and (8); SI 1991 No. 2000, reg. 3(1)(d)). A committee or subcommittee of the board may make listing rules but rules made thus must be confirmed by the board within 28 days (s. 142(8); SI 1991 No. 2000, reg. 3(1)(d)): this enables amendments to be made quickly in emergencies.

The Directives set out only minimum requirements: member States can make more stringent rules provided they are applied uniformly (Admission Directive, art. 5; Interim Reports Directive, art. 3; Listing Particulars Directive, art. 5, para. 1). In fact the London Stock Exchange's listing rules are in some respects more stringent than the Directives.

Listing rules must be made by an instrument in writing which must be printed and made available to the public (FSA 1986, s. 156(3) and (4)). A person is not to be taken as contravening any provision of listing rules if the provision had not been published at the time of the alleged contravention (s. 156(5)). (The certificate of an officer of the Exchange endorsed on a printed copy of the rules is prima facie evidence of the date of publication stated in the certificate: s. 156(6).) The first version of the Stock Exchange's listing rules was published in November 1984 in a loose-leaf book called *Admission of Securities to Listing,* which was popularly known as the 'Yellow Book' from the colour of its binder. A new version, entitled *The Listing Rules,* was published in September 1993 and came into force on 1 December 1993 — the traditional yellow binder has been retained and it continues to be known as the Yellow Book.

7.4.3 Application

7.4.3.1 *Application procedure*

An application for listing must be made in the manner required by the Listing Rules (FSA 1986, s. 143(1)). An application for the listing of securities cannot be made without the permission of the issuer of the securities (s. 143(2)) and no application may be made in respect of securities to be issued by a private company (s. 143(3)).

The London Stock Exchange may charge fees for applications for listing and for maintenance of listing (s. 155; the current fees are set out at the end of the Listing Rules).

The Exchange may refuse an application to list a company's securities (s. 144(3)):

(a)   if it considers that by reason of any matter relating to the company the admission of the securities would be detrimental to the interests of investors; or

(b)   in the case of securities already officially listed in another European Union country, if the company has failed to comply with any obligations imposed by that listing.

The Exchange must notify an applicant of its decision on the application within six months of receiving it (or within six months of receiving any further information it has requested) (s. 144(4)) and a failure to inform within this time will be taken as a refusal of the application (s. 144(5)).

Once a security has been listed, the listing cannot be called into question on the ground that any requirement or condition for admission to listing has not been complied with (s. 144(6)).

7.4.3.2   *Circumstances in which an application for listing may be made*

If a company's securities are already widely held and actively traded, e.g., on foreign stock exchanges, the London Stock Exchange may grant them official listing — this is called listing by 'introduction'. It is possible, as a concession, only in limited circumstances (Listing Rules, paras 4.12 and 4.13).

Usually an application for listing is made in respect of a new issue of securities, usually with allotment of those securities being conditional on listing being granted. The forms of new issues most commonly made are:

(a)   A public offer for subscription, in which there is a general invitation to the public to subscribe for the securities (i.e., to contribute capital or make a loan directly to the company that is issuing the securities). This is the most important circumstance in which listing is granted and the listing rules are drafted with that in mind. The information the public needs about the company and its securities should be in the listing particulars, which must, therefore, be made available to all intending subscribers.

(b)   A selective marketing (or 'placing'). This is where the bulk, or often all, of a new issue of securities is allotted to a small number of large investors who have been approached privately by the sponsor without any public offer being made.

In a 'vendor consideration' placing, a company acquires a major asset (such as all the issued shares of another company it is taking over) from a vendor or vendors and treats the acquired asset as contributed capital for which it issues new shares to the vendor. These new shares are immediately placed and the cash proceeds go to the vendor. If there is more than one vendor (as in a takeover), listing will not be granted unless all vendors have had an opportunity to participate in the placing (Listing Rules, para. 4.30(a)).

(c)   An intermediaries offer, in which shares are offered to a number of brokers and securities houses for them to place with their clients. An intermediaries offer is intended to create a wider spread of holdings than a placing.

(d)   A rights issue. This is an offer by a company of new shares to its existing shareholders in proportion to their present holdings and is made by means of renounceable allotment letters (see 6.2.2, 6.2.3 and 6.2.6). This is the normal method by which a company that is already listed raises extra capital.

(e)   An open offer. This is an invitation to existing shareholders of a company to subscribe for a new issue in which they can take up as many or as few as they wish, rather than being restricted to a number in proportion to their existing holdings as in a rights issue.

An application for listing may also be made in relation to an 'offer for sale'. This is a general invitation to the public to buy a large block of shares already issued, either because a major shareholder has decided to realise his investment or because a new issue has been made to an intermediary who takes the risk of the issue not succeeding with the public. A major shareholder wishing to sell may sell first to an intermediary for the same reason. Offers for sale through intermediaries are called 'secondary offers'.

If a new issue of equity shares is made by a company for a wholly cash consideration and it is not a rights issue then the members of the company must vote to disapply their pre-emption rights (see 6.2.6). This applies to a public offer, a selective marketing (other than a vendor consideration placing, which, as far as the issuing company is concerned, is not for cash) and an open offer.

An application for listing may also be made when a listed company increases its share capital by a capitalisation issue (see 10.4) or when holders of convertible securities exercise their right to convert or holders of subscription warrants exercise their right to subscribe for new shares. An application for listing will also be necessary when a company that has had its listing suspended wishes to return to the market.

7.4.3.3 Continuing obligations

Companies that apply for listing of their shares must accept the continuing obligations (which will apply following listing) to disclose to the Exchange all information necessary to protect investors and maintain an orderly market. These obligations are set out in ch. 9 of the Listing Rules, and incorporate requirements of the Admission Directive and the Interim Reports Directive. Principal provisions of these requirements are noted at appropriate points in this book (see especially 13.2.6).

Inclusion of continuing obligations in the listing rules is authorised by FSA 1986, s. 153. Section 153(1) states that listing rules may specify requirements to be complied with by issuers of listed securities and may authorise the London Stock Exchange to publicise transgressions and, if the transgression was a failure to publish information, to publish that information. This provision is retroactive in that it is deemed to apply equally to issuers already listed at the time that part IV of the Act became operative and to issuers listed since that date (s. 153(2)).

7.4.4 Discontinuance and suspension of listing

The London Stock Exchange may permanently discontinue or temporarily suspend a listing in accordance with the listing rules if it is satisfied that there are special circumstances which preclude normal regular dealings in the securities (FSA 1986, s. 145(1) and (2)). Listing would be discontinued only in exceptional circumstances which absolutely preclude normal, regular dealings in the securities in question. Suspension of listing, on the other hand, is not unusual and often occurs at the issuer's request, but it also can be used if the normal market in the shares is temporarily distorted or impaired, e.g., where there are rumours of an imminent takeover bid.

The Exchange does not have to inform the shareholders of a company that it is considering suspending or discontinuing the company's listing, and does not have to give them an opportunity to make representations (*R* v *International Stock Exchange of the United Kingdom and the Republic of Ireland Ltd, ex parte Else (1982) Ltd* [1993] QB 534). Shareholders in a company do not have a right under the Admission Directive to appeal to a court against a decision by the Exchange to suspend or discontinue the company's listing (ibid.).

If the listing of securities of a company is temporarily suspended the company is nevertheless subject to the continuing obligations to disclose information and is still liable to pay fees for maintenance of listing (s. 145(3)).

7.4.5   Listing particulars and prospectuses

7.4.5.1   When listing particulars and prospectuses are required

Like all markets, the market for company shares depends on the circulation of information about the securities being traded. The London Stock Exchange has for many years required companies to publish essential information about themselves when their shares are listed and has specified the matters on which information must be provided. Rules on information to be provided when shares are offered to the public are now the subject of European Directives. Under the Listing Particulars Directive (80/390/EEC), shares cannot be admitted to official listing on stock exchanges in member States unless there is a publicly available document called 'listing particulars' which gives standard details of the listed shares and of their issuer (art. 3) and which has been approved by the competent authority in the State where the shares are listed (art. 18(2)). In the United Kingdom the competent authority is the London Stock Exchange (see 7.4.1). The listing particulars must be submitted for approval as part of the process of applying for listing. The Listing Particulars Directive specifies the minimum information which must be contained in listing particulars.

Under Directive 89/298/EEC, when shares are offered to the public for the first time in a member State, whether or not they are going to be listed, a prospectus containing standard information about the shares and their issuer must be made available to investors (art. 4). When shares are offered to the public for the first time and an application is made for them to be listed (as in a public offer for subscription of shares which are to be listed), the prospectus must contain the same information and be subject to the same approval process as listing particulars (art. 7). If shares being offered to the public for the first time are not to be listed then the prospectus can be a simpler and cheaper document (see 7.5).

The provisions of these Directives are implemented in United Kingdom law by the Listing Rules (see 7.4.2) and by the FSA 1986 as amended by the Public Offers of Securities Regulations 1995 (POSR 1995) (SI 1995 No. 1537).

When an issuer applies for listing of its securities which are to be offered to the public in the United Kingdom for the first time before admission (as in a public offer for subscription), a prospectus must be submitted to and approved by the London Stock Exchange (FSA 1986, s. 144(2)(a); Listing Rules, para. 5.1(a)). When an issuer applies for listing of its securities in any other circumstances, listing particulars or a prospectus must be submitted to and approved by the Exchange (FSA 1986, s. 144(2A)(a); Listing Rules, para. 5.1(b)). Prospectuses for shares to be listed and listing particulars must be prepared in accordance with ch. 5 of the Listing Rules.

Prospectuses for shares to be listed and listing particulars must be published (FSA 1986, s. 144(2)(b) and (2A)(b)) by making them available (in printed form and free of charge) in sufficient numbers to satisfy public demand at the issuer's registered office and at the Exchange's Company Announcements Office (Listing Rules, paras 5.1(c) and 8.4) but they must not be published until they have received the formal approval of the Exchange (Listing Rules, paras 5.12 and 8.1). Where it is necessary to publish a prospectus for shares for which an application is being made for listing, it is unlawful to offer those shares to the public in the United Kingdom before the prospectus is published (FSA 1986, s. 156B). A copy of a prospectus for shares to be listed or listing particulars must be delivered to the registrar of companies on or before the date of publication and the published document must state that a copy has been delivered to the registrar (s. 149(1)). Publishing a prospectus for shares to be listed or listing particulars knowing that a copy has not been delivered to the registrar is an offence triable either way (s. 149(3)).

The Listing Rules provide some exemptions from the obligation to prepare prospectuses for shares to be listed or listing particulars. (The Listing Rules may make provision for exemptions by virtue of FSA 1986, s. 156(1) and (2).) In all the circumstances in which exemption is available under the Listing Rules, information equivalent to a prospectus or listing particulars will already have been published. For example, a complete prospectus is not required for a subscription offer if the issuer has published a full prospectus in the United Kingdom for some other securities in the preceding 12 months: in that case the issuer need only publish an abbreviated prospectus setting out changes that have occurred since the last prospectus was issued (Directive 89/298/EEC, art. 6; Listing Rules, para. 5.23). Listing particulars are not required for securities which have already been the subject of a public issue or are issued in connection with a takeover offer or merger, if a document containing information equivalent to that required in listing particulars has been published in the United Kingdom in the preceding 12 months (Listing Particulars Directive, art. 6(1); Listing Rules, para. 5.23A(a)). Listing particulars are not required if the securities have been listed elsewhere in the European Union for the past three years (para. 5.23A(b)) or traded on the Alternative Investment Market and the Unlisted Securities Market for the past two years (para. 5.23A(c)). Listing particulars are not required in the circumstances set out in para. 5.27 (which implements some of the exemptions in art. 6 of the Listing Particulars Directive) where there is a further issue (e.g., on capitalisation or conversion or to an employees' share scheme) of shares that are already listed.

A prospectus for shares to be listed is necessary only if the shares are to be offered to the public in the United Kingdom for the first time. What constitutes an offer to the public in the United Kingdom is defined in FSA 1986, s. 142(7A) and sch. 11A, in substantially the same way, and with substantially the same exemptions, as in the POSR 1995, regs 5, 6 and 7, discussed in 7.5.2. The only notable difference relevant to company law is that FSA 1986, sch. 11A, does not make an exemption for offers of private company shares since such shares cannot be listed and so could not be the subject of a prospectus for shares to be listed anyway.

7.4.5.2 Content of listing prospectuses and particulars

The content of prospectuses for shares to be listed and listing particulars is dictated by the Listing Rules (FSA 1986, s. 144(2)(a) and (2A)(a)). The requirements are specified in detail in ch. 5 and ch. 6 of the rules. In addition, prospectuses for shares to be listed and listing particulars must disclose all the information which investors and their professional advisers would reasonably require, and reasonably expect to find, in order to make an informed assessment of: the assets and liabilities of the company, its financial position, profits and losses and its prospects as well as what rights are attached to the securities (ss. 146(1) and 154A).

A person responsible for a prospectus or listing particulars is only liable to include information of which that person is aware or which that person could reasonably have obtained by making enquiries (s. 146(2)). To help in deciding what information should be included, s. 146(3) states that regard should be had to:

(a)   The nature of the securities and the issuer.

(b)   The nature of the potential purchasers. This means that less information may be given to experienced or sophisticated investors, though the category of persons and the amount of information they require will need to be judged objectively.

(c)   The fact that certain matters may reasonably be expected to be within the general knowledge of the type of professional advisers which the potential customer is likely to consult.

(d)   Any information available to investors or their professional advisers by virtue of the continuing obligations of listed companies to supply information to the London Stock Exchange or similar obligations imposed by any other investment exchange or under any other enactment.

7.4.5.3   *Omission of information from prospectuses and listing particulars*
In accordance with the Listing Particulars Directive, art. 7, the London Stock Exchange may authorise the omission from the prospectus or listing particulars for a company's securities of information otherwise required in any of the following circumstances (Listing Rules, para. 5.18):

(a)   If the information is of minor importance only and is not such as will influence assessment of the assets and liabilities, financial position, profits and losses and prospects of the company.

(b)   If disclosure of the information would be contrary to the public interest (FSA 1986, s. 148(1)(a)). The Exchange may rely on a certificate to that effect issued by the Secretary of State or the Treasury (s. 148(3)).

(c)   If disclosure of the information would be seriously detrimental to the company, though authorisation can be given on this ground only if not disclosing the information would not be likely to mislead a person considering acquiring the securities about any facts, knowledge of which it is essential for him to have in order to make an informed assessment (s. 148(1)(b) and (2)).

7.4.5.4   *Supplementary prospectuses and listing particulars*
A supplementary prospectus or supplementary listing particulars will need to be submitted to the London Stock Exchange and, with its approval, published if, between finalisation of the prospectus or listing particulars for a company's securities and the start of dealings, either (FSA 1986, ss. 147(1) and 154A):

(a)   there is a significant change affecting any matter included in the original particulars; or

(b)   a significant new matter arises that would have had to have been included had it arisen when the particulars were being prepared. The interpretation to be given to the term significant is any thing which affects the making of an informed assessment of the company's assets and liabilities, financial position, results and prospects or the rights attaching to the securities (ss. 146(1) and 147(2)).

The issuer, however, is only duty bound to disclose these changes or new matters if aware of them (s. 147(3)). A duty is placed by s. 147(3) on any other person who is responsible with the company for the prospectus or listing particulars, who becomes aware of such matters, to notify the company which itself will then be duty bound to publicise them, where significant, and if approved, in a supplementary document.

7.4.6   Advertising an application for official listing

7.4.6.1   *Statutory controls on advertising*
Before an advertisement relating to an application for listing can be issued in the UK, the London Stock Exchange must have checked and approved its contents, or, alternatively, authorised its issue without approval (FSA 1986, s. 154(1)).

When listing particulars are published for a class of shares not already listed then, no later than the next business day after publication of the particulars, a formal notice containing the information set out in para. 8.10 of the Listing Rules must be published in at least one national newspaper (Listing Rules, para. 8.7). If the shares are being offered for sale or subscription then the issuer may elect instead to publish in a national newspaper the listing particulars in full, or extracts in what is known as a mini-prospectus, or an offer notice complying with para. 8.11 of the Listing Rules. The Exchange must approve a formal notice or an offer notice before it is issued (Listing Rules, para. 8.23). A mini-prospectus must be authorised for issue before it is issued but the Exchange will not approve its contents (Listing Rules, para. 8.24).

Publication of an advertisement by a person authorised (under FSA 1986) to carry on investment business (see 7.3.3), without obtaining approval or authorisation will constitute a breach of the conduct of business rules to which that person is subject and the civil remedies provided in part I of the Act may be invoked (s. 154(2)).

An unauthorised person who issues an advertisement or other information concerning listing without approval or authorisation will commit a criminal offence triable either way (s. 154(3)). If a company is charged with this offence, then any of its officers or controllers who consented to or connived at the offence, or through whose neglect the offence occurred, shall be guilty together with the company and punishable in like manner (s. 202). No one, however, will be liable for issuing information or an advertisement on behalf of someone else, for example, as a publisher or advertising agent, if he proves that he believed on reasonable grounds that approval or authorisation of its publication had been obtained from the London Stock Exchange (s. 154(4)).

Immunity from civil liability is provided to the persons responsible for the publication of any approved or authorised information which, together with the listing particulars, would not be likely to mislead potential investors in those securities (s. 154(5)).

7.4.6.2 *Definition of issuing an advertisement in the United Kingdom*
By FSA 1986, s. 207(2), for the purposes of the Act's controls on advertising, 'advertisement' is to be interpreted as including:

> . . . every form of advertising, whether in a publication, by the display of notices, signs, labels or showcards, by means of circulars, catalogues, price lists or other documents, by an exhibition of pictures or photographic or cinematographic films, by way of sound broadcasting or television, by the distribution of recordings, or in any other manner.

By s. 207(3), an advertisement issued outside the UK is to be treated as issued inside the UK if it is directed to persons in the UK unless it is in a newspaper or periodical circulating principally outside the UK or in a sound or television broadcast transmitted for reception principally outside the UK.

7.5 PUBLIC OFFERS OF UNLISTED SHARES

7.5.1 Need for prospectuses for unlisted shares

When shares of a company are offered to the public for the first time in a European Union State and no application is made for an official listing on a stock exchange, then the person making the offer must publish a prospectus complying with Directive 89/298/EEC, which is implemented in the United Kingdom by the Public Offers of Securities Regulations 1995

(POSR 1995) (SI 1995 No. 1537). Regulations 3 to 16 of the POSR 1995 apply to shares that are not admitted to official listing nor the subject of an application for listing (reg. 3(1)).

Regulation 4 of the POSR 1995 provides that when unlisted shares are offered to the public in the United Kingdom for the first time, the offeror must publish a prospectus by making it available to the public, free of charge, at an address in the United Kingdom, from the time the shares are first offered until the offer closes. An advertisement, notice, poster or document which announces a public offer of unlisted securities for which a prospectus is required, and is issued to, or caused to be issued to, the public in the United Kingdom by the offeror, must state that a prospectus is or will be published and give an address in the United Kingdom where it can be obtained (reg. 12).

7.5.2   Definition of offer to the public; exemptions

It is the offeror of shares who has the obligation to publish a prospectus and POSR 1995, reg. 5, provides that only the following acts amount to 'offering' shares:

(a)   making an offer which, if accepted, would give rise to a contract for the issue or sale of the shares by the person making the offer or by another person with whom the person making the offer has made arrangements for the issue or sale of the shares;

(b)   inviting a person to make such an offer.

A prospectus is necessary only if an offer is made to the public. Regulation 6 provides that an offer is made to the public in the United Kingdom if, to the extent that it is made to persons in the United Kingdom, it is made to the public. Regulation 6 also states that an offer which is made to any section of the public is to be regarded as made to the public and cites as examples of 'sections of the public', members or debenture holders of a body corporate, and clients of the offeror. It is difficult to see from these examples what distinguishes a group of people which is a section of the public from a group which is not. However, the 21 subparagraphs of reg. 7(2) offer a wide variety of exemptions from the need to publish a prospectus including an exemption where the shares are offered to no more than 50 persons (reg. 7(2)(b)) which will probably make arguments about the meaning of 'section of the public' unnecessary. The 50-persons exemption can only be used once every 12 months by an offeror in relation to shares of the same class (reg. 7(6)).

Some other important exemptions from the obligation to publish a prospectus are where:

(a)   the shares are offered to persons whose ordinary activities involve them in acquiring, holding, managing or disposing of investments (as principal or agent) for the purposes of their businesses, or who it is reasonable to expect will deal in investments in that way (reg. 7(2)(a));

(b)   the shares are offered to persons in the context of their trades, professions or occupations (reg. 7(2)(a));

(c)   the shares are offered to the members of a club or association who have a common interest in what is to be done with the proceeds of the offer (reg. 7(2)(c));

(d)   the shares are offered to a restricted circle of persons whom the offeror reasonably believes to be sufficiently knowledgeable to understand the risks involved in accepting the offer (reg. 7(2)(d));

(e)   the shares are shares of a private company and are offered by the company to its members or employees or their families (as defined in reg. 7(8)) or its debenture holders (reg. 7(2)(f));

(f)   the total consideration payable for the shares cannot exceed ecu 40,000 (reg. 7(2)(h)) or the minimum amount which an investor can invest is ecu 40,000 or more (reg. 7(2)(i)) or the nominal value of each share is ecu 40,000 or more (reg. 7(2)(j)), or, in each case, the equivalent of ecu 40,000 calculated in accordance with reg. 7(9) (the para. (h) exemption can be used only once every 12 months by an offeror in relation to shares of the same class: reg. 7(6));

(g)   the shares are offered in connection with a takeover offer or a merger (reg. 7(2)(k) and (l) and (10));

(h)   the shares are bonus shares (reg. 7(2)(m) and (11));

(i)   the shares are not transferable (reg. 7(2)(u)).

7.5.3   Content

A prospectus for unlisted shares must (by POSR 1995, reg. 8(1)) contain the information specified in sch. 1 to the Regulations, or (by reg. 8(2)) equivalent information where sch. 1 is inappropriate to the issuer's sphere of activity or legal form. In addition, reg. 9 imposes a general duty of disclosure in the same terms as the duty imposed by FSA 1986, s. 146, in relation to prospectuses for listed shares and listing particulars (see 7.4.5.2). The only matters to which regard should be had in determining what information must be included in a prospectus for unlisted shares is the nature of the shares and of their issuer (reg. 9(3)). The information in a prospectus for unlisted shares must be presented 'in as easily analysable and comprehensible form as possible' (reg. 8(3) quoting from Directive 89/298/EEC, art. 11(2)).

The Treasury or the Secretary of State may authorise the omission from a prospectus of information otherwise required by the Regulations if they or he consider that disclosure of that information would be contrary to the public interest (reg. 11(1)).

If the offeror of the shares is not their issuer and is not acting in pursuance of an agreement with the issuer then information about the issuer can be omitted from the prospectus if it is not available to the offeror despite making reasonable efforts to obtain it (reg. 11(2)).

7.5.4   Supplementary prospectus

As with prospectuses for shares to be listed and listing particulars, there is an obligation under POSR 1995, reg. 10, to publish a supplementary prospectus for unlisted shares when:

(a)   there is a significant change affecting any matter which is in the prospectus because it is required by reg. 8 or reg. 9;

(b)   a significant new matter arises about which information would have to have been given if it had arisen when the prospectus was prepared; or

(c)   there is a significant inaccuracy in the prospectus.

A supplementary prospectus must be delivered to the registrar of companies and must be published in the same manner as a prospectus. Regulation 11 (see 7.5.3) applies to supplementary prospectuses.

7.5.5   Optional London Stock Exchange approval

Unlike prospectuses for listed shares and listing particulars, prospectuses for unlisted shares are not normally approved by a competent authority in the State where they are published and this helps to reduce costs to the offeror. However, arts 8 and 12 of Directive 89/298/EEC require member States to make official approval of prospectuses available to offerors of unlisted shares, principally so that prospectuses approved in one State can be recognised in other States. Provision for approval of prospectuses for unlisted shares by the London Stock Exchange is made by FSA 1986, s. 156A, and the Exchange's rules for approval of prospectuses where no application for listing is made are printed after ch. 26 of the Listing Rules.

7.5.6   Restriction on public offers by private companies

A private limited company commits an offence if it offers any of its unlisted shares to the public (CA 1985, s. 81), though an allotment made following an illegal offer is not invalid (s. 81(3)). As in the POSR 1995, there is a provision in CA 1985 that 'offering shares to the public' includes offering to any section of the public (s. 59) but important exceptions are made by s. 60.

An offer is not made to the public if the only persons who are able to take it up are the persons who receive the offer or if the offer can otherwise be regarded as being a 'domestic concern' of the persons making and receiving it (s. 60(1)). By s. 60(4), an offer is to be regarded as being a domestic concern if it is made to:

(a)   an existing member of the company making the offer,
(b)   an existing employee of the company,
(c)   a member of the family of such a member or employee (as defined in s. 60(5)), or
(d)   an existing debenture holder.

Section 60(7) permits an offer which is within s. 60(4) to provide for renunciation of allotment as long as the renunciation can only be in favour of another person in the list in s. 60(4). A prospectus is not required for an offer falling within s. 60(4) (POSR 1995, reg. 7(2)(f)). Offers made in relation to employees' share schemes are to be regarded as being of domestic concern (s. 60(6)).

7.5.7   Time for consideration of a prospectus for unlisted shares

No allotment of a company's unlisted shares may be made in pursuance of a prospectus until the beginning of the third day after the day on which it was first issued generally, or until such later time as may be specified in the prospectus (CA 1985, s. 82(1)). If, before the third day after that on which a prospectus is issued generally, it is, for the first time, issued as a newspaper advertisement then the day of the advertisement is regarded for the purposes of s. 82(1) as the day on which it was first issued generally (s. 82(3)). Saturdays, Sundays and bank holidays are not counted in reckoning what is the third day after a day (s. 82(4)). The beginning of the first day on which allotment is permitted under s. 82(1) is called 'the time of the opening of the subscription lists' (s. 82(2)).

If an allotment is made before the first time allowed by s. 82(1) then the contract of allotment is not void or voidable but the company, and every officer of the company who knowingly and wilfully authorised or permitted the allotment, will have committed an offence triable either way (ss. 82(5) and 730(5) and sch. 24).

Also s. 82(7) provides that an application to take shares made in pursuance of a prospectus for unlisted shares may not be revoked by the applicant until after the expiration of the third day after the time of the opening of the subscription lists. This provision was originally intended to limit the activities of speculators, known as stags, who apply for large numbers of shares in a public issue intending that if the issue is popular then they will be able to resell their allotments at a profit and if it is unpopular they will be able to withdraw their applications.

7.5.8 Minimum subscription for a first public offer

CA 1985, s. 83, provides that when a company makes its first public offer of unlisted shares for subscription it must not allot any unless, within 40 days of issuing the prospectus, it receives in cash the minimum subscription specified in the prospectus. The minimum subscription is the amount which, in the opinion of the directors, must be raised by the issue of share capital in order to provide for the matters specified in sch. 3, para. 2, namely:

(a)   the purchase price of any property purchased or to be purchased which is to be defrayed in whole or in part out of the proceeds of the issue,

(b)   any preliminary expenses and underwriting commission payable by the company,

(c)   the repayment of any money borrowed by the company in respect of (a) and (b), and

(d)   working capital.

The minimum amount required for these matters is required to be stated in the prospectus by POSR 1995, sch. 1, para. 21.

If, 40 days after the prospectus was issued, the minimum subscription has not been received then any application money that has been received must be returned within eight days, after which the directors become jointly and severally liable for repaying it (s. 83(5)). It is not possible to contract out of the minimum subscription provisions (s. 83(6)).

The offers to subscribe that are made within 40 days are not automatically made void by failure to obtain the minimum subscription. It is up to the allottees to serve notice on the company that they regard their allotments as void but this must be done within one month after the date of the allotment (s. 85(1)).

CA 1985, s. 85(2), makes any director of a company who knowingly contravenes, or permits or authorises the contravention of, any of the provisions of s. 83 with respect to allotment liable to compensate the company and any allottee for any loss, damages or costs they sustain or incur as a result. Proceedings under this provision must be taken within two years of the allotment (s. 85(3)).

7.5.9   Failure to obtain a stock exchange listing

If a prospectus states that an application has been, or will be, made for the shares that it is offering to be listed on any stock exchange other than the London Stock Exchange then any allotment made under the prospectus is void if the application is not in fact made before the third day after the first issue of the prospectus or if the application is refused within the three weeks following the closing of the subscription lists (CA 1985, s. 86).

If there is a failure to apply for or obtain a stock exchange listing within the time-limits set by s. 86 then any application money that has been received must be returned within eight days, after which the directors become jointly and severally liable for repaying it (s. 86(4)). It is not possible to contract out of these provisions (s. 86(7)). While any money received from applicants may have to be returned to them it must be kept in a separate bank account and failure to do so is an offence triable either way (s. 86(6) and sch. 24).

7.6 MISLEADING STATEMENTS AND OMISSIONS IN LISTING PARTICULARS OR PROSPECTUSES

7.6.1 Introduction

In 6.7 it was explained that the common law and the Misrepresentation Act 1967 provide some remedies to a person who has been induced to subscribe for shares by a misrepresentation and these remedies are available in all circumstances in which shares are issued. This section will describe the remedies provided by legislation to persons who suffer loss as a result of any untrue or misleading statement in, or omission from, a prospectus, supplementary prospectus, listing particulars or supplementary listing particulars.

Sections 150 to 152 of the FSA 1986 deal with listing and supplementary listing particulars and, by virtue of s. 154A, prospectuses and supplementary prospectuses for shares to be listed. Regulations 14 and 15 of POSR 1995 deal with prospectuses and supplementary prospectuses for unlisted shares. The two sets of provisions are substantially the same and will be dealt with together here. The provisions are expressly stated not to affect liability under any other legislation or at common law (FSA 1986, s. 150(4); POSR 1995, reg. 14(4)) so that the remedies described in 6.7 may be available in addition to the remedies described here.

7.6.2 Misrepresentation and omission

The first head of liability, in FSA 1986, s. 150(1), and POSR 1995, reg. 14(1), is for loss suffered as a result of:

(a) any untrue or misleading statement in a prospectus or listing particulars or supplement, or

(b) the omission from such a document of any matter required to be included by FSA 1986, s. 146, or POSR 1995, reg. 9 (the general duty of disclosure), or by FSA 1986, s. 147, or POSR 1995, reg. 10 (the duty to publish in a supplement details of any significant new matter, change or, in the case of a prospectus for unlisted shares, correction).

Where the Listing Rules or the provisions of sch. 1 to the POSR 1995 require a statement of information about some matter or a statement that there is no such matter then omitting information is to be regarded as a statement that there is no such matter (FSA 1986, s. 150(2); POSR 1995, reg. 14(2)).

By FSA 1986, s. 150(6), no one can be liable for an omission from listing particulars, or from a prospectus for shares to be listed, which has been authorised by the London Stock Exchange under s. 148 (omission because of public interest or serious detriment to the issuer).

7.6.3 Responsibility for listing particulars and prospectuses

Compensation under the first head of liability (see 7.6.2) is payable by the 'person or persons responsible for' the prospectus, listing particulars or supplement which contained the untrue or misleading statement or from which required information was omitted. In relation to a prospectus or listing particulars for company shares, or a supplement to such a document, the persons responsible are identified by FSA 1986, s. 152, and POSR 1995, reg. 13, as follows:

(a)   The issuer of the shares (FSA 1986, s. 152(1)(a); POSR 1995, reg. 13(1)(a)).

(b)   Every director of the issuer at the time of submission of the document to the Stock Exchange or, if it relates to unlisted shares, publication of the document (FSA 1986, s. 152(1)(b); POSR 1995, reg. 13(1)(b)), unless the document was published without the director's knowledge or consent and, on becoming aware of its publication, the director forthwith gives reasonable public notice that it is published without knowledge or consent (FSA 1986, s. 152(2); POSR 1995, reg. 13(2)).

(c)   Every person named in the document as a director or as having agreed to become a director (either immediately or in the future), provided this was done with the person's authorisation (FSA 1986, s. 152(1)(c); POSR 1995, reg. 13(1)(c)).

Paragraphs (a), (b) and (c) do not apply to a prospectus or supplementary prospectus for an offer of unlisted shares not made or authorised by the issuer (POSR 1995, reg. 13(2)).

(d)   Every person who accepts, and is stated in the document as accepting, responsibility for the document or any part of it (FSA 1986, s. 152(1)(d); POSR 1995, reg. 13(1)(d)), and every person who has authorised the contents of the document or any part of it (FSA 1986, s. 152(1)(e); POSR 1995, reg. 13(1)(g)). A person who has accepted responsibility for, or authorised only part of a document is responsible only for that part and only if it is included in (or substantially in) the form and context to which that person has agreed (FSA 1986, s. 152(3); POSR 1995, reg. 13(3)).

In addition, where a prospectus or supplementary prospectus is published by an offeror who is not the issuer of the shares then that offeror is responsible for the document (POSR 1995, reg. 13(1)(e)) and, if the offeror is a body corporate, every director of the offeror at the time the document is published is also responsible for it unless the offer was made in association with the issuer (reg. 13(1)(f)).

A person is not responsible for a document by reason only of giving advice about its contents in a professional capacity (FSA 1986, s. 152(8); POSR 1995, reg. 13(4)).

In relation to a prospectus for shares to be listed or listing particulars, FSA 1986, s. 152(5), empowers the London Stock Exchange to issue an exemption certificate to a director of the issuer, or a person named in the document as a present or future director, if, 'by reason of his having an interest, or any other circumstances', it is inappropriate for the person to be made responsible.

7.6.4   Defences in relation to misrepresentations and omissions

7.6.4.1   Reasonable belief

It is a defence to liability for a misrepresentation or omission to prove that, after making reasonable enquiries, the defendant reasonably believed, at the time the document was submitted to the London Stock Exchange (in the case of a prospectus for shares to be listed or listing particulars) or at the time it was delivered for registration (in the case of a prospectus for unlisted shares), that the statement in question was true and not misleading or that the matter which was omitted was properly omitted (FSA 1986, s. 151(1); POSR 1995, reg. 15(1)). One of the following four circumstances must also be proved:

(a)   that the defendant continued in that belief until the shares were acquired; or

(b)   that they were acquired before it was reasonably practicable to bring a correction to the attention of persons likely to acquire the shares in question; or

(c)   that before the shares were acquired the defendant had taken all reasonable steps to secure that a correction was brought to the attention of persons likely to acquire the shares in question; or

(d)   that the shares were acquired after such a lapse of time that the defendant ought in the circumstances to be reasonably excused, provided that the defendant continued to believe that the statement or omission was proper until after dealings in the shares commenced on the Exchange (if the statement or omission was in a prospectus for shares to be listed or listing particulars and the shares were admitted to listing) or until after commencement of dealings on an approved exchange (if the statement or omission was in a prospectus for unlisted shares dealt in on such an exchange).

7.6.4.2   Expert's statement

It is a defence to liability for a loss caused by a statement purporting to be made, as an expert, by or on the authority of someone other than the defendant, which statement is, and is stated to be, included in the prospectus or particulars with that expert's consent, to prove that the defendant reasonably believed, on reasonable grounds, at the time the document was submitted to the London Stock Exchange (in the case of a prospectus for shares to be listed or listing particulars) or at the time it was delivered for registration (in the case of a prospectus for unlisted shares), that the expert was competent to make or authorise the statement and had consented to its inclusion in the form and context in which it was included (FSA 1986, s. 151(2); POSR 1995, reg. 15(2)). One of the following four circumstances must also be proved:

(a)   that the defendant continued in that belief until the shares were acquired; or

(b)   that they were acquired before it was reasonably practicable to bring the fact that the expert was not competent or had not consented to the attention of persons likely to acquire the shares in question; or

(c)   that before the shares were acquired the defendant had taken all reasonable steps to secure that that fact was brought to the attention of persons likely to acquire the shares in question; or

(d)   that the shares were acquired after such a lapse of time that the defendant ought in the circumstances to be reasonably excused, provided that the defendant continued to believe in the expert until after dealings in the shares commenced on the London Stock Exchange (if the statement was in a prospectus for shares to be listed or listing particulars and the shares were admitted to listing) or until after commencement of dealings on an approved exchange (if the statement was in a prospectus for unlisted shares dealt in on such an exchange).

The term 'expert' includes any engineer, valuer, accountant or other person whose statements are given authority by his or her profession, qualifications or experience (FSA 1986, s. 151(7); POSR 1995, reg. 15(7)).

7.6.4.3   Reasonable steps taken to correct defect

Without prejudice to the defences in 7.6.4.1 and 7.6.4.2 it is a defence to prove that the defendant took reasonable steps to bring a correction, or the fact of an expert's lack of competence or consent, to the attention of potential investors before the plaintiff's shares were acquired (FSA 1986, s. 151(3); POSR 1995, reg. 15(3)).

7.6.4.4   Official statements and documents

It is a defence to prove that the statement which caused the loss accurately and fairly reproduces a statement made by an official person or contained in a public official document (FSA 1986, s. 151(4); POSR 1995, reg. 15(4)).

7.6.4.5 *Plaintiff's knowledge of the circumstances*

It is a defence to prove that the person claiming compensation acquired the shares in question with knowledge, as the case may be, that the statement was false or misleading or of the omission (FSA 1986, s. 151(5); POSR 1995, reg. 15(5)).

7.6.5 Failure to issue supplements

The second head of liability, in FSA 1986, s. 150(3), and POSR 1995, reg. 14(3), is loss suffered in respect of a failure to comply with FSA 1986, s. 147, or POSR 1995, reg. 10, which require:

(a) publication of a supplementary prospectus or listing particulars in certain circumstances; and

(b) notification of any matter for which a supplementary document would be required.

The person who has the duty of publishing a supplement, and who would be liable under this head for not publishing when aware that one is required, is:

(a) the issuer of the shares in the case of a prospectus for shares to be listed or listing particulars; or

(b) the offeror in the case of a prospectus for unlisted shares.

Any person who is responsible for a prospectus or listing particulars has the duty to inform the issuer or offeror on becoming aware of any matter which requires a supplementary document (FSA 1986, s. 147(3); POSR 1995, reg. 10(4)).

It is a defence to liability under this head to show:

(a) that the person claiming compensation acquired the shares in question with knowledge of the change or new matter or (in the case of a prospectus for unlisted shares) inaccuracy for which a supplement should have been published (FSA 1986, s. 151(5); POSR 1995, reg. 15(5));

(b) reasonable belief that the change etc. was not such as to call for a supplement (FSA 1986, s. 151(6); POSR 1995, reg. 15(6)).

7.6.6 Persons to whom compensation is payable

The provisions of FSA 1986, s. 150(1) and (3), and POSR 1995, reg. 14(1) and (3) (see 7.6.4 and 7.6.5), impose a liability to any person who has 'acquired' shares, which includes both original allottees and persons who have purchased shares in the market. This improves on the common law rule that only original allottees could sue for a misrepresentation made in a prospectus inviting subscriptions for new shares (*Peek* v *Gurney* (1873) LR 6 HL 377). This common law rule depended on the court finding that prospectuses were intended only for subscribers and not for subsequent purchasers. In *Possfund Custodian Trustee Ltd* v *Diamond* [1996] 1 WLR 1351, the plaintiffs claimed that the court should now recognise that stock market practice has since changed and that prospectuses are now intended to encourage subsequent trading in shares so that those responsible for prospectuses should be liable at common law to subsequent purchasers for negligent or deceitful misrepresentations. In preliminary proceedings, Lightman J refused to strike out this claim. At p. 1360, Lightman J seized on a difference in wording between FSA 1986, s. 150(1) (which imposes liability to pay compensation to any person 'who has acquired any of the securities in question') and POSR 1995, reg. 14(1) (which, like FSA 1986, s. 166(1), before it, imposes liability to any person 'who has acquired the securities to which the prospectus relates'). His lordship held, *obiter*, that this difference in wording means that POSR 1995, reg. 14(1), applies only to original allottees and not to subsequent purchasers, and applied the same reasoning to FSA 1986, s. 166(1). With the greatest respect it is very difficult to see that the slightly different wording could have such a dramatic consequence. In any case, his lordship ignored the fact that FSA 1986, s. 150(3), and POSR 1995, reg. 14(3), both use the 'any of the securities in question' formula (as did FSA 1986, s. 166(3)). If his lordship's interpretation were correct, subsequent purchasers could claim under reg. 14(3) for failure to publish a supplementary prospectus but not under reg. 14(1) for a misrepresentation in or omission from the principal prospectus, which cannot have been the Treasury's intention when making the Regulations.

Making a contract to acquire shares or an interest in shares is deemed to be an 'acquisition' of the shares (FSA 1986, s. 150(5); POSR 1995, reg. 14(5)).

These provisions of FSA 1986 and POSR 1995 replace similar provisions first enacted in the Directors Liability Act 1890. In relation to the earlier provisions it was held in *Clark* v *Urquhart* [1930] AC 28 that the measure of the 'compensation' for which they provided was the same as the measure of damages in an action for the tort of deceit (see 6.7.5). The term 'compensation' is used in FSA 1986, s. 150(1) and (3), and POSR 1995, reg. 14(1) and (3), and there is no reason to doubt that the measure of this compensation is still the same as in a tort action.

7.7 INVESTMENT ADVERTISEMENTS

Under s. 57 of FSA 1986, an 'investment advertisement' issued or caused to be issued in the UK (see 7.4.6.2) must be issued by, or approved by, an authorised person (see 7.3.3); otherwise a criminal offence triable either way is committed by the person who issued the advertisement (s. 57(3)), and a person who issued the advertisement or caused it to be issued cannot enforce any 'investment agreement' entered into as a result of the advertisement, and any such agreement may be rescinded at the option of the other party (s. 57(5) and (9)). (For a defence for publishers, see 7.8.4.) Advertising by approved persons is subject to conduct of business rules.

An 'investment advertisement' (ss. 57(2) and 207(1)) is, *inter alia,* any advertisement inviting persons to enter (or offer to enter) into an investment agreement or containing information calculated to lead (directly or indirectly) to persons doing so.

An 'investment agreement' (ss. 44(9) and 207(1)) is any agreement the making or performance of which by either party constitutes an activity which is investment business as defined by FSA 1986, sch. 1, part II (or would be apart from the exceptions provided in parts III and IV of the schedule) (*Re Chez Nico (Restaurants) Ltd* [1992] BCLC 192 at pp. 210–11). Buying, selling, subscribing for or underwriting investments or offering or agreeing to do so, either as principal or agent, constitutes investment business by para. 12 in part II of sch. 1. (The issue by a company of its own securities does not constitute carrying on investment business but subscribing for that issue is investment business, and if what is done by either party to an agreement constitutes investment business then the agreement is an investment agreement.)

An advertisement approved or authorised by the London Stock Exchange is not subject to s. 57 (s. 58(1)(d)).

Under s. 58(3), orders have been made providing exemptions from the requirements of s. 57. The most significant exemptions relevant to company law are:

(a) advertisements issued or caused to be issued by a company to persons whom it reasonably believes to be its members or creditors (including holders of its debentures) or holders of subscription warrants for its shares, stock or debentures, or persons connected in any of those ways with any other company in the same group (SI 1996 No. 1586, art. 3(1));

(b) advertisements issued in connection with employee share schemes (art. 6);

(c) advertisements issued by one member of a group of companies to other companies in the group (art. 7);

(d) advertisements issued in connection with a takeover of a private company provided the terms of the takeover offer have been recommended by all the directors of the offeree company (other than one who is the offeror or a director of the offeror). Such advertisements must comply with extensive conditions set out in SI 1995 No. 1536, sch. 4;

(e) advertisements issued in connection with arranging a transfer of control of a company in the circumstances contemplated by FSA 1986, sch. 1, para. 21 (see 7.3.2) (SI 1995 No. 1536, art. 5);

(f) advertisements issued to persons sufficiently expert to understand the risks involved (SI 1996 No. 1586, art. 11);

(g) advertisements directed at informing or influencing:

  (i) a government, local authority or public authority;

  (ii) persons whose ordinary business is trading in securities, or giving investment advice to others, and employees of such persons (SI 1995 No. 1536, art. 8).

7.8 CRIMINAL LIABILITY

7.8.1 Liability for offences by companies

Where an offence under FSA 1986 is committed by a company and it is proved to have been committed with the consent or connivance of, or to be attributable to any neglect on the part of:

(a) any director, manager, secretary or other similar officer of the company, or any person who was purporting to act in any such capacity; or

(b) a controller of the company

he, as well as the body corporate, shall be guilty of that offence and liable to be proceeded against and punished accordingly (s. 202(1)).

A person is a controller of a company if, either alone or with any associate or associates, the person is entitled to exercise, or control the exercise of, 15 per cent or more of the voting power at any general meeting of the company or another corporation of which it is a subsidiary (s. 207(5)). The following persons are 'associates' of a person for this purpose: the person's wife, husband, minor child or stepchild; corporations of which the person is a director; any employee or business partner of the person and, if the person is a corporation, any subsidiary of that corporation and any employee of any such subsidiary (s. 207(5)).

7.8.2 False and misleading statements

A person commits an offence triable either way under FSA 1986, s. 200, if he furnishes information which he knows to be false or misleading in a material particular or recklessly furnishes information which is false or misleading in a material particular:

(a)   for the purposes of or in connection with any application under the Financial Services Act (e.g., an application for listing), or

(b)   in purported compliance with any requirement imposed on him by or under that Act (e.g., compliance with the listing or the prospectus rules).

The use of the term 'reckless' in the section means that it is a crime of basic intention and the mental element of the offence can be satisfied by proof either of intention or recklessness, and recklessness may be shown by proving either that the defendant knew the risk but consciously chose to go ahead regardless and run that risk (*R* v *Cunningham* [1957] 2 QB 396) or that the defendant failed even to consider the risk in circumstances where any reasonable person would have taken the risk into account (*Metropolitan Police Commissioner* v *Caldwell* [1982] AC 341).

7.8.3   False statements by company directors

The Theft Act 1968, s. 19, provides that an officer of a body corporate (or person purporting to act as such) who, with intent to deceive members or creditors about its affairs, publishes or concurs in publishing a written statement or account which to his knowledge is or may be misleading, false or deceptive in a material particular, is liable to seven years' imprisonment. Any person who has entered into a security for the benefit of a body corporate is considered to be a creditor of it but, unlike the forerunner to this section which was contained in the now repealed Larceny Act 1861, there is no mention of any intent to induce any person to become a shareholder; consequently the scope of the s. 19 offence is considerably restricted and of little use in relation to false listing particulars or prospectuses, at least insofar as it has an application to new investors who do not already hold securities in the company concerned.

7.8.4   Unauthorised advertising

An unauthorised person (see 7.3.3) commits an offence under FSA 1986 triable either way if he issues in the UK an advertisement:

(a)   If it is an investment advertisement that has not been approved by an authorised person (s. 57(1) and (3)).

(b)   If it is an advertisement relating to an application for listing for which listing particulars are or are to be published and the advertisement has not been approved or authorised by the London Stock Exchange (s. 154(1) and (3)).

A person (e.g., the publisher of a newspaper) who, in the ordinary course of a business other than investment business, issues an advertisement to the order of another person is not guilty of an offence under any of these provisions if he proves that he believed on reasonable grounds that the advertisement did not contravene the relevant provision (ss. 57(4) and 154(4)).

7.8.5   Misleading statements and practices

Persons involved in carrying on investment business in the UK who are not authorised or exempt under FSA 1986 commit a criminal offence (s. 4). Part I of that Act provides offences in ss. 47 and 48 which are of particular relevance to persons dealing in securities and those involved in issues or offers for sale of company securities.

In particular s. 47 creates an offence of issuing, *inter alia,* false listing particulars or a false prospectus. It provides that it is an offence for a person to make a statement, promise or forecast which he knows to be misleading, false or deceptive, or to dishonestly conceal any material facts, or to recklessly make (dishonestly or otherwise) a statement, promise or forecast which is misleading, false or deceptive if it is for the purpose of inducing another to enter into any investment agreement (s. 47(1)). 'Investment agreement' is defined in 7.5.2.2.

Section 47 also makes it an offence to do any act or engage in any course of conduct which creates a false or misleading impression as to the market in or value of any investment if done to induce another to acquire, dispose of, subscribe for or underwrite those investments or to refrain from doing so or to exercise, or refrain from exercising, any rights conferred by those investments (s. 47(2)).

The maximum penalty for either offence is seven years' imprisonment and/or a fine (s. 47(5)).

7.9 UNDERWRITING

7.9.1 Definition

In relation to an offer of securities, an underwriting agreement is a contract by which a person, called an underwriter, agrees to take any shares that are not taken by the persons to whom the offer is made. The consideration is normally a percentage of the total price for which all the shares in the issue are being offered, and is called an underwriting commission. The underwriter receives the commission whether he has to take any shares or not. An underwriting agreement for a share offer is, of course, made before the offer is made.

From his own commission an underwriter may pay a commission to a sub-underwriter to take some shares if necessary. Alternatively there may be several underwriters to an offer, each agreeing to take a specific fraction of the shares that are not taken by the persons to whom the offer is made.

(For brokerage, see 6.4.1.)

7.9.2 Company's power to pay underwriting commission

If the members of a company, by a provision in their articles, authorise it to pay underwriting commission then a payment is lawful (CA 1985, s. 97(1) and (2); authorisation given by Table A, art. 4). This presumably means that payment of authorised underwriting commission does not contravene CA 1985, s. 100 (prohibition of allotment of shares at a discount), or CA 1985, s. 151 (prohibition of assistance for acquisition of shares).

7.9.3 Limits on underwriting commission

A company may not pay more in underwriting commission than is authorised by its articles and, in any case, not more than 10 per cent of the total price of the issue being underwritten (CA 1985, s. 97(2)). Table A does not make any provision in this respect.

7.9.4 Methods of payment

Underwriting commission may be paid by a company either from cash in hand (including cash received from subscribers for the issue) or by set-off from the money due from the underwriter for shares he has to take.

As a matter of accounting an underwriting commission may be written off share capital account, or profit and loss account, or (CA 1985, s. 130(2)(b)) share premium account. But there must be a writing-off because underwriting commission must not be treated as an asset in a balance sheet prepared in accordance with CA 1985, sch. 4 (CA 1985, sch. 4, para. 3(2)(b)).

7.9.5 Underwriting firm

An underwriting agreement may provide that the underwriter is to take a certain number of shares in any case. These shares are said to be underwritten firm, and, in effect, the underwriter obtains them at a discount. Where underwriting is shared the underwriting agreements should specify whether shares underwritten firm by one underwriter are to be regarded as taken by persons to whom the offer was made (thus reducing all underwriters' liabilities), or as credited against the individual underwriter's liability.

7.9.6 Disclosure

The Listing Rules, para. 6.B.15(h) and (i), require that listing particulars for a company's issue of shares must state:

(a)   Names, addresses and descriptions of the persons underwriting or guaranteeing the issue for the issuer.

(b)   Where not all the issue is underwritten or guaranteed, a statement of the portion not covered.

(c)   Indication or estimate of the overall amount and/or the amount per share, of all charges relating to the issue payable by the issuer, including underwriting commission.

7.10 INADEQUATE RESPONSE

By CA 1985, s. 84, whenever a public company offers shares for subscription it must not allot any of the shares if the issue is not subscribed for in full unless it has stated in the offer either that it will proceed to allotment in any event or that it will allot if certain conditions (such as a minimum proportion being subscribed for) are met and those conditions have been met.

If an offer is not fully subscribed as required by s. 84 the consequences in terms of repayment of application money, avoidance by allottees of contracts of allotment and directors' liability are the same as when there is a failure to achieve the minimum subscription required by s. 83 — see 7.5.8.

In practice the requirement of s. 84 would normally be met by an underwriting agreement for an issue on the London Stock Exchange.

8 Transfer of Shares

8.1 INTRODUCTION

This chapter describes some of the procedures involved when some or all of a company member's shares are transferred to another person. The procedure to be followed depends on three important factors: first whether or not the transfer is by a sale on the London Stock Exchange; second whether the whole of the member's holding is being transferred or only part of it; third whether the shares are certificated or uncertificated.

CA 1985, s. 182(1)(b), provides that shares in a company are to be transferable. This legislative provision states an essential feature of registered companies: that their shares are transferable. The shares of a registered company are transferable by virtue of the statutory provision and there is no need for any specific authority or permission to transfer to be stated in the company's memorandum or articles (*Re Smith, Knight & Co., Weston's Case* (1868) LR 4 Ch App 20). Buckley LJ said in *Re Discoverers Finance Corporation Ltd, Lindlar's Case* [1910] 1 Ch 312, CA, at p. 316:

> The regulations of the company may impose fetters upon the right of transfer. In the absence of restrictions in the articles the shareholder has by virtue of the statute the right to transfer his shares without the consent of anybody to any transferee.

However, the articles of nearly all (if not all) private companies restrict their members' right to transfer their shares (see 8.3.4).

Specific performance of contracts for the sale of company shares will be ordered unless there is a ready market in the shares, so that a plaintiff could make a substitute contract and would be adequately compensated by damages for the additional cost of (or lower receipts from) the alternative contract (*Re Schwabacher* (1907) 98 LT 127). If a seller of shares on the London Stock Exchange fails to deliver the shares then an Exchange official will buy the contracted number of shares in the market and the seller must bear any extra cost. Similarly any shares which a person has contracted to buy on the Exchange but has failed to pay for will be sold and the buyer will be liable for any loss this occasions. The procedure is known as buying-in and selling-out.

8.2 SHARE CERTIFICATES; UNCERTIFICATED SHARES

8.2.1 Description

A member's share certificate states the name, and in many cases the address, of the member and certifies that the member is the registered holder of a specified number of shares of a certain class. It either states that the shares are fully paid or, if they are partly paid, how much of their nominal value has been paid up. If all the shares of one class are fully paid, and rank equally for all purposes, then they do not have to be individually numbered (CA 1985, s. 182(2)). Otherwise shares do have to be numbered and a share certificate should state the distinguishing numbers of the shares it represents (as is required by Table A, art. 6).

The primary record of legal title to a company's shares is in the company's register of members (see 14.3). Share certificates provide convenient evidence of ownership of shares to facilitate members' share dealings. However, a person who owns shares in a company may sell the share certificate (for example, to a collector of such documents) without transferring the shares (*Re Baku Consolidated Oilfields Ltd* [1994] 1 BCLC 173).

Share transfers on the London Stock Exchange have been revolutionised by the introduction of CREST in July 1996. This is a system in which shares can be transferred by alterations in computer records which serve as evidence of title, so that share certificates are unnecessary. The operation of CREST is governed by the Uncertificated Securities Regulations 1995 (SI 1995 No. 3272). The Regulations provide for the approval of a person as 'Operator' of the system. The Operator must satisfy the requirements of sch. 1 to the Regulations. The Operator is CREST Co. Ltd. CREST is a voluntary system. Companies can choose whether to participate and allow their shares to be held in uncertificated form: normally a resolution of the directors of a company that it should participate will be sufficient to allow its shares to be transferred through CREST despite any provisions on transfer of shares in the company's articles (SI 1995 No. 3272, reg. 16), but such a resolution is subject to veto by the company's members (reg. 16(6)). Alternatively, a company can provide expressly in its articles for transfer of shares through CREST (reg. 15). Members of a company which participates in CREST can choose whether or not to hold their shares in uncertificated form. It is expected that persons who hold large numbers of shares and deal frequently will choose uncertificated form but persons who have small long-term holdings will continue to use certificates.

By CA 1985, s. 185, a company must issue certificates for any of its shares which are in certificated form when it allots them (see 6.2.9) or registers transfers of them (see 8.3.4 and 8.3.5).

The London Stock Exchange requires that a share certificate for listed shares be dated (Listing Rules, para. 13.20(e)). Table A, art. 6, requires a share certificate to be sealed with the company's common seal. But a company now does not have to have a common seal and listed companies are not required to seal their share certificates. By CA 1985, s. 40, if a company has a common seal then it may have, for sealing share certificates, an official seal which is a facsimile of the company's common seal with the addition of the word 'Securities'. When duly affixed to a document, such an official seal has the same effect as the company's common seal.

8.2.2 Estoppel

A share certificate under the common seal or securities seal of a company is prima facie evidence of the title of the named member to the shares specified in the certificate (CA 1985, ss. 40 and 186). So the onus is on the person who disputes the member's title to prove that the title is defective.

Companies issue share certificates so as to provide their members with convenient evidence of ownership of shares to facilitate selling the shares. In issuing a share certificate a company must be taken to intend that people will act on the assumption that the statements in the certificate are true. If a company issues a share certificate which misstates facts and a person acts in reliance on the truth of the statement and suffers a detriment as a result then, in legal proceedings between the company and that person, the company cannot rely on the true facts but must accept the statement made on the certificate (*Re Bahia & San Francisco Railway Co. Ltd* (1868) LR 3 QB 584; *Balkis Consolidated Co. Ltd* v *Tomkinson* [1893] AC 396, which is discussed in 8.4). This is an application of the doctrine of estoppel by representation: the company is estopped (precluded) from denying its representation on which the other party relied.

If a share certificate names the wrong person as owner of the shares then the company will have to refuse to register any transfer of the shares by that person. A disappointed buyer who relied on the false share certificate as evidence of the seller's title to the shares may sue for the value of the shares (as in *Re Bahia & San Francisco Railway Co. Ltd*). However, the company may be able to recover the damages from the person who caused it to issue the erroneous share certificate, see 8.4.

If a share certificate states that shares are fully paid when in fact they are not and a holder of the shares has suffered a detriment by acting in reliance on the statement (e.g., by parting with money to buy them or becoming a mortgagee of the shares as security for a loan) then that shareholder cannot be called upon to pay the unpaid part of the nominal value of the shares (*Burkinshaw* v *Nicolls* (1878) 3 App Cas 1004; *Bloomenthal* v *Ford* [1897] AC 156).

A statement creates an estoppel against a company only if it is made with the company's authority. In the following two cases it was held that the erroneous share certificates had been issued without authority and so did not create any estoppel.

In *Ruben* v *Great Fingall Consolidated* [1906] AC 439, the secretary of the defendant company issued what purported to be a share certificate of the company, having forged a transfer of shares belonging to one of the company's members. The purported share certificate bore the company's seal and the signatures of two directors, which the secretary had signed without their knowledge, and the secretary's signature. The certificate had been issued to a firm of stockbrokers to whom the secretary was pretending to mortgage the shares as security for money they had lent him. When the forgery was discovered the company refused to register the stockbrokers as holders of the shares and they sued for damages claiming that the company was estopped from denying the truth of the certificate. Lord Loreburn LC, however, said, at p. 443:

> I cannot see upon what principle your lordships can hold that the defendants are liable in this action. The forged certificate is a pure nullity.

In *South London Greyhound Racecourses Ltd* v *Wake* [1931] 1 Ch 496, a document purporting to be a share certificate of the company had been given to Mr Wake. It bore the company's seal and had been countersigned by the company's managing director and secretary. It related to shares which were owned by the English & Foreign Investment Trust Ltd, which in fact had never transferred the shares. The articles of association of South London Racecourses Ltd stated that the company's seal could be put on documents only when authorised by a resolution of the board of directors but the board had never authorised the issue of the certificate. Clauson J characterised the purported certificate as a forgery, which was of no effect.

It is disconcerting to find the concept of forgery being brought into a situation where one might have thought that officers of a company had an ostensible authority which the company could not deny (see 19.5.3 and 19.5.4). However, the House of Lords in *Ruben* v *Great Fingall Consolidated* was convinced that a company secretary had no ostensible authority to represent that a share certificate he or she issued was genuine. Lord Macnaghten said (at p. 444):

The secretary of the company, who is a mere servant, may be the proper hand to deliver out certificates which the company issues in due course, but he can have no authority to guarantee the genuineness or validity of a document which is not the deed of the company.

Similarly, in *South London Greyhound Racecourses Ltd* v *Wake,* Clauson J pointed out that the managing director had no ostensible authority to seal documents for the company, and that the company had never represented that he had such authority.

By Table A, art. 7, a member will be supplied with a replacement for a certificate that is defaced, worn out, lost or destroyed. The company's reasonable expenses of investigating title must be paid by the member. This replacement service is required of listed companies by the Stock Exchange (Listing Rules, ch. 13, app. 1, para. 10).

When issuing a replacement certificate for one supposed to have been lost or destroyed it is necessary to take precautions against fraudulent claims. It is usual to require:

(a)   a statutory declaration from the shareholder setting out the circumstances of the loss or destruction of the original certificate;

(b)   an indemnity under which the shareholder promises to make good to the company and its directors any loss they may suffer as a result of issuing a replacement certificate;

(c)   if the sum involved is large, a guarantee from a bank or insurance company.

When a replacement certificate is issued it should be marked 'duplicate' and a note should be made on the register of members so that any future transfer of the shares concerned is made only on production of the duplicate certificate.

8.3   TRANSFER PROCEDURES

8.3.1   Instrument of transfer

CA 1985, s. 183(1), requires that a transfer of certificated shares must be made in writing by 'a proper instrument of transfer'. This provision was enacted to ensure that a transfer of shares is made by a document on which stamp duty may be charged (stamp duty is levied on documents rather than transactions) (*Re Greene* [1949] Ch 333 per Harman J at p. 339; *Re Paradise Motor Co. Ltd* [1968] 1 WLR 1125). Accordingly, any instrument that will attract stamp duty is a 'proper' instrument for the purposes of s. 183(1). However, a document is capable of being a proper instrument of transfer for the purpose of s. 183(1) even though the amount of duty cannot be assessed from the document itself (because, for example, it gives insufficient information about the consideration for the transfer) (*Nisbet* v *Shepherd* [1994] 1 BCLC 300). A provision in a company's articles purporting to transfer shares of the company is not a proper instrument of transfer and so is void (*Re Greene*).

By the Stock Transfer Act 1963, s. 1(1) and (4)(a), fully paid company shares may be transferred by executing a document in one of the forms set out in sch. 1 to the Act (as amended by SI 1974 No. 1214, SI 1979 No. 277, SI 1990 No. 18 and SI 1996 No. 1571). By s. 2(1) of the 1963 Act such a form may be used to transfer fully paid shares of a company notwithstanding a provision in the company's articles requiring the use of some other form (Table A, art. 23, refers to the use of 'any usual form or . . . any other form which the directors may approve') and may be executed under hand only notwithstanding a provision in the articles requiring execution under seal.

The Stock Transfer Act 1963 does not apply to partly paid shares, and a company that has issued such shares may in its articles specify a transfer procedure for them.

A transfer of uncertificated shares may be registered without a proper instrument of transfer if the transfer is in accordance with the Uncertificated Securities Regulations 1995 (SI 1995 No. 3272) governing CREST (see SI 1995 No. 3272, reg. 40(2)).

8.3.2 Transaction not on the London Stock Exchange

The procedure by which a holder of fully paid shares in a company transfers them, when the transaction is not being carried out on the London Stock Exchange, is as follows. The transferor makes out and signs a stock transfer form on which is stated:

(a) the name of the company whose shares are being transferred;

(b) the number, nominal value and class of the shares being transferred (shares of different classes should not be transferred on the same form — see Table A, art. 24(b));

(c) the consideration being paid;

(d) the transferor's name and address;

(e) the name and address of the transferee.

If all the shares represented on a share certificate are being transferred to one transferee then the share certificate is sent with the transfer form to the transferee. The transferee pays the stamp duty and then sends the stock transfer form and the share certificate to the company for registration.

If only part of the holding represented by a share certificate is being transferred, or different parts of the holding are being transferred to different persons, then the transferor will not want to send the certificate to one transferee, for fear of it being used fraudulently to obtain a transfer of the whole holding. Instead the transferor sends the certificate and all transfer forms to the company so that it can certify on the transfer forms that the transferor has produced a certificate covering the shares being transferred and forward the forms to the transferees. This procedure is known as 'certification' of the transfer forms. If some of the shares represented by the transferor's share certificate are not being transferred then the company will send the transferor a 'balance ticket', which is a temporary certificate for the shares not being transferred. A new certificate for those shares would not normally be issued until the transfers were registered.

If a transfer is falsely certificated and the false certification was made fraudulently then any person to whom detriment has been caused by acting in reliance on the false certification can sue the person who made it for damages for deceit. Actions for deceit are discussed in more detail in 6.7.5. By statute, a company which makes a false certification negligently is under the same liability as if it had been made fraudulently (CA 1985, s. 184(2)) — this is a statutory liability for economic loss caused by negligent misstatement introduced before the courts recognised such a liability in common law.

The common law took the view that, as in the cases on forged share certificates (see 8.2.2), a company was not liable for a false certification of a transfer unless it had been made by someone with actual or ostensible authority to guarantee the authenticity of certifications, and that a company secretary does not have ostensible authority to do such a thing (*George Whitechurch Ltd* v *Cavanagh* [1902] AC 117; *Kleinwort Sons & Co.* v *Associated Automatic Machine Corporation Ltd* (1934) 151 LT 1). However, this has been affected by statute. CA 1985, s. 184(3)(b), deems a certification to have been made by a company if it was issued and signed by a person authorised to issue certifications.

8.3.3   Stamp duty

The stamp duty on an instrument of transfer of company shares by sale is $\frac{1}{2}$ per cent of the value transferred, rounded up to the nearest 50p (Finance Act 1963, s. 55(1A); Finance Act 1986, s. 64). There are exemptions. For example, if the transfer is to a body of persons established for charitable purposes only, or to the trustees of a trust so established, then no duty is payable (Finance Act 1982, s. 129). Transfers to the trustees of the National Heritage Memorial Fund and the Historic Buildings and Monuments Commission for England are also exempt (Finance Act 1982, s. 129; Finance Act 1983, s. 46).

Any person who registers an instrument chargeable with stamp duty when it is not duly stamped is liable to a fine (Stamp Act 1891, s. 17). Accordingly, a company is justified in refusing to register an improperly stamped transfer. However, if an incorrectly stamped transfer is registered then the shares are effectively transferred (*Nisbet* v *Shepherd* [1994] 1 BCLC 300).

If there are any doubts about the correct duty then the company can require the Inland Revenue to 'adjudicate' whether the correct amount has been paid.

A transfer not by way of sale is not subject to *ad valorem* duty. Previously it was necessary to submit such a transfer to the Inland Revenue who would check that it was exempt, and a fixed duty of 50p was payable. The Revenue would mark such a transfer with the words 'Transfer passed for 50p duty'. The Stamp Duty (Exempt Instruments) Regulations 1987 (SI 1987 No. 516) provide for self-certification by the transferor or his solicitor that a transfer is within one of the categories listed in the schedule to the regulations. A transfer thus certified is exempt from both *ad valorem* duty and the 50p duty.

Parliament has provided, in the Finance Act 1990, s. 108, for stamp duty on share transactions to be abolished, but has left it to the Treasury to appoint the abolition day, which has never been done.

8.3.4   Directors' approval, restrictions on transfer, and pre-emption rights

Entries in the register of members are acts of the company which may only be taken with the approval of the directors (see, for example, *South London Greyhound Racecourses Ltd* v *Wake* [1931] 1 Ch 496) or of all the members (*Re Zinotty Properties Ltd* [1984] 1 WLR 1249). The company secretary, for example, does not have authority to make entries in the register (*Chida Mines Ltd* v *Anderson* (1905) 22 TLR 27; *Re Indo-China Steam Navigation Co.* [1917] 2 Ch 100; *Re Zinotty Properties Ltd*).

Because it is an essential feature of registered companies that their shares are freely transferable, the directors of a company have no power to refuse to register a transfer unless they have been given such a power by the company's constitution (*Re Cawley & Co.* (1889) 42 ChD 209; *Re Bede Steam Shipping Co. Ltd* [1917] 1 Ch 123; *Re Copal Varnish Co. Ltd* [1917] 2 Ch 349). Table A, art. 24, entitles the directors to refuse to register a transfer of a partly paid share to a person of whom they do not approve (e.g., because the person is clearly unable to pay the amount outstanding on the shares). As shares are prima facie transferable, a restriction on transfer must be clearly expressed and will not usually be implied by the courts (*Greenhalgh* v *Mallard* [1943] 2 All ER 234 per Lord Greene MR at p. 237). The articles cannot be altered with retrospective effect so as to allow the directors to refuse to register a transfer that has already taken place (*W. & A. M'Arthur Ltd* v *Gulf Line Ltd* 1909 SC 732).

In a private company the directors are normally empowered by the articles to refuse to register any transfer. (There is no such power in Table A.) It is usually provided that the directors have absolute and unlimited discretion when exercising this power and are not bound to give reasons for refusing a transfer.

If the directors of a company have a power to refuse to register a transfer of the company's shares then they must always exercise that power 'bona fide in what they consider — not what a court may consider — is in the interests of the company' (*Re Smith & Fawcett Ltd* [1942] Ch 304 per Lord Greene MR at p. 306 — this principle applies to all acts of directors, see 16.4.1). When deciding whether to register a transfer the directors can consider only factors which the company's constitution allows them to consider. Unless permitted to do so by the constitution, they cannot, for example, refuse to register a transfer because they believe the transferee will be acting as a trustee for the transferor (*Moffat* v *Farquhar* (1878) 7 ChD 591) or because they believe the transferee will be acting as a trustee for a person of whom they disapprove (*Re Bell Bros Ltd* (1891) 65 LT 245) or because the transferee is not a member of a particular family (*Re Bell Bros Ltd*) or because the transferee will hold only one share (*Re Bede Steam Shipping Co. Ltd*). In practice it is difficult to challenge a decision by directors not to register a transfer because the courts have adopted a rule that directors are not bound to give a reason for refusal, and the court will presume that they have acted rightly (*Re Gresham Life Assurance Society, ex parte Penney* (1872) LR 8 Ch App 446; *Re Coalport China Co.* [1895] 2 Ch 404).

A renunciation of allotment in favour of another person is not a transfer for the purposes of provisions in articles empowering directors to refuse to register a transfer (*Re Pool Shipping Co. Ltd* [1920] 1 Ch 251; *System Controls plc* v *Munro Corporate plc* [1990] BCLC 659).

It is common for the articles of a private company to provide that a member may not sell shares without first offering them to existing members for sale at a price to be determined by independent valuation, or according to a formula set out in the articles. (This is called a right of pre-emption.) In practice, the other members of a private company often do not have enough cash to make such a purchase and so the provisions of CA 1985 enabling the company itself to buy out a member who wishes to depart are very welcome (see 10.6). It is the duty of directors to refuse to register a transfer to an outsider if the transferor has breached the company's articles by not offering the shares to other members first (*Tett* v *Phoenix Property & Investment Co. Ltd* [1986] BCLC 149).

In *Heron International Ltd* v *Lord Grade* [1983] BCLC 244 there was a takeover bid for Associated Communications Corporation plc, of which Lord Grade was chairman and chief executive. Lord Grade and his fellow directors agreed to transfer their own shares to the bidder but Heron International Ltd had acquired shares in the company and wished to launch a rival bid at a higher price. If the transfer of the directors' shares went through it would give the first bidder a majority of the votes in the company and Heron's bid would inevitably fail. Lawton LJ said (at pp. 264–5):

This duty to determine which person shall acquire and be registered as the holder of [shares] is a fiduciary power which the directors must exercise in the interests of the company and in the interests of the shareholders of the company. . . .

Where directors have decided that it is in the interests of a company that the company should be taken over, and where there are two or more bidders, the only duty of the directors, who have powers [to refuse to register transfers], is to obtain the best price. The directors should not commit themselves to transfer their own voting shares to a bidder unless they are satisfied that he is offering the best price reasonably obtainable. Where the directors must only decide between rival bidders, the interests of the company must be the interests of the current shareholders. The future of the company will lie with the successful bidder. The directors owe no duty to the successful bidder or to the company after it has passed under the control of the successful bidder. The successful bidder can look after himself, and the shareholders who reject the bid and remain as shareholders do so with their eyes open, having rejected that price which the directors consider to be the best price reasonably obtainable.

By art. 27 of Table A, no fee is to be charged for registering a transfer.

If the directors decline to register a transfer then the transferee must be informed and, by CA 1985, s. 183(5), the company must, under penalty, send notice of refusal within two months of a transfer being lodged for registration (penalty in s. 183(6) and sch. 24). Because a transferee has a prima facie right to be registered unless refused, the board of directors must positively adopt a resolution to refuse to register: inaction does not amount to refusal (*Re Hackney Pavilion Ltd* [1924] 1 Ch 276; *Moodie* v *W. & J. Shepherd (Bookbinders) Ltd* [1949] 2 All ER 1044). A decision not to register must be taken within a reasonable time and prima facie this is the two months allowed for sending the notice of refusal (*Re Swaledale Cleaners Ltd* [1968] 1 WLR 1710). Equally the transferee must wait a reasonable time, which is again prima facie two months, for a decision (*Re Zinotty Properties Ltd* [1984] 1 WLR 1249). Provided a decision to refuse registration has been taken within a reasonable time, the fact that notice of it was not sent within the statutory two-month period does not render the decision invalid (*Popely* v *Planarrive Ltd* [1997] 1 BCLC 8). If the directors fail to exercise a right to refuse to register a transfer within a reasonable time (prima facie, two months) then the right to refuse will be lost and the transferee will have the right to be registered as a member in respect of the shares. If the directors still refuse to register the transfer then the transferee can take proceedings for rectification of the register of members (see 14.3.3) and to compel the issue of a share certificate (see the next paragraph). If there is no board of directors to exercise a right of refusal then the transferee will be entitled to be registered after two months (*Re New Cedos Engineering Co. Ltd* [1994] 1 BCLC 797, in which the acting directors had not been validly appointed).

If the company does not refuse to register a transfer then it must, under penalty, within two months of the transfer being lodged for registration, have ready for delivery a new share certificate (CA 1985, s. 185(1) and (5) and sch. 24). The transferee may serve a notice on the company requiring it to supply a certificate and if the company does not do so within 10 days of service of the notice then the transferee may apply to the court to make an order requiring the company, and any officer, to make good the default (CA 1985, s. 185(6)). Failure to comply with such an order would be punishable as contempt of court.

8.3.5 Transactions on the London Stock Exchange

It is an essential feature of securities listed on the London Stock Exchange that they are freely transferable. This is required by the Admission Directive, Sch. A. II(2), incorporated in the Listing Rules, para. 3.15. The directors of a listed company must not have any power to refuse to approve transfers of shares other than in exceptional circumstances, approved by the Exchange, in which the market will not be disturbed (Listing Rules, para. 3.15). No charge may be made by a company for registering a transfer of listed shares (Listing Rules, ch. 13, app. 1, para. 5; cf. Table A, reg. 27). The articles of association of a listed company must provide that a member who sells part of a holding of listed shares is entitled to a certificate for the retained balance free of charge (Listing Rules, ch. 13, app. 1, para. 10). Table A makes all these provisions. CA 1985, s. 185(1), does not apply to transfers of uncertificated shares within CREST (SI 1995 No. 3272, reg. 32(2)).

The work of maintaining the register of members of a company with a large number of members is, in many cases, performed by a specialist firm of company registrars.

8.3.6 Stamp duty reserve tax

It is not possible to charge stamp duty on share sales in paperless trading on the London Stock Exchange, because stamp duty is a tax on documents. Part IV of the Finance Act 1986 therefore introduced stamp duty reserve tax. This is charged on an agreement to transfer shares for consideration in money or money's worth (s. 87) and is charged at the rate of 0.5 per cent on the consideration (s. 87(6)). The tax is payable by the purchaser (s. 91), though it is normally collected by a Stock Exchange intermediary. Although stamp duty reserve tax is charged on any agreement to transfer shares, the charge is cancelled (or any tax paid is repayable) if the agreement is carried out by means of an instrument on which stamp duty is paid (s. 92). A sale to a market maker in the ordinary course of business is exempt from stamp duty reserve tax (s. 88A).

Parliament has provided, in the Finance Act 1990, s. 110, for stamp duty reserve tax to be abolished on the same day as stamp duty on share transactions, but has left it to the Treasury to appoint the abolition day, which has never been done.

8.4 FORGED OR FRAUDULENT TRANSFERS

If the signature of a shareholder is forged on an instrument of transfer of those shares then the instrument is void; the shares are not transferred; and the original holder still holds them.

A person who presents a forged or fraudulent transfer of shares for registration (whether knowing it is a forgery or not) and who receives a share certificate cannot use the doctrine of estoppel by representation (see 8.2.2) to require the company to stand by its statement in the share certificate of who owns the shares because the representation merely repeated the information which that person provided (*Simm* v *Anglo-American Telegraph Co.* (1879) 5 QBD 188).

In *Balkis Consolidated Co. Ltd* v *Tomkinson* [1893] AC 396, the plaintiff had sent a transfer to the company for registration relying on the company's certification of the transfer. In fact the certification was false and the shares had already been sold to other buyers. Nevertheless the company issued the plaintiff with a share certificate, but when the plaintiff in turn tried to sell the shares the company had discovered the error and refused to register the purchasers, so the plaintiff had to buy equivalent shares to fulfil the contracts of sale. It was held that the plaintiff could rely on the representation of ownership in his share certificate because it repeated the representation made by the company in the certification of the transfer. This is now affected by statute. By CA 1985, s. 184(1), a company's certification of a transfer of shares is not to be taken as a representation that the transferor has any title to the shares: it is only a representation that documents have been produced to the company showing prima facie that the transferor has title to the shares. If a case like *Balkis Consolidated Co. Ltd* v *Tomkinson* occurred today, the plaintiff could claim damages under s. 184(2) for negligent false certification.

A person who presents a transfer for registration is required by common law to indemnify the company against any liability it incurs to other persons as a result of registering the transfer (*Sheffield Corporation* v *Barclay* [1905] AC 392, HL; *Yeung* v *Hong Kong & Shanghai Banking Corporation* [1981] AC 787, PC). So if A sends a forged or fraudulent transfer of a company's shares to the company for registration and receives a share certificate and subsequently B relies on the share certificate to buy the shares from A then

B can sue the company for the value of the shares (*Re Bahia & San Francisco Railway Co. Ltd* (1868) LR 3 QB 584, see 8.2.2) but the company can recover the damages from A, even if A did not know of the fraud or forgery. In *Royal Bank of Scotland plc* v *Sandstone Properties Ltd* (1998) *The Times*, 12 March 1998 a client of a stockbroker forged a transfer of shares, which he did not in fact own, to a company which the broker used to hold shares as nominee for its clients. (Subsequently the shares were sold by the broker at the instance of its fraudulent client.) It was held that the stockbroker had to indemnify the issuer of the shares for the losses which it incurred as a result of registering the transfer. The broker was liable despite acting in reliance on an erroneous share certificate given by the issuing company to the fraudulent client. It was said that giving the erroneous certificate had made it possible for the issuing company's loss to be caused but was not the cause of the loss: the cause of the loss was the forged transfer presented by the broker.

It is usual for a public company to insure itself against the consequences of acting on a forged instrument of transfer, or other document (such as a forged power of attorney) affecting share transfer.

If, as a result of a forged instruction within CREST, there is an error in a person's entry in a company's register of members which causes loss to that person, the court may make a compensation order against the CREST Operator (SI 1995 No. 3272, reg. 30). There are several limitations in reg. 30 on compensation orders. Perhaps the most significant is the rule that if the perpetrator of the forgery is identified, no compensation order can be made against CREST even if the loss cannot be recovered from the perpetrator (reg. 30(4)(a)).

8.5 TRANSMISSION OF SHARES

The term 'transmission' is used to describe the automatic transfer of ownership of an individual shareholder's shares which occurs by operation of law when the individual dies or is adjudged bankrupt. On death, an individual's shares are transmitted to his or her personal representatives or, if the individual was a co-owner of the shares, to the surviving co-owner or co-owners. In bankruptcy, shares go to the individual's trustee in bankruptcy (IA 1986, s. 306).

Transmission of a share of a company to a personal representative or trustee in bankruptcy does not by itself make that person a member of the company: the status of membership is not achieved until the person has agreed to be registered as a member (*Re Bowling and Welby's Contract* [1895] 1 Ch 663 per Lindley LJ at p. 670). Nevertheless, in the absence of a contrary provision, 'member' in articles of association must be read, as far as possible, as including the estate of a deceased member (*New Zealand Gold Extraction Co. (Newbery-Vautin Process) Ltd* v *Peacock* [1894] 1 QB 622, CA; *James* v *Buena Ventura Nitrate Grounds Syndicate Ltd* [1896] 1 Ch 456, CA). Table A, art. 31, provides that a person to whom a share is transmitted on death or bankruptcy has the rights to which that person would be entitled if registered as the holder of the share except that, unless actually registered as the holder of the share, the person has no right to attend or vote at a general or class meeting.

The personal representatives of a deceased shareholder, as representing his or her estate, are entitled to all the profits and advantages attaching to the deceased's shares, and are subject to all the incidental liabilities (*James* v *Buena Ventura Nitrate Grounds Syndicate Ltd*; *Llewellyn* v *Kasintoe Rubber Estates Ltd* [1914] 2 Ch 670). Under Table A, art. 30, the personal representatives of a deceased shareholder may elect either to become the registered holders of the shares themselves or to have some person nominated by them registered as member in succession to the deceased (the nominated person would normally be the person entitled to the shares under the deceased member's will or the law on intestate succession).

If there are no directors to register the changes of membership it may be necessary to apply to the court for rectification of the company's register of members.

The trustee in bankruptcy of a bankrupt shareholder in a company has a right to be registered as the holder of the bankrupt's shares in place of the bankrupt unless the company's articles restrict that right (*Wood* v *W. & G. Dean Pty Ltd* (1929) 43 CLR 77). The only reason for registering as the holder of the shares is that it enables the trustee to vote at general meetings but in practice it is rare for the trustee in bankruptcy of a shareholder in a company to wish to take part in the company's affairs. See further 14.4.9.1.5. Table A, art. 30, specifies the procedure to be followed by a trustee wishing to be registered but does not restrict the right to be registered unless the share is partly paid or the company has a lien on it (in which case art. 24 gives the directors power to refuse the registration).

8.6 SHARE WARRANTS

There are two methods of evidencing title to company shares. The method that is normally adopted in Britain is for the company to enter each shareholder's name in its register of members: as the shareholder's name is the vital element of this system the shares are said to be in 'nominative' form. The alternative system, which has been more popular in many continental European countries, is for title to be evidenced by possession of a title document which states that the bearer of the document is the owner of the shares specified in the document: shares under this system are said to be in 'bearer' form.

A British registered company cannot issue shares directly in bearer form: instead it may, if there is a provision to that effect in its articles (Table A does not make such provision), issue 'share warrants' to bearer for fully paid shares under CA 1985, s. 188. The bearer of a share warrant issued under the company's common seal is entitled to the shares specified in the warrant, and those shares may be transferred by delivery of the warrant (s. 188(2)). Share warrants to bearer are judicially recognised as being negotiable instruments (*Webb, Hale & Co.* v *Alexandria Water Co. Ltd* (1905) 21 TLR 572). The bearer of a share warrant may surrender it for cancellation to the company which must then register the bearer's name in its register of members in respect of the shares specified in the warrant (s. 355(2)). The articles may place conditions on the surrender of warrants (ibid.).

On issuing a share warrant to one of its members a company must pay stamp duty of three times the duty that would be payable if the shares were then being transferred by sale, i.e., $1\frac{1}{2}$ per cent of the value (rounded up to the nearest £1.50) (Stamp Act 1891, sch. 1, heading 'Bearer instrument' (inserted by Finance Act 1963, s. 59)). The Finance Act 1990, s. 107, abolishes stamp duty charges on share warrants to bearer but had not been brought into force when this edition went to press.

Share warrants to bearer were virtually prohibited under exchange controls from the time of the Second World War until 1979. Although they can at present be issued freely, it is unlikely that they will be very common, partly because of a fear of reimposition of exchange controls, partly because bearer documents attract thieves and forgers, and partly because it is considered important to know who a company's shareholders are.

8.7 THIRD-PARTY INTERESTS IN SHARES

8.7.1 No notice to company of third-party interests

Like any other item of property, it is possible for more than one person to have a property interest in a company share. For example, the owner of the legal title may be holding it in trust for one or more beneficiaries, or may be a mortgagee who is required to recognise the morgagor's equity of redemption. In a listed public company it is common for shares to be held by a 'nominee' — that is, a bare trustee who has no active duties of trusteeship to perform and holds the shares in name only, having agreed to do nothing with them except under the direction of the person for whom the shares are being held. It is common to form a company to act as a nominee shareholder and it is usually easy to identify such companies because they have the word 'nominees' in their names. An examination of the registers of members of 222 listed companies, reported in *The Stock Exchange Survey of Share Ownership* (1983), found that one-third of the shares in the companies were held by nominees.

It is an important principle of company law that if a person is named in a company's register of members as the owner of a share in the company then the company is entitled to regard that person as the only person interested in the share and to ignore the claims of anyone else, even if informed of those claims, unless the court intervenes. This is provided by Table A, art. 5, which is justified by CA 1985, s. 360:

> No notice of any trust, expressed, implied or constructive, shall be entered on the register, or be receivable by the registrar, in the case of companies registered in England and Wales.

The mysterious phrase 'receivable by the registrar' in s. 360 first appeared in CA 1862, s. 30, and from its context in that Act it clearly means the registrar of companies. However, the provision enacted in the section first appeared in the Joint Stock Companies Act 1856, s. 19, where the phrase used is 'receivable by the company'. it is pretty clear that the word 'registrar' was put in by mistake when the provision was re-enacted in 1862. In *Société Générale de Paris* v *Tramways Union Co. Ltd* (1884) 14 QBD 424, Lindley LJ, commenting on CA 1862, s. 30, said:

> The section in question appears to me . . . to relieve [registered companies] from the duty of attending to mere notices of equitable interests.

His lordship rejected the argument that the wording of the provision in the 1862 Act meant only that a company must not record a notice of an equitable interest in the register of members but that it is affected by such notice and should record it somewhere else. See also the remarks of the Earl of Selborne in the same case in the House of Lords (1885) 11 App Cas 20. In effect Lindley LJ's interpretation of the provision as enacted in 1862 (and re-enacted in 1985) gives it the meaning that its predecessor in the 1856 Act plainly had (see also *Re T. H. Saunders & Co. Ltd* [1908] 1 Ch 415 per Warrington J at p. 422).

If large numbers of shareholders in listed public companies start to have their shares held by nominees, because the nominees are able to use CREST which the beneficial owners of the shares cannot, it may be necessary to amend the law to enable companies to communicate with beneficial owners of shares held by nominees. See Department of Trade and Industry and HM Treasury, *Private Shareholders: Corporate Governance Rights* (URN 96/983) (London: DTI, 1996).

8.7.2 Stop notices

A person claiming to be interested in shares in a company may apply to the High Court to serve a 'stop notice' (Charging Orders Act 1979, s. 5(2)(b); Rules of the Supreme Court

1965, ord. 50, r. 12). A stop notice requires the company to refrain from registering a transfer of the shares in question and to refrain from paying any dividend without first sending a notice by first-class post to the person on whose behalf the stop notice was served and then waiting 14 days to see whether that person takes any action. If the company has heard nothing at the end of the 14 days it may safely go ahead with registering the transfer or paying the dividend.

A stop notice is also served by the High Court or a county court if the court has made a charging order on shares (Rules of the Supreme Court 1965, ord. 50, r. 5; County Court Rules 1981, ord. 31, r. 2(3)). A charging order imposes a charge in order to secure payment of a judgment debt (Charging Orders Act 1979, s. 1(1)) and while one is in force in relation to shares, the shares may not be transferred and no payment of dividend on them may be made without the court's authority.

8.7.3 Stop orders

A person claiming to be interested in shares in a company may apply to the High Court to make a 'stop order' (Charging Orders Act 1979, s. 5(2)(a); Rules of the Supreme Court 1965, ord. 50, r. 15). This orders the company not to register a transfer of the shares or pay any dividend on them.

8.7.4 Freezing orders

The Secretary of State or, in relation to public companies only, the court, may impose restrictions on the transfer of shares in a company under part XV (ss. 454 to 457) of CA 1985, which is discussed in 8.9.7.

8.8 TAKEOVERS

8.8.1 Takeovers and the City Code

If company A acquires sufficient shares in company B to control the board of directors and policies of B then there is a takeover of B by A. If B is a private company then it will probably have a provision in its articles authorising the directors to refuse to register a transfer of shares. So a takeover of a private company inevitably requires the approval of the directors. It is normally not possible to control a private company without holding more than 50 per cent of the voting shares. If B is a listed company with a large number of members then A will not normally be able to acquire sufficient shares to give it control merely by purchases on the Stock Exchange. So it is usually necessary to send a circular to B's shareholders offering to buy their shares. An offer of this kind is called a takeover bid; the company making the offer (A) is called the offeror company and the company whose shares it is sought to acquire is called the offeree or target company. It is common for the offeror to offer to allot new shares as the consideration for purchasing shares in the offeree company.

A letter sent to shareholders of a company, public or private, offering to buy their shares, or inviting them to offer to sell their shares is an investment advertisement which is subject to FSA 1986, s. 57 (see 7.7), and so such a letter must be issued or approved by a person authorised under FSA 1986 to conduct investment business (*Re Chez Nico (Restaurants) Ltd* [1992] BCLC 192) though SI 1995 No. 1536 exempts such letters sent to shareholders of private companies in certain circumstances (see 7.7).

The most significant control of takeovers is by way of the voluntary self-regulatory rules contained in the City Code on Takeovers and Mergers which is issued by the Panel on Takeovers and Mergers. That body was conceived by the Bank of England, which appoints the Panel's chairman and deputy chairman, and representatives of the leading City institutions are its members. One of those institutions is the London Stock Exchange, and clearly one of the most powerful compliance weapons is the threat that permission for the company's shares to be traded on the Exchange may be withdrawn.

The City Code on Takeovers and Mergers 'represents the collective opinion of those professionally involved in the field of takeovers as to good business standards and as to how fairness to shareholders can be achieved'. It applies to offers for any public company resident in the United Kingdom, the Channel Islands or the Isle of Man, or any private company so resident whose shares have been dealt in publicly in the preceding 10 years. The responsibilities described in the Code apply:

    (a)   most directly to persons actively engaged in the securities markets,

    (b)   to directors of companies subject to the Code,

    (c)   to persons or groups of persons who seek to gain or consolidate effective control of companies subject to the Code,

    (d) to all professional advisers insofar as they advise on the transactions in question.

The introduction to the Code states:

The Code has not, and does not seek to have, the force of law. It has, however, been acknowledged by both government and other regulatory authorities that those who seek to take advantage of the facilities of the securities markets in the United Kingdom should conduct themselves in matters relating to takeovers in accordance with best business standards and so according to the Code.

    Therefore, those who do not so conduct themselves may find that, by way of sanction, the facilities of those markets are withheld.

The day-to-day work of the Panel on Takeovers and Mergers is carried out by its executive, headed by the Director General. If there appears to have been a material breach of the Code, the executive invites the person concerned to appear before the Panel for a hearing. If the Panel finds that there has been a breach, it may have recourse to private reprimand or public censure or it may report the offender's conduct to another regulatory authority (such as the Department of Trade and Industry, the Stock Exchange, the Financial Services Authority or a relevant SRO) and/or require further action to be taken, as it thinks fit. There is a right of appeal against a decision of the Panel to the Appeal Committee of the Panel. The decisions of the Panel are subject to judicial review, though the court is aware that it is important for the Panel to give firm decisions quickly and may exercise discretion to give declarations of the meaning of rules in the Code for future guidance rather than reverse past decisions of the Panel (*R* v *Panel on Takeovers & Mergers, ex parte Datafin plc* [1987] QB 815, CA; *R* v *Panel on Takeovers & Mergers, ex parte Guinness plc* [1990] 1 QB 146). For a description of the administration of the Code, see D. Calcutt, 'Company Law Lecture — the work of the Takeover Panel' (1990) 11 Co Law 203.

In *R* v *Spens* [1991] 1 WLR 624, the prosecution wished to prove that the accused had breached the City Code, claiming that this showed that the accused acted dishonestly. The accused contended that they honestly believed that the Code did not prohibit what they did and that the question of the proper construction of the Code was a question of fact which should be left to the jury. The Criminal Division of the Court of Appeal described the Code as 'a form of consensual agreement between affected parties with penal consequences' (at p. 632) and took the view that the Code 'sufficiently resembles legislation as to be likewise regarded as demanding construction of its provisions by a judge'.

According to Calcutt, op. cit., at p. 205:

There are essentially four principles which underlie the Code. They are as follows:

(1)   shareholders should have full information in order to enable them to consider the merits of a bid, and should have it in proper time to enable them to reach a decision;

(2)   there should be equal treatment of all shareholders of a particular class;

(3)   frustrating action by the management of a target company can only be taken with the consent of shareholders in general meeting;

(4)   the Code seeks to ensure a fair market through the disclosure of appropriate dealings.

The Code recognises that a listed company may be controlled by the holders of less than 50 per cent of its voting rights because the fact that shares are dispersed among a large number of holders means that most members do not act in coordinated groups with agreed policies and voting strategies. The Code therefore states that a person controls a company if he holds 30 per cent or more of its voting rights.

When a person holds 30 per cent of the voting rights in a public company other shareholders will find that they are effectively in a minority and may feel that their interest in the company has been devalued. The City Code therefore requires that a person who gains 30 per cent control must make a takeover bid for all of the voting shares. This is known as a mandatory offer (rule 9.1). The price that has to be offered in a mandatory offer is the highest price at which the offeror (or persons acting in concert with it) has dealt in the offeree company's shares in the 12 months preceding the time when its holding reached 30 per cent (rule 9.5). This rule is intended to prevent an offeror obtaining a controlling interest at a premium price from a few large shareholders and then later buying out all the small shareholders cheaply.

In any takeover bid, if the holders of 90 per cent in value of the shares which are the subject of the bid accept it within four months then the offeror may compulsorily acquire the remainder under CA 1985, part XIIIA (see 8.8.2).

8.8.2   Compulsory acquisition of minority shareholdings

CA 1985, part XIIIA (ss. 428 to 430F), provides a procedure by which a takeover bidder whose bid is almost completely successful can acquire the remaining shares compulsorily. It also provides a procedure by which a small minority left after an almost completely successful takeover bid can force the bidder to buy them out. Part XIIIA was inserted by FSA 1986, s. 172 and sch. 12, to replace provisions with the same effect which had been found to be not detailed enough to deal with the wide variety of takeovers that occur in practice.

8.8.2.1   Meaning of 'takeover offer'
The provisions of CA 1985, part XIIIA, can be invoked only where there is a 'takeover offer' as defined in s. 428(1). This is an offer to acquire all the shares, or all the shares of any class or classes, in a company, other than:

(a)   Shares already held by the offeror at the date of the offer (including shares the offeror has contracted to buy, unless the contract either provides no consideration and is only enforceable by virtue of being under seal or the only consideration is a promise by the offeror to make the takeover offer: s. 428(5)).

(b)   Shares already held by 'associates' of the offeror (see 8.8.2.8) at the date of the offer (including shares that associates have contracted to acquire) (s. 430E(1)).

The terms of the offer must be the same in relation to all the shares being bid for (or the same for all shares of the same class where different classes are being bid for) though allowance is made in s. 428(4) for an offer to provide special terms to comply with the laws of foreign countries in which shares are held (as in *Mutual Life Insurance Co. of New York v Rank Organisation Ltd* [1985] BCLC 11).

If a person invites shareholders to offer their shares for purchase then the person is not making a takeover offer as defined in s. 428(1) (*Re Chez Nico (Restaurants) Ltd* [1992] BCLC 192).

8.8.2.2   *Conditions for compulsory acquisition*

The offeror can invoke part XIIIA if, within four months of the date of the offer, he has acquired, or contracted to acquire, *by virtue of the offer,* 90 per cent or more (in value) of the shares to which the offer relates (s. 429(1) and (3)), or, if the offer is for more than one class, 90 per cent or more (in value) of a class (s. 429(2)). If the 90 per cent limit is reached within four months then the offeror can acquire compulsorily the remaining shares (or the remaining shares of the particular class if the limit is reached only in relation to one class).

If the terms of the offer make provision for their revision, and for acceptances on the previous terms to be treated as acceptances on the revised terms, then a revision of the offer is not a fresh offer and the four-month time-limit runs from the date of the original offer (s. 428(7)). If an offer does not provide for the revision of its terms then the 90 per cent limit must be reached by virtue of the unrevised offer. In *Re Chez Nico (Restaurants) Ltd* [1992] BCLC 192, the original offer unwisely specified a deadline earlier than four months after the date of the offer; the 90 per cent limit was not reached by the deadline and the offerors' extension of the deadline was held to be a new offer because they had originally not provided for any variation of the terms of their offer.

The 90 per cent acceptance limit is 90 per cent of the shares that are the subject of the offer, which excludes shares held or contracted for by the offeror or his associates at the time of the offer, as described in 8.8.2.1. It also excludes any shares which the offeror, or any of his associates, acquires or contracts to acquire during the period within which the takeover offer can be accepted but otherwise than by virtue of the offer and at a price exceeding the offer price (or the highest offer price if it is revised) (ss. 429(8) and 430E(1)). However, shares acquired (or contracted for) otherwise than by virtue of the offer at a price less than the offer price (or the highest offer price if it is revised) can be counted as acquired or contracted for by virtue of the offer (ss. 429(8) and 430E(2)).

If the 90 per cent limit cannot be reached because the offeror has been unable, after reasonable enquiry, to trace one or more of the persons holding shares to which the offer relates, and the 90 per cent limit would be reached if such holders accepted it, then the court may authorise the offeror to carry out the compulsory purchase procedure if it is satisfied that the consideration offered is fair and reasonable (s. 430C(5)). However, the court must not make an order under this subsection unless it considers that it is just and equitable to do so having regard, in particular, to the number of shareholders who have been traced but who have not accepted the offer.

8.8.2.3 Procedure for compulsory acquisition

A notice in prescribed form must be sent by the offeror to each shareholder whose shares are to be compulsorily acquired and a copy must be given to the company together with a statutory declaration that the conditions for giving the notice are satisfied (CA 1985, s. 429(2) and (4)). The notice must be given within two months of reaching the 90 per cent limit (s. 429(3)). The procedure for giving the notice is specified in SI 1987 No. 752, reg. 4, which provides, *inter alia,* for advertisement where the shares to be acquired are represented by share warrants to bearer.

The offeror is bound to acquire the shares on the terms of the offer (s. 430(2)).

At the end of six weeks from the date of the notice the offeror must send a copy of it to the company, pay or transfer to the company the consideration for the shares and, if the shares are not uncertificated, provide an instrument of transfer of the shares executed by a person appointed by the offeror (or a statement that the shares are transferable by delivery) (s. 430(5), (6) and (7); SI 1995 No. 3272, reg. 35). The company must then register the offeror as the holder of the shares or issue it with a share warrant to bearer (s. 430(6) and (7)).

Consideration received by the company is held by it on trust for the former holder of the shares acquired and monetary consideration must be paid into a separate interest-bearing bank account (s. 430(9) and (10)). The company must make reasonable inquiries at reasonable intervals to locate the person to whom the money is due (s. 430(11); the cost comes out of the money held in trust: s. 430(15)) but if the person is not located after 12 years then the money must be paid into court (s. 430(11)).

Within six weeks from the date of a notice to a shareholder, he may apply to the court under s. 430C:

(a)   to order that the offeror shall not be entitled and bound to acquire the shares, or
(b)   to specify terms of acquisition different from those of the offer.

The offeror cannot carry out the transfer procedure until such an application is disposed of.

The onus is on the applicant to convince the court that it should interfere, and, in the absence of special circumstances, it must be shown that, despite acceptance by 90 per cent of the shareholders, the offer is unfair (*Re Hoare & Co. Ltd* (1933) 150 LT 374; *Re Press Caps Ltd* [1949] Ch 434, CA; *Nidditch v Calico Printers' Association Ltd* 1961 SLT 282). The test is of fairness to the body of shareholders, not the individual applicant (*Re Grierson, Oldham & Adams Ltd* [1968] Ch 17). It is not enough that the offer is open to criticism and could be improved; it must be 'obviously unfair, patently unfair, unfair to the meanest intelligence' (*Re Sussex Brick Co. Ltd* [1961] Ch 289 n per Vaisey J at p. 292) though this has been described as a 'rather enthusiastic statement of what is required' (*Re Deans* [1986] 2 NZLR 271 per Hardie Boys J; his honour went on to say that he was sure the applicant did not have to show the majority were morons).

If the shareholders who have accepted did so on the basis of advice from their board of directors then a dissentient shareholder may succeed if he can show that those who accepted were misled by erroneous advice (*Re Lifecare International plc* [1990] BCLC 222). If the shareholders who accepted did so without the benefit of information which they should have received under the provisions of the City Code on Takeovers and Mergers then the fact that 90 per cent have accepted cannot be decisive (*Re Chez Nico (Restaurants) Ltd* [1992] BCLC 192).

The fact that 90 per cent of the shareholders have accepted the offer will carry little weight as evidence that the court should not stop the compulsory purchase if in fact there is a substantial identity of interest between the offeror and the shareholders who have accepted (*Re Bugle Press Ltd* [1961] Ch 270, CA; *Esso Standard (Inter-America) Inc.* v *JW Enterprises Inc.* (1963) 37 DLR (2d) 598, Supreme Court of Canada). In most cases of substantial identity of interest, the accepting shareholders will be associates of the offeror and so their shares will not count in the calculation of the 90 per cent acceptance limit. This would have been the case had *Esso Standard (Inter-America) Inc.* v *JW Enterprises Inc.* been decided under the present British legislation. In that case, the offeror was a wholly owned subsidiary of a company which owned 96.75 per cent of the shares being bid for; it was not permitted to compulsorily purchase the remaining shares, even though some independent shareholders had accepted the offer. (Under the present British legislation, a holding company of the offeror is an associate of it: s. 430E(4)(b).) In *Re Bugle Press Ltd,* the offeror was a company whose only members and directors were two individuals who held 90 per cent of the shares being bid for (they would not be associates of the offeror under the current legislation): the offeror was not permitted to compulsorily purchase the remaining shares.

If an applicant is unsuccessful, s. 430C(4) requires the court not to make an order for costs against him unless the court considers that the application was unnecessary, improper or vexatious; or that there has been unreasonable delay in making the application, or unreasonable conduct on the applicant's part in conducting proceedings on the application. The only applications that this provision is intended to discourage are applications which ought not properly to engage the attention of the court. An application is not vexatious unless it is so obviously unsustainable or so impossible of success as to amount to an abuse of the process of the court (*Re Britoil plc* [1990] BCC 70, CA).

8.8.2.4   *Requirement by shareholder to be bought out*

If, in a takeover offer, the 90 per cent limit described in 8.8.2.2 is reached before the end of the period within which the offer can be accepted (the four-month time-limit does not apply), then a shareholder who has not accepted the offer can require the offeror to acquire his shares (CA 1985, s. 430A(1) and (2)). The requisition must be made in a written communication addressed to the offeror but there is no prescribed form. The offeror is bound to acquire the shares on the terms of the offer or on such other terms as may be agreed (s. 430B(2)) but either the holder or the offeror may apply to the court to fix the terms of acquisition (s. 430C(3)).

Within one month of reaching the 90 per cent limit, the offeror must either issue a compulsory purchase notice under s. 429 to every shareholder who has not accepted the offer or give notice in prescribed form (see SI 1987 No. 752) of the right to insist on being bought out under s. 430A (s. 430A(3) and (5)). Failure to do so is an offence triable either way (s. 430A(6) and sch. 24) and, if the offeror is a company, every officer of the company who is in default, or to whose neglect the failure is attributable, is liable to a fine (s. 430A(6)). (If the offeror is not a company then it is a defence for him to prove that he took all reasonable steps to secure compliance: s. 430A(7).)

If the offeror's notice is issued before the time for acceptance of the takeover offer has expired then the notice must state that fact (s. 430A(3)). It may specify a time-limit for insisting on being bought out under s. 430A(3) but that time-limit must not be less than three months after the end of the period in which the takeover offer itself could be accepted: if a time-limit is stated then a shareholder cannot require the offeror to buy him out after the time-limit has expired (s. 430A(4)).

8.8.2.5   *Choice of consideration*

If CA 1985, part XIIIA, is invoked after a takeover offer the terms of which provided for a choice of consideration then:

(a) A compulsory acquisition notice to a shareholder by the offeror must give him six weeks in which to make a choice in respect of his own shares and must state which consideration will be given in default of a choice being made (s. 430(3)).

(b) A shareholder insisting on being bought out may indicate his choice (s. 430B(3)).

(c) A notice to a shareholder of his right to insist on being bought out must give particulars of the choice and must state that a holder may indicate his choice when requiring the offeror to acquire his shares, and may state which consideration will be given in default of a choice being made (s. 430B(3)).

(d) If a time-limit or other conditions set in the offer for making a choice has expired then the rules stated in (a), (b) and (c) apply nevertheless (ss. 430(4) and 430B(4)).

(e) If the consideration chosen by a holder, either in response to a compulsory acquisition notice or on insisting on being bought out, is not cash and the offeror is no longer able to provide it, or was to have been provided by another person who is no longer bound or able to provide it, then the shareholder must be paid a cash equivalent (ss. 430(4) and 430B(4)).

8.8.2.6   Joint offers

CA 1985, s. 430D, states how part XIIIA is to operate when a takeover offer is made by two or more persons jointly.

8.8.2.7   Convertible securities

Securities of a company convertible into the company's shares are to be treated as 'shares' for the purposes of CA 1985, part XIIIA (s. 430F(1)). However, convertibles must be treated as a separate class from the shares into which they may be converted (s. 430F(2)).

8.8.2.8   Associates of the offeror

CA 1985, s. 430E(4) to (8), defines in detail who is an associate of an offeror for the purposes of part XIIIA. Briefly, any of the following is an associate of the offeror:

(a) A nominee of the offeror.

(b) A company in the same group as the offeror or a nominee of a company in the same group.

(c) A corporation in which the offeror has (or can control the exercise of) one-third or more of the voting rights.

(d) A corporation which is (or whose directors are) accustomed to act in accordance with the offeror's directions or instructions.

(e) Any party to an agreement with the offeror to acquire the shares that are the subject-matter of the takeover offer (or any nominee of such a party) if the agreement imposes obligations or restrictions on any one or more of the parties with respect to their use, retention or disposal of shares acquired.

8.8.3   Takeovers by share exchange

There are two methods of effecting a takeover by share exchange between companies A and B:

(a) The members of company B contribute to company A their shares in company B as assets in exchange for an allotment of A's shares. The result is that the members of B become members of A, and A not only owns its own business but also has B as a subsidiary.

Neither A nor B is dissolved in this method. The members of A must approve an allotment of shares in their company (see 6.2.5). However, the members of B do not have to meet to approve the merger because it necessarily involves the individual consent of each member to the exchange of his particular shares. If in fact the holders of 90 per cent of the shares in B accept the share exchange over a period of four months then the remainder may be compulsorily acquired by A under CA 1985, s. 429 (see 8.8.2). One possible problem is that the objects of B must be within the objects of A, otherwise A's long-term ownership of B will be *ultra vires* (*Joint Stock Discount Co.* v *Brown* (1866) LR 3 Eq 139) unless holding shares is itself an object of A (*Re Barneds Banking Co., ex parte Contract Corporation* (1867) LR 3 Ch App 105).

(b)   The members of B may agree to surrender their shares in B and for those shares to be cancelled. As compensation they will receive shares allotted by A. Meanwhile the reserve created by the cancellation of B's shares is used to pay up a capitalisation issue of shares which are all allotted to A. The result is the same as in method (b) but there may be a considerable saving in stamp duty because there are no transfers of shares to A. The surrender and cancellation of shares in B is a reduction of capital which must be carried out under the procedure of CA 1985, s. 135 (see 10.2). The whole scheme is an arrangement between B and its members which may be put through under the procedure of CA 1985, s. 425. The advantage of the s. 425 procedure is that it requires the approval of only the shareholders of B who attend (in person or by proxy) a meeting, and the majority at the meeting need hold only 75 per cent of the shares represented at the meeting (though shares already belonging to A cannot be counted — see *Re Hellenic & General Trust Ltd* [1976] 1 WLR 123). This contrasts with the 90 per cent approval needed before a compulsory purchase scheme may be put through under s. 429. However, s. 425 may only be used if the board of B approve the scheme (*Re Savoy Hotel Ltd* [1981] Ch 351) and the scheme may not be put into effect until it is approved by the court whereas a compulsory acquisition under s. 429 goes ahead unless a successful application is made to the court to stop it under s. 430C. Therefore, in *Re National Bank Ltd* [1966] 1 WLR 819 Plowman J was prepared to sanction a s. 425 takeover scheme which he was satisfied was fair despite the objection of the holders of just over 5 per cent of the shares of the company being taken over whereas in *Re Hellenic & General Trust Ltd* [1976] 1 WLR 123 Templeman J exercised his discretion the other way and refused to sanction a scheme objected to by the holders of 13.95 per cent of shares in the company being taken over.

The powers conferred on the court by CA 1985, s. 427, are available for a court-sanctioned arrangement made in connection with the amalgamation of companies.

8.9   REGISTER OF SUBSTANTIAL SHAREHOLDINGS

8.9.1   Need to identify substantial interests

The register of members of a public company may not reveal the true identity of its shareholders. If a share in a company is held by a nominee of the beneficial owner then the company is forbidden to state the name of the beneficial owner in the register even if it is informed of the beneficial owner's identity (CA 1985, s. 360; see 8.7.1). It may not be obvious from a company's register of members that a group of its members are in fact business associates, who together control a sizeable proportion of the company's voting rights. Such groups are called by the City Code 'persons acting in concert' and are colloquially known as 'concert parties'. A concert party may be used to hold more than 30 per cent of a company's voting rights secretly so that a mandatory bid does not have to be made, or it may be used to build up a powerful position from which a takeover bid can be launched without warning. A group holding more than 25 per cent of a company's voting rights would be able to block the adoption of a special resolution.

Identification of who really controls substantial numbers of shares in a company helps the company, its management and its shareholders to find out who has the ability to control the company and helps the market to assess how the distribution of shareholdings and demand for the shares might affect their price.

8.9.2 Obligation to notify substantial interests

Part VI (ss. 198 to 220) of CA 1985 makes very detailed provision for the disclosure of substantial interests in the shares of public companies. Part VI does not apply to private companies. Part VI has been amended by SI 1993 Nos. 1819 and 2689 to implement Directive 88/627/EEC on the information to be published when a major holding in a listed company is acquired or disposed of.

Part VI is concerned with interests in 'relevant share capital' of any public company and this means (s. 198(2)): 'the company's issued share capital of a class carrying rights to vote in all circumstances at general meetings of the company' disregarding temporary suspensions of voting rights.

A distinction is drawn between 'interests' and 'material interests' in shares. By s. 199(2A), interests are not material interests if they are held by various people listed in that subsection who manage investments on behalf of others, for example, operators of authorised unit trusts.

A person who has material interests in shares of a public company's relevant share capital has a 'notifiable interest' when the material interests are in 3 per cent or more of the nominal value of relevant share capital (s. 199(2)(a)). A person who has interests that are not material interests has a notifiable interest when the aggregate of that person's interests (whether or not material) reaches 10 per cent (s. 199(2)(b)).

A public company must be notified of the extent of any notifiable interest in its shares:

(a)   when the notifiable interest is first acquired (s. 199(4)),

(b)   whenever the amount of the notifiable interest changes (s. 199(5)(b)) — all percentages are rounded down to the nearest whole number (s. 200(1) and (2)) so there is a notifiable change only when the whole number part of the percentage changes,

(c)   when there ceases to be a notifiable interest (s. 199(5)(a)).

The company must record this information in a register kept for the purpose (s. 211).

Sections 208 and 209 define whether a person has a notifiable interest in shares (s. 208(1)). According to s. 208(2), 'A reference to an interest in shares is to be read as including an interest of any kind whatsoever in the shares'. It might be thought that nothing more need be said but s. 208 goes on to make further statements about what counts as an interest, while s. 209 (as substituted by SI 1993 No. 1819, reg. 8) allows various interests to be disregarded. Some of the rules are:

(a)   Restraints or restrictions on the exercise of any right attached to an interest do not prevent it being an interest (s. 208(2)).

(b)   If an interest in shares is held on trust then a beneficiary of the trust is interested in the shares (s. 208(3)) though various unit trusts and collective investment schemes are exempt (s. 209(1)(b)). However, a discretionary interest may be disregarded (s. 209(1)(a)).

(c)   A person who has made a contract to purchase shares (whether for cash or otherwise) has an interest in them (s. 208(4)(a)), whether they are identified or not (s. 208(8)). A person who has an option to purchase shares has an interest in them (s. 208(5)).

(d)   A person who is not registered as the holder of shares but is entitled to exercise any right conferred by holding them or to control the exercise of any such right has an interest in them (s. 208(4)(b)). Thus a person whose shares are held by another as nominee is interested in those shares. The interest of the nominee, as a 'bare trustee', may be disregarded (s. 209(1)(a) and (5)). Being appointed as a proxy for a shareholder for one meeting and any adjournments, or being appointed a representative of a corporate shareholder, is not a notifiable interest (s. 209(12)).

(e)   If an interest is held jointly then it must be counted as an interest of each of the joint holders (s. 208(7)).

(f)   An interest in shares held as security for the purposes of a transaction in the ordinary course of business of an authorised bank or securities dealer may be disregarded, provided the holder of the interest is not entitled to vote the shares or has not evinced any intention of voting (s. 209(1)(c), (2) and (6)).

(g)   Provided the shares in which the interests are held cannot be voted (s. 209(5)), interests in shares held by virtue of being a personal representative of a deceased individual may be disregarded (s. 209(1)(g); for the voting rights of personal representatives see 14.4.9.1.5). Similarly the interests of trustees of various unit trusts and collective investment schemes may be disregarded provided the trustees in question cannot vote the shares (s. 209(1)(h) and (5)).

(h)   An interest in shares of a company may be disregarded if it is held by a market maker who deals on a stock exchange in the European Union for the purpose of that market-making business, provided the market maker does not use the shares to intervene in the management of the company (s. 209(8) and (9)).

8.9.3   Details to be notified

A person who is under an obligation to notify a public company of an acquisition of an interest or a material interest in its relevant share capital or of any change in the level of that interest must do so in writing within the period of two days next following the day on which that obligation arises (CA 1985, s. 202(1)). Notification to the company must identify the person and give the person's address, and if the person is a director of the company it must state that it is a notice for the purposes of the register of interests in shares (and not one for the register of directors' interests) (s. 210(2)).

The notification must state:

(a)   The number of shares in which, to that person's knowledge, the person's material interests subsist (if the notifiable interest is 3 per cent or more) (s. 202(2)(a)) or interests subsist (if the level is 10 per cent or more) (s. 202(2A)). It is unnecessary to distinguish which interests are material interests and which are only interests (s. 202(2B)).

(b)   The number of shares in which the person is interested by virtue of s. 208(5) (that is, by virtue of having an option to acquire shares or an interest in shares) (s. 202(3)).

(c)   The names of the registered holders of the shares and the number held by each of those persons (s. 202(3)).

(d)   That the person is party to a concert party agreement, if that is the case, and the names and addresses of the other parties, and the number of shares in which the person is deemed to be interested by virtue of the agreement (s. 205(4)).

The nature of the interest does not have to be stated. Any subsequent changes in items (b) and (c) must be notified (s. 202(4)). Failure to fulfil an obligation of disclosure or giving false information is an offence triable either way (s. 210(3) and sch. 24).

8.9.4 Register

Every public company must keep a register of interests in shares in which it must enter all information disclosed to it about substantial shareholdings within three days of receiving such information (CA 1985, s. 211). See 4.4.1(c) for rules about inspection and so on.

A company listed on the London Stock Exchange must immediately communicate the information about substantial interests that it receives for registration to the Company Announcements Office of the Exchange (Listing Rules, paras 9.11 and 9.12). A listed company must also disclose in its annual report and accounts details of all substantial interests in its shares as at a date not more than one month before the date of the meeting before which the accounts are to be laid (Listing Rules, para. 12.43(1)). Details of substantial interests must also be given in listing particulars (Listing Rules, para. 6.C.16).

8.9.5 Company's notice requiring information

If a public company knows or has reasonable cause to believe that a person is interested in shares in its relevant share capital (see 8.9.1) then it may serve a written notice on the person requiring the person to confirm the company's knowledge or indicate whether or not its belief is true (CA 1985, s. 212(1)).

By s. 212(5), a person is regarded as 'interested' in shares for this purpose even if the person's interest may be disregarded by virtue of s. 209 (see 8.9.2). Not recognising the disregards means, for example, that notice may be served on a nominee shareholder or a person who has been appointed proxy for a shareholder (cf. s. 209(1)(a) and (12)). A notice issued under this provision may require the person to whom it is addressed to state whether there is subsisting in the shares an interest belonging to any other person and, if so, to identify that person and to state whether any person interested in the shares is party to a notifiable concert party arrangement (s. 212(2)(b) and (3)). The notice may also ask for information about other persons who have been interested in the shares at the same time as the person addressed at any time within the three years preceding the date of the notice. A notice may ask for the nature of any interest to be disclosed (*Re TR Technology Investment Trust plc* [1988] BCLC 256).

As well as persons presently interested in shares, notices may be served on persons who are known or reasonably believed to have been interested at any time within the preceding three years (s. 212(1)), and also on persons who have, or have had, options to subscribe for shares (s. 212(6)).

A company is empowered by s. 212 to address notices to persons domiciled abroad who have no connection with the UK (*Re F. H. Lloyd Holdings plc* [1985] BCLC 293).

A s. 212 notice must specify a 'reasonable time' within which a reply must be given. In the case of a person in the UK dealing in a listed company's shares on a large scale, it would be reasonable to require a reply within one working day, but foreigners must be given a further time to ask English solicitors to advise on what information must be provided: two clear working days is the longest period that need be allowed in all but very exceptional circumstances (*Re Lonrho plc (No. 2)* [1989] BCLC 309, which includes an interesting description of the way in which a large company uses s. 212).

If, in response to a notice given under s. 212, a company receives information about any person's present interests in its relevant share capital then it must record that information in a separate section of the register of substantial interests with a note that it was received in response to a notice and the date of the notice (s. 213). The company is not entitled to add comments or information derived from sources other than a response to a s. 212 notice (*Re TR Technology Investment Trust plc*). If the information concerns the interest of a person other than the person to whom the notice was addressed then the company must, within 15 days of being given the information, notify the other person of the entry to be made in the register and inform that person that there is a right to apply to the company to have the entry removed from the register (s. 217(2)). The person may apply to have the entry removed and the company must remove it if satisfied that it was made in pursuance of incorrect information (s. 217(3)). If the company refuses to remove the entry then the person may apply to the court for an order directing removal of the entry, and the court may make such an order if it thinks fit (s. 217(5)).

A person may be exempted by the Secretary of State from having to reply to notices under s. 212 but the Secretary of State must be satisfied that there are special reasons why the person should not be subject to the obligations imposed by s. 212 and must consult with the Governor of the Bank of England (s. 216(5)).

A person who fails to comply with a s. 212 notice, and who is not exempt from replying, is guilty of an offence triable either way (s. 216(3) and sch. 24) though it is a defence to prove that the requirement to give the information was frivolous or vexatious (s. 216(4)).

8.9.6 Members' requisition of investigation of share ownership

The holders of shares representing one-tenth or more of the amount paid up on shares carrying a right to vote at general meetings of a public company may, under CA 1985, s. 214, requisition it to exercise its powers under s. 212 (see 8.9.5). The requisition must specify the manner in which the powers are to be exercised and give reasonable grounds for requiring the company to exercise its powers in that manner (s. 214(2)).

On deposit of a requisition complying with s. 214 the company must exercise its powers under s. 212 as required and if it does not then the company and every officer of the company who knowingly and wilfully authorises or permits the failure to comply is guilty of an offence triable either way (ss. 214(5) and 730(5) and sch. 24).

On the conclusion of investigations made in response to a requisition, the company must prepare a report, which must be 'made available at the company's registered office within a reasonable period after the conclusion of that investigation' (s. 215(1)). Within three days of making a report available at the registered office, the company must inform the requisitionists of its availability (s. 215(5)). A report must be kept for six years and be available for inspection under the same conditions as the register of substantial interests (s. 215(7)).

Alternatively 200 or more members of a company, or members holding 10 per cent or more of the company's issued shares, may, under s. 442(3), ask the Secretary of State to investigate ownership and control of the company — see 18.10.2.2.

8.9.7 Freezing orders

If a company has served a notice on a person under CA 1985, s. 212, and that person has failed to give the company any information required by the notice then the company may apply to the court for an order (a 'freezing order') imposing restrictions on the shares in question (s. 216(1)). A person fails to give information if he does not, so far as lies within his knowledge, give a full and truthful answer to the question (*Re TR Technology Investment Trust plc* [1988] BCLC 256).

Similarly, if the Secretary of State is conducting an investigation into a company's share ownership under s. 442 or s. 444 (see 18.10.2.2) and it appears that there is difficulty in finding out the relevant facts then the Secretary of State may order that the shares be subject to restrictions (s. 445).

If a person has been convicted of an offence under s. 210 of failing to comply with an obligation to register a substantial interest in relevant share capital of a public company then the Secretary of State may order that the shares in relation to which the offence was committed shall be subject to restrictions (s. 210(5)).

Provisions about restrictions are contained in Part XV (ss. 454 to 457) of CA 1985. If restrictions are imposed on a share then the share may not be transferred, the votes attached to it may not be exercised, no dividend may be paid on it, there can be no return of capital unless the company is wound up, and no preemptive subscription rights may be exercised (s. 454).

A freezing order may declare that particular acts are permitted despite the provisions of part XV if necessary to protect the rights of third parties in respect of shares where those third-party rights would be unfairly affected by those provisions (ss. 210(5A), 216(1B) and 455(1A) inserted by SI 1991 No. 1646, regs 3, 4(a) and 5(a)).

If restrictions have been imposed by the Secretary of State then he may be asked to disapply them by making a further order under s. 210(5) or s. 445(1) as appropriate, and if he refuses, an application may be made to the court under s. 456(1) to lift the restrictions. If restrictions were imposed by the court then any application to disapply the restrictions must be made to the court under s. 456(1). On an application under s. 456(1), the court may direct that particular acts are permitted despite the provisions of part XV if necessary to protect the rights of third parties in respect of shares where those third-party rights would be unfairly affected by those provisions (s. 456(1A) inserted by SI 1991 No. 1646, reg. 8(a)). In addition, either the company itself or the Secretary of State (if he imposed the restrictions) may ask the court to order that shares subject to restrictions be sold (CA 1985, s. 456(4)).

An application to disapply restrictions (other than under s. 456(1A)) will be granted only if (s. 456(3)):

(a) the relevant facts about the shares have been disclosed to the company and no unfair advantage has accrued to any person as a result of the earlier failure to make that disclosure; or

(b) the shares are to be transferred for valuable consideration and the court or the Secretary of State (whichever is considering the application) approves the transfer.

The wording of this provision does not mean that the shareholder can choose either to disclose facts or sell the shares; the court will normally not permit a sale if the company requires information and it has not been given (*Re Geers Gross plc* [1987] 1 WLR 1649, CA) whether that information relates to the frozen shares or to other shares (*Re Lonrho plc* [1988] BCLC 53). On the other hand, a freezing order is imposed as a sanction to compel the provision of information to which the company is entitled and once the information is supplied there is no justification for continuing the sanction (*Re Ricardo Group plc* [1989] BCLC 566, in which Millett J reviewed in detail the procedure for making orders *ex parte*).

It is not sufficient that information can be obtained from other sources because such information cannot be entered on the register of substantial interests (*Re TR Technology Investment Trust plc*).

Restrictions may be imposed in respect of the interests of any person, even a person domiciled outside the UK having no connection with the UK (*Re F.H. Lloyd Holdings plc*

[1985] BCLC 293). Restrictions may be imposed on shares that the holder has contracted to sell, and the buyer cannot then be registered as the new holder (*Re Geers Gross plc*).

For more details see D. Milman and D. Singh, 'The evolution of the freezing order in UK company law' (1992) 13 Co Law 51.

8.9.8 Reform

The Department of Trade and Industry has issued a consultative document, *Proposals for Reform of Part VI of the Companies Act 1985* (URN 95/633) (London: DTI, 1995), listing a number of mainly technical reforms. Two proposals for basic changes are that part VI should no longer apply to all public companies but only to companies listed on the London Stock Exchange or traded on other organised markets and that, above a certain level, perhaps 15 per cent, the interval between disclosure levels could be increased from 1 per cent to as much as 25 per cent.

8.10 SHARES BOUGHT ON THE BASIS OF ERRONEOUS ACCOUNTS OR PROFESSIONAL ADVICE

A person who buys shares in a company on the basis of accounts which erroneously suggest the shares are worth more than they are may try to seek compensation for the error. The usual target has been the company's auditors for negligently failing to notice the errors in the accounts. However, liability to a person in negligence for damage which that person has suffered depends on the existence of a duty of care to save that person harmless from that kind of damage. A person's negligence may have unending consequences. The common law has always sought to limit the scope of the tort of negligence so as to make the system workable. As Lord Bridge of Harwich said in *Caparo Industries plc* v *Dickman* [1990] 2 AC 605 at pp. 617–18, a necessary ingredient in any situation giving rise to a duty of care is that: '. . . the situation should be one in which the court considers it fair, just and reasonable that the law should impose a duty of a given scope upon the one party for the benefit of the other'. An important consideration is that the law should not impose on a person 'liability in an indeterminate amount for an indeterminate time to an indeterminate class' (per Cardozo CJ in *Ultramares Corporation* v *Touche* (1931) 174 NE 441 at p. 444). Courts have said that liability will not be imposed for losses which are characterised as being too 'remote' or 'unforeseeable'. In circumstances in which the law does impose a duty of care there is said to be a relationship of 'proximity' between the person owing the duty and the person to whom it is owed. The common law has been especially reluctant to impose a duty of care to save a person from what are called 'economic losses', that is, damage other than injury to individuals' health or injury to tangible property (see *Murphy* v *Brentwood District Council* [1991] 1 AC 398). Since the landmark case of *Hedley Byrne & Co. Ltd* v *Heller & Partners Ltd* [1964] AC 465, it has been possible to sue for purely economic losses caused by a person's negligent misstatements if there was proximity between the person who made the misstatement and the person who suffered loss. Liability for negligent misstatements is treated as a special category of the tort of negligence. In *Caparo Industries plc* v *Dickman,* Lord Bridge said, at p. 621, that in order to establish a relationship of proximity between the defendant and the plaintiff in an action for negligent misstatement, the plaintiff must prove:

> that the defendant knew that his statement would be communicated to the plaintiff, either as an individual or as a member of an identifiable class, specifically in connection with

a particular transaction or transactions of a particular kind (e.g. in a prospectus inviting investment) and that the plaintiff would be very likely to rely on it for the purpose of deciding whether or not to enter upon that transaction or upon a transaction of that kind.

In *Murphy* v *Brentwood District Council,* Lord Keith of Kinkel suggested (at p. 466F) that liability for economic loss arises wherever the tortious liability arises 'out of a contractual relationship with professional people'.

In *Caparo Industries plc* v *Dickman,* the House of Lords decided that auditors of a company's accounts owe no duty of care to members of the public at large who rely upon the accounts in deciding to buy shares in the company. Nor do they owe a duty to save existing members from losses caused by buying further shares at an overvalue. In *Morgan Crucible plc* v *Hill Samuel & Co. Ltd* [1991] Ch 295, the Court of Appeal said, at pp. 318–19, that the reason why there is no duty of care in these circumstances is that an auditors' report on the annual accounts of a company is not given for the purpose of advising people how much they should pay for the company's shares: a plaintiff cannot sue for damage caused by relying on a statement which was not given for the purpose for which the plaintiff had relied on it.

Between 8 June 1984 and October 1984, Caparo Industries plc acquired all the issued shares of Fidelity plc, a public company listed on the Stock Exchange. The accounts of Fidelity plc for the year to 31 March 1984 were issued to Fidelity plc's members on 12 June 1984. Those accounts showed a pretax profit of about £1.3 million. Caparo Industries plc alleged that the accounts should have shown a loss of about £400,000 and that the auditors, Touche Ross & Co., had been negligent in not noticing this. The House of Lords held that whether or not this was so, Caparo Industries plc could not sue Touche Ross & Co. in negligence because there was no duty of care on which such an action could be based.

The fact that a company is vulnerable to a takeover bid does not mean that the auditors owe a duty of care to potential takeover bidders who would very probably rely on the audited accounts. (On this point the Law Lords disagreed with the view of the majority of the New Zealand Court of Appeal in *Scott Group Ltd* v *McFarlane* [1978] 1 NZLR 553 and with the Scottish case of *Twomax Ltd* v *Dickson, McFarlane & Robinson* 1982 SC 113. The Law Lords in *Caparo Industries plc* v *Dickman* considered that in these cases, the courts had wrongly decided that there was a relationship of proximity between the auditors and the takeover bidders. See at pp. 623–4 per Lord Bridge of Harwich and p. 647 per Lord Oliver of Aylmerton on *Scott Group Ltd* v *McFarlane* and at pp. 662–3 per Lord Jauncey of Tullichettle on *Twomax Ltd* v *Dickson, McFarlane & Robinson.*)

Similarly, the fact that it is highly probable that the company will need to borrow money does not make the auditors liable to potential lenders (*Al Saudi Banque* v *Clark Pixley* [1990] Ch 313, approved by Lord Bridge in *Caparo Industries plc* v *Dickman* at p. 623 and by Lord Jauncey at p. 662; *R. Lowe Lippmann Figdor & Franck* v *AGC (Advances) Ltd* [1992] 2 VR 671; *Berg Sons & Co. Ltd* v *Adams* [1993] BCLC 1045). Auditors of a company do not owe a duty of care to the beneficiaries of a trust of which the company is trustee (*Anthony* v *Wright* [1995] 1 BCLC 236).

It would be different if accountants were asked to prepare a special report specifically for a person to whom the controllers of a company wished to sell their shares: the accountants would be liable to that investor for negligent misstatements in that report, even if it was commissioned by the company rather than the investor. In *Caparo Industries plc* v *Dickman,* Lord Bridge, at p. 625, and Lord Oliver, at p. 648, thought that this might have been the situation in *JEB Fasteners Ltd* v *Marks, Bloom & Co.* [1983] 1 All ER 583. In that case, JEB Fasteners Ltd had taken over a company whose accounts were erroneous: the error had not been detected by the company's auditors. However, it was found that the real reason JEB Fasteners took over the company was to acquire the services of its directors, and the amount paid was not determined by the company's financial position, which was well known to be poor, so the plaintiff company's loss was not *caused* by the auditors' negligence, and the auditors were not liable for it.

In *James McNaughton Paper Group Ltd* v *Hicks Anderson & Co.* [1991] 2 QB 113, there had been a takeover by the plaintiff company of a group of companies known as the MK Paper group. This takeover had been negotiated by the chairman of the plaintiff company and the chairman of MK. In deciding on the takeover the plaintiff company's chairman had relied on draft annual accounts prepared by Hicks Anderson & Co. These accounts were erroneous and the plaintiff company claimed £75,000 damages for the accountants' negligence. The Court of Appeal held that in this case there was no relationship of proximity between the accountants and the plaintiff company. Although the chairman of the MK group had asked for the draft accounts to be prepared quickly when the negotiations were underway, they were prepared for him, not for any potential buyer of the group, according to Neill LJ. They were clearly labelled 'draft' accounts and, again according to Neill LJ, the chairman of the plaintiff company was not entitled to treat them as final accounts, and the accountants could not be expected to foresee that they would be so treated.

In *Lloyd Cheyham & Co. Ltd* v *Littlejohn & Co.* [1987] BCLC 303, the plaintiff company wished to invest in a company called Trec Rentals Ltd. It was made clear that no binding commitment would be made until the audited accounts for the year ended 31 December 1980 had been examined. In an action against the auditors for negligently auditing those accounts, it was conceded that the auditors owed a duty of care to the plaintiff company in those circumstances, but the auditors were found not to have been negligent.

In two reported cases at first instance, purchasers of shares in a company who relied on erroneous accounts have been able to make the company's accountants liable: in both cases the accountants attended meetings between the vendors of the shares and the purchasers and were persuaded to give verbal assurances to the purchasers that the accounts were accurate. In *Peach Publishing Ltd* v *Slater and Co.* [1996] BCC 751 the accounts relied on were unaudited but in *ADT Ltd* v *BDO Binder Hamlyn* [1996] BCC 808 they were audited annual accounts. In *ADT Ltd* v *BDO Binder Hamlyn* the accountants were held liable to pay £65 million in damages. However, on appeal in *Peach Publishing Ltd* v *Slater and Co.* [1998] BCC 139 it was held that the accountants were not liable for the representation made at the meeting: it was found that the partner who attended the meeting did so as an adviser to the vendor of the shares, not as an independent expert, and did not assume responsibility to the purchaser. The partner's statement verifying the accuracy of the accounts was elicited by the purchaser only for the purpose of persuading the vendor to warrant that the accounts were accurate and did not directly persuade the purchaser to buy the shares. This seems to be a very fine distinction. These cases will make accountants very wary about commenting on the work they have done for a company or its controlling shareholders when attending meetings with potential purchasers of shares.

In *Morgan Crucible Co. plc* v *Hill Samuel & Co. Ltd* [1991] Ch 295, Morgan Crucible had made an unsolicited takeover bid for First Castle Electronics plc, a listed company. In response, the directors of First Castle Electronics retained Hill Samuel to advise them and issued circulars to First Castle Electronics shareholders saying that the bid was inadequate given the financial position of the company as shown by its last audited annual accounts and the directors' forecast of profits for the current year. The accounts had been audited by Judkins & Co., and the circular included a letter from Judkins stating that the profit forecast had been properly compiled and on a basis consistent with the accounting policies normally adopted by the company. All parties concerned on the First Castle Electronics side were aware that r. 19.7 of the City Code on Takeovers and Mergers requires that copies of all documents and announcements bearing on an offer must be lodged with the advisers to all other parties to the offer. As a result of these circulars very few shareholders of First Castle Electronics accepted the bid, and Morgan Crucible decided to increase its offer, which was eventually successful. Subsequently, Morgan Crucible alleged that the audited accounts and the profit forecast were wrong, and that if the true position had been known, the bid would not have been made. It sued the directors of First Castle Electronics and their advisers, Hill Samuel, and the auditors of First Castle Electronics. Morgan Crucible's legal advisers realised that the original statement of claim in the case had not properly alleged that the various defendants owed a duty of care to Morgan Crucible and wished to amend the statement of claim. The defendants sought to prevent this amendment on the ground that it could not reasonably be argued that there was a duty of care. The Court of Appeal allowed the amendment, deciding that whether or not there was a duty of care was a serious issue to be decided by the judge at the trial. Earlier, in *Lonrho plc* v *Fayed* [1990] 1 QB 490, Pill J had struck out a very similar statement of claim on the ground that no duty of care was owed and there was no appeal against this aspect of his judgment.

In *Soden* v *British and Commonwealth Holdings plc* [1998] AC 298, British and Commonwealth Holdings plc ('B & C') had made a successful takeover bid to acquire all the shares in Atlantic Computers plc, which turned out to be worthless. B & C claimed that it had been induced to buy the shares by negligent misrepresentations made by Atlantic Computers and sued for damages. Under the Insolvency Act 1986, s. 74(2)(f), when a company is being wound up, a sum due to any member of the company, 'in his character of a member', cannot be paid until after all other creditors have been paid. The House of Lords held that B & C was not claiming anything due to it in its character of a member: although its claim was concerned with how it had acquired the shares which made it a member of Atlantic, the claim did not arise from the contract created by Atlantic's memorandum and articles — it was an entirely separate claim in tort which would have to be treated like other creditors' claims against the company. Thus a successful claim for negligent misrepresentation would convert B & C's worthless holding of shares into a claim as an unsecured creditor which would reduce the amount payable to other unsecured creditors.

9 Accounts

9.1 INTRODUCTION

An important feature of the companies legislation is the requirement that the directors of a company must, once a year, prepare accounts and present them to the company's members and (unless the company is unlimited) file them with the registrar of companies. In *Caparo Industries plc* v *Dickman* [1990] 2 AC 605, Lord Jauncey of Tullichettle said, at p. 662:

> . . . the purpose of annual accounts, so far as members are concerned, is to enable them to question the past management of the company, to exercise their voting rights, if so advised, and to influence future policy and management.

Financial results are required to be presented in a balance sheet and profit and loss account, and there are elaborate technical rules, on the preparation of these accounts. This book does not attempt to deal with the details of the accounting rules, which are covered in books for accountants, such as *The Companies Acts 1985 and 1989: Accounting and Related Requirements — the KPMG Guide*, 3rd ed. (Central Milton Keynes: Accountancy Books, 1998).

The accounting requirements of CA 1985 are contained in part VII (ss. 221 to 262A) of the Act.

The elaborate requirements calling for directors to account to members seem highly unrealistic for the typical private company whose directors and members are the same persons. For such companies the more important purpose of insisting on annual accounts is so that outsiders can look at them to assess creditworthiness, assess taxes or investigate financial dealings. Every limited company is required to file annual accounts with the registrar where they form part of the documentation available for inspection by anyone. However, most private companies that are not in a group in which there is a public company can summarise their accounts before filing them with the registrar (see 9.5) and small private companies can, if they wish, prepare accounts that are less detailed than those required from other companies (see 9.3.7.4).

The fact that a limited company has to reveal its financial affairs by filing accounts with the registrar is often regarded as a price that must be paid for limited liability: people who trade with unlimited liability — whether as sole traders, in partnerships or in unlimited companies — do not have to make their financial affairs public. Accordingly business people who use limited companies to conduct their businesses and act as directors but persistently fail to discharge their statutory obligations in respect of accounting must expect to be disqualified from being directors or taking part in the management of companies so that they will have to trade with unlimited liability (per Nicholls V-C in *Secretary of State for Trade & Industry* v *Ettinger* [1993] BCLC 896 at p. 900). (If all the members of a partnership or unlimited company are legal persons with limited liability then the accounts of the partnership or unlimited company do have to be published, by the Partnerships and Unlimited Companies (Accounts) Regulations 1993 (SI 1993 No. 1820), which implement Council Directive 90/605/EEC.)

Examining arguments for and against mandatory public disclosure of accounts, the Department of Trade and Industry has recently said that in its view the accounts of all limited companies should continue to be available at a central registry and that this should apply in all European Union member States (*Accounting Simplifications: a Consultative Document* (URN 95/669) (London: DTI, 1995), para. 4.18). Those dealing with limited companies should have access to this information, and normal business practice in the UK, especially in the provision of credit, depends on public availability of accounts in standardised form.

9.2 ACCOUNTING RECORDS

9.2.1 Every company must have accounting records

CA 1985, s. 221, requires every company to keep accounting records which are sufficient to show and explain the company's transactions and also to disclose, with reasonable accuracy, the financial position of the company at any time. The accounting records must also be adequate to enable the directors to ensure that any balance sheet and profit and loss account prepared under CA 1985, part VII, complies with the requirements of CA 1985.

R v Bennett (1985) 2 NZCLC 99,279 concerned a similarly worded provision in the New Zealand companies legislation. The New Zealand Court of Appeal held that the obligation to cause accounting records to be 'kept' was not merely an obligation to retain and store records but also to create records conforming with the requirements of the section (see 9.2.3) It was also held that dealings between a company and its members, for example, contributions of capital and payments of dividend, are transactions of the company that must be included in its accounting records.

An officer of a company who knowingly and wilfully authorises or permits it to keep accounting records that do not conform with s. 221 is guilty of an offence punishable by a fine or imprisonment for up to two years or both, unless it can be shown that the officer acted honestly and that inadequacies of accounting were excusable in the circumstances in which the company was operating (CA 1985, ss. 221(5) and (6) and 730(5) and sch. 24). The extent of a person's responsibility for any failure of a company to comply with its duty to keep accounting records in accordance with s. 221 is a matter to which the court must have regard in deciding whether that person's conduct as a director or shadow director of that company makes him or her unfit to be concerned in the management of a company (Company Directors Disqualification Act 1986, s. 9 and sch. 1, para. 4(a)).

If a company's auditors are of opinion that proper accounting records have not been kept by the company then they must state that fact in their report (s. 237(2)).

9.2.2 Preservation of records

The accounting records of a private company must be preserved for three years from the date on which they are made; those of a public company must be kept for six years (CA 1985, s. 222(5)). An officer of a company who does not take all reasonable steps to ensure that the company complies with these requirements is guilty of an offence (s. 222(6)). The extent of a person's responsibility for any failure of a company to comply with its duty to keep accounting records for the periods specified in s. 222 is a matter to which the court must have regard in deciding whether that person's conduct as a director or shadow director of that company makes him or her unfit to be concerned in the management of a company (Company Directors Disqualification Act 1986, s. 9 and sch. 1, para. 4(b)).

9.2.3   Contents of accounting records

By CA 1985, s. 221(2) and (3), the accounting records of a company must contain:

(a)   Entries from day to day of all sums of money received and expended by the company and the matters in respect of which the receipts and expenditures took place (a cash book).
(b)   A record of the assets and liabilities of the company.
(c)   If the company's business involves dealing in goods:

    (i)   statements of stock held by the company at the end of each financial year;
    (ii)   records of the stocktakings from which the statements in (i) are derived;
    (iii)   statements of all goods sold (except by ordinary retail trade) and purchased,

in sufficient detail to enable the goods and buyers and sellers to be identified.

9.2.4   Access to accounting records

A company's accounting records must, at all times, be open to inspection by the company's officers, and must be kept at the company's registered office or such other place as the directors think fit (CA 1985, s. 222(1)). If the directors decide to keep the accounting records outside Great Britain then accounts and returns complying with s. 222(3) must be sent to and kept at a place in Great Britain where they must be open to inspection by the company's officers at all times (s. 222(2)). If a company fails to comply with either of these provisions then an officer of the company who knowingly and wilfully authorised or permitted the failure is guilty of an offence triable either way unless it is shown that the officer acted honestly and that in the circumstances in which the company's business was carried on the default was excusable (ss. 222(4) and 730(5) and sch. 24). The extent of a person's responsibility for any failure of a company to comply with its duty to keep accounting records available for inspection in accordance with s. 222 is a matter to which the court must have regard in deciding whether that person's conduct as a director or shadow director of that company makes him or her unfit to be concerned in the management of a company (Company Directors Disqualification Act 1986, s. 9 and sch. 1, para. 4(b)).

The court will order a company to allow one of its directors to inspect its accounting records (*Burn v London & South Wales Coal Co.* (1890) 7 TLR 118; *Edman v Ross* (1922) 22 SR (NSW) 351; both decided before there was any statutory obligation to keep accounts open to inspection). The sole statutory provision for enforcing s. 222 is the criminal sanction imposed by s. 223: the court grants orders for inspection under the common law as stated in *Burn v London & South Wales Coal Co.* and, as with any injunctive relief, an order is granted at the court's discretion (*Conway v Petronius Clothing Co. Ltd* [1978] 1 WLR 72, in which an interlocutory order was refused in the circumstances of the case). It has been argued that s. 222 does create a statutory right to an order for inspection (*M'Cusker v M'Rae* 1966 SC 253, in which the petition was granted by consent; D.D. Prentice, 'A director's right of access to corporate books of account' (1978) 94 LQR 184; *Berlei Hestia (NZ) Ltd* v *Fernyhough* [1980] 2 NZLR 150 — in which a common law interlocutory injunction was granted — per Mahon J at p. 163).

Members of a company do not have a right of access to its accounting records (*R* v *Merchant Tailors' Co.* (1831) 2 B & Ad 115; *Edman* v *Ross*; *Lonrho Ltd* v *Shell Petroleum Co. Ltd* [19801 1 WLR 627 per Lord Diplock at p. 634; *Murray's Judicial Factor* v *Thomas Murray & Sons (Ice Merchants) Ltd* [1993] BCLC 1437) though under Table A, art. 109, a member may be given such a right by ordinary resolution of the members. Article 109 also entitles the directors to authorise a member to inspect accounting records.

An auditor has a right of access to the company's accounting records (s. 389A(1)) — see 9.8.

9.3 ANNUAL ACCOUNTS AND REPORTS FOR MEMBERS

9.3.1 Annual accounts

CA 1985, s. 226, requires the directors of a company to prepare, for each financial year (see 9.3.2) of the company:

(a) a balance sheet as at the last day of the year, and
(b) a profit and loss account.

Those accounts are called the company's 'individual accounts'. If at the end of the financial year, the company was a parent company then the directors must also prepare group accounts (s. 227(1)) (see 9.6) unless one of the exemptions provided by ss. 228 (see 9.6.4), 248 (see 9.6.5) and 229(5) (see 9.6.6) applies. A company which does not trade for profit is required to prepare an income and expenditure account instead of a profit and loss account (s. 262(2)). According to s. 262(1), the 'annual accounts' of a company are its individual accounts required by s. 226 and any group accounts required by s. 227. The amounts set out in the annual accounts of a company may also be shown in the same accounts translated into ecus using the exchange rate on the balance sheet date (s. 242B(1) and (3) inserted by SI 1992 No. 2452, reg. 3). The exchange rate used must be disclosed in notes to the accounts (s. 242B(3)).

A company's annual accounts must be approved by its board of directors, and signed on behalf of the board by a director of the company (s. 233(1)). The signature must be on the company's balance sheet (s. 233(2)). It is an offence to circulate, publish or issue a copy of an unsigned balance sheet (s. 233(6)). SSAP 17, para. 26, suggests that the date on which the directors approved the accounts should be stated, and it is convenient to note this next to the signature on the balance sheet.

The extent of a person's responsibility for any failure of the directors of a company to comply with s. 226, s. 227 or s. 233 is a matter to which the court must have regard in deciding whether that person's conduct as a director or shadow director of that company makes him or her unfit to be concerned in the management of a company (Company Directors Disqualification Act 1986, s. 9 and sch. 1, para. 5).

A company's accounts must give a true and fair view of its financial position (see 9.3.7 and 9.3.8):

. . . the responsibility for the preparation of accounts giving a true and fair view of the company's financial state is placed fairly and squarely on the shoulders of the directors (per Lord Jauncey of Tullichettle in *Caparo Industries plc* v *Dickman* [1990] 2 AC 605 at p. 660).

Copies of a company's annual accounts must be laid before the company in general meeting (s. 241, see 9.3.6.1) unless, in the case of a private company, the members have elected under s. 252 to dispense with the laying of accounts. By s. 238(1), copies of a company's annual accounts must be sent to every member of the company (see 9.3.6.2): this requirement cannot be dispensed with.

9.3.2 Accounting reference periods

The timetable for the production of the successive annual accounts of a company is based on the company's 'accounting reference periods'. Accounting reference periods are consecutive periods of, normally, one year each, ending on a date called the 'accounting reference date' (CA 1985, s. 224(5)). Normally, this is the last day of the month in which the anniversary of its incorporation falls (s. 224(3A) inserted by SI 1996 No. 189).

The successive annual accounts of a company refer to consecutive periods known as 'financial years', each of which must end not more than seven days before or after the end of an accounting reference period (s. 223).

A company may change its accounting reference date by following the procedure set out in s. 225 as amended by SI 1996 No. 189. Under s. 223(5), it is the duty of directors of a parent company to ensure that the financial years of their company and its subsidiary undertakings coincide, unless in their opinion there are good reasons to the contrary.

9.3.3 Directors' report

CA 1985, s. 234, requires the directors of a company to prepare, for each financial year, a directors' report containing a fair review of the developments of the business of the company and its subsidiary undertakings during the financial year and of their position at the end of it. The report must also state the dividend recommended by the directors (s. 234(1)).

The directors' report of a company for a financial year must be approved by the board of directors and signed on behalf of the board by a director or the secretary of the company (s. 234A(1)).

Copies of the directors' report of a company for a financial year must accompany the annual accounts laid before the company in general meeting (s. 241, see 9.3.6.1) and the copies of the annual accounts which must, under s. 238(1), be sent to every member of the company (see 9.3.6.2). Laying the accounts and directors' report before a general meeting can be dispensed with by a private company under s. 252 but sending the accounts and report to the members cannot be dispensed with.

For the contents of the directors' report see 9.7.

9.3.4 Auditors' report

It is usually assumed in company law that the members of a company are not directly active in managing the company. The annual accounts are prepared for the members by people who are directly concerned in management and there is an obvious danger that the accounts will deliberately or accidentally misrepresent the company's financial affairs. So members could benefit from an independent check on the adequacy of the accounts. Independent checks of financial accounts are normally provided by the process known as 'auditing' which has become a highly developed branch of accountancy. Under CA 1862, it was assumed that the members of a company would want to have its annual accounts audited and a provision to that effect was included in the model set of articles of association in Table

A (CA 1862, sch. 1) but, like any provision in the articles, this could be varied. CA 1900, ss. 21 to 23, made the audit of companies' annual accounts a mandatory requirement of company law and this requirement is now contained in part VII of CA 1985. Since 1900, users of accounts have demanded increasingly high standards of auditing, and the audit function has become more and more expensive. It has recently been recognised that in most small companies the members are directly concerned in management and regard a sophisticated audit of accounts as an unnecessarily costly protection. So ss. 249A to 249E of CA 1985 (inserted by SI 1994 No. 1935) have introduced exemptions from the mandatory audit requirement.

If a company is not exempt from the mandatory auditing requirement then it must appoint an auditor or auditors in accordance with the rules set out in 17.4.

The company's auditors are required by s. 235(1) to report to the members on all annual accounts which are, during the auditors' tenure of office, to be laid before the company in general meeting (see 9.3.6.1), or, if the company has elected under s. 252 to dispense with laying accounts (see 9.3.6.5), sent to the members under s. 238 (see s. 252(3)). The auditors' report must state the names of the auditors and be signed by them (s. 236(1)). Copies of the auditors' report on annual accounts must be sent with the copies of the accounts and directors' report to the members under s. 238 (see 9.3.6.2) and, if copies of the accounts and report are laid before a general meeting, must be laid with them.

In *Caparo Industries plc* v *Dickman* [1990] 2 AC 605, Lord Oliver of Aylmerton said, at p. 630:

> It is the auditors' function to ensure, so far as possible, that the financial information as to the company's affairs prepared by the directors accurately reflects the company's position in order, first, to protect the company itself from the consequences of undetected errors or, possibly, wrongdoing (by, for instance, declaring dividends out of capital) and, secondly, to provide shareholders with reliable intelligence for the purpose of enabling them to scrutinise the conduct of the company's affairs and to exercise their collective powers to reward or control or remove those to whom that conduct has been confided.

If a private company qualifies as a small company for a financial year (see 9.5.2 for the definition of a small company) then it will, under s. 249A, be exempt from the audit requirements of CA 1985, part VII, for that year if:

(a)   its turnover for that year is not more than £350,000 (or a proportionate amount if the financial year is not 12 months: s. 249A(6)) and

(b)   its balance sheet total is not more than £1.4 million.

But if such a company is in a group as a parent company or a subsidiary undertaking (defined in 9.6.2), it is exempt from being audited only if the group is a small group which is not an ineligible group (defined in 9.6.5), the group's aggregate turnover is not more than £350,000 net (or £420,000 gross) and its aggregate balance sheet total is not more than £1.4 million net (or £1.68 million gross) (s. 249B(1)(f), (1B) and (1C)). If a company is a charity, it cannot qualify for exemption from auditing if its gross income is more than £250,000, and if its gross income is more than £90,000, its directors must obtain from a 'reporting accountant' a report on unaudited accounts conforming with s. 249C. For accounts for any financial year ending before 15 June 1997, the requirement to obtain an accountant's report when turnover was more than £90,000 applied to all small companies, but by SI 1997, No. 936, this requirement has been restricted to charities.

Various financial services companies, including banking and insurance companies, cannot qualify for exemption under s. 249A — see s. 249B(1)(b) to (d).

A balance sheet of a company which is exempt from the audit requirements must include a statement by the directors to the effect that the conditions for exemption have been met and that they acknowledge their responsibility for keeping proper accounting records and preparing proper accounts (s. 249B(4) and (5)).

If, because of s. 249A, a company's accounts for a financial year will not be audited then, under s. 249B(2), any member or members holding 10 per cent or more in nominal value of the company's issued share capital, or any class of it, may require the company to obtain an audit of those accounts. A written notice requiring an audit must be deposited at the company's registered office during the financial year and not later than one month before the end of the year. Once such a notice has been deposited the company ceases to be exempt from the audit requirements (s. 249B(3)).

Exemption from auditing requirements is also available to dormant companies — see 17.4.1.7.

9.3.5   Period allowed for delivering accounts and reports

Copies of a company's annual accounts and reports must be laid before the company in general meeting (CA 1985, s. 241) unless, in the case of a private company, the members have elected under s. 252 to dispense with the laying of accounts. By s. 238(1), copies of a company's annual accounts and reports must be sent to every member of the company. By s. 242(1), the directors must deliver a copy of the company's annual accounts and reports to the registrar.

The period allowed for laying and delivering accounts and reports is defined in s. 244. In normal circumstances the period allowed is (s. 244(1)):

(a)   for a private company, 10 months after the end of the relevant accounting reference period, and

(b)   for a public company, seven months after the end of the relevant accounting reference period.

The relevant accounting reference period is the accounting reference period by reference to which the financial year for the accounts in question was determined (s. 244(6)).

The Secretary of State may allow a company an extension of the time-limit applying to it, provided it applies for an extension before the expiry of that time-limit and gives a 'special reason' (s. 244(5)). A company which carries on business, or has interests, outside the United Kingdom, the Channel Islands and the Isle of Man may claim an automatic extension of three months provided the directors give notice to the registrar before the normal time-limit has expired (s. 244(3)).

The London Stock Exchange requires a listed company to issue accounts for a financial year within six months of the end of the financial year, though in exceptional circumstances an extension may be granted (Listing Rules, para. 12.42(e)).

9.3.6   Laying accounts before a general meeting and sending accounts to members

9.3.6.1   *Laying before a general meeting*
The directors of a company must, under penalty, lay before a general meeting copies of the company's annual accounts, the directors' report and the auditors' report on those accounts

(CA 1985, s. 241), unless, in the case of a private company, the members have elected under s. 252 to dispense with the laying of accounts. If the company is a small private company and it is totally exempt from the auditing requirements then no auditors' report is required (s. 249E(1)(b)). An auditors' report is also not required if the company is a dormant company exempt from the auditing requirements (s. 250(4)). Laying accounts and reports before a general meeting must be done before the end of the 'period allowed for laying and delivering accounts and reports' — see 9.3.5.

If the directors of a company fail to lay copies of its accounts and reports before a general meeting before the end of the period allowed then every person who was a director of the company immediately before the period ended is guilty of an offence and may be fined (s. 241(2)). It is a defence to prove that one took all reasonable steps to get the accounts presented on time (s. 241(3)) but not that the accounts were not in fact prepared in time (s. 241(4)).

Exactly what has to be done to annual accounts and reports to constitute 'laying before' a general meeting partly depends on the practice of the company concerned. CA 1985, s. 238, requires the accounts and reports to be sent to the members before the meeting at which they are to be laid. Copies of the balance sheet and directors' report must not, under penalty, be laid before a general meeting unless the originals have been signed in accordance with ss. 233(1) and 234A(1) respectively (ss. 233(6) and 234A(4)). They must, under penalty, state the name of the persons who signed the original on behalf of the board (ss. 233(3) and (6), and 234A(2) and (4)). The copy of the auditors' report must, under penalty, state the names of the auditors (s. 236(2) and (4)). Usually, the notice convening the meeting will state that its business will include 'receiving' the accounts but no other action by the members is required or even possible. The meeting cannot, for example, 'adopt' the accounts: they are the accounts of the directors not of the members. If the members do not like what they read in the accounts then their remedy is to convene a further general meeting to dismiss the directors, or to instruct them to take a particular course of action (but see 15.7.1).

9.3.6.2 Sending copies before general meeting

A copy of a company's annual accounts for each financial year (together with the relevant directors' and auditors' reports) must be sent to each of the company's members and debenture holders (s. 238(1)). Copies of the accounts and reports must also be sent to anyone else entitled to receive notices of general meetings (s. 238(1)), which includes the company's auditors (s. 390(1)). If the company is a small private company and it is totally exempt from the auditing requirements then no auditors' report is required (s. 249E(1)(a)). An auditors' report is also not required if the company is a dormant company exempt from the auditing requirements (s. 250(4)).

If the company is not subject to an election to dispense with the laying of accounts and reports at general meetings then the accounts and reports must be sent not less than 21 days before the date of the general meeting at which they are to be laid (s. 238(1)). If an election is in force then the accounts and reports must be sent not less than 28 days before the end of the period allowed (see 9.3.5) for laying and delivering them (s. 253(1)).

Copies of the balance sheet and directors' report must not, under penalty, be circulated unless the originals have been signed in accordance with ss. 233(1) and 234A(1) respectively (ss. 233(6) and 234A(4)). They must, under penalty, state the name of the person who signed the original on behalf of the board (ss. 233(3) and (6), and 234A(2) and (4)). Copies circulated of the auditors' report must, under penalty, state the names of the auditors (s. 236(2) and (4)).

The copy of the balance sheet sent out must, under penalty, be a copy of a balance sheet that has been signed by a director on behalf of the board in accordance with s. 233(1) and must state the name of the person who signed the balance sheet on behalf of the board (s. 233(3) and (6)).

The time limit for sending a company's annual accounts and reports depends on whether there is an election in force to dispense with the laying of accounts and reports at general meetings (see 9.3.6.5).

If no election is in force then the accounts and reports must be sent not less than 21 days before the date of the general meeting at which they are to be laid (s. 238(1)). Normally the accounts will be presented at the annual general meeting, and normally 21 days' notice has to be given to convene the AGM (s. 369(1)(a)). However, s. 369(3)(a) permits an AGM to be held with a shorter period of notice provided every person entitled to attend and vote at the meeting agrees. So s. 238(4) permits a company to send its accounts less than 21 days before a meeting if all the members entitled to attend and vote at the meeting agree.

If an election is in force then the accounts and reports must be sent not less than 28 days before the end of the period allowed (see 9.3.5) for laying and delivering them (s. 253(1)).

If, without proper approval of members, a company fails to send annual accounts in time, or fails to send them at all, then an offence triable either way is committed by the company and by each of its officers who knowingly and wilfully authorised or permitted the failure (CA 1985, ss. 238(5) and 730(5) and sch. 24).

9.3.6.3   Right to demand copies of accounts and reports

Any member of a company and any holder of its debentures is entitled to demand a copy of its most recent annual accounts and reports free of charge (CA 1985, s. 239(1)). Failure to comply with such a demand within seven days renders the company and each of its officers who knowingly and wilfully authorised or permitted the failure liable to a fine (ss. 239(3) and 730(5) and sch. 24).

One person may demand only one copy of the annual accounts and reports for a year under s. 239 but that is in addition to any right under s. 238 to receive a copy (s. 239(2)).

9.3.6.4   Listed public company's summary financial statement

A listed public company is empowered by CA 1985, s. 251(1), and the Companies (Summary Financial Statement) Regulations 1995 (SI 1995 No. 2092) to prepare a summary financial statement which may be sent in substitution for the full annual accounts and reports required to be sent by s. 238, provided the company is not prohibited from doing so by its memorandum or articles of association (SI 1995 No. 2092, reg. 3). A summary financial statement can be sent instead of full accounts and reports only to a person who the company has ascertained does not wish to receive full accounts and reports. Wishes must be ascertained in the manner specified in SI 1995 No. 2092, regs 4, 5 and 6.

A summary financial statement must be derived from the company's annual accounts and directors' report (s. 251(3)) and must contain the information specified in SI 1995 No. 2092 and the Listing Rules, para. 12.45. It must have been approved by the board of directors, and the original statement must be signed on behalf of the board by one of the company's directors (SI 1995 No. 2092, reg. 4(4)(b)). Copies of the statement must state the name of the person who signed on behalf of the board (reg. 7(2)). It must contain a statement by the company's auditors of their opinion as to whether the summary financial statement is consistent with the full accounts and directors' report and whether it complies with the 1995 Regulations (CA 1985, s. 251(4)(b)). The auditors must also state whether their report on the annual accounts was qualified or not, and if it was qualified they must set out the report in full (s. 251(4)(c)). A summary financial statement must contain prominent statements that the summary does not contain sufficient information to allow for a full understanding of the results and state of affairs of the company or group and that members and debenture holders have a right, under CA 1985, s. 239, to demand, free of charge, a copy of the company's latest full accounts and reports (SI 1995 No. 2092, reg 7(3) and (4)).

A summary financial statement for a year must not be sent out if the period allowed for laying and delivering accounts and reports for the year has expired (reg. 4(4)(a)).

9.3.6.5   *Election to dispense with laying accounts and reports*

The members of a *private company* may elect under CA 1985, s. 252, to dispense with the laying of accounts and reports before the company in general meeting. An election must be made by elective resolution (unanimous approval) under s. 379A (see 14.4.8.4). It is likely that such an election will be made if there has been an election under s. 366A to dispense with the holding of annual general meetings.

If a private company has made an election to dispense with laying accounts and reports before general meetings then a copy of the company's annual accounts and reports for each financial year must be sent to members and others as described in 9.3.6.2. Once the accounts and reports for a financial year have been sent out then, within 28 days of them being sent out, any member or auditor of the company is entitled to require that a general meeting be held for the purpose of laying the accounts and reports before the company (s. 253(2)). A copy of accounts and reports sent to a member must be accompanied by a notice pointing out the right to require a meeting (s. 253(1)). The procedure is that the member or auditor must deposit a notice in writing at the company's registered office requiring that a general meeting be held (s. 253(2)). If the directors do not proceed duly to convene a meeting, the person who deposited the notice may do so personally (s. 253(3)) and must be repaid by the company the reasonable expenses of doing so (s. 253(5)). The company can, in turn, deduct the expenses from any fees or other remuneration due to the defaulting directors (s. 253(5)).

The directors are deemed to have failed duly to convene a meeting in either of the following circumstances:

(a)   If they do not proceed to convene a meeting within 21 days of deposit of the notice (s. 253(3)).

(b)   If the meeting is convened for a date more than 28 days after the date of the notice convening it (s. 253(6)).

9.3.7   Form and content of annual accounts

9.3.7.1   *Schedules 4, 4A, 9 and 9A*

CA 1985 prescribes the information that must be included in the annual accounts that the directors of a registered company must prepare for its members.

The requirements for individual accounts are contained in CA 1985, sch. 4, which is in accordance with the Fourth Directive. In individual accounts, the balance sheet must give a true and fair view of the state of affairs of the company as at the end of the financial year, and the profit and loss account must give a true and fair view of the profit or loss of the company for the financial year (s. 226(2)). By s. 226(3), individual accounts must comply with the provisions of sch. 4 unless complying with those provisions would be inconsistent with the requirement to give a true and fair view, in which case the directors must depart from the requirements to the extent necessary to give a true and fair view (s. 226(5)). If complying with the requirements would not be sufficient to give a true and fair view then the necessary additional information must be given in the accounts or in a note to them (s. 226(4)).

A large quantity of information is required by part III (paras. 35 to 58) of sch. 4 to be given in notes to a company's annual accounts if it is not given in the accounts. Also, by s. 232(1), notes to the accounts must give information, relating to the company's directors, specified in sch. 6, which is considered in 16.6.6 and 16.6.8.8.

The requirements for group accounts are contained in sch. 4A which is in accordance with the Seventh Directive. A company's group accounts must give a true and fair view of the state of affairs as at the end of the financial year, and the profit or loss for the financial year, of the undertakings included in the consolidation, as a whole, so far as concerns members of the company (s. 227(3)). Subsections (4) to (6) of s. 227 require group accounts to comply with sch. 4A subject to an overriding requirement to give a true and fair view, in the same way as subsections (3) to (6) of s. 226 provide for individual accounts.

Under CA 1985, s. 233(5), if annual accounts are approved which do not comply with the requirements of CA 1985 then every director of the company who is a party to their approval and who knows that they do not comply or is reckless as to whether they comply is guilty of an offence triable either way. Every director of the company at the time the accounts are approved is to be taken to be a party to their approval unless he shows that he took all reasonable steps to prevent their being approved.

A company's accounting records must be such as to enable the company's directors to ensure that any balance sheet and profit and loss account prepared under part VII of CA 1985 complies with the requirements of the Act (s. 221(1)(b)). An officer of a company who knowingly and wilfully authorises or permits it to keep accounting records that are not sufficient for this purpose is guilty of an offence triable either way (for which a prison sentence of up to two years may be imposed) unless he can show that he acted honestly and that inadequacies of accounting were excusable in the circumstances in which the company was operating (ss. 221(5) and (6) and 730(5) and sch. 24).

Banking and insurance companies are subject to special rules.

Directive 86/635/EEC on the annual accounts and consolidated accounts of banks and other financial institutions harmonises the accounting rules of Community States for credit institutions (including banks and building societies) — whether they are companies or partnerships. The Directive is implemented in English and Scots law by SI 1991 No. 2705, which amends CA 1985. By the new CA 1985, s. 255(1), which is inserted by SI 1991 No. 2705, reg. 3, a banking company (which, by CA 1985, s. 744, means a company which is authorised under the Banking Act 1987) must prepare its individual accounts in accordance with part I of sch. 9 to CA 1985 rather than sch. 4, and by the new s. 255A(1), the parent company of a banking group must prepare its group accounts in accordance with part II of sch. 9. The text of the new sch. 9 is set out in sch. 1 to SI 1991 No. 2705. By the new s. 255A(4) as amended by SI 1992 No. 3178, reg. 5, and SI 1993 No. 3246, reg. 3(2), the term 'banking group' means a group where:

> . . . the parent company is a banking company or where—
>   (a)   the parent company's principal subsidiary undertakings are wholly or mainly credit institutions, and
>   (b)   the parent company does not itself carry on any material business apart from the acquisition, management and disposal of interests in subsidiary undertakings.

A credit institution is an undertaking whose business is to receive deposits or other repayable funds from the public and to grant credits for its own account (s. 262(1); SI 1992

No. 3178, reg. 7). For the purposes of (b), the management of interests in subsidiary undertakings includes the provision of services to such undertakings, and a parent company's principal subsidiary undertakings are those subsidiary undertakings of the company whose results or financial position would principally affect the figures shown in the group accounts (s. 255A(5A)).

The accounts of insurance undertakings in the European Union are governed by Directive 91/674/EEC which is implemented by SI 1993 No. 3246. By CA 1985, s. 255(2), an insurance company must prepare its individual accounts in accordance with part I of sch. 9A to the Act and by s. 255A(2) the parent company of an insurance group (defined in s. 255A(5) in much the same way as a banking group is defined in s. 255A(4)) must prepare group accounts in accordance with part II of sch. 9A. The text of sch. 9A is set out in sch. 1 to SI 1993 No. 3246. Some small mutual associations and friendly societies are exempted by SI 1993 No. 3246, reg. 6.

9.3.7.2 Formats

Companies preparing their accounts in accordance with CA 1985, sch. 4, must present the balance sheet and profit and loss account in one of the standard formats prescribed in sch. 4, part I, section B. These formats are prescribed for use throughout the European Union by the Fourth Directive. The formats are lists of headings and subheadings naming categories of assets, liabilities, capital, income and charges against income. The main headings are identified by capital letters, subheadings either by roman numerals or by arabic numerals. There are two alternative formats for balance sheets and four for profit and loss accounts.

The directors of a company must choose one of the allowable formats for their balance sheets and one for their profit and loss accounts and use the formats consistently from year to year unless there are, in their opinion, special reasons for change, in which case they must explain why they have changed in a note to the first accounts prepared after a change (CA 1985, sch. 4, para. 2). In practice, balance sheets are usually in format 1.

Using their chosen formats the directors must show figures for all the headings and subheadings, in the order in which the items are given in the Act (CA 1985, sch. 4, para. 1) though the identifying letters and numerals need not be used (para. 1(2)). However, the subheadings identified by arabic numerals may be adapted to the needs of the particular business in which the company is engaged and such subheadings may be combined if individual amounts are not material (CA 1985, sch. 4, para. 3(3) and (4)).

In respect of every item shown in the accounts for a financial year of a company, the corresponding amount for the immediately preceding financial year must also be shown (CA 1985, sch. 4, para. 4).

There are no prescribed formats for the accounts of banking and insurance companies prepared in accordance with CA 1985, sch. 9.

9.3.7.3 Accounting principles

CA 1985, sch. 4, para. 9, requires that sch. 4 accounts of a company must be drawn up in accordance with five principles set out in paras 10 to 14 of the schedule, unless (para. 15) it appears to the directors of the company that there are special reasons for departing from them. If directors draw up accounts that depart from any of the principles then they must give particulars of the departure, the reasons for it and its effect (para. 15).

The first four of the five principles are familiar to British accountants as the 'fundamental accounting concepts' defined in SSAP 2. The five principles are:

(a)   The company shall be presumed to be carrying on business as a going concern (para. 10). In SSAP 2 this is not unexpectedly called the 'going concern concept'.

(b)   Accounting policies shall be applied consistently within the same accounts and from one financial year to the next (para. 11). The Act does not state what is meant by 'accounting policies' and the terminology is slightly unfortunate because 'accounting policy' is given a meaning in SSAP 2 which may not be the same as the meaning in the Act. The corresponding provision of the Fourth Directive is art. 31, para. 1:

> The Member States shall ensure that the items shown in the annual accounts are valued in accordance with the following general principles: . . .
> (b)   the methods of valuation must be applied consistently from one financial year to another.

This may be compared with the 'consistency concept' in SSAP 2: '[T]here is consistency of accounting treatment of like items within each accounting period and from one period to the next'.

(c)   The amount of any item shall be determined on a prudent basis (para. 12), and in particular:

> (i)   only profits realised at the balance sheet date shall be included in the profit and loss account; and
> (ii)   all liabilities and losses which have arisen or are likely to arise in respect of the financial year to which the accounts relate or a previous financial year shall be taken into account, including those which only become apparent between the balance sheet date and the date on which it is signed on behalf of the board of directors (see 9.3.1).

The recognition of profits and losses is considered further in 10.5.4. This principle is basically the concept of 'prudence' in SSAP 2 but it also includes rules on post balance sheet events which are given in SSAP 17.

(d)   All income and charges relating to the financial year to which the accounts relate shall be taken into account, without regard to the date of receipt or payment (para. 13). This is the 'accruals concept' in SSAP 2; see 10.5.4 for further discussion.

(e)   In determining the aggregate amount of any item the amount of each individual asset or liability that falls to be taken into account shall be determined separately (para. 14). There is no corresponding statement in any SSAP probably because this is merely a statement of the methodology of accounting in which each individual transaction is recorded in accounting records from which financial statements are derived.

9.3.7.4   *Small companies*

Under CA 1985, s. 246(2) (inserted by SI 1997 No. 220, reg. 2), the directors of a small company (defined in 9.5.2) may prepare its individual accounts in accordance with sch. 8 instead of sch. 4. Schedule 8 (inserted by SI 1997 No. 220, sch. 1) is a simplified version of sch. 4 appropriate to small companies, but the simplifications are optional: it is permissible under s. 246(2) to include in a small company's individual accounts prepared under sch. 8 some of the extra information required by sch. 4. If directors of a small company have prepared its individual accounts in accordance, wholly or partially, with sch. 8 and they also have to prepare group accounts then, by s. 248A inserted by SI 1997 No. 220, reg. 6, the group accounts can be in accordance with sch. 8 as modified by s. 248A. (Most small companies are exempt from preparing group accounts, see 9.6.5.) Individual and group accounts of a company prepared in accordance with sch. 8 must contain a statement in a prominent position on the balance sheet that they are prepared in accordance with the provisions of part VII of CA 1985 relating to small companies (ss. 246(8) and 248A(5)), but this statement is not required if the company is a dormant company exempt from the obligation to appoint auditors (s. 246(9)).

9.3.8 'True and fair view'

The phrase 'true and fair view' (of the state of affairs of a company, in relation to a balance sheet, and of the profit or loss of a company, in relation to a profit and loss account) was introduced into British company law in 1948 (CA 1948, s. 149(1)). The phrase has since been adopted in the European Union. The Fourth Directive requires that 'The annual accounts shall give a true and fair view of the company's assets, liabilities, financial position and profit or loss' (art. 2(2)). Earlier, the Companies (Consolidation) Act 1908, s. 113(2), had required a company's auditors to certify whether in their opinion its balance sheet 'is properly drawn up so as to exhibit a true and correct view of the state of the company's affairs'. This repeated a phrase used in CA 1900, s. 23. CA 1900 had reintroduced the requirement that every company must appoint an auditor. Under the Joint Stock Companies Act 1856 and CA 1862, auditing was a matter for the articles of association but the phrase 'true and correct view' was used in art. 94 of the model set of articles, Table A in CA 1862, sch. 1, though that article also referred to a 'full and fair balance sheet'. The phrase 'full and fair balance sheet' had appeared in the Joint Stock Companies Act 1844, s. 35. R.J. Chambers and P. W. Wolnizer have found that in partnership agreements and deeds of settlement before 1844, phrases such as 'full, true and explicit' and 'fair, accurate and just' were used ('A true and fair view of financial position' (1990) 8 C&SLJ 353 at p. 359). In *Re London & General Bank (No. 2)* [1895] 2 Ch 673, Rigby LJ said, at p. 692, that it was not easy to define what else was required of a 'full and fair' balance sheet for it to show a 'true and correct view'. His lordship thought that:

> A full and fair balance sheet must be such a balance sheet as to convey a truthful statement as to the company's position. It must not conceal any known cause of weakness in the financial position, or suggest anything which cannot be supported as fairly correct in a business point of view.

Clearly there has been some difficulty in finding the right words to express what is expected of accounts, and it may be that the present phrase, 'true and fair', cannot withstand too much analysis. H. Evans, 'True and fair revisited' [1990] LMCLQ 255, for example, suggests that 'fair' could mean either 'tolerable, passable, of moderate quality, average', or 'impartial, just, unbiased, equitable', and, remarkably, prefers the first meaning: it seems unlikely that this is correct.

The most significant feature of the true and fair view of financial position and of profit and loss required by CA 1985 is that it is an accountant's view expressed through the medium of a balance sheet and profit and loss account. A statement that a company is hopelessly insolvent may well be a true and fair view of its financial position but it is not the view required by CA 1985 because it is not a balance sheet.

The view of a company's state of affairs and profit and loss that is given by its accounts for a financial year is an accountants' view and will be fully appreciated only by people who are familiar with the way in which accountants prepare financial statements. The view is made clearer by knowing how the states of affairs of other companies are presented in their accounts. It follows that if the accounts of a company are not prepared in the way that accountants usually prepare financial statements of companies then a user is likely to have great difficulty in appreciating the view they are presenting. The basic methods of double-entry bookkeeping and preparation of financial statements are set out with few variations in numerous accounting textbooks. However, there are many matters that can be treated in several different ways in financial statements and choosing the most appropriate way may involve a lengthy consideration of the implications of each possible presentation. In recent years accountants have recognised the need to cooperate in making a thorough examination of these problems, choosing a most appropriate method of treatment and promulgating it as a standard to be followed throughout their profession.

In Britain and Ireland the Accounting Standards Committee was set up in January 1970 to develop definitive standards for financial reporting: it was a joint committee of six major professional institutes of accountants. The Committee prepared Statements of Standard Accounting Practice (SSAPs) for adoption by the six institutes.

In August 1990, the Accounting Standards Committee was replaced by the Accounting Standards Board, which issues standards (called Financial Reporting Standards, FRSs) itself rather than merely recommending them for issue by the accountancy institutes, and will thus be seen to be more independent from the accountancy profession. Members of the Accounting Standards Board are appointed by an independent body called the Financial Reporting Council, which arranges the funding of the Accounting Standards Board and guides its work. The Accounting Standards Board has formally adopted as its own standards all SSAPs issued by the Accounting Standards Committee.

The Accounting Standards Board's *Foreword to Accounting Standards* (1993), para. 16, says:

Accounting standards are authoritative statements of how particular types of transaction and other events should be reflected in financial statements and accordingly compliance with accounting standards will normally be necessary for financial statements to give a true and fair view.

Standard setting is undertaken by accountancy bodies all over the world and with particular seriousness in the USA. International cooperation is ensured by the International Accounting Standards Committee (based in London) which prepares International Accounting Standards (IAS). In most cases compliance with an FRS automatically ensures compliance with the relevant IAS (*Foreword to Accounting Standards*, para. 36).

Clearly the standards that have been established have formidable authority. However, they do not cover all areas of controversy. Work on setting standards began comparatively recently and will clearly go on for some time. The standard-setting bodies also acknowledge that there may be special circumstances in which their standards are inapplicable. However, if, in financial statements, there is a significant departure from applicable standards then the *Foreword to Accounting Standards*, para. 19, states that the departure should be disclosed and explained, and the financial effects estimated and disclosed.

The legal status of Financial Reporting Standards has been enhanced by provisions introduced into CA 1985 by CA 1989. Accounts prepared in accordance with CA 1985, sch. 4, have to state whether they have been prepared in accordance with 'applicable accounting standards', and particulars of any material departure from those standards and the reasons for the departure must be given (sch. 4, para. 36A). However, small companies (see 9.5.2) do not have to comply with this rule, because they have the option, under s. 246, of preparing their accounts in accordance with sch. 8, from which the rule is omitted.

Medium-sized companies (see 9.5.2) are also given the option not to comply with the rule, by s. 246A(2). The accounting standards 'applicable' to a company's annual accounts are the standards issued by the Accounting Standards Board which are, in accordance with their terms, relevant to the company's circumstances and to the accounts (s. 256(1) and (2); SI 1990 No. 1667).

If a court ever had to decide whether a set of accounts gave a true and fair view it is difficult to see what other criteria could be applied than whether the accounts are drawn up in accordance with the considered practice of accountants generally. There is no legal principle involved. As Viscount Haldane said in *Sun Insurance Office v Clark* [1912] AC 443, HL, 'It is plain that the question of what is or is not profit or gain must primarily be one of fact, and of fact to be ascertained by the tests applied in ordinary business'. In *Edward Collins & Sons Ltd v Commissioners of Inland Revenue* 1925 SC 151, Lord President Clyde said: 'It is a commonplace that . . . no particular method of computing profits is a part of the law universal'.

Most of the cases involving accounting in the past have been revenue cases in which the problem has been that tax is not charged simply on the profit as determined by accounts that show a true and fair view of profit, but on taxable income (and, more recently, on chargeable capital gains). In addition certain expenditures, though they have cost money and reduced profit, are not to be deducted from gross income or gains in computing taxable profit (for example, expenditure on entertaining customers: Income and Corporation Taxes Act 1988, s. 577). Determining taxable income involves matters of law. For example, '. . . the question whether an expenditure is for tax purposes on revenue or on capital account is ultimately a question of law' (per Orr LJ in *Heather v P-E Consulting Group Ltd* [1973] Ch 212 at p. 224). However, such questions of revenue law do not affect consideration of accounts that are not drawn up for taxation purposes. In *Odeon Associated Theatres Ltd v Jones* [1971] 1 WLR 442, Pennycuick V-C said:

> It is necessary to consider . . . the principle upon which the profit of a trader falls to be ascertained for the purpose of income tax . . . .
>
> . . . first one must ascertain the profits of the trade in accordance with ordinary principles of commercial accountancy. . . . Secondly, one must adjust this account by reference to the express prohibitions contained in the relevant [income tax] statute. . . . I believe that to be the true principle upon which the profit of the taxpayers' trade must be ascertained for the present purpose.
>
> [Counsel for the Crown] contended that there is a third and distinct requirement, namely, that the profit of the trade must be ascertained for the purpose of income tax. It was not clear to me (I do not suppose that it is [counsel's] fault) precisely what standard the court should adopt, apart from that of the ordinary principles of commercial accountancy, in arriving at the profit of a trade for the purpose of income tax. [Counsel] used the word 'logic'. If by that he intended no more than to say that one must apply the correct principles of commercial accountancy, I agree with that. . . . I think, however, he intended to go beyond that, and meant that the court must ascertain the profit of a trade on some theoretical basis divorced from the principles of commercial accountancy. If that is what is intended, I am unable to accept the contention, which I believe to be entirely novel.

Some commentators doubt whether current accountancy methods ever provide a true and fair view. See, for example, R. J. Chambers and P. W. Wolnizer, 'A true and fair view of financial position' (1990) 8 C & SLJ 353, criticising the use of historical cost accounting, and R. Instone, 'Realised profits: unrealised consequences' [1985] JBL 106, criticising the use of accrual accounting. C. Noke, 'Realised profits: unrealistic conclusions' [1989] JBL 37 is a reply to Instone.

See further K.P.E. Lasok and E. Grace, 'The true and fair view' (1989) 10 Co Law 13; A. McGee, 'The "true and fair view" debate: a study in the legal regulation of accounting' (1991) 54 MLR 874.

9.4 ANNUAL ACCOUNTS AND REPORTS FOR THE REGISTRAR

9.4.1 Delivery of accounts and reports to the registrar

In respect of each financial year, the directors of a company must deliver a copy of the company's annual accounts and reports to the registrar (CA 1985, s. 242(1)). Small and medium-sized companies are entitled to exemptions from the requirement to deliver copies of the full accounts and reports prepared for members: they may instead deliver abbreviated accounts and reports (see 9.5). The registrar notifies receipt of a company's accounts and reports (or abbreviated accounts and reports) in the *Gazette* (s. 711(1)(k)).

Delivery of accounts and reports to the registrar must be done before the end of the 'period allowed for laying and delivering accounts and reports' — see 9.3.5. If the company is a dormant company exempt from the auditing requirements then the balance sheet that is delivered must state that the company was dormant throughout the financial year (s. 250(4)).

If the directors of a company fail to deliver copies of its accounts and reports to the registrar before the end of the period allowed then every person who was a director of the company immediately before the period ended is guilty of an offence and may be fined (s. 242(2)). It is a defence for a director to prove that he took all reasonable steps to get the accounts delivered on time (s. 242(4)) but not that the accounts and reports were not in fact prepared in time (s. 242(5)).

In addition to the possibility of a fine for failure to deliver accounts and reports to the registrar, a notice can be served on the directors requiring compliance, and if they have failed to make good the default within 14 days after service of the notice then the court may order them to make good the default (s. 242(3)). Failure to comply with such an order would be punishable as a contempt of court. Application for such an order may be made by any member or creditor of the company, or the registrar.

Under s. 242A, fixed penalties, recoverable by the registrar in civil proceedings, are imposed for filing accounts late. The penalties are on two scales (one for public and one for private companies) related to the length of time by which the accounts are overdue — from £100 for a private company up to 1 month late to £5,000 for a public company more than 12 months late.

The copy of the balance sheet delivered to the registrar must, under penalty, be signed on behalf of the board by a director of the company (s. 233(3) and (6)). The copy of the directors' report must, under penalty, be signed on behalf of the board by a director or the secretary of the company (s. 234A(3) and (4)). The copy of the auditors' report must state the names of the auditors and be signed by them (s. 236(3) and (4)).

Annual accounts delivered to the registrar may be in any language but if they are not in English then they must be accompanied by a translation into English which is certified to be correct (s. 242(1); the certification requirements are prescribed in SI 1990 No. 572, reg. 5). This does not apply to a company (other than a listed company) whose memorandum states that its registered office is to be in Wales and which delivers annual accounts in Welsh (s. 710B(3)(a), (6) and (7); SI 1994 No. 117, reg. 4). Such Welsh accounts need not be accompanied by a translation but the registrar must have them translated (s. 710B(4)).

9.4.2 Exemption for unlimited companies

An unlimited company is exempt from the requirement to deliver accounts to the registrar and can therefore keep its financial affairs confidential in the same way that a partnership can (CA 1985, s. 254(1)). To prevent avoidance, an unlimited company cannot claim this exemption if at any time during the accounting reference period (see 9.3.2) for the financial year being reported on (s. 254(2) and (3)):

(a) The company has been, to its knowledge, a subsidiary undertaking of an undertaking which was then limited.

(b) There have been, to its knowledge, exercisable by or on behalf of two or more undertakings which were then limited rights which if exercisable by one of them would have made the company a subsidiary undertaking of it.

(c) The company has been a parent company of an undertaking which was then limited.

(d) It was the promoter of a trading stamp scheme.

This exemption does not apply to a banking or insurance company or to the parent company of a banking or insurance group (s. 254(3); SI 1993 No. 1820, reg. 10; SI 1993 No. 3246, sch. 2, para. 2). The terms 'banking company' and 'banking group' are explained in 9.3.7.1.

The exemption also does not apply to an unlimited company (called a 'qualifying company') if all its members are limited companies (or other unlimited companies, or Scottish firms, whose members are all limited companies) (s. 254(3); SI 1993 No. 1820, regs 9(1) and 10). The terms 'limited company', 'other unlimited company' and 'Scottish firm' are to be interpreted as including any comparable undertaking incorporated in or formed under the law of any country or territory outside Great Britain (SI 1993 No. 1820, reg. 9(2)).

9.5 ABBREVIATED ACCOUNTS AND REPORTS OF PRIVATE COMPANIES

9.5.1 Option to deliver abbreviated accounts to the registrar

Instead of delivering to the registrar copies of the accounts and reports for a financial year that they have prepared for members, the directors of most *private companies* may, if they wish, deliver abbreviated accounts and reports so that some details of the company's affairs remain confidential. National legislation giving these exemptions is permitted by arts 11 and 27 of Directive 78/660/EEC. The modifications permitted depend on whether, in respect of the financial year reported on, the company qualifies as a small or as a medium-sized company. If a company does not qualify as a small or as a medium-sized company then its directors must deliver to the registrar the full accounts they have prepared for their members.

9.5.2 Definition of small company and medium-sized company

For a particular financial year, a private company qualifies as a *small company* if, in respect of that year and the preceding financial year (CA 1985, s. 247(1)(b)) (or that year alone if it is the company's first financial year: s. 247(1)(a)), the company satisfies any two or more of the following conditions (s. 247(3); SI 1992 No. 2452, reg. 5(3)):

(a) Its turnover does not exceed £2.8 million (or a proportionate amount if the financial year is not 12 months: s. 247(4)).

(b)   Its balance sheet total (i.e., total assets) does not exceed £1.4 million.

(c)   Its weekly average number of employees during the financial year does not exceed 50.

For a particular financial year, a private company qualifies as a *medium-sized company* if, in respect of that year and the preceding financial year (s. 247(1)(b)) (or that year alone if it is the company's first financial year: s. 247(1)(a)), the company satisfies any two or more of the following conditions (s. 247(3); SI 1992 No. 2452, reg. 5(4)):

(a)   Its turnover does not exceed £11.2 million (or a proportionate amount if the financial year is not 12 months: s. 247(4)).

(b)   Its balance sheet total does not exceed £5.6 million.

(c)   Its weekly average number of employees during the financial year does not exceed 250.

Having once qualified under the foregoing rules as a small or a medium-sized company, the directors of a private company are entitled to claim the same status in future years if the company satisfies the relevant conditions at least every other year, but if it fails to satisfy the conditions for two consecutive years then they lose their entitlement in the second of those years (s. 247(2)).

If a company is a parent company then it does not qualify as a small company unless the group headed by it qualifies as a small group and does not qualify as a medium-sized company unless the group headed by it qualifies as a medium-sized group (see 9.6.5) (s. 247A(3) inserted by SI 1997 No. 220, reg. 4).

The directors of a company cannot take advantage of the exemptions for small or medium-sized companies if the company is, or was at any time during the financial year reported on:

(a)   A public company (s. 247A(1)(a)(i)).

(b)   A banking or insurance company (see 9.3.7.1) (s. 247A(1)(a)(ii)).

(c)   A company that is an authorised person under the Financial Services Act 1986 (s. 247A(1)(a)(iii)).

(d)   A company that is, or was, a member of an ineligible group (see below) (s. 247A(1)(b)) unless it was, at the end of the financial year reported on, a dormant company exempt from auditing requirements (s. 250(4)(d)).

By s. 247A(2), a group (that is, a parent undertaking and its subsidiary undertakings: s. 262(1)) is ineligible if any of its members is:

(a)   a public company, or a body corporate (other than a registered company), which has power under its constitution to offer its shares or debentures to the public and may lawfully exercise that power,

(b)   an authorised institution under the Banking Act 1987 (i.e., a banking company),

(c)   an insurance company to which part II of the Insurance Companies Act 1982 applies, or

(d)   an authorised person under the Financial Services Act 1986.

The definitions of small and medium-sized company are based on the definitions in arts 11 and 27 of Directive 78/660/EEC where the figures for turnover and balance sheet total are expressed in ecu and are revised every five years in accordance with art. 53(2). In the most recent revision (Directive 94/8/EC) the figures were increased by one quarter but this latest revision has not yet been reflected in the British legislation. Because of the decline in value of sterling against the ecu, the sterling figures could be increased by 50 per cent. The Department of Trade and Industry estimates that of the 956,700 companies on the register at the end of March 1994, 870,000 were small companies (*Accounting Simplifications: a Consultative Document* (URN 95/669) (London: DTI, 1995), para. 3.6). However, only 308,000 companies filed abbreviated accounts in 1993/94 (ibid., para. 4.14). It may be, as the DTI suggests, that many companies do not consider it worthwhile to incur extra costs in preparing abbreviated accounts. It may also be that many small companies are members of ineligible groups, most often because they are the subsidiaries of public companies.

9.5.3 Form of abbreviated accounts and reports

If a company qualifies as a *medium-sized company* then, under CA 1985, s. 246A inserted by SI 1997 No. 220, reg. 3, its directors have to file with the registrar the same accounts as they lay before members except that, in the profit and loss account, certain items may be combined to give a single figure for gross profit or loss, and the analysis of total turnover into turnovers for different businesses of the company need not be given.

If a company qualifies as a *small company* then, by s. 246(5) inserted by SI 1997 No. 220, reg. 2(1), the directors do not have to file either their profit and loss account or their directors' report, and may file only an abbreviated balance sheet complying with sch. 8A. Such an abbreviated balance sheet must be signed by a director on behalf of the board (see 9.4.1) (s. 246(7)). Small companies are given further options by s. 246(6) to omit information, notably details of directors' and auditors' remuneration.

Abbreviated accounts must contain a statement in a prominent position on the balance sheet that they are prepared in accordance with the provisions of part VII of CA 1985 relating to small or medium-sized companies, as appropriate (ss. 246(8) and 246A(4)), but a small company does not have to give this statement if it is a dormant company exempt from the obligation to appoint auditors (s. 246(9)). If abbreviated accounts are filed with the registrar for a company which is not exempt from the obligation to appoint auditors then they must, by s. 247B inserted by SI 1997 No. 220, reg. 5, be accompanied by a special auditors' report stating that in the auditors' opinion:

(a) the company is entitled to deliver abbreviated accounts prepared in accordance with s. 246(5) and/or (6) (if it is a small company) or s. 246A(3) (if it is a medium-sized company), and

(b) the accounts delivered are properly prepared in accordance with the relevant provision.

For abbreviated accounts delivered to the registrar the special auditors' report takes the place of the auditors' report prepared for the members, unless that report was qualified, in which case it must be set out in full in the special report, together with any further material necessary to understand the qualification (s. 247B(3)(a)). If the report to the members contains a statement that the company has not kept proper accounting records or that the auditors have failed to obtain information and explanations which they needed then that statement must be set out in full in the special auditors' report (s. 247B(3)(b)).

9.6   GROUP ACCOUNTS

9.6.1   Group accounts of a parent company

When a company conducts parts of its business through separate undertakings that it owns or controls then its members will want an overall picture of the financial position of the whole business, not just the part that is carried out by the company they are members of. Group accounts for a number of related undertakings treat them as one single entity and ignore transactions between undertakings within the group.

'Undertaking' in this context means (CA 1985, s. 259(1)):

(a)   a body corporate or partnership firm, or

(b)   an unincorporated association carrying on a trade or business, with or without a view to profit.

If at the end of a financial year, a company is a parent company then the directors must, as well as preparing individual accounts for the year, prepare group accounts (s. 227(1)) unless one of the exemptions provided by ss. 228 (see 9.6.4), 248 (see 9.6.5) and 229(5) (see 9.6.6) applies. Group accounts must, by s. 227(2), be consolidated accounts comprising:

(a)   a consolidated balance sheet dealing with the state of affairs of the parent company and its subsidiary undertakings, and

(b)   a consolidated profit and loss account dealing with the profit or loss of the parent company and its subsidiary undertakings.

9.6.2   Parent and subsidiary undertakings; group undertakings

The relationship of parent undertaking and subsidiary undertaking is defined in s. 258 in a way that is similar to the definition of the relationship of holding company and subsidiary in ss. 736 and 736A (see 14.7). A 'parent company' is a parent undertaking which is a company.

The relationship of parent undertaking and subsidiary undertaking may arise in the following ways:

(a)   under s. 258(2)(a), where the parent undertaking holds a majority of the voting rights in the subsidiary undertaking,

(b)   under s. 258(2)(b), where the parent undertaking is a member of the subsidiary undertaking and has the right to appoint or remove a majority of its board of directors,

(c)   under s. 258(2)(c), where the parent undertaking has the right to exercise a dominant influence over the subsidiary undertaking:

(i)   by virtue of provisions contained in the subsidiary undertaking's memorandum or articles, or

(ii)   by virtue of a control contract,

(d)   under s. 258(2)(d), where the parent undertaking is a member of the subsidiary undertaking and controls alone, pursuant to an agreement with other shareholders or members, a majority of the voting rights in the subsidiary undertaking,

(e)   under s. 258(4), where the parent undertaking has a participating interest in the subsidiary undertaking and:

    (i)   it actually exercises a dominant influence over it, or

    (ii)   it and the subsidiary undertaking are managed on a unified basis,

(f)   under s. 258(5), where the subsidiary undertaking is a subsidiary undertaking of an undertaking which is itself a subsidiary undertaking of the parent undertaking.

The definition of the relationship of parent undertaking and subsidiary undertaking corresponds to the definition of subsidiary and holding company, except for s. 258(2)(c) and (4) (items (c) and (e) in the above list), which have no equivalent in the definition of subsidiary and holding company.

The definition in s. 258 is explained and supplemented by sch. 10A, which corresponds to s. 736A in the definition of subsidiary and holding company and also, in para. 4, explains s. 258(2)(c).

Under sch. 10A, para. 4(1), an undertaking is not to be regarded as having the right to exercise a dominant influence over another undertaking unless it has a right to give directions with respect to the operating and financial policies of that other undertaking which its directors are obliged to comply with whether or not they are for the benefit of that other undertaking.

'Control contract' is defined by sch. 10A, para. 4(2), to mean a written contract conferring a right to exercise a dominant influence over another undertaking which:

(a)   is of a kind authorised by the memorandum or articles of the undertaking in relation to which the right is exercisable, and

(b)   is permitted by the law under which that undertaking is established.

In relation to an undertaking which is not a company, expressions appropriate to companies in s. 258 and sch. 10A (and other provisions of CA 1985, part VII (ss. 221 to 262A)) are to be construed as references to the corresponding persons, officers, documents or organs, as the case may be, appropriate to undertakings of that description (s. 259(3)).

By sch. 10A, para. 4(3), the concept of actual dominant influence of one undertaking over another in s. 258(4) is not to be interpreted by reference to sch. 10A, para. 4. Actual dominant influence or the management of undertakings on a unified basis creates the relationship of parent undertaking and subsidiary undertaking unders. 258(4) only if the parent undertaking has a 'participating interest' in the subsidiary. This term is defined at length in s. 260.

A 'participating interest' means an interest held by an undertaking in the shares of another undertaking which it holds on a long-term basis for the purpose of securing a contribution to its activities by the exercise of control or influence arising from or related to that interest (s. 260(1)). This includes the purposes and activities of any of the parent undertaking's other subsidiary undertakings and of the group as a whole (s. 260(5)). A holding of 20 per cent or more of the shares of an undertaking shall be presumed to be a participating interest unless the contrary is shown (s. 260(2)). Interests that are convertible into interests in shares and options to acquire shares must be counted as interests in shares for the purposes of this definition (s. 260(3)) and an interest held on behalf of an undertaking must be treated as held by it (s. 260(4)). Any interests held by any other subsidiary undertakings of the parent undertaking must be treated as held by it (s. 260(5)). Section 259(2) defines how the reference to 'shares' in s. 260 is to be interpreted in relation to various types of undertaking.

A company that is required to prepare group accounts must state in notes to its accounts, with respect to each of its subsidiary undertakings, which of the conditions specified in

s. 258(2) or (4) is the reason for it being a subsidiary undertaking of its immediate parent undertaking (sch. 5, para. 15(5)). It is not necessary to state expressly that the reason is the holding of a majority of voting rights if the immediate parent undertaking holds the same proportion of shares in the subsidiary undertaking as it holds voting rights. This is because the proportion of shares held by the parent (and by the group, if different) in each subsidiary must be shown in the accounts anyway (sch. 5, para. 16).

In relation to an undertaking A, another undertaking B is a 'group undertaking' if (s. 259(5)):

(a) B is a parent undertaking or a subsidiary undertaking of A, or
(b) B is a subsidiary undertaking of any parent undertaking of A.

9.6.3 Effect on individual accounts

A company that prepares group accounts does not have to include an individual profit and loss account for itself in its published annual accounts, provided there is a note to its individual balance sheet showing the company's profit or loss for the financial year, and provided the accounts disclose that the exemption applies (s. 230). However, by s. 230(3), the full individual profit and loss account (apart from some notes) must be considered and approved by the board, and signed in accordance with s. 233(1). In practice a separate profit and loss account for a parent company rarely gives useful information and is normally omitted.

9.6.4 Exemption for subgroups

Under CA 1985, s. 228, a company is exempt from the requirement to prepare group accounts if it is itself a subsidiary undertaking, and its immediate parent undertaking is established under the law of a European Union State (s. 228(1)). So if there are subgroups within an EU group of undertakings, it is unnecessary to prepare group accounts for each subgroup.

The exemption does not apply to a company if any of its securities are listed on a stock exchange in any EU State (s. 228(3)).

The exemption is available to a company only if it is in fact included in consolidated accounts for a larger group drawn up to the same date, or to an earlier date in the same financial year, by a parent company established under the law of an EU State (s. 228(2)(a)) and those accounts have been drawn up and audited in accordance with the provisions of the Seventh Directive (s. 228(2)(b)). The company must state in its individual accounts that it is exempt under s. 228 from preparing group accounts (s. 228(2)(c)) and must name the parent company which has prepared the group accounts in which it is included (s. 228(2)(d)). It must also deliver to the registrar, within the period allowed for delivering its individual accounts, copies of those group accounts and of the parent undertaking's annual report, together with the auditors' report on them (s. 228(2)(e)).

This exemption is qualified by s. 228(1)(b) where the company is not a wholly owned subsidiary, that is, where there are minority interests. First, it is only available if the immediate parent undertaking holds more than 50 per cent of the shares in the company. Secondly, it does not apply if a notice requesting the company to prepare group accounts has been served by shareholders holding in aggregate:

(a) more than half the remaining shares in the company, or
(b) 5 per cent of the total shares in the company.

Such notice must be served not later than six months after the end of the financial year *before* that to which it relates.

9.6.5 Exemption for small and medium-sized groups

Under CA 1985, s. 248, if a parent company is a *private company* then it need not prepare group accounts for a financial year in relation to which the group headed by that company qualifies as a small or medium-sized group and is not an ineligible group (s. 248(1)).

The definition of 'ineligible group' given for this purpose in s. 248(2) is the same as the definition in s. 246(4) — see 9.5.2. (Note that if the parent company is a public company then the group is an ineligible group by s. 248(2)(a).)

The conditions for qualifying as a small or medium-sized group are set out in s. 249. They correspond to the conditions under which a company qualifies as a small or medium-sized company except that the relevant figures for turnover, assets and employees are aggregate figures for all the undertakings in the group. The aggregates of turnover and assets may be either the figures (described as 'net') that would appear in group accounts (that is, after set-offs and other adjustments to eliminate transactions within the group) or 'gross' (that is, without such adjustments) (s. 249(4)). Two or more of the following requirements must be met (s. 249(3); SI 1992 No. 2452, reg. 6(3) and (4)):

Small group

1.	Aggregate turnover	Not more than £2.8 million net (or £3.36 million gross)
2.	Aggregate balance sheet total	Not more than £1.4 million net (or £1.68 million gross
3.	Aggregate number of employees	Not more than 50

Medium-sized group

1.	Aggregate turnover	Not more than £11.2 million net (or £13.44 million gross
2.	Aggregate balance sheet total	Not more than £5.6 million net (or £6.72 million gross)
3.	Aggregate number of employees	Not more than 250

9.6.6 Subsidiaries that may be excluded from group accounts

The general rule is that every subsidiary undertaking of a parent company must be included in the consolidation when group accounts are prepared (s. 229(1)). However, s. 229 allows for some subsidiaries to be excluded. A company that is required to prepare group accounts must state in notes to its accounts, in relation to each of its subsidiary undertakings, whether the subsidiary is included in the consolidation and, if it is not, the reasons for excluding it (sch. 5, para. 15(4)). Under s. 229(2) and (3), a subsidiary undertaking may be excluded from consolidation in the following circumstances:

(a) Under s. 229(2) if including the subsidiary is not material for the purpose of giving a true and fair view; but two or more undertakings may be excluded on this ground only if they are not material taken together.

(b) Under s. 229(3)(a) if severe long-term restrictions substantially hinder the exercise of all the rights of the reporting company over the assets or management of the subsidiary by virtue of which it is deemed to be the parent company.

(c) Under s. 229(3)(b) if the information necessary for the preparation of group accounts cannot be obtained without disproportionate expense or undue delay.

(d) Under s. 229(3)(c) if the interest of the parent company in the subsidiary undertaking by virtue of which it is deemed to be the parent company is held exclusively with a view to subsequent resale and the undertaking has not previously been included in consolidated group accounts prepared by the parent company.

Section 229(4) requires that subsidiary undertakings must be excluded from the consolidation if their activities are so different from those of other undertakings to be included in the consolidation that their inclusion would be incompatible with the obligation to give a true and fair view. If an undertaking excluded under this subsection is incorporated outside Great Britain and does not have an established place of business in Great Britain or is unincorporated then its latest individual and group accounts and auditors' report must be delivered to the registrar in accordance with s. 243.

If all the subsidiary undertakings of a parent company fall within these exclusions then no group accounts are required (s. 229(5)). The parent company must state in notes to its accounts that this is the reason why it does not prepare group accounts and must state which exclusion applies to each subsidiary (sch. 5, para. 1(4) and (5)).

9.6.7 Disclosure of information on related undertakings

Under CA 1985, s. 231, the information specified in sch. 5 to the Act must be given in notes to a company's annual accounts (s. 231(1)). Part I of sch. 5 (paras 1 to 13) applies to a company that is not required to prepare group accounts. Part II (paras 14 to 32) applies to a company that is required to prepare group accounts. Schedule 5 has been extensively amended by SI 1996 No. 189, sch. 3.

The name of each of the company's subsidiary undertakings must be stated (para. 1(2) in part I; para. 15(2) in part II). With respect to each subsidiary undertaking there must (by paras 1(3) and 15(3)) be stated:

(a) if it is incorporated outside Great Britain, the country in which it is incorporated;

(b) if it is unincorporated, the address of its principal place of business.

FRS 2 suggests that the nature of the business of each principal subsidiary should be indicated.

In relation to each subsidiary undertaking, the notes must state what proportion of each class of its shares is held by the company (para. 2 in part I; para. 16 in part II; para. 16 also requires this information to be given in respect of the group's holdings if they are different).

In part I, paras 3 and 4 require financial information about subsidiary undertakings. A small company need not give the information specified in para. 4 (s. 246(3) inserted by SI 1997 No. 570, reg. 6(1)). Similar information in respect of subsidiary undertakings not included in the consolidation is required by para. 17 in part II. In part I, para. 6, and in part II, para. 20, require the number, description and amount of the shares in the company held by or on behalf of its subsidiary undertakings to be disclosed.

In part II only, para. 21 requires information about any unincorporated joint venture which an undertaking included in the consolidation manages jointly with one or more undertakings not included in the consolidation, and para. 22 requires information about associated undertakings. An associated undertaking is an undertaking in which an undertaking included in the consolidation has a participating interest and over whose operating and financial policy it exercises a significant influence, but which is neither a subsidiary undertaking of the parent company nor a joint venture (sch. 4A, para. 20). An undertaking holding 20 per cent or more of the voting rights in another undertaking is presumed to exercise a significant influence over the other's operating and financial policy unless the contrary is shown (para. 20(2)).

In part I, paras 7, 8 and 9, and in part II, paras 23 to 38, require information about undertakings in which the reporting company has a significant holding (more than 20 per cent, or a holding whose value is more than 20 per cent of the reporting company's assets) and which are not otherwise dealt with in the accounts.

In part I, para. 9A, and in part II, para. 28A (both added by SI 1993 No. 1820, reg. 11), require information about any 'qualifying undertaking' of which the company is a member. A qualifying undertaking is an unlimited company (a 'qualifying company' as defined in 9.4.2) or partnership (a 'qualifying partnership' as defined in 9.11), all of whose members are legal persons with limited liability so that accounts have to be prepared for it under SI 1993 No. 1820.

In part I, paras 11 and 12, and in part II, paras 30 and 31, apply where the reporting company is itself a subsidiary undertaking. The parent undertaking that draws up group accounts must be identified, and the directors must state the name of the company (which includes any body corporate) regarded by the directors as being their company's ultimate parent company (if there is one). If it is incorporated outside Great Britain, they must state where it is incorporated, if they know.

9.7 CONTENTS OF DIRECTORS' REPORT

9.7.1 Introduction

The directors' report for a financial year of a company must comply with CA 1985, ss. 234 and 234A and sch. 7. Schedule 7 has been amended by SI 1996 No. 189, reg. 14(4) and (5) and SI 1997 No. 571. Listed companies, as part of their continuing obligations, must circulate a large quantity of additional information to members with the statutory directors' report (Listing Rules, para. 12.43). In practice a listed company prepares a single document complying with both statutory and London Stock Exchange requirements.

A company that qualifies as a small company need not deliver a directors' report to the registrar (see 9.5.3). In many such companies the only members are directors (or are nominees of directors) and it would seem completely unnecessary to require such directors to prepare a report for themselves which no one else is entitled to see. Under CA 1985, s. 246(4) (inserted by SI 1997 No. 220, reg. 2(1)), the directors of a small company (defined in 9.5.2) may omit from their report some or all of the information listed in that subsection: the provisions are noted at appropriate points below. A report which omits information as permitted by s. 246(4) must contain a statement in a prominent position that it is prepared in accordance with the provisions of part VII of CA 1985 relating to small companies (s. 246(8)), unless the company is a dormant company exempt from the obligation to appoint auditors (s. 246(9)).

9.7.2 General

The directors' report must contain a fair review of the development of the business of the company, and its subsidiary undertakings, during the financial year, and of their position at the end of it, and must state the directors' recommendations on dividend (CA 1985,

s. 234(1)). The report must state the principal activities of the company and its subsidiary undertakings during the year and any significant changes that occurred in those activities (s. 234(2)). It must contain particulars of any important events affecting the company or any of its subsidiary undertakings which have occurred since the end of the financial year and it must indicate likely future developments in the business of the company and its subsidiary undertakings (CA 1985, sch. 7, para. 6(a) and (b)). Unless the company is unlimited, the directors' report must indicate the existence of branches of the company outside the United Kingdom (para. 6(d) inserted by SI 1992 No. 3178, reg. 3) — 'branch' has the same meaning as in the EC 11th Directive (CA 1985, s. 698(2)(b) inserted by SI 1992 No. 3179, sch. 2, para. 13). The information required by s. 234(1) and sch. 7, para. 6, may be omitted from the directors' report of a small company (s. 246(4) inserted by SI 1997 No. 220, reg. 2(1)).

The London Stock Exchange requires an explanation from the directors in the event of results shown by the accounts differing by 10 per cent or more from any forecast published by the company (Listing Rules, para. 12.43(b)).

9.7.3   Valuation of fixed assets

In the case of land, if the market value at the end of the year differs substantially from the amount indicated in the balance sheet, and the directors consider the difference requires the attention of members or debenture holders, then the difference must be indicated in the report (sch. 7, para. 1(2)). Usually, the fact that a company's land has increased in value does not require the attention of users of the accounts and so does not have to be mentioned in the directors' report (*Re a Company, ex parte Burr* [1992] BCLC 724 at pp. 728–9). The information required by sch. 7, para. 1(2), may be omitted from the directors' report of a small company (s. 246(4) inserted by SI 1997 No. 220, reg. 2(1)).

9.7.4   Directors

The report must state the names of all persons who, at any time during the financial year reported on, were directors of the company (CA 1985, s. 234(2)). Directors of subsidiary undertakings do not have to be named.

For each person who was a director at the end of the year, the report must state whether or not he was interested in shares in, or debentures of, the company or its holding company, or a subsidiary of the company, or a subsidiary of the company's holding company (CA 1985, sch. 7, para. 2). If a director did have an interest at the end of the year then the number of shares or debentures in which he was interested must be stated. The report must also state each director's interests at the beginning of the year, or at the time he first became a director during the year. The interests that must be reported are the same as those which must be recorded in the register of directors' interests under CA 1985, ss. 324 to 328 (see 13.6).

The London Stock Exchange requires a note stating any change in directors' interests that occurred between the end of the financial year and a date not more than one month prior to the date of the notice of the general meeting before which the accounts are to be laid (the notice would normally be circulated with the accounts) (Listing Rules, para. 12.43(k)). Particulars must also be given of any arrangement under which a director has waived or agreed to waive any emoluments (Listing Rules, para. 12.43(d)).

The information on directors' interests may be given by way of notes to the balance sheet and profit and loss account instead of in the directors' report (CA 1985, sch. 7, para. 2(1)).

9.7.5 Holdings of own shares

Details of holdings of own shares must be disclosed in the directors' report. The requirements are discussed in 6.4.2, 10.3.6, 10.6.4, 10.8.1, 10.8.2, and 10.8.6.

9.7.6 Research and development

A directors' report is required to contain an indication of the activities (if any) of the company and its subsidiary undertakings in the field of research and development (CA 1985, sch. 7, para. 6(c)). The information required by sch. 7, para. 6, may be omitted from the directors' report of a small company (s. 246(4) inserted by SI 1997 No. 220, reg. 2(1)).

9.7.7 Political and charitable contributions

By CA 1985, sch. 7, para. 3, if a company and its subsidiaries have given more than £200 during the financial year reported on for charitable or political purposes then the directors' report must state the amount donated for each purpose. Money given for a charitable purpose to a person who, at the time of the gift, was ordinarily resident outside the UK may be ignored.

If an individual donation for a political purpose was more than £200 then the name of the person or political party to whom it was given, and the amount given, must be stated.

Because the directors' report of a holding company discloses information on the gifts of its subsidiaries, information about charitable and political contributions does not have to be given in the directors' report of a company that is the wholly owned subsidiary of an English or Scottish registered company.

9.7.8 Employment of disabled persons

By CA 1985, sch. 7, para. 9, if the average number of employees of a company exceeds 250 then the directors' report must contain a statement describing such policies as the company has applied during the financial year:

(a) for giving full and fair consideration to applications for employment by the company made by disabled persons, having regard to their particular aptitudes and abilities;

(b) for continuing the employment of, and for arranging appropriate training for, employees of the company who have become disabled persons during the period when they were employed by the company;

(c) otherwise for the training, career development and promotion of disabled persons employed by the company.

9.7.9 Employee involvement

By CA 1985, sch. 7, para. 11, the directors' report of a company that employed on average more than 250 employees during the financial year reported on must contain a statement describing:

the action that has been taken during the financial year to introduce, maintain or develop arrangements aimed at—

(a) providing employees systematically with information on matters of concern to them as employees,

(b)   consulting employees or their representatives on a regular basis so that the views of employees can be taken into account in making decisions which are likely to affect their interests,

(c)   encouraging the involvement of employees in the company's performance through an employees' share scheme or by some other means,

(d)   achieving a common awareness on the part of all employees of the financial and economic factors affecting the performance of the company.

The information required by sch. 7, para. 11, may be omitted from the directors' report of a small company (s. 246(4) inserted by SI 1997 No. 220, reg. 2(1)).

9.7.10   Policy and practice on the payment of creditors

The directors' report of a *public* company for a financial year must state what its policy on the payment of creditors will be for the following financial year (CA 1985, sch. 7, para. 12 inserted by SI 1997 No. 571). This statement is also required in the directors' report of a company which, at any time during the year reported on, was a member of a group of which the parent company was a public company, unless the reporting company qualified as small or medium-sized for that year (para. 12(1)(b)). As well as identifying the company's future policy, the report must reveal present practice by giving the creditor days ratio for the financial year being reported on. This is the ratio of the amount owed to suppliers at the end of the financial year to the average amount per day invoiced by suppliers during the year. It is an indicator of the average number of days' credit being taken by the company, though a ratio calculated only once a year can be misleading because of seasonal variation. Paragraph 12 specifies in detail what the statement on payment policy and practice must contain.

9.8   PUBLICATION OF ACCOUNTS

If a company wishes to publish financial statements relating to one of its financial years then, under CA 1985, s. 240, it has two options. It may publish either its 'statutory accounts' or 'non-statutory accounts'. In this context, a company 'publishes' a document if it publishes, issues or circulates it or otherwise makes it available for public inspection in a manner calculated to invite members of the public generally, or any class of members of the public, to read it (s. 240(4)).

The statutory accounts for a financial year are the individual accounts or group accounts that are required to be delivered to the registrar (bearing in mind that these may be abbreviated) (CA 1985, s. 240(5)).

If a company publishes any of its statutory accounts they must be accompanied by the relevant auditors' report or special auditors' report (s. 240(1); s. 247B(5); SI 1994 No. 1935, sch. 1, para. 1(2)). If it is required to prepare group accounts then it must not publish its statutory individual accounts without also publishing with them its statutory group accounts (s. 240(2)). (But it can publish its group accounts without its individual accounts.)

Copies of the balance sheet and directors' report must not, under penalty, be published unless the originals have been signed in accordance with ss. 233(1) and 234A(1) respectively (ss. 233(6) and 234A(4)). They must, under penalty, state the name of the person who signed the original on behalf of the board (ss. 233(3) and (6), and 234A(2) and (4)). Every published copy of an auditors' report or special auditors' report must, under penalty, state the names of the auditors (ss. 236(2) and (4) and 247B(4)).

The term 'non-statutory accounts' means (s. 240(5)):

(a)   any balance sheet or profit and loss account relating to, or purporting to deal with, a financial year of the company, or

(b)   an account in any form purporting to be a balance sheet or profit and loss account for the group consisting of the company and its subsidiary undertakings relating to, or purporting to deal with, a financial year of the company.

If a company publishes non-statutory accounts, then, by ss. 240(3) and 247B(5) and SI 1994 No. 1935, sch. 1, para. 1(3), it must not publish with them the auditors' report or special auditors' report but it must publish with them a statement indicating:

(a)   that they are not the company's statutory accounts,

(b)   whether statutory accounts dealing with any financial year with which the non-statutory accounts purport to deal have been delivered to the registrar,

(c)   whether the statutory accounts for any such financial year have been reported on by the company's auditors or reporting accountant, and

(d)   whether the report was qualified, or (in the case of an auditors' report) criticised the company's accounting records, or stated that the auditors had failed to obtain all the information and explanations necessary for the purposes of their audit.

9.9   REVISION OF ACCOUNTS

CA 1989 introduced a new procedure for the revision of defective accounts and reports, which is contained in the new ss. 245, 245A, 245B and 245C of CA 1985.

Under s. 245, directors of a company are empowered to prepare revised annual accounts or a revised directors' report if they find that the accounts or report they have previously prepared did not comply with the Act (s. 245(1)). The detailed procedure is set out in the Companies (Revision of Defective Accounts and Report) Regulations 1990 (SI 1990 No. 2570).

Under s. 245B, an application may be made to the court for a declaration that annual accounts of a company do not comply with the requirements of the Act and for an order requiring the company's directors to prepare revised accounts (s. 245B(1)). This modifies the decision in *Devlin* v *Slough Estates Ltd* [1983] BCLC 497 that, in the absence of bad faith or fraud, the court would not make declarations of how matters should be reported in a company's annual accounts. If the court orders revision of accounts it may give directions with respect to the auditing of the accounts, the revision of any directors' report or summary financial statement (if the company is a public company), and publicising the revision (s. 245B(3)). It may also make the directors liable for the costs of the application (s. 245B(4) and (5)).

Under s. 245A, the Secretary of State is empowered to notify directors of a company that he believes something is wrong with their annual accounts (but not a directors' report) and give them one month to give him an explanation of the accounts or prepare revised accounts (s. 245A(1) and (2)). He can exercise this power only after accounts have been sent out under s. 238 or laid before a general meeting or delivered to the registrar (s. 245A(1)). If the Secretary of State is not satisfied with the explanation he is given or with revised accounts (or if there is no response to his notice within the time-limit) then he may, if he thinks fit, apply to the court (s. 245A(3)) under the provisions of s. 245B.

Only the Secretary of State or the Financial Reporting Review Panel Ltd (which is authorised for the purpose by SI 1991 No. 13) may apply to the court under s. 245B.

Members of a company do not have standing to apply. If they have complaints about their company's accounts they must try to interest the review body in the matter: *Devlin* v *Slough Estates Ltd* would prevent them making an application to the court outside of s. 245B.

9.10   HALF-YEARLY REPORTS

The Interim Reports Directive is a Directive of the Council of the European Communities (Directive 82/121/EEC, OJ No. L48, 20 February 1982, p. 26). The Directive requires member States to ensure that listed companies publish half-yearly reports on their activities and profits and losses during the first six months of each financial year. In the UK the London Stock Exchange has been designated as the competent authority for implementing the Directive (under art. 9, para. 1) and the Exchange is permitted to add its own requirements to those of the Directive (art. 3).

The Exchange's requirements are set out in the Listing Rules, paras 12.46 to 12.59, and hardly differ from the requirements of the Directive.

A listed company must publish its half-yearly report within four months of the end of the period reported on (para. 12.48). The report must either be sent to the holders of the company's listed securities or inserted as a paid advertisement in at least one national newspaper (para. 12.50). A copy must be sent to the Company Announcements Office of the Exchange (para. 12.49).

A half-yearly report must either state that the figures contained in it have not been audited, if that is the case, or, if they have been audited, set out the auditors' report in full (para. 12.54).

A company's half-yearly report must include an explanatory statement which must give any significant information enabling investors to make an informed assessment of the trend of the activities and profit or loss of the company and its subsidiaries (para. 12.56(a)). The explanatory statement must also indicate any special factor which has influenced activities and profit or loss during the period reported on (para. 12.56(b)), and must enable a comparison to be made with the corresponding period of the preceding financial year (para. 12.56(c)). It must also, as far as possible, refer to the prospects of the company and its subsidiaries in the current financial year (para. 12.56(d)).

Paragraph 12.52 specifies the minimum financial data that must be set out in a half-yearly report.

No sanction, either civil or criminal, is imposed by law for failure to produce a half-yearly report though the Council of the Stock Exchange would probably suspend the listing of a company that failed to produce a report.

9.11   ACCOUNTS OF A PARTNERSHIP COMPOSED OF ENTITIES WITH LIMITED LIABILITY

The Partnerships and Unlimited Companies (Accounts) Regulations 1993 (SI 1993 No. 1820) implement Council Directive 90/605/EEC. The purpose of the Directive is to ensure that if a partnership is composed of legal persons with limited liability then accounts are prepared for the partnership on the same basis as for limited companies. The British implementing regulations apply to what are called 'qualifying partnerships'. By reg. 3(1), a partnership is a qualifying partnership if each of its members is:

(a)   a limited company, or

(b)   an unlimited company, or a Scottish firm, each of whose members is a limited company.

The terms 'limited company', 'unlimited company', 'Scottish firm' and 'another partnership' are to be interpreted as including any comparable undertaking incorporated in or formed under the law of any country or territory outside Great Britain (reg. 9(2)).

By reg. 4, the persons who are members of a qualifying partnership at the end of any financial year of the partnership must prepare annual accounts and an annual report for the partnership and cause an auditors' report to be prepared, all in the same form as if the partnership were a company (subject to modifications set out in the schedule to the regulations). There is an exemption from this rule if any member of the partnership which is established under the law of an EC member State, or a parent undertaking of any member of the partnership which is so established, deals with the partnership 'on a consolidated basis' (a term which is defined in reg. 2(1)) in its group accounts and those group accounts are prepared in accordance with the Seventh Directive and disclose that advantage has been taken of the exemption (reg. 7).

Special obligations are placed by the regulations on limited companies which are members of qualifying partnerships. By reg. 5, each limited company which is a member of a qualifying partnership at the end of any financial year of the partnership must append the partnership's accounts for that year to the next annual accounts of its own that it delivers to the registrar. Again, this procedure need not be followed if the partnership's accounts have been consolidated in group accounts prepared by an EC undertaking (reg. 7). If advantage is taken of reg. 7 in relation to a qualifying partnership then every limited company which is a member of the partnership must disclose on request the name of at least one of the undertakings whose group accounts deal with the partnership (reg. 7(3)). If advantage is not taken of reg. 7 then such a company must supply to any person on request the name of each member of the partnership which is to deliver, or has delivered, to the registrar a copy of the latest accounts of the partnership, plus the names of all members incorporated in other European Union States which are to publish, or have published, those accounts (reg. 5(2)).

10 Distributions and the Maintenance of Capital

10.1 CONTROLS ON PAYMENTS OUT OF CAPITAL

The statutory liability of a member of a limited company is, under the Insolvency Act 1986, s. 74, to contribute to its assets when it is wound up. The nominal value of the shares held by a member is the limit on this liability, and it is expected that all, or perhaps some, of the contribution will be made before winding up to form the company's capital while it is a going concern (s. 74(2)(d)). If a member could contribute capital in respect of shares before winding up and have it returned before winding up, on the basis that, having made a contribution once, there is no requirement to make it again in winding up, then this would evade the statutory liability. In *Guinness* v *Land Corporation of Ireland* (1882) 22 ChD 349, Cotton LJ said, at pp. 375–6 :

> That section [i.e., what is now the Insolvency Act 1986, s. 74] provides that in the case of a company limited by shares being wound up, no contribution shall be required from any member exceeding the amount if any unpaid on the shares in respect of which he is liable as a present or past member; that the capital of the company as mentioned in the memorandum is to be the fund which is to pay the creditors in the event of the company being wound up. From that it follows that whatever has been paid by a member cannot be returned to him. . . . [What is described in the memorandum as the capital] is, of course, liable to be spent or lost in carrying on the business of the company, but no part of it can be returned to a member so as to take away from the fund to which the creditors have a right to look as that out of which they are to be paid. . . . no part of the capital mentioned in the memorandum can be taken out of the fund to which the creditors have to look except for the purpose of employing it for the objects of the company.

Accordingly there are controls on operations which have the effect of returning to a member the capital which that member has contributed. The controls are somewhat complicated because the whole purpose of putting capital into a company is that the company will use the capital to make profits to be distributed among the members. The great problem is to distinguish between a legal distribution of profits and an illegal return of capital, and the problem is made worse by the wide variety of ways in which assets may be moved from a company to its members. Apart from a simple declaration of a dividend there are several ways in which members can rearrange the company's contributed capital, and these will be examined in this chapter. Whether or not a transaction is permissible under the rules to be discussed in this chapter is determined almost entirely by objective analysis of accounts.

The law was summarised by Lord Russell of Killowen giving the opinion of the Privy Council in *Hill* v *Permanent Trustee Co. of New South Wales Ltd* [1930] AC 720 at p. 731:

A limited company not in liquidation can make no payment by way of return of capital to its shareholders except as a step in an authorised reduction of capital [see 10.2]. Any other payment made by it by means of which it parts with moneys to its shareholders must and can only be made by way of dividing profits. Whether the payment is called 'dividend' or 'bonus', or any other name, it still must remain a payment on division of profits.

At the time Lord Russell was speaking, the courts had arrived, after initial uncertainty, at an absolute prohibition on a company purchasing its own shares (*Trevor* v *Whitworth* (1887) 12 App Cas 409). This prohibition has been relaxed by statute, and redemption (see 10.3) and repurchase (see 10.6) of shares are now additional ways in which a company may legally return capital to its members.

The law would be much simpler and easier to understand if every company was intended to run a business for a definite number of years and was not permitted to make payments to its members until the end of the period, when it would sell the business and be wound up. On winding up, a company's resources must be devoted first to paying its debts. Only the money left after paying debts (including long-term loans) is profit for distribution to the members. In practice the members of a company do not wish to wait until its liquidation before receiving a share of its profits: they wish to have a regular dividend income from the company. Although the payment of annual profit dividends to members is recognised as an essential feature of the financing of companies, the difficulty is to find a way of paying profit dividends before liquidation without jeopardising the order of priority of payment in liquidation. The answer adopted by CA 1985 depends on the concept of 'distributable profits' (see 10.5).

In a small private company, the members may all be directors or employees of the company. They can remove the company's assets by paying themselves large salaries and directors' fees. A holding company can require its subsidiary to pay large fees for 'group services'. Whether such practices are permissible or not cannot normally be determined objectively but depends on a subjective assessment of the intentions of those involved. If the members of a company genuinely resolve to pay remuneration to a director for service as a director then the court will not enquire whether the remuneration is reasonable, though if it finds that the so-called remuneration is in fact a repayment of capital it will order the money to be returned to the company (*Re Halt Garage (1964) Ltd* [1982] 3 All ER 1016). There is no rule that directors' fees can be paid only out of profits (*Re Lundy Granite Co. Ltd, Harvey Lewis's Case* (1872) 26 LT 673).

In the CA 1985 there are accounting rules for determining the 'distributable profits' of a company. Dividends may be legally paid out of distributable profits but any other payment to members is considered a return of capital and is illegal unless it is an authorised return of capital or a permitted redemption or repurchase of shares.

There is a more general rule that it is illegal for a company to make a gift to anyone of any of its assets otherwise than out of distributable profits or in furtherance of its objects. The rule is exemplified by *Re George Newman & Co.* [1895] 1 Ch 674, in which a man who had been a director and chairman of the company had used £3,500 of its money for improvements to his own house. The Court of Appeal said, at p. 686:

The shareholders . . . can, if they think proper, remunerate directors for their trouble or make presents to them for their services out of assets properly divisible amongst the shareholders themselves. . . . But to make presents out of profits is one thing and to make them out of capital or out of money borrowed by the company is a very different matter. Such money cannot be lawfully divided amongst the shareholders themselves, nor can it be given away by them for nothing to their directors so as to bind the company in its corporate capacity.

10.2 REDUCTION OF CAPITAL

10.2.1 Power to reduce

The term 'reduction of capital' is used in CA 1985, ss. 135 to 141, to describe a reduction of a company's issued and/or authorised share capital otherwise (by virtue of s. 121(5)) than by cancelling unissued shares under s. 121(1)(e) (for which see 6.1.13). A reduction of capital is generally illegal unless authorised by statute (*Trevor* v *Whitworth* (1887) 12 App Cas 409, HL). A reduction of a company's authorised capital involves an alteration of its memorandum but by CA 1985, s. 2(7), no alteration of the memorandum of a company may be made except in the mode and to the extent for which express provision is made by CA 1985. Section 135 permits a company to carry out a reduction of capital but only if its articles authorise it to do so (provision is made in Table A by art. 34), and only if the reduction is confirmed by the court (s. 135(1)).

This procedure for reducing capital applies to the amounts recorded in share capital accounts, a share premium account (s. 130(3); see 6.4.4) and a capital redemption reserve (s. 170(4); see 10.3.1). There are limited ways in which share premium account and capital redemption reserve may be reduced apart from going through the s. 135 procedure (see 6.4.4 and 10.4) and a company's issued share capital may be reduced by the redemption or repurchase of its own shares (see 10.3.1, 10.3.5 and 10.6.5).

Section 135(1) says that capital may be reduced under the section 'in any way'. Section 135(2) suggests that sums may be written off accounts or nominal values so that some contributed capital may be returned to members, or so as to reduce members' liability to pay uncalled capital, or so as to reflect a diminution in the value of the company's assets. But a company may have other reasons for making a change of this kind. For example, a share premium account may be reduced to create a reserve which can be set off against purchased goodwill under SSAP 22 as and when it arises (*Re Ratners Group plc* [1988] BCLC 685; *Re Thorn EMI plc* [1989] BCLC 612). However, the court will not approve a reduction that has no discernible purpose (per Harman J in *Re Ratners Group plc* and in *Re Thorn EMI plc* at p. 616).

A cancellation of shares is a form of reduction of the nominal value of the shares (*Re Northern Engineering Industries plc* [1994] 2 BCLC 709).

It is for the members to decide how to carry out a reduction of capital. In *Ex parte Westburn Sugar Refineries Ltd* [1951] AC 625, Lord Normand said, at p. 629: 'The general rule is that the prescribed majority of the shareholders are entitled to decide whether there should be a reduction of capital and if so in what manner and to what extent it should be carried into effect'. Any method of reducing capital is legal if carried out in accordance with the provisions of ss. 135 to 141, and the court has jurisdiction to confirm any kind of reduction. As Lord Herschell LC said in *British & American Trustee & Finance Corporation Ltd and reduced* v *Couper* [1894] AC 399 at p. 405: '. . . the statute has not prescribed the manner in which the reduction is to be carried out, nor has it prohibited any method of effecting that object'. For example, in *British & American Trustee & Finance Corporation Ltd and reduced* v *Couper,* it was held that a reduction could be carried out by purchasing the company's own shares, a procedure which was otherwise illegal at common law (*Trevor v Whitworth* (1887) 12 App Cas 409). In the statutory provision forbidding a company to purchase its own shares now made by CA 1985, s. 143, there is an express exemption for the acquisition of shares in a reduction of capital duly made (s. 143(3)(b)). It is possible to arrange for a 'deferred' reduction by converting shares into redeemable shares, which will be redeemed at some time in the future in a way that will reduce capital (*Forth Wines Ltd* [1991] BCC 638).

It is not necessary that all the issued shares of a class should be treated in exactly the same way. For example, a reduction may involve the company purchasing the shares of specific shareholders (*British & American Trustee & Finance Corporation Ltd and reduced* v *Couper*). However, if a reduction of capital involves treating different members of a class of equity shareholders differently then, unless all members of the class have consented to the reduction, there should be a court-sanctioned arrangement under the procedure of CA 1985, ss. 425 to 427, because that procedure offers better protection to minorities than the procedure in ss. 135 to 141 does (*Re Robert Stephen Holdings Ltd* [1968] 1 WLR 522).

If surplus capital is to be returned to members, it is not necessary that it be returned in cash, and the value of what is returned may exceed the amount by which the nominal values of the shares are reduced (*Ex parte Westburn Sugar Refineries Ltd,* in which members of Westburn Sugar Refineries Ltd whose shares in that company were being reduced from £1 to 90p each in nominal value received 10p shares in another company to which assets of Westburn Sugar Refineries Ltd had been transferred).

If a company has, by a provision in its articles, adopted the s. 135 power to reduce its capital then no provision of its articles or memorandum or of any contract made by the company can restrict its exercise of that power (*Russell* v *Northern Bank Development Corporation Ltd* [1992] 1 WLR 588, see 2.4.8.3). Existing members of a company may make an enforceable contract between themselves that they will not adopt a resolution to exercise the power unless certain conditions are satisfied (for example, that they have all given their written consent) but such a contract will not bind future members unless they expressly agree to it, and the company cannot be a party to the contract (ibid.). A company whose articles authorise it to exercise the s. 135 power can renounce that statutory power by altering its articles (under s. 9) to delete the authorisation.

In *Re Transatlantic Life Assurance Co. Ltd* [1980] 1 WLR 79, the company had issued shares in contravention of the law on exchange control then in force, so that the issue had been illegal and therefore void. It was held that the company's accounts could be corrected by removing references to the illegally issued shares, and the capital subscribed for those shares could be returned to the member concerned, without going through the s. 135 procedure for reduction of capital: as the share issue was void it had no legal effect so there was nothing to be reduced.

10.2.2 Role of the court

A reduction of capital can be made by a company only if it is confirmed by the court. In deciding whether or not to confirm a resolution for the reduction of capital the primary concern of the court is to be assured that the interests of existing creditors are protected (see 10.2.3) and that the procedure by which the reduction is carried out is formally correct (per Lord Simonds in *Scottish Insurance Corporation Ltd* v *Wilsons & Clyde Coal Co. Ltd* [1949] AC 462 at p. 486). The court must be satisfied that in obtaining the special resolution of members for reducing capital, the cause of the reduction was properly put to the members so that they could exercise an informed choice, and that the cause is proved by the evidence before the court (per Harman J in *Re Jupiter House Investments (Cambridge) Ltd* [1985] 1 WLR 975 at p. 978). Information should be given to the members in a circular accompanying the notice of the meeting at which the special resolution is to be proposed (per Harman J in *Re Thorn EMI plc* [1989] BCLC 612 at p. 616). In *Re European Home Products plc* [1988] BCLC 690, the court confirmed a reduction despite a significant error in the circular sent to members (a sum of US$38 million had been mistakenly treated as £38 million) because members had been informed of the error and invited to appear at the hearing to object but had not done so. The court will also consider the public interest (per Lord Reid in *Ex parte Westburn Sugar Refineries Ltd* [1951] AC 625 at p. 632), which will include the interests of members of the public who may be induced to take shares in the company (per Lord Macnaghten in *Poole* v *National Bank of China Ltd* [1907] AC 229 at p. 239; per Lord Normand in *Ex parte Westburn Sugar Refineries Ltd* at p. 629 and Lord Reid at p. 632) and future creditors of the company (per Lord Reid in *Ex parte Westburn Sugar Refineries Ltd* at p. 632). Normally, future investors and creditors are adequately protected by the statutory requirements for publicising the reduction and the requirement that accounts must show a true and fair view of the company's position (*Re Grosvenor Press plc* [1985] 1 WLR 980).

As far as the existing members of a company proposing a reduction of capital are concerned, the court will refuse its sanction if the scheme is unfair (*Poole* v *National Bank of China Ltd* per Lord Loreburn LC at p. 236). The court must consider whether the scheme is 'fair and equitable', either as between different classes of shareholders (ibid., per Lord Macnaghten at p. 239; *Scottish Insurance Corporation Ltd* v *Wilsons & Clyde Coal Co. Ltd* per Lord Simonds at p. 486) or as between different shareholders of the same class (*British & American Trustee & Finance Corporation Ltd and reduced* v *Couper* [1894] AC 399 per Lord Herschell LC at p. 406). In *Re Jupiter House Investments (Cambridge) Ltd* [1985] 1 WLR 975, Harman J said, at p. 978, that the court had to be satisfied that a proposed reduction affects all shareholders of equal standing in a similar manner, or that those treated in a different manner from their equals have consented to that different treatment. The onus is on those opposing the reduction to show that it is unfair: the company is not bound to satisfy the court that its proposals are not unfair (per Lord Normand in *Scottish Insurance Corporation Ltd* v *Wilsons & Clyde Coal Co. Ltd* at p. 498; per Evershed MR in *Re Old Silkstone Collieries Ltd* [1954] Ch 169).

In *Re Old Silkstone Collieries Ltd,* the company's business had been nationalised and the board had adopted a policy of returning capital to shareholders as and when it became available under the lengthy process of negotiating compensation. It was intended that when the compensation was finally obtained the company would be put into liquidation. Two reductions of capital had already been approved in pursuance of this policy. Each time the preference stockholders (who were not entitled to a share of surplus assets on liquidation) had been promised that they would not be bought out entirely but would be kept on as members of the company so that they would be entitled to claim compensation under a special scheme which was thought to be available to preference stockholders. The company proposed a third reduction which would return all remaining capital to the preference stockholders so that they would no longer be members of the company and could no longer claim compensation. (It was widely believed that in practice such compensation would not be forthcoming.) The Court of Appeal held that this reduction should not be approved.

10.2.3 Interests of creditors

There is a statutory procedure by which the interests of creditors are considered (CA 1985, ss. 136(2) to (6) and 137(1)). It comes into operation if the reduction involves either diminution of members' liability to pay uncalled capital, or repayment of capital to members (s. 136(2)). The court has discretion to dispense with it (s. 136(6)) but will do so only in special circumstances: the fact that the company is amply solvent is not a special circumstance (*Practice Note* [1930] WN 78). The court is empowered by s. 136(2), to direct that the creditors' procedure be followed in any other type of capital reduction, but if the company is not parting with a means of paying its creditors then creditors must show a very strong reason why they should be heard in objection to the company's petition (*Re Meux's Brewery Co. Ltd* [1919] 1 Ch 28).

The procedure in relation to creditors is that a list of the company's creditors as at a date fixed by the court is drawn up. The court may advertise for claims to be made, but generally the information will come from the company and so s. 141, makes it an offence triable either way for an officer of the company wilfully to conceal the company's creditors, or misrepresent the nature of their claims (penalty in CA 1985, sch. 24). The creditors to be included on the list are those who would be able to prove against the company for their debts if the company commenced winding up on the day fixed by the court (s. 136).

The court may make an order confirming the reduction only when it is satisfied that every creditor on the list has either been paid in full or has positively consented to the reduction (s. 137(1)). Alternatively the court may dispense with the consent of a creditor if satisfied that the company has made a provision for paying him, or has made what the court considers an adequate provision where the company disputes the claim (s. 136(5)). Any creditor on the list is entitled to be heard by the court in opposition to the proposed reduction.

In Australia it has been said that if subsidiaries of a company seeking to reduce its capital are creditors of the company and it has obtained their consent to the reduction by its control of them then the court should investigate whether the proposed reduction is likely to have a substantial effect on creditors of those subsidiaries (*Re Tolltreck Systems Ltd (No. 2)* (1991) 4 ACSR 804).

10.2.4 Treatment of different classes

When a company issues preference shares it is usual to provide that if the company is wound up, any surplus after paying debts is to be devoted first to repaying the capital contributed for the preference shares. Where this is so then, on a reduction of capital to reflect a loss of capital, the preference shares should be the last to be reduced (*Re Floating Dock Co. of St Thomas Ltd* [1895] 1 Ch 691). But on a return of surplus capital, the capital contributed for the preference shares should be returned first (*Scottish Insurance Corporation Ltd* v *Wilsons & Clyde Coal Co. Ltd* [1949] AC 462, HL; *Prudential Assurance Co. Ltd* v *Chatterley-Whitfield Collieries Ltd* [1949] AC 512, HL).

If a company has a share capital divided into shares of different classes and it is desired to vary the rights attached to a particular class, in connection with a reduction of the company's share capital under CA 1985, s. 135, using a provision for the variation of class rights contained in the company's memorandum or articles then s. 125(3) requires that the variation must be approved by a three-quarters majority of that class. Class approval may be given either at a class meeting by extraordinary resolution (three-quarters majority of those voting, see 14.4.8.3) or in writing by the holders of three-quarters in nominal value of the issued shares of the class. The requirement for a three-quarters majority is in addition to any other procedure specified in the memorandum or articles for variation of class rights. 'Variation' of rights in this context includes abrogation of rights (s. 125(8)).

There are special rules for the conduct of a class meeting to sanction a variation in class rights — see 14.6.2.4. If a majority agree to a variation then a dissentient minority may apply to the court to cancel it — see 14.6.2.5.

If, as is usual, the preference shareholders in a company are not entitled, when the company is wound up, to any share in a surplus beyond the return of their capital for which they have priority, then a reduction of capital which involves returning capital to, and cancelling the shares of, the preference shareholders will be in accordance with their rights and not in abrogation of them, so it is unnecessary to follow the procedures for the variation of rights contained in the company's constitution and s. 125(3) (*Re Saltdean Estate Co. Ltd* [1968] 1 WLR 1844; *House of Fraser plc* v *ACGE Investments Ltd* [1987] AC 387). This means that, provided it has the resources, a company can buy out its preference shareholders when it finds that it can obtain fresh capital more cheaply elsewhere, which means that the preference shareholders will have their investment terminated just when it starts to show better returns than would be available on new investments. In *Re Northern Engineering Industries plc* [1994] 2 BCLC 709, the preference shareholders in a company had sought to protect themselves by having a provision inserted in the company's articles that a reduction of capital paid up on their shares was deemed to be a variation of their rights which had to be approved by them in a separate class meeting. It was held that this was effective to prevent them being bought out without their permission because 'reduction' was held to include 'extinction'.

10.2.5 Procedure

A company may reduce its issued capital only if power to do so is provided by its articles (provision is made in Table A by art. 34); the power may only be exercised by special resolution of the members (or, in the case of a private company, by written resolution in accordance with CA 1985, ss. 381A to 381C, see 14.5.3); and a resolution has no effect until confirmed by the court (s. 135(1)). If the articles do not authorise the members to reduce capital then a special resolution to do so is not interpreted as impliedly altering the articles to provide the authorisation (*Re West India & Pacific Steamship Co.* (1868) LR 9 Ch App 11 n and other cases cited in 3.5.1). Authorisation in the memorandum is not effective. Except where it is done under ss. 381A to 381C, unanimous assent without meeting to a resolution for reduction of capital is not acceptable: as a matter of practice, the court requires the decision to be taken by special resolution at a meeting (*Re Barry Artist Ltd* [1985] 1 WLR 1305).

After the special resolution for a reduction has been passed, the company presents a petition to the court to confirm the reduction. If the court confirms the reduction it may do so on such terms and conditions as it thinks fit (CA 1985, s. 137). It may, for example, insist on the company adding 'and reduced' to its name or publishing an explanation of the reduction, but it is not now usual for this to be done. The court's order can correct an error in the resolution if it is insignificant, if no one will be prejudiced by the correction, and if it is clear how it should be corrected (*Re Willaire Systems plc* [1987] BCLC 67).

It is common for companies to carry out complicated rearrangements of capital of which a reduction of one capital account is only one step. It is convenient to adopt all the necessary resolutions together. However, if a scheme involving an increase of a capital account followed by its reduction is to be confirmed, the increase must have taken place by the time the court is asked to confirm the reduction (*Re Transfesa Terminals Ltd* (1987) 3 BCC 647; *Re TIP-Europe Ltd* (1987) 3 BCC 647).

When the court's confirmation of the reduction has been given, a copy of the court's order and a minute approved by the court showing the new particulars of the share capital must then be lodged with the registrar who will issue a certificate, which is conclusive evidence that all the requirements of the Act have been complied with, and the registered minute is then deemed to be substituted for the corresponding part of the memorandum of association (CA 1985, s. 138). The reduction of capital does not take effect until the minute is registered (s. 138(2); *Re Castiglione, Erskine & Co. Ltd* [1958] 1 WLR 688).

If a reduction of a public company's capital brings the nominal value of the company's allotted share capital below £50,000 then the company must be re-registered as a private company and the registrar must not register the reduction of capital unless the change of status takes place (CA 1985, ss. 139(1) and (2) and 118(1)) though the court is given a discretion to direct otherwise, for example, where the reduction is to be followed immediately by an increase of capital to the authorised minimum or more (as part of a scheme for changing the company's shares from one type to another) (*Re MB Group plc* [1989] BCLC 672; *Re Anglo-American Insurance Co. Ltd* [1991] BCLC 564). The change of status may be resolved by the company following the procedure of s. 53 (see 1.3.4.2) or it can be incorporated in the order of the court confirming the resolution for reducing share capital (CA 1985, s. 139(3)). If the court's order directs the change of status the registrar is authorised by CA 1985, s. 139(5), on receipt of the company's application for re-registration, to issue a new certificate of incorporation to the company which will be conclusive evidence that the requirements in respect of re-registration have been complied with and that the company is a private company. The court's order will specify the necessary changes in the company's memorandum and articles and these come into effect on the issue of the registrar's certificate.

If uncalled liability is reduced by reason of the court proceedings any creditor erroneously omitted from the list of creditors who is unable to get his money from the company may insist on members at the time of the reduction continuing to be liable to the extent of the capital formerly unpaid (CA 1985, s. 140).

In the consultation document introducing its review of company law (see 0.3.1.6) the DTI says: 'There is . . . a case for reform of the complicated and costly court procedures that companies must go through if they are to reduce their share capital' (*Modern Company Law for a Competitive Economy* (London: DTI, 1998), p. 7).

10.2.6 Alerting members to a serious loss of capital

CA 1985, s. 142, provides that if the net assets of a *public* company fall to half or less of its called-up share capital, the directors must, within 28 days of a director first becoming aware of this fact, convene an extraordinary general meeting. The meeting must take place not later than 56 days from the day on which a director became aware of the serious loss. The purpose of the meeting is to consider what measures should be taken to deal with that situation. Any director who knowingly and wilfully fails to comply with these requirements commits an offence triable either way (CA 1985, s. 142(2) and sch. 24).

10.3 REDEEMABLE SHARES

10.3.1 Description

The general rule stated in CA 1985, s. 143(1), is that a company must not acquire its own shares. However, s. 159(1) permits a company to issue redeemable shares provided it is authorised to do so by its articles. Table A, art. 3, provides such authorisation.

Redeemable shares in a company offer temporary membership of the company with repayment of the nominal value of the shares (and in some cases a redemption premium) at the end of the period of membership. The membership comes to an end either after a fixed period or at the company's option, depending on the terms of redemption of the shares. When the temporary membership ends the shares are said to be redeemed and they must be cancelled: this cancellation reduces the company's issued share capital but not its authorised share capital (s. 160(4)). However, when it repays the share capital on redemption it must normally replenish its capital fund either by making a fresh issue of shares or by transferring a sum from profit and loss account to a new capital account called capital redemption reserve (ss. 160(1) and 170(1) and (2)).

The amount recorded in a capital redemption reserve may be reduced by transfer to a share capital account to pay up fully paid bonus shares (see 10.4) but otherwise the amount cannot be reduced without court approval (see 10.2) until winding up (CA 1985, s. 170(4)).

An amount transferred from profit and loss account to capital redemption reserve must represent distributable profits of the company (see 10.5) (s. 160(1)(a)). However, s. 171(1) permits a *private company* to make a payment in respect of the redemption of its own shares otherwise than out of its distributable profits or the proceeds of a fresh issue of shares, provided it is authorised by its articles to do so (authorisation is given by Table A, art. 35). Such a payment is called a 'payment out of capital'.

10.3.2   Restrictions on issue

Redeemable shares may not be issued by a company at a time when none of its members holds any non-redeemable shares (e.g., because the company has repurchased all the non-redeemable shares) (CA 1985, s. 159(2)).

Redemption of a company's shares may be effected on such terms and in such manner as may be provided by the company's articles (s. 160(3)). Table A merely states that the terms and conditions of redemption of any redeemable shares are to be specified in the articles (that is, by amendment) (art. 3). Section 133 of CA 1989 provides a more detailed specification of what articles must state about redemption, but there are no plans to bring s. 133 into force.

10.3.3   Redemption premium

Redemption premium payable by a public company must be paid out of its distributable profits unless the premium effectively represents a repayment of capital because it was a share premium contributed when the shares were issued. In that case the amount may be deducted from the share premium account (provided, of course, that there is an adequate balance on the account — i.e., that it has not been used for other purposes, see 6.4.4) (CA 1985, s. 160(1)(b) and (2)). It is clear from the debates in committee, when what is now s. 160(2) was introduced as an amendment to the Bill that became CA 1981, that it was assumed that the amount written off share premium account under the subsection would have to be replaced by new contributed capital or share premium from a new issue of shares. However, this could only have been achieved by also amending what is now s. 170(2), and that was not done. Accordingly there are circumstances in which share premium account will be reduced on redemption of shares. See Jamieson, *Accountancy,* July 1983, p. 103; the reply by Anderson and Keenan, *Accountancy,* October 1983, p. 75 is unconvincing. The result is not much different from the position under CA 1948, see 10.3.4.

If a private company decides to pay for redemption otherwise than from the proceeds of a fresh issue of shares or from distributable profits then redemption premium may have to be written off any available capital account or the revaluation reserve (CA 1985, s. 171(5)).

10.3.4 Redeemable shares issued before 15 June 1982

The provisions relating to redeemable shares were brought into force on 15 June 1982. Under CA 1948, s. 58 (repealed by CA 1981, sch. 4), a company could issue redeemable preference shares (but not redeemable ordinary shares) and a share premium account, whatever the origin of the premium, could be written off to account for payment of a redemption premium (CA 1948, ss. 56(2) and 58(1)(c)). On and after 15 June 1982, a share premium account may still be used to pay a redemption premium on redeemable preference shares issued before 15 June 1982 (CA 1985, s. 180).

There was no provision in CA 1948 for a private company to redeem shares out of capital but on or after 15 June 1982 a payment out of capital may be used to redeem shares issued before that day (CA 1985, s. 180(1)).

10.3.5 Approval of a payment out of capital

When a redeemable share is redeemed it must be cancelled (CA 1985, s. 160(4)) and this means that its nominal value must be deducted from the balance on share capital account. (It must be the whole nominal value because only a fully paid share may be redeemed: s. 159(3).) The general policy is that the amount thus written off share capital account must be made up by a counterbalancing increase either in share capital and premium from the issue of new shares or in capital redemption reserve by a transfer from profit and loss. However, if a *private company* is authorised by its articles, under s. 171(1), to make a payment in respect of the redemption of its own shares otherwise than out of its distributable profits or the proceeds of a fresh issue of shares (authorisation is given by Table A, art. 35), then its members may adopt a special resolution to enable its shares to be redeemed with less than the full counterbalancing increase in capital accounts. This is called a resolution to make a 'payment out of capital' (s. 173(1) and (2)). It will mean that some or all of the cancelled capital written off will not be replaced and so the company will reduce its capital. The extent to which the counterbalancing is not done (i.e., the extent of the capital reduction) is limited to the 'permissible capital payment' (s. 171(3)) and this is computed in such a way that the company is forced to use all its distributable profits and all proceeds of a new issue of shares in making counterbalancing transfers to capital accounts (s. 171(3), (4) and (6)).

A special resolution to redeem shares with a payment out of capital must be adopted between five and seven weeks before the payment is to be made (s. 174(1)). When counting votes in favour of the resolution, votes attaching to the shares to be redeemed must be ignored (s. 174(2)) whether given in person or by proxy (s. 174(5)). However, if the resolution is to be adopted as a written resolution under s. 381A (see 14.5.3) then a member holding shares to which the resolution relates is regarded as not entitled to vote on it so that the resolution is effective without being signed by or on behalf of that member (sch. 15A, para. 6).

If a resolution for a payment out of capital is put to a general meeting then, notwithstanding anything in the company's articles, any member of the company may, in person or by proxy, demand a poll (s. 174(3) and (5)). Not more than a week before a resolution to make a payment out of capital is adopted by a company its directors must make a statutory declaration of the size of the permissible capital payment (ss. 173(3) and 174(1)). The directors must determine the size of the permissible capital payment by deducting from the amount of the redemption payment proposed:

(a)   the proceeds of any new issue of shares made for the purpose of raising money for the redemption;

(b)   the amount of the company's distributable profits as shown by accounts made up to a date not more than three months before the date of their declaration (s. 172(2), (3) and (6)) but allowing for appropriations from the profit and loss account made since the date of the accounts (s. 172(4) and (5)).

The directors' declaration must also state that in their opinion:

(a)   the company will be able to pay its other debts (including future and contingent debts) immediately after the redemption payment is made (i.e., the company's assets will be greater than its liabilities);

(b)   the company will continue in business as a going concern for the whole of the following year and during that year will be able to pay its debts as they fall due.

The declaration must give prescribed particulars of the company's business. The particulars are those set out in form 173, which is also the prescribed form for the purpose (Companies (Forms) Regulations 1985 (SI 1985 No. 854), reg. 4 and sch. 4, part II). Making such a declaration without having reasonable grounds for the opinion expressed in it is an offence triable either way; if tried on indictment the penalty is imprisonment for up to two years and/or a fine for which there is no limit (s. 173(6) and sch. 24).

If a company goes into liquidation insolvent within a year of making a payment out of capital then the member from whom the shares were purchased and the directors who made the statutory declaration of solvency are liable to repay the amount paid out of capital insofar as this is necessary to pay the company's debts — see IA 1986, s. 76.

The company's auditors must make a report to the directors (s. 173(5)) stating that, in their opinion:

(a)   the size of the permissible capital payment has been correctly determined;

(b)   the directors' view of the company's future solvency is not unreasonable.

If the resolution is to be adopted in general meeting then the directors' declaration and auditors' report must be available for inspection at the meeting (s. 174(4)). If the resolution is to be adopted as a written resolution under s. 381A (see 14.5.3) then the documents must be supplied to each member at or before the time at which the resolution is supplied to that member for signature (sch. 15A, para. 6).

If the resolution is adopted the company must deliver a copy of the directors' declaration and the auditors' report to the registrar (s. 175(5)). The special resolution must be filed with the registrar within 15 days of being adopted and must be included in any copy of the company's memorandum and articles issued while the resolution is in force (s. 380).

Within one week of adopting the special resolution the company must advertise its adoption in the *Gazette* (s. 175(1)) and must either insert a similar advertisement in a national newspaper or notify all of its creditors by letter (s. 175(2)). The registrar must receive his copy of the declaration and auditors' report on or before the day the first of these advertisements or notifications appears (s. 175(4) and (5)) and, from that day until five weeks after the special resolution was adopted, the declaration and report must be available at the company's registered office for inspection, free of charge, by any member or creditor of the company (s. 175(6)).

Within the period of five weeks following the adoption of the special resolution any creditor of the company, or any of its members who did not vote in favour of the resolution, may apply to the court for cancellation of the resolution (s. 176). The court may confirm or cancel the resolution, or alter its terms, or make any other kind of order that will equitably solve the dispute (s. 177).

10.3.6 Disclosure requirements

Whenever a company has members who hold redeemable shares it must, by CA 1985, sch. 4, para. 38(2), state in its balance sheet:

(a)   the earliest and latest dates on which the company has power to redeem those shares;
(b)   whether those shares must be redeemed in any event or are liable to be redeemed at the option of the company;
(c) whether any (and, if so, what) premium is payable on redemption.

Whenever a company redeems any of its shares it must within one month notify the registrar (s. 122) and the registrar must publish in the *Gazette* notice of receiving such notification (s. 711(1)(h)).

The directors' report of a company for a financial year must state the number and nominal value of its shares that it redeemed and cancelled during the financial year and the percentage of its paid-up share capital represented by them (sch. 7, paras 7(a) and 8(d) and (e)).

10.4   CAPITALISATIONS AND BONUS SHARES

Money that is reckoned in a company's accounts to be profit can be transferred to capital accounts and this is known as 'capitalisation'. Two ways of doing this are recognised in CA 1985, s. 280(2):

(a)   transferring the profits to capital redemption reserve (see 10.3.1);
(b)   transferring the profits to a share capital account and treating them as wholly or partly paying up unissued shares which are to be allotted to the company's members as 'bonus shares'.

An issue of bonus shares is known as a 'capitalisation issue' but bonus shares can also be paid up by a transfer from share premium account (s. 130(2)) or capital redemption reserve (s. 170(4)).

If profit that could be distributed to members is capitalised then it can no longer be distributed, and it is considered that such a use of profit should be specially authorised by the articles, as in art. 110 of Table A.

Table A, art. 110, specifies that the number of bonus shares to be allotted to a particular member is to be determined in the same way as entitlement to dividend.

Under art. 110 a decision to make a capitalisation issue is to be taken by the directors on the authority of an ordinary resolution of the members.

As bonus shares are paid up otherwise than in cash, a contract of allotment has to be filed with the registrar within one month of allotment (see 6.5.4). Table A, art. 110(d), authorises the directors to appoint any person to be the representative of the members for the purpose of making a contract of allotment with the company, and provides that a contract so made shall be binding on all members it affects. However, a valuation report does not have to be obtained by a public company (CA 1985, s. 103(2)). In *Re Cleveland Trust plc* [1991] BCLC

424, the company issued bonus shares paid up by capitalisation of the balance on its profit and loss account. It was not realised at the time of the issue that the accounts were wrong and that the balance on the profit and loss account was nowhere near enough to pay up the shares that were issued. It was held that the contract of allotment was void for mistake, and the court made an order rectifying the company's register of members by deleting all the holdings of the bonus shares.

Members may be issued with bonus shares of the same class as the shares they already hold or bonus shares of a different class (*White v Bristol Aeroplane Co. Ltd* [1953] Ch 65, CA).

10.5 DISTRIBUTIONS

10.5.1 Dividends

Commercial companies are formed to earn profits for their shareholders and no express power is needed in the memorandum to make distributions of profits. However, there is no rule that all profits must be distributed (*Burland v Earle* [1902] AC 83, PC) until, of course, the company is wound up.

Companies formed for charitable purposes usually have a provision in the articles or memorandum that no distributions are to be made to members. The memorandum or articles of an investment company must prohibit distribution of its capital profits (see 10.5.8).

A payment of the profits of a company to its members is called a 'dividend'. To a Latinist, 'dividend' means an amount to be divided but in its ordinary use now it means each person's portion of the amount to be divided (*Henry v Great Northern Railway Co.* (1857) 1 De G & J 606 per Lord Cranworth LC at pp. 636–7, Knight Bruce LJ at pp. 642–3).

Unless the articles provide otherwise, a dividend must be in cash (*Wood v Odessa Waterworks Co.* (1889) 42 ChD 636). Power to make a distribution in kind is given in Table A, art. 105.

CA 1985, s. 234(1), requires the directors of a company to state in the directors' report, which they must prepare for each financial year, their recommendations on dividend. A small company can avoid making its dividend recommendations public because it does not have to file its directors' report with the registrar of companies and is permitted by s. 246(4) inserted by SI 1997 No. 220, reg. 2(1), to omit the statement on recommended amount of dividend from its balance sheet. In recommending the amount of a dividend, the directors must have regard to the general interest of all classes of shareholders and not favour one class at the expense of another (*Henry v Great Northern Railway Co.* at p. 637). However, in Canada, a majority of the Supreme Court has held that a company with more than one class of ordinary shares may have in its articles a so-called 'discretionary dividend provision' giving the directors a discretion to choose which class or classes of shareholders are to receive any dividend declared (*McClurg v Canada* (1990) 76 DLR (4th) 217). In *McClurg's* case, the directors of the company held all the shares in two of the company's classes of shares and their wives held all the shares in the other class. Dividends were allocated to classes purely on the basis of which class of shareholders would pay the least tax. Clearly, in practice, the directors allocated the dividends with due regard to the interests of all classes of shareholders.

As from the time when a dividend is payable to a member, it is a debt owed by the company to the member and is subject to the Limitation Act 1980 (*Re Severn & Wye & Severn Bridge Railway Co.* [1896] 1 Ch 559). The limitation period is six years — see 3.4.2.9. No dividend is payable on a company's shares, even on preference shares, unless and until the company has decided to pay one (*Bond* v *Barrow Haematite Steel Co.* [1902] 1 Ch 353) — the decision is usually known as a 'declaration' of a dividend.

Table A, art. 102, provides that '. . . the company may by ordinary resolution declare dividends in accordance with the respective rights of the members, but no dividend shall exceed the amount recommended by the directors'. Although it is the members in general meeting who 'declare' a dividend, the actual payment can be made only on the authority of the directors, and they are responsible for seeing that the payment is properly made (*Re Exchange Banking Co, Flitcroft's Case* (1882) 21 ChD 519, CA).

10.5.2 Restrictions on dividends

The law has long sought to ensure that a dividend paid by a company to its members is not, in whole or in part, a return of the capital they have contributed, because this would enable the members to avoid their statutory liability to the company (see 10.1.1). This is seen as a protection for creditors of the company. In *Re Exchange Banking Co, Flitcroft's Case* (1882) 21 ChD 519 Jessel MR said, at pp. 533–4:

A limited company by its memorandum of association declares that its capital is to be applied for the purposes of the business. . . . The creditor has no debtor but that impalpable thing the corporation, which has no property except the assets of the business. The creditor, therefore, I may say, gives credit to that capital, gives credit to the company on the faith of the representation that the capital shall be applied only for the purpose of the business, and he has therefore a right to say that the corporation shall keep its capital and not return it to the shareholders, though it may be a right which he cannot enforce otherwise than by a winding-up order.

A creditor does not, however, have standing to restrain a wrongful distribution (*Mills* v *Northern Railway of Buenos Ayres Co.* (1870) LR 5 Ch App 621; see also *Lawrence* v *West Somerset Mineral Railway Co.* [1918] 2 Ch 250, which concerned a statutory company).

The great difficulty in controlling payments of dividends is that contributed capital is not kept by the company as a fund of cash: it is used to buy a continually changing set of assets whose value may go up or down but rarely stays the same. The assets of the company may be augmented by profits it makes or diminished by losses. Ascertaining whether any particular dividend payment represents a return of capital is not, therefore, straightforward. The courts attempted to lay down rules on a case-by-case basis but the result was not satisfactory, and CA 1980 introduced statutory rules, which are now set out in CA 1985, ss. 263 to 281.

The statutory rules restricting distributions apply to 'every description of distribution of a company's assets to its members, whether in cash or otherwise' (CA 1985, s. 263(2)) with the following exceptions:

(a) return of capital or distribution of surplus assets on winding up;
(b) return of capital to members in a properly authorised reduction of capital (including the cancellation or reduction of liability on partly paid shares);
(c) issue of fully or partly paid bonus shares;
(d) purchase or redemption of the company's own shares.

The most common form of distribution is a dividend paid to members on their shares (whether ordinary or preference). In *Aveling Barford Ltd* v *Perion Ltd* (1989) 5 BCC 677, a sale at an undervalue of an asset of Aveling Barford Ltd to another company controlled by the sole beneficial shareholder of Aveling Barford was held to be a distribution to him.

10.5.3 Profits available for distribution

The basic principle is that a company's profits available for distribution are (CA 1985, s. 263(3)):

its accumulated, realised profits, so far as not previously utilised by distribution or capitalisation, less its accumulated, realised losses, so far as not previously written off in a reduction or reorganisation of capital duly made.

10.5.4 Realised and unrealised profits

It is provided by CA 1985, s. 262(3), that whether or not a profit is a 'realised profit' is to be determined by the generally accepted accounting principles in use at the time the accounts showing the profit are prepared.

In the USA, the Financial Accounting Standards Board has said, in Statement of Financial Accounting Concepts 6, para. 143:

Realisation in the most precise sense means the process of converting non-cash resources and rights into money and is most precisely used in accounting and financial reporting to refer to sales of assets for cash or claims to cash. The related terms 'realised' and 'unrealised' therefore identify revenues or gains or losses on assets sold and unsold, respectively.

The realised profit of a company for a financial year, then, is the profit on its sales of assets — that is, the amount by which the income from its sales of assets exceeds associated expenses. If income from sales of assets for a financial year is less than expenses then there is a realised loss for that financial year. An unrealised profit occurs when there is no sale — for example, when an asset owned by the company is revalued upwards and the new value is recorded in the accounts. Similarly, in principle, when a provision is made for the depreciation of a fixed asset of the company this should be an unrealised loss, but CA 1985, s. 275(1), deems it to be a realised loss, thus imposing prudence on companies.

A related problem of accounting is when to recognise (that is, record in accounts) revenues and expenses (and hence profits or losses). The general rule is that expenses must be recognised when they are incurred (not when they are paid for). In respect of a cash sale, revenue is of course recognised at the time of the sale, which is the time when the cash is received. Most companies conduct their business on credit — that is, they allow their customers time to pay for goods and services supplied — but this does not affect the accounting recognition of the revenue from the sale: the revenue is recognised at the time of sale of goods or rendering of services, provided the amount to be charged is ascertained at that time, and provided it is not unreasonable to expect ultimate collection of the amount charged. These principles are stated in International Accounting Standard IAS 18, 'Revenue recognition', which also states how some special circumstances should be dealt with. See further C. Noke, 'Realised profits: unrealistic conclusions' [1989] JBL 37.

Some revenue recognised in accounts is not ultimately received in cash because some customers do not pay. At the end of each financial year a provision should be made for doubtful debts: this will be a percentage of the total outstanding trade debts reflecting the company's past experience of bad debts or the pattern of business in the industry in which the company operates. This provision is deemed to be a realised loss (CA 1985, s. 275(1)).

This way of treating revenues and expenses (usually described as 'accrual accounting') is fundamental to the preparation of financial statements. CA 1985, sch. 4, states accounting principles that must be followed in preparing accounts for a financial year of a company, unless the directors of the company believe that there are special reasons for departing from them. The fourth of these principles is: 'All income and charges relating to the financial year to which the accounts relate shall be taken into account, without regard to the date of receipt or payment' (para. 13).

If on a revaluation of an asset its value is increased, the increase is normally an unrealised profit. However, CA 1985, s. 275(2) and sch. 4, para. 32(3), permit a part of this profit to be treated as realised in each subsequent year of the asset's life: they permit the additional depreciation that has to be charged by virtue of the increase in valuation to be charged to revaluation reserve instead of profit and loss account, leaving the equivalent amount in profit and loss account as an untouched realised profit.

If the book value of a non-cash asset of a company includes an unrealised profit (because the asset has been revalued) then the asset itself may be distributed as a dividend in kind to members and, for that purpose only, the unrealised profit may be treated as a realised profit so as to make the distribution legal (CA 1985, s. 276).

10.5.5 Realised and unrealised losses

If a company decides that it has a future liability which cannot be precisely quantified then it can set aside for it a fund, which CA 1985, sch. 4, para. 89, calls a 'provision'. Clearly a provision does not represent a realised loss. Nevertheless, CA 1985, s. 275(1), requires a provision to be treated as a realised loss, thus preventing a company casting prudence aside by distributing a provision as a dividend.

The same rule applies to a provision in the form of an amount written off or retained by way of providing for depreciation, renewals or diminution in value of assets, *except* that if an amount has to be written off the value of an individual fixed asset because it is revalued downwards then this need not be treated as a realised loss if the decrease in the value of that asset is covered by an increase, overall, in the value of the company's other fixed assets (if necessary, ignoring goodwill) (CA 1985, s. 275(1)). It is not necessary to carry out a formal revaluation of all the company's fixed assets in order to treat an individual loss of value in this way, provided the directors satisfy themselves that this treatment is justified and are prepared to say so in a note to the accounts (CA 1985, s. 275(4), (5) and (6)).

Under certain conditions listed in SSAP 13, expenditure on the development of a specific product may be regarded as purchasing an asset the value of which will be systematically written down (amortised) over the period in which the developed product is sold. Instead of treating just the annual amortisation provisions as realised losses, CA 1985, s. 269, requires the whole of development expenditure to be treated as a realised loss. If development expenditure is treated as a fixed asset then SSAP 13 requires it to be separately disclosed and CA 1985, sch. 4, para. 20, requires a note to the accounts explaining why the expenditure is being treated that way and stating the period over which it is to be written off. CA 1985, s. 269(2), permits the directors to treat development expenditure as not being a realised loss if special circumstances justify such a decision and it is explained in a note to the accounts.

10.5.6 Accumulation

The rule that losses of previous years must be made good reverses the earlier view of the courts that it was legitimate to distribute profits of one year despite losses in previous years.

10.5.7 Public companies

A public company, like a private company, may not distribute more than its accumulated net realised profits but in addition, by CA 1985, s. 264, a distribution may not exceed the following limit:

net assets *minus* sum of called-up share capital plus undistributable reserves

The undistributable reserves of a company are various funds which are treated like contributed capital together with net unrealised profits, namely:

(a)   the share premium account;
(b)   the capital redemption reserve;
(c)   accumulated unrealised profits (so far as they have not been capitalised as bonus shares) less accumulated unrealised losses (so far as not written off in a reduction of capital);
(d)   any other reserve which the company is forbidden to distribute, under its memorandum or articles, or legislation, for example, a reserve for own shares (CA 1985, s. 148(4)).

If unrealised profits have in the past been transferred to capital redemption reserve or have been used to pay up amounts unpaid on previously issued shares (both these procedures are now forbidden) then the amounts have to be put back again into the calculation of undistributable reserves.

10.5.8 Investment companies

An investment company is a public company which has given notice to the registrar that it intends to operate as an investment company and has since complied with the requirements of CA 1985, s. 266(2). These are that:

(a)   the business of the company consists of investing its funds mainly in securities, with the aim of spreading risk and giving members of the company the benefit of the result of the management of its funds;
(b)   none of the company's holdings in companies (apart from other investment companies) represents more than 15 per cent by value of the company's total investments;
(c)   distribution of the company's capital profits is prohibited by its memorandum or articles of association;
(d)   the company does not retain more than 15 per cent of its income from securities.

These are virtually the same as the conditions under which a company will be recognised as an investment trust by the Board of Inland Revenue in order to be exempt from capital gains tax. An investment company must state on all its business letters and order forms that it is an investment company (CA 1985, s. 351(1)(c)).

Because a distribution of capital profits is forbidden, CA 1985, s. 265, expresses the limit for a distribution of an investment company, if it is listed on a recognised investment exchange in the UK, as:

assets *minus* $1\frac{1}{2}$ times liabilities

10.5.9 Accounts

To establish whether a distribution by a company is lawful it is necessary to check that it is within the amount permitted by statute as determined from the company's most recent annual accounts laid before the company in general meeting (CA 1985, s. 270(3)) (or, if the company has elected not to lay accounts before general meetings, sent to members in accordance with s. 238: see s. 252(3)). By s. 271, annual accounts cannot be relied upon for this purpose unless they have been properly prepared in accordance with CA 1985 (s. 271(2)). By s. 271(3), unless the company is exempt from the auditing requirements (s. 249E(1)(c)), the auditors must have reported on the accounts in accordance with s. 235. By s. 271(3) to (5), accounts cannot be relied upon if the auditors' opinion on whether they have been properly prepared in accordance with CA 1985 is qualified, unless the auditors have stated in writing whether the matter in respect of which the report is qualified is material for determining whether the distribution would contravene s. 263, s. 264 (in the case of a public company) or s. 265 (in the case of an investment company), and that statement has been laid before the company in general meeting (s. 271(3) and (4)) (or sent to members with the accounts if the company has elected not to lay accounts before general meetings: s. 252(3)). The members cannot waive this requirement (*Precision Dippings Ltd v Precision Dippings Marketing Ltd* [1986] Ch 447, CA).

If a distribution would not be justified according to the most recent annual accounts then the company may justify it on the basis of (more recent) *interim accounts* (s. 270(4)). In the case of a private company, the Act says nothing further about the way in which interim accounts used to justify a distribution should be prepared. In the case of a public company, interim accounts used to justify a distribution are required to be prepared as nearly as is practicable in the manner in which annual accounts are prepared under CA 1985, except that no auditors' report is required. Interim accounts used to justify a distribution of a public company must be filed with the registrar (s. 272(4)).

If a company wishes to make a distribution soon after it is incorporated, so that no annual accounts have yet been required, it can justify the distribution on the basis of *initial accounts* (s. 270(4)) to which the same conditions apply as for interim accounts (s. 273) except that an auditors' report is required in the case of a public company.

10.5.10 Consequences of an excessive distribution

If a company has made an illegal distribution then the directors who authorised the payment are liable to repay the money to the company (*Re National Funds Assurance Co.* (1878) 10 ChD 118; *Re Exchange Banking Co., Flitcroft's Case* (1882) 21 ChD 519). The fact that the illegal distribution was approved by the members does not cure its illegality, and the members' decision does not ratify the directors' act so as to absolve them from liability (*Re Exchange Banking Co., Flitcroft's Case*; *Aveling Barford Ltd* v *Perion Ltd* (1989) 5 BCC 677). However, a director who took reasonable care to secure that accounts were properly prepared and who exercised commercial judgment in assessing whether dividends were properly payable on the basis of those accounts will be relieved of liability. For example, in *Dovey* v *Cory* [1901] AC 477, John Cory, who was one of the directors of the National Bank of Wales Ltd, was held not to be liable for illegal dividend payments because he had justifiably relied on accounts which were prepared by the general manager and checked by the chairman (who was a brother of John Cory). In fact the general manager and chairman were defrauding the bank and were found guilty of criminal offences. They had concealed letters from the bank's auditors which questioned the accuracy of the accounts.

CA 1985, s. 277(1), makes a member liable to repay a distribution received if the member knew, or had reasonable grounds for knowing, that it was being paid in contravention of CA 1985, ss. 263 to 281. Section 277(2) states that the liability under s. 277(1) is without prejudice to any obligation imposed apart from s. 277 on a member of a company to repay a distribution unlawfully made to him. The position apart from s. 277 is that if a person has received money of a company that has been paid illegally (usually described as an '*ultra vires*' payment) then the money will be subject to a constructive trust for the benefit of the company if the person knew or ought to have known of the circumstances which made paying it improper (*Precision Dippings Ltd* v *Precision Dippings Marketing Ltd* [1986] Ch 447, CA; *Hilton International Ltd* v *Hilton* [1989] 1 NZLR 442; *Aveling Barford Ltd* v *Perion Ltd*). In *Moxham* v *Grant* [1900] 1 QB 88, CA, the directors of a company were ordered to compensate the company for the whole of an illegal dividend paid while they were directors. It was held that they could recover from each member who knew or ought to have known of the circumstances which made the dividend illegal the amount of dividend paid to that shareholder.

If an illegal dividend has been paid by a company in reliance on erroneous accounts which the company's auditors negligently failed to report were erroneous then the auditors are liable to the company for their negligence and must pay the company the amount of the illegal dividend (*Leeds Estate Building & Investment Co.* v *Shepherd* (1887) 36 ChD 787; *Re London & General Bank (No. 2)* [1895] 2 Ch 673; *Re Thomas Gerrard & Son Ltd* [1968] Ch 455; *Segenhoe Ltd* v *Akins* (1990) 29 NSWLR 569).

10.6 PURCHASE OF OWN SHARES

10.6.1 Authority to repurchase shares

The general rule stated in CA 1985, s. 143(1), is that a company must not acquire its own shares. However, s. 162(1) permits a company to purchase its own shares (including redeemable shares) in the circumstances prescribed in the Act, provided the company is authorised to do so by its articles. Table A, art. 35, provides such authorisation. Members are required to approve the terms of purchases (CA 1985, ss. 164(1) and 166(1)), and any authority given to a public company by its members to make purchases must not be valid for more than 18 months without renewal (CA 1985, ss. 164(4) and 166(4)). There are two kinds of approval depending on whether purchases are to be made on the London Stock Exchange of the listed shares of a public company (or on any other UK recognised investment exchange — see 7.3.4 — where the shares have been admitted to dealings) or are to be private deals with known sellers. Purchases made in trading on a recognised investment exchange are called 'market purchases' and other purchases are called 'off-market purchases' (s. 163).

Shares may not be purchased unless they are fully paid (CA 1985, s. 159(3) applied by s. 162(2)), which means that a company cannot subscribe for its own shares but can only repurchase them from existing members. This also follows from the use in s. 162(1) of the word 'purchase', which does not include subscription (*Re VGM Holdings Ltd* [1942] Ch 235).

If a company has a class of members with redeemable shares then it may not repurchase all its other shares leaving redeemable shares as the company's only issued shares (CA 1985, s. 162(3)).

The London Stock Exchange has made detailed rules governing purchases by listed companies of their own shares. These are in ch. 15 of the Listing Rules.

10.6.2 Authority for market purchases

The members of a company that is authorised by its articles to purchase its own shares may, by ordinary resolution, give authority for purchases on the London Stock Exchange Listed

Market (if the shares are listed) or any other UK recognised investment exchange where the shares have been admitted to dealings, but the resolution must state the maximum number of shares that may be purchased and the maximum and minimum prices to be paid. The resolution must also state a date on which the authority is to expire and this must not be more than 18 months after the resolution is adopted (CA 1985, s. 166). The maximum and minimum prices may be expressed as a formula, e.g., linking them to the average market quotation over a period (CA 1985, s. 166(6)(b)). The authority may be varied, revoked or renewed at any time by ordinary resolution of the members.

A copy of any resolution giving, varying, revoking or renewing authority for a London Stock Exchange or other recognised investment exchange purchase must be filed with the registrar within 15 days of adoption (CA 1985, s. 166(7), applying s. 380) and, while in force, must be attached to every copy of its memorandum and articles issued by the company (CA 1985, s. 380(2)).

An authorisation of this kind would enable a listed company to intervene in the market as a buyer in order to smooth out a sudden fall in its share price. Note that purchased shares have to be cancelled and cannot be reissued unless the members have given an authority to allot (see 6.2.5) so intervention to smooth out a sudden rise in the company's share price is less easy.

10.6.3 Authority for off-market purchases

A company cannot make an off-market purchase of its own shares unless the terms of the purchase contract have been approved in advance by the members (CA 1985, s. 164(1)). Authority to make an off-market purchase must be conferred by a special resolution under s. 164(2). In the case of a public company this resolution must specify a date on which the authority is to expire, which must not be later than 18 months after the date of adopting the resolution.

When counting votes in favour of a resolution to authorise the terms of an off-market contract, votes attaching to the shares to be purchased must be ignored whether given in person or by proxy (s. 164(5)). This would mean that such a resolution could not be adopted by unanimous assent without meeting (*Re R.W. Peak (Kings Lynn) Ltd* [1998] 1 BCLC 193). However, if such a resolution is to be adopted as a written resolution of a private company under s. 381A (see 14.5.3) then a member holding shares to which the resolution relates is regarded as not entitled to vote on it so that the resolution is effective without being signed by or on behalf of that member (sch. 15A, para. 5). In *Re R.W. Peak (Kings Lynn) Ltd* the requirements of s. 164 were completely ignored when the shares of the majority shareholder in a company were purchased by the company. The company was not authorised by its articles to purchase its own shares. There was a written contract signed by the majority shareholder as vendor of the shares and signed on the company's behalf by the only other shareholder, but clearly this contract did not alter the articles to give the company authority to purchase the shares. The fact that the company's two members had signed the contract in the belief that this would bring it into effect did not mean that they had approved it in advance, as required by s. 164. As s. 164(5) prohibits the vendor of the shares from voting on whether to approve the contract, it was not possible to treat the two members' signature of the contract as an agreement to waive the formalities of s. 164.

If a resolution to authorise the terms of an off-market contract is put to a general meeting then, notwithstanding anything in the company's articles, any member of the company may, in person or by proxy, demand a poll (s. 164(5)).

If a resolution to authorise the terms of an off-market contract is to be put to a general meeting then a copy of the proposed contract (or a memorandum of its terms if it is not in writing) must be available for inspection at the company's registered office for not less than 15 days ending with the day of the meeting, and at the meeting itself (s. 164(6)). The names of members holding shares to which the contract relates must be given (s. 164(6)). If a resolution is to be adopted by a private company as a written resolution under s. 381A (see 14.5.3) then the documents must be supplied to each member at or before the time at which the resolution is supplied to that member for signature (sch. 15A, para 5).

A company's authority to make an off-market purchase may be varied, revoked or renewed by special resolution under s. 164(3) following procedures similar to those for conferring authority. In particular, authority may be conferred under s. 164(7) to vary a contract already authorised.

A contingent purchase contract (e.g., a call option), whether market or off-market, may be made only if specifically authorised by special resolution under the same procedure as applies to off-market purchases (CA 1985, s. 165).

10.6.4 Publicity for purchases

Every purchase of its shares by a company must be reported to the registrar within 28 days of completion (CA 1985, s. 169(1)). A public company has to state how much it paid for the shares but a private company has to state only the number of shares and their nominal value (s. 169(1) and (2)).

The directors' report for a financial year of a company must state the number and nominal value of its own shares that the company purchased during the financial year, the total paid for them, the reasons for their purchase, and the percentage of the called-up share capital represented by the purchased shares (sch. 7, paras 7(a) and 8(a) and (e)).

A copy of every contract (or memorandum of the terms of an unwritten contract) made by a company to purchase its own shares (either absolutely or contingently) must be kept at its registered office, and made available for inspection to anyone if the company is public or to members only if the company is private, until 10 years from the date on which the transfer under the contract was completed or the contract otherwise determined (s. 169(4) and (5)).

A listed company must notify to the Company Announcements Office of the London Stock Exchange, for release to the market and the public, details of any purchases it makes of its own shares and any purchases of those shares by other companies in the same group (Listing Rules, para. 15.9).

10.6.5 Effect on capital accounts

After a company has purchased its own shares it must cancel them (CA 1985, s. 160(4) applied by s. 162(2)). The reduction in share capital account caused by the cancellation must be compensated either by new contributed capital from a new issue of shares made for the purpose or by transferring distributable profits from profit and loss account to capital redemption reserve (s. 160(1) applied by s. 162(2), and s. 170(1) and (2)).

If the price at which a company purchases its shares is greater than their nominal value then the excess is treated in the same way as a redemption premium on the redemption of own shares (see 10.3.3) (s. 160(1)(b) and (2) applied by s. 162(2)).

A private company may make a payment out of capital to repurchase its own shares under the same conditions as it may redeem shares out of capital (see 10.3.1 and 10.3.5) (s. 171(1); Table A, art. 35).

The Department of Trade and Industry has suggested abolishing the rule that repurchased shares must be cancelled. This would enable companies to hold their own shares as what is known as 'treasury shares', which it could resell. This raises the spectre of companies manipulating the market in their own shares. See Department of Trade and Industry, *Share Buybacks* (URN 98/713) (London: DTI, 1998).

10.7 EMPLOYEES' SHARE SCHEMES

In recent years many companies have taken the view that their employees should also be shareholders and so be able to appreciate directly the financial circumstances of the enterprise for which they work. Accordingly companies have set up schemes under which some of their profits each year are devoted to assisting employees to purchase shares, either on the Stock Exchange or by subscription for new shares. Such schemes also provide an element of profit-sharing as part of employees' remuneration.

Other companies have provided employees (often only senior executives) with interest-free or low-interest loans to be used to acquire their companies' shares. Schemes of this kind are less attractive now that the forgone interest is treated as a taxable benefit (see Income and Corporation Taxes Act 1988, s. 160).

An employees' share scheme is defined in CA 1985, s. 743, as:

a scheme for encouraging or facilitating the holding of shares or debentures in a company by or for the benefit of:

(a) the bona fide employees or former employees of the company, the company's subsidiary or holding company or a subsidiary of the company's holding company, or

(b) the wives, husbands, widows, widowers or children or stepchildren under the age of 18 of such employees or former employees.

Because of taxation advantages the most commonly adopted schemes are of the following type involving shares listed on the London Stock Exchange. Each employee of the company who has a minimum period of employment is entitled to have shares of the company acquired on his or her behalf by trustees. The trustees may acquire shares either on the Exchange or by taking allotments of new shares. The total nominal value of shares acquired each year is related to the company's profits for the year, and the number acquired on behalf of a particular employee is related to his or her earnings for that year. The cost of the shares is taken from the company's profits, and may come only from distributable profits if the company is a public company (CA 1985, ss. 153(4)(b) and 154). An employee in the scheme is entitled to instruct the trustees either to transfer shares held on his behalf to him or to sell them and transfer the sale proceeds to him.

A scheme of this type may be submitted to the Inland Revenue for approval. If approved then the value of shares acquired for a particular employee's benefit will not be counted as his or her taxable income, provided the trustees hold the shares for seven years or more. If the trustees hold the shares for between four and seven years, income tax is payable on only part of the value of the shares.

The London Stock Exchange requires that an employees' share scheme to be introduced for the employees of a listed company or any of its subsidiaries must be approved by ordinary resolution of the company's members (Listing Rules, para. 13.13). Various associations of investment institutions have indicated that they will approve a scheme only if:

(a) the issued equity share capital cannot grow by more than one per cent a year by allotments to the scheme;

(b)   not more than five per cent of profits is appropriated to the scheme;

(c)   the capital contribution for a share allotted under the scheme is the middle market price of such a share on a specific day before the allotment, and the capital contribution must be paid on allotment;

(d)   dividends are to be passed by the trustees to the employees for whom the shares are held and the trustees are required to seek those employees' instructions before exercising any voting rights attached to the shares.

10.8   FINANCIAL ASSISTANCE FOR PURCHASE OF OWN SHARES

10.8.1   Permissible forms of assistance

This chapter has dealt with several methods by which a company's own resources may be used to assist persons to acquire the company's shares:

(a)   by financing an employees' share scheme;

(b)   by redeeming or repurchasing own shares under a scheme properly approved by the members — this assists the company itself to acquire the shares but they must be cancelled on acquisition;

(c)   by paying up an issue of bonus shares.

The Companies Act insists that when a company uses its own resources in this way the capital and reserves section of the balance sheet must be adjusted. An issue of bonus shares in fact does not involve a use of company assets, only an adjustment of the capital and reserves accounts. A *public company* can only use its own assets for the acquisition of its own shares to the extent that the value of the assets used can be transferred from profit and loss account to a capital account or is covered by the proceeds of a new issue of shares made for the purpose.

Provided there is a special resolution by the members and a declaration of solvency by the directors, a *private company* can redeem or repurchase its own shares with a payment that exceeds distributable profits and so has to be written off its capital accounts or its revaluation reserve.

The court has power to order a company to repurchase the shares of dissentient members who have petitioned for the cancellation of a resolution to alter the company's memorandum (CA 1985, ss. 5(5) and 17(3)), or a resolution of a public company to re-register as a private company (s. 54(6)), or a resolution to make a payment out of capital to redeem or repurchase shares (s. 177(3)), or who have petitioned for relief from unfairly prejudicial conduct of the company's affairs (s. 461(2)(d)) (see also s. 157(3), discussed in 10.8.7).

The directors' report of a company for a financial year must state the number and nominal value of its shares that it purchased and cancelled during the year in pursuance of a court order, the reason for the purchase and the percentage of its paid-up share capital represented by them (sch. 7, paras 7(a) and 8(d) and (e)).

10.8.2   Prohibition on other acquisitions by a company of its own shares

Except in the circumstances stated in 10.8.1 a limited company may not acquire its own shares for valuable consideration (s. 143) though it may acquire its partly paid shares by forfeiture (or surrender in lieu) or its fully paid shares by gift (CA 1985, s. 143(3)). CA 1985, s. 143, puts in statutory form a rule which had been established in the courts by the case of *Trevor* v *Whitworth* (1887) 12 App Cas 409, HL.

The reasoning behind the decision in *Trevor* v *Whitworth* was that a registered limited company was permitted to reduce its capital only in the manner permitted by statute. Purchase of its own shares by a registered limited company involves a reduction of capital and (apart from the provisions described in 10.6 which were introduced by CA 1981) is not permitted by statute and is therefore illegal. (There is no restriction in this respect on unlimited companies.)

By CA 1985, s. 143(2), a purported acquisition in contravention of s. 143 is void (that is, it is treated as never having taken place), but a company which purports to acquire its own shares is liable to a fine for which there is no limit, and any officer of the company who knowingly and wilfully authorised or permitted the acquisition commits an offence triable either way (ss. 143(2) and 730(5) and sch. 24).

A public company must not exercise any voting rights in respect of shares it has acquired by gift (s. 146(1)(b) and (4)). If it fails to sell such shares within three years of acquiring them then it must cancel the shares and reduce its share capital account accordingly (s. 146(1)(b), (2)(a) and (3)(a)). This may lead to loss of public-company status (s. 146(2); see 6.6.3).

In the accounts of a company the same information must be given about own shares acquired by gift as for own shares forfeited or surrendered (see 6.4.2).

10.8.3 Holding shares in a holding company

If a body corporate is a subsidiary of a registered company (see 14.7) then it is not permitted to be a member of that company and it must not appoint a nominee to membership of that company (CA 1985, s. 23(1) and (7)). Therefore, a subsidiary of a registered company with a share capital must not hold shares in its holding company.

This rule was introduced by CA 1947, s. 80, in order to prevent a registered company evading the rule against purchase of own shares (now CA 1985, s. 143) by having a subsidiary company buy its shares. Any allotment or transfer of shares of a registered company to any subsidiary or a nominee of any subsidiary is void (s. 23(1) and (7)). The section was not retrospective so a subsidiary which held shares (either directly or through a nominee) in its holding company before 1 July 1948 is permitted to continue holding them but must not exercise any voting rights attached to the shares (s. 23(4)). The same applies where a company held shares legally under s. 23 as originally enacted but the holding became illegal when a revision of s. 23 came into force on 20 October 1997. Similarly, where a company holds shares in another company legally but circumstances change to make the holding illegal, it may continue, under CA 1985, s. 23(5), to hold the shares but may not vote them. So the fact that company B owns shares in company A is not a bar to company A buying all shares in B and turning it into a subsidiary (*Acatos and Hutcheson plc* v *Watson* [1995] 1 BCLC 218). The fact that A becomes a member of B does not mean that it 'acquires' B's assets so it has not acquired B's shares in A in contravention of s. 143 (*Acatos and Hutcheson plc* v *Watson*; R. Nolan, 'The veil intact' (1995) 16 Co Law 180). Where a company is continuing to hold shares under s. 23(4) or (5), a capitalisation issue may be made to it but it must not vote the bonus shares (s. 23(6)).

The prohibition does not apply where the subsidiary holds shares in the ordinary course of a bona fide business of dealing in securities on an exchange in the UK or any other EEA State (s. 23(3) with some exceptions set out in s. 23(3A)).

There is an exception in favour (principally) of banks. It is quite common for a bank to take a mortgage of shares as security for a loan. The bank as mortgagee of shares in a company becomes a member of that company. As shares in the major British banks are widely held by the public, sooner or later a bank will find itself as mortgagee of its own shares. To avoid being a holder of its own shares, shares mortgaged to a bank are always held by a subsidiary company as nominee. By CA 1985, s. 23(2), this is a permissible exception to the rule that a subsidiary must not hold shares in its holding company. There is a similar exception for shares held by a subsidiary (or its nominee) as personal representative of a deceased individual.

There is a further exception under s. 23(2) for shares in a company held by a subsidiary of that company as a trustee unless the company has a beneficial interest in the trust (apart from the security interest mentioned in the preceding paragraph and various residuary interests that may exist when a subsidiary of a company holds its shares for the purposes of a pension scheme or employees' share scheme — see CA 1985, sch. 2).

Every company must disclose in a note to its annual accounts the number, description and amount of the shares in the company held by or on behalf of its subsidiary undertakings (CA 1985, sch. 5, paras 6 and 20).

10.8.4   Other forms of assistance

CA 1985, s. 151, makes it illegal for a company to give financial assistance, directly or indirectly, for the acquisition of its own shares or of shares in its holding company except in the circumstances listed in 10.8.1. No definition is given of the words 'financial assistance', though s. 152(1)(a) states that financial assistance given in various ways (including by gift, guarantee, security, indemnity or loan) is financial assistance prohibited by s. 151. In *Charterhouse Investment Trust Ltd* v *Tempest Diesels Ltd* [1986] BCLC 1, Hoffmann J said, at p. 10, that the words 'giving financial assistance':

> have no technical meaning and their frame of reference is in my judgment the language of ordinary commerce. One must examine the commercial realities of the transaction and decide whether it can properly be described as the giving of financial assistance by the company, bearing in mind that the section is a penal one and should not be strained to cover transactions which are not fairly within it.

In *British and Commonwealth Holdings plc* v *Barclays Bank plc* [1996] 1 WLR 1, Aldous LJ said, at p. 15:

> . . . the section requires that there should be assistance or help for the purpose of acquiring the shares and that that assistance should be financial.

But terms such as 'gift', 'guarantee', 'security' and 'indemnity' in s. 152(1)(a) must be restricted to their technical legal meaning (*British and Commonwealth Holdings plc* v *Barclays Bank plc*).

In *Catley* v *Herbert* [1988] 1 NZLR 606, the New Zealand Court of Appeal held that 'financial assistance' has a wider meaning than 'monetary assistance' and can include a transfer of any of a company's assets for use in buying shares.

An example of illegal financial assistance is provided by *Belmont Finance Corporation* v *Williams Furniture Ltd (No. 2)* [1980] 1 All ER 393. Belmont Finance Corporation bought all the issued shares of Maximum Finance Ltd from a Mr Grosscurth and his associates for £500,000. The shares were worth about £60,000. Grosscurth and associates used the money they got from Belmont to buy all the issued shares in Belmont from its parent company (so the directors of Belmont who caused it to give £500,000 to Grosscurth were also directors of the parent company which sold the shares in Belmont to Grosscurth). This was illegal financial assistance by Belmont for the purchase of its own shares. It made no difference that the Belmont directors genuinely believed that, under the direction of the persuasive Mr Grosscurth (who subsequently went bankrupt and left the country), Maximum Finance really was worth £500,000: the only purpose of buying Maximum Finance was to provide Grosscurth with funds to buy the Belmont shares and this was well-known to all concerned.

In *Heald* v *O'Connor* [1971] 1 WLR 497, Douglas and Margaret Heald sold Mr O'Connor all the shares in D.E. Heald (Stoke-on-Trent) Ltd for £35,000 but also lent him £25,000. The company gave the Healds a floating charge on all its assets as security for repayment of this loan (floating charges are described in 11.6), the effect being that if Mr O'Connor did not pay for the shares, the company would. This was illegal financial assistance. CA 1985, s. 152(1)(a)(ii), makes it clear that financial assistance includes assistance given by way of security and s. 151(2) provides that where a person has acquired shares in a company and incurred a liability for the purpose of that acquisition then it is not lawful for the company to give financial assistance for the purpose of discharging that liability.

Financial assistance is illegal if given either before or at the same time as an acquisition takes place (s. 151(1)). It is also illegal to give financial assistance after an acquisition has occurred (s. 151(2)).

However, s. 151 does not prohibit a distribution of a company's assets by way of dividend lawfully made (s. 153(3)(a)). So it is legal to borrow money with which to acquire a controlling interest in a company on the basis that the control will be used to declare a dividend from which the loan will be repaid. (But the loan must not come from the company itself or one of its subsidiaries.)

Section 151 does not have extraterritorial effect, so it does not, for example, prohibit a company incorporated in Gibraltar giving financial assistance for the acquisition of shares in its holding company incorporated in England (*Arab Bank plc* v *Merchantile Holdings Ltd* [1994] Ch 71). This does not mean that a holding company can transfer assets to a foreign subsidiary so that they can be used to buy the holding company's shares: that would be indirect financial assistance by the holding company, which is prohibited by s. 151.

Section 153(1) provides that s. 151(1) does not apply to financial assistance given by a company for the purchase of its shares (or shares in its holding company) if the assistance is given in good faith in the interests of the company and:

(a)   the company's principal purpose in giving that assistance is not to give it for the purpose of any such acquisition, or

(b)   the giving of the assistance for that purpose is but an incidental part of some larger purpose of the company.

Section 153(2) provides a similar exemption from s. 151(2).

In *Brady* v *Brady* [1989] AC 755, it was held that the fact that financial assistance given by a company will produce a benefit for the company does not mean that producing the benefit is a 'larger purpose' which will validate the assistance. *Brady* v *Brady* concerned the Brady family which owned various companies. The family had quarrelled and divided into two factions. They decided to divide the family businesses into two — one for each faction. To do this, all the existing operating companies were made wholly owned subsidiaries of a holding company called Ovalshield Ltd in which the two factions had equal shareholdings. Then two companies, Motoreal Ltd and Activista Ltd, were created, the plan being that the factions would take one of these companies each. Motoreal and Activista both issued all their shares to Ovalshield in return for shares in the operating companies so that each operating company became wholly owned by either Motoreal or Activista. Motoreal acquired the shares in the most valuable operating company, T. Brady & Sons Ltd, and had to acknowledge that it still owed Ovalshield part of the purchase price of those shares. The right to receive this money was transferred by Ovalshield to Activista to make up the difference between the value of the operating companies being acquired by Activista and the value of Activista's shares. Ovalshield ended up owning shares in two companies, Motoreal and Activista, of equal value. Ovalshield was then liquidated and its shares in Motoreal went to one faction (Jack and Robert Brady) while its shares in Activista went to the other faction (Bob and John Brady). The final stage was to be the transfer to Activista of some assets of T. Brady & Sons Ltd which Activista would accept as discharging the debt owed by Motoreal. In other words T. Brady & Sons Ltd would discharge a debt which had been incurred in order to buy its shares. This was illegal financial assistance.

The assets of a *private company* or of one of its subsidiaries (provided it is also a private company) may be used (by gift or loan, or by waiving an obligation owed) or committed (by giving a guarantee or indemnity) to assist someone else to acquire the company's shares, provided the assistance is approved in advance by special resolution of the company's members and a declaration of solvency is made by the company's directors (CA 1985, s. 155(1)). (If the assistance is to be provided by a subsidiary then its directors must also make a declaration of solvency and, if it is not a wholly owned subsidiary, its members must give approval by special resolution.)

A private company may give financial assistance for the purchase of its shares, or those of its holding company (if that is a private company), only from its distributable profits or by means of a loan (though a loan is not permitted if its liabilities exceed its assets immediately before the loan is made) (CA 1985, s. 155(2)).

For a detailed discussion, see M.J. Sterling, 'Financial assistance by a company for the purchase of its shares' (1987) 8 Co Law 99.

10.8.5 Penalties

If a company gives financial assistance for the acquisition of its shares or those of a holding company, without proper authorisation, then it commits an offence for which the penalty is a fine for which there is no limit; and every officer of the company who knowingly and wilfully authorised or permitted the financial assistance is guilty of an offence triable either way (CA 1985, ss. 151(3) and 730(5) and sch. 24).

As with an illegal excessive dividend (see 10.5.10), money given by a company as illegal assistance for share acquisition and which is in the hands of any person who knew or ought to have known of the circumstances which made paying it improper will be subject to a constructive trust in favour of the company. For example, in *Belmont Finance Corporation* v *Williams Furniture Ltd (No. 2)* [1980] 1 All ER 393 (the facts of which are set out in 10.8.4), the money received by Belmont's parent company for selling the shares to Grosscurth was held by it on constructive trust for Belmont because its directors knew that the money was paid to Grosscurth by Belmont as illegal assistance for the acquisition of Belmont's shares. (The knowledge of the directors of the parent company was treated as the parent company's knowledge under the identification theory, see 19.8.)

The courts always have great difficulty in deciding how far to allow illegal contracts to be enforced. In *Heald* v *O'Connor* [1971] 1 WLR 497 (the facts of which are set out in 10.8.4) it was held that any contract for the giving of illegal financial assistance is void (so the contract made by the company in *Heald* v *O'Connor* giving a floating charge on its assets as security was void). This disagreed with the earlier case of *Victor Battery Co. Ltd* v *Curry's Ltd* [1946] Ch 242. As both *Heald* v *O'Connor* and *Victor Battery Co. Ltd* v *Curry's Ltd* were High Court decisions, the difference would seem to be unresolved but in two subsequent cases in the House of Lords (*Brady* v *Brady* [1989] AC 755; *Neilson* v *Stewart* 1991 SC (HL) 22) it was assumed without argument that the rule stated in *Heald* v *O'Connor* was correct.

If a contract for the acquisition of a company's shares includes a provision for illegal financial assistance then the illegal provision may be severed and the contract may be enforced without it, provided the illegal provision was made for the exclusive benefit of the party seeking to enforce the contract (*Carney* v *Herbert* [1985] AC 301, PC; *Neilson* v *Stewart*). In *Carney* v *Herbert*, illegal financial assistance for the purchase of shares had been given by way of security for payment of the purchase price. The purchaser was a company called Ilerain Pty Ltd, which was controlled by the defendant, who guaranteed payment of the purchase price. The shares were resold at an enormous profit but the defendant refused to honour his guarantee on the ground that the contract of sale of the shares to Ilerain was illegal. It was held that the contract was valid despite the ancillary illegal security, so the defendant was liable on his guarantee. In *Neilson* v *Stewart*, illegal security was given for a loan to enable the defender to purchase shares: it was held that, despite the illegality of the security, the defender had to repay the loan.

In *Brady* v *Brady* [1989] AC 755, as explained in 10.8.4, various members of the Brady family had agreed to divide their companies in a way which involved illegal financial assistance. At the last moment, Bob and John Brady said that the shares for which the assistance was to be given had been undervalued and refused to complete the deal unless the amount of financial assistance to be given by T. Brady & Sons Ltd was increased. When Jack and Robert sued for specific performance, Bob and John said the agreement was unenforceable because it was illegal financial assistance, but after three years of litigation and just before the case was to be heard by the House of Lords, the lawyers noticed that as T. Brady & Sons Ltd was a private company with more than enough distributable profits to cover the proposed assistance, Jack and Robert could pass the necessary resolutions to make the assistance legal.

10.8.6   Restrictions and disclosure

A person who has been given financial assistance by a public company to acquire that company's shares, and holds those shares as trustee (e.g., as nominee) for the company, must not exercise any voting rights attached to the shares (CA 1985, s. 146(1)(d) and (4)). If the company fails to dispose of its interests in such shares within one year of their acquisition by its trustee then it must cancel the shares and reduce its share capital accordingly (s. 146(1)(d), (2)(a) and (3)(b)). If it shows its interest in such shares as an asset in a balance sheet then the value of that interest must be transferred from distributable profits to a reserve fund that will not be available for distribution (s. 148(4)). The fund is called a reserve for own shares.

A person who has been given financial assistance by a limited company (public or private) to subscribe for new shares of the company as the company's nominee is nevertheless regarded for all purposes as owning the shares himself, and the company's equitable interest is disregarded (s. 144(1)) unless the company is itself acting as trustee for another person or as personal representative (s. 145(2)(a)).

In the accounts of a company the same information must be given about own shares acquired by trustees for the company (whether with or without the company's financial assistance) as for own shares forfeited or surrendered (see 6.4.2).

10.8.7   Authorisation of assistance by a private company for the acquisition of its own shares

By CA 1985, ss. 155(6) and 156, the directors of a private company giving financial assistance for the purchase of its own shares must make a statutory declaration of the details of the proposed assistance, and must state that in their opinion:

(a)   The company will be able to pay its other debts (including future and contingent debts) immediately after the assistance is given (i.e., the company's assets will be greater than its liabilities).

(b)   Either that the company will be able to pay its debts as they fall due during the year following the giving of the assistance or that it is proposed to wind up the company during that year and all the company's debts will be paid in full within one year of commencing the winding up.

The declaration must give prescribed particulars of the company's business and of the financial assistance. The particulars are those set out in form 155(6)a, which is also the prescribed form for the purpose (Companies (Forms) Regulations 1985 (SI 1985 No. 854), reg. 4 and sch. 4 part II). Making such a declaration without having reasonable grounds for the opinion expressed in it is an offence triable either way (CA 1985, s. 156(7) and sch. 24).

The company's auditors must make a report to the directors (s. 156(4)) stating that in their opinion the directors'view of the company's future solvency is not unreasonable.

The financial assistance must be given not more than eight weeks after the directors make their declaration (s. 158(4)). However, before the assistance is given, and within one week of the making of the declaration, the assistance must be approved by the members by special resolution (ss. 155(4) and 157(1)). If this resolution is to be adopted in general meeting then the directors' declaration and auditors' report must be available for inspection by the members at the meeting (s. 157(4)(a)). If the resolution is to be adopted by a private company as a written resolution under s. 381A (see 14.5.3) then the documents must be supplied to each member at or before the time at which the resolution is supplied to that member for signature (sch. 15A, para. 4).

A copy of the special resolution, accompanied by the directors' declaration and auditors' report, must be delivered to the registrar within 15 days of adoption (ss. 156(5)(a) and 380). Failure to file these documents on time does not make the financial assistance to which they relate illegal (*Re NL Electrical Ltd* [1994] 1 BCLC 22).

Within 28 days of the adoption of the resolution an application may be made to the court to cancel it by the holders of at least ten per cent in nominal value of the company's issued share capital (or any class thereof), provided they did not vote in favour of the resolution. The court may confirm or cancel the resolution, or alter its terms, or make any other kind of order that will solve the dispute equitably including an order that the company must purchase the dissentients' shares (s. 157(2) and s. 54(3), (5) and (6) applied by s. 157(3)). If such an application is made the company must forthwith give notice of it to the registrar (s. 54(4) applied by s. 157(3)) and must give the registrar an office copy of the court's order within 15 days from the making of the order or such longer time as the court may direct (s. 54(7) applied by s. 157(3)).

The financial assistance must not be given during the time when an application to the court may be made, unless every member of the company who is entitled to vote at its general meetings voted in favour of the resolution (and therefore no one can object) (s. 158(2)).

10.8.8 Authorisation of assistance to be given by a subsidiary

If private company A is a subsidiary of public company B which is a subsidiary of private company C then A cannot give financial assistance for the acquisition of shares in C (CA 1985, s. 155(3)).

When it is proposed that an acquisition of shares in a company should be financially assisted by a subsidiary of that company then both the holding company and the subsidiary must go through the routines described in 10.8.7 (s. 155(5) and (6)), except that it is not necessary for the members of a wholly owned subsidiary to pass a special resolution (s. 155(4)).

In addition, if there is a chain of holding companies — for example if A is a subsidiary of B and B is a subsidiary of C, and A is to give assistance for the purchase of shares in C — then the 'intermediate' holding companies (B in the example just mentioned) must also go through the routines described in 10.8.7 (s. 155(5) and (6)), except that it is not necessary for the members of a wholly owned subsidiary to pass a special resolution (s. 155(5)).

Where shares in a holding company are being acquired with assistance from a subsidiary, the directors of the holding company, and the directors of any intermediate holding company, must make the statutory declaration required by s. 155(6) on form 155(6)b. They must swear to the solvency of the company of which they are directors: 'the company' in s. 156(2) must mean 'the company of which they are directors' mentioned in s. 156(1) — this point is overlooked by S. Sharma, 'Whose solvency is it anyway?' (1993) 137 SJ 318, who thinks the wording of s. 156(2) and form 155(6)b ambiguous.

The time-limit of eight weeks runs from the date of the first directors' declaration made (s. 158(4)).

A directors' declaration made by the directors of a wholly owned subsidiary must be filed (together with the relevant auditors' report) with the registrar within 15 days of being made (s. 156(5)(b)).

10.8.9 Review

In the consultation document introducing its review of company law (see 0.3.1.6) the DTI singles out the rules on financial assistance for purchase of shares as an example of the excessive complexity of company law causing companies to incur substantial costs in management time and professional fees:

> These rules are notoriously difficult, and legal and auditing fees are often incurred to ensure that innocent and worthwhile transactions (e.g. deals to bring new capital into companies, which involve the payment of fees to those who provide that capital) do not breach the rules. Fees can exceed £10,000 in individual cases and are estimated at some £20 million a year in total. (*Modern Company Law for a Competitive Economy* (London: DTI, 1998), p. 7.)

11   Borrowing, Credit and Security

11.1   INTRODUCTION

Borrowing is an important method of financing the activities of companies in Britain. Nowadays by far the most important form of borrowing is an overdraft at a bank, but this is quite a recent phenomenon and much of the law on borrowing by companies was developed to deal with loans from private individuals.

A lender of money to a company usually insists on being granted a right of recourse against property of the company if the loan is not repaid on time. The right of recourse is *security* for the repayment of the loan.

Among business people the word 'debenture' usually denotes a document by which a company gives security for the repayment of a loan. However, the courts have always held that 'debenture' means any document issued by a company acknowledging indebtedness, and this is the sense in which the word is used in CA 1985 (*Lemon v Austin Friars Investment Trust Ltd* [1926] Ch 1, CA).

In the second half of the 19th century small companies often took loans from private investors in units of, say, £100. For each £100 (say) lent an investor was given a certificate specifying his entitlement to interest and repayment of principal, and the holders of these certificates would all be given an equal right of recourse against the company's property if there was default in paying interest or repaying principal. A set of identical certificates like this issued by a company is called a *series of debentures*. Debentures in series feature in many court cases and are covered by provisions of CA 1985 but are now virtually extinct.

Until about 1970 it was common for listed companies to raise very large loans from members of the public. An investor is encouraged to contribute to such a loan if it is marketable — that is, if there are facilities for him to sell his own rights to interest, and to repayment of capital, should he find himself in need of cash. Special arrangements can be made so that large loans are marketable through the Stock Exchange. Marketable loans will be considered separately in chapter 12.

If a company is registered as a public company on its initial incorporation then it is an offence for it to exercise any borrowing powers unless the registrar has issued it a certificate to commence business or it has re-registered as a private company (CA 1985, s. 117(7); see 6.6.1).

11.2   SECURITY FOR FINANCIAL OBLIGATIONS

11.2.1   Security contracts

If A owes B a financial obligation then A and B may also make an associated contract under which, if A personally fails to meet the obligation then B can have recourse to property owned by A and can obtain what is due by selling the property, or by receiving income (such as rents or royalties) earned by the property. This kind of parallel contract is called a 'contract of direct security' for a financial obligation. The property covered by the contract is said to be 'charged' with meeting the obligation, and B is known as the 'chargee' of the property.

Creditors have developed many different forms of security arrangement and an unfortunate consequence of this is that there is little agreement on terminology. Words which some people use to describe particular forms of security arrangement are used by others as generic terms to refer to all kinds of security arrangement. For example, the term 'mortgage' is used by many people to refer to a particular kind of security, but in the Law of Property Act 1925, the draftsman used 'mortgage' throughout and in the 'definitions' (s. 205(1)(xvi)) said ' "Mortgage" includes any charge or lien on any property for securing money or money's worth'. CA 1985, part XII (ss. 395 to 420), though, is drafted using 'charge' as the generic term and s. 396(4) (as originally enacted) says that '. . . "charge" includes mortgage'. In IA 1986, an interpretation section (s. 248) provides: '. . ."security" means . . . any mortgage, charge, lien or other security'. In this book we employ the Companies Act terminology.

If A owes B a financial obligation then, instead of or in addition to taking a charge on A's property, B may make a contract with a third party C, under which C promises to meet A's obligation to B if A fails to do so. This is called a 'guarantee' and C is called a 'guarantor'. C's guarantee may be reinforced by a charge on C's property. Guarantees, and charges as security for guarantees, are called contracts of 'collateral security'. A guarantee cannot be enforced unless there is a written memorandum of the terms of the guarantee signed by the guarantor or by the guarantor's authorised agent (Statute of Frauds 1677, s. 4), though the memorandum need not state what consideration was to be given to the guarantor (Mercantile Law Amendment Act 1856, s. 3). It is also possible for C's property to be charged as security for an obligation owed by A to B without any personal promise by C to meet the obligation (*Re Bank of Credit and Commerce International SA (No. 8)* [1998] AC 214).

A person whose property is charged as direct security or who acts as guarantor for another's financial obligation is called a 'surety'. One financial obligation may be covered by any number of direct and collateral security contracts.

Security contracts are most commonly made to cover repayment of loans but they also occur in connection with other kinds of financial obligation, such as payment of rent or payment for goods or services supplied. Any company with the power to borrow money has an implied power to give security for its repayment (*Re Patent File Co.* (1870) LR 6 Ch App 83).

Normally the consideration that supports a contract of security is the granting of a loan, or the grant of time to pay an obligation presently due. Something given before a contract is made is not consideration for that contract, so a creditor cannot obtain security for an obligation he has already allowed to be incurred unless the security is given in a deed. (In practice, as will be seen shortly, many contracts of security are made in a deed.) A contract by which a person promises to give a charge over property that he is to acquire in the future, and has no interest in at the time of making the contract, is unenforceable unless consideration was given, even if it is in a deed (*Re Ellenborough* [1903] 1 Ch 697).

A charge is created at the time that the contract of charge is formed (*Esberger & Son Ltd* v *Capital & Counties Bank* [1913] 2 Ch 366) even if it is given in contemplation of an obligation that is not incurred until later.

11.2.2   Redemption

If a secured obligation is met without recourse to the security then the security contract automatically terminates, and the security is said to be *redeemed* or *discharged (Walker* v *Jones* (1866) LR 1 PC 50; *Rourke* v *Robinson* [1911] 1 Ch 480). Chancery developed the important principle that a person whose property has been charged as security for meeting some obligation and who fails to meet the obligation on the contracted day may nevertheless redeem the security by meeting the obligation on some later day (*Brown* v *Cole* (1845) 14 Sim 427). Preservation of the right to redeem means that a person whose property has been charged always retains an interest in that property and this interest (which is called the 'equity of redemption') comes to an end only if:

(a)   there is redemption, i.e., if the charge itself is ended because the secured obligation is met; or

(b)   the right to redeem is ended (or 'foreclosed') by court order; or

(c)   the chargee exercises a power to sell the charged property, or it is sold by court order.

The courts protect the equity of redemption by declaring void any provision in a charge contract that has the effect of excluding the right to redeem. (Such a provision is called a 'fetter' or 'clog' on the equity of redemption.) See *G & C Kreglinger* v *New Patagonia Meat & Cold Storage Co. Ltd* [1914] AC 25. However, if a registered company gives a charge and excludes its right to redeem the charge, or makes it redeemable only on the happening of a contingency (such as the winding up of the company) then the clog on the equity will not be void (CA 1985, s. 193). This provision was enacted so that companies could borrow on what are called 'perpetual debentures', with no fixed date for the repayment of principal. An investor with a perpetual debenture has a right to a regular payment of interest for as long as the company exists. (Perpetual debentures are rare. The few recent issues of so-called perpetual debentures by banks have in fact been unsecured marketable loans — see chapter 12.) Section 193 also makes enforceable a security contract under which the contractual date for payment of the secured debt (and therefore the earliest date for redemption of the security) is far distant — e.g., 40 years (*Knightsbridge Estates Trust Ltd* v *Byrne* [1940] AC 613, HL).

11.2.3   Realisation

No action can be taken by a creditor to realise any security until the secured obligation is actually due to be met and there has been failure to meet it. So if a secured loan is not due to be repaid until a certain date, the security cannot be realised until that date has passed without repayment of the loan. Banks are in an especially strong position because nearly all their lending to companies is on overdraft which is repayable on demand by the bank. In *Williams & Glyn's Bank Ltd* v *Barnes* [1981] Com LR 205 Mr Barnes contested the bank's claim against him in debt for some £2 million. The claim arose from the crash of his company, Northern Developments Holdings Ltd, which Mr Barnes alleged came about because the bank unreasonably refused to continue financing. In particular he alleged that the bank should not have demanded repayment of its overdraft when it knew that this would destroy the company whose future profits were actually the only means of paying the debt. Ralph Gibson J said:

Where money is lent on overdraft by a bank, and there is no agreed date for repayment, and no special terms which require implication of a further term as to the date of repayment, then it is clear to me that the overdraft is repayable on demand . . . .

When a bank lends money to a customer there is no reason to suppose that, in the absence of agreement to that effect, the bank must regard the fulfilment of the customer's known purpose as the agreed, or only, source of repayment. Borrowing from a bank may be replaced by borrowing from another bank or moneylender. If the borrowing cannot be replaced, because of the parlous state of the borrower's business, or of the market generally, I know of nothing in the ordinary contract of lending which requires the lender to share the borrower's misfortune.

11.3 REGISTRATION OF NON-POSSESSORY CHARGES

Probably the simplest way of making a debtor's goods security for payment of the debt is to give possession of the goods to the creditor on condition that possession will be returned on payment of the debt. This is called 'pledging' the goods. There are also various situations in which a person who has been given possession of goods so as, for example, to store, repair or transport them, has a right to hold them until paid for what has been done to them. This right is called a 'lien' on the goods. Charging property, otherwise than by pledge or lien, does not in practice involve giving possession of the charged property to the chargee. There is a danger that a person who charges property without giving up possession of it will pretend to future creditors that the property is unencumbered and will borrow money on the strength of the apparent wealth conferred by the property. To provide protection against this, statutes have set up government-administered registers for recording non-possessory charges on the following types of property:

(a)   Registered land — that is, any estate in land that has been registered in one of the district land registries in England and Wales under the Land Registration Act 1925. If land has been registered at a district land registry then a charge on it should be registered at the same registry.

(b)   Unregistered land in England and Wales. A charge on unregistered land should be registered at the Land Charges Registry at Plymouth under the Land Charges Act 1972 unless the chargee takes possession of the title deeds to the land.

(c)   British ships. A charge on a British ship or a share in a ship should be registered under the Merchant Shipping Act 1995, sch. 1, para. 7, with the Registrar General of Shipping and Seamen.

(d)   Registered trade marks (Trade Marks Act 1994, s. 25).

(e)   Registered designs (Registered Designs Act 1949, s. 19).

(f)   UK patents (Patents Act 1977, s. 32).

(g)   Aircraft and hovercraft registered in the UK (Mortgaging of Aircraft Order 1972 (SI 1972 No. 1268)).

In addition, if an individual or a partnership executes a document giving a non-possessory charge on things in possession (personal tangible property) then the document is a bill of sale and must be registered at the Supreme Court under the Bills of Sale Acts 1878 and 1882 (unless the charged property is a ship), and the charge will be void unless the document is in the form prescribed by the schedule to the 1882 Act. However, the provisions of the Bills of Sale Acts do not apply to a charge given by a registered company on its things in possession (Bills of Sale Act (1878) Amendment Act 1882, s. 17; *Re Standard Manufacturing Co.* [1891] 1 Ch 627).

A non-possessory charge on almost any kind of property of a registered company must be registered with the registrar of companies under CA 1985, part XII (ss. 395 to 420) (see 11.7). This registration is required in addition to any registration that may be necessary because of the nature of the property charged. For example, a charge on a UK-registered aircraft belonging to a company must be registered in the register of aircraft mortgages kept by the Civil Aviation Authority and in the register of charges kept by the registrar of companies.

All these registers are open to public inspection for a modest fee. If a charge is registered in one of these registers then a buyer of the charged property has to recognise the claim of the chargee to the property, and if the property is charged a second time then the second chargee has to recognise the prior claim of the chargee who is already registered. On the other hand, if a charge that could be registered in one of these registers is not then it can be ignored by a subsequent buyer of the property, or subsequent second chargee of the property whose charge is registered, even if notice of the existence of the prior charge is given by some other means.

If a registrable charge is not registered but the surety does not sell or charge again the property then the charge is still enforceable against the surety (unless it is a bill of sale given by an individual or partnership, which becomes void if not registered within the time-limit). However, if a charge on a company's property is not registered with the registrar of companies and the company commences winding up then the company's liquidator is entitled to ignore the charge and if an administration order is made in relation to the company then the administrator may ignore it (CA 1985, s. 399).

In December 1985, Professor A.L. Diamond was asked by the Minister for Corporate and Consumer Affairs to consider the case for a single scheme of registration of security interests in property other than land, and in particular to consider the position of the registration of charges created by companies in the context of such a scheme. For a review of Professor Diamond's report, see M. Lawson, 'The reform of the law relating to security interests in property' [1989] JBL 287.

11.4 LEGAL AND EQUITABLE CHARGES

A security interest in property, like any other interest in property, may be legal or equitable. If it is a legal interest then it must be recognised by any person who subsequently acquires title to the property or any interest in it. If it is an equitable interest then it may be ignored by any person who subsequently acquires, bona fide and for value, a legal interest in or legal title to the property without notice (actual or constructive), at the time of acquisition, of the existence of the equitable interest.

11.4.1 Legal security interests

A legal security interest in property other than land may be created by transferring the property to the chargee on condition that it will be transferred back to the surety if and when the secured obligation is met. This is known as a 'legal mortgage'. Many people prefer to reserve the term 'mortgage' for security arrangements which involve transferring title to property to the beneficiary, as in the legal mortgage just described, but, as explained in 11.2.1, many others use the term more generally. A legal security interest in a legal estate in land may be created under the Law of Property Act 1925, s. 85(1) (if the estate is freehold), or s. 86(1) (if it is leasehold), by a deed which is expressed to create a charge by way of legal mortgage on the estate. A charge by way of legal mortgage confers on the chargee a legal estate in the land. It is also possible to create a legal security interest in a legal estate in land by granting a lease to the chargee but this method is hardly ever used in practice.

The person in whose favour a mortgage, or charge by way of legal mortgage, is given is called the 'mortgagee' and the person whose property has been mortgaged is called the 'mortgagor'. Even though a mortgagor's legal interest in property is transferred to the mortgagee under a legal mortgage, it was held in *Cunliffe Engineering Ltd* v *English Industrial Estates Corp.* [1994] BCC 972 that mortgaged property is not correctly described as the mortgagee's property but remains the mortgagor's because the mortgagor's equity of redemption is superior to the mortgagee's legal interest by virtue of the principle that the rules of equity prevail over the common law (Supreme Court Act 1981, s. 49(1)). However, this may be compared with the decision in *Re ELS Ltd* [1995] Ch 11 discussed in 11.6.2.

11.4.2 Equitable security interests

In *Re Charge Card Services Ltd* [1987] Ch 150, Millett J said:

> . . . the essence of an equitable charge is that, without any conveyance or assignment to the chargee, specific property of the chargor is expressly or constructively appropriated to or made answerable for payment of a debt, and the chargee is given the right to resort to the property for the purpose of having it realised and applied in or towards payment of the debt.

11.4.3 Priorities

The distinction between a legal and an equitable charge may be important if the person who granted the charge (the surety) deals with property after charging it. If a surety sells charged property (for value) then:

(a)   if the chargee has a legal charge then the property remains charged in the hands of the new owner (i.e., the chargee can still have recourse to it if the obligation secured by the charge is not met);

(b)   if the chargee has an equitable charge then the property remains charged in the hands of the new owner only if, at the time of buying the property, the new owner had notice of the chargee's interest.

If a surety has charged property but then grants a legal charge over the property to a second chargee (for value) then:

(a)   if the first charge is a legal charge then the first chargee is entitled to have recourse to the property in priority to the second chargee;

(b)   if the first charge is an equitable charge then the first chargee is entitled to priority only if, at the time the third party obtained his charge, he had notice of the first chargee's interest.

If two equitable charges are created over the same property then they take priority in order of creation. Chargees may agree among themselves to vary these rules and do not need the surety's consent to any variation (*Cheah Theam Swee* v *Equiticorp Finance Group Ltd* [1992] 1 AC 472).

The rules on priorities of legal and equitable charges are of very much less importance where there is a system for registering charges, because registration is equivalent to notice to any subsequent buyer or chargee of the existence of the registered charge (whether it is legal or equitable), and failure to register means that the charge (whether legal or equitable) may be ignored by any subsequent chargee who does register or any subsequent buyer. Thus registration rather than the form of the charge is the key to enforcing the charge against third parties.

11.5 RECOURSE TO CHARGED PROPERTY

11.5.1 Right to sell charged property

A pledgee has a right to sell pledged property if the obligation secured by the pledge is not met (*Re Hardwick* (1886) 17 QBD 690, per Bowen LJ at p. 698 and Fry LJ at p. 701), though there are statutory restrictions on this right in some circumstances under the Consumer Credit Act 1974, ss. 116 to 121.

A legal mortgagee of stocks and shares traded on the London Stock Exchange has a right to sell them when the obligation secured by the mortgage is not met (*Wilson* v *Tooker* (1714) 5 Bro Parl Cas 193, HL; *Deverges* v *Sandeman Clark & Co.* [1902] 1 Ch 579, CA).

A chargee has no right to sell charged property under other types of charge contract, unless that right has been granted by a provision in the charge contract. If the charge contract is made by deed, then a right of sale is deemed by the Law of Property Act 1925, s. 101, to be given by the contract, unless the contract provides otherwise.

If no right of sale is granted by the charge contract, then the chargee may apply to the High Court or a county court for an order to sell the charged property.

The right of sale given by the Law of Property Act 1925, s. 101, has been held to be not available to the holders of debentures in series (*Blaker* v *Herts & Essex Waterworks Co.* (1889) 41 ChD 399, decided under legislation that was replaced by s. 101 of the Law of Property Act 1925 in substantially the same terms).

Any profit made on selling charged property, after the secured obligation is met, is held on trust for the surety (Law of Property Act 1925, s. 105).

Equity does not permit charged property to be sold under the chargee's power of sale to the chargee, either as a sole purchaser or jointly with others, or to a trustee for the chargee (*Downes* v *Grazebrook* (1817) 3 Mer 200), though there can be a sale to a company in which the chargee is interested (*Tse Kwong Lam* v *Wong Chit Sen* [1983] 1 WLR 1349, PC).

When exercising a power of sale of charged property a chargee has a duty to take reasonable care to obtain the true market value of the property (*Cuckmere Brick Co. Ltd* v *Mutual Finance Ltd* [1971] Ch 949, CA). However, a chargee is entitled to sell when the power of sale becomes exercisable (i.e., when the secured obligation is due and has not been paid). If the market happens to be depressed at that time, the chargee is under no obligation to wait until it improves (*Bank of Cyprus (London) Ltd* v *Gill* [1980] 2 Lloyd's Rep 51, CA). Liability for breach of this duty may be excluded by an appropriately worded provision of the charge contract (*Bishop* v *Bonham* [1988] 1 WLR 742, CA, in which the wording of the contract was not effective to exclude the liability).

11.5.2 Exercise of the s. 101 power of sale

The Law of Property Act 1925, s. 103, provides that the power of sale given by s. 101 of the Act may be exercised only if:

(a)   the surety has failed to comply with three months' notice to repay the principal debt secured; or

(b)   interest payable on the secured debt is unpaid two months after becoming due; or

(c)   there has been a breach of a term of the charge contract other than terms relating to repayment of principal or payment of interest.

Law of Property Act 1925, s. 101(3), permits the time-limits to be varied by a term in the charge contract. It is usual for a contract to state that the power of sale will be exercisable immediately there is default in paying interest or repaying principal.

11.5.3   Right to take possession of charged property

A legal chargee is given the legal title to the charged property (or, in the case of land, a legal estate) and therefore has an immediate right to possession of the property. As Harman J said in *Four-Maids Ltd* v *Dudley Marshall (Properties) Ltd* [1957] Ch 317 at p. 320:

> The mortgagee may go into possession before the ink is dry on the mortgage unless there is something in the contract, express or by implication, whereby he has contracted himself out of that right.

The right to possession is exercisable whether or not the surety has defaulted, unless there is a contrary agreement (*Western Bank Ltd* v *Schindler* [1977] Ch 1, CA). However, a chargee who takes possession of the charged property comes under a strict and heavy liability because of the 'wilful default rule' under which a chargee in possession must account to the surety for rents and profits which, but for the chargee's default or neglect, the surety might have received. As Romilly MR said in *Chaplin* v *Young (No. 1)* (1864) 33 Beav 330, at pp. 337–8:

> . . . if [a chargee of a business] enter into possession, he becomes the owner of the business, and he stands exactly, as regards his powers, in the place of the mortgagor, and, accordingly, he is accountable to the owner of the equity of redemption for everything which he either has received or might have received, while he continued in such possession.

Accordingly, creditors developed a procedure by which security interests were enforced by appointing a 'receiver' to take possession of the charged property and sell it, with a term in the charge contract deeming the receiver to be the agent of the surety — see per Rigby LJ in *Gaskell* v *Gosling* [1896] 1 QB 559, CA, at pp. 691–3.

An equitable chargee has no right to possession of the charged property unless granted the right by a provision of the charge contract (*Tennant* v *Trenchard* (1869) LR 4 Ch App 537; *Vacuum Oil Co.* v *Ellis* [1914] 1 KB 693, CA, per Buckley LJ at 703). (For a strongly expressed view to the contrary, see Wade (1955) 71 LQR 204.) However, on application by an equitable chargee, the court may appoint a receiver to take possession of the charged property, as an officer of the court, pending an order by the court to sell it to meet the obligation owed to the chargee.

The distinction between the rights of an equitable and a legal chargee was summarised by Buckley J in *Re London Pressed Hinge Co. Ltd* [1905] 1 Ch 576 at p. 583:

> A legal mortgagee may take possession simply because he chooses. In so doing he accepts the responsibility of a mortgagee in possession. An equitable mortgagee must show good reason why the court should at his instance take possession by its receiver.

From the chargee's point of view the problem with a court-appointed receiver is that such a receiver is a neutral officer of the court whose task is to administer property that is the subject of proceedings for the benefit of all parties to those proceedings. A chargee obviously wants the property administered solely for the chargee's benefit. One way of achieving this is to insert in a contract of equitable charge a provision that the chargee may appoint a receiver to take possession of the charged property and sell it for the chargee's benefit, but acting as agent of the surety. The device of appointing a receiver as agent of the surety is invariably adopted in the most common form of equitable charge given by companies, the floating charge, which will be discussed in detail in 11.6.

11.5.4 Right to appoint a receiver of income due to charged property

Where charged property is land that has been leased the best way of satisfying the chargee's claims may be to ensure that the rent is paid to the chargee instead of to the surety. This may be achieved by appointing a receiver of income. A power to appoint a receiver of income is given by the Law of Property Act 1925, s. 101, to any chargee whose charge has been given in a deed. A receiver of income appointed under this power is deemed to be the agent of the surety (Law of Property Act 1925, s. 109(2)) and so probably does not 'take' possession of the charged property, and so may be appointed by an equitable or a legal chargee. The s. 101 power to appoint a receiver of income may be exercised only if the chargee is entitled to exercise the s. 101 power of sale (Law of Property Act 1925, s. 109(1)).

Receivers of income are of limited importance in practice. They are useful, for example, if the income will cover outstanding interest payments and the chargee does not require repayment of principal, or where the charged property is unsaleable.

11.5.5 Right to foreclosure

In theory a chargee may ask the court to foreclose (bring to an end) the surety's right of redemption. A chargee granted foreclosure would become absolute owner of the charged property. However, in any action for foreclosure the court may instead direct a sale of the charged property (Law of Property Act 1925, s. 91(2)) and in practice usually does.

11.5.6 Right to sue for performance of the obligation

A creditor who has been given security cannot be forced to utilise that security, and is permitted to keep it in reserve and enforce the observance of the secured obligation by, for example, an ordinary action for debt. However, a contract which creates a charge as security for an obligation does not in itself confer a right to sue the surety for performance of that obligation. This is significant where the charge is given as collateral security for another person's obligation: the chargee's right under such a contract is against the charged property not the chargor personally (unless the charge contract provides otherwise) (*Tam Wing Chuen* v *Bank of Credit and Commerce Hong Kong Ltd* [1996] 2 BCLC 69; *Re Bank of Credit and Commerce International SA (No. 8)* [1998] AC 214).

Once a charge has been foreclosed, the chargee loses the right to sue on any express or implied covenant in the charge contract to repay the secured debt, unless prepared (and able) to return the charged property (*Kinnaird* v *Trollope* (1888) 39 ChD 636; *Lloyds & Scottish Trust Ltd* v *Britten* (1982) 44 P & CR 249). This is because the value of the property already received by the chargee is not known and cannot be deducted from the debt. If, however, instead of foreclosure, there has been a sale of the charged property, under the chargee's power of sale or a court order, then its value will be known and the chargee can sue for the balance of the debt (*Gordon Grant & Co. Ltd* v *Boos* [1926] AC 781, PC).

11.6 FLOATING CHARGES

11.6.1 Definition of floating charge

Much of the property of a trading company is in the form of a continually changing collection of current assets employed by the company in its business. The form of security arrangement known as a 'floating charge' was invented as a means of charging such property — current assets used to be known as 'floating assets'. In a floating charge given by a company, the subject-matter of the charge is a class of the company's assets — such as plant, machinery and tools, or stocks of goods for sale — and the charge confers on the chargee the right to take for payment of the secured debt all the assets of that type that the company owns at the time when the charge 'crystallises'. Normally a floating charge on a company's assets crystallises when, after the company has failed to comply with a demand to pay the secured debt, the chargee appoints a receiver under the charge contract. The receiver's task is to sell the assets on which the floating charge has crystallised and use the proceeds to pay the secured debt. For more on crystallisation see 11.6.2. It is an important characteristic of a floating charge that until it crystallises, the company may buy, sell, replace and otherwise deal with assets of the charged class in the normal course of its business without reference to the chargee.

A 'fixed charge' is a charge that is not a floating charge. The typical fixed charge granted by a company is a charge on a specific asset owned by the company (fixed charges are often called specific charges), which the company cannot deal with at all unless it has the permission of the chargee. The exact distinction between fixed and floating charges can be disputed and is discussed in 11.6.4.

A powerful creditor such as a bank usually tries to take a charge on all of a company's assets. This is usually a composite charge which is expressed to be a fixed charge on specified fixed assets and a floating charge on the company's whole undertaking and property other than the items covered by the fixed charge.

A company whose only asset is a major fixed asset such as a ship or a building may create a fixed charge on that asset which will effectively be a fixed charge on its entire property, but normally a charge on the 'undertaking' of a company must be a floating charge (*Re Panama, New Zealand & Australian Royal Mail Co.* (1870) LR 5 Ch App 318).

A floating chargee, being an equitable chargee, has no right to possession of the charged property unless the right is given by the charge contract. Floating charges never grant a right to possession so that the chargee never has the liability of a chargee in possession. Instead a contract of floating charge given by a company invariably has a provision by which the chargee can appoint a receiver to sell, as the company's agent, the charged assets in order to meet the company's obligations to the chargee. A receiver who is appointed under a charge which, as created, was a floating charge (or a composite fixed and floating charge) to take control of the whole (or substantially the whole) of a company's property (or who would have done so had it not been for the appointment of another receiver over part of the property) is called an 'administrative receiver' (IA 1986, s. 29(2)).

Under the charge contract, the chargee is given the right to appoint the administrative receiver. As the receiver's duty is to utilise the company's property and business to meet the obligation owed to the chargee, one cannot be appointed until the obligation is due and payable.

A floating charge is invariably given in a deed so a floating chargee has the power of sale conferred by s. 101 of the Law of Property Act 1925. Usually, though, the charged property is sold by an administrative receiver, acting as the agent of the company that gave the charge, and this is not an exercise of the chargee's power of sale (*Re Wood's Application* [1941] Ch 112).

If a contract of floating charge did not contain a provision for the appointment of an administrative receiver, the chargee's power of sale could be put into effect only by getting the court to appoint a receiver to take possession (as an officer of the court) of the property and business of the company.

In *Governments Stock and Other Securities Investment Co. Ltd* v *Manila Railway Co. Ltd* [1897] AC 81 Lord Macnaghten gave the following description of a floating charge, at p. 86:

A floating security is an equitable charge on the assets for the time being of a going concern. It attaches to the subject charged in the varying condition in which it happens to be from time to time. It is of the essence of such a charge that it remains dormant until the undertaking charged ceases to be a going concern, or until the person in whose favour the charge is created intervenes. His right to intervene may of course be suspended by agreement. But if there is no agreement for suspension, he may exercise his right whenever he pleases after default.

And in *Illingworth* v *Houldsworth* [1904] AC 355 his lordship said, at p. 358:

. . . what I said [in the passage from the *Manila Railway* case quoted above] was intended as a description, not as a definition, of a floating security. I should have thought there was not much difficulty in defining what a floating charge is in contrast to what is called a specific charge. A specific charge, I think, is one that without more fastens on ascertained and definite property or property capable of being ascertained and defined; a floating charge, on the other hand, is ambulatory and shifting in its nature, hovering over and so to speak floating with the property which it is intended to affect until some event occurs or some act is done which causes it to settle and fasten on the subject of the charge within its reach and grasp.

The essence of a floating charge on assets of a company is that the company is free to deal with those assets in the ordinary course of its business. In a series of cases it was held that this included being able to create fixed charges on assets within the class covered by the floating charge, having priority over the floating charge, in order to secure borrowing in the ordinary course of the company's business (see *Wheatley* v *Silkstone and Haigh Moor Coal Co.* (1885) 29 ChD 715). The courts have recognised that the nature of a floating charge precludes a company which has created one over its assets from creating another floating charge over the same assets ranking equally with, or in priority to, the first floating charge, except with the first chargee's permission (*Re Benjamin Cope and Sons Ltd* [1914] 1 Ch 800). However, it is possible to create a second floating charge over a part of the assets with priority over the first charge (*Re Automatic Bottle Makers Ltd* [1926] Ch 412). In response to this it has become standard practice to include in a contract of floating charge a 'negative-pledge' clause, providing that the company will not create any charge over the assets covered by the floating charge with priority over the floating charge.

If a company grants two floating charges over its property and business then, as equitable charges, they take priority in order of creation (*Re Benjamin Cope and Sons Ltd* [1914] 1 Ch 800) though priority may be lost by failure to register under CA 1985, part XII (ss. 395

to 424) (see 11.7) and see also the discussion of *Griffiths* v *Yorkshire Bank plc* [1994] 1 WLR 1427 in 11.6.2.

11.6.2 Crystallisation

A floating charge is a charge on a class of assets (usually, all the assets) of a company. The actual assets in that class owned by the company change from time to time. The assets that the chargee is entitled to utilise for payment of the secured debt are the assets in the class that the company owns at the time when the charge 'crystallises'. Crystallisation has been described as operating as an equitable assignment (by way of charge), to the chargee, of the assets that were subject to the floating charge at the time of crystallisation (*George Barker (Transport) Ltd* v *Eynon* [1974] 1 WLR 462 per Edmund Davies LJ at p. 467, Stamp LJ at p. 471 and Sir Gordon Willmer at p. 475). On crystallisation a floating charge becomes a fixed (or specific) equitable charge — that is, a charge on the specific assets of the charged class owned by the company at the time of crystallisation (*Re Griffin Hotel Co. Ltd* [1941] Ch 129). In *Re ELS Ltd* [1995] Ch 11 it was held that when a floating charge on a company's goods has become fixed by crystallisation the goods covered by it are no longer 'goods of' the company and so cannot be taken in distress by a local authority for the company's unpaid business rates. Other creditors entitled to levy distress (such as landlords) are not restricted to seizing only the debtor's goods as a local authority is. Accordingly, one of the many oddities of the law on distress is that precisely because a company's goods subject to a floating charge are considered not to be part of the company's estate or effects they can be taken in distress by a landlord after the commencement of the company's winding up despite the Insolvency Act 1986, s. 128(1) (which renders void any distress against the estate or effects of a company after commencement of its winding up) (*Re New City Constitutional Club Co., ex parte Purssell* (1887) 34 ChD 646; *Re Harpur's Cycle Fittings Co.* [1900] 2 Ch 731) though this does not apply where the goods are required to pay the company's preferential debts under the Insolvency Act 1986, s. 175(2)(b) (see 20.2.9) (*Re South Rhondda Colliery Co. (1898) Ltd* [1928] WN 126). These interpretations of terms of ownership may be compared with *Cunliffe Engineering Ltd* v *English Industrial Estates Corp.* [1994] BCC 972 discussed in 11.4.1. In *Griffiths* v *Yorkshire Bank plc* [1994] 1 WLR 1427, Morritt J held that if a company creates two floating charges at different times and the second crystallises before the first then the fixed charge created on crystallisation of the second takes priority over the first charge even after that has crystallised. The opposite conclusion was reached in the Ontario case of *Re Household Products Co. Ltd and Federal Business Development Bank* (1981) 124 DLR (3d) 325 which was not cited to Morritt J, whose decision seems to ignore the rule that equitable interests take priority in order of creation. See further A. Walters, 'Priority of the floating charge in corporate insolvency: *Griffiths* v *Yorkshire Bank plc*' (1995) 16 Co Law 291.

A floating charge crystallises:

(a) When a receiver is appointed to realise the charged assets so as to pay the secured debt. Such a receiver will be an administrative receiver if the charge covers the whole or substantially the whole of the company's property (Insolvency Act 1986, s. 29(2)). It is an essential feature of receivership under a floating charge that the receiver takes whatever property is subject to the floating charge at the time of his or her appointment (unless the charge crystallised earlier) and so the appointment must be regarded as crystallising the charge. The power to appoint an administrative receiver exists only by virtue of the charge contract, which must therefore specify the circumstances in which the power is exercisable.

The basic condition is that the debt secured by the charge has not been paid when due. If the charge secures a bank overdraft repayable on demand, the basic condition is that a demand has been made and not met. The charge contract will probably specify that the debt will become due for payment on the happening of various events (in addition to the expiry of the term of the loan if it is for a fixed term). These events typically include:

(i)   The company going into liquidation (this is an event that in itself crystallises a floating charge — see (b)).

(ii)   The appointment of an administrative receiver or receiver by another chargee (for the circumstances in which this event crystallises a floating charge, see (e)).

(iii)   The levy of execution or distress on the assets of the company.

(iv)   The company becoming unable to pay its debts within the meaning of IA 1986, s. 122(1) (see 20.6.3).

(v)   Cessation of business by the company (this event in itself crystallises a floating charge — see (c)).

(vi)   The giving of notice by the chargee converting the charge into a fixed charge, if provision is made in the charge contract for such notices to be given — see (d).

(b)   When the company goes into liquidation (*Wallace v Universal Automatic Machines Co.* [1894] 2 Ch 547, CA; *Re Panama, New Zealand & Australian Royal Mail Co.* (1870) LR 5 Ch App 318; *Re Crompton & Co. Ltd* [1914] 1 Ch 954). This is an implied term of a floating charge contract and can be excluded by an express provision to the contrary (*Re Brightlife Ltd* [1987] Ch 200 at p. 212).

(c)   When the company ceases business (*Re Woodroffes (Musical Instruments) Ltd* [1986] Ch 366; *William Gaskell Group Ltd v Highley* [1994] 1 BCLC 197). This is also an implied term which may be excluded by express agreement (*Re Real Meat Co. Ltd* [1996] BCC 254).

Cessation of business may occur when another floating charge on the company's assets crystallises. In *Re Woodroffes (Musical Instruments) Ltd* there were two floating charges and it was held that when one was crystallised by a notice converting it into a fixed charge (see (d)) this did not cause a cessation of business and so did not crystallise the other charge. Similarly, in *National Australia Bank Ltd v Composite Buyers Ltd* (1991) 6 ACSR 94, appointment of an administrative receiver under one floating charge did not cause another floating charge to crystallise because the company did not cease business. In *Federal Business Development Bank v Prince Albert Fashion Bin Ltd* [1983] 3 WWR 464, Saskatchewan, the other charge crystallised by the appointment of an administrative receiver and it was found by the Court of Appeal that the company ceased business and that this had caused the first floating charge to crystallise.

At first instance in *Federal Business Development Bank v Prince Albert Fashion Bin Ltd* [1981] 5 WWR 543, Estey J (whose decision the Court of Appeal affirmed) considered that it was not the cessation of business which caused the first floating charge to crystallise but the mere fact that the second charge had crystallised. Estey J based this on a consideration of *Re Benjamin Cope and Sons Ltd* [1914] 1 Ch 800, saying: 'The effect of Sargant J's judgment is, I believe, that crystallisation of the subsequent floating charge really crystallises the prior debenture'. This more general rule was firmly rejected by Nourse J (before whom the Saskatchewan case was not cited) in *Re Woodroffes (Musical Instruments) Ltd* [1986] Ch 366 at p. 375 as running 'contrary to fundamental principles of the law of contract'. It is difficult to see that it is an inevitable consequence of *Re Benjamin Cope and Sons Ltd.* Nevertheless it has been accepted as a correct statement of the law in Alberta, in

Northland Bank v *GIC Industries Ltd* (1985) 36 Alta LR (2d) 200, in which the appointment of a receiver under a second floating charge was held to crystallise a first floating charge without considering what effect the receivership had on the company's business activities.

The Cork Committee (Cmnd 8558, 1982) recommended (para. 1580) that a floating charge should crystallise on the appointment of a receiver under any other floating charge on any assets or property of the company, and did not mention what should happen if crystallisation of another floating charge occurred in some other way. If the decision in *Griffiths* v *Yorkshire Bank plc* [1994] 1 WLR 1427 that crystallisation of a second floating charge gives it priority over the first is correct then it will become normal for a floating charge contract to provide that it will crystallise if any other floating charge given by the company crystallises by any means, whether or not it causes cessation of the company's business.

(d) If the charge contract so provides, when the chargee gives notice that the charge is converted into a fixed charge on whatever assets of the charged class are owned by the company at the time the notice is given (*Re Brightlife Ltd* [1987] Ch 200).

(e) If the company deals with charged assets otherwise than with a view to carrying on its business (*Fire Nymph Products Ltd* v *Heating Centre Pty Ltd* (1992) 7 ACSR 365).

(f) On the occurrence of any other event which is defined in the charge contract to be an event which causes crystallisation (*Stein* v *Saywell* (1969) 121 CLR 529; *Re Manurewa Transport Ltd* [1971] NZLR 909; *Re Permanent Houses (Holdings) Ltd* [1988] BCLC 563; *Fire Nymph Products Ltd* v *Heating Centre Pty Ltd*; *Covacich* v *Riordan* [1994] 2 NZLR 502). A provision in a floating charge contract that the charge is to crystallise on the happening of a certain event without any action by the chargee is usually described as a provision for 'automatic crystallisation'.

It is often suggested that the ease with which a floating charge can crystallise, especially under a provision for automatic crystallisation, is inconvenient, both for persons dealing with the company, who can never be sure whether a floating charge on its assets has crystallised, and for the company itself, and even for the chargee, who may not want the charge to crystallise. See the discussion in the Cork Committee report (Cmnd 8558, 1982), paras 1570–81. Nevertheless courts have no grounds on which they can refuse to give effect to contractual provisions for automatic crystallisation — see the judgments in *Re Brightlife Ltd* [1987] Ch 200 and *Covacich* v *Riordan*.

11.6.3 Rights conferred by a floating charge before crystallisation

The floating charge was invented in order to provide a means of charging a company's current assets. The essential feature of a current asset of a company is that the company intends to bring its ownership of the asset to an end as quickly as possible and convert it into cash, or a claim to cash, which will be used to acquire a new current asset, and so on. The continual selling of current assets is the means by which the company will earn income from which it can meet the obligation secured by the floating charge. A company that has given a floating charge over its assets must nevertheless be able to sell them and, moreover, the assets must not remain subject to a charge after they have been sold, otherwise nobody would be able to buy from the company with certainty. However, the fact that an individual asset may be freely sold without consulting a chargee and is not subject to a charge in the hands of the buyer is inconsistent with the asset being charged at all.

Yet it is usual to say that, before a floating charge crystallises, it is an existing charge. In *Evans* v *Rival Granite Quarries Ltd* [1910] 2 KB 979 Fletcher Moulton LJ said, at p. 994:

[A floating charge] is an existing charge, and is rightly termed so, but care must be taken to remember that it has not settled down and fastened on the property which is the subject of the charge.

This raises the question whether, before a floating charge has crystallised, it gives the chargee any interest in, or rights over, the assets in the class charged. The courts have recognised that the holder of a floating charge has an interest in the charged property before crystallisation of the floating charge in the following cases:

(a)   If the class of assets covered by a floating charge includes land, the courts have recognised that, before the charge has crystallised, the chargee has an interest in land (*Driver v Broad* [1893] 1 QB 744; *Wallace v Evershed* [1899] 1 Ch 891; *Re Dawson* [1915] 1 Ch 626). In the last of these cases the Court of Appeal did acknowledge that the interest could properly be described as a contingent or future interest which would arise only if and when the charge crystallised, while emphasising that whether it was a present or future interest made no difference to the point raised in the case.

(b)   A person with a floating charge over a company's assets can, before the charge crystallises, obtain an injunction to prevent the company dealing with the assets otherwise than in the normal course of its business (*Re Woodroffes (Musical Instruments) Ltd* [1986] Ch 366 per Nourse J at p. 378).

(c)   A person with a floating charge over a company's assets may ask the court to appoint a receiver if something expected to be done to the assets threatens the security (*Re London Pressed Hinge Co. Ltd* [1905] 1 Ch 576, in which one of the company's creditors had obtained judgment against it and was in a position to have the property subject to the floating charge seized in execution).

(d)   When a floating charge crystallises it brings into effect an equitable interest which was created when the contract of floating charge was made and this takes precedence over any equitable interest created after the contract of floating charge was made. This is demonstrated by the cases of *Re Opera Ltd* [1891] 3 Ch 260, CA, and *Taunton v Sheriff of Warwickshire* [1895] 2 Ch 319, CA, in which the equitable interest created when a writ of *fieri facias* is delivered to a sheriff was held to be subordinate to the interest of the holder of a floating charge created before delivery of the writ and crystallising after delivery, but before the sheriff had sold the goods. The decision of the Divisional Court in *Davey & Co. v Williamson & Sons Ltd* [1898] 2 QB 194 that the same applied even if the floating charge has not crystallised was disapproved by the Court of Appeal in *Evans v Rival Granite Quarries Ltd.*

But the courts seem to be unwilling to give a floating chargee any further interest in, or rights over, assets in the class covered by the floating charge before it crystallises. In *Biggerstaff v Rowatt's Wharf Ltd* [1896] 2 Ch 93 a firm owed Rowatt's Wharf Ltd a debt which was, in common with the rest of the company's property, subject to a floating charge. Subsequently Rowatt's Wharf Ltd became liable to the firm for a larger sum in liquidated damages. Then the holder of the floating charge appointed a receiver, which crystallised the floating charge. The firm claimed it could set off the two debts and so did not have to pay anything to Rowatt's Wharf Ltd. Against this it was claimed that as soon as the firm became indebted to Rowatt's Wharf Ltd the debt was assigned to the chargees by virtue of the floating charge and this occurred before the liability to the firm arose so that set-off could not be allowed. The Court of Appeal held that there had been no assignment to the chargees before crystallisation of the floating charge and so the firm was entitled to set off the two debts.

In *Evans* v *Rival Granite Quarries Ltd* judgment had been given against the quarry company for a debt. The company was owed money by its bank so the judgment creditor obtained a garnishee order *nisi* against the bank. Evans had a floating charge on the quarry company to secure a debt which was due and payable, but Evans had never taken action to crystallise his charge. When he heard of the garnishee order he told the bank that as chargee of the company's property he was entitled to the money and it could not be attached by garnishee proceedings. It was held that Evans was not entitled to the money as he had no specific charge on any asset of the company. If he had wanted the money he should have appointed a receiver in order to crystallise his floating charge on the whole property of the company (including the money at the bank) but he could not claim one asset only.

Two alternative legal analyses of floating charges have been offered to explain how they affect assets before the charge has crystallised. The first is that a floating charge on a class of assets of a company is a charge on each and every asset in the class during the time that it is owned by the company, but that the charge is coupled with a licence to the company to deal with each asset without reference to the chargee, though only in the normal course of the company's business. The alternative analysis is that a floating charge is not a charge on any individual asset until the floating charge crystallises. In *Evans* v *Rival Granite Quarries Ltd* the Court of Appeal soundly rejected the first theory in favour of the second. Fletcher Moulton LJ said, at p. 997:

> While it is a floating security the company has a right, not a mere licence, to carry on its business until the debenture-holder intervenes.

Buckley LJ said, at pp. 999–1000:

> A floating security is not a future security; it is a present security, which presently affects all the assets of the company expressed to be included in it. On the other hand, it is not a specific security; the holder cannot affirm that the assets are specifically mortgaged to him. The assets are mortgaged in such a way that the mortgagor can deal with them without the concurrence of the mortgagee. A floating security is not a specific mortgage of the assets, plus a licence to the mortgagor to dispose of them in the course of his business, but is a floating mortgage applying to every item comprised in the security, but not specifically affecting any item until some event occurs or some act on the part of the mortgagee is done which causes it to crystallise. . . . [Counsel for Mr Evans] argued that it was competent to the mortgagee to intervene at any moment and to say that he withdrew the licence as regards any particular item. That is not in my opinion the nature of the security; it is a mortgage presently affecting all the items expressed to be included in it, but not specifically affecting any item till the happening of the event which causes the security to crystallise as regards all the items.

The idea that a floating charge gave any charge on specific assets before crystallisation was also rejected in cases involving debentures given by railway companies which conferred 'a charge upon the undertaking of the company' (*Attree* v *Hawe* (1878) 9 ChD 337) but it seems that an important factor in these cases was that it had been decided that an administrative receiver could not be appointed, only a receiver of income (because of the public importance of keeping the railway running) so that the debenture holders could never obtain possession of the charged property (see C. Stebbings, 'Statutory railway mortgage debentures and the courts in the 19th century' (1987) 8 J Legal Hist 36).

It is usually argued that the cases which have given floating chargees rights over the charged property before crystallisation have depended on the specific charge and licence theory, and that they could not be decided in the same way since the rejection of that theory by the Court of Appeal in *Evans* v *Rival Granite Quarries Ltd* (see D.M. Hare and D. Milman, 'Debenture holders and judgment creditors — problems of priority' [1982] LMCLQ 57). However, those cases have never been expressly overruled and must be regarded as still representing the law. It is also argued that since *Evans* v *Rival Granite Quarries Ltd* the courts will not give floating chargees any new rights over charged property before crystallisation. On this argument the decision in *Re Margart Pty Ltd* [1985] BCLC 314, New South Wales, that retention by a bank of money paid into the account of a company which had given the bank a floating charge over all its assets was not a disposition of the company's property, even if the floating charge had not crystallised, must be doubted. Helsham CJ in Eq said that a person with a floating charge over a company's property 'has a beneficial interest in the property the subject of the charge' (at p. 318) and that it is not a disposition of the company's property for a person with a beneficial interest in the property to obtain that property, or the proceeds of its realisation, from the company at a time when he is entitled to have it. Unfortunately his honour did not spell out how the entitlement to have the property arose in the case before him, but if the argument is that the entitlement arises just because the property is subject to a floating charge then it is respectfully submitted that this is contrary to the general understanding of the nature of a floating charge and contrary to *Evans* v *Rival Granite Quarries Ltd*. In subsequent Australian cases it has been held, following *Evans* v *Rival Granite Quarries Ltd*, that, before crystallisation, a floating charge over property does not confer any equitable interest in the property (*Tricontinental Corporation Ltd* v *Federal Commissioner of Taxation* (1987) 73 ALR 433; *Lyford* v *Commonwealth Bank of Australia* (1995) 130 ALR 267). But in an *obiter* discussion in *Wily* v *St George Partnership Banking Ltd* (1997) 150 ALR 329 the question was left open.

For discussion of these issues, see *R in Right of British Columbia* v *Federal Business Development Bank* [1988] 1 WWR 1, British Columbia; E. Ferran, 'Floating charges — the nature of the security' [1988] CLJ 213; K.J. Naser, 'The juridical basis of the floating charge' (1994) 15 Co Law 11.

S. Worthington, 'Floating charges — an alternative theory' [1994] CLJ 81 has suggested that the interest which a floating chargee of a class of assets of a company has in each asset in that class before crystallisation should be regarded in law as a fixed charge on each asset which is subject to defeasance when the company deals with the asset provided the dealing is in the ordinary course of business. However, it seems from *Re New Bullas Trading Ltd* [1994] 1 BCLC 485 (reported after Worthington's article went to press) that a defeasible fixed charge on a class of assets will be treated by the courts as a fixed charge not a floating charge. As will be explained in 11.6.4, creditors want their charges to be treated as fixed not floating charges and the idea of a defeasible fixed charge may enable them to achieve this.

11.6.4 Determining whether a charge is fixed or floating

From the chargee's point of view, a floating charge has the disadvantage that the chargee's debt may be subordinated to the company's preferential debts and expenses of liquidation (see 20.2.9). A chargee whose charge was created as a fixed charge may realise the security ignoring preferential creditors and liquidation expenses. Under a composite floating and fixed charge it is legitimate for the chargee to take the property subject to fixed charges and treat only the remainder as subject to the floating charge and therefore available to pay the preferential creditors and liquidation expenses (*Re Lewis Merthyr Consolidated Collieries*

Ltd [1929] 1 Ch 498, CA). Accordingly creditors want as many as possible of their security interests to be fixed charges, and it is common for contracts of charge to declare that they are creating fixed charges whether they are or not. However, the courts will not accept that the label that parties to a contract attach to it is a conclusive statement of its legal nature (*Street* v *Mountford* [1985] AC 809 per Lord Templeman at p. 819) and have sometimes found that contracts declared to be creating fixed charges in fact created floating charges. The courts have usually taken as their starting-point a passage in the judgment of Romer LJ in *Re Yorkshire Woolcombers Association Ltd* [1903] 2 Ch 284:

> ['Floating charge'] is not a legal term. It has recently been used in more than one statute; but when the courts have to consider whether the charge is a floating one within the meaning of the term as used in the Acts of Parliament, and in particular within the meaning of the Companies Act 1900 [which introduced the requirement to register charges at Companies House discussed in 11.7], one must, I think, deal with the question of substance to be answered according to the circumstance of each particular case. I certainly do not intend to attempt to give an exact definition of the term 'floating charge', nor am I prepared to say that there will not be a floating charge within the meaning of the Act, which does not contain all the three characteristics that I am about to mention, but I certainly think that if a charge has the three characteristics that I am about to mention it is a floating charge. (1.) If it is a charge on a class of assets of a company present and future; (2.) if that class is one which, in the ordinary course of the business of the company, would be changing from time to time; and (3.) if you find that by the charge it is contemplated that, until some future step is taken by or on behalf of those interested in the charge, the company may carry on its business in the ordinary way as far as concerns the particular class of assets I am dealing with.

If a contract of charge contemplates that the company will deal with the assets covered by the charge without reference to the chargee then it is likely to be a floating charge whereas if the assets can be dealt with only after being released from the charge by the chargee then it is likely to be a fixed charge. (See per Vaughan Williams LJ in *Re Yorkshire Woolcombers Association Ltd* [1903] 2 Ch 284 at p. 294 and on appeal sub nom. *Illingworth* v *Houldsworth* [1904] AC 355 per the Earl of Halsbury LC at pp. 357–8.) For example, in *R in Right of British Columbia* v *Federal Business Development Bank* [1988] 1 WWR 1 (British Columbia), the bank had obtained a charge over the entire property of a company which was expressed to be 'a fixed and specific mortgage and charge'. However, a further term of the charge contract permitted the company to 'continue to make sales of the inventory and stock in trade . . . in the ordinary course of its business until the bank shall notify it in writing to cease so doing'. It was held that the charge was a floating charge. In *Re G.E. Tunbridge Ltd* [1995] 1 BCLC 34 the charge contract purported to create a fixed charge over all the company's assets apart from land and the company's trading stock of goods held for resale. This would have covered items such as office equipment, tools and book debts which would obviously be changing from time to time, and as the other two characteristics noted by Romer LJ were also present it was held that this was a floating charge. If it is contemplated that the company may carry on business in the usual way with the charged assets (Romer LJ's third characteristic) and Romer LJ's other two characteristics are also present then the fact that the company is required to obtain the chargee's permission before dealing with the assets does not in itself make the charge a fixed charge (*Re G.E. Tunbridge Ltd*). On the other hand, if the charge is on assets which do not, in the ordinary course of business, change from time to time, then Romer LJ's second characteristic is not present and the charge is a fixed charge even if the company can deal with the assets without the chargee's permission (*Re Cimex Tissues Ltd* [1994] BCC 626, in which the charged items were machines up to 11 m long some of which had been in use for 30 years).

It has been difficult for a creditor of a company to establish a fixed charge on the company's book debts. Although it is common for a charge contract to describe a charge on book debts as a 'fixed charge' it will actually be a floating charge if it contemplates that the company will be free to use in its business the money it collects from its debtors without reference to the chargee (*Illingworth* v *Houldsworth*): to create a fixed charge it is necessary to require that money collected from debtors must be paid to or held for the chargee (*Siebe Gorman & Co. Ltd* v *Barclays Bank Ltd* [1979] 2 Lloyd's Rep 142; *Re Brightlife Ltd* [1987] Ch 200; *Re a Company (No. 005009 of 1987)* [1989] BCLC 13). In *William Gaskell Group Ltd* v *Highley* [1994] 1 BCLC 197, a charge on book debts which required them to be paid into a special account from which withdrawals could not be made without the chargee's approval was a fixed charge. The fact that the chargee can in practice determine what is done with money received by the company because of being a director is not enough to turn a floating charge on book debts into a fixed charge: a director must act in the company's interests, not in his or her own interests as a creditor (*Re Double S Printers Ltd* (1998) *The Times*, 2 June 1998).

The difficulty of creating a charge on a company's book debts which avoids the Insolvency Act 1986, s. 40, but still allows the company to use the money it collects from debtors appears to have been ingeniously solved by the drafter of a charge contract considered in *Re New Bullas Trading Ltd* [1994] 1 BCLC 485. The charge contract in that case created what was called a fixed charge on book debts and provided that money collected from debtors was to be paid into an account at a named bank and then applied as directed by the chargee but that if no directions were given the money was 'released' from the fixed charge and made subject to a floating charge. No directions were ever given. The Court of Appeal held that, at the time when administrative receivers were appointed, uncollected debts were subject to a fixed charge and were therefore not covered by the Insolvency Act 1986, s. 40. It will be interesting to see whether the drafters of charge contracts can extend this idea, which seems to have similarities with the idea of the defeasible fixed charge (see 11.6.3), to charges on other classes of assets and whether this will be permitted by the courts. If creditors can evade the Insolvency Act 1986, s. 40, by drafting charge contracts to create what the courts will accept as being fixed charges, even if they have the same effect as floating charges, then the floating charge will be forgotten except as a danger to be avoided. If this works then the lawyers who drafted the contract in *Re New Bullas Trading Ltd* will have achieved a success comparable to the 19th-century invention of hire-purchase as a means of evading the Bills of Sale Acts 1878 and 1882. However, the government, whose debts are paid by s. 40, could get Parliament to change the statute law to regain what it might lose if creditors can stop using floating charges. Professor Goode, in 'Charges over book debts: a missed opportunity' (1994) 110 LQR 592, argues that it is wrong to divide a charge on a debt into separate charges on the debt before collection and the collected debt; for further discussion see S. Griffin, 'The effect of a charge over book debts; the indivisible or divisible nature of the charge?' (1995) 46 NILQ 163.

If a company leases an item of its property to another person and gives a charge on the lease then that charge is a fixed charge (*Re Atlantic Computer Systems plc* [1992] Ch 505) even if it is expressed to cover any future lease of the same item of property (*Re Atlantic Medical Ltd* [1993] BCLC 386). A charge on a lease charges the rental payments receivable by the lessor. The court will not analyse the charge into two separate charges: one on the lease and one on the payments due under the lease (*Re Atlantic Medical Ltd*) though presumably the charge contract could do that in the same way as the contract in *Re New Bullas Trading Ltd* separately charged a debt and payment of the debt.

In *Re CCG International Enterprises Ltd* [1993] BCLC 1428, a contract giving to a bank a floating charge on a company's assets required the company to insure all the charged assets and required any money received under the insurance policy to be paid into an account designated by the bank and used as the bank directed either to reduce the debt secured by the charge or to replace the lost assets. It was held that this created a fixed charge on the insurance money.

11.6.5 Avoidance of a floating charge securing a debt incurred before the charge was created

11.6.5.1 By a liquidator

The Insolvency Act 1986, s. 245, is intended to prevent an unsecured creditor of a company obtaining a floating charge to secure the existing debt and thus gain an advantage over other unsecured creditors. It enables a liquidator of a company to call in question floating charges created by the company in a certain period before the commencement of the winding up. The period is 12 months for charges granted to persons not connected with the company but two years for charges granted to persons who are connected.

The following are connected with a company (s. 249):

(a) a director or shadow director of the company;
(b) an associate of a director or shadow director of the company; and
(c) an associate of the company.

Section 435 of IA 1986 defines who is an associate of a person. The section is long and detailed, and should be read in its entirety, but, in summary, the associates of a person include that person's spouse and relatives, business partners and their spouses and relatives, and companies of which the person and his associates have control. Two companies are associates of each other if they are under the control of one person or of a number of associated persons. Employer and employee are associated with each other (s. 435(4)).

A liquidator cannot avoid a floating charge given to a person *not connected with* the company unless the company was unable to pay its debts when it gave the charge or became unable to do so 'in consequence of the transaction under which the charge is created' (s. 245(4)). Whether or not a company is unable to pay its debts is to be determined by the criteria set out in s. 123 (see 20.6.3). If a floating charge was given to a person *connected* with the company within the two years preceding commencement of winding up then it can be avoided regardless of the company's financial position at the time. (If the company has been under administration then financial position is also irrelevant when considering a charge given within the 12 months preceding commencement of winding up to a person not connected with the company if it was given in the period while the petition on which the administration order was made was pending.)

The effect of s. 245 is that, when a company is being wound up, the property charged by a floating charge that can be avoided under the section cannot be utilised by, or on behalf of, the chargee to pay anything other than:

(a) The value of so much of the consideration for the creation of the charge as consists of money paid, or goods or services supplied, to the company at the same time as, or after, the creation of the charge.

(b)   The value of so much of that consideration as consists of the discharge or reduction, at the same time as, or after, the creation of the charge, of any debt of the company.

(c)   The amount of such interest (if any) as is payable on amounts falling within (a) or (b) in pursuance of any agreement under which the money was so paid, the goods or services were so supplied or the debt was so discharged or reduced.

For the purposes of this provision, the value of goods or services supplied is the amount of money which, at the time they were supplied, could reasonably have been expected to be obtained for supplying them in the ordinary course of business on the same terms (apart from consideration) as those on which they were supplied to the company (s. 245(6)). In the past it had been thought that money paid, or goods or services supplied, before the charge was created but in anticipation of and in reliance on it being created would be covered by the charge (*Re Fairway Magazines Ltd* [1993] BCLC 643) but the Court of Appeal in *Power* v *Sharp Investments Ltd* [1994] 1 BCLC 111 has held that this is not so.

If the floating charge crystallised before commencement of winding up and the property has already been utilised for paying amounts not permitted by s. 245 then the liquidator cannot recover the money because s. 245 comes into operation only in liquidation (ss. 238(1)(b) and 245(1); *Mace Builders (Glasgow) Ltd* v *Lunn* [1987] Ch 191, CA; *Power* v *Sharp Investments Ltd*).

The debts which s. 245 does not permit to be paid using charged property are debts incurred before the floating charge was created. If the person who was granted a floating charge which is invalid under s. 245 was previously an unsecured creditor of the company then the charged property cannot be utilised to repay money advanced for the purpose of reducing the previously unsecured obligation. It is not permitted to substitute a secured loan for an unsecured one — see *Re G. T Whyte & Co. Ltd* [1983] BCLC 311, in which the new secured loan was made by a wholly owned subsidiary of the unsecured creditor but Nourse J found that the floating charge was 'in substance' created to secure the past indebtedness to the unsecured creditor: it is submitted that the case would be decided in the same way under the new legislation. In *Re Fairway Magazines Ltd* [1993] BCLC 643, the person who had been granted a floating charge which was invalid under s. 245 advanced money for the specific purpose of reducing a debt of the company which he had guaranteed: it was held that this was a substitution of a secured debt for an unsecured obligation (the obligation to reimburse whatever was paid under the guarantee) and the charged property could not be used to repay the advance.

Although charged property cannot be used for paying certain debts if a charge is avoided under this provision, the debts themselves are still payable (*Re Parkes Garage (Swadlincote) Ltd* [1929] 1 Ch 139).

The intention of the chargee is irrelevant to the question of whether the charge is valid, and a charge may be declared invalid even though the chargee was not connected with the company and did not know it was insolvent; likewise it is unnecessary to show that the conduct of the chargee was underhand (*Re G. T Whyte & Co. Ltd*).

The legislation permits an unsecured creditor of an insolvent company to obtain a fixed charge but not a floating charge. The Cork Report (Cmnd 8558, 1982) suggested that it was acceptable to allow a creditor to take a fixed charge on property already owned by the company but not to take a floating charge which, on crystallisation, will attach property acquired by the company after giving the charge and probably acquired on credit. The Report pointed out that there may be advantages in permitting a creditor to take a charge and allow the company to continue in business rather than press immediately for payment: this is in line with its view that companies in difficulty should be given the opportunity of working their way out of the difficulty wherever possible.

If a bank obtains a floating charge over the property of an insolvent company as 'continuing security' for 'all present or future indebtedness to the bank on current account' then each payment out of the account after the charge is given is money paid to the company in consideration for the charge. If the account was overdrawn at the time the charge was given, then payments into the account are presumed to pay off the existing overdraft on a first-in-first-out basis (*Devaynes* v *Noble, Clayton's Case* (1816) 1 Mer 572) and the bank will be left with debts incurred after the charge was created and for which the charge may be utilised (*Re Yeovil Glove Co. Ltd* [1965] Ch 148, CA).

11.6.5.2 By an administrator

The provisions of the Insolvency Act 1986, s. 245, invalidating floating charges given to secure existing debts (see 11.6.5.1) apply with the necessary changes to a company under administration (ss. 245(1) and 238(1)(a)). A chargee whose floating charge could be avoided under this provision cannot veto the making of an administration order (s. 9(3)(b)(ii); see 20.3.2).

A floating charge on a company's property may be avoided by the company's administrator if it was created at any time within the period of 12 months before the date of presentation of the petition on which the administration order was made, or during the time that the petition was pending, and this period is extended to two years for charges given to persons connected with the company (see 11.6.5.1).

11.7 REGISTRATION OF CHARGES ON COMPANY PROPERTY

11.7.1 Introduction

A person contemplating giving credit to a company may be encouraged to do so by the value of its assets, which could be seized in execution of any judgment obtained against the company. But the value of assets to one creditor is reduced or nullified if they have already been charged to another creditor. Accordingly, there is a system which requires every company to make available information about charges on its assets. Charges have to be recorded in a register kept by the company and in the companies charges register kept by the registrar of companies. The legislation on the subject is in part XII (ss. 395 to 424) of CA 1985.

Registration of charges with the registrar of companies began on 1 January 1901. CA 1862 had required each limited company to keep at its registered office a register of charges on its own property. However, only members of the company and existing creditors had a right to inspect this register, and if a charge was not entered in the register then it did not become ineffective in any way (*Wright* v *Horton* (1887) 12 App Cas 371, HL) though fines could be imposed on company officers for failure to register.

The introduction of the companies charges register, which may be inspected by anyone, together with a rule that an unregistered charge would be void against a liquidator or a subsequent chargee (and, since the introduction of the administration procedure, an administrator), was a great improvement in protection for creditors. There have long been problems in the operation of the companies charges register, particularly over discovering which arrangements had to be registered and which could not be registered, and how the system for registration of charges on company property interacted with the other systems for registration of charges on particular types of property. Parliament enacted a revised system for registration of company charges in CA 1989, part IV (ss. 92 to 107). However, it seems that some aspects of this revised system will cause problems, and it has been thought unfortunate that the revision was drafted without taking into consideration the reforms suggested by Professor Diamond (see 11.3). Accordingly part IV of CA 1989 has not been brought into force and the whole subject is under review by the Department of Trade and Industry. In this edition we will describe the law contained in part XII of CA 1985 as this was the law in force when this edition went to press. There was a brief description of part IV of CA 1989 in the 10th edition of this work, and a detailed discussion of it, and how it relates to the 1985 Act, can be found in E. Ferran and C. Mayo, 'Registration of company charges — the new regime' [1991] JBL 152. N.J.M. Grier, 'The Companies Act 1989 — a curate's egg?' (1995) 16 Co Law 3 lists some of the failings of CA 1989, part IV. The DTI has issued a consultative document, *Company Law Reform: Proposals for Reform of Part XII of the Companies Act 1985* (URN 94/635) (London: DTI, 1994).

11.7.2 Registration in the companies charges register

Under ss. 395(1) and 396(1) of CA 1985 the following charges must be registered with the registrar of companies in England and Wales within 21 days of being created by any company registered in England and Wales:

(a)   a charge securing an issue of debentures (see chapter 12);
(b)   a charge on uncalled share capital of the company;
(c)   a charge created or evidenced by an instrument which, if executed by an individual, would require registration as a bill of sale (see 11.3);
(d)   a charge on land or any interest in land, other than a rentcharge;
(e)   a charge on book debts of the company;
(f)   a floating charge on the undertaking or property of the company;
(g)   a charge on calls made but not paid;
(h)   a charge on a ship or aircraft, or any share in a ship;
(i)   a charge on goodwill, or on any intellectual property.

By s. 396(3A), the following are 'intellectual property':

(a)   any patent, trade mark, registered design, copyright or design right;
(b)   any licence under or in respect of any such right.

Charges on a company's property must be registered even if the property is situated outside England and Wales, but for a charge created outside the UK on property situated outside the UK the time-limit for registration is 21 days from the date on which the instrument creating the charge could have been received in the UK in due course of post (CA 1985, s. 398(2)).

It is the duty of a company to register any charges it creates, but registration may be effected by any person interested in a charge s. 399(1)). In practice the chargee normally performs the registration. There is now no fee for registering a charge.

If a company acquires property that is subject to a charge that would have been registrable if the company had created it then the company must register the charge within 21 days after the date on which the acquisition is completed (s. 400).

11.7.3 Effect of failure to register

If a registrable charge, which a company has created over its own property, is unregistered when the time-limit has expired then, as from the end of the time-limit the chargee's right of recourse against the charged property becomes 'void against the liquidator or administrator and any creditor of the company' (CA 1985, s. 395(1)). Another creditor who obtains a charge over the same property, and registers it, will be entitled to recourse against that property without regard to the unregistered chargee. If the company commences winding up then the liquidator can take the property and sell it without regard to the unregistered chargee: the proceeds of the sale will then be available for the benefit of the company's creditors generally, and the unregistered chargee loses the priority which would otherwise have been conferred by the charge. If an administration order is made in relation to the company then the administrator can sell the property without regard to the unregistered charge.

An unregistered registrable charge is void as against a liquidator, administrator or other creditor only; it is not, for example, void as against the company so that if the company has no unpaid creditors and is not in liquidation or under administration the charge is completely effective (though the company could instantly avoid it by going into liquidation).

The disabilities of non-registration do not apply until the time-limit for registration has expired. If a company creates a charge over its property and, before the time-limit for its registration has expired, sells the property or creates another charge over it then priorities will be determined by the rules set out in 11.4.3 (*Re Ehrmann Brothers Ltd* [1906] 2 Ch 697, CA; *Watson* v *Duff Morgan & Vermont (Holdings) Ltd* [1974] 1 WLR 450).

A liquidator, administrator or creditor may ingore an unregistered charge despite having specific notice of it by some other means. In *Re Monolithic Building Co.* [1915] 1 Ch 643, CA, the company charged its land to secure repayment of a loan made to it by a woman named Tacon. The joint managing directors were present when the company's seal was put on the charge contract. Because of an error in a standard textbook the charge was not registered by the solicitor who had arranged it. Nine months later the company gave a floating charge over its property to one of the joint managing directors and this charge was registered. It was held that the director was entitled to the company's property free of Tacon's charge.

If a registrable charge on the property of a company is not registered within the time-limit then the company, and every officer of the company who knowingly and wilfully authorised or permitted the failure to register, commits an offence triable either way (ss. 399(3) and 730(5) and sch. 24).

If when the time-limit for registration expires a registrable charge is not registered then the money secured by the charge becomes immediately payable (s. 395(2)).

If a company acquires property subject to a registrable charge created by a previous owner, and fails to register the charge, then the only sanctions are criminal (s. 400(4)); the charge itself remains effective as against all persons.

11.7.4 Registration procedure

To register a charge created by a company on its own property, the document creating or evidencing the charge must be sent to the registrar together with the 'prescribed particulars' of the charge (CA 1985, s. 395(1)), which are the particulars specified in form 395 (Companies (Forms) Regulations 1985 (SI 1985 No. 854), reg. 4(2)). If the charge was created outside the UK on property situated outside the UK then it is permissible to file a copy for the purposes of CA 1985, s. 395 (CA 1985, s. 398(1)).

The particulars asked for on form 395 are:

(a) name and number of the registering company;

(b)   date and description of the instrument creating or evidencing the charge;
(c)   names, addresses and descriptions of the chargees;
(d)   short particulars of the property charged.

If the charge is on property situated in Scotland or Northern Ireland and the original document has been registered there then, for the purposes of s. 395, it is only necessary to submit a copy of the original and a certificate that the original has been registered in Scotland or Northern Ireland (s. 398(4)).

If the charge was created by a previous owner on property that the company has acquired subject to the charge then it is necessary to file a certified copy of the document creating or evidencing the charge (s. 400(2)) plus the particulars set out in form 400, which asks for the same particulars as does form 395.

As well as filing the original of any document creating or evidencing a charge with the registrar of companies (or filing a copy if the original has to be filed elsewhere), a company must keep a copy of the document at its registered office (s. 406) and must allow it to be inspected by any creditor or member of the company, without fee, during at least two hours on every business day (s. 408(1)).

11.7.5   Registration of a charge does not give notice of the terms of the charge

Registration of a charge in the register of charges constitutes notice to the whole world that a charge of a particular type exists but does not constitute notice of the terms and conditions of the charge (*Re Standard Rotary Machine Co. Ltd* (1906) 95 LT 829; *Wilson v Kelland* [1910] 2 Ch 306). It is common, for example, to put a negative pledge in a contract giving a floating charge (see 11.6.1), but registration of such a floating charge has been held not to constitute notice of the prohibition to a third party who, for valuable consideration, actually obtains a charge on the company's assets with priority over the floating charge. In *G & T Earle Ltd v Hemsworth Rural District Council* (1928) 44 TLR 605, Wright J said:

> the debentures having been duly registered . . . the plaintiffs, like all the world, are deemed to have constructive notice of the fact that there are debentures. But it has never been held that the mere fact that persons in the position of the plaintiffs have constructive notice of the existence of debentures also affects them with constructive notice of the actual terms of the debentures or that the debentures are subject to the restrictive condition to which these debentures were subject. No doubt it is quite common for debentures to be subject to this limiting condition as to further charges, but that fact is not enough in itself to operate as constructive notice of the actual terms of any particular set of debentures.

This decision has been followed by the Supreme Court in the Republic of Ireland, where the registration system is essentially the same as in England and Wales (*Welch v Bowmaker (Ireland) Ltd* [1980] IR 251).

It is common for banks (and probably others) when registering floating charges granted to them to include in form 395 a statement that the charge contract prohibits the creation of prior fixed charges, even though this is not one of the prescribed particulars (though it is in Scotland — see form 410). Whether this will constitute constructive notice of the prohibition has yet to be tested in the courts.

In *Ian Chisholm Textiles Ltd v Griffiths* [1994] 2 BCLC 291, the learned deputy judge expressed a 'tentative view' that a person who acquires an interest in property of a company while actually, rather than constructively, informed that the property had been charged would be deemed to be informed of all provisions of the charge contract (in particular a negative pledge clause) because a reasonably prudent purchaser acting on skilled advice would have taken the trouble to read the contract.

11.7.6 Certificate of registration

After entering details of a charge in the register the registrar is required to give a certificate which is 'conclusive evidence that the requirements of [chapter I of part XII of CA 1985] as to registration have been complied with' (CA 1985, s. 401(2)(b)). If a person fills in form 395 incorrectly but the registrar nevertheless issues a certificate of registration then the certificate cannot be challenged. The details on the register (which are taken from form 395) will be wrong and persons inspecting the register will be misled but the actual charge as created by the company is deemed to have been duly registered and so must be observed by the company's creditors and its liquidator (*National Provincial & Union Bank of England* v *Charnley* [1924] 1 KB 431, CA; *Re Mechanisations (Eaglescliffe) Ltd* [1966] Ch 20). So in *Re C.L. Nye Ltd* [1971] Ch 442, CA, the Westminster Bank had lent money to C.L. Nye Ltd and obtained a charge on the company's land as security. The charge contract was not dated and the bank's solicitor forgot to register it with the registrar of companies. Several months later the company was in trouble and the bank decided to realise its security. The solicitor inserted that day's date on the charge contract, delivered it to the registrar of companies for registration and obtained a certificate under what is now s. 401(2). The company's liquidator contended he could ignore the charge because it was not registered within 21 days of creation. It was held that the certificate was conclusive evidence that 'the requirements . . . as to registration' had been fulfilled, which must mean that it was registered within 21 days of creation, since that was one of the requirements.

Because the registrar's certificate is deemed to be conclusive evidence that the requirements as to registration have been complied with, it is impossible for there to be proceedings for judicial review of the registrar's decision to register a charge, because such proceedings would involve giving evidence that the requirements as to registration were not complied with (*R* v *Registrar of Companies, ex parte Central Bank of India* [1986] QB 1114, CA). See G. McCormack, 'Conclusiveness in the registration of company charge procedure' (1989) 10 Co Law 175.

11.7.7 Memorandum of satisfaction

By CA 1985, s. 403 if a charge on any property of a company has been registered then, on receipt of prescribed evidence from the company, the registrar must note on the register any of the following facts:

(a) that the security has been discharged by meeting the obligation secured;
(b) that part of the obligation secured has been met;
(c) that part of the charged property has been released from the charge;
(d) that part of the charged property has ceased to belong to the company.

The prescribed evidence is a statement of the fact under the seal of the company together with a statutory declaration of the truth of the statement made jointly by a director and the secretary of the company.

11.7.8 Inspection of the register

Anyone may inspect the company charges register on payment of the appropriate fee (CA 1985, s. 401(3)).

11.7.9 Extension of time-limits and rectification of the register

Under CA 1985, s. 404, the court has power to permit registration outside the 21-day time-limit and also power to order rectification of an erroneous entry in the register of charges. It may do this if satisfied that the failure to register or the misstatement in the register was 'accidental, or due to inadvertence or to some other sufficient cause, or is not of a nature to prejudice the position of creditors or shareholders of the company, or that on other grounds it is just and equitable to grant relief'. This power is discretionary and an application to the court to exercise it must be supported by full evidence of the reasons for non-registration or mistaken registration (*Re Kris Cruisers Ltd* [1949] Ch 138).

If a charge has already been registered then s. 404 empowers the court only to correct errors within the register entry: the court does not have power, either under s. 404 or under its inherent jurisdiction, to order the removal from the register of an entire entry relating to a charge (*Exeter Trust Ltd* v *Screenways Ltd* [1991] BCLC 888).

If the court makes an order extending the time for registration of a charge and the charge is registered accordingly and a certificate of registration is issued then the certificate is conclusive evidence that the charge has been duly registered, even if the court's order permitting registration is overruled (*Wilde* v *Australian Trade Equipment Pty Ltd* (1981) 145 CLR 590; *Exeter Trust Ltd* v *Screenways Ltd*).

The court may impose 'such terms and conditions as seem to the court just and expedient'. When a late registration is permitted the court always makes the proviso that the registration is to be without prejudice to the rights of any parties acquired prior to the time when the charge is actually registered (*Re I.C. Johnson & Co. Ltd* [1902] 2 Ch 101, CA). For example, in *Re Monolithic Building Co.* (discussed in 11.7.3) Tacon had been permitted to register her charge 13 months after it was created but the director had acquired rights under his charge four months before that registration and so his charge continued to have priority over Tacon's charge. As a charge does not become ineffective until after the time-limit for registration has expired the standard proviso applies only to rights acquired after the normal time-limit expired (*Re Ehrmann Brothers Ltd* [1906] 2 Ch 697, CA; *Watson* v *Duff Morgan & Vermont (Holdings) Ltd* [1974] 1 WLR 450). A person who became an unsecured creditor of the company during the time that the charge was wrongly unregistered is not paid any attention by the court when permitting registration out of time, on the ground that an unsecured creditor of a company always takes the risk that a charge may be created over its assets (*Re MIG Trust Ltd* [1933] Ch 542, point not considered on appeal).

The court will not make an order under s. 404 extending time once a winding up has supervened unless there are exceptional circumstances. It is therefore the practice of the court to seek an assurance that the company is solvent and that no liquidation is impending before extending time (*Re Ashpurton Estates Ltd* [1983] Ch 110; *Re Resinoid & Mica Products Ltd* [1983] Ch 132; *Re L.H. Charles & Co. Ltd* [1935] WN 15) and to insert a term in the order giving a liquidator the right to challenge it (a '*Re Charles* term').

For a detailed discussion of this matter, see G. McCormack, 'Extension of time for registration of company charges' [1986] JBL 282.

11.7.10 Matters that do not require registration

If a person acquires rights over a company's property that do not have to be registered with the registrar of companiecs then the rights will not become void against subsequent chargees or an administrator or liquidator of the company. Arguments over whether or not an acquisition of rights should have been registered resolve into three questions:

(a)   Do the rights constitute a charge?
(b)   If the rights constitute a charge, is it one of the charges listed in CA 1985, s. 396(1)?
(c)   Were the rights created by the company?

11.7.10.1 Rights over property that are not charges

An agreement to give a charge is itself a charge (and so may be registrable) if it is immediately enforceable but not if it is contingent (*Re Jackson & Bassford Ltd* [1906] 2 Ch 467). For example, in *Williams* v *Burlington Investments Ltd* (1977) 121 SJ 424, HL, a landowner sold some farmland to a property development company. Under the sale contract the company was to pay £20,000 plus an additional amount if it should obtain planning permission for development of any of the land within the following 15 years. A term of the contract provided that if any additional amounts became payable then the landowner could, if he wished, require the development company to give a charge by way of legal mortgage of the land to secure payment of the additional amount. It was held that this contract did not require registration with the registrar of companies.

A contractual right to retain possession of a company's goods until payment has been received for transporting, storing or working on them (a contractual 'lien') is not a charge, even if the contract gives a right to sell the goods if the debt is not paid (*Re Hamlet International plc* (1998) *The Times*, 13 March 1998).

It is sometimes difficult to distinguish between a contract giving a mortgage or charge over property and a contract for the sale of property. In *Welsh Development Agency* v *Export Finance Co. Ltd* [1992] BCLC 148, Dillon LJ said (at p. 161) that 'there is no one clear touchstone' for making the distinction, though in the past it has been emphasised that a mortgage or charge is regarded by the parties as only one method of satisfying a financial obligation, and if the obligation is met in some other way then the mortgage or charge ceases to have any effect. As Slade J said in *Re Bond Worth Ltd* [1980] Ch 228 at p. 248:

> In my judgment, any contract which, by way of security for the payment of a debt, confers an interest in property defeasible or destructible upon payment of such debt, or appropriates such property for the discharge of the debt, must necessarily be regarded as creating a mortgage or charge, as the case may be.

The cases which have caused the greatest difficulty have been where a company has assigned to one of its creditors its right to receive money from one of its debtors. If this is done simply to pay the creditor, the assignment is not a charge on a book debt and need not be registered. If the assignment is made as security for payment of the creditor, contemplating that on payment of the creditor in some other way the assignment would be cancelled, the assignment is a charge on a book debt and will be void against a liquidator unless registered.

In *Re Kent & Sussex Sawmills Ltd* [1947] Ch 177, the company's bank allowed it an overdraft to finance work on a large contract for the Ministry of Fuel and Power. The bank required the company to write to the Ministry in the following terms:

we hereby authorise you to remit all moneys due [under the contract] direct to this company's account at Westminster Bank Ltd, Crowborough, whose receipt shall be your sufficient discharge. These instructions are to be regarded as irrevocable unless the said bank should consent to their cancellation in writing.

The bank contended that this was an outright assignment of the debts due under the contract and so the bank's failure to register the agreement as a charge on book debts was justified. The court held that the transaction was a charge, for otherwise there would be no need to make any statement about revocation.

By contrast, in *Siebe Gorman & Co. Ltd* v *Barclays Bank Ltd* [1979] 2 Lloyd's Rep 142, Siebe Gorman had supplied goods to a company called R.H. McDonald Ltd and was owed over £8,000 for them. But R.H. McDonald Ltd had bills of exchange, for just less than the amount of the debt, which were payable over a period of six months. These bills had been handed to the bank for collection. R.H. McDonald Ltd executed a deed assigning the bills to Siebe Gorman 'as security for' the debt owed to Siebe Gorman, and sent a letter to the bank instructing the bank to pay the proceeds of the bills direct to Siebe Gorman. The letter to the bank was expressed to be an irrevocable instruction. Slade J decided that the assignment was made in order to pay the debt and so held that the transaction was an absolute assignment and was not a contract of charge.

In *Orion Finance Ltd* v *Crown Financial Management Ltd* [1996] 2 BCLC 78, Atlantic Computer Systems Ltd had bought a computer on hire-purchase from Orion and leased it to Crown, assigning to Orion the rental payments due under the lease. The elaborate documents governing this deal (and numerous other similar transactions) repeatedly described the assignment as 'security' for the payment of the hire-purchase instalments, and stated that the rental payments were 'charged'. However, the contract had never been registered as a charge on Atlantic's book debts. The Court of Appeal held that there was no reason not to accept that the wording of the contract was the correct description of the transaction as intended by the parties, so the assignment was a charge on Atlantic's book debts and should have been registered as such (though this begs the question why, if it intended that the assignment should be by way of charge, Orion did not register it). The lease contract between Atlantic and Crown gave Crown an option to require Atlantic to make the lease payments for the last two years of the lease term. When Crown exercised this option, Atlantic was in insolvent liquidation. Orion's counsel put forward several extraordinarily ingenious arguments why Crown should be required to make the last two years' lease payments to Orion, but they were all rejected (*Orion Finance Ltd* v *Crown Financial Management Ltd (No. 2)* [1996] 2 BCLC 382).

In banking it is common for a bank to obtain security for a loan by means of a 'charge-back', which works as follows. A customer of a bank, with an account in credit, agrees that if a specified obligation owed to the bank, owed either by the customer or another person, is not met then the bank can use the balance in the account to meet it and is relieved from its contractual obligation to repay the credit balance to the customer. The legal categorisation of this agreement is difficult and has been the subject of much argument. In *Re Bank of Credit and Commerce International SA (No. 8)* [1996] Ch 245, CA; [1998] AC 214, HL, the question was argued by counsel and, though it was not necessary for the decision in the case, both the Court of Appeal and the House of Lords gave views on it. Unfortunately their views were totally opposed. In the Court of Appeal Millett LJ repeated the view he had expressed, when a High Court judge, in *Re Charge Card Services Ltd* [1987] Ch 150, at p. 175, that '. . . a charge in favour of a debtor of his own indebtedness to the chargor is conceptually impossible'. On this view a charge-back is merely a term of the banking contract between bank and customer and does not require registration as a charge. In the House of Lords Lord Hoffmann forcefully rejected this view and said that a charge-back is a charge. Lord Hoffmann saw a bank with a charge-back on a deposit as having an obligation to repay the deposit when required to do so by the customer and, separately, a charge on the customer's right to demand that repayment. The fact that the charge would be enforced merely by making entries in accounts does not, in Lord Hoffmann's view, mean that the banking contract and the security contract are merged. The other Law Lords said that they had read Lord Hoffmann's speech and agreed with his disposal of the appeal, without expressing any dissent from his view that a charge-back is a registrable charge, so that view carries great authority, even though it is *obiter*. For opposing commentaries see the casenotes by R. Calnan (1998) 114 LQR 174 (in favour of Lord Hoffmann) and R. Goode (1998) 114 LQR 178 (against Lord Hoffmann).

11.7.10.2 Charges that are not within s. 396(1)

CA 1985, s. 396(1), lists registrable charges. By implication, charges not on the list are not registrable. Some important examples of non-registrable charges are given in the following paragraphs.

A charge on any chose in action — other than the company's uncalled capital, calls made but not paid, goodwill, intellectual property and 'book debts' — is not registrable. For example, a charge on company shares or government stock owned by a company is not registrable, nor is a charge on an insurance policy owned by a company, nor is a charge on the benefit of a contract such as an option to purchase, nor is a charge on a share in a horse (*Re Sugar Properties (Derisley Wood) Ltd* [1988] BCLC 146). The DTI says that requiring registration of charges on shares owned by a company is impractical because actively traded share portfolios change so often (*Company Law Reform: Proposals for Reform of Part XII of the Companies Act 1985* (URN 94/635) (London: DTI, 1994), pp. 14–15).

The phrase 'book debts' in s. 396(1)(e) has never been satisfactorily defined. In *Independent Automatic Sales Ltd* v *Knowles & Foster* [1962] 1 WLR 974, Buckley J said, at p. 983:

> if it can be said of a debt arising in the course of a business and due or growing due to the proprietor of that business that such a debt would or could in the ordinary course of such a business be entered in well kept books relating to that business, that debt can properly be called a book debt whether it is in fact entered in the books of the business or not.

If, under a contract, a sum of money will become payable to a company if and when an uncertain event (a 'contingency') occurs, then the sum of money cannot be entered in the company's books as a debt due to it until the contingency occurs. Accordingly, a charge, created before the contingency has occurred, on the company's rights under such a contract has been held not to be a registrable charge on a book debt (*Paul & Frank Ltd* v *Discount Bank (Overseas) Ltd* [1967] Ch 348). But it has also been held that a charge, created before the contingency has occurred, on the amount payable under such a contract is a charge on a future book debt and is registrable (*Re Brush Aggregates Ltd* [1983] BCLC 320). The distinction drawn in these cases shows the arbitrariness of the present system of registering charges.

In normal commercial practice a company's 'cash at bank' is not considered to be a debt due to the company. Accordingly, a term in a charge contract providing for a charge on a company's book debts will normally be construed as not charging a credit balance on the company's bank account (*Re Brightlife Ltd* [1987] Ch 200; *Re Permanent Houses (Holdings) Ltd* [1988] BCLC 563; *Northern Bank Ltd* v *Ross* [1990] BCC 883). However, in law, the relationship between banker and customer is that of debtor and creditor, and the decisions just cited should not be taken as holding that a charge which is an effective charge on a company's bank balance is not registrable (*Re Permanent Houses (Holdings) Ltd*). The registrar considers that such a charge is registrable ((1985) 82 LS Gaz 2868).

If a company holds a negotiable instrument, such as a bill of exchange or promissory note, for the payment of a book debt owed to it then a charge on that instrument is a charge on the book debt and must be registered (*Chase Manhattan Asia Ltd* v *Official Receiver & Liquidator of First Bangkok City Finance Ltd* [1990] 1 WLR 1181). However, a charge created by deposit of such a negotiable instrument as security is exempt from registration (s. 396(2)) because the basis of such an arrangement is that the person with whom the instrument is deposited must be able to negotiate it.

The DTI has proposed that the term 'book debts' should be replaced by 'receivables' which should be given a statutory definition (*Company Law Reform: Proposals for Reform of Part XII of the Companies Act 1985* (URN 94/635) (London: DTI, 1994), p. 13).

All the charges that are not registrable with the registrar of companies do have to be entered in a company's own register of charges (see 11.7.12).

11.7.10.3   Retention of title by a seller
A contract of sale of goods may include a term stipulating that the property in the goods is not to pass until payment has been received by the seller (Sale of Goods Act 1979, s. 19(1)). Here 'property' means the general property in the goods (Sale of Goods Act 1979, s. 61), i.e., the legal title to them. Terms of sale of this nature are called retention of title agreements but they were little known in Britain until one was examined in the *Romalpa* case (*Aluminium Industrie Vaassen BV* v *Romalpa Aluminium Ltd* [1976] 1 WLR 676, CA) since when they have become common and are often called *Romalpa* clauses.

There have been several cases in which retention of title agreements have been examined but care must be exercised in drawing general conclusions from them because each decision has been made in the light of the wording of the particular contract involved and the commercial situation in which the dispute arose (per Robert Goff LJ in *Clough Mill Ltd* v *Martin* [1985] 1 WLR 111, CA).

If goods are sold to a buyer for resale by the buyer or for incorporation in the buyer's products then a retention of title agreement must include a provision permitting the buyer to use the goods in this way before title passes. Such a provision is not inconsistent with the legal title remaining with the seller (*Clough Mill Ltd* v *Martin*). Resale under such a provision is assumed to be for the first buyer's own account, not for the account of, or as agent for, the original supplier (*E. Pfeiffer Weinkellerei-Weineinkauf GmbH & Co.* v *Arbuthnot Factors Ltd* [1988] 1 WLR 150). Without such a provision a resale is without actual authority and is a conversion of the original seller's goods: nevertheless, provided the subpurchaser is acting in good faith, the contract of resale is made valid by the Factors Act 1889, s. 9, and the Sale of Goods Act 1979, s. 25, so that when its conditions concerning transfer of title are satisfied the subpurchaser acquires title to the goods and the original seller's retained title is extinguished.

This simple form of retention of title agreement does not constitute a charge on property of the buyer because rights are not granted over the buyer's own property: the goods are not the buyer's property until paid for (*Aluminium Industrie Vaassen BV* v *Romalpa Aluminium Ltd*; *Armour* v *Thyssen Edelstahlwerke AG* [1991] 2 AC 339, HL; see the definition in IA 1986, s. 251). Similarly, a conditional sale agreement is not a charge (*Paintin & Nottingham Ltd* v *Miller Gale & Winter* [1971] NZLR 164).

In *Re Bond Worth Ltd* [1980] Ch 228, a supplier of goods to Bond Worth Ltd had tried a different type of condition of sale. The sale contract provided that 'equitable and beneficial ownership shall remain with us [the supplier] until full payment has been received'. Slade J held that the supplier could not claim to pass legal title in goods to Bond Worth Ltd while retaining 'equitable and beneficial ownership'. He held that the 'equitable and beneficial ownership' must have been granted to the supplier by Bond Worth when Bond Worth became legal owner of the goods, and this was equivalent to creating a charge on the goods which should have been registered. As it had not been registered Bond Worth's liquidator could ignore it. It has been argued that the theoretical basis of this decision was removed by the House of Lords in *Abbey National Building Society* v *Cann* [1991] 1 AC 56 — see, for example, D. Turing, 'Retention of title: how to get value from a bad penny' (1995) 16 Co Law 119 — but this argument was rejected in *Stroud Architectural Systems Ltd* v *John Laing Construction Ltd* [1994] 2 BCLC 276.

In *Re Curtain Dream plc* [1990] BCLC 925, Curtain Dream plc sold its entire stock of curtaining fabric to Churchill Merchanting Ltd for cash under an arrangement which entitled Curtain Dream plc to repurchase the stock immediately on 90 days' credit (which is what happened) subject to retention of title by Churchill Merchanting Ltd until it received payment. There was no physical movement of the stock corresponding to the separate components of this transaction. Knox J held that what happened should be analysed as one global transaction, in which in fact the retention of title constituted a charge on Curtain Dream plc's fabric as security for a loan made by Churchill Merchanting Ltd. It was not a retention by Churchill Merchanting Ltd of title to its own fabric. As this charge had not been registered it was void as against the administrative receivers of Curtain Dream plc.

If goods subject to a retention of title agreement are used by the buyer in such a way that they lose their separate identity then there will be nothing in which the seller can retain title. It may be difficult to decide whether goods subject to a retention of title agreement lose their separate identity while in the buyer's possession. In *Hendy Lennox (Industrial Engines) Ltd* v *Grahame Puttick Ltd* [1984] 1 WLR 485, Staughton J held that an engine incorporated in a generator set could be so easily disconnected and removed that it remained separate and subject to a retention of title agreement. No case has yet been reported involving indistinguishable goods from different suppliers becoming mixed: in other contexts such mixtures have been held to be owned in common by the owners of the ingredients (see, e.g., *Gill & Duffus (Liverpool) Ltd* v *Scruttons Ltd* [1953] 2 All ER 977, in which it was said that such cases have to be dealt with *ad hoc*). It is possible to include a provision in a contract of sale of goods that anything made by the buyer from the goods will belong to the seller but this will normally be regarded as a charge on the buyer's goods (see the discussion of *Re Peachdart Ltd* [1984] Ch 131 and *Modelboard Ltd* v *Outer Box Ltd* [1993] BCLC 623 in the following paragraph). In *Ian Chisholm Textiles Ltd* v *Griffiths* [1994] 2 BCLC 291, an agreement that a seller of cloth should retain title to the cloth apparently contained no term specifying what was to happen when the cloth lost its separate identity by being made into garments. Curiously, the company conceded that the retention of title agreement still applied in some way to the garments, and David Neuberger QC (sitting as a deputy High Court judge) held that it created a charge on the garments in favour of the seller (which charge was void for non-registration). It is submitted that the true position is that the seller could not have had any interest in the garments unless the contract of sale provided for an interest to be created.

A supplier of goods who has stipulated for retention of title to the goods usually wishes to obtain some control over the proceeds of resale of the goods. A simple provision that the purchaser's rights against customers arising from reselling the goods are to be assigned to the supplier as security for the payment of the purchase price is a registrable charge on the book debts of the purchaser (*E. Pfeiffer Weinkellerei-Weineinkau GmbH & Co.* v *Arbuthnot Factors Ltd*; *Re Weldtech Equipment Ltd* [1991] BCLC 393). Some suppliers have tried a more sophisticated approach in which the purchaser, instead of being treated as trading on its own account, is turned into a mere agent for the supplier, or a mere bailee of the goods supplied, with a fiduciary obligation to account to the supplier for anything gained by dealing with the supplier's goods. There has to be an express provision to that effect: a retention of title agreement does not automatically make the buyer an agent or bailee of the seller (*Borden (UK) Ltd* v *Scottish Timber Products Ltd* [1981] Ch 25). However, the essence of such a contract is that the agency relationship is terminated when the debt to the supplier is paid and so it must be entered into as security for the payment of the debt. Accordingly the supplier's rights under such an arrangement, to money owed to the purchaser by its customers on dealing with the goods, constitute a registrable charge on the purchaser's book debts (*Tatung (UK) Ltd* v *Galex Telesure Ltd* (1988) 5 BCC 325; *Compaq Computer Ltd* v *Abercorn Group Ltd* [1993] BCLC 602). For further discussion, see S. Wheeler '*Pfeiffer* v *Arbuthnot;* good news for financiers of receivables' (1989) 10 Co Law 151; and J. de Lacy, 'Proceed with care' (1989) 10 Co Law 188. Similarly, a provision that any articles made by the buyer from the supplier's materials are to be the property of the supplier is really a charge because it is made on the basis that ownership of the articles will revert to the buyer as soon as the supplier has been paid (*Re Peachdart Ltd*; *Modelboard Ltd* v *Outer Box Ltd*). It seems that it is not possible for a retention of title agreement to give control over proceeds of resale without creating a charge that must be registered — see A. Hicks, '*Romalpa* is dead' (1992) 13 Co Law 217. For criticism of this result, asserting that the courts have misinterpreted such agreements, see J. de Lacy, 'When is a *Romalpa* clause not a *Romalpa* clause? When it is a charge on book debts' (1992) 13 Co Law 164.

11.7.10.4   *Rights arising by operation of law*
A right against the property of a company that arises by operation of law (such as a solicitor's lien or a vendor's lien) is not created by the company and so is not registrable (*London & Cheshire Insurance Co. Ltd* v *Laplagrene Property Co. Ltd* [1971] Ch 499).

In *Tatung (UK) Ltd* v *Galex Telesure Ltd* (1988) 5 BCC 325, Phillips J said that the fact that a retention of title agreement provided that the purchaser was to deal with the goods as agent of the supplier, as security for the payment of debts owed to the supplier, did not mean that the purchaser's obligation to account for the proceeds of reselling the goods arose only by operation of law (as one of the legal incidents of an agency relationship), and did not mean that it was not a right created by the purchaser. In his lordship's view the supplier's rights against resale proceeds arose out of the security arrangement created by the purchaser and therefore constituted a registrable charge created by the purchaser on its book debts.

11.7.11   Registration in property registers

If a company registered in England and Wales charges its land situated in England or Wales, its UK-registered aircraft, its British ships or its UK patents then the chargee should ensure that the charge is registered in the appropriate register for the kind of property charged as well as with the registrar of companies in England and Wales.

A floating charge is not a charge on any particular asset and so, even though a company that grants a floating charge may own land, ships, aircraft and patents, the charge cannot be registered in the registers for those kinds of property. (SI 1972 No. 1268, arts 2(2) and 4(1), expressly provide that a floating charge cannot be registered in the Register of Aircraft Mortgages.) Conversely, if a charge is registered in a property register as a charge on specific items of property, it would imply that dealing in those items could not take place without reference to the chargee, which would imply that the charge was a fixed charge on those items of property. The exception is unregistered land. The Land Charges Act 1972 permits the registration of 'a general equitable charge' (s. 2(4)(iii)) 'affecting land' (s. 2(1)), and this is wide enough to include a floating charge. Nevertheless in order to save work at the Land Charges Registry, the Land Charges Act 1972, s. 3(7) and (8), provide that registration of a floating charge with the registrar of companies in England and Wales is equivalent to registration in the Land Charges Register.

11.7.12   Company's own register of charges

Every company must keep at its registered office a copy of every instrument creating or evidencing a charge that has to be registered with the registrar of companies (CA 1985, s. 406). Every limited company must also keep at its registered office a register of 'all charges specifically affecting property of the company and all floating charges on the company's undertaking or any of its property' (s. 407(1)). The register must contain an entry for each charge giving a short description of the property charged, the amount of the charge and (unless it is a bearer security) the name of the persons entitled to it (s. 407(1)). Failure to comply with these provisions is an offence triable either way, even if the charge was given to the company officer who was responsible for the failure to register (s. 407(3) and sch. 24) but the failure does not affect the validity of the charge in any way (*Wright* v *Horton* (1887) 12 App Cas 371, HL).

A charge on a company's property that is created or evidenced by an instrument must be registered in the company's own register of charges whether or not it has to be registered with the registrar of companies. For example, in *Re South Durham Iron Co., Smith's Case* (1879) 11 ChD 579, it was held that it is necessary to register a negotiable warehouse warrant given as security for the repayment of a loan. Jessel MR said, 'The Act does not require you to register the instrument creating the charge, but the property charged'. A negotiable warehouse warrant is not registrable under s. 395 because (s. 396(1)(c)) if it were given by an individual it would not be registrable as a bill of sale (Bills of Sale Act 1878, s. 4). However, some charges have to be registered with the registrar but not in the company's own register. Only charges created by the company have to be registered in the company's own register of charges under s. 407, not, for example, a charge on property created before the company acquired the property (*Re General Horticultural Co. Ltd* (1885) 53 LT 699), whereas such a charge must be registered with the registrar by virtue of s. 400.

The register must be open to inspection by any person — see 4.4.1. The copies of instruments must be available for inspection by any member or creditor of the company — see 4.4.2.

12 *Marketable Loans*

12.1 INTRODUCTION

This chapter deals with arrangements by which a company borrows a large sum of money long term. The money is put up by a large number of investors who are entitled to receive interest payments (usually twice a year) and, at the end of the term of the loan, repayment of principal. Each investor in the loan is given the right to transfer all or part of his entitlements and the company would normally arrange for the loan to be listed on the London Stock Exchange. In recent years marketable loans have declined in importance as stock exchange investments though the highly specialised market for the form of marketable loan known as international bonds has grown considerably. Interests in marketable loans are called 'debt securities' or, in CA 1985, 'debentures'. Transfers of debt securities are generally exempt from stamp duty (Finance Act 1986, s. 79).

12.2 STOCK

For the purpose of measuring an individual investor's interest, when a company arranges a marketable loan it is nowadays usual to regard the whole amount borrowed as a 'stock' having a certain nominal value. This nominal value may be equal to, less than, or even greater than the amount actually loaned.

Each investor is regarded as being interested in a proportion of the stock, having a certain nominal value. He may transfer any proportion he wishes of his own interest.

The nominal value of a particular investor's stockholding is normally the same as the amount of principal to be paid to him by the company at the end of the term of the loan. In some marketable loans, the company promises that when it repays principal it will additionally pay a certain percentage of the principal as a bonus, known as a redemption premium. It is permissible to deduct an amount paid as a redemption premium from share premium account (CA 1985, s. 130(2)).

It is permissible to issue marketable loan securities at a discount, that is, for less than their nominal value (*Re Anglo-Danubian Steam Navigation & Colliery Co.* (1875) LR 20 Eq 339) and if this is done then it is permissible to deduct the shortfall from share premium account, i.e., to use share premium to repay part of the loan (s. 130(2)). Usually, however, the amount of the discount is written off over the term of the loan.

12.3 TRUSTEES

If debt securities are to be listed then it is usual for a trust to be constituted for the duration of the loan, with a trustee, or trustees, whose duty is to look after the interests of the stockholders. A trust for stockholders is invariably constituted in a deed.

A major advantage of a trust for a marketable loan is that security can be given for the loan by means of a contract between the company and the trustees. (Not all marketable loans are secured: those that are not are usually described as 'unsecured loan stock'.) The contract of security is normally incorporated in the deed constituting the trust, and it normally gives a floating charge on the company's business and property, and a fixed charge on the company's land.

When a trust has been constituted then the contract to pay interest and repay principal must be between company and trustee, not company and stockholder (*Re Uruguay Central & Hygueritas Railway Co. of Monte Video* (1879) 11 ChD 372; *Re Dunderland Iron Ore Co. Ltd* [1909] 1 Ch 446). The practical result of this is that only the trustee may take proceedings against the company, and this preserves the equality of the stockholders. Where security has been given in a contract with a trustee then only the trustee may enforce that security, for example, by appointing an administrative receiver under a floating charge. If a trustee is dilatory then any stockholder (as beneficiary of the trust) may ask the court to order the trustee to carry out his duties.

Any stockholder must, on request, be sent a copy, for which the company may charge a fee, of the trust deed covering his stock (whether secured or not) (CA 1985, s. 191(3)).

If the trust deed gives security then it must be sent to the registrar of companies for registration as a charge for the purpose of securing an issue of debentures (s. 396(1)(a) as originally enacted; see 11.7.2) and a copy must be kept available for inspection at the company's registered office.

12.4 STOCK CERTIFICATES

A stock certificate is a certificate given by a company that a person is the holder of stock to a specified nominal value.

A stock certificate issued in connection with a marketable loan is a written acknowledgement of a company's indebtedness and is therefore a 'debenture' for the purposes of CA 1985 (see 11.1). CA 1985, s. 744, says that the meaning of 'debenture' is to include debenture stock.

A stock certificate for a marketable loan may be made out to bearer and be transferable by delivery alone. Such a document is judicially recognised as being a negotiable instrument (*Bechuanaland Exploration Co.* v *London Trading Bank Ltd* [1898] 2 QB 658). In practice, bearer debentures are now as rare as share warrants to bearer (see 8.6) though bearer securities are normal in the market for international bonds (see 12.8). However, bearer debentures are exempt from stamp duty on issue and transfer (Finance Act 1986, s. 79(2)). Normally, issue and transfer of debenture stock and unsecured loan stock are through a register operated in the same way as a company's register of members. Normally a trust deed covering a marketable loan requires the company to maintain a register of stockholders.

If a company maintains a register of debenture holders then it must observe the same rules on where it must be kept, on provision of copies, and on permitting inspection of the register as apply to the register of members (see 4.4.1) except that a stockholder may not be charged a fee for inspecting the register (whereas, unless he is also a member, he may be charged a fee for inspecting the register of members).

12.5 CONTRACTS FOR THE ALLOTMENT OF DEBT SECURITIES

Company marketable loans are company securities and the law stated in chapter 7 applies to them, except that:

(a)   An allotment may be made however small a response there is to the offer — CA 1985, s. 84, does not apply to issues of debt securities.

(b)   There is no limitation on the payment of underwriting commission on marketable loans — CA 1985, s. 98, does not apply to marketable loans.

It was held in *South African Territories Ltd* v *Wallington* [1898] AC 309, HL, that a contract for the allotment of debentures would not be enforced by an order for specific performance, and so CA 1985, s. 195, gives a statutory power to the courts to order specific performance.

12.6   INFORMATION FOR DEBENTURE HOLDERS

The holder of any debenture of a company (i.e., any document it has issued evidencing indebtedness) is entitled to ask for a copy of the company's most recent annual accounts as submitted to its members (CA 1985, s. 239). Under s. 238(1), a company must send a copy of its annual accounts and reports to every holder of its debentures (unless it is unaware of a holder's address: s. 238(2)(a)) — see 9.3.6.2. Holders of debenture or loan stock are rarely, if ever, entitled to attend members' meetings.

12.7   CONVERTIBLES

Unsecured loan stock, or occasionally secured debenture stock, may carry a right to exchange the stock at a future date for shares of the company that issued the stock.

The trust deed covering the loan would specify how the number of shares to be allotted is to be related to the nominal value of stock given in exchange. Often there are several different dates on which conversion may be made, with a different exchange rate for each conversion period.

Convertible loan and debenture stocks are subject to stamp duty on transfer (Finance Act 1986, s. 79(5)). This is to be repealed by the Finance Act 1990, sch. 19, part VI, which had not been brought into force when this edition went to press. It was originally intended that the duty would be abolished when the London Stock Exchange introduced a paperless share transfer system.

The issue of convertible securities is subject to the rules on authority to allot discussed in 6.2.5 (CA 1985, s. 80(2)(b)). The issue of securities convertible into equity shares is subject to the rules on members' preemption rights discussed in 6.2.6 (CA 1985, s. 94(2)).

The terms of issue of a convertible security must not result in the company receiving less than the nominal value of the shares issued (*Mosely* v *Koffyfontein Mines Ltd* [1904] 2 Ch 108; CA 1985, s. 100).

12.8   INTERNATIONAL BONDS

A large company of undoubted creditworthiness may raise money in the specialised market for international bonds conducted by the Association of International Bond Dealers. A bond in this context is a bearer security of a certain nominal value issued for money by a company which promises payment of the nominal value at a certain date in the future and, usually, regular interest payments in the meantime. Attached to a bond is a sheet of 'coupons' which are detached and sent to the company (or a bank nominated by it as paying agent) to claim the interest payments. Some bonds are issued for much less than their nominal value and no interest is paid on them — the investor being content with the capital gain on redemption: such bonds are called 'zero-coupon bonds'.

In this market bonds issued by British companies are normally denominated in a currency other than sterling or in artificial units of account such as ecus or SDRs (European currency units, special drawing rights). It is expected that most buyers of an issue of bonds will be resident outside the UK, which is why they are called 'international' bonds. The market in international bonds has been associated with the market in Eurocurrencies and so they are sometimes called 'Eurobonds'.

13   Insider Dealing

13.1   REASONS FOR PROHIBITING INSIDER DEALING

The London Stock Exchange (see 7.2.3.1) is a market-place for buying and selling company shares and other securities. Like any market-place, people will be more inclined to use it if they believe that prices in it correctly represent the value of what is bought and sold. A person who buys something which turns out to be worth less than the price paid for it will feel aggrieved. So will a person who sells something for less than its real value.

In principle, deals in a market are more likely to be at a price correctly reflecting value if all the information used in valuation is available to both buyers and sellers. Two main kinds of information are used in valuing company shares:

(a)   Information about the economy of the nation, world trade, and the particular market in which the company is trading.
(b)   Information about how the company itself is handling its affairs.

Investors are expected to get information of type (a) from the financial press, reports of economists and government statistics, and it is assumed to be available to all. New information of type (b) is usually first known to people close to the company itself. They are therefore in a position to deal in the company's shares before the rest of the market has had an opportunity to revalue them in the light of the fresh information. Acting in this way is known as 'insider dealing'.

In recent years it has been increasingly realised that taking advantage of inside information is a fraud on other investors which is likely to lower public confidence in the Exchange. It is also seen as a breach of trust, especially when directors use the information they gain from their position to swindle the shareholders who appointed them. Accordingly, insider dealing was made a criminal offence by part V (ss. 68 to 73) of CA 1980. Those provisions were re-enacted in the Company Securities (Insider Dealing) Act 1985. The provisions concentrated on punishing misuse of unpublished information acquired in confidence from a company which would affect the price of that company's securities if made public. The provisions concentrated on persons who abused a confidential fiduciary relationship in a way which damaged the stock market. However, what damages the market is unequal access to information, and the means by which one trader acquires access to information which is denied to others is irrelevant to the damage caused by the use of the information. In 1989, a Directive (89/592/EEC) was adopted to coordinate regulations on insider dealing throughout the European Union. This has been implemented in UK law by part V (ss. 52 to 64) of the Criminal Justice Act 1993, which was brought into force on 1 March 1994 by SI 1994 No. 242. The new law is more focused on the control of securities markets than the abuse of confidential information. For a discussion of this change of emphasis see P. L. Davies, 'The European Community's Directive on insider dealing: from company law to securities markets regulation?' (1991) 11 Oxford J Legal Stud 92. There is a good deal of background information and further discussion in K. J. Hopt and E. Wymeersch, *European Insider Dealing — Law and Practice* (London: Butterworths, 1991). See also A. Alcock, 'Insider dealing — how did we get here?' (1994) 15 Co Law 67 and M. White, 'The implications for securities regulation of new insider dealing provisions in the Criminal Justice Act 1993' (1995) 16 Co Law 163.

The UK was the first European country to make insider dealing a criminal offence and the spread of control of insider dealing through Europe has been something of a shock to the culture of the financial markets which had previously regarded it as natural that anyone with an informational advantage should be able to profit from it. Insider dealing has been controlled for much longer in the USA, though always on the basis of abuse of fiduciary position (see L. Loss, 'The fiduciary concept as applied to trading by corporate ''insiders'' in the United States' (1970) 33 MLR 34; *United States* v *O'Hagan* (1997) 138 L Ed 2d 724). Abolition of controls on insider dealing was one of the earliest targets of the Chicago law and economics movement which regards profiting from inside information as a legitimate perk for managers and believes that it does not damage the economy (see, for example, H.G. Manne, 'In defence of insider trading' (1966) 44 (6) Harv Bus Rev 113; the arguments are reviewed briefly with references to original literature in Loss's article). This has shown starkly the conflict of opinion over whether the proper role of law in business is to enable business people to create wealth or to uphold standards of behaviour. For a sophisticated discussion of why the US law on insider dealing should be based on a theory of equal access to information and a response to the law and economics movement see K.L. Scheppele, ' ''It's just not right'': the ethics of insider trading' (1993) 56(3) Law & Contemp Prob 123.

13.2 DEFINITION OF THE OFFENCE OF INSIDER DEALING

13.2.1 Introduction

The offence of insider dealing is defined in the Criminal Justice Act 1993, s. 52, using a number of technical terms which are defined elsewhere in the Act. In the following discussion, the definitions of two of the most important terms, 'inside information' and 'having information as an insider', are examined first before looking at the definition of the offence of insider dealing.

The offence of insider dealing can be committed only by an individual, not a company or other entity.

13.2.2 Definition of inside information

Inside information is defined in the Criminal Justice Act 1993, s. 56(1), to mean information which:

(a) relates to particular securities or to a particular issuer of securities and not to securities generally or to issuers of securities generally;

(b) is specific or precise;

(c) has not been made public; and

(d) if it were made public would be likely to have a significant effect on the price of any securities.

Securities whose price would be likely to be significantly affected if an item of inside information were made public are known as 'price-affected securities' in relation to that information, and the information is called 'price-sensitive information' in relation to them (s. 56(2)).

In s. 56, 'price' includes value (s. 56(3)).

Information must be treated as relating to a company not only where it is about the company but also where it may affect the company's business prospects (s. 60(4)).

Section 58 gives some guidance on when information is to be regarded as made public, but s. 58(1) states that the section's provisions are not exhaustive. By s. 58(2), information is made public if:

(a) it is published in accordance with the rules of a regulated market for the purpose of informing investors and their professional advisers;

(b) it is contained in records which by virtue of any enactment are open to inspection by the public;

(c) it can be readily acquired by those likely to deal in any securities—

(i)   to which the information relates, or
(ii)   of an issuer to which the information relates; or

(d) it is derived from information which has been made public.

A 'regulated market' is a market identified as such in an order made by the Treasury under s. 60(1). The relevant order is SI 1994 No. 187 (as amended by SI 1996 No. 1561) which states that any market which is established under the rules of any of 45 investment exchanges in Europe listed in the schedule to the order is a regulated market. The list of exchanges running regulated markets includes the following UK institutions: the London Stock Exchange, LIFFE (the London International Financial Futures Exchange), OMLX (the London Securities and Derivatives Exchange) and Tradepoint Financial Networks plc. By s. 58(3) information may be treated as made public even though:

(a) it can be acquired only by persons exercising diligence or expertise;
(b) it is communicated to a section of the pubic and not to the public at large;
(c) it can be acquired only by observation;
(d) it is communicated only on payment of a fee; or
(e) it is published only outside the United Kingdom.

13.2.3 Having information as an insider

The basic idea of the definition of the offence of insider dealing in the Criminal Justice Act 1993, s. 52, is to restrict what may be done by a person who is described in the section as 'an individual who has information as an insider'. According to s. 57(1), an individual has information as an insider if and only if:

(a) the information is, and he or she knows that it is, inside information (which was defined in 13.2.2), and

(b) he or she has the information, and knows that he or she has it, from an inside source.

Section 57(2) goes on to explain that a person has information from an inside source if and only if:

(a) he or she has it through:

    (i) being a director, employee or shareholder of an issuer of securities; or

    (ii) having access to the information by virtue of his or her employment, office or profession; or

(b) the direct or indirect source of his or her information is a person within paragraph (a).

Paragraph (a)(i) covers persons who are directors, employees or shareholders of *an* issuer of securities, not necessarily the issuer of the securities whose price is affected by the inside information. Paragraph (a)(ii) is very wide-ranging: it would, for example, cover a financial journalist or an employee of a firm which prints offer documents for takeover bidders. Persons within para. (b) are sometimes known as 'tippees' (people who have been 'tipped off' by persons within para. (a)). An alternative terminology is to refer to people within para. (a) as 'primary insiders' and people within para. (b) as 'secondary insiders'. It is important to bear in mind that one essential element of the definition of inside information is that it is information which has not been made public. Once a primary insider makes his or her inside information public it ceases to be inside information and anyone who receives that information is not a secondary insider.

13.2.4 Restrictions on insiders

13.2.4.1 Restriction on dealing

The first restriction on an individual who has information as an insider is that he or she will commit an offence by *dealing* in 'securities that are price-affected securities in relation to the information' (Criminal Justice Act 1993, s. 52(1)). This is explained in s. 56(2):

> . . . securities are 'price-affected securities' in relation to inside information . . . if and only if the information would, if made public, be likely to have a significant effect on the price of the securities.

By s. 55(1), a person deals in securities if he or she:

(a) acquires or disposes of the securities (whether as principal or agent) or

(b) procures, directly or indirectly, an acquisition or disposal of the securities by any other person.

Other subsections of s. 55 extend the definition of dealing further, for example, prescribing that agreeing to acquire or dispose of securities counts as dealing.

Because it is market-places that are protected by the legislation, subsections (1) and (3) of s. 52 provide that an offence under s. 52(1) can be committed only if the acquisition or disposal in question occurs on a 'regulated market' (see 13.2.2), or the person dealing relies on a 'professional intermediary' or is acting as a professional intermediary.

The term 'professional intermediary' is defined in s. 59(1), (2) and (3) as follows:

> (1) For the purposes of this part, a 'professional intermediary' is a person—
>
>   (a) who carries on a business consisting of an activity mentioned in subsection (2) and who holds himself out to the public or any section of the public (including a section of the public constituted by persons such as himself) as willing to engage in any such business; or

(b)   who is employed by a person falling within paragraph (a) to carry out any such activity.

(2)   The activities referred to in subsection (1) are—

(a)   acquiring or disposing of securities (whether as principal or agent); or

(b)   acting as an intermediary between persons taking part in any dealing in securities.

(3)   A person is not to be treated as carrying on a business consisting of an activity mentioned in subsection (2)—

(a)   if the activity in question is merely incidental to some other activity not falling within subsection (2); or

(b)   merely because he occasionally conducts one of those activities.

Dealing in securities whose price would be affected by one's inside information if it were to be made public is what most people would consider to be the principal form of insider dealing. But dealing is punished only where necessary to protect a market-place identified by the Treasury as a regulated market. People who do not use regulated markets are not protected from insider dealing: any primary or secondary insider who is not a professional intermediary is at liberty to exploit his or her inside information in sales or purchases made outside a regulated market.

The dealing prohibited by s. 52(1) is an offence under the Act if the insider was within the UK at the time of doing any act constituting or forming part of the alleged dealing, no matter where in Europe the regulated market was on which the acquisition or disposal took place, or, if the dealing relied on a professional intermediary, no matter where the intermediary was (s. 62(1)(a)). Dealing is also an offence under the Act, wherever the insider was located, if the dealing occurred on a regulated market identified by the Treasury as a market regulated in the UK (s. 62(1)(b)). Those markets are identified in SI 1994 No. 187 as any market established under the rules of the London Stock Exchange, LIFFE (the London International Financial Futures Exchange) and OMLX (the London Securities and Derivatives Exchange). Dealing relying on a professional intermediary is an offence under the Act, wherever the insider was located, if the intermediary was within the UK at the time of doing anything by which the offence is alleged to have been committed (s. 62(1)(c)).

13.2.4.2   *Restriction on encouraging others to deal*

The second restriction on an individual who has information as an insider is that he or she will commit an offence by *encouraging another person to deal* in securities that are price-affected securities in relation to that information (Criminal Justice Act 1993, s. 52(2)(a)). Gain to the insider is irrelevant to this offence which clearly exists only to protect market-places. Accordingly, it is provided by s. 52(2)(a) and (3) that an offence under s. 52(2)(a) can be committed only by an insider who knows or has reasonable cause to believe that the dealing being encouraged would occur on a regulated market, or the person dealing would rely on a professional intermediary or would be acting as a professional intermediary.

The encouragement to deal prohibited by s. 52(2)(a) is an offence under the Act if the insider was within the UK at the time when he or she is alleged to have encouraged dealing, no matter where in Europe the regulated market was on which the dealing might occur or where the intermediary might be located (s. 62(2)(a)). Encouragement is also an offence under the Act, wherever the insider was located, if the alleged recipient of the encouragement was within the UK at the time of receiving it, again wherever the market or intermediary might be (s. 62(2)(b)).

13.2.4.3 Restriction on disclosing inside information

The third restriction on an individual who has information as an insider is that he or she will commit an offence by *disclosing the information* — otherwise than in the proper performance of the functions of his or her employment, office or profession — to another person (Criminal Justice Act 1993, s. 52(2)(b)). This is the widest form of restriction. Again it is intended to protect market-places, and an individual has a defence to a charge under s. 52(2)(b) by showing that he or she did not at the time expect any person, because of the disclosure, to deal in securities on a regulated market, or to deal in securities relying on a professional intermediary or to deal in them acting as a professional intermediary (s. 53(3)(a)).

The disclosure prohibited by s. 52(2)(a) is an offence under the Act if the insider was within the UK at the time when he or she is alleged to have disclosed the information, no matter where in Europe the regulated market was on which the dealing might occur or where the intermediary might be located (s. 62(2)(a)). Disclosure is also an offence under the Act, wherever the insider was located, if the alleged recipient of the information was within the UK at the time of receiving it, again wherever the market or intermediary might be (s. 62(2)(b)).

13.2.4.4 General defences

It is a defence to a charge of any form of insider dealing to show that one did not expect the dealing, which one had done, or encouraged others to do, or which might result from disclosing one's inside information, to result in a profit attributable to the fact that the information was 'price-sensitive information in relation to the securities' (Criminal Justice Act 1993, s. 53(1)(a), (2)(a) and (3)(b)). 'Profit' here includes avoidance of a loss (s. 53(6)). By s. 56(2) and (3), inside information is price-sensitive information in relation to securities if and only if the information would, if made public, be likely to have a significant effect on the price or value of the securities.

Under s. 53(1)(b) and (c) and (2)(b) and (c) it is a defence to a charge of dealing or encouraging others to deal while having information as an insider to show either:

(a) that one believed, on reasonable grounds, that the information had been disclosed widely enough to ensure that none of those taking part in the dealing would be prejudiced by not having the information, or

(b) that one would have done what one did even if one had not had the information.

13.2.4.5 Exemption for market makers

Market makers on regulated markets, and their employees, are exempt from the prohibitions on dealing or encouraging others to deal, provided they act in good faith in the course of the market-making business (Criminal Justice Act 1993, s. 53(4) and sch. 1, para. 1). They are not exempt from the prohibition on disclosure. Thus a market maker can encourage others to act on the basis of inside information but must not say what that information is.

13.2.4.6 Acting within price stabilisation rules

Individuals who act in accordance with price stabilisation rules have a defence to a charge of dealing or encouraging to deal (Criminal Justice Act 1993, s. 53(4) and sch. 1, para. 5). The rules are in part 10 of the Financial Services (Conduct of Business) Rules 1990 made by the Securities and Investments Board.

13.2.5   Use of market information

The term 'market information' is defined in the Criminal Justice Act 1993, sch. 1, para. 4. Essentially it is information about dealings in securities that have occurred or are being considered or negotiated, limited to the identity of the securities, the number involved, the price (or range of prices) and the identity of the buyers and sellers. It also covers information that an acquisition or disposal of securities will not take place. Schedule 1, para. 2(1), provides that an individual who has market information as an insider will have a defence to a charge of dealing or encouraging to deal if he or she can show that it was reasonable for an individual in his or her position to have acted as he or she did despite having that information as an insider at the time. Paragraph 2(2) says that, in determining the reasonableness of an individual dealing or encouraging to deal while having market information as an insider, account must be taken of:

(a)   the content of the information,
(b)   the circumstances and capacity in which the individual first had the information, and
(c)   the capacity in which the individual now acts.

It remains to be seen whether the Crown Prosecution Service will ever want to argue before a jury about what constitutes reasonable behaviour by stock market investors.

Schedule 1, para. 3, provides a defence to a charge of dealing or encouraging to deal for an individual whose inside information was only market information arising directly out of his or her involvement in the consideration or negotiation of an acquisition or disposal (or series of acquisitions and disposals) and that the dealing or encouragement to deal was in connection with, and was with a view to facilitating, that transaction or series of transactions.

13.2.6   Release of price-sensitive information to the London Stock Exchange

For many companies a London Stock Exchange listing is a valuable privilege which enables them to raise capital cheaply. In return for being granted the facilities of the Exchange, listed companies must ensure that investors get good value for the money put into their shares. This means that listed companies must ensure that all price sensitive information is published as rapidly as possible, and observance of this duty is the best way of preventing insider dealing.

Paragraph 9.1 of the Listing Rules requires a listed company to notify the Exchange's Company Announcements Office of any major new developments in its sphere of activity which are not public knowledge and which, by virtue of their effect on the company's assets and liabilities or financial position or on the general course of its business, may lead to substantial movement in the price of its listed securities.

Paragraph 9.2 requires a listed company to notify the Exchange without delay of all relevant information concerning any change known to its directors in its financial condition or in the performance of its business or in the company's expectation of its performance if knowledge of the change would be likely to lead to substantial movement in the price of its listed securities.

In addition to these general requirements a listed company must inform the Exchange of various specific matters including:

(a)   any proposed change in the company's capital structure (Listing Rules, para. 9.10(a));

(b)   any information received concerning substantial shareholdings (see 8.9) (Listing Rules, paras 9.11 and 9.12);

(c)   any information received concerning interests, or changes of interests, that directors or their spouses or children may have in the shares or debentures of the company or any other company in the same group (see 13.6.2 and 13.6.4) (Listing Rules, para. 16.13).

Any information received by the Exchange is immediately released to news services. If a listed company does not wish to reveal the exact nature of price-sensitive information then it may ask for a temporary suspension of listing until the information can be published (see Listing Rules, para. 1.19). See further P. Smith, 'Release of price-sensitive information: Stock Exchange guidance' (1994) 15 Co Law 89; A. Hofler, 'Publication of price-sensitive information' (1995) 16 Co Law 247.

A company is subject to the Traded Securities (Disclosure) Regulations 1994 (SI 1994 No. 188) if it is the issuer of a security which is not listed on the London Stock Exchange but which has been admitted to trading on any market in the UK which (a) is regulated and supervised by a recognised investment exchange, (b) operates regularly, and (c) is accessible directly or indirectly to the public (this covers the Alternative Investment Market). Such a market would be a regulated market regulated in the UK for the purposes of the insider trading legislation (see 13.2.4.1). The regulations require such a company to inform the public as soon as possible of any major new developments in the company's sphere of activity which are not public knowledge and which may, by virtue of their effect on the company's assets or liabilities or financial position, or on the general course of its business, lead to substantial movements in the price of the security (reg. 3(1)). Regulation 3(2) requires the investment exchange running the market to have rules which will enable it to suspend trading in a security if the issuer fails to comply with reg. 3(1).

13.2.7   Penalties

An offence under part V of the Criminal Justice Act 1993 is triable either way. On indictment the penalty can be imprisonment for up to seven years and/or a fine for which there is no limit (s. 61(1)). However, a prosecution can be instituted in England and Wales only by, or with the consent of, the Secretary of State or the Director of Public Prosecutions (s. 61(2)). A transaction entered into in contravention of the Act must stand: it is not void or even voidable (s. 63(2)). Nevertheless, the court will not enforce such a contract because of the doctrine *ex turpi causa non oritur actio* (an action does not arise from a base cause) (*Chase Manhattan Equities Ltd* v *Goodman* [1991] BCLC 897). See 13.5 for a discussion of possible civil remedies.

13.2.8   Investigation

The Secretary of State has a power to appoint inspectors if it appears that there are circumstances suggesting that there may have been a breach of part V of the Criminal Justice Act 1993 (FSA 1986, s. 177(1); see 18.8.2.5).

13.3   LONDON STOCK EXCHANGE MODEL CODE

The London Stock Exchange requires a listed company to adopt rules to govern dealings by its directors in its securities, and those rules must not be less stringent than the Exchange's model code for securities transactions by directors of listed companies (Listing Rules, para. 16.18).

The main features of this code (which is printed in the Listing Rules as an appendix to ch. 16) are:

(a) A director of a listed company must not deal in any securities of the company on considerations of a short-term nature (para. 2).

(b) Before dealing in the company's securities, a director of a listed company must notify the chairman (or some other director designated for the purpose) in advance and receive clearance (para. 6). (A dealing proposed by the chairman or designated director must be notified to and cleared by the board or another designated director.) A written record must be kept by the company of notifications and clearances (para. 8).

(c) A director of a listed company must not buy the company's securities during a 'close period' which is the two months before the preliminary announcements of its half-yearly and annual results or the month before the announcement of its quarterly results (para. 3).

13.4 OPTIONS

A director or a shadow director of a company commits an offence, triable either way, if he buys options (whether put, call, or put and call) on the shares or debentures (or debenture stock) of his company, its holding company, any of its subsidiaries, or any other subsidiary of its holding company, if such shares or debentures are listed on any stock exchange anywhere (CA 1985, s. 323). The penalty is up to two years in prison and/or a fine (CA 1985, s. 323(2) and sch. 24).

Such options must also not be bought by a director or shadow director's spouse or by his children and stepchildren under 18. However, it is a defence for such a relative to prove that he had no reason to believe his spouse or parent was a director or shadow director of a company in which he was buying options (or a company within the same group).

These provisions were an early attempt to penalise insider dealing, which the Insider Dealing Act now makes a criminal offence for anyone connected with a company, not just its directors. However, insider dealing is only an offence when carried out by someone who is knowingly in possession of confidential unpublished price sensitive information. It is not necessary to prove that a director or shadow director who purchased an option had any particular confidential information about the company: this is because option trading is essentially a speculative activity and it can be assumed that a director or shadow director would not buy an option unless he had a better idea than other investors of the future price of the company's shares.

Rights under a capitalisation issue and rights to convert debenture stock or unsecured loan stock are not options, nor are convertible warrants (CA 1985, s. 323(5)).

The Secretary of State has a power to appoint inspectors to investigate whether a contravention of s. 323 has occurred (CA 1985, s. 446(1); see 18.8.2.3).

13.5 CIVIL LIABILITY

If the occupation of a position imposes a fiduciary duty to a person then all profits made by occupying the position belong to the person to whom the duty is owed, unless that person has agreed otherwise. Agreement, in this context, is ineffective unless there has been full disclosure of the circumstances. See 16.5 and 16.8 for a full discussion.

It would seem to follow from these general principles that if a director of a company buys and sells its shares as a result of information about the company obtained by virtue of the directorship, then the profit made (perhaps, even, a loss avoided) belongs to the company unless the company agrees that the director should retain it. This has been held to be the law in the USA — see *Diamond* v *Oreamuno* (1969) 248 NE 2d 910.

It is doubtful whether English law can provide compensation to shareholders who buy or sell shares at wrong prices in ignorance of price sensitive information concerning the company.

A recognised investment exchange must place continuing obligations on companies whose securities are traded on the exchange to afford to persons dealing in the securities proper information for determining their current value (FSA 1986, sch. 4, para. 2(2)(b)), though the only penalty that can be imposed for a breach of such an obligation is suspension of trading which penalises the shareholders more than the company. The law does not impose any other duty on companies generally to reveal information to their shareholders to enable them to value their shares correctly.

The fact that Parliament has imposed stiff criminal penalties for insider dealing will probably stop the courts permitting actions for damages for breach of statutory duty brought by an uninformed buyer or seller of shares who has dealt at a wrong price with someone who was using unpublished price sensitive information. In theory, if a person were convicted of an offence of insider dealing the court could order him to compensate those who have suffered by his crime (Powers of Criminal Courts Act 1973, s. 35) but the difficulty of establishing the size of damages might well prevent the court awarding a compensation order in such a case.

In *Percival* v *Wright* [1902] 2 Ch 42 1, the joint holders of some shares in an unlisted colliery company offered them for sale to the company's chairman and two other directors. The price at which they were offered was determined by an independent valuer at £12 10*s* each. The sale of the shares was concluded but then it was discovered that while negotiating to purchase these shares the chairman had been discussing selling the whole colliery at a price that would have made each share in the company worth considerably more than £12 10*s*. In fact the colliery never was sold and the court found from the evidence that the board of directors never intended to sell it. Percival and his co-shareholder asked for the sale of their shares to be set aside on the ground that the chairman had a duty to disclose that he was negotiating for the sale of the colliery at a price which implied that the valuation price of the shares was wrong. It was held that there was no such duty. In a remarkable passage, Swinfen Eady J said, at p. 426:

> The contrary view would place directors in a most invidious position, as they could not buy or sell shares without disclosing negotiations, a premature disclosure of which might well be against the best interests of the company. I am of opinion that directors are not in that position.

The present-day opinion of investors as shown by the London Stock Exchange model code for securities transactions by directors of listed companies (see 13.3) is exactly the opposite: directors are in a difficult position and so they must not deal.

In *Re Chez Nico (Restaurants) Ltd* [1992] BCLC 192, Browne-Wilkinson V-C said, at p. 208, that he considered *Percival* v *Wright* to be 'very doubtful authority' for the proposition that directors of a company may purchase shares in the company without disclosing pending negotiations for the sale of the company's undertaking. His lordship continued: 'I consider the law to be that . . . in certain special circumstances fiduciary duties, carrying with them a duty of disclosure, can arise which place directors in a fiduciary capacity *vis-à-vis* the shareholders'. His lordship approved the decision of the New Zealand Court of Appeal in *Coleman* v *Myers* [1977] 2 NZLR 225. This concerned an old-established unlisted New Zealand company, Campbell & Ehrenfield Co. Ltd. Shares in the company were held by various members of three generations of the Myers family but very few shares were held by young Mr Douglas Myers, the chairman's son, when he took over as managing director. He indicated to his father that he did not want the tough job of chief executive unless he had a sizeable equity stake in the company. So Douglas, with his father's assistance, contracted to purchase two large blocks of shares in the company on condition that he did not have to pay for them for six months. During those six months he intended to use the control given to him by holding those blocks of shares to force the company to sell valuable buildings and lend him the cash obtained thereby: he would then use the cash to pay for the shares. Other shareholders began to attack him so he launched a full-scale takeover bid in order that he could compulsorily purchase the shares of the dissentient minority (see 8.8.2). The price at which he offered to purchase shares was arrived at by an independent valuer who, however, was unaware that the company's buildings were dramatically undervalued in the company's books. All the deals actually went through and Douglas made a small fortune because the sale of the company's buildings yielded vastly more money than was necessary to buy the shares at the price that had been agreed. Minority shareholders who had been compulsorily purchased eventually brought an action alleging fraud, breach of fiduciary duty, negligence, and breach of statutory duty (using the company's money to finance purchase of its shares). On the issue of fiduciary duty it was held that Douglas and his father, as managing director and chairman, owed fiduciary duties to the shareholders which arose from the family character of the company, their high degree of inside knowledge, and the way in which they conducted the takeover. Their duty was to disclose material facts. The court refused to follow *Percival* v *Wright,* on which Woodhouse J commented, at pp. 324–5:

> . . . the standard of conduct required from a director in relation to dealings with a shareholder will differ depending upon all the surrounding circumstances and the nature of the responsibility which in a real and practical sense the director has assumed towards the shareholder. In the one case there may be a need to provide an explicit warning and a great deal of information concerning the proposed transaction. In another there may be no need to speak at all. . . ., while it may not be possible to lay down any general test as to when the fiduciary duty will arise for a company director or to prescribe the exact conduct which will always discharge it when it does, there are nevertheless some factors that will usually have an influence upon a decision one way or the other. They include . . . dependence upon information and advice, the existence of a relationship of confidence, the significance of some particular transaction for the parties and, of course, the extent of any positive action taken by or on behalf of the director or directors to promote it.

Special circumstances justifying the imposition on a director of a fiduciary duty to a shareholder were found in *Glavanics* v *Brunninghausen* (1996) 19 ACSR 204, in which the company had only two members, who were its two directors, but one of them had not taken any part in the company's affairs for many years. The active director bought the other's one-sixth shareholding in the company for A$30,000 without disclosing that he was negotiating the sale of the company's business, which he concluded the next day at a price which valued the shares at about 12 times what he paid for them. Bryson J said, at p. 222:

> What in form was a company, with its invocation of *Percival* v *Wright,* was in substance a trading entity with two co-owners, conducted on what, for a company, was an artificial basis. A proposition that a fiduciary duty was owed by [the active director] as director only to the company as a whole and not to a particular shareholder is almost an absurdity

when an attempt is made to apply it to obligations in conscience owed to this company. The general body of shareholders is only the two of them.

In *Allen* v *Hyatt* (1914) 30 TLR 444, PC, directors of a company found a potential buyer of all its shares. They obtained from the company's other shareholders options to purchase their shares by representing that this would facilitate the sale to the potential buyer. In fact the price at which the directors exercised their options was lower than the price they had agreed with the purchaser, and the directors made a handsome profit. It was held that the directors were the agents of the shareholders for the purpose of selling their shares, and so owed the profit to their principals, the shareholders.

13.6 REGISTER OF DIRECTORS' INTERESTS

13.6.1 Introduction

It is inevitable that directors of a company should be suspected of lining their own pockets through the use of inside information and so it is important that the dealings in the securities of a company by the directors of that company should be open to inspection by members. Sections 325 to 329 of CA 1985 seek to ensure that full information about a director's dealings in his company's shares and debentures is available for inspection. The provisions apply to every registered company, not only public companies, and so they may also be considered as part of the general disclosure requirements of the companies legislation.

13.6.2 Obligation to report interests

A person who becomes a director or a shadow director of a company at a time when he is interested in shares in, or debentures of, the company (or a subsidiary of the company, or its holding company, or any other subsidiary of its holding company) commits an offence if he does not, within five days (excluding Saturdays, Sundays and bank holidays), give the company written notice of his interests and of the number of shares or debentures involved (CA 1985, s. 324(1) and (6) and sch. 13, paras 14 and 16).

A director or shadow director of a company must notify the company of any alteration — either in nature or extent — in his interest in shares in, or debentures of, the company or other companies in the group, within five days of the alteration (again ignoring weekends and holidays) (s. 324(2) and (6) and sch. 13, paras 14 and 16).

Failure to notify an interest is an offence triable either way with a possible prison sentence of two years on indictment (s. 324(7) and sch. 24). However, some of the interests that have to be notified are remote from the director who has to notify them so a director does not commit an offence by failing to notify an interest if he did not know of its existence but he must notify the interest within five days of becoming aware of its existence (s. 324(3)(b) and (7)(a) and sch. 13, para. 14). In England and Wales an offence under s. 324 cannot be prosecuted except by or with the consent of the Secretary of State or the Director of Public Prosecutions (ss. 324(8) and 732(1) and (2)(a)).

By s. 324(5), a notification of an interest is not effective unless it states that it is given in fulfilment of the obligation imposed by s. 324.

13.6.3 Register

Every company must, under penalty, maintain a register, and whenever it receives any information from a director or shadow director concerning his interests in shares or debentures it must, within three days (excluding Saturdays, Sundays and bank holidays) thereafter, record in the register, against the director's name, the information received from him and the date of making the entry (CA 1985, s. 325(1), (2), (5) and (6) and sch. 13, para. 22; penalty in s. 326 and sch. 24).

The entries against the names in the register must appear in chronological order (sch, 13, para. 21), and the names must appear in alphabetical order or the register must be provided with an index of names (sch. 13, para. 28).

The register must be kept at the company's registered office or at the place where its register of members is kept, and must be open for inspection. Members of the company must be allowed to inspect the register free of charge but other persons may be charged (sch. 13, para. 25). If the register is not kept at the registered office then notice must be given to the registrar of the place where it is kept and of any change in that place (sch. 13, para. 27).

The register may be kept in non-legible form (s. 723) provided it is available for inspection in legible form either at the registered office or at the place where the company's register of members is available for inspection (SI 1985 No. 724, sch. 1) and the registrar must be notified of the place where the register is available for inspection (SI 1985 No. 724, reg. 3(1) and (2)(c)).

The register must, under penalty, be available for inspection at, and be accessible during, every annual general meeting of the company (CA 1985, sch. 13, para. 29; penalty in ss. 326(5) and 730(5) and sch. 24).

When a company whose shares or debentures are listed on a UK recognised investment exchange is notified by a director of any interest in any of its listed securities then the company must, under penalty, notify the exchange before the end of the following day (disregarding Saturdays, Sundays and bank holidays) (ss. 329 and 730(5) and sch. 24). The exchange may publish information it receives under this provision as it thinks fit (s. 329(1)). An offence under s. 329 may not be prosecuted in England and Wales except by, or with the consent of, the Secretary of State or the Director of Public Prosecutions (ss. 329(3) and 732(1) and (2)(a)).

Any person may require a copy of the register or part of it on payment, and any copy requisitioned must be dispatched by the company within 10 days after receiving the request (sch. 13, para. 26).

If there is default in permitting inspection of the register or in despatching a requisitioned copy then the court may order compliance (s. 326(6)).

13.6.4   Interests to be notified

The interests that must be notified by a director or shadow director are defined in CA 1985, sch. 13, part I. A director or shadow director must notify these interests if they are his own or if they are interests of his spouse or of any of his children or stepchildren under 18 (s. 328).

It may be thought that most of CA 1985, sch. 13, part I, is unnecessary since para. 1(1) says: 'A reference to an interest . . . is to be read as including any interest of any kind whatsoever'. But the drafter has added the following rules:

(a)   A person who has made a contract to purchase (whether for cash or otherwise) shares or debentures has an interest in them (sch. 13, para. 3(1)(a)), whether they are identified or not (para. 8).

(b)   A person who is not registered as the holder of shares or debentures but is entitled to exercise any right conferred by holding them or to control the exercise of any such right has an interest in them (para. 3(1)(b)). This primarily covers shares held by another as nominee. Being appointed as a proxy for a shareholder for one meeting and its adjournment is not a notifiable interest (para. 3(3)).

(c) Paragraphs 4 and 5 of sch. 13 contain elaborate provisions for ensuring that a person who controls a company that is interested in shares is himself counted as being interested in those shares.

(d) A person who is a beneficiary of a trust is interested in any shares or debentures that are in the trust property (para. 2) except where the trust is an authorised unit trust or one of a number of unit trusts in which money held by public officials is invested (para. 11). An interest in reversion or remainder (or, in Scotland, in fee) need not be notified (para. 9).

(e) If an interest is held jointly then it must be counted as the interest of each of the joint holders (para. 7).

(f) An interest as a bare trustee or custodian trustee (or, in Scotland, as a simple trustee), or co-trustee or joint personal representative with the Public Trustee, may be disregarded (para. 10; S1 1985 No. 802, reg. 2(a)).

If a company is a wholly owned subsidiary of a company that is itself required to keep a register of its directors' interests then a director of both companies has to report only to the holding company (SI 1985 No. 802, reg. 3(1)(b)).

If a company is a wholly owned subsidiary of a corporation incorporated outside England, Wales and Scotland then a director of the company does not have to report to it his interests in the holding company's securities or in the securities of any other corporation incorporated outside England, Wales and Scotland (SI 1985 No. 802, reg. 3(1)(a)).

When a company grants a director or shadow director a right to subscribe for shares or debentures it must, within three days, record against his name in the register of directors' interests the date of the grant, the period during (or time at which) it is exercisable, the consideration (whether cash or kind) for the grant, description and number or amount of the securities, and the price (in cash or kind) to be paid. When the right is exercised the fact and the extent to which it is exercised must be recorded (CA 1985, s. 325(4) and (5)).

13.6.5 Investigations

The Secretary of State may appoint inspectors to investigate suspected contraventions of the obligation to notify directors' interests — see 18.8.2.3.

14 Shareholders

14.1 INTRODUCTION

The members of a company benefit, if it is successful, by taking annual profit dividends, or by sharing in a surplus of assets if the company is wound up while solvent. The members of a company have many important powers over the company's affairs (see 15.7.5), even though management of the company is assigned to directors. This chapter examines the question of who is a member, and how meetings of members are called and conducted.

14.2 DEFINITION

The definition of a member of a company is contained in CA 1985, s. 22:

(1) The subscribers of a company's memorandum are deemed to have agreed to become members of the company, and on its registration shall be entered as such in its register of members.

(2) Every other person who agrees to become a member of a company, and whose name is entered in its register of members, is a member of the company.

The fact that a person's name has been entered in a company's register of members is not in itself sufficient to make that person a member of the company: the person must have *agreed* to become a member. This means that entry of the person's name in the register must have been assented to or authorised by the person but it does not mean that the register entry must have been made as a result of a *contract* between the person and the company (*Re Nuneaton Borough Association Football Club Ltd* [1989] BCLC 454, CA). Agreement is deemed in the case of a subscriber of the memorandum (s. 22(1)). If the name of a person has been put on a company's register of members without that person's agreement then an application may be made to rectify the register (see 14.3.3). Equally, if the name of a person who has agreed to be a member of a company has not been entered on the company's register of members then rectification may be sought either by the person who wishes to be a member (so as to participate in the company or sell shares) or by the company (if it wishes to claim payment for shares). See the summary of the law by Slade J in *Re Compañía de Electricidad de la Provincia de Buenos Aires Ltd* [1980] Ch 146 at p. 182.

The fact that a person buys a share certificate as a scripophilist interested in the certificate as a collectable object does not in itself mean that the person has agreed to buy the shares and be a member of the company (*Re Baku Consolidated Oilfields Ltd* [1994] 1 BCLC 173).

Membership of a company limited by shares is normally based on shareholding but s. 22 is drafted to apply to any sort of company. This may have the unexpected result that a person may be a member of a company limited by shares by virtue of s. 22 without holding any shares. In *Re Nuneaton Borough Association Football Club Ltd*, Mr Shooter believed that he had been allotted 10,000 of the company's shares and that he had purchased a further 10,000 from a Mr Gallagher. His name was entered on the company's register of members accordingly. He believed that all 20,000 shares had been created by the company adopting a resolution to increase its authorised share capital. In fact, because of procedural irregularities, the authorised share capital had not been increased and Mr Shooter's shares did not exist. Nevertheless the Court of Appeal held that he was a member of the company by virtue of being registered as such.

A member who is registered in a false or fictitious name is nevertheless a member (*Re Hercules Insurance Co., Pugh and Sharman's Case* (1872) LR 13 Eq 566).

If a share in a company is held jointly by two or more persons then each of them is a member of the company (*Permanent Trustee Co. of New South Wales Ltd* v *Palmer* (1929) 42 CLR 277).

14.3   REGISTER

14.3.1   Requirement

By CA 1985, s. 352:

(1)   Every company shall keep a register of its members and enter in it the particulars required by this section.

(2)   There shall be entered in the register—

(a)   the names and addresses of the members;

(b)   the date on which each person was registered as a member; and

(c)   the date at which any person ceased to be a member.

(3)   The following applies in the case of a company having a share capital—

(a)   with the names and addresses of the members there shall be entered a statement—

(i)   of the shares held by each member, distinguishing each share by its number (so long as the share has a number) and, where the company has more than one class of issued shares, by its class, and

(ii)   of the amount paid or agreed to be considered as paid on the shares of each member.

If a company's shares can be held in uncertificated form then its register of members must state how many shares each member holds in uncertificated and certificated form (SI 1995 No. 3272, reg. 19(1)).

The register of members must be kept at the company's registered office or at the place at which it is made up, though it may not be kept at a place outside England and Wales if the company is registered in England and Wales, or at a place outside Scotland if it is registered in Scotland (CA 1985, s. 353(1)). Unless the register is at all times kept at the company's registered office, the company must notify the registrar of companies of the place where the register is kept and of any change in that place (s. 353(2) and (3)).

If a company has more than 50 members and the register is not in a form which constitutes an index of members, the company must also maintain and keep with the register an index of members which contains a sufficient indication to enable the account of each member in the register to be found readily (s. 354).

The entry relating to a person's membership may be removed from the register 20 years after the membership ceased (s. 352(6)).

The extent of a person's responsibility for any failure of a company to comply with its duty to keep a register of members in accordance with ss. 352 and 353 is a matter to which the court must have regard in deciding whether that person's conduct as a director or shadow director of that company makes him or her unfit to be concerned in the management of a company (Company Directors Disqualification Act 1986, s. 9 and sch. 1, para. 4(d) and (e)).

Under CA 1985, s. 352A (inserted by SI 1992 No. 1699), if the number of members of a private limited company (other than a hybrid company) falls to one then the company must, under penalty, enter in its register of members a statement that it has only one member and must state the date on which its membership fell to one (penalty in sch. 24). If the number of members of such a company increases from one to two or more then it must enter in its register of members a statement that it has ceased to have only one member, the date on which that happened and the name and address of the person who was formerly the sole member. The source of s. 352A is art. 3 of the EC 12th Company Law Directive.

There is no requirement that the addresses recorded for individual members in the register must be their residential addresses: for any member an accommodation address is sufficient (*Hemmerling* v *IMTC Systems* (1993) 109 DLR (4th) 582). However, the recorded address must be the one supplied by the member: the company cannot itself substitute an accommodation address so as to limit publicly available information about its members (*POW Services Ltd* v *Clare* [1995] 2 BCLC 435 at p. 451). The register may also record only the name and address of a nominee and not the beneficial owner of shares (see 8.7.1). These factors may reduce the usefulness of the register as a means of identifying and communicating with shareholders. In public companies, the register of substantial interests (see 8.9) may reveal more information about the beneficial ownership of shares.

In the consultation document introducing its review of company law (see 0.3.1.6) the DTI says that the requirement in s. 352(2)(b) and (c) to give the dates when a person became and ceased to be a member now probably serves no useful purpose (*Modern Company Law for a Competitive Economy* (London: DTI, 1998), p. 8).

14.3.2   Inspection

For the rules concerning inspection of the register of members see 4.4.1(g).

14.3.3   Effect and rectification

The effect of the register is stated in the following terms by s. 361 of CA 1985:

> The register of members is prima facie evidence of any matters which are by this Act directed or authorised to be inserted in it.

An entry recording a person as holding uncertificated shares provides the same evidence of title as would an entry relating to the same shares in certificated form (SI 1995 No. 3272, reg. 20(1)).

The register is thus not conclusive evidence of its contents, and if it is not correct then it may be rectified under s. 359:

> (1)   If—
>   (a)   the name of any person is, without sufficient cause, entered in or omitted from a company's register of members, or
>   (b)   default is made or unnecessary delay takes place in entering on the register the fact of any person having ceased to be a member,

the person aggrieved, or any member of the company, or the company, may apply to the court for rectification of the register.

(2) The court may either refuse the application or may order rectification of the register and payment by the company of any damages sustained by any party aggrieved.

The court has jurisdiction under s. 359 to rectify the register in respect of part only of a member's shareholding (*Re Transatlantic Life Assurance Co. Ltd* [1980] 1 WLR 79). The order may be retrospective so that the court can declare that a person was or was not a member of a company as from a particular date (*Re Sussex Brick Co.* [1904] 1 Ch 598; *Barbor* v *Middleton* 1988 SLT 288). However, the section only provides for summary jurisdiction and this will not be exercised where there is a difficult question, e.g., of dispute between two alleged owners of a share, which should be determined by an action commenced by writ (*Re Leon Needham Ltd* (1966) 110 SJ 652) and discretion will not be exercised if injustice would be caused to other members (*Re Sussex Brick Co.*)

In *Re Data Express Ltd* (1987) *Independent,* 13 April 1987, the company's register of members had been inadvertently deposited in a skip and irretrievably lost. The court treated the company as having a register which was erroneous because it was blank, and it rectified the register by inserting the names of the shareholders.

On an application under s. 359, the court is empowered to decide any question relating to the title to shares of any person who is a party to the application, and generally may decide any question necessary or expedient to the question of rectification (s. 359(3)). If the court orders rectification of the register, it will also order notice of the rectification to be given to the registrar of companies (s. 359(4)).

14.4 MEETINGS

14.4.1 Introduction

Meetings are held to provide an opportunity to communicate information and opinions, and to make decisions. It is an important feature of company law that it allows for changes in companies — directors may be dismissed and replaced; capital structure may be altered; a company may change its name, its objects, its articles of association; and so on. The legislation provides that decisions to make changes on many matters concerning a company may be taken only by the company's members (see 15.7.5).

If it is necessary for the members of a company to decide on some matter and all the members entitled to vote on that matter in fact assent to the decision then the decision is effective and it does not matter whether the members' assents were given separately or while they were gathered together (see 14.4.8.5). However, in any company with more than a handful of members it will often be difficult to get every member to assent to a decision. Therefore, as a general rule, the assent of a properly constituted meeting of members is effective to make a decision that binds all members whether present at the meeting or not. Furthermore, again as a general rule, a meeting will have assented to a decision if more votes are cast in favour of the decision than are cast against it.

However, in company law, decisions on a wide range of matters are required, if taken at meetings, to be taken by special or extraordinary resolutions which require the assent of three-quarters of the votes cast on the question (see 14.4.8.3). Also, on some particularly important matters, even though a special resolution is adopted, a dissentient minority can apply to the court to have the resolution cancelled (CA 1985, ss. 5 (alteration of objects clause of memorandum), 17 (alteration of condition of memorandum which could have been in articles), 54 (re-registration of public company as a private company), 127 (alteration of class rights), 157 (private company providing financial assistance for the purchase of its own shares) and 176 (private company making a payment out of capital for the redemption or purchase of its own shares)). Under s. 127 the court may only confirm or cancel the resolution; under the other provisions it may grant such other relief as appears just and equitable.

If there is dissension over whether a particular decision should be taken then the rules governing meetings may be of crucial importance. When legislation requires a decision to be taken at a meeting of members of a company, the decision must be taken at a meeting conducted in accordance with the company's articles (*Re Cambrian Peat, Fuel, & Charcoal Co. Ltd, De La Mott's and Turner's Case* (1875) 31 LT 773; *Howling's Trustees* v *Smith* (1905) 7 F 390).

If members who do not attend a meeting are to be bound by the meeting's decisions then all members must be given a reasonable opportunity of attending the meeting — that is, they must be given proper notice, see 14.4.5 — and the meeting itself must be properly conducted — there must be a quorum, see 14.4.6, and voting must be properly conducted, see 14.4.8 and 14.4.9.

Members attending a meeting have only themselves to blame if they do not use the rules governing the meeting to their own advantage: no one at a meeting has a duty to explain the rules to the members — in particular, the auditors do not have such a duty (*Re Hockerill Athletic Club Ltd* [1990] BCLC 921). A resolution is not invalid merely because members who disagreed with it might have made more effective opposition had they known the rules better (ibid.).

A meeting that all members of a company are entitled to attend is called a 'general' meeting whereas a meeting which only one class of members is entitled to attend is called a 'class' meeting.

There is no requirement in CA 1985 that a company registered under the Act must hold its meetings in the jurisdiction in which it is incorporated (England and Wales or Scotland), but the constitution of a company may specify where its meetings are to be held.

The underlying reason for requiring a company to hold meetings is that members shall be able to attend in person so as to debate and vote on matters affecting the company (*Byng* v *London Life Association Ltd* [1990] Ch 170, CA, per Browne-Wilkinson V-C). It is not necessary for all the persons attending the meeting to be together in the same room provided there are adequate audio-visual links to enable everyone attending to see and hear what is going on in all the rooms being used (ibid.). At first the courts were unwilling to accept that a telephone conversation, lacking a visual link, could be a meeting (*Re Associated Color Laboratories Ltd* (1970) 12 DLR (3d) 338, British Columbia; *Higgins* v *Nicol* (1971) 18 FLR 343 per Joske J at p. 357; *Magnacrete Ltd* v *Douglas-Hill* (1988) 48 SASR 567). However, in *Re GIGA Investments Pty Ltd* (1995) 17 ACSR 472, it was held in the Federal Court of Australia that two people can hold a meeting by ordinary telephone connection and more than two can meet using telephone conference facilities. It remains to be seen whether this will be accepted in England and Wales.

A company has a dual aspect as an association of its members and a person separate from its members. It is natural to think of a general meeting as representing the company in its association aspect but because the association and the separate person are but two aspects of the same thing, a decision of a general meeting must also be a decision of the company as a separate person. This would accord with the idea that a general meeting of members of a company is an 'organ' of the company by which the company acts, as suggested by the realist theory of corporate personality (see 5.3.1). In CA 1985, for example, s. 135(1) has the words '. . . a company . . . may . . . by special resolution reduce its share capital', treating a resolution adopted by the members as a resolution of the company, and the Act sometimes uses the phrase 'the company in general meeting', for example, in s. 121(4). In Table A, art. 102 says that '. . . the company may by ordinary resolution declare dividends', which enables a general meeting of the members to create a debt owed by the company, as a separate person, to each of its members who is entitled under the articles to participate in the dividend. In *Re Devala Provident Gold Mining Co.* (1883) 22 ChD 593, legal proceedings were being taken against a company, alleging that there had been a misrepresentation in its prospectus. It was sought to give evidence that the company's chairman, as its agent, had admitted, at a general meeting of the company, that there was an error in the prospectus. A statement by an agent is regarded as an admission by the principal if made to someone other than the principal, but it was held that in this case the chairman was only reporting to his own principal because the meeting was identified with the company as a separate person, and so his statement was not an admission by the company.

In *Northern Counties Securities Ltd* v *Jackson & Steeple Ltd* [1974] 1 WLR 1133, unusually, the company as a legal person was separated from its members who made its decisions. The defendant company had failed to fulfil its obligations under a contract and had been ordered by the court to perform those obligations. The company was required by the Stock Exchange to obtain its members' approval before performing the contract (a point which apparently had been overlooked by the directors when they made the contract). The plaintiff claimed that if the members failed to approve the contract then they would be in contempt of court but this was rejected by Walton J, who pointed out that it was the company as a separate person which was subject to the court order not the members. The members could take a decision that would effectively prevent the company complying with the order but it would then be the company that was in contempt not the members. The lack of liability of the members of a company for its contempt of court may be contrasted with the duty which its directors have to ensure that it complies with court orders (see 15.10) and a company's vicarious liability for contempt of court caused by its employees' actions (see 19.7). The *Northern Counties Securities* case may also be contrasted with *Re Arthur Rathbone Kitchens Ltd* [1997] 2 BCLC 280, in which the learned deputy High Court judge, Roger Kaye QC, held, at p. 295, that the members of a company which makes a voluntary arrangement (see 20.4) are bound by it, and referred to the members breaking the terms of the arrangement by adopting a resolution for voluntary winding up.

The circumstances in which a resolution of company members can create a contract binding the company is discussed at length in P. Jaffey, 'Contractual obligations of the company in general meeting' (1996) 16 LS 27. See also 3.5.3 and 3.5.4 on the interaction between contracts made by a company and resolutions by the company's members to alter its articles.

14.4.2 Annual general meeting

By CA 1985, s. 366:

(1) Every company shall in each year hold a general meeting as its annual general meeting in addition to any other meetings in that year, and shall specify the meeting as such in the notices calling it.

(2) However, so long as a company holds its first annual general meeting within 18 months of its incorporation, it need not hold it in the year of its incorporation or in the following year.

(3)   Not more than 15 months shall elapse between the date of one annual general meeting of a company and that of the next.

Where s. 366 is not complied with, s. 367 gives the Secretary of State power, on the application of any member, to call or direct the calling of a general meeting and to give such ancillary or consequential directions as he thinks fit.

The members of a *private company* may elect under s. 366A to dispense with the holding of annual general meetings. An election must be made by elective resolution (unanimous approval) under s. 379A (see 14.4.8.4). Any member of a company that has made such an election is entitled to require the holding of an annual general meeting for a year by giving notice not later than three months before the end of the year (s. 366A(3)). An election under s. 366A has effect for the year in which it is made and subsequent years but does not affect any liability already incurred for default in holding annual general meetings (s. 366A(2)).

14.4.2.1   Business of an annual general meeting

The annual general meeting of a company provides the opportunity for members to question the stewardship of the company during the preceding year. The following matters constitute the usual business of an annual general meeting of a company:

(a)   The directors lay before the company the annual accounts and reports for the most recent financial year of the company (see 9.3.6). The directors of a private company must lay accounts before a general meeting within 10 months of the end of an accounting reference period; for a public company the time-limit is seven months (see 9.3.5).

(b)   The auditors' term of office ends at the end of the meeting so they must be reappointed or new auditors appointed in their place (see 17.4.1).

(c)   The accounts for the financial year must include a directors' report which must contain the directors' recommendation of the dividend to be paid to shareholders (see 9.3.3), and a resolution will be proposed that the amount recommended be paid as dividend. (Table A, art. 102, requires dividends to be declared by ordinary resolution but without exceeding the amount recommended by the directors.)

(d)   In companies whose articles require directors to retire by rotation (as Table A does, see 15.3.2) some directors will retire at each annual general meeting and will have to be re-elected or replaced (see 15.2.3.2).

(e)   A resolution to pay an amount to the auditors as their fee may be proposed.

(f)   A resolution to pay the directors an amount as their fee may be proposed.

In most companies nowadays, directors' and auditors' fees are fixed by contract.

Members may be able to have their own resolutions placed on the agenda for an annual general meeting under CA 1985, s. 376 — see 14.4.5.7.

14.4.3   Extraordinary general meeting

By art. 36 of Table A, general meetings of the company which are not annual general meetings are known as 'extraordinary general meetings'. (In the past, annual general meetings used to be called 'ordinary'general meetings.) Under Table A, only the directors are empowered to call extraordinary general meetings except that if there are not enough directors present in the UK to form a quorum at a directors' meeting then any member may call an extraordinary general meeting (art. 37).

The directors' power to call general meetings is a fiduciary power which must (see 16.4) be exercised by the directors bona fide in what they consider is the interest of the company and not for any collateral purposes (*Pergamon Press Ltd* v *Maxwell* [1970] 1 WLR 1167). The directors of a public company must, under penalty, convene an extraordinary general meeting if half or more of the company's capital has been lost (CA 1985, s. 142; see 10.2.6).

Members of a company have a statutory right under CA 1985, s. 368, to deliver to the company's registered office a 'requisition' demanding that the company's directors proceed within 21 days to convene an extraordinary general meeting for objects specified in the requisition. The members making the requisition are called the 'requisitionists'. They must, at the time of depositing the requisition, hold between them at least 10 per cent of the company's voting shares (s. 368(2)). (The relevant percentage is the percentage of paid-up share capital.) A requisition must be signed by the requisitionists but may consist of several documents in like form each signed by one or more requisitionists (s. 368(3)).

On receipt of a requisition in proper form, notice must be given to the members of an extraordinary general meeting to be held on a date not more than 28 days after the date of the notice (s. 368(8)).

If the directors do not proceed duly to convene a meeting, the requisitionists may convene one instead (s. 363(4)) and must be repaid by the company the reasonable expenses of doing so (s. 368(6)). The company can, in turn, deduct the expenses from any fees or other remuneration due to the defaulting directors (s. 368(6)).

The directors are deemed to have failed duly to convene a meeting in any of the following circumstances:

(a) If they do not proceed to convene a meeting within 21 days of deposit of the requisition (s. 368(4)).

(b) If the requisition states that an object of the meeting is to consider a special resolution but the notice required for special resolutions (see 14.4.5.3 and 14.4.8.3) is not given (s. 368(7)).

(c) If the meeting is convened for a date more than 28 days after the date of the notice convening it (s. 368(8)).

If the directors recognise that they have failed in one or more of these ways, and the requisitionists have not yet exercised their right to convene a meeting then the directors may validly call a meeting for the objects stated in the requisition: the requisitionists are not given an exclusive right to call a meeting once the directors have failed (*Re Ariadne Australia Ltd* [1991] 2 QdR 377).

In Canada it has been held that, pending the holding of a requisitioned meeting, there is no rule to preclude the directors from exercising their powers in such a way as to render nugatory the stated purpose of the requisitionists, provided the directors are not otherwise abusing their powers (see 16.4) (*Shield Development Co. Ltd* v *Snyder* [1976] 3 WWR 44, British Columbia).

Members other than the requisitionists have no right to have resolutions put on the agenda for a requisitioned extraordinary general meeting, but the directors who convene the meeting may put their own business on the agenda (*Ball* v *Metal Industries Ltd* 1957 SC 315).

If the objects for which a meeting is requisitioned cannot be legally carried into effect in any manner then the directors are justified in refusing to act on the requisition (*Isle of Wight Railway Co.* v *Tahourdin* (1883) 25 ChD 320, CA, per Fry LJ at p. 334; *National Roads & Motorists' Association* v *Parker* (1986) 6 NSWLR 517) and the requisitionists cannot convene a meeting themselves following such a justified refusal (*Queensland Press Ltd* v *Academy Instruments No. 3 Pty Ltd* [1988] 2 QdR 575; *Windsor* v *National Mutual Life Association of Australasia* (1992) 106 ALR 282). If one of several objects cannot be legally effected then the directors are justified in omitting that object from the notice of the meeting they convene (*Turner* v *Berner* [1978] 1 NSWLR 66).

In Australia it has been held that the court will relieve the directors of their obligation to comply with a requisition if it is clear that the purpose of the meeting is something other than the passing of the resolutions contained in the requisition (*Humes Ltd* v *Unity APA Ltd (No. 1)* [1987] VR 467).

For the requisition of a general meeting of a private company under s. 253 for the purpose of laying accounts and reports, see 9.3.6.5. For the requisition of a general meeting of a private company under s. 393 to consider ending the appointment of the company's auditors, see 17.4.3. For the requisition by a resigning auditor of a general meeting under s. 392A to consider the circumstances of the resignation, see 17.4.3.

14.4.4   Court's power to order meetings

Under CA 1985, s. 371, if, for any reason, it is 'impracticable' to call a meeting of a company in any manner in which meetings of that company may be called, or to conduct a meeting in manner prescribed by the articles or by CA 1985, then the court may order a meeting to be called, held and conducted in any manner the court thinks fit. In particular the court may direct that one member of the company present in person or by proxy be deemed to constitute a meeting (s. 371(2)). The court may make such an order of its own motion or on the application of any director of the company or of any member who would be entitled to vote at the meeting (s. 371(1)). When making such an order, the court may give such ancillary or consequential directions as it thinks expedient (s. 371(2)).

This power only arises where it is 'impracticable' to call a meeting. In *Re El Sombrero Ltd* [1958] Ch 900 Wynn-Parry J said:

It is conceded that the word 'impracticable' is not synonymous with the word 'impossible'; and it appears to me that the question necessarily raised by the introduction of that word 'impracticable' is merely this: examine the circumstances of the particular case and answer the question whether, as a practical matter, the desired meeting of the company can be conducted, there being no doubt, of course, that it can be convened and held.

The power has been used to remove practical obstacles. For example, in *Edinburgh Workmen's Houses Improvement Co. Ltd* 1935 SC 56, the company had 54 members who were widely scattered geographically. Its articles required 13 members present in person to form a quorum at a general meeting. To enable the company to effect a reduction of capital, the court ordered extraordinary general meetings to be summoned at which five members present in person would be sufficient to form a quorum. In *Re Beckers Pty Ltd* (1942) 59 WN (NSW) 206, one member and director of the company had died, leaving only two members to attend general meetings for which the quorum was three and only one director to attend board meetings for which the quorum was two. Furthermore, the company's articles did not provide (as Table A, art. 90, does) for a surviving director to make appointments to the board to make up a quorum. The court ordered an extraordinary general meeting to be convened (to consider filling the vacancy on the board of directors) at which two members present in person or by proxy would be sufficient to constitute a quorum.

The power may also be used on the application of a member whose attempts to have a resolution adopted by a general meeting have been deliberately frustrated by other members. For example, in *Re El Sombrero Ltd*, the applicant held 900 of the company's 1,000 shares. The company's other two members each held 50 shares and were the company's only directors. The quorum for a general meeting was two. The applicant wished to exercise his power under what is now CA 1985, s. 303, to dismiss the two directors, so they defaulted in convening the company's annual general meeting and indicated that they would refuse to attend any meeting he convened under s. 368. The court ordered an extraordinary general meeting to be held which could be constituted by one member present in person or by proxy.

Re H.R. Paul & Son Ltd (1973) 118 SJ 166 and *Re Opera Photographic Ltd* [1989] 1 WLR 634 were similar cases in which a minority shareholder was not allowed to frustrate meetings. However, if the provisions of a company's articles and/or a unanimous shareholders' agreement show that the members have deliberately agreed that one of them is to have the ability to frustrate the holding of meetings then the court should not order a meeting to be held contrary to that member's wishes (*Harman* v *BML Group Ltd* [1994] 1 WLR 893; *Ross* v *Telford* (1997) *The Times*, 4 July 1997).

In *Re Sticky Fingers Restaurant Ltd* [1992] BCLC 84, the situation was similar to *Re Opera Photographic Ltd* but the minority shareholder/director had presented a petition under s. 459 for the relief of unfairly prejudicial conduct of the company's affairs (see 18.6). The court ordered a meeting, at which one member present in person or by proxy would constitute a quorum, to be called by the majority shareholder (Rolling Stones bass player Bill Wyman) for the purpose of appointing additional directors but on condition that any additional directors undertook not to act to prejudice the minority shareholder's position until the s. 459 petition was disposed of. A s. 459 petition cannot, however, be used to frustrate a pending s. 371 application (*Re Whitchurch Insurance Consultants Ltd* [1993] BCLC 1359).

There are statutory provisions empowering the court to order meetings of members to be summoned for specific purposes — for example, s. 425(1) (meeting to consider compromise or arrangement to be sanctioned by the court). However, outside these statutory provisions, the court will not order a general meeting of a company in any other circumstances, except to determine whether or not legal proceedings begun in the name of the company should be continued (*MacDougall* v *Gardiner* (1875) LR 10 Ch App 606).

14.4.5 Notice of meetings

14.4.5.1 Authority to call meetings
Under Table A, art. 37, the directors have authority to summon a general meeting but if there are not sufficient directors within the United Kingdom to do so, a general meeting may be summoned by any director or any member of the company.

If directors do not proceed duly to convene a meeting when required to do so by a member or auditor under CA 1985, s. 253(2) (requiring a general meeting of a private company for the purpose of laying accounts and reports), then the member or auditor who requisitioned the meeting may convene it (s. 253(3)). If directors do not proceed duly to convene a meeting requisitioned under s. 368 then the requisitionists may convene it (s. 368(4)). If directors do not proceed duly to convene a meeting after deposit of a notice under s. 393 (proposing that the appointment of the auditors of a private company which has elected to dispense with annual appointment of auditors be brought to an end) then the member who deposited the notice may convene a meeting (s. 393(4)). In any of these cases the meeting is to be convened in the same manner, as nearly as possible, as that in which meetings are to be convened by directors (ss. 253(4), 368(5) and 393(5)).

Section 367 empowers the Secretary of State to call an annual general meeting of a company if default is made in holding one. Alternatively the Secretary of State may direct the calling of a meeting.

A notice of a meeting issued by a person who does not have authority to issue such notices is void and even if the meeting takes place its decisions will be void (*Re Haycraft Gold Reduction & Mining Co.* [1900] 2 Ch 230; *Re State of Wyoming Syndicate* [1901] 2 Ch 431) though the court will not intervene if it is clear the decisions would have been the same had the correct procedure been followed (*Browne* v *La Trinidad* (1887) 37 ChD 1, CA; *Southern Counties Deposit Bank Ltd* v *Rider* (1895 73 LT 374, CA; *Bentley-Stevens* v *Jones* [1974] 1 WLR 638; see 18.5).

14.4.5.2   Who should be given notice and how?
Table A, art. 38, provides:

> Subject to the provisions of the articles and to any restrictions imposed on any shares, the notice [of a general meeting] shall be given to all the members [of the company], to all persons entitled to a share in consequence of the death or bankruptcy of a member and to the directors and auditors.

The phrase 'Subject . . . to any restrictions imposed on any shares' raises the controversial question of whether a member (such as a preference shareholder) who is only entitled to vote on certain matters is in law entitled to receive notice of a meeting at which none of those matters will be discussed. It may be that, at common law, a mere restriction on the right to vote disentitles a member from receiving notice. This seems to have been the view of Astbury J in *Re Mackenzie & Co. Ltd* [1916] 2 Ch 450 (though his lordship thought the point immaterial to the case before him). In *John Shaw & Sons (Salford) Ltd* v *Shaw* [1935] 2 KB 113, CA (which concerned the equivalent point in relation to a directors' meeting), Greer LJ thought such a member was not entitled to notice but Slesser LJ thought he was: the third member of the court expressed no opinion on the point. However, an express requirement that all members are to receive notice of meetings may override the common law rule: in *Royal Mutual Benefit Building Society* v *Sharman* [1963] 1 WLR 581 and in *Re Compaction Systems Pty Ltd* [1976] 2 NSWLR 477, such an express requirement was held to mean that members not entitled to vote at a meeting were nevertheless entitled to notice of it — however, there was no discussion of *Re Mackenzie & Co. Ltd* or *John Shaw & Sons (Salford) Ltd* v *Shaw*. We suggest that as art. 38 expressly requires notice to be given to all members, the 'restrictions' referred to in the article must be restrictions on the right to receive notice and not merely restrictions on the right to vote.

By Table A, art. 31, persons entitled to a share on the death or bankruptcy of a member are not entitled to vote at meetings unless they have their own names entered on the register of members. Table A does not require directors to be shareholders.

An auditor of a company is, by statute, entitled to receive a notice of any general meeting during the auditor's term of office (CA 1985, s. 390(1)) or, if removed from office, the general meeting at which the term of office would otherwise have expired and any general meeting at which it is proposed to fill the vacancy caused by the auditor's removal (CA 1985, s. 391(4)).

Table A, art. 111, requires a notice of a general meeting to be in writing. Table A, art. 112, sets out the main rules on giving notice:

> The company may give any notice to a member either personally or by sending it by post in a prepaid envelope addressed to the member at his registered address or by leaving it at that address. In the case of joint holders of a share, all notices shall be given to the joint holder whose name stands first in the register of members in respect of the joint

holding and notice so given shall be sufficient notice to all the joint holders. A member whose registered address is not within the United Kingdom and who gives to the company an address within the United Kingdom at which notices may be given to him shall be entitled to have notices given to him at that address, but otherwise no such member shall be entitled to receive any notice from the company.

Members of private companies with an international membership will probably wish to modify these provisions of Table A and may permit notice to be given by fax.

The provision of Table A, art. 112, that a member outside the UK may give a UK address for service of notices is required by the London Stock Exchange to be included in the articles of listed companies (Listing Rules, ch. 13, app. 1, para. 19), unless the articles provide for notice to be given to addresses outside the UK: airmail must be used when communicating with holders of listed securities residing outside the European Union (Listing Rules, para. 9.29).

Where shares are held by personal representatives or by a trustee in bankruptcy, notice may be given to them at the address supplied by them for the purpose, or (until such an address is supplied) by giving notice as if the death or bankruptcy had not occurred (art. 116).

14.4.5.3 *Length of notice*

The giving of notice of meetings of the company is a matter of domestic concern to be determined by the articles but, by CA 1985, s. 369(1), provisions in articles are void insofar as they provide for shorter notice than 21 days for an annual general meeting or 14 days for an extraordinary general meeting. Table A, art. 38, accordingly requires at least 21 clear days' notice of an annual general meeting and at least 14 clear days' notice of an extraordinary general meeting. The use of the phrase 'clear days' means, by art. 1, a period excluding the day when the notice is given or deemed to be given and the day for which it is given. If a provision in articles is avoided by s. 369(1) then s. 369(2) supplies a replacement provision complying with the minimum requirements.

In the case of an annual general meeting, all the members entitled to attend and vote at the meeting may agree that shorter notice than the period required by the articles shall not prevent the meeting from having been duly called (s. 369(3)(a)). Any other meeting can be deemed to have been duly called notwithstanding short notice, if a majority in number of the members entitled to attend and vote at the meeting so agree, provided that that majority together hold 95 per cent or more in nominal value of the shares which give a right to attend and vote at the meeting (s. 369(3)(b) and (4)).

If it is intended to propose a special resolution (see 14.4.8.3), not less than 21 days' notice of the meeting must be given, though, again, a majority in number of the members may agree to the proposing and adoption of such a resolution notwithstanding short notice provided that that majority together hold 95 per cent or more in nominal value of the shares giving the right to attend and vote at the meeting (s. 378(2) and (3)). The agreement must relate to the specific resolution or resolutions to be adopted and those agreeing must appreciate that they are agreeing to short notice (*Re Pearce Duff & Co. Ltd* [1960] 1 WLR 1014).

The statutory provisions for short notice are adopted by Table A, art. 38. The members of a *private* company may elect to substitute a lower percentage (but not less than 90 per cent) for the 95 per cent minimum required by s. 369(4) and/or s. 378(3). Such an election must be made by elective resolution (unanimous approval) under s. 379A (see 14.4.8.4).

Table A, art. 38, also requires at least 21 clear days' notice to be given of an extraordinary general meeting called for the adoption of a resolution appointing a person as a director, though a majority in number holding not less than 95 per cent of the shares may agree to shorter notice.

The rules in CA 1985 and Table A allowing members to accept short notice of a meeting require the approval of members entitled to attend and vote at the meeting, which includes members who, under Table A, art. 112, are not entitled to notice because of not having a UK address. On the other hand they make no provision for persons such as auditors who have a right to notice of meetings but not to vote.

14.4.5.4 *Effect of failure to give notice; waiver of notice*

There is a long-established rule of the law of meetings that failure to give notice of a meeting to a member entitled to notice invalidates the proceedings of the meeting (the rule was applied to companies in *Musselwhite* v *C.H. Musselwhite & Son Ltd* [1962] Ch 964). However, a person who does not receive proper notice of a meeting, or of a particular item of business, but who attends the meeting may waive the entitlement to notice. Accordingly, if all members entitled to attend a meeting are gathered together then they may agree to treat their gathering as a meeting of which they have all waived their entitlement to notice (*Re Oxted Motor Co. Ltd* [1921] 3 KB 32). If any one of those present does not consent to the gathering being treated as a meeting then it is not. For example, in *Barron* v *Potter* [1914] 1 Ch 895, the company had only two directors, Mr Potter and Canon Barron. Barron refused to attend any board meeting with Potter but Potter confronted him as he got off a train at Paddington Station and announced they were holding a board meeting and that Potter would exercise his casting vote to pass the resolutions he proposed. Barron walked away and it was held that the resolutions were invalid.

It has been held in Australia that a gathering of members without proper notice cannot be treated as a meeting if a person who was entitled to notice of meetings but was not entitled to vote (such as an auditor) did not attend and waive the entitlement to notice (*Re Compaction Systems Pty Ltd* [1976] 2 NSWLR 477). Paradoxically, it has also been held that a gathering without proper notice cannot be a valid meeting unless all persons entitled to attend meetings are present including those who are not entitled to notice (*Re Stanley W. Johnson Pty Ltd* [1936] VLR 59; cf. the statutory provisions on acceptance of short notice discussed in 14.4.5.3), which seems to confuse waiver of entitlement to notice with waiver of the need for a meeting (see 14.5.1).

Table A now contains a provision (art. 113) that a member present, either in person or by proxy, at a meeting shall be deemed to have had notice of it. It is submitted that this article makes no difference to the rule that a gathering of members without notice cannot subsequently be claimed by some of them to have been a meeting unless all consented to it being considered to be a meeting.

Table A, art. 39, provides that:

> The accidental omission to give notice of a meeting to, or the non-receipt of notice of a meeting by, any person entitled to receive notice shall not invalidate the proceedings at that meeting.

This article refers to accidental omission to give notice of meetings (as in *Re West Canadian Collieries Ltd* [1962] Ch 370 where a few members did not receive a notice because their address plates were inadvertently not put in an addressing machine). In *Musselwhite* v *C.H. Musselwhite & Son Ltd*, the company deliberately failed to give notice of its annual general meeting to the plaintiffs, in the mistaken belief that the plaintiffs were not entitled to attend the meeting because they had sold their shares in the company even though the purchaser had not yet been entered in the register of members. Russell J held that the plaintiffs, as registered holders of the shares, were entitled to attend the meeting and that, accordingly, the annual general meeting was invalid for want of notice to the plaintiffs.

It has been held in the past that the proceedings of a meeting of any kind will be invalid if a member did not attend and did not have notice of the meeting even if the member had indicated that he or she did not want to receive notices (*Re Portuguese Consolidated Copper Mines Ltd* (1889) 42 ChD 160; *Young v Ladies' Imperial Club Ltd* [1920] 2 KB 523). In the reported cases the waiver of notice has been less than definitive; nevertheless it is thought that as a general rule a member's request not to be sent notices must be ignored.

In *Re Pearce Duff & Co. Ltd* [1960] 1 WLR 1014, a special resolution for reduction of capital was adopted at a meeting for which the notice was shorter than is required by s. 378(2). The meeting was not attended by all members entitled to vote, and it was not realised at the time of the meeting that the notice was inadequate. After the meeting, all members entitled to vote on the matter agreed in writing (without meeting) that the special resolution should be treated as valid. It was held that the court could confirm the reduction of capital since no member was now entitled to object to it.

14.4.5.5 Contents of notice and circulars

Table A, art. 38, requires a notice of a meeting to specify the time and place of the meeting (known as the 'venue' of the meeting) and the general nature of the business to be transacted. CA 1985, s. 372(3), requires every notice calling a meeting of a company to state 'with reasonable prominence' that a member entitled to attend and vote is entitled to appoint a proxy (or proxies), and that a proxy need not also be a member of the company. If it is intended to propose a resolution as an extraordinary or a special resolution, this intention must be stated in the notice (CA 1985, s. 378(1) and (2); see 14.4.8.3).

It is not permissible to give conditional notice — that is, notice that a meeting will be held only if some condition is fulfilled (*Alexander v Simpson* (1889) 43 ChD 139, CA, a case concerning the requirement, now abolished, for confirmation of a special resolution, see 14.4.8.3). Once a meeting of a company has been summoned it cannot be postponed or cancelled unless the company's articles provide a power to do so, which Table A does not (*Smith v Paringa Mines Ltd* [1906] 2 Ch 193; *Bell Resources Ltd v Turnbridge Pty Ltd* (1988) 13 ACLR 429, Western Australia).

In construing the meaning of a notice of a company meeting, 'The test is, what is the fair business-like construction which business men in the position of shareholders would place on this document when they receive it?' (per Bowen LJ in *Alexander v Simpson*, at p. 147). In *Re Marra Developments Ltd* (1976) 1 ACLR 470, New South Wales, it was said that dicta referring to notices being appropriate for a 'businessman' should now be interpreted as referring to individuals generally since shareholding is more widespread than it used to be.

It is usual for the notice of a meeting to be a brief formal document but to send out with it a more discursive document, called a 'circular', setting out the background to items of business on the agenda. The London Stock Exchange requires a listed company to send an explanatory circular with a notice of any meeting that includes business other than routine business at an annual general meeting (Listing Rules, para. 14.17). If a notice is accompanied by a circular the two documents can and should ordinarily be treated as one document (*Tiessen v Henderson* [1899] 1 Ch 861 at p. 867; *Re Moorgate Mercantile Holdings Ltd* [1980] 1 WLR 227 at p. 242).

In England and Wales, the principle derived from the older cases is that the notice of a meeting and accompanying circular must give sufficient information to allow shareholders to decide whether they will attend the meeting or not. As Kekewich J said in *Tiessen* v *Henderson* at pp. 866–7 :

> A shareholder may properly and prudently leave matters in which he takes no personal interest to the decision of the majority. But in that case he is content to be bound by the vote of the majority; because he knows the matter about which the majority are to vote at the meeting. If he does not know that, he has not a fair chance of determining in his own interest whether he ought to attend the meeting, make further inquiries, or leave others to determine the matter for him.

And see similar remarks by the same learned judge in *Young* v *South African & Australian Exploration & Development Syndicate* [1896] 2 Ch 268.

In *Re Teede & Bishop Ltd* (1901) 70 LJ Ch 409, notice of an extraordinary general meeting described its purpose as consideration of a resolution for voluntary winding up in order to carry out a reconstruction. In fact only a resolution for voluntary winding up was adopted and this was held to be ineffective because it was not covered by the description of the business given in the notice: a shareholder might not have troubled to go to a meeting to consider reconstruction but would have gone to one proposing a complete liquidation of the company.

It is particularly important for directors to disclose in a circular their own interests in matters being put before a meeting (*Kaye* v *Croydon Tramways Co.* [1898] 1 Ch 358, CA; *Tiessen* v *Henderson*; *Baillie* v *Oriental Telephone & Electric Co. Ltd* [1915] 1 Ch 503, CA; *Pacific Coast Coal Mines Ltd* v *Arbuthnot* [1917] AC 607, PC). In *Baillie* v *Oriental Telephone & Electric Co. Ltd*, Lord Cozens-Hardy MR said, at p. 515, that in such circumstances a notice would not be effective unless it 'substantially put the shareholders in the position to know what they were voting about'.

In *Kaye* v *Croydon Tramways Co.*, a notice convened an extraordinary general meeting of the company to approve the sale of its undertaking to another company without disclosing that the members would have to approve the receipt by their directors of a large payment from the purchasing company. The meeting was held and the resolution adopted but the Court of Appeal held that it was ineffective because of what Lindley MR, in a much quoted phrase, described (at pp. 369–70) as a 'tricky notice'. See also *Baillie* v *Oriental Telephone & Electric Co. Ltd* [1915] 1 Ch 503 per Lord Cozens-Hardy MR at p. 515.

In *Pacific Coast Coal Mines Ltd* v *Arbuthnot*, Viscount Haldane noted that the uninformative notice in the case had been particularly inappropriate for the members who had appointed as their proxies at the meeting the directors who wanted the resolution adopted and who would benefit from it.

More recently the view has developed that directors have a duty to give to members sufficient information for them to make informed decisions about proposals which the directors recommend they approve at meetings.

Paragraph 14.1 of the Listing Rules requires that any circular sent by a company to holders of its listed securities must:

> (a)   provide a clear and adequate explanation of its subject-matter;
>
> (b)   if voting or other action is required, contain all information necessary to allow the holders of the securities to make a properly informed decision;
>
> (c)   where voting is required, contain a recommendation from the directors as to the voting action shareholders should take, indicating whether or not the proposal described in the circular is, in the opinion of the directors, in the best interests of the shareholders as a whole.

In *Rackham v Peek Foods Ltd* [1990] BCLC 895, Templeman J said, at p. 899, that directors owe 'a duty conscientiously to report to the shareholders and to furnish facts and information to enable the shareholders to decide whether to approve or disapprove' a resolution to be put to the meeting. The same view has been taken in Australia (for example, in *Residues Treatment & Trading Co. Ltd v Southern Resources Ltd* (1988) 14 ACLR 375 and *TNT Australia Pty Ltd v Poseidon Ltd* (1989) 52 SASR 379) and Canada (*Garvie v Axmith* (1961) 31 DLR (2d) 65).

When directors of a listed company arrange for it to enter into a significant transaction with another person, the Listing Rules require that the transaction must be conditional on the approval of the company's shareholders (see 15.7.6). It is usual for directors to promise to the other party that they will use all reasonable endeavours to obtain that approval. Such an undertaking is subject to the directors' duty to give their honest opinion of what is in the interests of the company to the company's members (*Rackham v Peek Foods Ltd*; *John Crowther Group plc v Carpets International plc* [1990] BCLC 460). In *Northern Counties Securities Ltd v Jackson & Steeple Ltd* [1974] 1 WLR 1133 the defendant company's directors had caused it to enter into a significant transaction unconditionally, apparently in ignorance of the Stock Exchange's requirements. The court ordered the company to complete the contract and its directors were ordered to issue a circular to members recommending that they approve the transaction because if they did not the company would be liable to damages for breach of contract.

Directors have a right and a duty to advise members about resolutions proposed or supported by the directors (*Campbell v Australian Mutual Provident Society* (1908) 77 LJ PC 117, PC) and accordingly the expenses of preparing and distributing information are payable from company funds (*Peel v London & North Western Railway Co.* [1907] 1 Ch 5, CA). However, the power to use company funds for this purpose is limited by directors' fiduciary duty to act in what they bona fide believe is in the company's interests and for a proper purpose (see 16.3.2). In *Advance Bank of Australia Ltd v FAI Insurances Australia Ltd* (1987) 9 NSWLR 464, five directors of the bank were due to retire at the next annual general meeting and offered themselves for re-election: they were supported by the other four directors but not by FAI Insurances Australia Ltd which had a substantial shareholding. The bank's board of directors resolved to promote the re-election of the five retiring directors by sending a letter to shareholders and by engaging a marketing company to telephone shareholders using a script approved by the board. Kirby P in the New South Wales Court of Appeal (at p. 487) said that neither the letter nor the telephone script made the 'slightest pretence to be a dispassionate presentation of information on policy questions such as the shareholders had an interest to receive and such as might have been expected of the directors in discharge of their duties'. Both were electioneering material. The directors would have to bear the cost themselves.

In *Dawson International plc v Coats Patons plc* 1988 SLT 854, Lord Cullen said, at p. 861:

> If . . . directors take it upon themselves to give advice to current shareholders, . . . they have a duty to advise in good faith and not fraudulently, and not to mislead whether deliberately or carelessly. If they fail to do so the affected shareholders may have a remedy, including the recovery of what is truly the personal loss sustained by them as a result.

See also *Gething v Kilner* [1972] 1 WLR 337 per Brightman J at p. 341 (duty to be honest and not to mislead) and *Goldex Mines Ltd v Revill* (1974) 54 DLR (3d) 672, Ontario, at

p. 679 ('shareholders have a right to expect that the information sent to them is fairly presented, reasonably accurate, and not misleading').

For statutory provisions requiring circulars in specific circumstances, see s. 95(5) in 6.2.6 (disapplication of pre-emption rights in relation to a particular allotment of equity shares), s. 304(2) in 15.3.3 (representations of director sought to be dismissed), s. 376(1) in 14.4.5.7 (members' statement concerning business of annual general meeting), s. 391A(3) and (4) in 17.4.3 (representations of retiring auditor whom it is not proposed to reappoint or of auditor sought to be dismissed), s. 394(3) in 17.4.3 (statement of circumstances connected with auditor's resignation) and s. 426 (effect of compromise or arrangement). See also Table A, art. 77, in 15.2.3.2 (circulation of details of persons sought to be appointed as directors).

14.4.5.6   Special notice
Special notice is required of resolutions:

(a)   to dismiss a director under CA 1985, s. 303, by ordinary resolution of a general meeting (s. 303(2)),

(b)   to appoint a person to fill the vacancy caused by the dismissal of a director under s. 303 at the same meeting (s. 303(2)),

(c)   in certain circumstances, to appoint or retain, or approve the appointment of, a director of a public company or subsidiary of either a public company or a Northern Ireland public company, who has attained the age of 70 (s. 293(5); see 15.2.4 and 15.3.6),

(d)   to fill a casual vacancy in the office of auditor (s. 388(3)),

(e)   to reappoint as auditor a retiring auditor who was appointed by the directors to fill a casual vacancy (s. 388(3)),

(f)   to dismiss an auditor (s. 391A(1)),

(g)   to appoint as auditor a person other than a retiring auditor (s. 391A(1)).

Special notice is notice to the company of the intention to move the resolution and must be given not less than 28 days before the meeting at which it is to be moved (CA 1985, s. 379(1)). If, after special notice of the intention to move a resolution at a meeting has been given to the company, that meeting is then called for a date 28 days or less after the notice has been given, the special notice is deemed to have been properly given (s. 379(3); *Fenning* v *Fenning Environmental Products Ltd* (1981) 79 LS Gaz 803). If a company has received special notice of intention to move a resolution at a meeting, and if that resolution is to be included in the business of the meeting, then the company must give its members notice of that resolution at the same time and in the same manner as it gives notice of the meeting or, if that is not practicable, by advertisement or in any other mode allowed by the company's articles, at least 21 days before the meeting (s. 379(2)). The fact that special notice of intention to move a resolution has been given does not in itself require the conveners of the meeting to put it on the agenda: only the requisitionists of an extraordinary general meeting under s. 368 (see 14.4.3) or of a resolution at an annual general meeting under s. 376 (see 14.4.5.7) can force an item on to the agenda (*Pedley* v *Inland Waterways Association Ltd* [1977] 1 All ER 209).

14.4.5.7   Circulation of members' resolutions etc.
The power and advantage given to a company's directors in relation to the calling of a meeting and the circulation of their reasoning among members was noted in 14.4.5.5. Any shareholder who wants himself to propose a resolution and put his case to his fellow members is correspondingly placed at a disadvantage, and may have to consider incurring

the expense involved in the production and circulation of notices of resolutions and accompanying circulars. Such a shareholder is helped to a degree by CA 1985, s. 376. This section allows any number of shareholders who together represent not less than one-twentieth (five per cent) of the total voting rights of all members having at the date of the requisition a right to vote at the meeting to which the requisition relates, or not less than 100 members holding shares on which there has been paid up an average of £100 or more per member, to require the company by requisition in writing (s. 376(1)):

(a) to give to members of the company entitled to receive notice of the next annual general meeting notice of any resolution which may properly be moved and is intended to be moved at that meeting;

(b) to circulate to members entitled to have notice of any general meeting sent to them any statement of not more than 1,000 words with respect to the matter referred to in any proposed resolution or the business to be dealt with at that meeting

and the expense of complying with the request is to be borne by the requisitionists unless the company resolves otherwise (s. 376(1) and (2)). Notice of the resolution and any statement to be circulated should be served in the same manner and at the same time as the notice of the meeting or as soon as practicable thereafter (s. 376(5)). In order to require the company to comply with s. 376, the requisitionists must deposit a signed copy of the requisition at the company's registered office not less than six weeks before the annual general meeting (if the requisition requires notice of a resolution) or not less than one week before a meeting (if the requisition relates to a circular) (s. 377(1)(a)). The fact that, after deposit of a requisition, an annual general meeting is called for a date within six weeks of the deposit of the requisition does not invalidate the deposit (s. 377(2)). The requisitionists are also required to deposit or tender with their requisition 'a sum reasonably sufficient to meet the company's expenses' in giving effect to the requisition (s. 377(1)(b)). By s. 376(6), the business which may be dealt with at an annual general meeting is to include any resolution of which notice is given pursuant to the section notwithstanding any provision in the company's articles, and for the purposes of the subsection notice is deemed to have been given in accordance with the section notwithstanding the accidental omission, in giving the notice, of one or more members. If directors deliberately failed to give notice to some members, knowing that this would invalidate proceedings, then they would be liable to a fine (s. 376(7) and sch. 24).

Any requisitioned resolution which, even if adopted by the annual general meeting, would not be legally effective is not a resolution 'which may be properly moved' as required by s. 376(1)(a), and so the company need not give the members notice of it (*Credit Development Pte Ltd* v *IMO Pte Ltd* [1993] 2 SLR 370, in which it was held that the company did not have to give notice of requisitioned resolutions which would have been inconsistent with the company's articles of association).

14.4.5.8 *Membership after notice of a meeting*

Under Table A, a person who becomes entitled to a share is 'bound' by any notice in respect of that share duly given to anyone from whom the person derives title to the share (art. 114) provided the notice was given before the person is registered as the new holder of the share. A company with uncertificated shares is permitted to specify in a notice of a meeting a time by which a person must be entered on the register of members to be eligible to attend or vote at the meeting: the time must not be more than 48 hours before the time fixed for the meeting (SI 1995 No. 3272, reg. 34(1) and (2)). A company with uncertificated shares is also permitted to determine that only persons on the register at the close of business on a day determined by the company are entitled to notice of a meeting (reg. 34(3)) though that day must not be more than 21 days before the day on which the notices of the meeting are sent (reg. 34(4)).

14.4.6   Quorum and single-member meetings

14.4.6.1   Quorum

The quorum for a meeting is the number of members who must be present at the meeting for its proceedings to be valid. Table A, art. 40, provides: 'Two persons entitled to vote upon the business to be transacted, each being a member or a proxy for a member or a duly authorised representative of a corporation, shall be a quorum'. Two persons who are both proxies for the same member (in respect of different parts of the member's shareholding) do not constitute a quorum under this provision (*Re Queensland Petroleum Management Ltd* [1989] 1 QdR 549).

A quorum can be formed only from persons entitled to vote (*Henderson* v *James Loutitt and Co. Ltd* (1894) 21 R 674; Table A, art. 40).

CA 1985, s. 370A (inserted by SI 1992 No. 1699), provides that notwithstanding anything in its articles, when a private limited company (other than a hybrid company) has only one member then one member present in person or by proxy is a quorum.

If a company does not have a quorum provision in its articles then it may be necessary to rely on CA 1985, s. 370, which contains provisions that 'have effect in so far as the articles of the company do not make other provision in that behalf' (s. 370(1)). Section 370(4) provides: 'Two members personally present are a quorum'. This does not allow for members to be present by proxy because it will mainly be applied to unlimited and guarantee companies without a share capital (Table A is not compulsory for such companies) and such companies are not required to permit proxies (CA 1985, s. 372(2)(a)).

An inquorate meeting is incapable of transacting business, by definition (*Re Cambrian Peat, Fuel, & Charcoal Co. Ltd, De La Mott's and Turner's Case* (1875) 31 LT 773). Accordingly, Table A, art. 41, provides that if, within half an hour from the time appointed as the commencement of a meeting, a quorum is not present, the meeting is adjourned to the same day and time in the next week and is to be held at the same place, or is adjourned to such time and place as the directors may determine.

In the 1985 version of Table A there is for the first time a specific provision (in art. 41) that if during a meeting a quorum ceases to be present then the meeting stands adjourned in the same way as if there had been no quorum at the beginning of the meeting (see the preceding paragraph).

14.4.6.2   Single-member meetings

A meeting is not properly constituted unless at least two individuals entitled to attend it are present. As Lord President Clyde said in *Neil M'Leod & Sons Ltd* 1967 SC 16 at p. 21: '. . . a meeting is not properly constituted if only one individual is present, for there is no one for him to meet'. The leading case is *Sharp* v *Dawes* (1876) 2 QBD 26 in which Mellish LJ said:

> It is clear that, according to the ordinary use of the English language, a meeting could no more be constituted by one person than a meeting could have been constituted if no shareholder at all had attended. No business could be done at such a meeting.

One individual alone does not constitute a meeting even if he or she represents two or more members, for example, by being both a member and a proxy for another member (*Re Sanitary Carbon Co.* [1877] WN 223; *Re M.J. Shanley Contracting Ltd* (1979) 124 SJ 239) or by being a member both in his or her own right and as trustee for another (*James Prain & Sons Ltd* 1947 SC 325).

Under CA 1985, s. 367(2) (see 14.4.2), a direction may be given by the Secretary of State that one member of a company present in person or by proxy is to consititute an annual general meeting of the company. A similar power is given to the court by s. 371(2) for use when it orders a meeting to be called where it is otherwise impracticable to do so (see 14.4.4). In *Re London Flats Ltd* [1969] 1 WLR 711, Plowman J described what are now ss. 367(2) and 371(2) as exceptional (at p. 719) and held that they did not displace the general rule that 'a single shareholder cannot constitute a meeting' (at p. 717).

The rule of law that a meeting is not properly constituted unless at least two individuals entitled to attend it are present must be modified (under SI 1992 No. 1699, reg. 2) in relation to a single-member private company. As s. 370A provides for the quorum of such a company to be one member present in person or by proxy, a meeting of such a company attended by one individual as a member or proxy would be properly constituted and its proceedings would be valid.

14.4.7 Chairman

It is usual to appoint a chairman to supervise the proceedings at a meeting. As with provisions on quorum (see 14.4.6.1) almost all companies will be subject to the provision of some version of Table A or will have substituted their own provision. By art. 42 of Table A:

> The chairman, if any, of the board of directors or in his absence some other director nominated by the directors shall preside as chairman of the meeting, but if neither the chairman nor such other director (if any) be present within fifteen minutes after the time appointed for holding the meeting and willing to act, the directors present shall elect one of their number to be chairman and, if there is only one director present and willing to act, he shall be chairman.

In Table A, art. 91 sets out the procedure for appointing a chairman of the board of directors (see 15.5.2).

Article 43 then supplements art. 42 by providing that:

> If no director is willing to act as chairman, or if no director is present within fifteen minutes after the time appointed for holding the meeting, the members present and entitled to vote shall choose one of their number to be chairman.

As with the provisions relating to quorum (see 14.4.6.1), CA 1985, s. 370, makes a provision for any company that does not have a provision in its articles for appointing a chairman of members' meetings. Section 370(5) provides: 'Any member elected by the members present at a meeting may be chairman of it'. An individual who is present as a proxy for a member may be appointed chairman under Table A, art. 43, or CA 1985, s. 370(5) (*Re Bradford Investments plc* [1991] BCLC 224). It may be necessary for someone to act as chairman temporarily for the purpose of organising the election of a chairman.

In *National Dwellings Society* v *Sykes* [1894] 3 Ch 159, Chitty J said, at p. 162:

Unquestionably it is the duty of the chairman, and his function, to preserve order, and to take care that the proceedings are conducted in a proper manner, and that the sense of the meeting is properly ascertained with regard to any question which is properly before the meeting.

The chairman of a meeting has authority to decide all incidental questions arising at the meeting concerning its proceedings which require decision at the time: the onus is therefore on a person challenging such a decision to show that it was wrong (*Re Indian Zoedone Co.* (1884) 26 ChD 70, CA). Traditionally companies manage their own affairs and do not call upon an independent outsider to chair meetings. The chairman of a company general meeting is usually a member, or at least a director, of the company and will therefore be personally interested in all the procedural questions he or she has to decide. Accordingly, it is misleading to describe the chairman of a company general meeting as occupying a quasi-judicial position because a person in a judicial position would not be permitted to be judge in his or her own cause whereas it is an inevitable consequence of the tradition of self-government that a company chairman is not disqualified by self-interest. When deciding questions a chairman must act honestly and fairly to all sectional interests, and in the interests of the company (*Blair* v *Consolidated Enfield Corp.* (1995) 128 DLR (4th) 73 at p. 87).

14.4.8   Resolutions

14.4.8.1   Introduction
Decisions of meetings are embodied in statements known as 'resolutions'. The normal rule is that a resolution is adopted if more votes are cast for it than against it (usually called a 'simple majority'): if the votes are equal then the resolution is not adopted. On a large number of matters, CA 1985 and IA 1986 require a larger majority: they require that three-quarters of the votes cast are in favour of the resolution. On these matters the Acts direct either that a 'special resolution' be adopted or an 'extraordinary resolution': the difference is that at least 21 days' notice must be given of intention to propose a special resolution whereas no notice period is specified for extraordinary resolutions. A company's memorandum or articles may specify additional matters requiring extraordinary or special resolutions.

14.4.8.2   Ordinary resolutions
A resolution is an 'ordinary resolution' if it is not an extraordinary, special or elective resolution. A simple majority is sufficient to adopt an ordinary resolution (*Bushell* v *Faith* [1970] AC 1099 per Lord Upjohn at p. 1108 and Lord Donovan at p. 1110).

14.4.8.3   Special and extraordinary resolutions
In order for a special or an extraordinary resolution to be adopted at a general meeting of a company, three-quarters of the votes cast (whether in person or by proxy) by members entitled to vote must be in favour of the resolution (CA 1985, s. 378(1) and (2)). Notice must have been given of intention to propose the resolution as a special or extraordinary resolution, as the case may be (s. 378(1) and (2)). The only point now distinguishing a special resolution from an extraordinary resolution is that normally the notice of intention to propose a special resolution must be given at least 21 days before the meeting (s. 378(2)) whereas no minimum notice period is specified for an extraordinary resolution. As explained in 14.4.5.3, the notice period for a special resolution can be shortened under s. 378(3). In *Re Moorgate Mercantile Holdings Ltd* [1980] 1 WLR 227 it was held that the notice must set out the text or the entire substance of the resolution, and the resolution actually adopted

by the meeting must be the same as that specified in the notice, though corrections of clerical or grammatical errors are allowed, or the resolution may be given a more formal wording provided nothing of substance is altered. This means that no amendments of substance, however trivial, can be made by the meeting. It follows that a minor error of substance in the notice of a special or extraordinary resolution may mean that a new meeting has to be convened. C. Baker, 'Amending special resolutions' (1991) 12 Co Law 64 discusses an unreported case (*Re Fenner plc* (1990)) in which the court did not follow *Re Moorgate Mercantile Holdings Ltd*.

Until 30 October 1929, a special resolution adopted by a meeting had to be confirmed by a simple majority at a second, separately convened meeting. This inconvenient requirement, which was originally the principal feature distinguishing special resolutions from extra-ordinary resolutions, was abolished by CA 1928, s. 25. In the consultation document introducing its review of company law (see 0.3.1.6) the DTI singles out the lingering distinction between extraordinary and special resolutions as an example of excessive detail in company law which makes the legislation more complicated than it needs to be (*Modern Company Law for a Competitive Economy* (London: DTI, 1998), p. 6).

The majority in favour of a special or extraordinary resolution is based on the numbers of votes cast for and against the motion — that is, abstentions and disallowed votes are not counted (s. 378(5)).

A special resolution is required in the following situations:

(a)   to change the objects of a company (CA 1985, s. 4);

(b)   to alter the articles of association of a company (CA 1985, s. 9(1));

(c)   to alter any condition contained in a company's memorandum which could lawfully have been contained in its articles (CA 1985, s. 17(1));

(d)   to change a company's name (CA 1985, s. 28(1));

(e)   to ratify action by the directors which is not capable of being within the objects of the company (CA 1985, s. 35(3));

(f)   to relieve any liability of directors or any other person incurred because the directors have acted outside the company's objects (CA 1985, s. 35(3));

(g)   to allow a private company to re-register as a public company (CA 1985, s. 43(1)(a));

(h)   to re-register an unlimited company as a private limited company (CA 1985, s. 51(1));

(i)   to allow a public company to re-register as a private company (CA 1985, s. 53(1)(a));

(j)   to give directors power to ignore or modify members' statutory pre-emption rights to subscribe for new shares or on the issue of options or convertibles, if the power is not given by the articles, or to renew such a power (CA 1985, s. 95(1), (2 and (3); this provision is irrelevant to a private company if the statutory pre-emption rights are excluded by its memorandum or articles under s. 91);

(k)   to decide that uncalled share capital shall not be called up except on winding up (CA 1985, s. 120);

(l)   to reduce share capital if so authorised by the company's articles (CA 1985, s. 135(1));

(m)   to approve the giving of financial assistance for the acquisition of shares in a private company or its holding company (CA 1985, s. 155(4) and (5));

(n)   to authorise the terms of a proposed contract for an off-market purchase by a company of any of its own shares; to vary, revoke or renew any such authority; and to vary an existing contract of purchase (CA 1985, s. 164(2), (3) and (7));

(o)   to authorise the terms of a contingent contract under which a company may become entitled or obliged to buy its own shares; to vary, revoke or renew any such authority; and to vary an existing contingent purchase contract (CA 1985, s. 165(2));

(p)   to authorise the proposed release by a company of its rights under a contract for an off-market purchase of its own shares or a contingent purchase contract; to vary, revoke or renew any such authority; and to vary an existing release agreement (CA 1985, s. 167(2));

(q)   to approve a payment out of a private company's capital for the redemption or purchase of any of its own shares (CA 1985, s. 173(2));

(r)   to make a dormant company exempt from auditing requirements (CA 1985, s. 250);

(s)   to alter a company's memorandum so as to render the directors' or managers' or any managing director's liability unlimited (CA 1985, s. 307(1));

(t)   to approve the assignment by a director or manager of his office to another person (CA 1985, s. 308);

(u)   to resolve to petition for compulsory liquidation (IA 1986, s. 122(1)(a); the directors also have power to petition: s. 124(1));

(v)   to resolve that a company be voluntarily wound up, unless the circumstances are such that an ordinary or extraordinary resolution is sufficient — see 20.5.2 (IA 1986, s. 84(1)(b));

(w)   to approve the acceptance by a liquidator in a members' voluntary winding up of shares of another company to which assets of the company in liquidation are to be transferred (IA 1986, ss. 110(2), (3) and (4) and 111(3)).

If the members of a company resolve by extraordinary resolution to the effect that it cannot by reason of its liabilities continue its business, and that it is advisable to wind up, then that is effective to commence voluntary liquidation (IA 1986, s. 84(1)(c)): in other circumstances, voluntary liquidation must be commenced by special resolution unless an ordinary resolution is justified by the articles — see 20.5.2.

An extraordinary resolution is required in the following situations:

(a)   in certain circumstances, at a class meeting, to vary class rights (CA 1985, s. 125(2) and (3); see 14.5.3.2);

(b)   to give the liquidator in a members' voluntary liquidation powers to pay a class of creditors in full or make a compromise or arrangement concerning any of the debts of the company or any debts owed to the company (IA 1986, s. 165(2)(a)).

In addition, Table A, art. 117, specifies an extraordinary resolution for giving sanction to a liquidator to distribute surplus assets in kind instead of realising them for cash.

The definitions of extraordinary and special resolutions in s. 378(1) and (2) refer to them as resolutions passed 'at a general meeting', but by s. 381A(6), the members of a *private company* may agree to a special or extraordinary resolution in writing without meeting, in accordance with s. 381A (see 14.5.3). Also s. 380(4)(c) (see 14.4.11) shows that it is contemplated in the CA 1985 that a decision which the Act requires to be taken by extraordinary or special resolution at a meeting may alternatively be taken by unanimous agreement without meeting (*Re M.J. Shanley Contracting Ltd* (1979) 124 SJ 239).

14.4.8.4   Elective resolutions

An elective resolution is not effective unless adopted at a meeting of which at least 21 days' notice in writing is given, stating that an elective resolution is to be proposed and stating the terms of the resolution (CA 1985, s. 379A(2)(a)). In addition, it must be agreed to at the meeting, in person or by proxy, by all the members entitled to attend and vote at the meeting (s. 379A(2)(b)). The requirement of 21 days' notice can be waived if all members entitled to attend and vote at the meeting agree (s. 379(2A) inserted by SI 1996 No. 1471, art. 2). Under s. 379A(1), an elective resolution is required in order for a private company to make an election under any of the following provisions of CA 1985:

(a)   s. 80A (duration of directors' authority to allot shares),
(b)   s. 252 (dispensing with laying of accounts and reports before general meeting),
(c)   s. 366A (dispensing with holding of annual general meeting),
(d)   s. 369(4) or s. 378(3) (majority required to authorise short notice of meeting),
(e)   s. 386 (dispensing with annual appointment of auditors).

As only a private company may make any of these elections, an elective resolution of a private company is automatically revoked on re-registration of the company as a public company (s. 379A(4)). By s. 381A(6), an elective resolution may be agreed to in writing, in accordance with s. 381A (see 14.5.3).

Members may revoke an elective resolution by adopting an ordinary resolution to that effect (s. 379(3)).

14.4.9   Voting

14.4.9.1   Right to vote

14.4.9.1.1   General principle.   Normally each individual at a meeting has one vote which is exercised by a show of hands. However, companies normally allow members to have a number of votes proportional to the number of shares held, but such weighted voting rights can be exercised only when voting is by poll (*Re Horbury Bridge Coal, Iron & Waggon Co.* (1879) 11 ChD 109; see 14.4.9.2).

Under Table A, art. 58, an objection to the qualification of any voter must be raised at the meeting or adjourned meeting at which the vote objected to is tendered. An objection must be referred to the chairman whose decision is final and conclusive. Every vote not disallowed at the meeting shall be valid. The provision for the finality of the chairman's decision on the admissibility of votes does not apply to the decision of a person acting as chairman for the purpose of organising the election of a chairman under Table A, art. 43, or CA 1985, s. 370(5) (*Re Bradford Investments plc* [1991] BCLC 224).

14.4.9.1.2   Members.   Under Table A, a shareholder is not entitled to vote in respect of a share if any money payable in respect of that share has not been paid (art. 57).

Under Table A, if a share is jointly held and votes are tendered by more than one of the joint holders then only the vote of the 'senior' will be accepted and seniority is determined by the order of the names in the register of members. Joint holders therefore have a right to instruct the company on the order in which their names are to appear in the register (*Re T.H. Saunders & Co. Ltd* [1908] 1 Ch 415).

If a share has been sold but, at the date of a meeting, the transfer has not been completed because the share has not been paid for then the unpaid vendor retains the right to vote in respect of the share (*Musselwhite* v *C.H. Musselwhite & Son Ltd* [1962] Ch 964). If a vendor of a share has not been paid for it but the transfer has been registered then the buyer must vote in accordance with the unpaid vendor's instructions (ibid.).

14.4.9.1.3 Proxies. At common law an individual who cannot attend a meeting does not have an absolute right to appoint a proxy to vote at the meeting in his or her stead — a proxy may be appointed only if permitted by the rules governing the meeting (*Harben* v *Phillips* (1882) 23 ChD 14 per Cotton LJ at p. 32 and Bowen LJ at pp. 35–6). In company law there is a mandatory requirement that proxy voting must be permitted by all companies (CA 1985, s. 372(1)) at general and class meetings (s. 372(7)), and notices of general and class meetings must state the right to appoint proxies (s. 372(3) and (7)). Moreover, a private company must give a member's proxy at a meeting the same right to speak at the meeting as the member would have (s. 372(1)). A company cannot require that only a member of the company can act as a proxy (s. 372(1)).

A proxy is not entitled to vote on a show of hands, but only on a poll, unless the articles provide otherwise, which Table A does not (s. 372(2)(c)). The instrument appointing a proxy to vote at a meeting is deemed to confer authority to demand, or join in demanding, a poll, and any provision of a company's articles preventing a proxy from demanding, or joining in demanding, a poll is void (s. 373).

A member of a private company who has more than one share in the company is not entitled to appoint more than one proxy (to represent different parts of the shareholding) to attend on the same occasion, unless the articles provide otherwise (s. 372(2)(b)). Table A, art. 59, makes such a provision.

Under Table A, an instrument appointing a proxy must be in writing under the hand of the appointer and be deposited at the company's registered office not less than 48 hours before the meeting to which it relates (arts 60 and 62). A provision in a company's articles requiring instruments appointing proxies to be deposited more than 48 hours before a meeting is void (CA 1985, s. 372(5)). Articles 60 and 61 of Table A set out forms for appointing proxies. Article 63 specifies the procedure for revoking the appointment of a proxy. Even if the art. 63 procedure has not been followed, a proxy who acts knowing that his or her authority has been revoked will be in breach of duty to his or her appointer (*Cousins* v *International Brick Co. Ltd* [1931] 2 Ch 90, CA, per Romer LJ at p. 104). The appointment of a proxy does not constitute an irrevocable decision by the appointer not to vote in person. If a member who has appointed a proxy for a meeting actually attends the meeting and tenders a vote then the chairman must take that vote and not any vote tendered by the proxy (*Cousins* v *International Brick Co. Ltd*).

Proxy voting is of great practical importance, in particular because very few members of public companies attend meetings. The Listing Rules require that every time a notice convening a meeting of holders of listed securities is sent out it must be accompanied by a form for the appointment of a proxy (para. 13.28(a)). Usually the directors convening a meeting will want one of their number appointed proxy and able to vote as they want, so proxy forms sent out with notices will have the name of the directors' preferred proxy already printed on them. CA 1985, s. 372(6), makes it an offence to send out such prepared proxy forms at the company's expense to some only of the members. The Listing Rules require that proxy forms must state that a member can choose a proxy and provide space for the member's choice to be written in (para. 13.28(c)). The Listing Rules also require that a proxy form must enable the appointer to specify how the proxy is to vote on each motion other than procedural motions (para. 13.28(b); this is the type of form specified in Table A, art. 61, and known as a 'two-way' proxy form).

The right given to a member by s. 372(1) is a right to appoint an agent to act for that member. In *Coachcraft Ltd* v *SVP Fruit Co. Ltd* (1980) 28 ALR 319, PC, some members of SVP Fruit Co. Ltd (a company registered in Victoria) had sold their shares to Coachcraft Ltd but, because of restrictions in the articles of SVP Fruit Co. Ltd, these shares were still registered in the sellers' names and not in the name of Coachcraft Ltd. Those sellers had irrevocably appointed a representative of Coachcraft Ltd to vote in respect of their shares. The Privy Council found that this representative had been appointed to act in the interests of Coachcraft Ltd as purchaser of the shares and so the appointment was not an exercise of the right to appoint a proxy. Accordingly the company could reject the representative's votes without contravening the Victorian equivalent of CA 1985, s. 372(1).

14.4.9.1.4 Corporate shareholders. The right to appoint proxies is conferred on all company members whether natural or legal persons but CA 1985, s. 375, also gives a corporate member of a company the more valuable right to appoint a human 'representative' who can act on behalf of the corporation at general or class meetings of the company with the same powers as the corporation could exercise if it were an individual. The appointment must be made by resolution of the corporate member's directors or other governing body.

14.4.9.1.5 Trustees in bankruptcy and personal representatives. A trustee in bankruptcy or a personal representative, though entitled under Table A to notice of company meetings (art. 38 discussed in 14.4.5.2) is not, unless registered as a member in respect of a share, generally entitled to exercise any right conferred by membership in relation to company meetings (art. 31 of Table A). A bankrupt who is still registered as a member in respect of his or her shares remains entitled to attend and vote at company meetings though obliged to vote in accordance with the directions of his or her trustee in bankruptcy because the trustee has the beneficial interest in the shares (*Wise* v *Lansdell* [1921] 1 Ch 420; *Morgan* v *Gray* [1953] Ch 83).

14.4.9.1.6 Trustees. Under Table A, art. 5, the only interest in one of its shares that a company will recognise is an absolute right of the registered shareholder to the whole share, except as otherwise provided by the articles or by law. By CA 1985, s. 360 (see 8.7.1), a company is not affected by notice that any of its shares are held in trust. Therefore, if a share in a company is held on trust, a beneficiary of the trust cannot insist that the company accept his vote instead of the vote of the trustee who is the registered holder of the share. However, this does not prevent the court ordering a company not to act on a resolution adopted by means of votes cast in breach of trust (*McGrattan* v *McGrattan* [1985] NI 28).

It is possible for a company to have provisions in its articles which entitle it to have regard to the beneficial as well as the legal ownership of shares. For example, in *Coachcraft Ltd* v *SVP Fruit Co. Ltd* (1980) 28 ALR 319, PC, the articles of SVP Fruit Co. Ltd provided that not more than 10,000 shares could be held by or on behalf of any one member. The Privy Council held that this meant that any one member could not exercise more than 10,000 votes at a general meeting and that, because the limit was expressed in terms of shares 'held by or on behalf of any one member', it was permissible for the chairman of a general meeting to consider the beneficial as well as the legal ownership of shares in the company when deciding whether or not to accept votes.

14.4.9.1.7 Freezing orders. While investigations are in progress about the true ownership of shares in a company those shares may be subjected to restrictions, imposed by the court or the Secretary of State, which, *inter alia*, prevent the votes attached to those shares being exercised. For details, see 8.9.7.

14.4.9.1.8 Non-members. It has been held in Australia that a provision in a company's articles cannot give a non-member a right to vote at members' meetings (other than as a proxy or corporate representative) because such a provision would be inconsistent with the companies' legislation (*Shears* v *Phosphate Co-operative Co. of Australia Ltd* (1988) 14 ACLR 747). The provisions of CA 1985 concerned with company meetings clearly contemplate that it is only members and their proxies or representatives who are entitled to vote. For example, the definition of extraordinary and special resolutions in s. 378 refer only to the votes of members, and s. 372(1) confers the right to appoint a proxy only on members. Furthermore, as Gibbs J pointed out in *Kolotex Hosiery (Australia) Pty Ltd* v *Federal Commissioner of Taxation* (1975) 132 CLR 535 at p. 569, a person who is not a member of a company would not be able to take legal action to enforce any voting right in the company's articles (see 3.4.2.3).

14.4.9.2   Method of voting
Under Table A, there are two methods of voting:

(a)   A show of hands. Voters in favour of a resolution are asked to raise a hand each and are counted; the same is done for voters against the motion. Each voter can be counted only once.

(b)   A poll. A written record is made of each voter's vote and the numbers for and against the motion are counted. By art. 54, on a poll, every member has one vote for every share held, subject to any rights or restrictions attached to shares.

By CA 1985, s. 372(2)(c), a proxy is not entitled to vote on a show of hands unless the articles provide otherwise, which Table A does not. But the right to appoint a proxy is a right to appoint someone entitled to vote on a poll (s. 372(1) and (2)(c)) and Table A, art. 59, confirms that on a poll votes may be given either personally or by proxy. On a poll, a member entitled to more than one vote need not use all of them, and may cast some for and some against the resolution (CA 1985, s. 374) — this enables a member holding shares as nominee for two or more beneficial owners to cast votes as they wish.

If there is an equality of votes on either a show of hands or a poll then, under Table A, art. 50, the chairman can exercise a casting vote 'in addition to any other vote he may have' — the quoted words mean that a chairman who does not have any other vote, for example, because he or she holds only non-voting shares or is not a member at all, does not have a casting vote (*Re Halcyon Heights Estates Ltd* [1980–84] LRC (Comm) 583 at p. 588). There is no common law right to a casting vote: if there is no provision in the articles for a casting vote then an ordinary resolution on which there is an equality of votes is lost. Sometimes two persons form a joint venture company on the basis of exactly equal control. In such a company it is important for no one to have a casting vote: see *Re Medefield Pty Ltd* (1977) 2 ACLR 406 discussed in 14.4.9.5 and *Daniels* v *Fielder* (1988) 52 DLR (4th) 424.

Because there is only one vote each on a show of hands but one vote per share on a poll and because proxies can vote on a poll but not on a show of hands, the two methods of voting can, and often do, produce opposite results. It is therefore very important to know which method of voting is to be used on any particular question. Under art. 46 of Table A, a decision is to be taken by show of hands unless there is a demand for a poll, either before there is a show of hands or on the declaration of the result of a show of hands. Under Table A, art. 47, if there is no demand for a poll then the chairman's declaration of the result of a show of hands and a statement of that declaration entered in the minutes are conclusive evidence of the fact stated. This extends a statutory provision in CA 1985, s. 378(5), that the chairman's declaration that a special or extraordinary resolution has been passed on a show of hands is conclusive evidence of that fact unless a poll is demanded.

In *Re Horbury Bridge Coal, Iron & Waggon Co.* (1879) 11 ChD 109, a question had to be decided at a company general meeting and only an ordinary resolution (simple majority) was required. On a show of hands, three voters holding altogether 50 shares voted in favour and two voters holding altogether 65 shares voted against. No poll was demanded but the chairman declared that those voting against had won. It was held that this was wrong because if no poll was demanded then the question had to be determined by show of hands only, ignoring the weighted voting rights which were available only when voting was by poll. The company's articles had no provision equivalent to Table A, art. 47, so the chairman's declaration of the result was not conclusive — see *Arnot v United African Lands Ltd* [1901] 1 Ch 518.

If a poll is demanded on a question after a vote on that question has been taken by show of hands then the vote on the show of hands is void and the question remains undecided until the poll has been held (*R v Wimbledon Local Board* (1882) 8 QBD 459, CA). Under Table A, art. 48, a demand for a poll may, with the consent of the chairman, be withdrawn before the poll is taken. If a demand for a poll is withdrawn and the question has not been decided by show of hands then the meeting continues as if the demand for a poll had not been made (art. 51); if the question has previously been decided by show of hands then that decision is reinstated (art. 48).

It is common for articles to provide that a demand for a poll is ineffective unless supported by a significant proportion of the membership. Section 373 permits such conditions within limits: the articles must at least provide that the following persons may demand a poll (s. 373(1)):

(a)   not less than five members having the right to vote at the meeting; or

(b)   a member or members representing not less than one tenth of the total voting rights of all the members having the right to vote at the meeting; or

(c)   a member or members holding shares in the company conferring a right to vote at the meeting, being shares on which an aggregate sum has been paid up equal to not less than one tenth of the total sum paid up on all the shares conferring that right.

The articles must also provide that a demand by a proxy for a member is the same as a demand by the member (s. 373(2)).

Table A, art. 46, is more generous in that it allows a poll to be demanded by two members rather than five and also allows a poll to be demanded by the chairman of the meeting. The chairman of a meeting is given a power to demand a poll in order that he or she can ascertain the sense of the meeting upon a matter before them (*Second Consolidated Trust Ltd v Ceylon Amalgamated Tea & Rubber Estates Ltd* [1943] 2 All ER 567). It would seem therefore that the chairman must exercise the power whenever he or she is aware that a poll would reverse a decision obtained by show of hands.

In private companies it is usual to modify Table A to provide that any one member present in person or by proxy may demand a poll: this modification is necessary because private companies usually have a small membership. For an example of extraordinary results that can follow from not having an article on demands for a poll that is appropriate to the company's circumstances, see *Siemens Brothers & Co. Ltd v Burns* [1918] 2 Ch 325, CA, discussed in 18.5.

In addition to the right to demand a poll conferred by CA 1985, s. 373, if rights attached to special classes of shares are to be varied pursuant to CA 1985, s. 125 (see 14.6.2), any holder of shares of the class in question who is present at a class meeting in person or by proxy may demand a poll (s. 125(6)(b)). Notwithstanding anything in the company's articles, any member of the company may, in person or by proxy, demand a poll on a special resolution to confer, revoke or renew authority for an off-market purchase of its own shares or a contingent purchase contract relating to any of its shares (ss. 164(5) and 165(2)) or on a special resolution approving a payment out of the company's capital for the redemption or purchase of any of its own shares (CA 1985, s. 174(3) and (5)).

When a vote is taken by poll, procedures are followed which have the following purposes:

(a)   To enable members to vote who are not present in the room where the meeting is being held.

(b)   To enable each voter to cast more than one vote.

(c)   To enable each voter's entitlement to vote to be verified.

The exact procedures used vary from company to company: they may be specified in more or less detail in the articles of association or left to be arranged by the company secretary. Table A, art. 49, leaves it to the chairman to direct how a poll is to be taken and empowers the chairman to appoint scrutineers, who need not be members. Because art. 59 says that votes on a poll may be given in person or by proxy, a chairman cannot under art. 49 direct a poll to be taken otherwise than by voting in person or by proxy — for example, postal voting is not allowed (*McMillan* v *Le Roi Mining Co. Ltd* [1906] 1 Ch 331).

One possible polling procedure is for members to call at a polling place to cast their votes at an appointed time: this is appropriate, for example, in the election of officers of a society but is inappropriate on procedural questions such as the election of a chairman or a motion to adjourn. CA 1985, s. 373, prohibits a company from excluding altogether the right to demand a poll at a general meeting on any question other than the election of the chairman of the meeting or the adjournment of the meeting. Table A does not exclude the right to demand a poll on those two procedural questions but instead art. 51 requires a poll on either of them to be taken forthwith. Otherwise, art. 51 requires the chairman to decide either to hold a poll forthwith or to direct the time and place at which it is to be held: the time must not be later than 30 days after the poll is demanded. Unless the time and place of polling are announced at the meeting, at least seven clear days' notice of them must be given (art. 52).

The fact that a poll has been demanded on a question does not prevent the meeting continuing with other business (art. 51).

Whenever and wherever it is taken, a poll on a question before a meeting is part of that meeting (*Shaw* v *Tati Concessions Ltd* [1913] 1 Ch 292) and the result of the poll is deemed to be the resolution of that meeting (Table A, art. 49). However, the date of the resolution is the date on which the result of the poll is ascertained (*Holmes* v *Keyes* [1959] Ch 199, CA). If a poll on a question considered by a meeting is conducted some time after the meeting has dispersed it nevertheless does not constitute an 'adjourned meeting': it is part of the meeting at which the poll was demanded. Accordingly, in the interval between the demand for and the holding of the poll new proxy appointments cannot be made (*Shaw* v *Tati Concessions Ltd*) unless the articles provide otherwise. Table A, art. 62, permits new proxy appointments in such circumstances if the poll is to be taken more than 48 hours after it is demanded: the proxy appointments must be deposited with the company at least 24 hours before the time appointed for taking the poll. Table A, art. 63, also provides for proxy appointments to be revoked in the interval between the demand for and the holding of a poll if the poll is not held on the day on which it was demanded.

14.4.9.3   *Conflict of interest and duty*

As will be explained in 16.5.1, a director of a company is in a fiduciary position and so is subject to the rule against conflict of interest and duty. However, it has often been stated that a member of a company is not, when voting as a member, subject to any rule against conflict of interest and duty because a member of a company is not a fiduciary for the company. In *Peters' American Delicacy Co. Ltd* v *Heath* (1939) 61 CLR 457, Dixon J said, at p. 504:

> The shareholders are not trustees for one another, and, unlike directors, they occupy no fiduciary position and are under no fiduciary duties. They vote in respect of their shares, which are property, and the right to vote is attached to the share itself as an incident of property to be enjoyed and exercised for the owner's personal advantage.

It follows that a member who is also a director is not subject to the rule against conflict of interest and duty when voting as a member (*North-West Transportation Co. Ltd* v *Beatty* (1887) 12 App Cas 589, PC; *Re Express Engineering Works Ltd* [1920] 1 Ch 466; *Baird* v *J. Baird & Co. (Falkirk) Ltd* 1949 SLT 368). In *North-West Transportation Co. Ltd* v *Beatty*, Sir Richard Baggallay said, at p. 593:

> Unless some provision to the contrary is to be found in the charter or other instrument by which the company is incorporated, the resolution of a majority of the shareholders, duly convened, upon any question with which the company is legally competent to deal, is binding upon the minority, and consequently upon the company, and every shareholder has a perfect right to vote upon any such question, although he may have a personal interest in the subject-matter opposed to, or different from, the general or particular interests of the company.

In the same vein, Jessel MR in *Pender* v *Lushington* (1877) 6 ChD 70 observed, at p. 75:

> . . . a man may be actuated in giving his vote by interests entirely adverse to the interests of the company as a whole. He may think it more for his particular interest that a certain course may be taken which may be in the opinion of others very adverse to the interests of the company as a whole, but he cannot be restrained from giving his vote in what way he pleases because he is influenced by that motive.

Also widely quoted is Lord Maugham's remark in *Carruth* v *Imperial Chemical Industries Ltd* [1937] AC 707 at p. 765:

> . . . the shareholders' vote is a right of property, and prima facie may be exercised by a shareholder as he thinks fit in his own interest.

These remarks focus on the freedom of a member of a company to benefit from membership. Majority members are not so free to use their voting power to damage the interests of the minority, as will be seen in 14.4.9.4, 14.4.9.5 and 14.4.9.6. One area in which a decision by members may be declared to be invalid by the courts, alteration of the articles of association, has already been discussed in 3.5.3.5. Two recent articles have noted that recently judges have been increasingly willing to intervene in corporate decision-making at the instance of dissentient members. J.G. MacIntosh, 'Minority shareholder rights in Canada and England: 1869–1987' (1989) 27 Osgoode Hall LJ 561, ascribes this to an increasing concern for the position of minorities in companies, which is reflected in the statutory provisions for relief from conduct of a company's affairs that is unfairly prejudicial to some of its members (see 18.6). L.S. Sealy, '"Bona fides" and "proper purposes" in corporate decisions' (1989) 15 Mon LR 265 is primarily concerned with decisions by directors but includes a discussion of the concept of acting bona fide in the interests of a company which is relevant both to decisions by members and decisions by directors (see 14.4.9.4 and 16.4).

There are two statutory restrictions on self-interested voting. When counting votes in favour of a special resolution of a private company to make a payment out of capital to redeem shares, votes attaching to the shares to be redeemed must be ignored (CA 1985, s. 174(2)). When counting votes in favour of a special resolution to confer, vary, revoke or renew authority to make an off-market purchase of its own shares, or to make a contingent purchase contract for its own shares, votes attaching to the shares to be purchased must be ignored (ss. 164(5) and 165(2)).

14.4.9.4 Bona fide for the benefit of the company and for a proper purpose
Courts have sometimes said that a resolution of the members of a company would be invalid if members voting for it did not vote bona fide in the interests of the company (e.g., *Allen* v *Gold Reefs of West Africa Ltd* [1900] 1 Ch 656, CA, see 3.5.3.4) or if the resolution was adopted for an improper purpose (*Re Western Mines Ltd* (1975) 65 DLR (3d) 307, British Columbia, at p. 313). These are conditions which are placed on any exercise of powers by directors (see 16.4). However, the courts are more ready to interfere with directors' exercise of their powers than with members (*Ngurli Ltd* v *McCann* (1953) 90 CLR 425 at pp. 438–9). In the case of directors the conditions are imposed to prevent abuse of a fiduciary position, but members of a company do not have a fiduciary relationship with the company — in their case the conditions are imposed to prevent misuse of the power of a majority to bind a minority (see per Lindley MR in *Allen* v *Gold Reefs of West Africa Ltd* quoted in 3.5.3.4). (The majority do not have a fiduciary relationship with the minority: *Brant Investments Ltd* v *KeepRite Inc.* (1991) 80 DLR (4th) 161.)

The courts have imposed conditions in the following situations:

(a)   When the members are exercising the company's statutory power to alter its articles of association: then an alteration must be bona fide for the benefit of the company as a whole (see 3.5.3.4 where it is noted that this condition may be inappropriate where the alteration affects only the rights of members *inter se*).

(b)   An appointment of a director must be made for the benefit of the company as a whole and not for any ulterior purpose (*Re H.R. Harmer Ltd* [1959] 1 WLR 62 per Jenkins LJ at p. 82). See further 15.2.3.2.

(c)   At a class meeting the power of the majority to bind the minority must be exercised for the purpose of benefiting the class as a whole, not only particular members (*British America Nickel Corporation Ltd* v *M.J. O'Brien Ltd* [1927] AC 369, PC, per Viscount Haldane at p. 371). The importance of this rule is illustrated by *Re Holders Investment Trust Ltd* [1971] 1 WLR 583. The company sought to reduce its capital by cancelling all of its redeemable preference shares (which were due for redemption in 10 months' time) and issuing unsecured loan stock (redeemable in 15–20 years' time) to the holders in exchange for their preference shares. The exchange had been approved at a class meeting of the preference shareholders but the majority voting in favour were also holders of ordinary shares in the company and it was proved that they voted in favour of the exchange only because it would improve the position of ordinary shareholders. Megarry J held that they had not given an effective approval of the reduction of capital. However, L.S. Sealy, 'Equitable and other fetters on the shareholder's freedom to vote', in N.E. Eastham and B. Krivy (eds), *The Cambridge Lectures 1981* (Toronto: Butterworths, 1982), has attacked the rule as wrong and based on a misinterpretation of previous authorities.

(d)   When voting on whether the company should take legal proceedings to enforce its rights against persons in control of the company in respect of a matter that is illegal or *ultra vires* or is of a fraudulent character, members must vote bona fide in the interests of the company and not for an improper purpose, in particular, a member must not vote with a view to supporting the intended defendants to the action rather than securing benefit to the company (*Taylor v National Union of Mineworkers (Derbyshire Area)* [1985] BCLC 237 at p. 255; *Smith v Croft (No. 2)* [1988] Ch 114 at p. 186) — see 18.4.2.

On the other hand, the power conferred by CA 1985, s. 719, to provide for employees on cessation or transfer of the company's business may be exercised notwithstanding that its exercise is not in the best interests of the company (s. 719(2)) — that is, of the members as a whole (*Re Halt Garage (1964) Ltd* [1982] 3 All ER 1016 per Oliver J at p. 1035). Thus the exercise of the power cannot be challenged by a dissentient minority as was done, before this provision was enacted, in *Hutton v West Cork Railway Co.* (1883) 23 ChD 654, CA, and *Parke v Daily News Ltd* [1962] Ch 927.

There have been two cases, *Phillips v Manufacturers' Securities Ltd* (1917) 86 LJ Ch 305 and *Harris v A. Harris Ltd* 1936 SC 183, in which the judges seem to have disagreed over whether it was appropriate to ask whether the resolution in question had been adopted bona fide for the benefit of the company and for a proper purpose, or whether it was sufficient to ask whether the resolution was *ultra vires*, fraudulent or oppressive (see 14.4.9.5). However, in both cases the resolutions in question were upheld by the courts so that the form of the test to be applied was not crucial to the outcome of the cases.

14.4.9.5   Ultra vires, *fraudulent or oppressive*

Minority members of a company may bring an action to question a decision of the majority that is *ultra vires*, fraudulent or oppressive (*MacDougall v Gardiner* (1875) 1 ChD 13 per James LJ at pp. 21–2). Actions to question *ultra vires* decisions will be considered in 18.4.10.

A decision that is fraudulent or oppressive towards shareholders who oppose it is often referred to as a 'fraud on the minority'. A leading example is *Menier v Hooper's Telegraph Works* (1874) LR 9 Ch App 350, CA, in which the major shareholder in a company had contracted to make and lay a submarine telegraph cable for the company but found that it was more advantageous to do the work for another person and so caused the company to abandon the contract. James LJ said, at p. 353:

> The minority of the shareholders say in effect that the majority has divided the assets of the company, more or less, between themselves, to the exclusion of the minority. I think it would be a shocking thing if that could be done, because if so the majority might divide the whole assets of the company, and pass a resolution that everything must be given to them, and that the minority should have nothing to do with it. Assuming the case to be as alleged . . ., then the majority have put something into their pockets at the expense of the minority. If so, it appears to me that the minority have a right to have their share of the benefits ascertained for them in the best way in which the court can do it, and given to them.

In *Clemens v Clemens Bros Ltd* [1976] 2 All ER 268, the two shareholders in Clemens Bros Ltd were Miss Clemens (who had 55 per cent of the votes) and her niece, the plaintiff in the case (who had 45 per cent). They had inherited their shares. The plaintiff had resigned her directorship after disagreements with her aunt. Miss Clemens had remained a director

and there were four other directors who the plaintiff thought aligned themselves with her
aunt against her.

Miss Clemens exercised her voting rights so as to secure the passing of a resolution
authorising the issue of new shares to directors other than herself and to an employee trust
scheme. The effect of the issue was to reduce the plaintiff's holding in the company to under
25 per cent (thus preventing her from being able to stop the passing of extraordinary and
special resolutions) and to reduce the value of her pre-emptive rights to purchase other
members' shares. She accordingly applied to the court to have the resolution set aside.
Foster J said, at p. 282:

> . . . in such a case as the present Miss Clemens is not entitled to exercise her majority
> vote in whatever way she pleases. The difficulty is in finding a principle, and obviously
> expressions such as 'bona fide for the benefit of the company as a whole', 'fraud on a
> minority' and 'oppressive' do not assist in formulating a principle.
>
> I have come to the conclusion that it would be unwise to try to produce a principle,
> since the circumstances of each case are infinitely varied. It would not, I think, assist to
> say more than that in my judgment Miss Clemens is not entitled as of right to exercise
> her votes as an ordinary shareholder in any way she pleases. To use the phrase of Lord
> Wilberforce [in *Ebrahimi* v *Westbourne Galleries Ltd* [1973] AC 360 at p. 379], that right
> is 'subject . . . to equitable considerations . . . which may make it unjust . . . to exercise
> [it] in a particular way'. Are there then any such considerations in this case?
>
> I do not doubt that Miss Clemens is in favour of the resolutions and knows and understands
> their purport and effect; nor do I doubt that she genuinely would like to see the other directors
> have shares in the company and to see a trust set up for long service employees. But I cannot
> escape the conclusion that the resolutions have been framed so as to put into the hands of
> Miss Clemens and her fellow directors complete control of the company and to deprive the
> plaintiff of her existing rights as a shareholder with more than 25 per cent of the votes and
> greatly reduce her [pre-emptive rights]. They are specifically and carefully designed to ensure
> not only that the plaintiff can never get control of the company but to deprive her of what has
> been called her negative control. Whether I say that these proposals are oppressive to the
> plaintiff or that no one could honestly believe they are for her benefit matters not. A court of
> equity will in my judgment regard these considerations as sufficient to prevent the
> consequences arising from Miss Clemens using her legal right to vote in the way that she has
> and it would be right for a court of equity to prevent such consequences taking effect.

Clemens v *Clemens Bros Ltd* may be contrasted with *Greenhalgh* v *Arderne Cinemas Ltd*
[1946] 1 All ER 512. The shares of Arderne Cinemas Ltd were originally all 10*s* (50p)
shares. Its articles provided that on a poll a member had one vote for each share held. Mr
Greenhalgh had contributed capital to the company under an agreement which provided that
the shares allotted to him would be subdivided into 2*s* (10p) shares so that he would have
five times as many votes for his money as the other members. Two other members of the
company made a contract with him that they would always vote their shares with him. Two
years later, however, they transferred nearly all their shares to opponents of Mr Greenhalgh.
In earlier proceedings, the Court of Appeal had held that this transfer was permitted by the
articles and was not a breach of the voting contract (*Greenhalgh* v *Mallard* [1943] 2 All ER
234). Then a general meeting of the company resolved to subdivide all the remaining 10*s*
shares into 2*s* shares so that in future Mr Greenhalgh would be outvoted. The Court of
Appeal refused to declare the subdivision resolution invalid, pointing out that when he
invested in the company Mr Greenhalgh could have protected himself from such a move by

insisting on changes being made in the articles. The case was argued on the basis of implying a term into Mr Greenhalgh's agreement with the company that the company would not alter his voting control and the court refused to imply such a term. In *Clemens* v *Clemens Bros Ltd* it was thought appropriate to invoke equitable principles of conscionability and fairness but *Greenhalgh* v *Arderne Cinemas Ltd* was confined to legal questions concerning the interpretation of contracts.

The idea that equitable considerations may make it unjust for a company member to exercise a vote in a particular way also appears in cases in which the court has given relief for conduct of a company's affairs in a manner unfairly prejudicial to the interests of a member. The court can give relief in cases where the exercise of the vote is contrary to non-contractual agreements and understandings between members in quasi-partnership companies (see 18.6.2 and 18.6.5).

In *Kounis* v *Kounis* (1987) 11 ACLR 854, Western Australia, the Kounis brothers, Paul and James, started a business in equal partnership. They later incorporated a company, in which each brother's family company held equal shares, to operate the business. For tax reasons, all shares except one in this original company were sold to another company called Industrial Management Pty Ltd (IM) in which again the two brothers' family companies had equal shareholdings and the two brothers were the only directors. The unsold share in the original company was held by Paul as trustee for IM. This was done purely because the company had to have a minimum of two members. However, because of the peculiar voting structure of the original company, this one share gave Paul 78 per cent of the votes. Having fallen out with his brother, Paul intended to hold a meeting of the members of the original company and dismiss his brother from his directorship of that company. An interlocutory injunction was granted restraining Paul from voting for a motion dismissing James and restraining the company from holding a meeting for this purpose. On appeal, Brinsden J said: 'It seems clearly arguable that for Paul to use [the share he held in trust for IM] in the manner which he proposes without the instructions of IM so to do, is contrary to the agreement the parties reached which was to be one of equal equity and equal control'.

Similarly, in *Re Medefield Pty Ltd* (1977) 2 ACLR 406, New South Wales, two men had agreed to participate in a joint venture company with the intention that they should have exactly equal interests. They acquired a shelf company for the purpose. One of them was informally appointed chairman without appreciating that the articles of the company gave its chairman the right to chair members' meetings and (like Table A, art. 50 — see 14.4.9.2) gave the chairman of a members' meeting a casting vote. An injunction was granted to prevent that casting vote being exercised because it would be contrary to the understanding between the two men that their interests in the company should be equal.

In *Estmanco (Kilner House) Ltd* v *Greater London Council* [1982] 1 WLR 2 the company had been formed to carry into effect an agreement with the council. The directors instituted an action in the company's name for specific performance of the agreement but a shareholders' meeting (at which the council was the only shareholder entitled to vote) instructed the directors to discontinue the action. It was accepted that this instruction was effective (for the controversy on this issue, see 15.7.3). Megarry V-C said, at p. 16:

No right of a shareholder to vote in his own selfish interests or to ignore the interests of the company entitles him with impunity to injure his voteless fellow shareholders by depriving the company of a cause of action and stultifying the purpose for which the company was formed.

His lordship therefore permitted a voteless shareholder to continue the action in her own name as a derivative action (see 18.4.4).

14.4.9.6   Mareva *injunction*

In *Standard Chartered Bank* v *Walker* [1992] 1 WLR 561, it seems that George Walker, the founder of Brent Walker plc, and his family company, Birdcage Walk Ltd, had been lent money by various banks to invest in Brent Walker. Their investments in that company were the only significant assets from which the loan could be repaid. The banks were also owed a vast amount of money by Brent Walker itself and had proposed a financial restructuring plan for the company which involved removing Mr Walker from his directorship. Mr Walker proposed to vote against the plan but the banks were granted an injunction to prevent him doing so because it was found that if that particular restructuring plan were not approved the company would collapse so that Mr Walker would be destroying the source of funds for repaying his debt to the banks. The injunction was analogous to a *Mareva* injunction. For an earlier stage in Mr Walker's battle to keep control of his company see 15.5.3.

14.4.9.7   *Further reading*

For further discussion of *Clemens* v *Clemens Bros Ltd* [1976] 2 All ER 268, see the casenotes by D.D. Prentice, 'Restraints on the exercise of majority shareholder power' (1976) 92 LQR 502 and V. Joffe, 'Majority rule undermined?' (1977) 40 MLR 71. The whole topic of restrictions on voting rights has been examined in three articles by P.G. Xuereb, 'The limitation on the exercise of majority power' (1985) 6 Co Law 199, 'Remedies for abuse of majority power' (1986) 7 Co Law 53 and 'Voting rights: a comparative review' (1987) 8 Co Law 16, and by G.R. Douglas, 'What are the voting duties of company members?' (1987) 131 SJ 796. L.S. Sealy, 'Equitable and other fetters on the shareholder's freedom to vote', in N.E. Eastham and B. Krivy (eds), *The Cambridge Lectures 1981* (Toronto: Butterworths, 1982), vigorously attacks such fetters.

S.J. Burridge, 'Wrongful rights issues' (1981) 44 MLR 40 describes and comments on an unreported case with many similarities to *Clemens* v *Clemens Bros Ltd*.

14.4.9.8   *Voting agreements*

Shareholders may enter into agreements restricting or determining the way in which they exercise their voting rights. Such agreements are valid and may be enforced by mandatory injunction (*Puddephatt* v *Leith* [1916] 1 Ch 200). Thus, in *Greenwell* v *Porter* [1902] 1 Ch 530, the defendants bound themselves by agreement to do all things within their power to secure the election of two named persons as directors of a company and thereafter to vote for their re-election. When the defendants subsequently tried to oppose the re-election of one of the two as a director, Swinfen Eady J granted an injunction restraining them from voting in any way inconsistent with the agreement.

It is clear that shareholder agreements of this nature bind only the parties to the agreement. As Lord Greene MR said in *Greenhalgh* v *Mallard* [1943] 2 All ER 234 at p. 239:

> If the contract is such that it only imposes an obligation to vote in respect of whatever shares the contracting parties happen to have available, it follows that directly they sell their shares the contract is at an end — until possibly they acquire more shares. . . .
>
> If the contract on its true construction ceases to operate when the shares are sold, then in the hands of the purchaser there can be no question of a continuing obligation which runs with the shares.

Shareholder agreements may be the subject of a separate contract between the shareholders involved, but they may also arise out of the contract formed by the articles. Thus, a director may be given a right of veto in relation to certain transactions, as in *Salmon* v *Quin & Axtens Ltd* [1909] AC 442 (see 3.4.2.7) or different voting rights may attach to certain shares on specified matters, as in *Bushell* v *Faith* [1970] AC 1099 (see 3.5.3.3). Contracts in the articles are, however, subject to the difficulties of enforcement and to the problems of alteration discussed in 3.4 and 3.5.

Shareholder agreements restricting, enlarging or determining the exercise of voting rights are generally concerned with specified matters. It is not uncommon, however, for different rights to be attached by agreement, to certain classes of shares. The protection of these class rights is considered in 14.6.

14.4.10 Adjournment

A meeting is said to be 'adjourned' if, at a time when its business has not been completed, the meeting is discontinued with the intention that there will be a continuation of the meeting at a subsequent time. When the meeting reassembles it is described as an 'adjourned meeting'. Article 45 of Table A provides:

> The chairman may, with the consent of a meeting at which a quorum is present (and shall if so directed by the meeting), adjourn the meeting from time to time and from place to place, but no business shall be transacted at an adjourned meeting other than business which might properly have been transacted at the meeting had the adjournment not taken place. When a meeting is adjourned for fourteen days or more, at least seven clear days' notice shall be given specifying the time and place of the adjourned meeting and the general nature of the business to be transacted. Otherwise it shall not be necessary to give any such notice.

The persons who attend an adjourned meeting may not be the same as the persons who attended when the meeting first assembled. In particular, it is possible under Table A to appoint new proxies to attend an adjourned meeting. Table A, art. 62, requires an instrument appointing a proxy to be deposited at the company's registered office not less than 48 hours before the time for holding an adjourned meeting. A provision in a company's articles requiring proxy appointments to be deposited more than 48 hours before an adjourned meeting is void (CA 1985, s. 372(5)).

The chairman of a meeting has a common law power to adjourn it but this power may be exercised only where necessary for the proper transaction of the business of the meeting, for example:

(a)   where there is disorder and it is impossible to arrange an adjournment with the meeting's consent (*John* v *Rees* [1970] Ch 345); or

(b)   if it is impossible for the meeting to continue because, for example, the meeting place has to be given up (*Jackson* v *Hamlyn* [1953] Ch 577); or

(c)   in order to facilitate the presence of those entitled to debate and vote on a resolution (*Byng* v *London Life Association Ltd* [1990] Ch 170, CA).

Article 45 applies only if the meeting is quorate. By art. 41, if a meeting is inquorate 30 minutes after the time appointed as the beginning of the meeting, it will stand adjourned 'to the same day in the next week at the same time and place or to such time and place as the directors may determine'.

Of course business cannot be transacted at an adjourned meeting unless it is quorate. Somewhat exceptionally, however, CA 1985, s. 125(6)(a), provides that at an adjourned meeting of a class of shareholders called to consider a variation of their class rights the necessary quorum is one person holding shares of the class in question or his proxy.

CA 1985, s. 381, prohibits a company from deeming that a resolution passed at an adjourned general or class meeting was adopted at an earlier date than the date on which it was in fact passed. If the question was decided by poll and the result of the poll was ascertained after the adjourned meeting then the date of the resolution is the date on which the result of the poll is ascertained (*Holmes* v *Keyes* [1959] Ch 199, CA).

14.4.11 Minutes and registration

A company must keep minutes in books of all proceedings of its general meetings (CA 1985, s. 382(1)). If such minutes are purported to be signed by the chairman of the meeting at which the proceedings minuted took place or of the next succeeding meeting, those minutes are evidence of the proceedings (s. 382(2)). Minutes must be kept in bound books from which leaves cannot be removed (*Hearts of Oak Assurance Co. Ltd* v *James Flower and Sons* [1936] Ch 76; *POW Services Ltd* v *Clare* [1995] 2 BCLC 435 at p. 444). Where minutes have been made in accordance with s. 382 then, until the contrary is proved, the meeting is deemed duly held and convened, and all proceedings at the meeting are deemed to be valid (s. 382(4)).

In the case of a private company, if a written resolution is agreed to under s. 381A as if it were a resolution of the company in general meeting, a record of the resolution and the signatures must be entered in a book in the same way as minutes of proceedings at the company's general meetings (s. 382A(1)). If such a record is purportedly signed by a director of the company or by the company secretary then it is evidence of the proceedings in agreeing to the resolution (s. 382A(2)). Where a record of a written resolution has been made in accordance with s. 382A then, until the contrary is proved, the requirements of CA 1985 with respect to the procedure for agreeing to the resolution are deemed to be complied with.

Where a private limited company (other than a hybrid company) has only one member and that member takes any decision which may be taken by the company in general meeting and which has effect as if agreed by the company in general meeting (under the principle of *East* v *Bennett Brothers Ltd* [1911] 1 Ch 163, see 14.5.1) then the member must, under penalty, provide the company with a written record of the decision (s. 382B, penalty in sch. 24, both inserted by SI 1992 No. 1699). Failure to provide a copy of a decision in accordance with s. 382B does not invalidate the decision (s. 382B(3)). The source of s. 382B is art. 4 of the EC 12th Company Law Directive.

A company must make the minutes of proceedings at its general meetings available for inspection by members without charge at the company's registered office (s. 383(1)). A private company must make available the record of its written resolutions (s. 382A(3)). Members are entitled, on payment of a fee, to copies of minutes or written resolutions (ss. 382A(3) and 383(3)). If any provision of s. 382, s. 382A or s. 383 is contravened then the company and any officer who knowingly and wilfully authorised or permitted the contravention will have committed a summary offence (ss. 382(5), 382A(3), 383(4) and 730(5) and sch. 24).

Certain resolutions of the company, however, are of such importance as to affect persons other than its members, for example, debtors, creditors, and prospective shareholders. Accordingly, CA 1985, s. 380 and some other sections require copies of certain resolutions or agreements to be forwarded to the registrar of companies within 15 days of being adopted or made (s. 380(1)), and a copy of every such resolution or agreement must be embodied in or annexed to every copy of the articles issued after the adoption of the resolution, or the making of the agreement, for as long as the resolution or agreement is in force (s. 380(2)). The resolutions or agreements involved are:

(a)   special resolutions (s. 380(4)(a); see 14.4.8.3);

(b)   extraordinary resolutions (s. 380(4)(b); see 14.4.8.3);

(c)   elective resolutions and resolutions revoking elective resolutions (s. 380(4)(bb); see 14.4.8.4);

(d)   resolutions agreed to by all the members of a company (see 14.5) which, if there had not been unanimity, would have been ineffective unless they were special or extra-ordinary resolutions (s. 380(4)(c));

(e)   resolutions or agreements agreed to by all the members of a class of shareholders which, if there had not been unanimity, would have been ineffective unless they had been adopted by some particular majority or otherwise in some manner, and all resolutions or agreements which effectively bind all members of any class of shareholders though not agreed to by all of them (s. 380(4)(d));

(f)   a directors' resolution adding 'Ltd' to a company's name in compliance with a direction by the Secretary of State (ss. 31(2) and 380(4)(e); see 2.4.2);

(g)   a resolution giving, varying, renewing or revoking directors' powers to allot shares or issue convertible securities or grant share options (ss. 80(8) and 380(4)(f); see 6.2.5);

(h)   a directors' resolution converting a public company into a private one because holdings of its own shares have reduced its allotted share capital below the authorised minimum (ss. 147(2) and 380(4)(g); see 6.4.2);

(i)   a resolution conferring, varying, revoking or renewing authorisation for market purchases of a company's own shares (ss. 166(7) and 380(4)(h); see 10.6.2);

(j)   a resolution requiring a company to be voluntarily wound up under the Insolvency Act 1986, s. 84(1)(a) (because the duration of the company fixed by its articles has expired or an event has occurred on which the articles provide that the company is to be dissolved) (s. 380(4)(j) and Insolvency Act 1986, s. 84(3));

(k)   a directors' resolution that an old public company should be re-registered as a public company (CA 1985, s. 380(4)(k) and Companies Consolidation (Consequential Provisions) Act 1985, s. 2(3));

(l)   a directors' resolution that a company's securities should be traded in uncertificated form through CREST and a members' resolution vetoing such a decision (CA 1985, s. 380(4)(l) and (m) inserted by SI 1995 No. 3272, reg. 40(3); see 8.2.1);

(m)   any resolution approving an acquisition by a public company of non-cash assets from certain founding members (CA 1985, s. 111(2); see 17.6.3.2);

(n)   resolutions increasing authorised share capital (s. 123(3); see 6.1.13);

(o)   a resolution of a meeting called by or at the direction of the Secretary of State that the meeting is to be the annual general meeting for a previous year (s. 367(5); see 14.4.2).

Section 380(4)(c) shows that it is contemplated in the CA 1985 that a decision which the Act requires to be taken by extraordinary or special resolution at a meeting may alternatively be taken by unanimous agreement without meeting (*Re M.J. Shanley Contracting Ltd* (1979) 124 SJ 239).

14.5   DECISION-MAKING WITHOUT MEETING

14.5.1   Unanimous assent

If all the members of a company who are entitled to vote on the matter actually agree to a particular decision then the decision is binding and effective without meeting. As Cotton LJ said in *Baroness Wenlock* v *River Dee Co.* (1883) 36 ChD 675 n at pp. 681–2 n:

. . . the court would never allow it to be said that there was an absence of resolution when all the shareholders, and not only a majority, have expressly assented to that which is being done.

In *Re Duomatic Ltd* [1969] 2 Ch 365, at p. 373, Buckley J stated the principle as follows:

. . . where it can be shown that all shareholders who have a right to attend and vote at a general meeting of the company assent to some matter which a general meeting of the company could carry into effect, that assent is as binding as a resolution in general meeting would be.

And as Astbury J observed in *Parker & Cooper Ltd* v *Reading* [1926] Ch 975:

I do not think it matters in the least whether that assent is given at different times or simultaneously.

The members of a company cannot, by unanimous agreement, overcome prohibitions imposed on the company by the general law or the Companies Acts, for example, they cannot alter conditions of the memorandum of association for which CA 1985 does not provide an alteration procedure. So in *Salomon* v *A. Salomon & Co. Ltd* [1897] AC 22, Lord Davey expressed the rule as: '. . . the company is bound in a matter *intra vires* by the unanimous agreement of its members' (at p. 57).

Various statements of the principle have differed over whether every member must agree or just the members entitled to vote on the matter. In *Re Duomatic Ltd* Buckley J held that it is only necessary to have the agreement of those who can vote on the matter and in this form the principle has come to be known as the '*Duomatic* principle'.

Unanimous agreement without meeting is not effective if the persons who give the assent could not have made the decision at a meeting, for example, because there are not enough of them to form a quorum, or there is only one person, who could not constitute a meeting (*Re New Cedos Engineering Co. Ltd* [1994] 1 BCLC 797).

Courts in the Commonwealth seem to have differed over what should happen if a share in a company is held on trust and it is sought to establish unanimous assent of the company's members without meeting. In Victoria, in *Re Action Waste Collections Pty Ltd* (1976) 2 ACLR 253, it was held that it must be shown that the trustee's assent was obtained (because the trustee is the registered member) and that assent by the beneficial owner only is inadequate. The same view was taken in Western Australia in *Poliwka* v *Heven Holdings Pty Ltd* (1992) 8 ACSR 747. But the Supreme Court of Canada seems to have taken the view that if the registered holder of the shares is a mere nominee who has a duty always to vote as instructed by the beneficial owner then only the beneficial owner's assent need be proved (*Walton* v *Bank of Nova Scotia* (1965) 52 DLR (2d) 506, see especially at p. 510).

In *Re Express Engineering Works Ltd* [1920] 1 Ch 466, a company was formed with five shareholders who were also directors. The company's articles prevented any director from voting on a contract in which he might be interested. At a meeting of the five, which was ostensibly a board meeting, they unanimously approved a contract by which the company purchased property from themselves and also approved the issue to themselves of debentures securing payment to them of the purchase money (the articles of the company did not permit directors to vote on the company giving security for debts owed to themselves as Table A, art. 94, now does — see 16.6.3). The company went into liquidation and the liquidator argued that as all the directors were disqualified from voting on the purchase and security contracts no board meeting had ever bound the company to those contracts. It was too late to repudiate the purchase contract because the company could not restore the property to the directors but the liquidator sought a declaration that the debentures were invalid. The Court of Appeal held that the company was bound by the unanimous assent of the shareholders. Warrington LJ said, at pp. 470–1:

> It happened that these five directors were the only shareholders of the company, and it is admitted that the five, acting together as shareholders, could have issued these debentures. As directors they could not but as shareholders acting together they could have made the agreement in question. It was competent to them to waive all formalities as regards notice of meetings, etc., and to resolve themselves into a meeting of shareholders and unanimously pass the resolution in question. Inasmuch as they could not in one capacity effectually do what was required but could do it in another, it is to be assumed that as businessmen they would act in the capacity in which they had power to act. In my judgment they must be held to have acted as shareholders and not as directors, and the transaction must be treated as good as if every formality had been carried out.

Counsel for the liquidator conceded that the members had power to issue the debentures but R. Grantham, 'The unanimous consent rule in company law' [1993] CLJ 245 points out that the juridical basis for this is unclear since members of a company are normally thought of as having no power to manage the company (see 15.7) and no authority to make contracts for it (see 15.1.1). It is submitted that there are two alternative ways of dealing with this problem. First, when there is no board capable of acting in a matter, the directors' powers of management revert to the members and the members must be regarded as agents of the company for the purpose of exercising those powers (see 15.7.7). Second, if directors of a company act outside their authority then the members may supply the missing authority by ratifying the act (see 19.5.8) and it might be considered that the five shareholder directors of Express Engineering Works Ltd were acting as its directors when they issued the debentures and simultaneously acted as members ratifying the unauthorised act of themselves as directors: this was the view taken by the New Zealand Court of Appeal in *Wairau Energy Centre Ltd* v *First Fishing Co. Ltd* (1991) 5 NZCLC 67,379. In *Walton* v *Bank of Nova Scotia* (1965) 52 DLR (2d) 506, Mr Ridout, who was the sole beneficial owner of all the issued shares of Ridout Real Estate Ltd, had signed and sealed documents on behalf of the company, charging some of its assets to the bank as security for a loan to himself and his brother, though he had not been authorised to do so by the board of directors. The Supreme Court of Canada held that the company was bound by the charge because it had been approved by Mr Ridout. The question of whether a member of a company has power to charge its assets was not raised though the court observed that if the transaction had been put to a board meeting it would obviously have been approved because Mr Ridout would have removed any directors who opposed his wishes.

Where all the members of a company are directors of it, the principle of *Re Express Engineering Works Ltd* that directors' meetings are *de facto* members' meetings is often applied. It has been extended to the situation in which all members of a company are either individuals who are directors or are corporations that have appointed directors: in such a situation a meeting of all the directors is a *de facto* meeting of all the members (*Bobbie Pins Ltd* v *Robertson* [1950] NZLR 301; *Multinational Gas & Petrochemical Co.* v *Multinational Gas & Petrochemical Services Ltd* [1983] Ch 258).

In *Re Duomatic Ltd*, two directors drew sums as salary according to their personal needs, and accounts showing these sums were signed and approved by them as directors at the time when they were also the only ordinary shareholders (though there were also non-voting preference shareholders). Subsequently the company went into liquidation and the liquidator sought repayment of the salaries on the ground that they had not been voted in general meeting as required by a provision of the company's articles in the same terms as art. 82 of Table A (see 15.6.1.2). Buckley J held that the payments were valid since they had been approved by the unanimous assent of all shareholders entitled to vote on the matter. On an earlier occasion, the same two directors had paid £4,000 to a third director in order to persuade him to leave the company. Under CA 1985, s. 312, such a payment is unlawful unless particulars of the payment are disclosed to, and approved by, 'members of the company' (see 15.6.2.1). Buckley J held in this instance that the preference shareholders were members who were entitled to approve or disapprove the payment to the third director and that since the payment had not been disclosed to them in accordance with s. 312 the payment was unlawful. The principle of unanimous assent therefore requires that all persons who are entitled to assent must be given the opportunity to do so, though it would seem that the assent of all joint holders of shares is not required since one joint holder can assent on behalf of the other or others (*Re Gee & Co. (Woolwich) Ltd* [1975] Ch 52).

In *Re Barry Artist Ltd* [1985] 1 WLR 1305 Nourse J emphasised that a resolution adopted unanimously without meeting does not satisfy the statutory definition of a special resolution and said that the court would not normally accept a unanimously adopted decision in place of the special resolution required to reduce a company's capital (see 10.2.5). The same argument could be applied to extraordinary resolutions. Nevertheless, unanimous assent without meeting has been accepted as effective in other circumstances where the legislation says that there should be a special resolution (*Ho Tung* v *Man On Insurance Co. Ltd* [1902] AC 232, PC; *Cane* v *Jones* [1980] 1 WLR 1451; *Re Home Treat Ltd* [1991] BCLC 705) or an extraordinary resolution (*Re M.J. Shanley Contracting Ltd* (1979) 124 SJ 239). Use of unanimous agreement in place of a special or extraordinary resolution is contemplated in CA 1985, s. 380(4)(c) (see 14.4.11). However, where additional procedures are prescribed it is doubtful whether a decision taken without following those procedures could be effective, even if there were an express agreement by members to waive the procedures. For example, the prescribed procedure for dismissing a director under s. 303 includes allowing the director an opportunity to speak at the meeting which considers the resolution to dismiss (s. 304(1)) so it is doubtful whether a resolution to dismiss under s. 303 could be adopted without holding a meeting (see 15.3.3 and the similar provision in s. 391A in relation to the dismissal of auditors discussed in 17.4.3). See also s. 164(6), which prescribes documents which must be available at a meeting adopting a resolution conferring authority for an off-market purchase of the company's own shares and is discussed in 10.6.3. In *Re R.W. Peak (Kings Lynn) Ltd* [1998] 1 BCLC 193, the requirements of s. 164 were completely ignored when the shares of the majority shareholder in a company were purchased by the company. There was a written contract signed by the majority shareholder as vendor of the shares and signed on the company's behalf by the only other shareholder. It was argued that this constituted a unanimous agreement to waive the formalities imposed by s. 164, but Lindsay J pointed out that s. 164(5) actually prohibits the vendor of the shares from voting on whether to approve the contract, so it is not possible for the vendor to decide whether or not the formalities of s. 164 should apply at all.

It seems that s. 121(4) imposes a mandatory requirement that a resolution altering a company's share capital must be adopted at a general meeting (see 6.1.13).

In *Re George Newman & Co.* [1895] 1 Ch 674, the company (which was in liquidation) did persuade the court that a decision taken by its members without meeting was not effective. Mr George Newman had been a director and chairman of the company and had made a profit of £3,000 selling to it property which he knew it required. Newman had also used £3,500 of the company's money for improvements to his own house. Keeping these sums was contrary to the rule against profiting (see 16.4.1) but Mr Newman claimed that all the shareholders (except those who were minors) approved of the payments so that they were ratified (see 16.4.6), which, if true, would have meant that the company was no longer entitled to recover the money. The Court of Appeal held that there had been no effective ratification, saying (at p. 686):

> Individual assents given separately may preclude those who give them from complaining of what they have sanctioned; but for the purpose of binding a company in its corporate capacity individual assents given separately are not equivalent to the assent of a meeting. The company is entitled to the protection afforded by a duly convened meeting, and by a resolution properly considered and carried and duly recorded.

However, this reason for finding the decisions were invalid was said to be only an alternative to the court's principal reason, which was that the payments were illegal gifts out of capital and so could not have been validated by the members at all (see 10.1). Subsequently, this principal reason has been taken to be the only *ratio* for the decision and it has been assumed that the court's remarks about decision-making without meeting were only saying that members could not make an *ultra vires* illegal decision without meeting (which would have been pointless: an *ultra vires* decision cannot be taken in any way).

It is unclear what the juridical basis is for the cases on the effectiveness of decisions taken by unanimous assent without meeting. Sometimes it is said, as in the passage from *Re George Newman & Co.* quoted above, that, in the absence of contrary provisions in the constitution of a company, decisions of its members ought to be taken at meetings. When members unanimously take a decision without meeting they are treated as waiving their right to have the company's affairs conducted constitutionally so that they cannot subsequently rely on the lack of formality to claim that the decision is invalid. But in the cases it is not usually the members of a company who seek to have their own decisions invalidated. Usually it is the company as a separate person which tries to have a decision taken by its members declared invalid, and usually the company is no longer under the control of the members who took the decision but is in liquidation. It is unclear how the waiver by the members becomes a waiver by the company as a separate person. In *Re George Newman & Co.* the Court of Appeal said that a waiver by the members does not affect the company, which 'is entitled to the protection afforded by a duly convened meeting'. It seems that the underlying reason for not allowing a company to rely on procedural defects in decision-making to excuse it from fulfilling obligations is really the desire for security of transaction: persons who deal with companies should not have to worry that their transactions will be upset by technicalities.

In *Herrman* v *Simon* (1990) 4 ACSR 81, it was emphasised that inability to question decisions taken unanimously without meeting depends on the fact that the members have waived the right to hold a meeting. In the case, the members of a company unanimously agreed without meeting to alter its articles without realising that they were altering class rights, for which the articles required a special procedure. The alteration was held to be ineffective. The reasoning of Meagher JA (with whom the other members of the court agreed) was that in order to make a decision by unanimous agreement without meeting, members had to waive their right to insist on a properly convened meeting but waiver could not be effective unless given with full knowledge and consent — in this case the members did not know that they had any rights to be waived and so their waiver was ineffective.

In *Re New Cedos Engineering Co. Ltd* [1994] 1 BCLC 797, Oliver J suggested what may be a more satisfactory basis for refusal to allow a company to have members' decisions declared invalid because they were taken without meeting. His lordship's view was that it is inequitable to allow the company to rely on a mere irregularity of procedure when exactly the same decision would have been reached if the correct procedure had been followed. He said, at p. 814:

. . . the *ratio* of Buckley J's decision [in *Re Duomatic Ltd*] is that where that which has been done informally could, but for an oversight, have been done formally and was assented to by 100 per cent of those who could have participated in the formal act, if one had been carried out, then it would be idle to insist upon formality as a precondition to the validity of the act which all those competent to effect it had agreed should be effected.

A similar view was taken by the New Zealand Court of Appeal in *Westpac Securities Ltd* v *Kensington* [1994] 2 NZLR 555 at p. 563. This view may be contrasted with the English Court of Appeal's opinion in *Re George Newman & Co.*, at p. 686, that:

It may be true, and probably is true, that a meeting, if held, would have done anything which Mr George Newman desired; but this is pure speculation, and the liquidator, as representing the company in its corporate capacity, is entitled to insist upon and to have the benefit of the fact that even if a general meeting could have sanctioned what was done, such sanction was never obtained.

However, it seems that the Court of Appeal's view in *Re George Newman & Co.* has been abandoned as a general principle.

It has also been said in Australia that company law does not demand that members' decisions must be taken at a meeting if the company's constitution does not make that requirement (*Perseus Mining NL* v *Landbrokers (Perth) Pty Ltd* [1972] WAR 12).

In *Re Compaction Systems Pty Ltd* [1976] 2 NSWLR 477, Bowen CJ in Eq said that he doubted whether *Re Duomatic Ltd* was correctly decided because it ignored the fact that the company's auditors were entitled to notice of and to attend general meetings. It is respectfully submitted that the whole point of *Re Duomatic Ltd* was that there was no meeting of which notice had to be given to the auditors. It is interesting that the new statutory procedure for written resolutions of private companies (see 14.5.3) provides for copies of such resolutions to be sent to auditors but does not make any provision for members who are entitled to notice of meetings but who are not entitled to vote.

In *Re New World Alliance Pty Ltd* (1994) 122 ALR 531 Gummow J said, *obiter*, that if the members of a company have, unconstitutionally, taken a decision unanimously without meeting which affects another person, A, then the decision will be treated as effective in legal proceedings between A and the company, but not in proceedings between A and another person.

A company's articles may contain express provision relating to unanimous assent. For example, art. 53 of Table A provides that:

A resolution in writing executed by or on behalf of each member who would have been entitled to vote upon it if it had been proposed at a general meeting at which he was present shall be as effectual as if it had been passed at a general meeting duly convened and held and may consist of several instruments in the like form each executed by or on behalf of one or more members.

It seems that this article cannot be used to take a decision for which formalities are prescribed which can be followed only if a meeting is held, for example, under s. 304(1) (see above). It is not clear whether the existence of this article prevents the giving of unanimous oral assents.

If there is only one member of a body of persons then a requirement that a decision of the body must be taken at a meeting will normally be interpreted as meaning that the decision can be taken by that one member without calling a meeting (*East* v *Bennett Brothers Ltd* [1911] 1 Ch 163, in which one person held all the preference shares of a company and a decision taken by him was as effective as a decision taken by a meeting of the preference shareholders). It is doubtful whether this principle can be applied where the decision must be taken with formalities which can be followed only if a meeting is held.

14.5.2 Acquiescence

The discussion of the principle of unanimous assent has so far proceeded on the basis that the assent has been actively and positively given, and it is clear in this situation that a shareholder who has positively assented cannot later object that the resolution in question was not validly passed (*Re Pearce, Duff & Co. Ltd* [1960] 1 WLR 1014). But what of acquiescence (for example, by abstention) and assent given negatively? In *Re Bailey Hay & Co. Ltd* [1971] 1 WLR 1357, the company had five shareholders. An extraordinary general meeting of the company was called by a notice which was one day short of the notice period required by the company's articles, though all five shareholders attended. At the meeting, an extraordinary resolution for voluntary winding up of the company was adopted. Three of the shareholders abstained from voting on the resolution, but over five years later questioned its validity. Brightman J held that the acquiescence of these shareholders must be taken as an assent to the resolution so that the resolution should be deemed to have been passed with the unanimous assent of all the shareholders. His lordship said at p. 1367:

> The conclusion is that they outwardly accepted the resolution to wind up as decisively as if they had positively voted in favour of it. If corporators attend a meeting without protest, stand by without protest while their fellow-members purport to pass a resolution, permit all persons concerned to act for years on the basis that that resolution was duly passed and rule their own conduct on the basis that the resolution is an established fact, I think it is idle for them to contend that they did not assent to the purported resolution.

To show assent by acquiescence it is not necessary to prove the acquiescence of each individual shareholder: it is sufficient to show circumstances which are reasonably calculated to satisfy the court that the matter to be approved came to the knowledge of all who chose to enquire, all having full opportunity and means of enquiry (*Phosphate of Lime Co. Ltd* v *Green* (1871) LR 7 CP 43). It would seem, however, that acquiescence can only be treated as tacit assent as a result of attendance at a meeting at which no objection was raised, and a failure to challenge the resolution within a reasonable time after the meeting.

14.5.3 Written resolutions of private companies

In relation to a *private company*, CA 1985, s. 381A(1), provides that anything which may be done by resolution in general meeting (apart from dismissing a director under s. 303 or dismissing an auditor under s. 391: s. 381A(7) and sch. 15A, para. 1) may be done by resolution in writing signed by or on behalf of all the members of the company who, at the date of the resolution, would be entitled to attend and vote at a general meeting. Such a resolution is effective despite the fact that no meeting was held and no notice was given. It has effect as if passed by the company in general meeting (s. 381A(4)). Similarly, anything which may be done by resolution of a meeting of any class of the company's members may be done by resolution in writing signed by or on behalf of all the members who, at the date of the resolution, would be entitled to attend and vote at such a class meeting, and such a written resolution has effect as if passed by a meeting of the relevant class of members.

In this context, the date of a written resolution is the date when the resolution is signed by or on behalf of the last member to sign (s. 381A(3)).

Members' signatures to a written resolution adopted under s. 381A need not be on a single document, provided each is on a document which accurately states the terms of the resolution (s. 381A(2)).

When it is proposed that the members of a company should agree to a written resolution under s. 381A, a copy of the resolution must be sent to the company's auditors, if it has auditors (s. 381B substituted by SI 1996 No. 1471, art. 3). Failure to notify the auditors does not invalidate the resolution (s. 381B(4)) but the directors or secretary of the company who failed to ensure that the auditors were informed will have committed an offence punishable by a fine (s. 381B). The new version of s. 381B, which has effect as from 19 June 1996, replaces elaborate provisions in s. 381B as originally enacted which gave auditors a right to veto written resolutions and which were soon found to be unnecessary.

The procedures of ss. 381A and 381B apply notwithstanding any provision in the company's articles or memorandum (s. 381C(1)). By s. 381A(6), the fact that a resolution is required to be adopted as a special, extraordinary or elective resolution does not prevent it being agreed to in accordance with s. 381A.

These provisions allow the members of a private company to take a decision by unanimous agreement without meeting where it would otherwise not be possible because formalities are prescribed which can only be followed if a meeting is held. Schedule 15A provides for the adaptation of these formalities when written resolutions are used. It deals with the formalities under s. 95 (see 6.2.6), s. 155 (see 10.8.7), ss. 164, 165 and 167 (see 10.6.3), s. 173 (see 10.3.5), s. 319 (see 15.6.4) and s. 337 (see 16.6.8.2). In other circumstances it seems that the members of a private company can take a decision by unanimous agreement without meeting under the common law without following the procedures prescribed in ss. 381A and 381B since those sections are declared by s. 381C(2) not to affect the common law. An amendment to s. 381C(1) made by SI 1996 No. 1471, art. 4, makes it clear that any provision of a private company's articles permitting the adoption of written resolutions (such as Table A, art. 53) continues to have effect notwithstanding the existence of the statutory procedure in s. 381A.

14.5.4 Single-member private companies

Article 4 of the EC 12th Company Law Directive requires member States to provide that the sole member of a single-member private limited company shall exercise the powers of the general meeting of the company. In Britain, the sole member of such a company may take decisions by written resolution under a provision in the company's articles like art. 53 of Table A, though probably not if the decision requires formalities which can only be carried out at a meeting (see 14.5.1). Even if there is no provision in the company's articles for written resolutions, a decision by the sole member will be effective under the principle in *East* v *Bennett Brothers Ltd* [1911] 1 Ch 163, again provided no special formalities are required (see 14.5.1) and provided a written record of the decision is given to the company

(CA 1985, s. 382B, see 14.4.11). A decision by a sole member can be given using the written resolution procedure in s. 381A (see 14.5.3) though that procedure cannot be used to dismiss a director under s. 303 or to dismiss an auditor under s. 391. For any kind of decision, a meeting may be held at which the quorum will be one by virtue of s. 370A.

14.6 ALTERATION OF CLASS RIGHTS

14.6.1 Class rights

The capital structure of a company may involve the existence of different classes of shares, for example, ordinary shares and preference shares. Class rights may be defined as the rights which attach to a particular class of shares but not to another class or to shareholders generally. Such rights may be created by the memorandum or articles of association of a company, and may relate to such matters as the right to a dividend, the right to share in surplus assets if the company is wound up, and the right to attend and vote at company meetings. If rights are given by a company's articles to a particular shareholder, but are not attached to particular shares, the shareholder may enforce those rights for as long as he holds any shares in the company (or at least the requisite holding specified by the articles), and those rights are class rights which can only be varied in accordance with the provisions discussed in 14.6.2.3 (*Cumbrian Newspapers Group Ltd* v *Cumberland and Westmorland Herald Newspaper and Printing Co. Ltd* [1987] Ch 1).

The very nature of class rights requires that safeguards be provided to prevent one class being deprived of its rights by the votes of other classes, and the problems posed by the variation of class rights must now be considered.

14.6.2 Variation of class rights

14.6.2.1 Introduction
Where a company's shares are of different classes, the variation of the class rights is now governed by s. 125 of CA 1985, which 'is concerned with the variation of the rights attached to any class of shares in a company whose share capital is divided into shares of different classes' (s. 125(1)). This section draws various distinctions, though the primary distinction adopted in the following discussion is between class rights created by the memorandum and class rights created otherwise than by the memorandum. Table A is drafted for a company with only one class of shares and so makes no provision for variation of class rights.

14.6.2.2 Class rights created by memorandum
If rights are attached to a class of shares in a company by the company's memorandum, and there is no provision for the variation of the rights in either the memorandum or the articles then the rights may be varied if all members of the company agree to the variation (CA 1985, s. 125(5)). Alternatively, class rights specified in a memorandum with no provision for variation in the memorandum or articles may be varied by a court-sanctioned arrangement under s. 425 (*Re Palace Hotel Ltd* [1912] 2 Ch 438; *Re J.A. Nordberg Ltd* [1915] 2 Ch 439; *City Property Investment Trust Corporation Ltd* 1951 SC 570).

Apparently, it is possible for a company to have a memorandum which itself provides for the variation of class rights specified in the memorandum (see 2.4.7) and nothing in s. 125 affects the operation of such a provision, except that s. 125(3) prescribes that if the variation is made in connection with authority for allotment (see 6.2.5) or reduction of capital (see 10.2.4) then the variation must be approved by a three-quarters majority of that class.

If rights are attached to a class of shares by the memorandum and there is in the articles a provision for the variation of the rights, and that provision was included in the articles at the time of the company's original incorporation then the rights may only be varied in accordance with that provision of the articles (s. 125(4)), though the basic procedure prescribed in s. 125(3) must be followed (in addition to the procedures specified in the articles) if the variation is made in connection with authority for allotment (see 6.2.5) or reduction of capital (see 10.2.4). The fact that s. 125 allows for a company's articles to provide for the alteration of a condition in the company's memorandum is apparently sufficient to enable an alteration to be made in that way despite CA 1985, s. 2(7) (see the discussion in 2.4.7).

14.6.2.3   *Class rights created otherwise than by memorandum*

Where class rights are created otherwise than by the company's memorandum, and the company's articles provide for the variation of those rights (whenever the provision was introduced into the articles) then the class rights may be varied only in accordance with those provisions of the articles (CA 1985, s. 125(4)), though s. 125(3) applies in addition if the variation is made in connection with authority for allotment (see 6.2.5) or reduction of capital (see 10.2.4).

If there is no provision in the articles for the variation of class rights created otherwise than by the company's memorandum then s. 125(2) provides that the rights may be varied if, but only if, the variation is approved by a three-quarters majority of that class. Class approval may be given either at a class meeting by extraordinary resolution (three-quarters majority of those voting, see 14.4.8.2) or in writing by the holders of three-quarters in nominal value of the issued shares of the class. The requirement for a three-quarters majority is in addition to any other procedure specified in the memorandum or articles for variation of class rights.

14.6.2.4   *Conduct of meetings*

Any meeting of shareholders of a company required by CA 1985, s. 125, or otherwise in connection with the variation of class rights must be conducted in accordance with the provisions in the company's articles relating to general meetings, so far as applicable and with the necessary modifications (s. 125(6)).

Also the provisions of CA 1985, ss. 369 (length of notice for calling meetings), 370 (general provisions about meetings and votes), and 376 and 377 (circulation of members' resolutions), apply to such meetings (s. 125(6)).

There are two special rules in s. 125(6) for such meetings:

(a)   The quorum, other than at an adjourned meeting, is two persons holding or representing by proxy at least one third in nominal value of the issued shares of the class in question. At an adjourned meeting the quorum is one person holding shares of the class in question or his proxy.

(b)   Any holder of shares of the class in question present in person or by proxy may demand a poll.

At a class meeting the power of the majority to bind the minority must be exercised for the purpose of benefiting the class as a whole, not only particular members (*Re Holders Investment Trust Ltd* [1971] 1 WLR 583, see 14.4.9.4).

14.6.2.5   *Application to cancel variation*

Notwithstanding the safeguards provided by s. 125 of CA 1985, a further right is given by s. 127. Where class rights have been varied, the holders of not less than 15 per cent of the issued shares of the class in question who did not consent to or vote in favour of the variation may apply to the court to have the variation cancelled, and the variation does not then take effect until it is confirmed by the court (s. 127(2)). The application must be made within 21 days after the variation was made, and may be made on behalf of the shareholders entitled to apply by one or more of their number appointed by them in writing (s.127(3)). The court must have regard to all the circumstances of the case and if it is satisfied that the variation would unfairly prejudice the holders of the class rights concerned it may disallow the variation, but must, if not so satisfied, confirm the variation, and in any event the court's decision is final (s. 127(4)).

The provisions of s. 127 apply to all the variations envisaged by s. 125 and described in 14.6.2.2 and 14.6.2.3 (CA 1985, s. 127(1)).

14.6.2.6 Meaning of variation
All statutory provisions in this area make it clear that 'variation' includes abrogation of rights (CA 1985, ss. 17(2)(b), 125(8) and 127(6)). Further, by s. 125(7):

> Any alteration of a provision contained in a company's articles for the variation of the rights attached to a class of shares, or the insertion of any such provision into the articles, is itself to be treated as a variation of those rights.

Apart from these express provisions, one must look to the judiciary for guidance on the meaning of 'variation', and it seems apparent that the judges are reluctant to describe most changes of class rights as a variation. It may be thought that one of the most drastic 'variations' would be to issue more shares of the same class, thereby 'diluting' or 'watering down' the effective rights of the existing members of that class. In *White v Bristol Aeroplane Co. Ltd* [1953] Ch 65, the company wanted to issue new preference shares and ordinary shares as bonus shares to the existing ordinary shareholders only and it was argued that this would vary the existing preference shareholders' voting rights since one vote would be a much smaller proportion of the total after the issue than before. The Court of Appeal held that there was no variation. Evershed MR explained at p. 74:

> It is no doubt true that the enjoyment of, and the capacity to make effective, those rights is in a measure affected; for as I have already indicated, the existing preference stockholders will be in a less advantageous position on such occasions as entitle them to register their votes, whether at general meetings of the company or at separate meetings of their own class. But there is to my mind a distinction, and a sensible distinction, between an affecting of the rights and an affecting of the enjoyment of the rights, or of the stockholders' capacity to turn them to account.

Romer LJ said at pp. 81–2:

> The position then will be precisely the same as now — namely, that the holder of preference stock will have on a poll one vote for every £1 of preference stock held by him. It is quite true that . . . the total voting power of the class, will, or may, have less force behind it, because it will *pro tanto* be watered down by reason of the increased total voting power of the members of the company; but no particular weight is attached to the vote, by the constitution of the company, as distinct from the right to exercise the vote, and certainly no right is conferred on the preference stockholders to preserve anything in the nature of an equilibrium between their class and the ordinary stockholders or any other class.

The same result will obtain if preference shares are issued to the detriment of ordinary shareholders (*Re John Smith's Tadcaster Brewery Co. Ltd* [1953] Ch 305, CA). Similarly, if shares of one class are subdivided, thereby increasing voting rights as against another class there will be no variation (*Greenhalgh* v *Arderne Cinemas Ltd* [1946] 1 All ER 512, CA, where 50p shares of one class were subdivided into 10p shares).

A class right is not varied by making it worthless. For example, if preference shareholders have a right to participate in surplus assets on winding up then the company does not vary that right by ensuring that all surplus assets are distributed to the ordinary shareholders before winding up (*Dimbula Valley (Ceylon) Tea Co. Ltd* v *Laurie* [1961] Ch 353). In *Adelaide Electric Supply Co. Ltd* v *Prudential Assurance Co. Ltd* [1934] AC 122 a preferential dividend payable in England became, as a result of an alteration, payable in Australia. The Australian pound was worth less than the pound sterling, so the preferential dividend diminished. The House of Lords held that this was not a variation of the preference shareholders' rights.

In *Re Mackenzie & Co. Ltd* [1916] 2 Ch 450, preference shareholders were entitled to a dividend of 4 per cent on the amount paid up on their shares. The full nominal value of £20 had been paid on each share but a general meeting of the company (at which preference shareholders were not entitled to vote) approved a reduction of capital which would reduce the nominal value of each share to £12 so that the preference dividend would be reduced from £8 per share to £4.80 per share. This was held not to be a variation of the preference shareholders' rights.

In all these cases, the class rights involved remained the same — to have one vote per share, to participate in surplus assets, to be paid a dividend in pounds, to be paid a 4 per cent dividend — and they could not therefore be said to be varied, even though as a result of a change those rights became worth less. In *House of Fraser plc* v *ACGE Investments Ltd* [1987] AC 387, HL, House of Fraser plc reduced its capital by returning all capital to a class of preference shareholders, thus expelling them from the company. It was held that this was not a variation of the preference shareholders' rights. Thus, for class rights to be protected in the event of a variation, the nature of those rights, rather than their enjoyment, must be affected, for example, by changing voting rights from one per share to one per member, or by removing completely the right to share in surplus assets on a winding up.

14.6.2.7   Registration of variations

Often a variation of class rights is made by a resolution of which a copy has to be forwarded to the registrar under CA 1985, s. 380 (see 14.4.11). Filing at Companies House under s. 380 of a copy of a resolution which varies rights attached to any shares in a public company or assigns a new name or designation to any class of shares in a public company must be notified by the registrar in the *Gazette* (s. 711(1)(l)). In addition, a company which varies the rights attached to any of its shares in a way that is not subject to notification under s. 380 must, within one month from the date on which the variation is made, deliver particulars of the variation to the registrar (s. 128(3)).

Where a company, by any means which is not registrable in accordance with s. 380, assigns a name or other designation, or a new name or designation, to any class of its shares, it must notify the registrar in the prescribed form within one month (s. 128(4)).

Filing at Companies House under s. 128 of any information relating to a public company must be notified by the registrar in the *Gazette* (s. 711(1)(j)).

Where an application is made under s. 127 (see 14.6.2.5), the company must deliver a copy of the court's order to the registrar within 15 days of the making of the order (s. 127(5)).

14.7 HOLDING AND SUBSIDIARY COMPANIES

For the purposes of CA 1985, the terms 'holding company', 'subsidiary' and 'wholly owned subsidiary' are defined in ss. 736 and 736A. The same definitions apply (see CA 1989, s. 144(2)) to IA 1986 (s. 251 of that Act), to CDDA 1986 (s. 22(9) of that Act) and to FSA 1986 (s. 207(8) of that Act).

By s. 736(2), a company is a wholly owned subsidiary of another company (which we will call the owning company) if all its members are in one or more of the following categories:

(a) the owning company,
(b) persons acting on behalf of the owning company,
(c) other wholly owned subsidiaries of the owning company,
(d) persons acting on behalf of other wholly owned subsidiaries of the owning company.

In this definition, 'company' includes any body corporate (s. 736(3)). Thus a body corporate that is not a registered company (for example, a company incorporated outside Great Britain) can be counted as one of a registered company's wholly owned subsidiaries if the exclusive membership criterion of s. 736(2) is met. A wholly owned subsidiary is obviously very closely tied to its owning company. The owning company is the only effective member of a wholly owned subsidiary.

Sometimes it is necessary to know whether two companies are in the relationship of subsidiary and holding company. A subsidiary is closely tied to its holding company but there may be one or more effective members or directors apart from the holding company. Under s. 736(1) there are four ways in which the relationship of holding company and subsidiary may arise:

(a) under s. 736(1)(a), where the holding company holds a majority of the voting rights in the subsidiary,
(b) under s. 736(1)(b), where the holding company is a member of the subsidiary and has the right to appoint or remove a majority of its board of directors,
(c) under s. 736(1)(c), where the holding company is a member of the subsidiary and controls alone, pursuant to an agreement with other shareholders or members, a majority of the voting rights in the subsidiary,
(d) under the final clause of s. 736(1), where the subsidiary is a subsidiary of a company which is itself a subsidiary of the holding company.

As with the definition of wholly owned subsidiary, 'company' includes any body corporate (s. 736(3)).

It is common to call a holding company and its subsidiaries a 'group' (for example, in CA 1985, ss. 153(5) and 319(7)(b)).

The definition of the relationship of subsidiary and holding company in s. 736 is explained and supplemented by s. 736A, in which, again, 'company' includes any body corporate (s. 736A(12)).

By s. 736A(4), rights which are exercisable only in certain circumstances shall be taken into account only:

(a) when the circumstances have arisen, and for so long as they continue to obtain, or
(b) when the circumstances are within the control of the person having the rights.

Also by s. 736A(4), rights which are normally exercisable but are temporarily incapable of exercise shall continue to be taken into account.

Rights held by a person in a fiduciary capacity (see 16.3.1) are to be treated as not held by that person (s. 736A(5)). If shares in a company are sold but the transfer is not completed by registration in the company's register of members, the seller remains entitled to exercise any votes attached to the shares. The seller, though holding the shares on trust for the buyer, is not bound to vote in accordance with the buyer's directions and so does not hold the voting rights in a fiduciary capacity for the purposes of s. 736A(5) (*Michaels v Harley House (Marylebone) Ltd* [1997] 1 WLR 967).

Subsections (6) to (11) of s. 736A attribute to a company rights held on its behalf by others or held by its subsidiaries.

Rights must be treated as held by a company if they are held by any of its subsidiaries (s. 736A(8)).

Rights held by a person as nominee for another must be treated as held by the other (s. 736A(6)). Rights are to be regarded as held as nominee for another if they are exercisable only on the other's instructions or with that other's consent or concurrence (s. 736A(6)). (Though this is not to be construed as requiring rights held by a company to be treated as held by any of its subsidiaries (s. 736A(8)).) By s. 736A(9), rights must be treated as being exercisable in accordance with the instructions or in the interests of a company if they are exercisable in accordance with the instructions of or, as the case may be, in the interests of:

(a)   any subsidiary or holding company of that company, or
(b)   any subsidiary of a holding company of that company.

Subsection (7) deals with rights attached to shares held by way of security (see 11.2).

Voting rights in a company must be reduced by any rights held by the company itself (s. 736A(10)).

References in any provision of subsections (5) to (10) to rights held by a person include rights falling to be treated as held by that person by virtue of any other provision in those subsections (s. 736A(11)). But references in any provision of subsections (5) to (9) to rights held by a person do not include rights which, by virtue of any other provision in those subsections, are to be treated as not held by that person (s. 736A(11)).

Another group of subsections define precisely what is meant by voting rights and rights to appoint directors.

'Voting rights' in a company are the rights conferred on shareholders in respect of their shares (or, in the case of a company not having a share capital, on members) to vote at general meetings of the company on all, or substantially all, matters (s. 736A(2)).

A 'right to appoint or remove a majority of a company's board of directors' means the right to appoint or remove directors holding a majority of the voting rights at meetings of the board on all, or substantially all, matters (s. 736A(3)). Subsection (3) further provides that a company must be treated as having the right to appoint to a directorship if:

(a)   a person's appointment to the directorship follows necessarily from his appointment as director of the company, or
(b)   the directorship is held by the company itself.

Also by subsection (3), a right to appoint or remove which is exercisable only with the consent or concurrence of another person shall be left out of account unless no other person has a right to appoint or, as the case may be, remove in relation to that directorship. The appointment and dismissal of directors, and voting at board meetings, are dealt with in chapter 15.

15 Directors

15.1 DIRECTORS IN THE LEGAL STRUCTURE OF THE COMPANY

15.1.1 The need for directors

A company as an artificial person cannot perform its own acts, and there must accordingly be someone who can represent and act on behalf of the company. In *Ferguson* v *Wilson* (1866) LR 2 Ch App 77, Cairns LJ said, at pp. 89–90: 'The company itself cannot act in its own person . . . it can only act through directors'. One of the features that distinguish incorporated companies from partnerships is that every member of a partnership is an agent of the firm who is presumed to have authority to bind the firm in the ordinary course of the firm's business (Partnership Act 1890, s. 5) whereas a member of an incorporated company is never presumed to have any authority at all to bind the company, which is a separate person and can be bound only by the persons who, under its constitution, are authorised to act for it. In *Ernest* v *Nicholls* (1857) 6 HL Cas 401, Lord Wensleydale said, at p. 419: '[The shareholders] can only act through their directors, and the acts of the individual shareholders have no effect whatever on the company at large'. And at p. 423 his lordship said:

> . . . for the purposes of contract, the company exists only in the directors and officers acting by and according to the deed [i.e., the deed of settlement, equivalent in those days to the memorandum and articles of association]; and by the statute law the company is no more liable than a corporation by charter for the act of one or more of its members, who are distinct persons by law.

It was not at first thought necessary to have a statutory rule that a registered company must have directors, but CA 1947, s. 26(1), imposed a requirement that every company must have at least one director, and this requirement was imposed on existing as well as new companies. An earlier requirement introduced by CA 1928, s. 28, that every public company had to have at least two directors affected only companies registered after it came into force, which was on 1 November 1929. Since 18 April 1977 it has been impossible to register a company without naming a person or persons to be the first director or directors of the company — see 15.2.2.

There is no requirement in CA 1985 that a company registered under the Act must appoint any directors domiciled in the jurisdiction in which it is incorporated (England and Wales or Scotland).

As well as representing the company in its external relations, the most significant part of the role of directors of a company is that they are required by Table A, art. 70, to manage the business of the company. Thus they are at the centre of what is known as 'corporate governance', that is, the system by which companies are directed and controlled.

15.1.2   The relationship between directors and members: the Combined Code

The reason for appointing directors of a company is to provide the company with persons who can act for it, but it is also necessary to define the purposes for which the directors must act. The courts have adopted the rule that directors of a company must act bona fide in what they consider is in the interests of the company, and not for any collateral purpose (see 16.4). As a company is incorporated to pursue the objects stated in its memorandum it is clear that the directors must act in pursuit of those objects but it is also necessary to ask what purpose the pursuit of the objects serves — in whose interests does the company pursue its objects? This brings up again the controversy discussed in 0.2.4. In the shareholder-centred vision a company is seen as owned by its shareholders and existing to serve their interests exclusively. But other people see companies as existing for other constituencies besides shareholders.

In the shareholder-centred view a company's directors are required to act in the interests of the shareholders exclusively. Shareholder primacy supports the idea that a company's shareholders are entitled to its profits, which continues the view of the capitalist held by the classical economists. For example, J.S. Mill, in a passage first published in 1848, talked of:

> . . . the share of the capitalist; the profits of capital or stock; the gains of the person who advances the expenses of production — who, from funds in his possession, pays the wages of the labourers, or supports them during the work; who supplies the requisite buildings, materials, and tools or machinery; and to whom, by the usual terms of the contract, the produce belongs, to be disposed of at his pleasure. After indemnifying him for his outlay, there commonly remains a surplus, which is his profit; the net income from his capital. (*Principles of Political Economy* (London: 1848), bk 2, ch. 15, sect. 1.)

Normally the directors of a company do not have to own any of its shares (see 15.2.9). Economists have analysed the problems which may arise when the people managing a business do not own all of it. Managers in this position are believed to manage the business less efficiently than if they did own it. Rather than treating this as a consequence of the fact that wealth owners are not necessarily good business managers and good business managers are not necessarily wealth owners, the analysis adopted in the shareholder-primacy view of the company is that the inefficiency of managers is a detriment for providers of capital, for whom the managers are treated as 'agents'. The role model for directors seems to be the eighteenth- or nineteenth-century steward or land-agent managing an estate for a temporarily absent landlord who might be expected to return to retake control. This was how the leading classical economist Adam Smith put it in a passage first published in 1784:

> The directors of such companies, however, being the managers rather of other people's money than their own, it cannot well be expected, that they should watch over it with the same anxious vigilance with which the partners in a private copartnery frequently watch over their own. Like the stewards of a rich man, they are apt to consider attention to small matters as not for their master's honour, and very easily give themselves a dispensation from having it. Negligence and profusion, therefore, must always prevail, more or less, in the management of the affairs of such a company. (*An Inquiry into the Nature and Causes of the Wealth of Nations*, ed. R.H. Campbell and A.S. Skinner (Oxford: Clarendon Press, 1976), p. 741.)

In this analysis, the efficiency losses, the costs incurred by investors in monitoring managers and the so-called 'bonding costs' incurred by managers to demonstrate that they really are working in the investors' interests are known collectively as 'agency costs'. Controlling agency costs is seen as central to the relationship between shareholders and directors of a company (see M.C. Jensen and W.H. Meckling, 'Theory of the firm: managerial behavior, agency costs and ownership structure' (1976) 3 J Fin Econ 305). In law, though, directors are not agents of members (see 15.9).

Law and economics analysts who favour explanations in terms of markets suggest that economic forces are significant in controlling the behaviour of directors of companies whose shares are publicly traded: they think that when the stock market is informed that the directors of a company are not acting in the best interests of its shareholders, the price of the company's shares will fall and it will be taken over by new owners who will install new directors to run the business more efficiently (H.G. Manne, 'Mergers and the market for corporate control' (1965) 73 J Pol Econ 110). They believe that directors will be so frightened of this happening, because they will lose their jobs and will not be employed in such good jobs again, that they will realise that it is in their own interests to act in the interests of the shareholders. It is said that the market for corporate control and the market for directors' employment will align the interests of directors and shareholders. However, it is admitted that in some cases a director may be able to make more by diverting money from the company than he or she can hope to make legitimately and that such a director would not be deterred from taking the company's money merely by fear of losing legitimate earnings (H.N. Butler, 'The contractual theory of the corporation' (1989) 11 Geo Mason U L Rev 99).

It is often claimed that the concept of shareholders as owners and directors as stewards does not correctly describe the actual relationship between directors and shareholders of public companies. The whole idea of the public company has always been that it offers the opportunity to invest in a company without any involvement in management. Public company shareholders treat their *shares* as their property which they can do what they like with, but they see ownership of shares in a company as separate from ownership of the company. Usually a person buying company shares on a stock exchange does not obtain them from the company and does not give the company money for them — normally shares are bought from other shareholders. It is alleged that in many public companies, the wide spread of ownership of shares means that no one shareholder or group of shareholders can exercise effective control over the directors and that if owners of the shares in a company do not like what its directors are doing then, rather than try to influence the directors, they sell the shares. This situation was described as a 'separation of ownership and control' in an influential book by A.A. Berle Jr and G.C. Means, *The Modern Corporation and Private Property* (New York, 1932). (The title of a more recent book by M.J. Roe, *Strong Managers, Weak Owners* (Princeton University Press, 1994), has provided another apt catchphrase.) Berle and Means noted that venturing capital in business and controlling or managing the business are two different functions, both of which need to be encouraged if economic activity is to be promoted. They argued that the shareholder-centred model of the company and the traditional view that the profits of an enterprise should go to the providers of its capital arose at a time when individual business people both provided capital for and directed their enterprises, so that profits, though the reward and incentive for both investment and direction, went to a single owner who combined both functions. The separation of ownership and control separated the two functions, which meant that the shareholder providers of capital could no longer claim the exclusive need to be incentivised by profits. Berle and Means made the not altogether obvious leap from this argument to the proposal that large American corporations in which ownership and control had been separated should serve 'all society' (p. 356) and that:

the 'control' of the great corporations should develop into a purely neutral technocracy, balancing a variety of claims by various groups in the community and assigning to each a portion of the income stream on the basis of public policy rather than private cupidity.

Once again the directors are given a self-effacing role working purely for others.

Even classical economists acknowledged that a business's profits reward the successful direction of the business, by what they called the 'entrepreneur', as well as the passive supply of funds. This became clearer when capital markets developed and appeared to establish a price (rate of return) for the supply of capital, dependent on the riskiness of the investment. Investors could be regarded as supplying capital for a fixed return (at least, fixed from time to time by the capital market) just as workers worked for a fixed wage, and, some would argue, the balance of profits should go to the entrepreneur, though there is much room for disagreement over exactly which entrepreneurial function deserves the reward.

A different approach sees a business organisation as a coalition of individuals, including managers, workers, shareholders, suppliers, customers, lawyers, tax collectors and industry regulators (R.M. Cyert and J.G. March, *A Behavioral Theory of the Firm*, 2nd ed. (Cambridge Mass: Blackwell, 1992), p. 31). Sharing the profits may be a matter of bargaining between these groups. For an exploration of companies in terms of bargaining between managers and shareholders, analysed using game theory, see M.A. Utset, 'Towards a bargaining theory of the firm' (1995) 80 Cornell L Rev 540.

E.F. Fama, 'Agency problems and the theory of the firm' (1980) 88 J Polit Econ 288 suggested that 'ownership of capital should not be confused with ownership of the firm' (at p. 290). Capital is just one input supplied to a company for the purpose of its operations and each input is owned by some person. Management is just another input. Using the nexus of contracts image discussed in 5.3.2, Fama went on to say (loc. cit.):

The firm is just the set of contracts covering the way inputs are joined to create outputs and the way receipts from outputs are shared among inputs. In this 'nexus of contracts' perspective, ownership of the firm is an irrelevant concept.

But in a later article, E.F. Fama and M.C. Jensen, 'Separation of ownership and control' (1983) 26 J Law & Econ 301, re-established shareholder primacy by describing the equity shareholders of a company as the 'residual claimants' — that is, they are entitled to whatever is left of the company's assets after its debts have been paid. They may receive any amount from zero upwards, but in a limited company, provided their shares are fully paid, they will not be required to pay anything more. Fama and Jensen offer the alternative description 'residual risk bearers' and this has become a popular description, but it may perhaps exaggerate the heroism of shareholders. Members of companies risk losing their investment, but this is no different from the risk that all creditors of limited companies bear of not being paid. The 'residual risk' that members bear is just the risk of not receiving the return that they expect on their investments. The idea of equity shareholders as residual claimants rather than owners allows for other claimants such as creditors in whose interests the company may be operated. But as residual claimants, equity shareholder members can argue that the company ought to be run in such a way as to maximise their residue and that may not be in the interests of other constituencies.

For a restatement of the view that the shareholders of a company should not be seen as its owners, either economically or legally, see R. Sappideen, 'Ownership of the large corporation: Why clothe the emperor?' (1996–7) 7 King's College LJ 27. Professor Sappideen argues that the only owner of a company is the company itself so that it is meaningless to talk of a separation of ownership and control.

In May 1991 the Financial Reporting Council, the Stock Exchange and the accountancy profession set up a committee chaired by Sir Adrian Cadbury (chairman of Cadbury Schweppes plc) to consider the financial aspects of corporate governance. The committee's report was published in December 1992 (*Report of the Committee on the Financial Aspects of Corporate Governance* (London: Gee, 1992)). The report noted that: 'Companies whose standards of corporate governance are high are the more likely to gain the confidence of investors and support for the development of their businesses' (para. 1.6). The report included a Code of Best Practice (known as the 'Cadbury Code'), which rapidly assumed great practical importance because the London Stock Exchange required every listed company to state in its annual report and accounts whether or not it had complied throughout the accounting period with the Cadbury Code, identifying the paragraphs of the code with which it had not complied and giving reasons for non-compliance (Listing Rules, para. 12.43(j)). In November 1995 a committee was established under the chairmanship of Sir Ronald Hampel, chairman of ICI plc, to review the implementation of the Cadbury Code. It published its final report in January 1998 (Committee on Corporate Governance, *Final Report* (London: Gee, 1998); see A. Dignam, 'A principled approach to self-regulation? The report of the Hampel Committee on Corporate Governance' (1998) 19 Co Law 141). In consultation with the London Stock Exchange, the Hampel Committee produced a new 'Combined Code' containing principles of good governance and a code of best practice, which is appended to the Listing Rules. For accounting periods ending on or after 31 December 1998, instead of stating how they have complied with the Cadbury Code, listed companies must state how they have applied the principles set out in the Combined Code (Listing Rules, para. 12.43A).

Some commentators prefer to think of control of a company as a variety of political process (A.A. Berle Jr, '"Control" in corporate law' (1958) 58 Colum L Rev 1212 at p. 1215; A.A. Berle, 'Modern functions of the corporate system' (1962) 62 Colum L Rev 433 at p. 445: 'In fact, a large corporation is a variety of non-statist [meaning, apparently, non-State] institution'). J. Pound, 'The rise of the political model of corporate governance and corporate control' (1993) 68 NYU L Rev 1003 observes that in democratic politics, influence may be exerted by discussion and lobbying as well as by intermittently changing the government by general election and claims that in the USA in the early 1990s changes in board personnel and policies were more often brought about by the lobbying of large investors than by takeovers, which Pound claims are an inefficiently drastic method of correcting mismanagement.

The increase in shareholder activism in the USA, where large public employee pension funds are particularly significant shareholders, is discussed by B.S. Black, 'Shareholder passivity reexamined' (1990) 89 Mich L Rev 520. Black notes that shareholding is becoming more concentrated as institutions such as pension funds invest large amounts in the leading companies whose shares are publicly traded. It is possible for large institutional shareholders to control enough shares to overcome the separation of ownership and control in large public companies and have a direct influence on their management. For similar comments in the British context see J. Farrar and M. Russell, 'The impact of institutional investment on company law' (1984) 5 Co Law 107. However, several commentators have pointed out that active participation in the management of companies is an inappropriate activity for many institutional investors, such as pension funds and insurance companies, which have duties to their own members or customers requiring them to avoid risk (see R. Sappideen, 'Ownership of the large corporation: Why clothe the emperor?' (1996–7) 7 King's College LJ 27; T.A. Smith, 'Institutions and entrepreneurs in American corporate finance' (1997) 85 Calif L Rev 1). The Combined Code, principle E.1, states that 'Institutional shareholders have a responsibility to make considered use of their votes'.

Principle E.2 states that 'Institutional shareholders should be ready, where practicable, to enter into a dialogue with companies based on the mutual understanding of objectives'.

15.1.3 Minimum number of directors

CA 1985, s. 282, requires every public company to have at least two directors unless it was registered before 1 November 1929. (The effect on the exception of the provision in s. 1(3) that a public company must have registered or re-registered as such on or after 22 December 1980 is questionable.)

In Australia it has been held that a company subject to a statutory requirement to have at least two directors may nevertheless have articles assigning all the directors' powers to one named person during the time that the person holds office as a director (*Whitehouse* v *Carlton Hotel Pty Ltd* (1987) 162 CLR 285). The residual power of the remaining directors to act if the named person leaves office and the fact that they must act under any statutory requirement not overridden by the articles (under British law, for example, IA 1986, s. 89(1)) are sufficient. Table A, art. 72, permits directors to delegate their powers to a managing director or a director who is also an employee.

CA 1985, s. 282, requires every private company to have at least one director.

Table A, art. 64, requires there to be at least two directors unless the company determines otherwise by ordinary resolution. The company may, by the same article, by ordinary resolution set a maximum number of directors.

If a company has fewer directors in office than the minimum number prescribed for the company by its articles then the directors in office cannot act at all (*Re Alma Spinning Co., Bottomley's Case* (1880) 16 ChD 681) unless there is a provision in the articles which permits them to act (*Re Scottish Petroleum Co.* (1883) 23 ChD 413, CA). Table A, art. 90, provides that 'The continuing directors or a sole continuing director may act notwithstanding any vacancies in their number'. This form of words occurred in the articles of the Scottish Petroleum Co., which required a minimum of four directors. Only two were left because of resignations. It was held that the acts of these two were valid. However, it seems that a provision in the articles of association worded in this way applies only when the number of directors has been reduced below the minimum and does not cover a situation in which the minimum number of directors never have taken office because of a failure to appoint the minimum number on registration of the company (*Re British Empire Match Co. Ltd* (1889) 59 LT 291; *Re Sly, Spink & Co.* [1911] 2 Ch 430).

There is no objection to a company or other corporation being appointed a director (*Re Bulawayo Market & Offices Co. Ltd* [1907] 2 Ch 458). In New Zealand the companies legislation now prohibits a body corporate from being a director of a company and in the context of this legislation it was held in *Commercial Management Ltd* v *Registrar of Companies* [1987] 1 NZLR 744 that the members of a partnership could not be appointed jointly as a director because that would be 'quite foreign to the concept of the office of director which calls for individual judgment and responsibility' (at p. 747). However, it would seem that as the British legislature has not prohibited corporate directors it does not share the New Zealand court's view of the nature of a directorship and so presumably a directorship of a British company may be jointly held.

15.1.4 Interpretation of 'director' in legislation

By CA 1985, s. 741(1), the expression 'director', when used in CA 1985, includes any person occupying the position of director, by whatever name called. The same provision is made in IA 1986, s. 251; CDDA 1986, s. 22(4); and FSA 1986, s. 207(1).

15.1.5 *De iure* and *de facto* directors

A person is described as a *de iure* director of a company if:

(a) the person has been appointed to the office of director in accordance with the rules governing such appointment (see 15.2);

(b) the person has agreed to hold office;

(c) the person is not disqualified from being a director of the company (see 15.2.5); and

(d) the person has not vacated office (see 15.3).

A person who acts as a director of a company but is not a *de iure* director of it is called a *de facto* director.

15.1.6 Shadow directors

In relation to a company, the term 'shadow director' means a person in accordance with whose directions or instructions the directors of the company are accustomed to act, but advice given in a professional capacity does not make the adviser a shadow director (CA 1985, s. 741(2)). The same definition is given in IA 1986, s. 251, and CDDA 1986, s. 22(5). In FSA 1986, the term 'director' is to be interpreted as including a shadow director (s. 207(1)). A shadow director of a company is not, and does not claim or purport to be, a director of the company, that is, a shadow director of a company is not a *de iure* or *de facto* director of the company (*Re Hydrodam (Corby) Ltd* [1994] 2 BCLC 180).

It is possible for a parent company to be a shadow director of its subsidiary companies (but not necessarily, see *Gramophone & Typewriter Ltd* v *Stanley* [1908] 2 KB 89, CA) and CA 1985, s. 741(3), makes some special provisions for such cases, see 15.6.4, 16.4.5, 16.6.7 and 19.5.9. If a parent company is a shadow director of one of its subsidiaries, it does not follow that the directors of the parent company must also be shadow directors of the subsidiary (*Re Hydrodam (Corby) Ltd*).

A person is a shadow director of a company only if 'the directors of the company' are accustomed to act in accordance with that person's directions or instructions. The fact that only a minority of the company's directors are accustomed so to act is not enough to make the person a shadow director (*Kuwait Asia Bank EC* v *National Mutual Life Nominees Ltd* [1991] 1 AC 187, PC, at p. 223; *Re Unisoft Group Ltd (No. 3)* [1994] 1 BCLC 609 at p. 620). A person will not be a shadow director of a company unless the directors of that company act on the person's directions or instructions as a matter of regular practice, over a period of time (*Re Unisoft Group Ltd (No. 3)* at p. 620).

In *Re a Company (No. 005009 of 1987)* [1989] BCLC 13, Knox J held that it was arguable that a bank had acted as shadow director of a company when the company was managed in accordance with the bank's recommendations as a condition of the bank not appointing an administrative receiver. However, at the hearing of the case (*Re MC Bacon Ltd* [1990] BCLC 372), the allegation was abandoned (rightly in the judge's view) after evidence was presented. In *Re PFTZM Ltd* [1995] 2 BCLC 354, PFTZM had operated a hotel but it was not as profitable as expected and its managing director thought it would be unable to pay the rent. The landlord company permitted PFTZM to continue trading provided one of its directors and/or a manager attended PFTZM's weekly management meetings and decided which of PFTZM's creditors were to be paid. Judge Paul Baker QC (sitting as a High Court judge) decided that there was not even a prima facie case that the landlord's director and manager were shadow directors of PFTZM. It seems that almost complete control of a company's affairs will be required before a person is to be reckoned a shadow director of the company (see G. Bhattacharyya, 'Shadow directors and wrongful trading revisited' (1995) 16 Co Law 313).

15.1.7 Executive and non-executive directors

In practice a distinction is often drawn between executive directors and non-executive directors. A non-executive director of a company typically does not devote his or her whole working time to the company and receives a relatively small director's fee. An executive director of a company typically devotes his or her whole working time to the company (or a number of companies in a group), often as an employee of the company, and has a significant personal interest in the company as a source of income. The distinction between executive and non-executive directors has no significance in company law though it may cause difficult problems in employment law.

Many people believe that non-executive directors (NEDs) can be effective in ensuring that the board of a company acts in the interests of the company rather than a member or members of the board. The Bank of England has sponsored an organisation called PRO NED to promote the appointment of non-executive directors. However, *Re Polly Peck International plc (No. 2)* [1994] 1 BCLC 574, which is discussed in 15.2.5.6, shows how unrealistic it is to expect non-executive directors to control a determined and powerful managing director. The Hampel Committee was probably more realistic in identifying one of the functions of non-executive directors as being to act as mentors to relatively inexperienced executives (Committee on Corporate Governance, *Final Report* (London: Gee, 1998), p. 25). The Hampel Committee saw the primary function of a company's non-executive directors as contributing to the development of the company's strategy (ibid., loc. cit.). The Combined Code for listed companies (see 15.1.2), principle A.3, states:

> The board should include a balance of executive and non-executive directors (including independent non-executives) such that no individual or small group of individuals can dominate the board's decision taking.

'Independent' here means independent of management and free from any business or other relationship which could materially interfere with the exercise of their independent judgment (Combined Code, para. A.3.2). The code of practice, para. A.3.1, says that a company's board 'should include non-executive directors of sufficient calibre and number for their views to carry significant weight in the board's decisions' and that at least one third of the board should be non-executive. The directors' report of a listed company must identify which of its directors are independent non-executive and give short biographical notes for them (Listing Rules, para. 12.43(i)).

15.2 APPOINTMENT TO OFFICE

15.2.1 Who appoints?

The Companies Act 1985 does not prescribe who is to be responsible for appointing the directors of a company though it requires the first directors to be appointed by a statement signed by, or on behalf of, the subscribers of the memorandum (see 15.2.2) and it gives the company's members an irremovable right to dismiss directors of the company (see 15.3.3). Provision for appointment is normally made in a company's articles. In the absence of any provision, directors are to be appointed by the company's members (*Woolf* v *East Nigel Gold Mining Co. Ltd* (1905) 21 TLR 660; *Harman* v *Energy Research Group Australia Ltd* [1986] WAR 123). An appointment of a person as a director of a company does not take effect unless the person agrees to the appointment (*Re British Empire Match Co. Ltd* (1888) 59 LT 291).

In Table A the power to appoint directors is given both to the members, by art. 78, and the directors, by art. 79. But art. 79 provides that a director appointed by the board can hold office only until the next annual general meeting, and points out that if a maximum number of directors has been fixed by, or in accordance with, the articles, the directors cannot enlarge the board beyond that maximum. Table A, art. 64, gives the members power to determine a maximum number of directors by ordinary resolution, but provides that there is no maximum number until such a resolution is passed.

15.2.2   First directors

When a company is registered, a statement in the prescribed form naming the person who is, or the persons who are, to be the first director or directors of the company must be delivered to the registrar (CA 1985, s. 10(2)(a)). The person or persons so named must sign the statement to show consent to the appointment and the statement must also be signed by or on behalf of the subscriber or subscribers of the memorandum (s. 10(3)). The person or persons named in the statement are deemed to have been appointed director or directors on the company's incorporation (s. 13(5)). These provisions were introduced by CA 1976. As the subscribers to a company's memorandum are, by definition, the company's first members (s. 22(1)), these provisions accord with the common law rule that, in the absence of any provision in a company's constitution about the appointment of its first directors, an appointment made by its members is valid, and if they are unanimous then they can make appointments without meeting (*Perseus Mining NL* v *Landbrokers (Perth) Pty Ltd* [1972] WAR 12). It used to be common for a company's first director or directors to be appointed in its articles: persons thus named would normally have full power to act as directors on registration of the articles (*Re Sly, Spink & Co.* [1911] 2 Ch 430 at p. 436). This procedure is less common now with the widespread use of shelf companies. If a company's articles appoint as director of the company a person who is not named as a first director in the statement delivered under s. 10(2) then the appointment in the articles is void (s. 10(5)).

If a company is registered with Table A as its articles of association then it must have at least two directors on registration (art. 64). If only one director is in office on registration then that director cannot act at all: the director cannot act under art. 79 (see 15.2.3.3) to appoint another director but must wait until the members appoint one under art. 78 (*Re British Empire Match Co. Ltd* (1888) 59 LT 291).

Under Table A, art. 73, at the first annual general meeting of the company all its directors must retire, though, under art. 80, anyone so retiring may seek reappointment by the members under art. 78. So none of the first directors can continue in office beyond the first annual general meeting without being approved by the members.

15.2.3   Subsequent directors

15.2.3.1   Circumstances in which appointments are made
After a company's first directors have been appointed, it may be necessary to make new appointments, either to fill a vacancy when a director vacates office (see 15.3) or to increase the size of the board by appointing one or more additional directors.

15.2.3.2   Appointment by the members
Table A, art. 78, empowers the members to appoint a person by ordinary resolution to be a director, either to fill a vacancy or as an additional director, but art. 78 says that only a person who is willing to act may be appointed.

The power of the majority to appoint directors must 'be exercised for the benefit of the company as a whole and not to secure some ulterior advantage' (*Re H.R. Harmer Ltd* [1959] 1 WLR 62 per Jenkins LJ at p. 82; *Re Broadcasting Station 2GB Pty Ltd* [1964–5] NSWR 1648 per Jacobs J at p. 1662). In *Theseus Exploration NL v Mining & Associated Industries Ltd* [1973] QdR 81, the court issued an interlocutory injunction to prevent members of a company electing certain persons as directors because there was sufficient evidence that those persons intended to use the company's assets solely for the benefit of the majority shareholder.

Table A, art. 73, provides that all the first directors must retire at the first annual general meeting. Article 73 also provides a system of retirement by rotation for non-executive directors, under which one third of them retire at each annual general meeting after the first (see 15.3.2).

A retiring director may, if willing to act, be reappointed (Table A, art. 80) and a director retiring by rotation will be deemed to have been reappointed if the company does not, at the general meeting at which the retirement takes effect, appoint someone else to fill the vacancy (art. 75), unless the retiring director's reappointment was put to the meeting and rejected, or the meeting expressly resolved not to fill the vacancy (art. 75). (The operation of provisions in articles of association like art. 75 is limited by CA 1985, s. 292(2) (see below) and s. 293(4) (see 15.3.6).) Article 76 of Table A is important:

> No person other than a director retiring by rotation shall be appointed or reappointed a director at any general meeting unless —
>
> (a)   he is recommended by the directors; or
> (b)   not less than 14 nor more than 35 clear days before the date appointed for the meeting, notice executed by a member qualified to vote at the meeting has been given to the company of the intention to propose that person for appointment or reappointment stating the particulars which would, if he were so appointed or reappointed, be required to be included in the company's register of directors [see 15.4.1] together with notice executed by that person of his willingness to be appointed or reappointed.

Although this provision of Table A makes the latest date for lodging notice of intention to propose someone not recommended by the board as a director 14 days before the meeting, the London Stock Exchange requires the articles of listed companies to make the latest date seven days before the meeting (Listing Rules, ch. 13, app. 1, para. 22). Table A, art. 77, requires the company to give notice, to every person entitled to receive notice of a general meeting, of particulars of persons to be proposed for election as directors at that meeting, other than a director retiring by rotation at the meeting. The particulars to be given are the particulars that would have to be included in the register of directors (see 15.4.1) if the person were elected. The notice is to be given not less than seven nor more than 28 clear days before the meeting.

Table A, art. 38, requires at least 21 clear days' notice to be given of an extraordinary general meeting called for the purpose of adopting a resolution appointing a person as a director. Proposals to appoint directors at extraordinary general meetings are also subject to arts 76 and 77 (see above).

The term of office of a director whose appointment has been put to the vote will not commence until it has been ascertained that the vote is in favour of the appointment (*Holmes v Keyes* [1959] Ch 199, CA).

At a general meeting of a public company, a motion for the appointment of two or more persons as directors by a single resolution must not be made, unless a resolution that it shall be so made has first been agreed to by the meeting without any vote being given against it (CA 1985, s. 292(1)). A resolution in contravention of s. 292(1) is void even if no one objected to it at the time (s. 292(2)). However, the fact that appointments of directors of a company are deemed to be void by s. 292(2) does not bring into operation a provision in the company's articles like Table A, art. 75, for the automatic reappointment of a retiring director in default of another appointment.

Principle A.5 of the Combined Code for listed companies (see 15.1.2) states that 'There should be a formal and transparent procedure for the appointment of new directors to the board'. The code of best practice says that a listed company's board, unless it is small, should establish a nomination committee, to make recommendations to the board on all new board appointments (para. A.5.1). A majority of the members of the nomination committee should be non-executive directors, and the chairman should be either the chairman of the board or a non-executive director. The chairman and members of the nomination committee should be identified in the annual report. Principle A.6 requires all directors of listed companies to submit themselves for re-election at least every three years, and the code of best practice says that sufficient biographical details should be supplied about persons submitted for election or re-election as directors to enable shareholders to take an informed decision on their election (para. A.6.2).

15.2.3.3 Appointment by the directors

Table A, art. 79, empowers the directors to appoint a person to be a director, either to fill a vacancy or as an additional director, but only a person who is willing to act may be appointed. If, because of the occurrence of a vacancy, the number of directors is less than the minimum number prescribed by the articles or is insufficient to form a quorum at a board meeting, the continuing director or directors may, under Table A, art. 90 (see 15.5.1), nevertheless make an appointment to fill the vacancy. The reference to 'directors' in art. 79 must therefore include the case of a sole director (*Channel Collieries Trust Ltd v Dover, St Margaret's & Martin Mill Light Railway Co.* [1914] 2 Ch 506, CA; *APT Group Services Pty Ltd v Ferguson* (1991) 6 ACSR 231, Victoria). A sole continuing director of a public company may make an appointment under arts 79 and 90 even though CA 1985, s. 282, requires the company to have two directors (*Macson Development Co. Ltd v Gordon* (1959) 19 DLR (2d) 465, Nova Scotia; *APT Group Services Pty Ltd v Ferguson*).

A director appointed by the directors under art. 79 holds office only until the next annual general meeting, whether the appointment was to fill a vacancy or as an additional director. At the annual general meeting such a person is not a director retiring by rotation and so cannot be reappointed unless the conditions of art. 76 are complied with (see 15.2.3.2). Furthermore a resolution to reappoint must be adopted: a director retiring other than by rotation may not continue in office by default under art. 75. The London Stock Exchange requires the articles of a listed company to include provisions on the retirement of a director appointed by the directors with the effect of Table A, art. 79 (Listing Rules, ch. 13, app. 1, para. 21).

The directors' power to fill a vacancy under a provision such as Table A, art. 79, continues for as long as the vacancy subsists (*Munster v Cammell Co.* (1882) 21 ChD 183, in which, after the vacancy occurred, a general meeting was held which made no appointment, and a subsequent appointment by the directors was held to be valid). However, a vacancy subsists only. while there are fewer directors than before the vacancy occurred. In *Zimmers Ltd* v *Zimmer* [1951] WN 600, a vacancy occurred when one director resigned. The sole continuing director appointed his wife as an 'additional' director. It was held that the vacancy then ceased to exist so that a later appointment of a third director was not made to fill that vacancy. (Under the company's articles, unlike Table A, art. 79, whether a director was appointed to fill a vacancy or as an additional director made a difference to when he was deemed to retire.)

15.2.4   Age

A company must record in its register of directors the dates of birth of its directors (CA 1985, s. 289(1)(a)(vii)). The dates of birth of the first directors of a company must be given in the statement delivered to the registrar under s. 10(2) (sch. 1, para. 1(a)). Unless a company's articles otherwise provide, there is no minimum age below which a director may not be appointed, nor, in the case of a private company that is not a subsidiary of a public company or of a Northern Ireland public company, is there any maximum age beyond which a director may not be appointed or continue to act.

In the case of a public company or a subsidiary of a public company or of a Northern Ireland public company, though, a person is not capable of being appointed a director if at the time of his appointment he has attained the age of 70 (CA 1985, s. 293(2)), unless the company's articles provide otherwise (s. 293(7)). If the company was registered before 1947 then, by s. 293(7), only provisions introduced into its articles since the beginning of 1947 are effective to exclude or modify s. 293(2). Even if the company's articles do not exclude or modify s. 293(2), an individual who has attained the age of 70 may be validly appointed a director of the company if his or her appointment is made or approved by a general meeting of the members, provided special notice (see 14.4.5.6) is given of the resolution to make or approve the appointment (s. 293(5)). In the notice given to the company, and by the company to its members, under the special notice procedure, the age of the individual to whom it relates must be stated.

An individual who is appointed, or to his or her knowledge is proposed to be appointed, director of a public company, or of a subsidiary of either a public company or a Northern Ireland public company, at a time when he or she has attained the age of 70 (or any other age limit set by the company's articles) must, under penalty, give notice of his or her age to the company (s. 294(1), (4) and (5); penalty in sch. 24). This rule applies even if the company has modified or excluded all or any of the provisions of s. 293 (s. 294(2)). This notice does not have to be given on reappointment on the termination of a previous appointment as director of the company (s. 294(3)).

See further 15.3.6.

15.2.5   Disqualification

A significant aspect of the control of companies for the public interest is the prohibition of certain persons from acting as company directors. In recent years Parliament has considerably extended the circumstances in which the courts can declare a person disqualified from directing or managing companies. Nevertheless the power to make a disqualification order is always discretionary and will not be exercised until months, perhaps years, after the misdeeds that justify the disqualification. It is notable that an individual who becomes personally insolvent and is declared bankrupt will automatically commit an offence if he or she acts as director of a company (see 15.2.5.1). However, an individual who directs a company into insolvency is entitled to set up a new company immediately unless and until a court, in its discretion, makes a disqualification order. This is a striking example of the way in which incorporation of a company to carry on a business separates an individual's personal and business affairs.

15.2.5.1 By personal insolvency

It is an offence triable either way for an undischarged bankrupt to act as director of, or directly or indirectly to take part in or be concerned in the management of a company unless he or she has the leave of the court that made the bankruptcy order (CDDA 1986, ss. 11 and 13; for discussion of sentencing see *R* v *Theivendran* (1992) 13 Cr App R (S) 601). The offence is one of strict liability, that is, the prosecution only have to prove that the accused did the prohibited act and do not have to prove an intention to offend (*R* v *Brockley* [1994] 1 BCLC 606). In four cases reported on applications by bankrupts for leave to take part in the management of companies, leave was refused (*Re Kingsgate Rare Metals Pty Ltd* [1940] QWN 42; *Re Altim Pty Ltd* [1968] 2 NSWR 762; *Re McQuillan* (1988) 5 BCC 137; *Re Ansett* (1990) 3 ACSR 357). In *Re Altim Pty Ltd,* Street J emphasised that the prohibition on bankrupts managing companies was not intended to punish bankrupts but was to protect the community. There was no evidence that the applicant in *Re Altim Pty Ltd* was in any way dishonest, but his long history of business failures in the building industry demonstrated an incompetence from which the community should be protected. In *Re McQuillan,* it seemed that the court would be acting in vain in giving leave to act as director of the company concerned because there was no chance that he would actually be appointed a director of the company because of the opposition of the company's only other member. The applicant had not demonstrated any need for him to act as a director of the company and no reason why the court should depart from the strong policy of the law that bankrupts should not act as company directors.

If an administration order (under which an individual's estate is administered by a court under the County Courts Act 1984, part VI) is revoked because the individual has failed to make a payment required by the order then the court may order that CDDA 1986, s. 12, is to apply to that individual (IA 1986, s. 429(2)(b)). The individual is then prohibited from acting as director of, or directly or indirectly taking part or being concerned in the management of, a company without leave of the court which ordered s. 12 to apply: contravention of the prohibition is an offence triable either way (CDDA 1986, s. 13).

In CDDA 1986, 'director' includes any person occupying the position of director, by whatever name called (CDDA 1986, s. 22(4); see 15.1.4).

15.2.5.2 By disqualification order

A disqualification order against a person is an order that the person shall not, without leave of a court (see 15.2.5.7), be a director of a company or in any way, whether directly or indirectly, be concerned or take part in the management of a company (CDDA 1986, s. 1(1)). The person is also banned from promoting companies and from acting as an insolvency practitioner. In effect a disqualification order prevents a person from trading with limited liability though a disqualified person may engage in business as a sole trader or in partnership.

The acts which a disqualified person is prohibited from doing are listed in four separate paragraphs in s. 1(1), but the only form of disqualification order which may be made is one disqualifying a person from doing all the things listed: it is not possible to disqualify from only a selection of them (*Official Receiver* v *Hannan* [1997] 2 BCLC 473; *R* v *Cole* [1998] BCC 87).

Acting in contravention of a disqualification order is an offence triable either way (CDDA 1986, s. 13). In addition a person who contravenes a disqualification order by being a director of a company, or being concerned, whether directly or indirectly, or taking part, in the management of a company, may be made personally liable for all debts and liabilities of the company incurred while so acting (CDDA 1986, s. 15(1)(a), (3)(a) and (4)). A person liable under s. 15 is jointly and severally liable with the company itself and with any other person who is also jointly and severally liable for the debts (whether under s. 15 or some other provision such as CA 1985, s. 24, see 1.3.2.6) (CDDA 1986, s. 15(2)).

Acting as a management consultant advising on financial management and restructuring of a company may constitute being directly or indirectly concerned in the management of the company for these purposes (*R* v *Campbell* (1983) 78 Cr App R 95). The concept of 'management' in this context includes activities which involve policy-making or decision-making affecting the company as a whole or a substantial part of it and which may have a significant effect on its financial standing (*Commissioner for Corporate Affairs* v *Bracht* [1989] VR 821). 'Taking part in' and 'being concerned in' are to be interpreted widely and include activities involving some responsibility and participation in the decision-making processes of the company as opposed to routine clerical or administrative duties which may be associated with management: to prove that a person contravened a disqualification order, it is not necessary to show that the person had ultimate control or responsibility (ibid.). There is obviously great difficulty in catching people who act as shadow directors, managing companies through people who do what they are told. CDDA 1986, s. 15, therefore also imposes personal liability for the debts of a company on any person involved in its management who is willing to act on instructions given by a person whom the person knows to be the subject of a disqualification order (s. 15(1)(b), (3)(b) and (4)).

15.2.5.3 Grounds for disqualification
A disqualification order may be made against a person on the following grounds:

(a) Under CDDA 1986, s. 2, if the person has been convicted (whether on indictment or summarily) of an offence triable either way or (on indictment) of an offence triable only on indictment and the offence was in connection with the promotion, formation, management, liquidation or striking off of a company, or with the receivership or management of a company's property. An order on these grounds may be made by the court which convicted the person. Disqualification of a person under s. 2 is a punishment for the offence of which the person has been convicted, and so it cannot be combined with a conditional discharge (*R* v *Young* (1990) 12 Cr App R (S) 262; but this decision was doubted in *R* v *Cole* [1998] BCC 87). It is wrong to combine a disqualification order with a compensation order where the effect of disqualifying would be to prevent the offender earning money to pay the compensation (*R* v *Holmes* (1991) 13 Cr App R (S) 29). Section 2 can be invoked on conviction of any indictable offence 'in connection with the . . . management . . . of a company'. '. . . in connection with' means having 'some relevant factual connection with' the management of a company, and includes insider dealing (*R* v *Goodman* [1993] 2 All ER 789). '. . . management . . . of a company' means the management of the company's affairs including both its internal affairs and its dealings with other persons (*R* v *Austen* (1985) 1 BCC 99,528). In *R* v *Austen*, Mr Austen's companies had operated car showrooms, and he had been convicted of making fraudulent hire-purchase arrangements for cars sold from the showrooms. He was disqualified for 10 years and the Court of Appeal dismissed his appeal against that disqualification. In *R* v *Georgiou* (1988) 87 Cr App R 207, the Court of Appeal held that a director who carried on an insurance business through a company without authorisation under the Insurance Companies Act 1982 was committing an offence in connection with the management of a company which warranted his being disqualified for five years by the trial court.

(b)   Under CDDA 1986, s. 3, if the person has been persistently in default in providing returns, accounts or other documents required to be filed with the registrar of companies. A person is conclusively proved to be a persistent defaulter if it is shown that within five years there have been three instances of conviction for failing to provide information or of orders made requiring delivery of information (s. 3(2) and (3)).

Evidence that an insolvency practitioner persistently ignored chasing letters from the Companies Registration Office but always supplied returns just in time to avoid a default order might be enough to merit a disqualification order (*Re Arctic Engineering Ltd* [1986] 1 WLR 686). The court held that the word 'persistently' required some degree of continuance or repetition either by persisting in the same default or in a series of defaults. Also the court held that culpability was not an essential ingredient of persistent default although that factor might be considered in deciding whether to exercise the discretion to disqualify.

(c)   Under CDDA 1986, s. 4, if the person has been guilty, while an officer or liquidator of a company now in liquidation, or receiver or manager of the company's property, of any fraud in relation to the company or of any breach of his duty as such officer, liquidator, receiver or manager, or has been guilty of an offence (whether convicted of it or not) of knowingly being a party to fraudulent trading in contravention of CA 1985, s. 458 (see 20.10).

(d)   Under CDDA 1986, s. 5, if the person has been found guilty in a magistrates' court of an offence triable only summarily that consists of failing to provide information to the registrar, and that, including the present offence, there have been three instances within the past five years of conviction for failing to provide information or of orders made requiring delivery of information.

(e)   Under CDDA 1986, s. 6, if the person is or has been a director or shadow director (s. 22(4)) of a company which has at any time during or after that person's directorship 'become insolvent' (see below) and the person's conduct as a director or shadow director of that company, or that company and one or more other companies, makes the person unfit to be concerned with the management of a company. For these purposes a company 'becomes insolvent' if (s. 6(2)):

(i) The company goes into liquidation (see 20.8) at a time when its assets are insufficient for the payment of its debts and other liabilities and the expenses of the winding up; or

(ii)   An administration order is made in relation to the company; or

(iii)   An administrative receiver of the company is appointed.

As to item (i) in the above list, post-liquidation interest, either payable or receivable, cannot be taken into account but the liquidator's remuneration, if properly approved, must be (*Official Receiver* v *Moore* [1995] BCC 293).

As to item (ii), the making of an interim order on a petition for an administration order does not count (*Secretary of State for Trade & Industry* v *Palmer* [1994] BCC 990).

In considering the conduct of a person as director or shadow director of a company that has become insolvent the court may take into account the person's conduct in relation to any matter connected with or arising out of the insolvency and the person's conduct as a director or shadow director of other companies, including conduct relating to other companies' insolvency (CDDA 1986, s. 6(1)(b) and (2)). The court is also required to have regard to the matters listed in CDDA 1986, sch. 1 (CDDA 1986, s. 9).

(f)   Under CDDA 1986, s. 8, if the person's conduct, as revealed by an inspectors' report made under CA 1985, s. 437, or FSA 1986, s. 177 (see 18.8.3.1), or a report on an investigation of a collective investment scheme under FSA 1986, s. 94, or as revealed by any documents obtained under CA 1985, ss. 447 or 448 (see 18.8.1), or FSA 1986, s. 105, or obtained by the Director of the Serious Fraud Office under Criminal Justice Act 1987, s. 2, in relation to a company of which the person is or has been a director or shadow director makes that person unfit to be concerned in the management of a company or it is otherwise considered by the Secretary of State to be expedient in the public interest that a disqualification order should be made. In considering a person's conduct as a director the court is required to have regard to the matters listed in CDDA 1986, sch. 1 (CDDA 1986, s. 9).

(g)   Under CDDA 1986, s. 10, if the person has been found liable by the court to contribute to the assets of a company being wound up, either under IA 1986, s. 213 (liability for fraudulent trading, see 20.10) or IA 1986, s. 214 (director's responsibility for company's wrongful trading, see 20.12).

The vast majority of disqualification orders are made under s. 6. In 1996–7, 1,040 orders were made under s. 6, 11 under s. 8, and 168 under all the other provisions.

15.2.5.4   *Proceedings for making a disqualification order*

The procedural rules envisage that in some cases a disqualification order will be made following an application to a court for the specific purpose of disqualifying a particular person, and in other cases the court will, of its own motion, disqualify a person as a result of other proceedings taken against that person.

A disqualification order under ss. 2, 3 or 4 of CDDA 1986 (grounds (a), (b) or (c) in the list in 15.2.5.3) may be made by a court that has jurisdiction to wind up any of the companies in relation to which offences or defaults were committed (CDDA 1986, ss. 2(2)(a), 3(4) and 4(2)). An application for the making of such a disqualification order may be made by the Secretary of State or an official receiver, or by the liquidator or any past or present member or creditor of any company in relation to which the person sought to be disqualified has committed or is alleged to have committed an offence or other default (CDDA 1986, s. 16(2)).

A disqualification order under s. 2 (ground (a)) may also be made by the court that convicts the person of the offence (s. 2(2)(b) and (c)).

A disqualification order against a person under s. 5 (ground (d)) can be made only by the court which convicted the person or by another magistrates' court acting for the same petty sessions area. No application is necessary.

An order under s. 6 can be applied for only by the Secretary of State (though she may direct the official receiver to apply if the company that has become insolvent is in compulsory liquidation) (s. 7(1)). If the company that has become insolvent is in creditors' voluntary liquidation or has been dissolved, the official receiver does not have standing to make an application qua official receiver for a disqualification order: the application must be in the name of the Secretary of State, and an application in the wrong name will be dismissed (*Re Probe Data Systems Ltd* [1989] BCLC 561; *Re NP Engineering and Security Products Ltd* [1995] 2 BCLC 586). However, official receivers, liquidators, administrators and administrative receivers who believe that directors or shadow directors or companies for which they are responsible deserve disqualification under s. 6 are required to report the matter to the Secretary of State (ss. 7(3) and 6(3)). The court to which the application must be made depends on the way in which the company has become insolvent (s. 6(3)). If the company is in compulsory liquidation then the application must be made to the court winding up the company. If it is in voluntary liquidation then the application is to any court having jurisdiction to wind up the company. If the company is in administration then application is to the court that made the administration order. In any other case the application is to the High Court.

An application for a person to be disqualified under s. 6 must be made within two years of the date on which the company of which the person was a director or shadow director became insolvent (ss. 7(2) and 6(3)). This is the date when one of the events mentioned in s. 6(2) occurred. If more than one of them occurred then it is the date when the first of them occurred (*Re Tasbian Ltd (No. 1)* [1991] BCLC 54). The court may grant leave for an application to be made out of time (s. 7(2)). In considering an application for leave to commence proceedings out of time the court should take into account: (a) the length of the delay, (b) the reasons for the delay, (c) the strength of the case against the director, and (d) the degree of prejudice caused to the director by the delay (*Re Probe Data Systems Ltd (No. 3)* [1992] BCLC 405 per Scott LJ at p. 416). In *Secretary of State for Trade & Industry* v *McTighe* [1994] 2 BCLC 284 the persons sought to be disqualified had been largely responsible for the delay and leave was given to commence proceedings out of time. In *Re Polly Peck International plc (No. 2)* [1994] 1 BCLC 574, it was found that the allegations were not serious enough to warrant disqualification and anyway the case was very weak, and the delay could not be excused and had prejudiced the persons sought to be disqualified. Mere administrative difficulties in the Department of Trade and Industry did not provide a good reason for extending time in *Re Crestjoy Products Ltd* [1990] BCLC 677 and *Re Cedar Developments Ltd* [1994] 2 BCLC 714.

Once an application has been made, it is up to the applicant to pursue the case and bring it to a hearing. If there is inordinate and inexcusable delay by the applicant then the court may dismiss the application for want of prosecution if the delay has substantially damaged the possibility of a fair trial or has otherwise prejudiced the person sought to be disqualified, as long as striking out the application would not be contrary to the public interest (*Re Noble Trees Ltd* [1993] BCLC 1185; *Official Receiver* v *B Ltd* [1994] 2 BCLC 1; *Re Manlon Trading Ltd* [1996] Ch 136).

By CDDA 1986, s. 16(1), any person intending to apply for the making of a disqualification order by the court having jurisdiction to wind up a company (i.e., where the application is for an order under ss. 2, 3, 4 or 6) must give not less than 10 days' notice of that intention to the person against whom the order is sought. Remarkably, a majority of the Court of Appeal in *Secretary of State for Trade & Industry* v *Langridge* [1991] Ch 402 held that the court can hear an application for a disqualification order even if the required notice has not been given.

By s. 8(1), only the Secretary of State may apply for an order under s. 8 (ground (f)). The application must be made to the High Court. In *R* v *Secretary of State for Trade and Industry, ex parte Lonrho plc* [1992] BCC 325, the Secretary of State had received an inspectors' report which criticised three businessmen, the Fayed brothers, but had decided not to apply for any disqualification orders to be made against any of them. The appointment of the inspectors had been made after representations by Lonrho plc, which had lost to the Fayed brothers in a takeover battle and believed the brothers had acted wrongly. It was held that because of its involvement in the circumstances leading up to the making of the report, Lonrho plc had standing to apply for judicial review of the Secretary of State's decision not to apply for disqualification orders. However, the court could not find that the Secretary of State's decision was unlawful in this case.

An application for a disqualification order under s. 6 or s. 8 must be made in accordance with the Insolvent Companies (Disqualification of Unfit Directors) Proceedings Rules 1987 (SI 1987 No. 2023).

A disqualification order under s. 10 may be made only by the court that makes the declaration of liability and may be considered a further sanction imposed by the court for the fraudulent or wrongful trading. No application is necessary.

Proceedings against a person under s. 6 or s. 8 should not be delayed to await the outcome of civil proceedings against the person in relation to matters relied on as evidence of unfitness (*Re Rex Williams Leisure plc* [1994] Ch 350). But hearings are often delayed until criminal proceedings have been concluded. When disqualification proceedings against several directors of one company are ordered to be heard together but have to be delayed because some of them are subject to criminal proceedings the delay can be unfair on the ones who are not defending criminal charges (see *EDC* v *United Kingdom* (application No. 24433/94) [1998] BCC 370; *Secretary of State for Trade and Industry* v *Tjolle* [1998] 1 BCLC 333). In *EDC* v *United Kingdom* the Human Rights Commission accepted that it is necessary to delay disqualification proceedings until related criminal proceedings are completed because of the danger of prejudicing those proceedings. In *Secretary of State for Trade and Industry* v *Tjolle* a former director of a holiday company faced criminal proceedings for fraudulent trading, was sent to prison for nine months and disqualified by the criminal court for 10 years. He then faced an adjourned application for disqualification under s. 6 and was disqualified for the maximum 15 years. The court refused to make a disqualification order against a fellow respondent to the s. 6 proceedings, who had not been charged with criminal offences, and who had been waiting three years for her case to be heard.

15.2.5.5   Period of disqualification
A court of summary jurisdiction (which might make an order on grounds (a) or (d) in the list in 15.2.5.3) may not make the period of disqualification longer than five years (CDDA 1986, ss. 2(3)(a) and 5(5)), and five years is also the maximum for an order made by any court on ground (b) (s. 3(5)). In all other cases the maximum is 15 years (ss. 2(3)(b), 4(3), 6(4), 8(4) and 10(2)). The disqualification period if the order is on ground (e) must not be less than two years (s. 6(4)).

In *Re Civica Investments Ltd* [1983] BCLC 456, Nourse J said that the length of the disqualification period in cases on ground (b) should depend on whether the defendant's conduct was deliberate and whether he or she had subsequently taken remedial action.

In *Re Sevenoaks Stationers (Retail) Ltd* [1991] Ch 164, Dillon LJ accepted (at p. 179) the following guidelines for disqualification under s. 6:

(i) the top bracket of disqualification for periods over 10 years should be reserved for particularly serious cases. These may include cases where a director who has already had one period of disqualification imposed on him falls to be disqualified yet again. (ii) The minimum bracket of two to five years' disqualification should be applied where, though disqualification is mandatory, the case is, relatively, not very serious. (iii) The middle bracket of disqualification for from six to 10 years should apply for serious cases which do not merit the top bracket.

In a case under s. 2, the Court of Appeal decided that fraudulent trading for four years resulting in losses of about £0.75 million was a middle-bracket offence meriting eight years' disqualification (*R* v *Millard* (1993) 15 Cr App R (S) 445). In *Secretary of State for Trade and Industry* v *McTighe (No. 2)* [1996] 2 BCLC 477, a case under s. 6, the Court of Appeal imposed disqualification for 12 years on a 'particularly serious case' in which a man had caused three companies successively to trade at the risk of their creditors, ultimately leaving unpaid debts of well over £1 million. Over £$\frac{1}{2}$ million had been misappropriated in a way that was 'tantamount to theft' and the director had failed to cooperate with the liquidator or official receiver.

In *Re Westmid Packing Services Ltd* [1998] 2 All ER 124 there is an extensive review by the Court of Appeal of the approach to be taken when determining the period of disqualification. The Court of Appeal wants the process to be kept simple and disapproves of extensive citation from previous cases. The court should exercise its jurisdiction 'in a summary manner' (p. 135). The Court of Appeal emphasised that determining the length of a period of disqualification is little different from determining the sentence in a criminal case:

> The period of disqualification must reflect the gravity of the offence. It must contain deterrent elements. That is what sentencing is all about, and that is what fixing the appropriate period of the disqualification is all about. (p. 132)

The fact that the court has already decided to grant leave to act as a director during the period of disqualification (see 15.2.5.7) should not affect the length of the period. The period of disqualification is a matter for the judge's discretion, which, like any exercise of judicial discretion, must be decided in the light of all relevant circumstances, which can include mitigating factors such as: 'the former director's age and state of health, the length of time he has been in jeopardy, whether he has admitted the offence, his general conduct before and after the offence, and the periods of disqualification of his co-directors that may have been ordered by other courts' (at p. 134).

15.2.5.6 Factors the court considers in an application under CDDA 1986, ss. 6 and 8

Unlike disqualification under CDDA 1986, ss. 2, 3, 4, 5 and 10, the court cannot disqualify a person under s. 6 or s. 8 unless it is satisfied that the person's conduct as a director or shadow director of a particular company makes him or her unfit to be concerned in the management of a company. This means unfit to be concerned in the management of companies generally, not unfitness in relation to any particular company: a director cannot escape disqualification by saying, for example, that he or she may be unfit to run public companies but can be left to manage private ones (*Re Polly Peck International plc (No. 2)* [1994] 1 BCLC 574). In *Re Polly Peck International plc (No. 2)*, Lindsay J thought that what had to be proved was unfitness at the time of the hearing so that the court could take into account changes of behaviour since the time of the conduct complained of. But in *Re Grayan Building Services Ltd* [1995] Ch 241, Hoffmann LJ rejected that approach, saying that if the conduct complained of made the director unfit then a disqualification order had to be made even if only as an example to others. In examining the past conduct of a person sought to be disqualified, CDDA 1986, s. 9, requires the court to have regard in particular to the matters mentioned in part I of sch. 1 to the Act. These matters include:

(a)   Any misfeasance or breach of any fiduciary or other duty by the director in relation to the company (sch. 1, para. 1).

(b)   Any misapplication or retention by the director of, or any conduct by the director giving rise to an obligation to account for, any money or other property of the company (sch. 1, para. 2).

(c)   The extent of the director's responsibility for any failure by the company to comply with various accounting and publicity requirements of CA 1985 (CDDA 1986, sch. 1, paras 4 and 5).

Where the company has become insolvent, the court is to have regard in particular to the matters mentioned in part II of sch. 1. These include:

(a)   The extent of the director's responsibility for the causes of the company becoming insolvent (sch. 1, para. 6).
(b)   The extent of the director's responsibility for any failure by the company to supply any goods or services which have been paid for (in whole or in part) (sch. 1, para. 7).

The applicant for a disqualification order under s. 6 or s. 8 must prove the case against the director — there is no procedure analogous to pleading guilty to a criminal charge (*Re New Generation Engineers Ltd* [1993] BCLC 435 at p. 436). However, in *Re Carecraft Construction Co. Ltd* [1994] 1 WLR 172, a case under s. 6, Ferris J was willing to adopt a 'summary procedure' in which the person sought to be disqualified submitted that a statement of agreed facts (ignoring disputed facts) showed that he was unfit but that the disqualification period should be no longer than the minimum period of two years, leaving the court the option of rejecting the submission and insisting on a full hearing which might result in a longer period of disqualification. This procedure is now regularly used, but Scott V-C has said that it still wastes court time and costs, and has suggested that the legislation should be amended to permit the Department of Trade and Industry to agree a period of disqualification in an undisputed case and simply register it without any court proceedings at all (*Practice Note* [1996] 1 All ER 442).
Some people against whom disqualification proceedings have been brought have sought to avoid a public trial and registration of a disqualification order by offering an undertaking never to act as a director again, while vigorously protesting their innocence on all charges. In *Re Homes Assured Corporation plc* [1996] BCC 297, with the agreement of the official receiver who was applying for the order, such an undertaking was accepted, and the disqualification proceedings stayed in the case of the former Conservative MP, Sir Edward du Cann, who was 72 years old and in poor health. But he perked up sufficiently to take the government to the European Commission of Human Rights, which ruled that taking more than four years to reach a substantive hearing of the application to disqualify him breached art. 6(1) of the European Convention on Human Rights, which declares that everyone is entitled to a hearing within a reasonable time to determine civil rights and obligations (*EDC v United Kingdom* (application No. 24433/94) [1998] BCC 370). In *Secretary of State for Trade and Industry v Cleland* [1997] 1 BCLC 437, an application to commence proceedings outside the two-year time limit was stayed because an undertaking never to be a director was given. Again the person concerned was in poor health. However, an application to stay proceedings on giving suitable undertakings was refused in *Re Blackspur Group plc* [1998] 1 WLR 422 in the case of a man who had no health problems and was sufficiently wealthy not to need to work again, but who claimed it would not be in the public interest to have a long and expensive trial of the application to disqualify him when his undertakings would have the same effect as a disqualification order.
The following discussion concentrates on disqualification under s. 6.
In *Re Sevenoaks Stationers (Retail) Ltd* [1991] Ch 164, Dillon LJ said at p. 176:

It is beyond dispute that the purpose of section 6 is to protect the public, and in particular potential creditors of companies, from losing money through companies becoming insolvent when the directors of those companies are people unfit to be concerned in the management of a company. The test laid down in section 6 — apart from the requirement that the person concerned is or has been a director of a company which has become insolvent — is whether the person's conduct as a director of the company or companies in question 'makes him unfit to be concerned in the management of a company'. These are ordinary words of the English language and they should be simple to apply in most cases. It is important to hold to those words in each case.

The past conduct that the court considers is conduct as a director whether properly appointed as such or not (*Re Eurostem Maritime Ltd* 1987 PCC 190; *Re Lo-Line Electric Motors Ltd* [1988] Ch 477; *Re Moorgate Metals Ltd* [1995] 1 BCLC 503). In *Re Lo-Line Electric Motors Ltd*, Browne-Wilkinson V-C said that Parliament's plain intention was to have regard to the conduct of a person acting as a director, whether validly appointed, invalidly appointed or just assuming to act as a director without any appointment at all. It may be very difficult to decide whether what a person has done amounts to acting as a director so as to make the individual liable to disqualification, though in practice the question may be inextricably linked with whether what he or she has done in itself merits disqualification — see *Secretary of State for Trade and Industry* v *Tjolle* [1998] 1 BCLC 333. The conduct relevant to future suitability to act as a director depended on the person's past record irrespective of the circumstances in which he or she came to act as a director. The conduct may have occurred outside England and Wales, and persons who are not British subjects or are not domiciled in England and Wales may be disqualified under s. 6 (*Re Seagull Manufacturing Co. Ltd (No. 2)* [1994] Ch 91).

An application under s. 6 to disqualify a person arises because the person has been a director of a company which has become insolvent (s. 6(1)(a)), but, under s. 6(1)(b), the court may consider the person's conduct as director both of that company (the 'lead company') and any other company or companies ('collateral companies'). Any conduct in relation to collateral companies which tends to show that the director is unfit may be considered: the court is not restricted to considering conduct which arises from or is in some way connected with the affairs of the lead company (*Secretary of State for Trade and Industry* v *Ivens* [1997] 2 BCLC 334). Conduct in relation to a collateral company may be considered even though it became insolvent more than two years before proceedings commenced (*Secretary of State for Trade and Industry* v *Ivens*). But if there is in fact nothing in the director's conduct in relation to the lead company which shows that the director is unfit, the court cannot consider anything done in relation to collateral companies (*Secretary of State for Trade and Industry* v *Ivens*).

Judges have offered some guidelines about the type of conduct that makes a person unfit. For example, in *Re Lo-Line Electric Motors Ltd*, Browne-Wilkinson V-C said, at p. 486:

> Ordinary commercial misjudgment is in itself not sufficient to justify disqualification. In the normal case, the conduct complained of must display a lack of commercial probity, although I have no doubt that in an extreme case of gross negligence or total incompetence disqualification could be appropriate.

In *Re Bath Glass Ltd* [1988] BCLC 329, Peter Gibson J thought (at p. 333) that it was necessary to show 'a serious failure or serious failures' of duty, 'whether deliberately or through incompetence'.

In *Re Firedart Ltd* [1994] 2 BCLC 340, Arden J said (at p. 351):

In my judgment there are a number of matters which if proved would generally lead me to the conclusion that a director was unfit to be concerned in the management of a company. They include: trading while insolvent; taking personal benefits over and above any proper remuneration; failing to keep proper accounting records.

In *Secretary of State for Trade and Industry* v *McTighe (No. 2)* [1996] 2 BCLC 477 Morritt LJ said that adoption by directors of a policy of not paying creditors who do not press for payment when the company could not otherwise continue in business would in itself demonstrate that the directors were unfit, even if they did not intend never to pay the debts. His lordship also said that persistent failure to cooperate with the liquidator and the official receiver would in itself show unfitness.

However, in *Re Sevenoaks Stationers (Retail) Ltd*, Dillon LJ pointed out, at p. 176, that whether or not a director's conduct makes him or her unfit is a question of fact, and judicial guidelines should not be regarded as laying down absolute criteria which have to be construed as matters of law. At p. 184, his lordship said that he did not think it was necessary for incompetence to be 'total', as suggested by Browne-Wilkinson V-C in the passage just quoted, to render a director unfit. Incompetence or negligence 'in a very marked degree' was sufficient in the case before him.

There is a lengthy discussion by Lindsay J in *Re Polly Peck International plc (No. 2)* [1994] 1 BCLC 574, of the nature of the misconduct which should lead to disqualification. His lordship said that, as two years is the minimum period of disqualification under s. 6, a person cannot be disqualified at all unless his or her conduct merits at least two years' disqualification. The court's power to give leave to act as a director etc. during a period of disqualification (see 15.2.5.7) is not something to be taken into account when deciding whether to disqualify. It is not right to deal with misconduct that is not serious enough to warrant two years' disqualification by disqualifying and then giving leave to act despite being disqualified: the right course is not to disqualify at all. His lordship also said that any breach of duty designed to benefit the director who owes the duty is likely to be regarded as serious enough to warrant disqualification, but a breach of duty which was not intended to benefit the director may not merit disqualification.

Many applications for disqualification orders have been reported at first instance but each case depends on its own peculiar facts and no one can be regarded as typical or as establishing a general principle. For some recent examples of disqualification under s. 6, see *Re Cladrose Ltd* [1990] BCLC 204; *Re Chartmore Ltd* [1990] BCLC 673; *Re Keypak Homecare Ltd* [1990] BCLC 440; *Re Austinsuite Furniture Ltd* [1992] BCLC 1047 (in which *The Sun* newspaper's Young Business Brain of the Year 1984 was disqualified for five years); *Re T & D Services (Timber Preservation & Damp Proofing Contractors) Ltd* [1990] BCC 592 (which Vinelott J said was the most serious he had encountered); *Re Melcast (Wolverhampton) Ltd* [1991] BCLC 288; *Re Sevenoaks Stationers (Retail) Ltd*; *Re Tansoft Ltd* [1991] BCLC 339; *Re City Investment Centres Ltd* [1992] BCLC 956 (in which the third Baron Broadbridge was disqualified for six years); *Re Cargo Agency Ltd* [1992] BCLC 686; *Re Godwin Warren Control Systems plc* [1993] BCLC 80; *Re New Generation Engineers Ltd* [1993] BCLC 435; *Re Burnham Marketing Services Ltd* [1993] BCC 518; *Re Linvale Ltd* [1993] BCLC 654; *Re Moonbeam Cards Ltd* [1993] BCLC 1099; *Re GSAR Realisations Ltd* [1993] BCLC 409; *Re A & C Group Services Ltd* [1993] BCLC 1297; *Re Synthetic Technology Ltd* [1993] BCC 549; *Re Brooks Transport (Purfleet) Ltd* [1993] BCC 766; *Re Moorgate Metals Ltd* [1995] 1 BCLC 503; *Re CSTC Ltd* [1995] BCC 173. See also *Re Wimbledon Village Restaurant Ltd* [1994] BCC 753 in which disqualification orders were refused. For surveys of earlier cases, see C.D. Drake, 'Disqualification of directors — the "red card"'' [1989] JBL 474; V. Finch, 'Disqualification of directors: a plea for competence' (1990) 53 MLR 385; J. Dine, 'Disqualification of directors' (1991) 12 Co Law 6; D. Milman, 'Personal liability and disqualification of company directors: something old, something new' (1992) 43 NILQ 1 at pp. 12–17.

If a disqualification order is refused at first instance it may be made on appeal as in *Re Hitco 2000 Ltd* [1995] 2 BCLC 63 and *Re Grayan Building Services Ltd* [1995] Ch 241.

In *Re Polly Peck International plc (No. 2)* [1994] 1 BCLC 574, the company had been dominated by Mr Asil Nadir, who owned 25 per cent of the shares and was widely regarded as one of the most successful entrepreneurs of his time. It was alleged that Mr Nadir had used the company, which was listed on the Stock Exchange, to raise enormous sums of money from shareholders and banks, which money was lent to subsidiary companies which did not in fact need much of the money but deposited it in banks in the Turkish Republic of Northern Cyprus (which is not recognised by the British government) from which the money could not be recovered. Mr Nadir had failed to appear for trial on criminal charges concerning his handling of the company's finances. The Secretary of State sought leave to commence proceedings out of time to seek the disqualification of the company's finance director, its former joint managing director and two non-executive directors. It was said that they should have made the company institute better financial controls to prevent Mr Nadir mishandling its funds and that they should have threatened to resign. Lindsay J pointed out that the four were a minority of the company's board of directors and could not have forced any decision. There was no evidence that a threat to resign would have had any effect on Mr Nadir, who was obviously planning to get rid of one of the four anyway. The finance director had in fact done a great deal to improve controls and was constantly pushing for better financial management. His lordship described the Secretary of State's case as 'at best speculative and very weak' (at p. 604) and refused leave to bring the proceedings out of time. Similarly in *Secretary of State for Trade and Industry v Taylor* [1997] 1 WLR 407 unfitness was not demonstrated by the fact that a director did not resign when his advice that the company could not avoid insolvent liquidation and should cease trading was ignored by the majority of the board. But in *Re Westmid Packing Services Ltd* [1998] 2 All ER 124 the Court of Appeal emphasised that former directors of a company could not claim to be excused from failure to keep themselves properly informed of the company's position just because the board was dominated by another person:

> It is of the greatest importance that any individual who undertakes the statutory and fiduciary obligations of being a company director should realise that these are inescapable personal responsibilities. The appellants may have been dazzled, manipulated and deceived by Mr Griffiths [who controlled the company and was disqualified for nine years] but they were in breach of their own duties in allowing this to happen.

Re Samuel Sherman plc [1991] 1 WLR 1070 was the first case under s. 8 to be brought to a hearing. Mr Bryans had acquired 28.75 per cent of the shares in the company, which was a listed public company in the clothing trade. This made him the largest of the company's 1,400 or so shareholders. The company's business was declining and so all its fixed assets were sold, leaving the company, in 1980, with cash of about £300,000. Between 1982 and 1988 when it went into liquidation, Mr Bryans used this money to make investments in oil and gas fields. These investments were outside the objects of the company and lost it about 90 per cent of its cash. During this period the company held only one annual general meeting and only one set of annual accounts was circulated to members. After November 1986, Mr Bryans was the sole director of the company and was also its secretary contrary to CA 1985, ss. 282 and 283. The Department of Trade and Industry investigated the company under CA 1985, s. 447 (see 18.8.1), and, as a result, the Secretary of State sought Mr Bryans's disqualification. Mr Bryans was disqualified for five years. For subsequent cases under s. 8 see *Re Looe Fish Ltd* [1993] BCLC 1160; *Re Aldermanbury Trust plc* [1993] BCC 598.

In a case where the Secretary of State has applied to disqualify a director under s. 8 following a report by investigating inspectors, a transcript of the evidence given to the inspectors by the director has been allowed to be put in evidence even though such evidence is given under the threat of being punished for contempt of court if the inspectors' questions are not answered and there is no privilege against self-incrimination (*R v Secretary of State for Trade and Industry, ex parte McCormick* [1998] BCC 379, see 18.8.2.6).

15.2.5.7 Leave to act during a period of disqualification
During the period of a disqualification order a disqualified person may apply for leave to do any of the things forbidden by the order (CDDA 1986, s. 1(1)). An application to be a director etc. of a particular company must be made to a court with jurisdiction to wind up that company (CDDA 1986, s. 17(1)). If the disqualification order was made on the application of the Secretary of State or an official receiver or a liquidator then that person may appear and give evidence at the hearing of the application for leave (CDDA 1986, s. 17(2)).

Leave may be given at the same time as the disqualification order is made (as in *Re Majestic Recording Studios Ltd* [1989] BCLC 1; *Re Chartmore Ltd* [1990] BCLC 673; *Re Cargo Agency Ltd* [1992] BCLC 686; *Secretary of State for Trade and Industry* v *Palfreman* [1995] 2 BCLC 301). Leave will be given only where there is a need for it (*Re Cargo Agency Ltd*) and that must be the need of the company for the director's services not the director's need to work (*Re Gibson Davies Ltd* [1995] BCC 11). Adequate protection of the public must be provided. For example, an independent chartered accountant or solicitor must act as co-director (*Re Majestic Recording Studios Ltd*; *Secretary of State for Trade and Industry* v *Palfreman*). In *Re Gibson Davies Ltd* 10 protective undertakings were given. The court does not tolerate imperfect compliance with such undertakings (*Re Brian Sheridan Cars Ltd* [1996] 1 BCLC 327). See further, D. Milman, 'Partial disqualification orders' (1991) 12 Co Law 224.

15.2.5.8 Register of disqualification orders
The Secretary of State maintains a register of disqualification orders, which is open to inspection free of charge (CDDA 1986, s. 18). The register may be inspected at the Companies Houses in London, Cardiff and Edinburgh, and at the Royal Courts of Justice in London. Within 14 days of a disqualification order being made by a court the chief clerk of the court must send prescribed particulars of the order to the Secretary of State for entry in the register (SI 1986 No. 2067). Variations of orders and grants of leave to act despite an order must also be reported.

15.2.5.9 By being auditor or secretary
An individual who is a director of a company is disqualified from acting as its auditor: in other words the individual must choose to be either auditor or director (CA 1989, s. 27(1)).

A sole director of a company cannot also be secretary of the company (CA 1985, s. 283).

15.2.5.10 By being a member of the Church of England clergy
A member of the Church of England clergy who holds any cathedral preferment, benefice, curacy or lectureship, or who is licensed or otherwise allowed to perform the duties of any

ecclesiastical office may not act as a director of a company that carries on a trade for gain or profit unless licensed to do so by the bishop in whose diocese the office is held (Pluralities Act 1838, s. 29; Clergy (Ordination and Miscellaneous Provisions Measure 1964, s. 11). Apart from curbing companies from using a 'vicar on the board' as a means of professing respectability, this provision must be borne in mind when establishing companies for charitable trading. However, the provision does not apply to giving instruction or education for profit or reward (Pluralities Act 1838, s. 30).

15.2.6 Defective appointments

By s. 285 of CA 1985:

The acts of a director or manager are valid notwithstanding any defect that may afterwards be discovered in his appointment or qualification; and this provision is not excluded by section 292(2) (void resolution to appoint).

This statutory validation is repeated and extended by art. 92 of Table A:

All acts done by a meeting of directors, or of a committee of directors, or by a person acting as a director shall, notwithstanding that it be afterwards discovered that there was a defect in the appointment of any director or that any of them were disqualified from holding office, or had vacated office, or were not entitled to vote, be as valid as if every such person had been duly appointed and was qualified and had continued to be a director and had been entitled to vote.

These provisions validate acts done by directors in relation to members (such as making calls and forfeiting shares) as well as transactions with outsiders (*Dawson* v *African Consolidated Land & Trading Co.* [1898] 1 Ch 6).

These provisions were considered by the House of Lords in *Morris* v *Kanssen* [1946] AC 459, where Lord Simonds said, at pp. 471–2:

There is, as it appears to me, a vital distinction between (a) an appointment in which there is a defect or, in other words, a defective appointment, and (b) no appointment at all. In the first case it is implied that some act is done which purports to be an appointment but is by reason of some defect inadequate for the purpose; in the second case there is not a defect, there is no act at all. The section does not say that the acts of a person acting as director shall be valid notwithstanding that it is afterwards discovered that he was not appointed a director. . . . These observations apply equally where the term of office of a director has expired, but he nevertheless continues to act as a director, and where the office has been from the outset usurped without the colour of authority. . . . the section and the article, being designed as machinery to avoid questions being raised as to the validity of transactions where there has been a slip in the appointment of a director, cannot be utilised for the purpose of ignoring or overriding the substantive provisions relating to such appointment.

In the case, Kanssen and Cromie were a company's only directors. Cromie claimed falsely that a third person, Strelitz, had been appointed a director and a minute of the appointment was falsely recorded. By the operation of the rule in *Re Consolidated Nickel Mines Ltd* [1914] 1 Ch 883 (see 15.3.2), all the company's directors (real or false) automatically vacated office when the company failed to hold annual general meetings. (The company's articles, unlike the present Table A, art. 92, did not validate the acts of directors afterwards found to have vacated office.) Subsequently, Cromie and Strelitz purported to hold a board meeting at which they appointed Mr Morris a 'director' of the company. Cromie, Strelitz and Morris then purported to hold a board meeting at which shares of the company were allotted which were acquired by Morris. Morris claimed that this allotment was validated by what is now s. 285. The House of Lords held that the provision did not apply because the persons whose acts were sought to be validated had not been appointed directors at all.

A person seeking to rely on validation provisions must have acted in good faith (*Channel Collieries Trust Ltd* v *Dover, St Margaret's & Martin Mill Light Railway Co.* [1914] 2 Ch 506, CA, per Lord Cozens-Hardy MR at p. 512). In particular, the defect must not have been known at the time of the appointment, though persons are not, in this context, presumed to know the law so the validation provisions can apply where the facts which rendered the appointment invalid were known to the people involved at the time of the appointment but they honestly failed to appreciate that the legal effect was to render the appointment invalid (*British Asbestos Co. Ltd* v *Boyd* [1903] 2 Ch 439; *Channel Collieries Trust Ltd* v *Dover, St Margaret's & Martin Mill Light Railway Co.*). As Farwell J put it in *British Asbestos Co. Ltd* v *Boyd* at pp. 444–5, the object of these provisions:

> is to make the honest acts of *de facto* directors as good as the honest acts of *de iure* directors. . . . although there may be some slip which has been overlooked, if it has been bona fide overlooked, then the acts of the *de facto* directors are as good as the acts of the *de iure* directors.

A person cannot rely on the validation provisions to validate some acts of a *de facto* director and also seek to denounce other acts of that director on the ground that he was not a director *de iure* (*Levin* v *Clark* [1962] NSWR 686).

Where minutes have been made in accordance with s. 382 of a general meeting or a board meeting at which a director was appointed then, until the contrary is proved, the meeting is deemed duly held and convened, and the director's appointment is deemed to be valid (s. 382(4)).

The acts of a director who has vacated office but who continues to act are not covered by CA 1985, s. 285, because the director is acting without having been appointed rather than acting under a defective appointment (*Tyne Mutual Steamship Insurance Association* v *Brown* (1896) 74 LT 283; *Morris* v *Kanssen*). The situation is, however, covered by Table A, art. 92. There is a statutory provision in CA 1985, s. 293(3), validating the acts of a director who should have vacated office at the annual general meeting following his or her seventieth birthday (see 15.2.4), but did not.

15.2.7 Alternate directors

Table A permits a director to appoint an alternate — that is, a person who can attend meetings that the appointing director is unable to attend, and can generally act in place of the appointing director. A director may appoint another present member of the board as alternate or may appoint another person, provided that other person is approved by resolution of the directors and is willing to act (Table A, art. 65). By art. 69, an alternate is not deemed to be the agent of the director by whom he was appointed but is responsible for his own acts and defaults. An alternate vacates office when the director who appointed him vacates office (art. 67) and an alternate cannot himself appoint an alternate (art. 65).

15.2.8 Nominee directors

A shareholder with a significant investment in a private company who is not an executive director of the company usually ensures that he has the right to appoint one or more directors. This can best be done by dividing the company's shares into two classes: class A being those of the major investor and class B those of the other members. The articles are then amended to exclude arts 76 to 80 of Table A and substitute a provision that a certain number of directors may be appointed and removed by notice given by holders of the majority of class A shares, and a certain number appointed similarly by the B shareholders. This creates class rights which can be altered only in accordance with CA 1985, s. 125 (see 14.6.2). Usually the articles will provide that the rights of a class of shareholders can be altered only by an extraordinary resolution of that class.

15.2.9 Share qualification

It was common at one time for a company's articles of association to require its directors each to hold a certain number of shares in the company. Share qualifications are now much less common and the 1985 version of Table A does not mention them. However, if the articles of a company impose a share qualification on directors then any person appointed a director of the company must obtain the qualification shares within two months of appointment (the articles may specify a shorter time) (CA 1985, s. 291(1)). A director who fails to acquire the specified qualification within the time-limit or who subsequently fails to keep it vacates office (s. 291(3)) and commits an offence by acting as a director while disqualified (s. 291(5)) and is disqualified from being re-elected until the necessary shares are obtained (s. 291(4)). The articles may not provide that shares represented by a share warrant to bearer count as qualification shares (ss. 291(2) and 355(5)).

15.3 TERMINATION OF OFFICE

15.3.1 Vacation of office deemed by the articles

By art. 81 of Table A, a director's office is vacated in the following circumstances:

(a) on ceasing to be a director by virtue of any provision of CA 1985 or becoming prohibited by law from being a director;

(b) on becoming bankrupt or making any arrangement or composition with his or her creditors generally;

(c) on becoming of unsound mind as evidenced by court order or hospital admission;

(d) on resigning office by notice in writing to the company; or

(e) after being absent without permission of the directors from meetings of the directors for a period of more than six months.

When one of these circumstances or events affects a director, the director's office is vacated automatically: there is no need for the other directors or the members to consider the matter or adopt a resolution. The other directors cannot waive the effect of art. 81 (*Re Bodega Co. Ltd* [1904] 1 Ch 276). A person who is removed from office by art. 81 can be reappointed a director when no longer affected by the disqualifying circumstance (ibid.). A director whose office is vacated for absence from board meetings for six months can be reappointed immediately since this is not a continuing circumstance.

For the statutory prohibition on undischarged bankrupts acting as company directors, see 15.2.5.1. For disqualification orders, see 15.2.5.2.

15.3.2   Retirement by rotation

Table A, art. 73, provides for retirement by rotation as follows:

> At the first annual general meeting all the directors shall retire from office, and at every subsequent annual general meeting one-third of the directors who are subject to retirement by rotation or, if their number is not three or a multiple of three, the number nearest to one-third shall retire from office; but, if there is only one director who is subject to retirement by rotation, he shall retire.

As to the choice of retiring directors, art. 74 provides:

> Subject to the provisions of the Act, the directors to retire by rotation shall be those who have been longest in office since their last appointment or reappointment, but as between persons who became or were last reappointed directors on the same day those to retire shall (unless they otherwise agree among themselves) be determined by lot.

For the purposes of a provision such as art. 74, the seniority of a director reappointed on vacating office at an annual general meeting under CA 1985, s. 293(3), because of reaching the age of 70 (see 15.3.6) dates from the time of his or her last appointment before so vacating office (s. 293(6)). A person appointed to replace a director retired because of reaching the age of 70 takes on the seniority which the retired director had (s. 293(6)). Otherwise, the fact that a director is to vacate office at an annual general meeting under CA 1985, s. 293(3), because of reaching the age of 70 is to be disregarded in determining when any other directors are to retire (s. 293(6)).

A person who is appointed by the directors to fill a vacancy or as an additional director under art. 79 (see 15.2.3.3) holds office until the next following annual general meeting and is not taken into account in determining retirement by rotation (art. 79).

If the members exercise their power under art. 78 to appoint an additional director then they may, under the same article, determine in what rotation the new director is to retire.

In *Re Consolidated Nickel Mines Ltd* [1914] 1 Ch 883 it was held that with articles like these if an annual general meeting for a particular year is not held in that year then the directors due to retire at that meeting automatically vacate office at the end of the year. The new form of Table A introduced in SI 1985 No. 805 deals with this by providing, in art. 92, that acts done by a meeting of directors, or of a committee of directors, or by a person acting as a director shall be valid even if it is afterwards discovered that any of the directors had vacated office.

A managing director and a director holding any other executive office are not subject to retirement by rotation under Table A (art. 84; see 15.5.3 and 15.5.4) though they cannot have service contracts for more than five years without shareholder approval (see 15.6.4).

The Combined Code for listed companies (see 15.1.2) requires all directors of listed companies to submit themselves for re-election at least every three years (principle A.6), and says that, ideally, the maximum term of an executive director's service contract should be one year (para. B.1.7).

15.3.3   Dismissal from office

Provision for the removal of directors is made by s. 303 of CA 1985. A company may, by ordinary resolution, remove a director before the expiration of his period of office, notwithstanding anything in its articles or in any agreement between the company and the director (s. 303(1)). Special notice (see 14.4.5.6) is required of any resolution under s. 303 to remove a director (s. 303(2)) and a copy of the notice must be sent by the company to the director concerned who is entitled to speak on the resolution at the meeting whether he is a member or not (s. 304(1)). Because of the director's right under s. 304(1) to speak at the meeting it is doubtful whether a decision to dismiss a director arrived at by unanimous agreement without meeting could be effective under s. 303. The procedure provided to private companies by s. 381A for agreement to written resolutions cannot be used to dismiss a director under s. 303 (s. 381A(7) and sch. 15A, para. 1(a)).

A director sought to be dismissed by a resolution under s. 303 is entitled to make representations in writing not exceeding a reasonable length which the company must send to every shareholder to whom notice of the meeting is sent, though if the representations are received by the company too late for distribution to members the director concerned may (in addition to his right to speak at the meeting) require that his written representations be read out at the meeting (s. 304(2) and (3)).

There seems to be no reason why the members for the time being of a company should not provide in a unanimous shareholders' agreement that they will not use s. 303 to dismiss some or all of the company's directors.

In *Bushell* v *Faith* [1970] AC 1099, the company's 300 shares were held equally between the plaintiff, the defendant and their sister. The plaintiff and defendant were the company's only directors. The company's articles weighted the voting rights attached to the shares from one per share to three per share where the issue before a general meeting of the company was the removal of the director holding those shares. The plaintiff and her sister purported to remove the defendant from his office. The House of Lords upheld the validity of the voting rights by a 4–1 majority, and the resolution seeking the defendant's removal was therefore defeated by 300 votes (the defendant's weighted votes) to 200 (the plaintiff and her sister's combined unweighted votes). Lord Upjohn explained:

> Parliament has never sought to fetter the right of the company to issue a share with such rights or restrictions as it may think fit. There is no fetter which compels the company to make the voting rights or restrictions of general application and it seems to me clear that such rights or restrictions can be attached to special circumstances and to particular types of resolution. This makes no mockery of [s. 303]; all that Parliament was seeking to do thereby was to make an ordinary resolution sufficient to remove a director. Had Parliament desired to go further and enact that every share entitled to vote should be deprived of its special rights under the articles it should have said so in plain terms by making the vote on a poll one vote one share.

This decision has been subjected to a good deal of criticism, but is clearly justified by the wording of s. 303. P.V. Baker said in a casenote (1970) 86 LQR 155, at p. 157: 'Either there are sound reasons of public policy why a bare majority of shareholders in general meeting should have ultimate control over the board of directors, or there are not. If there are, [*Bushell* v *Faith* shows] that [s. 303] needs strengthening. If there are not, it should be repealed.' It should be emphasised that this type of weighted voting would be entirely inappropriate in large companies, and the Stock Exchange would refuse a listing to any public company with articles which weighted voting rights in this way. Professor Schmitthoff saw the decision in *Bushell* v *Faith* as justified by the fact that the company in question was a quasi-partnership company. See C.M. Schmitthoff, 'How the English discovered the private company', in *Quo vadis ius societatum*, ed. P. Zonderland (Deventer: Kluwer, 1972), pp. 183–93.

A person cannot be appointed to fill the vacancy caused by the removal of a director under s. 303 *at the same meeting* unless special notice of the appointment resolution has been given (s. 303(2)). If, however, the vacancy is not filled at the same meeting then, under s. 303, 'it may be filled as a casual vacancy'. The term 'casual vacancy' means a vacancy occurring otherwise than by retirement by rotation (*Munster* v *Cammell Co.* (1882) 21 ChD 183 at p. 187). Table A does not make separate provision for filling casual vacancies so an appointment may be made by the members under art. 78 (see 15.2.3.2) or by the directors under art. 79 (see 15.2.3.3).

A person appointed a director in place of a director removed under s. 303 is treated for the purpose of determining retirement by rotation (see 15.3.2) as if he had become a director on the day on which the director in whose place he is appointed was last appointed (s. 303(4)).

Nothing in s. 303 derogates from any other power to remove a director (s, 303(5)). Thus articles could provide for dismissal of a director without special notice and without permitting the director to make representations (though the 1985 version of Table A does not make any such provision) (*Browne* v *Panga Pty Ltd* (1995) 120 FLR 34). If a company's articles provide for its directors to be dismissed by the members without formalities that can be carried out only at a meeting then the dismissal may be by unanimous agreement without meeting, and in a private company may be by written resolution under s. 381A. It is common for articles to provide that a director's office is to be vacated if all the other members of the board make a written request for the director's resignation. Directors must act in the best interests of the company, and not for an ulterior motive, when making such a request but the fact that they are acting for an ulterior motive does not invalidate a request (*Lee* v *Chou Wen Hsien* [1984] 1 WLR 1202, PC).

Removal of a person from the office of director of a company may be in breach of a contract between that person and the company. It may breach the contract under which the person acts as director if the contract is for a fixed period which has not expired or if the director is entitled to a period of notice. However, if the provision for a minimum period of service or notice is only in the articles of the company, rather than in a separate contract with the director concerned, then it may be held to be subject to any power of removal also provided by the articles so that using that power of removal does not breach the contract (as in *Shuttleworth* v *Cox Brothers & Co. (Maidenhead) Ltd* [1927] 2 KB 9, CA).

Removal of a person from the office of director of a company, whether or not breaching the contract under which the person serves as a director, may breach a second contract if the person can perform the second contract only by being a director. The leading cases have concerned removal from directorships of persons who served as managing director. Under a provision of articles of association like art. 84 of Table A (see 15.5.3) the appointment of a person as managing director of a company terminates if he or she ceases to be a director of the company. In *Southern Foundries (1926) Ltd* v *Shirlaw* [1940] AC 701 and in *Shindler* v *Northern Raincoat Co. Ltd* [1960] 1 WLR 1038, removal of a director from office prevented him from continuing as managing director and caused a breach of the contract of appointment as managing director because, in both cases, the appointment as managing director was for a fixed term of 10 years which had not expired. On the other hand, in *Read* v *Astoria Garage (Streatham) Ltd* [1952] Ch 637, CA, there was nothing in the contract under which the plaintiff served as managing director to give him a fixed term of employment or even a period of notice so that summary removal from his directorship did not cause any breach of the contract of appointment as managing director.

By s. 303(5), the fact that a company which dismisses a director under the s. 303 procedure is using a power which is statutory and therefore overrides any contract with the director does not absolve the company from liability to pay the director compensation or damages for the dismissal.

If a director of a company is an employee of the company then removing the director from the directorship may mean terminating the contract of employment, which may involve a large compensation payment. Accordingly, provision has been made to ensure that members can discover the terms of their directors' contracts of service (CA 1985, s. 318; see 4.4.3). Compensation payments may be particularly heavy if a director has a fixed-term contract and so fixed-term contracts (whether contracts of service or contracts for services) for terms in excess of five years are subject to approval by the members (s. 319; see 15.6.4). A non-contractual termination payment must be approved by the members (ss. 312 to 315; see 15.6.2).

15.3.4   Assignment of office

The articles of some private companies used to allow directors to assign their office to a person of their choice on their retirement. Such powers as exist today are subject to s. 308 of CA 1985, which requires any assignment to be approved by the members by special resolution.

15.3.5   Resignation

A director of a company is entitled to relinquish the office at any time by giving notice to the company. The director's resignation is effected by the notice and does not depend on acceptance of the resignation by the company because the company cannot refuse acceptance. However, once notice has been given it cannot be withdrawn except by agreement with the company (*Glossop* v *Glossop* [1907] 2 Ch 370). Although Table A directs that notice of resignation is to be in writing, an oral resignation is effective if accepted (*Latchford Premier Cinema Ltd* v *Ennion* [1931] 2 Ch 409). In *POW Services Ltd* v *Clare* [1995] 2 BCLC 435 a man who had been named in the company's statement of first directors wrote to another of those named saying that he was resigning. All this happened before the company was actually registered but the court held that the letter was a continuing representation of the man's wish to resign which became effective on the company's registration.

15.3.6   Retirement on reaching statutory age limit

A director of a public company or of a subsidiary of either a public company or a Northern Ireland public company is deemed to vacate office at the end of the annual general meeting commencing next after he or she attains the age of 70 (CA 1985, s. 293(3)), unless the company's articles provide otherwise (s. 293(7)). If the company was registered before 1947 then, by s. 293(7), only provisions introduced into its articles since the beginning of 1947 are effective to exclude or modify s. 293(3). Even if the company's articles do not exclude or modify s. 293(3), an individual who has attained the age of 70 is not deemed to vacate office under s. 293(3) if his or her appointment was made or approved by a general meeting of the members, provided special notice (see 14.4.5.6) was given of the resolution to make or approve the appointment (s. 293(5)). The notice given to the company, and by the company to its members, under the special notice procedure, must have stated the age of the individual to whom it related.

A director who is deemed to vacate office at an annual general meeting under s. 293(3) may be reappointed at that meeting provided the special notice procedure is followed (see 15.2.4) but no provision for the automatic reappointment of a director in default of another appointment (such as Table A, art. 75; see 15.2.3.2) is permitted to operate in favour of the retiring director (s. 293(4)).

15.3.7   Disputes about who holds office as a director

In a number of English cases a member of a company has successfully brought an action to restrain a person who is acting as a director of the company, but has not been properly appointed, from continuing to act (*Catesby* v *Burnett* [1916] 2 Ch 325; *Spencer* v *Kennedy* [1926] 1 Ch 125; see also *Oliver* v *Dalgleish* [1963] 1 WLR 1274 in which a declaration that the defendants were not directors was given). The company also may bring such an action (*Latchford Premier Cinema Ltd* v *Ennion* [1931] 2 Ch 409; *Worcester Corsetry Ltd* v *Witting* [1936] Ch 640). This raises the question whether the right of action in such a case belongs to the company or its members, see 18.4.9.

A person who has been properly appointed director of a company may obtain an injunction to restrain the company or other directors from preventing him acting as such (*Pulbrook* v *Richmond Consolidated Mining Co.* (1878) 9 ChD 610; *Munster* v *Cammell Co.* (1882) 21 ChD 183; *Foster* v *Greenwich Ferry Co. Ltd* (1888) 5 TLR 16). (In particular, an injunction may be issued to restrain directors from using their power to delegate to a committee as a device to exclude a particular director: *Kyshe* v *Alturas Gold Ltd* (1888) 4 TLR 331 and other cases cited in 15.5.5.) In deciding whether to grant an *interlocutory* injunction, the court will take into account the opinion of the members of the company, expressed in general meeting, on whether or not they wish the plaintiff to act as a director (*Harben* v *Phillips* (1883) 23 ChD 14; *Bainbridge* v *Smith* (1889) 41 ChD 462; *Clifton* v *Mount Morgan Ltd* (1940) 40 SR (NSW) 31). Such opinion would carry even more weight now that the members have a statutory right, under CA 1985, s. 303, to dismiss a director by ordinary resolution — a right which was not available when any of the three last-mentioned cases was decided. In *Currie* v *Cowdenbeath Football Club Ltd* 1992 SLT 407, the club had commenced proceedings to prevent two men acting as its directors, claiming that they had resigned. The other directors decided to resolve the situation by convening an extraordinary general meeting to consider a resolution to dismiss each of the men under CA 1985, s. 303, 'if, as a matter of fact, [he] is presently a director'. Remarkably, Lord Penrose granted the men interim interdict (the Scottish equivalent of an interlocutory injunction) against the holding of the meeting, saying that it was an attempt to usurp the court's jurisdiction over the dispute and that it is not possible to pass a contingent resolution under s. 303. In a similar case in Western Australia, though, Ipp J took the opposite view and held that members do have a power to decide whether or not they want particular persons to be directors (*Browne* v *Panga Pty Ltd* (1995) 120 FLR 34). It is submitted that Ipp J's view is preferable.

In *Hayes* v *Bristol Plant Hire Ltd* [1957] 1 WLR 499, the extent of a plaintiff's proprietary interest in his office as a director required to justify the court granting an injunction was questioned. It was held that, in Mr Hayes's case, his shareholding and the possibility of being paid fees as a director were sufficient. It remains questionable whether a non-shareholding director could have a sufficient interest.

Exclusion of a director may also be conduct of the company's affairs in a manner unfairly prejudicial to the interests of members (see the discussion of *Re H.R. Harmer Ltd* [1959] 1 WLR 62, CA, in 15.5.1).

15.4   PUBLICITY

The position occupied by directors is of such importance that disclosure of details relating to directors is required. This publicity is achieved by the maintenance of a register, and by notification to the registrar and in the *Gazette*.

15.4.1 Register

Every company is required to keep a register of directors and secretaries at its registered office (CA 1985, s. 288(1)). In respect of each individual who is a director (or shadow director — see 15.1.6: s. 288(6)) of the company, the register must state the individual's Christian name or forename and surname (and former names excluding the name or surname by which a married woman was known before the marriage, or names changed or disused before the individual became 18 or more than 20 years previously), the individual's usual residential address, nationality, business occupation (if any), particulars of other directorships held in the preceding five years, and date of birth (s. 289(1)(a), (2) and (3)(a)). For an individual who is a peer or is usually known by a title, the register may state the title instead of, or in addition to, Christian name or forename and surname, or either of them, and it is not necessary to give the name by which the director was known before the adoption of, or succession to, the title, unless it is not a British title (s. 289(2)(b)). In respect of each corporation that is a director or shadow director, the register must state the corporate name and registered or principal office (s. 289(1)(b)). In respect of a Scottish firm, the firm name and principal office must be given (ibid.).

In respect of an individual director or shadow director of the registering company it is not necessary to record another directorship held within the past five years (and not presently held) if it was a directorship of a corporation incorporated in England and Wales or Scotland that was one of the following types of corporation for the whole period during which the director was one of its directors (disregarding periods more than five years ago):

(a) A holding company of which the registering company is (or was during the director's directorship) a wholly owned subsidiary, and any other wholly owned subsidiaries of such a holding company.

(b) A wholly owned subsidiary of the registering company.

(c) A dormant company.

Details of a past directorship may be deleted from the register when five years have elapsed since it was held (CA 1985, s. 289(3) and (4)).

The Department of Trade and Industry has proposed abolishing the requirement to record a director's business occupation (which in practice is usually given as 'company director'), nationality (a requirement introduced during the First World War to force disclosure of enemy allegiance), particulars of other directorships (which can be discovered from the Companies House database) and residential address (which people do not want to disclose for security reasons). See *Disclosure of Directors' and Company Secretaries' Particulars* (URN 97/537) (London: DTI, 1997).

The register also includes details of the company's secretaries (see 17.3.2) and is therefore called the register of directors and secretaries.

The register must be open to inspection by members without charge or by others on payment of a fee (see 4.4.1) (s. 288(3)).

The company and its defaulting officers are liable to fines on conviction for any failure to comply with s. 288 (s. 288(4) and sch. 24), and in the event of a refusal to allow inspection of the register, the court may order an immediate inspection (s. 288(5)). The extent of a person's responsibility for any failure of a company to comply with its duty to keep a register of directors and secretaries in accordance with s. 228 is a matter to which the court must have regard in deciding whether that person's conduct as a director or shadow director of that company makes him or her unfit to be concerned in the management of a company (Company Directors Disqualification Act 1986, s. 9 and sch. 1, para. 4(c)).

15.4.2 Notification to the registrar and in the *Gazette*

When application is made to register a new company, a statement must be delivered to the registrar containing the names of the person who is, or the persons who are, to be the first director or directors of the company (CA 1985, s. 10(2)). The statement must give the particulars of each person named that are set out in sch. 1 to the Act. These particulars are the same as the particulars of directors that must be recorded in the company's register of directors and secretaries (see 15.4.1).

A company must notify the registrar within 14 days of any change in its directors or in the particulars contained in the register, and any notification of the appointment of a new director must contain a consent signed by that person to act as director (s. 288(2)). Filing at Companies House of any notification of a change among the directors of a company must be notified by the registrar in the *Gazette* (s. 711(1)(c)). Section 42 (see 4.3) prevents a company from relying on a change in its directors until there has been notification in the *Gazette*.

The Department of Trade and Industry has proposed that some of the details of directors currently recorded in a company's register should no longer be required (see 15.4.1), and that those details should no longer be sent to the registrar. However, it considers that the registrar should have a record of directors' residential addresses. It is proposed that a director could ask for his or her residential address to be kept in a secure record available only to the police and other regulatory authorities, provided the director supplied an address for service which would be available for public inspection.

The fact that a person is (or is not) recorded at the companies registry as being a director of a company does not determine whether the person actually is (or is not) a director of that company (*POW Services Ltd* v *Clare* [1995] 2 BCLC 435). However, the fact that a company has permitted a person to be registered as one of its directors is a representation to others that the person is a director which the company may not be allowed to deny.

15.4.3 Business documents

By s. 305 of CA 1985, on any business letter of a company on which the company's name appears, the company may not state in any form the name of any of its directors or shadow directors (otherwise than in the text or as a signatory) unless it states in legible characters the name of every director and shadow director. This provision does not apply to a company registered before 23 November 1916.

15.5 THE BOARD OF DIRECTORS

15.5.1 Proceedings of directors

The word 'board' — originally referring to the table around which a council sat — was sometimes used in the 19th century to refer to a meeting of directors: when directors met they were said to 'hold a board' — hence the term 'boardroom' for a room in which directors meet. Now 'board' has come to be used as a collective noun for directors and they are said to hold a 'board meeting', which once would have been tautologous.

Table A, art. 88, provides:

Subject to the provisions of the articles, the directors may regulate their proceedings as they think fit. A director may, and the secretary at the request of a director shall, call a meeting of the directors. It shall not be necessary to give notice of a meeting to a director who is absent from the United Kingdom. Questions arising at a meeting shall be decided by a majority of votes. In the case of an equality of votes, the chairman shall have a second or casting vote. A director who is also an alternate director shall be entitled in the absence of his appointor to a separate vote on behalf of his appointor in addition to his own vote.

Many companies will wish to delete the provision that a director outside the UK is not to be given notice. Many companies will wish to have a provision permitting directors' meetings to be conducted by telephone or other telecommunications media — see 14.4.1.

There is no requirement in CA 1985 that the directors of a company registered under the Act must hold board meetings in the jurisdiction in which the company is incorporated (England and Wales or Scotland), but the constitution of a company may specify where board meetings are to be held.

Unlike meetings of members, it is not necessary to state in the notice of a directors' meeting what business is to be transacted at the meeting. Unlike members, directors have a duty to attend to the transaction of the company's affairs (*La Compagnie de Mayville* v *Whitley* [1896] 1 Ch 788).

In *Re H.R. Harmer Ltd* [1959] 1 WLR 62, CA, Romer LJ said, at p. 87:

> Members are entitled to expect that their board shall perform its functions as a board, and that the proceedings of the directors shall be carried out in a normal and orthodox manner. They are entitled to the benefit of the collective experience of the directors and to expect that the directors and each of them can freely express their views at board meetings, and that regard shall be had to what they say and to resolutions duly passed.

Accordingly, exclusion of a director from participation in board meetings may be conduct unfairly prejudicial (see 18.6) to the interests of that director as a member or of the members who appointed him under a right of appointment conferred by the articles (per Romer LJ, loc. cit.).

Conversely, a director 'has a right by the constitution of the company to take part in its management, to be present, and to vote at the meetings of the board of directors' (*Pulbrook* v *Richmond Consolidated Mining Co.* (1878) 9 ChD 610 per Jessel MR at p. 612 — see further 15.3.6).

It is unsettled whether a director who is not entitled to vote at a board meeting must nevertheless be given notice of it. In *John Shaw & Sons (Salford) Ltd* v *Shaw* [1935] 2 KB 113, CA, Greer LJ thought such a director was not entitled to notice but Slesser LJ thought he was: the third member of the court expressed no opinion on the point. See the discussion in 14.4.5.2.

In Table A, art. 89 provides that the quorum for the transaction of the business of the directors is to be fixed by them, but if it is not fixed by them it will be two. A decision taken at an inquorate board meeting is invalid and does not bind the company (*Re Greymouth Point Elizabeth Railway & Coal Co. Ltd* [1904] 1 Ch 32; *Re North Eastern Insurance Co. Ltd* [1919] 1 Ch 198). However, if the decision is to enter into a transaction with some person who is not a director then usually the company will be precluded by the indoor management rule from claiming that it is not bound by the transaction (*County of Gloucester Bank* v *Rudry Merthyr Steam & House Coal Colliery Co.* [1895] 1 Ch 629, CA; *Re Bank of Syria, Owen and Ashworth's Claim* [1901] 1 Ch 115, CA; see 19.5.4.1).

A quorum can be formed only by directors capable of voting on the business of the meeting (Table A, art. 95; *Re Greymouth Point Elizabeth Railway & Coal Co. Ltd* [1904] 1 Ch 32; see 16.6.3).

A quorum can be formed only from a properly constituted board. In particular, if the articles specify a minimum number of directors then a quorum cannot be formed if there are fewer than the minimum number in office (*Faure Electric Accumulator Co. Ltd* v *Phillipart* (1888) 58 LT 525; *Re British Empire Match Co. Ltd* (1888) 59 LT 291) unless there is a provision in the articles like Table A, art. 90, which permits the continuing directors or a sole continuing director to act notwithstanding any vacancies in their number (*Re Scottish Petroleum Co.* (1883) 23 ChD 413, CA). However, it seems that the form of words in Table A, art. 90, applies only when the number of directors has been reduced below the minimum and does not cover a situation in which the minimum number of directors never has taken office because of a failure to appoint the minimum number on registration of the company (*Re British Empire Match Co. Ltd*).

Table A, art. 90, also provides that the continuing directors or a sole continuing director may act notwithstanding any vacancies in their number even if the number of directors is less than the number required to form a quorum, but then they may act only for the purpose of (a) appointing sufficient directors (under art. 79) to increase their number to the number required to form a quorum, or (b) calling a general meeting (under art. 37), but not for any other purpose. A sole continuing director of a public company may act under this provision even though CA 1985, s. 282, requires the company to have two directors (*Macson Development Co. Ltd* v *Gordon* (1959) 19 DLR (2d) 465, Nova Scotia; *APT Group Services Pty Ltd* v *Ferguson* (1991) 6 ACSR 231, Victoria).

The requirements of CA 1985, s. 382, relating to keeping minutes of general meetings (see 14.4.11) apply, with necessary changes, to directors' meetings (s. 382(1)). So art. 100 of Table A requires that:

The directors shall cause minutes to be made in books kept for the purpose—

    (a)   of all appointments of officers made by the directors; and

    (b)   of all proceedings at meetings . . . of the directors, and of committees of directors, including the names of the directors present at each such meeting.

A decision of directors is not invalidated by failure to minute it (*Re North Hallenbeagle Mining Co., Knight's Case* (1867) LR 2 Ch App 321).

It used to be thought that the decisions of the directors of a company with more than one director had to be taken at a meeting (*D'Arcy* v *Tamar, Kit Hill, & Callington Railway Co.* (1867) LR 2 Ex 158; *Re Haycraft Gold Reduction & Mining Co.* [1900] 2 Ch 230; *Re Associated Color Laboratories Ltd* (1970) 12 DLR (3d) 338). However, it would often be the case that the indoor management rule would preclude a company from claiming that it was not bound by a transaction not decided on at a meeting (*Re Bonelli's Telegraph Co., Collie's Claim* (1871) LR 12 Eq 246; see 19.5.4.1). Recently, decisions of directors of a company have been accepted as binding the company even though not taken at a meeting, provided all the directors agreed to or acquiesced in the decision (*Charterhouse Investment Trust Ltd* v *Tempest Diesels Ltd* [1986] BCLC 1 at p. 9; *Runciman* v *Walter Runciman plc* [1992] BCLC 1084). In *Mulcon Pty Ltd* v *MYT Engineering Pty Ltd* (1996) 20 ACSR 606, Bryson J in the Supreme Court of New South Wales said, at p. 610:

Subject to the obvious difficulties of establishing what happened, there is nothing wrong in principle, and no lack of validity, in directors' reaching agreement in exercise of the powers of management under [a provision in articles like Table A, art. 70] by informal conversation over the telephone without any written record.

Procedural informality is acceptable when all the directors agree to a decision. For a decision of some only of a company's directors to be effective it must be taken at a meeting convened and conducted in accordance with the company's constitution.

Table A, art. 93, makes express provision for directors to take decisions without meeting, by providing that a resolution in writing, signed by all the directors who are entitled to receive notice of a board meeting, is as valid and effective as if adopted at a board meeting duly convened and held. This article validates a decision taken by some only of the directors if the others were not entitled to notice, for example, under Table A, art. 88, because of being absent from the United Kingdom. However, a written resolution is 'business of the directors' for which a quorum is necessary under Table A, art. 89 (*Davidson and Begg Antiques Ltd* v *Davidson* [1997] BCC 77; *Hood Sailmakers Ltd* v *Axford* [1997] 1 WLR 625).

15.5.2 Chairman

If there is an equality of votes for and against a board resolution then it is not adopted (*Moodie* v *W. & J. Shepherd (Bookbinders) Ltd* [1949] 2 All ER 1044, HL), so the identity of the chairman of a meeting of directors may be crucial because of the casting vote given to the chairman by a provision in articles like the fifth sentence of art. 88 in Table A (quoted in 15.5.1). In practice it is common for one director to be permanent chairman. In Table A, art. 91 provides:

The directors may appoint one of their number to be the chairman of the board of directors and may at any time remove him from that office. Unless he is unwilling to do so, the director so appointed shall preside at every meeting of directors at which he is present. But if there is no director holding that office, or if the director holding it is unwilling to preside or is not present within five minutes after the time appointed for the meeting, the directors present may appoint one of their number to be chairman of the meeting.

The appointment of a chairman must be noted in the minutes (art. 100(a), see 15.5.1). Where, as in art. 91, the power to appoint a chairman is vested in the board, the members cannot appoint a chairman (*Clark* v *Workman* [1920] 1 IR 107).

Table A, art. 42, gives the chairman the right to preside over general meetings of the company (see 14.4.7) with a consequent right to a casting vote at such a meeting (art. 50, see 14.4.9.2).

15.5.3 Managing director

It is usual for the articles of a company to provide that one of its directors may be appointed 'managing director' of the company, to whom powers of the directors may be delegated. The managing director of a company is its chief executive officer.

Article 84 of Table A provides:

Subject to the provisions of the Act, the directors may appoint one or more of their number to the office of managing director or to any other executive office. . . . Any such appointment . . . may be made upon such terms as the directors determine. . . . Any appointment of a director to an executive office shall terminate if he ceases to be a director but without prejudice to any claim to damages for breach of the contract of service between the director and the company. A managing director . . . shall not be subject to retirement by rotation.

Under art. 84, a director who has been appointed managing director by the board may be removed from that office at any time by the board (*Foster* v *Foster* [1916] 1 Ch 532). Where, as in art. 84, the power to appoint a managing director is vested in the board, the members cannot appoint a managing director (*Thomas Logan Ltd* v *Davis* (1911) 104 LT 914; affirmed (1911) 105 LT 419). However, the members can, by ordinary resolution, dismiss a managing director from his or her directorship (CA 1985, s. 303; see 15.3.3) and then his or her appointment as managing director will automatically cease under art. 84. A managing director who is dismissed by the board but remains a director is likely to disrupt future board meetings, and opponents will usually wish to convene an early general meeting to remove the ex managing director from the board. In *Walker* v *Standard Chartered Bank plc* [1992] BCLC 535, Mr Walker had been removed by the board from his position as chief executive of Brent Walker plc. He alleged that this dismissal had been procured by Standard Chartered Bank in breach of an agreement with him. He sought an injunction to prevent the bank voting at a general meeting in favour of removing him from the board altogether. However, the court pointed out that the alleged agreement covered only his position as chief executive and had already been broken. The only remedy he could have against the bank was damages for breach of the alleged agreement.

Removal of a managing director from his or her directorship, so that, because of a provision like art. 84 of Table A, it is impossible to continue as managing director, may be a breach of the contract governing the appointment as managing director (see *Southern Foundries (1926) Ltd* v *Shirlaw* [1940] AC 701 and *Shindler* v *Northern Raincoat Co. Ltd* [1960] 1 WLR 1038 discussed in 15.3.3).

Under Table A, the appointment of a managing director must be noted in the directors' minutes (art. 100(a), see 15.5.1).

By art. 72 of Table A:

The directors may . . . delegate to any managing director . . . such of their powers as they consider desirable to be exercised by him. Any such delegation may be made subject to any conditions the directors may impose, and either collaterally with or to the exclusion of their own powers and may be revoked or altered.

It has been common for a company to have one individual as both managing director and chairman, giving that individual a clearly dominant position in the company. It was the view of the Cadbury Committee (see 15.1.2) that chairman and chief executive have different roles and the offices should be held by different persons. 'Chairmen should be able to stand sufficiently back from the day-to-day running of the business to ensure that their boards are in full control of the company's affairs and alert to their obligations to their shareholders' (Cadbury Report, para. 4.7). Principle A.2 of the Combined Code for listed companies (see 15.1.2) states that 'There should be a clear division of responsibilities at the head of the company which will ensure a balance of power and authority, such that no one individual has unfettered powers of decision'. The code of best practice says that a decision to combine the posts of chairman and chief executive officer should be publicly justified (para. A.2.1). The non-executive directors should include a recognised senior member, other than the chairman, to whom concerns can be conveyed. The senior non-executive director should be identified in the annual report.

If the board of directors acquiesce in one of their number acting as a managing director then that person will have the ostensible authority of a managing director (*Freeman &*

Lockyer v *Buckhurst Park Properties (Mangal) Ltd* [1964] 2 QB 480, CA; *Hely-Hutchinson* v *Brayhead Ltd* [1968] 1 QB 549, CA).

The courts have taken differing views on the role of a managing director. In *Re Newspaper Proprietary Syndicate Ltd* [1900] 2 Ch 349, Cozens-Hardy J said that 'A managing director is only an ordinary director entrusted with some special powers'. Other judges have seen a managing director as a manager who happens also to be a director (Lord President Normand in *Anderson* v *James Sutherland (Peterhead) Ltd* 1941 SC 203 at p. 217). In *Southern Foundries (1926) Ltd* v *Shirlaw* [1940] AC 701, Viscount Maugham said, at p. 712, that '. . . the two positions, that of director and that of manager, involve different qualifications, duties and responsibilities'. These differing opinions reflect the fact that the position of managing director of a company is defined not so much by company law as by the company's articles, the managing director's service contract and what the managing director makes of the position. A managing director's role can vary from autocrat to hired functionary. For example, in *Harold Holdsworth & Co. (Wakefield) Ltd* v *Caddies* [1955] 1 WLR 352, HL, Mr Caddies was appointed managing director of the appellant company under an agreement which required him to 'perform the duties and exercise the powers in relation to the business of the company and the businesses (howsoever carried on) of its existing subsidiary companies at the date hereof which may from time to time be assigned to or vested in him by the board of directors'. The board of the appellant company subsequently resolved that Mr Caddies should devote his attentions entirely to one of its subsidiaries. It was held that this was not a breach of the company's agreement with him.

15.5.4 Executive directors

Table A, art. 84, empowers the directors to appoint one or more of their number to any executive office under the company and to enter into an agreement or arrangement with any director for his or her employment by the company. Article 72 permits the directors to delegate to a director holding executive office such of their powers as they consider desirable to be exercised by him or her. Any such delegation may be made subject to any conditions the directors may impose, and either collaterally with or to the exclusion of their own powers. Delegated powers may be altered or revoked. A director holding executive office does not retire by rotation under Table A (art. 84) but his or her appointment as an executive automatically terminates on ceasing to be a director (without prejudice to a claim for damages for breach of the contract of service) (art. 84).

15.5.5 Committees

It may not always be possible or convenient for the full board of directors to consider certain issues relating to the company's affairs, or it may happen that the expertise of some directors lends itself to a separate consideration by them of various problems and decisions. Table A, art. 72, therefore permits the directors to delegate any of their powers to any committee consisting of one or more directors. Delegation of powers to a committee may be made subject to any conditions the directors may impose, and either collaterally with or to the exclusion of their own powers. These powers may be altered or revoked (art. 72). Subject to any conditions imposed by the directors the proceedings of a committee with two or more members are governed by the articles regulating the proceedings of the full board of directors, so far as they are capable of applying (art. 72). Minutes must be kept of the proceedings of a committee (art. 100(b), see 15.5.1).

The power to delegate to a committee must not be used as a device to exclude a particular director (*Great Western Railway Co.* v *Rushout* (1852) 5 De G & Sm 290, which concerned a statutory company; *Kyshe* v *Alturas Gold Ltd* (1888) 4 TLR 331; *Bray* v *Smith* (1908) 124 LT Jo 293; *Trounce* v *NCF Kaiapoi Ltd* (1985) 2 NZCLC 99,422).

The Combined Code for listed companies (see 15.1.2) says that the board of a listed company should establish:

(a) a nomination committee, with a majority of non-executive directors, to make recommendations to the board on all new board appointments (para. A.5.1);

(b) a remuneration committee, composed exclusively of independent non-executive directors (paras B.2.1 and B.2.2), to make recommendations on the remuneration of executive directors; and

(c) an audit committee of at least three non-executive directors, the majority of whom are independent, to review the scope and results of audits (paras D.3.1 and D.3.2).

For the American experience of these committees see Committee on Corporate Laws, 'The overview committees of the board of directors' (1979) 34 Bus Law 1837.

15.6 REMUNERATION

15.6.1 Remuneration

15.6.1.1 No prima facie entitlement to remuneration
A director of a company does not have a right to be remunerated for any services performed for the company except as provided by its constitution or approved by the company's members (*Dunston* v *Imperial Gas Light & Coke Co.* (1832) 3 B & Ad 125; *Hutton* v *West Cork Railway Co.* (1883) 23 ChD 654; *Guinness plc* v *Saunders* [1990] 2 AC 663). This is an aspect of the general principle that a director is not allowed to make a profit unless expressly permitted (see 16.5.1).

In *Hutton* v *West Cork Railway Co.* (1883) 23 ChD 654, CA, Bowen LJ said (at p. 672):

A director is not a servant. He is a person who is doing business for the company, but not upon ordinary terms. It is not implied from the mere fact that he is a director, that he is to have a right to be paid for it. In some companies . . . there is a special provision for the way in which the directors should be paid; in others there is not. If there is a special provision for the way in which they are to be paid, you must look to the special provision to see how to deal with it. But if there is no special provision their payment is in the nature of a gratuity.

The directors of a company have no authority to pay the company's money to themselves or any one of their number, unless they are given authority by the company's constitution or the payment is approved by the members (*Re George Newman & Co.* [1895] 1 Ch 674, CA). This rule was extended to cover a payment to the widow of a director in *Re Lee Behrens & Co. Ltd* [1932] 2 Ch 46.

15.6.1.2 Provisions in articles for payment of directors' fees
In practice it is accepted that the directors of a company are to be paid fees for holding office, and provision for such fees is usually made in the articles of association. Table A, art. 82, provides:

The directors shall be entitled to such remuneration as the company may by ordinary resolution determine and, unless the resolution provides otherwise, the remuneration shall be deemed to accrue from day to day.

It is not necessary under art. 82 for remuneration to be determined at a general meeting: it is sufficient if all the members entitled to vote on the matter assent to the amount of the directors' remuneration (*Re Duomatic Ltd* [1969] 2 Ch 365).

If the articles of a company provide how the remuneration of its directors is to be determined then the court will not make its own determination of remuneration (*Re Richmond Gate Property Co. Ltd* [1965] 1 WLR 335; *Guinness plc* v *Saunders* [1990] 2 AC 663). The court will not award a *quantum meruit* (see 3.4.4) nor will it make an 'equitable allowance' by analogy with its power to authorise a trustee to charge for services rendered. In both *Re Richmond Gate Property Co. Ltd* and *Guinness plc* v *Saunders* the remuneration of the director concerned was to be determined by the company's board of directors but no determination was made: in each case therefore the director concerned was not entitled to anything. It follows that in a company with Table A as its articles, if the members do not determine the directors' remuneration under art. 82, the directors will not be entitled to anything.

15.6.1.3 Expenses
Table A, art. 83, authorises the payment of all travelling, hotel and other expenses properly incurred by the directors in connection with the discharge of their duties and attendance at meetings.

15.6.1.4 Remuneration for other services
Under Table A, art. 84, the directors may (a) enter into an agreement or arrangement with any director for the employment of that director by the company, (b) enter into an agreement or arrangement with any director for the provision by that director of any services outside the scope of the ordinary duties of a director. The article further provides that the directors may determine the terms of any such agreement or arrangement, and that any director with whom such an agreement or arrangement has been made may be remunerated by the directors 'as they think fit'.

The directors of a company should limit payments to executive directors to what the company can afford. Failure by a director to ensure that the board fixes affordable salaries may show the director's unfitness and be a ground for a disqualification order, as in *Secretary of State for Trade and Industry* v *Van Hengel* [1995] 1 BCLC 545. It is not correct that the company must pay the going rate for the job (ibid.).

Principle B.2 of the Combined Code for listed companies (see 15.1.2) states:

> Companies should establish a formal and transparent procedure for developing policy on executive remuneration and for fixing the remuneration packages of individual directors. No director should be involved in deciding his or her own remuneration.

Principle B.3 states that:

> The company's annual report should contain a statement of remuneration policy and details of the remuneration of each director.

The statement required by principle B.3 is known as a remuneration report. The code of best practice suggests that a listed company's board of directors should establish a remuneration committee, consisting only of independent non-executive directors, to determine the remuneration of executive directors (paras B.2.1 and B.2.2). The remuneration of the non-executive directors should be set by the board itself, unless the articles require their remuneration to be determined by the shareholders (para. B.2.4). The members of the remuneration committee should be listed in the remuneration report (para. B.2.3). The committee should have access to professional advice inside and outside the company (para. B.2.5). See further 15.6.3.1.

Highly paid 'fat cat' directors, whose pay increases regularly outstrip their employees', are a popular target for adverse comment. In the consultation document introducing its review of company law (see 0.3.1.6) the DTI notes (at p. 11) that:

> . . . there have been many calls for [directors'] pay to be made subject to the specific approval of shareholders. The Government has made it plain that it is watching developments closely. The review will provide an opportunity to examine the responsibilities of shareholders in this and other areas.

15.6.1.5 Employment status of directors

The fact that a person is a director of a company does not in itself make that person an employee (what used to be called a 'servant') of the company (*Dunston v Imperial Gas Light & Coke Co.* (1832) 3 B & Ad 125; *Hutton v West Cork Railway Co.* (1883) 23 ChD 654). Being a director of a company is usually categorised as 'holding an office' rather than being an employee (*McMillan v Guest* [1942] AC 561, HL). The same applies to being a managing director (*Goodwin v Brewster* (1951) 32 TC 80, CA). (For an explanation of the term 'public company' as used in the income tax legislation discussed in *McMillan v Guest* and *Goodwin v Brewster*, see 4.6. For a discussion of the distinction between office and employment, see J. Ward '''What can it matter? Why should it matter?'':the taxation of offices and employments' [1989] BTR 281.) Whereas an employee serves under a contract of service, the appointment of a person as a director of a company does not in itself form any contract between the person and the company (*Newtherapeutics Ltd v Katz* [1991] Ch 226). Indeed the non-contractual nature of an appointment as a director is an indicator that it is an office rather than an employment. However, it is possible for the holder of an office to be considered to be also an employee. Whether a person who provides services is an employee depends on the conditions under which the services are provided, and is a notoriously difficult question of employment law. Deciding whether a particular director is serving under a contract of service is especially difficult (see, for example, *Parsons v Albert J. Parsons & Sons Ltd* [1979] ICR 271) though some guidance has been given by the Employment Appeal Tribunal in *Eaton v Robert Eaton Ltd* [1988] ICR 302. In *Secretary of State for Trade and Industry v Bottrill* [1998] IRLR 120 the Employment Appeal Tribunal emphasised that whether or not a person is an employee is a question of fact, and there is no rule of law that an individual who is able, by reason of a beneficial interest in the shares of a company, to prevent the company dispensing with his or her services to the company cannot be an employee of the company, as was suggested in *Buchan v Secretary of State for Employment* [1997] IRLR 80.

If a director of a company makes a contract with the company establishing the terms on which he will serve (under Table A, art. 84, for example) and the director is not serving under a contract of service then the contract is a contract for the supply of a service (also called a contract for services).

There is no implied term in a contract for the supply of services as a director in which remuneration is not settled that the company will pay a reasonable charge (Supply of Goods and Services Act 1982, ss. 15 and 16(1)). If a person performs services as a director of a company without there being any agreement about remuneration then a *quantum meruit* (see 3.4.4) will not be awarded (*Woolf v East Nigel Gold Mining Co. Ltd* (1905) 21 TLR 660).

In *Craven-Ellis* v *Canons Ltd* [1936] 2 KB 403, Mr Craven-Ellis was one of the first directors of Canons Ltd. He and all the company's other directors automatically vacated office on failing to acquire qualification shares. Nevertheless they continued to act as directors. Eighteen months after vacating office, the acting directors appointed Mr Craven-Ellis managing director and purported to make a contract with him agreeing his remuneration. The Court of Appeal held that there was no binding contract between the company and Mr Craven-Ellis, and awarded him a *quantum meruit*. There was no argument about whether the fact that he had acted as a director of the company made him subject to the fiduciary duties of a director so that he was not entitled to profit from his office. In *Guinness plc* v *Saunders* [1990] 2 AC 663, Lord Templeman said, at p. 693, that because Mr Craven-Ellis was not a director, there was no conflict between his claim to remuneration and the rule against profiting.

15.6.1.6 Prohibition of net-of-tax agreements
By CA 1985, s. 311, it is unlawful for a company to agree to give a certain amount of remuneration to a director net of income tax, or to agree to vary a director's remuneration in line with changes in rates of income tax. Any such agreement operates as an agreement to pay a gross sum (on which the director must pay tax) of the same amount as the agreed net after-tax sum. See also the Income and Corporation Taxes Act 1988, s. 164.

15.6.2 Compensation for loss of office

15.6.2.1 Payments requiring approval
The Companies Act 1985 requires certain payments by way of compensation for loss of office to be approved. Section 312 provides that:

> It is not lawful for a company to make to a director of the company any payment by way of compensation for loss of office, or as consideration for or in connection with his retirement from office, without particulars of the proposed payment (including its amount) being disclosed to members of the company and the proposal being approved by the company.

Where the loss of office arises because the company is wound up or sold off, s. 313(1) provides:

> It is not lawful, in connection with the transfer of the whole or any part of the undertaking or property of a company, for any payment to be made to a director of the company by way of compensation for loss of office, or as consideration for or in connection with his retirement from office, unless particulars of the proposed payment (including its amount) have been disclosed to members of the company and the proposal approved by the company.

Any payment received in breach of s. 313(1) is held by the director in trust for the company (s. 313(2)). In connection with takeover bids etc. resulting in loss of office, s. 314 provides:

> (1) This section applies where, in connection with the transfer to any persons of all or any of the shares in a company, being a transfer resulting from—
> (a) an offer made to the general body of shareholders; or
> (b) an offer made by or on behalf of some other body corporate with a view to the company becoming its subsidiary or a subsidiary of its holding company; or

(c)   an offer made by or on behalf of an individual with a view to his obtaining the right to exercise or control the exercise of not less than one-third of the voting power at any general meeting of the company; or

(d)   any other offer which is conditional on acceptance to a given extent,

a payment is to be made to a director of the company by way of compensation for loss of office, or as consideration for or in connection with his retirement from office.

(2)   It is in those circumstances the director's duty to take all reasonable steps to secure that particulars of the proposed payment (including its amount) are included in or sent with any notice of the offer made for their shares which is given to any shareholders.

By s. 315(1), the making of the proposed payment within s. 314(1) must, before the transfer of any shares in pursuance of the offer, be 'approved by a meeting (summoned for the purpose) of the holders of the shares to which the offer relates and of other holders of shares of the same class as any of those shares'. Any sum received without such approval is held in trust by the director for the persons who have sold their shares as a result of the offer made (s. 315(1)).

Since these provisions require disclosure to members as such, even non-voting shareholders must be informed (*Re Duomatic Ltd* [1969] 2 Ch 365; see 14.5.1).

15.6.2.2   *Payments not requiring approval*

The provisions of ss. 312 to 315 do not apply to 'any bona fide payment by way of damages for breach of contract or by way of pension in respect of past services' (s. 316(3)). Furthermore s. 312 applies only to voluntary payments: it does not, for example, apply to any payment which the company is obliged to make by virtue of the director's service contract (*Taupo Totara Timber Co. Ltd* v *Rowe* [1978] AC 537; *Lander* v *Premier Pict Petroleum Ltd* [1998] BCC 248). Table A, art. 87, expressly authorises directors to pay gratuities or make provision for the payment of pensions to any director who has held, but no longer holds, any executive office or employment with the company or any of its subsidiaries.

15.6.3   Disclosure in accounts of payments to directors

15.6.3.1   *Emoluments*

The Companies Act 1985 does not require a company's accounts for a financial year to disclose the remuneration of each director by name. However, s. 232(1) and sch. 6, part I, require a company to show, in a note to its annual accounts, the aggregate amount of directors' salary, fees and other benefits. Schedule 6 has been amended by SI 1997 No. 570. A company is required to show:

(a)   The aggregate amount of emoluments paid to or receivable by directors (sch. 6, para. 1(1)(a)). By para. 1(3) 'emoluments' includes salary, fees, bonuses, expenses that are chargeable to UK income tax and the estimated money value of non-cash benefits, but does not include share options, pension-scheme contributions and benefits or amounts receivable under long-term incentive schemes, which are covered by other provisions of para. 1(1).

(b)   Unless the company is a listed company, the number of directors who exercised share options and the number who received or were entitled to receive shares under long-term incentive schemes (para. 1(2)), though this information need not be given by a small company (s. 246(3)). If the company is listed, instead of these numbers, the aggregate of the amount of gains made by directors on the exercise of share options must be disclosed (sch. 6, para. 1(1)(b)). The share options that have to be reported are options to acquire shares in either the company or any group undertaking (defined in 9.6.2) (para. 1(5)).

(c) The aggregate amount of money paid to or receivable by the directors under long-term incentive schemes and the net value of assets other than money and share options so received or receivable (para. 1(1)(c)) — unless the company is listed, shares are not assets that have to be included in this figure (para. 1(2)). An incentive scheme is long-term if the conditions under which rewards are payable cannot be fulfilled in one financial year (para. 1(4)).

(d) The aggregate value of company contributions paid, or treated as paid, in respect of directors to pension schemes for money-purchase benefits (para. 1(1)(d)).

(e) The number of directors to whom retirement benefits are accruing under (i) money-purchase schemes and (ii) defined-benefit schemes (para. 1(1)(e)).

Amounts need to be included in these aggregates only so far as they relate to 'qualifying services'. A director's qualifying services are services as director of the company and of any of its subsidiary undertakings or otherwise in connection with the management of the affairs of the company or of any of its subsidiaries (para. 1(5)). Small companies need only give the total of items (a), (c) and (d) (s. 246(3)) but other companies must report each item separately.

Any payments receivable in respect of the financial year reported on (whenever paid) must be included together with payments made during the financial year but not receivable in respect of a period (para. 11(1)).

If one of the company's directors is nominated (directly or indirectly) by it to be director of any other undertaking then the amounts payable to, or receivable by, that director from that undertaking must be included in the total even if it is not a subsidiary undertaking (para. 13(2)(a)).

References to amounts paid to or receivable by a person include amounts paid to or receivable by a person connected with, or a body corporate controlled by, that person (but not so as to require an amount to be counted twice) (para. 10(4)). See 16.6.8.10 for the meanings of connection and control.

If the total of the figures that have to be reported under para. 1(1)(a), (b) (which applies only to listed companies) and (c) is £200,000 or more, the company must show how much of that total and how much of the para. 1(1)(d) aggregate are attributable to its highest-paid director (para. 2), though it does not have to reveal which director that is. In addition, if the highest-paid director is in a defined-benefit pension scheme, his or her accrued retirement benefits must be stated (para. 2(2)), and if he or she exercised any share options or received or became entitled to receive shares under a long-term incentive scheme, those facts must be stated (para. 2(3) and (4)). None of the information about the highest-paid director need be given by a small company (s. 246(3)).

Whether or not a small company takes advantage of the exemptions provided by s. 246(3) in the accounts supplied to members, none of the information required by sch. 6, paras 1 and 2, need be included in the accounts it files with the registrar (s. 246(6)).

The annual report and accounts of a listed company must include a remuneration report. For accounting periods ending before 31 December 1998 this must contain the information specified in the Listing Rules, para. 12.43(x). For subsequent periods it must comply with para. 12.43A(c). Among the matters required to be reported by para. 12.43A(c) are:

(a) a statement of the company's policy on executive directors' remuneration;

(b) the amount of each element in the remuneration package, for the period under review, of each director by name;

(c)   information on share options for each director by name;

(d)   details of long-term incentive schemes for each director by name;

(e)   details of any director's service contract with a notice period in excess of one year, or with provision for predetermined compensation on termination exceeding one year's salary and benefits in kind, giving the reason for the notice period;

(f)   a statement of the company's policy on the granting of options or awards under its employees' share schemes and other long-term incentive schemes, explaining and justifying any departure from that policy in the period under review and any change in the policy from the preceding year.

15.6.3.2   Excess retirement benefits

A company is required by CA 1985, s. 232(1) and sch. 6, para. 7, to show in a note to its accounts the aggregate amount by which directors' or past directors' pensions paid in, or payable in respect of, the financial year being reported on (para. 11(1)) exceed the pensions to which they were entitled on the later of 31 March 1997 or when the pensions first became payable. Increases do not have to be included in this figure if they were paid to all members of the pension scheme and were paid without recourse to additional contributions. A small company does not have to give this information in the accounts presented to members (s. 246(3)) and, even if it does give the information to members, it can omit it from the copy of the accounts filed with the registrar (s. 246(6)).

15.6.3.3   Compensation for loss of office

A company is required by CA 1985, s. 232(1) and sch. 6, para. 8, to show in a note to its annual accounts the aggregate amount of any compensation to directors or past directors in respect of loss of office (see 15.6.2). A small company may omit this information from the copy of its accounts filed with the registrar (s. 246(6)).

15.6.3.4   Sums paid to third parties in respect of directors' services

A company is required by CA 1985, s. 232(1) and sch. 6, para. 9, to show in a note to its annual accounts the aggregate amount of any consideration paid to or receivable by third parties for making available the services of any person as a director of the reporting company; services, while a director of the reporting company, as director of any of its subsidiary undertakings; or services, while a director of the reporting company, in connection with the management of the affairs of the company or any of its subsidiary undertakings (para. 9(1)). 'Third parties' means persons other than the director himself or a person connected with him or body corporate controlled by him and does not include the reporting company or any of its subsidiary undertakings (para. 9(3)). A small company may omit this information from the copy of its accounts filed with the registrar (s. 246(6)).

15.6.3.5   Directors' and auditors' duties

A director of a company, and any person who has been an officer of a company at any time in the preceding five years, must, under penalty, notify the company of his emoluments, pensions or compensation for loss of office or amounts payable for his services to third parties required to be disclosed in the company's annual accounts (CA 1985, s. 232(3) and sch. 24). A company is required to give information on these matters in its accounts only so far as the information is contained in the company's books and papers or the company has the right to obtain it from the person concerned (sch. 6, para. 14). If the requirements of CA 1985, sch. 6, concerning disclosure in accounts of payments to directors have not been complied with then the auditors must include in their report, so far as they are reasonably able to do so, a statement giving the required particulars (s. 237(4)).

15.6.4 Inspection and approval of directors' service contracts

The terms of a company's contracts of service with its directors (that is, contracts of service as employees — see 15.6.1.5) must be made available for inspection by the members under CA 1985, s. 318 (see 4.4.3). This provision also applies to shadow directors (s. 318(6)). In addition, a listed company is required by the Stock Exchange to make available for inspection by any person, at its registered office or transfer office, copies of all directors' service contracts. The copies must also be available for inspection at the place of the annual general meeting at least 15 minutes before the meeting and at the meeting (Listing Rules, para. 16.9).

By CA 1985, s. 319, if an agreement is made whereby a director (or shadow director: s. 319(7)) of a company is to provide services to the company or any of its subsidiaries (whether under a contract of service or a contract for services: s. 319(7)) for more than five years and it contains a term under which the company cannot terminate the employment by notice, or can do so only in specified circumstances (s. 319(1)), then that term is void (and the company is deemed to be able to terminate the employment by giving reasonable notice) (s. 319(6)) unless it is 'first approved by a resolution of the company in general meeting' (s. 319(3)). Presumably this means that the term must be approved before the contract is made. In relation to employment within a group of companies of a director of the holding company, the section contemplates that the agreement may be made either by the holding company or a subsidiary: if it is made by a subsidiary that is not a wholly owned subsidiary then the non-termination term must be approved by a general meeting of the subsidiary as well (s. 319(3) and (4)). If the contract is to be approved in general meeting then a written memorandum of the contract must be available for inspection by the members at the company's registered office for the 15 days ending with the day of the meeting at which it is to be approved and at the meeting itself (s. 319(5)). If the resolution is to be adopted as a written resolution under s. 381A (which applies only to private companies; see 14.5.3) then the documents must be supplied to each member at or before the time at which the resolution is supplied to that member for signature (sch. 15A, para. 7).

A contract for services supplied by a parent company to its subsidiary does not have to be approved in accordance with s. 319 if the only reason for treating the parent company as a shadow director of the subsidiary is that the subsidiary's directors are accustomed to act in accordance with the parent company's directions or instructions (s. 741(3)).

The Cadbury Code, which must be observed by all listed companies (see 15.1.2), insists that directors' service contracts should not exceed three years without shareholders' approval (para. 3.1). The Cadbury Code is being replaced by the Combined Code, in which the code of best practice, para. B.1.7, says that listed companies should now move to a one-year maximum term.

Section 318 applies only to contracts of service (i.e., service as an employee, e.g., as a managing director or executive director) whereas s. 319 applies also to contracts for services (e.g., a contract covering service as a director simply) (s. 319(7)(a)).

15.7 POWERS OF MANAGEMENT

15.7.1 Division of power between members and directors

Directors' authority to manage their company has been reinforced by the principle, which the courts have adopted, that the articles divide the company's powers between the directors and the members, and the members cannot instruct the directors on how to exercise the powers assigned to them.

In *Howard Smith Ltd* v *Ampol Petroleum Ltd* [1974] AC 821 Lord Wilberforce, delivering the judgment of the Privy Council, said, at p. 837:

> The constitution of a limited company normally provides for directors, with powers of management, and shareholders, with defined voting powers having power to appoint the directors, and to take, in general meeting, by majority vote, decisions on matters not reserved for management . . . it is established that directors, within their management powers, may take decisions against the wishes of the majority of shareholders, and indeed that the majority of shareholders cannot control them in the exercise of these powers while they remain in office.

In *Grundt* v *Great Boulder Proprietary Mines Ltd* [1948] Ch 145, Cohen LJ said, at p. 157:

> . . . there is nothing unusual in the shareholders not being allowed to interfere in matters which have been deliberately placed under the control of the directors.

The principle of division of powers is often described as achieving a 'separation of ownership and control'. It is important to bear in mind that only some companies are affected by this: in the vast majority of private companies the directors and the members are the same persons.

The law gives directors freedom to exercise the powers assigned to them but this freedom is granted to the directors as *fiduciaries* and is subject to the control that the courts have over the exercise of fiduciary powers (see chapter 16). This control places limits on the *purposes* for which directors' powers may be exercised: directors must act in the interests of the company (or, at least, what they bona fide consider to be in the company's interests) and they must exercise their powers for the purpose for which they were given. Within these limits, directors' actions cannot be controlled by the members.

The members are not, however, entirely without influence: since 1948 the members of a company have had a statutory right to dismiss any of the company's directors, by ordinary resolution (CA 1985, s. 303; see 15.3.3). Cases decided before 1948 should always be considered in the light of the rule in force at that time that directors could not be removed unless there was a power in the articles to dismiss (*Imperial Hydropathic Hotel Co., Blackpool* v *Hampson* (1882) 23 ChD 1, CA) and where such a power was given by the articles it was usual to require a special resolution.

No statutory power of dismissal was available to the members in *Teck Corporation Ltd* v *Millar* (1972) 33 DLR (3d) 288, British Columbia, in which the majority of members of a company authorised legal proceedings against its directors, seeking to halt an allotment of shares by the directors on the ground that it would be a misuse of their powers. Berger J, however, found that the allotment would not be an abuse of the directors' powers so that it could not be prevented. Berger J, at pp. 307–8, adopted the following statement by Barwick CJ in *Ashburton Oil NL* v *Alpha Minerals NL* (1971) 123 CLR 614 at p. 620:

> Directors who are minded to do something which in their honest view is for the benefit of the company are not to be restrained because a majority shareholder or shareholders holding a majority of shares in the company do not want the directors so to act.

15.7.2 Directors' general power of management

15.7.2.1 Table A, article 70
In Table A, the directors' general power of management is conferred by art. 70:

Subject to the provisions of [the Companies Act 1985 as amended], the memorandum and the articles and to any directions given by special resolution, the business of the company shall be managed by the directors who may exercise all the powers of the company.

This general power of management applies only to managing the company as a going concern (see 15.7.2.2) and is expressed to be subject to legislation and the provisions of the company's memorandum and articles (see 15.7.2.3). It does not imply a power to pay bribes to secure business for the company (*E. Hannibal & Co. Ltd* v *Frost* (1987) 4 BCC 3, CA). What is controversial is whether the members have a general supervisory power: the courts have, as indicated above, generally adopted the theory that they do not (see 15.7.2.4).

15.7.2.2 Management as a going concern

It has been said that the general power of management conferred by Table A, art. 70, and similar provisions is a power only to carry on the company's business as a going concern (*Re Standard Bank of Australia Ltd* (1898) 24 VLR 304; *Re Galway & Salthill Tramways Co.* [1918] 1 IR 62 — a case concerning a statutory company with power of management governed by the Companies Clauses Consolidation Act 1845, s. 90, see 15.7.1.1.3). Accordingly it does not give the directors power to petition for the winding up of the company (*Re Galway & Salthill Tramways Co.*; *Re Emmadart Ltd* [1979] Ch 540) or to oppose the restoration to the register of a company struck off by the registrar (*Re Regent Insulation Co. Ltd* (1981) *The Times*, 5 November 1981). However, the directors of a company now have a statutory power to petition for its winding up (IA 1986, s. 124(1)) or for an administration order (IA 1986, s. 9(1)). The decision to present a petition must be taken at a properly constituted board meeting (*Re Equiticorp International plc* [1989] 1 WLR 1010) or agreed to by all the directors without meeting (*Re Instrumentation Electrical Services Ltd* [1988] BCLC 550). The suggestion by some commentators that these powers conferred directly by statute are nevertheless subject to the limitations of the powers conferred by Table A, art. 70, seems to be misconceived.

15.7.2.3 Subject to the articles

The general power of management conferred by Table A, art. 70, is expressed to be subject to the articles. In *Salmon* v *Quin & Axtens Ltd* [1909] 1 Ch 311, the articles of Quin & Axtens Ltd conferred a general power of management on the directors (art. 75) but art. 80 made directors' decisions on certain matters subject to the veto of either of two named shareholders (who between them held the bulk of the company's shares). These two named shareholders were also appointed directors and managing directors of the company by the articles. The Court of Appeal upheld the validity of a veto issued by one of the named shareholders under art. 80 and held that an ordinary resolution of the members was ineffective to override the veto because it was an attempt to alter art. 80 by ordinary resolution instead of special resolution. The Court of Appeal's decision was affirmed by the House of Lords (sub nom. *Quin & Axtens Ltd* v *Salmon* [1909] AC 442).

Matters which the articles allot to the members, such as determination of the directors' fees under Table A, art. 82, are not within art. 70 (*Foster* v *Foster* [1916] 1 Ch 532).

15.7.2.4 Members' general supervisory power

In versions of Table A prior to 1985, the general power of management (e.g., in art. 80 of Table A in CA 1948) was expressed to be subject 'to such regulations . . . as may be prescribed by the company in general meeting' (i.e., by ordinary resolution). The articles of some companies provided that the general power of management was subject to regulations made by extraordinary resolution. Such provisions would appear to give members a general supervisory power over directors. However, judges have taken the view that these provisions are not enough to confer on members a general supervisory power: to do that it would be necessary to use the formula adopted for statutory companies in the Companies Clauses Consolidation Act 1845, s. 90, which makes directors' exercise of their powers 'subject also to the control and regulation of any general meeting specially convened for the purpose' (for the operation of this provision, see *Exeter & Crediton Railway Co.* v *Buller* (1847) 5 Ry & Can Cas 211; *Isle of Wight Railway Co.* v *Tahourdin* (1883) 25 ChD 320, CA). The absence of words as strong as this in Table A shows that directors of a registered company have a different status from those of statutory companies and that the members of registered companies do not have a general supervisory power (*Automatic Self-Cleansing Filter Syndicate Co. Ltd* v *Cuninghame* [1906] 2 Ch 34 per Collins MR at p. 43 and per Cozens-Hardy LJ at p. 46; *Salmon* v *Quin & Axtens Ltd* [1909] 1 Ch 311, CA, per Farwell LJ at p. 320; *Breckland Group Holdings Ltd* v *London & Suffolk Properties Ltd* [1989] BCLC 100; see also *Charter Oil Co. Ltd* v *Beaumont* (1967) 65 DLR (2d) 112, British Columbia at pp. 119–20 where it was said that a majority of members do not have a right to manage the company).

Directors of registered companies are not regarded as delegates of the members; the members cannot hold meetings to tell the directors what to do. As Buckley LJ said in *Gramophone & Typewriter Ltd* v *Stanley* [1908] 2 KB 89, CA, at pp. 105–6:

> The directors are not servants to obey directions given by the shareholders as individuals; they are not agents appointed by and bound to serve the shareholders as their principals.

The courts have generally ruled provisions in articles making the general management power of directors subject to directions given by ordinary resolution ineffective because they are inconsistent with the principle of division of powers (*John Shaw & Sons (Salford) Ltd* v *Shaw* [1935] 2 KB 113, CA; *Scott* v *Scott* [1943] 1 All ER 582; *Macson Development Co. Ltd* v *Gordon* (1959) 19 DLR (2d) 465, Nova Scotia, at p. 470; *Black White & Grey Cabs Ltd* v *Fox* [1969] NZLR 824; *Winthrop Investments Ltd* v *Winns Ltd* [1975] 2 NSWLR 666, per Samuels JA at p. 683; *National Roads & Motorists' Association* v *Parker* (1986) 6 NSWLR 517). To the contrary are *Marshall's Valve Gear Co. Ltd* v *Manning Wardle & Co. Ltd* [1909] 1 Ch 267 and *Dowse* v *Marks* (1913) 13 SR (NSW) 332 following an *obiter* remark by Warrington J in *Thomas Logan Ltd* v *Davis* (1911) 104 LT 914 — see below. Also to the contrary is *Credit Development Pte Ltd* v *IMO Pte Ltd* [1993] 2 SLR 370.

Similarly, a provision making the general power subject to extraordinary resolution is ineffective (*Queensland Press Ltd* v *Academy Instruments No. 3 Pty Ltd* [1988] 2 QdR 575).

It is a significant new feature of the 1985 version of Table A that it contemplates the members giving directions to the directors by special resolution. However, it would seem unlikely that the courts would hold that to be any more effective than the provisions for directions to be given by ordinary or extraordinary resolution. In *Re Coachman Tavern (1985) Ltd* [1988] 2 NZLR 635, Gallen J said, at p. 639: 'In terms of the theories enunciated in the leading cases, it would be difficult to justify a contention that the company in general meeting could usurp powers reserved to the directors by using a special resolution'. It might be argued that a direction given by special resolution should be construed as altering art. 70 so as to give the directors powers of management except on the subject-matter of the direction, and being by special resolution this would be an effective alteration under CA 1985, s. 9. However, the direction should be stated explicitly to be an alteration of the articles because *ad hoc* special resolutions are not generally construed as altering the articles by implication (*Imperial Hydropathic Hotel Co., Blackpool* v *Hampson* (1882) 23 ChD 1, CA). Since the members could alter the articles in this way under the general power conferred by CA 1985, s. 9, it would seem that this part of art. 70 is superfluous.

The principles of division of powers, and separation of ownership and control, are not universally popular. Many critics believe that directors should be subject to members' control and should be regarded more as members' delegates than as company officers. This is, in particular, crucial to proposals that in some companies, directors should be appointed to represent the interests of employees — see G.R. Sullivan, 'The relationship between the board of directors and the general meeting in limited companies' (1977) 93 LQR 569.

Critics of the division of powers principle have regarded statements of the principle by judges as *obiter*. This was the view taken by Neville J in *Marshall's Valve Gear Co. Ltd* v *Manning Wardle & Co. Ltd*, in which his lordship held that members of a company have an inherent right to supervise directors by ordinary resolution unless the articles specify otherwise. According to this theory, a provision in articles that the power of management is subject to regulations prescribed by the company in general meeting merely restates the general law, and so does s. 90 of the Companies Clauses Consolidation Act 1845. His lordship distinguished *Automatic Self-Cleansing Filter Syndicate Co. Ltd* v *Cuninghame* on the ground that the general management article in that case had subjected the power of management to regulations made by extraordinary resolution and thereby disentitled the members from interfering by ordinary resolution.

However, Neville J was answered within a month by Farwell LJ in the Court of Appeal in *Salmon* v *Quin & Axtens Ltd* [1909] 1 Ch 311, who argued that a minority who had become members of a company 'on the footing that the business should be managed by the board of directors' should not have to suffer that management being interfered with by 'a bare majority very inimical to [their] interests'. Farwell LJ was deploying an argument used by Neville J himself in *Horn* v *Henry Faulder & Co. Ltd* (1908) 99 LT 524 to hold that directors could not agree to someone who was not a director having autonomous control over a division of the company's business.

Treating the principle of division of powers as a mere *obiter dictum*, critics assert that there is no basis for the decisions that provisions in articles subjecting directors' powers of management to regulations made by ordinary resolution are ineffective. Several commentators offer lengthy discussions of the true construction of such articles and conclude that they do give members the right to control directors. This was the view taken by the learned judicial commissioner in *Credit Development Pte Ltd* v *IMO Pte Ltd* [1993] 2 SLR 370. In our view, however, the principle of division of powers is the reason for holding such provisions ineffective.

In *Salmon* v *Quin & Axtens Ltd* at first instance (1908) 25 TLR 64 and in *Thomas Logan Ltd* v *Davis* at first instance (1911) 104 LT 914, Warrington J, apparently differing from his view in *Cuninghame's* case at first instance, said that an express provision that the members could give directions by ordinary resolution on matters of general management was effective. In *Salmon* v *Quin & Axtens Ltd* his lordship was overruled on appeal. In *Thomas Logan Ltd* v *Davis*, he said that the directors had not acted under the general power of management but under a specific power granted by a different article which was not expressly subject to a power of the members to give directions: therefore, the directors' decision could not be altered by the members by ordinary resolution. This seems to contradict Neville J's theory that the members have an inherent right to control the directors by ordinary resolution. It is a pity that the Court of Appeal is not reported as saying anything about this when it affirmed ((1911) 105 LT 419) Warrington J's decision on the substantive point of the case.

The principle of separation of powers seems to have been generally adopted by the courts in recent years (see, for example, *Breckland Group Holdings Ltd* v *London & Suffolk Properties Ltd*) but criticism of it has continued in academic writings. In addition to the article by Sullivan mentioned above, discussion of the point will be found in the following articles: K.A. Aickin, 'Division of power between directors and general meeting as a matter of law, and as a matter of fact and policy' (1967) 5 MULR 448; B. Slutsky, 'The relationship between the board of directors and the shareholders in general meeting', *Univ. of Br. Columbia Law Rev.*, vol. 3, No. 3 (1968), pp. 81–95; G.D. Goldberg, 'Article 80 of Table A of the Companies Act 1948' (1970) 33 MLR 177; C.J. Cohen, 'The distribution of powers in a company as a matter of law' (1973) 90 SALJ 262; M.S. Blackman, 'Article 59 and the distribution of powers in a company' (1975) 92 SALJ 286; J-A. MacKenzie, '"Who controls the company?" — the interpretation of Table A' (1983) 4 Co Law 99; M. Stokes, 'Company law and legal theory', in W. Twining (ed.), *Legal Theory and Common Law* (Oxford: Blackwell, 1986), pp. 155–83; L. Flynn, 'The power to direct' (1991) 13 DULJ 101.

In debates about how companies should be governed by their members and directors, the company is often viewed, consciously or unconsciously, as a microcosm of the State and writers on the topic often take over political theories. For a discussion of this, see R. Romano, 'Metapolitics and corporate law reform' (1984) 36 Stan L Rev 923. The literature on how companies should be governed is extensive: for a recent addition, with references to other material, see C.S. Axworthy, 'Corporate directors — who needs them?' (1988) 51 MLR 273.

15.7.3 Power to litigate

The power to litigate in the name of a registered company is one of the general powers of management assigned to the directors by Table A, art. 70, and, therefore, cannot be controlled by the members (*John Shaw & Sons (Salford) Ltd* v *Shaw* [1935] 2 KB 113, CA; *Alexander Ward & Co. Ltd* v *Samyang Navigation Co. Ltd* [1975] 1 WLR 673, HL; *Breckland Group Holdings Ltd* v *London & Suffolk Properties Ltd* [1989] BCLC 100; *Mitchell and Hobbs (UK) Ltd* v *Mill* [1996] 2 BCLC 102).

John Shaw & Sons (Salford) Ltd v *Shaw* concerned an established family company. Two members of the family, Peter and John Shaw, who were directors of the company, had admitted responsibility for 'deficiencies' of just over £25,000. Their brother, Percy, also a director, had previously admitted responsibility for a deficiency of £13,150. There were two other directors. (The brothers had presumably been putting the company's takings direct into their own pockets in order to evade tax.)

Part of a complicated arrangement for repaying these deficiencies to the company was that three additional directors were appointed and the articles of association were changed so that these three were named 'permanent directors'. The other five directors remained in office but as 'ordinary directors' and at board meetings they were to have 'such rights of voting . . . as may from time to time be conferred upon them by the permanent directors' (art. 87). In addition, Peter, John and Percy Shaw had no control over, and no right to deal with, the debts due from them (art. 86A). Article 95 was the article conferring general powers of management on the directors, in this company subject to 'regulations' adopted by ordinary resolution.

The three permanent directors held a board meeting and resolved to sue Peter and John Shaw for their debt to the company. They did not give notice of this meeting to the other directors on the ground that they were not entitled to vote on the matter (see 14.4.5.2). A shareholders' meeting resolved that the action against Peter and John should be discontinued and the Court of Appeal had to consider Peter and John's motion that the action should be struck out on the grounds, *inter alia*, that:

(a) The directors' meeting was not properly convened.
(b) The directors' decision had been overruled by the members.

Greer LJ (at p. 133) held that the directors' meeting was properly convened but Slesser LJ (at pp. 138–42) held that it was not. Roche LJ said that the defendants had failed to fulfil their burden of proof that the meeting was improperly convened.

On point (b), both Greer and Slesser LJJ held that the members had no power to overrule the directors (at pp. 134 and 143). Roche LJ did not mention the point but it is implicit in his lordship's conclusion that the action should not be struck out that he agreed with Greer and Slesser LJJ.

In *Duckett* v *Gover* (1877) 6 ChD 82, a member of a company (who was also a director) commenced a derivative action (see 18.4.2) with the company as co-defendant but was allowed to amend the pleadings to make the company co-plaintiff. Later the directors resolved to sanction the proceedings (25 WR 554 at p. 555). (See also the comments on the case by Jessel MR in *Mason* v *Harris* (1879) 11 ChD 97 at p. 106.)

However, in *Harben* v *Phillips* (1883) 23 ChD 14, Harben, who was a member of a company, claimed to have been elected a director and so joined the company as co-plaintiff in his action to restrain the other directors from excluding him from board meetings. But the company's name was struck out after a shareholders' meeting disapproved of the company's name being used (per Cotton LJ at p. 38).

Furthermore, in *Marshall's Valve Gear Co. Ltd* v *Manning Wardle & Co. Ltd* [1909] 1 Ch 267 the majority of the directors of a company were not allowed to have struck out an action brought in the company's name by the majority of its members, Neville J taking the view that the members could instruct the directors to bring the action (cf. *Pender* v *Lushington* (1877) 6 ChD 70 per Jessel MR at p. 79). (In relation to statutory companies governed by the Companies Clauses Consolidation Act 1845, s. 90 — see 15.7.2.4 — it was established that the members could maintain an action in the company's name to restrain directors from acting contrary to the members' ordinary resolutions: *Exeter & Crediton Railway Co.* v *Buller* (1847) 5 Ry & Can Cas 211.)

In *Breckland Group Holdings Ltd* v *London & Suffolk Properties Ltd*, the facts were similar to those in *Marshall's Valve Gear Co. Ltd* v *Manning Wardle & Co. Ltd*. An action had been brought in the name of London & Suffolk Properties Ltd by solicitors acting on the instructions of a man who controlled a company which owned 51 per cent of the shares in London & Suffolk Properties Ltd. It was admitted that the action was not properly authorised but contended that either a board meeting or a general meeting of members of London & Suffolk Properties Ltd could adopt it. Harman J held that the general meeting did not have power to adopt the action, only the board of directors had that power. His lordship chose not to follow *Marshall's Valve Gear Co. Ltd* v *Manning Wardle & Co. Ltd* and the view taken in that case must now be regarded as abandoned.

In *Club Flotilla (Pacific Palms) Ltd* v *Isherwood* (1987) 12 ACLR 387, New South Wales, the entire board of directors (known as the committee) of the company (which was a holiday timeshare club) had automatically vacated office because of the rule in *Re Consolidated Nickel Mines Ltd* [1914] 1 Ch 883 (see 15.3.2). It was contended that the secretary of the company had authority to instigate litigation in its name. In rejecting that contention, Needham J said, at p. 390:

This particular company . . . has vested in its committee full powers of management of the company and, in my opinion, it is only the committee which may give instructions for the institution of proceedings in which that company has an interest.

(See also *Daimler Co. Ltd* v *Continental Tyre & Rubber Co. (Great Britain) Ltd* [1916] 2 AC 307, HL in which it was held that the secretary of a company does not have authority to institute litigation in the company's name unless authority has been delegated to him by the directors.)

15.7.4 Powers conferred on directors by articles other than an article conferring a general power of management

In addition to an article such as Table A, art. 70, conferring a general power of management on directors there may be other articles conferring specific powers. For example, Table A, art. 84, gives the directors a power to appoint one of their number to be managing director. In *Thomas Logan Ltd* v *Davis* (1911) 104 LT 914 Warrington J held that this was a power separate from the general power of management conferred by a different article and therefore was not subject to any limitations contained in the article conferring the general power. (His lordship considered that the limitation on the general power — that it was subject to 'regulations' prescribed by ordinary resolution of the members — was effective, but see 15.7.2.4.)

In *Blair Open Hearth Furnace Co. Ltd* v *Reigart* (1913) 108 LT 665 Eve J held that the company's articles conferred a separate power on the directors to appoint additional directors (cf. Table A, art. 79) and moreover that the members were thereby excluded from appointing additional directors. (Table A, art. 78, however, confers on the members a parallel power to appoint additional directors.) See also Table A, art. 91, discussed in 15.5.2.

G. Hornsey, 'Some aspects of the law relating to company control' (1950) 13 MLR 470 at p. 476, claimed that the decision in *Automatic Self-Cleansing Filter Syndicate Co. Ltd* v *Cuninghame* [1906] 2 Ch 34, CA, that the members of the company did not have power by ordinary resolution to instruct the directors to sell the company's property (see 15.7.2.4) depended on the fact that the power to sell the company's property was a separate power given by an article (art. 97) other than the article conferring the general power of management (art. 96). This argument was not raised before the court and it is very doubtful that it is correct. Article 96 referred to 'the powers and authorities by these presents expressly conferred upon [the directors]' and stated that the directors 'may exercise all such powers', thus treating art. 97 as merely an enumeration of some of the general powers of management. This is the way the matter was treated by Collins MR in *Cuninghame's* case at p. 42. Hornsey's view is, however, shared by Goldberg (1970) 33 MLR 177 at p. 179 and Sullivan (1977) 93 LQR 569 at p. 574.

Table A, art. 101, provides that the company's seal 'shall *only* be used by the authority of the directors or of a committee of directors authorised by the directors' (emphasis added). This is a very definitely expressed allocation of power exclusively to the directors.

15.7.5 Powers exercisable only by the members

The general power of management conferred by Table A, art. 70, is expressly subject to the provisions of CA 1985 as amended. The members of a company are given by CA 1985, and by IA 1986, a large number of powers, which cannot be exercised by the directors (or by any other person). These powers may be exercised in general meeting (in which case many require an extraordinary or special resolution) or by unanimous agreement. The powers are:

(a) to alter the objects of the company (CA 1985, s. 4 — special resolution required);

(b) to alter the company's articles of association (s. 9(1) — special resolution required);

(c) to alter any condition in the company's memorandum which could have been contained in its articles (s. 17(1) — special resolution required);

(d) to change the company's name (s. 28(1) — special resolution required);

(e) to resolve to re-register (ss. 43(1)(a) (private to public); 51(1) (unlimited to private limited); 53(1)(a) (public to private) — all requiring a special resolution; a decision to re-register a private limited company as an unlimited company requires the consent of all the members (s. 49(8));

(f) if the company is public, to approve an agreement to acquire non-cash assets from founder members, in certain circumstances (s. 104(4)(c) — see 17.6.3.3);

(g) to decide that uncalled share capital shall not be called up except on winding up (s. 120 — special resolution required);

(h) to alter share capital pursuant to s. 121 (s. 121(4); authorisation in articles required; see 6.1.13);

(i) to reduce share capital (s. 135(1) — authorisation in articles and special resolution required);

(j) if the company is a private company, to approve the company giving financial assistance for the purchase of its shares or (unless it is a wholly owned subsidiary (shares of its holding company (s. 155(4) — special resolution required);

(k) if the company is a private company, to approve financial assistance for the purchase of the company's shares or (unless it is a wholly owned subsidiary) shares of its holding company, where the financial assistance is to be provided by a subsidiary of the company (s. 155(5) — special resolution required);

(l) to authorise the terms of a proposed contract for an off-market purchase by the company of any of its own shares; to vary, revoke or renew any such authority; and to vary an existing contract of purchase (s. 164(2), (3) and (7) — special resolution required);

(m) to authorise the terms of a contingent contract to purchase shares under which the company may become entitled or obliged to buy its own shares; to vary, revoke or renew any such authority; and to vary an existing contingent purchase contract (s. 165(2) — special resolution required);

(n) to approve a market purchase by the company of its own shares (s. 166(1));

(o) to authorise the proposed release by the company of its rights under a contract for an off-market purchase or a contingent purchase contract; to vary, revoke or renew any such authority; and to vary an existing release agreement (s. 167(2) — special resolution required);

(p) to approve a payment out of the company's capital for the redemption or purchase of any of its own shares (s. 173(2); special resolution required — such payments may not be made by public companies);

(q) to alter the company's memorandum so as to impose unlimited liability on directors, managers or any managing director (s. 307(1) — special resolution required);

(r) to approve the assignment by a director or manager of his or her office to another person (s. 308 — special resolution required);

(s) to approve compensation to directors on loss of office (ss. 312 and 313(1), and cf. s. 315(1));

(t) to approve directors' and shadow directors' service contracts for periods in excess of five years which make no provision for termination by notice or provide for such termination only in specified circumstances (s. 319(3));

(u) to approve substantial property transactions with directors (s. 320(1));

(v) to approve loans to directors to meet expenditure on company business (s. 337);

(w) to resolve that the company be wound up voluntarily (IA 1986, s. 84(1));

(x) to approve the acceptance by a liquidator in a members' voluntary liquidation of shares of another company to which assets of the company in liquidation are to be transferred (IA 1986, ss. 110(2), (3) and (4) and 111(3) — special resolution required);

(y) to give the liquidator in a members' voluntary liquidation powers to pay a class of creditors in full or make a compromise or arrangement concerning any of the debts of the company or any debts owed to the company (IA 1986, s. 165(2)(a); extraordinary resolution required).

For control by members over allotment of shares by directors see 6.2.5 and 6.2.6.

If the directors of a company act outside their authority then only the members can ratify their unauthorised acts — see 19.5.8 — and ratification must be by special resolution if the act was outside the company's objects (CA 1985, s. 35(3)).

The members of a company also have statutory powers which, although not unique to them, cannot be taken away from them, and may be important in controlling their directors. These include the power to dismiss directors (CA 1985, s. 303 — see 15.3.3) and the power to petition for a compulsory liquidation (IA 1986, s. 122(1)(a) — special resolution required). In addition, any member may petition the court for relief of unfairly prejudicial conduct of the company's affairs under CA 1985, ss. 459 to 461 (see 18.6) or (provided the company is solvent) for compulsory liquidation on the ground that it is just and equitable (IA 1986, s 122(1)(g) — see 18.7). Members holding 5 per cent of the total voting rights may insist on their resolution being put on the agenda of an annual general meeting (CA 1985, s. 376 — see 14.4.5.7) and members holding 10 per cent of votes may requisition an extraordinary general meeting (s. 368 — see 14.4.3) or ask the Secretary of State to appoint inspectors (s. 431 — see 18.8.2.1).

15.7.6   Approval by members of a listed company's large-scale transaction

The Listing Rules require that a listed company must not undertake a large-scale transaction without the prior approval of its shareholders in general meeting, and any agreement effecting the transaction must be conditional upon such approval being obtained (para. 10.37). The transactions which require shareholder approval are known as 'super class 1 transactions' and 'reverse takeovers'. A transaction is a super class 1 transaction if any one of five financial ratios associated with the transaction is 25 per cent or more; it is a reverse takeover if any of the ratios is 100 per cent or more or if the transaction would result in a fundamental change in the company's business or a fundamental change in board or voting control of the company (paras 10.4 and 10.5). The most significant of the ratios used to classify a transaction is the ratio of the net assets which are the subject of the transaction to the company's total net assets — the other ratios are listed in para. 10.5 of the Listing Rules. In the typical reverse takeover of a company, the company acquires new assets (usually another company) by issuing so many of its own shares to the vendors that they end up with voting control of the company. A reverse takeover used to be a way for a financier to acquire a company with a stock exchange listing without having to disclose any information about himself. Now the London Stock Exchange will suspend the listing of any company which announces a reverse takeover and will require new listing particulars as if the company were a new applicant for listing (Listing Rules, para. 10.39).

15.7.7   Reversion of powers to the members

If for some reason the directors are unable or unwilling to exercise their powers of management, those powers revert to and can be exercised by the members of the company.

For instance, if no board of directors exists, the members may assume control of management (*Alexander Ward & Co. Ltd* v *Samyang Navigation Co. Ltd* [1975] 1 WLR 673, HL). In this case, the respondent company had been registered in Hong Kong and its articles contained a provision that:

> The business of the company shall be managed by the directors, who . . . may exercise all such powers of the company as are not by the [Hong Kong] Ordinance or by these articles required to be exercised by the company in general meeting.

It was argued that this provision meant that, at a time when the company had no directors, it did not have capacity to take legal proceedings. This was rejected by the House of Lords. Lord Hailsham of St Marylebone said, at pp. 678–9:

> In my opinion, at the relevant time the company was fully competent . . . to raise proceedings. . . . The company could have done so either by appointing directors, or, as I think, by authorising proceedings in general meeting, which in the absence of an effective board, has a residual authority to use the company's powers.

Power similarly reverts to the general meeting where the board cannot act because its meetings are inquorate (*Foster* v *Foster* [1916] 1 Ch 532). It seems that the members must be regarded as agents of the company for the purpose of transacting any business when there are no directors.

In *Barron* v *Potter* [1914] 1 Ch 895, the company had two directors who were given power to appoint additional directors. The company's business came to a halt because one of the directors refused to attend any board meeting at which the other was present! Warrington J said:

> If directors having certain powers are unable or unwilling to exercise them — are in fact a non-existent body for the purpose — there must be some power in the company to do itself that which under other circumstances would be otherwise done. The directors in the present case being unwilling to appoint additional directors under the power conferred on them by the articles, in my opinion, the company in general meeting has power to make the appointment.

It would therefore seem that power reverts to the general meeting where a deadlock exists between the directors which renders them incapable of exercising their powers of management. The situation in *Barron* v *Potter*, where the deadlock arose from an inability to act, must be distinguished from a situation like that in *Salmon* v *Quin & Axtens Ltd* [1909] AC 442, HL.

In *Berlei Hestia (NZ) Ltd* v *Fernyhough* [1980] 2 NZLR 150, Mahon J suggested, at p. 155, that the powers of the directors of a company can revert to the members in general meeting only if the members in general meeting have the power to appoint directors. The articles of Berlei Hestia (NZ) Ltd, provided for each of two classes of shareholders to appoint equal numbers of directors and made no provision for a casting vote at directors' meetings. Because of disagreement between the two classes of shareholders and their respective directors, the company was deadlocked. R. Grantham, 'The unanimous consent rule in company law' [1993] CLJ 245 argues that to allow the members of a company to exercise the directors' powers of management is a denial of the company's separate personality.

15.8   LEGAL CATEGORISATION OF DIRECTORS

In *Imperial Hydropathic Hotel Co., Blackpool* v *Hampson* (1882) 23 ChD 1, CA, Bowen
LJ said, at p. 12:

> . . . when persons who are directors of a company are from time to time spoken of by
> judges as agents, trustees, or managing partners of the company, it is essential to recollect
> that such expressions are used not as exhaustive of the powers or responsibilities of those
> persons, but only as indicating useful points of view from which they may for the moment
> and for the particular purpose be considered — points of view at which they seem for the
> moment to be either cutting the circle or falling within the category of the suggested kind.
> It is not meant that they belong to the category, but that it is useful for the purpose of
> the moment to observe that they fall *pro tanto* within the principles which govern that
> particular class.

In chapter 19 we will look at directors as agents of the company, a viewpoint that is useful
when considering the company's liability for its directors' acts; in chapter 16 we will look
at directors as fiduciaries for the company, a viewpoint that is useful when considering the
duties of directors.

In the 19th century it used to be said that directors of a company were trustees of the
company's property, especially in the context of what is now IA 1986, s. 212, which provides
for 'misfeasance proceedings' to be taken against any past or present officer of a company in
liquidation. Before 1986, misfeasance proceedings could be taken for any 'breach of trust'. In
Re National Funds Assurance Co. (1878) 10 ChD 118, Jessel MR said (at p. 128) that directors
who had paid dividends out of capital had been guilty of a breach of trust for the purposes of
misfeasance proceedings. However, unlike true trustees, directors of a company do not hold
the legal title to the company's property, and in *Re Exchange Banking Co., Flitcroft's Case*
(1882) 21 ChD 519, another case of dividends being paid out of capital, Jessel MR preferred to
call the directors 'quasi trustees' (at p. 534). In *Regal (Hastings) Ltd* v *Gulliver* [1967] 2 AC
134, Lord Porter said, at p. 159: 'Directors, no doubt, are not trustees, but they occupy a
fiduciary position towards the company whose board they form'. The misfeasance provision
has now been reworded, and instead of 'breach of trust' now refers to 'breach of fiduciary or
other duty'. It would seem to be no longer necessary to refer to directors as trustees.

15.9   DIRECTORS ARE NOT AGENTS OF MEMBERS

As Buckley LJ pointed out in the passage from *Gramophone & Typewriter Ltd* v *Stanley*
[1908] 2 KB 89 quoted in 15.7.2.4, directors of a company do not, when acting as such, act
as agents of the members of the company. Even a director who is an employee of a
shareholder and was nominated to his directorship by that shareholder does not act as agent
for that shareholder when acting as a director of the company (*Kuwait Asia Bank EC* v
National Mutual Life Nominees Ltd [1991] 1 AC 187). It follows that a member of a
company cannot be vicariously liable for wrongs committed by a director of the company
on the basis of being a principal liable for the wrongs of his agent.

It is possible that particular circumstances may make a director of a company the agent
of members of the company. This occurred, for example, in two cases where directors acted
for members in selling their shares: *Allen* v *Hyatt* (1914) 30 TLR 444 and *Briess* v *Woolley*
[1954] AC 333. In *Allen* v *Hyatt* the directors of a company made an undisclosed profit from
selling the shares of the members of the company and were held liable to them (see 13.5).

In *Briess* v *Woolley*, the managing director of a company made a fraudulent misrepresentation when arranging the sale of the shares of members of the company and the members were held liable as principals to the purchasers for their agent's fraud.

15.10 DIRECTORS' LIABILITY FOR A COMPANY'S WRONGS

A director of a company is not automatically liable for wrongs committed by the company. In relation to torts committed by a company, Slade LJ, giving the judgment of the Court of Appeal in *C. Evans & Sons Ltd* v *Spritebrand Ltd* [1985] 1 WLR 317, said at p. 329:

> . . . a director of a company is not automatically to be identified with his company for the purpose of the law of tort, however small the company may be and however powerful his control over its affairs. . . . In every case where it is sought to make him liable for his company's torts, it is necessary to examine with care what part he played personally in regard to the act or acts complained of.

If a company has committed a tortious act then it may be that it did so as agent for, or jointly with, a director who will then be liable, either vicariously as a principal for an agent's acts, or as a joint tortfeasor. In *Mancetter Developments Ltd* v *Garmanson Ltd* [1986] QB 1212, a director of Garmanson Ltd was held liable for an act of waste (i.e., damage to property leased to the company) which was an act of the company but which was procured and directed by him. In *A.P. Besson Ltd* v *Fulleon Ltd* [1986] FSR 319, a director of a company was held liable, as a joint tortfeasor, for damages for an infringement of copyright committed by his company because of his personal involvement in the actual ordering or physical commission of the tort. In *Fairline Shipping Corporation* v *Adamson* [1975] QB 180, Mr Adamson owned a refrigerated store, which was used by a company of which he was managing director. That company contracted with Fairline Shipping Corporation to store perishable goods in Mr Adamson's store but the goods were ruined because of Mr Adamson's negligence. He was held to be personally liable to Fairline for his negligence. (The company which actually made the contract with Fairline had gone into liquidation and could not have paid any damages.)

In *Williams* v *Natural Life Health Foods Ltd* [1998] 1 WLR 830 the plaintiffs sued for damages for negligent advice given to them under a franchise agreement they had made with Natural Life Health Foods Ltd. They contended that the company's managing director was personally liable for this negligent advice, because the company's own advertising made clear that it relied on his expertise. The plaintiffs had not dealt with the managing director personally, though he had helped to prepare the negligent advice. The House of Lords held that the managing director had never assumed personal responsibility for giving the advice and so was not liable.

For the liability of a director of a company for crimes committed by the company, see 19.8.4.

Where a court has ordered a company to do or not to do something then a director of the company who has been notified of the order has a positive duty to ensure that the order is complied with and may be guilty of contempt of court if the order is not complied with (*Attorney-General for Tuvalu* v *Philatelic Distribution Corporation Ltd* [1990] 1 WLR 926).

15.11 TWO-TIER BOARDS

In Britain and America, the non-executive directors of a company participate in regular board meetings equally with the executive directors, though they meet separately in the remuneration and audit committees from which executive directors are normally excluded. In Germany and the Netherlands, the general idea is that the non-executive directors form a separate board, known as the 'supervisory board' (the board of executive directors being known as the 'management board'). In those countries a two-tier structure of supervisory and management boards is mandatory for large public companies, and a supervisory board has statutory functions, notably, the function of appointing the members of the management board and determining their remuneration.

In Germany, supervisory boards have an important role in the German system of worker participation in management, known as 'co-determination'. In most German public companies, one third of the members of the supervisory board must be elected by the employees of the company while the other two thirds are elected by the shareholders. In the Netherlands, appointments to a company's supervisory board are by co-optation but the company's works council may veto an appointment.

British society has always been based on a tribal separation of workers and management, and managers accordingly view with horror the idea of supervisory boards with employee members. However, L. Miles, 'UK company shareholder protection — a call for reform' (1994) 15 Co Law 202, proposes the adoption of supervisory boards in Britain (without mentioning employee participation) as a means by which shareholders can monitor the performance of executive directors and ensure they act in the interests of their company.

16 Directors' Duties

16.1 INTRODUCTION

Directors of a company normally have the exclusive power to manage the company's business and exercise its powers. Company law gives the directors all this power but says that they must exercise it as fiduciaries for the company and without negligence. This chapter examines first directors' liability for negligence — the so-called 'duty of skill and care' — and then the fiduciary duties of directors.

16.2 DUTY OF SKILL AND CARE

16.2.1 Liability of directors for negligence

16.2.1.1 Statement of directors' duty

If directors of a company are negligent in the performance of their duties as directors then they will be liable to the company for the damage caused by their negligence. For example, in *Dorchester Finance Co. Ltd* v *Stebbing* [1989] BCLC 498, Dorchester Finance Co. Ltd was a moneylending company and had three directors, Stebbing, Parsons and Hamilton. No board meetings were ever held. Parsons and Hamilton left all the affairs of the company to Stebbing: their only contribution was to sign blank cheques on the company's account and leave them for Stebbing to do what he liked with. Stebbing lent the company's money to companies controlled by himself, his clients or his brother but without complying with the statutory controls on moneylending then in force, so that the loans were all unenforceable. All three directors were held liable to the company for their negligence.

According to the general analysis of liability for negligence made by the House of Lords in *Henderson* v *Merrett Syndicates Ltd* [1995] 2 AC 145, the duty of care owed by a director of a company to the company arises from the circumstance that the director assumes responsibility for the property or affairs of the company (per Lord Browne-Wilkinson at p. 205). It is a duty in the law of tort and does not depend on any contract. It could be modified by contract but CA 1985, s. 310 (see 16.9.1), limits contracting out by directors of a company from liability for breach of duty to the company.

The classic statement of a director's duty of care is to be found in the judgment of Romer J in *Re City Equitable Fire Insurance Co. Ltd* [1925] Ch 407. Romer J expressed (at pp. 428–9) three propositions which he thought were supported by reported cases:

(1) A director need not exhibit in the performance of his duties a greater degree of skill than may reasonably be expected from a person of his knowledge and experience. . . . It is perhaps only another way of stating the same proposition to say that directors are not liable for mere errors of judgment. (2) A director is not bound to give continuous attention

to the affairs of his company. His duties are of an intermittent nature to be performed at periodical board meetings, and at meetings of any committee of the board upon which he happens to be placed. He is not, however, bound to attend all such meetings, though he ought to attend whenever, in the circumstances, he is reasonably able to do so. (3) In respect of all duties that, having regard to the exigencies of business, and the articles of association, may properly be left to some other official, a director is, in the absence of grounds for suspicion, justified in trusting that official to perform such duties honestly.

There is no statutorily implied term in a contract for the supply of services as a director that the director will carry out the services with reasonable care and skill, because directors have been exempted from s. 13 of the Supply of Goods and Services Act 1982 by SI 1982 No. 1771. Members of a company have no right to expect a reasonable standard of general management from the company's managing director: it is one of the normal risks of investing in a company that its management may turn out not to be of the highest quality (*Re Elgindata Ltd* [1991] BCLC 959 at p. 994).

The London Stock Exchange has made it a condition of the listing of a company's securities that the directors of the company must have *collectively* appropriate expertise and experience for the management of its business (Listing Rules, para. 3.8).

For an extended discussion, see M.J. Trebilcock, 'The liability of company directors for negligence' (1969) 32 MLR 499. See also Mr Justice Ipp, 'The diligent director' (1997) 18 Co Law 162 on moves to raise the standards by which directors are judged.

16.2.1.2 *Skill required of a director*

Probably the most important aspect of the standard of care imposed by the law on a director is that a director of a company is not required to have any special qualifications. In particular, a director of a company is not required to have any expertise at all in the business in which the company is engaged. In *Re Brazilian Rubber Plantations and Estates Ltd* [1911] 1 Ch 425, Neville J said, at p. 437:

A director's duty has been laid down as requiring him to act with such care as is reasonably to be expected from him, having regard to his knowledge and experience. He is, I think, not bound to bring any special qualifications to his office. He may undertake the management of a rubber company in complete ignorance of everything connected with rubber, without incurring responsibility for the mistakes which may result from such ignorance.

Such reasonable care must, I think, be measured by the care an ordinary man might be expected to take in the same circumstances on his own behalf. He is clearly, I think, not responsible for damages occasioned by errors of judgment.

However, as Neville J went on to say, if a director does have special knowledge relevant to the company's business then he is bound to give the company the advantage of his knowledge when transacting the company's business.

In *Norman* v *Theodore Goddard* [1991] BCLC 1028, Hoffmann J (as he then was) accepted, without hearing argument, counsel's suggestion (based on s. 214(4) of the Insolvency Act 1986 — see 20.12) that the degree of care which a director of a company owes a duty to take when carrying out functions in relation to the company is the care that may reasonably be expected of a person carrying out those functions. It would seem that this could be different from the care that may be reasonably expected from the director, having regard to his knowledge and experience, which was the standard stated by Neville

J in the passage quoted above and accepted by Romer J in *Re City Equitable Fire Insurance Co. Ltd* [1925] Ch 407 (see 16.2.1.1). The director's knowledge and experience may be less than the knowledge and experience that may reasonably be expected of a person who carries out the director's functions. The true nature of the test was not crucial to the case before Hoffmann J, in which negligence was not proved: his lordship held that a director of a property development company was not required to be an expert in tax planning (for more on the case, see 16.2.1.4). In *Re D'Jan of London Ltd* [1994] 1 BCLC 561, Hoffmann LJ again said that the Insolvency Act 1986, s. 214(4), correctly states the common law duty of care of a director but again it was not crucial since his lordship held that the director had acted negligently having regard only to his own knowledge and experience. See C. Nakajima, 'Signing without reading' (1994) 15 Co Law 123; A. Boyle, 'The common law duty of care and enforcement under s. 459' (1996) 17 Co Law 83. Speaking extra-curially, Lord Hoffmann (as he now is) seems now to accept that the standard of care and skill expressed in *Re Brazilian Rubber Plantations and Estates Ltd* and *Re City Equitable Fire Insurance Co. Ltd* is correct ('The fourth annual Leonard Sainer lecture' (1997) 18 Co Law 194).

16.2.1.3 Attendance to the company's affairs

Unless a director is contractually bound to perform specific duties (for example, under a contract of employment) he is, in general, only liable for negligence in what he or she actually does do, not for omitting to attend to the company's business. In *Re Brazilian Rubber Plantations and Estates Ltd* [1911] 1 Ch 425, Neville J said, at p. 437:

> [A director of a company] is not, I think, bound to take any definite part in the conduct of the company's business, but so far as he does undertake it he must use reasonable care in its dispatch.

16.2.1.4 Reliance on company officials and others

In *Dovey* v *Cory* [1901] AC 477, the facts of which are given in 10.5.10, the Earl of Halsbury LC said, at pp. 485–6 :

> The charge of neglect appears to rest on the assertion that Mr Cory, like the other directors, did not attend to any details of business not brought before them by the general manager or the chairman [who were both defrauding the company], and the argument raises a serious question as to the responsibility of all persons holding positions like that of directors, how far they are called upon to distrust and be on their guard against the possibility of fraud being committed by their subordinates of every degree. It is obvious if there is such a duty it must render anything like an intelligent devolution of labour impossible. . . . I cannot think that it can be expected of a director that he should be watching either the inferior officers of the [company] or verifying the calculations of the auditors himself. The business of life could not go on if people could not trust those who are put into a position of trust for the express purpose of attending to details of management.

In *Norman* v *Theodore Goddard* [1991] BCLC 1028, Mr Quirk, a chartered surveyor, was a director of a property company. The shares in the company were the principal assets of a trust administered by Theodore Goddard, a leading firm of solicitors. It was held that it was not negligent for Mr Quirk to rely on the advice of a partner in Theodore Goddard that tax would be saved if the company's surplus cash were lent on deposit to a company which the partner claimed was controlled by Theodore Goddard. In fact the company was controlled by that partner personally and was one of the devices he used to steal money from trust funds administered by his firm.

16.2.2   Forgiveness by members

Provided there has been no fraud or bad faith, and provided their actions have not been illegal, the negligence of directors of a company may be forgiven by unanimous decision of the members, even if that decision has been procured by the negligent directors through their control of voting shares (*Multinational Gas & Petrochemical Co.* v *Multinational Gas & Petrochemical Services Ltd* [1983] Ch 258, CA). All the members must actually approve or ratify the directors' negligence. In *Re D'Jan of London Ltd* [1994] 1 BCLC 561 the negligent director owned 99 per cent of the company's shares. His wife owned the other 1 per cent and had never disagreed with her husband on business matters. Nevertheless, as she had never specifically considered the act of negligence in question she could not be taken to have approved it.

Directors' negligence may be forgiven by a majority of the members provided there is no fraud on the minority (*Pavlides* v *Jensen* [1956] Ch 565; *Daniels* v *Daniels* [1978] Ch 406).

16.3   FIDUCIARY DUTY

16.3.1   Nature of a director's fiduciary duty

The word 'fiduciary' refers to trust and confidence. A fiduciary is a person who agrees, or undertakes, to act for, or on behalf of, or in the interests of, another person in the exercise of a power or discretion which will affect the interests of that other person in a legal or practical sense (per Mason J in *Hospital Products Ltd* v *United States Surgical Corporation* (1984) 156 CLR 41 at pp. 96–7). A fiduciary acts in a representative capacity. There are numerous fiduciary relationships recognised by the law and the categories are not closed (*English* v *Dedham Vale Properties Ltd* [1978] 1 WLR 93 per Slade J at p. 110). The best known examples are the relationships of trustee to beneficiary, agent to principal, solicitor to client, and director to company (*Imperial Mercantile Credit Association* v *Coleman* (1873) LR 6 HL 189; *Regal (Hastings) Ltd* v *Gulliver* [1967] 2 AC 134 in which Lord Porter said, at p. 159: 'Directors, no doubt, are not trustees, but they occupy a fiduciary position towards the company whose board they form').

Fiduciaries have duties imposed on them by equity for the protection of the persons for whom they act. These duties are intended to prevent fiduciaries from exercising their powers or discretions in a manner detrimental to those for whom they act (see 16.4) and to prevent them from abusing the trust and confidence reposed in them (see 16.5 to 16.7). Directors' fiduciary duties are a mandatory element of company law: they are imposed by the courts on all directors of all companies.

The fiduciary duties of the directors of a company considered in this chapter are owed to the company itself and it is the company that can enforce them. Shareholders and creditors cannot enforce the duties (per Dillon LJ in *Multinational Gas & Petrochemical Co.* v *Multinational Gas & Petrochemical Services Ltd* [1983] Ch 258 at p. 288; *Brant Investments Ltd* v *KeepRite Inc.* (1991) 80 DLR (4th) 161), nor can fellow directors (*Lee* v *Chou Wen Hsien* [1984] 1 WLR 1202, PC). In *Western Finance Co. Ltd* v *Tasker Enterprises Ltd* (1979) 106 DLR (3d) 81, it was alleged that a director of a company called Red River Road Builders Ltd had breached his fiduciary duties to the company. The allegation was made in an action brought by another company which was a creditor of Red River (and so had suffered from Red River's insolvency) and had the same shareholders and directors but it was held that this company was not entitled to bring the action.

A company does not owe fiduciary duties to its members (*Esplanade Developments Ltd v Dinive Holdings Pty Ltd* [1980] WAR 151).

It is possible for the directors of a company to owe fiduciary duties to one or more members of the company by virtue of special transactions the directors enter into involving those members. Some examples are given in 13.5. Another example is *Elliott v Wheeldon* [1993] BCLC 53, in which it was held to be arguable that where two persons pursue a joint venture as partners through the medium of a company of which they are directors then each person's actions as a director are subject to the fiduciary duties owed to the other as a partner. However, these are duties arising from special circumstances and are quite separate from the duties considered in this chapter which are duties owed by all directors to their companies by virtue of being a company director.

Fiduciary duties are owed by persons who act as directors but have not been formally appointed as such (*Canadian Aero Service Ltd v O'Malley* (1973) 40 DLR (3d) 371 Supreme Court of Canada; *DPC Estates Pty Ltd v Grey* [1974] 1 NSWLR 443). However, a person who has been elected a director of a company but has not yet taken up office does not owe fiduciary duties to the company, nor does a director of a holding company owe fiduciary duties to a subsidiary of the company if the subsidiary has an independent board (*Lindgren v L & P Estates Ltd* [1968] Ch 572, CA).

Some people argue that it is inappropriate to apply the concept of a fiduciary, which is derived from the concept of a trustee, to company directors. Trustees are supposed to be prudent, risk-averse people whose priority is to preserve the capital value of trust assets whereas company directors are supposed to be risk-taking entrepreneurs. In response it may be argued that prohibition of risk-taking is not central to the law on fiduciary duties — it is a feature of the law on trustees, but in the law on company directors, courts have consistently stated that they will not judge the commercial sense of directors' decisions (see 16.4.3 and 18.3.3.1). What is, and should be, central to the law on fiduciaries is that fiduciaries should be prevented from exercising their powers or discretions in a manner detrimental to those for whom they act and from abusing the trust and confidence reposed in them. It may also be said that economic theory suggests that executive directors of public companies should be more risk-averse than shareholders. An executive director has only one job which he or she will be careful to preserve whereas the typical shareholder has a diversified portfolio of investments so as to be more able to withstand losses on individual shares.

16.3.2   Further reading

The classic text on this subject is P.D. Finn, *Fiduciary Obligations* (Sydney: Law Book Co., 1977). See also two articles by L.S. Sealy, 'Fiduciary relationships' [1962] CLJ 69 and 'The director as trustee' [1967] CLJ 83. There has recently been considerable interest in attempts to give a comprehensive description of the circumstances in which relationships are fiduciary. For recent discussions see D.A. DeMott, 'Beyond metaphor: an analysis of fiduciary obligation' (1988) Duke LJ 879 and J.R.M. Gautreau, 'Demystifying the fiduciary mystique' (1989) 68 Can Bar Rev 1.

16.4   CONSTRAINTS ON THE EXERCISE BY DIRECTORS OF THEIR POWERS

16.4.1   General statement of duty

The general statement of the duty of directors when exercising their directorial powers is normally taken from the judgment of Lord Greene MR in *Re Smith & Fawcett Ltd* [1942] Ch 304, CA. The Master of the Rolls said, at p. 306, that directors of a company must act:

... bona fide in what they consider — not what a court may consider — is in the interests of the company, and not for any collateral purpose.

In *Teck Corporation Ltd* v *Millar* (1972) 33 DLR (3d) 288, British Columbia, Berger J put it as follows (at p. 290):

> The law says that the directors of a company, in exercising their powers, must act bona fide in what they consider to be the best interests of the company. . . . But their purpose must be one countenanced by the law. They cannot exercise their power for an extraneous purpose.

It is noticeable that Berger J expressed the test in terms of the 'best interests' of the company whereas Lord Greene MR spoke only of the 'interests' of the company. In Canada there is a legislative requirement that the directors of a company incorporated under Dominion law must act 'with a view to the best interests of the corporation' (Canada Business Corporations Act, s. 122(1)). In giving the judgment of the Privy Council in *Lee* v *Chou Wen Hsien* [1984] 1 WLR 1202, Lord Brightman, at p. 1206, said that a director of a company had to act in what the director believed to be the best interests of the company. There seems to be a great deal of difference between requiring a director of a company to act in the interests of the company and requiring the director to act in the company's best interests. A duty to act in a company's best interests seems to be a duty always to make the best possible decisions, which seems to be an impossibly high standard. Whether the adjective 'best' is part of the legal requirement in England and Wales does not seem to have been discussed in any reported case (though see *Re Welfab Engineers Ltd* [1990] BCLC 833 discussed in 16.4.9). In the remainder of the discussion here, Lord Greene's formulation without the adjective will be used.

In *Rolled Steel Products (Holdings) Ltd* v *British Steel Corporation* [1986] Ch 246, Slade LJ, at p. 288, said that the tests formulated by Eve J in *Re Lee Behrens & Co. Ltd* [1932] 2 Ch 46 at p. 51 of whether a company has an implied power to enter into a transaction (see 2.3.5.7) 'may well be helpful in considering whether or not in any given case directors have abused the powers vested in them by the company'. These tests are:

(i) Is the transaction reasonably incidental to the carrying on of the company's business? (ii) Is it a bona fide transaction? and (iii) Is it done for the benefit and to promote the prosperity of the company?

If the directors of a company have exercised their powers in breach of this duty the court may intervene. An injunction may be issued to prevent the improper exercise of a power being put into effect; any contract made between the company and a director in breach of the director's fiduciary duty may be rescinded if possible; the directors are liable to replace any of the company's money they have improperly expended; a constructive trust may be imposed on any company property transferred (*Rolled Steel Products (Holdings) Ltd* v *British Steel Corporation*).

In *Bishopsgate Investment Management Ltd* v *Maxwell (No. 2)* [1994] 1 All ER 261, Mr Ian Maxwell was a director of Bishopsgate Investment Management Ltd, which was the trustee of the assets of a number of pension schemes for employees of companies controlled by his father, Robert Maxwell. As a director of Bishopsgate he signed a transfer of five parcels of its shares, for nil consideration, to Robert Maxwell Group plc, of which he was also a director. He offered no evidence that it was in Bishopsgate's interests to make this gift, the sole purpose of which was to provide funds for the Maxwell family companies. It was held that Ian was liable to pay damages for the loss caused to Bishopsgate by the gift.

Provided the directors of a company do not cause it to enter into an illegal transaction, an exercise of their powers in breach of fiduciary duty is nevertheless an *intra vires* exercise of the powers: it is not an action in excess of powers. Therefore, any contract made is voidable, not void (*Spackman* v *Evans* (1868) LR 3 HL 171 per Lord Romilly at p. 244; *Bamford* v *Bamford* [1970] Ch 212, CA; *Winthrop Investments Ltd* v *Winns Ltd* [1975] 2 NSWLR 666 per Samuels JA at pp. 679–80 and per Mahoney JA at pp. 688–9). As Megarry J put it in *Gaiman* v *National Association for Mental Health* [1977] Ch 317 at p. 330, 'A breach of trust is not a nullity but a ground for complaint'.

16.4.2 One duty or two?

In *Hogg* v *Cramphorn Ltd* [1967] Ch 254, Buckley J held that the statement of Lord Greene MR in *Re Smith & Fawcett Ltd* [1942] Ch 304, CA, quoted in 16.4.1 meant that directors of a company will be at fault if they act *either:*

(a)   not bona fide in the interests of the company (subjective element), *or*

(b)   for an improper purpose (objective element) *even if* they reasonably and accurately believe they are acting bona fide in the interests of the company.

In *Teck Corporation Ltd* v *Millar* (1972) 33 DLR (3d) 288, British Columbia, however, Berger J said, at pp. 312–17, that the purpose for which directors acted would not be improper if the directors honestly believed that they were acting in the best interests of the company and there were reasonable grounds for that belief, thus reducing the test to the simple one of whether the directors were acting bona fide in the interests of the company (see the casenote by B.V. Slutsky, 'Canadian rejection of the *Hogg* v *Cramphorn* "improper purposes" principle — a step forward?' (1974) 37 MLR 457 and J.S. Ziegel, 'Directors' powers and the proper purposes' [1974] JBL 85).

In *Howard Smith Ltd* v *Ampol Petroleum Ltd* [1974] AC 821, PC, Lord Wilberforce rejected Berger J's approach and emphasised that, in a case in which the court has found that directors have believed they were acting bona fide in the interests of the company, the court must find whether the purpose for which the directors acted was objectively proper or improper, though his lordship also made it clear that the range of proper purposes may be wider than was previously thought. (Lord Wilberforce's judgment is considered in detail in 16.4.10.) See the casenote by J.R. Birds, 'Proper purposes as a head of directors' duties' (1974) 37 MLR 580. Interestingly, in *Teck Corporation Ltd* v *Millar,* Berger J, at p. 331, said that if his approach was wrong it would not affect his decision because in his view the directors in the case had acted for a proper purpose. This was confirmed by Lord Wilberforce in *Howard Smith Ltd* v *Ampol Petroleum Ltd* at pp. 836–7 , and the preferability of that reasoning is argued in a detailed article by F. Iacobucci, 'The exercise of directors' powers: — the battle of Afton Mines' (1973) 11 Osgoode Hall LJ 353. See further, M.E. Bennun, 'Directors' powers to issue shares: two contrasting decisions' (1975) 24 ICLQ 359.

In England and Wales, the Privy Council's statement of the law has been accepted by Goulding J in *Mutual Life Insurance Co. of New York* v *Rank Organisation Ltd* [1985] BCLC 11 and by Harman J in *Re a Company (No. 00370 of 1987)* [1988] 1 WLR 1068, and is the basis of the remaining discussion in this book. It is also the law in Singapore (*Goh Kim Hai Edward* v *Pacific Can Investment Holdings Ltd* [1996] 2 SLR 109 per Judith Prakash J at p. 140). In Canada, however, Berger J's approach has been accepted in *Olson* v *Phoenix Industrial Supply Ltd* (1984) 9 DLR (4th) 451, Manitoba, in which directors' exercise of powers for an improper purpose was held to be valid because the directors believed they were acting in the best interests of the company, but rejected in *Exco Corporation Ltd* v *Nova Scotia Savings & Loan Co.* (1987) 78 NSR (2d) 91, in which such an exercise of powers for an improper purpose was held invalid despite the directors' bona fides. For a discussion of this conflict in Canadian law, see M. St P. Baxter, 'The fiduciary obligations of directors of a target company in resisting an unsolicited takeover bid' (1988) 20 Ottawa L Rev 63.

For a detailed discussion of the way in which increasing judicial intervention in corporate decision-making has been facilitated by putting more emphasis on an objective assessment of whether directors' decisions are taken for proper purposes rather than on whether their decisions are bona fide in the interests of their company, see L.S. Sealy '"Bona fides" and "proper purposes" in corporate decisions' (1989) 15 Mon LR 265. See also N.C.A. Franzi, 'The subjective and objective elements of a company board's power to issue shares' (1976) 10 MULR 392; S. Burridge, 'Wrongful rights issues' (1981) 44 MLR 40, at pp. 50–2 ; and the discussion by Powell J in *Russell Kinsela Pty Ltd* v *Kinsela* [1983] 1 NSWLR 452 at pp. 458–62.

16.4.3 Bona fide in the interests of the company

In *Charterbridge Corporation Ltd* v *Lloyds Bank Ltd* [1970] Ch 62, Pennycuick J said, at p. 74, 'The proper test, I think, [of whether a director of a company has acted bona fide in the interests of the company] . . . must be whether an intelligent and honest man in the position of a director of the company concerned, could, in the whole of the existing circumstances, have reasonably believed that the transactions were for the benefit of the company'.

In *Richard Brady Franks Ltd* v *Price* (1937) 58 CLR 112, the High Court of Australia expressed the criterion to be applied to directors' actions as 'bona fide for the benefit of the company as a whole' — the same terms as were used in *Allen* v *Gold Reefs of West Africa Ltd* [1900] 1 Ch 656 to state the limitation on the members' power to alter the articles of the company (see 3.5.3.5). Latham CJ in *Richard Brady Franks Ltd* v *Price* said, at p. 136, that a person challenging an action of directors must show 'that they did not honestly act for what they regarded as the benefit of the company'.

In examining a bona fide exercise of a power for a proper purpose in the interests of the company, the court (as Lord Greene MR suggested in the dictum quoted in 16.4.1) does not inquire whether the directors took the optimum decision. As Lord Wilberforce said in *Howard Smith Ltd* v *Ampol Petroleum Ltd* [1974] AC 821 at p. 832:

> There is no appeal on merits from management decisions to courts of law: nor will courts of law assume to act as a kind of supervisory board over decisions within the powers of management honestly arrived at.

As Latham CJ put it in *Richard Brady Franks Ltd* v *Price*, at p. 136, 'It is not for a court to determine whether or not the action of the directors was wise'.

A company has a dual aspect as an association of its members and as a person separate from its members. As with the members' exercise of their power to alter articles, the idea that directors' powers must be exercised bona fide in the interests of the company inevitably raises the question whether it is the interests of the company as a separate entity or the interests of members, or both, that must be considered.

In *Mutual Life Insurance Co. of New York* v *Rank Organisation Ltd* [1985] BCLC 11, Goulding J said, at p. 21, that provisions of a company's constitution conferring powers on its directors are subject to two implied terms:

First, the time-honoured rule that the directors' powers are to be exercised in good faith in the interests of the company, and secondly, that they must be exercised fairly as between different shareholders.

The directors of the Rank Organisation had decided to issue new shares and part of the issue was made available to existing shareholders at a favourable price, but shareholders living in North America were excluded so as to save the company the high cost of complying with US and Canadian legislation concerning public offers of shares in those countries. It was held that the directors had not acted in breach of duty in preferring the interests of the company as a separate person to the interests of some of its members. This was followed by Arden J in *Re BSB Holdings Ltd (No. 2)* [1996] 1 BCLC 155. Her ladyship said, at p. 251: 'The law does not require the interests of the company to be sacrificed in the particular interests of a group of shareholders'.

In *Gaiman* v *National Association for Mental Health* [1971] Ch 317, Megarry J observed, at p. 330, that as a company is an artificial legal entity, it is not easy to determine what is in its best interests without paying due regard to its present and future members as a whole. Nevertheless his lordship went on to decide, at pp. 335–6, that whereas persons exercising a power of expelling members from an unincorporated association may have a duty to the persons sought to be expelled to observe the rules of natural justice, what distinguished a registered company from an unincorporated association is precisely that:

Where there is corporate personality, the directors or others exercising the powers in question [in this case, the board of directors was described as the 'council'] are bound not merely by their duties towards the other members, but also by their duties towards the corporation. These duties may be inconsistent with the observance of natural justice. . . . Where, as in the present case, their duty [to the corporation] may impel the council to exercise the power with great speed, whereas natural justice would require delay, I think that that indicates that the council is intended to be able to exercise its powers unfettered by natural justice.

In a similar case in Australia, though, the court decided that the directors' duties to the company as a separate person did not permit them to ignore the rules of natural justice (*Australian Securities Commission* v *Multiple Sclerosis Society of Tasmania* (1993) 10 ACSR 489).

In relation to the fiduciary duties of directors of a business company to act in the interests of the company as an association of its members, it is usually assumed that the only interest the members have is in maximising the return on their investments. However, this is not necessarily easy to define. Do the directors have to ensure the company pays the highest possible annual dividends, or that the market price for its shares is as high as possible, or should they ensure the long-term growth and stability of the company? How risky should the shareholders' investment be?

In Delaware, in *Paramount Communications Inc.* v *Time Inc.* (1990) 571 A 2d 1140, the court accepted that it was legitimate for the directors of Time Inc. to decide that it was in the best interests of their company to go ahead with a merger with another company and not to allow shareholders the opportunity of selling their shares to an unwelcome takeover bidder, even though the bidder was offering considerably more than the current market price for the company's shares and many shareholders would have found the bid attractive. It is possible to interpret this case in terms of a preference for long-term increase in the company's value over short-term gain for the shareholders, but the court said, at p. 1150:

> . . . we think it unwise to place undue emphasis upon long-term versus short-term corporate strategy. . . . the question of 'long-term' versus 'short-term' values is largely irrelevant because directors, generally, are obliged to chart a course for a corporation which is in its best interests without regard to a fixed investment horizon.

It seems that the court was defining the directors' duties in terms of the interests of the company as a separate person ('*its* best interests'). The court expressly rejected the idea that the directors' duty was simply to maximise shareholder value in the short term.

A common criticism of British business people is that their approach is too short term, preferring immediate profits to long-term growth, and that this is bad for the British economy. See Commission on Public Policy and British Business, *Promoting Prosperity: a Business Agenda for Britain* (London: Vintage, 1997).

The interests of a company as a separate person and the interests of its members are enforced in different ways. The fiduciary duty of the directors of a company to act in the interests of the company is owed to the company as a separate person, and the company is the proper plaintiff to enforce that duty: the duty is not owed to individual members (per Dillon LJ in *Multinational Gas & Petrochemical Co.* v *Multinational Gas & Petrochemical Services Ltd* [1983] Ch 258 at p. 288). The members of a company have a statutory right under CA 1985, s. 459, to petition for relief of conduct of the company's affairs which is unfairly prejudicial to their interests (see 18.6). The existence of the unfair prejudice remedy makes it unnecessary to extend directors' fiduciary duties to members (*Brant Investments Ltd* v *KeepRite Inc.* (1991) 80 DLR (4th) 161).

16.4.4   Consideration of the interests of other persons

In recent years the courts and Parliament have formulated the fiduciary duties of directors so as to require them to consider the interests of persons other than the company as a separate entity and/or as an association of its members (see 16.4.3). These other interests will be considered in 16.4.5 to 16.4.8.

The principal problem with imposing on directors a duty to consider the interests of persons other than the company is whether that duty should be owed directly to those persons or whether the company can be entrusted with enforcing its directors' duty to consider their interests. It may be that if the directors of a company take a decision without considering some interest which they ought to consider then the decision will be unlawful and could be challenged by a member under the principle discussed in 18.4.12. The situation is made more difficult by confusion over whether the interests which the directors of a company have to consider are interests that the company must promote. Accordingly it is not clear that acting in favour of these other interests is acting in the company's interests.

16.4.5   Interests of employees

CA 1985, s. 309 (first enacted in 1980), provides that:

> (1)   The matters to which the directors of a company are to have regard in the performance of their functions include the interests of the company's employees in general, as well as the interests of its members.

(2)   Accordingly, the duty imposed by this section on the directors of a company is owed by them to the company (and the company alone) and is enforceable in the same way as any other fiduciary duty owed to a company by its directors.

A shadow director also owes this duty (s. 309(3)) but a holding company does not owe the duty to its subsidiary if the only reason for treating the holding company as a shadow director of that subsidiary is that the subsidiary's directors are accustomed to act in accordance with the holding company's directions or instructions (s. 741(3)).

Section 309 specifically states that the duty it imposes on directors is owed only to the company. This must mean that the duty to consider the interests of employees is not owed to, and is not enforceable by, the employees themselves. It also does not state that a company must promote the interests of its employees so raising the question whether directors of a company who act in the interests of its employees are acting in the company's interests.

For discussions of directors' duties to have regard to the interests of employees, see Anthony Boyle and Barry J. Mordsley. 'The Companies Act 1980 (4)' (1980) 1 Co Law 280 at pp. 284–5, and P.G. Xuereb, 'The juridification of industrial relations through company law reform' (1988) 51 MLR 156. The interests of employees have traditionally been given scant attention in British company law: see B. Bercusson, 'Workers, corporate enterprise and the law', in R. Lewis (ed.), *Labour Law in Britain* (Oxford: Basil Blackwell, 1986); Lord Wedderburn of Charlton, 'Companies and employees: common law or social dimension?' (1993) 109 LQR 220.

16.4.6   Interests of creditors

16.4.6.1   Common law duty
In *West Mercia Safetywear Ltd* v *Dodd* [1988] BCLC 250, the Court of Appeal held that a director of an insolvent company must have regard to the interests of its creditors. The court adopted into English law a principle which had previously been enunciated in Australia and New Zealand in such cases as *Walker* v *Wimborne* (1976) 137 CLR 1; *Nicholson* v *Permakraft (NZ) Ltd* [1985] 1 NZLR 242; and *Kinsela* v *Russell Kinsela Pty Ltd* (1986) 4 NSWLR 722. Dillon LJ in *West Mercia Safetywear Ltd* v *Dodd* approved the following statement by Street CJ in *Kinsela* v *Russell Kinsela Pty Ltd* at p. 730:

In a solvent company the proprietary interests of the shareholders entitle them as a general body to be regarded as the company when questions of the duty of directors arise. If, as a general body, they authorise or ratify a particular action of the directors, there can be no challenge to the validity of what the directors have done. But where a company is insolvent the interests of the creditors intrude. They become prospectively entitled, through the mechanism of liquidation, to displace the power of the shareholders and directors to deal with the company's assets. It is in a practical sense their assets and not the shareholders' assets that, through the medium of the company, are under the management of the directors pending either liquidation, return to solvency, or the imposition of some alternative administration.

Earlier in *Lonrho Ltd* v *Shell Petroleum Co. Ltd* [1980] 1 WLR 627, HL, Lord Diplock had explained, at p. 634, that in relation to the principle that directors of a company must act in the best interests of the company, 'These are not exclusively those of its shareholders but may include those of its creditors'.

Accordingly, if directors of a company, at a time when the company is insolvent, deal with its property in a way that is prejudicial to the interests of creditors then they are in breach of their fiduciary duty to the company. This is especially so if the purpose of the transaction is to place the company's assets beyond the reach of the creditors (*Kinsela* v *Russell Kinsela Pty Ltd*; *Australian Growth Resources Corporation Pty Ltd* v *Van Reesema* (1988) 13 ACLR 261, South Australia). For the facts of *West Mercia Safetywear Ltd* v *Dodd*, see 20.11.3.

In *Re Halt Garage (1964) Ltd* [1982] 3 All ER 1016, Oliver J said, at p. 1039, that those who deal with a limited company: 'are entitled to have the capital kept intact'.

If a solvent company is regarded as serving the interests of its members so that acting in the company's interests means acting in the members' interests then the view that the creditors of an insolvent company replace the members as the 'owners' or at least residual claimants implies that an insolvent company must serve the interests of its creditors so that directors of an insolvent company who act in the interests of its creditors are acting in the company's interests.

It has been held in Australia that a director of a company also has a duty to the company to consider the interests of the company's creditors when the company is not insolvent but where, to the knowledge of the director, there is a real risk of insolvency (*Grove* v *Flavel* (1986) 43 SASR 410).

As well as a duty to the company to consider the interests of its creditors when the company is insolvent or there is a real risk of insolvency, it appeared for a short time that directors might owe a duty directly to the creditors in such circumstances. In *Winkworth* v *Edward Baron Development Co. Ltd* [1986] 1 WLR 1512, HL, Lord Templeman (with whom the other Law Lords agreed) said, at p. 1516:

> . . . a company owes a duty to its creditors, present and future . . . to keep its property inviolate and available for the repayment of its debts. The conscience of the company, as well as its management, is confided to its directors. A duty is owed by the directors to the company and to the creditors of the company to ensure that the affairs of the company are properly administered and that its property is not dissipated or exploited for the benefit of the directors themselves to the prejudice of the creditors.

His lordship added that breaches of this duty do not matter if the directors can maintain the company's solvency and see that all its creditors are paid in full. In *Multinational Gas & Petrochemical Co.* v *Multinational Gas & Petrochemical Services Ltd* [1983] Ch 258, CA, Dillon LJ made the stronger statement that, when a company is solvent, neither it nor its directors owe any duty to creditors. In *Re Joshua Shaw & Sons Ltd* (1988) 5 BCC 188, Hoffmann J assumed that the New South Wales Court of Appeal had formulated a duty to creditors in *Kinsela* v *Russell Kinsela Pty Ltd*, though it is respectfully submitted that the court in that case was concerned only with a duty to the company to consider the interests of creditors.

However, in *Kuwait Asia Bank EC* v *National Mutual Life Nominees Ltd* [1991] 1 AC 187, Lord Templeman was a member of the Judicial Committee of the Privy Council which stated (at p. 217 per Lord Lowry) that: 'A director does not by reason only of his position as director owe any duty to creditors or to trustees for creditors of the company'. This seems finally to dispose of the possibility of creditors of a company taking action against its directors, and this has been confirmed in *Yukong Line Ltd* v *Rendsburg Investments Corporation (No. 2)* [1998] 1 WLR 294.

See further, V. Finch, 'Directors' duties towards creditors' (1989) 10 Co Law 23; C.A. Riley, 'Directors' duties and the interests of creditors' (1989) 10 Co Law 87; R. Grantham,

'The judicial extension of directors' duties to creditors' [1991] JBL 1; J.S. Ziegel, 'Creditors as corporate stakeholders: the quiet revolution — an Anglo-Canadian perspective' (1993) 43 UTLJ 511. For criticism of the concept of a duty to consider the interests of creditors see an article and a casenote by L.S. Sealy, 'Directors' "wider" responsibilities — problems conceptual, practical and procedural' (1987) 13 Mon LR 164; *f*Directors' duties — an unnecessary gloss' [1988] CLJ 175. *f*

16.4.6.2 *Statutory duty*

In Britain, the common law duty of directors of a company to consider the interests of the company's creditors has, since 28 April 1986, been put on a statutory basis by what is now IA 1986, s. 214 (wrongful trading). Under this section, the court may declare a director or shadow director of a company in liquidation liable to contribute to the assets of the company if the director knew, or ought to have concluded, that the company had no reasonable prospect of not going into insolvent liquidation and did not take every step he or she ought to have taken to minimise the potential loss to the company's creditors.

This duty arises only where the company has no reasonable prospect of not going into insolvent liquidation, which is similar to the limitation on the circumstances in which the common law duty arises.

This provision is considered in more detail in 20.12.

16.4.7   Interests of persons for whom the company is a fiduciary

In *Hurley* v *BGH Nominees Pty Ltd* (1984) 37 SASR 499, South Australia, Walters J said, at p. 510:

> I do not think it can rightly be said that the fiduciary responsibility of a director is owed simply to the company by virtue of his status as a director and that it does not extend to responsibility to shareholders or, indeed, to beneficiaries of a trust of which the company is trustee.

In England it has been held that directors of a company are not directly in a fiduciary relationship with persons for whom the company is a fiduciary (*Bath* v *Standard Land Co. Ltd* [1911] 1 Ch 618, CA). However, this case has not been followed in New Zealand (*Lion Breweries Ltd* v *Scarrott* (1986) 3 NZCLC 100,042) and may be compared with *Re The French Protestant Hospital* [1951] Ch 567 in which it was held that directors of a chartered corporation which held property on charitable trusts should themselves be treated as trustees of the charity. See further A.R. Coleman, 'Duties of directors of corporate trustees to beneficiaries' (1984) 2 C & SLJ 147; R.I. Barrett (1985) 59 ALJ 46.

The fiduciary duties of the directors of a company may be enforced by the beneficiaries of a trust of which the company is trustee (*Baden* v *Société Générale pour Favoriser le Développement du Commerce et de l'Industrie en France SA* [1993] 1 WLR 509, point not considered on appeal).

16.4.8   Other constituencies

For a long time there has been discussion over whether the directors of a company should consider the interests of persons other than the company as a separate person and the members of the company. The introduction into British company law in the 1980s of duties to consider the interests of employees (see 16.4.5) and creditors (see 16.4.6) was a notable development but there have been many suggestions that directors should consider the interests of other groups (or 'constituencies' or 'stakeholders'). In the USA many state legislatures, beginning with Pennsylvania in 1983, have enacted provisions allowing corporate directors to consider the interests of employees, customers, creditors, suppliers, and communities in which the corporation has facilities, as well as national and state economies and other community and societal considerations. These 'other constituencies statutes' have usually been enacted to enable directors to take action in defence against hostile takeover bids where it is expected that the bidder, if successful, will change drastically the taken-over company's operations on which the other constituencies depend. However, the statutes are not expressed to be limited to that situation. As explained in 16.4.12, the British position under the City Code is that directors cannot take action to frustrate a takeover offer without the approval of existing members.

Other constituencies statutes acknowledge the continuing importance that a company may have for many persons other than its members. It is argued that companies must acknowledge these responsibilities and act as good citizens in a socially responsible way (see E.M. Dodd, 'For whom are corporate managers trustees?' (1932) 45 Harv L Rev 1145; J.B. White, 'How should we talk about corporations? The languages of economics and of citizenship' (1985) 94 Yale LJ 1416). If acting in a socially responsible way is a citizenship duty of a company as a separate person then directors who cause it to act in that way are acting in the interests of the company. Dodd's article prompted a response by A.A. Berle, 'For whom corporate managers *are* trustees' (1932) 45 Harv L Rev 1365, who vigorously opposed the idea that corporate managers should have a free hand to use shareholders' money to promote the managers' own ideas of what was socially desirable (see also M. Friedman, *Capitalism and Freedom* (University of Chicago Press, 1962), pp. 133–6). Berle's 1932 view was maintained by the courts in the USA but arguments for and against social responsibility continued: see, for example, Lord Wedderburn of Charlton, 'The social responsibility of companies' (1985) 15 MULR 4; Lord Wedderburn of Charlton, 'Trust, corporation and the worker' (1985) 23 Osgoode Hall LJ 203; C.D. Stone, 'Corporate social responsibility: what it might mean if it were really to matter' (1986) 71 Iowa L Rev 557; H.J. Glasbeek, 'The corporate social responsibility movement — the latest in Maginot Lines to save capitalism' (1988) 11 Dalhousie LJ 363. Berle eventually admitted that in practice when corporate managers in the USA had acted in the public interest they had acted wisely and had forestalled the need for government action ('Modern functions of the corporate system' (1962) 62 Colum L Rev 433 at pp. 442–4). The Committee on Corporate Laws, 'Other constituencies statutes: potential for confusion' (1990) 45 Bus Law 2253 asserts that Berle's 1932 view should still prevail and points out that the other constituency statutes which have been enacted may not have much practical significance because, like the British provision requiring directors to consider the interests of employees, they do not provide any mechanism by which representatives of the other constituencies can require directors to take them into consideration. It seems that the stock market in the USA has not reduced share prices in response to the enactment of other constituencies statutes, possibly because of a general perception that they are practically ineffective (R. Romano, 'Comment: what is the value of other constituency statutes to shareholders?' (1993) 43 UTLJ 533). For a full discussion see the special issue of the *University of Toronto Law Journal* entitled 'The corporate stakeholder debate: the classical theory and its critics', vol. 43, No. 3 (Summer 1993).

In the consultation document introducing its review of company law (see 0.3.1.6) the DTI displays an ambivalent attitude to extending the duties of directors to other constituencies. On p. 17 of the document it says that the review will 'identify in which areas there should be mandatory rules to protect the interests of shareholders, creditors, employees, and other participants', and the draft terms of reference (p. 14) speak of company law protecting, 'through regulation where necessary, the interests of those involved with the enterprise, including shareholders, creditors and employees'. But on p. 10 of the document it says:

A wider issue for the review is whether directors' duty to act in the interests of their company should be interpreted as meaning simply that they should act in the interests of their shareholders, or whether they should also take account of other interests, such as those of employees, creditors, customers, the environment, and the wider community. . . . The review hopes to stimulate wider discussions of such concerns to see if there is common ground on whether and how they need to be further addressed — whether they just represent interesting philosophical ideas and ideals or whether they lead to concrete proposals that should be pursued.

The Commission on Public Policy and British Business, *Promoting Prosperity: a Business Agenda for Britain* (London: Vintage, 1997) recommended that British companies legislation should be amended along the lines of the Pennsylvania law, to enable directors to take a broader view of their responsibilities (p. 107).

16.4.9 Conflict of interests

A great problem for a director who is required to consider the interests of several different persons is what to do where those interests conflict, whether it is a conflict between groups, for example, between members and creditors, or a conflict within a group, for example, between different members.

As far as a conflict of interest between creditors and any other group is concerned, it seems that creditors' interests have to be given priority where there is no reasonable prospect of the company not going into insolvent liquidation and that this is the only situation in which there is a duty to consider creditors' interests. Also, if a company goes into insolvent liquidation, the creditors have the right to appoint the liquidator and thus take control of the company. Nevertheless, in *Re Welfab Engineers Ltd* [1990] BCLC 833, Hoffmann J held that it is not correct to say that the duty of directors is to act 'to the best advantage of creditors': their duty is not to act in a way that would leave creditors in a worse position than on liquidation. See further R. Grantham, 'Directors' duties and insolvent companies' (1991) 54 MLR 576.

In both *Mutual Life Insurance Co. of New York* v *Rank Organisation Ltd* [1985] BCLC 11 and *Re BSB Holdings Ltd (No. 2)* [1996] 1 BCLC 155 the directors of a company were permitted to prefer the interests of the company as a separate person to the interests of a minority of its members (see 16.4.3).

Where there is a conflict between members it seems that the favoured solution is to require one group to buy out the other on an application for relief of unfairly prejudicial conduct of the company's affairs (see 18.6).

16.4.10 The proper-purposes doctrine

Directors of a company have authority to exercise powers in their management of the company's affairs. But there may be limits on the purposes for which those powers may be exercised and thus limits on their authority. When a power is exercised for a purpose outside its limits (variously described as an improper, extraneous or collateral purpose), the court may intervene.

In *Re Cameron's Coalbrook Steam Coal, & Swansea & Lougher Railway Co, Bennett's Case* (1854) 5 De G M & G 284, Turner LJ said, at p. 298:

> . . . in the exercise of the powers given to them . . . [directors] must, as I conceive, keep within the proper limits. Powers given to them for one purpose cannot, in my opinion, be used by them for another and different purpose. To permit such proceedings on the part of directors of companies would be to sanction not the use but the abuse of their powers. It would be to give effect and validity to an illegal exercise of a legal power.

Use of a power for a purpose which is outside the objects of the company is a special example of using a power for an improper purpose and is considered in 19.5.7.

Sometimes the limits on the exercise of a power may be found in the articles of association. In general, however, it is not possible to lay down in advance, as rules of law, the limits beyond which directors may never pass in exercising a particular power. Every case depends upon a scrutiny, in context, of its own relevant facts (*Advance Bank of Australia Ltd v FAI Insurances Australia Ltd* (1987) 9 NSWLR 464 per Kirby P at p. 485).

In *Howard Smith Ltd v Ampol Petroleum Ltd* [1974] AC 821, Lord Wilberforce, giving the judgment of the Privy Council, said, at p. 835:

> To define in advance exact limits beyond which directors must not pass is, in their lordships' view, impossible. This clearly cannot be done by enumeration, since the variety of situations facing directors of different types of company in different situations cannot be anticipated. No more, in their lordships' view, can this be done by the use of a phrase — such as 'bona fide in the interest of the company as a whole', or 'for some corporate purpose'. Such phrases, if they do anything more than restate the general principle applicable to fiduciary powers, at best serve, negatively, to exclude from the area of validity cases where the directors are acting sectionally, or partially: i.e., improperly favouring one section of the shareholders against another . . .
>
> In their lordships' opinion it is necessary to start with a consideration of the power whose exercise is in question. . . . Having ascertained, on a fair view, the nature of this power, and having defined as can best be done in the light of modern conditions the, or some, limits within which it may be exercised, it is then necessary for the court, if a particular exercise of it is challenged, to examine the substantial purpose for which it was exercised, and to reach a conclusion whether that purpose was proper or not. In doing so it will necessarily give credit to the bona fide opinion of the directors, if such is found to exist, and will respect their judgment as to matters of management; having done this, the ultimate conclusion has to be as to the side of a fairly broad line on which the case falls.

In many cases, directors' exercise of a power leads to two or more effects, achieving one or more of the effects is a proper purpose and achieving the remainder is an improper purpose. The court is therefore required to find whether achieving the improper effects was the 'substantial' purpose, or the 'dominant' purpose (a phrase used in *Whitehouse v Carlton Hotel Pty Ltd* (1987) 162 CLR 285 at p. 294) or 'the moving cause' (a phrase used by Lord Shaw in *Hindle v John Cotton Ltd* (1919) 56 SLR 625, HL, at p. 631). Thus the fact that a directors' exercise of power benefits themselves does not invalidate the exercise of the power if the self-benefit was not the dominant purpose (*Hirsche v Sims* [1894] AC 654, PC; *Richard Brady Franks Ltd v Price* (1937) 58 CLR 112; *Mills v Mills* (1938) 60 CLR 150). In *Hindle v John Cotton Ltd,* Viscount Finlay said, at pp. 630–1 :

Where the question is one of abuse of powers, the state of mind of those who acted, and the motive on which they acted, are all important, and you may go into the question of what their intention was, collecting from the surrounding circumstances all the materials which genuinely throw light upon that question of the state of mind of the directors so as to show whether they were honestly acting in discharge of their powers in the interests of the company or were acting from some by-motive, possibly of personal advantage, or for any other reason.

It has been said in the High Court of Australia that an improper purpose would invalidate the exercise of a power if the power would not have been exercised had that purpose not been present (*Mills* v *Mills,* per Dixon J at p. 186; *Whitehouse* v *Carlton Hotel Pty Ltd,* per Mason, Dean and Dawson JJ at p. 294). The concept of a dominant purpose is not easy to apply in practice. For a discussion see D.M.J. Bennett, 'The ascertainment of purpose when bona fides are in issue — some logical problems' (1989) 12 Syd LR 5.

Acting bona fide in the interests of the company is not an excuse for acting for a dominant improper purpose, especially where the directors are acting in their own self-interest (*Ashburton Oil NL* v *Alpha Minerals NL* (1971) 123 CLR 614 per Menzies J at p. 627; *Howard Smith Ltd* v *Ampol Petroleum Ltd* at p. 834 though the contrary was held in *Olson* v *Phoenix Industrial Supply Ltd* (1984) 9 DLR (4th) 451). In *Advance Bank of Australia Ltd* v *FAI Insurances Australia Ltd,* Kirby P said, at p. 485:

. . . statements by the directors about their subjective intention, whilst relevant, are not conclusive of the bona fides of the directors or of the purposes for which they acted as they did. In this sense, although the search is for the subjective intentions of the directors, it is a search which must be conducted objectively as the court decides whether to accept or discount the assertions which the directors make about their motives and purposes: cf. Megarry V-C in *Cayne* v *Global Natural Resources plc* (12 August 1982 unreported); affirmed on another point [1984] 1 All ER 225.

In *Howard Smith Ltd* v *Ampol Petroleum Ltd,* Lord Wilberforce said, at p. 832:

. . . when a dispute arises whether directors of a company made a particular decision for one purpose or for another, or whether, there being more than one purpose, one or another purpose was the substantial or primary purpose, the court, in their lordships' opinion, is entitled to look at the situation objectively in order to estimate how critical or pressing, or substantial or, *per contra,* insubstantial an alleged requirement may have been. If it finds that a particular requirement, though real, was not urgent, or critical, at the relevant time, it may have reason to doubt, or discount, the assertions of individuals that they acted solely in order to deal with it, particularly when the action they took was unusual or even extreme.

16.4.11 Power to allot shares

Many of the cases in which the question of an improper use of a power has arisen are concerned with directors using their power to allot shares in order to give votes to their friends and so prevent a change in the control of the company, and it is in these cases that the proper-purposes doctrine has been most fully explored in recent years.

In British company law the directors' power to allot shares is now restricted by CA 1985 as described in 6.2.5 and 6.2.6. Before these restrictions came into force it was established that:

(a)   If directors allot shares for the dominant purpose of preserving their own control of the management of the company (by ensuring that there is a majority of votes in their favour) then the allotment is invalid (*Fraser* v *Whalley* (1864) 2 Hem & M 10; *Punt* v *Symons & Co. Ltd* [1903] 2 Ch 506; *Piercy* v *S. Mills & Co. Ltd* [1920] 1 Ch 77; *Hogg* v *Cramphorn Ltd* [1967] Ch 254; *Ashburton Oil NL* v *Alpha Minerals NL* (1971) 123 CLR 614).

(b)   If directors allot shares for the dominant purpose of manipulating voting power by favouring one shareholder or group of shareholders at the expense of another non-consenting shareholder or group, the allotment will be invalid (*Howard Smith Ltd* v *Ampol Petroleum Ltd* [1974] AC 821, PC; *Whitehouse* v *Carlton Hotel Pty Ltd* (1987) 162 CLR 285).

(c)   If directors allot shares for the dominant purpose of benefiting themselves financially, the allotment will be invalid (*Ngurli Ltd* v *McCann* (1953) 90 CLR 425).

See further, K.E. Lindgren, 'The fiduciary nature of a company board's power to issue shares' (1971–2) 10 West Aust L Rev 364.

In *Re Looe Fish Ltd* [1993] BCLC 1160, a director who allotted himself shares in order to provide himself with sufficient votes to defeat a motion to appoint further directors of whom he disapproved was disqualified from being a director for two and a half years.

In the *Howard Smith Ltd* case (an appeal from New South Wales), a company was being threatened with a takeover by two associates who between them held 55 per cent of the company's shares. The company needed more capital but proposed to obtain it by issuing $4\frac{1}{2}$ million shares to members other than the takeover bidders: this allotment would have reduced the takeover bidders to a minority in the company and was held to be a misuse of the directors' powers. (Pre-emption rights, see 6.2.6, are important in preventing manoeuvres like this.)

16.4.12   Response to takeover bids

A takeover bid is an offer to acquire the shares of a company's members and it is up to them to decide whether or not to accept. Directors who seek to prevent a bid succeeding will almost inevitably be thought to be acting primarily with a view to maintaining themselves in office. Many of the cases on directors' exercise of their power to allot shares have concerned allotments made to defeat unwelcome takeover bids. In Britain, the pre-emption rules which ensure that new shares are allotted to members in proportion to their existing shareholdings have reduced the incidence of such cases. Also significant is the City Code on Takeovers and Mergers, general principle 7:

> At no time after a bona fide offer has been communicated to the board of the offeree company, or after the board of the offeree company has reason to believe that a bona fide offer might be imminent, may any action be taken by the board of the offeree company in relation to the affairs of the company, without the approval of the shareholders in general meeting, which could effectively result in any bona fide offer being frustrated or in the shareholders being denied an opportunity to decide on its merits.

This restriction imposed by the City Code goes further than the common law: there is no legal principle that it is improper for directors to take action designed to defeat a takeover offer (per Clarke JA in *Darvall* v *North Sydney Brick & Tile Co. Ltd* (1989) 16 NSWLR 260 at p. 335).

Where there are rival takeover bids the directors must not exercise their powers in such a way as to prevent the members obtaining the best price for their shares (*Heron International Ltd* v *Lord Grade* [1983] BCLC 244, CA (use of power to refuse to register transfers); *Re a Company (No. 008699 of 1985)* [1986] BCLC 382 (use of power to provide information)). In *Howard Smith Ltd* v *Ampol Petroleum Ltd* [1974] AC 821, PC, Lord Wilberforce said, at pp. 837–8:

> The right to dispose of shares at a given price is essentially an individual right to be exercised on individual decision. . . . Directors are of course entitled to offer advice, and bound to supply information, relevant to the making of such a decision.

However, where there are competing offers, the directors are not under a positive duty to recommend and facilitate the implementation of the higher offer (*Re a Company (No. 008699 of 1985)*; *Dawson International plc* v *Coats Patons plc* 1988 SLT 854).

The question has been posed whether directors can validly issue shares in order to defeat a takeover by an asset-stripper, a rival or an incompetent manager who would ruin the company. In *Cayne* v *Global Natural Resources plc* (12 August 1982 unreported) Megarry V-C said:

> I cannot see why that should not be a perfectly proper exercise of fiduciary powers by the directors of [the company]. The object is not to retain control as such, but to prevent [the company] from being reduced to impotence and beggary, and the only means available to the directors for achieving this purpose is to retain control. This is quite different from directors seeking to retain control because they think they are better directors than their rivals would be.

On the other hand, Hoffmann J, in *Re a Company (No. 005136 of 1986)* [1987] BCLC 82 said that: 'The company is not particularly concerned with who its shareholders are' (at p. 84). A sale of shares in a company by one of its members is not something that relates to the conduct of the company's affairs for the purposes of CA 1985, s. 459 (*Re Leeds United Holdings plc* [1996] 2 BCLC 545). But in *Dawson International plc* v *Coats Patons plc* 1988 SLT 854, Lord Cullen said, at p. 860:

> I do not accept as a general proposition that a company can have no interest in the change of identity of its shareholders upon a takeover. It appears to me that there will be cases in which its agents, the directors, will see the takeover of its shares by a particular bidder as beneficial to the company. For example, it may provide the opportunity for integrating operations or obtaining additional resources. In other cases the directors will see a particular bid as not in the best interests of the company.

See also per Mahoney JA in *Darvall* v *North Sydney Brick & Tile Co. Ltd* (1989) 16 NSWLR 260 at pp. 324–5. These conflicting opinions raise the crucial issue of how a company's interests are to be judged.

If directors of a company allow the company to be taken over by persons who ruin it then the company cannot, it seems, sue those directors because members are free to pursue foolish or even negligent policies (*Multinational Gas & Petrochemical Co.* v *Multinational Gas & Petrochemical Services Ltd* [1983] Ch 258, CA). See further the discussion of *Heron International Ltd* v *Lord Grade* [1983] BCLC 244, CA, in C. Baxter, 'The true spirit of *Foss* v *Harbottle*' (1987) 38 NILQ 6 at p. 29, n. 96.

16.4.13   Other powers subject to the fiduciary duty

Although the most extensive discussion recently of directors' duties when exercising powers has been in relation to the power to allot shares, the duties have been examined in other cases, notably in relation to:

   (a)   Power to refuse to register a transfer of shares (the subject-matter of *Re Smith & Fawcett Ltd* [1942] Ch 304, in which Lord Greene MR stated the definition of fiduciary duties quoted in 16.4.1). This is considered in 8.3.4.

   (b)   Power to circulate information to shareholders (see 14.4.5.5).

   (c)   Power to borrow and give security (see *Rolled Steel Products (Holdings) Ltd* v *British Steel Corporation* [1986] Ch 246).

   (d)   Power to forfeit shares (see 6.4.2).

   (e)   Power to make calls on partly paid shares (*Anglo-Universal Bank* v *Baragnon* (1881) 45 LT 362, CA; *Savoy Corporation Ltd* v *Development Underwriting Ltd* [1963] NSWR 138).

   (f)   Power to determine which competing bids from members for shares being offered by a member under pre-emption provisions of articles should succeed (*T.C. Newman (Qld) Pty Ltd* v *DHA Rural (Qld) Pty Ltd* [1988] 1 QdR 308).

   (g)   Power to call general meetings (*Pergamon Press Ltd* v *Maxwell* [1970] 1 WLR 1167).

   (h)   Power to cause the company to enter into contracts (*Lee Panavision Ltd* v *Lee Lighting Ltd* [1992] BCLC 22; *Neptune (Vehicle Washing Equipment) Ltd* v *Fitzgerald (No. 2)* [1995] BCC 1000).

16.4.14   Ratification by members

If directors of a company breach their fiduciary duty by exercising powers in a way not bona fide in the company's interests or if they exercise their powers for an improper purpose (other than a purpose outside the objects of the company) then the members may, by ordinary resolution, ratify the action (*Hogg* v *Cramphorn Ltd* [1967] Ch 254, in which the directors acted bona fide in the company's interests but for an improper purpose; *Bamford* v *Bamford* [1970] Ch 212, CA, in which it was assumed for the sake of argument that the directors did not act bona fide in the company's interests). *Bamford* v *Bamford* was followed by the New South Wales Court of Appeal in *Winthrop Investments Ltd* v *Winns Ltd* [1975] 2 NSWLR 666, in which it was assumed for the sake of argument that the directors had acted in breach of duty though in subsequent proceedings ((1979) 4 ACLR 1) it was held that they had not. In earlier proceedings ((1975) 1 ACLR 219), Helsham J said that his own decision in *Provident International Corporation* v *International Leasing Corporation* (1969) 89 WN (Pt 1) (NSW) 370 that an exercise of power not bona fide in the company's interests was not ratifiable was wrong.

   The term 'ratification' is used not in the restricted sense of validating a transaction by making good a deficiency of authority (see 19.5.8) but in the more general sense of precluding legal action by deeming that a right of action has not arisen. A directors' act in breach of fiduciary duty is voidable, not void, so the effect of ratification is to end the company's right to avoid: it is not an independent new decision on the matter by the members (*Bamford* v *Bamford*; *Winthrop Investments Ltd* v *Winns Ltd* in the Court of Appeal; and see the casenotes on these cases by D.D. Prentice, 'Company law — directors' duties — collateral use of power — ratification of directors' wrongs' (1969) 47 Can Bar

Rev 648; 'Jurisdiction of shareholders' meetings' (1977) 40 MLR 587). Because ratification means that there is no right of action at all, it is not the same as a compromise of an action and does not have to be supported by consideration (R.J.C. Partridge, 'Ratification and the release of directors from personal liability' [1987] CLJ 122 argues to the contrary). It would seem that directors can ask for prospective ratification of a proposed act that, if unratified, would be a breach of duty (per Buckley J in *Hogg* v *Cramphorn Ltd* at p. 269).

A ratification is not effective if it is a fraud on the minority (*Ngurli Ltd* v *McCann* (1953) 90 CLR 425; *Hannes* v *MJH Pty Ltd* (1992) 7 ACSR 8). However, it would seem that not every exercise of directors' powers in breach of fiduciary duty is a fraud on the minority — the question was not raised in *Bamford* v *Bamford* or *Hogg* v *Cramphorn Ltd*. What was also not raised in those cases was whether a ratification by the members would be effective if made for an improper purpose (see per Mahoney JA in *Winthrop Investments Ltd* v *Winns Ltd* [1975] 2 NSWLR 666 at pp. 701–2). But it is not obvious that there should be any limits on the purposes for which the power of ratification may be exercised. The power to ratify must at least be wider than the power being ratified, otherwise the members would be subject to exactly the same fiduciary duties as the directors. Nevertheless, in Australia it has been held that if the directors of a company exercise their power for an improper purpose then the members cannot ratify for the same purpose (*Gray Eisdell Timms Pty Ltd* v *Combined Auctions Pty Ltd* (1995) 122 FLR 253, in which the act in question was the allotment of sufficient shares in a company to its managing director to give him permanent control of the company).

Ratification by the members will be ineffective if the directors' breach of duty prejudiced the interests of creditors at a time when the company was insolvent (*Kinsela* v *Russell Kinsela Pty Ltd* (1986) 4 NSWLR 722; approved by Dillon LJ in *West Mercia Safetywear Ltd* v *Dodd* [1988] BCLC 250, CA).

For ratification of an act outside a company's objects, see 19.5.8. See also 19.5.9.

16.4.15 Nominee directors

A nominee director of a company may be put into an impossible position by a conflict of interests of the company and his nominator. In *Scottish Cooperative Wholesale Society Ltd* v *Meyer* [1959] AC 324, HL, the Scottish CWS owned 4,000 of the 7,900 issued shares of Scottish Textile & Manufacturing Co. Ltd. The society exercised its right under the company's articles of association to appoint three of its five directors. The other two directors were the minority shareholders in the company. The society decided to operate in the company's line of business in competition with the company, and deliberately set out to destroy the company. The society's nominee directors did nothing to protect the company's interests. Lord Denning said, at p. 366, '. . . so soon as the interests of the two companies were in conflict, the nominee directors were placed in an impossible position'. At p. 367, his lordship said:

> They probably thought that 'as nominees' of the co-operative society their first duty was to the co-operative society. In this they were wrong.

There was no attempt in this case to make the nominee directors personally liable. The result of their wrongful preference of the interests of their nominator was that a petition by the minority shareholders for relief of prejudicial conduct of the company's affairs — see 18.6 — succeeded and the society was required to purchase the minority's shares.

In *Kuwait Asia Bank EC* v *National Mutual Life Nominees Ltd* [1991] 1 AC 187, Kuwait Asia Bank EC was beneficially interested in about 40 per cent of the shares of a New

Zealand company called AIC Securities Ltd ('AICS') and appointed its employees House and August as two of the five directors of AICS. The Privy Council said (at p. 222):

> In the performance of their duties as directors . . . House and August were bound to ignore the interests and wishes of their employer, the bank. They could not plead any instruction from the bank as an excuse for breach of their duties to AICS.

However, in *Re Broadcasting Station 2GB Pty Ltd* [1964–5] NSWR 1648, Jacobs J expressed the view that a nominee director of a company is entitled to follow the wishes of his nominator, provided he bona fide believes that the interests of the nominator are identical with the interests of 'the company as a whole'. A nominee director would be wrong, however, to act in his nominator's interests either when they are contrary to the company's interests or without any regard to the interests of the company. His honour said, at p. 1663:

> I realise that, upon this approach, I deny any right in the company as a whole to have each director approach each company problem with a completely open mind, but I think that to require this of each director is to ignore the realities of company organisation. Also, such a requirement would, in effect, make the position of a nominee or representative director an impossibility.

See further P. Redmond, 'Nominee directors' (1987) 10 UNSWLJ 194; E. Boros, 'The duties of nominee and multiple directors' (1989) 10 Co Law 211, (1990) 11 Co Law 6; P. Crutchfield, 'Nominee directors: the law and commercial reality' (1991) 12 Co Law 136.

16.4.16 Contractual restrictions on directors

It is legitimate for the directors of a company to enter into a binding agreement that they will act as directors in a particular way if, at the time of making the agreement, they bona fide consider that it is in the interests of the company (*Thorby* v *Goldberg* (1964) 112 CLR 597; *Fulham Football Club Ltd* v *Cabra Estates plc* [1994] 1 BCLC 363). Having made such an agreement bona fide in the interests of the company, the directors will be held to it even if they consider that circumstances have changed and it would be in the interests of the company for them to act in a different way. In *Fulham Football Club Ltd* v *Cabra Estates plc*, the plaintiff company, at a time when it was called Bannerton Ltd, agreed that, in return for substantial payments, its football club, Fulham, would cease to use its traditional home ground, Craven Cottage, which would be redeveloped by a subsidiary of the defendant company. Additionally, the plaintiff company was permitted to change its name to Fulham Football Club Ltd, which was then the defendant company's name. The directors of the plaintiff company executed a deed by which they covenanted not to object to the grant of planning permission for the redevelopment. Subsequently, they formed the view that it would be in the best interests of the club if the ground was not redeveloped in the way the defendant company proposed. They sought a declaration that they were entitled to object to the granting of planning permission for the redevelopment and could not be bound by the deed to act in a way that was not for the benefit of the company. The Court of Appeal held that such a declaration should not be made. The directors had entered into a contract which conferred substantial benefits on their company and they could not renege.

A company director who makes a contract to carry out directorial duties in a certain way regardless of whether it is in the interests of the company to do so would be agreeing to act, if required by the contract, in a way that was not in the interests of the company, and the courts would not enforce the contract by ordering the director to act contrary to the interests of the company. It has sometimes been said that the whole of such a contract would be illegal and void and such contracts are described as 'fettering' a director's discretion. In *Boulting* v *Association of Cinematograph, Television & Allied Technicians* [1963] 2 QB 606, Lord Denning MR said, at p. 626:

> It seems to me that no one, who has duties of a fiduciary nature to discharge, can be allowed to enter into an engagement by which he binds himself to disregard those duties or to act inconsistently with them. No stipulation is lawful by which he agrees to carry out his duties in accordance with the instructions of another rather than on his own conscientious judgment; or by which he agrees to subordinate the interests of those whom he must protect to the interests of someone else.

But in *Motherwell* v *Schoof* [1949] 4 DLR 812 it was held that the only circumstance in which such a contract would not be enforced is where an injunction was being sought to order the director to act against the company's interests. In *Thorby* v *Goldberg* (1964) 112 CLR 597, Menzies J said that if all the members of a company agreed that its directors should carry out their duties in a certain way (which is a common feature of unanimous shareholders' agreements) then they cannot rely on the contract being illegal and in *Davidson* v *Smith* (1989) 15 ACLR 732, Ipp J said (at p. 736) that the court would enforce such an agreement by a decree of specific performance. For a detailed discussion see T. B. Courtney, 'Fettering directors' discretion' (1995) 16 Co Law 227.

16.5 CONFLICT OF INTEREST AND DUTY

16.5.1 Rules against profiting and against conflict of interest and duty

The courts adopt a severe method of ensuring that the trust and confidence reposed in a fiduciary such as a director are not abused. The fundamental principle was stated by Lord Herschell in *Bray* v *Ford* [1896] AC 44 at pp. 51–2 :

> It is an inflexible rule of a court of equity that a person in a fiduciary position . . . is not, unless otherwise expressly provided, entitled to make a profit; he is not allowed to put himself in a position where his interest and duty conflict. It does not appear to me that this rule is, as has been said, founded upon principles of morality. I regard it rather as based on the consideration that, human nature being what it is, there is danger, in such circumstances, of the person holding a fiduciary position being swayed by interest rather than by duty, and thus prejudicing those whom he was bound to protect. It has, therefore, been deemed expedient to lay down this positive rule.

Furthermore a fiduciary for one person must not enter into a position which imposes conflicting duties to another person (*Re Haslam & Hier-Evans* [1902] 1 Ch 765, CA; *Transvaal Lands Co.* v *New Belgium (Transvaal) Land & Development Co.* [1914] 2 Ch 488, CA, discussed in 16.5.3). These rules are often, especially in the USA, described as the duty of loyalty. It is not, however, accurate to say that the director owes a *duty* to the company not to make an unauthorised profit and not to be in a position in which interest and duty, or duty to the company and duty to another, conflict. The law should not be analysed as imposing duties at two different levels. The correct analysis is that if a director does make unauthorised profits from the directorship, or is in a position of conflict of interest and duty, or conflict of duty to the company and duty to another, then the company will be given a remedy by the courts (see 16.5.5) (*Tito* v *Waddell* (*No. 2*) [1977] Ch 106 at pp. 248–9; *Movitex Ltd* v *Bulfield* (1986) 2 BCC 99,403 at p. 99,440).

The principle can be traced back to the case of *Keech* v *Sandford* (1726) Sel Cas t King 61 in which, under the will of a deceased lessee of some property, the leasehold interest had been given to a trustee to hold for the benefit of a minor. When the lease came up for renewal the lessor refused to grant a new lease to the minor because of the minor's contractual incapacity so the trustee obtained a renewal of the lease for himself. Lord King LC ordered the trustee to assign the new lease to the minor. His lordship said:

> I must consider this as a trust for the infant; for I very well see, if a trustee, on the refusal to renew, might have a lease to himself, few trust estates would be renewed to cestui que use; though I do not say there is a fraud in this case, yet he should rather have let it run out, than to have had the lease to himself. This may seem hard, that the trustee is the only person of all mankind who might not have the lease: but it is very proper that rule should be strictly pursued, and not in the least relaxed; for it is very obvious what would be the consequence of letting trustees have the lease, on refusal to renew to cestui que use.

For further discussion of the origins of the rules against profiting and against conflict of interest and duty, see G. Jones, 'Unjust enrichment and the fiduciary's duty of loyalty' (1968) 84 LQR 472.

16.5.2   One rule or two?

In *Boardman* v *Phipps* [1967] 2 AC 46 Lord Upjohn, at p. 123, described the rule against profiting as 'part of the wider rule' against conflict of interest and duty; and Lord Herschell, in the passage quoted in 16.5.1 from *Bray* v *Ford* [1896] AC 44, spoke of 'this rule' against profiting and against conflict of interest and duty as if there were only one rule. This echoes the words of Lord Cranworth LC in *Broughton* v *Broughton* (1855) 5 De G M & G 160:

> The rule applicable to the subject has been treated at the bar as if it were sufficiently enunciated by saying, that a trustee shall not be able to make a profit of his trust, but that is not stating it so widely as it ought to be stated. The rule really is, that no one who has a duty to perform shall place himself in a situation to have his interests conflicting with that duty.

Nevertheless the rules against profiting and against conflict of interest and duty are, as Deane J pointed out in *Chan* v *Zacharia* (1984) 154 CLR 178 at pp. 198–9, two aspects or themes which, while overlapping, are distinct. Thus a transaction of a company will be set aside because it involved a director of the company in a conflict of interest and duty even though the director did not profit from it (*Movitex Ltd* v *Bulfield* (1986) 2 BCC 99,403) and the rule against profiting is not analysed as a conflict between an interest in making the profit and a duty not to make it (or a duty to make the profit for the company). In *Regal (Hastings) Ltd* v *Gulliver* [1967] 2 AC 134, directors were held liable to account for profits they had made on shares that they had acquired by virtue of their office. Lord Macmillan said, at p. 153:

> The point was not whether the directors had a duty to acquire the shares in question for the company and failed in that duty. They had no such duty. . . . However, that does not

absolve them from accountability for any profit which they made, if it was by reason and in virtue of their fiduciary office as directors.

Lord Porter said, at p. 159:

> Directors, no doubt, are not trustees, but they occupy a fiduciary position towards the company whose board they form. Their liability in this respect does not depend upon breach of duty but upon the proposition that a director must not make a profit out of property acquired by reason of his relationship to the company of which he is director.

See further, A.J. McClean, 'The theoretical basis of the trustee's duty of loyalty' (1969) 7 Alta L Rev 218.

16.5.3 Actual or potential conflict

The rule against conflict of interest and duty is often formulated to comprehend actual and potential conflicts as if they were distinguishable. Lord Cranworth LC, in *Aberdeen Railway Co.* v *Blaikie Bros* (1854) 1 Macq 461, HL, said, at p. 471:

> . . . it is a rule of universal application, that no one, having [fiduciary] duties to discharge, shall be allowed to enter into engagements in which he has, or can have, a personal interest conflicting, or which possibly may conflict, with the interests of those whom he is bound to protect.

Other formulations emphasise that a conflict which is so small that it will not affect observance of a fiduciary duty will be ignored. Thus in *Queensland Mines Ltd* v *Hudson* (1978) 52 ALJR 399 the Privy Council referred to 'a real sensible possibility of conflict', and in *Chan* v *Zacharia* (1984) 154 CLR 178, Deane J, at pp. 198–9, referred to 'a conflict or significant possibility of conflict'. In *Movitex Ltd* v *Bulfield* (1986) 2 BCC 99,403, Vinelott J, at p. 99,433, referred to the interest of the fiduciary being 'so small that it can as a practical matter be disregarded'. An interest as a bare trustee with no duties to perform does not give rise to any conflict (*Cowan de Groot Properties Ltd* v *Eagle Trust plc* [1991] BCLC 1045). However, if an interest is sufficiently large to be capable of influencing the fiduciary's mind the strict rule applies. For instance, in *Transvaal Lands Co.* v *New Belgium (Transvaal) Land & Development Co.* [1914] 2 Ch 488, CA, the plaintiff company had contracted to buy from the defendant company shares in a third company. The plaintiff company had three directors and the quorum for board meetings was two. One of the directors could not vote on the contract because he was a director of the defendant company and owned 5 per cent of its shares. A second director, Harvey, did vote in favour of the contract without disclosing that he held 0.5 per cent of the defendant company's shares as trustee for the estate of his father-in-law. It was held that there was a conflict between his duty to the plaintiff company and his duty to the beneficiaries of the trust and so the contract was set aside. It may be that the court was influenced by the fact that Harvey was appointed a director of the defendant company at the time of the transactions (see pp. 490–1 of the report).

The idea that the rule against conflict of interest and duty should not be applied absolutely without regard to the significance of the conflict appeared in the important dissenting speech of Lord Upjohn in *Boardman* v *Phipps* [1967] 2 AC 46 at p. 124:

The phrase 'possibly may conflict' [in the dictum of Lord Cranworth quoted above] requires consideration. In my view it means that the reasonable man looking at the relevant facts and circumstances of the particular case would think that there was a real sensible possibility of conflict; not that you could imagine some situation arising which might, in some conceivable possibility in events not contemplated as real sensible possibilities by any reasonable person, result in a conflict.

16.5.4 Disapplication of the rules

In *Boulting* v *Association of Cinematograph, Television & Allied Technicians* [1963] 2 QB 606, Upjohn LJ (as he was then) at p. 636 described how the rules against profiting and against conflict of duty and interest (which he treated as a single rule) could be relaxed:

> The rule . . . is one essentially for the protection of the person to whom the duty is owed. Thus the company is entitled to the undivided loyalty of its directors . . . But the person entitled to the benefit of the rule may relax it, provided he is . . . *sui iuris* and fully understands not only what he is doing but also what his legal rights are, and that he is in part surrendering them. Thus the company may, in its articles of association, permit directors to be interested in contracts with the company [cf. Table A, arts. 85 and 86; see 16.6.2]. It may go further, and articles may validly permit directors to be present at board meetings and even to vote when proposed contracts in which they are interested are being discussed; provided, of course, that they make full disclosure of their interests [cf. Table A, art. 94; see 16.6.3].

Thus the members of a company can, by ordinary resolution, relax the rules against profiting and against conflict of duty and interest, provided there has been full and frank disclosure of all material facts (see 16.8). The articles referred to by Upjohn LJ provide that the rules will not be invoked against a director if he enters into a transaction in which interest and duty conflict, or from which he profits, provided he fulfils conditions concerning disclosure of interest and not voting on the transaction at board meetings. The articles therefore provide a general disapplication of the rules.

A public company applying for listing on the London Stock Exchange must ensure that each of its directors is free of conflicts between duties to the company and private interests and other duties, unless it can demonstrate that arrangements are in place to avoid detriment to its interests (Listing Rules, para. 3.9).

16.5.5 Remedies

16.5.5.1 Rescission

If a transaction between a company and one of its directors profits the director or involves a conflict between the director's duty to the company and personal interest or duty to another, then the transaction is voidable at the company's option. The transaction is not, however, void (*Hely-Hutchinson* v *Brayhead Ltd* [1968] 1 QB 549, CA). If the company repudiates the contract this may be confirmed by a court order for rescission of the contract. The rule that rescission is always granted in such circumstances is known as the 'self-dealing rule'. See per Vinelott J in *Movitex Ltd* v *Bulfield* (1986) 2 BCC 99,403 at p. 99,432.

If a director of a company profits from a transaction between the company and another person, or such a transaction involves a conflict between the director's duty to the company and personal interest or duty to another, then the transaction is voidable at the company's option if it can show that the other party to the transaction was informed of, or wilfully refused to receive information about, the director's profit or conflict of interest (*Logicrose Ltd v Southend United Football Club Ltd* [1988] 1 WLR 1256). The fact that the director has accounted to the company for any profit made does not mean that the company has affirmed the transaction so that it is no longer voidable: the remedies of rescission and account (see 16.5.5.2) are independent (ibid.). Furthermore, the profit which the director gained from the transaction was not paid by the other party under its contract with the company and so is not returnable when that contract is rescinded (ibid.).

16.5.5.2   Liability to account
The liability to account was set out in the High Court of Australia by Deane J in *Chan v Zacharia* (1984) 154 CLR 178 at p. 199:

> . . . the principle of equity is that a person who is under a fiduciary obligation must account to the person to whom the obligation is owed for any benefit or gain (i) which has been obtained or received in circumstances where a conflict or significant possibility of conflict existed between his fiduciary duty and his personal interest in the pursuit or possible receipt of such a benefit or gain or (ii) which was obtained or received by use or by reason of his fiduciary position or of opportunity or knowledge resulting from it.

Furthermore, as Lord Radcliffe said in *Gray v New Augarita Porcupine Mines Ltd* [1952] 3 DLR 1, PC, at p. 15: '. . . a trustee who is accountable is not the less accountable if he shows that the transaction impugned is both reasonable and fair'. In *Parker v McKenna* (1874) LR 10 Ch App 96, Lord Cairns LC, at p. 118, said:

> No man can in this court, acting as an agent, be allowed to put himself into a position in which his interest and his duty will be in conflict. . . . The court will not inquire, and is not in a position to ascertain, whether the bank has lost or not lost by the acts of [its] directors. All that the court has to do is to examine whether a profit has been made by an agent, without the knowledge of his principal, in the course and execution of his agency, . . . these agents in the course of their agency have made a profit, and for that profit they must, in my opinion, account to their principal.

The remedy is given without any need to prove that the director acted dishonestly or *mala fide* but it is confined to recovery for the company of the director's profits not those made by others (see *Regal (Hastings) Ltd v Gulliver* [1967] 2 AC 134, HL, discussed in 16.7.1).

16.5.5.3   Constructive trust
In *Chan v Zacharia* (1984) 154 CLR 178, High Court of Australia, Deane J continued the statement quoted in 16.5.5.2 by saying:

> Any such benefit or gain is held by the fiduciary as constructive trustee. . . . That constructive trust arises from the fact that a personal benefit or gain has been so obtained or received and it is immaterial that there was no absence of good faith or damage to the person to whom the fiduciary duty was owed.

See also *Carlton v Halestrap* (1988) 4 BCC 538.

16.5.5.4   Criminal liability

The fact that equity would regard a director as constructive trustee of benefits or gains made in the circumstances described in 16.5.5.2 does not mean that the director's taking of those benefits or gains constitutes the offence of theft (*Attorney-General's Reference (No. 1 of 1985)* [1986] QB 491, CA). However, an agreement by a director with others dishonestly to conceal such benefits or gains so as to prevent the company recovering them does constitute the offence of conspiracy to defraud (*Adams* v *The Queen* [1995] 1 WLR 52).

16.5.5.5   Refusal to grant remedies

The remedies of rescission, account and imposition of a constructive trust are equitable remedies which will not be granted if granting them would be inequitable. Because the rules against profiting and against conflict of interest and duty are regarded as 'inflexible' (see per Lord Herschell in *Bray* v *Ford* [1896] AC 44 quoted in 16.5.1) and 'universal' (see per Lord Cranworth LC in *Aberdeen Railway Co.* v *Blaikie Brothers* (1854) 1 Macq 461 quoted in 16.5.3) it is to be expected that the courts will very rarely find it inequitable to grant the remedies. However, this did occur in *Runciman* v *Walter Runciman plc* [1992] BCLC 1084 which is discussed in 16.6.2.

16.5.6   Circumstances in which the rules apply

The circumstances in which the rules against profiting and against conflict of interest and duty are applied may be divided into two classes:

  (a)   where the director benefits from a transaction that the company enters into (see 16.6);
  (b)   where the director benefits from a transaction to which the company is not a party (see 16.7).

In cases in the second class it will normally not be possible to set aside the transaction but the director will have to account for profits and will be treated as a constructive trustee for the company of any property acquired.

16.6   TRANSACTIONS TO WHICH THE COMPANY IS A PARTY

16.6.1   Introduction

The strict application of the rules against profiting and against conflict of interest and duty to a transaction entered into by a company from which a director of that company may benefit was established in *Aberdeen Railway Co.* v *Blaikie Brothers* (1854) 1 Macq 461, HL. Mr Blaikie was chairman of the board of directors of the railway company. He used this position to make a contract under which the company would buy components for railway tracks from a partnership called Blaikie Brothers of which he was managing partner. The railway company repudiated the contract but the partnership claimed this was unjustifiable because the contract was on ordinary commercial terms and the company would not suffer by it. Lord Cranworth LC said, at p. 471:

  A corporate body can only act by agents, and it is of course the duty of those agents so to act as best to promote the interests of the corporation whose affairs they are conducting. Such agents have duties to discharge of a fiduciary nature towards their principal. And it is a rule of universal application, that no one, having such duties to discharge, shall be allowed to enter into engagements in which he has, or can have, a personal interest conflicting, or which possibly may conflict, with the interests of those whom he is bound to protect.

So strictly is this principle adhered to, that no question is allowed to be raised as to the fairness or unfairness of a contract so entered into.

The members of a company can, by ordinary resolution, permit a director to benefit from a transaction with the company, provided there has been full and frank disclosure of all material facts (see 16.8).

In practice, company directors often have numerous business connections from which all the enterprises concerned could benefit. It is therefore usual for the members of a company to declare in their articles of association that the rules against profiting and against conflict of interest and duty will be excluded from applying to specified transactions in which any of the company's directors is interested, provided the director concerned complies with conditions relating to provision of information about his interests. Articles normally assign the management of the company, and therefore the decision whether to enter into a transaction in which a director is interested, to the directors and so the normal condition for disapplying the rules is that the director's interest is declared to the board (see 16.6.2). Such articles are backed up by CA 1985, s. 317, which makes it a criminal offence for a director of a company to fail to declare to a board meeting an interest in a transaction of the company (see 16.6.5).

Parliament has intervened to require certain transactions (known as 'substantial property transactions') between a company and one of its directors (or a director of its holding company) to be approved not just by the board of directors but by the members in general meeting (see 16.6.7) and to make a transaction by which a company gives credit to one of its directors (or a director of its holding company) illegal and even, where a public company is involved, a criminal offence (see 16.6.8).

16.6.2 Articles excluding the rules against profiting and against conflict of interest and duty

Table A, art. 85, allows a director to be a party to any transaction or arrangement with the company or in which the company is otherwise interested and provides that the contract is not voidable and the director concerned is not liable to account to the company for any benefit derived, provided the nature and extent of any material interest of the director is disclosed to the directors.

If all the directors are interested in a transaction, it seems that disclosure to themselves will satisfy this condition. Although Vinelott J had reservations about the validity of self-disclosure in *Movitex Ltd* v *Bulfield* (1986) 2 BCC 99,403 at pp. 99,428–9, it was contemplated in *Neptune (Vehicle Washing Equipment) Ltd* v *Fitzgerald (No. 2)* [1995] BCC 1000 that disclosure by a sole director to himself would have been sufficient, though in that case it was found that disclosure had not been made in the manner required by the company's articles. The articles of Neptune (Vehicle Washing Equipment) Ltd required disclosure to be made at a meeting of the directors in accordance with what is now CA 1985, s. 317 (see 16.6.5). It was held that in order for a sole director to comply with those requirements there had to be a distinct declaration of interest at a board meeting with a pause for thought about the existence of a conflict of interest and about the director's duty to prefer the company's interests to his or her own. Table A, art. 85, merely requires disclosure and does not refer to meetings or statutory requirements. It remains to be seen what form of self-disclosure will be required by the courts to comply with the present art. 85.

Runciman v *Walter Runciman plc* [1992] BCLC 1084 is another case concerning a requirement to disclose at a board meeting in accordance with CA 1985, s. 317, but, unlike *Neptune (Vehicle Washing Equipment) Ltd* v *Fitzgerald (No. 2)*, was not a case of self-disclosure by a sole director. In *Runciman* v *Walter Runciman plc* the defendant had failed to disclose his interest in his own service contract before he and the other directors agreed to change the terms of the contract. Simon Brown J refused to rescind the variation of the contract, saying, at p. 1097:

> To hold in these circumstances that what was at most a merely technical breach of a statutory duty of disclosure should render that variation unenforceable would to my mind involve the most patent injustice.

An interest which does not give rise to a conflict of interest and duty, such as an interest as a bare trustee with no duties to perform, does not have to be disclosed (*Cowan de Groot Properties Ltd* v *Eagle Trust plc* [1991] BCLC 1045).

A director who must declare an interest must state what the interest is and quantify it. As Lord Cairns said in *Imperial Mercantile Credit Association* v *Coleman* (1873) LR 6 HL 189: 'a man declares his interest, not when he states that he has an interest, but when he states what his interest is'. See also *Gray* v *New Augarita Porcupine Mines Ltd* [1952] 3 DLR 1, PC, at p. 14.

Table A, art. 86(a), deals with a situation in which, for example, a company is likely to have regular dealings with a company or partnership of which one of its directors is a member. The director can, under art. 86(a), give a general notice to the board that if a specified person (or class of persons) is interested in a transaction or arrangement with the company then the director is to be regarded as having an interest in the transaction or arrangement. The notice must specify the nature and extent of the director's interest. This general notice is deemed to be a disclosure of the specified interest in relation to each transaction or arrangement entered into with the specified person (or class of persons).

Table A, art. 86(b), provides that 'an interest of which a director has no knowledge and of which it is unreasonable to expect him to have knowledge shall not be treated as an interest of his'.

16.6.3 Prohibition on voting

Table A, art. 94, forbids a director of the company from voting at any meeting of the directors or of a committee of directors on any resolution concerning a matter in which the director, or a person with whom the director is connected (see 16.8.10), has a material interest or duty which conflicts or may conflict with the interests of the company. The article cannot be evaded by appointing an alternate director to vote instead because an alternate is deemed by art. 94 to have the interests of his or her appointor as well as his or her own interests. A director who is disqualified by an interest from voting on a resolution cannot be counted towards the quorum for the meeting at which that resolution is discussed (Table A, art. 95; *Re Greymouth Point Elizabeth Railway & Coal Co. Ltd* [1904] 1 Ch 32; *Re North Eastern Insurance Co. Ltd* [1919] 1 Ch 198). It is not permissible for the board to reduce its quorum (as permitted by Table A, art. 89) temporarily to overcome this difficulty (*Re North Eastern Insurance Co. Ltd*). Accordingly private companies with a small number of directors often delete art. 94 from their articles and permit directors to vote on contracts in which they are interested. Such a permission to vote is effective (*A.M. Spicer & Son Pty Ltd* v *Spicer* (1931) 47 CLR 151).

Table A, art. 94, specifies four exemptions from the prohibition on voting and art. 96 empowers the members, by ordinary resolution, to suspend or relax the prohibition either generally or in respect of any particular matter. In *Re Greymouth Point Elizabeth Railway & Coal Co. Ltd, Cox* v *Dublin City Distillery (No. 2)* [1915] 1 IR 345 and *Re North Eastern Insurance Co. Ltd* directors voted in favour of their companies giving them security for debts owed to them (and see *Re Express Engineering Works Ltd* [1920] 1 Ch 466 discussed in 14.5.1). Voting on such a matter is now permitted under exemption (a) in Table A, art. 94. In *Victors Ltd* v *Lingard* [1927] 1 Ch 323, directors voted in favour of the company giving security for a debt which the directors had guaranteed: this is now covered by exemption (b) in art. 94.

A listed company is required to have an article in similar terms to Table A, art. 94, but prohibiting voting only when the director has knowledge of having a material interest, and providing two further exemptions (Listing Rules, ch. 13, app. 1, para. 20). One of the further exemptions required by the Listing Rules allows a director to vote on a resolution relating to any company in which the director holds an interest provided the interest is less than 1 per cent of any class of the company's equity capital or less than 1 per cent of the company's voting rights. The other extra exemption allows a director to vote on a resolution relating to insurance which the company proposes to purchase or maintain for the benefit of directors.

It seems that as the prohibition in art. 94 is only from voting at a meeting of directors or of a committee of directors, it does not extend to signing a written resolution under art. 93. Indeed in *Re Charles Atkins & Co. Ltd* [1929] SASR 129, it was said (at p. 134) that signing a written resolution is not voting.

The prohibition in art. 94 is from voting at board meetings: it does not apply, where the director is a member of a company, to voting at members' meetings (*Re Express Engineering Works Ltd* discussed in 14.5.1; *Baird* v *J. Baird & Co. (Falkirk) Ltd* 1949 SLT 368; see 14.4.9.3).

16.6.4 Effect of articles excluding the rules

The effect of articles such as those in Table A discussed in 16.6.2 is that if a company enters into a transaction from which one of its directors benefits or may benefit but the director has complied with the conditions specified in the articles then the rules against profiting and against conflict of interest and duty are excluded and the company cannot avoid the transaction or recover any benefits or gains made by the director. For an example, see *Joint receivers & managers of Niltan Carson Ltd* v *Hawthorne* [1988] BCLC 298. Under Table A, art. 85, the two conditions are that the director's interest must be disclosed and the director cannot vote on the contract or be counted towards the quorum except in the cases specified in art. 94. If a director's interest is not disclosed in accordance with art. 85 or if, apart from that director's vote, the resolution would not have been passed or if the meeting would otherwise have been inquorate, the rules are not excluded and the company has the remedies set out in 16.5.5: in particular, the transaction is voidable, not void (*Hely-Hutchinson* v *Brayhead Ltd* [1968] 1 QB 549, CA).

The onus is on the director to prove that the conditions have been complied with (*Gray* v *New Augarita Porcupine Mines Ltd* [1952] 3 DLR 1, PC). A director who has an interest in a company transaction should ensure that the compliance with the articles (i.e., the declaration of interest if required and the names of the directors who voted) is recorded in the minutes of board meetings. As Vinelott J said in *Movitex Ltd* v *Bulfield* (1986) 2 BCC 99,403 at p. 99,443:

> . . . if a director enters into a self-dealing transaction which is challenged, the burden is on him to show that full disclosure was made and that the requirements of the company's articles were otherwise complied with. If he fails to ensure that formal disclosure is minuted, he exposes himself to the risk that after some years he may be unable to show by positive evidence that there was disclosure.

Articles such as those discussed in 16.6.2 deal only with the rules against profiting and against conflict of interest and duty. They do not give a board of directors freedom to make any contracts they like for their own benefit because they are always subject to the rule discussed in 16.4.1 that they must act bona fide in the interests of the company and not for a collateral purpose such as their own enrichment (*Neptune (Vehicle Washing Equipment) Ltd* v *Fitzgerald (No. 2)* [1995] BCC 1000).

16.6.5   Statutory duty to declare an interest

A director of a company who is in any way, whether directly or indirectly, interested in a contract, or proposed contract, with the company must declare the nature of the interest at a meeting of directors of the company (CA 1985, s. 317(1)).

A declaration of interest by a director of a company under s. 317(1) does not in itself relieve the director from the operation of the rules against profiting and against conflict of interest and duty (s. 317(9)): only the members of the company can disapply those rules, either by a general provision in the articles (see 16.6.2) or by ratifying a particular transaction (see 16.8). A general provision in the articles may itself prescribe that declaring an interest is a condition for disapplying the rules: under Table A, declaration of an interest is required by art. 84 but that article only requires disclosure of any 'material interest' whereas s. 317(1) requires disclosure of any interest.

If company A proposes to contract with company B and a director of company A is a member of company B then the membership is an interest which must be disclosed under s. 317(1) (*Re British America Corporation Ltd* (1903) 19 TLR 662). A director's interest in his or her own service contract is an interest which has to be disclosed under s. 317(1) (*Toms* v *Cinema Trust Co. Ltd* [1915] WN 29; *Runciman* v *Walter Runciman plc* [1992] BCLC 1084). By s. 317(6), disclosure of an interest in a contract must be made under s. 317 even if the contract is a loan or other transaction which is illegal under s. 330 (see 16.6.8). Section 317 also extends to the disclosure of substantial property transactions (see 16.6.7) and (by s. 317(8)) to the interests of shadow directors.

A director who is interested in a proposed contract must declare that interest at the first board meeting which considers entering into the contract (s. 317(2)). A director who becomes interested in a contract after it has been entered into, or becomes interested in a proposed contract after the board has considered entering into it, must disclose the interest at the next board meeting after becoming interested (ibid.).

Disclosure is not limited to contracts which are considered by the board, and a director who is interested in a contract which was made without board consideration must, if necessary, call a board meeting so as to disclose the interest: in particular, a sole director of a company who is interested in a company contract must hold a board meeting and record the interest in the minutes in order to comply with s. 317(1) (*Neptune (Vehicle Washing Equipment) Ltd* v *Fitzgerald* [1996] Ch 274).

For the purposes of s. 317, a general notice to the effect that a director is a member of a specified company or firm and is to be regarded as interested in any contract which may, after the date of the notice, be made with that company or firm (e.g., under art. 86(a) of Table A discussed in 16.6.2), or that the director is to be regarded as interested in any contract which may after the date of the notice be made with a specified person with whom the director is connected (see 16.8.10), is deemed to be a sufficient declaration of the director's interest (s. 317(3)). However, such a general notice is not effective unless it is given at a directors' meeting or the director concerned takes reasonable steps to secure that it is brought up and read at the next meeting of the directors after it is given (s. 317(4)). Thus, s. 317 envisages either a general or a specific notice of a director's interest, though the circumstances of a general notice are somewhat limited. If a company has made a contract in which a director is interested then that interest must be declared when a variation of the contract is considered (*Runciman* v *Walter Runciman plc*).

The way in which a declaration of interest should be made by a shadow director (who will not be entitled to attend board meetings) is set out in s. 317(8).

Failure to disclose interests in accordance with s. 317 is an offence triable either way (s. 317(7) and sch. 24). It used to be common for company articles to require compliance with s. 317 as a condition for disapplying the rules against profiting and against conflicts of interest and duty but this is not now required by Table A (see 16.6.2). In cases dealing with the old form of articles judges have said that failure to declare an interest in a contract under s. 317 would render the contract voidable (per Lord Denning MR in *Hely-Hutchinson* v *Brayhead Ltd* [1968] 1 QB 549 at p. 585; per Lord Templeman in *Guinness plc* v *Saunders* [1990] 2 AC 663 at p. 694), but this is only because in those cases failure to comply with s. 317 meant failure to comply with the company's articles. It is not accurate to say that, in general, failure to comply with s. 317 renders a contract voidable. Section 317 does not say anything about the effect of non-compliance on a contract (see per Lord Wilberforce in *Hely-Hutchinson* v *Brayhead Ltd* at p. 589 and Lord Pearson at p. 594). The correct position is as stated by Lord Goff of Chievely in *Guinness plc* v *Saunders* at p. 697 that breach of s. 317 does not affect the contract (per Samuels JA in *Woolworths Ltd* v *Kelly* (1991) 22 NSWLR 189 at pp. 209–10; per Harman J in *Lee Panavision Ltd* v *Lee Lighting Ltd* at first instance [1991] BCLC 575 at p. 583 (though on appeal Dillon LJ refused to express any opinion on the question: [1992] BCLC 22 at p. 33); per Knox J in *Cowan de Groot Properties Ltd* v *Eagle Trust plc* [1991] BCLC 1045 at p. 1113).

There is no prescribed form of disclosure under s. 317. In *Neptune (Vehicle Washing Equipment) Ltd* v *Fitzgerald*, Lightman J said, at p. 283:

> Where a director is interested in a contract, the section secures that three things happen at a directors' meeting: first, all the directors should know or be reminded of the interest; second, the making of the declaration should be the occasion for a statutory pause for thought about the existence of the conflict of interest and of the duty to prefer the interests of the company to their own; third, the disclosure or reminder must be a distinct happening at the meeting which therefore must be recorded in the minutes of the meeting.

The first point is not entirely clear. One would expect it to read: '. . . all the directors should be told or reminded of the interest'. The main point of the case was that a declaration of interest has to be made even if all the directors already know of the interest or where it is obvious (such as a director's interest in his or her own service contract). There has been disquiet about this ruling (see, for example, *Neptune (Vehicle Washing Equipment) Ltd* v *Fitzgerald (No. 2)* [1995] BCC 1000 at pp. 1002–3) and in Australia, the majority of the court in *Woolworths Ltd* v *Kelly* (1991) 22 NSWLR 189 took a different view.

16.6.6 Disclosure in accounts

A company is required by CA 1985, s. 232(1) and sch. 6, paras 15(c) and 16(c), to disclose, in notes to its annual accounts, details of any transaction or arrangement with the company subsisting during the financial year reported on in which a director or shadow director of the company or of its holding company had, directly or indirectly, a material interest.

A holding company is required by s. 232(1) and sch. 6, para. 15(c), to disclose in notes to its annual accounts details of any transaction or arrangement with any of its subsidiaries in which a director or shadow director of the company or of its holding company had, directly or indirectly, a material interest. This must be done whether or not the company produces group accounts (sch. 6, para. 15).

The question whether or not an interest in a transaction or arrangement is material may be decided by a majority vote of the directors of the reporting company (but without the participation of the person whose interest is being considered if that person is a director of the reporting company) (sch. 6, para. 17(2)).

Disclosure of a material interest is required in respect of any person who was a director at any time during the financial year reported on (sch. 6, paras 15(c) and 16(c)) even if not a director at the time the transaction or arrangement was entered into (para. 19(b)). A transaction or arrangement with a director personally (apart from a service contract, by para. 18(b)) is one in which the director is 'interested' (para. 17(1)). A transaction or arrangement with a person connected with a director (see 16.6.8.10) is one in which the director is interested (para. 17(1)).

To avoid having to list contracts between members of a group of companies, sch. 6, para. 18(a), provides that it is not necessary to disclose particulars of transactions or arrangements with another company in which a director is interested only by virtue of being a director of that other company; and para. 21 provides that if a director is associated with the reporting company (see 16.6.8.10) and the reporting company is a wholly owned subsidiary then it need not disclose transactions or arrangements in which the director had a material interest by virtue of the association if they would not otherwise be disclosable. If a director is associated with the reporting company then it need not disclose transactions or arrangements between itself and its subsidiaries in which the director had a material interest by virtue of the association if they would not otherwise be disclosable (para. 21).

Most important of all the exemptions is that if the reporting company, and/or another company in the same group as the reporting company, became a party to a transaction or arrangement in the ordinary course of business and did not do so on specially favourable terms because a person interested in the transaction or arrangement was a director of the reporting company or its holding company then the transaction or arrangement need not be reported (para. 20).

CA 1985, sch. 6, para. 22, requires the following particulars of a transaction or arrangement to be disclosed:

(a) The principal terms of the transaction or arrangement.
(b) The name of the interested director and the nature of the interest.
(c) The 'value' of the transaction or arrangement, as defined by s. 340, which is, in effect, the market value of whatever is being supplied.

Disclosure of transactions with a director is not required if, during the financial year reported on, the total value of transactions or arrangements with that director by the reporting company and its subsidiaries did not exceed £1,000. For most companies disclosure is required only if the total value of transactions and arrangements exceeded 1 per cent of the net assets shown in the reporting company's balance sheet for the financial year reported on but a company with net assets of more than £½ million must disclose transactions if the total value exceeds £5,000 (sch. 6, para. 25).

16.6.7 Substantial property transactions

Under the articles in Table A discussed in 16.6.2, a company director's interests in a company transaction need be disclosed only to the other directors. CA 1985, s. 320 (first enacted in CA 1980, s. 48), has gone further and made certain 'substantial property transactions' between a company and any of its directors or any person connected with any of its directors (see 16.6.8.10) illegal (s. 322) unless the company in general meeting first approved the transaction (s. 320(1)). If the director or connected person in the transaction is also a director of the company's holding company then the transaction must also have been approved by the holding company in general meeting. The same rule applies to a substantial property transaction with a director of a company's holding company (even if not a director of the company itself) and furthermore shadow directors are treated as directors for the purposes of the provisions (s. 320(3)) though a parent company is not to be treated as a shadow director of its subsidiary only because the subsidiary's directors are accustomed to act in accordance with its directions or instructions (s. 741(3)).

A substantial property transaction will not be saved from illegality by shareholders' approval unless they approved all important terms of the transaction, especially the price (*Demite Ltd* v *Protec Health Ltd* (1998) *The Times*, 25 July 1998).

A 'substantial property transaction' is any arrangement (s. 320(1)):

(a) whereby a director of the company or its holding company or a person connected with such a director is to acquire from the company one or more non-cash assets of the requisite value (except where the director or person concerned acquires the asset as a shareholder of the company), or

(b) whereby the company acquires from a director of the company or its holding company or a person connected with such a director one or more non-cash assets of the requisite value.

The section does not, however, apply to an arrangement between a holding company and any of its wholly owned subsidiaries or between wholly owned subsidiaries of the same holding company (s. 321(2)(a)) nor if the value of the non-cash asset is less than £2,000 (s. 320(2); SI 1990 No. 1393).

A non-cash asset is any property or interest in property other than cash (including foreign currency) (CA 1985, s. 739(1)), and will be of the requisite value if its value at the time of the arrangement exceeds the lesser of £100,000 or 10 per cent of the amount of the company's net assets as shown in its most recent annual accounts (or of its called-up share capital if it has not yet produced accounts) (s. 320(2); SI 1990 No. 1393; *Joint receivers & managers of Niltan Carson Ltd* v *Hawthorne* [1988] BCLC 298). In *Duckwari plc* v *Offerventure Ltd* [1995] BCC 89, Offerventure Ltd had contracted to buy land for £495,000 and had paid the usual 10 per cent deposit to stakeholders. Offerventure was connected with a director of Duckwari plc, who arranged for the benefit of the purchase contract to be assigned to Duckwari plc without obtaining the approval of a general meeting of Duckwari's members. It was held that the value of the transaction was the value of the land (which was agreed to be at least £495,000 at the time of the deal) less the balance of the purchase price (for which the vendor would have a lien on the land), that is, at least £49,500. As this was more than 10 per cent of Duckwari's net assets, the transaction was a substantial property transaction.

A transaction effected by a director on a recognised investment exchange (see 7.3.4) is not a substantial property transaction prohibited by s. 320 if it is effected through the agency of an 'independent broker' — that is, a person who, independently of the director, selects the person with whom the transaction is to be effected (s. 321(4)). Similarly a transaction effected on a recognised investment exchange by a person connected with a director is not prohibited by s. 320 if it is effected through the agency of an independent broker who, independently of that person or of the director with whom that person is connected, selects the person with whom the transaction is to be effected (ibid.).

An arrangement entered into in contravention of s. 320 (and any other transaction entered into in pursuance of the arrangement) is voidable at the company's instance unless restitution is impossible, or rights have been acquired by a bona fide third party for value without actual notice of the contravention, or the arrangement is affirmed by the company (and, if appropriate, its holding company) in general meeting within a reasonable period (s. 322(1) and (2)). In addition, if the arrangement was with a director then the director concerned, and any other director who authorised the arrangement, are liable to account to the company for any gain which they make whether directly or indirectly by the arrangement or transaction, and are liable (jointly and severally) to indemnify the company for any loss or damage resulting from the arrangement or transaction (s. 322(3)), though an authorising director who, at the time the arrangement was entered into, did not know the relevant circumstances constituting the contravention will not be liable (s. 322(6)). If the arrangement was with a person connected with a director then that director and the connected person and any other director who authorised the arrangement are liable to account to the company for any gain which they make whether directly or indirectly by the arrangement or transaction, and are liable (jointly and severally) to indemnify the company for any loss or damage resulting from the arrangement or transaction (s. 322(3)), though the director with whom the person was connected will not be liable if all reasonable steps were taken by that director to secure the company's compliance with s. 320 (s. 322(5)), and neither the connected person nor an authorising director will be liable if they can show that at the time the arrangement was entered into they did not know the relevant circumstances constituting the contravention (s. 322(6)).

Where a company has acquired an asset in contravention of s. 322, the loss or damage which it may claim under s. 322(3) may include losses resulting from the subsequent decline in value of the asset: if the company had not acquired the asset, that loss would have been borne by the director and/or connected person from whom the asset was acquired, so they should not be able to pass that loss on to the company by a prohibited transaction (*Re Duckwari plc* (1998) *The Times*, 18 May 1998).

In *British Racing Drivers' Club Ltd* v *Hextall Erskine and Co.* [1996] 3 All ER 667, the company, which was a guarantee company whose members were present or former motor racing drivers, was persuaded by one of its directors, Mr Walkinshaw, to invest £5.3 million in his retail motor business. The business had been making losses for some years in a period of recession in the motor trade. The judge described the director as having a 'dominant position' on the board, whose members regarded him as having a 'Midas touch'. Walkinshaw did not want the members of the company consulted about the investment in advance because he said that some of them were his commercial rivals who would be prejudiced against him. The company's solicitors negligently advised that it was not necessary to obtain the members' approval for the transaction. After the investment was made and revealed to the members (without disclosing the price paid), dissenting members were advised by Mary Arden QC (now Arden J) that the approval of a general meeting should have been obtained under s. 320. At a subsequent extraordinary general meeting, a motion to approve the transaction was defeated by 82 per cent of those voting. Eventually, litigation against Mr Walkinshaw was settled by him repurchasing the investment for £3.2 million, so the club lost £2.1 million. It was, however, able to recover this from its solicitors in an action for damages for their negligence.

A director of a company who has an interest in property sold to the company must disclose that interest, both under the general law of fiduciary duties and under CA 1985, s. 317 (see 16.6.5), and if disclosure is not made then, even if it is not a substantial property transaction, the company may repudiate the purchase or obtain a court order for rescission (*Great Luxembourg Railway Co.* v *Magnay (No. 2)* (1858) 25 Beav 586). However, the company cannot, instead of having the transaction rescinded, recover the profit the director has made on it unless the profit was made in circumstances to which the rule against profiting or the rule against conflict of interest and duty apply (*Furs Ltd* v *Tomkies* (1936) 54 CLR 583, per Rich, Dixon and Evatt JJ at p. 599; *Peninsular & Oriental Steam Navigation Co.* v *Johnson* (1938) 60 CLR 189).

Before the legislation on substantial property transactions was enacted, the courts held that a company director selling property to the company was not in a position of conflict of interest and duty, or of making a profit from the directorship, if the director did not acquire the asset in the knowledge that it was required by the company. There is no liability to account for profit made on a sale of property already owned before the company's need became known (*North-West Transportation Co. Ltd* v *Beatty* (1887) 12 App Cas 589, PC), or property acquired in the course of the director's own business as a dealer in such property (as in *Peninsular & Oriental Steam Navigation Co.* v *Johnson*).

The distinction is commonly expressed in the words of Lord Buckmaster LC in *Cook* v *Deeks* [1916] 1 AC 554 at p. 563 as a distinction between: '. . . the case of a director selling to his company property which was in equity as well as at law his own, and which he could dispose of as he thought fit' and 'the case of a director dealing with property which, though his own at law, in equity belonged to his company'. It is a distinction that is also important in the liability of promoters (see 17.6.4).

For an example of a case in which a director of a company did acquire property in the knowledge that the company required it and was accordingly liable to the company for the profit made on reselling the property to the company see *Canada Safeway Ltd* v *Thompson* [1951] 3 DLR 295, in which the director also utilised his position as a director to obtain information about the property before purchasing it for himself and deliberately concealed his interest.

In *Burland* v *Earle* [1902] AC 83, in which the Privy Council reversed a decision of the Court of Appeal of Ontario, the defendant director purchased equipment and immediately resold it at a profit to his company. He was said to have had no commission or mandate from his company to purchase the equipment so there was no conflict of interest and duty. The case has been heavily criticised in Canada — see per Manson J in *Canada Safeway Ltd* v *Thompson* at pp. 321–2 ; Prentice (1972) 50 Can Bar Rev 623 at p. 632; Beck (1975) 53 Can Bar Rev 771 at p. 787.

Because of CA 1985, s. 322(3), these restrictions on suing for the director's profit no longer apply where the sale was a substantial property transaction.

16.6.8 Loans and other credit transactions

16.6.8.1 Loans and collateral

It is illegal for a company to lend money to one of its directors unless the amount of the loan, together with the total outstanding on all other loans made to that director by the company and all its subsidiaries is £5,000 or less (CA 1985, ss. 330(2)(a), 334, 339 and 341(1)).

It is illegal for a company to lend money to a director of its holding company unless the total amount of the loan, together with the total outstanding on all other loans made to that director by the holding company and all its subsidiaries is £5,000 or less (ibid.).

It is illegal for a company to give a guarantee or provide collateral security for a loan made by another person to one of its directors or a director of its holding company (ss. 330(2)(b) and 341(1)). The same applies to an indemnity (s. 331(2)).

The legislation describes these illegal transactions as 'prohibited'.

These prohibitions apply to loans and collateral provided during a director's term of office. A person can be appointed director of a company despite owing the company or one of its subsidiaries money lent before the appointment, and the loan does not have to be repaid on appointment. However, the loan will have to be disclosed in the company's accounts after the appointment (see 16.6.8.8), and the amount outstanding must be taken into consideration when a new loan is proposed under the £5,000 exemption.

A shadow director is treated as a director for the purposes of these provisions (s. 330(5)).

The rules cannot be avoided by the company taking an assignment from another person of rights, obligations or liabilities under a transaction which would have been prohibited if entered into by the company itself (ss. 330(6) and 339(2)(b)), nor can the company give any benefit to another person in return for the other person entering into an arrangement which would have been a prohibited transaction if entered into by the company itself (ss. 330(7) and 339(2)(b)).

16.6.8.2   Exceptions to the prohibitions on loans and collateral

A subsidiary may make a loan to its holding company and enter into a guarantee or provide security in connection with a loan made by another person to its holding company (CA 1985, s. 336(a)). This exception covers a situation in which a holding company is a director of its subsidiary.

The prohibitions on loans and collateral do not affect any transaction by a money-lending company in the normal course of its business, provided the loan or security would be given on the same terms to someone of the same financial status unconnected with the company (s. 338(1), (2) and (3)). (A loan on specially favourable terms may be made by a money-lending company for the purchase or improvement of a director's principal private residence, provided such loans are usually available to the company's employees for this purpose and the total amount outstanding on loans for this purpose to the director does not exceed £100,000 (s. 338(6): we believe that the reference in s. 339(1) to s. 338(4) should be a reference to s. 338(1) if the pre-consolidation legislation is to be reproduced accurately).) If a money-lending company is a public company or a subsidiary of a public company then this exception is subject to a financial limit (see 16.6.8.4) unless the company is a banking company (s. 338(4)).

The prohibitions do not affect any transaction to provide funds needed for the performance of a director's duties, provided the transaction is approved by the members in general meeting (s. 337). If the company is a public company or the subsidiary of a public company then this exception is subject to a financial limit (see 16.6.8.4). At a general meeting approving such a transaction, certain matters prescribed in s. 337(4) must be disclosed. If the approval is given by the members of a private company by means of a written resolution under s. 381A then the matters must be disclosed to each member at or before the time at which the resolution is supplied to that member for signature (sch. 15A, para. 9).

16.6.8.3 *Additional restrictions on relevant companies*

CA 1985, s. 330, also prohibits various types of credit transactions, other than straight loans, between a company and its directors and the directors of its holding company. These additional restrictions apply only to 'relevant companies'. 'Relevant companies', for this purpose, are public companies and those private companies which belong to a group in which any one of the member companies is a public company (s. 331(6)). In addition s. 342 makes it a criminal offence for a relevant company to contravene the prohibitions on loans and credit facilities.

The additional prohibitions applying to relevant companies prevent them entering into the following kinds of transactions with their directors or directors of their holding companies:

(a)   Credit sales (e.g., on hire-purchase or by leasing) of land or goods or services to such a director or anyone connected with such a director (ss. 330(4)(a), 331(7) and (8)) unless made in the normal course of business on credit terms which the company would have extended to a person of the same financial status unconnected with the company (s. 335(2)).

(b)   Entering into a guarantee or otherwise giving collateral security for a credit sale by a third party to such a director or anyone connected with such a director, with the same exception as in (a) (ss. 330(4)(b), 331(7) and (8), 335(2)).

Transactions of types (a) and (b) may be entered into otherwise than in the normal course of business if the total outstanding on all such transactions from one director and all the persons connected with him does not exceed £10,000, counting transactions with the company of which he is a director and all its subsidiaries (ss. 335(1) and 339; SI 1990 No. 1393).

(c)   Quasi-loans to such a director (s. 330(3)(a)). 'Quasi-loan' means an arrangement under which a company meets some financial obligations of a director on the understanding that it will be reimbursed later (s. 331(3)). Quasi-loans may be made to a director if reimbursement is to occur within two months and the total outstanding does not exceed £5,000, counting quasi-loans by the company of which he is a director and by all its subsidiaries (s. 332).

(d)   Loans or quasi-loans to a person connected with such a director (s. 330(3)(b)). But a company may make a loan or quasi-loan to another company in the same group even if a director is associated with that company (s. 333).

(e)   Entering into a guarantee or otherwise giving collateral security for a loan or a quasi-loan given by a third party to a person connected with such a director with the same exception as in (d) (ss. 330(3)(c) and 333).

For a list of the persons connected with a director see 16.6.8.10.

16.6.8.4 *Exceptions*

The exceptions noted in 16.6.8.2 apply in similar terms to the types of transactions listed in 16.6.8.3. However, relevant companies are allowed the second and third of the exceptions only within certain monetary limits.

If a money-lending company is a public company, or the subsidiary of a public company, then it may make loans or quasi-loans, or act as surety for loans or quasi-loans, on its normal terms of business. But, unless it is a banking company, the total amount outstanding on such transactions from one director and all the persons connected with him must not exceed

£100,000, counting arrangements with the company of which he is a director and all its subsidiaries (CA 1985, ss. 338(1) to (5) and 339).

Credit arrangements given by a relevant company to enable a director to carry out his duties must not total more than £20,000, counting arrangements with the company of which he is a director and all its subsidiaries (ss. 337 and 339; SI 1990 No. 1393).

16.6.8.5   Anti-avoidance provisions
Subsections (6) and (7) of CA 1985, s. 330, prevent the prohibitions on credit transactions being avoided by getting another person to provide the credit.

Under s. 330(6), an assignment taken by a company from another person of rights, obligations or liabilities under any arrangement which, if entered into by the company, would have been a prohibited transaction is itself a prohibited transaction.

Under s. 330(7) any benefit given by a company to another person in return for it entering into an arrangement which, if entered into by the company would have been a prohibited transaction is itself a prohibited transaction.

16.6.8.6   Criminal penalties
If a public company or a subsidiary of a public company enters into any of the arrangements described in 16.6.8.1, 16.6.8.3 and 16.6.8.5 (and not within the exceptions) then it commits an offence triable either way (CA 1985, s. 342(2) and (4) and sch. 24). It is a defence for the company to show that it did not know the relevant circumstances (s. 342(5)). Any director of the company who authorised or permitted the company to enter into the arrangement knowing, or having reasonable cause to believe, that the company was thereby contravening s. 330 is guilty of an offence triable either way (CA 1985, s. 342(1) and (4) and sch. 24) as is a person who knowingly procured the company to enter into the transaction (s. 342(3)).

16.6.8.7   Civil remedies
Any transaction or arrangement entered into in contravention of CA 1985, s. 330, is voidable at the company's option unless restitution is impossible or rights have been acquired by a bona fide third party for value without actual notice of the contravention (s. 341(1)). In addition, if the arrangement was with a director then the director concerned, and any other director who authorised the transaction or arrangement, are liable to account to the company for any gain which they made whether directly or indirectly by the transaction or arrangement, and are liable (jointly and severally) to indemnify the company for any loss or damage resulting from the transaction or arrangement (s. 341(2)), though an authorising director will not be liable if he can show that at the time the transaction or arrangement was entered into he did not know the relevant circumstances constituting the contravention (s. 341(5)). If the arrangement was with a person connected with a director then that director and the connected person and any other director who authorised the arrangement are liable to account to the company for any gain which they made whether directly or indirectly by the arrangement or transaction, and are liable (jointly and severally) to indemnify the company for any loss or damage resulting from the arrangement or transaction (s. 341(2)). However, the director with whom the person was connected will not be liable if he can show that he took all reasonable steps to secure the company's compliance with s. 330 (s. 341(4)), and neither the connected person nor an authorising director will be liable if he can show that at the time the arrangement was entered into he did not know the relevant circumstances constituting the contravention (s. 341(5)).

16.6.8.8 Disclosure in annual accounts
CA 1985, s. 232(1) and sch. 6, paras 15(a) and 16(a), require every company to disclose in notes to its annual accounts details of all transactions and arrangements, of the types described in CA 1985, s. 330 (loans, guarantees, quasi-loans and credit transactions), which it has entered into, during the financial year reported on, for:

(a) Any of its directors or shadow directors.
(b) Any directors or shadow directors of its holding company.
(c) Persons connected with such directors or shadow directors.

CA 1985, sch. 6, para. 15(b), requires disclosure of any agreement to enter into a s. 330 transaction or arrangement in the future for any of these persons.
   CA 1985, s. 232(1) and sch. 6, para. 15(a) and (b), require a holding company to disclose in notes to its accounts all the s. 330 transactions and arrangements and agreements to enter into such transactions and arrangements provided by any of its subsidiaries for any of the persons listed above. This must be done whether or not the company produces group accounts (sch. 6, para. 15).
   Disclosure must be made whether or not the transaction is illegal (sch. 6, para. 19(a)) and must therefore be made for transactions entered into before the person concerned became a director or became connected with a director (para. 19(b)) and before a company became a subsidiary of the reporting company (para. 19(c)). However, it is not necessary to report credit sales and guarantees of credit sales to a director and the persons connected with him if the total outstanding on such sales from that group of persons never exceeded £5,000 during the financial year reported on (counting arrangements with the reporting company and all its subsidiaries) (sch. 6, para. 24).
   The details to be disclosed in the accounts are specified in sch. 6, paras 22 and 23. The name of the director concerned must be stated. For a loan, the amounts outstanding at the beginning and end of the financial year, and (to avoid window-dressing) the maximum amount outstanding during the year, the amount of interest currently in arrear, and a statement of any provision made against non-repayment. In the case of a guarantee, the company's liability at the beginning and end of the year (and the maximum during the year) and any payments made under the guarantee. In the case of a credit sale, the market value of the goods sold.
   There are special provisions for banks (s. 255B(2) and sch. 9, part IV).

16.6.8.9 Disclosure of transactions with officers other than directors
All companies are required to disclose in notes to annual accounts details of loans, quasi-loans and credit transactions entered into by the company or by any of its subsidiaries to or on behalf of officers of the company other than directors (CA 1985, s. 232(1) and sch. 6, paras 28 to 30). Also included are related guarantees, securities and arrangements of the kind described in s. 330(6) or (7) (see 16.6.8.5).
   The accounts are required to disclose, in respect of loans, quasi-loans and credit transactions separately, the aggregate amounts outstanding at the end of the financial year and the number of officers for whom they were made.
   If the aggregate amount outstanding at the end of the financial year reported on in respect of all transactions and arrangements made for a particular officer is £2,500 or less then all the transactions and arrangements for him can be left out of account for the purpose of this disclosure (sch. 6, para. 29(2)).

16.6.8.10   Connected persons

By CA 1985, s. 346, the persons 'connected with' a director are:

(a)   The director's spouse.

(b)   The director's legitimate or illegitimate children and stepchildren under 18.

(c)   Any company if the director and persons connected with him are interested in more than 20 per cent of its equity share capital (or control more than 20 per cent of its voting rights). (The director is said to be 'associated' with such a company.)

(d)   A trustee of any trust under which any person mentioned in (a), (b) or (c) could benefit, apart from an employees' share scheme or a pension scheme.

(e)   Any partner (in a business or profession) of the director or of any person mentioned in (a), (b), (c) or (d).

However, any such person who is also a director of the same company is not treated as being connected (otherwise one would go round in circles).

If a director of a company, together with his fellow directors and all the persons connected with him, are interested in more than 50 per cent of the equity share capital of a body corporate (or control more than 50 per cent of its voting rights) then the director is deemed to 'control' that body corporate (s. 346(5)). However, this does not apply if neither the director himself nor any person connected with him is interested in any part of the equity share capital of the body corporate (or can control any of its voting power) (s. 346(5)(a)).

16.7   TRANSACTIONS TO WHICH THE COMPANY IS NOT A PARTY

16.7.1   Rule against profiting

A director of a company must account to the company for profits made not only from the director's transactions with the company but also from some transactions to which the company is not a party. The immediate problem is to define which transactions are subject to the rule. The leading case is *Regal (Hastings) Ltd* v *Gulliver* [1967] 2 AC 134. According to the Law Lords in that case, a director's profit from a transaction to which the company is not a party is subject to the rule if the profit arises 'by reason and in course of [the director's] fiduciary relationship' (per Lord Russell of Killowen at p. 143), or 'by reason and in virtue of [the] fiduciary office as [director]' (per Lord Macmillan at p. 153), or 'by reason of [the director's] fiduciary position, and by reason of the opportunity and the knowledge, or either, resulting from it' (per Lord Wright at p. 154) or 'only by use of [the director's] fiduciary position' (per Lord Porter at p. 158). Lord Wright's formulation appears to be the most comprehensive.

The narrower view of Lord Blanesburgh in *Bell* v *Lever Brothers Ltd* [1932] AC 161, at p. 194, that a company could only be interested in a profit made by one of its directors from a transaction to which the company was not a party if 'in earning that profit he has made use either of the property of the company or of some confidential information which has come to him as a director of the company' has not been generally accepted as fully stating the law.

Whether or not the company itself was capable of making the profit is irrelevant to the application of the rule against profiting. However, the director will be allowed to retain a profit if the directors of the company decided bona fide that the company itself should not pursue the transaction (see 16.7.3.4), or if the articles have disapplied the rule against profiting (see 16.7.5) or if the members give their fully informed consent to the director making the profit (see 16.8).

In *Regal (Hastings) Ltd* v *Gulliver,* the company owned and managed a freehold cinema. It set up a wholly owned subsidiary, called Hastings Amalgamated Cinemas Ltd ('Amalgamated'), to acquire leases of two other cinemas in the same town. All the directors of Regal (Hastings) Ltd were directors of the new subsidiary. The landlords of those two other cinemas said that unless this subsidiary had a paid-up share capital of £5,000, personal guarantees of payment of rent would be required from directors. However, the directors knew that another person wished to acquire all three cinemas.

At a meeting the directors decided that the parent company should subscribe for 2,000 £1 shares in Amalgamated and that the company's five directors (including the chairman, Gulliver) and the company's solicitor should subscribe for 500 shares each. (In the event, Gulliver did not subscribe for shares personally but persuaded a friend of his and two companies in which he was interested to subscribe.) Three weeks later all the shares in the company and in Amalgamated were sold: subscribers for Amalgamated shares, including the four directors other than Gulliver, made a profit of £2 16s 1d on each Amalgamated share. The House of Lords held that each director except Gulliver had to account for this profit to the company. (Gulliver escaped liability because it was found as a fact that he had not personally profited from the allotments to the subscribers he had introduced as they were not acting as his nominees.) Lord Russell of Killowen said (at p. 147) that the directors' profit was made 'by reason, and only by reason of the fact that they were directors of Regal, and in the course of their execution of that office'. His lordship said, at pp. 144–5:

> The rule of equity which insists on those, who by use of a fiduciary position make a profit, being liable to account for that profit, in no way depends on fraud, or absence of bona fides; or upon such questions or considerations as whether the profit would or should otherwise have gone to the plaintiff, or whether the profiteer was under a duty to obtain the source of the profit for the plaintiff, or whether he took a risk or acted as he did for the benefit of the plaintiff, or whether the plaintiff has in fact been damaged or benefited by his action. The liability arises from the mere fact of a profit having, in the stated circumstances, been made.

At their meeting the directors had decided that the parent company could not afford to subscribe more than £2,000 for Amalgamated shares. Had the parent company raised the other £3,000 for itself by making a rights issue of its own shares to its shareholders (including its directors) and itself subscribed for all the shares in Amalgamated then there would have been nothing to complain of.

16.7.2 Rule against conflict of interest and duty

The rule against conflict of interest and duty applies to a transaction from which a director of a company benefits even if the company itself is not a party to the transaction provided the company has what has been called a 'specific interest' in the transaction (*Cook* v *Deeks* [1916] 1 AC 554, PC; *Regal (Hastings) Ltd* v *Gulliver* [1967] 2 AC 134, HL, per Viscount Sankey at p. 137; *Canada Safeway Ltd* v *Thompson* [1951] 3 DLR 295, British Columbia; *Zwicker* v *Stanbury* [1954] 1 DLR 257, Supreme Court of Canada; *Consul Development Pty Ltd* v *DPC Estates Pty Ltd* (1975) 132 CLR 373, per Gibbs J at p. 393). The limitation to transactions in which the company has a specific interest was pointed out by Falconer J in *Balston Ltd* v *Headline Filters Ltd* [1990] FSR 385 at p. 412.

The wide range of circumstances in which the rule has been applied can be seen from the long list of cases cited in the preceding paragraph. However, the rule has been particularly important in a group of cases in which directors have taken for themselves business opportunities of their companies, and these are considered in 16.7.3.

16.7.3   The corporate opportunity doctrine

16.7.3.1   Introduction

There may be a conflict of interest and duty if a director of a company pursues for his or her own benefit a business opportunity in the company's line of business (*Cook* v *Deeks* [1916] 1 AC 554, PC; *G.E. Smith Ltd* v *Smith* [1952] NZLR 470; *DPC Estates Pty Ltd* v *Grey* [1974] 1 NSWLR 443). This conflict is not necessarily resolved by resigning the directorship (*Industrial Development Consultants Ltd* v *Cooley* [1972] 1 WLR 443; *Canadian Aero Service Ltd* v *O'Malley* (1973) 40 DLR (3d) 371, Supreme Court of Canada; *Roper* v *Murdoch* (1987) 39 DLR (4th) 684, British Columbia).

The director must account to the company for the profits made and is also a constructive trustee for the company of any property acquired (*Carlton* v *Halestrap* (1988) 4 BCC 538).

This has come to be known as the 'corporate opportunity doctrine'.

16.7.3.2   Examples

In *Cook* v *Deeks* [1916] 1 AC 554, PC, the holders of three quarters of the shares in the Toronto Construction Co. Ltd, who were three of the company's directors, fell out with the fourth director and shareholder, Cook. The company had completed several successful contracts for the Canadian Pacific Railway Co. and the majority directors were only known to the railway company because of their association with Toronto Construction Co. Negotiations for a new contract with the railway company were conducted by the majority directors without informing Cook and when the contract was awarded the majority directors formed a new company to carry it out. The Privy Council ordered the majority directors and the new company to account to the Toronto Construction Co. for the profits made out of the contract. Lord Buckmaster LC said, at p. 563:

> . . . the real question [is] whether [the transaction] was one into which, consistently with their duty, they were at liberty to enter.
>
> . . . men who assume the complete control of a company's business must remember that they are not at liberty to sacrifice the interests which they are bound to protect, and, while ostensibly acting for the company, divert in their own favour business which should properly belong to the company they represent.

In *Industrial Development Consultants Ltd* v *Cooley* [1972] 1 WLR 443, Mr Cooley was managing director of the plaintiff company, which acted as project managers in the construction industry. During 1968 he had sought contracts for the company from the Eastern Gas Board. However, at that time the Gas Board decided not to go ahead with the work. In the next year the Gas Board reconsidered the position and this became known to Cooley personally through discussion with the Gas Board's deputy chairman. The Gas Board objected 'in principle to the set-up' of Industrial Development Consultants and other companies in the same group but were willing to employ Cooley himself. During the weekend of 14/15 June 1969, Cooley prepared a tender for the contracts. On 16 June he went to see the chairman of Industrial Development Consultants and pretended that he was on the verge of a breakdown and had to be released from his job immediately — this was agreed to. On 17 June he submitted the tender. He was awarded the contract, which Roskill J found was substantially the same contract as Industrial Development Consultants had been trying to get the previous year. His lordship said, at p. 446:

There can be no doubt that the defendant got this Eastern Gas Board contract for himself as a result of work which he did whilst still the plaintiffs' managing director.

And at p. 451:

From the time he embarked upon his course of dealing with the Eastern Gas Board . . . he embarked upon a deliberate policy and course of conduct which put his personal interest as a potential contracting party with the Eastern Gas Board in direct conflict with his pre-existing and continuing duty as managing director of the plaintiffs.

It did not make any difference that when talking to the Gas Board in early June, Cooley said that he was acting for himself, not for Industrial Development Consultants. Roskill J said, at p. 451:

The defendant had one capacity and one capacity only in which he was carrying on business at that time. That capacity was as managing director of the plaintiffs.

Accordingly Cooley was trustee for the plaintiffs of his profits on the Gas Board contract. Incidentally, it should be pointed out that Roskill J's extempore judgment is reported in some respects more fully in [1972] 2 All ER 162.

In *Canadian Aero Service Ltd* v *O'Malley* (1973) 40 DLR (3d) 371, the first two defendants, O'Malley and Zarzycki, had the job titles of 'president and chief executive officer' and 'executive vice-president and director' of Canadian Aero Service Ltd (usually referred to as 'Canaero'), which was a wholly owned subsidiary of an American company. Because of failure by the parent company to comply with formalities of Canadian company law, the defendants had not formally been appointed directors of Canaero. The Supreme Court of Canada, however, held this made no difference since they were clearly 'top management' of the company and so should be subject to the same fiduciary obligations as directors. (Liability was imposed in a similar situation in *DPC Estates Pty Ltd* v *Grey* [1974] 1 NSWLR 470.)

Canaero was engaged in aerial surveying and had been attempting to get a government contract for this work in Guyana from 1962 to 1966. Zarzycki, a widely respected expert on aerial survey techniques, visited Guyana on Canaero's behalf in 1962 and 1965 and prepared a proposal which was submitted to the relevant government agencies. On 9 July 1966, O'Malley and Zarzycki met the prime minister of Guyana and reported to Canaero that it was certain to get the contract. The next month the two men resigned from the company and set up a new company of their own, which tendered for the Guyana contract the following month and was awarded it in November 1966. The tender price was exactly that stated by Zarzycki in his 1965 proposal.

The Supreme Court of Canada awarded damages to Canaero.

16.7.3.3 Limits of the doctrine

The liability of a company director for personally pursuing one of the company's business opportunities is not diminished by the fact that the company itself would not have pursued the opportunity (*Industrial Development Consultants Ltd* v *Cooley* [1972] 1 WLR 443; *Consul Development Pty Ltd* v *DPC Estates Pty Ltd* (1975) 132 CLR 373 per Gibbs J at p. 395) unless there is a bona fide decision by the board not to pursue it (see 16.7.3.4). As in any circumstance where the rule against conflict of interest and duty might apply, a company director will not be liable for personally pursuing one of the company's business opportunities if the articles have disapplied the rule (see 16.7.5) or if the members give their fully informed consent to the director's action (see 16.8).

The main problem for the courts in corporate opportunity cases is to decide whether the company has a specific interest in the opportunity which conflicts with the director's interest. In many cases a company's interest in an opportunity which one of its directors has personally pursued arises because the director found the opportunity and is held to have been under a duty to inform the company of it. In *DPC Estates Pty Ltd* v *Grey* [1974] 1 NSWLR 443, Huntley JA said, at p. 465:

[Grey's] agreement required him to devote himself exclusively to the business of working manager of the associated companies, and one of his principal duties was to find avenues for real estate development. It is a notorious fact that such information comes from many sources, for example, from tips in clubs and on social occasions. In my opinion, any information which he obtained in relation to real estate matters within the scope of the business of the associated companies could only be used by him for the benefit of those companies.

In *Industrial Development Consultants Ltd* v *Cooley*, Roskill J said, at p. 451:

Information which came to [Cooley] while he was managing director and which was of concern to [the company of which he was managing director] and was relevant for the [company] to know, was information which it was his duty to pass on to the [company] because between himself and the [company] a fiduciary relationship existed.

However, in *Canadian Aero Service Ltd* v *O'Malley* (1973) 40 DLR (3d) 371, Laskin J, giving the judgment of the Supreme Court of Canada, took, at p. 391, a more general approach to the problem:

The general standards of loyalty, good faith and avoidance of a conflict of duty and self-interest to which the conduct of a director or senior officer must conform, must be tested in each case by many factors which it would be reckless to attempt to enumerate exhaustively. Among them are the factor of position or office held, the nature of the corporate opportunity, its ripeness, its specificness and the director's or managerial officer's relation to it, the amount of knowledge possessed, the circumstances in which it was obtained and whether it was special or, indeed, even private, the factor of time in the continuation of fiduciary duty where the alleged breach occurs after termination of the relationship with the company, and the circumstances under which the relationship was terminated, that is whether by retirement or resignation or discharge.

It is certainly a breach of duty for a director of a company, while still a director, to invite its existing customers to cease dealing with the company and to deal instead with the director's own business (*Aubanel & Alabaster Ltd* v *Aubanel* (1949) 66 RPC 343; *Mordecai* v *Mordecai* (1988) 12 NSWLR 58).

Where a former director of a company pursues one of the company's corporate opportunities after leaving the company, liability is limited by the law's policy against restraints on trade (*Island Export Finance Ltd* v *Umunna* [1986] BCLC 460).

In *Canadian Aero Service Ltd* v *O'Malley,* Laskin J said, at p. 382:

An examination of the case law in this court and in the courts of other like jurisdictions on the fiduciary duties of directors and senior officers shows the pervasiveness of a strict ethic in this area of the law. In my opinion, this ethic disqualifies a director or senior officer from usurping for himself or diverting to another person or company with whom or with which he is associated a maturing business opportunity which his company is actively pursuing; he is also precluded from so acting even after his resignation where the resignation may fairly be said to have been prompted or influenced by a wish to acquire for himself the opportunity sought by the company, or where it was his position with the company rather than a fresh initiative that led him to the opportunity which he later acquired.

In *Island Export Finance Ltd* v *Umunna* [1986] BCLC 460, Hutchinson J said, at p. 481:

> It appears to me, if I may say so with respect, that the judges in the *Canaero* case were absolutely right to conclude that on the facts of that case there was a breach of fiduciary duty by the defendants: and that in so holding they were consistently applying the principles laid down in the line of authorities of which *Regal (Hastings) Ltd* v *Gulliver* [1967] 2 AC 134 is an example.

His lordship approved the passage from Laskin J's judgment quoted above apart from the last 42 words in so far as they:

> . . . could justify holding former directors accountable for profits wherever information acquired by them as such led them to the source from which they subsequently, perhaps as the result of prolonged fresh initiative, acquired business.

A director's position with a company will naturally provide the director with information about the markets in which the company operates. However, such information becomes part of the director's general fund of knowledge and stock in trade, and, because of the policy of the law against restraints on trade, after leaving the company, the director cannot be held accountable for exploiting that information for his or her own or a new employer's benefit. In *Balston Ltd* v *Headline Filters Ltd* [1990] FSR 385, Falconer J said, at p. 412:

> In my judgment an intention by a director of a company to set up business in competition with the company after his directorship has ceased is not to be regarded as a conflicting interest within the context of the [rule against conflict of interest and duty], having regard to the rules of public policy as to restraint of trade, nor is the taking of any preliminary steps to investigate or forward that intention so long as there is no actual competitive activity, such as, for instance, competitive tendering or actual trading, while he remains a director.

Another way of ameliorating the corporate opportunity doctrine has been found by the High Court of Australia. It has ruled that, even if it is found that the setting up of a business by a company director exploiting one of the company's corporate opportunities was in breach of fiduciary duty to that company, it may not be equitable to compel the director to account for all profits made from pursuing the business indefinitely: some allowance may be made for the director's own input of effort and capital (*Warman International Ltd* v *Dwyer* (1995) 182 CLR 544).

16.7.3.4 *Investments the board has decided not to make*
If the board of directors of a company considers a new venture and concludes bona fide that the company shall not pursue it then individual directors can pursue the venture on their

own account (*Peso Silver Mines Ltd (NPL)* v *Cropper* (1966) 58 DLR (2d) 1, Supreme Court of Canada; *Queensland Mines Ltd* v *Hudson* (1978) 52 ALJR 399, PC; *Joint receivers & managers of Niltan Carson Ltd* v *Hawthorne* [1988] BCLC 298). (In *Regal (Hastings) Ltd* v *Gulliver* [1967] 2 AC 134, Lord Russell of Killowen said, at pp. 152–3, that this had certainly not happened in that case.) In *Queensland Mines Ltd* v *Hudson*, Lord Scarman said that in the case of Queensland Mines Ltd it did not matter whether it was said (a) that the board's decision meant that the venture was put outside the scope of the director's fiduciary relationship because it was outside the scope of the company's business or (b) that the company had given its fully informed consent to the director making the profit for himself. However, it is submitted that, generally, it is not appropriate for the board of directors to give their consent to one of their number making a profit which the company could claim (see *Furs Ltd* v *Tomkies* (1936) 54 CLR 583) whereas it is within the powers of the board of directors to decide which ventures the company should invest in. It would be better, it is submitted, to regard the matter as no longer within the scope of the fiduciary relationship, and this analysis would explain *Peso Silver Mines Ltd (NPL)* v *Cropper*, in which there was no express consent by the members to the directors' profit. See also the remark of Lord Buckmaster LC in *Cook* v *Deeks* [1916] 1 AC 554 (see 16.7.3.2) at p. 565 that if the directors had 'decided on a matter of policy' the outcome of the case would have been different. The possibility that there may be a limit to the subject-matter of a director's fiduciary relationship is mentioned by Lord Wilberforce in *New Zealand Netherlands Society 'Oranje' Incorporated* v *Kuys* [1973] 1 WLR 1126, PC, at p. 1131 and by Gibbs CJ in *Hospital Products Ltd* v *United States Surgical Corporation* (1984) 156 CLR 41, at p. 73. See also per Gibbs J (as he then was) in *Consul Development Pty Ltd* v *DPC Estates Pty Ltd* (1975) 132 CLR 373, at pp. 399–400. As it happens the only two shareholders of Queensland Mines Ltd (both of them companies) were represented on the board so that directors' meetings were *de facto* members' meetings (see 14.4.8.4) and it is clear that the fully informed consent of the members to a director's action excludes the rule against profiting (see 16.8).

The *Peso Silver Mines* decision has been heavily criticised in a lengthy analysis by Beck, 'The saga of Peso Silver Mines: corporate opportunity reconsidered' (1971) 49 Can Bar Rev 80. See also Beck (1975) 53 Can Bar Rev 771 and D.D. Prentice, '*Regal (Hastings) Ltd* v *Gulliver* — the Canadian experience' (1967) 30 MLR 450. *Queensland Mines Ltd* v *Hudson* is criticised in a casenote by G.R. Sullivan, 'Going it alone — *Queensland Mines* v *Hudson*' (1979) 42 MLR 711.

16.7.3.5 *Further reading*

The two articles by Beck, 'The saga of Peso Silver Mines: corporate opportunity reconsidered' (1971) 49 Can Bar Rev 80 and 'The quickening of fiduciary obligation: *Canadian Aero Services* [sic] v *O'Malley*' (1975) 53 Can Bar Rev 771, offer a very full discussion of the corporate opportunity doctrine, including a comparison with the position in the USA. The first of them was reprinted with slight changes as 'Corporate opportunity revisited', in Jacob S. Ziegel (ed.), *Studies in Canadian Company Law*, vol. 2 (Toronto: Butterworths, 1973), pp. 193–238. Further commentary will be found in three casenotes by D.D. Prentice, 'Directors' fiduciary duties — the corporate opportunity doctrine'(1972) 50 Can Bar Rev 623 (on *Industrial Development Consultants Ltd* v *Cooley* [1972] 1 WLR 443), 'The corporate opportunity doctrine' (1974) 37 MLR 464 (on *Canadian Aero Service Ltd* v *O'Malley* (1973) 40 DLR (3d) 371) and 'Corporate opportunity — windfall profits' (1979) 42 MLR 215 (on *Abbey Glen Property Corporation* v *Stumborg* (1978) 85 DLR (3d) 35). The casenote on *Industrial Development Consultants Ltd* v *Cooley* by H. Rajak, 'Fiduciary

duty of a managing director' (1972) 35 MLR 655 takes a wide-ranging and critical view.
J.P. Lowry, '*Regal (Hastings)* 50 years on: breaking the bonds of the *ancien régime*?' (1994)
45 NILQ 1 takes up the criticism noted in 16.3.1 of directors being subject to fiduciary
duties and suggests that they should not be liable if the company has not suffered a loss.
Lowry approves of *Peso Silver Mines Ltd (NPL)* v *Cropper* (1966) 58 DLR (2d) 1 and *Island
Export Finance Ltd* v *Umunna* [1986] BCLC 460, which he thinks display the necessary
flexibility in their treatment of fiduciary obligations. See also G.M.D. Bean, 'Corporate
governance and corporate opportunities' (1994) 15 Co Law 266.

16.7.4 Competing directorships

London & Mashonaland Exploration Co. Ltd v *New Mashonaland Exploration Co. Ltd*
[1891] WN 165 is usually cited as authority for the proposition that a director of a company
may be a director of a competing company. It may be that the *Mashonaland* case depends
on the fact that the director concerned was an inactive figurehead (a 'Lord on the board')
whom the judge thought owed no duties to his company other than not to divulge
confidential information (cf. *Waite's Auto Transfer Ltd* v *Waite* [1928] 3 WWR 649 and
Glavanics v *Brunninghausen* (1996) 19 ACSR 204 at p. 228, which were also cases of
inactive directors). A competing directorship will not be wrong unless there is a 'real
sensible possibility of conflict' (see 16.5.3) (cf. D.C. McDonald J in *Abbey Glen Property
Corporation* v *Stumborg* at first instance (1975) 65 DLR (3d) 235 at p. 278; Beck (1975)
53 Can Bar Rev 771 at pp. 789–92; Mahon J in *Berlei Hestia (NZ) Ltd* v *Fernyhough* [1980]
2 NZLR 150, at pp. 160–1). See E. Boros, 'The duties of nominee and multiple directors.
Part II' (1990) 11 Co Law 6; M. Christie, 'The director's fiduciary duty not to compete'
(1992) 55 MLR 506 (which argues that the *Mashonaland* case was wrongly decided).

16.7.5 Articles disapplying the rules

Table A, art. 85, permits a director of the company to be a director, or other officer or
employee, of any corporation promoted by the company or in which the company is
otherwise interested, provided that the nature and extent of the director's interest is disclosed
to his fellow directors. If that disclosure is made then the rules against profiting and against
conflict of interest and duty are disapplied.

16.8 RATIFICATION OF PROFITING AND CONFLICT OF INTEREST

The members of a company can effectively exclude the rules against profiting and against
conflict of interest and duty in relation to any transaction in which one of the company's
directors is interested by giving their fully informed consent to the transaction, after full and
frank disclosure of all material facts (*North-West Transportation Co. Ltd* v *Beatty* (1887) 12
App Cas 589, PC; *New Zealand Netherlands Society 'Oranje' Incorporated* v *Kuys* [1973]
1 WLR 1126, PC; *Queensland Mines Ltd* v *Hudson* (1978) 52 ALJR 399, PC; cf. *Boulting*
v *Association of Cinematograph, Television & Allied Technicians* [1963] 2 QB 606 per
Upjohn LJ at p. 636).

 This applies whether the company is a party to the transaction (e.g., *North-West
Transportation Co. Ltd* v *Beatty*; *Grant* v *United Kingdom Switchback Railways Co.* (1888)
40 ChD 135, CA) or not (e.g., *New Zealand Netherlands Society 'Oranje' Incorporated* v
Kuys). However, in most British companies nowadays, a vote of members is unnecessary in
relation to a transaction to which the company is a party because a provision in the articles

like those discussed in 16.6.2 will exclude the rules against profiting and against conflict of interest and duty provided there is disclosure of the interest (and the interest must be disclosed in any case under CA 1985, s. 317 — see 16.6.5).

Consent must be given by the members: consent by the board of directors is insufficient (*Furs Ltd* v *Tomkies* (1936) 54 CLR 583, per Latham J at p. 590, Rich, Dixon and Evatt JJ at p. 599) unless the members and the directors are the same persons (*Attorney-General for the Dominion of Canada* v *The Standard Trust Co. of New York* [1911] AC 498, PC; *Re Express Engineering Works Ltd* [1920] 1 Ch 466, CA; and see the discussion of *Queensland Mines Ltd* v *Hudson* in 16.7.3.4).

Consent given without full disclosure is ineffective. In *Kaye* v *Croydon Tramways Co.* [1898] 1 Ch 358, CA, a resolution approving a contract of sale of the company's undertaking was set aside because the notice convening the meeting and a circular sent by the directors to shareholders had failed to disclose that the purchaser would make a substantial payment to the selling company's directors. In *Baillie* v *Oriental Telephone & Electric Co. Ltd* [1915] 1 Ch 503, CA, a resolution authorising the company's directors to receive remuneration from one of the company's subsidiaries was set aside because the directors had failed to disclose that it would allow them to keep more than £40,000 that they had already received. See also *Tiessen* v *Henderson* [1899] 1 Ch 861.

Consent to a transaction with a director is ineffective if the transaction is a fraud on creditors (*Re DKG Contractors Ltd* [1990] BCC 903, see 20.11.4).

Consent by the members is often called 'ratification', meaning precluding legal action by deeming that a right of action has not arisen — see 16.4.14.

In *North-West Transportation Co. Ltd* v *Beatty* (1887) 12 App Cas 589, PC, Sir Richard Baggallay said, at pp. 593–4:

The general principles applicable to cases of this kind are well-established. . . .

. . . a director of a company is precluded from dealing, on behalf of the company, with himself, and from entering into engagements in which he has a personal interest conflicting, or which possibly may conflict, with the interests of those whom he is bound by fiduciary duty to protect. . . . Any such dealing or engagement may, however, be affirmed or adopted by the company, provided such affirmance or adoption is not brought about by unfair or improper means, and is not illegal or fraudulent or oppressive towards those shareholders who oppose it.

If an informed consent is freely given then, as Vinelott J put it in *Movitex Ltd* v *Bulfield* (1986) 2 BCC 99,403 at p. 99,430, 'the conflict between duty and interest is dissolved'. His lordship went on to say:

The resolution in general meeting protects the director not because it operates to release him from the consequences of a breach of the self-dealing rule but because, to the extent that the company in general meeting gives its informed consent to the transaction there is no breach; the conflict of duty and interest is avoided.

A director interested in a transaction who is also a member can, as a member, vote at the general meeting in favour of ratifying the transaction (*North-West Transportation Co. Ltd* v *Beatty*; *Attorney-General for the Dominion of Canada* v *Standard Trust Co. of New York*; *Re Express Engineering Works Ltd*). The resolution will then be an effective ratification, even if the vote would have gone the other way if the director/member had not voted (*North-West Transportation Co. Ltd* v *Beatty*), unless the resolution was a fraud on the minority (*Cook* v *Deeks* [1916] 1 AC 554, PC; *Daniels* v *Daniels* [1978] Ch 406 — see 18.4.4).

For wide-ranging criticism of the current law on ratification see J. Lowry, 'Directorial self-dealing: constructing a regime of accountability' (1997) 48 NILQ 211.

16.9 RELIEF FROM LIABILITY

16.9.1 Relief by the company

In *Re Brazilian Rubber Plantations and Estates Ltd* [1911] 1 Ch 425, the terms of directors' appointments, contained in the company's articles of association, provided that the company could not sue a director for 'any . . . loss, damage, or misfortune whatever which shall happen in the execution of the duties of his office or in relation thereto, unless the same happen through his own dishonesty'. Neville J held that this was lawful and prevented the company's liquidator from taking misfeasance proceedings against the directors for alleged negligence (though his lordship also found that there was no negligence). *Re City Equitable Fire Insurance Co. Ltd* [1925] Ch 407 concerned a company with a similar provision in its articles of association so that, although directors were found to have been negligent in some respects, they were not liable to the company. Following these cases, CA 1928, s. 78, was enacted to limit contracting out from directors' liability. The provision is now CA 1985, s. 310, which is as follows:

(1)   This section applies to any provision, whether contained in a company's articles or in any contract with the company or otherwise, for exempting any officer of the company or any person (whether an officer or not) employed by the company as auditor from, or indemnifying him against, any liability which by virtue of any rule of law would otherwise attach to him in respect of any negligence, default, breach of duty or breach of trust of which he may be guilty in relation to the company.

(2)   Except as provided by the following subsection [see below], any such provision is void.

An indemnity given by a person other than the company is not covered by the section: 'or otherwise' in s. 310 must be interpreted *eiusdem generis* (*Burgoine* v *London Borough of Waltham Forest* [1997] 2 BCLC 612).

Articles that disapply the rules against profiting and against conflict of interest and duty (see 16.6.2) and decisions to disapply the rules (see 16.8) are not subject to s. 310 because it is not a 'breach of duty' for a director to make unauthorised profits from his directorship or put himself in a position in which his duty to the company and his personal interest or duty to another conflict (*Movitex Ltd* v *Bulfield* (1986) 2 BCC 99,403; see 16.5.1). In the past this question was a matter of considerable controversy — see J. Birds, 'Excluding the duties of directors' (1987) 8 Co Law 31.

Section 310(3) is in the following terms:

This section does not prevent a company—

(a)   from purchasing and maintaining for any such officer or auditor insurance against any such liability, or

(b)   from indemnifying any such officer or auditor against any liability incurred by him—

(i)   in defending any proceedings (whether civil or criminal) in which judgment is given in his favour or he is acquitted, or

(ii)   in connection with any application under section 144(3) or (4) (acquisition of shares by innocent nominee) or section 727 (general power to grant relief in case of honest and reasonable conduct) in which relief is granted to him by the court.

An indemnity in the terms of para. (b) is given by Table A, art. 118.

16.9.2   Relief by the court

CA 1985, s. 727, empowers a court which finds an officer of a company or a person employed by a company as auditor (whether he is or is not an officer of the company) liable in respect of negligence, default, breach of duty or breach of trust to relieve him, either wholly or partly, from his liability if it finds that he has acted honestly and reasonably, having regard to the circumstances of the case, including those connected with his appointment.

Section 727 was considered by the Court of Appeal in *Commissioners of Customs & Excise* v *Hedon Alpha Ltd* [1981] QB 818. The circumstances in which the section cannot apply were explained by Stephenson LJ:

> I would . . . hold that [s. 727] . . . is inapplicable to any claim by third parties to enforce any liability except a director's liability to his company or his director's duties under the Companies Acts. Wide and general though the opening words of [s. 727] are, read in their context they do not allow an officer or auditor of a company to claim relief in 'any' legal proceedings which may be brought against him in his capacity as an officer or auditor of a company by the rest of the world.

Or, as Ackner LJ put it:

> I accept that the true ambit of [s. 727], with one limited exception, is restricted to claims by or on behalf of the company or its liquidator against the officer or auditor for their personal breaches of duty. The only exception relates to the criminal process for the enforcement of certain specific duties imposed by [CA 1985] on the company's officers.

The Court of Appeal also considered the meaning of the word 'default' in s. 727. The conclusion reached by Ackner LJ was that:

> In the context in which it appears in [s. 727], it signifies a species of misconduct by an officer of a company or a person employed by a company as auditor, against a liability for which a court may relieve him either wholly or in part.

In a similar vein, Griffiths LJ said:

> The word 'default', where it appears in the section, is to be construed as a failure to conduct himself properly as a director of the company in discharge of his obligations pursuant to the provisions of [CA 1985].

Re Duomatic Ltd [1969] 2 Ch 365 is an example of the operation of s. 727. The articles of Duomatic Ltd prescribed that directors' remuneration had to be approved by the members. Mr Elvins was a director of the company and, until part way through its last financial year, held the majority of the ordinary shares. Directors drew salaries from the company without prior authorisation by a general meeting, but in every year except the last all members entitled to attend and vote at general meetings in fact approved the directors' drawings and this was held to be equivalent to approval by a general meeting (see 14.5.1). In the last year, Mr Elvins continued to draw a salary at a rate agreed with his fellow directors at the beginning of the year, but there was no approval by the members with or without meeting. It was not suggested that Mr Elvins had acted dishonestly. Buckley J held that he had acted reasonably and ought fairly to be relieved of liability to repay the agreed final year's salary. However, the judge refused to excuse Mr Elvins in respect of another breach of duty: Mr Elvins and a co-director wished to dismiss a third director, Mr Hanly, with whom they had quarrelled; Hanly threatened to sue the company and so Elvins agreed that the company should make Hanly a severance payment of £4,000. This was illegal because it was not approved under CA 1985, s. 312 (see 15.6.2.1). Buckley J held that Elvins should not have agreed to this payment without seeking legal advice to discover whether Hanly actually had any claim against the company. Because he had not sought legal advice, Mr Hanly had not acted reasonably and ought not to be excused.

If a person acquires shares in a company as the company's nominee and he fails to pay an amount due in respect of those shares, the directors of the company may become jointly and severally liable with the nominee for payment (CA 1985, s. 144(2)), though the court may relieve any director from liability if it is satisfied 'that he has acted honestly and reasonably and, having regard to all the circumstances of the case, he ought fairly to be excused from liability' (s. 144(3)). This relieving provision bears a very close similarity to s. 727.

17 Corporate Officers and Promoters

17.1 INTRODUCTION

A company may have many people who together perform its functions — a fact which is recognised by the Companies Act when it refers to 'officers of the company'. The purpose of this chapter is to identify who is or is not an officer of the company, what the duties of various officers are, and how they are appointed.

CA 1985, s. 744, offers a definition (unless the contrary intention appears) of 'officer' as including 'a director, manager or secretary'. The position of directors, including the chairman of the directors and the managing director, was discussed in the two preceding chapters. This chapter will therefore consider managers, the secretary and auditors.

The chapter ends with a short discussion of the law relating to promoters of companies.

17.2 MANAGERS

The meaning of the term 'manager', when used in legislation in relation to a company, may vary according to context. In a provision fixing a manager with criminal responsibility, it should be interpreted narrowly to mean only a person who has the management of the whole affairs of the company, is in a position of real authority and has the power and responsibility to decide corporate policy and strategy (*R* v *Boal* [1992] QB 591). On the other hand, in *Re a Company* [1980] Ch 138, it was necessary to determine whether a departmental manager of a company was, by virtue of the definition of 'officer' in CA 1985, s. 744 (see 17.1), an officer of the company in relation to whom s. 721 could be invoked. The Court of Appeal held that he was. Shaw LJ said, at p. 144, that for the purposes of s. 721:

> The expression 'manager' should not be too narrowly construed. It is not to be equated with a managing or other director or a general manager. As I see it, any person who in the affairs of the company exercises a supervisory control which reflects the general policy of the company for the time being or which is related to the general administration of the company is in the sphere of management. He need not be a member of the board of directors. He need not be subject to specific instructions from the board.

The acts of a defectively appointed manager are validated by CA 1985, s. 285 (see 15.2.6).

A manager of a company may be sufficiently senior to be in a fiduciary relationship with the company. In *Agip (Africa) Ltd* v *Jackson* [1991] Ch 547, the chief accountant of a company was held to be in a fiduciary relationship with it. In *Canadian Aero Service Ltd* v *O'Malley* (1973) 40 DLR (3d) 371, Supreme Court of Canada, two employees of the company (which was a wholly owned subsidiary) who had the jobs of 'president and chief executive officer' and 'executive vice-president and director', but whose appointments as directors were formally defective, were held to owe the same fiduciary duties as directors. In *DPC Estates Pty Ltd* v *Grey* [1974] 1 NSWLR 470 the defendant was employed as 'manager' of a group of companies and acted as director of one of them though his appointment as director was formally defective. He was held to owe the same fiduciary duties as a director. In *Green* v *Bestobell Industries Pty Ltd* [1982] WAR 1, the company was organised in four divisions and each division had a branch in each State of Australia. The branches were operated separately and to some extent autonomously. Mr Green was the manager of the Victoria branch of one of the divisions with 'the complete control of all human, financial and contractual resources within the branch' according to his letter of appointment. He was held to owe the same fiduciary duties as a director. In *Manley Inc.* v *Fallis* (1977) 38 CPR (2d) 74, Ontario, the sales manager of a company was held to owe fiduciary duties not only to the company but also to its parent company, the court applying the theory of enterprise entity (see 5.2.2.9).

Senior managers are therefore subject to the same fiduciary rules against profiting and against conflict of interest and duty as directors (see 16.5). There is a difference, however, in that the rule that a director of a company is not entitled to remuneration except as provided by its constitution or approved by the company's members does not apply to senior managers or even to persons who act as directors without being properly appointed — see the discussion of *Craven-Ellis* v *Canons Ltd* [1936] 2 KB 403 in 15.6.1.5.

17.3 THE SECRETARY

17.3.1 Appointment and qualifications

By s. 283 of CA 1985:

(1) Every company shall have a secretary.
(2) A sole director shall not also be secretary.

A company with only one director, X, may not have as secretary a company whose only director is also X (CA 1985, s. 283(4)(a)). Apart from this, there is no objection to another company carrying out the duties of company secretary, nor to those duties being carried out by joint secretaries.

When a company is registered, a statement in the prescribed form of the person who is, or the persons who are, to be the first secretary or joint secretaries of the company must be delivered to the registrar (CA 1985, s. 10(2)(b)). The person or persons so named must sign the statement to show consent to the appointment and the statement must also be signed by or on behalf of the subscriber or subscribers of the memorandum (s. 10(3)). The person or persons named in the statement are deemed to have been appointed secretary or joint secretaries on the company's incorporation (s. 13(5)). These provisions were introduced by CA 1976. Previously it was common for a company's first secretary to be appointed in its articles. Now any appointment in the articles which is inconsistent with the statement delivered on registration is void (CA 1985, s. 10(5)).

Under Table A, art. 99, the directors are to appoint the company's secretary and may remove any secretary so appointed. CA 1985, s. 286(1), imposes a duty on the directors of a public company to ensure that the company's secretary is adequately qualified and experienced, and lists specific qualifications which a public company secretary should have.

Paragraph A.1.4 of the Combined Code for listed companies (see 15.1.2) states:

All directors should have access to the advice and services of the company secretary, who is responsible to the board for ensuring that board procedures are followed and that applicable rules and regulations are complied with. Any question of the removal of the company secretary should be a matter for the board as a whole.

If the office of secretary is vacant, or for any reason the secretary is not capable of acting, then, under s. 283(3), an assistant or deputy secretary may act or the directors can authorise any officer of the company to act in place of the secretary generally or specially.

The rule that a sole director of a company cannot also be its secretary is reinforced by s. 284 which enacts that any provision requiring or authorising a thing to be done by or to a director and the secretary is not satisfied by being done by or to the same person acting both as director and as, or in place of, the secretary.

17.3.2   Register and notification to the registrar

Every company is required to keep at its registered office a register of its directors and secretaries (CA 1985, s. 288(1); see 15.4.1). In respect of each individual who is a secretary or joint secretary of the company, the register must state the individual's Christian name or forename and surname (and former names excluding the name or surname by which a married woman was known before the marriage or names changed or disused before the individual became 18 or more than 20 years previously) and his usual residential address (s. 290(1)(a) and (3)). For an individual who is a peer or is usually known by a title, the register may state the title instead of, or in addition to, his Christian name or forename and surname, or either of them, and it is not necessary to give the name by which he was known previous to the adoption of, or succession to, the title, unless it is not a British title (s. 290(3)). If a corporation is a secretary or joint secretary, the register must state the corporate name and registered or principal office (s. 290(1)(b)). Where all the partners in a firm are joint secretaries, the register may give the name and principal office of the firm instead of details of each individual partner (s. 290(2)). In respect of a Scottish firm, the firm name and principal office must be given (s. 290(1)(b)).

When application is made to register a new company, CA 1985, s. 10(2), requires a statement to be delivered to the registrar naming the person who is to be the company's first secretary (or the persons who are to be its first joint secretaries), and giving the particulars of each person named that are set out in sch. 1. These particulars are the same as the particulars of secretaries that must be recorded in the company's register of directors and secretaries.

The company is required to notify the registrar of companies of any change in its secretary or of any change in the particulars in the register within 14 days of the change, and if the change is the appointment of a new secretary or joint secretary, the notice must contain a consent to act as secretary signed by the person so appointed (s. 288(2)). For rules relating to inspection of the register, see 4.4.1.

17.3.3   Duties

The company secretary performs many of the administrative duties imposed upon companies, for instance delivering documents to the registrar of companies and engaging office staff. In *Re Maidstone Buildings Provisions Ltd* [1971] 1 WLR 1085, Pennycuick V-C said:

So far as the position of a secretary as such is concerned, it is established beyond all question that a secretary, while merely performing the duties appropriate to the office of secretary, is not concerned in the management [of] the company. Equally I think he is not concerned in carrying on the business of the company. On the other hand, it is equally well established, indeed it is obvious, that a person who holds the office of secretary may in some other capacity be concerned in the management of the company's business.

The Cadbury Committee saw the company secretary as a kind of impartial civil servant offering advice to the board on procedures and responsibilities. In its report the committee said, at para. 4.25:

The company secretary has a key role to play in ensuring that board procedures are both followed and regularly reviewed. The chairman and the board will look to the company secretary for guidance on what their responsibilities are under the rules and regulations to which they are subject and on how those responsibilities should be discharged. All directors should have access to the advice and services of the company secretary. . . . It should be standard practice for the company secretary to administer, attend and prepare minutes of board meetings.

And at para. 4.27:

The committee expects that the company secretary will be a source of advice to the chairman and to the board on the implementation of the Code of Best Practice.

17.4 AUDITORS

17.4.1 Appointment and reappointment

17.4.1.1 General requirement
By CA 1985, ss. 384(1) and 388A(1), every company must appoint an auditor or auditors in accordance with chapter V of part XI of the Act (ss. 384 to 394A) unless it is a small private company which is exempt from the auditing requirements of CA 1985 or a dormant company that has adopted a special resolution under s. 250 to exempt the company from those requirements.

A person appointed as auditor under chapter V of part XI is called a 'company auditor' (CA 1989, s. 24(2)). Where a partnership firm is appointed the appointment is of the firm and not of the partners even if the firm does not have legal personality (CA 1989, s. 26(2)).

17.4.1.2 Public companies
A public company's first auditors may be appointed by its directors, or, in default, by a general meeting, to hold office until the conclusion of the first general meeting of the company at which the company's accounts and reports are laid (CA 1985, s. 385(1), (3) and (4)). Thereafter, a public company must, at each general meeting of the company at which accounts are laid, appoint an auditor or auditors to hold office from the conclusion of that meeting until the conclusion of the next general meeting at which accounts are laid (s. 385(1) and (2)). However, special notice (see 14.4.5.6) is required of a resolution to appoint as auditor a person other than a retiring auditor (s. 391A(1)). If there is a general meeting of a public company at which accounts are laid but no appointment is made of an auditor or auditors to hold office from the conclusion of that meeting then the company must within one week give notice to the Secretary of State, who may then appoint a person to fill the vacancy (s. 387).

17.4.1.3   Private companies

A private company is subject to the same rules concerning appointment of auditors as a public company (see 17.4.1.1) unless:

(a)   It has elected to dispense with the obligation to appoint auditors annually (CA 1985, ss. 384(4) and 386; see 17.4.1.4).

(b)   It has elected to dispense with the laying of accounts before the company in general meeting (ss. 384(2), 385(1) and 385A; see 17.4.1.5).

(c)   It is a small company which is, under s. 249A, exempt from the auditing requirements of CA 1985 (see 17.4.1.6).

17.4.1.4   Election to dispense with annual appointment

The members of a private company may elect under s. 386 to dispense with the obligation to appoint auditors annually, that is, to dispense with the obligation to consider once a year whether to reappoint as auditors of the company the persons who were the company's auditors at the time of making the election. An election must be made by elective resolution (unanimous approval) under s. 379A (see 14.4.8.4). When such an election is in force the company's auditors are deemed to be reappointed for each succeeding financial year (s. 386(2)).

17.4.1.5   Election to dispense with laying of accounts

A private company that has elected under CA 1985, s. 252, to dispense with the laying of accounts before the company in general meeting (and which is not dormant) must appoint its auditors in accordance with s. 385A, unless it has also elected to dispense with annual appointments of auditors (see 17.4.1.4). Section 385A requires an annual appointment by the company in general meeting within 28 days of circulating copies of the accounts to members. As the holding of a meeting following circulation of accounts is the very thing that an election under s. 252 is intended to avoid it is likely that a company making an election under s. 252 will also make an election to dispense with annual appointments of auditors.

17.4.1.6   Exempt small companies

If, under CA 1985, s. 249A, a small private company is exempt from the auditing requirements of CA 1985 then it is exempt from the obligation to appoint auditors (s. 388A(1)). The conditions for exemption are set out in 9.3.4. Subsections (2) to (5) of s. 388A detail what must be done to appoint auditors of such a company if and when it ceases to be exempt.

17.4.1.7   Dormant companies

By CA 1985, s. 250(3), a company is 'dormant' during a period in which no 'significant accounting transaction' occurs — meaning a transaction that has to be entered in its accounting records by virtue of s. 221 (see 9.2.1 and 9.2.3) apart from transactions relating to the issue of shares to the subscribers of the company's memorandum in pursuance of their undertaking in the memorandum (under s. 2(5)(b) and (c); see 1.3.2.1). A company ceases to be dormant as soon as a significant accounting transaction occurs (s. 250(3)).

The members of a dormant company may adopt a special resolution under s. 250 to make the company exempt from the provisions of CA 1985, part VII, relating to the audit of accounts. This may not be done if the company is a banking or insurance company or an authorised person under the Financial Services Act 1986 (CA 1985, s. 250(2)).

If a company has been dormant from the time of its formation then a special resolution under s. 250 may be adopted at any time (s. 250(1)(a)).

If a company has been active but becomes dormant, then, under s. 250(1)(b), a resolution under s. 250 cannot be adopted until after the accounts for the last active financial year have been sent in accordance with s. 238(1), and three conditions must be satisfied:

(a) The company must have been dormant since the end of the financial year to which the accounts relate.

(b) The company must be entitled, in respect of its individual accounts for that year, to the exemptions available to a small company (see 9.5.2) (or be disentitled from such exemptions only by reason of being a public company or a member of an ineligible group).

(c) The company must not be required to prepare group accounts for that year.

A company that has adopted a special resolution under s. 250 ceases to be exempt from the provisions of CA 1985, part VII, relating to the audit of accounts if (s. 250(5)):

(a) it ceases to be dormant, or

(b) it would no longer qualify (for any other reason) to be exempted under s. 250.

A dormant company that has adopted a special resolution under s. 250 is exempt from the obligation to appoint auditors (s. 388A(1)). Subsections (2) to (5) of s. 388A detail what must be done to appoint auditors of such a company if and when it ceases to be dormant.

17.4.2 Eligibility for appointment as a company auditor

17.4.2.1 New system of eligibility
CA 1989, part II (ss. 24 to 54), has created a new system for controlling the training and supervision of company auditors, to conform with the European Community Eighth Company Law Directive on regulation of auditors. The new system was brought into force on 1 October 1991.

17.4.2.2 Recognised supervisory bodies
Under the new system of eligibility, by CA 1989, s. 25(1), a person is eligible for appointment as a company auditor only if:

(a) a member of a recognised supervisory body, and

(b) eligible for appointment under the rules of that body.

A person is treated as a member of a supervisory body if subject to its rules in seeking appointment or acting as a company auditor, whether or not a member of the body (s. 30(2)).

A supervisory body is 'recognised' by means of a recognition order made under CA 1989, sch. 11. The recognised bodies are the Institute of Chartered Accountants in England and Wales, the Institute of Chartered Accountants of Scotland, the Chartered Association of Certified Accountants, the Association of Authorised Public Accountants, and the Institute of Chartered Accountants in Ireland.

17.4.2.3 Qualification
Under CA 1989, sch. 11, para. 4, a recognised supervisory body must have rules to the effect that a person is not eligible for appointment as a company auditor unless:

(a)   in the case of an individual, he or she holds an appropriate qualification;

(b)   in the case of a 'firm' (which means a partnership firm or a body corporate: s. 53(1)):

(i)   the individuals responsible for company audit work on behalf of the firm hold an appropriate qualification, and

(ii)   the firm is controlled by qualified persons.

Paragraph 5 of sch. 11 explains what is meant by 'controlled by qualified persons'.
CA 1989, s. 35, and SI 1991 No. 1566 require the setting up of a register of:

(a)   the individuals and firms eligible for appointment as company auditor, stating the name of the relevant supervisory body, and

(b)   the individuals holding an appropriate qualification who are responsible for company audit work on behalf of such firms.

It is an offence for a person whose name does not appear on the register to describe himself as a registered auditor or so to hold himself out as to indicate, or be reasonably understood to indicate that he is a registered auditor (s. 41(2); penalty in s. 41(5); diligence defence in s. 41(6)).

Initially, for the vast majority of individuals the 'appropriate qualification' will be that they were, both immediately before 1 January 1990 and immediately before 1 October 1991, members of one of the professional accountancy bodies whose members were eligible for appointment as company auditors under the old law (CA 1989, s. 31(1)(a)). Those bodies are all recognised supervisory bodies under the new law. In future most individuals wishing to work as auditors will obtain, from a qualifying body, a professional qualification recognised under CA 1989, s. 32 and sch. 12 (s. 31(1)(b)). All the recognised supervisory bodies except the Association of Authorised Public Accountants are also qualifying bodies, and the Association of International Accountants is a qualifying body but not a supervisory body. There are special arrangements for people who were in training on 1 January 1990 (s. 31(4)), and for the approval of overseas qualifications (s. 33). There are also special provisions allowing a small group of otherwise unqualified individuals who were auditors of private companies in 1966 to work as auditors of unquoted companies (s. 34).

17.4.2.4   *Ineligibility for lack of independence*
A person is, by CA 1989, s. 27(1), ineligible for appointment as auditor of a company if:

(a)   an officer or employee of the company, or

(b)   a partner or employee of such a person, or a partnership of which such a person is a partner, or

(c)   ineligible by virtue of (a) or (b) for appointment as auditor of any associated undertaking of the company.

So that two partners can be appointed auditors of the same company, it is provided that, for the purposes of the subsection, an auditor of a company is not to be regarded as an officer or employee of the company.
By s. 27(3), an 'associated undertaking' of a company is:

(a)   a parent undertaking or subsidiary undertaking of the company, or

(b)   a subsidiary undertaking of any parent undertaking of the company.

Subsection (2) of s. 27 empowers the Secretary of State to make supplementary regulations specifying when a person is ineligible for appointment as auditor of a company because of lack of independence.

17.4.2.5 Effect of ineligibility

No person may act as a company auditor if ineligible for appointment to the office (CA 1989, s. 28(1)). A person who acts as company auditor though ineligible commits an offence triable either way (s. 28(3)), though it is a defence to show that he did not know and had no reason to believe that he was ineligible for appointment (s. 28(5)).

CA 1989, s. 29, makes provisions for requiring a company whose auditing has been conducted by a person who was ineligible for appointment to have the audit work reviewed or done again by an eligible person.

17.4.3 Removal, resignation and replacement

A company may, by ordinary resolution, at any time, remove an auditor from office, notwithstanding anything in any agreement between it and the auditor (CA 1985, s. 391(1)). Special notice (see 14.4.5.6) must be given of such a resolution (s. 391A(1)) and the company must send a copy of the notice to the auditor sought to be removed (s. 391A(2)). The auditor is entitled to make representations in writing (not exceeding a reasonable length) which the company must send to every member of the company to whom notice of the meeting is sent, though if the representations are received by the company too late for distribution to members the auditor may (in addition to a right under s. 390(1) to be heard at the meeting) require that the written representations be read out at the meeting (s. 391A(3), (4) and (5)). Because of the auditor's right under s. 391A to make representations to members it is doubtful whether a decision to dismiss an auditor arrived at by unanimous agreement without meeting could be effective. The procedure provided to private companies by s. 381A for agreement to written resolutions cannot be used to dismiss an auditor under s. 391 (s. 381A(7) and sch. 15A, para. 1(b)).

Notice of removal of an auditor at a general meeting must, under penalty, be given to the registrar within 14 days (s. 391(2)).

If an election is in force under s. 386 dispensing with annual appointment of auditors then, under s. 393, any member of the company may deposit notice in writing at the company's registered office proposing that the appointment of the company's auditors be brought to an end. No member may deposit more than one such notice in any financial year of the company (s. 393(1)). On receipt of a notice in proper form proposing the ending of the auditors' appointment, the directors must convene a general meeting to be held on a date not more than 28 days after the date of the notice, and propose at that meeting a resolution enabling the company to decide whether the auditors' appointment should be ended (s. 393(2)). If the directors do not proceed duly to convene a meeting, the person who gave the notice to the company may convene one instead (s. 393(4)) and must be repaid by the company the reasonable expenses of doing so (s. 393(6)). The company can, in turn, deduct the expenses from any fees or other remuneration due to the defaulting directors (s. 393(6)). The directors are deemed to have failed duly to convene a meeting if they do not proceed to convene a meeting within 14 days of deposit of the notice (s. 393(4)).

The policy of CA 1985 is that auditors of a company who are critical of the company have a statutory right to bring that criticism to the attention of members: they cannot be got rid of silently. The provisions are elaborately detailed to deal with a variety of different circumstances in which an auditor may cease to hold office, and only the main points will be given here.

An auditor of a company who ceases for any reason to hold office must, under penalty, deposit at the company's registered office a statement of any circumstances connected with ceasing to hold office which the ex-auditor considers should be brought to the attention of the members or creditors of the company or, if the ex-auditor considers that there are no such circumstances, a statement that there are none (s. 394(1); penalty in s. 394A(1) to (3) and sch. 24). If the statement is of circumstances to be brought to the members' or creditors' attention then the company must, under penalty, send a copy of it to every person who, under s. 238, is entitled to be sent copies of the accounts (s. 394(3); penalty in s. 394A(4) and sch. 24), and the auditor may requisition an extraordinary general meeting to consider the circumstances (s. 329A). There are supplementary provisions in s. 394(3) to (7).

An auditor of a company may resign by depositing a notice in writing to that effect at the company's registered office (s. 392(1)). However, the notice is not effective unless it is accompanied by the statement required by s. 394(1) and (2).

A person who has been appointed auditor of a company but who becomes ineligible to hold that office must thereupon vacate the office, and must forthwith give written notice to the company of vacating the office because of ineligibility (CA 1989, s. 28(2)). Failure to do so is an offence triable either way (s. 28(3)) though it is a defence to show that one did not know and had no reason to believe that one had become ineligible for appointment (s. 28(5)).

If there is a casual vacancy in the office of auditor of a company then any surviving or continuing auditor may continue to act while the vacancy continues (CA 1985, s. 388(2)). Either the directors or the company in general meeting may make an appointment to fill the vacancy (s. 388(1)).

By s. 388(3), special notice (see 14.4.5.6) is required for a resolution at a general meeting of a company (a) filling a casual vacancy in the office of auditor, or (b) reappointing as auditor a retiring auditor who was appointed by the directors to fill a casual vacancy. By s. 391A(1) special notice is required for a resolution at a general meeting appointing as auditor a person other than a retiring auditor. A copy of notice of any such intended resolution must be sent by the company to the person proposed to be appointed (ss. 388(4) and 391A(2)).

An auditor who has resigned must be sent a copy of notice of an intended general-meeting resolution to fill the vacancy caused by the resignation or to reappoint an auditor appointed by the directors to fill the vacancy (s. 388(4)). The auditor who has resigned may attend that general meeting and is entitled to be heard at the meeting on matters concerning him or her as a former auditor (ss. 390(1) and 392A(8)), and the auditor may requisition an extraordinary general meeting to consider the circumstances (s. 392A).

17.4.4 Remuneration

The remuneration of the auditors of a company appointed by the company in general meeting must be fixed by the company in general meeting or in such manner as the company in general meeting may determine (CA 1985, s. 390A(1)). The remuneration of the auditors of a company appointed by the company's directors must be fixed by the directors (s. 390A(2)). The Secretary of State fixes the remuneration of any auditors he appoints (s. 390A(2)).

The amount of the remuneration of a company's auditors in their capacity as such must be stated in a note to the company's annual accounts (s. 390A(3)). Expenses and benefits in kind must also be reported (s. 390A(4) and (5)).

17.4.5 Duties

The principal function of a company's auditors is to report on the accounts for a financial year of the company, as described in 9.3.4. It is sufficient if they deliver their report to the company secretary: they are not required personally to ensure it is supplied to the members (*Re Allen, Craig & Co. (London) Ltd* [1934] Ch 483). The auditors' report must state whether in their opinion the accounts have been properly prepared in accordance with CA 1985 and give a true and fair view (CA 1985, s. 235(2)). If they express doubts about certain matters in the accounts then they must state whether they doubt the legality of the dividend proposed in the directors' report (see 10.5.9). If the requirements of CA 1985, sch. 6, concerning disclosure in accounts of payments to directors (see 15.6.3) have not been complied with then the auditors must include in their report, so far as they are reasonably able to do so, a statement giving the required particulars (s. 237(4)).

The auditors must consider whether the information given in the directors' report is consistent with the annual accounts: if they are of the opinion that it is not consistent they must state that fact in their report (s. 235(3)).

In order to prepare their report, auditors must, by CA 1985, s. 237(1), carry out investigations sufficient to enable them to form an opinion on whether proper accounting records have been kept by the company and on whether the accounts for the financial year agree with those accounting records. They must state in their report any reservations they have on these matters (s. 237(2)).

By CA 1985, s. 389A(1):

> The auditors of a company have a right of access at all times to the company's books, accounts and vouchers, and are entitled to require from the company's officers such information and explanations as they think necessary for the performance of their duty as auditors.

By s. 237(3) the auditors must state in their report if they have failed to obtain information and explanations needed by them. By s. 389A(2), any officer of a company who knowingly or recklessly gives information or an explanation required by auditors which is misleading, false or deceptive in a material particular is guilty of an offence triable either way. The punishment can be imprisonment for up to two years and/or a fine (unlimited) (CA 1985, sch. 24).

The auditors of a company which is a subsidiary undertaking must supply the parent company's auditors with such information and explanations as they may reasonably require for the purposes of their duties as auditors of the parent company (s. 389A(3)). If a company's auditors require information and explanations about one of its subsidiary undertakings which is not a body corporate incorporated in Great Britain then the company must take all steps reasonably open to it to obtain the required information (s. 389A(4)). Auditors of a foreign subsidiary who provide the parent company with information for its group accounts may be liable to the parent company for losses caused by their negligence in providing that information (*Barings plc* v *Coopers and Lybrand* [1997] 1 BCLC 427).

The duty of an auditor in the performance of his or her work was considered by Lopes LJ in *Re Kingston Cotton Mill Co. (No. 2)* [1896] 2 Ch 279 at pp. 288–9:

> It is the duty of an auditor to bring to bear on the work he has to perform that skill, care, and caution which a reasonably competent, careful, and cautious auditor would use. What is reasonable skill, care, and caution must depend on the particular circumstances of each

case. An auditor is not bound to be a detective, or, as was said, to approach his work with suspicion or with a foregone conclusion that there is something wrong. He is a watchdog, but not a bloodhound. He is justified in believing tried servants of the company in whom confidence is placed by the company. He is entitled to assume that they are honest, and to rely upon their representations, provided he takes reasonable care. If there is anything calculated to excite suspicion he should probe it to the bottom; but in the absence of anything of that kind he is only bound to be reasonably cautious and careful.

. . . [An auditor] does not guarantee the discovery of all fraud.

As Lord Denning put it in *Fomento (Sterling Area) Ltd* v *Selsdon Fountain Pen Co. Ltd* [1958] 1 WLR 45, HL:

An auditor is not to be confined to the mechanics of checking vouchers and making arithmetical computations. He is not to be written off as a professional 'adder-upper and subtractor'. His vital task is to take care to see that errors are not made, be they errors of computation, or errors of omission or commission, or downright untruths. To perform this task properly he must come to it with an inquiring mind — not suspicious of dishonesty, I agree — but suspecting that someone may have made a mistake somewhere and that a check must be made to ensure that there has been none.

In *Barings plc* v *Coopers and Lybrand* Leggatt LJ said at p. 435:

The primary responsibility for safeguarding a company's assets and preventing errors and defalcations rests with the directors. But material irregularities, and a fortiori fraud, will normally be brought to light by sound audit procedures, one of which is the practice of pointing out weaknesses in internal controls. An auditor's task is so to conduct the audit as to make it probable that material misstatements in financial documents will be detected.

Auditors can refute a charge of negligence by showing that they have acted in accordance with a practice accepted as proper by a body of responsible and skilled professional opinion (*Lloyd Cheyham & Co. Ltd* v *Littlejohn & Co.* [1987] BCLC 303). Statements of Standard Accounting Practice 'are very strong evidence as to what is the proper standard which should be adopted and unless there is some justification, a departure from this will be regarded as constituting a breach of duty' (per Woolf J in *Lloyd Cheyham & Co. Ltd* v *Littlejohn & Co.* at p. 313).

If company auditors perform their work negligently then it is the company that is the proper plaintiff to sue for loss: members of the company are not proper plaintiffs. In *Caparo Industries plc* v *Dickman* [1990] 2 AC 605, Lord Bridge of Harwich said, at p. 626:

The shareholders of a company have a collective interest in the company's proper management and insofar as a negligent failure of the auditor to report accurately on the state of the company's finances deprives the shareholders of the opportunity to exercise their powers in general meeting to call the directors to book and to ensure that errors in management are corrected, the shareholders ought to be entitled to a remedy. But in practice no problem arises in this regard since the interest of the shareholders in the proper management of the company's affairs is indistinguishable from the interest of the company itself and any loss suffered by the shareholders, e.g., by the negligent failure of the auditor to discover and expose a misappropriation of funds by a director of the company, will be recouped by a claim against the auditors in the name of the company, not by individual shareholders.

In *Berg Sons & Co. Ltd* v *Adams* [1993] BCLC 1045, the auditors of a company were found to have carried out their audit negligently in that they failed to state in their report that an important part of the company's assets consisted of bills payable by a person whose creditworthiness could not be evaluated by the auditors. However, this fact was well-known to Mr Golechha, who was the only person beneficially interested in the company's shares and who was its only active director. Accordingly the company had not suffered from the auditors' negligence (because Mr Golechha was identified with the company — see 19.8) and so was entitled only to nominal damages. In *Galoo Ltd* v *Bright Grahame Murray* [1994] 1 WLR 1360 it was alleged that a company's auditors had negligently failed to recognise that its accounts were erroneous in showing that it was solvent when in fact it was insolvent and that the company would have ceased trading had it been known that it was insolvent. The company tried to sue the auditors for the losses incurred in continuing to trade when insolvent. It was held that the auditors had not caused these losses: failure to report that the company was insolvent merely gave the company an opportunity to continue trading and incur losses.

For auditors' liabilities to other persons, see 8.10.

17.4.6   Is an auditor an officer of a company?

The auditors that companies are required to appoint under CA 1985, s. 384(1), are appointed to 'hold office' (see ss. 385(2) and (3) and 385A(2) and (3)). CA 1985, s. 744, which explains how the term 'officer' is to be interpreted, says that it includes 'a director, manager or secretary' but does not mention auditors. It is clear that the statement in s. 744 is not meant to be an exhaustive listing of all the persons who are to be treated as officers. The probable explanation is that although an auditor appointed in accordance with s. 384(1) is an officer (*R* v *Shacter* [1960] 2 QB 252; *Mutual Reinsurance Co. Ltd* v *Peat Marwick Mitchell and Co.* [1997] 1 BCLC 1), it is possible for a company to appoint other people called 'auditors' (for example, internal auditors or people who conduct transfer audits in connection with registration of shareholdings) who are not officers of the company.

17.4.7   Audit committees

Although the auditors of a company are supposed to be appointed by, and are required to report to, the members of the company, in practice their only communication is with the directors. It is potentially easy for the auditors to adopt the board's attitudes to the company and to overlook negligence and fraud which the board overlooks or is party to. One way of guarding against this is for the board to appoint a committee, consisting wholly of non-executive directors, to deal with the auditors. This is required by para. D.3.1 of the Combined Code for listed companies (see 15.1.2), which says that the majority of the committee should be independent non-executive directors. Paragraph D.3.2 of the Code says:

> The duties of the audit committee should include keeping under review the scope and results of the audit and its cost effectiveness and the independence and objectivity of the auditors. Where the auditors also supply a substantial volume of non-audit services to the company, the committee should keep the nature and extent of such services under review, seeking to balance the maintenance of objectivity and value for money.

17.5   RELIEF FROM LIABILITY

The provisions relating to relief from liability of a company's directors discussed in 16.5 apply equally to other officers and auditors of the company. It is interesting that s. 727(1) (relief by the court, see 16.5.2) refers to 'a person employed by a company as auditor (whether he is or is not an officer of the company)' (cf. 17.4.6). An administrator (see 20.3) of a company is an officer for the purposes of s. 727(1) (*Re Home Treat Ltd* [1991] BCLC 705).

17.6 PROMOTERS

17.6.1 Introduction

When an individual has an idea for a new business venture, he or she may set about interesting others in the venture and persuade them to contribute capital to a company to be incorporated for the purpose of carrying on the venture. The individual will then be described as a 'promoter' of the company. In the 19th century there were no restrictions on advertising immediately to the public inviting them to take shares in new companies, and some promoters took advantage of their position and the gullibility of the public. The most common forms of misbehaviour were:

(a)   A promoter of a company would transfer his own property to the company for a consideration — either in cash (i.e., the capital contributed by others) or in fully paid shares — that greatly overvalued the property. By taking shares with a nominal value greater than the value of the property sold, the promoter could obtain for himself a large cash profit by reselling the shares if a sufficient public demand for them could be stimulated or, if he kept the shares, a disproportionate share of dividends if the company was successful; deeming the shares to be fully paid meant he had no liability for the company's debts if it was unsuccessful. Most promoters took a combination of cash and shares. (It is now an offence for a plc to allot shares for a non-cash consideration unless an independent valuation report has certified that there is no overvaluation — see 6.5.4.)

(b)   A promoter of a company would undertake to acquire for the new company an essential asset, such as land for development, mining rights or a patent, without disclosing that he personally would profit from the deal, either by buying the asset first on his own account and then reselling at a profit to the company or by taking a commission from the vendor. Often an individual promoter did not have sufficient resources to purchase a property and resell it to the promoted company, so he would form a 'syndicate' of investors to finance that stage of the promotion. Sometimes the syndicate would itself be incorporated as a company.

During most of the 20th century people have refused to buy shares in newly incorporated companies with no trading history and so disreputable company promoters have disappeared. An important factor in eliminating them has been the London Stock Exchange's refusal (other than in exceptional cases) to list the shares of a company until it can show the results of a substantial period of trading (currently three years: Listing Rules, paras 3.3(a) and 3.6). However, this has meant that genuine new businesses have been unable to use contributed capital, beyond the usually small resources of their founders, and have had to rely instead on bank overdrafts as finance in their early years. There has been an increase in public offers of shares outside the listed market including shares in companies with new businesses and it may be that the law relating to company promoters is due for a revival.

17.6.2 Definition

The activities of a promoter are so varied that no comprehensive definition of the term has ever been formulated, though judges have from time to time offered broad guidelines. For example, in *Whaley Bridge Calico Printing Co.* v *Green* (1880) 5 QBD 109, Bowen J said:

The term promoter is a term not of law, but of business, usefully summing up in a single word a number of business operations familiar to the commercial world by which a company is generally brought into existence.

Generally, therefore, a promoter is any person who complies with the necessary formalities of company registration (or acquires a company off the shelf), finds directors and shareholders for the new company, acquires business assets for use by the company, negotiates business contracts on behalf of the new company, and the like. It is not necessary that a person should be involved in every stage of a company's formation for him to be regarded as a promoter.

The technicalities of forming a company may induce the promoters to engage the services of a lawyer or an accountant or other professional adviser. Such a person does not himself become a promoter merely by carrying out his professional duties (*Re Great Wheal Polgooth Co.* (1883) 53 LJ Ch 42), though he may if he does anything beyond this, for example, by becoming or finding a director (*Bagnall v Carlton* (1877) 6 ChD 371, CA).

For how long a person remains a promoter is apparent from the judgment of Cockburn CJ in *Twycross v Grant* (1877) 2 CPD 469 (at p. 541):

A promoter, I apprehend, is one who undertakes to form a company with reference to a given project and to set it going, and who takes the necessary steps to accomplish that purpose. . . . and so long as the work of formation continues, those who carry on that work must, I think, retain the character of promoters. Of course, if a governing body, in the shape of directors, has once been formed, and they take, as I need not say they may, what remains to be done in the way of forming the company, into their own hands, the functions of the promoter are at an end.

In *Lagunas Nitrate Co.* v *Lagunas Syndicate* [1899] 2 Ch 392, CA, the syndicate of promoters had been incorporated as a registered company. The directors of that company were also the directors of the company they promoted. Lindley MR said, at p. 428:

The [promoted] company, although, in one sense, formed when registered, was not completely formed, as contemplated by the promoters, until a prospectus had been issued and a large capital had been subscribed. The issue of the prospectus was the last act of promotion.

For a detailed discussion, see J.H. Gross, 'Who is a company promoter?' (1970) 86 LQR 493.

17.6.3 Duties of promoters

17.6.3.1 Fiduciary duty

The special position which a promoter occupies in relation to an unformed company has since the early days persuaded the courts to cast a discerning eye over their activities. As Lord Cairns LC pointed out in *Erlanger* v *New Sombrero Phosphate Co.* (1878) 3 App Cas 1218, at p. 1236:

They have in their hands the creation and moulding of the company; they have the power of defining how, and when, and in what shape, and under what supervision, it shall start into existence and begin to act as a trading corporation.

Implicit in this degree of power is the opportunity for abuse, and accordingly the courts have sought to counter this opportunity by holding that the relationship between a promoter and the company he promotes is fiduciary (per Lord Cairns LC, loc. cit.). The meaning of this equitable concept is examined in more detail in 16.3 because nowadays its most important application in company law is to the relationship between a director and his company. For present purposes it is sufficient to note two rules that have been derived from the law on fiduciaries and applied to promoters of companies:

(a) If a company enters into a transaction in which its promoter is interested then the transaction is voidable if it was not properly approved by the company after full disclosure of the promoter's interest (*Erlanger* v *New Sombrero Phosphate Co.*). The company may repudiate the transaction or obtain a court order for rescission. Rescission of a contract involves each party returning to the other what was transferred under the contract and therefore will not be ordered if complete restitution (*restitutio in integrum*) is no longer possible. What the promoter returns to the company will include any profit the promoter has made. It is not necessary to prove that any profit has been made in order to obtain an order for rescission though, in practice, of course, it would not be asked for unless the property was not worth what the company paid for it. The fact that property has declined in value since it was acquired is no bar to rescission of the acquisition (*Armstrong* v *Jackson* [1917] 2 KB 822).

(b) If a company enters into a transaction in which its promoter has an interest and the promoter acquired that interest while acting as promoter of the company then the company can recover any profit made by the promoter on the transaction that was not disclosed to and approved by the company (usually described as a 'secret profit') (*Gluckstein* v *Barnes* [1900] AC 240, HL).

Judicial control of promoters appeared early in company law. In *Hichens* v *Congreve* (1828) 4 Russ 562, Sir William Congreve and his associates promoted an unincorporated joint stock company to work coal mines in Ireland and invited the public to take shares. Congreve and his associates bought the mines for £10,000 and sold them to the company for £25,000, pretending that they were not involved in the deal as intermediate purchasers. Lord Lyndhurst LC said, at p. 574, that he could not help considering this fraudulent and, at p. 575: 'Such a transaction is so incorrect, that it is impossible that any court of justice could permit it to stand'. The characterisation of promoters as fiduciaries seems to have been first made by Wigram V-C in *Foss* v *Harbottle* (1843) 2 Hare 461 at p. 489. *Foss* v *Harbottle* concerned an incorporated company and established the important rule that any wrong done by a promoter of an incorporated company is done to the company as a separate person so that action against the promoter must be taken by the company not by its members.

17.6.3.2 *Disclosure and approval*

The rules on disclosure and approval of a promoter's interest and profit are based on the idea that everyone whom the promoter intends should become members of the promoted company must be involved in the disclosure and approval process. If the promoter's scheme is that the company is to be a private company with only certain persons as members then disclosure to and approval by all those persons is sufficient, even if subsequently other persons become members (*Re Ambrose Lake Tin & Copper Mining Co.* (1880) 14 ChD 390, CA; *Re British Seamless Paper Box Co.* (1881) 17 ChD 467, CA; *Salomon* v *A. Salomon & Co. Ltd* [1897] AC 22, HL).

Where the promoter's scheme is to invite the general public to become members of the company then the promoter may either disclose to and obtain approval from a board of directors whose members are independent of the promoter or make the disclosure to the subscribers of the memorandum and in the material published to prospective shareholders inviting them to take shares so that persons only become members of the company in full knowledge of the promoter's interest (*Erlanger* v *New Sombrero Phosphate Co.* (1878) 3 App Cas 1218, HL; *Lagunas Nitrate Co.* v *Lagunas Syndicate* [1899] 2 Ch 392, CA; *Gluckstein* v *Barnes* [1900] AC 240, HL).

In the old cases the document in which information was given to prospective shareholders was always called the 'prospectus'. The present-day procedures for offering shares to the public are described in chapter 7. A large issue of shares will normally be listed on the London Stock Exchange and full information must be published in listing particulars. The listing particulars must include the name of any promoter and the amount of any cash, securities or benefits paid, issued or given within the past two years (or proposed to be given) to any promoter, and the consideration received (Listing Rules, para. 6.C.21).

In *Erlanger* v *New Sombrero Phosphate Co.*, a syndicate headed by the Paris banking firm of Erlanger & Co. acquired a lease of Sombrero Island, one of the Leeward Islands chain in the Caribbean, for £55,000. John Marsh Evans was nominated by the syndicate to be the leaseholder. At this stage the syndicate was not promoting a company but later they did incorporate the New Sombrero Phosphate Co. and appointed its first five directors: two of them were abroad, one was John Marsh Evans, one was a friend of Baron Erlanger and the fifth was the Lord Mayor of London of whom it was charitably assumed by Lord Selborne (at p. 1260) that he was 'too much occupied with other duties to be able to give much attention'. At a board meeting attended by the three directors who were not abroad, it was agreed to purchase the lease from Evans for £80,000 in cash and £30,000 in fully paid shares. A prospectus was issued which did not mention that anyone other than Evans had an interest in the lease. The House of Lords dismissed an appeal against the Court of Appeal's order rescinding the purchase of the lease. Lord Cairns LC said, at p. 1236:

> I do not say that the owner of property may not promote and form a joint stock company, and then sell his property to it, but I do say that if he does so he is bound to take care that he sells it to the company through the medium of a board of directors who can and do exercise an independent and intelligent judgment on the transaction, and who are not left under the belief that the property belongs, not to the promoter, but to some other person.

Lord Blackburn, at p. 1239, said that the purchase was voidable 'because there was not the exercise upon it of the intelligent judgment of an independent executive'. See also per Lord Penzance at p. 1229, Lord O'Hagan at p. 1255 and Lord Gordon at p. 1284.

In *Lagunas Nitrate Co.* v *Lagunas Syndicate,* the promoters were the first directors of the promoted company so that it did not have an independent board but they (and two associates) were the subscribers of the memorandum, and the prospectus inviting the public to take shares in the company disclosed the promoters' interest in the property which they had sold to it. A majority of the Court of Appeal held this to be sufficient disclosure (Rigby LJ thought that there ought to have been an independent board). Lindley MR said, at p. 426:

> No one need join a company unless he likes, and if a person knows that if he becomes a member he will find as directors persons who, in his opinion, ought not to be directors, he should not join the company.

In *Gluckstein* v *Barnes*, Mr Gluckstein and three others formed a syndicate to promote a company called Olympia Ltd to run the Olympia exhibition hall in London. The previous owner of the hall was a company which had become insolvent and was being compulsorily wound up. The hall had been mortgaged by its previous owner and the syndicate persuaded the various mortgagees to transfer the debts they were owed and the mortgages securing payment of the debts to the syndicate at a substantial discount. As a result, when the syndicate purchased the hall at the agreed price of £140,000 they only had to pay £120,000 because part of the price was set off against the debts now owed to them. The prospectus inviting the public to take shares in Olympia Ltd disclosed that the syndicate would sell the hall to the new company for £180,000 but gave the impression that they had actually paid £140,000 for it so that there was a secret profit of £20,000. The members of the syndicate appointed themselves as the only directors of the new company.

The following vivid description is taken from the speech of Lord Macnaghten in that case, at p. 248:

> These gentlemen set about forming a company to pay them a handsome sum for taking off their hands a property which they had contracted to buy with that end in view. They bring the company into existence by means of the usual machinery. They appoint themselves sole guardians and protectors of this creature of theirs, half-fledged and just struggling into life, bound hand and foot while yet unborn by contracts tending to their private advantage, and so fashioned by its makers that it could only act by their hands and only see through their eyes. They issue a prospectus representing that they had agreed to purchase the property for a sum largely in excess of the amount which they had, in fact, to pay. On the faith of this prospectus they collect subscriptions from a confiding and credulous public. And then comes the last act. Secretly, and therefore dishonestly, they put into their own pockets the difference between the real and the pretended price.

Mr Gluckstein (who was the only promoter proceeded against) was ordered to pay the company his share of the secret profit.

17.6.3.3 *Statutory duty*

A person who is a member of a public company at the time of its incorporation (i.e., a subscriber of its memorandum) or at the time of its re-registration as a public company is prevented by CA 1985, s. 104, from profiting by selling non-cash assets to it within two years after the date of its certificate to commence business or its re-registration (apart from a sale in the normal course of the company's business or a sale for a consideration that is less than 10 per cent of the nominal value of the company's allotted share capital). This is because the property to be sold to the company in such circumstances must be independently valued and the valuer's report must state that it is worth at least as much as the consideration being given for it by the company (ss. 104(4)(a) and 109(2)(d)). In addition, the agreement for sale must be approved by ordinary resolution of the members (s. 104(4)(c)) and a copy of this resolution and the valuation report must be sent to the registrar within 15 days of adoption (s. 111(2); penalty in s. 111(4)). The registrar publishes notice of receipt of the report in the *London Gazette* (s. 711(1)(f)). If an agreement is made without following this procedure then the company is entitled to recover any consideration it has given, and the agreement, so far as unperformed, is void (s. 105(1) and (2)). These provisions mean that a promoter of a public company intending to sell property to it at a profit must find persons to act as first members of the company who will not profit themselves from the sale. These provisions also mean that investors in public companies can have considerable confidence where the company was formed to take over property from persons who were founder members of the company.

17.6.4 Legitimate and wrongful profits of promoters

There is an important distinction between a promoter who enters into a transaction in his capacity as a promoter and profits from it, and one who acquired an interest in property before promoting and makes a profit when the property is sold to the promoted company. In the former circumstance the profit is made in breach of fiduciary duty whereas in the second circumstance the profit is legitimate. As James LJ said in *Re Coal Economising Gas Co., Gover's Case* (1875) 1 ChD 182, CA, at p. 187:

> It is surely open to any man, in point of law, to sell his property to a joint stock company, and to invite persons to form themselves into a joint stock company to purchase from him, just as it is open to any man to sell to any persons in the world the right to become his partners in any property or undertaking. Until the formation of the partnership he is simply a vendor of the wares; he may ask what price he likes, and obtain what price he can, and he is under no obligation whatever to say what price he gave, or has to give, for them in order to complete his title to the goods.

(In *Re Lady Forrest (Murchison) Gold Mine Ltd* [1901] 1 Ch 582, however, Wright J said that the amount of a legitimate profit must be disclosed when the promoter discloses his interest.)

The distinction between the two types of profit is set out clearly by Lord Parker in *Jacobus Marler Estates Ltd v Marler* (1913) 85 LJ PC 167 n.

The difficulty of deciding whether or not a promoter entered into a transaction while he was a promoter will be apparent from nearly all the cases on promoters' liabilities, but see especially *Re Coal Economising Gas Co., Gover's Case*; *Ladywell Mining Co. v Brookes* (1887) 35 ChD 400, CA; *Omnium Electric Palaces Ltd v Baines* [1914] 1 Ch 332, CA.

If a promoter of a company fails to disclose his interest in property sold to the company then the contract of sale is voidable and will be rescinded if possible whether the promoter acquired his interest before or after becoming a promoter. Thus he will have to repay his profit whether it is legitimate or not. In some cases this may be thought to be a harsh penalty for failure to disclose an interest. If rescission is not possible, then the company can only recover a promoter's profit if the promoter acquired his interest after becoming a promoter, i.e., the company can only recover a profit made in breach of fiduciary duty. If the profit was legitimate then the company cannot recover it: the court will not attempt to decide the price at which the property should have been sold to the company (*Re Cape Breton Co.* (1885) 29 ChD 795, CA, affirmed by HL (1887) sub nom. *Bentinck v Fenn* (1887) 12 App Cas 652; *Ladywell Mining Co v Brookes*; *Re Lady Forrest (Murchison) Gold Mine Ltd*).

For further discussion of the liabilities of promoters, see J. Gold, 'The liability of promoters for secret profits in English Law' (1943) 5 UTLJ 21 and B.E. McCrea, 'Disclosure of promoters' secret profits', *Univ. of Br. Columbia Law Rev.,* vol. 3, No. 3 (1968), pp. 183–216.

18 Remedies for Maladministration

18.1 INTRODUCTION

In very general terms, we have seen that responsibility for a company's acts and affairs will rest either with its officers (normally the directors) or with its shareholders (normally a simple majority). The purpose of this chapter is to consider what action may be taken and by whom to remedy any acts of maladministration. It is proposed to consider in turn action by the company itself, action by the shareholders, and action by the Secretary of State.

The practical problem here is that usually the people who are causing the harm to the company also control it and so can prevent it taking action to remedy the harm. A minority shareholder who wishes to take action will not be allowed to do so without first establishing that it is wrong of those in control of the company not to take action. This can make action by aggrieved shareholders very difficult and expensive. The Law Commission, which has already done some preliminary work in this area (see 18.6.1), has been asked to review the whole subject of shareholders' rights and remedies.

18.2 ACTION BY THE COMPANY

18.2.1 Action against company officers

If an actionable wrong has been done to a company by its officers then the company has a cause of action which it can pursue like any other person in legal proceedings. In practice the major difficulty is that the offending officers may themselves be able to block action through being in control of board meetings and/or holding sufficient shares to control members' meetings. Often, action is taken only when a company goes into liquidation and comes under the control of an independent liquidator. In liquidation it is possible to take action against officers by special summary proceedings called 'misfeasance proceedings' — see 20.11.

As with any other person who has suffered an actionable wrong, there is no legal requirement that a company must pursue the wrongdoer through the courts to the bitter end. It may decide that no purpose would be served by pursuing an action, and even if it does commence an action it may compromise it or even abandon it. As Vinelott J said in *Taylor* v *National Union of Mineworkers (Derbyshire Area)* [1985] BCLC 237 at pp. 254–5:

> . . . it is open to a majority of the members, if they think it is right in the interests of the corporate body to do so, to resolve that no action should be taken to remedy the wrong done to the corporate body and such a resolution, if made in good faith and in what they considered to be for the benefit of the corporate body, will bind the minority. The majority of the members of a trading company, for instance, might properly take the view that the

publicity, costs, and the inevitable loss, let us say, of the services of a managing director, who would be the defendant, would outweigh the benefit to the company of successfully prosecuting an action and might properly decide not to pursue it; although, of course, a contractual release of the right of action, as compared with a decision simply not to institute proceedings, would require to be supported by some consideration.

As explained in 16.4.14 and 16.8, a company may preclude a cause of action arising by ratifying a director's actions or by disapplying the rule against profiting or the rule against conflict of duty and interest.

In most companies the directors have control of the company's litigation (see 15.7.3). The considerations outlined by Vinelott J apply to decisions by directors as well as to decisions by members.

Of course, some members may disapprove of the company not pursuing an action against a delinquent officer. The possibility of action being taken at the instance of a dissentient member is discussed in 18.4.

18.2.2   Constructive trust of wrongfully disposed property

If directors of a company act in breach of their fiduciary duties to the company then a person outside the company may be made liable as a constructive trustee of property misappropriated by the directors in two circumstances:

(a)   where, in breach of the directors' fiduciary duties, company property is transferred to the outsider who knows that the transfer is a breach of duty or where the outsider receives company property otherwise than as a bona fide purchaser for value and deals with the property in a manner inconsistent with such fiduciary duties (usually called 'knowing receipt or dealing');

(b)   where the outsider dishonestly assists in or procures the directors' breach of fiduciary duty even though not personally receiving company property (liability as an accessory).

This is a general principle of the law on trusts which applies wherever there is a breach of fiduciary duty. In *Barnes* v *Addy* (1874) LR 9 Ch App 244, Lord Selborne LC said, at pp. 251–2:

. . . strangers are not to be made constructive trustees merely because they act as the agents of trustees in transactions within their legal powers . . . unless those agents receive and become chargeable with some part of the trust property, or unless they assist with knowledge in a dishonest and fraudulent design on the part of the trustees.

It used to be thought, as Lord Selborne said, that liability as an accessory could arise only if the fiduciaries' breach of duty was dishonest and the outsider knew of their dishonesty. Accordingly, liability as an accessory used to be known as liability for 'knowing assistance in a fraudulent design'. However, in *Royal Brunei Airlines Sdn Bhd* v *Tan* [1995] 2 AC 378 the Privy Council held that dishonesty on the part of the fiduciaries was not necessary for liability as an accessory and that knowledge 'is better avoided as a defining ingredient'. The Privy Council said that the essential element that has to be established to make an outsider liable as an accessory is that the outsider was acting dishonestly. Nevertheless, in order to make an outsider liable as an accessory to a breach of fiduciary duty it must be proved that the outsider knew that the duty was being breached (*Brinks Ltd* v *Abu-Saleh (No. 3)* (1995) *The Times*, 23 October 1995; but questioned by J. Stevens [1996] Conv 447).

The law on liability for knowing receipt or dealing was summarised in the following terms by Buckley LJ in *Belmont Finance Corporation Ltd* v *Williams Furniture Ltd (No. 2)* [1980] 1 All ER 393 at p. 405:

> . . . in consequence of the fiduciary character of their duties the directors of a limited company are treated as if they were trustees of those funds of the company which are in their hands or under their control, and if they misapply them they commit a breach of trust (*Re Lands Allotment Co.* [1894] 1 Ch 616 per Lindley LJ at p. 631 and Kay LJ at p. 638). So, if the directors of a company in breach of their fiduciary duties misapply the funds of their company so that they come into the hands of some stranger to the trust who receives them with knowledge (actual or constructive) of the breach, he cannot conscientiously retain those funds against the company unless he has some better equity. He becomes a constructive trustee for the company of the misapplied funds.

In *Rolled Steel Products (Holdings) Ltd* v *British Steel Corporation* [1986] Ch 246, Slade LJ said, at p. 298:

> The *Belmont* principle thus provides a legal route by which a company may recover its assets in a case where its directors have abused their fiduciary duties and a person receiving assets as a result of such abuse is on notice that they have been misapplied.
>   . . . the *Belmont* principle must, in my opinion, be equally capable of applying in a case where the relevant misapplication of the company's assets by the directors has consisted either of an application for purposes not authorised by its memorandum or an application in breach of the company's articles of association, e.g., pursuant to a board resolution passed at an inquorate meeting of the directors.

For cases in which persons have been held liable as constructive trustees of companies under the knowing receipt or dealing head see *Belmont Finance Corporation Ltd* v *Williams Furniture Ltd (No. 2)*; *International Sales & Agencies Ltd* v *Marcus* [1982] 3 All ER 551; and *Rolled Steel Products (Holdings) Ltd* v *British Steel Corporation*.

In *Agip (Africa) Ltd* v *Jackson* [1991] Ch 547, the chief accountant of a company (who was held to owe fiduciary duties to the company because of the seniority of his managerial position) stole money from it. Two of the defendants dishonestly assisted in laundering that money and were liable as accessories. In *Royal Brunei Airlines Sdn Bhd* v *Tan*, unusually, a company was itself a trustee. The defendant was the managing director and principal shareholder of the company and was found to have dishonestly caused it to commit breaches of trust by using trust funds for its own purposes. He was therefore liable to the beneficiary of the trust as an accessory.

In order to be liable as a constructive trustee of company property transferred in breach of directors' fiduciary duties, an outsider must know that the property is the subject-matter of directors' fiduciary duties and that the transfer of the property is in breach of those duties. The most controversial area of the law on constructive trusts is the definition of the circumstances in which an outsider who does not have actual knowledge of these matters is nevertheless to be held liable as a constructive trustee. In *Baden* v *Société générale pour favoriser le développement du commerce et de l'industrie en France SA* [1993] 1 WLR 509 Peter Gibson J reviewed the authorities and decided that liability will be imposed if there was: (a) actual knowledge, (b) a wilful shutting of one's eyes to the obvious, (c) a wilful and reckless failure to make inquiries that an honest and reasonable man would have made. His lordship added two further categories: (d) knowledge of circumstances which would have indicated the facts to an honest and reasonable man and (e) knowledge of circumstances which would have put an honest and reasonable man on inquiry. (In circumstances (b) to (e) there is said to be 'constructive knowledge'.) In *Agip (Africa) Ltd* v *Jackson* [1991] Ch 547, Fox LJ said that he accepted Peter Gibson J's formulation but added (at p. 567): 'It is, however, only an explanation of the general principle and is not necessarily comprehensive'. Other judges have, however, suggested that the last two categories are too widely stated in that they could include mere carelessness whereas it is lack of probity which is the essential fault warranting the imposition of a constructive trust — see per Megarry V-C in *Re Montagu's Settlement Trusts* [1987] Ch 264; May LJ in *Lipkin Gorman* v *Karpnale Ltd* [1989] 1 WLR 1340 at p. 1355 (point not considered on appeal) and Knox J in *Cowan de Groot Properties Ltd* v *Eagle Trust plc* [1992] 4 All ER 700 at pp. 754–60; C. Harpum, 'Liability for intermeddling with trusts' (1987) 50 MLR 217; P.L. Loughlan, 'Liability for assistance in a breach of fiduciary duty' (1989) 9 Oxford J Legal Stud 260; P.J. Millett, 'Tracing the proceeds of fraud' (1991) 107 LQR 71. Peter Gibson J's analysis was made primarily for the purpose of deciding whether the defendants in the case before him were liable as accessories under the old 'knowing assistance in a fraudulent design of fiduciaries' category (it was found that they did not know of the fraudulent design and so were not liable). Most of the academic comment cited focuses on that aspect of the problem, which has now been dealt with by the decision in *Royal Brunei Airlines Sdn Bhd* v *Tan* that it is an accessory's own dishonesty which makes the accessory liable, not the accessory's knowledge of any dishonesty of the fiduciary. Nevertheless, proving that an accessory assisted a fiduciary despite knowing that the fiduciary was acting dishonestly would be prima facie evidence of the accessory's own dishonesty, as in *Agip (Africa) Ltd* v *Jackson*, where the defendants offered no evidence to excuse their behaviour. According to Knox J in *Cowan de Groot Properties Ltd* v *Eagle Trust plc*, knowledge in the last two categories of Peter Gibson J's list is insufficient by itself to prove the dishonesty of an accessory. In *Eagle Trust plc* v *SBC Securities Ltd (No. 2)* [1996] 1 BCLC 121, Arden J held that knowledge in the last two categories is insufficient to impose liability in a 'knowing receipt' case where the receipt occurs in the discharge of a lawful debt (at least one arising out of a transaction which does not itself constitute a breach of trust).

An agreement by two or more persons dishonestly to conceal a transfer of a company's property to a person who would be liable as a constructive trustee so as to prevent the company recovering the property is a criminal conspiracy to defraud (*Adams* v *The Queen* [1995] 1 WLR 52).

For a general discussion see B. Strong, 'Civil asset recovery procedures: how equity deters fraud' (1992) 13 Co Law 44.

18.3 THE RULE IN *FOSS* v *HARBOTTLE*

18.3.1 Statement of the rule

The big problem for a member of a company seeking to cure maladministration of the company by legal action is that the courts have usually tried to avoid hearing such actions. The term 'the rule in *Foss* v *Harbottle*' is used to describe the policy of the courts of not hearing an action concerning the affairs of a company brought by a member or members of the company.

From the statement of Lord Davey in *Burland* v *Earle* [1902] AC 83, PC, at pp. 93–4 (quoted below), it seems that this policy is manifested in three principles:

(a)   If a wrong is done to a company (as a person separate from its members) then only the company may sue for redress. This is the significant principle stated by Wigram V-C in *Foss* v *Harbottle* (1843) 2 Hare 461 itself and is known as the 'proper plaintiff' principle. There are exceptions to this principle which are considered in 18.4.2.

(b)   The court will not interfere with the internal management of companies acting within their powers. This is called the 'internal management' principle. The internal management principle has a 'proper plaintiff aspect' which is that the court will not determine a question concerning what it regards as the internal management of a company except in proceedings brought by the company itself. This is considered in 18.4.8.

(c)   A member cannot sue to rectify a mere informality or irregularity if the act when done regularly would be within the powers of the company and if the intention of the majority of members is clear. This is called the 'irregularity' principle. It is considered in 18.5.

Lord Davey said:

> It is an elementary principle of the law relating to joint stock companies that the court will not interfere with the internal management of companies acting within their powers, and in fact has no jurisdiction to do so. Again, it is clear law that in order to redress a wrong done to the company or to recover moneys or damages alleged to be due to the company, the action should prima facie be brought by the company itself. . . . It should be added that no mere informality or irregularity which can be remedied by the majority will entitle the minority to sue, if the act when done regularly would be within the powers of the company and the intention of the majority of shareholders is clear.

The proper plaintiff principle and the proper plaintiff aspect of the internal management principle apply to any association that can sue in its own name, for example, a trade union (*Cotter* v *National Union of Seamen* [1929] 2 Ch 58, CA), a building society (*Farrow* v *Registrar of Building Societies* [1991] 2 VR 589) or a partnership (*Watson* v *Imperial Financial Services Ltd* (1994) 111 DLR (4th) 643).

In *Edwards* v *Halliwell* [1950] 2 All ER 1064, CA, Jenkins LJ referred to the rule in *Foss* v *Harbottle* as applying only where a wrong had been done to the company as a separate person and said that it had two elements: (a) the proper plaintiff principle and the proper plaintiff aspect of the internal management principle, as above, and (b) a principle that if a wrong done to a company is ratifiable by a simple majority of members (see, e.g., 16.4.14 and 16.8) then a member cannot sue in respect of it because when it has been ratified it is no longer a wrong and if the members decide against ratification then there is no valid reason why the company itself should not sue (the 'ratifiability principle').

In *Prudential Assurance Co. Ltd* v *Newman Industries Ltd (No. 2)* [1982] Ch 204, the Court of Appeal said, at pp. 210–11, that Jenkins LJ's judgment in *Edwards* v *Halliwell* stated the 'classic definition of the rule in *Foss* v *Harbottle*' but pointed out that the rule 'also embraces' the irregularity principle as a 'related principle'. Australian courts, on the other hand, still regard the judgment of the Privy Council in *Burland* v *Earle* as containing the 'classic statement' of the rule (per Street J in *Hawkesbury Development Co. Ltd* v *Landmark Finance Pty Ltd* (1969) 92 WN (NSW) 199 at p. 206; King CJ in *Hurley* v *BGH Nominees Pty Ltd* (1982) 31 SASR 250 at p. 252).

18.3.2   Academic and judicial comment

The rule in *Foss* v *Harbottle* is the deepest mystery of company law but is of great practical importance: a lawyer must be able to determine whether his or her client's claim will or will not be heard by the court and if the client's claim concerns the affairs of a company of which the client is a member then the lawyer must determine whether the claim is an exception to the rule. Unfortunately there is disagreement over defining the rule itself, let alone its exceptions, and the topic has been, and will continue to be, the subject of a vast amount of academic and judicial comment.

The best recent discussion is the lucid and comprehensive account in Law Commission, *Shareholder Remedies* (Consultation Paper No. 142) (London: Stationery Office, 1996).

Some cases and articles are particularly important. K. W. Wedderburn, 'Shareholders' rights and the rule in *Foss* v *Harbottle*' [1957] CLJ 194, [1958] CLJ 93 is a very important article as are two articles by S.M. Beck, 'An analysis of *Foss* v *Harbottle*', in J. S. Ziegel (ed.), *Studies in Canadian Company Law* (Toronto: Butterworths, 1967) and 'The shareholders' derivative action' (1974) 52 Can Bar Rev 159. Leading cases include *Foss* v *Harbottle* (1843) 2 Hare 461; *Burland* v *Earle* [1902] AC 83, PC; *Edwards* v *Halliwell* [1950] 2 All ER 1064, CA; and the lengthy and expensive suit of *Prudential Assurance Co. Ltd* v *Newman Industries Ltd (No. 2)*, in which at first instance ([1981] Ch 257) Vinelott J examined previous case law in great detail. However, his lordship's analysis and judgment were attacked by Professor Lord Wedderburn of Charlton, 'Derivative actions and *Foss* v *Harbottle*' (1981) 44 MLR 202, and by the Court of Appeal ([1982] Ch 204). (See also the casenotes by L.S. Sealy [1981] CLJ 29, [1982] CLJ 247.) Subsequently, Vinelott J has been defended by G.R. Sullivan, 'Restating the scope of the derivative action' [1985] CLJ 236, and Colin Baxter has carried out a very interesting review of the whole area in 'The true spirit of *Foss* v *Harbottle*' (1987) 38 NILQ 6.

The most recent case, also of great interest, is *Smith* v *Croft (No. 2)* [1988] Ch 114, of which the proceedings beginning at p. 139 of the report are of the most general interest. See C. Graham. 'Minority rights: further problems arise' (1987) 8 Co Law 128; D.D. Prentice, 'Shareholder actions: the rule in *Foss* v *Harbottle*' (1988) 104 LQR 341 M. Stamp, 'Minority shareholders: another nail in the coffin' (1988) 9 Co Law 134.

For the history of the rule, see B.S. Prunty Jr, 'The shareholders' derivative suit: notes on its derivation' (1957) 32 NYU L Rev 980; A.J. Boyle, 'The minority shareholder in the 19th century: a study in Anglo-American legal history' (1965) 28 MLR 317 and D. Linehan, 'Derivative suits in American, English and Irish law' (1974) 9 Irish Jurist 265. Linehan makes the point that the derivative action is much more important in the USA than in England or Ireland because English jurisprudence has placed greater emphasis on the so-called 'personal rights' of members — see 18.4.2.6 and 18.5.1. Accordingly the US experience is not always relevant to the law on this side of the Atlantic.

18.3.3 Reasons for the rule

There appear to be three reasons for the court's policy of not hearing an action by a member of a company concerning the affairs of the company:

(a) refusal to be involved in disputes over business policy;
(b) disputes among members should be settled by the members themselves in general meeting where the majority should prevail;
(c) a fear of multiplicity of actions.

18.3.3.1 Refusal to decide business policy
Judges have repeatedly said that a court determines questions of law not questions of business judgment. A court will not review the merits of a lawful decision of the members

or directors of a company. See, in particular, the remarks of Scrutton LJ in *Shuttleworth* v *Cox Brothers & Co. (Maidenhead) Ltd* [1927] 2 KB 9, CA, at pp. 22–4, and those of Lord Wilberforce and Latham CJ quoted in 16.4.3. The view is an old one. Lord Eldon LC was clearly horrified when, in *Waters* v *Taylor* (1808) 15 Ves Jr 10, the endlessly disputing partners of the Italian Opera asked him to appoint a manager to carry on the opera house and decide their disputes. Making such an appointment, said his lordship (at p. 25) would 'justify an expectation, that this court is to carry on every brewery, and every speculation in the kingdom'. Four years later, in *Carlen* v *Drury* (1812) 1 Ves & B 154, his lordship *was* asked to appoint a manager of the Bankside Brewery and made his much-quoted remark (at p. 158): 'This court is not to be required on every occasion to take the management of every playhouse and brewhouse in the kingdom'.

Thus, in *Lord* v *Governor & Co. of Copper Miners* (1848) 2 Ph 740 the court would not review a decision by the members to make an assignment for the benefit of creditors generally. In *Inderwick* v *Snell* (1850) 2 Mac & G 216, the members had dismissed directors under a provision in the company's articles that directors could be removed for 'reasonable cause': the court held that this meant what the members considered a reasonable cause not what the court thought was reasonable. In both cases the plaintiffs attempted to characterise the members' decisions as fraudulent but failed to convince the courts that any fraud was involved. See also *Odessa Tramways Co.* v *Mendel* (1878) 8 ChD 235 and *Anglo-Universal Bank* v *Baragnon* (1881) 45 LT 362, which concerned directors' decisions and are discussed in 6.4.2.

A more recent example is *Sandys* v *House of Fraser plc* 1985 SLT 200, in which a director of House of Fraser plc, who represented Lonrho plc's interest in the company, failed to obtain an interim interdict requiring an extraordinarily detailed analysis of the company's activities to be put before its board of directors as part of Lonrho's attempts to buy from House of Fraser the London department store Harrods.

18.3.3.2   Majority rule

There is a long-standing opinion that membership of any kind of association involves an obligation to settle disputes within the association and to abide by majority decisions. In *Cooper* v *Gordon* (1869) LR 8 Eq 249 (a case concerning a dissenting congregation), Stuart V-C said:

> The submission of the minority is the principle on which civil society is founded. It is a principle essential for that reasonable harmony which is necessary for the coherence of all societies, great or small, civil or religious.

As Lord Wilberforce said in *Re Kong Thai Sawmill (Miri) Sdn Bhd* [1978] 2 MLJ 227, PC, at p. 229: 'Those who take interests in companies limited by shares have to accept majority rule'.

The principle of majority rule is thought by commentators to be the basis of the rule in *Foss* v *Harbottle*.

Wedderburn's theory is that the ratifiability principle applies both where the company could be plaintiff and where it could be defendant: a member cannot complain to a court about an act that is ratifiable by a simple majority of members but there is a class of acts which cannot be ratified by a simple majority, and a member can complain to a court about any act of that class. So he says ([1957] CLJ 194 at p. 198): '. . . there is, after all, one "rule in *Foss* v *Harbottle*"; and the limits of that rule lie along the boundaries of majority rule'. The two problems with this approach are, first, that one is left to find out what is and is not 'ratifiable' — see especially the controversy over ratification of directors' breaches of duty (16.4.14 and 16.8) of which Wedderburn said: 'We know that a shareholder can sue to challenge [directors' breaches of duty] and that they can be ratified, but not why' ('Unreformed company law' (1969) 32 MLR 563 at p. 564). The second problem is that it seems to assume that the effectiveness of a ratification depends only on the nature of the act being ratified and not at all on the circumstances of the ratifiers, whereas it will be suggested in 18.4.5 and 18.4.11 that in some circumstances a ratification can be ineffective if it is a fraud on the minority but effective if it is not.

Beck's theory is that majority rule is the foundation of the rule in *Foss* v *Harbottle* because the internal management principle is based on the idea that matters of internal management are conclusively settled by majority decision and so not reviewable by the courts and the proper plaintiff principle is based on a supposed common law rule that the majority in general meeting have the right to decide on whether or not to litigate in the company's name (see 15.7.3).

18.3.3.3 Multiplicity of actions

Of the many judicial comments on this, perhaps the most frequently quoted is that of Mellish LJ in *MacDougall* v *Gardiner* (1875) 1 ChD 13 at p. 25:

> Looking to the nature of these companies, looking at the way in which their articles are formed, and that they are not all lawyers who attend these meetings, nothing can be more likely than that there should be something more or less irregular done at them — some directors may have been irregularly appointed, some directors as irregularly turned out, or something or other may have been done which ought not to have been done according to the proper construction of the articles. Now, if that gives a right to every member of the company to file a bill to have the question decided, then if there happens to be one cantankerous member, or one member who loves litigation, everything of this kind will be litigated; whereas, if the bill must be filed in the name of the company, then, unless there is a majority who really wish for litigation, the litigation will not go on. Therefore, holding that such suits must be brought in the name of the company does certainly greatly tend to stop litigation.

And see per Lord Campbell LC in *Orr* v *Glasgow, Airdrie & Monklands Junction Railway Co.* (1860) 3 Macq 799 at pp. 802–3, and per James LJ in *Gray* v *Lewis* (1873) LR 8 Ch App 1035 at pp. 1050–1.

18.3.3.4 Floodgates

The reasons for the rule in *Foss* v *Harbottle* are typical 'floodgates' arguments which the courts use to refuse jurisdiction — that courts should not deal with matters with which they are not familiar, and for which a domestic settlement procedure exists, and that allowing one action would lead to an overwhelming number of similar actions. As in other circumstances in which floodgates arguments are used to justify not hearing a class of cases: (a) the courts make exceptions, and (b) the legislature has intervened to require the courts to deal with cases. We have already said that it is difficult to state what the exceptions are but that will be the topic of 18.4. The major legislative intervention is now in part 17 of CA 1985 (protection of company's members against unfair prejudice) — see 18.7. There are also provisions for a dissentient minority to apply to the court in respect of decisions on certain matters — see the list in 14.4.1.

Despite the function of the rule in *Foss* v *Harbottle* of holding back a flood of litigation, it may be that sometimes a case which could have been barred by the rule has been heard simply because no defendant sought to invoke the rule to have the case stopped. In *Advance Bank of Australia Ltd* v *FAI Insurances Australia Ltd* (1987) 9 NSWLR 464, counsel for Advance Bank of Australia Ltd conceded that, on appeal, it was too late to challenge the standing of a member of the company to bring an action in respect of the company's affairs when standing had not been questioned at first instance (see per Kirby P at pp. 470–1 and Mahoney JA at p. 492). See also per Mahoney JA in *Darvall* v *North Sydney Brick & Tile Co. Ltd* (1989) 16 NSWLR 260 at p. 332. So not every case in which a company's affairs were considered by a court at the instance of a member can be regarded as a precedent on the applicability of the rule in *Foss* v *Harbottle*.

18.3.4   The ratifiability principle

In *Edwards* v *Halliwell* [1950] 2 All ER 1064, CA, Jenkins LJ took the view that the ratifiability principle is a vital component of the rule in *Foss* v *Harbottle* (see 18.3.1). Academic discussions of the rule often accord the ratifiability principle the central position which Jenkins LJ thought it had. See, for example, R. Gregory, 'What *is* the rule in *Foss* v *Harbottle*?' (1982) 45 MLR 584.

The ratifiability principle was stated by Wigram V-C in *Bagshaw* v *Eastern Union Railway Co.* (1849) 7 Hare 114 at p. 130 in the following form:

> . . . if the act, though it be the act of the directors only, be one which a general meeting of the company could sanction, a bill by some of the shareholders, on behalf of themselves and others, to impeach that act cannot be sustained, because a general meeting of the company might immediately confirm and give validity to the act of which the bill complains.

See also *Davidson* v *Tulloch* (1860) 3 Macq 783, HL, per Lord Campbell LC at p. 792 and Lord Cranworth at p. 796.

As will become clear in the following discussion, our view is that the ratifiability principle is not central to the rule in *Foss* v *Harbottle* and we will not use it as the basis of our discussion.

18.4   PROPER PLAINTIFF PRINCIPLE

18.4.1   The company is the proper plaintiff to enforce its rights

The legal rights of a company belong to the company as a separate person and not to its members. The members of a company do not have standing to enforce its rights by legal action. As the Court of Appeal explained in *Prudential Assurance Co. Ltd* v *Newman Industries Ltd (No. 2)* [1982] Ch 204, at p. 210, it is an:

> elementary principle that A cannot, as a general rule, bring an action against B to recover damages or secure other relief on behalf of C for an injury done by B to C. C is the proper plaintiff because C is the party injured, and, therefore, the person in whom the cause of action is vested. This is sometimes referred to as the rule in *Foss* v *Harbottle* (1843) 2 Hare 461 when applied to corporations, but it has a wider scope and is fundamental to any rational system of jurisprudence.

Whether or not a company sues to enforce its legal rights must be decided by the persons who, under the company's constitution, have authority to institute legal proceedings in the company's name. This will normally be the directors under Table A, art. 70 (*Breckland Group Holdings Ltd* v *London & Suffolk Properties Ltd* [1989] BCLC 100; see 15.7.3).

In *Foss* v *Harbottle* itself, Mr Foss and Mr Turton, who were members of a statutory company called the Victoria Park Co., alleged that various people, including five directors of the company (one of whom was Mr Harbottle), had made secret profits as promoters of the company (see 17.6.3) and that the directors had breached their fiduciary duties to the company by causing it to enter into improper and fraudulent transactions. Foss and Turton commenced an action against the alleged wrongdoers, 'on behalf of themselves and all other the proprietors of shares except the defendants'. Wigram V-C said (at p. 490):

> The Victoria Park Co. is an incorporated body, and the conduct with which the defendants are charged in this suit is an injury not to the plaintiffs exclusively; it is an injury to the whole corporation.

His honour observed that there was no doubt that proceedings to remedy this wrong could have been brought in the name of the company but these proceedings had been:

> brought by two individual corporators, professedly on behalf of themselves and all other members of the corporation, except those who committed the injuries complained of — the plaintiffs assuming to themselves the right and power in that manner to sue on behalf of and represent the corporation itself.

The plaintiffs were treating the company just as an association of its members, so that they could represent the company if they represented the members, but this ignored the fact that the company was also a separate person:

> It was not, nor could it successfully be, argued that it was a matter of course for any individual members of a corporation thus to assume to themselves the right of suing in the name of the corporation. In law the corporation and the aggregate members of the corporation are not the same thing for purposes like this.

The proper plaintiff principle applies even if a majority of members support action by a member to enforce a right of the company (*Mozley* v *Alston* (1847) 1 Ph 790) and even if all the members are suing (*Hawkesbury Development Co. Ltd* v *Landmark Finance Pty Ltd* (1969) 92 WN (NSW) 199).

18.4.2 Derivative actions

Sometimes the court permits a right of action of a company to be pursued in proceedings brought in the name of a member of the company, as an exception to the proper plaintiff principle. At first such proceedings were treated, like the unsuccessful proceedings in *Foss* v *Harbottle* (1843) 2 Hare 461 (see 18.4.1), as being brought by the company as an association of its members, and were expressed to be brought on behalf of the plaintiff and all other members of the company except (if they were also members) the defendants. More recently, following United States jurisprudence, a member of a company bringing proceedings to enforce a right of the company is said to be deriving a right of action from the company. Accordingly such proceedings are called 'derivative actions' (*Schiowitz* v *IOS Ltd* (1971) 23 DLR (3d) 102, New Brunswick, at p. 121; *Estmanco (Kilner House) Ltd* v *Greater London Council* [1982] 1 WLR 2 at p. 10) and it is not essential that a derivative action be expressed to be brought on behalf of the plaintiff and other members (*Wallersteiner* v *Moir (No. 2)* [1975] QB 373 per Lord Denning MR at p. 391). The company must be joined as a co-defendant so that if its rights are vindicated it will be able to enforce the judgment (*Russell* v *Wakefield Waterworks Co.* (1875) LR 20 Eq 474; *Spokes* v *Grosvenor & West End Railway Terminus Hotel Co. Ltd* [1897] 2 QB 124; *Ferguson* v *Wallbridge* [1935] 3 DLR 66, PC; *Prudential Assurance Co. Ltd* v *Newman Industries Ltd (No. 2)* [1982] Ch 204, CA, at p. 220).

The Law Commission has proposed the following legislative definition:

A derivative action is an action by a member of a company where the cause of action is vested in the company and relief is sought on its behalf.

See Law Commission, *Shareholder Remedies* (Law Com. No. 246, Cm 3769) (London: Stationery Office, 1997), app. A.

The need for a derivative action arises only where action cannot be taken in the company's name. Authority to institute litigation normally lies with the directors (see 15.7.3). On a petition under CA 1985, s. 459 (relief of unfairly prejudicial conduct of a company's affairs, see 18.6), the court may authorise civil proceedings to be brought in the name and on behalf of the company by such person or persons and on such terms as the court may direct (s. 461(2)(c)). Thus matters which could be the subject of a derivative action may be raised in s. 459 proceedings (*Re a Company (No. 005287 of 1985)* [1986] 1 WLR 281; *Lowe* v *Fahey* [1996] 1 BCLC 262). In *Whyte* 1984 SLT 330, a minority shareholder in, and managing director of, a company called Liquid Gas Equipment Ltd (LGE) petitioned under what is now s. 459 and obtained an interim order to restrain the group of companies which controlled the majority of shares in LGE from acting to obtain the discontinuance of an action by LGE against another company in the group.

The Secretary of State may bring an action in the name of a company if, from any report made or information obtained under CA 1985, part XIV (ss. 431 to 453), it appears to be in the public interest to do so (s. 438, see 18.8.3.4).

An administrator or administrative receiver of a company also has power to institute litigation in its name (IA 1986, sch. 1, para. 5).

In the liquidation of a company the liquidator has power to institute litigation (IA 1986, ss. 165(3) (voluntary liquidation) and 167(1)(a) (compulsory liquidation) and sch. 4, para. 4). A member of a company in liquidation is not permitted to bring a derivative action but must apply to the court under IA 1986, ss. 112 (voluntary liquidation) or 167(3) (compulsory liquidation), to reverse any decision by the liquidator not to bring proceedings (*Ferguson* v *Wallbridge*; *Fargro Ltd* v *Godfroy* [1986] 1 WLR 1134).

A derivative action, then, is necessary only where there is a dispute between a member of a company not in liquidation and those in control of the company's litigation over the merits of litigating to enforce a right of the company (or of ratifying a wrong so as to preclude litigation) and that dispute is not dealt with in an application under CA 1985, s. 459. A dissentient member must normally accept the decision of those who under the company's constitution have the authority to decide on litigation or ratification. So a derivative action is allowed only if the court is willing to ignore the company's decision to ratify or not to sue. Under the present common law the court will do that if it regards the decision as a 'fraud on the minority' (the 'minority' being the member or members who want the company to sue).

There will be a particular suspicion of fraud where the persons sought to be sued use their own influence over the company (for example, as directors or major shareholders) to prevent the company suing them. In *Burland* v *Earle*, Lord Davey said, at p. 93:

But an exception is made to the [proper plaintiff principle], where the persons against whom the relief is sought themselves hold and control the majority of the shares in the company, and will not permit an action to be brought in the name of the company. In that case the courts allow the shareholders complaining to bring an action in their own names. This, however, is mere matter of procedure in order to give a remedy for a wrong which would otherwise escape redress.

Conversely, a decision not to sue which is taken independently of those sought to be sued will not be a fraud on the minority and a derivative action will not be allowed (*Burrows* v *Becker* (1968) 70 DLR (2d) 433; *Smith* v *Croft (No. 2)* [1988] Ch 114), provided the decision not to sue is taken in good faith and for the benefit of the company (*Taylor* v *National Union of Mineworkers (Derbyshire Area)* [1985] BCLC 237 per Vinelott J at p. 255). As Knox J said in *Smith* v *Croft (No. 2)* at p. 185:

Ultimately the question which has to be answered in order to determine whether the [proper plaintiff principle] applies to prevent a minority shareholder seeking relief as plaintiff for the benefit of the company is 'Is the plaintiff being improperly prevented from bringing these proceedings on behalf of the company?' If it is an expression of the corporate will of the company by an appropriate independent organ that is preventing the plaintiff from prosecuting the action he is not improperly but properly prevented and so the answer to the question is no. The appropriate independent organ will vary according to the company concerned and the identity of the defendants who will in most cases be disqualified from participating by voting in expressing the corporate will.

His lordship used the following test to determine whether there was an independent majority in favour of the company not taking action (at p. 186):

. . . votes should be disregarded if, but only if, the court is satisfied either that the vote or its equivalent is actually cast with a view to supporting the defendants rather than securing benefit to the company, or that the situation of the person whose vote is considered is such that there is a substantial risk of that happening.

His lordship added that: 'The court should not substitute its own opinion but can, and in my view should, assess whether the decision-making process is vitiated by being or being likely to be directed to an improper purpose.' It may be difficult for the court to decide whether votes are cast truly independently, especially where the company's controllers have transferred their shares in anticipation of proceedings (Mr Justice Ipp, 'Problems with "control" in fraud-on-the-minority actions' (1997) 18 Co Law 88 and see *Biala Pty Ltd* v *Mallina Holdings Ltd (No. 4)* (1993) 13 WAR 11 discussed in 18.4.13).

When considering whether to allow a member of a company to bring a derivative action the common law considers not only the circumstances of the company's refusal to bring an action itself, but also the nature of the cause of action (see 18.4.4).

In the Commonwealth it has been held that it is necessary to be a member of a company to be able to sue on its behalf by a derivative action: so if the membership of company A includes another company, B, then a member of company B cannot take a derivative action on A's behalf (*Ruralcorp Consulting Pty Ltd* v *Pynery Pty Ltd* (1996) 134 FLR 188). Similarly a person with only an equitable interest in shares in a company cannot bring a derivative action on its behalf (*Hooker Investments Pty Ltd* v *Email Ltd* (1986) 10 ACLR 443 per Young J at p. 445; *Fulloon* v *Radley* [1992] 2 QdR 290; *Svanstrom* v *Jonasson*

(Cayman Islands CA, 4 April 1997, unreported)). In its report, *Shareholder Remedies* (Law Com. No. 246, Cm 3769) (London: Stationery Office, 1997), the Law Commission proposes that only present members of a company should be able to bring a derivative action on its behalf (para. 6.50).

18.4.3   The company's decision not to sue

A member of a company seeking to enforce a right of the company by a derivative action must show that authority cannot be obtained for proceedings to be brought in the company's name (*Birch* v *Sullivan* [1957] 1 WLR 1247).

A company's decision not to sue may take one of three forms:

(a)   A decision by the directors not to sue where the directors have authority to litigate in the company's name, as is usual.

(b)   A decision by the members not to sue where the members have authority to litigate in the company's name.

(c)   A decision by the members to ratify the act in question. (This option is not available if the act is contrary to the general law or the Companies Acts.) If a decision by the members to ratify an act is effective then a derivative action is not possible: the act will be deemed by the ratification not to be a wrong to the company and so there is no right of action that a member can derive from the company (*Kent* v *Jackson* (1851) 14 Beav 367; affirmed (1852) 2 De G M & G 49).

If a decision not to sue was effected by the votes of those sought to be sued then a derivative action will be allowed (*Atwool* v *Merryweather* (1868) LR 5 Eq 464 n at p. 468 n). In particular, if a ratification was effected by the votes of those sought to be sued then the ratified act will nevertheless be treated as a wrong to the company for which a derivative action may be brought (*Prudential Assurance Co. Ltd* v *Newman Industries Ltd (No. 2)* [1982] Ch 204, CA, at p. 219).

It would seem that the form of the decision not to sue is irrelevant: if the persons sought to be sued prevent whichever body has the power to litigate from suing them then a derivative action is possible. If, on the other hand, the decision not to sue is not effected by the votes of those sought to be sued then the decision not to sue is effective (*Smith* v *Croft (No. 2)* [1988] Ch 114 at p. 139).

It is unnecessary to show that there has been a positive decision not to sue if it is not possible to reach a decision on the question because the parties sought to be sued can block decision-making, for example, because they have exactly the same number of votes as the parties seeking to sue or they can prevent meetings being quorate by refusing to attend (*Ingre* v *Maxwell* (1964) 44 DLR (2d) 764, British Columbia; *Glass* v *Atkin* (1967) 65 DLR (2d) 501; *Fargro Ltd* v *Godfrey* [1986] 1 WLR 1134; *Anglo-Eastern (1985) Ltd* v *Knutz* [1988] 1 HKLR 322). In such a case the plaintiff may not have a minority of votes but will be in the same position as a minority (*Glass* v *Atkin* at p. 504).

So far we have expressed the conditions in which a derivative action is permitted in terms of the persons sought to be sued using votes to prevent action being taken by the company itself against them. Sometimes a more general approach is taken. In *Edwards* v *Halliwell* [1950] 2 All ER 1064, Jenkins LJ, at p. 1067, referred to the wrongdoers being 'in control of the company', and in *Prudential Assurance Co. Ltd* v *Newman Industries Ltd (No. 2)*, the Court of Appeal said, at p. 219:

['Control'] embraces a broad spectrum extending from an overall absolute majority of votes at one end, to a majority of votes at the other end made up of those likely to be cast by the delinquent himself plus those voting with him as a result of influence or apathy.

In *Farrow* v *Registrar of Building Societies* [1991] 2 VR 589, the concept of control by the person sought to be sued was extended when a member of a building society incorporated in the State of Victoria was permitted to take a derivative action against the State's Registrar of Building Societies, its Attorney-General and the State itself for wrongfully appointing an administrator of the building society (who displaced the directors) and for wrongfully not removing the administrator for misconduct. Marks J (at p. 592) said that it was obvious that the administrator himself would not take action in the name of the building society against those who appointed him to challenge his own appointment. At p. 594, his honour said:

Application of the exception to the *Foss* v *Harbottle* rule does not depend, in my view, on the wrongdoer being a party to the proceeding or, if a party, that relief is sought against him or her. What is necessary is that the proceeding is to redress injury to the company and that it would not be brought by the company because it is controlled by the wrongdoers who have done the damage; alternatively, by persons who, as a matter of reality, will, for obvious reasons, not bring it.

18.4.4 Causes for which derivative actions are allowed

18.4.4.1 Present position
The general principle is that a member of a company may take a derivative action to redress an infringement of the company's rights if the company itself has decided not to sue those who acted against it but the decision not to sue was a fraud on the minority. The fact that the decision not to sue was effected by the votes of those sought to be sued is an indication that it is a fraud on the minority. But even if the decision not to sue was taken under the influence of those sought to be sued, the court may accept that, because of the character of the act complained of, the decision not to sue is not a fraud on the minority. For example, if a company has acquired an asset from one of its directors who is also a member of the company then a ratification of the purchase carried by the votes of the director-member concerned is not a fraud on the minority provided the director-member did not acquire the asset in the knowledge that it was required by the company (*North-West Transportation Co. Ltd* v *Beatty* (1887) 12 App Cas 589; *Burland* v *Earle* [1902] AC 83; as explained in *Cook* v *Deeks* [1916] 1 AC 554; see 16.6.7). Here the director-member's self-interested voting is not regarded as defrauding the minority.

Saying that a member of a company must abide by the majority's decision not to sue in respect of one sort of act detrimental to the company's interests (sometimes called 'ratifiable' acts), but may bring a derivative action in respect of other sorts of acts, implies that ratifiable detriments to the company are merely normal hazards of business which members of the company must put up with, whereas acts for which derivative actions may be brought do offend the public business morality which the courts enforce.

The courts have not defined what characterises a ratifiable act, in respect of which a derivative action will not be allowed, but, according to Lord Davey in *Burland* v *Earle* at p. 93, what characterises acts in respect of which a derivative action can be taken is that they: 'are of a fraudulent character or beyond the powers of the company'. He continued:

A familiar example is where the majority are endeavouring directly or indirectly to appropriate to themselves money, property, or advantages which belong to the company, or in which the other shareholders are entitled to participate, as was alleged in the case of *Menier* v *Hooper's Telegraph Works* (1874) LR 9 Ch App 350.

In *Menier* v *Hooper's Telegraph Works*, the major shareholder in a company had contracted to make and lay a submarine telegraph cable for the company but found that it was more advantageous to do the work for another person and so caused the company to abandon the contract. A minority shareholder in the company was permitted to pursue a derivative action to recover for the company from the majority shareholder the profits to be made from the alternative contract. *Kerry* v *Maori Dream Gold Mines Ltd* (1898) 14 TLR 402, CA, is a similar case. See also *Cook* v *Deeks*, the facts of which are given in 16.7.3.2.

Unfortunately, beyond giving one example, Lord Davey did not precisely define what is and is not of a fraudulent character for the purpose of the exception from the proper plaintiff principle and recent cases have permitted derivative actions in respect of acts for which 'fraudulent' does not seem to be an apt description.

As Megarry V-C said in *Estmanco (Kilner House) Ltd* v *Greater London Council* [1982] 1 WLR 2, at p. 12:

> It does not seem to have yet become very clear exactly what the word 'fraud' means in this context [i.e., in the phrase 'fraud on a minority']; but I think it is plainly wider than fraud at common law, in the sense of *Derry* v *Peek* (1889) 14 App Cas 337.

(a)   *Acts that are not of a fraudulent character*. It has already been noted that a purchase by a company from one of its directors of property which the director acquired without knowing that it was required by the company is not of a fraudulent character and cannot be the subject of a derivative action. In *Pavlides* v *Jensen* [1956] Ch 565 directors of a company were alleged to have sold company property negligently at an undervalue but there was no evidence that they had personally benefited from the transaction. A derivative action was not allowed. Danckwerts J said, at p. 576:

> There is no allegation of fraud on the part of the directors or appropriation of assets of the company by the majority shareholders in fraud of the minority . . . it was open to the company by a vote of the majority to decide that, if the directors by their negligence or error of judgment had sold the company's mine at an undervalue, proceedings should not be taken by the company against the directors.

Contrasting this with *Daniels* v *Daniels* [1978] Ch 406 discussed below, it seems that negligence by directors which does not benefit them personally is not of a fraudulent character.

(b)   *Acts that are of a fraudulent character*.   In *Alexander* v *Automatic Telephone Co.* [1900] 2 Ch 56, the company's directors allotted shares to themselves and others. They had a controlling interest in the company and, although they paid nothing for their shares, required the other allottees to make payments on application and on allotment. The Court of Appeal allowed a derivative action to succeed even though the directors had acted in the belief that they were doing nothing wrong and the plaintiffs did not allege 'deliberate fraud'. It was sufficient that the directors were in breach of their duty to the company by depriving it of the use of money which they ought to have paid up sooner than they did and giving themselves the advantage of not having to pay without disclosure to the members.

In *Daniels* v *Daniels*, a husband and wife were the directors and majority shareholders of a company. In 1970, the company sold some land to the wife for £4,250 which, some four years later, she sold for £120,000. There was no intention to defraud the minority shareholders, but Templeman J held that there had been a misappropriation of the company's land in respect of which a derivative action would lie. His lordship distinguished *Pavlides* v *Jensen* on the basis that, in that case, although a company asset had been sold by directors at an undervalue, no benefit had accrued to the directors. His lordship concluded (at p. 414):

> The principle which may be gleaned from *Alexander* v *Automatic Telephone Co.* (directors benefiting themselves), from *Cook* v *Deeks* (directors diverting business in their own favour) and from dicta in *Pavlides* v *Jensen* (directors appropriating assets of the company) is that a minority shareholder who has no other remedy may sue where directors use their powers, intentionally or unintentionally, fraudulently or negligently, in a manner which benefits themselves at the expense of the company.

In *Prudential Assurance Co. Ltd* v *Newman Industries Ltd (No. 2)* [1981] Ch 257, Vinelott J surveyed the cases and concluded, at p. 316, that:

> . . . the authorities show that the exception applies not only where the allegation is that directors who control a company have improperly appropriated to themselves money, property or advantages which belong to the company or, in breach of their duty to the company, have diverted business to themselves which ought to have been given to the company, but more generally where it is alleged that directors though acting 'in the belief that they were doing nothing wrong' (per Lindley MR in *Alexander* v *Automatic Telephone Co.* [1900] 2 Ch 56 at p. 65) are guilty of a breach of duty to the company, including their duty to exercise proper care, and as a result of that breach obtain some benefit. In the latter case it must be unnecessary to allege and prove that the directors in breaking their duty to the company acted with a view to benefiting themselves at the expense of the company; for such an allegation would be an allegation of misappropriation of the company's property. On the other hand, the exception does not apply if all that is alleged is that directors who control a company are liable to the company for damages for negligence it not being shown that the transaction was one in which they were interested or that they have in fact obtained any benefit from it. It is not easy to see precisely where the line between these cases is to be drawn.

In *Estmanco (Kilner House) Ltd* v *Greater London Council* the plaintiff company had been formed by the defendant council for the purpose of managing a block of 60 flats. The company had 60 shares which were initially vested in the defendant council. The defendant council had agreed with the company to endeavour to sell each of the flats and each purchaser of a flat was to be given one share in the company, though all voting rights were to remain in the council until all the flats had been disposed of. When 12 flats had been sold, the council decided that the remaining flats should be let to council tenants. The council used its voting power to direct the company's directors to discontinue an action in the company's name against the council for the performance of the agreement, so one of the 12 shareholders applied to be substituted as plaintiff in the action so that she could continue it as a derivative action. Megarry V-C allowed the application, saying:

> All that I need say is that in my judgment the exception usually known as 'fraud on a minority' is wide enough to cover the present case, and that if it is not, it should now be

made wide enough. There can be no doubt about the 12 voteless purchasers being a minority; there can be no doubt about the advantage to the council of having the action discontinued; there can be no doubt about the injury to the applicant and the rest of the minority, both as shareholders and as purchasers, of that discontinuance; and I feel little doubt that the council has used its voting power not in order to promote the best interests of the company but in order to bring advantage to itself and disadvantage to the minority. Furthermore, that disadvantage is no trivial matter, but represents a radical alteration in the basis on which the council sold the flats to the minority. It seems to me that the sum total represents a fraud on the minority in the sense in which 'fraud' is used in that phrase, or alternatively represents such an abuse of power as to have the same effect. . . .

No right of a shareholder to vote in his own selfish interests or to ignore the interests of the company entitle him with impunity to injure his voteless fellow shareholders by depriving the company of a cause of action and stultifying the purpose for which the company was formed.

In *Farrow* v *Registrar of Building Societies* [1991] 2 VR 589, discussed in 18.4.3, Marks J said, at p. 595: '. . . allegations of fraud or misappropriation are not necessary for the operation of the exception to the *Foss* v *Harbottle* rule, although it is likely that allegation of a wrongdoing amounting to unlawfulness is'. This case, like *Estmanco (Kilner House) Ltd* v *Greater London Council*, seems to have extended the availability of the derivative action.

(c)   Ultra vires *acts*. In *Cockburn* v *Newbridge Sanitary Steam Laundry Co. Ltd* [1915] 1 IR 237, the company alleged that it had agreed with its managing director that he should obtain work for the company from the local army barracks and pay the company out of the money he received, leaving him free to use the balance to bribe the people who gave him the work. Minority shareholders were permitted to bring a derivative action to recover the balance of the contract price from the managing director because the alleged agreement was illegal.

In *Smith* v *Croft (No. 2)* [1988] Ch 114, there was a prima facie case that a company had given illegal assistance for the purchase of its shares by a company controlled by its executive directors. Minority shareholders were not permitted to pursue a derivative action against the other company and the directors because a majority of the independent shareholders were against taking the action. The derivative action would have been permitted if there had not been an independent majority against it.

18.4.4.2   Proposed reform

In its report, *Shareholder Remedies* (Law Com. No. 246, Cm 3769) (London: Stationery Office, 1997), the Law Commission has proposed replacing the common law set out in 18.4.4.1 with a statutory provision specifying the causes in respect of which a derivative action may be brought. The proposed provision is that a derivative action may be brought by a member of a company only if:

the cause of action arises as a result of an actual or proposed act or omission involving—
(a)   negligence, default, breach of duty or breach of trust by a director of the company, or
(b)   a director putting himself in a position where his personal interests conflict with his duties to the company.

It is proposed that 'director' here should include *de facto* directors and shadow directors. The proposed provision makes it clear that, although the cause of a derivative action must arise out of something done or proposed to be done by a director, the derivative action itself may be taken against some other person, for example, to recover wrongfully transferred property.

The laudable purpose of this proposal is to end wasteful litigation about what may or may not be the subject of a derivative action. By referring to 'negligence' without qualification the proposal would end the rule derived from *Pavlides* v *Jensen* [1956] Ch 565 that a derivative action cannot be brought in respect of negligence by directors which has not benefited them personally. The proposal is intended to prevent a derivative action being brought in respect of a wrong done to a company by anyone other than a director. For example, the action permitted in *Estmanco (Kilner House) Ltd* v *Greater London Council* would not be allowed under the Commission's proposal, because it arose from conduct of the majority shareholder rather than the directors. The Commission argues (para. 6.34):

> The decision on whether to sue a third party (i.e. someone who is not a director and where the claim is not closely connected with a breach of duty by a director) is clearly one for the board. If the directors breach their duty in deciding not to pursue the claim then . . . a derivative claim can be brought against them. To allow shareholders to have involvement in whether claims should be brought against third parties in our view goes too far in encouraging excessive shareholder interference with management decisions.

18.4.5 Ratifiability as the basis of the fraud on the minority exception

A derivative action can never be taken in respect of an act which can be ratified by interested votes because a decision not to sue the perpetrator cannot be a fraud on the minority. In the past it has been asserted that if a wrong to a company cannot be ratified by interested votes then it cannot be ratified at all and so can always be the subject of a derivative action — this may be called the 'ratifiability theory'. However, it seems that the true position is that a wrong which cannot be ratified by interested votes can be ratified by disinterested votes (*Smith* v *Croft (No. 2)* [1988] Ch 114; *Taylor* v *National Union of Mineworkers (Derbyshire Area)* [1985] BCLC 237). As Vinelott J said in *Prudential Assurance Co. Ltd* v *Newman Industries Ltd (No. 2)* [1981] Ch 257 at p. 307:

> . . . there is no obvious limit to the power of the majority to authorise or ratify an act or transaction whatever its character provided that the majority does not have an interest which conflicts with the company.

(Lord Wedderburn of Charlton has been a leading proponent of the ratifiability theory (see 'Shareholders' rights and the rule in *Foss* v *Harbottle*' [1958] CLJ 93 at p. 96) and so is critical of the remark by Vinelott J just quoted: see 'Derivative actions and *Foss* v *Harbottle*' (1981) 44 MLR 202 at pp. 207–8.)

It follows that the fact that a valid decision not to sue may be taken in respect of a wrong done to a company and will prevent a derivative action in respect of that wrong does not mean that the wrong is not of a fraudulent character. In *Regal (Hastings) Ltd* v *Gulliver* [1967] 2 AC 134, HL, the company was, properly, the plaintiff in an action concerning a wrong done to it. Lord Russell of Killowen, at p. 143, said that the defendants' liability was considered on the footing that they acted with bona fides, intending to act in the interest of the company and that an attempt at first instance to make out a case of wilful misconduct or fraud on their part had failed. At p. 150 his lordship said that the five directors against whom the case had been brought '. . . could, had they wished, have protected themselves by a resolution (either antecedent or subsequent) of the Regal shareholders in general meeting'. There were (according to his lordship at p. 140) 20 shareholders in all and they never considered whether to resolve to allow the directors to keep their profit from the transaction in question: accordingly, whether there had been a fraud on the minority was never an issue in the case. Deducing from this that a director's profit from a transaction to which the company is not a party is not of a fraudulent character for the purposes of the exception to the proper plaintiff principle (Lord Wedderburn of Charlton, 'Derivative actions and *Foss* v *Harbottle*' (1981) 44 MLR 202 at pp. 206 and 210–11) assumes that the ratifiability of an act depends only on the nature of the act and not at all on the circumstances of the ratification.

For critical discussion of various suggested methods of deciding whether ratification is a fraud on the minority based only on the character of the act, see F.H. Buckley, 'Ratification and the derivative action under the Ontario Business Corporations Act' (1976) 22 McGill LJ 167 and Sullivan [1985] CLJ 236 at pp. 239–44, and for a recent suggestion, see P. St J. Smart, 'Misuse of confidential information: the company's and minority shareholder's remedies' [1987] JBL 464. At p. 248 of his article, Sullivan attempts to unravel the mystery surrounding Lord Russell's remark in *Regal (Hastings) Ltd* v *Gulliver*. The rest of his article defends Vinelott J's analysis, which Smart dismisses as wrong (n. 42).

18.4.6   Suing for loss of value of shares

If a company has a right of action against a person to recover compensation for damage which it has suffered, this does not in itself give members of the company a right of action to sue the person for the loss in value of their shares arising from the same damage: the members' loss is only a reflection of the company's loss and when the company as the proper plaintiff recovers its loss the shares will return to their former value (*Prudential Assurance Co. Ltd* v *Newman Industries Ltd (No. 2)* [1982] Ch 204, CA, at pp. 222–3).

In *Stein* v *Blake* [1998] 1 All ER 724 the plaintiff owned half the shares in a number of companies. The first defendant owned the other half and was sole director of the companies. It was alleged that the first defendant misappropriated assets from the companies and he was sued for the loss in value of the plaintiff's shares resulting from that misappropriation. The companies could have sued the first defendant for the value of the misappropriated assets. It seems that the plaintiff brought his personal action because all the companies had gone into liquidation and the liquidators were not taking action. The plaintiff's action was struck out because the companies were the proper plaintiffs in respect of the wrong allegedly done to them. As all the companies were insolvent it was their creditors who were primarily interested in recovery of its assets, not the plaintiff. It made no difference that the plaintiff alleged that the other director owed him a duty personally: the damage allegedly caused by breach of that duty was to the companies and was caused in breach of the defendant's duty to the companies. The loss caused to the plaintiff was only a reflection of the companies' loss, which the companies were the proper plaintiffs to recover.

In *O'Neill* v *Ryan* [1993] ILRM 557, a former chief executive of an airline operator, Ryanair Ltd, sued another airline operator, Aer Lingus plc, and other people in the industry, claiming that the value of his shares in Ryanair (which he had sold) had been diminished by anticompetitive practices which contravened directly applicable European Community law. It was held that he had no cause of action because any damage caused by the alleged wrongdoing was damage to the company.

In *Verderame* v *Commercial Union Assurance Co. plc* [1992] BCLC 793, Mr and Mrs Verderame were the only shareholders in and directors of VA Garage (Cardiff) Ltd. Thieves entered the company's premises and stole so much that the company was unable to carry on business so that Mr and Mrs Verderame lost their income as employees, shareholders and directors of the company. An insurance policy covering losses from theft and consequential loss of business had been taken out with Commercial Union. This had been arranged by an insurance broker on the Verderames' instructions. When a claim was made on the policy it was discovered that it insured the Verderames' property, not the company's property. The Verderames then sued the insurance broker for the tort of negligence claiming damages for their loss of income. The Court of Appeal said that the company should sue the insurance broker for negligently carrying out its contract to effect insurance for the company (a contract which the company had entered into through the agency of its directors, the Verderames). To allow the Verderames a separate cause of action in tort would be to make the broker liable twice over for the same loss.

An action by a holder of shares in a company to recover damages for loss in value of the shares will be permitted if the shareholder is the proper plaintiff to recover the damages and double recovery by both shareholder and company can be avoided. For example, in *George Fischer (Great Britain) Ltd* v *Multi Construction Ltd* [1995] 1 BCLC 260 a company sued for breach of contract to supply equipment for its warehouse. The breach of contract had disrupted the activities of its wholly owned subsidiaries which used the warehouse, and the company sued for the resulting loss in value of its shares in those subsidiaries. It was held that damages for breach of contract could be recovered for this loss. The only person who could sue for the breach was the parent company which was party to the contract. Although the subsidiaries had suffered loss because of the breach of contract they were not the proper plaintiffs in respect of that loss because they were not parties to the contract. *Christensen* v *Scott* [1996] 1 NZLR 273 was a more complicated example which is difficult to reconcile with *Stein* v *Blake*. Mr and Mrs Christensen were the only members of a company which suffered disastrous losses allegedly because of negligence by a firm of accountants and a firm of solicitors. The Christensens claimed that these firms acted as their advisers as well as the company's advisers so that they could claim for damages in contract or tort for loss of value in their shares caused by the negligent advice. The New Zealand Court of Appeal (unusually constituted by five judges) refused to strike out this claim even though the company had already settled its own claim against the firms. (The settlement was made by the company's liquidator and the Christensens thought it inadequate.) The court observed that care would have to be taken to prevent double recovery. The Christensens were also allowed to sue for the losses they had sustained as guarantors of the company's liabilities. See also *Barings plc* v *Coopers and Lybrand* [1997] 1 BCLC 427.

For further discussion of the possibility of suing for loss of value of shares, see M.J. Sterling, 'The theory and policy of shareholder actions in tort' (1987) 50 MLR 468.

18.4.7 Leave to continue a derivative action

The Rules of the Supreme Court 1965 were amended in 1994 to provide that if a defendant in a derivative action gives notice of intention to defend then the plaintiff must apply to the court for leave to continue the action (ord. 15, r. 12A). If there is a material change of circumstances after leave to proceed has been given then a defendant may ask the court to review the case (r. 12A(12)). The new rule does not specify how the court is to decide whether or not to give leave but it specifies that the plaintiff must provide evidence verifying the facts of the claim and the entitlement to sue on behalf of the company (r. 12A(3)). This implies that, as suggested by the Court of Appeal in *Prudential Assurance Co. Ltd* v *Newman Industries Ltd (No. 2)* [1982] Ch 204, a plaintiff must establish a prima facie case

(a) that the company is entitled to the relief claimed, and (b) that the action falls within the proper boundaries of the exception to the proper plaintiff principle.

The court will not allow a derivative action to proceed if, rather than being pursued bona fide for the benefit of the company, the action has been brought for an ulterior purpose, or if there is another adequate remedy (*Barrett* v *Duckett* [1995] 1 BCLC 243). In *Barrett* v *Duckett* the plaintiff was pursuing a derivative action against her former son-in-law primarily in retribution for his treatment of her daughter, but she apparently could not afford to continue with the action and it was found that putting the company into liquidation, so that an independent liquidator could take over the litigation, would be better than continuing with the derivative action.

The court will not allow a derivative action to be brought by a person who participated in the wrongful act complained of (*Whitwam* v *Watkin* (1898) 78 LT 188). In *Towers* v *African Tug Co.* [1904] 1 Ch 558, the company had paid an illegal dividend because of an honest mistake by its directors. Two shareholders, who had received the illegal dividend in respect of their shares, sought to bring a derivative action against the directors to compel them to pay the amount of the illegal dividend to the company. It was held that they were not entitled to bring the action. For another example see *Nurcombe* v *Nurcombe* [1985] 1 WLR 370, CA.

It is possible for a derivative action to be brought in respect of a wrong which the company suffered before the plaintiff became a member of the company because it is the company's and not the plaintiff member's rights that are being enforced (*Seaton* v *Grant* (1867) LR 2 Ch App 459).

If a derivative action is successful or legal action was a reasonable and prudent course to take in the circumstances, the company for whose benefit the action was taken should pay the costs incurred by the plaintiff on the company's behalf (*Wallersteiner* v *Moir (No. 2)* [1975] QB 373, CA; *Jaybird Group Ltd* v *Greenwood* [1986] BCLC 319; *Farrow* v *Registrar of Building Societies* [1991] 2 VR 589). The plaintiff in a derivative action may ask the court to order the company to give such an indemnity when asking for leave to continue the action (Rules of the Supreme Court 1965, r. 12A(13)). However, it is very difficult for the court to decide whether to make an order that the company should indemnify the plaintiff at a very early stage in the plaintiff's action — see *Smith* v *Croft* [1986] 1 WLR 580 in which an order was refused. See further D.D. Prentice, 'Wallersteiner v Moir: a decade later' [1987] Conv 167.

In its report, *Shareholder Remedies* (Law Com. No. 246, Cm 3769) (London: Stationery Office, 1997), the Law Commission has proposed new rules of court which will, among other things, state certain matters which the court must take into account when considering an application for leave to continue a derivative claim. These matters are:

(a)   whether the plaintiff is acting in good faith in bringing the derivative claim;

(b)   whether the derivative claim is in the interests of the company, taking account of the views of the company's directors on commercial matters;

(c)   whether the director's activity as a result of which the cause of action is alleged to arise may be approved by the company in general meeting and (if it may be) whether it has been;

(d)   whether the company in general meeting has resolved not to pursue the cause of action;

(e)   the opinion (if any) of an independent organ that for commercial reasons the derivative claim should or (as the case may be) should not be pursued;

(f)   whether a remedy is available as an alternative to the derivative claim.

18.4.8 The company is the proper plaintiff in a matter concerning its internal management

The internal management principle is that the court will not interfere with the internal management of companies acting within their powers. The proper plaintiff aspect of this principle is that the court will not determine a question concerning what it regards as the internal management of a company except in proceedings brought by the company itself.

The proper plaintiff aspect of the internal management principle is derived from the Court of Appeal's decision in *MacDougall* v *Gardiner* (1875) 1 ChD 13, in which James LJ said, at pp. 21–2:

> I think it is of the utmost importance in all these companies that the rule which is well known in this court as the rule in . . . *Foss* v *Harbottle* should be always adhered to; that is to say, that nothing connected with internal disputes between the shareholders is to be made the subject of a bill by some one shareholder on behalf of himself and others, unless there be something illegal, oppressive, or fraudulent — unless there is something *ultra vires* on the part of the company qua company, or on the part of the majority of the company, so that they are not fit persons to determine it; but that every litigation must be in the name of the company, if the company really desire it. [In the Chancery procedure of the time, a bill was the equivalent of a writ and statement of claim.]

Actions to challenge majority decisions that are fraudulent or oppressive are considered in 14.4.9.5; see also 18.4.2 on decisions not to sue company controllers. Actions in respect of a company's *ultra vires* acts are considered in 18.4.10.

In *MacDougall* v *Gardiner*, Colonel Gardiner had chaired a meeting of members of a company. He knew that he and his colleagues would win votes taken by show of hands but lose votes taken by poll. So, before any resolutions that he did not like could be put to the meeting, Colonel Gardiner accepted a resolution to adjourn the meeting which had been adopted by show of hands, and refused a demand for a poll on the resolution. (As was usual at that time, the articles of the company did not contain a provision like art. 51 of the present Table A that a poll on a question of adjournment must be taken forthwith. Some lawyers thought that it was unnecessary to make this provision explicitly because in their view it merely stated a common-law rule. Other lawyers — including those advising Colonel Gardiner — said that there was no such common-law rule, and argued that as, without such a provision, any demand for a poll on a question of adjournment could be rendered ineffective by directing that the poll be held after the meeting, it followed that not making such a provision implied that a poll could not be demanded on a question of adjournment. The disagreement has never been settled. See *R* v *Vestry of St Pancras* (1839) 11 Ad & El 15; *R* v *D'Oyly* (1840) 12 Ad & El 139.) The Court of Appeal in *MacDougall* v *Gardiner* dismissed a member's action seeking to question Colonel Gardiner's refusal of the demand for a poll. The court had two reasons for dismissing the action. First, it observed that the member did not seek any substantive relief. At that time, the court had no power to make a declaration on a question of law where the plaintiff was not seeking any other relief. Accordingly the court did not have jurisdiction. Secondly, and more controversially, the court said that the company was the only proper plaintiff because, as James LJ put it at p. 23:

> The whole question comes back to a question of internal management; that is to say, whether the meeting ought or ought not to be held in a particular way. . . . if [the affairs of the company] are being managed in a way in which they ought not to be managed,

the company are the proper persons to complain of that. . . . this was a bill which, if it was to be sustained at all, could only be sustained by the company.

In *Cotter* v *National Union of Seamen* [1929] 2 Ch 58, CA, it was said that the internal management principle applied to everything '*intra vires* the corporation' (per Laurence LJ at pp. 107–8 and Russell LJ at p. 111). (Incidentally the plaintiffs' action in *Cotter* v *National Union of Seamen* could have been dismissed by invoking the irregularity principle without reference to the internal management principle. Lord Hanworth MR, at p. 100, described the plaintiffs' complaints as 'matters really of irregularity, and no more'.)

The importance of the internal management principle in relation to an action by a member of a company against the company has been considerably diminished by the courts recognising 'personal rights' exceptions (see 18.4.9).

18.4.9   Action by a member to vindicate a personal right

Despite the internal management principle, the courts do sometimes allow a member of a company to take legal proceedings in respect of matters internal to the company and which are not regarded as vindicating the company's rights.

A person is not debarred from obtaining damages or other compensation from a company by reason only of holding or having held shares in the company (CA 1985, s. 111A). In *Prudential Assurance Co. Ltd* v *Newman Industries Ltd (No. 2)* [1982] Ch 204, the Court of Appeal, at p. 222, gave the following example:

> . . . if directors convene a meeting on the basis of a fraudulent circular, a shareholder will have a right of action to recover any loss which he has been personally caused in consequence of the fraudulent circular; this might include the expense of attending the meeting.

If proceedings taken by a member of a company are not in respect of the company's rights (so the member is not pursuing a derivative action) they must be enforcing the legal rights of the member. Accordingly the cases in which members of companies are allowed to bring proceedings in respect of their companies' internal affairs are often regarded as being concerned with the 'personal rights' of the members. For example, a member of a company may bring an action in respect of:

(a)   A decision to enter into a transaction beyond the company's objects (*Simpson* v *Westminster Palace Hotel Co.* (1860) 8 HL Cas 712).

(b)   A decision to enter into a transaction contrary to the general law or the Companies Acts (*Hope* v *International Financial Society* (1876) 4 ChD 327; *Bisgood* v *Henderson's Transvaal Estates Ltd* [1908] 1 Ch 743).

(c)   A members' resolution which was required to be adopted as a special resolution but had not received the requisite majority (*Young* v *South African & Australian Exploration & Development Syndicate* [1896] 2 Ch 268; cf. *Edwards* v *Halliwell* [1950] 2 All ER 1064).

(d)   A members' decision to pay dividends in the form of bonds though the articles required dividends to be paid in cash (*Wood* v *Odessa Waterworks Co.* (1889) 42 ChD 636).

(e)   A directors' decision which, under a provision in the articles, had been effectively vetoed (*Quin & Axtens Ltd* v *Salmon* [1909] AC 442).

(f)   A special resolution to alter the company's articles (*Allen* v *Gold Reefs of West Africa Ltd* [1900] 1 Ch 656, CA, and other cases discussed in 3.5.3.5).

(g) A resolution that was not properly adopted because votes against it were improperly rejected (*Pender* v *Lushington* (1877) 6 ChD 70 and other cases discussed in 18.5).

(h) A decision by directors to allot shares where the decision is not bona fide in the company's interests or is for an improper purpose (*Fraser* v *Whalley* (1864) 2 Hem & M 10; *Punt* v *Symons & Co. Ltd* [1903] 2 Ch 506; *Residues Treatment & Trading Co. Ltd* v *Southern Resources Ltd* (1988) 51 SASR 177).

(i) Failure of directors to provide adequate notice of meetings (*Baillie* v *Oriental Telephone & Electric Co. Ltd* [1915] 1 Ch 503, CA, and other cases discussed in 14.4.5.5).

(j) Whether or not a preference dividend was cumulative under the articles and terms of issue (*Webb* v *Earle* (1875) LR 20 Eq 556) or by the company's memorandum (*Staples* v *Eastman Photographic Materials Co.* [1896] 2 Ch 303, CA). (In neither of these cases was the rule in *Foss* v *Harbottle* pleaded as a defence.)

(k) A decision of the members to pay a dividend that was less than was required to be paid by the memorandum (*Evling* v *Israel & Oppenheimer Ltd* [1918] 1 Ch 101) or by the articles (per Wynn-Parry J in *Godfrey Phillips Ltd* v *Investment Trust Corporation Ltd* [1953] Ch 449 at p. 457).

(l) An irregular forfeiture of shares by directors (*Sweny* v *Smith* (1869) LR 7 Eq 324 and other cases discussed in 6.4.2).

(m) The proper conduct of elections of directors or other officers (*Ryan* v *South Sydney Junior Rugby League Club Ltd* (1974) 3 ACLR 486; *Pappaioannoy* v *The Greek Orthodox Community of Melbourne* (1978) 3 ACLR 801; but *Watt* v *Commonwealth Petroleum Ltd* [1938] 4 DLR 701 shows that a contrary view is taken in Canada).

(n) Decision-making by the board of directors contrary to natural justice (*St Johnstone Football Club Ltd* v *Scottish Football Association Ltd* 1965 SLT 171).

Although cases in which members challenge a decision to act *ultra vires* or a decision not taken by special majority which should have been ((a), (b) and (c) in the above list) are traditionally discussed separately, it would seem that they are examples of the personal rights exception. In *Fulloon* v *Radley* [1992] 2 QdR 290, it was held that a person with only an equitable interest in shares of a company could not bring a derivative action in respect of a wrong alleged to have been done to the company. It was argued that in 19th-century cases, such as *Bagshaw* v *Eastern Union Railway Co.* (1850) 2 Mac & G 389, equitable owners had been permitted to bring derivative actions but the court observed that they were all cases to prevent companies acting *ultra vires* and therefore were not derivative actions but were actions to protect the personal rights of shareholders.

There does not seem to be any generally accepted test of what is and what is not a personal right in respect of which an exception will be made to the internal management principle.

In some situations it is disputed whether wrongful conduct of a company's affairs is a wrong to the company or to its members or both. For example, if a person acts as a director of a company without being properly appointed then in Canada it has been held that the wrong is to the company only (*Watt* v *Commonwealth Petroleum Ltd* [1938] 4 DLR 701; *Schiowitz* v *IOS Ltd* (1971) 23 DLR (3d) 102). But in Australia it has been held that such a situation affects the personal rights of the company's members for which they may take action personally (*Australian Coal and Shale Employees' Federation* v *Smith* (1937) 38 SR (NSW) 48; *Kraus* v *J.G. Lloyd Pty Ltd* [1965] VR 232). In the English cases on a person wrongfully acting as a director of a company, both the company (*Latchford Premier Cinema Ltd* v *Ennion* [1931] 2 Ch 409; *Worcester Corsetry Ltd* v *Witting* [1936] Ch 640) and members (*Catesby* v *Burnett* [1916] 2 Ch 325; *Spencer* v *Kennedy* [1926] 1 Ch 125; *Oliver* v *Dalgleish* [1963] 1 WLR 1274) have been plaintiffs but the standing of the members who brought proceedings was never questioned.

The Law Commission, *Shareholder Remedies* (Consultation Paper No. 142) (London: Stationery Office, 1996) considered whether CA 1985 should include a statutory list of circumstances in which an action may be brought under the personal rights exception but recommended against doing so.

18.4.10   *Ultra vires* transactions

Any one member of a company may take action to restrain it from doing something that is *ultra vires*, in the sense of being beyond the company's objects (*Simpson* v *Westminster Palace Hotel Co.* (1860) 8 HL Cas 712; see 2.3.5.2) or because it is contrary to the general law or the Companies Acts (*Hope* v *International Financial Society* (1876) 4 ChD 327). Such an action is permitted as an exception to the proper plaintiff aspect of the internal management principle. This is an example of the court permitting an action in respect of a member's interest in having the affairs of the company conducted constitutionally — see 18.4.12 — and it seems that such an action should not be classified as a derivative action (see *Fulloon* v *Radley* [1992] 2 QdR 290 discussed in 18.4.9).

In *Powell* v *Kempton Park Racecourse Co. Ltd* [1899] AC 143, in order to determine whether the company was breaking the law by allowing bookmakers to operate at its racecourse, a member of the company brought an action to restrain the company, its agents and employees from permitting bookmakers to use the course. The House of Lords decided by a majority that the company was not breaking the law and so refused to grant the injunction.

There are, it seems, limits on the standing of a member of a company to prevent the company acting illegally. In *Anderson* v *Midland Railway Co.* [1902] 1 Ch 369, a member of the company alleged that the company was charging one of its regular customers less than the company's standard rate for carrying freight and that this was forbidden by a statutory provision which required all customers to be treated alike. Under the relevant statutory provision, a customer who suffered from undue preference to another customer was entitled to bring the matter before the Railway and Canal Commissioners. Buckley J held that the member did not have standing to complain because (at p. 377):

> The breach, if there be a breach, of the Act of Parliament is not one which gives rise to any rights as between the corporator and the corporation, but one which gives rise to rights as between the corporation and other customers of the corporation. There is nothing *ultra vires* in the act which is done by the corporation towards the particular customer of which the corporator can complain; it is an act of which other customers of the corporation may complain.

It is not obvious what distinguishes breaches of law by a company which can be restrained by its members (as in *Powell* v *Kempton Park Racecourse Co. Ltd*) and breaches which cannot be restrained (as in *Anderson* v *Midland Railway Co.*). See also the discussion of *Australian Agricultural Co.* v *Oatmont Pty Ltd* (1992) 106 FLR 314 in 2.3.5.10. It may be doubted, for example, whether a member of a company could restrain the company from trading contrary to consumer protection or environmental protection legislation.

If an *ultra vires* transaction has been completed then the proper plaintiff in an action for the recovery of property transferred under the transaction is the company itself (*Russell* v *Wakefield Waterworks Co.* (1875) LR 20 Eq 474 at p. 479; *Nankivell* v *Benjamin* (1892) 18

VLR 543; *Hawkesbury Development Co. Ltd* v *Landmark Finance Pty Ltd* (1969) 92 WN (NSW) 199). It is competent for the company to decide not to recover property which has been transferred *ultra vires*, provided the decision is taken in good faith in the company's interests (*Taylor* v *National Union of Mineworkers (Derbyshire Area)* [1985] BCLC 237; *Smith* v *Croft (No. 2)* [1988] Ch 114 at 139; cf. *Gray* v *Lewis* (1873) LR 8 Ch App 1035; *Cockburn* v *Newbridge Sanitary Steam Laundry Co. Ltd* [1915] 1 IR 237 seems to be to the contrary). Nevertheless, derivative actions have been allowed to recover such property (e.g., *Salomons* v *Laing* (1850) 12 Beav 377; *Simmonds* v *Heffer* [1983] BCLC 298; see the discussion in *Russell* v *Wakefield Waterworks Co.* and in *Smith* v *Croft (No. 2)* [1988] Ch 114 at pp. 168–77). However, in *Smith* v *Croft (No. 2)* it was held that a derivative action will not be allowed if the decision not to sue was taken by an independent majority in good faith in the interests of the company.

18.4.11 Ratifiability as the basis of the personal rights exceptions

Jenkins LJ in *Edwards* v *Halliwell* [1950] 2 All ER 1064 observed that a decision that a company should enter into an *ultra vires* transaction, which is not regarded as a question of internal management, cannot be ratified by the company's members. The same observation was made by Wigram V-C in *Bagshaw* v *Eastern Union Railway Co.* (1849) 7 Hare 114. (The law has subsequently been changed in one respect. CA 1985, s. 35(3), now permits a decision to enter into a transaction which is not capable of being within a company's objects to be ratified by special resolution.) The ratifiability principle asserts that the converse is true: any matter which can be ratified by the members must be one which the court will consider only in proceedings brought by the company, either because it is a question of internal management or because a derivative action is not allowed. Our view is that the question whether a matter can be ratified by the members of a company and the question whether members of a company have standing to sue in respect of the matter are separate issues which are not logically connected, and that the ratifiability principle does not accurately summarise the law on standing to sue.

It has now been held in South Australia that the fact that a decision, though unlawful, is capable of being ratified is not a bar to an action until the infringement has been expunged by ratification (*Residues Treatment & Trading Co. Ltd* v *Southern Resources Ltd* (1988) 51 SASR 177 at p. 205). Even where ratification has occurred it is still open to challenge as a fraud on the minority.

In *Hogg* v *Cramphorn Ltd* [1967] Ch 254, a member of a company challenged the lawfulness of an allotment of shares by the directors of the company. Having found that the allotment was unlawful, Buckley J stood over the action so that a meeting of the members could be held to ratify the allotment, the allottees having undertaken not to vote their shares at that meeting. In *Southern Resources Ltd* v *Residues Treatment & Trading Co. Ltd* (1990) 56 SASR 455, a member of Southern Resources Ltd challenged a decision of its directors to take over a company in which the chairman of Southern Resources had a substantial interest. The takeover was to be by share exchange which would give the chairman a controlling interest in Southern Resources Ltd. A general meeting of Southern Resources Ltd ratified the directors' decision but it was held that the decision was unlawful because it was made for the improper purpose of increasing the directors' control over the company, and the ratification by the members was held to be an oppressive fraud on the minority. Accordingly Southern Resources Ltd was ordered not to go ahead with the takeover. These two cases show that it is not the ratifiability of a decision which determines whether the court will hear a member's action to question the decision. However, in the past, commentators have usually proposed that ratifiability should be the criterion: see K.W. Wedderburn, 'Shareholders' control of directors' powers: a judicial innovation?' (1967) 30 MLR 77 and 'Unreformed company law' (1969) 32 MLR 563; C.J.H. Thomson, 'Share issues and the rule in *Foss* v *Harbottle*' (1975) 49 ALJ 134; H. Mason, 'Ratification of directors' acts: an Anglo-Australian comparison' (1978) 41 MLR 161; R. Baxt, 'Judges in their own cause: the ratification of directors' breaches of duty' (1978) 5 Mon LR 16.

For other discussions of the personal rights exceptions to the rule in *Foss* v *Harbottle* see N.A. Bastin, 'The enforcement of a member's rights' [1977] JBL 17; R.J. Smith, 'Minority shareholders and corporate irregularities' (1978) 41 MLR 147; C. Baxter, 'The role of the judge in enforcing shareholder rights' [1983] CLJ 96.

18.4.12 Lawfulness of decision-making as the basis of the personal rights exceptions

A decision of a company (either of the members or of the directors) may be unlawful in the sense that it fails to comply with the general law or with the constitution of the company or with the Companies Acts. If the lawfulness of a decision of a company is in question then two separate interests are usually involved:

(a)   The interests of the company as a separate person. If the decision has already been implemented the company has an interest in any property lost as a result of the decision, which it may be able to recover by having the decision rescinded. If the decision has not been implemented the company has an interest in not having to enter into transactions that are voidable.

(b)   The interests of the members who disagree with the decision. As Romer LJ said in *Re H.R. Harmer Ltd* [1959] 1 WLR 62, CA, at p. 87:

. . . shareholders are entitled to have the affairs of a company conducted in the way laid down by the company's constitution.

So both the company and a member may be plaintiff in respect of their separate interests (as in *Pender* v *Lushington* (1877) 6 ChD 70). The company is the proper plaintiff in respect of its interests and a member is not permitted to bring a derivative action to enforce the company's rights unless there has been a fraud on the minority (see 18.4.2). An action to enforce the interests of the members is an action against the company. One would expect such an action to be barred by the proper plaintiff aspect of the internal management principle but in fact it rarely is — see 18.4.9.

For example, if directors propose to allot shares for an improper purpose or not bona fide in the interests of the company (that is, in breach of their fiduciary duty) then a member has standing to bring an action to prevent the proposed allotment (*Fraser* v *Whalley* (1864) 2 Hem & M 10; *Punt* v *Symons & Co. Ltd* [1903] 2 Ch 506; *Residues Treatment & Trading Co. Ltd* v *Southern Resources Ltd* (1988) 51 SASR 177). If an allotment has been made in breach of fiduciary duty then the company is the proper plaintiff to sue for rescission of it (*Bamford* v *Bamford* [1970] Ch 212, CA, per Harman LJ at p. 238, Russell LJ at p. 242). If an allotment made in breach of fiduciary duty has been ratified by the members then a member is not permitted to bring a derivative action for rescission unless there has been a fraud on the minority (see 18.4.2) as there was in *Ngurli Ltd* v *McCann* (1953) 90 CLR 425 (see further *Residues Treatment & Trading Co. Ltd* v *Southern Resources Ltd*; *Re a Company (No. 005136 of 1986)* [1987] BCLC 82 and J. Birds, 'No costs for minority shareholder' (1987) 8 Co Law 131).

It is especially difficult to analyse cases where the chairman of a meeting of members has made a wrong decision. In *MacDougall* v *Gardiner* (1875) 1 ChD 13, James LJ (at p. 22) thought that the wrong in such a case was only to the company as a separate person, but in *Pender* v *Lushington*, Jessel MR said that a wrongful refusal to count a member's votes was a wrong to the member personally. In *Breay* v *Browne* (1897) 41 SJ 159, DC, Wright J said that the wrongful refusal of the chairman of a members' meeting to put to the meeting a motion proposed by a member did not damage the member personally: her right was not a personal one but belonged to her as a member of the company. The appropriate remedy was an order compelling the company to convene a fresh meeting and forbidding the chairman of the fresh meeting repeating the mistake. The chairman of a meeting is not personally liable to pay damages for his or her mistaken decisions (*Breay* v *Browne*; *Bluechel* v *Prefabricated Buildings Ltd* [1945] 2 DLR 725, British Columbia). Thus the action is properly against the company to prevent it acting on the wrong decision: there is no order for the court to make against the chairman who made the wrong decision (*Turner* v *Canadian Pacific Ltd* (1979) 107 DLR (3d) 142, Ontario).

We suggest that the common factor in the personal rights cases is that a member is alleging that a decision is unlawful in the sense that it fails to comply with the general law or with the constitution of the company or with the Companies Acts. We suggest that a member of a company has standing to challenge the lawfulness of any decision of the members or the directors or the chairman of a meeting of members, subject only to the irregularity principle (see 18.5). The recognition of a member's standing to challenge the lawfulness of company decisions would, we suggest, provide a means of enforcing the entitlement of shareholders 'to have the affairs of a company conducted in the way laid down by the company's constitution' which Romer LJ recognised in *Re H.R. Harmer Ltd* [1959] 1 WLR 62, CA, at p. 87.

In *Dunn* v *Banknock Coal Co. Ltd* (1901) 9 SLT 51, Lord Stormonth Darling said, at p. 52, '. . . any shareholder is entitled to object to a material deviation from what is the law of the company, without the necessity of showing that the thing done is hurtful to the interests of the company'. His lordship identified 'the law of the company' as its memorandum and articles and the Companies Acts. We would add that deviation from the general law, such as breaches of the rule that a decision must be taken in the interests of the company, can also be grounds for a member's action. We would also explain the term 'material deviation' as meaning a breach to which the irregularity principle does not apply.

18.4.13 Jenkins LJ's four (or five?) exceptions to the proper plaintiff principle

Discussions of the circumstances in which the courts will permit a member of a company to bring a derivative action or proceedings concerning the company's internal affairs are usually based on a list of exceptions to the proper plaintiff principle taken from the judgment of Jenkins LJ in *Edwards* v *Halliwell* [1950] 2 All ER 1064 at p. 1067. The exceptions stated by Jenkins LJ are (with relevant quotations from his lordship's judgment):

(a) *Ultra vires* acts. '. . . in cases where the act complained of is wholly *ultra vires* the company . . . the rule has no application because there is no question of the transaction being confirmed by any majority.' These are matters which are not regarded as questions of internal management.

(b) Special majorities. 'Romer J in *Cotter* v *National Union of Seamen* [1929] 2 Ch 58 . . . pointed out that the rule did not prevent an individual member from suing if the matter in respect of which he was suing was one which could validly be done or sanctioned, not by a simple majority of the members of the company, . . . but only by some special majority, as, for instance. . . . a special resolution duly passed as such.' These are matters which are not regarded as questions of internal management.

(c)   Personal rights. Where 'personal and individual rights of membership . . . have been invaded . . . the rule in *Foss* v *Harbottle* has no application at all, for the individual members . . . sue, not in the right of the [company], but in their own right'. These are matters which are not regarded as questions of internal management.

(d)   Fraud on the minority. '. . . where what has been done amounts to what is generally called in these cases a fraud on the minority and the wrongdoers are themselves in control of the company, the rule is relaxed in favour of the aggrieved minority who are allowed to bring what is known as a minority shareholders' action on behalf of themselves and all others. The reason for this is that, if they were denied that right, their grievance could never reach the court because the wrongdoers themselves, being in control, would not allow the company to sue.' These are situations in which a derivative action is permitted to vindicate the rights of the company as a separate person.

In our discussion we have used only two categories of exception, corresponding to (c) personal rights and (d) fraud on the minority in Jenkins LJ's list. We regard the special majorities cases as examples of personal rights. We divide the *ultra vires* cases into cases concerned with preventing *ultra vires* transactions, which are personal rights cases, and cases concerned with recovering property from completed *ultra vires* transactions, which we group with the fraud on the minority cases.

Jenkins LJ also made a comment that has caused considerable controversy. He said: '[Exceptions (a) and (d)] show, especially the last one, that the rule is not an inflexible rule and it will be relaxed where necessary in the interests of justice'. The problem is whether the list of exceptions given above is exhaustive and the reason for making them is to serve the interests of justice (per Megarry V-C in *Estmanco (Kilner House) Ltd* v *Greater London Council* [1982] 1 WLR 2 at p. 11) or whether there is a 'fifth exception' which 'will be made where the justice of the case demands it' as is implied by Harman LJ in *Heyting* v *Dupont* [1964] 1 WLR 843, CA, at p. 854 and by numerous authorities cited by Russell LJ in the same case at pp. 850–1. In *Prudential Assurance Co. Ltd* v *Newman Industries Ltd (No. 2)* [1982] Ch 204, the Court of Appeal said, at p. 221, that they were 'not convinced that [the justice of the case] is a practical test', though at p. 220 they had said: '. . . it so happens that this court cannot properly on this appeal decide the scope of the exception to the rule in *Foss* v *Harbottle*' and so their remark must be treated as *obiter*. The court particularly objected to the circular reasoning that if a derivative action is heard and the case is proved against the defendant then that in itself will show that it was just to allow the derivative action and so it is right to hear a derivative action in order to determine whether it should be brought. The new rules requiring leave to continue a derivative action should deal with this problem.

In the Commonwealth, courts have been favourable to the idea of making an exception to the proper plaintiff principle whenever the justice of the case requires it.

In *Hawkesbury Development Co. Ltd* v *Landmark Finance Pty Ltd* (1969) 92 WN (NSW) 199, Street J said, at p. 208, that an exception where justice so requires 'is, perhaps, a useful door to be left open lest in some extremely unusual circumstances injustice would result from applying the [proper plaintiff principle]'. Nevertheless his honour had not had cited to him any case in which such an exception had been made and he was not going to make it in the case before him. Similarly, in *Ellis* v *McQueen* (1967) 63 DLR (2d) 678, Ontario, no case could be found in which a fifth exception had been necessary. In *Scarel Pty Ltd* v *City*

Loan & Credit Corporation Ltd (1988) 79 ALR 483, Gummow J thought that *Campbell* v *Kitchen & Sons Ltd* (1910) 12 CLR 513, was an example of the 'fifth exception' being applied but unfortunately his honour was not referred to the appeal in the case ((1910) 12 CLR 515 at 517) in which Griffith CJ made it clear that it was a case of fraud on the minority. In *Biala Pty Ltd* v *Mallina Holdings Ltd (No. 4)* (1993) 13 WAR 11, the defendants to a derivative action, who controlled a majority of shares when the action was commenced, sold those shares to apparently independent persons before the trial of the action. Nevertheless the trial took place, the case against the defendants was proved, and the court held that the justice of the case required that the plaintiffs be permitted to succeed in their derivative action. On appeal (sub nom. *Dempster* v *Mallina Holdings Ltd* (1994) 13 WAR 124) the case against the defendants was upheld but there was no appeal against the decision that the plaintiffs had standing. In Australia, it has been thought necessary to invoke the fifth exception where the plaintiff's interest in the company is equal to the defendant's, because it is not appropriate to refer to the plaintiff as being in a 'minority' in such a case (*Ruralcorp Consulting Pty Ltd* v *Pynery Pty Ltd* (1996) 134 FLR 188; this was apparently the reason why the fifth exception was invoked in *Mesenberg* v *Cord Industrial Recruiters Pty Ltd* (1996) 39 NSWLR 128). But, as pointed out in *Glass* v *Atkin* (1967) 65 DLR (2d) 501, such a plaintiff is in the same position as a minority because the defendant has negative control over the company's litigation. The existence of a fifth exception was conceded in *Cope* v *Butcher* (1996) 20 ACSR 37, but the report does not make it clear why the plaintiff sought to invoke it, and the claim was struck out because the plaintiff had failed to plead a failure by the company to take the action sought.

In *Smith* v *Croft (No. 2)* [1988] Ch 114 at 139, Knox J said, at p. 170:

> . . . the fact that such a yardstick [i.e., the justice of the case] would or might be unsatisfactory because it does not give a practical guide to the limits of the rule and its exceptions does not detract from the fact that the whole doctrine whereby a minority shareholder is permitted to assert claims on behalf of the company is rooted in a procedural expedient and adopted to prevent a wrong going without a redress.

18.4.14 Reform

The Law Commission, *Shareholder Remedies* (Consultation Paper No. 142) (London: Stationery Office, 1996) concludes that having to prove that there is a fraud on the minority before being allowed to bring a derivative action is too restrictive, and proposes that, when deciding whether to give leave to continue a derivative action, the court should be permitted to consider all the circumstances of the case. However, this would apply only if the cause of action arose from a breach or threatened breach of a director's duty to the company.

18.5 IRREGULARITY PRINCIPLE

A member of a company may not bring an action questioning the lawfulness of a decision taken by the members (or directors) of a company if the only factor alleged to make it unlawful is a mere informality or irregularity and the intention of the members (or directors) is clear (*Burland* v *Earle* [1902] AC 83, PC, per Lord Davey at pp. 93–4). This principle is often expressed in terms of ratification: where only a mere informality or irregularity is alleged to invalidate a decision, a member may not bring an action questioning its validity if it is clear that, on going through the correct procedure, the decision would be ratified.

In particular, a court will not consider actions that attempt to invalidate the proceedings of meetings on the ground of mere mistakes in procedure if there is no evidence that the decision would have been different had the correct procedure been observed. As Cotton LJ said in *Browne* v *La Trinidad* (1887) 37 ChD 1 at p. 10:

> . . . a court of equity refuses to interfere where an irregularity has been committed, if it is within the power of the persons who have committed it at once to correct it by calling a fresh meeting and dealing with the matter with all due formalities.

In *Browne* v *La Trinidad*, there was a purported meeting of directors of La Trinidad Ltd at which it was resolved to summon an extraordinary general meeting of the members. At first instance it was found that the directors' meeting itself had been improperly convened because inadequate notice was given to one of the directors, Mr Browne, who was ultimately removed from office by the extraordinary general meeting of the members. The Court of Appeal judges doubted that the notice to Mr Browne was inadequate but were unwilling to overturn the finding of the judge below on this ground. The Court of Appeal refused to rule that the proceedings of the members' meeting had been invalidated by the irregularity. They observed that Mr Browne had had plenty of time to call another directors' meeting and argue his point of view but had not done so and that the decision of the members had been unanimous. Clearly there was no point in going through the procedure again.

In *Southern Counties Deposit Bank Ltd* v *Rider* (1895) 73 LT 374, CA, a decision of a directors' meeting to summon a general meeting of members was challenged. Two directors had acted as a quorum at the board meeting though the directors' decision that their quorum should be two was in fact invalid, and the quorum should have been three. As the directors had previously acted with two as a quorum for six years without challenge, the court held that the irregularity did not affect the decision taken at the members' meeting.

In *Bentley-Stevens* v *Jones* [1974] 1 WLR 638, a director of a company alleged that the extraordinary general meeting which had removed him from office was invalid because convened by a director who was not acting in pursuance of any board resolution. Plowman J dismissed a motion in interlocutory proceedings to restrain the company from acting on the removal resolution. The company was a wholly owned subsidiary of a holding company. A majority of the members and board of the holding company instructed its representative to vote for the plaintiff's removal; by definition the only other members of the company must have been nominees of the holding company (or other wholly owned subsidiaries) who would have voted the same way, so the irregularity of notice was irrelevant to the result of the meeting.

In *MacDougall* v *Gardiner* (1875) 1 ChD 13, CA, Mellish LJ said, at p. 25:

> In my opinion, if the thing complained of is a thing which in substance the majority of the company are entitled to do, or if something has been done irregularly which the majority of the company are entitled to do regularly, or if something has been done illegally which the majority of the company are entitled to do legally, there can be no use in having a litigation about it, the ultimate end of which is only that a meeting has to be called, and then ultimately the majority gets its wishes.

In both *Re Haycraft Gold Reduction & Mining Co.* [1900] 2 Ch 230 and *Re State of Wyoming Syndicate* [1901] 2 Ch 431 a meeting of members had been summoned and had adopted a resolution for voluntary winding up. However, in both cases the notice convening the meeting had been issued by the secretary of the company without the authority of the directors, which was not permitted by the articles of association. In both cases the court held it would be going too far to hold that this was a mere irregularity and so the resolutions for voluntary winding up were declared to be invalid.

In *Boschoek Proprietary Co. Ltd* v *Fuke* [1906] 1 Ch 148, all the three men acting as the company's directors had, for one reason or another, not been properly appointed. They held a board meeting and instructed the secretary to summon a general meeting for the purpose of ratifying their acts as directors. The general meeting was held and adopted the ratification resolution unanimously. Swinfen Eady J said that, in the circumstances, the directors' lack of authority to summon the meeting should be treated as a mere irregularity which was not sufficient to invalidate any resolution adopted at the meeting.

In *Pappaioannoy* v *The Greek Orthodox Community of Melbourne* (1978) 3 ACLR 801, Victoria, King J said that the irregularity principle means 'that where it is clear that if the proper procedure had been followed the result would have been the same the court will not interfere merely to ensure mere regularity of procedure' and it does not apply if it is not clear that the correct procedure would produce the same result. Other Australian courts have adopted a rule that the onus is on the defendant to show that it is unnecessary to go through the procedure again (*Ryan* v *South Sydney Junior Rugby League Club Ltd* (1974) 3 ACLR 486; *Scullion* v *Family Planning Association of Queensland* (1985) 10 ACLR 249; *Rivers* v *Bondi Junction-Waverley RSL Sub-Branch Ltd* (1986) 5 NSWLR 362).

If an irregularity changes the outcome of a vote then the court will intervene.

In *Pender* v *Lushington* (1877) 6 ChD 70 the chairman of a meeting of shareholders disallowed 649 votes that had been cast against an amendment to a proposed resolution. Accordingly the chairman declared the resolution (which was proposed by Pender) amended whereas if the 649 votes had been allowed the amendment would have been defeated. Jessel MR held that the chairman's decision to disallow the votes was wrong.

In *Henderson* v *Bank of Australasia* (1890) 45 ChD 330 (which concerned a chartered company), a general meeting of the company had debated a resolution and Mr Henderson indicated that he wished to move an amendment to the resolution. The chairman ruled that the resolution could not be amended as notice of the amendment had not been given, and refused to put the amendment to the meeting, which then adopted the unamended resolution. The Court of Appeal held that the chairman's ruling had been wrong and granted an injunction preventing the company acting on the unamended resolution.

Another case in which the court intervened in the proceedings of a members' meeting because the decision would make a difference to the outcome of the meeting was *Shaw* v *Tati Concessions Ltd* [1913] 1 Ch 292, in which the chairman of a meeting directed that a poll demanded at the meeting was to be held about six weeks later. Because he had proxies for about 58,000 shares, Shaw would win the poll unless his opponents were permitted to use proxies they held for over 99,000 shares. On the day before the poll was to be taken, the court ruled that the documents appointing proxies for the 99,000 shares opposing Shaw had not been delivered within the time-limit set by the company's articles and so had to be disallowed, thus ensuring that the vote would go in Shaw's favour and not against him.

Another example is *Siemens Brothers & Co. Ltd* v *Burns* [1918] 2 Ch 324, CA, which concerned a company called Siemens Brothers Dynamo Works Ltd, which had been registered at a time when every company had to have at least seven members. Of its 20,000 shares, seven were held by seven individuals who held one share each. The remaining 19,993 were in the joint names of Burns (whose name was first on the register) and another person. By the company's articles if shares were in joint names then only the person named first in the register could vote in respect of the shares. A meeting was held at which it was proposed to pass a special resolution to alter the company's articles. The matter was voted on by a show of hands on which the alteration was adopted by seven votes (those of the members with one share each) to one (that of Burns with 19,993 shares). Burns demanded a poll but the chairman ruled that he lacked entitlement under the articles to demand a poll.

The Court of Appeal held that for the purposes of the article relating to a demand for a poll, Burns and his co-holder were 'members holding . . . together at least 300 shares' and so could demand a poll. Clearly this case involved a procedural error that affected the outcome of a very important decision of the meeting.

For another case in which the result of a meeting was affected by the court's decision see *Marks* v *Financial News Ltd* (1919) 35 TLR 681.

18.6   UNFAIRLY PREJUDICIAL CONDUCT OF THE COMPANY'S AFFAIRS

18.6.1   Petition for relief of unfairly prejudicial conduct

By s. 459(1) of CA 1985:

> A member of a company may apply to the court by petition for an order under this Part [i.e., ss. 459 to 461] on the ground that the company's affairs are being or have been conducted in a manner which is unfairly prejudicial to the interests of its members generally or of some part of its members (including at least himself) or that any actual or proposed act or omission of the company (including an act or omission on its behalf) is or would be so prejudicial.

In addition, the section applies to a person who is not a member of the company but to whom shares in the company have been transferred or transmitted by operation of law (for example, personal representatives or trustees in bankruptcy who are not on the register of members), and references to a member or members must be construed accordingly (s. 459(2)).

The word 'transferred' in s. 459(2) requires at least that a proper instrument of transfer should have been executed and delivered to the transferee or the company in respect of the shares in question. It is not sufficient that there is an agreement for transfer (*Re a Company (No. 003160 of 1986)* [1986] BCLC 391; *Re Quickdome Ltd* [1988] BCLC 370). A person who cannot show prima facie evidence of standing will not be allowed to petition: the question of standing must be settled first. In *Re Quickdome Ltd*, a company had been bought off the shelf and the original members (the company registration firm which had sold it) had executed transfers of their shares without naming the transferees. Unfortunately the purchasers never registered any share transfers and when one of them petitioned under s. 459 she could not prove any agreement that she should be a shareholder. Mervyn Davies J ruled that the dispute over who should be the company's shareholders would have to be settled before a petition under s. 459 could be presented. (This does not mean that disputes over the ownership of shares cannot be the subject of s. 459 proceedings. In *Re Garage Door Associates Ltd* [1984] 1 WLR 35, a person who was the registered holder of one share in the company was permitted to bring s. 459 proceedings to challenge the allotment of 799 of the company's other 800 shares: the one share registered in his name gave him standing.)

The phrase 'transmitted by operation of law' in s. 459(2) refers to a legal process by which the legal title passes and does not cover the creation of an equitable interest, for example, under a trust (*Re a Company (No. 007828 of 1985)* (1985) 2 BCC 98,951).

The legislation does not give a former member standing to petition (*Re a Company (No. 00330 of 1991)* [1991] BCLC 597). Prentice (1988) 8 Oxford J Legal Stud 55 argues (at p. 64) that it should. In *Re a Company (No. 00330 of 1991)*, an injunction was granted to prevent the other members of the company operating a provision in the company's articles entitling them to compulsorily purchase the petitioner's shares and thus deprive him of his standing before the petition was heard.

A petition for relief of unfairly prejudicial conduct of a company's affairs may be presented by a person who joined the company in the knowledge that its affairs were being conducted in the manner complained of (*Bermuda Cablevision Ltd* v *Colica Trust Co. Ltd* [1998] AC 198).

Under s. 460(1) the Secretary of State has standing to present a petition for the relief of what appears to him, from an inspectors' report or from inspection of books and papers, to be unfairly prejudicial conduct of a company's affairs (see 18.9.3.5).

Sections 459 to 461 of CA 1985 were originally enacted as CA 1980, s. 75, to replace a provision in CA 1948, s. 210, which provided a remedy only if the affairs of a company were being conducted in a manner oppressive to some part of the members. The term 'oppressive' was given a restricted interpretation by the courts which also insisted that relief could be given only in respect of continuing conduct. Furthermore, it was necessary under s. 210 to show that the circumstances of the company were such that it was just and equitable that the company should be wound up (see 18.7). These restrictions meant that only a handful of petitions under s. 210 succeeded. The new provisions have given the courts power to intervene in relation to a much wider range of conduct and similar provisions have been enacted in many Commonwealth jurisdictions. There are surveys of cases decided under CA 1985, ss. 459 to 461, so far in D.D. Prentice, 'The theory of the firm: minority shareholder oppression: sections 459–461 of the Companies Act 1985' (1988) 8 Oxford J Legal Stud 55; B. Hannigan, 'Section 459 of the Companies Act 1985 — a code of conduct for the quasi-partnership?' [1988] LMCLQ 60; C.A. Riley, 'Contracting out of company law: section 459 of the Companies Act 1985 and the role of the courts' (1992) 55 MLR 782. Vastly more petitions have been litigated under the unfair prejudice provisions than under the old oppressive conduct s. 210 but there has been some disquiet about the way the provisions operate in practice. In *Re Unisoft Group Ltd (No. 3)* [1994] 1 BCLC 609, Harman J said, at p. 611:

Petitions under s. 459 have become notorious to the judges of this court — and I think also to the Bar — for their length, their unpredictability of management, and the enormous and appalling costs which are incurred upon them particularly by reason of the volume of documents liable to be produced.

The unreported case of *Re Freudiana Music Co. Ltd* (1993) occupied 165 days of court time. Unfortunately lawyers presenting a case on unfair prejudice in a company often deal with the whole history of the company in detail so as to build up an overall picture of prejudice and this is countered by equally extensive evidence and cross-examination from the other side. The result can easily be that costs exceed the value of the assets being fought over, as in *Re Elgindata Ltd* [1991] BCLC 959, discussed in 18.6.4, where costs of £320,000 were incurred arguing over shares worth a mere £24,600. The fact that litigants continue with these cases may reflect more on the depth of personal animosity involved than a desire for compensation for financial loss but it is an important criticism of the legal system that it cannot provide a simpler method of dealing with such disputes and requires so much publicly funded court resources to be devoted to them (see L. Sealy, 'No relief for the minority shareholder' (1995) 16 Co Law 178). In *Re a Company (No. 00836 of 1995)* [1996] 2 BCLC 192, the petition was struck out because a reasonable offer to buy the petitioner's shares had been made, but Judge Weeks QC commented (at p. 205) that striking out might also be justified if it appeared that the proceedings were being conducted in pursuit of a family feud rather than for commercial reasons. The two sides in the case had already incurred costs of between £1 million and £2 million in another case, *Re Macro (Ipswich) Ltd* [1994] 2 BCLC 354, which is discussed in 18.6.4.

In its report, *Shareholder Remedies* (Law Com. No. 246, Cm 3769) (London: Stationery Office, 1997), the Law Commission has considered ways of reforming unfair prejudice proceedings. Its principal recommendation is that the problems of excessive length and cost should be dealt with primarily by active case management by the courts. This reflects the view that the civil justice system generally will benefit from more case management (Lord Woolf, *Access to Justice: Final Report* (London: HMSO, 1996)). The Law Commission has also recommended that there should be a time limit within which proceedings for unfair prejudice may be brought, time starting to run from the date when the petitioner ought reasonably to have known the relevant facts. It also recommends that in the most common type of case, exclusion from the management of a quasi-partnership, statutory presumptions should apply, which it hopes will simplify proceedings (see 18.6.5).

The differences between CA 1985, s. 459, and the equivalent provisions in other jurisdictions (except British Columbia and Hong Kong) mean that comments of judges in those other jurisdictions are not necessarily apposite to the British legislation. In particular it should be noted that other jurisdictions usually provide for relief of conduct that is unfairly discriminatory, which CA 1985, s. 459, does not provide for. There is some discussion of the legislation in other jurisdictions in L. Griggs and J.P. Lowry, 'Minority shareholder remedies: a comparative view' [1994] JBL 463.

Most of the cases on ss. 459 to 461 have concerned quasi-partnership companies but the sections apply to all types of company (*Re a Company (No. 00314 of 1989)* [1991] BCLC 154).

18.6.2 Meaning of 'interests'

The conduct, act or omission complained of in a petition under CA 1985, s. 459, must be unfairly prejudicial to the interests of members in their capacity as members (*Re a Company (No. 004475 of 1982)* [1983] Ch 178). A member is not entitled to complain about prejudice to any interest he may happen to have — for example, he cannot complain that the company is carrying out operations on land adjoining his house which has caused a lowering of the market value of that house (per Lord Grantchester QC sitting as a deputy High Court judge in *Re a Company (No. 004475 of 1982)* at p. 189). In *Re J.E. Cade & Son Ltd* [1992] BCLC 213, the petitioner owned the freehold of land which the company occupied for the purposes of its farming business. The petitioner was not permitted to add to his petition a claim for possession of the farm because his interest as freeholder of land which the company occupied was not an interest of his as a member of the company which could be the subject of a petition under s. 459. (For criticism of this case see S. Griffin, 'Defining the scope of a membership interest' (1993) 14 Co Law 64.) Disputes among members of a company about dealings in their shares cannot normally involve unfairly prejudicial conduct of the company's affairs (*Re Unisoft Group Ltd (No. 3)* [1994] 1 BCLC 609).

The rights of a member of a company are defined by the company's constitution and the Companies Acts but the word 'interests' is wider than the term 'rights' and members may have different interests even if their rights as members are the same (*Re Sam Weller & Sons Ltd* [1990] Ch 682).

Conduct that affects all members may be prejudicial to the interests of some of them only (as in *Re Cumana Ltd* [1986] BCLC 430, CA, in which it was known that a rights issue on apparently favourable terms could not be taken up by a minority shareholder because of his financial position and would have had the desired effect of squeezing him out of the company — see also the earlier proceedings in the same case [1985] BCLC 80). However, until s. 459 was amended by CA 1989, sch. 19, para 11, the court did not have jurisdiction under s. 459 to deal with conduct that was indiscriminately prejudicial to the interests of all the members of a company (*Re a Company (No. 00370 of 1987)* [1988] 1 WLR 1068; cf. *Re Carrington Viyella plc* (1983) 1 BCC 98,951 at p. 98,959). It may be that the court in *Re a Company (No. 00370 of 1987)* was mistaken in not recognising that the conduct complained of affected different members in different ways and could have been found to have been unfairly prejudicial to some of them — see *Re Sam Weller & Sons Ltd* [1990] Ch 682; *McGuiness* v *Black* 1990 SC 21 at p. 24.

In *Jaber* v *Science & Information Technology Ltd* [1992] BCLC 864, a number of persons claimed that they had been wrongfully excluded from membership of a company. They could not petition under s. 459 in respect of that wrong because they were not members. An individual who supported them and was actually a member could not petition in respect of that wrong because it was held that a member of a company does not have an interest in the recognition of voting rights of other persons claiming to be members. Disputes about membership have to be resolved either by a claim for rectification of the register of members (see 14.3.3) or, in a complicated case, by action begun by writ.

18.6.3 Meaning of 'unfairly prejudicial'

In *Re Saul D. Harrison & Sons plc* [1995] 1 BCLC 14, Neill LJ said, at pp. 30–1:

> The words 'unfairly prejudicial' are general words and they should be applied flexibly to meet the circumstances of the particular case. . . .
>
> The conduct [being complained of] must be both prejudicial (in the sense of causing prejudice or harm to the relevant interest) and also unfairly so: conduct may be unfair without being prejudicial or prejudicial without being unfair, and it is not sufficient if the conduct satisfies only one of these tests.

But in *Bermuda Cablevision Ltd* v *Colica Trust Co. Ltd* [1998] AC 198 the Privy Council agreed with the judge at first instance that unfairness is inherent in the concept of prejudice so that prejudicial conduct must be unfair.

In *Re R.A. Noble & Sons (Clothing) Ltd* [1983] BCLC 273, Nourse J adopted the following statement by Slade J in *Re Bovey Hotel Ventures Ltd* (ChD 31 July 1981, unreported):

> I do not think it necessary or appropriate in this judgment to attempt any comprehensive exposition of the situations which may give rise to the court's jurisdiction under [CA 1985, s. 459]. Broadly, however, I would say this. Without prejudice to the generality of the wording of the section, which may cover many other situations, a member of a company will be able to bring himself within the section if he can show that the value of his shareholding in the company has been seriously diminished or at least seriously jeopardised by reason of a course of conduct on the part of those persons who have had *de facto* control of the company, which has been unfair to the member concerned. The test of unfairness must, I think, be an objective, not a subjective, one. In other words it is not necessary for the petitioner to show that the persons who have had *de facto* control of the company have acted as they did in the conscious knowledge that this was unfair to the petitioner or that they were acting in bad faith; the test, I think, is whether a reasonable bystander observing the consequences of their conduct, would regard it as having unfairly prejudiced the petitioner's interests.

The harm must be 'harm in a commercial sense, not in a merely emotional sense' (per Harman J in *Re Unisoft Group Ltd (No. 3)* [1994] 1 BCLC 609 at p. 611). However, s. 459 cannot be limited to cases in which the value of members' shareholdings has been seriously diminished or jeopardised (per Nourse J in *Re R.A. Noble & Sons (Clothing) Ltd* at p. 291; *Re Elgindata Ltd* [1991] BCLC 959). In *Re Saul D. Harrison & Sons plc*, Hoffmann LJ (at pp. 17–18) was not keen on invoking the reasonable bystander:

> For one thing, the standard of fairness must necessarily be laid down by the court. . . . An appeal to the views of an imaginary third party makes the concept seem more vague than it really is. It is more useful to examine the factors which the law actually takes into account in setting the standard.
> In deciding what is fair or unfair for the purposes of s. 459, it is important to have in mind that fairness is being used in the context of a commercial relationship. . . . the starting-point in any case under s. 459 will be to ask whether the conduct of which the shareholder complains was in accordance with the articles of association.

An infringement of a member's rights under the articles may not in itself be unfairly prejudicial (*Re Carrington Viyella plc* (1983) 1 BCC 98,951). Section 459 was not intended to cover trivial or technical infringements of the articles (per Hoffmann LJ in *Re Saul D. Harrison & Sons plc* at p. 19).

In some cases the court recognises that a member of a company has a legitimate expectation that the company's affairs will be conducted in a particular way, even though there is nothing to that effect in the company's constitution or the Companies Act 1985, and that failure to run the company in that way is unfairly prejudicial to that member's interests. It is the nature of the company which determines whether the court will take account of legitimate expectations outside the constitution. The type of company in which such expectations will be taken into account is known as the 'quasi-partnership company' (see 1.3.5). In *Re a Company (No. 00477 of 1986)* [1986] BCLC 376, Hoffmann J, applying the dictum of Lord Wilberforce in *Ebrahimi* v *Westbourne Galleries Ltd* [1973] AC 360 quoted in 1.3.5, held that the use of the word 'unfairly' in s. 459(1) enables the court to have regard to wider equitable considerations and to recognise that members of quasi-partnership companies may have legitimate rights, expectations and obligations *inter se* that are not stated in the company's constitution or the Companies Act 1985. In relation to a quasi-partnership company a petitioner under s. 459 is not confined to alleging infringement of rights under the company's constitution.

A person who invests capital in a company on the basis of taking part in its management has an interest in continuing to take part in management, so that, for example, being dismissed from a directorship may be unfairly prejudicial — see 18.6.5.

If the provisions of the articles do not conflict with other rights, expectations and obligations, then a member cannot complain about conduct in accordance with those articles, especially provisions that have been deliberately inserted, unless it can be shown that there is bad faith or impropriety or, possibly, that the articles themselves are unfair (per Hoffmann J in *Re a Company (No. 004377 of 1986)* [1987] 1 WLR 102 at p. 110). In *Re Posgate & Denby (Agencies) Ltd* [1987] BCLC 8, Hoffmann J said:

> Section 459 enables the court to give full effect to the terms and understandings upon which the members of the company became associated but not to rewrite them.

Similarly, where there are agreements and understandings between the members which are not set out in the articles, the court does not rewrite those agreements and understandings to make them accord with an objective standard of fairness (*Re J.E. Cade & Son Ltd* [1992] BCLC 213).

Where the petitioner became a member of the company by virtue of a complex set of formal written agreements, it will be assumed that the petitioner's rights and expectations are defined exhaustively in those agreements (*Re Elgindata Ltd* [1991] BCLC 959 per Warner J at p. 985).

In the case of a public company, the court is highly unlikely to pay attention to understandings and agreements that are not recorded in the documents available to outside investors (*Re Blue Arrow plc* [1987] BCLC 585; *Re Tottenham Hotspur plc* [1994] 1 BCLC 655).

The court will only take into account understandings between the members, not a belief by some members that others will be externally constrained to act in a particular way. Thus in *Re Carrington Viyella plc* (1983) 1 BCC 98,951, the holder of 49.36 per cent of the issued ordinary shares of the company had given undertakings to the government to reduce its holding to not more than 35 per cent, and not to exercise votes in excess of 35 per cent meanwhile, in return for the government not making a reference to the Monopolies and Mergers Commission. Vinelott J held that a petition could not be presented for relief of unfairly prejudicial conduct based on allegations of past and proposed breaches of these undertakings because the undertakings should not be treated as part of the constitution of the company or as in any way affecting the rights of shareholders *inter se*. In any case, other shareholders must have known that the undertakings 'were never intended to be immutable' and were always 'subject to change in the light of changed circumstances'.

A situation which a member can get rid of immediately by exercising voting control (for example, by dismissing a director) cannot be unfairly prejudicial to that member's interests (*Re Baltic Real Estate Ltd (No. 2)* [1993] BCLC 503).

18.6.4 Conduct on which a petition may be grounded

In *Re London School of Electronics Ltd* [1986] Ch 211, a petition was presented under what is now CA 1985, s. 459, by the holder of 25 per cent of the shares in the company, whose business was providing further-education courses. The other 75 per cent of the shares were held by a company called City Tutorial College Ltd. Two directors of London School of Electronics Ltd, who were also directors and principal shareholders in City Tutorial College Ltd, caused London School of Electronics to transfer many of its students to City Tutorial College thus depriving the petitioner of his 25 per cent share in the profits to be made from those students. This was held to be prejudicial conduct and the court ordered City Tutorial College to buy the petitioner's shares, which should be valued as if the students had not been transferred.

In *Re Cumana Ltd* [1986] BCLC 430, CA, the court gave effect to an oral agreement between the two owners of the company that they should share the profits of their business ventures in the ratio two thirds to one third. The man who was to get two thirds devised various schemes to cut the other out of his share. One (as in *Re London School of Electronics Ltd*) was to divert some of the company's business to another company controlled by himself. Another scheme was to make a large rights issue of shares, which, although priced favourably, he knew the minority member could not afford to take up. Thirdly he got the company to pay him an excessive bonus and to pay an excessive contribution to his pension fund. All three matters were held to be unfairly prejudicial conduct. The rights issue was restrained in interlocutory proceedings ([1985] BCLC 80).

In *Re Little Olympian Each-Ways Ltd (No. 3)* [1995] 1 BCLC 636, the petitioner was Supreme Travel Ltd, which was a substantial but minority holder of preference shares in the company which was the subject of the petition. The controller of Supreme had lost interest in the investment, because of its poor performance, and then died, after which the company was unable to contact Supreme. The majority of the shares in the company came under the control of three new directors who improved its business greatly though it suffered from heavy debts. In a restructuring they transferred their shares to a new company (referred to in the judgment as 'Newco') which they controlled and then caused the company to sell all its assets to Newco for £1. Subsequently they sold their shares in Newco for £10 million. It was found that this was conduct prejudicial to the interests of Supreme, and Newco was ordered to buy Supreme's shares and to pay for them what Supreme would have got if the company had itself received the £10 million and then been wound up. The directors acted negligently and in breach of trust when they sold the assets for only £1 and their knowledge of this breach of trust would be attributed to Newco because they were directors of Newco and under a duty to inform it that the transaction was tainted by breach of trust (see *Belmont Finance Corporation* v *Williams Furniture Ltd (No. 2)* [1980] 1 All ER 393 discussed in 19.8.3). That made Newco responsible.

The hearing in *Re Elgindata Ltd* [1991] BCLC 959 lasted 43 days during which almost every aspect of the company's affairs was minutely examined. The petitioners made numerous allegations of bad management by the company's managing director and principal shareholder. Warner J said (at p. 993) that although, in an appropriate case, serious mismanagement of a company's affairs would constitute unfairly prejudicial conduct, the court would normally be very reluctant to accept that managerial decisions can amount to unfairly prejudicial conduct. It is not for the court to resolve differences of commercial judgment (see 18.3.3.1). It is not unfair for a member of a company to suffer the consequences of poor management of the company: it is one of the normal risks of investing in a company that its management may turn out not to be of the highest quality. The petitioners had no right to expect a reasonable standard of general management from the managing director. However, the evidence showed that the managing director used assets of the company for his personal benefit and for the benefit of his family and friends. This was unfairly prejudicial conduct by its very nature rather than because it reduced the value of the petitioners' shares, and the managing director was ordered to buy the petitioners' shares. In *Re Macro (Ipswich) Ltd* [1994] 2 BCLC 354, though, it was found that mismanagement of the two companies involved had been so serious that the court should order the majority shareholder and sole director of the two companies to buy out the minority and that the value of the shares should be increased to take account of what the companies had lost through the mismanagement. The hearings in *Re Macro (Ipswich) Ltd* occupied 25 days and ranged over 40 years of the companies' history. The difference between the mismanagement in *Re Macro (Ipswich) Ltd* (where the companies had shown a consistent growth in profits) and that in *Re Elgindata Ltd* (which had declined into loss-making) is difficult to characterise and shows how difficult it is for legal advisers to predict the outcome of these lengthy and expensive proceedings.

It is prejudicial to the interests of a holder of shares in a company to be prevented from selling those shares at the best price. Thus a misleading letter from the chairman of a company asserting that the lower of two rival takeover bids for the company should be accepted because the other 'cannot succeed' (when this was not in fact the case) is capable of being unfairly prejudicial conduct (*Re a Company (No. 008699 of 1985)* [1986] BCLC 382).

A policy of paying excessive remuneration to director shareholders and not distributing profits as dividends despite the company not having any use for retained profits in its business (apart from paying the directors) is unfairly prejudicial to shareholders who are not directors (*Re a Company (No. 004415 of 1996)* [1997] 1 BCLC 479).

It is permissible for a petition to complain that a company's affairs are being conducted in contravention of criminal law: such a petition does not infringe the principle that the criminal law should not be enforced by civil proceedings (*Bermuda Cablevision Ltd* v *Colica Trust Co. Ltd* [1998] AC 198).

Under CA 1948, s. 210, it was necessary to show that the affairs of a company were being conducted in a manner oppressive to some part of the members. It would seem that conduct which is oppressive must be unfairly prejudicial so that conduct which was held to be oppressive under CA 1948, s. 210, would certainly be unfairly prejudicial under CA 1985, s. 459 (per Slade J in *Re Bovey Hotel Ventures Ltd* (ChD 31 July 1981, unreported; adopted by Nourse J in *Re R.A. Noble & Sons (Clothing) Ltd* [1983] BCLC 273).

In *Scottish Cooperative Wholesale Society Ltd* v *Meyer* [1959] AC 234, the Scottish CWS appealed to the House of Lords against the Scottish court's decision that it should purchase from Dr Meyer and Mr Lucas their minority interest in its subsidiary, Scottish Textiles & Manufacturing Co. Ltd, on the ground that its affairs had been conducted in a manner oppressive to Dr Meyer and Mr Lucas. The subsidiary had been formed in 1946 to exploit Dr Meyer's ability to obtain a government licence to produce rayon, production of which was strictly controlled at the time. The CWS controlled the company by holding a majority of shares and appointing a majority of directors. The arrangement was that a factory owned by CWS would weave cloth which the subsidiary would dye and finish. The subsidiary made considerable profits for five years but when production controls were lifted the CWS decided that it had served its purpose and should be liquidated. Accordingly it diverted its supplies of woven cloth to its own dyeing and finishing department, to which it sold cloth at low prices, leaving the subsidiary to buy cloth (which was then in short supply) at uneconomically high prices. The House of Lords dismissed the appeal, finding that the CWS's policy of destroying the company was, in effect, carried out by its nominee directors who failed to do anything to defend the company and failed to use their own position in the CWS to persuade the CWS to change its policy: the conduct of the subsidiary's affairs was in the hands of these nominee directors because they were in a majority on the board.

In *Nicholas* v *Soundcraft Electronics Ltd* [1993] BCLC 360, the petitioner was a minority shareholder in a subsidiary company. The parent company acted as overseas agent for the subsidiary and also effectively controlled its finances — for example, all cheques drawn on the subsidiary's bank account had to be signed by a director of the parent company. The parent company got into grave financial difficulties and refused to pass on to the subsidiary money earned from overseas sales of the subsidiary's products. The Court of Appeal held that this amounted to conduct of the subsidiary's affairs but that it was not unfairly prejudicial to the petitioner because the subsidiary depended on the parent company, and the parent company was entitled to use the resources of the group to keep both companies going.

In *Re H.R. Harmer Ltd* [1959] 1 WLR 62, CA, the company had been formed in 1947 to conduct the long-established philatelic business of Mr Harmer, then aged 77. The shares were owned by Mr Harmer, his two sons (who had spent their working lives in the business) and their wives. Mr Harmer senior and his wife held 78.6 per cent of the voting shares but only about 10 per cent of the total share capital (most of the shares were non-voting). By the time the petition was heard, Mr Harmer senior was 88, very deaf, and had difficulty comprehending questions put to him at the hearing. He took the view that he was entitled to disregard board decisions because he controlled so many voting shares. He often acted against the board's wishes in important matters which were detrimental to the interests of the company and acted foolishly, doubtless because of his advancing age. The Court of Appeal upheld Roxburgh J's order that the company should appoint Mr Harmer senior its salaried philatelic consultant and give him the title of president for life (an office carrying no rights or duties) in return for him not interfering with the business of the company except in accordance with board decisions.

For another example of a finding of oppressive conduct, see *Caratti Holding Co. Pty Ltd v Zampatti* (1978) 52 ALJR 732, PC, discussed in 3.4.3.

A petition will complain of conduct by persons in *de facto* control of the company but it can only complain of their conduct of the company's affairs, not of their own affairs which happen to affect the company (*Re a Company (No. 001761 of 1986)* [1987] BCLC 141, in which it was held that the fact that a director had purchased a debt owed by the company without informing the company and the fact that she had asked other members of the company to transfer their shares to her and resign as directors could not support a petition under s. 459; *Re Leeds United Holdings plc* [1996] 2 BCLC 545, in which it was held that an alleged understanding that major shareholders would not sell their shares without consulting each other could not relate to conduct of the company's affairs).

A petition may be grounded on conduct that has occurred in the past as well as conduct that is continuing (*Re a Company (No. 005287 of 1985)* [1986] 1 WLR 281).

A petition may be grounded on proposed prejudicial conduct (*Whyte* 1984 SLT 330), and it is no answer to such a petition to say that the immediate threat of the proposal was withdrawn before the petition was heard: the proposal might be made again and it is for the court to decide, on hearing the petition, whether an order is necessary to protect the petitioner's interests (*Re Kenyon Swansea Ltd* [1987] BCLC 514; D. Milman, 'Anticipated unfair prejudice' (1987) 8 Co Law 272).

It is not necessary to allege a course of action — a single act or omission is sufficient.

18.6.5   Exclusion from a quasi-partnership company

Many petitions under CA 1985, s. 459, arise because of a disagreement among members of quasi-partnership companies (see 1.3.5). As will be seen in 18.7, one method of dealing with a dispute in a quasi-partnership company is to wind up the company but in many cases this is an undesirably drastic remedy. What is usually required is for one of the disputing factions to leave the company, but this involves fixing an acceptable price at which the departing interest is to be bought out. Dismissal of a member of a quasi-partnership company from a directorship is capable of being unfairly prejudicial conduct (*Re a Company (No. 00477 of 1986)* [1986] BCLC 376). However, s. 459 is not necessarily relevant in such situations. The fact that members of a company disagree with each other, even to the extent of an irretrievable breakdown in relations, does not necessarily mean that the company's affairs have been conducted in a manner that is unfairly prejudicial to any member. A member cannot force other members to buy him out simply because he wants to realise his interest in the company (*Re a Company (No. 004475 of 1982)* [1983] Ch 178). If it is clear that one of the disputing factions must leave the company then the fact that one of the members has been excluded from membership and employment is not in itself conduct prejudicial to that member's interests: the question is whether, if there is to be a parting, it is reasonable that he should leave rather than the other member or members and whether the terms on which he is bought out are unfairly prejudicial (*Re a Company (No. 007623 of 1984)* [1986] BCLC 362; *Re a Company (No. 004377 of 1986)* [1987] 1 WLR 102). It is nearly always clear from the outset which party should leave the company (*Re a Company (No. 004377 of 1986)* at p. 110) and the decision of Peter Gibson J in *Re a Company (No. 003096 of 1987)* (1987) 4 BCC 80 shows that even where there was originally equality between the factions the one that has lost practical control to such an extent as to think it necessary to petition the court for relief is likely to be the one that will have to go. It would be very unusual for the court to order a majority shareholder in a company actively concerned in the management of the company to sell his shares to a minority shareholder when the majority shareholder is willing and able to buy out the minority shareholder at a fair price (*Re a Company (No. 006834 of 1988)* [1989] BCLC 365).

In *Re Ghyll Beck Driving Range Ltd* [1993] BCLC 1126, the petitioner had joined three other men who were all to be equal partners in a joint venture in which they would each invest £25,000. All were to take part in management but the petitioner thought the others were not pulling their weight financially or managerially and quarrelled with them after which he was excluded from management. The other three were ordered to buy his shares for a quarter of the going-concern value of the company.

In its report, *Shareholder Remedies* (Law Com. No. 246, Cm 3769) (London: Stationery Office, 1997), the Law Commission recommends that if a member of a private company who is petitioning under s. 459 shows that he or she has been removed as a director, or has been prevented from carrying out substantially all functions as a director, the court must presume there has been unfairly prejudicial conduct of the company's affairs unless the contrary is shown. This presumption would apply only if the petitioner held at least 10 per cent of the voting rights in the company and substantially all other members of the company were directors. The Law Commission further recommends that if, in such a case, the court decides to make an order for the purchase of the petitioner's shares, a statutory formula for fixing the price will be used unless the court orders otherwise. The Commission hopes that these presumptions will focus the parties' attention on the real dispute between them and reduce the cost of solving that dispute.

18.6.6 Orders the court may make

If the court is satisfied that the applicant's petition is well-founded, it is empowered by CA 1985, s. 461(1) to 'make such order as it thinks fit for giving relief in respect of the matters complained of'. More particularly, under s. 461(2), the court may:

(a) regulate the conduct of the company's affairs in the future; this could include an alteration of the company's memorandum or articles or preventing the company from making any, or any specified, alteration to the memorandum or articles without the court's leave;

(b) require the company to refrain from doing or continuing an act complained of by the petitioner or to do an act which the petitioner has complained it has omitted to do;

(c) authorise civil proceedings to be brought in the name and on behalf of the company by such person or persons and on such terms as the court may direct: whatever doubts may exist generally in relation to the power to bring a derivative action (see 18.4), this provision removes them in this situation, and the power of the court to direct the terms on which the action is to be brought may also remove any doubt as to the burden of the derivative plaintiff's costs;

(d) provide for the purchase of the shares of any members of the company by other members or by the company itself and, in the case of a purchase by the company itself, the reduction of the company's capital accordingly.

The petitioner must specify the relief sought, and it must be appropriate to the conduct of which the petition complains (*Re J.E. Cade & Son Ltd* [1992] BCLC 213 at p. 223) though it need not be directed solely towards remedying the particular things that have happened (*Re Hailey Group Ltd* [1993] BCLC 459 at p. 472). The court is required to make the order that is appropriate at the time of the hearing (ibid., loc. cit.). The court can only enforce the actual agreement between the members, taking into account, if appropriate, legitimate understandings of how that agreement would be implemented: it cannot substitute a different agreement which is thought to be fairer (*Re J.E. Cade & Son Ltd*). The court has jurisdiction to make orders against persons who are not members of the company or who are not involved in the conduct complained of (provided they have been made parties to the proceedings) but it is inconceivable that the court would order a person who was not a member of the company to buy the petitioner's shares (*Re Little Olympian Each-ways Ltd* [1994] 2 BCLC 420).

The court has a power under s. 461(1) to make such orders as it considers will enable the company, for the future, to be properly run, and for its affairs to be under the conduct of somebody who shareholders generally can be confident will conduct the affairs of the company properly (*Re a Company (No. 00789 of 1987)* [1990] BCLC 384 per Harman J at p. 395, followed in *Re Hailey Group Ltd*).

In *Re Hailey Group Ltd*, the company had become insolvent and an administrative receiver had been appointed in the time between presentation and hearing of an s. 459 petition which had asked for an order that the petitioner should buy out the other shareholders. It was held that the court could not make any order on the petition except that the parties who had forced the hearing of the case should pay the petitioner's costs.

The most common order is that the majority shareholders must buy the petitioner's shares. Exceptionally, in *Re Brenfield Squash Racquets Club Ltd* [1996] 2 BCLC 184, the majority shareholder was ordered to sell its shares to the petitioner.

For discussion of the way in which shares are priced when purchase is ordered under s. 461(2)(d) see G. Shapira, 'Valuation of shares in buyout orders' (1995) 16 Co Law 11; D.D. Prentice, 'Minority shareholder oppression: valuation of shares' (1986) 102 LQR 179.

If it is plain that the appropriate solution to the situation which the petitioner is complaining about is sale of the petitioner's shares, if other members of the company are willing to buy them, and if the articles provide a procedure for determining the price to be paid on a sale from one member to another then the petitioner is nevertheless entitled to pursue the petition in order to obtain the court's valuation of the shares if there is any risk that the procedure provided by the articles will undervalue them (*Re a Company (No. 00330 of 1991)* [1991] BCLC 597). This risk may be present, for example, if:

(a) The articles provide for some arbitrary or artificial method of valuation (*Re a Company (No. 004377 of 1986)* [1987] 1 WLR 102).

(b) There has been some impropriety in the management of the company which has significantly affected the value of its shares (*Re a Company (No. 006834 of 1988)* [1989] BCLC 365, in which allegations of such impropriety were rejected as they were in *Re a Company (No. 003843 of 1986)* [1987] BCLC 562).

(c) The person who will value the shares is not, or cannot be seen to be, wholly independent (*Re Boswell & Co. (Steels) Ltd* (1988) 5 BCC 145).

(d) There is no procedure for making representations to the valuer and the valuer has inadequate means of evaluating claims against the company (*Re a Company (No. 00330 of 1991)*).

If an offer is made which proposes a genuinely independent valuation dealing with the objections listed above, the court will strike out the petition as an abuse of process: the petitioner is not entitled to insist on the court carrying out a valuation which can be performed more cheaply by an accountant (*Re a Company (No. 00836 of 1995)* [1996] 2 BCLC 192).

It is desirable that the status quo should be preserved in the time between presentation and hearing of a petition and the court will grant injunctions to achieve this (*Re a Company (No. 002612 of 1984)* [1985] BCLC 80; *Re a Company (No. 00330 of 1991)*; *Re a Company (No. 003061 of 1993)* [1994] BCC 883). See also *Re Sticky Fingers Restaurant Ltd* [1992] BCLC 84 discussed in 14.4.4. As usual when considering whether to grant an interlocutory injunction, the court will not grant an injunction if the balance of convenience is against it (*Rutherford* [1994] BCC 876).

Where a petition for the relief of unfairly prejudicial conduct of a company's affairs arises from a personal dispute between members of the company, it is a misapplication of the company's money to pay any costs of the proceedings except for those necessarily incurred in representing the company as a separate person (*Re Kenyon Swansea Ltd* [1987] BCLC 514; *Re Elgindata Ltd* [1991] BCLC 959). An injunction will be granted to prevent the company paying such costs (*Re Milgate Developments Ltd* [1993] BCLC 291; *Re a Company (No. 004502 of 1988)* [1992] BCLC 701).

18.6.7   Exit rights in articles

In its report, *Shareholder Remedies* (Law Com. No. 246, Cm 3769) (London: Stationery Office, 1997), the Law Commission recommends that Table A should include a provision providing a minority shareholder with 'exit rights' to demand to be bought out by the other members at a fair valuation in certain circumstances, such as on being dismissed from a directorship. A draft article is set out in app. C to the report. The Commission believes that many unfair-prejudice petitions litigated so far would have been unnecessary if such exit rights had been available.

18.7   JUST AND EQUITABLE WINDING UP OF QUASI-PARTNERSHIPS

By s. 122(1)(g) of IA 1986, a 'company may be wound up by the court if the court is of the opinion that it is just and equitable that the company should be wound up'. As Lord Wilberforce pointed out in *Ebrahimi* v *Westbourne Galleries Ltd* [1973] AC 360, HL, in a passage quoted in 1.3.5, the words 'just and equitable' enable the court to recognise rights, expectations and obligations of members *inter se* and to wind up a company where such rights and obligations are being thwarted or obligations not observed even if what is being done is strictly within the law. Lord Wilberforce said, at p. 379:

> It would be impossible, and wholly undesirable, to define the circumstances in which these considerations may arise. Certainly the fact that a company is a small one, or a private company, is not enough. There are very many of these where the association is a purely commercial one, of which it can safely be said that the basis of association is adequately and exhaustively laid down in the articles. The superimposition of equitable considerations requires something more, which typically may include one, or probably more, of the following elements: (i) an association formed or continued on the basis of a personal relationship, involving mutual confidence — this element will often be found where a pre-existing partnership has been converted into a limited company; (ii) an agreement, or understanding, that all, or some (for there may be 'sleeping' members), of the shareholders shall participate in the conduct of the business; (iii) restriction upon the transfer of the members' interest in the company — so that if confidence is lost, or one member is removed from management, he cannot take out his stake and go elsewhere.

For the facts of *Ebrahimi* v *Westbourne Galleries Ltd* see 1.3.5.

A winding-up order will not be made on a member's petition unless he has a sufficient interest in having the company wound up (*Re Rica Gold Washing Co.* (1879) 11 ChD 36). The interest that a member must have is known as a 'tangible interest', a phrase used by Jessel MR in *Re Rica Gold Washing Co.* at p. 43. Thus a member whose shares are all fully paid up cannot petition unless it appears there will be a dividend for him in the winding up (*Re Rica Gold Washing Co.*; *Re Bellador Silk Ltd* [1965] 1 All ER 667; *Re Othery Construction Ltd* [1966] 1 WLR 69; *Re Expanded Plugs Ltd* [1966] 1 WLR 514; *Re Chesterfield Catering Co. Ltd* [1977] Ch 373).

Those opposing a member's petition may point out to the court that even if the court takes the view that the petitioner is entitled to relief from a situation that is unjust and inequitable to him, there is a remedy available to him other than winding up the company. However, IA 1986, s. 125(2), requires the court, if it is of opinion that the petitioner is entitled to relief, to decide whether it is just and equitable that the company should be wound up, *ignoring* the possibility of other forms of relief. If it comes to the conclusion that in the absence of any other remedy it would be just and equitable that the company should be wound up then it *must* make a winding-up order unless it is of opinion that the petitioner is acting unreasonably in seeking a winding-up order rather than pursuing some alternative remedy (see *Re a Company (No. 002567 of 1982)* [1983] 1 WLR 927 per Vinelott J at p. 932; *Vujnovich* v *Vujnovich* [1990] BCLC 227 at p. 232). It cannot be unreasonable of the petitioner not to pursue an alternative remedy that the court has itself refused him (*Vujnovich* v *Vujnovich*). The alternative remedy that is usually appropriate is an application under CA 1985, s. 459 (see 18.6), but a reasonable offer by other members of the company to buy out the petitioner's interest is also an alternative remedy (*Re a Company (No. 002567 of 1982)* [1983] 1 WLR 927; *Re a Company (No. 003843 of 1986)* [1987] BCLC 562; *Re a Company (No. 003096 of 1987)* (1987) 4 BCC 80).

It is not unreasonable to refuse an offer to buy the petitioner's shares if the person who will value them is not, or cannot be seen to be, wholly independent (*Re Boswell & Co. (Steels) Ltd* (1988) 5 BCC 145). In *Re a Company (No. 001363 of 1988)* [1989] BCLC 579, it was not unreasonable of the petitioner to refuse an offer to buy the one share registered in his name because one of the claims of his petition was that he was entitled to 3,250 shares. It is not unreasonable of a petitioner to refuse an offer to buy his shares if he fears that the valuation will be wrong, because, for example, the valuer will apply a discount to reflect the fact that the shareholding is not large enough to give control of the company or will be unable to deal properly with disputed claims against the company (*Virdi* v *Abbey Leisure Ltd* [1990] BCLC 342).

Even so, as Lord Wilberforce said in *Cumberland Holdings Ltd* v *Washington H. Soul Pattinson & Co. Ltd* (1977) 13 ALR 561, PC, at pp. 566–7: '. . . to wind up a successful and prosperous company and one which is properly managed must clearly be an extreme step and must require a strong case to be made'.

In *Ebrahimi* v *Westbourne Galleries Ltd* [1973] AC 360, Lord Cross of Chelsea said at p. 387:

A petitioner who relies on the 'just and equitable' clause must come to court with clean hands, and if the breakdown in confidence between him and the other parties to the dispute appears to have been due to his misconduct he cannot insist on the company being wound up if they wish it to continue.

However, in the Republic of Ireland, in *Re Vehicle Buildings & Insulations Ltd* [1986] ILRM 239, it was held that the objective fact that the shareholders/directors of a company could not legally or practically administer the company without the cooperation of each other but in practice neither would cooperate meant that it was just and equitable for the company to be wound up even though it was alleged that the deadlock had been caused by the petitioner's own misconduct, including dubious financial dealings which had caused the company to be investigated by the police and the revenue authorities. In *Morgan* v *45 Flers Avenue Pty Ltd* (1986) 10 ACLR 692, New South Wales, Young J said, at p. 708, that he thought it better to say that the plaintiff's conduct was one of the factors to be taken into consideration in deciding whether it is just and equitable to wind up the company.

18.7.1 Failure of personal relationship

Perhaps the most striking illustration of the breakdown of a personal relationship and the loss of mutual confidence occurred in *Re Yenidje Tobacco Co. Ltd* [1916] 2 Ch 426. Two tobacconists and cigarette manufacturers, who had previously traded separately, amalgamated their businesses by forming a private company of which they were the only shareholders and directors. Differences arose between them and eventually neither would speak to the other, though the company continued to trade and make large profits. The Court of Appeal upheld Astbury J's decision to make a winding-up order. Lord Cozens-Hardy MR explained:

Is it possible to say that it is not just and equitable that that state of things should not be allowed to continue, and that the court should not intervene and say that this is not what the parties contemplated by the arrangement into which they entered? They assumed, and it is the foundation of the whole of the agreement that was made, that the two would act as reasonable men with reasonable courtesy and reasonable conduct in every way towards each other, and arbitration was only to be resorted to with regard to some particular dispute between the directors which could not be determined in any other way. Certainly, having regard to the fact that the only two directors will not speak to each other, and no business which deserves the name of business in the affairs of the company can be carried on, I think the company should not be allowed to continue. . . . We are told that we ought not to do it because the company is prosperous, making large profits, rather larger profits than before the disputes became so acute. . . . Whether such profits would be made in circumstances like this or not, it does not seem to me to remove the difficulty which exists. It is contrary to the good faith and essence of the agreement between the parties that the state of things which we find here should be allowed to continue.

In *Loch* v *John Blackwood Ltd* [1924] AC 783, the Privy Council held that a just and equitable winding-up order was justified where the directors failed to call general meetings, to submit accounts, to recommend a dividend and had generally kept the petitioners in ignorance of the company's affairs. The petitioners had lost confidence in management and suspected that the directors hoped to acquire their shares for less than they were in fact worth.

18.7.2 Loss of management participation

Ebrahimi v *Westbourne Galleries Ltd* [1973] AC 360 itself shows that a just and equitable winding-up order may be made where a person is ousted from a management position and thereby loses his say in the company's affairs, the more so, where, as in that case, the removal also entails the loss of an income or right to participate in company profits. But removal by itself is not sufficient. A director must accept that he may be dismissed under CA 1985, s. 303, or under the company's articles, or that the articles may provide for retirement by rotation subject to re-election (see 15.3.2). In addition, as Lord Wilberforce said in the *Ebrahimi* case:

> The just and equitable provision nevertheless comes to his assistance if he can point to, and prove, some special underlying obligation of his fellow member(s) in good faith, or confidence, that so long as the business continues he shall be entitled to management participation, an obligation so basic that, if broken, the conclusion must be that the association must be dissolved.

A winding-up order was also made in *Re Lundie Bros. Ltd* [1965] 1 WLR 1051 where the petitioner was excluded from management following the termination of his employment as a working director. Similarly, in *Re A & BC Chewing Gum Ltd* [1975] 1 WLR 579, Plowman J referred to the above-quoted words of Lord Wilberforce and applied them to a situation where, although there had been no pre-existing partnership, the petitioners were entitled by agreement with the company's directors, to appoint a director to represent them on the board, and the directors subsequently refused to recognise an appointment by the petitioners.

18.7.3 Restriction on transfer of shares

Where a petitioner is dependent on the approval of the directors or shareholders in whom he has lost confidence or who have excluded him from participation in management for the transfer of his shares to another person, it seems that this restriction on his ability to realise his investment and go elsewhere will weigh heavily in his favour when the court is deciding whether or not it is just and equitable to wind up the company. It was certainly a factor emphasised by Lord Wilberforce in *Ebrahimi* v *Westbourne Galleries Ltd* [1973] AC 360 since Mr Ebrahimi could not dispose of his interest in Westbourne Galleries Ltd without the consent of Mr Nazar and his son.

18.7.4 Further discussion

Ebrahimi v *Westbourne Galleries Ltd* [1973] AC 360 provoked a considerable amount of academic comment. See M.R. Chesterman, 'The "just and equitable" winding up of small private companies' (1973) 36 MLR 129; D.D. Prentice, 'Winding up on the just and equitable ground: the partnership analogy' (1973) 89 LQR 107; B.A.K. Rider, 'Partnership law and its impact on "domestic companies"' [1979] CLJ 148. Since then the provisions that are now CA 1985, ss. 459 to 461, have been enacted (see 18.6) and it may be that the court can provide better remedies for disputes in quasi-partnership companies under those provisions than by the drastic method of winding up. However, there is still uncertainty over the precise scope of the jurisdictions to remedy prejudicial conduct and to order winding up on the just and equitable ground: in some quasi-partnership cases prejudicial conduct cannot be found but a just and equitable winding up can be ordered as in *Re R.A. Noble (Clothing) Ltd* [1983] BCLC 273 and *Re a Company (No. 00370 of 1987)* [1988] 1 WLR 1068. On the other hand, a petitioner seeking a just and equitable winding up may be defeated by the clean hands rule or the tangible interest rule, neither of which applies to a petition for relief of unfairly prejudicial conduct (see 18.6.1).

18.8 COMPANY INVESTIGATIONS

The Secretary of State has extensive powers to examine a company's affairs. Broadly speaking these powers divide into two types: a power to inspect company documents, and a power to appoint investigative inspectors. These powers will be discussed together with a consideration of the consequences of such inspections or investigations.

The power to inspect a company's documents is exercised by officers of the Department of Trade and Industry who can use it to conduct a brief discreet inquiry into a company about which complaints have been received. The appointment of inspectors is a much more serious matter. The fact of appointment is always publicly announced. In the case of public companies it is usual to appoint two inspectors: one a senior partner in a firm of accountants and the other senior counsel. Inspectors' reports on public companies are usually published. More general information will be found in the Department of Trade and Industry's publication, *Handbook of the Companies Inspection System* (London: HMSO, 1980).

18.8.1 Inspection of documents

The Companies Act 1985, s. 447, gives the Secretary of State power to require a company to produce documents for inspection. A requirement can be made either in directions given to the company by the Secretary of State under s. 447(2) or by a Department of Trade and Industry officer or other competent person authorised by the Secretary of State under s. 447(3). The term 'documents' includes information recorded in any form (s. 447(9)). Information not in legible form must be produced in legible form if required (s. 447(9)). If a company carrying on the business of banking is the subject of a requirement under s. 447(1) or (2) then it can be required to produce documents relating to its customers if it appears to the Secretary of State to be necessary in order to investigate the affairs of the bank (s. 452(3)). The Secretary of State or authorised person also has power to require the production of a company's documents from any person who appears to be in possession of them (s. 447(4)), except (s. 452(2)) a lawyer who would be able to claim legal professional privilege in respect of the documents. This power may be used to require a person carrying on the business of banking to produce documents relating to the affairs of the company under investigation but not documents relating to any other customer of the bank (s. 452(3)). When the documents are produced, copies of or extracts from them may be taken, and the person producing them or any present or past officer or employee of the company may be required to provide an explanation of any of them (s. 447(5)(a)). If the documents are not produced, the person who was required to produce them may be required to state to the best of his or her knowledge and belief where they are (s. 447(5)(b)). It is an offence under s. 451 for a person knowingly or recklessly to give a false explanation or statement in response to a requirement imposed under s. 447(5). The power to require documents to be produced for inspection may be exercised if the Secretary of State thinks there is good reason to do so (s. 447(2) and (3)). Although the Secretary of State is not required to observe the rules of natural justice when deciding whether to make an investigation under s. 447 (*Norwest Holst Ltd* v *Department of Trade* [1978] Ch 201, CA), the Secretary of State or the authorised officer or other person when exercising the powers to require production or statements under s. 447 must not exceed or abuse the discretion given by the section (for example, by not acting bona fide or by acting dishonestly) and must not exercise the discretion for some purpose outside the statute (*R* v *Secretary of State for Trade, ex parte Perestrello* [1981] QB 19). Failure to comply with a requirement to produce documents is an offence under s. 446(6) (though it is a defence under s. 446(7) to prove that the accused did not have possession of or control over the documents and that it was not reasonably practicable to comply with the requirement). It is also an offence under s. 447(6) to fail to give an explanation or statement required under s. 447(5).

A search warrant for documents may be obtained under s. 448. Such a warrant may require a named person to provide an explanation of documents.

It is an offence to obstruct the lawful exercise of a right of entry or search conferred by a warrant or for a person named in a warrant to fail to provide explanations of documents (s. 448(7)). It is an offence for an officer of a company to destroy, mutilate or falsify, or be privy to the destruction, mutilation or falsification of, a document affecting or relating to the company's property or affairs, or to make or be privy to the making of a false entry in such a document, unless it can be proved that the accused had no intention to conceal the company's state of affairs or to defeat the law (s. 450(1)). It is also an offence for an officer of a company fraudulently to part with, alter or make an omission in any document affecting or relating to the company's property or affairs or be privy to the fraudulent parting with, altering or making of an omission in any such document (s. 450(2)).

18.8.2 Investigation by inspectors

The Secretary of State has several powers permitting the appointment of inspectors to investigate and report on a company or on suspected insider dealing in a company's securities. Before considering these extensive powers, it may be useful to consider the function of an inspector and the nature of an investigation. First, it must be realised that an inspector's function is purely investigative or inquisitorial and is in no way judicial (*Re Pergamon Press Ltd* [1971] Ch 388, CA; *Fayed* v *United Kingdom* (1994) 18 EHRR 393). Secondly, an investigation is conducted in private. Thirdly, no one presents a case to the inspector. As Lord Denning MR said in *Maxwell* v *Department of Trade & Industry* [1974] QB 523, CA:

> The inspector has to do it all himself. He has himself to seek out the relevant documents and to gather the witnesses. He has himself to study the documents, to examine the witnesses and to have their evidence recorded. He has himself to direct the witnesses to the relevant matters. He has himself to cross-examine them to test their accuracy or their veracity. No one else is there to cross-examine them. Even if a witness says things prejudicial to someone else, that other does not hear it and is not there to cross-examine him.

Finally, the inspectors have to report. As to this, Lord Denning MR said:

> They should state their findings on the evidence and their opinions on the matters referred to them. If their report is to be of value, they should make it with courage and frankness, keeping nothing back. The public interest demands it. It may on occasion be necessary for them to condemn or criticise a man. Before doing so, they must act fairly by him. But what does fairness demand?

The answer is best expressed by Lawton LJ in the same case:

> Those who conduct inquiries have to base their decisions, findings, conclusions or opinions (whichever is the appropriate word to describe what they have a duty to do) on the evidence. In my judgment they are no more bound to tell a witness likely to be

criticised in their report what they have in mind to say about him than has a judge sitting alone who has to decide which of two conflicting witnesses is telling the truth. The judge must ensure that the witness whose credibility is suspected has a fair opportunity of correcting or contradicting the substance of what other witnesses have said or are expected to say which is in conflict with his testimony. Inspectors should do the same but I can see no reason why they should do any more.

18.8.2.1 *Investigation into a company's affairs*

The Secretary of State may appoint one or more inspectors to investigate a company's affairs and to report thereon on an application by the company itself or of either 200 or more shareholders or shareholders holding at least 10 per cent of the company's issued share capital (CA 1985, s. 431(1) and (2)). The application must be supported by such evidence as the Secretary of State may require for the purposes of showing that the applicants have good reason for requiring the investigation (s. 431(3)). If an investigation is undertaken then the applicants may be liable to pay for it (s. 439(5)) and so the Secretary of State may require applicants to give security for up to £5,000 (s. 431(4)).

The Secretary of State may also appoint one or more inspectors to investigate and report on a company's affairs if it appears to the Secretary of State that (s. 432(2)):

(a)   the company's affairs are being or have been conducted with intent to defraud its creditors or the creditors of any other person or otherwise for a fraudulent or unlawful purpose or in a manner which is unfairly prejudicial to some part of its members (including a person who is not a member but to whom shares have been transferred or transmitted by operation of law, such as a personal representative or trustee in bankruptcy: s. 432(4)), or any actual or proposed act or omission of the company or on its behalf is or would be so prejudicial, or it was formed for any fraudulent or unlawful purpose; or

(b)   persons concerned with the company's formation or management of its affairs have been guilty of fraud, misfeasance or other misconduct towards the company or its members; or

(c)   the company's shareholders have not been given all the information with respect to its affairs which they might reasonably expect.

The Secretary of State may exercise this power even if the company is in the course of being voluntarily wound up (s. 432(3)).

The Secretary of State *must* appoint one or more inspectors to investigate and report on a company's affairs if the court by order declares that its affairs ought to be investigated by an inspector (s. 432(1)).

The rules of natural justice (i.e., the right to a fair hearing, which includes the right to know the case against you, conducted before an unbiased tribunal) do not apply to the process of taking a decision to appoint inspectors under s. 432(2) (*Norwest Holst Ltd* v *Department of Trade* [1978] Ch 201). In *Norwest Holst Ltd* v *Department of Trade*, the company claimed the appointment was invalid because none of the grounds in s. 432 were present or stated to be present by the Secretary of State. The court held that he was not under an obligation to reveal his reasons for the investigation and, furthermore, that the investigation might not be directed at the company anyway but at persons who were acting against it or its members.

18.8.2.2 *Investigation of ownership or control*

The Secretary of State, if satisfied that there is good reason to do so, may appoint one or more inspectors to investigate and report on the 'membership of any company, and otherwise with respect to the company, for the purpose of determining the true persons who are or have been financially interested in the success or failure (real or apparent) of the company or able to control or materially to influence its policy' (CA 1985, s. 442(1)). Any such appointment may define the scope of the investigation and in particular may confine it to particular shares or debentures (s. 442(2)).

An application may be made to the Secretary of State by members of the company for such an investigation to be undertaken with respect to particular shares or debentures of the company (s. 442(3)). If the application is by 200 or more members of the company, or by members holding 10 per cent or more of the company's issued shares, then the Secretary of State must appoint inspectors unless satisfied that the application is vexatious or that it would be sufficient to carry out an investigation under s. 444 (see the following paragraph) (s. 442(3), (3A) and (3C)). The Secretary of State is entitled to exclude from the inspectors' terms of reference any matter which the members want included if satisfied that it is unreasonable for the matter to be investigated (s. 442(3A)). If an investigation is undertaken, either by inspectors or under s. 444, then the applicants may be liable to pay for it (s. 439(5)) and so the Secretary of State may require applicants to give security for up to £5,000 (s. 442(3B)).

Where the Secretary of State is satisfied that there is good reason to investigate the ownership of any shares in or debentures of a company but that it is unnecessary to appoint an inspector for the purpose, a requirement may be imposed under s. 444 on persons to give information which they have, or are able to obtain, about the present and past interests in those shares or debentures, and the names and addresses of the persons interested and of any persons who act or have acted on their behalf in relation to those shares or debentures. Such a requirement may be imposed on any person whom the Secretary of State has reasonable cause to believe has or is able to obtain the information. Under s. 444(2), the persons who are deemed to be interested in shares and debentures include persons who have any right to acquire or dispose of them, or of any interest in them, or to vote in respect of them, and any person whose consent is necessary for the exercise of any of the rights of other persons interested in them. If persons interested in shares or debentures can be required, or are accustomed, to exercise their rights in accordance with another person's instructions then that other person is deemed to be interested in those shares or debentures. It is an offence not to give information required by s. 444 or, in giving it, knowingly or recklessly to make a statement which is false in a material particular (s. 444(3)).

Where an investigation is proceeding under ss. 442 or 444 and it appears to the Secretary of State that there is some difficulty in finding out the relevant facts about any shares or debentures, a freezing order may be imposed on the shares (s. 445). For details, see 8.9.7.

18.8.2.3 Investigation of directors' share dealings

One or more inspectors may be appointed by the Secretary of State under CA 1985, s. 446(1), if it appears that there are circumstances suggesting that contraventions may have occurred, in relation to shares in or debentures of a company, of s. 323 (dealing by director in options to buy or sell listed shares in or listed debentures of the company or associated companies: see 13.4) or s. 324 (obligation of director to notify company of interests in shares in or debentures of the company or associated companies: see 13.6.2) or s. 328(3) to (5) (extension of s. 324 to director's spouse and children: see 13.6.4). Inspectors are appointed under s. 446(1) to carry out such investigations as are requisite to establish whether or not contraventions have occurred and to report the result to the Secretary of State. Sections 434, 436 and 437 of CA 1985 (discussed in 18.8.2.6 and 18.8.3.1) apply with modifications (s. 446(3) and (4)).

18.8.2.4 *Investigation of related companies*

An inspector appointed to investigate a company under CA 1985, ss. 431, 432, 442 or 446 may, if he or she thinks it necessary, extend the investigation to the company's holding company or any subsidiary of the company or of its holding company. The inspector may also investigate any corporation which, at any relevant time, has been a subsidiary or holding company of the company under investigation, or a subsidiary of its holding company or (unless the investigation is under s. 446) a holding company of its subsidiary (ss. 433(1), 443(1) and 446(3)). A related company may be investigated whether it is incorporated in Great Britain or elsewhere (s. 740).

18.8.2.5 *Investigation into insider dealing*

Under FSA 1986, s. 177, the Secretary of State may appoint one or more inspectors to carry out an investigation if it appears that an offence under part V of the Criminal Justice Act 1993 (insider dealing) may have been committed. The inspectors are asked to carry out such investigations as are requisite to establish whether or not any such offence has been committed and to report the result of the investigation to the Secretary of State.

A search warrant for documents may be obtained under s. 199. It is an offence triable either way for anyone to obstruct the exercise of any rights conferred by the warrant or to fail without reasonable excuse to comply with any requirement imposed under this section (s. 199(6)).

It is an offence triable either way for a person, in purported compliance with a requirement imposed by ss. 177 or 199, to furnish information which the person knows to be false or misleading in a material particular or recklessly to furnish information which is false or misleading in a material particular (s. 200(1) and (5)).

18.8.2.6 *Collection of evidence*

An investigating inspector has a right to call on persons:

(a) To produce all documents of, or relating to, a company under investigation (or relating to the company in whose securities insider dealing is suspected, or the securities of that company).

(b) To attend before the inspector.

(c) Otherwise to give the inspector all reasonable assistance with the investigation which they are reasonably able to give.

In any investigation an inspector has a right to call on any person if the inspector considers that person may be able to provide relevant information (CA 1985, ss. 434(2) (investigation under ss. 431, 432 or 433(1)), 443(1) (investigation under s. 442) and 446(3) (investigation under s. 446; FSA 1986, s. 177(3) (investigation under FSA 1986, s. 177)).

In some investigations an inspector has an absolute right to call on certain persons. In an investigation under CA 1985, ss. 431, 432, 433(1), 442 or 446, an inspector may call on all past and present officers and agents (including auditors, solicitors and bankers) of the company under investigation (s. 434(1)). In an investigation under s. 442, an inspector may call on all persons who are or have been: (a) financially interested in the success or failure (or apparent success or failure) of the company under investigation, or (b) able to control or materially influence its policy (s. 443(2)). In an investigation under s. 446, an inspector may call on any individual who is an authorised person, or an officer of a corporation that is an authorised person, or a partner in a firm that is an authorised person (i.e., authorised under FSA 1986 to carry on investment business in the UK) (CA 1985, s. 446(4)).

An inspector may examine on oath any person, and may personally administer oaths (CA 1985, s. 434(3); FSA 1986, s. 177(4)).

A person is not required to disclose any information that is subject to legal professional privilege except, in an investigation under CA 1985, a client's name and address (CA 1985, s. 452(1)(a); FSA 1986, s. 177(7)).

Inspectors may not require a bank to disclose information about the affairs of any customer other than the company under investigation unless the Secretary of State authorises the requirement (CA 1985, s. 452(1A); FSA 1986, s. 177(8)). This does not apply if the bank is the subject of the investigation, provided the investigation is under CA 1985, ss. 431, 432 or 433 (s. 452(1B)).

Persons questioned by inspectors cannot claim privilege against self-incrimination (*R* v *Seelig* [1992] 1 WLR 148; *Re London United Investments plc* [1992] Ch 578).

Any person who fails to cooperate with an inspector when properly required to do so may be reported to the court by the inspector and the court may punish the person as if he or she were in contempt of court (CA 1985, s. 436; FSA 1986, s. 178(1) and (2)(a)). In an investigation under FSA 1986, s. 177, if the refusal is by an authorised person then the court may, under s. 178(2)(b), direct that either the Secretary of State or the Financial Services Authority may remove or limit the person's authorisation. Before punishing for contempt, the court must first inquire into the case and hear witnesses and a statement in defence (CA 1985, s. 436(2); FSA 1986, s. 178(2)). This gives an opportunity to question whether the inspectors were right to ask for the information which has been refused by the alleged contemnor.

A journalist who refuses to disclose his or her sources of information to an inspector may be in contempt despite the Contempt of Court Act 1981, s. 10, if it is proved that the evidence is really needed for the prevention of crime (*Re an Inquiry under the Company Securities (Insider Dealing) Act 1985* [1988] AC 660).

Evidence given by a person to an inspector may include a confession that the person has committed a criminal offence. Evidence that the person made the confession may be admitted at the person's trial for that offence under the Police and Criminal Evidence Act 1984, s. 76, despite being hearsay, but not (by s. 76(2)) if it was obtained by oppression or in circumstances likely to render it unreliable. Under the common law, before the Police and Criminal Evidence Act 1984, evidence of a confession made under threat of punishment for not making it was not admissible but this did not apply where the statute imposing the punishment expressly provided that the evidence should be admissible, as CA 1985, s. 434(5), does in relation to evidence given to inspectors (see J.D. Heydon, 'Statutory restrictions on the privilege against self-incrimination' (1971) 87 LQR 214). In *R* v *Seelig* [1992] 1 WLR 148, the Criminal Division of the Court of Appeal ruled that s. 434(5) meant that evidence of a person's confession made to inspectors under threat of punishment for contempt for not making it is admissible under the Police and Criminal Evidence Act 1984, s. 76. The court also would not overrule the judge's refusal to exclude the evidence under the Police and Criminal Evidence Act 1984, s. 78 (which gives a general discretion to exclude prosecution evidence which would have an adverse effect on the fairness of the proceedings because of the circumstances in which it was obtained). The same line was taken by the court in *R* v *Saunders* [1996] 1 Cr App R 463, but in *Saunders* v *United Kingdom* (1996) 23 EHRR 313 the European Court of Human Rights held that failure to prevent the use at Ernest Saunders's trial of answers he had given to inspectors' questions was an infringement of his right to a fair trial under art. 6 of the European Convention for the Protection of Human Rights. The Court of Human Rights said, at para. 74:

[The court] does not accept the [United Kingdom] government's argument that the complexity of corporate fraud and the vital public interest in the investigation of such fraud and the punishment of those responsible could justify such a marked departure as that which occurred in the present case from one of the basic principles of a fair procedure. . . . it considers that the general requirements of fairness contained in art. 6, including the right not to incriminate oneself, apply to criminal proceedings in respect of all types of criminal offences without distinction, from the most simple to the most complex.

But the court would not speculate on whether excluding the evidence would have made a difference to the outcome of Saunders's trial, and refused to award compensation for wrongful conviction. Despite this ruling by the Court of Human Rights, British courts must still apply the British statutory provisions which authorise the use in a criminal trial of answers the accused has given to inspectors' questions (*R* v *Morrissey* (1997) *The Times*, 1 May 1997) leaving a convicted person to apply to the European Court for redress. The Secretary of State has now adopted a policy of not using against the accused in criminal proceedings transcripts of evidence which the accused was compelled to give to inspectors (*R* v *Secretary of State for Trade and Industry, ex parte McCormick* [1998] BCC 379 at pp. 383 and 390–1). But it has been decided that transcripts of compelled evidence will still be used in director disqualification proceedings, and in *R* v *Secretary of State for Trade and Industry, ex parte McCormick* the Court of Appeal refused to declare that this decision is unlawful. The court found that it was not irrational, unreasonable or inconsistent for the Secretary of State to take the view that director disqualification proceedings are not criminal proceedings and that what is required by art. 6 of the Human Rights Convention to achieve a fair trial in civil proceedings is not the same as in criminal proceedings. In our view such an important question relating to human rights should not be left to ministerial policy but should be spelled out in a statutory provision.

In *R* v *Seelig* the court also refused to overturn the trial judge's finding that inspectors appointed under CA 1985, ss. 432 and 442, were not charged with the duty of investigating offences or charging offenders and so were not required by the Police and Criminal Evidence Act 1984, s. 67(9), to have regard to the codes of practice under the Act, in particular the provisions of Code of Practice C relating to questioning of persons by police officers.

18.8.2.7 Interruption of investigations
The Secretary of State may direct inspectors to take no further steps in their investigation, or take only such steps as are specified in the direction (CA 1985, ss. 437(1B), 443(1) and 446(3); FSA 1986, s. 177(5A)). The Secretary of State may not interrupt a CA 1985 investigation unless it appears that matters have come to light in the investigation suggesting the commission of criminal offences and those matters have been referred to the appropriate prosecuting authority.

18.8.2.8 Assistance of overseas regulatory authorities
Sections 82 to 91 of CA 1989 introduce new powers under which the Secretary of State can, in person or by authorising any Department of Trade and Industry officer or any other competent person, interrogate any person and require the production of documents in order to assist an overseas regulatory authority. The kinds of regulatory authority that may be assisted are listed in s. 82(2). They include bodies concerned with the investigation of insider dealing, supervision of insurance and banking, supervision of listing on stock exchanges, and 'any function corresponding to . . . a function of the Secretary of State under . . . the Companies Act 1985'.

The Secretary of State, or an authorised officer or other person, may, under s. 83(2), require any person:

(a)   to attend before him or her at a specified time and place, and answer questions or otherwise furnish information with respect to any matter relevant to the inquiries,

(b)   to produce at a specified time and place any specified documents, and

(c)   otherwise to give such assistance as the person is reasonably able to give.

These powers may be exercised if the Secretary of State considers there is good reason for their exercise (s. 83(1)) following a request from the overseas regulatory authority (s. 82(1)).

There are supplementary provisions concerning information covered by legal professional privilege (s. 83(5)) and a banker's obligation of confidence (s. 84(4)); penalties for failure to comply (ss. 85, 89, 90 and 91); and operation in Northern Ireland (s. 88).

18.8.3   Consequences of inspection or investigation

18.8.3.1   Investigating inspectors' reports

Investigating inspectors must make a final report to the Secretary of State at the end of an investigation; they may also make interim reports and must do so if the Secretary of State directs them to (CA 1985, ss. 437(1), 443(1) and 446(3); FSA 1986, s. 177(5)). The Secretary of State must send a copy of any report prepared by an inspector appointed by order of the court under s. 432(1) to the court (s. 437(2)). When inspectors are appointed under s. 432(2), their terms of appointment may specify that their report is not for publication (s. 432(2A)). If their appointment was not on those terms, or if they were appointed under any other provision of CA 1985, then the Secretary of State may have their report printed and published, send a copy of the report to the company's registered office, and send a copy, on request and payment of a fee, to any member of the company which was the subject of the report, the applicants for the investigation, the company's auditors, any person whose conduct is referred to in the report, and any person whose financial interests appear to be affected by matters dealt with in the report (ss. 437(3), 443(1) and 446(3)).

It has long been the practice to publish reports submitted by inspectors under s. 437 as being matters of public interest. However, the Department of Trade and Industry has always been cautious to delay publication until any legal proceedings arising from the issues dealt with in the report are complete. In practice, this may mean many years' delay in the publication of inspectors' reports, by which time the affair which caused the inspection has been largely forgotten. In *R* v *Secretary of State for Trade & Industry, ex parte Lonrho plc* [1989] 1 WLR 525 Lonrho plc attempted to challenge this cautious practice by means of judicial review of the Secretary of State's decision that publication of a report into House of Fraser Holdings plc should be delayed until after the report had been considered by the Serious Fraud Office and the completion of any prosecutions. Lonrho plc had lost to the brothers Mohamed, Ali and Salah Fayed in their rival attempts to take over House of Fraser plc (which owned the famous London department store, Harrods). Lonrho plc considered that it had been defeated by unfair means and mistaken government decisions concerning references to the Monopolies and Mergers Commission: it wished to maintain public awareness of its grievances. The House of Lords, however, found no fault in the way in which the Secretary of State exercised his discretion. He was entitled and obliged to decide for himself whether or not to publicise or postpone publication of the report in the public interest. The report was eventually published in March 1990 after the Serious Fraud Office decided not to prosecute anyone and the Secretary of State decided not to apply for disqualification orders against the Fayed brothers (see *R* v *Secretary of State for Trade and Industry, ex parte Lonrho plc* [1992] BCC 325 discussed in 15.2.5.4). The Fayed brothers objected to the criticisms made of them in the report but were unable to sue the inspectors for libel because publication of the report was privileged. The European Court of Human Rights ruled in *Fayed* v *United Kingdom* (1994) 18 EHRR 393 that it is in the public interest that inspectors should be able to report freely. The inspectors' procedure was fair and the Fayeds had been given adequate opportunities to respond to the allegations made against them. The investigation did not involve a denial of the Fayeds' right of access to a court because judicial review was available to control any unfairness in the inspectors' procedure. As the inspectors' findings were not a judicial determination, they were not subject to art. 6(1) of the European Convention on Human Rights requiring a fair and public hearing for the determination of civil rights and obligations. The report is discussed by G. McCormack, 'The House of Fraser inspectors' report' (1994) 15 Co Law 40.

There is no provision for publication of FSA 1986 investigations. The results of an inspection of documents are never collected in a formal report but may be used as a basis for further action.

18.8.3.2 Cooperation with other regulatory authorities

Under s. 449, as a general rule, any information or document relating to a company obtained under s. 447 must be treated as confidential, and it is an offence to publish or disclose it without the company's prior written consent (s. 449(1) and (2)). But s. 449 makes a large number of exceptions to this general rule. There may be publication or disclosure if required for the purposes of criminal proceedings (s. 449(1)(a)) or an application for a director disqualification order (s. 449(1)(ba)). Information may also be disclosed to any other person authorised to inspect documents under s. 447 and to an investigating inspector appointed under the provisions discussed in 18.8.2 (s. 449(1)(c) and (cc)). Section 449(1)(d) authorises disclosure for the purpose of enabling or assisting the Secretary of State or the Treasury to exercise any of their functions under CA 1985, the insider dealing legislation, the Insurance Companies Act 1982, the Insolvency Act 1986, the Company Directors Disqualification Act 1986, FSA 1986 or the parts of CA 1989 concerning qualification of auditors (part II), assistance of overseas regulatory authorities (part III) and the insolvency of parties to transactions in financial markets (part VII). Section 449 also authorises disclosure to a large number of regulatory authorities, such as the Occupational Pensions Regulatory Authority and the recognised supervisory and qualifying bodies for auditors, for the purpose of enabling or assisting them to discharge their functions: all these bodies are themselves bound by statutory restrictions on disclosure of information in similar terms to s. 449.

Inspectors appointed under FSA 1986, s. 177, are subject to similar rules contained in FSA 1986, s. 179.

Investigating inspectors appointed under CA 1985 may inform the Secretary of State, at any time, of any matters coming to their knowledge as a result of their investigations (and can be directed by the Secretary of State to do so) (CA 1985, ss. 437(1A), 443(1) and 446(3)). By s. 451A the Secretary of State may disclose any information obtained from inspectors to any person to whom, or for any purpose for which, disclosure is permitted under s. 449. The Secretary of State can also authorise such disclosure directly by the inspectors. An investigating inspector is authorised by s. 451A(3) to disclose information to any other investigating inspector or to any person authorised to inspect documents under s. 447.

18.8.3.3   Just and equitable winding up
The Secretary of State may petition for the compulsory liquidation of a company under
Insolvency Act (IA) 1986, s. 124(4)(b), if the case falls within IA 1986, s. 124A. A case
falls within s. 124A if the company is not already in compulsory liquidation (s. 124A(2))
and it appears to the Secretary of State that it is expedient in the public interest that the
company should be wound up, this being apparent from, among other matters (s. 124A(1)):

   (a)   any report made or information obtained under CA 1985, part XIV (ss. 431 to 453)
(company investigations etc.),
   (b)   any report made under FSA 1986, s. 177 (investigation into insider dealing), or
   (c)   any information obtained under CA 1989, s. 83 (powers exercisable for purpose of
assisting overseas regulatory authorities).

   Petitions in cases falling within s. 124A are called 'public-interest petitions'. Whereas
creditors and contributories petition in their own interests as members of a class, the
Secretary of State necessarily acts not in his own interest but in the interests of the public
at large (per Megarry J in *Re Lubin, Rosen & Associates Ltd* [1975] 1 WLR 122 at pp.
128–9). Section 124A defines cases in which the Secretary of State has standing to present
a public-interest petition. However, the court has jurisdiction to make a winding-up order
only if one of the circumstances listed in IA 1986, s. 122(1), is proved to exist, and s.
124A(1) confines the court, when considering a public-interest petition, to considering
whether it is just and equitable that the company should be wound up (s. 122(1)(g)).
   The Secretary of State has standing to present a petition for the compulsory liquidation
of a company only if he has formed and holds the opinion that it is expedient in the public
interest that the company be wound up. In accordance with general principles of constitutional law, it is competent for an official of the Department of Trade and Industry to form
that opinion and decide to present a petition: the matter does not have to be considered by
the Secretary of State personally (*Re Golden Chemical Products Ltd* [1976] Ch 300). A
decision to present or not present a petition is subject to judicial review. In *Re Walter L.
Jacob & Co. Ltd* [1989] BCLC 345, Nicholls LJ observed, at p. 352, that judicial review of
a decision to present a petition would probably be pointless because if no reasonable
Secretary of State could have formed the opinion that it was in the public interest that the
company be wound up then the petition would presumably fail.
   The court must be careful not to be influenced too much by the very fact that a
public-interest petition is presented by a person of such significance as the Secretary of
State. This fact means that it is highly unlikely that the petition has been presented
frivolously or vexatiously but it does not mean that the court is relieved of its function of
determining judicially whether or not a winding-up order should be made. Nicholls LJ in
Re Walter L. Jacob & Co. Ltd said, at p. 353:

   . . . the court will take note that the source of the submissions that the company should
   be wound up is a government department charged by Parliament with wide-ranging
   responsibilities in relation to the affairs of companies. The department has considerable
   expertise in these matters and can be expected to act with a proper sense of responsibility
   when seeking a winding-up order. But the cogency of the submissions made on behalf of
   the Secretary of State will fall to be considered and tested in the same way as any other
   submissions. His submissions are not *ipso facto* endowed with such weight that those
   resisting a winding-up petition presented by him will find the scales loaded against them.

Equally the court should not indulge a prejudice against civil servants as being incapable of understanding the realities of business life.

It may be in the public interest to wind up a company as a matter of punishment for past misbehaviour and to set an example to others (*Re Walter L. Jacob & Co. Ltd* [1989] BCLC 345). Undertakings by the company to discontinue its previous mode of trading are of no value since neither the court nor the Department of Trade and Industry can be expected to supervise such undertakings (*Re Bamford Publishers Ltd* (1977) 74 LS Gaz 711). Even the fact that a company is no longer able to continue its former business because, for example, of the withdrawal of a licence should not persuade the court that a winding-up order is not required in order to express disapproval and serve as an example. The wishes of the company's controllers, that the company should remain extant for other purposes, should normally carry little weight (*Re Walter L. Jacob & Co. Ltd* per Nicholls LJ at p. 360).

Several recent public-interest petitions have concerned companies running so-called pyramid or snowball schemes, in which people are persuaded to pay to join a scheme on the basis that they can take a proportion of the joining fees of people whom they persuade to join after them. Such schemes are usually found to be illegal lotteries and a company running one will be wound up because its business is illegal. There are full examinations of these schemes in *Secretary of State for Trade and Industry* v *Hasta International Ltd* 1998 SLT 73, which was a hearing of a winding-up petition, and *Re Senator Hanseatische Verwaltungsgesellschaft mbH* [1996] 2 BCLC 562, which was concerned with steps to protect the public pending the hearing of a petition.

There have been several reported cases of petitions against companies conducting insurance business illegally. In *Re Secure and Provide plc* [1992] BCC 405, *Re a Company (No. 007923 of 1994) (No. 2)* [1995] 1 BCLC 594 and *Re a Company (No. 007816 of 1994)* [1995] 2 BCLC 539 the petitions failed because the court refused to accept that the breaches were serious enough to justify winding up. In *Re Sentinel Securities plc* [1996] 1 WLR 316, on the other hand, a company was wound up for carrying on insurance business without being authorised to do so.

In *Re Market Wizard Systems (UK) Ltd* (1998) *The Times*, 31 July 1998 a company was wound up for giving investment advice without being authorised under the Financial Services Act 1986.

18.8.3.4 Civil proceedings in company's name

The Secretary of State has power under CA 1985, s. 438, to bring civil proceedings in the name and on behalf of a company, if it appears from any report made or information obtained under CA 1985, part XIV (ss. 431 to 453), that such proceedings ought to be brought in the public interest. The Secretary of State must indemnify the company against any costs or expenses incurred by it in or in connection with those proceedings (s. 438(2)).

18.8.3.5 Unfair prejudice

The Secretary of State has power under CA 1985, s. 460, to petition under s. 459 (see 18.6) for the relief of any prejudicial conduct of a company's affairs which is revealed by a report under s. 437 (see 18.8.3.1) or documents produced under ss. 447 or 448. It seems that this power has never been exercised (Law Commission, *Shareholder Remedies* (Consultation Paper No. 142) (London: Stationery Office, 1996), p. 118, n. 20).

18.8.3.6 Application for a disqualification order

The Secretary of State may, under CDDA 1986, s. 8, apply for a disqualification order (see 15.2.5) to be made against a person if it appears, from a report made under CA 1985, s. 437

(investigating inspectors' reports, see 18.8.3.1), or FSA 1986, s. 177 (insider dealing investigation, see 18.8.2.5), or from information or documents obtained under CA 1985, ss. 447 or 448, to be expedient in the public interest. An application may be made in respect of a person who is or has been a director or shadow director of any company, not just a company that has been investigated.

18.8.3.7   Recovery of expenses

The expenses of, and incidental to, a CA 1985 investigation are in the first instance borne by the Secretary of State. However, the Secretary of State is entitled to demand reimbursement from any person who is convicted of an offence as a result of the investigation (to such extent as the convicting court may order), by any company dealt with by an inspectors' report (unless the company itself applied for the investigation or the inspectors were appointed on the Secretary of State's own motion), or by the applicants under s. 431 or s. 442(3) (to such extent as the Secretary of State may direct) (s. 439(1) to (5)).

19 Dealings with a Company

19.1 INTRODUCTION

A company's property is owned by the company as a separate person, not by the members; the company's business is conducted by the company as a separate person, not by the members. Therefore it is the company as a separate person that enters into contracts in relation to the company's business and property.

Any physical act that has to be done in order to make a company a party to a voluntary transaction has to be done by a human being acting on the company's behalf. It is necessary to establish rules which determine the circumstances in which the acts of one or more individuals are to be regarded as the acts of a company. In *Meridian Global Funds Management Asia Ltd* v *Securities Commission* [1995] 2 AC 500, Lord Hoffmann described these rules as 'rules of attribution' (at p. 506). For each company, what Lord Hoffmann called 'primary rules of attribution' are established by its constitution, which will state, for example, the rules governing general meetings, at which the members may take decisions which are the decisions of the company as a separate person (see 14.4.1), and the rules on appointment of directors, who are given authority by a provision like Table A, art. 70, to exercise all the powers of the company in the management of its business. Lord Hoffmann also included in the category of primary rules, general rules of company law such as those on decision-making without meeting (see 14.5). In many companies, dealings with persons outside the company are on such a scale that they cannot all be handled by the board of directors and so employees and other agents must be appointed to act on the company's behalf. The rules on the attribution of an employee's acts to his or her employer and the rules of agency apply whether the employer or principal is a company or a natural person. Agency rules are considered in 19.5 and rules on vicarious liability for employees in 19.7. Unfortunately these rules of attribution do not cover all the situations in which attribution is required, and the courts are often left with the difficult task of filling the gaps (see 19.8).

In relation to company contracts, there has always been great difficulty in reconciling two opposing principles: the first is that the members of a company should be protected from misapplication of the money they have invested in it; the second is that dealings with a company should not be hindered or discouraged. Companies would be less useful as means of carrying on business if people would not deal with them because of uncertainty about the security of their transactions, or if security of transaction could be ensured only by making extensive enquiries.

The early attitude of the courts was that members' investments in a company should be protected by insisting that every person was deemed to be informed of the contents of the memorandum and articles of the company (or, under the Joint Stock Companies Act 1844, its deed of settlement) (per Lord Wensleydale in *Ernest* v *Nicholls* (1857) 6 HL Cas 401 at p. 419; per Lord Hatherley in *Mahony* v *Easy Holyford Mining Co. Ltd* (1875) LR 7 HL 869 at p. 893). Having made every person who dealt with a company cognisant of the restrictions which its constitution placed on the use of its funds, the courts could then make such persons responsible for seeing that the restrictions were observed by insisting that they bear the loss when those restrictions were not observed. One important consequence of this philosophy was the '*ultra vires* rule' which is discussed in 19.4.1.

People who dealt with companies naturally thought it unfair that they should have the burden of making enquiries to ensure that companies' funds were not misapplied. The courts responded initially with the 'rule in *Turquand's* case', subsequently developed as the 'indoor management rule', which limited the enquiries that had to be made (see 19.5). The indoor management rule was largely replaced by the concept of the ostensible authority of a person acting for a company, but complete reform had to wait until Parliament enacted CA 1989, which abolishes the doctrine of deemed notice of the company's memorandum and articles (CA 1989, s. 142, which had not been brought into force when this edition went to press) and abolishes the *ultra vires* rule (s. 108) (see 19.4).

19.2 AUTHENTICATION AND EXECUTION OF DOCUMENTS

An individual shows that a document expresses his or her intention by signing it and thereby authenticating it. Where the document is intended to have some legal effect, this is an expression of an intention to accept that legal effect. Acceptance of the legal effect of a document may be expressed more strongly by executing it as a deed. If a company as a separate person is to accept the legal effect of documents, ways have to be found of showing that acceptance which are equivalent to those used by individuals. This is the topic that will be considered in 19.2. The topic is currently being reviewed by the Law Commission, which has issued a consultation paper, *The Execution of Deeds and Documents by or on behalf of Bodies Corporate* (Consultation Paper No. 143) (London: Stationery Office, 1996).

19.2.1 Signature

A document or proceeding requiring authentication by a company is sufficiently authenticated by the signature of a director, secretary or other authorised officer of the company (CA 1985, s. 41).

A document is 'signed by' a company if it is signed by a duly authorised human agent or officer of the company (signing his or her own name) acting within the scope of his or her authority and on behalf of the company in the course of the company's business (*UBAF Ltd* v *European American Banking Corporation* [1984] QB 713, CA). There is controversy over whether a document is signed by a company when the company's own name has been put on it by a human agent or officer. One view is that putting a company's name on a document is no different from putting on the name of an individual who is incapacitated from signing. The contrary view is that this cannot be putting the company's signature on because a company cannot be said to have a signature of its own for someone else to use: a company can only ever sign documents through a human agent. In *Chapman* v *Smethurst* [1909] 1 KB 927, Vaughan Williams and Kennedy LJJ referred to the rubber-stamped name of a company on a promissory note as the company's signature but Joyce J described it as a 'signature (if it can properly be so called)'. In *McDonald* v *John Twiname Ltd* [1953] 2 QB 304, Evershed MR said, at p. 315, that rubber-stamping a company's name on a document is an effective way of executing it, but in *Lazarus Estates Ltd* v *Beasley* [1956] 1 QB 702, Denning LJ said, at p. 710, that it is not.

An individual who signs a company document with his or her own name for the purpose of authenticating it as an act of the company or in order to make it signed by the company does not incur any personal liability. However, it must be clear that it is a company document that is being signed, otherwise there is a danger that the individual's signature on the document will be taken as establishing personal liability.

In *Badgerhill Properties Ltd* v *Cottrell* [1991] BCLC 805, Badgerhill Properties Ltd used the trading name 'The Plumbing Centre'. Mrs Cottrell entered into a contract on the basis of an estimate written on notepaper headed 'The Plumbing Centre' with the company's name (misspelled) at the bottom. The estimate ended 'Yours faithfully, The Plumbing Centre, B. Twigg, Director'. All Mrs Cottrell's dealings had been with Mr Twigg, and she argued that she had contracted with him personally (it seemed likely that the company would be unable to pay the damages she claimed). The Court of Appeal rejected this argument. Woolf LJ said, at p. 809:

> So far as those documents are concerned, their contents establish that Mrs Cottrell was accepting the estimates of the Plumbing Centre and that she was contracting with whoever was trading as the Plumbing Centre.

Once it was established that the documents were the documents of the company which was trading as the Plumbing Centre, Mr Twigg's signature could be on them only for the purpose of authenticating them as company documents.

If there is no other evidence that a document signed by an individual is a company document then words added to the signature which merely describe the signer ('AB, director of CD Ltd') may be insufficient to exclude personal liability. It is necessary to add words which establish that the signer has signed only as an agent or in a representative capacity, and is not personally liable ('AB, director of CD Ltd, for and on behalf of CD Ltd'). See, for example, the Bills of Exchange Act 1882, s. 26, quoted in 19.2.6.

19.2.2 A company's common seal

As a body corporate a company is entitled to a 'common seal' for authenticating documents, usually taking the form of a die used to reproduce an engraved design when pressed on to paper. However, a company need not have a common seal (CA 1985, s. 36A(3)).

A company which has a common seal must, under penalty, have its name engraved in legible characters on the seal (s. 350(1)). Affixing a company's common seal to a document is sufficient to execute it as a document of the company (s. 36A(2)), and a company may be made a party to a written contract by affixing its common seal to the contract (s. 36). Table A, art. 101, prescribes that the company's seal may be used only by the authority of the directors or of a committee of directors authorised by the directors, and that any document to which the seal is affixed must also be signed by either a director and the secretary of the company or by two directors, unless the directors determine otherwise. When a company's seal has been attached to a document, officers of the company sign under art. 101 as part of the process of attaching the company's seal: they are not attesting witnesses (*Deffell* v *White* (1866) LR 2 CP 144), nor do their signatures mean that the document is signed by the company (*UBAF Ltd* v *European American Banking Corporation* [1984] QB 713, CA, at pp. 722–3).

Under a provision like Table A, art. 101, the authority of the directors may be given by any means: it is not necessary to have a resolution of a board meeting (*J. W. Broomhead (Vic) Pty Ltd* v *J. W. Broomhead Pty Ltd* [1985] VR 891; *Magnacrete Ltd* v *Douglas-Hill* (1988) 48 SASR 567). If the seal is to be affixed to a document in connection with a matter which some directors are disqualified from voting on then it is sufficient to have the authority of the directors who are qualified even if that authority is given without adopting a resolution at a board meeting (*Magnacrete Ltd* v *Douglas-Hill*).

CA 1985, s. 36A(2), does not mention signatures by company officers when a document is sealed, but it is generally assumed that the subsection does not override a provision in articles like Table A, art. 101, and provide authority for a document to be executed by sealing without signature even though the articles specify that use of the seal must be accompanied by signatures. The Law Commission, *The Execution of Deeds and Documents by or on behalf of Bodies Corporate* (Consultation Paper No. 143) (London: Stationery Office, 1996) has, however, asked whether this needs clarification. The Commission has also asked whether it is necessary to require a company to put its name on its seal.

For the use of the seal on share certificates see 8.2.1.

19.2.3 Contractual formalities

Any formalities required by law in the case of a contract made by an individual also apply, unless a contrary intention appears, to a contract made by or on behalf of a company (CA 1985, s. 36). Few formal requirements are nowadays imposed in relation to contracts, but, for instance, a legal estate in land can be created or conveyed only by deed (Law of Property Act 1925, s. 52(1), with the exceptions noted in ss. 52(2), 54(2) and 55), and a disposition of an equitable interest must be in writing (Law of Property Act 1925, s. 53(1)(c)). Bills of exchange and promissory notes are by definition written (Bills of Exchange Act 1882, ss. 3(1) and 83(1)).

19.2.4 Execution of documents

A document is executed by a company by the affixing of its common seal (CA 1985, s. 36A(2)). However, a company need not have a common seal (s. 36A(3)). Whether or not a company has a common seal, a document signed by a director and the secretary of the company, or by two directors, and expressed (in whatever form of words) to be executed by the company has the same effect as if executed under the company's common seal (s. 36A(3) and (4)).

In favour of a 'purchaser', a document is deemed to have been duly executed by a company if it purports to be signed by a director and the secretary of the company, or by two directors of the company (s. 36A(6)). A 'purchaser' for this purpose means a purchaser in good faith for valuable consideration and includes a lessee, mortgagee or other person who for valuable consideration acquires an interest in property (ibid.).

Under the Law of Property Act 1925, s. 74(2), the board of directors of a company may, by resolution or otherwise, appoint an agent, either generally or in any particular case, to execute on behalf of the company any agreement or other instrument which is not a deed in relation to any matter within the company's powers.

19.2.5 Deeds

Section 1 of the Law of Property (Miscellaneous Provisions) Act 1989 altered the law relating to deeds. Subsection (2) of s. 1 provides that an instrument is not a deed unless:

(a) it makes it clear on its face that it is intended to be a deed by the person making it or, as the case may be, by the parties to it (whether by describing itself as a deed or expressing itself to be executed or signed as a deed or otherwise); and

(b) it is validly executed as a deed by that person or, as the case may be, one or more of those parties.

In order to be effective, a deed must be 'delivered' as the act and deed of the party expressed to be bound by it. Lord Denning MR explained in *Vincent v Premo Enterprises (Voucher Sales) Ltd* [1969] 2 QB 609 at p. 619:

> A deed is binding on the maker of it . . . as long as it has been signed, sealed and delivered. 'Delivery' in this connection does not mean 'handed over' to the other side. It means delivered in the old legal sense, namely, an act done so as to evince an intention to be bound.

In s. 1 of the Law of Property (Miscellaneous Provisions) Act 1989, the term 'execution' is used as it often is in relation to deeds to refer to the whole process of signing (and/or sealing) and delivery (see s. 1(3) concerning execution of deeds by individuals). (The old law that a seal is required for the valid execution of an instrument as a deed by an individual is abolished by s. 1(1)(b) of the Act.) Unfortunately the new provisions of CA 1985, s. 36A, relating to the signing, sealing and delivery of deeds by companies use 'execution' in a different sense. Section 36A is expressed to 'have effect with respect to the execution of documents by a company' (s. 36A(1)) and the section as a whole is drafted to apply to all documents whether or not they are deeds, and so in s. 36A delivery is not regarded as part of the process of execution of a deed, just as it is not part of the process of executing documents that are not deeds.

CA 1985, s. 36A(5), provides that a document executed by a company which makes it clear on its face that it is intended by the person or persons making it to be a deed has effect, upon delivery, as a deed. Furthermore, unless a contrary intention is proved, it is presumed to be delivered upon its being so executed (ibid.). Subsections (2), (3) and (4) of s. 36A, which are discussed in 19.2.4, define what constitutes 'execution' of a document by a company. They provide that a document may be executed by the affixing of the company's common seal (if it has one) or, provided the document is expressed to be executed by the company, by being signed by a director and the secretary or by two directors. It is submitted that s. 36A(5) makes sense only if 'executed' is interpreted by reference to s. 36A(2), (3) and (4) as meaning signed or sealed but not delivered. The Law Commission has suggested that the wording of s. 36A should be clarified (*The Execution of Deeds and Documents by or on behalf of Bodies Corporate* (Consultation Paper No. 143) (London: Stationery Office, 1996), paras 15.2–15.4). See further D.N. Clarke, 'Delivery of a deed: recent cases, new statutes and altered practice' [1990] Conv 85; City of London Law Society, 'Execution of deeds by companies' (1992) 89(1) LS Gaz 28 — the second of these articles examines the new provisions with the traditional abundant caution of conveyancers.

In favour of a 'purchaser', a document executed by a company which makes it clear on its face that it is intended by the person or persons making it to be a deed is deemed to have been delivered upon execution (s. 36A(6)). A 'purchaser' for this purpose means a purchaser in good faith for valuable consideration and includes a lessee, mortgagee or other person who for valuable consideration acquires an interest in property (ibid.).

Also, the Law of Property Act 1925, s. 74(1), provides that, in favour of a 'purchaser' (defined by s. 205(1)(xxi) of the 1925 Act almost in the same way as in CA 1985, s. 36A(6)), a deed shall be deemed to have been duly executed by a company if the company's seal is affixed to it in the presence of and attested by its secretary and a director, and where a seal purporting to be the seal of a company has been affixed to a deed, attested by persons purporting to be persons holding the offices of secretary and director, the deed shall be presumed to have been executed in accordance with the requirements of s. 74, and to have taken effect accordingly. As in CA 1985, s. 36A, 'executed' in s. 74 of the Law of Property Act 1925 does not include delivery (*Longman* v *Viscount Chelsea* (1989) 58 P & CR 189).

The Law Commission has identified several inconsistencies between the Law of Property Act 1925, s. 74(1), and CA 1985, s. 36A(6), and has suggested reforms (*The Execution of Deeds and Documents by or on behalf of Bodies Corporate*, paras 15.11–15.26).

19.2.6 Bills of exchange, cheques and promissory notes

A bill of exchange must, by definition, be signed by its drawer (Bills of Exchange Act 1882, s. 3(1)) and a promissory note must be signed by its maker (s. 83(1)). An acceptance of a bill must be signed by the drawee (s. 17(2)) and an endorsement must be signed by the endorser (s. 32(1)). No person is liable as drawer, endorser, or acceptor of a bill who has not signed it as such (s. 23). To make a company liable on a bill or note, the normal practice is for it to be signed by one or more individuals signing for and on behalf of the company. A bill of exchange or promissory note is deemed to have been made, accepted or endorsed on behalf of a company if made, accepted or endorsed in the name of, or by or on behalf or on account of, the company by a person acting under its authority (CA 1985, s. 37). (The Bills of Exchange Act 1882, s. 91(2), provides that where any instrument is required by the Act to be signed it is sufficient if it is sealed by a company but in practice it is rare for bills or notes to be sealed.) Any holder of a bill or note is entitled to know who is liable on it and so any signature made as a representative for another must clearly express that fact. Section 26 of the 1882 Act provides:

(1) Where a person signs a bill as drawer, endorser, or acceptor, and adds words to his signature, indicating that he signs for and on behalf of a principal, or in a representative character, he is not personally liable thereon; but the mere addition to his signature of words describing him as an agent, or as filling a representative character, does not exempt him from personal liability.

(2) In determining whether a signature on a bill is that of the principal or that of the agent by whose hand it is written, the construction most favourable to the validity of the instrument shall be adopted.

A cheque is defined by s. 73 as a bill of exchange drawn on a banker payable on demand. The fact that a cheque is expressed to be drawn on the account of a company at a particular bank is normally sufficient to make it the company's cheque and not the cheque of an individual who signed it for the company, even if words such as 'for and on behalf of [the company]' have not been added to the signature (*Electrical Equipment of Aust. Ltd* v *Peters* [1957] SR (NSW) 361; *Bondina Ltd* v *Rollaway Shower Blinds Ltd* [1986] 1 WLR 517). The practice now is for a cheque issued by a company to be drawn on a standard printed form supplied by its bank overprinted with the company's account number and with the company's name above the space where the signature is written. Such a cheque is plainly the cheque of the company (*Bondina Ltd* v *Rollaway Shower Blinds Ltd*). So is a cheque drawn on a form specially printed for the company with the company's name incorporated in the printed design (*Allprint Co. Ltd* v *Erwin* (1982) 136 DLR (3d) 587, Ontario). In the older case of *Electrical Equipment of Aust. Ltd* v *Peters,* two directors of a company had signed a cheque and put the company's name above their signature by a rubber stamp; neither of the directors had an account with the bank on which the cheque was drawn, and it was held to be the company's cheque on which they were not liable.

There may be more difficulty with a bill of exchange other than a cheque, or with a promissory note, because the existence of a bank account is not essential to the validity of such an instrument, and care needs to be taken to word such an instrument to show that the individual signing it for the company is not liable on it. See, for example, *Chapman* v *Smethurst* [1909] 1 KB 927.

Section 26 of the Bills of Exchange Act 1882, like the rest of the Act, does not affect 'the provisions of . . . any Act relating to . . . companies' (s. 97(3)). In particular it does not affect the operation of CA 1985, s. 349(4), under which a person who has signed or authorised to be signed a bill of exchange, promissory note or cheque which does not have on it the company's name in legible characters is personally liable on the instrument unless the company honours it (see 4.5.1). A minor mistake in naming the company for which an agent is signing would probably be tolerated under s. 26 of the 1882 Act so that the agent would not have liability under that provision (see the discussion in *Arab Bank Ltd* v *Ross* [1952] 2 QB 216). But no mistakes at all are permitted under CA 1985, s. 349(4), under which liability can arise despite there being no liability under s. 26 of the 1882 Act.

19.3 COMPANY CONTRACTS

CA 1985, s. 36, sets out two ways in which a company may become contractually bound to another person (a 'contractor'). The first is by a written contract to which the company's common seal is affixed (CA 1985, s. 36(a)). Whether or not a company has a common seal, if a written contract is signed by a director and the secretary of the company, or by two directors, and is expressed (in whatever form of words) to be executed by the company then it has the same effect as if executed under the common seal of the company (s. 36A(3) and (4)).

The second means by which a company may become contractually bound to a contractor is where a person who was acting under the express or implied authority of the company has made a contract on behalf of the company (CA 1985, s. 36(b)). The main problem for the contractor is to know whether the person who has acted for the company did so with the company's authority. There used to be another danger for a contractor in that a contract might be beyond the company's contractual capacity because it was outside the company's objects. This difficulty has been removed by CA 1989 but, because of its historical importance, will be discussed briefly in 19.4.

19.4 CONTRACTUAL CAPACITY

19.4.1 The *ultra vires* rule

In *Ashbury Railway Carriage and Iron Co. Ltd* v *Riche* (1875) LR 7 HL 653, the House of Lords decided that a registered company did not have the contractual capacity to enter into contracts outside the company's objects. This came to be known as the '*ultra vires* rule'. A similar rule had been established in relation to statutory companies (see, e.g., *East Anglian Railways Co.* v *Eastern Counties Railway Co.* (1851) 11 CB 775 and the general discussion by Lord Cranworth LC in *Shrewsbury & Birmingham Railway Co.* v *North-Western Railway Co.* (1857) 6 HL Cas 113 at pp. 135–8).

A transaction entered into by a company outside of its legal capacity is not enforceable in law. The company does not have to carry out its side of the bargain even if the other party's obligations have been completely performed. The fact that the members of the company approve the transaction cannot cure the company's lack of capacity, even if they approve it unanimously (*Ashbury Railway Carriage and Iron Co. Ltd* v *Riche*). However, since the Companies (Memorandum of Association) Act 1890, the members of a company have been able to alter its objects under what is now CA 1985, s. 4 (see 2.4.4).

The objects of the Ashbury Railway Carriage and Iron Co. Ltd were to make and sell, or lend on hire, railway carriages and wagons, and all kinds of railway plant, fittings, machinery and rolling stock; to carry on the business of mechanical engineers etc. The directors entered into a contract to buy a concession for the construction of a railway in Belgium, subcontracting the construction work to Mr Riche's firm. The company's shareholders disapproved of the deal and the company repudiated Mr Riche's contract. The House of Lords held that constructing a railway, as opposed to railway carriages and rolling stock, was not within the objects of the company and that the company did not have capacity to enter into a contract to build a railway. As the contract was void, Mr Riche was not entitled to damages for breach of it.

In *Rolled Steel Products (Holdings) Ltd* v *British Steel Corporation* [1986] Ch 246, the Court of Appeal held that if an act was capable of being within the objects of a company then it would be within the company's contractual capacity. This covers acts such as borrowing money which do not have an implicit purpose so that the contractor does not know whether the act is for the purpose of pursuing the company's objects or not.

Although the Law Lords in *Ashbury Railway Carriage and Iron Co. Ltd* v *Riche* were convinced that they were protecting creditors by insisting on certainty about the extent of a company's capacity, in practice the *ultra vires* rule was very unfair to persons contracting with companies. It assumed that a person contracted with a company only after reading its memorandum to ascertain whether the contract was for a purpose within its objects. In practice, however, few persons have ever bothered to read the memorandum of a company they were contracting with, and drafters of objects clauses have tried to counter the *ultra vires* rule by producing lengthy and wide-ranging objects clauses.

CA 1989 abolished the *ultra vires* rule by substituting in CA 1985 a new s. 35(1):

The validity of an act done by a company shall not be called into question on the ground of lack of capacity by reason of anything in the company's memorandum.

CA 1989 also abolishes the doctrine of deemed notice of the contents of a company's memorandum and articles (by inserting a new s. 711A to that effect into CA 1985) but this provision had not been brought into force when this edition went to press. These important reforms have been much discussed. Abolition of the *ultra vires* rule was first recommended in 1945 by the Committee on Company Law Amendment (Cmd 6659, para. 12). At the end of 1985 the government appointed Dr D. Prentice to conduct a study of the legal and commercial implications of abolishing the *ultra vires* rule. See Department of Trade and Industry, *Reform of the* Ultra Vires *Rule: A Consultative Document* (London: DTI, 1986), which includes Dr Prentice's report. For comments on the report, see [1986] JBL 346; M. Stamp (1986) 136 NLJ 962; B.M. Hannigan, 'The reform of the *ultra vires* rule' [1987] JBL 173; S.N. Frommel, 'Reform of the *ultra vires* rule: a personal view' (1987) 8 Co Law 11; R. Pennington, 'Reform of the *ultra vires* rule' (1987) 8 Co Law 103. CA 1989 did not follow exactly Dr Prentice's recommendations and commentators have suggested that there may be difficulties with the new law; see J. Poole, 'Abolition of the *ultra vires* doctrine and agency problems' (1991) 12 Co Law 43; E. Ferran, 'The reform of the law on corporate capacity and directors' and officers' authority' (1992) 13 Co Law 124 and 177.

19.4.2 Charitable companies

Under s. 65 of the Charities Act 1993, the new s. 35 of CA 1985 (which generally abolishes the *ultra vires* rule, see 19.4.1) does not apply to the acts of a company which is a charity, except in favour of a person who:

(a)   gives full consideration in money or money's worth in relation to the act in question, and

(b)   does not know that the act is not permitted by the company's memorandum,

or who does not know at the time the act is done that the company is a charity.

Accordingly, charitable companies are now required to make it clear to persons who deal with them that they are charities (see 4.5.5).

In *Rosemary Simmons Memorial Housing Association Ltd* v *United Dominions Trust Ltd* [1986] 1 WLR 1440, Mervyn Davies J held that it was beyond the capacity of an incorporated charity to give away its assets to a non-charitable body (presumably this does not refer to gifts to the objects of the charity). See J. Warburton, 'Charitable companies and the *ultra vires* rule' [1988] Conv 275.

See also 19.5.11.

19.5   AUTHORITY

19.5.1   Acting under a company's authority

The concept in CA 1985, s. 36(b), of a person who is acting under the authority of a company making a contract on behalf of the company is a concept of agency law. The person making the contract on behalf of the company is an agent of the company, and the company is the person's principal.

The rule of agency law is that an agent can act only within what is known as the agent's 'authority': the principal of an agent is not bound by any legal relationship which the agent purports to put the principal into if it was outside the agent's authority (though the principal may choose to 'ratify' — that is, adopt the contract and retrospectively supply the missing authority). The authority under which a contract made by an agent on behalf of a company will become binding on the company may be actual (see 19.5.2) or ostensible (see 19.5.3 and 19.5.4). Any legal relationship which a company is put into by an agent within the actual or (with exceptions) ostensible authority of the agent is binding on the company. But an agent of a company who purports to make a contract on behalf of the company which is outside the scope of the agent's actual or ostensible authority has not made a contract by which the company is bound: a contractor who suffers loss as a result may sue the agent for breach of warranty of authority.

19.5.2   Actual authority

19.5.2.1   Definition

The actual authority of an agent of a company is the authority conferred on the agent by the contract governing the agency which has been agreed between the agent and the company. As Diplock LJ said in *Freeman & Lockyer* v *Buckhurst Park Properties (Mangal) Ltd* [1964] 2 QB 480, CA, at pp. 502–3:

An 'actual' authority is a legal relationship between principal and agent created by a consensual agreement to which they alone are parties. Its scope is to be ascertained by applying ordinary principles of construction of contracts, including any proper implications from the express words used, the usages of the trade, or the course of business between the parties. To this agreement the contractor is a stranger; he may be totally ignorant of the existence of any authority on the part of the agent. Nevertheless, if the agent does enter into a contract pursuant to the 'actual' authority, it does create contractual rights and liabilities between the principal and the contractor.

Thus if any person acting within the scope of his or her actual authority makes a contract on behalf of a company then the company will be bound by it.

19.5.2.2   Limitations on actual authority by the company's constitution
The most notable limitation on the actual authority of the directors of a company (and so, on any agent to whom the directors might delegate authority) is that they do not have actual authority to put it into any transaction which is not for the purpose of, or reasonably incidental to, attaining or pursuing the company's objects as set out in its memorandum (*Rolled Steel Products (Holdings) Ltd* v *British Steel Corporation* [1986] Ch 246, CA, per Slade LJ at p. 295). There may be other constitutional limitations. For example, it used to be common for the articles of association of a company to limit the amount that its directors could commit it to borrowing.

CA 1985, s. 35A (see 19.5.5), has severely curtailed the effect on the enforceability of a company's contracts of limitations made by a company's constitution on the actual authority of its agents.

19.5.3   Ostensible authority

Ostensible, or apparent, authority is the authority of an agent as it appears to others. As Byles J said in *Totterdell* v *Fareham Blue Brick & Tile Co. Ltd* (1866) LR 1 CP 674 at pp. 677–8:

> . . . a principal is bound, not only by such acts of the agent as are within the scope of the agent's *actual* authority, but by such acts as are within the larger margin of an apparent or *ostensible* authority derived from the representations, acts, or default of the principal.

In *Armagas Ltd* v *Mundogas SA* [1986] AC 717, HL, Lord Keith of Kinkel said at p. 777:

> Ostensible authority comes about where the principal, by words or conduct, has represented that the agent has the requisite actual authority, and the party dealing with the agent has entered into a contract with him in reliance on that representation.

Having represented that the agent has the requisite authority, the principal is precluded (or 'estopped') from claiming that the agent actually did not have authority.

19.5.4   Protection of the contractor when actual authority is less than ostensible authority: common law

19.5.4.1   The common law rule; the rule in Turquand's case; the indoor management rule
The common law developed rules under which a contract made by an agent (or a person who was represented to be an agent) of a company within the agent's ostensible authority but outside that person's actual authority would nevertheless be binding on the company. These rules were summarised by Diplock LJ in *Freeman & Lockyer* v *Buckhurst Park Properties (Mangal) Ltd* [1964] 2 QB 480 at p. 506. Such a contract would be binding if:

(a)   The ostensible authority of the person acting as agent to make such a contract was represented to the contractor.

(b)   The representation was made by a person or persons who had actual authority to manage the business of the company, either generally or in respect of the matters to which the contract relates.

(c)   The contractor actually relied on the representation as a reason for entering into the contract.

(d)   Under its constitution:

   (i)   the company had capacity to enter into the contract (this is no longer relevant by virtue of CA 1985, s. 35 — see 19.4.1 — except in relation to charitable companies — see 19.4.2), and

   (ii)   the company was not precluded from authorising the person acting as agent to make the contract in question on its behalf (this is no longer relevant, by virtue of CA 1985, ss. 35A and 35B, if the contractor dealt with the company in good faith — see 19.5.5).

The first two conditions were elaborated upon by Diplock LJ in *Freeman & Lockyer* v *Buckhurst Park Properties (Mangal) Ltd* at p. 505:

> The commonest form of representation by a principal creating an 'apparent' authority of an agent is by conduct, namely, by permitting the agent to act in the management or conduct of the principal's business. Thus, if in the case of a company the board of directors who have 'actual' authority under the memorandum and articles of association to manage the company's business permit the agent to act in the management or conduct of the company's business, they thereby represent to all persons dealing with such agent that he has authority to enter on behalf of the corporation into contracts of a kind which an agent authorised to do acts of the kind which he is in fact permitted to do usually enters into in the ordinary course of such business. The making of such a representation is itself an act of management of the company's business. Prima facie it falls within the 'actual' authority of the board of directors.

In this case, Kapoor and Hoon formed a company to buy and resell the Buckhurst Park estate. The two of them, and a nominee of each, were appointed directors. The company's articles conferred full powers of management on the directors, and also gave power to appoint a managing director, though none was ever appointed. Kapoor instructed the plaintiff architects to carry out certain work in connection with the development of the estate, and the plaintiffs subsequently sued the company for the payment of their fees. In holding the company liable, the Court of Appeal explained that the directors knew that Kapoor had in fact been acting as managing director and had permitted him to do so, and by that conduct had represented that he had authority to enter into contracts of a kind which a managing director or an executive director would in the normal course be authorised to enter into on the company's behalf. The board had actual authority to manage the business under the terms of the articles. The two conditions were thus satisfied.

There is a problem, however, identified by Lord Pearson in *Hely-Hutchinson* v *Brayhead Ltd* [1968] 1 QB 549, CA, at p. 593, in showing how a representation by conduct is made by the directors to the contractor:

> Now there is not usually any direct communication in such cases between the board of directors and the outside contractor. The actual communication is made immediately and directly, whether it be express or implied, by the agent to the outside contractor. It is,

therefore, necessary in order to make a case of ostensible authority to show in some way that such communication which is made directly by the agent is made ultimately by the responsible parties, the board of directors. That may be shown by inference from the conduct of the board of directors in the particular case by, for instance, placing the agent in a position where he can hold himself out as their agent and acquiescing in his activities, so that it can be said they have in effect caused the representation to be made. They are responsible for it and, in the contemplation of law, they are to be taken to have made the representation to the outside contractor.

In determining what representations have been made of the apparent authority of a company's agent it is necessary to look at the entire conduct of those making the representations (*Ebeed* v *Soplex Wholesale Supplies Ltd* [1985] BCLC 404, CA).

In *First Energy (UK) Ltd* v *Hungarian International Bank Ltd* [1993] BCLC 1409, the manager of the bank's Manchester branch had made an offer of financing facilities to First Energy (UK) Ltd. He did not have either actual or ostensible authority to decide to make such an offer himself but it was found that he had ostensible authority to communicate such offers. Accordingly the bank was bound when the offer was accepted.

The common law rule had been developing for a century before *Freeman & Lockyer* v *Buckhurst Park Properties (Mangal) Ltd.* Early cases were not expressed in terms of ostensible authority, and it is sometimes difficult to fit them in to the modern rules based on that concept. The first case to deal with the protection of a person contracting with agents of a company who were exceeding their actual authority was *Royal British Bank* v *Turquand* (1856) 6 El & Bl 327. The 'rule in *Turquand's* case' was expressed by Wood V-C in *Fountaine* v *Carmarthen Railway Co.* (1868) LR 5 Eq 316 at p. 322 as follows:

> If, . . . as in the case of *Royal British Bank* v *Turquand,* the directors have power and authority to bind the company, but certain preliminaries are required to be gone through on the part of the company before that power can be duly exercised, then the person contracting with the directors is not bound to see that all these preliminaries have been observed. He is entitled to presume that the directors are acting lawfully in what they do.

The rule in *Turquand's* case was originally intended to limit the enquiries that persons dealing with companies had to make. In *Royal British Bank* v *Turquand,* the directors of a company had, on its behalf, borrowed money from the Royal British Bank and had affixed the company's seal to a bond for £2,000 to secure repayment of the borrowing. Under the company's deed of settlement, borrowings had to be approved by resolution of the members, and the company (through its liquidator, Mr Turquand) claimed that no resolution had been adopted to cover this borrowing. When the bank sued on the bond, it was argued that the company should not be liable because the bank was deemed to be informed of the contents of the company's deed of settlement and should have enquired whether the appropriate resolution had been adopted. As it had not enquired it should bear the loss. The court thought this was requiring too many enquiries from persons dealing with companies: they were at that time, as Jervis CJ said, at p. 332, 'bound to read the statute and the deed of settlement. But they are not bound to do more.' The Chief Justice explained that:

> . . . the party here, on reading the deed of settlement, would find not a prohibition from borrowing, but a permission to do so on certain conditions. Finding that the authority might be made complete by a resolution, he would have a right to infer the fact of a resolution authorising that which on the face of the document appeared to be legitimately done.

It would seem that the rule in *Turquand's* case has been completely replaced by CA 1985, s. 35A. In addition, CA 1989, s. 142, will abolish the doctrine of deemed notice of a company's memorandum and articles but s. 142 had not been brought into force when this edition went to press.

The rule in *Turquand's* case was subsequently developed by the courts as the indoor management rule, which was described in the following terms by Lord Hatherley in *Mahony v East Holyford Mining Co. Ltd* (1875) LR 7 HL 869 at p. 894:

> . . . all that the directors do with reference to what I may call the indoor management of their own concern, is a thing known to them and known to them only.
>
> . . . when there are persons conducting the affairs of the company in a manner which appears to be perfectly consonant with the articles of association, then those so dealing with them, externally, are not to be affected by any irregularities which may take place in the internal management of the company. They are entitled to presume that that of which only they can have knowledge, namely, the external acts, are rightly done, when those acts purport to be performed in the mode in which they ought to be performed.

Under the indoor management rule, if a decision that a company should enter into an obligation has purportedly been made by the company's board of directors, the company cannot escape from the obligation by claiming that the board meeting was inquorate (*County of Gloucester Bank v Rudry Merthyr Steam & House Coal Colliery Co.* [1895] 1 Ch 629, CA; *Re Bank of Syria, Owen and Ashworth's Claim* [1901] 1 Ch 115, CA) or that there was no board meeting (*Re Bonelli's Telegraph Co., Collie's Claim* (1871) LR 12 Eq 246). As Atkin LJ said in *Kreditbank Cassel GmbH v Schenkers Ltd* [1927] 1 KB 826 at p. 844:

> When . . . a certain thing . . . can be done by the company in board meeting, and there purports to be a resolution authorising it, you are not obliged to inquire whether or not the forms of the company required by the articles as to the constitution of the board, the quorum and so forth, have been actually complied with.

A person dealing with a company can use the ostensible authority doctrine to prevent the company denying the contract but a company cannot use the doctrine to ratify a contract made without its authority where ratification by resolution of the directors or members is no longer possible because, for example, a quorum cannot be assembled (*Re Qintex Ltd (No. 2)* (1990) 2 ACSR 479, which is discussed in 19.5.4.3) or ratification will not be allowed because it would prejudice another person (*NM Superannuation Pty Ltd v Baker* (1992) 7 ACSR 105).

19.5.4.2 Ostensible authority conferred by position or job title

A person's job title or official position is nowadays the most important factor determining the content of his or her ostensible authority. Business people generally expect that a managing director of a company, for example, has a certain range of authority to make contracts on the company's behalf by virtue of being its managing director. As Lord Keith of Kinkel said in *Armagas Ltd v Mundogas SA* [1986] AC 717 at p. 777:

> In the commonly encountered case, the ostensible authority is general in character, arising when the principal has placed the agent in a position which in the outside world is generally regarded as carrying authority to enter into transactions of the kind in question. Ostensible general authority may also arise where the agent has had a course of dealing

with a particular contractor and the principal has acquiesced in this course of dealing and honoured transactions arising out of it.

A person appointed to an office in a company has ostensible authority to make contracts on behalf of the company that are usually made by persons in that office. This ostensible authority exists whether or not an express delegation of authority has been made by the board of directors under a provision of the articles like art. 71 or art. 72 of Table A. A person who is permitted by a company to act as though holding a particular office in the company also has the ostensible authority of that office (*Freeman & Lockyer* v *Buckhurst Park Properties (Mangal) Ltd* [1964] 2 QB 480). If, for example, it is not intended that a particular individual associated with a company should have the authority associated with the title 'managing director' then the individual must not be given that title, or allowed to act as a managing director: if the company gives the individual the title of 'managing director' or allows him or her to act as such then it will be bound by all contracts that the individual enters into on its behalf within the usual authority that managing directors have.

Normally the actual authority of a person in a particular position is the same as the ostensible authority which people in such a position usually have. There are two possible reasons for the actual authority of a person in a particular position being less than the person's ostensible authority:

(a)   when the person was never in fact appointed to the position which the principal represents that the person holds;
(b)   when the person's authority has actually been limited by the principal so that it is less than the person's ostensible authority.

In *Re County Life Assurance Co.* (1870) LR 5 Ch App 288, the company was held to be bound to pay the sum assured by a life assurance policy which was signed by three men who acted as directors of the company but had never been appointed as such, and countersigned by a man who acted as secretary but had never been appointed: the court heard that about 350 other policies had been issued in the same way. Giffard LJ said, at p. 293:

The company is bound by what takes place in the usual course of business with a third party where that third party deals bona fide with persons who may be termed *de facto* directors, and who might, so far as he could tell, have been directors *de iure*.

In *Mahony* v *East Holyford Mining Co. Ltd* (1875) LR 7 HL 869 it was held that the bank at which the East Holyford Mining Co. Ltd had its account was justified in honouring cheques drawn by persons who had been represented as being the directors and secretary of the company even though they had never been appointed as such. See also *Totterdell* v *Fareham Blue Brick & Tile Co. Ltd* (1866) LR 1 CP 674 and *Duck* v *Tower Galvanizing Co. Ltd* [1901] 2 KB 314, DC.

For an example of a case in which the ostensible authority conferred by a job title was found not to cover the transaction which the contractor wanted the company to be bound by, see *British Bank of the Middle East* v *Sun Life Assurance of Canada (UK) Ltd* [1982] BCLC 78, HL, which concerned the ostensible authority of a branch manager of an insurance company. See also *Kreditbank Cassel GmbH* v *Schenkers Ltd* [1927] 1 KB 826 discussed in 19.5.6.

Sometimes a company may represent that a person's authority to act for the company is greater than that normally conferred by the person's job title or position in the company. For example, *Ebeed* v *Soplex Wholesale Supplies Ltd* [1985] BCLC 404, CA, concerned a transaction entered into by the documentary credit manager of a bank. There was conflicting evidence over whether the transaction in question would be within the ostensible authority of a documentary credit manager of a merchant bank or trading bank, but it was also found that in this instance the directors had regularly allowed their documentary credit manager to act for the company over a wide field of business beyond that normally associated with the work of an official with that job title, and so he did have ostensible authority in relation to the transaction in question. In *Commissioners of Inland Revenue* v *Ufitec Group Ltd* [1977] 3 All ER 924, Mr Zhilka was a director of Ufitec Group Ltd and chairman of the board. On 10 March 1971, Mr Zhilka signed a contract, in which he was described as 'the duly authorised representative' of Ufitec Group Ltd, to sell one of its major assets. The contract had been drawn up by the company's solicitors, a well-known London firm, and the sale had been negotiated by Mr Zhilka and by a partner in that firm of solicitors over a period of months. The negotiations were known to the other directors of the company. Unfortunately it had been forgotten that the company was supposed to retain beneficial ownership of the asset until 18 April 1971 in order to qualify for an important tax relief. When the Revenue denied the company the tax relief, the company pointed out that making a contract to sell a company's major asset is outside the ostensible authority of one member of the company's board of directors and that the Revenue could not prove that Mr Zhilka had ever been given actual authority to make the contract by Ufitec's board, and so could not prove that the contract was effective. However, it was held that by allowing Mr Zhilka and the solicitor to conduct the negotiations the company had represented that Mr Zhilka had authority to make the contract and he therefore had ostensible authority to make it so that the contract was effective.

19.5.4.3 *Ostensible authority or implied actual authority*
An alternative way of looking at the authority of a person in a particular office or job in a company is to say that in making the appointment the company impliedly authorised the person to do everything within the usual scope of the office or job. Such implied authority would be *actual* authority. This was the line taken by the Court of Appeal in *Hely-Hutchinson* v *Brayhead Ltd* [1968] 1 QB 549. The difference between these two ways of looking at the authority attached to an office is crucial if the company itself wishes to show that it is bound by the act of a particular officer. For example, in *Re Qintex Ltd (No. 2)* (1990) 2 ACSR 479, the managing director of Qintex Ltd instructed solicitors to oppose a petition for the compulsory winding up *of* his company which had been presented to the Tasmania Supreme Court by a company claiming to be a creditor of Qintex Ltd. On the application of another creditor supporting the petition, it was held that the managing director of a company does not have implied actual authority to make crucial decisions following the presentation of a petition to wind up the company, and, in particular, does not have implied actual authority to instruct solicitors to oppose the petition. As there was no decision of the board of directors to give the instructions, it was held that the court could not recognise the solicitors as acting for the company and could not hear the counsel they had instructed. (The board was unable to ratify the managing director's acts because there were no longer enough directors to form a quorum.) The company could not rely on the doctrine of ostensible authority because that doctrine can only be invoked to bind the company to a contract by the other party to that contract. It cannot be invoked by the company itself to make itself bound by a contract purportedly made by an agent of the company outside his actual authority.

19.5.4.4 No representation by the company
If a person purporting to act as agent of a company acts outside any actual or ostensible authority then the company is not bound. If such a person acts by way of making and issuing a document purporting to be a document of the company when it is not (because of the person's lack of actual authority to make the document) then the document is a forgery and, provided the company has never represented that the person has ostensible authority to make the document, the company is not bound by it. This is what happened in *Ruben* v *Great Fingall Consolidated* [1906] AC 439, HL, and *South London Greyhound Racecourses Ltd* v *Wake* [1931] 1 Ch 496, which are discussed in 8.2.2. In *Ruben* v *Great Fingall Consolidated,* the stockbrokers who had been issued the forged share certificate argued that the company was bound by it because of the indoor management rule. Lord Loreburn LC said, at p. 443:

> I cannot see upon what principle your lordships can hold that the defendants are liable in this action. The forged certificate is a pure nullity. It is quite true that persons dealing with limited liability companies are not bound to inquire into their indoor management, and will not be affected by irregularities of which they had no notice. But this doctrine, which is well established, applies only to irregularities that otherwise might affect a genuine transaction. It cannot apply to a forgery.

In *Northside Developments Pty Ltd* v *Registrar-General* (1990) 170 CLR 146, a mortgage of the company's land was purportedly executed by Robert Sturgess, who was one of the company's three directors, and by a person acting as the company secretary who had never been appointed as such. They attached the company's seal to the mortgage deed and countersigned it though they did not have the requisite authority of a board resolution to do so. The mortgage was given not to secure any indebtedness of the company but to secure debts of other companies controlled by Sturgess. A majority of the High Court of Australia held that the mortgage was a forgery which did not bind the company. The minority preferred to say that the indoor management rule did not apply to bind the company to observe the mortgage because a person taking a mortgage of a company's property that was not for the benefit of the company should make inquiries to satisfy itself that the persons who executed the mortgage were authorised to do so, and the bank had not made such inquiries. This division of opinion reflects a long-running debate about the nature of the 'forgery exception' to the indoor management rule — the debate is fully explored in the judgments delivered by the High Court in the case.

If the representation that a person holds a particular office in a company is made falsely by that person, and there is no representation to that effect by the company, then the person does not have the ostensible authority of that office. In *First City Capital Ltd* v *105383 BC Ltd* (1985) 28 BLR 274, a man who was secretary and general manager of a company pretended to be its president for the purpose of leasing a car. The British Columbia Court of Appeal held that the company was not bound by the lease. Curiously, according to *Panorama Developments (Guildford) Ltd* v *Fidelis Furnishing Fabrics Ltd* [1971] 2 QB 711 (see 19.5.10) the man would have had ostensible authority as company secretary to bind the company to a contract for the hire of a car.

19.5.4.5 Failure to ask questions about authority
The internal management rule is subject to a rather unpredictable limitation. A claim that a lack of authority is a matter of internal management on which the company cannot rely may be denied if, in the court's opinion, because of the circumstances of the transaction, the claimant should have asked whether authority had been properly given, but did not. In

Mahony v *East Holyford Mining Co. Ltd* (1875) LR 7 HL 869 Lord Hatherley said, at p. 895, that the internal management rule is subject to the assumption that 'All those ordinary inquiries which mercantile men would, in the course of their business make . . . would have to be made on the part of the persons dealing with the company'. For cases in which it was held that the rule could not be relied on because of failure to ask questions that the court decided should have been asked see *A.L. Underwood Ltd* v *Bank of Liverpool and Martins* [1924] 1 KB 775 and *B. Liggett (Liverpool) Ltd* v *Barclays Bank Ltd* [1928] 1 KB 48.

Now CA 1985, s. 35B, provides:

> A party to a transaction with a company is not bound to enquire as to whether it is permitted by the company's memorandum or as to any limitation on the powers of the board of directors to bind the company or authorise others to do so.

The fact that the questions specified in s. 35B have not been asked cannot be a reason for denying the benefit of the internal management rule, whatever the circumstances of the case. However, it may be that the court can deny the benefit of the rule if other questions, not covered by s. 35B, have not been asked and the court finds that, in the circumstances of the case, they should have been asked. For example, it may be that s. 35B does not apply in a case like *B. Liggett (Liverpool) Ltd* v *Barclays Bank Ltd* where the persons who purported to cause the company to enter into the transaction were not in fact the board of directors though they acted as such and the court finds that the person claiming the benefit of the internal management rule should have asked whether the directors had been properly appointed.

A person trying to enforce a contract with a company made without its actual authority, who was, at the time the contract was purportedly made, a director of the company, or acting as such, cannot rely on the internal management rule (*Re Patent Ivory Manufacturing Co.* (1888) 38 ChD 156; *Morris* v *Kanssen* [1946] AC 459). As Lord Simonds said in *Morris* v *Kanssen* at p. 476:

> His duty as a director is to know; his interest, when he invokes the rule, is to disclaim knowledge. Such a conflict can be resolved in only one way.

Transactions to which directors are party are now subject to statutory rules discussed in 19.5.9.

19.5.4.6 Articles of association do not confer ostensible authority

At first, cases on ostensible authority were argued in the context of provisions in companies' articles for delegation of authority. The indoor management rule was interpreted as meaning that any contractor with whom a contract was made on behalf of the company by a person to whom authority *could have been delegated* under a provision in the articles was entitled to assume that it had been, and this meant that the person had ostensible authority to make the contract on behalf of the company. For example, in *Biggerstaff* v *Rowatt's Wharf Ltd* [1896] 2 Ch 93, which concerned the ostensible authority of Mr Davy, the managing director of the defendant company, to assign to other persons debts owed to the company, Lopes LJ said, at pp. 103–4:

> There is no doubt that Mr Davy was the managing director and acted as such, and according to the articles the directors could have given him the power which he purported to exercise. . . .

It cannot be said but that Mr Davy was acting within the limits of his apparent authority.

In *Dey* v *Pullinger Engineering Co.* [1921] 1 KB 77, DC, this argument was adopted to hold that the managing director of a company had what was called 'implied authority' to draw and endorse a bill of exchange on behalf of the company.

However, in *J.C. Houghton & Co.* v *Nothard, Lowe & Wills Ltd* [1927] 1 KB 246 and *Kreditbank Cassel GmbH* v *Schenkers Ltd* [1927] 1 KB 826, the Court of Appeal switched to the view that it is the general understanding of the authority usually held by a person in a particular position which determines the ostensible authority of a person in that position. If a person in a particular position acts outside the usual authority of a person in such a position then the act was outside the person's ostensible authority and it makes no difference that under the articles of that particular company there was a theoretical possibility that actual authority for the act could have been conferred. In *J.C. Houghton & Co* v *Nothard, Lowe & Wills Ltd*, Sargant LJ said, at p. 267, that in *Biggerstaff* v *Rowatt's Wharf Ltd*:

> . . . the act done was one within the ordinary ambit of the powers of a managing director in the transaction of the company's affairs. It is I think clear that the transaction there would not have been supported had it not been in this ordinary course, or had the agent been acting merely as one of the ordinary directors of the company.

Similarly, in *Freeman & Lockyer* v *Buckhurst Park Properties (Mangal) Ltd* [1964] 2 QB 480, CA, Diplock LJ said, at p. 509, that the contract in *Biggerstaff* v *Rowatt's Wharf Ltd* 'was a normal contract, that is of a kind which a director managing the affairs of the company . . . would be authorised to enter into'. Accordingly the only relevance of the articles of association was that there was nothing in them to *prevent* delegation of authority to enter into such a contract on behalf of the company.

It seems that the argument based on the internal management rule was dropped because, as articles usually permit delegation to any agent, the argument would lead to the result that any agent could make any contract on the company's behalf and this was contrary to the principle that the members of a company should be protected from misapplication of the money they have invested in it. As Sargant LJ said in *J.C. Houghton & Co.* v *Nothard, Lowe & Wills Ltd* at p. 266:

> . . . in my opinion this is to carry the doctrine of presumed power far beyond anything that has hitherto been decided, and to place limited companies, without sufficient reason for so doing, at the mercy of any servant or agent who should purport to contract on their behalf. On this view, not only a director of a limited company with articles founded on Table A, but a secretary or any subordinate officer might be treated by a third party acting in good faith as capable of binding the company by any sort of contract, however exceptional, on the ground that a power of making such a contract might conceivably have been entrusted to him.

See also per Atkin LJ in *Kreditbank Cassel GmbH* v *Schenkers Ltd* [1927] 1 KB 826 at pp. 842–3.

In *J.C. Houghton & Co.* v *Nothard, Lowe & Wills Ltd*, the plaintiffs were a firm of fruit brokers. They had wanted to gain the right to sell all fruit imported by the defendant company and retain 70 per cent of the net proceeds of sale of that fruit as repayment of a loan they had made to a company associated with the defendant company. They had an oral agreement with the chairman of the board of the defendant company to that effect but wanted written confirmation from the company. The only document they ever received, though, was a letter from the company's secretary purporting to confirm the arrangement. The secretary had no actual authority to make such a contract on behalf of the company and the Court of Appeal rejected the argument that as there was a power in the articles to delegate such an authority the plaintiffs were entitled to assume under the indoor management rule that it had been delegated.

In *Kreditbank Cassel GmbH* v *Schenkers Ltd,* the manager of the defendant company's branch office in Manchester had purported to draw and endorse bills of exchange on behalf of the company but did not have actual authority to do so. The defendant company's articles empowered its directors to determine who should be entitled to draw and endorse bills on its behalf. The Court of Appeal held that the plaintiff bank could not argue that because of the indoor management rule it could assume that authority to draw and endorse bills had been delegated to the Manchester branch manager. The manager of a branch of a business does not have ostensible authority to draw and endorse bills of exchange on behalf of the owner of the business.

These two cases show that it is the nature of the office which determines the ostensible authority of an officer of a company not the existence in the company's articles of a provision for the delegation of authority.

It follows that a contractor may be able to rely on the ostensible authority attaching to a particular company office whether or not the contractor was aware that the authority could have been expressly delegated. For example, in *British Thomson-Houston Co. Ltd* v *Federated European Bank Ltd* [1932] 2 KB 176, CA, the chairman of the board of directors of the bank made a contract on behalf of the bank to guarantee some debts owed to the plaintiff company. It was held that the plaintiff company dealt with the chairman in a matter in which normally a director would have power to act and therefore the bank was bound by the guarantee. Under the bank's articles, the board could have expressly delegated authority to the chairman to enter into guarantees on the bank's behalf but had never done so. The plaintiff company had not actually been informed of the contents of the bank's articles and so did not rely on the possibility of delegation. *Freeman & Lockyer* v *Buckhurst Park Properties (Mangal) Ltd* is a similar case.

In both *J.C. Houghton & Co.* v *Nothard, Lowe & Wills Ltd* and *Kreditbank Cassel GmbH* v *Schenkers Ltd,* the plaintiffs were not informed of the contents of the companies' articles when dealing with them and so could not even claim that there was a representation on which they had relied that the officers with whom they dealt had, under the articles, been delegated the authority on which they relied.

19.5.5 Protection of the contractor when actual authority is less than ostensible authority: statute

The old attitude of the law was that the investments of the members of a company should be protected by making everyone who dealt with a company responsible for seeing that restrictions imposed by its constitution on the use of its assets were observed. The present-day attitude is that a person dealing in good faith with a company should not have to be concerned at all with its constitution. The common law had moved some way in this direction by developing the rule in *Turquand's* case, the indoor management rule and the doctrine of ostensible authority. In CA 1989, Parliament made a further important move in favour of security of transaction of persons dealing with companies by abolishing the *ultra vires* rule (s. 108) and the doctrine of deemed notice of the company's memorandum and articles (s. 142) though the second of these reforms had not been brought into force when this edition went to press. The move in favour of security of transaction is required by the First Company Law Directive of the EEC (68/151/EEC). The preamble to that Directive states that:

. . . the protection of third parties must be ensured by provisions which restrict to the greatest possible extent the grounds on which obligations entered into in the name of the company are not valid.

Article 9(2) of that Directive provides:

The limits on the powers of the organs of the company, arising under the statutes or from a decision of the competent organs, may never be relied on as against third parties, even if they have been disclosed.

It seems that the articles of association of a British company are its 'statutes', the memorandum of such a company being its 'instrument of constitution'. Article 9(2) of the Directive is implemented by CA 1985, ss. 35A and 35B. The Directive was drafted before the UK joined the Community and uses the unfamiliar concept of an 'organ' of a company, in the sense of an instrumentality by which acts of the company are performed. In the British implementing legislation the board of directors of a company is given the role of the 'competent organ'. See further 19.5.6 and V. Edwards, '*Ultra vires* and directors' authority — an EC perspective' (1995) 16 Co Law 202. CA 1985, s. 35A, provides:

(1) In favour of a person dealing with a company in good faith, the power of the board of directors to bind the company, or authorise others to do so, shall be deemed to be free of any limitation under the company's constitution.

(2) For this purpose—

(a) a person 'deals with' a company if he is a party to any transaction or other act to which the company is a party;

(b) a person shall not be regarded as acting in bad faith by reason only of his knowing that an act is beyond the powers of the directors under the company's constitution; and

(c) a person shall be presumed to have acted in good faith unless the contrary is proved.

(3) The references above to limitations on the directors' powers under the company's constitution include limitations deriving—

(a) from a resolution of the company in general meeting or a meeting of any class of shareholders, or

(b) from any agreement between the members of the company or of any class of shareholders.

Also, by s. 35B:

A party to a transaction with a company is not bound to enquire as to whether it is permitted by the company's memorandum or as to any limitation on the powers of the board of directors to bind the company or authorise others to do so.

If the board of directors of a company purport to exercise a power to bind the company to a transaction or act, or authorise others to do so, outside a limitation under the company's constitution then the company cannot claim that, for the purposes of s. 35A(2), it is not a party to the transaction or act so that any other party to the transaction or act has not dealt with the company and so cannot claim the protection of s. 35A — the purpose of the section is to validate purported transactions and acts (*TCB Ltd* v *Gray* [1986] Ch 621, point not considered on appeal). However, it has been suggested that ss. 35A and 35B cannot apply if persons who act as if they are the board of directors of a company but in fact are not (because they were not properly appointed, or because their decision was taken at an inquorate board meeting) purport to cause the company to enter into a transaction (E. Ferran, 'The reform of the law on corporate capacity and directors' and officers' authority: part 2' (1992) 13 Co Law 177 at p. 178). If the sections do not apply in these circumstances then the contractor would have to rely on the common law indoor management rule. The distinction, if it exists, is hard to justify.

Sections 35A and 35B replace the provisions of CA 1985, s. 35, as originally enacted. (The provision first appeared as European Communities Act 1972, s. 9(1), which was the first attempt to comply with the First Company Law Directive.) Section 35 as originally enacted had caused some problems of interpretation, which the new provisions attempt to solve.

The definition of 'deals with' a company in s. 35A(2)(a) overrules the decision in *International Sales & Agencies Ltd* v *Marcus* [1982] 3 All ER 551. In that case, cheques were drawn on the company's bank account by a director in order to pay a debt incurred by a deceased fellow director for which the director who drew the cheques felt responsible but for which the company was not responsible. Lawson J held that the recipient of the cheques was not a person dealing with the company under s. 35 as originally enacted. The new s. 35A(2)(a) has overruled that.

The provision of s. 35A(2)(b) that a person is not to be regarded as acting in bad faith by reason only of his knowing that an act is beyond the directors' powers overrules the opinion of Lawson J in *International Sales & Agencies Ltd* v *Marcus* at p. 559. It is reinforced by the provision in s. 35B that a party to a transaction with a company has no duty to enquire whether it is permitted by the company's memorandum or whether there is any limitation on the powers of the board of directors to bind the company or authorise others to do so. Section 35B means that when a person invokes s. 35A to validate an irregular transaction of a company, it cannot be said that s. 35A does not apply because the circumstances were such that the person ought to have enquired about the regularity of the transaction. Section 35B applies to a party to a transaction with a company whether or not that party was acting in good faith. However, s. 35B applies only to 'transactions' and not to any 'other act' to which s. 35A would extend by virtue of s. 35A(2)(a).

On the other hand, an *obiter* comment of Nourse J on s. 35 as originally enacted still seems to be relevant to the new s. 35A. His lordship said, in *Barclays Bank Ltd* v *TOSG Trust Fund Ltd* [1984] BCLC 1, at p. 18, that '. . . a person acts in good faith if he acts genuinely and honestly in the circumstances of the case', but in order to show that he acted in good faith it is not necessary to show that he acted reasonably. (The remark was *obiter* because his lordship found that it was unnecessary to rely on s. 35 as originally enacted to validate the transactions in question in the case and this was not pursued on appeal.)

In *TCB Ltd* v *Gray* [1986] Ch 621, a company's articles provided that whenever the company's seal was put on a document it had to be attested by the signature of a director. The company's seal was put on a debenture giving a floating charge on the company's property but was signed by an attorney for a director and not by a director. The company's articles did not permit a director to act by attorney in the matter. Browne-Wilkinson V-C held that the power of the directors to bind the company was deemed by the equivalent at the time of s. 35A(1) to be free from the limitation under the company's articles that they could not do so by attorney when attesting the sealing of a document. If this were not so then a person dealing with the company in good faith would have to assure himself that the directors had acted in accordance with the articles whereas the equivalent at the time of s. 35B says that he is not bound to enquire into any limitation under the memorandum or articles on the powers of the directors. (This point was not considered on appeal.)

Article 9 of Directive 68/151/EEC is concerned to prevent the validity of a transaction with a company from depending on the company's own constitution: it does not affect laws which make company contracts invalid for other reasons, such as conflict of duty and interest on the part of the directors who made the contract (see 16.5; *Coöperatieve Rabobank 'Vecht en Plassengebied' BA* v *Minderhoud* (case C-104/96) [1998] 1 WLR 1025).

19.5.6 Authority of a board of directors

In *Heiton* v *Waverley Hydropathic Co. Ltd* (1877) 4 R 830, Lord President Inglis said, at p. 843:

> The fundamental doctrine of the law of partnership in the case of ordinary mercantile companies is, that every individual partner of the company may bind the company in all ordinary transactions, and that each partner has an implied mandate to that effect. But in the case of a joint-stock company . . . there is no room for such a presumption as that, because the very nature of the association renders it indispensable that there should be a directorial body to carry on the business of the company, and the constitution of the body of directors of course takes away at once the power of any individual member of the company to bind the company. But it does more than that, for it creates a presumption of a different kind — a presumption that the whole business of the company is to be done by the directors and by nobody else, and in no other way; and the public are entitled to expect that everything that the directors do shall be valid and binding upon the company.

In *Ferguson* v *Wilson* (1866) LR 2 Ch App 77, Cairns LJ said at pp. 89–90:

> The company itself cannot act in its own person . . . it can only act through directors, and the case is, as regards those directors, merely the ordinary case of principal and agent.

This statement is not consistent with the idea that the board of directors of a company is an organ of the company which acts as the company rather than as agent for it, as suggested by the realist theory of corporate personality (see 5.3.1).

The directors must act as a board, unless they delegate their powers. In *Re Marseilles Extension Railway Co., ex parte Crédit Foncier & Mobilier of England* (1871) LR 7 Ch App 161, Mellish LJ said, at p. 168, '. . . a director is simply a person appointed to act as one of a board, with power to bind the company when acting as a board, but having otherwise no power to bind them'. Table A, art. 72, permits the board to delegate their powers to a committee, a managing director or an executive director. In *Mitchell and Hobbs (UK) Ltd* v *Mill* [1996] 2 BCLC 102, one of two directors of a company instructed solicitors to bring legal proceedings in the name of the company. There was no evidence that he had been delegated authority to do this by the board and there had been no board meeting to ratify his action, which was in fact opposed by the other director. Accordingly the proceedings were struck out as unauthorised.

CA 1985 treats the board of directors of a company as primarily authorised to make contracts on behalf of the company. By virtue of s. 35A(1), in favour of a person dealing with a company in good faith, the company cannot claim that the actual authority of its board to make contracts on its behalf is limited in any way by the company's constitution or (s. 35A(3)) by a resolution of or agreement between the members.

Under Table A, art. 70, '. . . the business of the company shall be managed by the directors who may exercise all the powers of the company'. This is stated to be 'Subject to the provisions of [the Companies Act 1985 as amended], the memorandum and the articles and to any directions given by special resolution'. Thus if a company has Table A as its articles of association and its board of directors make any kind of contract that directors can make with a person dealing with the company in good faith, either the contract is within the board's actual authority under art. 70, or any limitations on their actual authority permitted by art. 70 are deemed by s. 35A(1) not to exist.

19.5.7 Actual authority limited by the company's objects

The actual authority of the directors of a company to act on its behalf is limited to acting for the purpose of, or reasonably incidental to, attaining or pursuing the company's objects.

Under the common law, a person making a contract with a company through an agent of the company, knowing or having constructive notice that the contract was outside the company's objects, and therefore outside the agent's actual authority, would not be able to rely on the agent's ostensible authority (*Re Introductions Ltd* [1970] Ch 199; *Rolled Steel Products (Holdings) Ltd* v *British Steel Corporation* [1986] Ch 246, CA). However, under CA 1985, s. 35A, a contract between a company and a contractor made through the agency of the company's board of directors, or any person authorised by the board, is enforceable by the contractor despite being outside the company's objects even if the contractor was informed, or had constructive notice, that the contract was outside the objects. Section 35A provides that, in favour of a person dealing in good faith with a company, the power of the board of directors to bind the company, or authorise others to do so, is deemed to be free of any limitation under the company's constitution, such as a limitation to act within the objects specified in the company's memorandum. A person is not to be regarded as acting in bad faith in this context by reason only of knowing that an act is beyond the powers of the directors under the company's constitution (s. 35A(2)(b)). Furthermore, a party to a transaction with a company, whether acting in good faith or not, has no duty to enquire whether it is permitted by the company's memorandum (s. 35B). It follows that a company cannot now repudiate a transaction with a contractor on the ground that it is outside the company's objects (and therefore outside the actual authority of the person who acted on the company's behalf in the transaction), unless the contractor was acting in bad faith or the transaction is covered by s. 322A — see 19.5.9 — or, in certain circumstances, if the company is a charity — see 19.5.11. If a transaction with a company is in one of these exceptional classes then it may be necessary to analyse the company's memorandum to establish whether the transaction is outside the company's objects.

The company object for which a transaction is entered into is not always implicit in the transaction itself. For example, when a company borrows money there is normally no implication that the money will be used for any particular purpose. If a particular act of the directors is of a category which is *capable* of being performed as reasonably incidental to the attainment or pursuit of the company's objects then it is within their ostensible authority (*Rolled Steel Products (Holdings) Ltd* v *British Steel Corporation* per Slade LJ at p. 295, Browne-Wilkinson LJ at p. 306). In *Rolled Steel Products (Holdings) Ltd* v *British Steel Corporation*, Slade LJ summarised the law as follows, at p. 295:

A company holds out its directors as having *ostensible* authority to bind the company to any transaction which falls within the powers expressly or impliedly conferred on it by its memorandum of association. . . . a person dealing in good faith with a company . . . is entitled to assume that its directors are properly exercising such powers for the purposes of the company as set out in its memorandum. Correspondingly, such a person in such circumstances can hold the company to any transaction of this nature.

For example, in *Re David Payne & Co. Ltd* [1904] 2 Ch 608, David Payne & Co. Ltd borrowed money which was not used for its own purposes but to pay the personal debts of its controller. It was held that the company could not avoid the loan. The lender was not bound to inquire how the borrowing company would use the borrowed money.

19.5.8   Ratification of acts outside actual authority

If an act of a company's agent is outside the agent's actual authority then it is possible for the act to be ratified by the company: ratification supplies the lacking authority and adopts the act as an act of the company.

The general rule is that if the board of directors of a company have acted on behalf of the company outside their actual authority then the act may be ratified by the members in general meeting by ordinary resolution (*Grant v United Kingdom Switchback Railways Co.* (1888) 40 ChD 135, CA).

If some person other than the board of directors has acted outside actual authority then the board of directors may ratify the act if it is within the board's actual authority. Similarly, the acts of an agent appointed, under delegated authority, by any person other than the board of directors may be ratified by that person if within that person's actual authority.

The exception to the general rule is that if an unauthorised act of any agent of a company would have been beyond the company's capacity but for CA 1985, s. 35(1) (under which a company's capacity is not limited by its memorandum), then ratification must be by a special resolution of the members (s. 35(3)). A special resolution ratifying an act which would have been beyond the company's capacity but for s. 35(1) does not affect any liability incurred by the directors or any other person; relief from any such liability must be agreed to separately by special resolution (s. 35(3)).

The usual reason why an act would be beyond a company's capacity but for s. 35(1) is that the act is not capable of being within the company's objects (the old *ultra vires* rule, see 19.4.1).

If an agent of a company causes it to enter into a transaction for a purpose outside its objects then there are two possibilities:

(a)   The transaction is not capable of being within the objects and so would have been beyond the company's capacity under the old *ultra vires* rule. Such a transaction is described as '*ultra vires* in the narrow sense'.

(b)   The transaction is capable of being within the company's objects. Such a transaction would have been within the company's capacity under the old *ultra vires* rule but is still outside the agent's actual authority. This second kind of transaction is described as '*ultra vires* in the wider sense'.

Acts which are *ultra vires* in the narrow sense are, by s. 35(1), no longer void for lack of capacity but they are nevertheless beyond actual authority. Section 35(3) empowers the members of a company to ratify by special resolution an act of the company's directors which is *ultra vires* in the narrow sense. Such a resolution would cure the directors' lack of actual authority.

Acts which are *ultra vires* in the wider sense never have been void for lack of contractual capacity. Accordingly s. 35(3) does not apply to them so they can be ratified by ordinary resolution and only an ordinary resolution is necessary to relieve directors of liability for them.

For example, in *Irvine* v *Union Bank of Australia* (1877) 2 App Cas 366 there was no limitation on the company's borrowing powers but the directors were limited to borrowing a sum equal to half the company's paid-up capital. The Privy Council held that the company in general meeting could ratify borrowing by the directors in excess of their borrowing powers. It would also seem that a public company is required to ratify any business done or borrowing power exercised in breach of CA 1985, s. 117 (s. 117(8), see 6.6.1). Ratification by the members of a contract in respect of which the directors were disqualified from voting was allowed by the Court of Appeal in *Grant* v *United Kingdom Switchback Railways Co.* Corporate litigation which is instituted without authority may be ratified by the company in general meeting (*Danish Mercantile Co. Ltd* v *Beaumont* [1951] Ch 680, CA).

It is necessary in this connection to distinguish the ratification of past acts which were not authorised by the articles, and which is effected by ordinary resolution, and the authorisation of future acts which are not permitted by the articles, which is not ratification but an alteration of the articles and must be effected by special resolution (see 3.5.1) (*Irvine* v *Union Bank of Australia* at pp. 375–6). As Cotton LJ said in *Grant* v *United Kingdom Switchback Railways Co.* at p. 138:

> The ratifying a particular contract which had been entered into by the directors without authority, and so making it an act of the company, is quite a different thing from altering the articles. To give the directors power to do things in future which the articles did not authorise them to do, would be an alteration of the articles, but it is no alteration of the articles to ratify a contract which has been made without authority.

The members may ratify a contract which an individual director has entered into when it should have been decided on by the entire board (*Re Horsley & Weight Ltd* [1982] Ch 442, CA).

19.5.9 Transactions to which directors are party

In general, if the board of directors of a company enter into a transaction, on the company's behalf, with a person who is dealing with the company in good faith then the fact that the board have exceeded any limitation on their powers under the company's constitution does not entitle the company to repudiate the transaction. This is because, by virtue of CA 1985, s. 35A(1), the power of the board of directors to bind the company is, in such circumstances, deemed to be free of any limitation under the company's constitution. However, by s. 322A, a transaction is voidable, at the option of the company, on the ground that the directors have exceeded a limitation on their powers under the company's constitution (such as the limitation to act only within the company's objects) if the parties to the transaction include:

(a) a director of the company or of its holding company, or

(b) a person connected with such a director or a company with whom such a director is associated (for the meaning of 'connection' and 'association' in this context see 16.6.8.10).

The persons listed in paragraphs (a) and (b) will be referred to in this discussion as 'insiders'.

'Transaction' includes any act (s. 322A(8)).

The section makes a transaction to which an insider is a party voidable if, in connection with the transaction, the board of directors exceeded any limitation on their powers under the company's constitution. This includes, by s. 322A(8), any limitations deriving:

(a)   from a resolution of the company in general meeting or a meeting of any class of shareholders, or

(b)   from any agreement between the members of the company or of any class of shareholders.

The provision clearly applies where the directors have acted without actual authority — for example, where they have acted outside the company's objects. It is questionable, however, whether it operates when the directors misuse their authority and act in a way that is not bona fide in the interests of the company or for an improper purpose other than a purpose outside the company's objects (see 16.4).

If an insider is party to a transaction in connection with which the board exceeded their powers under the company's constitution then the transaction ceases to be voidable if (s. 322A(5)):

(a)   restitution of any money or other asset which was the subject-matter of the transaction is no longer possible, or

(b)   the company is indemnified for any loss or damage resulting from the transaction, or

(c)   rights acquired bona fide for value and without actual notice of the directors' exceeding their powers by a person who is not party to the transaction would be affected by the avoidance, or

(d)   the transaction is ratified by the company in general meeting, by ordinary or special resolution or otherwise as the case may require.

A special resolution is required to ratify a transaction which was not capable of being within the company's objects (s. 35(3)).

Whether or not a transaction of a company to which an insider is a party is avoided, any insider who is party to the transaction, and any director of the company who authorised the transaction is liable by s. 322A(3):

(a)   to account to the company for any gain which he has made directly or indirectly by the transaction, and

(b)   to indemnify the company for any loss or damage resulting from the transaction.

A person other than a director of the company is not liable under s. 322A(3) if he shows that at the time the transaction was entered into he did not know that the directors were exceeding their powers.

The fact that a transaction to which an insider is a party which is outside the company's objects has been ratified by special resolution (that is, the company has supplied the lack of authority and adopted the transaction) does not affect any liability under s. 322A(3): relief from such liability must be agreed to separately by special resolution (s. 35(3)).

If the board of directors of a company have exceeded their powers under the company's constitution in relation to a transaction of the company then the fact that an insider was a party to the transaction, so bringing it within s. 322A, does not affect the protection given by s. 35A to any party who is not an insider (s. 322A(7)). If a transaction is voidable under s. 322A but valid under s. 35A then an application may be made to the court, which may affirm, sever or set aside the transaction on such terms as appear to it to be just (s. 322A(7)).

If a private limited company (other than a hybrid company) has only one member who is also a director or shadow director of the company then s. 322B (inserted by SI 1992 No. 1699) requires that any contract between the company and the director/member otherwise than in the ordinary course of the company's business must be recorded in writing. If the contract itself is not in writing, its terms must be set out in a written memorandum or recorded in the minutes of the first board meeting after the contract is made. Failure to comply does not affect the validity of the contract (s. 322B(6)) but the company and every officer who knowingly and wilfully authorised or permitted the default will have committed an offence (ss. 322B(4) and 730(5); penalty in sch. 24). A contract between a subsidiary company and its holding company is not subject to s. 322B if the only reason for treating the holding company as a shadow director of the subsidiary is that the subsidiary's directors are accustomed to act in accordance with the holding company's directions or instructions (s. 741(3)). The source of s. 322B is art. 5 of the 12th Company Law Directive.

19.5.10 Authority of a company secretary

In *Panorama Developments (Guildford) Ltd* v *Fidelis Furnishing Fabrics Ltd* [1971] 2 QB 711, the plaintiff company carried on a car hire business. The defendant company's secretary hired cars from the plaintiff company apparently for use in the course of the defendant company's business. The hire agreements were in the secretary's name and signed by him as 'Company Secretary'. The cars were used for the secretary's own purposes and not by the defendant company. The plaintiff company sued the defendant company for non-payment of the hire charges. The Court of Appeal held that the company secretary had apparent or ostensible authority to enter into contracts connected with the administrative side of the defendant company's affairs, including the hiring of cars. The defendant company was accordingly liable to pay the hire charges. Lord Denning MR said of a company secretary:

> He is an officer of the company with extensive duties and responsibilities. This appears not only in the modern Companies Acts, but also by the role which he plays in the day-to-day business of companies. He is no longer a mere clerk. He regularly makes representations on behalf of the company and enters into contracts on its behalf which come within the day-to-day running of the company's business. So much so that he may be regarded as held out as having authority to do such things on behalf of the company. He is certainly entitled to sign contracts connected with the administrative side of a company's affairs, such as employing staff, and ordering cars, and so forth. All such matters now come within the ostensible authority of a company's secretary.

Panorama Developments (Guildford) Ltd v *Fidelis Furnishing Fabrics Ltd* has not altered the rule that the secretary of a company does not have authority, other than by specific delegation, to institute legal proceedings in the company's name (*Daimler Co. Ltd* v *Continental Tyre & Rubber Co. (Great Britain) Ltd* [1916] 2 AC 307, HL; *Club Flotilla (Pacific Palms) Ltd* v *Isherwood* (1987) 12 ACLR 387) nor the rule that the secretary does not have authority to make entries in the company's register of members (*Re Zinotty Properties Ltd* [1984] 1 WLR 1249, see 8.3.4).

19.5.11   Charitable companies

By s. 65 of the Charities Act 1993, the new ss. 35 and 35A of CA 1985 do not apply to the acts of a charity which is a company (see also 19.4.2) except in favour of a person who:

(a)   gives full consideration in money or money's worth in relation to the act in question, and

(b)   does not know that the act is not permitted by the company's memorandum or, as the case may be, is beyond the powers of the directors,

or who does not know at the time the act is done that the company is a charity (see 4.5.5).

However, CA 1985, s. 35B (no duty to enquire as to capacity of company or authority of directors), does apply to a charitable company.

By the Charities Act 1993, s. 65(4), a ratification under CA 1985, s. 35(3), or a ratification of a transaction to which s. 322A applies, is ineffective without the prior written consent of the Charity Commissioners.

19.6   PRE-INCORPORATION AND POST-DISSOLUTION CONTRACTS

19.6.1   Personal liability

When people wish to pursue a business opportunity and incorporate a company for the purpose they may make contracts before the company is incorporated. These are called 'pre-incorporation contracts' and they may be made in the following circumstances:

(a)   Where promoters make arrangements which they intend that the company, when incorporated, will carry out.

(b)   Where people make contracts for the company, perhaps even describing themselves as 'directors', unaware of, or disregarding, the fact that the company is not yet incorporated.

The common law attempted to distinguish whether it was intended that the contract should be with the company (in which case, the company being non-existent, there would be no contract at all) or directly with the person who was acting in relation to the company (in which case that person would be liable on the contract). In *Kelner* v *Baxter* (1866) LR 2 CP 174, the person acting in relation to the non-existent company was held liable on the contract, and it used to be thought that this imposed an absolute rule that a person purporting to make a contract for a non-existent company would always be personally liable. However, in *Newborne* v *Sensolid (Great Britain) Ltd* [1954] 1 QB 45, the supposed contract was held to have been with the non-existent company and therefore not a contract at all. That the position depends on the intention of the parties when the contract was formed was suggested by Oliver LJ in *Phonogram Ltd* v *Lane* [1982] QB 938, CA, and has been applied by the Court of Appeal in *Cotronic (UK) Ltd* v *Dezonie* [1991] BCLC 721.

The law relating to pre-incorporation contracts was altered on 1 January 1973 when European Communities Act 1972, s. 9(2), came into force, enacted to implement art. 7 of the EEC First Company Law Directive. That provision has been re-enacted, with slight changes, as CA 1985, s. 36C(1):

A contract which purports to be made by or on behalf of a company at a time when the company has not been formed has effect, subject to any agreement to the contrary, as one made with the person purporting to act for the company or as agent for it, and he is personally liable on the contract accordingly.

The subsection applies to both of the situations distinguished by the common law (*Phonogram Ltd* v *Lane*). It applies to the making of a deed under the law of England or Wales as it applies to the making of a contract (s. 36C(2)). It applies even if the company is never in fact registered (*Phonogram Ltd* v *Lane*). It does not apply to a contract purportedly made on behalf of a company which is subsequently incorporated outside Great Britain (*Rover International Ltd* v *Cannon Film Sales Ltd* [1987] BCLC 540, in which the point was not pursued on appeal and the question of whether the liability of the individual who purported to act for the company might be governed by the law of the place in which the company was eventually incorporated was not argued).

In *Phonogram Ltd* v *Lane,* it was suggested that, for the purpose of s. 36C(1), a contract is only 'purported' to be made by a company when there has been a representation that the company is already in existence. Lord Denning MR (with whom Shaw and Oliver LJJ agreed) said, at p. 943:

I do not agree. A contract can purport to be made on behalf of a company, or by a company, even though that company is known by both parties not to be formed and that it is only about to be formed.

It may be concluded, therefore, that, subject to any agreement to the contrary, promoters are now personally liable in respect of all pre-incorporation contracts made for the benefit of their unformed company, irrespective of the capacity in which they purport to contract and irrespective of their subjective beliefs.

If promoters make contracts before buying a company off the shelf then, provided the company they buy was in existence at the time the contracts were made, CA 1985, s. 36C, does not apply and the company can ratify the contracts, though the promoters must have made it clear that they were acting as agents for the company when they made the contracts. It makes no difference that the shelf company did not have the right name at the time the contracts were made (*Oshkosh B'Gosh Inc.* v *Dan Marbel Inc. Ltd* [1989] BCLC 507, CA). It is, however, easy to make mistakes in this situation. In *Cross* v *Aurora Group Ltd* (1988) 4 NZCLC 64,909, Mr Cross made a contract on behalf of 'Cross Property Management Ltd a company currently being formed'. He then bought a shelf company, which was in existence at the time the contract was made, and changed its name to Cross Properties Management Ltd. It was held that this company could not adopt the contract. It was not the company Mr Cross was purporting to act for because it had already been formed when the contract was made.

Persons who work together to form a registered company and order goods for the company and open a bank account, are not carrying on a business so as to be in partnership (*Keith Spicer Ltd* v *Mansell* [1970] 1 WLR 333, CA).

CA 1985, s. 36C, does not apply when a person purports to make a contract for a company which once existed but has been dissolved (*Cotronic (UK) Ltd* v *Dezonie*). However, the person purporting to represent the non-existent company can sue for a *quantum meruit* for any work he or she does under the supposed contract (*Cotronic (UK) Ltd* v *Dezonie*) or, if the obligations apparently undertaken by the non-existent company under the supposed contract are not performed, the person who purported to represent it can be sued for damages for breach of warranty of authority (*Royal Bank of Canada* v *Starr* (1985) 31 BLR 124, Ontario).

19.6.2　Agreement to the contrary and novation

A person who makes a pre-incorporation contract, purporting to act for, or as agent for, the company may avoid personal liability for the contract by entering into an 'agreement to the contrary' (CA 1985, s. 36C(1)). In *Phonogram Ltd* v *Lane* [1982] QB 938, it was suggested that if it was stated that a person making a pre-incorporation contract was acting as agent for the future company then it could be inferred that an agreement had been made excluding what is now s. 36C. The Court of Appeal firmly rejected this idea. Oliver LJ pointed out, at p. 946, that the provision was specifically expressed to apply to a contract which purported to be made by a person as agent so that, rather than excluding the provision, stating that one is acting as agent in fact brings it into operation.

An express agreement simply to exclude s. 36C from operating on a contract seems unlikely because it would mean that there would be no enforceable contract at all. What may be provided in a pre-incorporation contract is that the person making the pre-incorporation contract will be released from liability on it if the company, after it has been incorporated, enters into a second contract with the contractor in the same terms as the pre-incorporation contract. This is known as a 'novation'. The problem for the contractor is to prove that the company did make a new contract after incorporation — the general attitude of the courts seems to be to require very clear evidence (*Bagot Pneumatic Tyre Co.* v *Clipper Pneumatic Tyre Co.* [1902] 1 Ch 146, CA). Simply acting in the mistaken belief that a pre-incorporation contract is binding is not enough (*Re Northumberland Avenue Hotel Co.* (1886) 33 ChD 16, CA). However, if a company, after incorporation, takes possession of property transferred to it in a pre-incorporation contract, the court may be able to infer that the only possible explanation is that a new contract was made after incorporation (*Re Patent Ivory Manufacturing Co.* (1888) 38 ChD 156; *Heinhuis* v *Blacksheep Charters Ltd* (1987) 46 DLR (4th) 67, British Columbia).

The fact that the terms of a pre-incorporation contract are stated in the company's articles, giving authority to adopt the contract, is not in itself evidence that there actually was a novation (*Melhado* v *Pôrto Alegre, New Hamburgh, & Brazilian Railway Co.* (1874) LR 9 CP 503; *Eley* v *Positive Government Security Life Assurance Co. Ltd* (1876) 1 ExD 88, CA; *Re Hereford & South Wales Waggon & Engineering Co.* (1876) 2 ChD 621, CA; *Browne* v *La Trinidad* (1887) 37 ChD 1, CA; *Re Dale & Plant Ltd* (1889) 61 LT 206).

A company cannot simply ratify a contract purportedly made on its behalf before it was incorporated so as to make the contract in its original form valid: the contract could not have been a valid contract within the company when it was made because the company did not exist then, and the company cannot retrospectively supply the person who made the contract with authority to act as its agent because the company could not have had any agents when it did not exist (*Kelner* v *Baxter* (1866) LR 2 CP 174; *Re Empress Engineering Co.* (1880) 16 ChD 125, CA; *Natal Land & Colonization Co. Ltd* v *Pauline Colliery & Development Syndicate Ltd* [1904] AC 120, PC).

19.6.3　Further reading

J.H. Gross, 'Pre-incorporation contracts' (1971) 87 LQR 367 gives an extensive survey of the law as it was before 1973, with references to the situation in the USA and Canada. When the new law was first enacted it was commented on in D.D. Prentice, 'Section 9 of the European Communities Act' (1973) 89 LQR 518 at pp. 530–3 . For an extended discussion of the new law, see N.N. Green, 'Security of transaction after *Phonogram*' (1984) 47 MLR 671 and A. Griffiths, 'Agents without principals: pre-incorporation contracts and section 36C of the Companies Act 1985' (1993) 13 LS 241.

19.7 VICARIOUS LIABILITY FOR TORTS

A company is liable for any torts it commits, for example, by publishing a newspaper containing a defamatory libel. Like any other employer, a company is vicariously liable for torts committed by its employees in the course of their employment. A company's vicarious liability for another's tort does not mean that the company is regarded as having committed the tort: the company is liable for someone else's commission of the tort under a liability which arises because of the company's employment of that other person. The company's capacity to commit the tort is therefore irrelevant. For example, in *Citizens' Life Assurance Co. Ltd* v *Brown* [1904] AC 423, the insurance company was held to be vicariously liable for a defamatory libel which one of its employees published in the course of his employment. The jury found that the employee had acted with what is known in libel law as 'express malice' so that he would not have been able to claim the defence of qualified privilege had he been sued personally. It was argued for the company that 'malice' had no meaning in relation to a company so it could claim the defence, but this missed the point that the company was being made liable for its employee's actions and motives, not its own. Lord Lindley, giving the judgment of the Privy Council, said, at p. 426:

> To talk about imputing malice to corporations appears to their lordships to introduce metaphysical subtleties which are needless and fallacious. Their lordships concur with the view of the Acting Chief Justice [of New South Wales] in this case that, if [the employee] published the libel complained of in the course of his employment, the company are liable for it on the ordinary principles of agency.

In *W.B. Anderson and Sons Ltd* v *Rhodes (Liverpool) Ltd* [1967] 2 All ER 850, Rhodes (Liverpool) Ltd acted as agent for a company called Taylors (Corn and Produce) Ltd making contracts by which Taylors bought potatoes. The employee of Rhodes who made the contracts told the sellers that Taylors was creditworthy but in fact it was not. That employee would only have known that Taylors was a bad payer if either Rhodes's manager or its bookkeeper had told him but they negligently did not. The manager and bookkeeper were not liable for negligent misrepresentation because they made no representations. The employee who did make the representations was not negligent. Even so Rhodes was held vicariously liable for negligent misrepresentation. The court aggregated the negligence of two employees with the representation made by the third to create the employer's liability.

Vicarious liability for crimes is considered in 19.8.4.

19.8 IDENTIFICATION OF HUMANS WITH A COMPANY

19.8.1 Introduction

A company as a separate person is not a human person and therefore it cannot itself do things which require human thought or action. A legal penalty or detriment for an act — particularly a criminal liability — is usually thought of as deserved only by a person who consciously chose to act in the way that attracts the penalty. This is at the heart of the concept of *mens rea* in criminal law and is often reflected in the wording of legislation imposing penalties. Nevertheless it has been found to be expedient to make companies liable to penalties for wrongful acts by attributing to a company the wrongful acts and thoughts of humans identified with the company.

Many civil law rights and liabilities attach only to persons who have requisite knowledge. To make these concepts applicable to companies as separate persons it is necessary to attribute to companies the knowledge of humans identified with them.

The rules of attribution discussed so far in this chapter are not intended to cover these situations and so it is necessary for the courts to devise appropriate rules.

For example, in *Lennard's Carrying Co. Ltd* v *Asiatic Petroleum Co. Ltd* [1915] AC 705, a shipowning company, Lennard's Carrying Co. Ltd, attempted to claim the protection of the Merchant Shipping Act 1894, s. 502, which provided that a shipowner was not liable for fire damage to goods on board the ship which happened 'without his actual fault or privity'. The company owned a ship which had carried a cargo of benzine consigned to the Asiatic Petroleum Co. Ltd. The ship ran aground because its boilers were in such a poor state that there was not enough power to navigate the vessel. Grounding the ship damaged the cargo holds. The benzine escaped and exploded when it came into contact with the boiler fires. The evidence showed that Mr J.M. Lennard, a director of the shipowning company, knew, or ought to have known, that the ship was unseaworthy. Viscount Haldane LC said, at pp. 713–14:

> . . . did what happened take place without the actual fault or privity of the owners of the ship who were the appellants? . . . a corporation is an abstraction. It has no mind of its own any more than it has a body of its own; its active and directing will must consequently be sought in the person of somebody who for some purposes may be called an agent, but who is really the directing mind and will of the corporation, the very ego and centre of the personality of the corporation. . . . If Mr Lennard was the directing mind of the company, then his action must, unless a corporation is not to be liable at all, have been an action which was the action of the company itself within the meaning of s. 502. . . . It must be upon the true construction of that section in such a case as the present one that the fault or privity is the fault or privity of . . . somebody for whom the company is liable because his action is the very action of the company itself.

The company could have had the benefit of s. 502 if it had shown that Mr Lennard's position was such that his fault was not the company's fault or a fault to which the company was privy. However, the burden of proving this was on the company and as it had not discharged that burden it was liable.

The Admiralty Court developed an extensive case law on the liability of companies under s. 502 of the Merchant Shipping Act 1894, and the similar s. 503 (which limited liability for various matters including damage caused by improper navigation of the ship). See, for example, *The Lady Gwendolen* [1965] P 294 and *The Ert Stefanie* [1987] 2 Lloyd's Rep 371. In *The Lady Gwendolen*, Sellers LJ said, at p. 333, that in order to show that something had been done without the actual fault or privity of a shipowning company it is necessary to show that it was done without the actual fault or privity of the person or persons in the company who were 'in charge of and responsible, in the capacity of the owners, for the running of the ships'. Willmer LJ, at p. 343, said that this did not have to be a director, though in this case the court approved the finding of the judge at first instance that it was one of the company's assistant managing directors. Sections 502 and 503 have since been repealed and shipowners' liability is now governed by an international convention.

The principle that one or more humans associated with a company can be identified with it for the purpose of attributing a human thought or action to the company is usually known as the 'identification theory'. Some commentators, however, refer to it as the 'organic theory', which was the terminology used in *Gower's Principles of Modern Company Law* (see 5th ed., pp. 193–8, where it is explained that individuals identified with a company are treated as organic parts of the company), though it has been dropped in favour of 'identification' in the 6th ed. Other commentators refer to it as the 'alter ego theory', saying either that the person identified with the company is its alter ego (second self) or that the company is the alter ego of the person identified with it. See for example, G. Virgo, 'Stealing from the small family business' [1991] CLJ 464 at p. 478, n. 67. In *UBAF Ltd* v *European American Banking Corporation* [1984] QB 713, the Court of Appeal said, at pp. 719–20, that it found the description of a person as a company's 'alter ego', '. . . largely meaningless, save as an indication of some very wide but undefined authority'. In *Cristina* v *Seear* [1985] 2 EGLR 128, Purchas LJ was equally dubious about describing a company as an alter ego of its members.

19.8.2 Enemy character

In time of war it is illegal for any person bound in loyalty to the Crown to trade with the enemy power or its subjects. This is now largely governed by statutory provisions in the Trading with the Enemy Act 1939. Under s. 2(1) of that Act, any corporation controlled by an enemy is deemed to be an enemy itself. In the First World War, there was no legislative provision for determining whether a body corporate was an enemy and there were no common law rules because the use of registered companies for trading had developed since Britain was last engaged in a large-scale European war. The question came before the courts in the controversial case of *Daimler Co. Ltd* v *Continental Tyre & Rubber Co. (Great Britain) Ltd* [1916] 2 AC 307. Daimler Co. Ltd claimed that it did not have to pay money it owed to the respondent company because to do so would be trading with the enemy (namely Germany). The respondent company was incorporated in England to sell tyres made by a German company. Of its 25,000 shares, only one was held by a person who was not German. All the directors were German and none of them had been in England since the outbreak of war. The company secretary had issued a writ in the company's name against Daimler Co. Ltd but the House of Lords held he had no authority to control the company's litigation so that the writ was of no effect. The Law Lords also dealt with the question whether the company was an enemy. Lord Parker of Waddington said, at pp. 344–5:

(1)   A company incorporated in the United Kingdom is a legal entity, a creation of law with the status and capacity which the law confers. It is not a natural person with mind or conscience. To use the language of Buckley LJ, 'it can be neither loyal nor disloyal. It can be neither friend nor enemy.'

(2)   Such a company can only act through agents properly authorised, and so long as it is carrying on business in this country through agents so authorised and residing in this or a friendly country it is prima facie to be regarded as a friend, and all His Majesty's lieges may deal with it as such.

(3)   Such a company may, however, assume an enemy character. This will be the case if its agents or the persons in *de facto* control of its affairs, whether authorised or not, are resident in an enemy country, or, wherever resident, are adhering to the enemy or taking instructions from or acting under the control of enemies. A person knowingly dealing with the company in such a case is trading with the enemy.

His lordship went on to say that if the question was not settled by looking at the directors of the company then it was necessary to consider whether the members of the company were enemies in order to discover 'whether the company's agents, or the persons in *de facto* control of its affairs, are in fact adhering to, taking instructions from, or acting under the control of enemies'. (The case was heard by eight Law Lords and Lord Parker's judgment represented the views of four of them: himself, Lord Sumner, who helped to draft it,

Viscount Mersey and Lord Kinnear. The Earl of Halsbury LC thought that the company was a sham. Lord Parmoor and Lord Shaw of Dunfermline thought that it could not be an enemy.)

In *The Polzeath* [1916] P 241 and *The St Tudno* [1916] P 291, ships owned by English companies whose shareholders were enemy aliens were held to be enemy ships. (See also *The Hamborn* [1919] AC 993, PC, in which the shareholding was indirect.)

Even though a company registered in England and Wales has enemy character it is still an English company subject to English law: in particular it is not free to trade with the enemy (*Kuenigl v Donnersmarck* [1955] 1 QB 515).

19.8.3   Attribution of knowledge

If an individual can be identified with a company then that individual's knowledge may be regarded as the knowledge of the company if he or she is under a duty to communicate that knowledge to the company. For example, in *Belmont Finance Corporation v Williams Furniture Ltd (No. 2)* [1980] 1 All ER 393 (the facts of which are given in 10.8.4), the directors of Belmont Finance Corporation, in breach of their fiduciary duty, caused it to give illegal financial assistance for the purchase of its shares from its holding company, City Industrial Finance Ltd. Two directors and the secretary of City Industrial Finance Ltd knew about this (one of the directors and the secretary were directors of Belmont) and their knowledge was attributed to City Industrial Finance Ltd so that it could be declared to be a constructive trustee of the money it received for selling the shares. Buckley LJ said (at p. 404):

> . . . an officer of a company must surely be under a duty, if he is aware that a transaction into which his company or a wholly owned subsidiary is about to enter is illegal or tainted with illegality, to inform the board of that company of the fact.

See also *Re Little Olympian Each-Ways Ltd (No. 3)* [1995] 1 BCLC 636 discussed in 18.6.4. On the other hand, in *Re David Payne & Co. Ltd* [1904] 2 Ch 608 (the facts of which are given in 19.5.7), a company which lent money to David Payne & Co. Ltd was not bound to inquire how the borrowed money was to be used. Accordingly, one of the lending company's directors, who knew that the money was not going to be used within the objects of the borrowing company, was not under a duty to communicate that information to the lending company so the knowledge could not be imputed to the lending company.

An individual's knowledge of his or her own wrongdoing (whether it was fraudulent or merely an irregularity) cannot be imputed to a company with which the individual is identified (*Re Hampshire Land Co.* [1896] 2 Ch 743). In particular, knowledge of matters relevant to a fraud being perpetrated by the individual against the company itself cannot be imputed to the company and so the company cannot be guilty of conspiring with the individual to defraud itself (*Belmont Finance Corporation Ltd v Williams Furniture Ltd* [1979] Ch 250). But *Meridian Global Funds Management Asia Ltd v Securities Commission* [1995] 2 AC 500 and *Bank of Credit and Commerce International SA v Dawson* 1987 FLR 342, discussed in 19.8.6.1, are to the contrary. See also 19.8.6.3.

19.8.4   Criminal liability

Two early cases involving statutory companies established that it is possible to bring criminal proceedings against a body corporate (*R v Birmingham & Gloucester Railway Co.* (1842) 3 QB 223; *R v Great North of England Railway Co.* (1846) 9 QB 315).

It may be argued that there is something about a particular offence which prevents a company being charged with it. For example, it may be said that the offence can be committed only by someone performing some physical action, which a company is incapable of — for example, a company cannot be convicted of an offence which can be committed only by driving a lorry (*Richmond London Borough Council* v *Pinn & Wheeler Ltd* [1989] RTR 354). It has been said that where the only punishment that can be ordered for an offence is corporal (such as the mandatory sentence of life imprisonment, custody for life or detention during Her Majesty's pleasure which must be ordered for murder), a court would not 'stultify itself by embarking on a trial [of a company for the offence] in which, if a verdict of guilty is returned, no effective order by way of sentence can be made' (*R* v *ICR Haulage Ltd* [1944] KB 551 at p. 554). Whether or not a company may be guilty of a crime must be decided for each crime separately (*R* v *P & O European Ferries (Dover) Ltd* (1990) 93 Cr App R 72 per Turner J at p. 84) except where the question is settled by statutory definition of a particular crime. Many would say that Parliament is the proper forum for deciding such fundamental questions of criminal liability but Parliament has given no general guidance on the question, and the courts have proceeded cautiously.

It used to be thought that a company could not be charged with an offence which had a mental element requiring proof of a criminal state of mind (*mens rea*) (see per Channell J in *Pearks, Gunston & Tee Ltd* v *Ward* [1902] 2 KB 1 at p. 11). However, in *Director of Public Prosecutions* v *Kent & Sussex Contractors Ltd* [1944] KB 146, it was held that the identification theory could be used to make a company liable for such an offence.

In *Director of Public Prosecutions* v *Kent & Sussex Contractors Ltd,* the company's transport manager had signed a false statement of the distance that had been travelled by one of the company's vehicles, presumably in order to obtain an increased allocation of petrol under the rationing scheme then in force. The company was charged with two offences under the Defence (General) Regulations 1939: that, for the purposes of the petrol-rationing scheme, it had made use of a document which was false in a material particular, with intent to deceive; and that, in furnishing information for the purposes of the scheme, it made a statement which it knew to be false in a material particular. The magistrates' court refused to convict, saying that a limited company could not have an 'intent to deceive' and could not 'know' that a statement was false. The divisional court allowed the prosecutor's appeal. Macnaghten J, at p. 156, said:

It is true that a corporation can only have knowledge and form an intention through its human agents, but circumstances may be such that the knowledge and intention of the agent must be imputed to the body corporate.

Viscount Caldecote CJ said, at p. 155: 'The officers are the company for this purpose'. See further *R* v *ICR Haulage Ltd* [1944] KB 551, in which the Court of Criminal Appeal held that the company had been rightly convicted of a common-law conspiracy to defraud. Use of the identification theory to make a company criminally liable had been approved in the Canadian courts before it was adopted in England; see *R* v *Fane Robinson Ltd* [1941] 3 DLR 409, Alberta, which was also a case of conspiracy to defraud. The possibility of using the identification theory to make a company criminally liable had been put forward in an article by C.R.N Winn, 'The criminal responsibility of corporations' (1929) 3 CLJ 398.

In *Tesco Supermarkets Ltd* v *Nattrass* [1972] AC 153, Lord Reid said, at p. 170:

A living person has a mind which can have knowledge or intention or be negligent and he has hands to carry out his intentions. A corporation has none of these: it must act through living persons, though not always one or the same person. Then the person who acts is not speaking or acting for the company. He is acting as the company and his mind which directs his acts is the mind of the company. . . . He is an embodiment of the company or, one could say, he hears and speaks through the persona of the company, within his appropriate sphere, and his mind is the mind of the company. If it is a guilty mind then that guilt is the guilt of the company.

At p. 173, Lord Reid criticised a statement in *R* v *ICR Haulage Ltd* at p. 559 that the liability of a company for a criminal act of an individual identified with the company depends on the nature of the charge. In Lord Reid's view:

If the guilty man was in law identifiable with the company then whether his offence was serious or venial his act was the act of the company but if he was not so identifiable then no act of his, serious or otherwise, was the act of the company itself.

A company may be guilty of manslaughter. In *R* v *P & O European Ferries (Dover) Ltd*, the company which operated the cross-Channel ferry *Herald of Free Enterprise*, which capsized off Zeebrugge on 6 March 1987 with the loss of 192 lives, was indicted for manslaughter. The trial judge, Turner J, held that the indictment was valid. Five senior managers of the company were also indicted and tried with the company but the prosecution were unable to prove that any single one of those managers, who could be identified with the company, had the *mens rea* necessary to be guilty of manslaughter, and accordingly the necessary *mens rea* could not be attributed to the company. The judge rejected the argument that the company could be found guilty because of the collective fault of the individuals who could be identified with it (the principle of aggregation) and ruled that the company could be guilty only if one individual who could be identified with it was guilty. This contrasts with the use of aggregation in establishing vicarious liability for tort (see 19.7). On 19 October 1990 the judge directed the jury to find the company and the individual defendants not guilty (*R* v *Stanley*: details of the judge's ruling (which is otherwise unreported) are given in Law Commission, *Criminal Law: Involuntary Manslaughter* (Consultation Paper No. 135) (London: HMSO, 1994), paras 4.31 to 4.45).

The first ever conviction in England and Wales of a company for manslaughter was of OLL Ltd on 8 December 1994 at Winchester Crown Court. In that case, one individual who could be identified with the company, its managing director, Peter Kite, was found guilty of manslaughter so that his proven *mens rea* could be attributed to the company. OLL Ltd operated an activity centre. During a course at the centre a group of sixth-formers were sent on a canoeing trip across Lyme Bay on the south coast of England with hopelessly inadequate supervision and organisation so that four of them were drowned, having been wrongly instructed that they should not inflate their life-jackets if their canoes capsized. Evidence was given that the company routinely employed unqualified instructors and did not train them. The company was fined £60,000, which was said to represent its entire assets. Its managing director was sentenced to three years in prison, which was reduced on appeal to two years (*R* v *Kite* [1996] 2 Cr App R (S) 295).

R v *Stanley* and the OLL case show that if a crime is committed in the course of a company's business then conviction of the company will be easier the smaller it is, because a large company will be better able to claim that blame should be shared among more than one senior manager, none of whom is individually guilty of the crime. This situation is an affront to justice. The Law Commission has proposed the creation of a new offence of corporate killing, in which a death would be regarded as having been caused by the conduct of a corporation if it was caused by a failure, in the way in which the company's activities were managed or organised, to ensure the health and safety of persons employed in or affected by those activities. A company would be guilty of the proposed offence only if its conduct in causing the death fell far below what could reasonably be expected. The Commission has proposed that the offence should be formulated in such a way that it is not necessary to identify any individual with the company in order to convict it. Thus a company of any size could be convicted of the offence. It is also proposed that if a company is found guilty of corporate killing, the court should have power to order it to remedy the failures of management or organisation which caused the death. See Law Commission, *Legislating the Criminal Code: Involuntary Manslaughter* (Law Com. No. 237, House of Commons Papers, Session 1995–96, 171) (London: HMSO, 1996).

Just as an individual can be guilty of a crime if he or she instructs another to commit it, so a company which obtains the commission of a crime by an agent can be guilty of the crime. The agent who commits the criminal act may have no criminal intent and so be innocent but the company will be guilty if an individual identified with the company has the necessary criminal intent. In *Deutsche Genossenschaftsbank* v *Burnhope* [1995] 1 WLR 1580 it was accepted (though ultimately the point was not necessary for the decision in the case) that a company had been guilty of theft of property from a bank because the chairman of the company (who was identified with it) had the dishonest intention of permanently depriving the bank of the property, though the actual appropriation of the property was carried out by an innocent employee who was unaware of the chairman's plan. However, this point was *obiter* because the case was concerned with an insurer's liability for the bank's loss and it was held that the insurance policy did not cover thefts by companies. The policy referred to thefts by persons present on the bank's premises. The innocent employee had performed the appropriation on the bank's premises but the chairman was not with him. The bank argued that in the policy, the word 'person' included a company because of the Law of Property Act 1925, s. 61, which provides that in contracts 'person' includes a corporation unless the context otherwise requires. But a majority of the House of Lords held that the context of this insurance policy did otherwise require: the policy was concerned only with physically present thieves not a thief deemed in law to be present by an application of the identification theory, and in any case Lords Keith of Kinkel, Lloyd of Berwick and Nicholls of Birkenhead thought that the innocent employee was not identified with the company so that it was not present on the bank's premises.

In New Zealand, homicide is defined by statute as the killing of a human being by another human being, and it was held in *R* v *Murray Wright Ltd* [1970] NZLR 476 that this statutory wording precluded the indictment of a non-human entity for manslaughter. Using the reasoning in *R* v *Murray Wright Ltd,* it would seem that if the statutory definition of an offence is in terms of an act of 'a man' then a company cannot commit the offence. Accordingly it would seem that a company cannot be indicted for rape (Sexual Offences Act 1956, s. 1(1): 'It is an offence for a man to rape a woman or another man').

In Canada it has been held that a company on trial for a criminal offence cannot call evidence that it is of good character: it is in the nature of a corporation that it does not have a character and the character of humans identified with the corporation cannot be attributed to it (*R* v *Deslauriers* [1993] 2 WWR 401).

The usual principle of English criminal law is that there cannot be a conviction of a person accused of a crime without proving that the person had a criminal state of mind when performing the prohibited act. The identification theory enables a company to be given a criminal state of mind by attributing to it the state of mind of individuals associated with it. But there are many offences which do not have any mental element. They are often called offences of strict liability. For example, in *Alphacell Ltd* v *Woodward* [1972] AC 824, the company operated a factory in which paper was made. The layout of the plant was such that if two pumps failed, waste material from the paper-making process would be discharged into a river. The pumps failed and the river was polluted by the waste material. The House of Lords dismissed the company's appeal against conviction for causing polluting matter to enter a stream contrary to the Rivers (Prevention of Pollution) Act 1951, s. 2 (since repealed and replaced by the Water Resources Act 1991, s. 85). The company had caused the pollutant to enter the river and this was sufficient to make it guilty of the offence: it was not necessary to ask whether the company 'knew' that it was polluting the river.

If a company is accused of an offence of strict liability, it is unnecessary to prove that individuals who can be identified with the company were responsible for committing the offence. In *R* v *Gateway Foodmarkets Ltd* [1997] 3 All ER 78 the Court of Appeal dismissed Gateway's appeal against conviction of the offence of failing to ensure, so far as is reasonably practicable, the health, safety and welfare at work of all its employees, contrary to the Health and Safety at Work etc. Act 1974, ss. 2(1) and 33(1). The court held that this is an offence of strict liability. So it was irrelevant that (a) the failure that had caused the commission of the offence was of a shop manager who, Gateway claimed, could not be identified with the company and (b) it was not reasonably practicable for anyone who could be identified with the company to do more to comply with the Act. See also *R* v *British Steel plc* [1995] 1 WLR 1356 on s. 3(1) of the 1974 Act.

Unless the question is settled by statute it is for the courts to decide whether an offence is one of strict liability. The courts have found strict liability particularly appropriate where criminal penalties are invoked to enforce regulation of economic activity of general public importance. This is the type of offence with which companies are most often charged and so strict liability is particularly important to companies. Nevertheless strict liability is a characteristic of an offence and is a general concept of criminal law not company law. If an offence is one of strict liability, it is unnecessary to examine the mental state of any person on trial for the offence, whether the accused is a natural person or a company. Deciding to make an offence one of strict liability will facilitate the conviction of companies but will also affect the trials of natural persons.

Another concept of criminal law that is of great significance for companies is vicarious liability, which imposes criminal liability on the employer of an individual who commits an offence while acting within the course and scope of his or her employment. A company employer may be convicted of a vicarious-liability offence committed by its employee (see, for example, *Pearks, Gunston and Tee Ltd* v *Ward*). As with strict liability, whether an offence is one of vicarious liability must be decided by the courts unless the question is settled by statute. The courts tend to impose vicarious liability for the same sort of regulatory offences for which strict liability is imposed. For example, in *National Rivers Authority* v *Alfred McAlpine Homes East Ltd* [1994] 4 All ER 286 it was held that if a company's employees, acting within the course and scope of their employment, had caused polluting matter to enter controlled waters contrary to the Water Resources Act 1991, s. 85, then the company would be guilty of an offence under that section regardless of whether the employees were sufficiently senior to be identified with the company. The company would be vicariously liable for its employees' breach of the law, not directly liable because of being identified with those employees. Nevertheless, in *Seaboard Offshore Ltd* v *Secretary of State for Transport* [1994] 1 WLR 541, in which the offence of failure by a shipowner to secure that a ship is operated in a safe manner (Merchant Shipping Act 1995, s. 100) was held not to be a vicarious-liability offence, Lord Keith of Kinkel (at p. 546) emphasised that vicarious and strict liability are separate concepts.

In relation to many vicarious-liability offences, Parliament has provided employers with a 'due diligence' defence — that is, the employer is relieved of liability if it is shown that the employer had exercised all due diligence to avoid commission of the offence; see *Tesco Supermarkets Ltd* v *Nattrass* [1972] AC 153 discussed in 19.8.6.

In *Mousell Bros* v *London & North-Western Railway Co.* [1917] 2 KB 836 a company was made vicariously liable for an offence committed by its employee even though the definition of the offence required it to be committed 'with intent'. According to Atkin J, at p. 846, it was sufficient that the employee had the intent so that the offence was committed: the employer was then vicariously liable for the offence that had been committed. However, in *Vane* v *Yiannopoullos* [1965] AC 486 the House of Lords held that, unless otherwise specified by statute, there could be no vicarious liability for an offence with a mental element unless the employer's proprietary or managerial functions had been delegated to the employee who committed the offence. In *Vane* v *Yiannopoullos* Lord Evershed glossed over *Mousell Bros* v *London & North-Western Railway Co.*, saying that intent, unlike knowledge, was not '*mens rea* in a real sense'.

Sometimes a statute creating an offence with strict and vicarious liability creates a defence for an employer which depends on the state of mind of the employee who carried out the prohibited act. For example, in *Tesco Stores Ltd* v *Brent London Borough Council* [1993] 1 WLR 1037, Tesco was convicted of supplying an 18 certificate video to a person under 18 contrary to the Video Recordings Act 1984, s. 11. This is a strict-liability offence but s. 11(2)(b) provides a defence if 'the accused' neither knew nor had reasonable grounds to believe that the person supplied was under 18. Tesco was vicariously liable for a supply made by a check-out operator but claimed that it was entitled to the s. 11(2)(b) defence because none of the individuals who could be identified with it knew anything at all about the person supplied. It was held that 'the accused' in s. 11(2)(b) had to be construed as meaning the employee who did the prohibited act, because otherwise a large company like Tesco could never be convicted. Indeed any owner of a business, whether a natural or a legal person, who did not serve customers personally could escape prosecution. The same view was taken in Australia in *Woolworths Ltd* v *Luff* (1988) 77 ACTR 1 (in relation to an offence of selling alcohol to a person under 18) and in England in *Chuter* v *Freeth and Pocock Ltd* [1911] 2 KB 832, which was not cited in either the *Tesco* or the *Woolworths* case. For further discussion see C. Wells, 'Corporate liability and consumer protection: *Tesco* v *Nattrass* revisited' (1994) 57 MLR 817.

As with strict liability, vicarious liability is a concept of criminal law not company law. Whether an offence should be one of vicarious liability depends on whether employers generally should be required to control and take responsibility for the actions of their employees.

The discussion so far in 19.8.4 has been concerned with the ways in which the criminal law makes a company liable for criminal acts committed in the course of its activities. Another problem for the criminal law is to ensure that when a criminal offence is committed in the course of a company's business, liability can be imposed on the human beings who caused it to commit the offence. Under the common law it is an offence to aid, abet, counsel or procure the commission of any offence. Nevertheless, it is nowadays standard practice in statutes creating offences to make a provision like CA 1985, s. 733(2), that the fact that a company is guilty of the offence does not preclude prosecution of 'any director, manager, secretary or other similar officer . . . or any person who was purporting to act in any such capacity' if the offence 'occurred with the consent or connivance of, or was attributable to any neglect' on his or her part. Such officer is deemed to be liable as a principal. Under such a provision, it would seem that if an individual who is identified with a company commits an offence then that individual and the company can both be convicted as principals in respect of the same act. This has been accepted under somewhat different provisions of Australian law (*Hamilton* v *Whitehead* (1988) 166 CLR 121). 'Manager' in such a provision means a person who has the management of the whole affairs of the company, is in a position of real authority and has the power and responsibility to decide corporate policy and strategy (*R* v *Boal* [1992] QB 591).

In two recent cases the Queen's Bench Divisional Court has gone out of its way to impose criminal liability on company directors. *Brown* v *Director of Public Prosecutions* (1998) 162 JP 333 concerned the Sexual Offences (Amendment) Act 1976, s. 4, which provides that if the name or address of the victim of a rape offence is published in England and Wales in a written publication available to the public, any proprietor, any editor and any publisher of the newspaper or periodical shall be guilty of an offence. A newspaper owned by a company published information in contravention of the provision and it was held that the company's managing director, who did not take part in the editing of the newspaper, had been rightly convicted as the 'publisher' of the newspaper. In *Jones* v *Hellard* (1998) *The Times*, 23 March 1998 a letter had been written by an individual on a company's notepaper. If the letter had been written in the course of carrying on the individual's business, an offence would have been committed, because the individual signed his name followed by 'FRIBA', meaning fellow of the Royal Institute of British Architects, but had ceased to be registered under the Architects Registration Act 1938. If the letter had been written in the course of the company's business, there would have been no offence, because the company's name did not contain the word 'architect'. Remarkably the Divisional Court held that the individual had been rightly convicted of an offence under ss. 1 and 3 of the 1938 Act of practising or carrying on business under a name, style or title containing the word 'architect' while not registered under the Act. The Divisional Court rejected the argument that he was carrying on business under his company's name not his own, saying that he was offering his personal services not his company's services.

19.8.5   Double-counting; theft from a company

The act of an individual who is identified with a company, because of being the directing mind and will of the company, the very ego and centre of the personality of the company, is attributed to the company and creates the liability of the company. The individual in question cannot then be guilty of conspiring with the company to commit the act: conspiracy requires two or more guilty minds but under the identification theory there is only one guilty mind, the mind of the human whose guilty thoughts are attributed to the company (*R* v *McDonnell* [1966] 1 QB 233). For a detailed exploration of this topic, including the difficult question of whether a company can conspire with two or more of its directors, see M.R. Goode, 'Corporate conspiracy: problems of *mens rea* and the parties to the agreement' (1975) 2 Dalhousie LJ 121.

Whether people who own all the shares in a company and who have taken its money, otherwise than in a way permitted by company law (as a dividend, authorised reduction of capital, repurchase or redemption of shares, payment for services or goods, or distribution of surplus on winding up), should be convicted of theft has been the subject of much debate, following the decisions of the Court of Appeal in *Attorney-General's Reference (No. 2 of 1982)* [1984] QB 624 and *R* v *Philippou* (1989) 89 Cr App R 290 that conviction for theft is possible if the accused have acted dishonestly, which is a question for the jury. The Theft Act 1968, s. 1(1), provides that a person is guilty of theft 'if he dishonestly appropriates property belonging to another with the intention of permanently depriving the other of it'.

If persons, who between them represent the directing mind and will of a company, dishonestly appropriate the company's property then they cannot rely on the doctrine that their minds are the minds of the company to deem that the company has consented to what they have done (*Attorney-General's Reference (No. 2 of 1982)*) or authorised it (*R v Philippou*). As the Court of Appeal made clear in *Attorney-General's Reference (No. 2 of 1982)* at p. 640, the identification theory does not apply to offences committed against the company itself or to illegal or dishonest actions in relation to the company. In particular, they cannot rely on the Theft Act 1968, s. 2(1)(b), which provides that 'A person's appropriation of property belonging to another is not to be regarded as dishonest . . . if he appropriates the property in the belief that he would have the other's consent if the other knew of the appropriation and the circumstances of it'. Persons who between them represent the directing mind and will of a company cannot rely on s. 2(1)(b) to negate the dishonesty of their appropriation of the company's property if the only consent they can allege is the consent of themselves which they say should be deemed to be the company's consent by virtue of the identification theory, for in those circumstances there is no consent by an 'other', only their own consent (*Attorney-General's Reference (No. 2 of 1982)*).

The Court of Criminal Appeal of Victoria took the opposite view in *R v Roffel* [1985] VR 511, saying that the accused can not only say that the company 'consented' to what they did because their consent can be attributed to the company, but also that the consent means that there has been no 'appropriation' as that term is used in the statutory definition of theft. The House of Lords has since made it clear in *Director of Public Prosecutions v Gomez* [1993] AC 442 that an action can be an appropriation of an owner's property for the purposes of the Theft Act 1968 despite the owner's consent to the action. Lord Browne-Wilkinson said, at pp. 496–7, that in his judgment *R v Roffel* was wrongly decided and the law was correctly stated in *Attorney-General's Reference (No. 2 of 1982)* and *R v Philippou*.

Two articles discuss the question further. D.W. Elliott, 'Directors' thefts and dishonesty' [1991] Crim LR 732 suggests that where people who own all the shares in a company have taken its money, otherwise than in a way permitted by company law, then they have not been dishonest so that there can be no conviction of theft. G. Virgo, 'Stealing from the small family business' [1991] CLJ 464, on the other hand, believes that conviction for theft is possible and is a proper deterrent to abuse of the corporate form, especially where creditors are prejudiced.

19.8.6 Who will be identified with a company?

The most obvious problem with the identification theory is discovering who will be identified with a company.

19.8.6.1 Purpose of the identification

In *Meridian Global Funds Management Asia Ltd v Securities Commission* [1995] 2 AC 500 at p. 507, Lord Hoffmann emphasised that choosing who to identify with a company for the purpose of applying a rule of law to it depends on interpreting that rule:

Whose act (or knowledge, or state of mind) was *for this purpose* intended to count as the act etc. of the company? One finds the answer to this question by applying the usual canons of interpretation, taking into account the language of the rule (if it is a statute) and its content and policy.

Lord Hoffmann said that it was a mistake to seize on the phrase 'directing mind and will' which had been used by Viscount Haldane LC in *Lennard's Carrying Co. Ltd v Asiatic*

Petroleum Co. Ltd [1915] AC 705 quoted in 19.8.1 and use that as a criterion for determining who to identify with a company. In *Meridian Global Funds Management Asia Ltd* v *Securities Commission* the Privy Council held that when determining whether a company had failed to comply with a New Zealand statute which required it to give notice of being a substantial holder of securities in a public company as soon as it knew or ought to have known that it had become one, the knowledge that had to be attributed to the company was the knowledge of the individual who had authority to acquire the securities for the company, regardless of whether that individual was the company's directing mind and will. However, Lord Hoffmann said, at p. 511:

> But their lordships would wish to guard themselves against being understood to mean that whenever a servant of a company has authority to do an act on its behalf, knowledge of that act will for all purposes be attributed to the company. It is a question of construction in each case as to whether the particular rule requires that the knowledge that an act has been done, or the state of mind with which it was done, should be attributed to the company.

There have been circumstances in which an individual who was not part of a company's directing mind and will was identified with the company (or at least the identification was made without mentioning whether the court had inquired whether the individual was part of the directing mind and will). For example, as mentioned in 19.8.2, courts have found companies to have an enemy character because their shareholders were enemy aliens. See also *Bank of Credit and Commerce International SA* v *Dawson* 1987 FLR 342, *Director General of Fair Trading* v *Pioneer Concrete (UK) Ltd* [1995] 1 AC 456 and *R* v *Rozeik* [1996] 1 WLR 159, which are discussed below. *Meridian Global Funds Management Asia Ltd* v *Securities Commission* is unusual in that it identifies with a company an individual who is not part of the company's directing mind and will for the purpose of imposing criminal liability on the company. This was also done in *Moore* v *I. Bresler Ltd* [1944] 2 All ER 515, in which the Divisional Court held that a company had been rightly convicted of publishing false documents with intent to deceive (and so avoid tax). The documents in question had been prepared by the company's secretary and a branch manager, and Viscount Caldecote CJ said, at p. 516:

> These two men were important officials of the company, and when they made statements and rendered returns . . . they were clearly making those statements and giving those returns as the officers of the company, the proper officers to make the returns.

In *Bank of Credit and Commerce International SA* v *Dawson* a banking company sued the drawer of three cheques which one of its customers had paid into his overdrawn account, having received the cheques in payment for goods. The drawer had stopped payment of the cheques because the goods were not delivered. In fact the customer had never intended to deliver the goods but needed the cheques to be paid into his account to disguise the fact that it was heavily overdrawn. The branch manager knew about and encouraged this deceit because he had taken bribes from the customer to misreport the state of his account so that the customer could run up a huge overdraft of which the manager's superiors were unaware. It was held that the bank was not, as it claimed to be, a holder in due course of the cheques, as defined in the Bills of Exchange Act 1882, s. 29, because it had not taken them in good faith. The branch manager's lack of good faith was attributed to the banking company even though he was not part of its directing mind and will.

In *Director General of Fair Trading* v *Pioneer Concrete (UK) Ltd* the Director General of Fair Trading had obtained a court order under the Restrictive Trade Practices Act 1976, s. 35(3), against Pioneer Concrete and other companies restraining them from giving effect to agreements which restricted competition among them in the supply of ready-mixed concrete and which had not been registered as required by the Act. The companies had been fined for being in contempt of court by disobeying these orders. By s. 35(4) an order could only have been made against any of the companies if it was a 'person party to the agreement'. Pioneer claimed that the agreements in question had been entered into by its employees (an area manager and plant manager) with employees of the other companies, against the express prohibition of their employers. So it was claimed that Pioneer was not a party to the agreement and no order could have been made against it. The House of Lords rejected this argument. Lord Nolan said, at p. 475:

> The Act is not concerned with what the employer says but with what the employee does in entering into business transactions in the course of his employment. The plain purpose of s. 35(3) is to deter the implementation of agreements or arrangements by which the public interest is harmed, and the subsection can only achieve that purpose if it is applied to the actions of the individuals within the business organisation who make and give effect to the relevant agreement or arrangement on its behalf.

In *R* v *Rozeik* Mr Rozeik had received cheques from two companies and was convicted of obtaining them dishonestly, by deceiving the companies. On appeal the issue was whether the prosecution had proved that the companies had been deceived. To do this the prosecution had to prove that an individual who could be identified with the company was deceived. Which individuals might count for this purpose? The court said, at p. 165 per Leggatt LJ:

> In cases in which the company is the victim the person or persons who stand for its state of mind may differ from those who do so in cases in which a company is charged with the commission of a criminal offence. The latter are [more] likely to represent what Viscount Haldane LC in *Lennard's Carrying Co. Ltd* v *Asiatic Petroleum Co. Ltd* called 'the directing mind and will' of the company. [Leggatt LJ has kindly confirmed to us that he meant 'more' rather than 'less' as printed in the report quoted.]

For the purposes of this particular crime, many junior employees who had been deceived did not count because it could not be said that the cheques had been 'obtained' from them. As the court said, at p. 165:

> . . . a cheque could only be obtained from the company from an employee who had authority to provide it. The deception had to operate on the mind of the employee from whom the cheque was obtained.

Employees who checked and typed a cheque were not persons from whom the cheque was obtained, but employees who signed it were. If an employee who signed a cheque knew that it was being issued fraudulently then that knowledge would be attributed to the company so that the company was not deceived and it did not matter that the employee was not part of the directing mind and will of the company. It was part of the prosecution's case that a branch manager who had signed a cheque knew of the fraud. As this would have meant that the company was not deceived, the jury should not have convicted.

19.8.6.2   Directing mind and will

Although, as indicated in 19.8.6.1, there have been cases in which a person who was not part of the directing mind and will of a company was identified with it, being part of the directing mind and will has always been the most common criterion for identification, especially, as Leggatt LJ indicated in the passage from *R* v *Rozeik* [1996] 1 WLR 159 quoted in 19.8.6.1, when what is being considered is the attribution of a state of mind to a company so as to make it liable for a criminal offence.

A famous description of the nature of a company's directing mind and will comes from a civil case. In *H.L. Bolton (Engineering) Co. Ltd* v *T.J. Graham & Sons Ltd* [1957] 1 QB 159, a company applied for renewal of its lease of business premises under the provisions of the Landlord and Tenant Act 1954. The landlord, T.J. Graham & Sons Ltd, sought to rely on s. 30(1)(g) of the Act under which a landlord can oppose renewal of a lease on the ground that 'the landlord intends to occupy the holding for the purposes, or partly for the purposes, of a business to be carried on by him therein'. The tenant objected that the landlord did not in fact have that intention. There were three directors of the landlord company, which was a wholly owned subsidiary of another company. The three directors only held board meetings once a year but they had all on many occasions discussed and approved an extensive redevelopment of the site in question. The county court judge found that the landlord company had evinced the necessary intention, and this finding was affirmed by the Court of Appeal, where Denning LJ, in a much quoted passage at p. 172, indulged in some medieval anthropomorphism:

> A company may in many ways be likened to a human body. It has a brain and nerve centre which controls what it does. It also has hands which hold the tools and act in accordance with directions from the centre. Some of the people in the company are mere servants and agents who are nothing more than hands to do the work and cannot be said to represent the mind or will. Others are directors and managers who represent the directing mind and will of the company, and control what it does. The state of mind of these managers is the state of mind of the company and is treated by the law as such.

(For medieval anthropomorphic (or 'organological') conceptions of Church and State, see M. Wolff, 'On the nature of legal persons' (1938) 54 LQR 494 at pp. 498–9; E.H. Kantorowicz, *The King's Two Bodies* (Princeton University Press, 1957), ch. 5.)

In *Tesco Supermarkets Ltd* v *Nattrass* [1972] AC 153, Lord Reid said, at p. 171:

> There have been attempts to apply Lord Denning's words to all servants of a company whose work is brain work, or who exercise some managerial discretion under the direction of superior officers of the company. I do not think that Lord Denning intended to refer to them. He only referred to those who 'represent the directing mind and will of the company, and control what it does'.
>
> I think that is right for this reason, Normally the board of directors, the managing director and perhaps other superior officers of a company carry out the functions of management and speak and act as the company. Their subordinates do not. They carry out orders from above and it can make no difference that they are given some measure of discretion. But the board of directors may delegate some part of their functions of management giving to their delegate full discretion to act independently of instructions from them. I see no difficulty in holding that they have thereby put such a delegate in their place so that within the scope of the delegation he can act as the company. It may not always be easy to draw the line but there are cases in which the line must be drawn.

In *Tesco Supermarkets Ltd* v *Nattrass,* the company was charged under the Trade Descriptions Act 1968, s. 11, with the offence of advertising goods for sale at a price less than that at which they were in fact offered for sale. The offence was committed at the company's store at Northwich near Manchester. The company would have had a defence to the charge if it could prove that the commission of the offence was due to the act or default of 'another person' and that it took all reasonable precautions and exercised all due diligence to avoid the commission of such an offence by itself or any person under its control (Trade Descriptions Act 1968, s. 24(1)). The prosecutor said that the company could not claim this defence because the manager of its Northwich store, who the prosecutor claimed should be identified with the company, had clearly not avoided committing the offence. The House of Lords allowed Tesco's appeal against conviction, saying that the store manager was not identified with the company but was 'another person', and the people who were identified with the company had taken all reasonable precautions and exercised all due diligence. The crucial factor in these findings seems to have been that the company had more than 800 store managers. The bigger the company the easier it is to escape liability. The Trade Descriptions Act 1968, s. 11, has since been repealed. Provisions concerning misleading pricing are now made by the Consumer Protection Act 1987, part III (ss. 20 to 26). The 1987 Act provides a due diligence defence in s. 39. An offence under the new provisions can be committed by a person only 'in the course of any business of his'. Where a business owner has employees, anything they do which results in misleading pricing of the business's goods will be done in the course of the owner's business not the employees' business and so the employees cannot be guilty of offences under the new provisions (*R* v *Warwickshire County Council, ex parte Johnson* [1993] AC 583). As a large corporate employer (in *Ex parte Johnson* it was Dixons) will usually be able to escape liability under the principles laid down in *Tesco Supermarkets Ltd* v *Nattrass,* many instances of misleading pricing cannot now be prosecuted (see I. Brown, 'Corporate criminal liability and consumer protection' [1993] LMCLQ 158).

When determining whether a company has criminal liability the courts have been unwilling to make the knowledge of an employee about some subject the knowledge of the company merely because it was the employee's job to deal with that subject. *Moore* v *I. Bresler Ltd* [1944] 2 All ER 515 and *Meridian Global Funds Management Asia Ltd* v *Securities Commission* [1995] 2 AC 500 are rare exceptions. In *John Henshall (Quarries) Ltd* v *Harvey* [1965] 2 QB 233, a weighbridge operator employed by John Henshall (Quarries) Ltd at one of its quarries permitted a lorry to leave the quarry even though it exceeded the maximum permitted weight. One of his duties was to see that lorries were not overweight, and the quarry manager periodically checked that this rule was being observed. The haulage contractor was convicted of the offence of using an overweight lorry and the quarry company was charged with aiding, abetting, counselling and procuring the contractor's offence. It was accepted that the weighbridge operator took no part in the general management of the company. The Divisional Court held that therefore he could not be identified with the company so that his knowledge that an offence had been committed by the contractor could not be attributed to the company. Accordingly the company could not be guilty of aiding, abetting, counselling and procuring the contractor's offence. In *Airtours plc* v *Shipley* (1994) 158 JP 835, the directors of a company had established what was admitted to be a good system for ensuring that no errors appeared in the company's holiday brochures but they never checked any brochures themselves, leaving that to persons employed to perform that task. When a mistake did appear in a brochure, contravening the Trade Descriptions Act 1968, s. 14, it was held that the directors had not delegated to the responsible employee their management functions as envisaged in the statement by Lord

Reid in *Tesco Supermarkets Ltd* v *Nattrass* quoted above. Accordingly no one who could be identified with the company had committed the offence and the company was not guilty of it.

It is often suggested that crimes are committed in the course of business conducted by companies because of organisational failures. This is what the Law Commission seeks to deal with in its proposed offence of corporate killing (see 19.8.4). But the organisation which is seen to fail is the organisation of the company's business, not the association of members which forms the company in law. The traditional approach of the courts has been to find a company liable for the criminal failings of its business organisation if either the crime was one for which the company could be held vicariously liable or the crime was intended by the directors who are at the interface of the company as it is conceived in law and the organisation which conducts the company's business.

19.8.6.3 Acting against the company
In *Moore* v *I. Bresler Ltd* [1944] 2 All ER 515, the Divisional Court held that a company had been rightly convicted of making false tax returns with intent to deceive when the company officials who had prepared the returns had falsified them in order to disguise their own fraud against the company. This seems to be inconsistent with *Belmont Finance Corporation Ltd* v *Williams Furniture Ltd* [1979] Ch 250 (discussed in 19.8.3): the officials' intent to deceive should not have been imputed to the company because the officials were acting dishonestly against the company. The Law Commission has proposed in its draft Criminal Code Bill (Law Com. No. 177) that a company should not be guilty of an offence by virtue of one of its officers acting with the intention of doing harm, or of concealing harm done by him or another, to the corporation (see clause 30(6) of the draft Bill).

19.8.7 Further discussion of corporate criminal liability

A great deal of law breaking goes on in the conduct of business by companies but it causes little public concern and is not a high priority for law-enforcement agencies and prosecuting authorities (see C.D. Stone, *Where the Law Ends: The Social Control of Corporate Behavior* (New York: Harper & Row, 1975); H.J. Glasbeek, 'Why corporate deviance is not treated as a crime — the need to make "profits" a dirty word' (1984) 22 Osgoode Hall LJ 393; C. Wells, 'The decline and rise of English murder: corporate crime and individual responsibility' [1988] Crim LR 788). The central importance of the concept of *mens rea* makes English criminal law unsuitable for attaching criminal liability to a company as a person separate from its members. The courts have adopted the identification theory to deal with the problem of attaching criminal liability to companies for offences when liability normally depends on a state of mind. It may be feared that because the identification theory concentrates on top management it is inadequate to deal with the situation in large companies where junior employees are influenced to break the law by the company's system of work and its internal decision-making processes (see P.A. French, 'The corporation as a moral person' (1979) 16 Am Philos Q 207). The decision in *Tesco Supermarkets Ltd* v *Nattrass* [1972] AC 153 is thought to have deterred prosecutions of large companies. The larger a company is, the less likely it is that a member of top management is specifically responsible for any crimes committed in the company's operations. For a discussion of possible organisational criteria for corporate criminal liability, see S. Field and N. Jörg, 'Corporate liability and manslaughter: should we be going Dutch?' [1991] Crim LR 156. They examine the idea that the faults of several individuals identified with the company may be aggregated to prove the overall fault of the company, and the idea that a company's criminal liability for its employee's act should be based on the power and acceptance criteria: (a) did the company have the power to determine whether the employee acted in this way, and (b) did the employee's act belong to a category of acts accepted by the company as being in the course of normal business operations? See also D. Burles, 'The criminal liability of corporations' (1991) 141 NLJ 609. B. Fisse, 'The attribution of criminal liability to corporations' (1991) 13 Syd LR 277 suggests that a company should be liable for a criminal act of one of its employees where it has been at fault by, among other things, having a policy that expressly or impliedly authorises or permits the commission of the offence. Professor Fisse's article includes a comprehensive draft of a statute embodying his ideas on corporate criminal liability.

The problems of finding an appropriate form of punishment are discussed in G. Slapper, 'Corporate punishment' (1994) 144 NLJ 29.

There is a very good discussion of the principles of corporate criminal liability in Law Commission, *Legislating the Criminal Code: Involuntary Manslaughter* (Law Com. No. 237, House of Commons Papers, Session 1995–96, 171) (London: HMSO, 1996).

The identification theory of corporate criminal liability sometimes seems too fragile to survive. Some commentators argue that it is merely a restricted version of the theory of vicarious liability (G.R. Sullivan, 'The attribution of culpability to limited companies' [1996] CLJ 515; R.J. Wickins and C.A. Ong, 'Confusion worse confounded: the end of the directing mind theory?' [1997] JBL 524). Some argue that a company is a person capable of moral responsibility and accountability, which can therefore be criminally liable (P.A. French, *Collective and Corporate Responsibility* (New York: Columbia University Press, 1984); M.B. Metzger and D.R. Dalton, 'Seeing the elephant: an organisational perspective on corporate moral agency' (1996) 33 Am Bus LJ 489; P.A. French, 'Integrity, intentions, and corporations' (1996) 34 Am Bus LJ 141), but this is rejected by Sullivan, op. cit. For some, companies should never be subject to criminal proceedings (D.R. Fischel and A.O. Sykes, 'Corporate crime' (1996) 25 J Legal Stud 319).

For other extensive discussions see L.H. Leigh, *The Criminal Liability of Corporations in English Law* (LSE Research Monographs 2) (London: London School of Economics and Political Science; Weidenfeld & Nicolson, 1969); *Tesco Supermarkets Ltd v Nattrass* [1972] AC 153; L.H. Leigh, 'The criminal liability of corporations and other groups' (1977) 9 Ottawa L Rev 247; *Canadian Dredge & Dock Co. Ltd v R* (1985) 19 DLR (4th) 314; B. Fisse and J. Braithwaite, 'The allocation of responsibility for corporate crime: individualism, collectivism and accountability' (1988) 11 Syd LR 468; C. Wells, *Corporations and Criminal Responsibility* (Oxford: Clarendon Press, 1993); C.M.V. Clarkson, 'Kicking corporate bodies and damning their souls' (1996) 59 MLR 557.

19.8.8 Identification of religious belief

In *Adelaide Company of Jehovah's Witnesses Incorporated v Commonwealth* (1943) 67 CLR 116, Latham CJ said, at p. 147, 'It is obvious that a company cannot exercise a religion'. A body corporate is incapable of public worship and cannot exercise itself in 'the duties of piety and true religion' as required by the Sunday Observance Act 1677 before it was repealed (*Rolloswin Investments Ltd v Chromolit Portugal Cutelarias e Produtos Metálicos SARL* [1970] 1 WLR 912). A statement that a company does or does not have a particular opinion is really only a statement that an individual who can be identified with the company has or does not have that opinion (*Lloyd v David Syme & Co. Ltd* [1986] AC 350). In *Edwards Books & Art Ltd v R* (1986) 35 DLR (4th) 1, Dickson CJC said, at p. 53:

I have no hesitation in remarking that a business corporation cannot possess religious beliefs. . . . A more difficult question is whether a corporate entity ought to be deemed in certain circumstances to possess the religious values of specified natural persons. If so, should the religion of the directors or shareholders or even employees be adopted as the appropriate test. What if there is a divergence of religious beliefs within the corporation?

The Chief Justice did not find it necessary to rule on this question in the case before the court.

In *Re Northern Ireland Electricity Service's Application* [1987] NI 271, the High Court of Northern Ireland was concerned with Northern Ireland legislation which renders unlawful certain kinds of discrimination on the grounds of religious belief or political opinion. The Fair Employment Agency for Northern Ireland wished to investigate an allegation that, in making contracts with companies, the Northern Ireland Electricity Service (NIES) had unlawfully discriminated on the ground of religious belief or perceived political opinion NIES sought to stop the investigation saying that there could be no discrimination to investigate because the dealings were with companies and companies could not have religious beliefs or political opinions. Nicholson J held that discrimination under the legislation was not restricted to discrimination against a person for that person's own beliefs: a person who is adversely affected by discrimination against others can complain about that discrimination. Accordingly a company could complain about being affected by discrimination against people connected with it. As this disposed of the case it was unnecessary for his lordship to go on to deal with the question of whether a company could hold a religious belief or political opinion. However, he did so, at pp. 288–9 , saying that in his view the identification theory could be used to attribute to a company 'the religious belief (or supposed religious belief) of its governing body or chief officer or other superior officers who speak and act as' the company, and similarly a company can have a political opinion.

19.8.9   Ethnicity

Courts have always refused to attribute the ethnicity of a company's members to the company itself. Thus a company whose members are all American Indians is itself neither an Indian nor a band of Indians (*Reference re Stony Plain Indian Reserve No. 135* (1981) 130 DLR (3d) 636 at p. 657). A company whose members are all Indians entitled to exemption from taxation on their property is not itself a tax-exempt Indian (*Re Kinookimaw Beach Association* (1979) 102 DLR (3d) 333; *Northwest/Prince Rupert Assessor, Area No. 25 v N. & V. Johnson Services Ltd* [1991] 1 WWR 527). A company whose members are all Africans is not an African entitled to sue in a court whose jurisdiction is limited to disputes between Africans (*Kajubi v Kayanja* [1967] EA 301). A company whose members are all Afro-Americans is not a 'person of African descent' or a 'coloured person' (*People's Pleasure Park Co. Inc. v Rohleder* (1908) 61 SE 794, in which owners of land had covenanted not to sell it to such persons). The State of California is not a white person, and so a Chinese person could give evidence for another Chinese defending a criminal prosecution by the State despite a California statute (presumably now repealed) prohibiting members of various races from giving evidence for or against a white person (*People v Awa* (1865) 27 Cal 638).

19.9   COMPANIES IN COURT

In superior courts, the usual rule of court practice is that a litigant may appear to address the court and examine witnesses either in person or through the agency of a legally qualified advocate who has been granted a right of audience by the court, but representation by an unqualified person is not allowed because it is usually inefficient. A company cannot appear in person and so must employ a qualified advocate. This is the rule in the House of Lords (*Tritonia Ltd* v *Equity & Law Life Assurance Society* [1943] AC 584), in the Court of Appeal (*Re International Securities Corporation Ltd* (1908) 25 TLR 31) and in the High Court (*Re an Arbitration between London County Council and London Tramways Co.* (1897) 13 TLR 254, DC; *Scriven* v *Jescott (Leeds) Ltd* (1908) 53 SJ 101; *Frinton & Walton Urban District Council* v *Walton & District Sand & Mineral Co. Ltd* [1938] 1 All ER 649). For a detailed discussion of the rule, see *Re G.J. Mannix Ltd* [1984] 1 NZLR 309. The rule is subject to a court's inherent right to regulate its own proceedings: a judge has a discretion to allow an unqualified advocate to appear for a company in an exceptional case. In *ALI Finance Ltd* v *Havelet Leasing Ltd* [1992] 1 WLR 455 and *Arbuthnot Leasing International Ltd* v *Havelet Leasing Ltd (No. 2)* [1990] BCC 636, the managing director and sole beneficial shareholder of three companies, who was also himself a party to the proceedings, was permitted to address the court on behalf of himself and his companies. The companies were forbidden by a *Mareva* injunction from spending money on legal expenses and the managing director had no money to pay those expenses himself. In *Collins Bros Stationers Pty Ltd* v *Zebra Graphics Pty Ltd* (1985) 10 ACLR 267, the managing director of a company was permitted to speak (successfully) on its behalf having been unable to obtain professional representation at short notice. In county courts, leave is often given for companies to be represented by their officers. However, a company being represented by its officer is not a litigant in person able to claim the officer's remuneration as costs under the Litigants in Person (Costs and Expenses) Act 1975 (*Jonathan Alexander Ltd* v *Proctor* [1996] 1 WLR 518, in which Hirst LJ said, at p. 523, that this is a considerable injustice).

Under the Rules of the Supreme Court 1965, ord. 5. r. 6(3), a body corporate may not begin or carry on any proceedings in the High Court otherwise than by a solicitor, except as expressly authorised by or under any enactment. Under ord. 12, r. 1(2), acknowledgement of service of a writ on a body corporate and notice of intention to defend the action may be given by any person duly authorised to act on the defendant's behalf but otherwise a corporate defendant may not take steps in an action otherwise than by a solicitor. The reason for these rules seems to be that the court must be assured that a qualified legal representative is responsible for ascertaining that all steps taken in proceedings are properly authorised. However, there are no such rules in county courts (*Charles P. Kinnell & Co. Ltd* v *Harding, Wace & Co.* [1918] 1 KB 405). A company must employ a solicitor to present a petition to the High Court for the compulsory winding up of another company (*Re a Company (No. 001029 of 1990)* [1991] BCLC 567).

The need for a court to deal with a body corporate through a responsible legal representative was recognised as long ago as the *Abbot of Hulme's Case* (1491) YB 21 Edw IV, f. 12, Mich., pl. 4; see H. Lubasz, 'The corporate borough in the late Year-Book period' (1964) 80 LQR 228 at p. 237.

According to Bingham MR in *Radford* v *Freeway Classics Ltd* [1994] 1 BCLC 445, it is necessary to restrict the way in which companies litigate because the costs which a company litigant can cause other parties to incur may not be recoverable from a company whose members have limited liability for its debts. If a limited company is a plaintiff in any action or other legal proceeding in a court then, under CA 1985, s. 726, that court can make it a condition of allowing the proceeding to go on that the company must put up security for the payment of the defendant's costs in the event of being ordered to pay them. The defendant must produce 'credible testimony' that there is reason to believe that the plaintiff company would be unable to pay the defendant's costs. However, a company *defending* legal proceedings does not have to give security for costs.

If a company has been an unsuccessful party to legal proceedings then it is possible in principle for the directors or members of the company who caused successful parties to incur costs in the proceedings to be ordered to pay those costs. The directors or members sought to be made responsible for costs must be given an opportunity to make representations and present relevant evidence (*Re Land and Property Trust Co. plc (No. 4)* [1994] 1 BCLC 232). Normally, however, when a company has unsuccessfully defended legal proceedings it would be contrary to the principles of separate personality and limited liability to make anyone other than the company liable for costs, unless, perhaps, the defence was not bona fide (*Taylor* v *Pace Developments Ltd* [1991] BCC 406). In *Morgan* v *Morgan Insurance Brokers Ltd* [1993] BCC 145, Millett J said that when a member of a company had been forced by its directors to litigate to vindicate his rights as a member then it would be unfair for the value of the member's interest in the company to be reduced by the company having to pay the costs of that litigation, and so the directors were ordered to pay the costs.

Companies are not entitled to legal aid (Legal Aid Act 1988, s. 2(10)). An individual suing on behalf of a company in a derivative action is also not entitled to legal aid (*Wallersteiner* v *Moir (No. 2)* [1975] QB 373). After a spate of cases in which companies assigned their rights of action to individuals who could pursue them with legal aid (see *Norglen Ltd* v *Reeds Rains Prudential Ltd* [1997] 3 WLR 1177) a new reg. 33A was added to the Civil Legal Aid (General) Regulations 1989 (SI 1989 No. 339) authorising refusal of legal aid in such circumstances.

A company may be required to provide evidence concerning its affairs for the purposes of legal proceedings to which it is a party. Such evidence may be in the form of documents or written answers to interrogatories (*Penn-Texas Corporation* v *Murat Anstalt (No. 2)* [1964] 2 QB 647). A company cannot be ordered to attend, by an officer, for oral examination (*Penn-Texas Corporation* v *Murat Anstalt* [1964] 1 QB 40). Documents or answers to interrogatories have to be transmitted and attested by an officer or other agent of the company but will bind the company (*Welsbach Incandescent Gas Lighting Co.* v *New Sunlight Incandescent Co.* [1900] 2 Ch 1). Accordingly, privilege against incriminating the company can be claimed (*Triplex Safety Glass Co. Ltd* v *Lancegaye Safety Glass (1934) Ltd* [1939] 2 KB 395). If the evidence would incriminate the particular officer or agent nominated to transmit it then that individual can refuse to provide it but the court can nominate another person to provide it (*Sociedade Nacional de Combustiveis de Angola UEE* v *Lundqvist* [1991] 2 QB 310).

Evidence about a company's affairs can also be given by an individual with knowledge of those affairs as the evidence of that individual and not as the evidence of the company (*Macmillan Inc.* v *Bishopsgate Investment Trust plc (No. 2)* [1993] ICR 385): the fact that the individual could be identified with the company does not in itself mean that he or she is giving evidence as or for the company (*R* v *N.M. Paterson & Sons Ltd* (1980) 117 DLR (3d) 517). So such an individual is not entitled to claim any privilege to which the company is entitled, such as the privilege against self-incrimination. For example, in *R* v *N.M. Paterson & Sons Ltd,* the company was charged with an offence. The prosecution wished to call as a witness a manager who could be regarded as the directing mind and will of the company under the identification theory. It was contended for the manager that his evidence would be the company's evidence and so he could refuse to testify because of the rule that a person charged with an offence cannot be compelled to give evidence at his own trial for that offence. However, the Supreme Court of Canada rejected this contention and held that the manager would be giving his own evidence not the company's evidence and so could be compelled to testify.

In *Environment Protection Authority* v *Caltex Refining Co. Pty Ltd* (1993) 118 ALR 392 the High Court of Australia has refused to follow the English rule that companies can claim privilege against self-incrimination. The division of opinion on this issue reflects different views of the nature of corporate personality which are explored at length in the judgments of the members of the court.

20 Company Insolvency and Liquidation

20.1 INTRODUCTION

20.1.1 Nature of company insolvency and liquidation procedures

The governance of a company is normally entrusted to its directors. In certain circumstances, notably when a company is insolvent, the directors may be displaced by a qualified insolvency practitioner or (in a more restricted range of circumstances) an official receiver.

Several different procedures are available for putting a qualified insolvency practitioner or an official receiver in charge of a company. The different procedures are suitable for different circumstances. All but one of them are used to deal with insolvent companies and may conveniently be referred to as 'insolvency procedures'.

The insolvency procedures are administrative receivership, administration, voluntary arrangement, creditors' voluntary liquidation, compulsory liquidation and the appointment of a provisional liquidator. Of these, only creditors' voluntary liquidation and compulsory liquidation involve the liquidation of the company and may be called 'liquidation procedures'. The other procedure available for putting a qualified insolvency practitioner in charge of a company, members' voluntary liquidation, is a procedure for the liquidation of a solvent company.

All the company insolvency and liquidation procedures involve the appointment of a qualified insolvency practitioner (or in some circumstances an official receiver) to a named office in relation to a company — the offices being those of administrative receiver, administrator, supervisor of a voluntary arrangement, liquidator and provisional liquidator.

20.1.2 Liquidation

The end-result of the liquidation (or winding up, the terms are used interchangeably) of a company is that the company ceases to exist. The purpose of a liquidation procedure is to ensure that, before the company's existence ceases, all its affairs are dealt with (or 'wound up'), which means removing the company from all its legal relationships. Its contracts must be completed, transferred or otherwise brought to an end; it must cease carrying on business; its liabilities must be met, as far as possible; legal proceedings to which it is a party must be determined.

The members are entitled to benefit from any property remaining unless the articles provide otherwise. Surplus non-cash assets may be sold and the proceeds distributed to the members or, under Table A, art. 117, if the members adopt an extraordinary resolution sanctioning such a course, the property may be distributed in kind.

Finally the company must be removed from the register.

20.1.3   Legislation on company insolvency and liquidation

The statute law on company insolvency and liquidation is now contained principally in the Insolvency Act 1986 (IA 1986), which came into force on 29 December 1986 (IA 1986, s. 443; SI 1986 No. 1924, art. 3). (Sections 252 to 385 of IA 1986 are concerned with the insolvency of natural persons (bankruptcy) and are not relevant to this work.)

IA 1986 is a consolidation Act, which was enacted in order to tidy up the statute book following the passing of an important amending Act, the Insolvency Act 1985 (IA 1985), which amended the previous law contained in parts 18 to 25 of the Companies Act 1985 (CA 1985). Apart from a few provisions which were brought into force earlier in 1986, the provisions of IA 1985 concerning company insolvency and liquidation were brought into force on 29 December 1986 (SI 1986/1924, art. 2) and were immediately replaced by IA 1986.

In a supplementary consolidation, a small group of sections from CA 1985 and IA 1985 were re-enacted in the Company Directors Disqualification Act 1986 (CDDA 1986), which also came into force on 29 December 1986 (CDDA 1986, s. 25).

The primary legislation is supplemented by secondary legislation made by the Lord Chancellor and the Secretary of State under IA 1986, s. 411. The principal item of secondary legislation is the Insolvency Rules 1986 (SI 1986/1925) (IR 1986). Company insolvency rules are made after consultation with the Insolvency Rules Committee (IA 1986, s. 413). The committee was established in 1976. Its members are judges particularly concerned with insolvency matters, and an accountant, a barrister and a solicitor specialising in insolvency work.

20.2   ADMINISTRATIVE RECEIVERSHIP

20.2.1   Summary description

Administrative receivership is an insolvency procedure: it is usually invoked in relation to insolvent companies and not solvent companies.

Administrative receivership is not a liquidation procedure.

Except in rare cases, the involvement of the court is not required for initiating or confirming the use of this procedure.

An administrative receiver takes control of the whole (or substantially the whole) of a company's property so as to realise it for the purpose of paying one creditor who is secured by a floating charge (or sometimes a group of creditors who have common security in the form of a floating charge). No other interest groups are involved. Administrative receivership arises because of the security contract made between a company and one or more of its creditors (or a trustee for a group of creditors): by agreeing to a contract of that type with a creditor, the company confers on that creditor a special advantage over other creditors.

20.2.2   Definition of administrative receiver

In relation to England and Wales, the term 'administrative receiver' is defined in IA 1986, s. 29(2), to mean:

(a)   a receiver or manager of the whole (or substantially the whole) of a company's property appointed by or on behalf of the holders of any debentures of the company secured by a charge which, as created, was a floating charge, or by such a charge and one or more other securities; or

(b)   a person who would be such a receiver or manager but for the appointment of some other person as the receiver of part of the company's property.

A 'receiver' is an individual appointed to take control of property. A receiver of property may be appointed, for example, by a court to collect and protect the property until its fate can be determined by the court, or by a chargee to utilise the property in meeting the obligation secured by the charge. If by its nature the property to be controlled by a receiver requires management, for example, because it is a business, a second individual may be appointed 'manager' of the property or the receiver may be appointed 'receiver and manager'. In practice it is difficult to draw a line between the tasks of a receiver and those of a manager.

The power of the civil courts to appoint receivers is now stated expressly in statutes — see Supreme Court Act 1981, s. 37(1); County Courts Act 1984, s. 38, and County Court Rules 1981, ord. 32.

In the past the usual practice with a floating charge was to ask the court to appoint a receiver when it became necessary to enforce the charge. The procedure was called a 'debenture-holder's action'. A receiver or manager of the whole (or substantially the whole) of a company's property appointed by a court in a debenture-holder's action would be appointed 'on behalf of' the debenture holder (cf. IA 1986, s. 32) and therefore would be an administrative receiver. It is now very rare for a charge to be enforced by a court-appointed receiver in Britain and so the procedure of debenture-holders' actions will not be considered here.

Nowadays the practice is to include in the charge contract a provision entitling the chargee to appoint a receiver, and a receiver appointed under such a provision is sometimes described as a receiver 'appointed out of court'. IA 1986 also uses the phrase 'appointed under powers contained in an instrument' (e.g., in s. 35(1)), and by s. 29(1)(b) this refers also to a receiver appointed under powers which, by virtue of any enactment, are deemed to be contained in an instrument, e.g., the power to appoint a receiver of income deemed by the Law of Property Act 1925, s. 101, to be included in every contract of charge made by deed.

In *Re Croftbell Ltd* [1990] BCLC 844, the company had granted a floating charge over 'the whole of its undertaking and all its property and assets'. It was held that a receiver appointed to enforce the charge was an administrative receiver despite the fact that at the time of appointment, the company's only asset (apart from a relatively small sum of money owed to it by its parent company) was charged separately and would not come under the receiver's control.

The Insolvency Service has proposed that the holder of a floating charge on a company's property should be required by statute to give five days' notice of intention to appoint an administrative receiver unless the company consents or the court gives leave. This is to give the company time to consider whether to propose a voluntary arrangement (see 20.4). See *The Insolvency Act 1986: Revised Proposals for a New Company Voluntary Arrangement Procedure: a Consultative Document* (London: Insolvency Service, 1995). In Britain the standard practice is to act very quickly in appointing an administrative receiver so as to prevent controllers of the company doing anything about the appointment. Banks have been able to persuade the courts that if a secured loan is repayable on demand (as overdrafts normally are) then the borrower must at all times keep the cash in some convenient place ready to meet a demand by the lender so that the only time that need be allowed between making a demand and regarding the borrower as being in default so that the charge can be enforced is the time necessary to effect the mechanics of payment. If it is known that the borrower has not got the money then no time at all need be allowed (*Sheppard and Cooper Ltd* v *TSB Bank plc* [1996] 2 All ER 654). Of course, a bank would be horrified to find that money it had lent to an industrial or commercial company was just being kept on the company's premises or at another bank to await a demand for repayment instead of being used to earn profits from which the bank's interest could be paid. The courts have permitted the wording of charge contracts to prevail over the reality of the underlying transaction so as to give banks the best possible security for their lending.

20.2.3 Effect on directors

From the time of appointment an administrative receiver of a company has sole authority to deal with the charged property. The directors of the company no longer have any authority to deal with charged property. However, they continue in office and are still liable, for example, to submit returns and documents to the registrar. In *Newhart Developments Ltd* v *Cooperative Commercial Bank Ltd* [1978] QB 814, CA, it was held that the appointment of a receiver does not divest the directors of their power to institute proceedings in the company's name (see 15.7.3) provided they do not interfere with the receiver's work of realising the charged assets (cf. *Shanks* v *Central Regional Council* 1987 SLT 410, affirmed 1988 SLT 212). In *Tudor Grange Holdings Ltd* v *Citibank NA* [1992] Ch 53, Browne-Wilkinson V-C said that he had substantial doubts that *Newhart Developments Ltd* v *Cooperative Commercial Bank Ltd* was correctly decided, and thought that, at present, it should only be followed in cases where, as in the *Newhart Developments* case, the directors proposing litigation undertook to meet any award of costs against the company if the litigation should fail. The Vice-Chancellor had two specific criticisms of the *Newhart Developments* decision. First, he pointed out that any cause of action of a company in administrative receivership would be covered by the charge under which the receiver was appointed and should therefore be under the control of the receiver. Second, allowing directors to start proceedings of their own but leaving the receiver to defend any counterclaim would be chaotic. Directors of a company in receivership may, of course, take proceedings to challenge the validity of the receiver's appointment (*Hawkesbury Development Co. Ltd* v *Landmark Finance Pty Ltd* (1969) 92 WN (NSW) 199; *Paramount Acceptance Co. Ltd* v *Souster* [1981] 2 NZLR 38, CA). Directors of a company in receivership may oppose a petition to wind up the company (*Re Reprographic Exports (Euromat) Ltd* (1978) 122 SJ 400) or cause the company to sue an administrative receiver for breach of duty (*Watts* v *Midland Bank plc* [1986] BCLC 15).

An administrative receiver of a company must, on request, supply its directors with whatever information they require to carry out their residual duties. For example, they still have a duty to prepare annual accounts for the members and the registrar, and they must be provided with the information necessary to compile those accounts. If they propose to arrange for new finance for the company they may require information about assets that the receiver has not yet realised. See *Smiths Ltd* v *Middleton* [1979] 3 All ER 842 and *Gomba Holdings UK Ltd* v *Homan* [1986] 1 WLR 1301.

20.2.4 Administrative receiver's powers

A professionally drafted contract of floating charge will confer on an administrative receiver appointed under the contract a wide range of powers. Now, s. 42(1) of, and sch. 1 to,

IA 1986 confer on every administrative receiver a standardised list of powers (though a charge contract may exclude any of them). A person dealing with an administrative receiver of a company in good faith and for value is entitled to assume that the receiver is acting within his powers (IA 1986, s. 42(3)).

20.2.5   Administrative receiver as agent of the company

Section 44(1)(a) of IA 1986 provides that an administrative receiver of a company is deemed to be an agent of the company unless and until the company goes into liquidation. This puts in statutory form a provision that has, in practice, always been inserted in contracts of floating charge. Because an administrative receiver is agent of the company, not of the chargee by whom he was appointed, the chargee avoids incurring the onerous duties of a mortgagee in possession — indeed, the chargee escapes all liability unless the chargee meddles in the receivership in which case the chargee will become liable for the results of the meddling (*Re Della Rocella's Estate* (1892) 29 LR Ir 464; *Standard Chartered Bank Ltd v Walker* [1982] 3 All ER 938, CA).

If an administrative receiver of a company carries on its business then the business is nonetheless the business of the company not the receiver (*Gosling v Gaskell & Grocott* [1897] AC 575, HL). The actions of an administrative receiver of a company are 'affairs' of the company which may be investigated by inspectors appointed under CA 1985, s. 432 (*R v Board of Trade, ex parte St Martins Preserving Co. Ltd* [1965] 1 QB 603, DC).

As agent of the company an administrative receiver must not cause it to breach any injunction to which it is subject. For example, in *Cretanor Maritime Co. Ltd v Irish Marine Management Ltd* [1978] 1 WLR 966, an administrative receiver appointed by an Irish chargee could not transfer the company's money to Ireland because the company was subject to a *Mareva* injunction forbidding it to remove its assets from England and Wales.

20.2.6   Information about the affairs of a company in receivership

20.2.6.1   Statement of affairs

20.2.6.1.1   Requirement to submit a statement.   Under IA 1986, s. 47, an administrative receiver of a company may require one or more persons connected with the company to make out and submit to the receiver a statement of the affairs of the company. The receiver is allowed to choose whom he will require to submit the statement from a wide variety of persons though in practice the directors (or ex directors) are usually chosen. The chosen person must be given notice in prescribed form and any person chosen may try to persuade the receiver to release him from the obligation to make out a statement and may appeal to the court if the receiver refuses to release him (s. 47(5)). The requirement to submit a statement of affairs must be fulfilled within 21 days of receiving notice of the requirement, or within such longer time as is specified in the notice or is subsequently allowed by the receiver or the court (s. 47(4) and (5)). It is an offence triable either way to fail to comply with a requirement to prepare a statement of affairs (s. 47(6) and sch. 10).

20.2.6.1.2   Contents of statement.   The principal information to be given in a statement of affairs is (IA 1986, s. 47(2)):

(a)   Particulars of the company's assets, debts and liabilities.
(b)   The names and addresses of its creditors.

(c)   The securities held by the creditors.

(d)   The dates when the securities were given.

A statement of affairs must be verified by affidavit by the persons required to submit it (s. 47(2)).

A statement of affairs may be used in evidence against any person who made it and may be so used in any proceedings (s. 433).

The administrative receiver must send a copy of the statement of affairs to the registrar of companies (IR 1986, r. 38(3) and (4)). If the administrative receiver thinks that it would prejudice the conduct of the receivership for the whole or part of the statement of affairs to be disclosed, he may apply to the court, under IR 1986, r. 3.5, for an order of limited disclosure. This is an order that the statement, or part of it, is not to be open to inspection otherwise than with the leave of the court.

20.2.6.2   Report to creditors

Within three months of his appointment, an administrative receiver of a company must, under penalty, prepare a report for the company's creditors in accordance with IA 1986, s. 48. The court may extend the time-limit. The principal matters on which the receiver must report are (IA 1986, s. 48(1)):

(a)   The events leading up to his appointment, so far as he is aware of them.

(b)   The disposal or proposed disposal by him of any property of the company and the carrying on or proposed carrying on by him of any business of the company.

(c)   The amounts payable to the chargee by whom he was appointed and the amounts of preferential debts payable (see 20.2.9).

(d)   The amount, if any, likely to be available to pay other creditors.

The report must also include a summary of the statement of affairs submitted to the receiver and a summary of the receiver's comments (if any) on the statement (IA 1986, s. 48(5)). The report may omit any information which, if disclosed, would seriously prejudice the carrying out of the receiver's functions (s. 48(6)).

Within three months after being appointed, the administrative receiver must, under penalty, send copies of the report to the registrar, to any trustees for secured creditors (see 12.3) and to all secured creditors of whose addresses he is aware (s. 48(1)). He is also required to send a copy of the report to all unsecured creditors of whose addresses he is aware, unless he publishes a notice stating an address to which unsecured creditors may write for copies of the report to be sent to them free of charge (s. 48(2)). However, he is relieved of the requirement to inform unsecured creditors if a liquidator of the company is appointed within the three months following his own appointment (s. 48(4)).

20.2.6.3   Meeting of unsecured creditors

An administrative receiver of a company that is not in liquidation must, having prepared the report discussed in 20.2.6.2, either (IA 1986, s. 48(2) and (3)):

(a)   Summon a meeting of unsecured creditors, giving not less than 14 days' notice, before which he will lay a copy of the report; or

(b)   State in the report that he intends to apply to the court for a direction that no meeting be held.

As mentioned in 20.2.6.2, the report must either be sent to all unsecured creditors whose addresses are known to the administrative receiver or he must advertise that the report is available. If the administrative receiver decides to apply to the court for a direction that no unsecured creditors' meeting need be held then the application cannot be heard until 14 days have elapsed since the report was published or advertised to the unsecured creditors (s. 48(3)(b)).

If a meeting of unsecured creditors is held then it is entitled to establish a committee of creditors (s. 49). The committee may require the administrative receiver to attend before it at any reasonable time and furnish it with information about the carrying out of his functions provided it gives him not less than seven days' notice (s. 49(2)).

If the administrative receiver was appointed to a company already in liquidation, or if the company has gone into liquidation, and the receiver delivers a copy of his report to the liquidator within three months after being appointed receiver then the report need not be sent to unsecured creditors and no advertisement of it need be published and no meeting of unsecured creditors need be held (s. 48(4)).

20.2.6.4   Other information for the receiver

Even if they are not required by the administrative receiver to prepare the statement of affairs, directors, ex directors and other persons connected with the company are, by IA 1986, ss. 234(1) and 235, under an obligation:

(a)   To give to the administrative receiver such information concerning the company and its promotion, formation, business dealings, affairs or property as the administrative receiver may at any time after his appointment reasonably require.

(b)   To attend on the administrative receiver at such times as he may reasonably require.

Failure, without reasonable excuse, to comply with an obligation imposed by s. 235 is an offence triable either way (s. 235(5) and sch. 10).

The court has a power to order delivery to a company's administrative receiver of books, papers or records to which the company appears to be entitled (s. 234(1) and (2)).

An administrative receiver of a company has, under ss. 234(1) and 236, the same power as a liquidator to ask the court to summon persons for private examination — see 20.9.3.

20.2.7   Effect of administrative receivership on contracts of the company

20.2.7.1   Contracts made before the administrative receiver was appointed

If a contract entered into by a company is of a type for which specific performance will be ordered (e.g., a contract for the sale of land) then the appointment of an administrative receiver makes no difference and the court will still make an order for specific performance (*Freevale Ltd* v *Metrostore (Holdings) Ltd* [1984] Ch 199; *AMEC Properties Ltd* v *Planning Research & Systems plc* [1992] BCLC 1149). Similarly, it has been held in Australia that the court will grant an injunction to prevent a company in administrative receivership breaching an express negative covenant in a contract entered into before the receivership (*Schering Pty Ltd* v *Forrest Pharmaceutical Co. Pty Ltd* [1982] 1 NSWLR 286) since such an injunction is always granted (*Doherty* v *Allman* (1878) 3 App Cas 709 per Lord Cairns LC at p. 720). In *Telemetrix plc* v *Modern Engineers of Bristol (Holdings) plc* [1985] BCLC 213, Peter Gibson J said that an administrative receiver cannot ignore the equitable rights of third parties.

Apart from these situations, an administrative receiver of a company may cause it to repudiate any contract it entered into before he was appointed (that is, he may cause the company to fail to perform its obligations under the contract) (*Ardmore Studios (Ireland) Ltd* v *Lynch* [1965] IR 1). The only remedy of the injured party to the contract is damages in an action against the company for breach of contract, but the administrative receiver is unlikely to leave the company with any money with which to pay damages (*Airlines Airspares Ltd* v *Handley Page Ltd* [1970] Ch 193).

As an agent of the company when it breached its contract the administrative receiver has not committed the tort of inducing another to breach a contract because agent and principal are treated as one so that there is no persuasion by one person of another (*Said* v *Butt* [1920] 3 KB 497; *Welsh Development Agency* v *Export Finance Co. Ltd* [1992] BCLC 148). (This will not apply to acts outside the scope of the agent's authority, e.g., when acting fraudulently: *Einhorn* v *Westmount Investments Ltd* (1970) 11 DLR (3d) 509, Saskatchewan; *Kepic* v *Tecumseh Road Builders* (1985) 29 BLR 85, Ontario.)

A court-appointed receiver is a neutral officer of the court appointed to protect the company's property for the benefit both of the company and the chargee. Therefore, he will not be allowed by the court to cause the company to breach its contracts if to do so would injure the goodwill of the company (*Re Newdigate Colliery Ltd* [1912] 1 Ch 468, CA). The court will authorise its receiver to cause the company to breach its contracts if the company's goodwill is worthless (*Re Great Cobar Ltd* [1915] 1 Ch 682). However, as a court-appointed receiver is not an agent of the company, it seems he will commit the tort of causing another to breach a contract, and will be personally liable in damages.

In *Re B. Johnson & Co. (Builders) Ltd* [1955] Ch 634, CA, Evershed MR said that an administrative receiver of a company does not owe a duty to the company to preserve the goodwill and business of the company but in *R* v *Board of Trade, ex parte St Martins Preserving Co. Ltd* [1965] 1 QB 603, DC, Phillimore J said that an administrative receiver does have that duty. Both were speaking *obiter*. The problem arises only where the goodwill is of value to the company, e.g., where the receiver is selling the business as a going concern or where the receiver will have a surplus after meeting the secured debt and will leave the company to continue in business (cf. *Kernohan Estates Ltd* v *Boyd* [1967] NI 27).

An administrative receiver of a company who does not cause the company to repudiate an unexecuted contract entered into by the company before the receiver's appointment is said to 'adopt' the contract (*Powdrill* v *Watson* [1995] 2 AC 394, HL). The terminology is misleading because the receiver does not become a party to an adopted contract — the adoption is on behalf of the company. A contract adopted by an administrative receiver is still the contract that the company originally entered into; it is not a new contract made by the receiver (*Forster* v *Nixon's Navigation Co. Ltd* (1906) 23 TLR 138; *Parsons* v *The Sovereign Bank of Canada* [1913] AC 160, PC) and it continues with the terms and conditions agreed between the company and the other party when the contract was made.

Thus in *George Barker (Transport) Ltd* v *Eynon* [1974] 1 WLR 462, CA, a company had a contract with a carrier for the transportation of its goods. The contract gave the carrier a lien on the company's goods in the carrier's hands to secure the payment of 'any moneys whatsoever due from [the company] to the carrier'. An administrative receiver of the company was appointed and he asked the carrier to complete the job it was engaged on. The carrier refused to deliver the goods in its possession unless it was paid what it was owed for previous jobs. The Court of Appeal held that the carrier was entitled to do this. The receiver had adopted the contract as it had been made by the company before his appointment including the term giving the carrier a lien.

Similarly, in *Rother Iron Works Ltd* v *Canterbury Precision Engineers Ltd* [1974] QB 1, CA, an administrative receiver of a company caused it to complete a contract for the supply of goods which had been formed before he was appointed. Unfortunately for the receiver the company also owed money to the customer and this debt was due and payable before the receiver was appointed. It was held that the customer was entitled to set off the company's debt against the price of the goods supplied and pay only the balance to the receiver.

20.2.7.2 Contracts of employment

In *Reid* v *Explosives Co. Ltd* (1887) 19 QBD 264, CA, it was held that when the court appoints a receiver of a company's property, the company's contracts of employment are automatically terminated immediately. As summary dismissal is almost always a breach of a contract of employment the employees have a right to damages. Dismissal by a court-appointed receiver occurs because a contract of employment is a personal relationship between employer and employee, and the receiver is a stranger.

Appointment of an administrative receiver of a company as agent for the company does not alter the personal relationship and so does not terminate the company's contracts of employment (*Griffiths* v *Secretary of State for Social Services* [1974] QB 468; *Nicoll* v *Cutts* [1985] BCLC 322, CA). If an administrative receiver of a company can see no hope of selling its business as a going concern (in practice it is usually possible to decide this within one or two weeks) then he or she will dismiss the employees forthwith. Such dismissal will almost undoubtedly be because of redundancy and (provided there is no unfair selection of persons to be dismissed) will almost certainly not be unfair dismissal.

An administrative receiver who wants any of the company's employees to continue working for it during the receivership may either adopt their existing contracts of employment or, acting as agent of the company, negotiate new contracts between them and the company. An administrative receiver who adopts existing contracts of employment is, by statute, personally liable for the company's liability to pay wages or salary and contributions to an occupational pension scheme in respect of services rendered wholly or partly after the adoption (IA 1986, s. 44(1)(b) and (2A) as amended by the Insolvency Act 1994, s. 2). Subsections (2B) to (2D) of s. 44 explain how liability for holiday and sick pay is to be allocated. An administrative receiver is entitled under s. 44(1)(c) to an indemnity out of the assets of the company for the liability imposed by s. 44(1)(b). An administrative receiver cannot contract out of personal liability for adopted contracts of employment but can, it seems, do so for newly negotiated contracts (s. 44(1)(b)). Nothing done or omitted to be done during the first 14 days after a receiver's appointment is to be taken as showing that the receiver has adopted any contract of employment (s. 44(2)). An administrative receiver of a company who continues to employ persons after the first 14 days and to pay them in accordance with their previous contracts will be held impliedly to have adopted those contracts (*Powdrill* v *Watson* [1995] 2 AC 394, HL). Until *Powdrill* v *Watson* it was thought that an administrative receiver could easily avoid liability for contracts of employment by writing to employees and telling them that their contracts were not being adopted, a procedure which was apparently approved in the unreported case of *Re Specialised Mouldings Ltd* (ChD 13 February 1987). It seems that receivers appointed on or after 29 December 1986 (when the rules on liability for adopted contracts of employment first came into force) who relied on *Re Specialised Mouldings Ltd* may now be unexpectedly liable for large amounts of employees' wages. The Insolvency Act 1994 clarified exactly what an administrative receiver who adopts contracts of employment is liable for but it has effect only in relation to contracts of employment adopted on or after 15 March 1994 (s. 2(4)). The extent of the liability of receivers appointed on or after 29 December 1986 on contracts adopted before 15 March 1994 was determined by the House of Lords in an appeal which was consolidated with *Powdrill* v *Watson* from a decision of Lightman J (sub nom.

Re Leyland DAF Ltd [1995] 2 WLR 312). Lightman J had ruled that an administrative receiver who adopted a contract of employment before the 1994 Act came into force was liable for all payments due under the contract including payments in respect of services rendered before the receiver was appointed. However, the House of Lords decided that although this appeared to be the literal meaning of IA 1986, s. 44(1)(b), as originally enacted, it was so absurd that it could not have been Parliament's intention. The correct construction must be that such a receiver was personally liable only for services rendered during the receiver's term of office. The government has announced that it will not propose legislation to relieve receivers of this liability retrospectively ((1995) 16 Co Law 186).

20.2.7.3 New contracts
By IA 1986, s. 44(1)(b), an administrative receiver is personally liable on any contract entered into in the performance of his or her functions, except insofar as the contract otherwise provides. This applies to contracts made with the chargee as well as contracts with third parties (*Hill Samuel & Co. Ltd* v *Laing* 1988 SLT 452). Exclusion of liability may be express or implied (ibid.). In practice, administrative receivers always try to contract out of this liability. An administrative receiver of a company who does undertake liability for its contracts is entitled to an indemnity out of the assets of the company (s. 44(1)(c)) and, in practice, will usually also have an indemnity from the chargee.

It would seem that this provision applies to new contracts of employment so that an administrative receiver can contract out of liability for them.

20.2.8 Property available to an administrative receiver

20.2.8.1 Property subject to other security arrangements; preferential debts
An administrative receiver who finds that property of which he or she is receiver is also subject to another charge ranking equally with or in priority to the one under which he or she was appointed may apply to the court, under IA 1986, s. 43, for an order authorising disposal of the property as if it were not subject to the other charge. It must be a condition of an order under s. 43 that the proceeds of disposal must go first to discharging the debt secured by the other charge (s. 43(3)). If the proceeds are less than the market value of the property then the court may order that the deficiency be paid to the other chargee (and presumably no receiver would seek an order without checking that the other assets of the company could be used to pay the deficiency). Before making an order under s. 43 the court must be satisfied that it will enable the company's assets to be realised more advantageously than if the order were not made (s. 43(1)). An administrative receiver must, under penalty, send an office copy of any order made under s. 43 to the registrar within 14 days of the making of the order (s. 43(5) and (6)).

The property coming to the hands of a company's administrative receiver must be devoted first to paying the company's preferential debts before being used to pay the debt secured by the charge under which the receiver was appointed (IA 1986, s. 40). If any of that property is also subject to a charge that ranks equally with or has priority over the charge under which the receiver was appointed and was created as a fixed charge then the preferential debts do not have priority over the debt which that other charge secures (*Re Lewis Merthyr Consolidated Collieries Ltd* [1929] 1 Ch 498). But there is disagreement over what happens if a prior charge was created as a floating charge. In *Griffiths* v *Yorkshire Bank plc* [1994] 1 WLR 1427 it was held that a floating charge created after the one under which the receiver was appointed acquired priority over it by crystallising first (the opposite conclusion was reached in *Re Household Products Co. Ltd and Federal Business*

Development Bank (1981) 124 DLR (3d) 325; see 11.6.2), and, because no receiver was appointed under it, what is now IA 1986, s. 40, did not apply to it and the preferential debts did not have priority over the debt it secured. This would seem to open the way for any floating chargee to collaborate with another creditor to avoid the operation of s. 40. In *Re H and K (Medway) Ltd* [1997] 2 All ER 321 the chargee who had appointed the receiver had agreed (for legitimate business reasons) that another floating charge was to have priority and it was held that s. 40 gave the preferential debts priority over both floating charges. The interpretation of s. 40 adopted in *Re H and K (Medway) Ltd*, though very strained, would prevent avoidance of the section.

In *Cretanor Maritime Co. Ltd* v *Irish Marine Management Ltd* [1978] 1 WLR 966, an administrative receiver was appointed of a company that was subject to a *Mareva* injunction. This injunction had been obtained by a plaintiff in an action against the company and it prohibited the company from removing its assets from the jurisdiction of the High Court. Its purpose was to ensure that if the plaintiff succeeded in the legal action there would be assets available to pay the amount claimed. However, the legal proceedings were not completed at the time of crystallisation of the charge under which the receiver was appointed so the plaintiff had no claim on the company's assets. The court found that the chargee had sufficient interest in the matter to apply for the injunction to be discharged, and the court so ordered. A plaintiff who seeks a *Mareva* injunction usually ensures that it includes a provision forbidding the creation of charges over the defendant's assets, but this will have no effect where there is already a floating charge as in *Cretanor Maritime Co. Ltd* v *Irish Marine Management Ltd.*

20.2.8.2 Property acquired after crystallisation

If a floating charge on a company's assets of a particular class is expressed to charge all present and future assets of that class then, after the floating charge has crystallised, any asset of that class acquired by the company will be subject to a fixed equitable charge as from the time of acquisition (*N.W. Robbie and Co. Ltd* v *Witney Warehouse Co. Ltd* [1963] 1 WLR 1324). For example, if a floating charge on a company's book debts has crystallised, any debt which becomes due after crystallisation is subject to a fixed charge as from the time it becomes due. Provided notice of this charge is given to the debtor, any amount which subsequently becomes due from the company to the debtor cannot be set off against the charged debt (*Business Computers Ltd* v *Anglo-African Leasing Ltd* [1977] 1 WLR 578).

20.2.8.3 Property seized in execution

If execution is levied on company property at the instance of judgment creditors then the sheriff must observe the rights of others to that property if those rights were created before delivery of the writ to the sheriff. So any execution levied after crystallisation of a floating charge will yield nothing for the judgment creditor; the sheriff cannot seize an equity of redemption (*Scott* v *Scholey* (1807) 8 East 467).

Similarly if a pre-existing floating charge crystallises after the writ is delivered, but before the execution is completed, then the judgment creditor gets nothing. This is because the chargee's equitable right to the property was created before the writ bound the property even though it only came into force afterwards (*Re Opera Ltd* [1891] 3 Ch 260, CA; *Taunton* v *Sheriff of Warwickshire* [1895] 2 Ch 319, CA). This rule applies even if the execution is put in to enforce a judgment given before the floating charge was created since the judgment itself creates no rights over property (*Geisse* v *Taylor & Hartland* [1905] 2 KB 658, DC). However, if crystallisation does not occur until after the execution is completed then the floating chargee will never have had any rights over the seized property (*Royal Bank of Canada* v *Mohawk Moving & Storage Ltd* (1985) 16 DLR (4th) 434, Ontario).

Similarly if a judgment creditor of a company seeks to execute the judgment by garnishee (attachment) proceedings in respect of a debt owed to the company then a floating charge created before the proceedings will take priority if it crystallises at any time before the garnishor actually receives payment (*Robson* v *Smith* [1895] 2 Ch 118; *Cairney* v *Back* [1906] 2 KB 746).

Because these are problems of priorities of equitable interests it is irrelevant that a judgment creditor has not had notice of the appointment of an administrative receiver before attempting to obtain payment by execution or garnishment (*MacKay & Hughes (1973) Ltd* v *Martin Potatoes Inc.* (1984) 9 DLR (4th) 439, CA of Ontario).

20.2.8.4   Court orders to deliver property

The court has a power to order delivery to a company's administrative receiver of property to which the company appears to be entitled (IA 1986, s. 234(1) and (2)). The court may also order delivery of property discovered during a private examination under IA 1986, ss. 236 and 237 (see 20.2.6.4 and 20.9.3).

20.2.8.5   Wrongful seizure of property

An administrative receiver of a company who seizes or disposes of property that does not belong to the company is not liable for loss or damage arising from the seizure or disposal provided he was not negligent and provided he believed, and had reasonable grounds for believing, that he was entitled to seize or dispose of the property at the time that he did so (IA 1986, s. 234(1), (3) and (4)). There is no relief from liability for wrongly taking intangible property because the provision refers to 'seizure' of property and intangible property cannot be seized (*Welsh Development Agency* v *Export Finance Co. Ltd* [1992] BCLC 148).

20.2.9   Preferential creditors

One disadvantage of a floating charge, as far as the chargee is concerned, is that if an administrative receiver is appointed, or if the company is wound up before an administrative receiver is appointed, then certain of the company's debts, called its 'preferential debts', must be paid out of the assets subject to the floating charge in priority to the chargee's debt (IA 1986, ss. 40 and 175(2)(b)). The preferential debts are defined in s. 386 and sch. 6 (see 20.13.1).

A second disadvantage of floating charges is that any assets of a company in liquidation which are subject to a charge which was created as a floating charge are assets from which the expenses of the liquidation (including the liquidator's remuneration) are payable in priority to any other claim (*Re Barleycorn Enterprises Ltd* [1970] Ch 465; *Re Portbase Clothing Ltd* [1993] Ch 388).

If, in addition to the floating charge under which a receiver is appointed, property of the company is charged under a fixed charge that ranks in priority to, or equally with, the receiver's floating charge then that property cannot be utilised to pay the preferential debts or liquidation expenses, even if it is charged to secure the same debt as is secured by the receiver's charge (*Re Lewis Merthyr Consolidated Collieries Ltd* [1929] 1 Ch 498, CA; *Re G.L. Saunders Ltd* [1986] 1 WLR 215). Creditors exploit this rule by obtaining a charge that combines a fixed charge over as many assets as possible and a floating charge on the remainder. A receiver can be appointed under both fixed and floating elements of the charge but preferential debts are paid only out of the property charged by the floating charge. However, property subject to a floating charge and also a fixed charge which ranks *after* the floating charge must be utilised to pay preferential debts (*Re Portbase Clothing Ltd*).

The expenses of the receivership are payable in priority to the preferential debts (*Woods* v *Winskill* [1913] 2 Ch 303; *Re Glyncorrwg Colliery Co. Ltd* [1926] Ch 951). The principle, as explained in *Batten* v *Wedgwood Coal & Iron Co.* (1884) 28 ChD 317, is that: 'The man who has actually produced the fund for distribution is to have his costs of producing it paid in priority'.

However, a receiver has a duty not to incur expenses if to do so would lessen the amount available to pay preferential creditors (*Woods* v *Winskill*; *Westminster Corporation* v *Haste* [1950] Ch 442 — both of which were concerned with liabilities incurred in carrying on the company's business).

A receiver who pays preferential debts is entitled to recoup the payment out of any assets of the company available for payment of general creditors (s. 40(3)).

For a detailed study see H. Anderson, 'Receivership preferential creditors' (1994) 15 Co Law 195.

20.2.10   Liability for maladministration

In *Downsview Nominees Ltd* v *First City Corporation Ltd* [1993] AC 295, the Privy Council made a detailed examination of the liability of administrative receivers for negligence. Reflecting the present reluctance of the English courts to impose negligence liability, the Privy Council held that an administrative receiver of a company does not owe any duty of care to the company or to persons who have charges over the company's property ranking after the one under which the administrative receiver was appointed. It follows that an administrative receiver appointed under a charge given by a company also owes no duty of care to guarantors of the obligation secured by the charge, despite the Court of Appeal's view to the contrary in *Standard Chartered Bank Ltd* v *Walker* [1982] 1 WLR 1410.

The Privy Council confirmed that an administrative receiver appointed under a charge given by a company has the same duty as the chargee has to take reasonable care to obtain the true market value of the property (*Downsview Nominees Ltd* v *First City Corporation Ltd* at p. 315; see *Cuckmere Brick Co. Ltd* v *Mutual Finance Ltd* [1971] Ch 949 and 11.5.1).

An administrative receiver appointed under a charge given by a company must exercise his or her powers in good faith and for the purpose of obtaining payment of the obligation secured by the charge. This duty is owed to the company and to persons who have charges over the company's property ranking after the one under which the administrative receiver was appointed. This duty was breached in *Downsview Nominees Ltd* v *First City Corporation Ltd*. A company called Glen Eden Motors Ltd had issued a first debenture to a bank and a second debenture to First City Corporation. The company traded at a loss and the second debenture holder appointed an administrative receiver who proposed to sell the company's assets. The principal of the company, Mr Pedersen, then persuaded Downsview Nominees Ltd to purchase the first debenture and appoint its own administrative receiver apparently for the sole purpose of keeping the company intact for Mr Pedersen. Downsview Nominees Ltd and its administrative receiver were held to be liable to First City Corporation for the damage caused by this misuse of the administrative receiver's powers.

20.3   ADMINISTRATION

20.3.1   Summary description

Administration is an insolvency procedure: it can be invoked only in relation to a company that is, or is likely to become, insolvent. Most of the law on administration is contained in IA 1986, part II (ss. 8 to 27).

Administration is not a liquidation procedure.

This procedure can be initiated only by court order.

An administrator is appointed by the court on the petition of the company as a separate person or of a creditor of the company. The company's directors are empowered to present a petition on behalf of the company as a separate person. A company's administrator is asked to formulate, if possible, a plan for dealing with the company otherwise than by putting it into liquidation. The administrator's proposals must, within three months of his or her appointment, be submitted for the approval of the company's unsecured creditors.

For a detailed discussion of administration see D. Prentice et al., 'Administration: the Insolvency Act 1986, part II' [1994] LMCLQ 487.

20.3.2 Application for an administration order

An administrator can be appointed to deal with a company only by the court and, initially, an appointment is made in an 'administration order' (IA 1986, s. 13), which is defined in IA 1986, s. 8(2), as:

> an order directing that, during the period for which the order is in force, the affairs, business and property of the company shall be managed by a person (the 'administrator') appointed for the purpose by the court.

A petition applying for the court to make an administration order in relation to a company may be presented by the company or its directors, or by a creditor or creditors (including any contingent or prospective creditor) (s. 9(1)) or by the supervisor of a voluntary arrangement (see 20.4) (s. 7(4)(b)). A decision by the directors to present a petition must be taken at a properly constituted board meeting (*Re Equiticorp International plc* [1989] 1 WLR 1010) or agreed to by all the directors without meeting (*Re Instrumentation Electrical Services Ltd* [1988] BCLC 550). The clerk to a magistrates' court may petition for an administration order if a company has failed to pay a fine (Magistrates' Courts Act 1980, s. 87A; Criminal Justice Act 1988, s. 62). However, there are restrictions on the circumstances in which an administration order may be made in relation to a company. The court must be satisfied that the company is, or is likely to become, unable to pay its debts (IA 1986, s. 8(1)(a)) but the company must not be in liquidation (s. 8(4)).

By IA 1986, s. 8(1)(a), a company is deemed to be unable to pay its debts in any of the circumstances specified in IA 1986, s. 123, which states the circumstances in which the court may make an order to wind up a company on the ground that it is unable to pay its debts (see 20.6.3).

The court may only make an administration order in relation to a company if it considers that making the order would be likely to achieve one or more of the purposes specified in IA 1986, s. 8(3), and the court must specify in the order the purpose or purposes it is intended to achieve (ibid.). The purposes listed in s. 8(3) are:

(a) The survival of the company, and the whole or any part of its undertaking, as a going concern.

(b) The approval of a voluntary arrangement under IA 1986, part I (ss. 1 to 7).

(c) The sanctioning under CA 1985, s. 425, of a compromise or arrangement between the company and its members or creditors.

(d) A more advantageous realisation of the company's assets than would be effected on a winding up.

In deciding whether it is 'likely' that one or more of these purposes will be achieved the court must be satisfied that there is a real prospect of achievement but does not have to be satisfied that achievement is more likely than not (*Re Harris Simons Construction Ltd* [1989] 1 WLR 368; *Re SCL Building Services Ltd* [1990] BCLC 98).

In *Re Imperial Motors (UK) Ltd* [1990] BCLC 29, a creditor presented a petition which was opposed by the company. The purpose intended to be achieved was the more advantageous realisation of the company's assets than in a winding up. Hoffmann J said that he had to balance the interests of the creditor in achieving a more advantageous realisation and the interests of the company, its shareholders and management in not having the business taken out of their hands and sold to a third party. As the creditor had adequate security for its debt anyway, his lordship thought that on balance he should refuse to make an order.

If there is already an administrative receiver dealing with the affairs of a company then the court cannot make an administration order in relation to that company unless the chargee who appointed the receiver has consented to an order being made or the court is satisfied that if an order were made then the floating charge under which the receiver was appointed would be discharged or avoided or declared invalid by the court under IA 1986, ss. 238 to 240 or 245 (see 11.6.5) (IA 1986, s. 9(3)). Accordingly notice of a petition for an administration order must be served on any person who has appointed, or is or may be entitled to appoint, an administrative receiver of the company (s. 9(2)(a)). While a petition for an administration order is pending a chargee may appoint an administrative receiver who may function without reference to the court (s. 10(2)(b) and (c)). These provisions enable the holder of a floating charge to frustrate the making of an administration order by putting in his own administrative receiver. Accordingly it has become the practice for a creditor secured by a fixed charge to take in addition a floating charge over remaining assets — a so-called 'lightweight' floating charge — purely to prevent an administration order being made (see *Re Croftbell Ltd* [1990] BCLC 844; J.B.C. Simmonds, 'Rebirth of the floating charge' (1990) 134 SJ 32; F. Oditah, 'Lightweight floating charges' [1991] JBL 49). On the making of an administration order any administrative receiver of the company shall vacate office (s. 11(1)(b)) and thereafter no administrative receiver may be appointed while the administration order is in force (s. 11(3)(b)).

20.3.3 Administrator's proposals

The principal duty of an administrator is to prepare proposals for achieving the purposes for which the administration order was made. The administrator of a company may at any time apply to the court for the administration order to be varied so as to specify an additional purpose or to be discharged because it appears to him that a purpose cannot be achieved (IA 1986, s. 18). Within three months after the administration order is made (unless the court extends the time) the administrator must, under penalty, make a statement of proposals for achieving the purposes of the order, send copies of that statement to the registrar and the company's creditors and lay a copy of the statement before a meeting of the company's creditors summoned for the purpose on not less than 14 days' notice (s. 23(1) and (3)). Copies of the statement must also be sent to all the company's members unless the administrator publishes a notice stating an address to which members may write for copies of the statement to be sent to them free of charge (s. 23(2)). However, no meeting of members is summoned.

The meeting of creditors is required to decide whether or not to approve the administrator's proposals (s. 24(1)). It is an important feature of administration that proposals must be approved by a creditors' meeting *before* they are implemented (*Re Consumer & Industrial Press Ltd (No. 2)* (1987) 4 BCC 72). If it is among the purposes of the administration order, the administrator may propose a composition or arrangement, but the creditors' meeting in administration cannot impose a composition or arrangement: it can only approve the administrator's proposals — further steps must be taken under IA 1986, ss. 1 to 7, or CA 1985, ss. 425 to 427, as appropriate (*Re St Ives Windings Ltd* (1987) 3 BCC 634).

Decisions to adopt resolutions at the meeting of creditors are taken by a simple majority, *in value,* of the creditors who are present and vote, in person or by proxy (IR 1986, r. 2.28(1)). Only unsecured creditors can vote — a secured creditor is entitled to vote only in respect of the balance (if any) of his debt after deducting the value of his security as estimated by him (IR 1986, r. 2.24). Debts are valued as at the date of the administration order except that amounts paid since that date must be deducted (IR 1986, r. 2.22(4)).

The meeting may modify the proposals but only if the administrator consents to each modification (IA 1986, s. 24(2)). The administrator must report the result of the meeting to the court and the registrar (s. 24(4)).

If the meeting approves the administrator's proposals then the administrator is required to manage the affairs, business and property of the company in accordance with those proposals (s. 17(2)(b)). If the meeting declines to approve the proposals then the court may discharge the administration order (s. 24(5)). If members of the company object to what is happening then their only course is to apply to the court under IA 1986, s. 27, for an order regulating the administrator's future management of the company on the ground that his or her present or proposed actions unfairly prejudice the interests of the members. However, unless they can show that the company is actually solvent so that they have a financial interest in it then (unless they have only partly paid shares) it is unlikely that the members can claim that they have any interests that are affected by the administrator's actions.

If the meeting of creditors approves the administrator's proposals then it is entitled to establish a creditors' committee (s. 26). The committee may require the administrator to attend before it at any reasonable time and furnish it with information about the carrying out of his or her functions provided it gives the administrator not less than seven days' notice (s. 26(2)).

If an administrator's proposals are accepted by a creditors' meeting but the administrator subsequently wishes to make amendments 'which appear to him substantial' (s. 25(1)(b)) then the revised proposals must be circulated and a fresh meeting of creditors called to consider the changes, which the administrator must not act on until they have been approved by the meeting (s. 25). If there is an urgent need to implement a substantial amendment before a meeting of creditors can be summoned to consider it then the court may give the administrator directions under s. 14(3) to implement the amendment (*Re Smallman Construction Ltd* (1988) 4 BCC 784, in which the amendment was unanimously approved by the creditors' committee).

20.3.4 Powers of an administrator

The very wide powers of an administrator are stated in IA 1986, s. 14(1):

The administrator of a company—
(a) may do all such things as may be necessary for the management of the affairs, business and property of the company, and
(b) without prejudice to the generality of paragraph (a), shall have the powers specified in Schedule 1 to this Act.

By s. 14(1), in applying sch. 1 to an administrator of a company, the words 'he' and 'him' refer to the administrator.

In exercising his or her powers an administrator of a company is deemed to be acting as agent of the company (s. 14(5)) like an administrative receiver. Unlike an administrative receiver an administrator is not burdened with a statutory liability on contracts (see 20.2.7.2 and 20.2.7.3). A person dealing with an administrator of a company in good faith and for value is entitled to assume that the administrator is acting within his or her powers (s. 14(6)).

The administrator of a company has power to call meetings of its members or creditors (s. 14(2)(b)).

The administrator of a company may dispose of any of its property that is subject to a charge which as originally created was a floating charge as if the property were not subject to the charge (s. 15(1) and (3)) but then the chargee shall have the same priority in respect of any property of the company directly or indirectly representing the property disposed of as he would have had in respect of the property disposed of (s. 15(4)).

The administrator of a company may apply to the court for authority to dispose of property subject to any charge other than a floating charge as if it were free from the charge, provided the proceeds of disposal go first to paying the obligation owed to the chargee (s. 15). This is similar to the procedure available to administrative receivers under IA 1986, s. 43 — see 20.2.8.1. As with that procedure if the proceeds of disposal are less than the market value of the property, the court may order that the deficiency be paid to the chargee and the court must in any case be satisfied that making an order under s. 15 would be likely to promote the purpose of the company's administration order (s. 15(2)). For a detailed discussion, see *Re ARV Aviation Ltd* [1989] BCLC 664. Unlike an administrative receiver an administrator may apply for an order in respect of property in the possession of the company under hire-purchase, conditional sale, chattel leasing or retention of title agreements (s. 15(2) and (9)) — for such property the court's order will enable it to be sold as if the company owned it provided the true owner is paid what is owed to him out of the proceeds of sale (s. 15(2) and (5)). An administrator may ignore a charge that should have been registered with the registrar of companies but was not registered (see 11.7).

Debts or liabilities incurred during administration are payable out of the property under the administrator's custody or control in priority to the receiver's own remuneration and expenses, and both have priority over any charge on that property which was, as created, a floating charge (ss. 19(3), (4) and (5) and 15(1) and (3)). Sums payable under contracts of employment adopted by the administrator have the same priority (s. 19(6) inserted by the Insolvency Act 1994, s. 1(4)) but limited to sums payable in respect of services rendered wholly or partly after the adoption of the contract. Subsections (7) to (10) of s. 19 explain how liability for holiday and sick pay is to be allocated. Nothing done or omitted to be done during the first 14 days after an administrator's appointment is to be taken as showing that the administrator has adopted any contract of employment (s. 19(6)). For discussion of the meaning of 'adoption' and the background to the 1994 Act see 20.2.7.2. Unlike an administrative receiver, an administrator does not incur personal liability for adopted contracts of employment. An administrator will probably seek an indemnity for his or her remuneration from the creditors or other persons who are promoting the administration.

20.3.5 Effect on directors

As with an administrative receiver, the appointment of an administrator of a company leaves its directors with very little to do. IA 1986, s. 14(4), provides that any power of the company or its officers that could be exercised in such way as to interfere with the administrator's exercise of his powers is not exercisable except with the consent of the administrator. (This subsection offers the curious possibility of an administrator consenting to the company interfering with his powers.) Furthermore the administrator of a company is given a power to remove any of its directors from office and a power to appoint directors either to fill vacancies on the board or as additional directors (s. 14(2)(a)).

20.3.6 Moratorium

While an administration order is in force in relation to a company, IA 1986, s. 11, prevents creditors, unless they have the leave of the court, from enforcing security, putting in execution, distraining on the company's goods or taking legal proceedings. Also, no steps may be taken to repossess goods in the company's possession under any hire-purchase agreement, conditional sale agreement, chattel leasing agreement or retention of title agreement except with the leave of the court. The company cannot adopt a resolution to wind up and the court cannot make a winding-up order. The same immunity is given while a petition for an administration order is pending — that is, from the time the petition is presented until the order is made or the petition is dismissed (s. 10). However, if a petition for an administration order is presented in relation to a company at a time when there is an administrative receiver of the company then the period of immunity does not begin unless and until the person who appointed the receiver consents to the making of an order (s. 10(3)). A winding-up petition can be presented while a petition for an administration order is pending but it will be dismissed if an administration order is made (s. 11(1)(a)). In effect there is a moratorium on action to enforce payment of a company's debts as from the time a petition for an administration order is presented, except that a creditor with a floating charge may appoint an administrative receiver while a petition is pending (though not after an order has been made).

Guidance on dealing with applications for leave to exercise security rights against a company under administration was given by the Court of Appeal in *Re Atlantic Computer Systems plc (No. 1)* [1992] Ch 505 at pp. 541–4).

An administrator cannot pay one creditor in preference to others (*Re Manlon Trading Ltd* (1988) 4 BCC 455).

20.3.7 Information about the affairs of the company

20.3.7.1 Statement of affairs
Section 22 of IA 1986 makes the same provision for the preparation of a statement of affairs on the appointment of an administrator as s. 47 does in relation to the appointment of an administrative receiver (see 20.2.6.1). An administration statement of affairs must be filed in court (IR 1986, r. 2.12(6)) as well as with the registrar (IR 1986, r. 2.16(d)). If the administrator thinks it would prejudice the conduct of the administration for the whole or part of the statement of affairs to be disclosed, he may apply to the court under IR 1986, r. 2.13, for an order of limited disclosure. This is an order that the statement, or a part of it, is to be filed separately and not be open to inspection otherwise than with the leave of the court.

20.3.7.2 Other information for the administrator
Section 235 of IA 1986 applies in relation to administrators as it does in relation to administrative receivers (see 20.2.6.4).

20.3.7.3   *Private examination*

An administrator may apply for a private examination of a person under IA 1986, s. 236, in the same way as an administrative receiver (see 20.2.6.4) or a liquidator (see 20.9.3 for full details).

20.3.7.4   *Unenforceability of liens on books*

A lien or other right to retain possession of any of the books, papers or other records of a company that is under administration is unenforceable to the extent that it would deny possession of them to the company's administrator (IA 1986, s. 246). This affects, for example, the right of an accountant in public practice or a solicitor to retain the books and records of a client until paid for work done for the client. There is an exception for 'a lien on documents which give a title to property and are held as such' (s. 246(3)). In *Brereton* v *Nicholls* [1993] BCLC 593, Morritt J decided that 'held as such' means 'held in circumstances giving rise to a lien' rather than 'held for the purpose of giving title to property'. A lien on books is unenforceable against an administrator or a liquidator but is enforceable against an administrative receiver. The court has a power to order delivery to a company's administrator of books, papers or records to which the company appears to be entitled (IA 1986, s. 234(1) and (2)).

20.4   VOLUNTARY ARRANGEMENTS

20.4.1   Summary description

Voluntary arrangement is an insolvency procedure: it is usually invoked in relation to insolvent companies and not solvent companies. Most of the law on voluntary arrangements is contained in IA 1986, part I (ss. 1 to 7).

Voluntary arrangement is not a liquidation procedure.

A proposal for a voluntary arrangement must be reported to the court but does not require the court's approval.

In a voluntary arrangement a three-quarters majority of a company's unsecured creditors voting at a meeting of creditors imposes on all unsecured creditors a composition or scheme of arrangement that has been proposed by the company's directors (or its liquidator or administrator) and approved by its members.

20.4.2   Proposal for a voluntary arrangement

If a company is not in liquidation or under administration then its directors may propose a composition or scheme (IA 1986, s. 1(1)). The directors must nominate a qualified insolvency practitioner to be supervisor and the nominee must, within 28 days after he is given notice of the proposal, submit a report to the court stating whether, in his opinion, the proposal should be put to meetings of creditors and members of the company (s. 2(1) and (2)). The directors must provide the nominee with a statement of the company's affairs (s. 2(3)) and any further information he requires (IR 1986, r. 1.6). If the nominee's opinion is that the scheme is not worth putting to meetings then the court cannot overrule him (IA 1986, s. 3(1)) but if it does not then the nominee must summon a meeting of all the creditors of the company of whose addresses he is aware and a meeting of the company's members (s. 3(1) and (3)).

If a company is in liquidation or under administration then its liquidator or administrator (who must be a qualified insolvency practitioner) may propose a composition or scheme to be supervised by himself (s. 1(3)). The administrator or liquidator may then summon meetings of creditors and members for such time, date and place as he thinks fit (s. 3(2)) without reference to the court. Alternatively a liquidator or administrator may nominate another insolvency practitioner to be supervisor and then a report is made to the court as if the proposal had been made by the directors using the procedure described in the preceding paragraph.

In practice, one of the likely difficulties for a company not under administration or in liquidation of preparing a proposal for a composition or scheme will be that once creditors become aware of the preparations they may present a winding-up petition. To prevent this, it is likely that the directors of a company preparing a proposal will petition for an administration order to be made in relation to the company. From the time of presentation of the petition there is a moratorium on payment of the company's debts except that an administrative receiver can be appointed (see 20.3.6). So, provided they have the agreement of every person entitled to appoint an administrative receiver, directors can buy time by petitioning for administration. The approval of a composition or scheme of arrangement is one of the specific purposes an administration order may be made to achieve (s. 8(3)). The Insolvency Service has proposed a new procedure in which a 28-day moratorium is available while proposals for a voluntary arrangement are formulated so that the expense and complication of going into administration can be avoided (*The Insolvency Act 1986: Revised Proposals for a New Company Voluntary Arrangement Procedure: a Consultative Document* (London: Insolvency Service, 1995)).

20.4.3   Approval of a proposal

The meetings of a company's members and creditors summoned by the insolvency practitioner nominated to be supervisor of a composition or scheme of arrangement (see 20.4.2) must decide whether to approve the proposal, with or without modifications (IA 1986, s. 4(1)).

A meeting cannot approve a proposal or a modification that deprives a secured creditor of his right to enforce the security unless that creditor agrees (s. 4(3)). This means that, as with administration orders, no proposal can go forward without the consent of the holders of floating charges over the company's property.

A meeting cannot approve a proposal that affects the priority of any preferential debt (or any debt that would be preferential if the company had gone into liquidation when its administration order, if there is one, was made or when the proposal is approved, if there is no administration order and the company is not in liquidation) (ss. 4(4) and 387(2)). Preferential debts are discussed in 20.13.1.

The chairman of each meeting must report its result to the court and must give notice of the result to all persons who were summoned to the meeting (IA 1986, s. 4(6); IR 1986, r. 1.24(4)). If each of the meetings approves the proposal (either with the same modifications or without modification) then the composition or scheme takes effect as if made at the creditors' meeting and it binds every person who had notice of, and was entitled to vote at, that meeting (IA 1986, s. 5(1) and (2)). However, during the period of 28 days beginning with the day on which the first of the chairmen's reports required by s. 4(6) is made to the court, any person entitled to vote at either the members' or the creditors' meeting, the nominee, or the company's liquidator or administrator (if there is one) may apply to the court under IA 1986, s. 6, on the ground:

(a)   that the approved composition or scheme unfairly prejudices the interests of a creditor, member or contributory of the company; and/or

(b) that there has been some material irregularity at or in relation to either of the meetings.

The court may then revoke or suspend the approvals given by the meetings and make directions for revised proposals to be put before further meetings (s. 6(4)). An approval is not invalidated by any irregularity at or in connection with the meetings unless the approval is successfully challenged by proceedings under IA 1986, s. 6 (s. 6(7)).

If a proposal is approved for a company that is in liquidation or under administration then, when the 28-day period for lodging an objection has expired, and after the court has disposed of any objections that are made, the court may order that the proceedings in the winding up be stayed (i.e., that it shall proceed no further) or discharge the administration order (s. 5(3) and (4)).

20.5 VOLUNTARY LIQUIDATION

20.5.1 Summary description

20.5.1.1 *Members' voluntary liquidation*

Members' voluntary liquidation is not an insolvency procedure: it can be invoked only in relation to solvent companies.

Members' voluntary liquidation is a liquidation procedure.

The involvement of the court is never required for initiating or confirming the use of this procedure.

It is initiated when the members of a company adopt a resolution for voluntary winding up following a statutory declaration of solvency by the company's directors. The members appoint a qualified insolvency practitioner to act as liquidator of the company.

20.5.1.2 *Creditors' voluntary liquidation*

Creditors' voluntary liquidation is an insolvency procedure: it is usually invoked in relation to insolvent companies and not solvent companies.

Creditors' voluntary liquidation is a liquidation procedure.

The involvement of the court is never required for initiating or confirming the use of this procedure.

It is initiated when the members of a company adopt a resolution for voluntary winding up without a statutory declaration of solvency by the company's directors. The company's unsecured creditors have the right to appoint a qualified insolvency practitioner to act as liquidator of the company.

20.5.2 Resolution for voluntary winding up

For the members of a company to commence its voluntary winding up they must, unless there are exceptional circumstances, adopt a special resolution that the company be wound up (IA 1986, s. 84(1)) but there are less stringent requirements in two exceptional circumstances:

(a) If, by reason of its liabilities, the company cannot continue its business, and it is advisable to wind up, then an extraordinary resolution is sufficient (s. 84(1)(c)).

(b) If the articles (not the memorandum) of the company provide that it should cease operations on the expiry of a certain time, which has now expired, or on the happening of a particular event, which has now happened, then an ordinary resolution is sufficient (s. 84(1)(a)). A company has no power to provide in its memorandum or articles that it will commence winding up on the happening of a specified event, or after a specified time, *without* a resolution of the members.

If an extraordinary resolution is appropriate then the company will probably be insolvent and there will be a creditors' voluntary winding up. In other circumstances it is more likely that the liquidation will proceed as a members' voluntary winding up.

20.5.3 Declaration of solvency

After the adoption of a resolution to wind up, the liquidation may proceed as a members' voluntary winding up only if, within the five weeks *preceding* the adoption of the resolution, a majority of the directors of the company made, at a board meeting, a statutory declaration of the company's solvency (IA 1986, s. 89). The declaration may be made on the same day as the members' meeting provided it is made before the meeting (s. 89(2)(a)).

If a directors' declaration of solvency is not made then the liquidation is a creditors' voluntary winding up (s. 90).

The directors must, under penalty, file their declaration with the registrar before the expiry of the period of 15 days immediately following the date on which the winding-up resolution is adopted (s. 89(3) and (6) and sch. 10).

The requirement that the declaration must be made by a majority of directors means that there must be more directors making the declaration than not making it. So if the company has only two directors then both must make the declaration; and if it has only one director then that director must make the declaration (s. 89(1)).

The declaration must state that the declaring directors have made a full inquiry into the affairs of the company, and have formed the opinion that the company will be able to pay its debts (including post-liquidation interest) in full within a specified period after the commencement of winding up. The specified period must not exceed 12 months (s. 89(1)).

A declaration is of no effect unless it embodies a statement of the company's assets and liabilities as at the latest practicable date before the making of the declaration (s. 89(2)(b)). It is not required that the statement be correct in every detail provided it can be fairly described as being a statement of assets and liabilities (*De Courcy* v *Clement* [1971] Ch 693).

A director making a declaration of solvency without reasonable grounds for the opinion expressed in it commits an offence triable either way (s. 89(4) and sch. 10). If the company's debts are not paid or provided for within the period stated in the declaration then the makers of the declaration are presumed not to have had reasonable grounds for making it (s. 89(5)).

20.5.4 Appointment of a members' liquidator

In a members' voluntary winding up the members in general meeting must appoint one or more liquidators (IA 1986, s. 91(1)). The appointment would normally be made at the meeting at which the resolution to wind up is adopted and no notice is required of intention to propose a resolution to appoint a liquidator at that meeting (*Re Trench Tubeless Tyre Co.* [1900] 1 Ch 408, CA).

On the appointment of a liquidator of a company all the powers of its directors cease, though either the company in general meeting or the liquidator may allow some or all of the directors to continue to exercise some or all of their powers (s. 90(2)). However, after the resolution to wind up is adopted, if the members fail to appoint a liquidator then the directors commit a summary offence if they exercise any of their powers without the sanction of the court (s. 114) except for the purpose of disposing of goods that are perishable or likely to diminish in value if not immediately disposed of and for the purpose of protecting the company's assets (s. 114(3)).

20.5.5 Resolution for a creditors' voluntary liquidation

If no declaration of solvency is made by the directors of a company in the five weeks preceding the meeting at which it is proposed to adopt a resolution to wind up then the liquidation will be a creditors' voluntary winding up (IA 1986, s. 90). The creditors are given the right to appoint a liquidator and also to appoint a liquidation committee to assist the liquidator and receive reports on the progress of the liquidation. However, the members are also given some say in the appointment of the liquidator and may appoint members of the liquidation committee. Parliament has had some difficulty in balancing the interests of members and creditors. The key to involving creditors in the voluntary liquidation of a company is to force the company to hold a meeting of its creditors. IA 1986, s. 166, achieves this by making it an offence for a liquidator nominated by the members in a creditors' voluntary liquidation to exercise any powers (except for the purpose of taking control of the company's property, disposing of perishable goods and goods likely to diminish in value unless immediately disposed of and protecting the company's assets) until a creditors' meeting has been held. At the creditors' meeting, if the creditors do not approve of the members' choice of liquidator then they may nominate a liquidator and their nominee becomes liquidator unless the court otherwise directs (IA 1986, s. 100).

20.5.6 Liquidation committee

In a creditors' voluntary liquidation, the creditors may appoint a committee (known as a 'liquidation committee') of not more than five persons to act with the liquidator. If they do so then the members of the company may appoint up to five persons to the committee to represent shareholders' interests. However, the creditors may then veto any or all of the persons appointed by the shareholders and this veto is effective unless the court orders otherwise, though the court may appoint some other person in place of a vetoed appointee (IA 1986, s. 101).

The function of the liquidation committee is to assist and supervise the work of the liquidator and in particular it may:

(a)	sanction a proposal by the liquidator (IA 1986, s. 165(2)(b) and sch. 4, paras 1–3):

(i)	to pay any class of creditors in full;
(ii)	to make any compromise or arrangement with creditors;
(iii)	to compromise any claim the company has against others;

(b)	sanction the sale of the company's business to another company in exchange for shares of the purchasing company (IA 1986, s. 110);

(c)	sanction the continuance of the powers of the directors of the company (IA 1986, s. 103);

(d)	approve payment of the expenses of the statement of affairs to the liquidator or an associate of the liquidator (IR 1986, r. 4.38(4));

(e)	approve payment of the expenses of the first meeting of creditors to the liquidator or an associate of the liquidator (r. 4.62(4));

(f)   fix the liquidator's remuneration (r. 4.127);

(g)   receive reports and information from the liquidator (rr. 4.155 and 4.168) and inspect the liquidator's financial records (Insolvency Regulations 1986 (SI 1986 No. 1994), reg. 27(2));

(h)   sanction committee members' dealings with the company (r. 4.170);

(i)   permit the liquidator to distribute the company's assets in kind to creditors (r. 4.183);

(j)   resolve that the liquidator is to require costs, charges or expenses payable by the company to be taxed (r. 7.34(2)).

The committee must, from time to time, review the adequacy of the liquidator's security (r. 12.8(2)).

If the liquidator disposes of any property of the company to a person who is connected with the company (for the meaning of 'connected with' a company, see 11.6.5.1) the liquidator must notify the liquidation committee (IA 1986, s. 165(6)).

20.6   COMPULSORY LIQUIDATION

In practice, compulsory liquidation is mostly invoked in relation to insolvent companies and so may be considered an insolvency procedure, but there are also significant circumstances in which solvent companies may be subject to compulsory liquidation.

Compulsory liquidation is a liquidation procedure.

The involvement of the court is required for initiating this procedure.

It is a liquidation of a company by virtue of an order of a court (with appropriate jurisdiction) that the company be wound up by that court under the provisions of the relevant legislation, currently the Insolvency Act 1986. A petition for the court to order the compulsory liquidation of a company may be presented by a secured or unsecured creditor or a member of the company, by the company as a separate person, by the directors of the company or by the Secretary of State representing the public interest. The company's unsecured creditors have the right to appoint a qualified insolvency practitioner to act as liquidator of the company.

20.6.1   Petition

An application to the court for a winding-up order must be made by petition under IA 1986, s. 124 (*Re Brooke Marine Ltd* [1988] BCLC 546). If an order is made then the winding up is deemed to have commenced when the petition was presented (s. 129(2)) unless the company was then already in voluntary liquidation in which case it is deemed to have commenced when the resolution for voluntary winding up was adopted (s. 129(1)).

The court's power to order a winding up is discretionary. On hearing a winding-up petition the court may dismiss it, or adjourn the hearing conditionally or unconditionally, or make an interim order, or any other order that it thinks fit (IA 1986, s. 125(1)). The discretion of the judge whether or not to make an order cannot be interfered with on appeal unless he erred in law (*Re P. & J. Macrae Ltd* [1961] 1 WLR 229; *Re J.D. Swain Ltd* [1965] 1 WLR 909). A petition must be dismissed if an administration order was made while the petition was pending (IA 1986, s. 11(1)(a)).

The presentation of a petition to wind up a company may seriously inconvenience it but a petitioner is never required to give an undertaking in damages unless he asks for the appointment of a provisional liquidator (*Re Highfield Commodities Ltd* [1985] 1 WLR 149).

For full details of the process of petitioning for winding up see D. French, *Applications to Wind up Companies* (London: Blackstone, 1993).

20.6.2 Petitioners

A person may petition for the compulsory liquidation of a company only if given standing to do so by legislation (*Mann* v *Goldstein* [1968] 1 WLR 1091 at p. 1094). The persons who may petition for the compulsory liquidation of any company under IA 1986 are (s. 124(1)):

(a) any creditor or creditors of the company (including any contingent or prospective creditor or creditors),

(b) any contributory or contributories of the company,

(c) the company itself,

(d) the directors of the company,

(e) a supervisor of a voluntary arrangement of the company (s. 7(4)(b)),

(f) the clerk of a magistrates' court (if the company has failed to pay a fine) (category added by Criminal Justice Act 1988, s. 62(2)),

(g) all or any of the parties listed in (a) to (f) together or separately,

(h) the Secretary of State (see 18.8.3.3) (s. 124(4)),

(i) an official receiver (though only if the company is already in voluntary liquidation) (s. 124(5)),

(j) an administrator of the company (s. 14(1); sch. 1, para. 21) — an administrator of a company is deemed to act as the company's agent (s. 14(5)),

(k) an administrative receiver of the company (s. 42(1) and (2); sch. 1, para. 21) — an administrative receiver of a company is deemed to act as the company's agent (s. 44(1)).

In practice, the most important classes of petitions are those by creditors and those by contributories (though about 95 per cent of petitions are by creditors). The significant difference between these two classes of petitions is that, in general, creditors petition to wind up insolvent companies whereas contributories petition to wind up solvent companies.

Other statutes confer standing on other persons to petition in relation to special classes of companies, such as charitable companies, banks and insurance companies, but this book will concentrate on the provisions of IA 1986.

20.6.3 Circumstances in which compulsory liquidation may be ordered

By IA 1986, s. 122(1) as amended by SI 1992 No. 1699:

A company may be wound up by the court if—

(a) the company has by special resolution resolved that the company be wound up by the court,

(b) being a public company which was registered as such on its original incorporation, the company has not been issued with a certificate under section 117 of the Companies Act [1985] (public company share capital requirements) and more than a year has expired since it was so registered,

(c) it is an old public company, within the meaning of the [Companies Consolidation (Consequential Provisions) Act 1985],

(d) the company does not commence its business within a year from its incorporation or suspends its business for a whole year,

(e) except in the case of a private company limited by shares or by guarantee, the number of members is reduced below two,

(f) the company is unable to pay its debts,

(g)   the court is of the opinion that it is just and equitable that the company should be wound up.

A petitioner does not have to present accounts to the court in order to prove that a company 'is unable to pay its debts' (IA 1986, s. 122(1)(f)) because subsections (1) and (2) of s. 123 define a series of circumstances which the court will take as sufficient evidence of inability to pay debts. The section provides:

(1)   A company is deemed unable to pay its debts—

(a)   if a creditor (by assignment or otherwise) to whom the company is indebted in a sum exceeding £750 then due has served on the company, by leaving it at the company's registered office, a written demand in the prescribed form requiring the company to pay the sum so due and the company has for three weeks thereafter neglected to pay the sum or to secure or compound for it to the reasonable satisfaction of the creditor, or

(b)   if, in England and Wales, execution or other process issued on a judgment, decree or order of any court in favour of a creditor of the company is returned unsatisfied in whole or in part, or

(c)   if, in Scotland, the induciae of a charge for payment on an extract decree, or an extract registered bond, or an extract registered protest, have expired without payment being made, or

(d)   if, in Northern Ireland, a certificate of unenforceability has been granted in respect of a judgment against the company, or

(e)   if it is proved to the satisfaction of the court that the company is unable to pay its debts as they fall due.

(2)   A company is also deemed unable to pay its debts if it is proved to the satisfaction of the court that the value of the company's assets is less than the amount of its liabilities, taking into account its contingent and prospective liabilities.

A written demand served under s. 123(1)(a) is known as a 'statutory demand'.

IA 1986, s. 123(1)(a), comes into operation only when a creditor of a company has served a statutory demand on the company 'by leaving it at the company's registered office' (IA 1986, s. 123(1)(a)). This contrasts with the provision of the Companies Act 1985, s. 725(1), that: 'A document may be served on a company by leaving it at, or sending it by post to, the company's registered office'. Accordingly, Nourse J, in *Re a Company* [1985] BCLC 37, took the view that IA 1986, s. 123(1)(a), does not operate if a statutory demand has been sent by post. The same view was taken (without reference to *Re a Company* [1985] BCLC 37) by Sheriff Principal N.D. MacLeod QC in *Craig v Iona Hotels Ltd* 1988 SCLR 130, ruling that a statutory demand sent by recorded delivery was not effective. However, in *Re a Company (No. 008790 of 1990)* [1991] BCLC 561, Morritt J observed that s. 123(1)(a) does not specify who is to leave the demand at the registered office, and held that it can be left there by any agent of the person making the demand, including the Post Office: the important point is that it must be proved that the demand was left; there is no presumption that a posted demand has been delivered; however, a demand sent by registered post which the company admitted had been delivered was effective. It is submitted that Morritt J's decision is correct. It accords with the view of Wynn-Parry J in *Stylo Shoes Ltd v Prices Tailors Ltd* [1960] Ch 396 that the act of sending a letter by ordinary post is equivalent to leaving it for the proposed recipient at the place to which the letter is delivered. In *Re a Company* [1985] BCLC 37, Nourse J held that a demand transmitted by telex was not properly served.

Showing that there has been a neglect to comply with a statutory demand (s. 123(1)(a)) or that there has been an unsatisfied execution (s. 123(1)(b), (c) or (d)) or that the company's assets are less than its liabilities (s. 123(2)) is sufficient for the company to be deemed to be unable to pay its debts. However, as Dillon LJ pointed out in *Taylors Industrial Flooring Ltd* v *M & H Plant Hire (Manchester) Ltd* [1990] BCLC 216 at p. 219:

> The practice for a long time has been that the vast majority of creditors who seek to petition for the winding up of companies do not serve statutory demands. The practical reason for that is that if a statutory demand is served, three weeks have to pass until a winding-up petition can be presented. If, after the petition has been presented, a winding-up order is made, the winding up is only treated as commencing at the date of the presentation of the petition; thus, if the creditor takes the course of serving a statutory demand, it would be giving the company an extra three weeks' grace in which such assets as the company may have may be dissipated in attempting to keep an insolvent business afloat, or may be absorbed into the security of a debenture-holder bank. So there are practical reasons for not allowing extra time, particularly where commercial conditions and competition require promptness in the payment of companies' debts so that the creditor companies can manage their own cash flow and keep their own costs down.

20.6.4   Liquidator on making an order

If a winding-up order is made immediately upon the discharge of an administration order then the court may appoint as liquidator of the company the person who was its administrator (s. 140(1)). Similarly, if there is a supervisor of a voluntary arrangement in office at the time that a company is ordered to be wound up then the court may appoint that supervisor to be liquidator (IA 1986, s. 140(2)). A creditors' meeting can remove a liquidator appointed in this way though in order to remove an ex supervisor a meeting must be requested by not less than one-quarter, in value, of the company's creditors (s. 172(1), (2) and (3)).

In any other case when the court makes an order to wind up a company in England and Wales the official receiver attached to the court becomes liquidator of the company ex officio (s. 136(1) and (2)). The official receiver's appointment renders the company liable to pay an administration fee, which is now £490 (SI 1986 No. 2030). An official receiver may act as liquidator despite not being a qualified insolvency practitioner (IA 1986, ss. 230(3) and (5), 388(1)(a) and (5) and 389).

20.6.5   First meetings

The first task of an official receiver who becomes liquidator of a company is to inquire whether it has any assets or any affairs that require investigation. If it appears to the official receiver that the realisable assets of the company are insufficient to cover the expenses of liquidation and that the affairs of the company do not require further investigation then the official receiver may give notice to the creditors and contributories of intention to apply for the company to be dissolved. The notice must be given 28 days before the application for dissolution is made and, if there is an administrative receiver of the company then 28 days' notice must also be given to the receiver (IA 1986, s. 202(1), (2) and (3)). Having given such notice the official receiver is not required to perform any duties in relation to the company other than apply for its dissolution (s. 202(4)). For the procedure after notice of intention to seek dissolution has been given see 20.14.2.6.

If an official receiver is liquidator of a company in compulsory liquidation and has not given notice of intention to apply for dissolution then, at any time, one-quarter, in value, of the company's creditors may request the official receiver to summon separate meetings (called 'first meetings') of the company's contributories and creditors for the purpose of choosing someone else to be liquidator in place of the official receiver (s. 136(5)(c)). However, if the official receiver becomes liquidator of a company ex officio when a winding-up order is made then it is his duty (if he has not given notice of intention to apply for dissolution), as soon as practicable within the 12 weeks beginning on the day the winding-up order is made, to decide whether he will himself summon first meetings (s. 136(5)(a)). (He is relieved of this duty once the creditors have requested meetings (s. 136(5)).) If the official receiver decides against summoning meetings (and the creditors have not requested him to do so) then he must notify this decision — before the end of the 12-week period — to the court and to the company's creditors and contributories (s. 136(5)(b)), and the notice to creditors must include a statement of their right to request him to summon first meetings (s. 136(6)).

Under the law prior to IA 1986, first meetings of contributories and creditors had to be summoned in every case but, in practice, about 80 per cent of such meetings failed to appoint a liquidator in place of the official receiver. The new Act has recognised that, in most liquidations, first meetings are unnecessary. However, IA 1986 also gives a new power to the official receiver to apply to the Secretary of State to appoint another person as liquidator in his place. The official receiver may make such an application either after deciding not to summon meetings himself or if he thinks it is necessary to do so after summoning first meetings that fail to appoint a liquidator in his place (s. 137). The Secretary of State may either appoint a liquidator or decline to appoint one (s. 137(3)).

If meetings of creditors and contributories are held then each meeting may nominate a person to be liquidator in place of the official receiver (s. 139(2)). The person nominated by the creditors becomes the liquidator but if they do not nominate anyone then the person nominated by the members becomes liquidator (s. 139(3)). However, if the two meetings nominate different persons then any contributory or even creditor may, within seven days after the date on which the nomination was made by the creditors, apply to the court to have the contributories' nominee appointed instead of or jointly with the creditors' nominee or to have someone else appointed instead of the creditors' nominee (s. 139(4)). It is important to remember that only unsecured creditors vote at a creditors' meeting.

20.6.6 Liquidation committee

Where a winding-up order has been made and first meetings have been summoned (see 20.6.5) those meetings may establish a liquidation committee (IA 1986, s. 141(1)). Such a committee cannot exercise any functions while the official receiver is liquidator (s. 141(4)). If a compulsory liquidator of a company is not an official receiver and there is no liquidation committee then he may at any time, if he thinks fit, summon meetings of creditors and contributories to consider establishing one, and he is required to summon such meetings if one-tenth, in value, of the creditors request him to do so (s. 141(2)). If a liquidator has been appointed by the Secretary of State under IA 1986, s. 137(3) (see 20.6.5), then that liquidator must give notice of his appointment and state in the notice either that he intends to call meetings to consider establishing a liquidation committee or that he does not intend to do so but that the creditors have a right to requisition such meetings (s. 137(4) and (5)).

In a compulsory liquidation, where the official receiver is not the liquidator, the function of a liquidation committee is to assist and supervise the work of the liquidator. In particular, it may:

(a)   approve a proposal by the liquidator (s. 167(1)(a)):

    (i)   to bring or defend any action or other legal proceeding in the name and on behalf of the company;
    (ii)   to carry on the business of the company;
    (iii) to pay any class of creditors in full;
    (iv) to make any compromise or arrangement with creditors;
    (v)   to compromise any claim the company has against others;

(b)   sanction the making of a call by the liquidator (IA 1986, s. 160(2));
(c)   fix the liquidator's remuneration (IR 1986, r. 4.127);
(d)   receive reports and information from the liquidator (rr. 4.155 and 4.168) and inspect his financial records (Insolvency Regulations 1986 (SI 1986 No. 1994), reg. 9(2));
(e)   sanction committee members' dealings with the company (r. 4.170);
(f)   permit the liquidator to distribute the company's assets in kind to creditors (r. 4.183);
(g)   resolve that the liquidator is to require costs, charges or expenses payable by the company to be taxed (r. 7.34(2)).

The committee must, from time to time, review the adequacy of the liquidator's security (r. 12.8(2)).

If the liquidator disposes of any property of the company to a person who is connected with the company (for the meaning of 'connected with' a company, see 11.6.5.1), or if he employs a solicitor to assist him in carrying out his functions, he must notify the liquidation committee (IA 1986, s. 167(2)).

20.6.7   Effect on directors

The functions of a compulsory liquidator of a company are to secure that the assets of the company are got in, realised and distributed to the company's creditors and, if there is a surplus, to the persons entitled to it (IA 1986, s. 143(1)). The compulsory liquidator of a company 'shall take into his custody or under his control all the property and things in action to which the company is or appears to be entitled' (s. 144(1)). He has the power to sell the company's property, use the company's seal, draw cheques on its bank account (s. 167(1)(b)) and, with the sanction of the court, to carry on the business of the company so far as may be necessary for its beneficial winding up (s. 167(1)(a)). Clearly there is little left for the company's directors to do in these circumstances, but the Act never explicitly makes the important point that the powers of the directors cease on a compulsory winding up as it does on a voluntary winding up. In *Re Farrow's Bank Ltd* [1921] 2 Ch 164, CA, Lord Sterndale MR said:

There is no express provision in the Act in the case of a compulsory liquidation as there is in the case of a voluntary liquidation, that the powers of the directors shall cease on the appointment of a liquidator, but they do in fact cease on the appointment of a liquidator in a compulsory liquidation. In that case the liquidator is imposed upon the company compulsorily by the court to do acts on behalf of the company and to carry on the business of the company so far as it shall be necessary for the purposes of the winding up. It is quite true that the company does not choose him; he is put there by the court; but he is put there to do the acts which the directors of the company did before their powers ceased: with this restriction, of course, that in all that he does he must have regard to the interests of the creditors of the company.

However, the directors may appeal against the winding-up order, because the suspension of their powers derives from the very order they dispute (*Re Diamond Fuel Co.* (1879) 13 ChD 400, CA).

As in a voluntary winding up the company cannot deny the apparent authority of its directors until the suspension of their powers is notified in the *Gazette* but in the case of a compulsory winding up the relevant notification is of the making of a winding-up order (CA 1985, s. 42).

In *Madrid Bank Ltd* v *Bayley* (1866) LR 2 QB 37, the bank was in compulsory liquidation and there was a dispute between its liquidator and a contributory over liability to calls. In legal proceedings concerning this dispute the contributory sought pre-trial discovery by interrogatories. Since the other party to the dispute was a company its 'officers' could be required to answer these interrogatories. Blackburn J held that individuals who were directors of the company when it went into liquidation 15 months previously still held office and so were required to answer the interrogatories. However, in *Re Ebsworth & Tidy's Contract* (1889) 42 ChD 23, CA, Lord Esher MR said, at p. 43, that he thought that on the appointment of a liquidator in the compulsory winding up of a company, the directors of the company 'have ceased to exist', and the decision in *Madrid Bank Ltd* v *Bayley* is inconsistent with the views of the Court of Appeal in *Measures Brothers Ltd* v *Measures* [1910] 2 Ch 248. Mr Measures had a fixed-term contract to be a director of the company until 26 June 1910, which he could then renew at his option for a further seven years. A winding-up order was made on 13 October 1909. Buckley LJ said (at p. 256):

> . . . by the operation of a winding-up order . . . the office itself came to an end. . . . after that order was made the company could not employ him in the office. . . . He has ceased to hold his office.

Kennedy LJ said (at p. 257):

> The effect of the events of 1909 . . . was unquestionably . . . to render the company admittedly and finally unable to fulfil its agreement for the continuance of the defendant as a director.

One problem with the theory that an order for the compulsory liquidation of a company abolishes the offices of the directors of the company is to determine what happens if the liquidation is stayed. Australian judges have taken the view that when a winding-up order is made, the directors remain in office but their powers are removed, and therefore if proceedings in the winding up are stayed, the directors continue in office and their powers are returned to them (*Re Country Traders Distributors Ltd* [1974] 2 NSWLR 135; *Austral Brick Co. Pty Ltd* v *Falgat Constructions Pty Ltd* (1990) 2 ACSR 766; *McAusland* v *Deputy Commissioner of Taxation* (1993) 118 ALR 577). In *Re Country Traders Distributors Ltd*, however, it was held that the directors of a company in liquidation could not be required to sign a document which the company was required by statute to prepare and which the statute directed should be signed by the company's directors: they could not be responsible for the preparation of the document and so should not be forced to authenticate it. And in *Lord Corporation Pty Ltd* v *Green* (1991) 22 NSWLR 532 it was held that a director of a company no longer holds a fiduciary position with respect to the company after it has gone into compulsory liquidation. It is submitted that these decisions show that it is artificial to regard directors of a company as still holding office after it has gone into compulsory liquidation and that the better view is that the winding-up order has the effect of removing them from office.

20.7 APPOINTMENT OF A PROVISIONAL LIQUIDATOR

At any time after a petition for the compulsory liquidation of a company has been presented to the court, and before the court disposes of the petition, any person with standing to petition for the company's compulsory liquidation may apply for the appointment by the court of a provisional liquidator. Like compulsory liquidation, to which it is closely linked, the procedure for appointing a provisional liquidator is mostly invoked in relation to insolvent companies and so may be considered an insolvency procedure, but there are also significant circumstances in which it may be applied to solvent companies.

Appointment of a provisional liquidator is not a liquidation procedure.

A provisional liquidator can be appointed only by the court.

A provisional liquidator is appointed to take charge of the company's affairs, maintain the status quo and prevent prejudice either to those supporting the winding-up petition or to those against it, pending the court's decision on the petition.

20.8 COMMENCEMENT OF WINDING UP: GOING INTO LIQUIDATION

As winding up is a distinct and special period in the history of a company it is important to know when it commences. This is determined by two sections of IA 1986. By s. 86, a voluntary winding up is deemed to commence at the time of the passing of the resolution for voluntary winding up. By s. 129(1), if a winding-up order is made in respect of a company on a petition presented when the company was already in voluntary liquidation then the winding up is still deemed to have commenced at the time the resolution for voluntary winding up was passed. By s. 129(2), in any other compulsory winding up, the date of commencement is the day on which the petition for winding up was presented.

The provision in s. 381 of CA 1985, that a resolution passed at an adjourned meeting of a company is to be treated as having been passed on the date on which it was in fact passed, was enacted in CA 1928 to stop companies backdating the commencement of winding up (see Report of the Company Law Amendment Committee 1925–26 (Cmd 2657, 1926), paras 36–7).

IA 1986 also uses the phrase 'to go into liquidation'. By s. 247(2), a company goes into liquidation when it adopts a resolution for voluntary winding up or when a winding-up order is made against it (unless it had already passed a resolution for voluntary winding up in which case the date of that resolution is the date of going into liquidation).

A company subject to compulsory winding up (not preceded by voluntary winding up) 'goes into liquidation' when the winding-up order is made but the winding up 'commenced' when the petition for the order was presented (*Re Walter L. Jacob & Co. Ltd* [1993] BCC 512).

20.9 INVESTIGATION OF THE AFFAIRS OF A COMPANY IN LIQUIDATION

The matters considered in 20.9 apply in both voluntary and compulsory liquidations.

20.9.1 Duty to cooperate with the liquidator

Certain persons connected with a company in liquidation are, by IA 1986, ss. 234(1) and 235, under an obligation:

(a) To give to the company's liquidator such information concerning the company and its promotion, formation, business dealings, affairs or property as the liquidator may, at any time after his appointment, reasonably require.

(b) To attend on the liquidator at such times as he may reasonably require.

'Reasonably' in this context means that the liquidator's request must be proportionate and relevant to the achievement of his or her objective (*Bishopsgate Investment Management Ltd v Maxwell* [1993] Ch 1 per Mann LJ at p. 57).

Failure, without reasonable excuse, to comply with an obligation imposed by s. 235 is an offence triable either way (s. 235(5) and sch. 10).

The persons who have a duty under s. 235 to cooperate with the liquidator are (s. 235(3) and (4)):

(a) Persons who are or have at any time been officers of the company.

(b) Persons who have taken part in the formation of the company at any time within one year before the company went into liquidation (see 20.8).

(c) Persons who are in the employment of the company, or have been in its employment within that year, and are, in the liquidator's opinion, capable of giving information which he requires.

(d) Persons who are, or have within that year been, officers of, or in the employment of, another company which is, or within that year was, an officer of the company in liquidation.

For these purposes, 'employment' includes employment under a contract for services.

There is a similar duty to cooperate with a provisional liquidator (ss. 234(1)(d) and 235(1)) but then the period within which one must have been connected with the company in order to be subject to the duty is one year before the appointment of the provisional liquidator (s. 235(3) and (4)).

IA 1986, s. 208(1)(a) to (c), makes it an offence, triable either way, for a past or present officer or shadow director (s. 208(3)) of a company in liquidation to keep from its liquidator any property, books or papers of the company. A sentence of up to seven years' imprisonment may be imposed (sch. 10). It is a defence to prove that there was no intent to defraud (s. 208(4)(a)).

20.9.2 Court orders to deliver property

The court has a power to order delivery, to a company's liquidator or provisional liquidator, of any property, books, papers or records to which the company appears to be entitled (IA 1986, s. 234(1) and (2)).

20.9.3 Private examination

Under IA 1986, s. 236, the liquidator of a company may apply to the court for an order requiring a person:

(a)   to appear before the court for oral examination on oath or by interrogatories (ss. 236(2) and 237(4));

(b)   to submit an affidavit to the court containing an account of his dealings with the company (s. 236(3));

(c)   to produce any books, papers or other records in his possession or under his control relating to the company or the promotion, formation, business, dealings, affairs or property of the company (s. 236(3)).

The court's order may be backed by a warrant for arrest and seizure of books, papers, records, money and goods (s. 236(5)).

A provisional liquidator may apply for an order under s. 236 (ss. 234(1)(d) and 236(1)), as may an administrative receiver (see 20.2.6.4) or an administrator (see 20.3.7.3).

The persons who may be required to provide information under s. 236 are:

(a)   Any officer of the company.

(b)   Any person known or suspected to have in his possession any property of the company or supposed to be indebted to the company.

(c)   Any person whom the court thinks capable of giving information concerning the promotion, formation, business, dealings, affairs or property of the company.

An inquiry under s. 236 is intended primarily to obtain information and is not a stage in civil or criminal proceedings against the person summoned. Accordingly attendance at an oral examination is limited by the court and such an examination is known as a 'private examination' (*Re Greys Brewery Co.* (1883) 25 ChD 400; *Re Norwich Equitable Fire Insurance Co.* (1884) 27 ChD 515). An examinee is entitled to be attended and advised by solicitor and counsel who may re-examine the examinee and make representations on his or her behalf (IR 1986, r. 9.4(5)). A written record must be made of the examination in such form as the court thinks proper (r. 9.4(6)). It must be read over, either to or by the examinee, and signed by the examinee (r. 9.4(6)). An examinee is not entitled to privilege against self-incrimination (*Bishopsgate Investment Management Ltd* v *Maxwell* [1993] Ch 1). The written record may be used in any proceedings as evidence against the examinee of any statement made by him or her in the course of the examination (IA 1986, s. 433; IR 1986, r. 9.4(7); *R* v *Kansal* [1993] QB 244).

The written record of an examination under s. 236 is a private document for the use of the insolvency office-holder. Unless the court otherwise directs, the record is not filed in court and is not made available for public inspection (IR 1986, r. 9.5). The court may give directions concerning the custody of the record (r. 9.5(4)).

The court will order disclosure of the record of a private examination if the Director of the Serious Fraud Office has, under the Criminal Justice Act 1987, s. 2(2), required it to be produced for the purposes of an investigation (*Hamilton* v *Naviede* [1995] 2 AC 75). Material obtained by the Serious Fraud Office in this way could be used as evidence at the trial of the examinee, even though the same evidence obtained directly by the Serious Fraud Office itself interviewing the examinee could not be so used because of the provisions of the Criminal Justice Act 1987, s. 2(8). The court giving leave for disclosure of the record cannot control its use as evidence in a criminal trial (*Hamilton* v *Naviede*). However, the criminal court might exclude the evidence under the Police and Criminal Evidence Act 1984, s. 78. Similar problems arise with evidence collected in investigations (see 18.8.2.6).

Disclosure will also be ordered if it is required by the Secretary of State under the Company Directors Disqualification Act 1986, s. 7(4), so that the Secretary of State may consider whether to institute disqualification proceedings against a present or past director of the company (*Re Polly Peck International plc* [1994] BCC 15). In *R v Clowes* [1992] 3 All ER 440, persons on trial on serious fraud charges in relation to the affairs of two companies were granted witness summonses ordering production of the record of private examinations conducted by the liquidators of the companies: the public interest in affording the accused every opportunity to defend themselves on serious charges outweighed the advantages of privacy of the examinations. A liquidator of a company may disclose information obtained under s. 236 to the company's subsidiaries to enable them to recover or defend their assets for the benefit of themselves and the parent company (*Re Esal (Commodities) Ltd* [1989] BCLC 59).

The court can order a person within the jurisdiction to produce books, papers or records held outside the jurisdiction (*Re Mid East Trading Ltd* [1998] 1 All ER 577). In *McIsaac* [1994] BCC 410 it was held in Scotland that an order under s. 236 may be made against an individual outside the jurisdiction, whereas in England in *Re Tucker, ex parte Tucker* [1990] Ch 148 it was held that such an order could not be made under the corresponding provision in bankruptcy. If the court has ordered that a person attend for oral examination then it may order the person not to leave the jurisdiction until the examination is completed (*Re Oriental Credit Ltd* [1988] Ch 204, in which the man sought to be examined was offered the alternative of posting a bond for £250,000; in *Re Bank of Credit and Commerce International SA (No. 7)* [1994] 1 BCLC 455 security of £500,000 was required).

The court has a discretion whether or not to make an order under s. 236. The exercise of that discretion was examined by the House of Lords in *British & Commonwealth Holdings plc v Spicer & Oppenheim* [1993] AC 426. In *Re Castle New Homes Ltd* [1979] 1 WLR 1075, Slade J had pointed out that the power to make an s. 236 order is necessary because the office-holder is 'a stranger to relevant events' (at p. 1080), and in *Cloverbay Ltd v Bank of Credit & Commerce International SA* [1991] Ch 90, Browne-Wilkinson V-C said that where a company's records are missing or defective, s. 236 enables the company's liquidator or other insolvency office-holder to 'reconstitute the state of knowledge that the company should possess'. But that is not a limit on the purposes for which the section may be invoked (*British & Commonwealth Holdings plc v Spicer & Oppenheim*). The powers conferred by s. 236 are there to enable the court to help a liquidator or other insolvency office-holder to discover the truth of the circumstances connected with the affairs of the company so that the insolvency office-holder can complete his or her functions as effectively as possible and with as little expense as possible (*British & Commonwealth Holdings plc v Spicer & Oppenheim* per Lord Slynn of Hadley at p. 438, approving a statement by Buckley J in *Re Rolls Razor Ltd* [1968] 3 All ER 698 at p. 700). The discretion to make an order must be exercised only after a careful balancing of the reasonable requirements of the insolvency office-holder against the oppressive effect that an order may have on the person sought to be examined (*British & Commonwealth Holdings plc v Spicer & Oppenheim* at p. 439).

In *British & Commonwealth Holdings plc v Spicer & Oppenheim,* British & Commonwealth was under administration and its administrators were investigating the company's recent acquisition of Atlantic Computers plc. Atlantic had been bought for £420 million on the basis of accounts, which had been audited by Spicer & Oppenheim. About 18 months after the acquisition, Atlantic had to be put into administration and it was revealed to have a deficiency in assets of about £279 million. The administrators of British & Commonwealth sought an order that Spicer & Oppenheim produce all books, papers and other records relating to their last two audits of Atlantic and to advice given to Atlantic in relation to the takeover. The House of Lords granted the order, saying that the administrators' need to find out how such a massive sum of money had been lost outweighed the interest of Spicer &

Oppenheim in not providing the administrators with information which might reveal that their audits had been negligent and the disruption that would be caused by providing the documents sought. In *Re Arrows Ltd (No. 2)* [1994] 1 BCLC 355, examination was ordered of a man who had been the chairman, managing director and sole beneficial shareholder of a company which had collapsed owing approximately £103 million and who had been arrested and charged with serious offences in relation to the company. The public interest in discovering what had happened to many millions of pounds outweighed the fact that the examinee might have to give incriminating answers to questions relating to the offences with which he had been charged. In *Re Brook Martin & Co. (Nominees) Ltd* [1993] BCLC 328, two solicitors, who were the only directors and shareholders of the company, were ordered to produce documents despite the fact that they were being sued for negligence by the company's liquidator. The documents were necessary for the liquidator to carry out his work in relation to the company and it was only incidental that they might reveal information which would be useful to the liquidator in his proceedings against the solicitors.

In *Cloverbay Ltd* v *Bank of Credit & Commerce International SA,* the balance was the other way. The administrators of Cloverbay Ltd suspected that BCCI had knowingly assisted Cloverbay's former managing director to defraud Cloverbay. Oral examination of officers of BCCI was refused since its apparent purpose was to force them to admit the fraud, whereas in an action against BCCI the burden would be on the company to prove the fraud. (The case was heard before the widespread malpractices in BCCI were revealed to the public.)

Deciding whether examination is primarily required to assist the office-holder's work, and so allowable, or is primarily intended to give the office-holder an unfair advantage in litigation against the examinee, and so not allowable, seems to be a virtually impossible task, especially as it is legitimate for an office-holder to seek information in order to determine whether or not there is a case worth pursuing against the examinee (because if the office-holder can discover that there is no such case then he or she will have avoided wasting money on commencing proceedings) (see *Re Bishopsgate Investment Management Ltd (No. 2)* [1994] BCC 732).

An application for an order under s. 236 must be made in writing with a brief statement of the grounds on which it is made (IR 1986, r. 9.2(1)). The application may be made *ex parte* (r. 9.2(4)). The application is not made available for public inspection unless the court orders otherwise (r. 9.5(3)). If the court decides to make an order under s. 236 it must be served personally forthwith (r. 9.3(5)) and the person who has been ordered to provide information may then apply for the order to be set aside on the ground, for example, that the discretion has been exercised wrongly. The court may then allow the person against whom the order has been made to inspect the application for the order if withholding the evidence would, or might, prevent the court from fairly and properly disposing of the application (*Re British & Commonwealth Holdings plc* [1992] Ch 342). In *Re Bishopsgate Investment Management Ltd (No. 2)* [1994] BCC 732, inspection of the application was refused because it would have disclosed the applicant's suspicions against the person sought to be examined and the source of those suspicions.

If an order is sought that a person produce documents which, though in that person's possession, in fact belong to another person then the true owner must be informed and the effect of production on the true owner is a factor which the court will take into consideration when deciding whether to make an order (*Morris* v *Director of Serious Fraud Office* [1993] Ch 372). The court will not order the Secretary of State to produce transcripts of evidence given during an investigation of a company under CA 1985, s. 432 (see 18.8.2.1), without allowing the person who gave the evidence an opportunity to be heard by the court (*Soden* v *Burns* [1996] 1 WLR 1512).

A person who has a lien on documents may nevertheless be ordered to produce them (*Re South Essex Estuary & Reclamation Co., ex parte Paine & Layton* (1869) LR 4 Ch App 215; *Re Aveling Barford Ltd* [1989] 1 WLR 360). An order under s. 236 is, however, for production of documents for inspection only so a person who has a lien on documents does not have to give up possession of them and lose the lien. This is now only relevant to an application by an administrative receiver because, by virtue of s. 246, liens on documents are now of no effect against the other insolvency office-holders who may apply under s. 236.

20.9.4 Unenforceability of liens on books

A lien or other right to retain possession of any of the books, papers or other records of a company that has gone into liquidation (see 20.8) is unenforceable to the extent that it would deny possession of them to the company's liquidator or provisional liquidator (IA 1986, s. 246; see also 20.3.7.4).

20.9.5 Official receiver's investigation and report

In a compulsory liquidation of a company, the official receiver attached to the court that made the winding-up order has a duty to investigate the promotion, formation, business, dealings and affairs of the company, and, if the company has failed, the causes of the failure (IA 1986, s. 132(1)). The official receiver may, if he thinks fit, make a report to the court on these matters (ibid.). Such a report is prima facie evidence of facts stated in it (s. 132(2)) and is absolutely privileged so that an official receiver always has a complete defence to an action for defamation based on statements made in a report (*Bottomley* v *Brougham* [1908] 1 KB 584).

In a compulsory liquidation an official receiver may apply for a private examination (see 20.9.3) whether or not he is the liquidator of the company (s. 236(1)).

20.9.6 Statement of affairs

On the making of a winding-up order against a company, or on the appointment of a provisional liquidator (see 20.7), the official receiver may require one or more persons connected with the company to make out and submit to him a statement of the affairs of the company (IA 1986, s. 131). The provisions in s. 131 are almost the same as the provisions for statements of affairs on the appointment of an administrative receiver made in IA 1986, s. 47 (see 20.2.6.1). Only the official receiver may require a statement of affairs in compulsory liquidation, even if someone else is appointed liquidator or provisional liquidator. A statement of affairs obtained by the official receiver must be filed in court (but not with the registrar of companies (IR 1986, r. 4.33(6)). If the official receiver thinks that it would prejudice the conduct of the liquidation for the whole or part of the statement of affairs to be disclosed, he may apply to the court under IR 1986, r. 4.35, for an order of limited disclosure. This is an order that the statement, or a part of it, is to be filed separately and not be open to inspection otherwise than with leave of the court.

In a creditors' voluntary liquidation it is the duty of the directors to make out a statement of affairs for submission to the creditors' meeting (IA 1986, s. 99).

If an administrative receiver is appointed of a company already in liquidation then the administrative receiver may require a statement of affairs for himself whether or not one has been prepared for the official receiver (s. 46(3)).

It is an offence triable either way for a past or present officer or shadow director of a company to make a material omission in a statement of affairs of a company that goes into liquidation (whether before or after the making of the statement), and on trial on indictment a prison sentence of up to seven years may be imposed (s. 210 and sch. 10). It is a defence if the accused proves he had no intent to defraud (s. 210(4)).

20.9.7 Suspected criminal offences

By IA 1986, s. 218(4), if it appears to a voluntary liquidator of a company that any past or present officer, or any member, of the company has been guilty of any offence in relation to the company for which he is criminally liable, then the liquidator must forthwith report the matter to the Director of Public Prosecutions. The liquidator must assist the Director by providing information and access to documents in his possession as required by the Director. The Director may refer the matter to the Secretary of State for further inquiry, and the Secretary of State may then exercise all the powers of inspectors appointed under CA 1985, ss. 431 or 432 (see 18.8.2.1) for the purpose of investigating the allegations (IA 1986, s. 218(5)). An answer given by a person to a question put to him in such an investigation may be used in evidence against him (s. 219(2)). If the prosecuting authority institutes criminal proceedings then it is the duty of the liquidator, and every officer and agent of the company past and present (other than the defendant in the proceedings), to give to the Director all assistance which he is reasonably able to give (s. 219(3) and (4)). The court may direct a voluntary liquidator to make a s. 218(4) report, either of its own motion or on the application of anyone interested in the winding up (s. 218(6)).

If it appears to the court in the course of a compulsory winding up that any past or present officer, or any member, of the company being wound up has been guilty of an offence in relation to the company for which he is criminally liable, the court may direct the liquidator to refer the matter to the Director of Public Prosecutions. The court may do this of its own motion or on the application of any person interested in the winding up (s. 218(1) and (2)). If the Director institutes criminal proceedings then it is the duty of the liquidator, and every officer and agent of the company past or present (other than the defendant in the proceedings), to give the Director all assistance which he is reasonably able to give (s. 219(3) and (4)).

In a compulsory liquidation the court will normally be alerted to possible criminal charges by its official receiver. If a compulsory liquidator is not an official receiver then IA 1986, s. 218(3), imposes a duty on the liquidator to report any suspected criminal offence to the official receiver.

20.9.8 Public examination of officers

In a compulsory liquidation of a company, an officer or promoter of the company may be ordered to attend the court for a public examination on the promotion, formation or management of the company, or the conduct of its business and affairs or his conduct and dealings in relation to the company (IA 1986, s. 133). The Cork Committee believed that public examinations (which had not taken place in company liquidations since 1935) were very valuable and should be revived. The Committee took the view that a public examination should serve three purposes (Cmnd 8558, 1982, para. 655):

(a) To form the basis of reports by the official receiver, e.g., on possible offences (see 20.9.7) or disqualification of directors (see 15.2.5).

(b) To obtain material information for the administration of the liquidation.

(c) To give publicity, for the information of creditors and the community at large, to the salient facts and unusual features connected with the company's failure.

A public examination is applied for by the official receiver (IA 1986, s. 133(1)) and the official receiver must make an application if requested to do so by one-half, in value, of the company's creditors or three-quarters, in value, of the company's contributories (s. 133(2)). The following persons may be summoned for public examination (s. 133(1)):

(a) Any person who is or has been an officer of the company.

(b) Any person who has acted as liquidator or administrator of the company, or as receiver or manager of its property.

(c) Any other person who is or has been concerned, or has taken part, in the promotion, formation or management of the company.

An individual who is among those specified in s. 133(1) may be summoned for a public examination in England and Wales whether or not he or she is within the jurisdiction at the time, and whether or not he or she is a British subject (*Re Seagull Manufacturing Co. Ltd* [1993] Ch 345).

The following may put questions during a public examination (IA 1986, s. 133(4)):

(a) The official receiver.

(b) The liquidator of the company.

(c) Any person who has been appointed special manager of the company's property or business.

(d) Any creditor of the company who has tendered a proof.

(e) Any contributory of the company.

The person being examined may not claim privilege against self-incrimination (*Bishopsgate Investment Management Ltd* v *Maxwell* [1993] Ch 1 per Dillon LJ at pp. 24–5; Stuart-Smith LJ at p. 46; Mann LJ at p. 62).

It seems that where a company is in voluntary liquidation, its liquidator or any creditor or contributory may apply under IA 1986, s. 112(1), for the court to exercise its power under s. 133 to order a public examination as if the company were in compulsory liquidation (*Re Campbell Coverings Ltd (No. 2)* [1954] Ch 225; *Bishopsgate Investment Management Ltd* v *Maxwell* [1993] Ch 1 per Dillon LJ at p. 24; Stuart-Smith LJ at p. 46).

20.10 LIABILITY FOR FRAUDULENT TRADING

20.10.1 Introduction

A person who is found to have been knowingly party to the carrying on of a business of a company with intent to defraud its creditors, or creditors of any other person, or for any fraudulent purpose, may be declared by the court to be liable to make such contributions (if any) to the company's assets as the court thinks proper (IA 1986, s. 213). Furthermore a disqualification order (see 15.2.5) may be made under CDDA 1986, s. 10.

A declaration may be made only in the course of winding up the company and it is for the company's liquidator to apply for a declaration.

A person who was knowingly party to a company's fraudulent trading may be made liable to contribute to its assets only when it is wound up but such a person may at any time be prosecuted for the criminal offence of knowingly being a party to fraudulent trading (CA 1985, s. 458). The offence may be tried either way and on indictment a prison sentence of up to seven years may be imposed (CA 1985, sch. 24) and a disqualification order may be made under CDDA 1986, s. 2.

It was held in *R* v *Kemp* [1988] QB 645, CA that the provisions of CA 1985, s. 458, and IA 1986, s. 213, are concerned with three different practices (and so s. 458 creates three separate offences), namely, carrying on the business of a company:

(a)   with intent to defraud the creditors of the company,

(b)   with intent to defraud the creditors of any person,

(c)   for any fraudulent purpose (which is not limited to fraudulence against creditors but may be, for example, against customers of the company as in *Kemp's* case).

Under (a) or (b) the provisions may be invoked even if the fraudulence was against only one creditor or was in relation to only one transaction. As Templeman J said in *Re Gerald Cooper Chemicals Ltd* [1978] Ch 262 at p. 268:

> It does not matter for the purposes of [CA 1985, s. 458, and IA 1986, s. 213] that only one creditor was defrauded, and by one transaction, provided that the transaction can properly be described as a fraud on a creditor perpetrated in the course of carrying on business.

Under (a), 'creditors' includes persons whose debts are payable in the future as well as those presently payable (*R* v *Smith* [1996] 2 Cr App R 1).

Under (c), the fraudulent purpose does not have to be the sole or even the dominant purpose for which the company carries on business. The crucial question is whether what is done for a fraudulent purpose is carried out in the course of business. In *R* v *Philippou* (1989) 89 Cr App R 290, the two accused were the sole shareholders and directors of a company in the travel trade which could not carry on its business without an Air Travel Organiser's Licence issued by the Civil Aviation Authority. The Authority has to be satisfied that the persons to whom it issues licences have adequate financial resources. The accused concealed from the Authority the true financial position of their companies to avoid having the licence cancelled. Dismissing the accused's appeals against conviction for offences under what is now CA 1985, s. 458, the Court of Appeal held that applying for, maintaining and renewing the licence were integral parts of the company's business, and doing those things fraudulently could amount to carrying on the company's business for a fraudulent purpose.

If, in the course of winding up a company, it appears that a person has been guilty of an offence for which he is liable (whether he has been convicted or not) under CA 1985, s. 458, then the court may make a disqualification order (see 15.2.5) against him (CDDA 1986, s. 4(1)(a)).

20.10.2   What amounts to fraud?

The phrases 'intent to defraud' and 'fraudulent purpose' used in IA 1986, s. 213 imply that a person should be made responsible only for 'actual dishonesty involving, according to current notions of fair trading among commercial men, real moral blame' (*Re Patrick & Lyon Ltd* [1933] Ch 786 per Maugham J), that is, only if there was conduct which was deliberately and actually dishonest according to the notions of ordinary decent business people (*Re EB Tractors Ltd* [1986] NI 165). It is also essential to prove dishonesty in order to secure a conviction under CA 1985, s. 458 (*R* v *Cox* (1982) 75 Cr App R 291) though more recently it has been held that in a criminal case the jury should be directed to consider the standards of ordinary and honest people rather than 'commercial men' (*R* v *Lockwood* (1985) 2 BCC 99,333, CA).

The Court of Appeal, in *R* v *Grantham* [1984] QB 675, considered the meaning of the phrase 'intent to defraud' in CA 1985, s. 458, and IA 1986, s. 213, and noted a relevant dictum of Lord Radcliffe in *Welham* v *DPP* [1961] AC 103:

> Now, I think that there are one or two things that can be said with confidence about the meaning of this word 'defraud'. It requires a person as its object: that is, defrauding involves doing something to someone. Although in the nature of things it is almost invariably associated with the obtaining of an advantage for the person who commits the fraud, it is the effect upon the person who is the object of the fraud that ultimately determines its meaning.

In *R* v *Grantham* the Court of Appeal also noted that it had said in *R* v *Allsop* (1977) 64 Cr App R 29 that a person is guilty of fraud if he intends by deceit to induce a course of conduct in another which puts that other's economic interests in jeopardy, even though he does not intend that actual loss should ultimately be suffered by that other.

Probably the commonest form of fraudulent trading is allowing a company to continue to trade when insolvent. Deceitfully inducing people to give credit to a company when it is known that they will not be paid when they expect to be paid puts their economic interests in jeopardy and amounts to fraudulent trading: it is not necessary to prove an intention that the creditors should never be paid at all (*R* v *Grantham*). There is intent to defraud if liability to 'involuntary creditors' such as the Inland Revenue or Customs and Excise is incurred when there is no honest belief that the liability will be discharged when due, or shortly thereafter (*Re a Company (No. 001418 of 1988)* [1991] BCLC 197).

In *Re White & Osmond (Parkstone) Ltd* (30 June 1960, ChD, unreported) Buckley J formulated what has become known as the 'sunshine' test:

> . . . there is nothing to say that directors who genuinely believe that the clouds will roll away and the sunshine of prosperity will shine upon them again and disperse the fog of their depression are not entitled to incur credit to help them get over the bad time.

In *R* v *Grantham,* the Court of Appeal said:

> Insofar as Buckley J was saying that it is never dishonest or fraudulent for directors to incur credit at a time when, to their knowledge, the company is not able to meet all its liabilities as they fall due, we would respectfully disagree.

In *Re Sarflax Ltd* [1979] Ch 592, Sarflax Ltd had supplied a metalworking press to an Italian customer but the press did not work and the customer started proceedings in Italy to recover compensation from Sarflax. Three months after these proceedings started Sarflax ceased to trade and began realising its assets in order to pay its debts. The company withdrew from the Italian proceedings. By the time the Italian court delivered judgment for about £86,000 against Sarflax, the company had used all its assets in paying its other debts and had adopted a resolution for voluntary winding up so there was nothing to satisfy the judgment. The liquidator (who was, of course, a creditors' liquidator) then claimed that the collection of the company's assets and their distribution in defraying the debts of the company without making *pari passu* provision for the Italian customer's claim constituted the carrying on of the company's business with intent to defraud a creditor, for which the directors of Sarflax and its parent company should be made liable. Oliver J held that where a debtor, knowing or having good grounds to suspect that he does not have and will not have sufficient assets to pay all his creditors in full, pays some but not others, or pays them in unequal proportions, with the consequence that some creditor either is not paid at all or is paid a lesser proportion of his debt than others, this is not of itself fraudulent conduct within CA 1985, s. 458 and IA 1986, s. 213. However, his lordship did not decide that there never could arise 'circumstances of a very peculiar nature involving preferential payments from which the intention required by [ss. 458 and 213] could be inferred'.

In *Re Augustus Barnett & Son Ltd* [1986] BCLC 170, the company was a wholly owned subsidiary of a Spanish company, Rumasa SA. The subsidiary traded at a loss for some time but the parent company repeatedly issued statements that it would continue to support the subsidiary. Some of these statements were made in letters (known as 'comfort letters') written to the subsidiary's auditors and published in the subsidiary's annual accounts for three successive years. Eventually the parent company allowed the subsidiary to go into liquidation. Hoffmann J held that these facts did not show that the parent company intended to defraud the subsidiary's creditors; they were consistent with the parent company having an honest intention, at the time of making the statements, to support the subsidiary — the fact that it later altered this intention did not prove that its original statements were fraudulent.

According to Murray J in *Re EB Tractors Ltd* [1986] NI 165, the badges of fraud are:

(a)   badly kept accounts that are not up to date, and
(b)   blatantly self-serving manoeuvres.

In *Re EB Tractors Ltd*, the directors' unrealistic hopes of survival were not dishonest, and the fact that they paid debts unpunctually or not at all was not fraud given that they did not know that the company was insolvent. Their use of money received to pay one debt in preference to others was also not fraudulent trading.

The meaning of 'intent to defraud' is considered at length in M. Beckman and S. Ross, 'Fraudulent or wrongful trading' (1991) 141 NLJ 1744, (1992) 142 NLJ 62, 100.

20.10.3   Who are parties to the carrying on of the business?

In *Re Maidstone Buildings Provisions Ltd* [1971] 1 WLR 1085 it was held that a company secretary, who knew that the company was insolvent but failed to advise the company's directors that the company should cease trading, was not included among 'parties to the carrying on of the business' with intent to defraud creditors. Pennycuick V-C said:

> The expression 'parties to the carrying on of the business' is not, I think, a very familiar one but, so far as I can see, the expression 'party to' must on its natural meaning indicate no more than 'participates in', 'takes part in' or 'concurs in'. And that, it seems to me, involves some positive steps of some nature. I do not think it can be said that someone is party to carrying on a business if he takes no positive steps at all. So in order to bring a person within the section you must show that he is taking some positive steps in the carrying on of the company's business in a fraudulent manner.

The term 'parties to the carrying on of the business' includes both the directors and so on who actively carried on the company's business for a fraudulent purpose and persons such as financiers who encouraged the carrying on of the business for the fraudulent purpose without carrying on the business themselves. It is essential to show that a person who actively carried on the business did so with fraudulent intent before any other party can be made liable (*Re Augustus Barnett & Son Ltd* [1986] BCLC 170). In a criminal case, *R v*

Miles [1992] Crim LR 657, the Court of Appeal said that s. 458 does not apply to persons who do not exercise a controlling or managerial function or who are not 'running the business'.

20.10.4 Nature of liability

What is now IA 1986, s. 213, has been described as 'in the nature of a punitive provision' (*Re William C. Leitch Brothers Ltd* [1932] 2 Ch 71 per Maugham J at p. 79). Accordingly the sum which the court may order a person to pay under the section is not limited to the amount that the company owes to persons who have been defrauded. In *Re a Company (No. 001418 of 1988)* [1991] BCLC 197 the liability was the amount of the company's trading losses apart from extraordinary items but plus a 'punitive element' of £25,000. The court is allowed to give such further directions as it thinks proper for the purpose of giving effect to the declaration, and may in particular make the liability under its declaration a charge on any debt or obligation due from the company to the person liable or on any mortgage or charge on any of the company's assets held by that person (s. 215(2)). Furthermore it can order that any debt owed by the company to the person declared liable shall rank in priority after all its other debts and the interest owed on all other debts (s. 215(4)).

Although a person is, by a declaration under IA 1986, s. 213(2), made liable to contribute to the assets of a company, he is not one of the 'contributories' of the company (s. 79(2)) and so does not acquire any right to influence the winding up.

20.11 MISFEASANCE PROCEEDINGS

20.11.1 Nature of misfeasance proceedings

IA 1986, s. 212, provides an important means, commonly called 'misfeasance proceedings', by which a liquidator may recover company property that has been misapplied by persons who formed or managed the company.

The persons who may be made liable in misfeasance proceedings in the winding up of a company are:

(a)   Any person who is or has been an officer of the company.

(b)   Any person who has acted as liquidator, administrator or administrative receiver of the company.

(c)   Any person who is, or has been, concerned, or has taken part, in the promotion, formation or management of the company.

Such a person may be made liable if he or she 'has misapplied or retained, or become accountable for, any money or other property of the company, or been guilty of any misfeasance or breach of any fiduciary or other duty in relation to the company' (s. 212(1)). Someone who has been a liquidator or administrator may also be made liable for misfeasance or breach of duty in connection with the carrying out of his or her functions as liquidator or administrator (s. 212(2)).

Misfeasance proceedings may be commenced by the liquidator or an official receiver or any creditor or (with the leave of the court) any contributory of the company. They are essentially summary proceedings, for recovering money, provided by the Act as an alternative to commencing an action for any of the wrongs enumerated in s. 212(1) and (2). In *Bentinck v Fenn* (1887) 12 App Cas 652, HL, Lord Macnaghten said:

The 165th section of the Act of 1862 [now IA 1986, s. 212] has often come under discussion, and it has been settled, and I think rightly settled, that that section creates no new offence, and that it gives no new rights, but only provides a summary and efficient remedy in respect of rights which apart from that section might have been vindicated either at law or in equity.

Misfeasance proceedings cannot be used for matters not listed in s. 212(1) and (2), so they cannot be used instead of an action for debt (*Re Etic Ltd* [1928] Ch 861) but, as the wording of the legislation was changed in IA 1986, misfeasance proceedings have been taken for negligence in *Re D'Jan of London Ltd* [1994] 1 BCLC 561.

If misfeasance proceedings in a company's liquidation are taken to enforce a right of action of the company that is an asset subject to a floating charge, anything recovered in the proceedings will be subject to the charge (*Re Anglo-Austrian Printing and Publishing Union, Brabourne* v *the Company* [1895] 2 Ch 891).

20.11.2 Examples of misfeasance proceedings

Misfeasance proceedings have been used to recover from directors dividends that were paid otherwise than from distributable profits (*Re National Funds Assurance Co.* (1878) 10 ChD 118; *Re Exchange Banking Co., Flitcroft's Case* (1882) 21 ChD 519, CA). In *Re Thomas Gerrard & Son Ltd* [1968] Ch 455 dividends were paid otherwise than from the company's distributable profits because the accounts had been falsified by the managing director to show larger profits than had in fact been made. The company's auditors were held liable in misfeasance proceedings to make up the dividends wrongly paid because they had failed to audit the accounts properly.

In *Re VGM Holdings Ltd* [1942] Ch 235, CA, the company had been registered in April 1938. At its first board meeting, the directors (Vanbergen, Glass and Miller) resolved that the company should buy all the issued shares of Century Refrigeration Ltd for £8,301 12s 3d and should also lend Century £7,678 7s 9d so that Century could pay off debts it owed to its directors, who were, not surprisingly, Vanbergen, Glass and Miller. Vanbergen was beneficial owner of all of Century's shares. VGM Holdings made out a cheque for £15,980 to Century Refrigeration. Century Refrigeration made out cheques to Vanbergen, Glass and Miller in payment of the debts owed to them and in payment for the shares. Vanbergen, Glass and Miller then indorsed these cheques in favour of VGM Holdings and used them to pay for the shares in VGM Holdings for which they had subscribed. Century was in fact insolvent and its shares were worthless. It was held that Vanbergen (the only director against whom proceedings were taken) was guilty of misfeasance in respect of the payment of £15,980. He was ordered to contribute to the assets of VGM Holdings an amount sufficient (with the company's other assets) fully to discharge the company's debts (other than any debt to himself).

20.11.3 Creditors' interests

Misfeasance proceedings may be taken against a director of a company in relation to a breach of his duty to consider the interests of creditors when the company was insolvent (see 16.4.6) (*West Mercia Safetywear Ltd* v *Dodd* [1998] BCLC 250, CA).

In *West Mercia Safetywear Ltd* v *Dodd,* Mr Dodd was a director of A.J. Dodd & Co. Ltd and of its wholly owned subsidiary, West Mercia Safetywear Ltd. The parent company was owed £30,000 by the subsidiary. The parent company had a large overdraft at the bank which Mr Dodd had personally guaranteed. Both companies got into financial difficulties and Mr Dodd was advised by an accountant that they were both insolvent and should go into creditors' voluntary liquidation. West Mercia Safetywear Ltd was then paid £4,000 by one of its debtors. Mr Dodd transferred that money from West Mercia's bank account to the overdrawn account of the parent company apparently in part payment of the £30,000 debt but really so as to reduce his liability under his guarantee. The transfer was obviously a preference of the parent company (or, to be precise, a fraudulent preference, having been made before the new law on preferences was enacted) but the money could not be recovered because of the parent company's insolvency. Accordingly, the liquidator took misfeasance proceedings against Mr Dodd personally and Mr Dodd was ordered to pay the £4,000 to West Mercia Safetywear Ltd.

In *Walker* v *Wimborne* (1976) 137 CLR 1, a father and his sons were directors of several companies and administered them as a group though there was no holding company. Among other transactions challenged by the liquidator of one of these companies, called Asiatic Electric Co. Pty Ltd, was a payment by it of A$10,000 to another of the companies, Australian Sound & Communications Pty Ltd, for which the only reason was that the other company 'needed the money': the other company was clearly incapable of repaying the money. Mason J, speaking for the majority of the court, said:

> . . . it should be emphasised that the directors of a company in discharging their duty to the company must take account of the interest of its shareholders and its creditors. Any failure by the directors to take into account the interests of creditors will have adverse consequences for the company as well as for them. . . .

> The transaction offered no prospect of advantage to Asiatic, it exposed Asiatic to the probable prospect of substantial loss, and thereby seriously prejudiced the unsecured creditors of Asiatic. It was more than an improvident transaction reflecting an error of judgment; it was undertaken in accordance with a policy adopted by the directors in total disregard of the interests of the company and its creditors.

> The payment to Australian Sound was in my view a 'misfeasance'.

In New Zealand, Cooke J, presiding in the Court of Appeal, has said, *obiter*, that a payment made to the prejudice of current or continuing creditors when a likelihood of loss to them ought to have been known, is capable of constituting misfeasance by the directors (*Nicholson* v *Permakraft (NZ) Ltd* [1985] 1 NZLR 242, in which the court unanimously held that there had been no misfeasance).

20.11.4 Ratification by members

After a company has gone into liquidation, its members have no power to ratify to the detriment of creditors anything done previously by the company's directors (*Precision Dippings Ltd* v *Precision Dippings Marketing Ltd* [1986] Ch 447 per Dillon LJ at p. 456; *Re D'Jan of London Ltd* [1994] 1 BCLC 561).

In *Rolled Steel Products (Holdings) Ltd* v *British Steel Corporation* [1986] Ch 246, Slade LJ said, at p. 296, that approval by all the members of a company, given before it went into liquidation, could not bind the company to 'a transaction which constitutes a fraud on its creditors'. His lordship cited as an example *Re Halt Garage (1964) Ltd* [1982] 3 All ER 1016. In *Re Halt Garage (1964) Ltd,* Oliver J said, at p. 1039, that those who deal with a limited company 'are entitled to have the capital kept intact'. In *Re DKG Contractors Ltd* [1990] BCC 903, work which the company had contracted to do was carried out by a director of the company, using his own equipment and workers but the company purchased materials. Money paid to the company by its customers was almost entirely paid out to the director. For the last 10 months of its existence the company was insolvent, and during that time paid the director over £400,000. In misfeasance proceedings, the company's liquidator claimed this money back from the director, saying that it was paid in breach of the directors' duties to the company. It was argued for the director that the company could not reclaim the money because payment had been approved by all the company's members (the director and his wife). John Weeks QC said, at p. 908, that the rule that an *intra vires* act is binding on a company if approved by all the members is subject to two exceptions: 'One of them is that creditors are entitled to have the company assets kept intact. Another is that the rule does not extend to cases involving a fraud on creditors.' Mr Weeks found that the transactions in this case fell within both these exceptions and ordered repayment of the money.

The majority (Lawton and Dillon LJJ) of the Court of Appeal in *Multinational Gas & Petrochemical Co.* v *Multinational Gas & Petrochemical Services Ltd* [1983] Ch 258 held that if all the members of a company agreed to decisions by its directors then the company (which in this case had gone into liquidation) could not maintain an action for negligence against the directors, though May LJ (at pp. 280–2) strongly disagreed. In *Re Horsley & Weight Ltd* [1982] Ch 442, CA, Cumming-Bruce and Templeman LJJ doubted whether if all the members of a company approved an action by the directors which involved more than mere negligence, the approval would bind the company not to sue. In *Multinational*, Dillon LJ said that nothing more than mere negligence was alleged in the case before him so that the remarks of Cumming-Bruce and Templeman LJJ did not apply but Lawton LJ said that he did not share the doubts of Cumming-Bruce and Templeman LJJ.

In *Kinsela* v *Russell Kinsela Pty Ltd* (1986) 4 NSWLR 722, the Court of Appeal of New South Wales emphasised that there was a difference between a solvent and an insolvent company. If the actions of directors damage a solvent company then it is the interests of the members that are damaged and the members can decide whether or not to forgive the directors. In an insolvent company, however, actions of directors that damage the company damage the interests of the creditors, not the members, and therefore the members cannot be allowed to preclude action being taken against the directors to recover property for distribution amongst the creditors. This approach was approved by Dillon LJ in *West Mercia Safetywear Ltd* v *Dodd* [1988] BCLC 250, CA (see 20.11.3).

It is submitted that if directors of a company are its only members then their ratification, as members, of their misfeasance as directors is not effective because the 'approval' is then just part of the misfeasance (cf. *Belmont Finance Corporation Ltd* v *Williams Furniture Ltd* [1979] Ch 250; *Attorney-General's Reference (No. 2 of 1982)* [1984] QB 624; see 10.1.2). Harman LJ said in *Bamford* v *Bamford* [1970] Ch 212, CA, at p. 238:

> . . . directors can, by making a full and frank disclosure and calling together the general body of the shareholders, obtain absolution and forgiveness of their sins.

But to pursue the theological analogy further, it is not to oneself that one looks for forgiveness. Thus in *Re VGM Holdings Ltd* [1942] Ch 235, CA, discussed in 20.11.2, all the members of the company approved of the transaction in question but they were all the directors who benefited from the transaction and it does not even seem to have been suggested that their approval released them from liability.

20.12 WRONGFUL TRADING

According to its marginal note, s. 214 of IA 1986 is concerned with 'wrongful trading', though the phrase 'wrongful trading' is not used in the section. Briefly, the section empowers the court to declare a director or shadow director (s. 214(7)) of a company liable to contribute to the assets of the company if the director knew, or ought to have concluded, that the company had no reasonable prospect of not going into insolvent liquidation and did not take every step that ought to have been taken by that director to minimise the potential loss to the company's creditors. The section applies to *de facto* directors as well as *de iure* directors (*Re Hydrodam (Corby) Ltd* [1994] 2 BCLC 180).

The section comes into operation only if a company goes into liquidation (see 20.8) at a time when its assets are insufficient for the payment of its debts and other liabilities and the expenses of winding up (IA 1986, s. 214(1), (2)(a) and (6)) and it is for the company's liquidator to apply to the court for a declaration (s. 214(1)). The test of insufficiency of assets is the same as in the Company Directors Disqualification Act 1986, s. 6, which was interpreted in *Official Receiver* v *Moore* [1995] BCC 293 (see 15.2.5.3).

It has to be proved to the court that a director or shadow director against whom a declaration is sought 'knew or ought to have concluded that' insolvent liquidation was unavoidable. However, the director or shadow director may in defence prove that he 'took every step . . . he ought to have taken' to minimise creditors' losses.

The phrases 'ought to have concluded that' and 'ought to have taken' imply that the legislation is referring to a standard of thinking and behaviour, and a director is to be penalised for not meeting that standard. IA 1986, s. 214(4) and (5), attempts to specify what that standard is. The court is asked to consider the facts which would be known or ascertained, the conclusions which would be reached and the steps which would be taken by a reasonably diligent person having both:

(a) the general knowledge, skill and experience that may reasonably be expected of a person carrying out the same functions as are carried out by the person against whom a declaration is sought in relation to the company that is in liquidation; and

(b) the general knowledge, skill and experience that that person has.

In other words, a person who is not sufficiently qualified for his job is to be tested by the standards of someone who is ideally qualified while someone who is overqualified is to be tested by the higher standards he happens to possess. Subsection (5) emphasises this by requiring the court to look at the ideal qualifications of a person doing the job with which the person against whom the declaration is sought was entrusted, even if he did not in fact carry out some or all of its functions.

In *Secretary of State for Trade and Industry* v *Taylor* [1997] 1 WLR 407 Chadwick J said, at p. 414, in relation to an application to disqualify a director:

The companies legislation does not impose on directors a statutory duty to ensure that their company does not trade while insolvent; nor does that legislation impose an obligation to ensure that the company does not trade at a loss. . . . Directors may properly take the view that it is in the interests of the company and of its creditors that, although insolvent, the company should continue to trade out of its difficulties. They may properly take the view that it is in the interests of the company and its creditors that some loss-making trade should be accepted in anticipation of future profitability. They are not to be criticised if they give effect to such views, properly held. But the legislation imposes on directors the risk that trading while insolvent may lead to personal liability. Section 214 imposes that liability where the director knew, or ought to have concluded, that there was no reasonable prospect that the company would avoid going into insolvent liquidation.

A director or shadow director may escape liability by showing that he took 'every step with a view to minimising the potential loss to the company's creditors as . . . he ought to have taken' (IA 1986, s. 214(3)). This provision is likely to cause considerable difficulty in application, especially by its use of the word 'every'. It implies that there is an exhaustive list of steps to be taken on discovering that insolvent liquidation is unavoidable so that a defendant may prove he took all of them. Moreover, s. 214(4) assumes that such lists exist for each possible type of director that the court may have to judge. In reality no such list exists for any kind of director, partly, of course, because most directors are never directors of insolvent companies and have no experience on which to base a standard procedure (if they did develop such an experience they would be disqualified).

It is suggested that if directors of a company conclude that its insolvent liquidation is inevitable then they should immediately consult a qualified insolvency practitioner. This will, at least, provide them with the advice of someone who is trained in insolvency matters. Following the advice of the insolvency practitioner should be a good protection against action under this section, though whether creditors will be able to persuade courts that other steps ought to be taken remains to be seen. See R. Whitehouse and T. Arnold, 'Protecting yourself as director of a company in difficulties' (1993) 137 SJ 218.

CA 1985, s. 727 (see 16.9.2), does not apply to proceedings for wrongful trading (*Re Produce Marketing Consortium Ltd* [1989] 1 WLR 745).

If the court makes a declaration against a person then it may give such further directions as it thinks proper for the purpose of giving effect to the declaration and may in particular make the liability under its declaration a charge on any debt or obligation due from the company to the person liable or on any mortgage or charge on any of the company's assets held by him (IA 1986, s. 215(2)). Furthermore it can order that any debt owed by the company to the person declared liable shall rank in priority after all its other debts and the interest owed on all other debts (IA 1986, s. 215(4)).

The court may make a disqualification order (see 15.2.5) against a person when making a declaration under s. 214(1) (CDDA 1986, s. 10).

Although a person is, by a declaration under IA 1986, s. 214(1), made liable to contribute to the assets of a company, he is not one of the 'contributories' of the company (IA 1986, s. 79(2)) and so does not acquire any right to influence the winding up.

In the first wrongful trading case to be reported, *Re Produce Marketing Consortium Ltd (No. 2)* [1989] BCLC 520, the liquidator of the company sought an order under s. 214 declaring that two directors were liable to contribute to the assets of the company. It had acted as agent in relation to the import of fruit and, although it traded successfully for some time, gradually the number of directors, the turnover and the profitability shrank until it went into creditors' voluntary liquidation with an estimated deficit of £317,694 after approximately 16 years' trading. The general drift towards insolvency was evident from the audited accounts. They showed a decline from no overdraft, excess assets over liabilities and no trading loss in 1980 to a large overdraft, excess of liabilities over assets and a trading loss by 1984. These all continued to deteriorate until the liquidation in 1987. The gradual decrease in the company's overdraft in the later years was financed by increased indebtedness to the company's most important shipper who was owed £175,062 in the liquidation.

One of the directors admitted knowing in February 1987 that the liquidation of the company was inevitable but put forward, as justification for its continuing to trade until October of that year, that it enabled an advantageous realisation of the company's stock of perishable fruit in cold store. This was said to be an attempt within s. 214(3) to minimise the potential loss to creditors.

Knox J held that the two directors were liable to contribute £75,000 to the company's assets. They ought to have concluded back in July 1986 that there was no reasonable prospect of avoiding insolvent liquidation because, although they did not have the accounts until January 1987, they had an intimate knowledge of the business and must have known that turnover was well down on the previous year, which would inevitably lead to an increase in the deficit of assets over liabilities. Furthermore, s. 214 refers not only to facts which directors ought to know but also to facts which they ought to ascertain. Therefore the court assumed that the financial results for the year ending September 1985 were known at the end of July 1986. His lordship said, at p. 551:

> [Counsel for one of the directors] was not able to advance any particular calculation as constituting a basis for concluding that there was a prospect of insolvent liquidation being avoided. He is not to be criticised for that for in my judgment there was none available. Once the loss in the year ending 30 September 1985 was incurred PMC was in irreversible decline, assuming (as I must) that the [directors] had no plans for altering the company's business and proposed to go on drawing the level of reasonable remuneration that they were currently receiving.

In short, they should not have continued trading after July 1986. Also the directors had not taken the steps they ought to have taken under s. 214(3) because they continued trading after July 1986 and even after February 1987 and that conduct was compounded by the fact that trading from February 1987 was not limited to realising the fruit in cold store as claimed.

Re Sherborne Associates Ltd [1995] BCC 40 concerned three men who had set up a company to run an advertising agency. None of them had worked in an advertising agency but one of them was an accountant who had considerable business experience at a high level and had identified advertising as a profitable area to invest in. They relied on hiring employees with the necessary skills and client contacts but in fact none of the people they hired was able to contribute enough to make the business profitable and it was put into liquidation two years after it commenced trading. The liquidator alleged that at a date one year before the liquidation, the directors ought to have concluded that there was no reasonable prospect that the company would avoid going into insolvent liquidation but Judge Jack QC, sitting as a High Court judge, decided that the liquidator had not shown that the directors were not entitled at that time to believe that the company could become profitable. This seems to have been a generous application of the sunshine test (see 20.10.2).

In *Re Produce Marketing Consortium Ltd*, Knox J decided that the appropriate amount which the directors were to be ordered to contribute to the company's assets was the amount by which its assets could be seen to have been depleted by the director's conduct which caused the discretion to arise. In effect the jurisdiction under s. 214 is primarily compensatory rather than penal.

In *Re Purpoint Ltd* [1991] BCLC 491, Vinelott J rejected a submission that a director held liable for wrongful trading should pay all the company's creditors whose debts were incurred after he should have known that the company would go into insolvent liquidation. Money ordered to be paid under s. 214 goes into the general assets of the company for distribution among all creditors: the court has no power to direct payment of the money to particular creditors. The right measure of the director's liability for wrongful trading in this case was the increase in the net liabilities of the company caused by the company continuing to trade after the director should have known that it would go into liquidation.

In *Re DKG Contractors Ltd* [1990] BCC 903, the facts of which are given in 20.11.4, both directors of the company were held liable for wrongful trading but it was accepted that the amount for which they were liable was covered by the amount ordered to be paid in the misfeasance proceedings. The amount which the directors of DKG Contractors Ltd were declared liable to pay for wrongful trading was the amount of trade debts incurred since they should have known that the company would go into insolvent liquidation, but this seems to be the wrong measure according to the decisions in *Re Produce Marketing Consortium Ltd (No. 2)* and *Re Purpoint Ltd.*

It seems that liquidators have been encouraged by the introduction of the wrongful trading provision to make much more detailed investigations into the past activities of directors — the judge in *Re Purpoint Ltd* was concerned with what kind of car it was appropriate for the company to buy its director — and to make composite misfeasance and wrongful trading claims. It may be that misfeasance and wrongful trading claims carry rather less stigma than fraudulent trading claims or disqualification orders, and are therefore easier to sustain (see 'Company directors and insolvent companies: a new reality?' (1991) 12 Co Law 82). On the other hand it must be recognised that most individuals against whom misfeasance and wrongful trading claims are upheld will be bankrupted by them.

For detailed discussions of s. 214, see F. Oditah, 'Wrongful trading' [1990] LMCLQ 205; D. Milman, 'Personal liability and disqualification of company directors: something old, something new' (1992) 43 NILQ 1 and A. Hicks, 'Advising on wrongful trading' (1993) 14 Co Law 16, 55.

20.13   ORDER OF APPLICATION OF ASSETS

The matters considered in 20.13 apply in both voluntary and compulsory liquidations.

20.13.1   Principles

In a compulsory liquidation, IA 1986, s. 143(1), provides:

> The functions of the liquidator of a company which is being wound up by the court are to secure that the assets of the company are got in, realised and distributed to the company's creditors and, if there is a surplus, to the persons entitled to it.

This provision is repeated by IA 1986, s. 148(1), and IR 1986, r. 4.179, under which a compulsory liquidator must discharge the court's duty to 'cause the company's assets to be collected, and applied in discharge of its liabilities'.

In a compulsory liquidation, IA 1986, s. 154, provides that: 'The court shall adjust the rights of the contributories among themselves and distribute any surplus among the persons entitled to it.'

In principle, if a company is insolvent so that creditors cannot be paid in full then all creditors must be paid equal percentages of their debts (IA 1986, s. 107 (voluntary liquidation); IR 1986, r. 4.181 (compulsory liquidation)). However, three further principles have to be taken into account. The first is the principle of salvage, that the expenses of collecting and realising the assets and distributing the proceeds must be paid out of those proceeds (*Batten* v *Wedgwood Coal & Iron Co.* (1884) 28 ChD 317). The second principle is that certain debts are, by statute, made preferential and payable before other debts (though not before expenses). The provisions on preferential debts are contained in IA 1986, ss. 175, 386 and 387 and sch. 6. In IA 1986, s. 175(2)(a), though, it is provided that the expenses of the winding up must be paid before the preferential payments. By IA 1986, s. 115, all expenses properly incurred in a voluntary winding up, including the remuneration of the liquidator, are payable out of the assets of the company in priority to all other claims. The third principle is set-off of mutual debts. A creditor of an insolvent person who is also owed money by that person is likely to be very aggrieved if forced to pay the whole of the debt owed to the insolvent person in return for only a percentage of the debt owed by the insolvent. Accordingly insolvency law has long allowed for mutual debts to be set off. In the winding up of companies the provision currently permitting set-off of mutual debts is IR 1986, r. 4.90. This rule normally benefits a creditor of a company being wound up who is also a debtor to the company but it also aids the administration of the winding up and it cannot be excluded by any agreement between a creditor and a company (*National Westminster Bank Ltd* v *Halesowen Presswork and Assemblies Ltd* [1972] AC 785).

From what has been said so far it emerges that, rather than all a company's liabilities being treated *pari passu,* there are at least three groups — expenses of the liquidation, preferential payments, other liabilities — each subject to its own rules. And it must not be forgotten that secured creditors with charges may take whatever property has been charged with payment of their debts and pay themselves out of the proceeds of sale of that property.

The result is that, ignoring secured creditors who look after themselves, a liquidator of a company is required to classify the claims against the company into groups. The groups are paid off one by one in an order prescribed by law. When the liquidator comes to a group that cannot be paid in full, all claimants in the group receive the same proportion (called a 'dividend') of their claims — that is, claimants in that group are treated *pari passu* — and subsequent groups receive nothing.

The groups and their order of priority are:

(a) Expenses properly incurred in the winding up, including the remuneration of the liquidator (IA 1986, s. 115 (voluntary liquidation); IA 1986, s. 175(2)(a) (compulsory and voluntary liquidation)). Assets required to pay these expenses are released from any charge which was created as a floating charge (*Re Barleycorn Enterprises Ltd* [1970] Ch 465, CA; *Re Portbase Clothing Ltd* [1993] Ch 388).

(b) The preferential debts (IA 1986, s. 175). The preferential debts of a company are listed in IA 1986, sch. 6; they are money owed to the Inland Revenue for income tax deducted at source; VAT, insurance premium tax, car tax, betting and gaming duties, beer duty, lottery duty, air passenger duty; social security and pension scheme contributions; remuneration etc. of employees; and levies on coal and steel production.

(c) Other unsecured liabilities, unless they are in categories (d) to (l).

(d) Post-liquidation interest on debts in categories (b) and (c) (IA 1986, s. 189; see 20.13.2).

(e) If the court so orders, any debt owed to a person who has been declared liable to contribute to the company's assets under IA 1986, s. 213 (liability for fraudulent trading, see 20.10) or s. 214 (responsibility for wrongful trading, see 20.12) (s. 215(4)).

(f) Post-liquidation interest on debts in category (e) (s. 215(4)).

(g) Amounts to be paid by the company to purchase its own shares, in pursuance of a contract entered into before commencement of the winding up, and amounts to be paid to redeem redeemable shares issued on or after 15 June 1982. However, if any other class of shares of the company has priority in respect of income or capital over the shares being repurchased or redeemed then amounts due in satisfaction of those preferred rights (categories (i) to (l)) must be paid before the repurchase or redemption of the subordinated shares (CA 1985, s. 178(6)).

(h) Post-liquidation interest on debts in category (g). Interest payable in categories (d), (h) and (j) ranks equally, in principle (IA 1986, s. 189(3)).

(i)   Debts owed to members or past members in their character as members incurred before the commencement of the liquidation (IA 1986, s. 74(2)(f); *Re Consolidated Goldfields of New Zealand Ltd* [1953] Ch 689; *Re Compañía Electricidad de la Provincia de Buenos Aires Ltd* [1980] Ch 146). Dividends declared before liquidation but not paid are in this category. (The obligation to divide up the company's ultimate surplus among members is not a debt incurred before commencement.)

(j)   Post-liquidation interest on debts in category (i). In principle such interest ranks equally with interest in categories (d) and (h) (IA 1986, s. 189(3)).

(k)   Expenses of summoning and holding a meeting of contributories on the requisition of contributories, if the meeting resolves that they are to be paid out of the assets (IR 1986, r. 4.61(4)).

(l)   Any surplus is distributed to members (IA 1986, ss. 107 (voluntary liquidation) and 154 (compulsory liquidation)). The company's articles may prescribe the order in which different classes of members are to be treated.

If there is enough to pay group (a) in full but not enough to pay group (b) in full then the liquidator must pay group (a) and distribute whatever is left among the claimants in group (b) in such a way that all claimants receive the same proportion of their claims (IA 1986, s. 175(2)(a)).

If groups (a) and (b) can be paid in full but group (c) cannot then all claimants in group (c) must receive the same proportion of their claims, and so on.

It is possible for a creditor of a company to agree that if the company should go into liquidation, payment of the creditor's debt will be postponed until other specified debts, which would normally have equal or lower priority, are paid. This is known as 'subordination' of the debt. The creditors who are to be paid before the subordinated creditor are known as 'senior' creditors. A subordination agreement will be enforced by the courts (*Re Maxwell Communications Corporation plc* [1993] 1 WLR 1402; *United States Trust Co. of New York* v *Australia and New Zealand Banking Group Ltd* (1995) 37 NSWLR 131). The effect of a subordination agreement is that any dividend due to the subordinated creditor is paid instead to the senior creditors. However, this does not mean that the subordination agreement is a charge on the subordinated debt (*United States Trust Co. of New York* v *Australia and New Zealand Banking Group Ltd*).

Where shares are partly paid and different amounts have been paid up, a call may have to be made on some shareholders (*Re Anglo-Continental Corporation of Western Australia* [1898] 1 Ch 327) and at this stage any amount owed by the company to a shareholder may be set off against a call made on him (IA 1986, s. 149(3)).

20.13.2   Post-liquidation interest

Under the law in force before 29 December 1986, if a debt owed by a company in liquidation carried interest contractually agreed between the company and the creditor then that interest had to be paid for the period between the commencement of the winding up and the payment of the debt, if the company could afford to do so (*Bower* v *Marris* (1841) Cr & Ph 351; *Re Humber Ironworks & Shipbuilding Co., Warrant Finance Co.'s Case* (1869) LR 4 Ch App 643) but if no interest had been contractually agreed then no interest was payable, however long it took the liquidator to pay the debt (*Re Fine Industrial Commodities Ltd* [1956] Ch 256; *Re Rolls-Royce Ltd* [1974] 1 WLR 1584).

By IA 1986, s. 189, interest is now payable on all debts proved in a liquidation once the proved debts have been paid. The rate payable is either the contractually agreed rate, if there is one, or the rate specified in the Judgments Act 1838, s. 17, on the day the company went into liquidation, whichever is greater. The rate in the 1838 Act is altered from time to time by order of the Lord Chancellor under the Administration of Justice Act 1970, s. 44. As from 16 April 1985 the rate is 15 per cent a year (SI 1985 No. 437). The interest is paid on the amount of debt proved (which may include pre-liquidation interest) and the interest is payable for the period during which the debts have been outstanding since the company went into liquidation (IA 1986, s. 189(2)).

In a complicated liquidation several dividends may be paid so that debts are repaid by instalments. The old law in relation to contractual interest was that each dividend was regarded as first paying off interest accrued to the date of payment of the dividend and then to reduction of the principal debt (*Bower* v *Marris* (1841) Cr & Ph 351; *Re Lines Bros Ltd (No. 2)* [1984] Ch 438). Under the new law, however, no post-liquidation interest is payable until the principal debts have been completely repaid and it is submitted that the law now is that each dividend goes to reducing the principal debt and only when all debts are paid can any dividend be regarded as paying interest. It is submitted that the wording of s. 189(1): 'In a winding up interest is payable in accordance with this section', means that it shall not be payable in accordance with *Bower* v *Marris* and *Re Lines Bros Ltd (No. 2)*.

If a debt on which post-liquidation interest is payable was a debt in a foreign currency then, initially, the interest payable is a sterling amount calculated with reference to the sterling value of the principal debt on the date of going into liquidation (*Re Lines Bros Ltd (No. 2);* IR 1986, r. 4.91). If there is a surplus after paying all the company's interest on this basis then the creditor's full contractual rights can be enforced and it must be paid any exchange losses. It is questionable what should be done if the foreign currency has lost value since the company went into liquidation.

20.13.3 Provision for employees

The liquidator of a company is empowered by IA 1986, s. 187, to make provision for the benefit of persons employed or formerly employed by the company or any of its subsidiaries on the cessation or transfer of its business, though only after the company's liabilities have been fully satisfied and provision has been made for the costs of the winding up. Whether the winding up is compulsory or voluntary the liquidator must have the sanction of an ordinary resolution of the company, unless the company's articles or memorandum impose more restrictive conditions on the exercise of the power in which case those restrictions must be complied with. In a compulsory liquidation the liquidator's exercise of this power is subject to the court's control and any creditor or contributory may apply to the court in respect of it (s. 187(4)) and this provision applies also to a voluntary liquidation by virtue of s. 112. If the company resolved to make provision for employees under CA 1985, s. 719, before the commencement of liquidation then the liquidator is empowered to put the resolution into effect (IA 1986, s. 187(1)).

20.14 DISSOLUTION

20.14.1 Introduction

In the sense in which the term is used in Britain, the dissolution of a company is effected by the registrar removing the name of the company from the register. Dissolution of a company ends its legal personality and dissolves the relationship between company and members. The company ceases to be party to any legal relationship: if it has property at the time of dissolution then that property passes to the Crown or a royal duchy in the same way as the property of an intestate deceased individual who has no heirs (CA 1985, s. 654). If a company was holding property on trust for another at the time of its dissolution then a new trustee must be appointed to replace the company. If an individual has given a company property in his or her will but the company is dissolved before he or she dies then the gift lapses (*Re Servers of the Blind League* [1960] 1 WLR 564) unless the court can infer a general charitable intention so that it can make a scheme for applying the gift cy pres (*Re Finger's Will Trusts* [1972] Ch 286). If an insurer compensated a company for a loss it suffered then, after dissolution of the company, the insurer loses the right of subrogation to sue in the company's name for recovery of the loss from the person who caused it (*M.H. Smith (Plant Hire) Ltd* v *Mainwaring* [1986] BCLC 342, CA).

The people who bring about the dissolution of a company may do so in ignorance of some important legal relationship of the company with some other person. CA 1985 therefore provides a number of methods by which other people may complete their dealings with a dissolved company.

In European Union documents the term 'dissolution' is used in the sense in which that term is understood in Continental legal systems — that is, for what in Britain is called the commencement of winding up. On the Continent the transition from going concern to company in winding up is thought of as the point at which the company is 'dissolved'. In Britain the final end of a company's legal personality on completion of winding up is regarded as the point of dissolution but on the Continent this is regarded simply as the end of winding up.

20.14.2   Methods of dissolution

20.14.2.1   By Act of Parliament
Occasionally a statute is necessary to end the legal relationships or duties of a company. A statute is usually necessary, for example, to transfer the business of one bank to another, so as to transfer to the acquiring bank the obligations owed to customers by the taken-over bank. The Lloyds Bank Act 1981, for example, was obtained so that the business of Lewis's Bank Ltd (a wholly owned subsidiary of Lloyds) could be transferred to Lloyds. Section 12(2) of the Act provides that at the request of Lloyds the registrar will strike Lewis's Bank Ltd off the register of companies and it will thereupon be dissolved. However, dissolution has not been requested, and subsequent bank merger Acts have not made similar provisions. A statute that moves a company from one domicile to another (see 2.4.3) will provide for the company to be struck off the register but this will not dissolve the company which continues in its new domicile.

20.14.2.2   By cancellation of registration
On an application by the Attorney-General for judicial review of the registrar's decision to register a company, the court may order the registrar to cancel the company's registration (see 1.2.1).

Paragraph 2 of art. 11 of the EC First Company Law Directive requires the laws of member States to provide that what the Directive calls 'nullity' of limited companies may be ordered by a court only on six grounds listed in the paragraph, namely:

(a)   that no instrument of constitution (i,e., memorandum of association) was executed or that the rules of preventive control (e.g., the rules for vetting of sensitive names) or the requisite legal formalities were not complied with;

(b)   that the objects of the company are unlawful or contrary to public policy (this was the ground relied on in *R* v *Registrar of Companies, ex parte Attorney-General* [1991] BCLC 476 discussed in 1.2.1);

(c)   that the instrument of constitution (i.e., the memorandum of association) or the statutes (i.e., the articles of association) do not state the name of the company, the amount of the individual subscriptions of capital, the total amount of the capital subscribed or the objects of the company;

(d)   failure to comply with the provisions of the national law concerning the minimum amount of capital to be paid up;

(e)   the incapacity of all the founder members;

(f)   that, contrary to the national law governing the company, the number of founder members is less than two.

No UK legislation has been passed to implement this requirement. However, a UK court, as an authority of the State which was required to implement the Directive, must interpret its national law in the light of the wording and purpose of the Directive, and so must not declare the registration of a company to have been void on any ground other than those listed in para. 2 of art. 11 (*Marleasing SA* v *La Comercial Internacional de Alimentación SA* (case C-106/89) [1990] ECR I-4135). The 'objects of the company' referred to in art. 11(2)(b) are the objects stated in its memorandum of association, not (if they are different) the objects actually pursued by the company (ibid.).

The registration of a trade union as a company is void (Trade Union and Labour Relations (Consolidation) Act 1992, s. 10(3)) and the annual reports of the Department of Trade and Industry on companies since 1974 show that three companies have been removed from the register because they were trade unions. It would seem that this was contrary to para. 1 of art. 11 of the First Directive which requires that nullity must be ordered by a court of law: the registrar, as an authority of the State which was required to implement the Directive, should have complied with this provision.

Article 12, para. 3, of the First Directive requires that nullification of the incorporation of a company shall not of itself affect the validity of any commitments entered into by or with the company and art. 12, para. 2, requires that nullification shall entail the winding up of the company. No UK legislation has been enacted to implement the requirements of these paragraphs. It is submitted that the reversal by legal process of a decision on the ground that it was wrong operates to substitute a new decision as from the date of reversal but that acts done before that date which depend on the original decision remain valid. This point was made, in the context of an appeal reversing a judicial decision, by Megarry V-C in *Re D (J)* [1982] Ch 237 and it is submitted that it applies equally to judicial review reversing an administrative decision (see per Donaldson MR in *R* v *Panel on Takeovers & Mergers, ex parte Datafin plc* [1987] QB 815).

The problems of void registration are considered in more detail in R.R. Drury, 'Nullity of companies in English law'(1985) 48 MLR 644.

20.14.2.3   *By order of the court*

Under CA 1985, s. 427, the court may make an order dissolving without winding up any company which, under a compromise or arrangement sanctioned by the court under s. 425, is transferring its business and property to another registered company. A company in relation to which such an order is made must, under penalty, deliver an office copy of it to the registrar within seven days (s. 427(5) and sch. 24).

20.14.2.4   *By the registrar*

The registrar may strike a defunct company off the register under CA 1985, s. 652.

If a company has not gone into liquidation but the registrar has reasonable cause to believe it is not carrying on business or is not in operation then he sends a letter to the company enquiring whether it is in operation; if no reply is received then, between four and six weeks after the first letter, he sends a second letter by registered post warning that if no reply is received within one month then he will take the next step in the process. The next step is the publication of a notice in the *Gazette* that, three months after the date of the notice, the final step will be taken to dissolve the company unless cause is shown to the contrary. A copy of this notice is sent to the company. The final step is to strike the name of the company off the register and to publish a notice in the *Gazette* that it has been struck off. The company is dissolved when this final notice is published (s. 652(5)).

If a company has commenced winding up but the registrar has reasonable cause to believe either that no liquidator is acting or that the affairs of the company are fully wound up, and six months have passed without the liquidator making any returns, then the registrar can go straight to the publication of the three-month warning notice in the *Gazette* without writing to the company first (s. 652(4)). He must send a copy of the notice to the company or, if there is one, to the liquidator at his last known place of business.

Under s. 652A (which was inserted by the Deregulation and Contracting Out Act 1994, sch. 5), the directors of a *private company*, or a majority of them, may apply to the registrar to have the company struck off the register provided it has been inactive for three months. An application cannot be made unless a long list of activities specified in s. 652B have not occurred in the previous three months. These include trading or otherwise carrying on business or being the subject of any other insolvency or liquidation procedure. So, for example, a company cannot escape from a winding-up petition by applying to be dissolved. The registrar must give three months' notice in the *Gazette* of intention to act on an application to have a company struck off (s. 652A(3)). The company is dissolved when the registrar publishes a notice in the *Gazette* that it has been struck off (s. 652A(4) and (5)).

It is expressly provided that if a company is struck off by the registrar under s. 652 or s. 652A the liability, if any, of every director, managing officer and member of the company shall continue and may be enforced as if the company had not been dissolved (ss. 652(6)(a) and 652A(6)).

20.14.2.5   *On completion of voluntary liquidation*

The final stage of a voluntary winding up should be the filing with the registrar of the liquidator's account of the winding up plus a return that a final meeting was either held or was summoned but was inquorate (IA 1986, ss. 94(3), (4), (5), 106(3), (4) and (5)).

On receiving the account and return the registrar must register them, and three months from the date of registration the company is dissolved unless the court orders deferment of dissolution (IA 1986, s. 201(2) and (3)). Filing at Companies House of a liquidator's account and return of final meeting must be notified by the registrar in the *Gazette* (CA 1985, s. 711(1)(r)).

An application to the court to defer dissolution may be made by the liquidator or by any other person who appears to the court to be interested (IA 1986, s. 201(3)). If the court grants the application then the applicant must, under penalty, within seven days, file an office copy of the court's order with the registrar (IA 1986, s. 201(4) and sch. 10), but the registrar does not have to advertise it in the *Gazette*.

The process of dissolution under s. 201 is effective even if the liquidator was mistaken in filing final accounts because the company actually had property that had not been dealt with in the liquidation (*Re Cornish Manures Ltd* [1967] 1 WLR 807).

20.14.2.6 *On application by the official receiver for early dissolution*

An official receiver who is liquidator in the compulsory winding up of a company may apply to the registrar for 'early dissolution' of the company under IA 1986, s. 202. This may be done only if it appears to the official receiver that the realisable assets of the company are insufficient to cover the expenses of liquidation and that the affairs of the company do not require further investigation (IA 1986, s. 202(2)). The official receiver must give 28 days' notice of intention to apply for early dissolution to the company's creditors and contributories and, if there is one, its administrative receiver ((IA 1986, s. 202(3)). Once that notice has been given the official receiver has no obligation to do anything else in relation to the company except put in an application for dissolution to the registrar ((IA 1986, s. 202(4)).

During the 28-day notice period fresh information may become apparent: the official receiver, any creditor, any contributory or an administrative receiver of the company may apply to the Secretary of State for directions to enable the liquidation to proceed as if no notice had been given (IA 1986, s. 203).

If the official receiver proceeds to make application for early dissolution, the registrar must register the application and, at the end of three months beginning with the day of registration, the company will be dissolved (IA 1986, s. 202(5)). Again, however, if new information becomes apparent, the official receiver, or any person who appears to the Secretary of State to be interested, may apply to the Secretary of State for directions to enable the winding up to continue and for the date of dissolution to be deferred (IA 1986, ss. 202(5) and 203).

20.14.2.7 *On completion of compulsory liquidation*

If a liquidator in a compulsory liquidation who is not the official receiver forms the opinion that the winding up is for practical purposes complete then he or she must summon a final meeting of the creditors under IA 1986, s. 146. The liquidator must notify the registrar that the final meeting was held, or was summoned but was inquorate (s. 172(8); form 4.43 in IR 1986, sch. 4). On receipt of that notice the registrar must register it, and at the end of the period of three months beginning with the day of registration the company is dissolved unless the Secretary of State or, on appeal, the court, directs deferment of dissolution (s. 205(1) to (4)).

An official receiver who is a compulsory liquidator does not have to hold a final meeting but will send the registrar a notice that the winding up is complete. The procedure is the same as with a notice of final meeting of creditors (s. 205(1) to (4)).

Application for deferment of dissolution may be made by the official receiver or any other person who appears to the Secretary of State to be interested. A person for whom deferment of dissolution is directed must, under penalty, send the registrar a copy of the direction within seven days of it being given (s. 205(6) and (7) and sch. 10).

Index

Abbreviated accounts
  form   277
  medium-sized companies   276–7
  option to deliver   275
  private companies   275–7
  small companies   270–1, 275–7, 467
Acceptance of shares   180
Accounting reference periods   262, 264
Accounts   258–89
  abbreviated *see* Abbreviated accounts
  accounting principles   269–70
  accounting records *see* records
  accrual accounting   270, 304–5
  annual filing with register
    delivery of accounts   274
    unlimited company exceptions   275
  auditor's report attached   262–4
  director's report attached   262
  disclosure in
    allotments   184
    borrowing other than directors'   523
    directors' borrowing   523
    directors' interests   516–17
  distribution in   306–7
  erroneous, shares bought on basis of   254–7
  formats   269
  group accounts   268
  half-yearly reports   288
  laying before general meeting   262, 264–5
    election to dispense with   267
  members, for   261–73
  partnerships of entities with limited liability
    288–9
  period for delivery   264
  profits realised and unrealised   304–5
  publication   286–7
  records
    access to   260–1
    contents   260
    legal requirement   259
    preservation   259–60
  revenue recognition   304
  revision   287–8
  right to demand copies   266
  schedules 4, 4A, 9 and 9A   267–9
  sending copies before meeting   265–6

Accounts – *continued*
  small companies exemption   263, 270–1,
    275–7, 467
  summary financial statements   266–7
  true and fair view   271–4
  see also Balance sheet; Group accounts;
    Profit and loss account
Accrual accounting   270, 304–5
Accumulation   305
Acquiescence of members *see* Ratification
Act of Parliament, incorporation by   4
Actual dominant influence   279
Adjournment of meetings   400, 407–8
Administration   676–82
  administrator's proposals   678–9
  application for order   677–8
  effect on directors   680–1
  moratorium   681
  powers of administrator   564, 680–1
  private examination   682
  statement of affairs   681
  unenforceability of liens on books   682
Administration orders *see* Administration;
    Administrative receiver; Administrator
Administrative receiver   329–30, 665–76
  as agent of company   668
  contracts of company and
    employment contracts   672–3
    made before appointment   670–2
    new contracts   673
  definition   665–7
  effect on directors   667
  liability for maladministration   676
  meeting of unsecured creditors   669–70
  powers   667–8
    to institute litigation   564
  preferential creditors   675–6
  property available to
    acquired after crystallisation   674
    court orders to deliver   675
    seized in execution   674–5
    subject to other security arrangements
      673–4
    wrongful seizure   675
  report to creditors   669
  statement of affairs   699–700

Administrative receiver – *continued*
  content 668–9
  requirement to submit 668
  unsecured creditors meeting 669–70
  see also Administrator
Administrator
  avoidance of charge securing debt incurred
      before charge created 341
  powers 564, 680–1
  proposals 678–9
  see also Administration orders:
      Administrative receivers
Admission for securities listing (Yellow Book)
    205, 209, 228, 251, 310, 311, 364
Advertising *see* Investment advertisements
Agency
  administrative receiver as agent 668
  corporate entity and 144–6
  signature on bill of exchange 127–8
Aggregate theory 162
Agreement
  in exercising voting right 406–7
  members *inter socios* agreement 104–7
  oral 591
  retention of title 350–2
Allotment of shares 176–7
  acceptance 180
  allottee 177
  authorisation 181–3
  by directors 182–3, 499–500
  contract 100–1
    failure to carry out 184–5
    registration 194
  convertibles 181, 356
  disclosure in accounts 184
  offer 180
  options 181
  pre-emption rights 183–4
  registration of contract 194
  remedy for misrepresentation
    criminal liability 201–2
    damages 200–1
  remedy for wronged allottee 196–7
  renunciation 180–1, 235
  rescission of misrepresentation 197
  returns of 184
    bonus shares 301–2
    notification in *Gazette* 121
  rights issue 210
  share certificates *see* Share certificates
  to subscribers 202
  vendor consideration issue 192
Alteration of articles
  benefit of company as a whole 113–17
  fraud on minority 113–17
  notification 111
  power to alter 110
  'proper purposes test' 116

Alteration of articles – *continued*
  restrictions
    imposed by company or members
        112–13
    imposed by contract 113
    imposed by court 112
    statutory 111
  special resolution to alter 110
  terms of another contract 117–18
  unanimous assent 110
Alternative Investment Market 205
Amalgamations *see* Takeovers
Annual general meeting 377–8
  business of 378
  members' own resolutions 378
  see also Meetings
Annual returns
  disclosure 130–2
  membership list 131, 132
Application of assets 712–15
  order of priorities 713–14
  post-liquidation interest 714–15
  principles 712–14
  provision for employees 715
Appointed representatives 208
Appointment of directors 430–49
  by directors 433–4
  by members 432–3
  defective 447–8
  upon terms of articles 107–9
Arrangements *see* Voluntary arrangements
Articles of association 38
  alteration
    benefit of company as a whole 113–17
    fraud on minority 113–17
    notification 111
    power to alter 110
    'proper purposes test' 116
    restrictions
      imposed by company or members
          112–13
      imposed by contract 113
      imposed by court 112
      statutory 111
    special resolution to alter 110
    terms of another contract 117–18
    unanimous assent 110
  alternative articles 91
  authority for otherwise prohibited acts 92
  construction 92
  constructive notice 59
  contents 90–2
  contractual effects of s.14
    academic analysis 103–4
    category 3 rights 102
    company and members 96–104
    contract of allotment of shares 100–1
    contractual analysis 92–6

Articles of association – *continued*
  debts under contract formed by articles
    104
  director appointment upon terms of articles
    107–9
  enforcing provision of articles   102–3
  history of provisions   94–5
  members *inter socios* agreement   104–7
  nature of contract   96–8
  outsider rights   98–100, 104
  provisions relating to membership only
    98
  copies for members   118
  deemed notice   624
  exit rights   597
  listed companies   92
  ostensible authority not conferred by
    629–31
  power of management
    authority for otherwise prohibited acts   92
    general   469–74
    other than general   476
  registration   88–90
  Stock Exchange stipulations   92
  Table A   88–9, 90–1
  Table G   90
Artificial entities   2–3
Assets
  in accounts   185
  fixed   186–7, 305
    valuation in director's report   284
  net   185
  non-cash
    book value   305
    shares in return for   193–4, 196
    valuation of   193–4
  provision   305
  unclaimed, valuation   305, 306
  see also Application of assets
Assignment of director's office   453
Association of Authorised Public Accountants
    541
Association of International Bond Dealers
    207, 356
Audit committees   547
Auditor
  access to accounting records   261
  appointment
    dispensing with annual   540
    eligibility   541–3
    private company   540
    public company   539
  dispensing with annual appointment   540
  dispensing with laying of accounts   540
  dormant companies and   540–1
  duties   545–7
    disclosure of payments   468
    f iduciary   468, 470

Auditor – *continued*
  erroneous accounts, takeovers and   254–7
  lack of independence   542–3
  negligence   546–7
  notice of meetings   382
  officer of company   547
  qualification   541–2
  recognised supervisory bodies   541
  relief from liability   547–8
  removal from office   543–4
  remuneration   544
  replacement   544
  resignation   543–4
  small companies   540, 545
  valuation of non-cash assets   193–4
Auditor's report
  attached to annual report   262–4
  inspection before purchase of own shares
    125
  small companies   277
Australian companies   28, 29, 38
Authentication of documents   614–19
  bills of exchange   618–19
  cheques   618–19
  contractual formalities   616
  deeds   616–18
  execution of documents   616
  promissory notes   618–19
  sealing   615–16
  signature   614–15
Authorised persons, FSA definition   206,
    207–8
Authorised share capital   42, 44, 49–50, 171
  alteration   177–8
  authorised minimum   49–50, 195–6
    reduction below   297
  increase   178
  reduction of capital
    creditors' interests   294–5
    power to reduce   292–3
    preference shareholder and   294
    procedure   296–7
    role of court   293–4
    serious loss of capital   297
    treatment of different classes   293, 295–6
Authority
  acting under company's authority   621
  actual
    definition   621–2
    less than ostensible authority   631–4
    limited by company objects   622, 635–6
    ratification of acts outside   636–7
  charitable companies   640
  company secretary   639
  express powers   76–7
  failure to ask questions   628–9
  implied actual authority   627
  implied powers   71–3

Authority – *continued*
  indoor management rule 614, 622–5
  lack of, knowledge or notice of 628–9
  no representation by company 628
  ostensible
    articles of association and 629–31
    board of directors 634–5
    conferred by position or job title 625–7
    definition 622
    directors party to transactions 637–9
    implied actual authority 627
    limited by company objects 635–6
    protection of contractor
      common law 622–31
      statute law 631–4
  for otherwise prohibited acts 92
  rule in *Turquand's case* 614, 622–5
  see also Borrowing: Management power of
    directors
Autopoietic (self-creating) theory 164

Balance sheet
  accounting method 185
  depreciation 186–7, 305
  formats 269
  net assets in 185
  provisions in 185, 186
  requirements of annual 261
  true and fair view 271–4
  see also Accounts
Balance ticket 233
Bank of England, FSA exempted 208
Banking companies 268, 275, 276
  holding shares of holding companies
    313–14
Bearer debentures 354
Bills of exchange 127, 128
  authentication 618–19
Board of directors
  chairman 391–2, 459
  ostensible authority 634–5
  proceedings 456–9
  quorum 457–8
  two-tier boards 481–2
  written resolution 459
Bona fide in company's interest 487–8, 490–2
Bonds
  eurobonds 357
  international 356–7
  zero-coupon 356
Bonus shares 301–2, 312
Book debts 348, 349–50, 352
Borrowing 320–53
  by directors 519–24
    anti-avoidance provision 522
    civil remedies 522
    credit sales 521
    criminal penalties 522
    disclosure in accounts 523

Borrowing – *continued*
    quasi loans 521
  cash at bank 349
  guarantees
    for directors' loans 520
    security for borrowing 321, 521
  implied powers to borrow 71
  marketable loans 354–7
  mortgage 324–5
  other than by directors 523
  security for 520
    clog on equity 322
    equity of redemption 322
    fetter on equity 322
    guarantees 321, 521
    realisation 322–3
    redemption 322
    security contracts 320–1
  see also Debts: Guarantees for borrowing:
    Security for financial obligations
Bracket theory 162
Brokers and brokerage 188, 203–4
  market maker 203, 204
  matching broker 203, 204
Business address 36, 38
  disclosure 131
  in memorandum 68
Business documents
  authentication *see* Authentication of
    documents
  bills of exchange 127, 128, 618–19
  charitable status disclosure 130–1
  cheques 127–8, 618–19
  deeds 616–18
  directors' names in 129, 456
  disclosure of information 126–30
  execution of 616
  insolvency disclosure 129–30
  name of company 126–9
  promissory notes 618–19
  signatures 614–15
  see also Company registers and information
Business name *see* Name of company

Cadbury Code
  company secretary 537–8, 539
  directors 423–8, 460, 462
Call option 310
Called up share capital 171
  in balance sheet 185
Capacity of company to act *see* Ultra vires rule
Capital *see* Share capital
Capital duty, on conversion 356
Capital redemption reserves 297–8
  bonus shares paid from 301–2
  undistributable 306
Capitalisation/capitalisation issues 301–2
Case law 22–6
  judicial supervision 22–4

Case law – *continued*
reports 24–5
Cash at bank 349
Certificate of incorporation
altered 80–1, 86
evidence of compliance with CA 1985 38,
39, 52, 133
notification in *Gazette* 52, 53, 86–7, 121
Certificate to commence business 50, 53,
195–6
Chairman
board of directors 459
meetings 391–2
Charges
book debts 348, 349–50, 352
chose in action 349
company property *see* Register of charges
contract under seal 328
distress 331
equitable 325–6, 327–8
fixed 336–9
floating *see* Floating charges
land 323
legal 324–5, 327–8
negative pledges 330
non-possessory, registration 323–4
priorities 325–6
registration of particulars *see* Register of
charges
rights of lender
action for performance 328–9
appointment of receiver 328
foreclosure 328
possession 327–8
sale 326
rights over property that are not charges
347–9
see also Creditors *and* Debts
Charitable companies
authority 640
contractual liability 620–1
status disclosure 130–1
Charitable contributions 285
Charities 12
Chartered Association of Certified Accountants
(Ireland) 541
Cheques 128
authentication 618–19
signing 127
Chicago law and economics movement
32–5
Chinese walls 208
Chose in action 175–6
charges on 349
Circulars
accompanying notice of meeting 385–8
directors' 387
City Code on Takeovers and Mergers 242–3,
248

Claims
priority 293, 295–6
see also Debts
Class meetings 376
conduct of 418
quorum 390
Class rights
abrogation 83
reduction of capital 293, 295–6
variation 83, 182, 417–20
cancellation 418–19
conduct of meetings 418
created by memorandum 417–18
created other than by memorandum 418
meaning 419–20
registration 420
Clearing houses, FSA recognised 208
Collateral liability 44–5
Collateral security 321, 520, 521
Commission, underwriting *see* Underwriting
Committees of directors 461–2
Commonwealth 28, 29
Communitarians 35
Community law 26–31
Companies
as a whole *see* Corporate personality
Australian 28, 29, 38
change of status 51–4
from private to public
limited by guarantee 53
limited by shares 53
from public to private 52–3
from unlimited to limited 54
hybrid companies 52, 53–4
charges register *see* Register of charges
classification 41–56
collateral liability 44–5
in courts 660–3
dealings with *see* Dealings with company
dormant 540–1
existing registration of 57–8
groups, as separate entity 154–7
guarantee 41, 42, 44, 52, 53
holding *see* Holding companies
hybrid 45, 49, 52, 53–4
in Ireland 28
legislation *see* Company law
limited 41–9
by guarantee 41, 42, 44, 52, 53
by shares 43–4, 53
listed 92
litigation 660–3
medium-sized 276–7
money lending 521–2
no liability company 49
numbers 56–7
off-the-shelf, or ready-made 39–40
offeree 241
offeror 241

Companies – *continued*
  old public companies 50–1
  partnership companies 56, 89
  patent companies 63
  phoenix companies 67
  quasi-partnerships 54–6, 98, 594–5,
    597–600
  registration *see* Registration
  relevant 521–2
  Scotland 27–8, 36, 38
  single-member 12, 47, 390–1, 416–17
    decision-making 416–17
  small *see* Small companies
  subsidiary *see* Subsidiaries
  target 241
  unlimited 41
  in USA 28–9, 48
  see also Banking, Insurance, Private *and*
    Public companies
Company law
  Acts 17–22
  criticism 20
  governance 14–17
  history 17–18
  importance 17
  legislative process 19–20
  mandatory content 13–14
  purpose 11–17
  review 20–1
  shareholder primacy 14–15
  sources *see* Sources
Company registers and information, inspection
    122–6
  by any person 123–4
  by members and creditors only 125
  by members only 125–6
  by officers only 126
Company secretary
  in annual returns 131
  appointment 537–8
  authority 639
  Cadbury Code 537–8, 539
  duties 538–9
  first 37, 538
  qualifications 537–8
  register 538
    inspection 124
  subsequent 538
Compensation for loss of office
  disclosure in accounts 468
  not requiring approval 466
  requiring approval 465–6
Compulsory winding up 687–94
  circumstances for ordering 688–90
  dissolution after 719
  effect on directors 692–4
  first meetings 690–1
  liquidation committee 691–2

Compulsory winding up – *continued*
  liquidator on making order 690
  petition 687
  petitioners 688
  provisional liquidator appointment 694
  public examination of officers 700–1
  statutory demand 689–90
  staying of proceedings 693–4
Computers
  evidence of share title 230
  see also Talisman system: TAURUS
Concert parties 248, 250
Concession theory 9–10, 13
Conduct of business rules, FSA 207–8
Conflict of interest
  circumstances in which rules apply 510
  company not party to transactions
    articles disapplying rules 531
    competing directorships 531
    corporate opportunity doctrine 526–31
    investments 529–30
    rule against conflict of interest and duty
      525–6
    rule against profiting 524–5
  company transactions benefiting directors
    510–14
  constructive trust 509
  criminal liability 510
  interests of other parties 497
  remedies
    constructive trust 509
    liability to account 509
    no criminal liability 510
    rescission 508–9
  rules against 505–8
    circumstances of application 510
    disapplication 508, 531
  voting prohibition 512–13
Connected persons 521, 524
Consensual security 321
Consistency concept 270
Constructive trust 509, 555–7
Contingent purchase contract 310
Contractarians 166–8
Contracts of company 619
  administrative receiver and 670–3
    employment contracts 672–3
    new contracts 673
  charitable companies 620–1
  damages 200–1
  pre-incorporation
    agreement to the contrary 642
    personal liability 640–1
    ratification and novation 642
  purchase of own shares 310
  relational 95
  security contracts 320–1
  see also Ultra vires rule

Contractual effect of memorandum
  alteration of articles
    contracts and   113
    fraud on minority   113–17
    'proper purpose test'   116
  benefit of company as whole   113–17
  category 3 rights   102
  company and members   96–104
  contract of allotment of shares   100–1
  debts under contract formed by articles   104
  director appointment upon terms of articles
    107–9
  enforcing provision of articles   102–3
  members *inter socios* agreement   104–7
  nature of contract   96–8
  outsider rights   98–100, 104
  producers' cooperatives   101–2
  provisions relating to membership only   98
  s.14   92–109
    academic analysis   103–4
    contractual analysis   92–6
    history of provisions   94–5
Control of company property   150–1
Control contract   278, 279
Convertibles   247
  allotment   181, 356
  conversion rights   356
  marketable loans   356
  stamp duty on transfer   356
Corporate law theory   161–8
  contractarians   166–8
  criticism of separate personality   161–6
  economic theories   166–8
  influence of theories   168
Corporate manslaughter   648
Corporate opportunity doctrine   526–31
  limits   527–9
Corporate personality
  company information and   122–6
  disclosure   119–32
  inspection   123–4
  lifting the veil *see* Veil of incorporation
  registry information   119–21
    inspection   121
  singular or plural term   169
  see also Legal personality: Separate legal
    personality
Corporate quasi-partnership   594–5
Corporate veil *see* Veil of incorporation
Corporation sole   3–4
  see also Single-member companies
Courts
  jurisdiction   23–4
  practice in   660–3
Credit
  sales to directors   521
  see also Borrowing: Debts
Credit union   62

Creditors
  directors' responsibility to
    common law duty   493–5
    statutory duty   495
  interests in capital reduction   294–5
  liquidation *see* Liquidation, voluntary
  meetings *see* Creditors meetings
  preferential   675–6
  unsecured   669
  see also Borrowing: Debts
Creditors meetings
  administrative receiver and   669–70
  administrator's proposals and   678–9
Crest settlement system   230, 236, 238
Criminal liability of company   646–52, 658–9
  criminal state of mind   649–50
Crystallisation   331–3
  events causing   331–3

Damages
  deceit   200–1
  negligent misrepresentation   200–1
Dealings with company   613–63
  authentication of documents
    bills of exchange   618–19
    cheques   618–19
    contractual formalities   616
    deeds   616–18
    execution of documents   616
    promissory notes   618–19
    sealing   615–16
    signature   614–15
  authority *see* Authority
  identification theory *see* Identification theory
  liability for torts   643
Death of all members   137–8
Debenture holders
  information for   356
  inspection of register   123–4
Debentures
  bearer   355
  perpetual   322
  share premium and   191
  see also Debt securities
Debt securities
  allotment   355–6
  see also Debentures: Security for financial
    obligations
Debts
  subordination   714
  under contract formed by article   104
  see also Borrowing: Claims: Credit
Deceit, damages for   200–1
Declaration of solvency   685
Deed of settlement   59, 90, 94
Deeds   616–18
Deemed notice   624
Default, of directors   534

Deferred shares 175
Depreciation 186–7, 305
  straight line method 186
Derivative actions 563–6
  causes 567–70
  company's decision not to sue 566–7
  leave to continue action 573–4
  loss of value of shares 572–3
  present position 567–70
  proposed reform 570–1
  ratifiability
    as basis of fraud on minority exception
    571–2
    as basis of personal rights exceptions
    579–80
Devolution of shares 176
Directing mind and will 652, 656–8
Directors
  access to accounting records 260–1
  action to restrain person acting as 454
  administrative receiver and 667
  administrator and 680–1
  age 434
  agents of members 480–1
  allotment of shares by 182–3, 499–500
  alternate 448
  in annual returns 131
  appointment 430–49
    by directors 433–4
    by members 432–3
    defective 447–8
    upon terms of articles 107–9
  approval of share transfer required 234–6
    refused 234–5, 236
  assignment of office 453
  board
    chairman 391–2, 459
    ostensible authority 634–5
    proceedings 456–9
    quorum 457–8
    two-tier boards 481–2
    written resolution 459
  borrowing 519–24
    anti-avoidance provision 522
    civil remedies 522–3
    credit sales 521
    criminal penalties 522
    disclosure in accounts 523
    quasi loans 521
  Cadbury Code 423–8, 460, 462
  calls on partly paid shares 188–9
  care, duty of 483–6
    attendance to company's affairs 485
    forgiveness by members 486
    liability for negligence 483–6
    reliance on 485–6
    skill required 484–5
    statement of 483–4
  change notification in *Gazette* 122

Directors – *continued*
  committees 461–2
  compensation for loss of office
    disclosure in accounts 468
    not requiring approval 466
    requiring approval 465–6
  competing directorships 531
  compulsory liquidator and 692–4
  conflict of interest
    actual or potential conflict 507–8
    circumstances in which rules apply 510
    company not party to transactions
      articles disapplying rules 531
      competing directorships 531
      corporate opportunity doctrine 526–31
      investments 529–30
      rule against conflict of interest and duty
      525–6
      rule against profiting 524–5
    company transactions benefiting directors
      510–14
    constructive trust 509
    criminal liability 510
    interests of other parties 497
    remedies
      constructive trust 509
      liability to account 509
      no criminal liability 510
      rescission 508–9
    rules against 505–8
      circumstances of application 510
      disapplication of 508, 531
    voting prohibition 512–13
  connected persons 521, 524
  contractual restrictions 504–5
  credit sales to 521
  de facto 429
  de iure 429
  declaration of payment out of capital
    299–300
  declaration of solvency 685
  default of 534
  disclosure in accounts
    compensation for loss of office 468
    emoluments 466–8
    omission from small companies accounts
    467
    pensions 468
    sums paid to third parties 468
  dismissal 450–3
    by members 470
  disputes about holders of office 454
  disqualification *see* Disqualification of
    directors
  employment status 464–5
  executive 430, 461
  false statements by 226
  fiduciary duty 468, 470
    'best interests of company' 488

Directors – *continued*
   bona fide in interests of company 487–8,
     490–2
   general statement 487–9
   improper purpose 489
   interests of other parties 492
     conflict of interests 497
     creditors 493–5
     members and employees 492–3
     other constituencies 495–7
     persons to whom company is fiduciary
      495
   nature of 486–7
   other powers 502
   power to allot shares 499–500
   proper-purpose doctrine 497–9
   ratification by members 502–3
   takeover bids and 500–1
   see also conflict of interest
   first 431
   registration 37
   Gazette
     notification in 454, 456
     of change 122
   holding or subsidiary companies 422
   interests 284
     conflict *see* conflict of interest
     disclosure 511–12
      in accounts 516–17
     register *see* Register of directors' interests
   interpretation of 'director' in legislation
     428
   investigation of share dealings 604
   legal categorisation 480
   liability
     for company's wrongs 481
     relief by company 533–4
     relief by court 534–5
   loans and guarantees *see* Borrowing
   managing 459–61
   minimum numbers 428
   names 129
   need for 423
   negligence 483–6
     see also care, duty of: fiduciary duty
   nominee 449, 503–4
   non-executive 430
   payment out of capital declaration 299–300
   pensions for widows 74
   power *see* Management power of directors
   profiting *see* conflict of interest
   purchase of own shares 125
   quantum meruit 109, 465
   register 455
     inspection 124
     notification 456
   removal *see* dismissal: Disqualification of
     directors: termination of office
   remuneration 462–9, 537

Directors – *continued*
   committee 461–2
   compensation for loss of office 465–6,
     468
   disclosure 466–8
   employment status 464–5
   expenses 463
   net of tax agreement prohibition 465
   no entitlement 462
   other services 463–4
   provision in articles for fees 462–3
   report *see* Directors' report
   resignation 453
   retirement
     by rotation 450
     on reaching statutory age 453–4
   self dealing rule 532–3
   service contracts 125
     approval 469
     inspection 125, 469
   severance payments 73
   shadow 429–30, 493, 515, 520, 523, 709
   share qualification 449
   signature on share certificate 230, 231
   subsequent 431–4
   substantial property transactions 511, 514,
     517–19
   termination of office
     assignment 453
     dismissal 450–3
     resignation 453
     retirement
      by rotation 450
      on reaching statutory age 453–4
     vacation deemed by articles 449
   transactions
     benefiting 510–14
     substantial property transactions 511,
      514, 517–19
     to which are party 637–9
   unauthorised acts, ratification 502–3, 531–3
   vacation of office 449
   voting prohibition 512–13
   wrongful trading 708–12
   see also Management power of directors
Directors' report 283–6
   allotment disclosure 184
   annual reports to be attached 262
   charitable contributions 285
   details of directors 284
   disabled persons employment 285
   employee involvement 285–6
   holding of own shares 285
   political contributions 285
   repurchase of own shares 312
   research and development activities 285
   shares 190
   valuation of fixed assets 284
Disabled persons employment 285

Discharge of contract, agreement   104
Disclosure   119–32
  allotments   184
  annual returns   131–2
  business documents   126–30
  company information   122–6
  directors' details   455
  directors' interests in contracts   513–15
  directors' remuneration   466–8
  insolvency   129–30
  listing particulars   228
  notification in *Gazette*   121–2
  promoter's profit   550–2
  purchase of own shares   317
  redeemable shares   301
  registry information
    inspection   121
    registration   119–21
  related undertakings information   282–3
  underwriting   228
  see also Company registers and information
Discounts   187–8
Discrimination test   115–16
Dismissal of directors   450–3, 470
Disqualification of directors   434–47
  application for order   438–40
  by being auditor or secretary   446
  by being C of E clergyman   446–7
  by order   435–6, 611–12
  by personal insolvency   435
  failure to keep accounts and   259–60, 261
  grounds   436–8
  leave to act   446
  period of disqualification order   440–1
  register of orders   446
Dissentient minority
  cancellation of resolution   375
  compulsory share purchase   243–7, 312
  objections to articles change   110
  objections to memorandum change   83–4,
    85
  questioning decisions   403–5
  status change of company   52
  voting and   401
  see also Fraud on the minority; Shareholders
Dissolution   6, 715–19
  by Act of Parliament   716
  by cancellation of registration   716–17
  by order of court   717
  by registrar   718
  on completion of liquidation
    compulsory   719
    voluntary   718–19
  early   719
  notice in *Gazette*   121, 122, 718
  Official receiver and   719
Distress   331
Distribution
  accounts   306–7

Distribution – *continued*
  accumulation   305
  controls on payments out of capital   290–2
  dividends
    illegal excessive   316–17
    meaning   302–3
    preference   174
    shareholders' rights   172, 173
  excessive   307–8
  investment companies   306
  meaning   302–3
  profits
    available for   304
    realised and unrealised   304–5
  public companies   306
  realised and unrealised losses   305
  restrictions   303–4
  see also Reduction of capital
Dividends
  illegal excessive   316–17
  meaning   302–3
  preference   174
  shareholders' rights   172, 173
Dormant companies   540–1
Duplicate certificates   232

EC Directives
  Admissions Directive   209
  formation   27
  Fourth Directive   267–8, 271
  insider dealing   358–9
  Interim Reports Directive   209
  Listing Particulars Directive   209, 213
  Second Directive   49
  Seventh Directive   268
Employee share schemes   311–12, 314
Employees
  involvement, in directors' report   285–6
  provision for   715
Employment contracts
  adoption by administrative receiver   672–3
  directors'   125, 469
Equitable charges   325–6, 327–8
  two on same property   325–6
Equity
  of redemption   322
  shares   175
Estoppel   230–2
Ethnicity   660
Eurobonds   357
European Community
  Community law   26–31
  Directives *see* EC Directives
  single market   30
  subsidiaries and competition law   158
European company   27
Examination
  private   682, 695–9
  public   700–1

Execution, *fieri facias* writ   334
Executive directors   461
Express powers, separate objects provision and 76–7
Extraordinary general meeting   378–80
  courts power to call   380–1
  quorum for   381
  requisitioned   379
  serious loss of capital   297
  see also Meetings

Fiction theory   164–5, 168
Fiduciary duty   468, 470
  'best interests of company'   488
  bona fide in interests of company   487–8, 490–2
  general statement   487–9
  improper purpose   489
  interests of other parties   492
    conflict of interests   497
    creditors   493–5
    members and employees   492–3
    other constituencies   495–7
    persons to whom company is fiduciary   495
  nature of   486–7
  other powers   502
  power to allot shares   499–500
  proper-purpose doctrine   497–9
  ratification by members   502–3
  takeover bids and   500–1
Fieri facias writ   334
Financial Reporting Standards   272–3
Financial Services Act 1986   206–8
  authorised persons   206, 207–8
  conduct of business rules   207–8
  exempted persons   208
  investment business, definition   206, 207
  investments, definition   206
  recognised clearing houses   208
  recognised investment exchanges   208
  see also Offering shares to the public
Fixed assets   186–7, 305
  valuation, in directors' report   284
Fixed charges   336–9
Floating charges   336–9
  administrative receiver appointment   329–30
  crystallisation   331–3
    events causing   331–3
    rights conferred before   333–6
  for debt incurred before charge created   339–41
    avoidance by administrator   341
    avoidance by liquidator   339–41
  definition   329–30
  fixed or floating   336–9
  present interest   335
  specific charges not created by   333–6

Floating charges – *continued*
  see also Charges
Foreclosure   328
Forfeiture of shares   189–90
Forgery
  forged transfer   237–8
  share certificates   231–2
Foss v Harbottle rule
  academic comment   558–9
  'flood gates' arguments   561–2
  judicial comment   558–9
  majority rule   558, 560–1
  multiplicity of actions   561
  'proper plaintiff' principle   557–8
  ratifiability principle   558, 560–1, 562
  reasons for rule   559–62
  refusal to decide business policy   559–60
  statement of   557–8
  see also Proper plaintiff principle
Founders' shares *see* Deferred shares
Fraud on the minority   503, 567–8, 582
  company as a whole   113–17
  discrimination test   115–16
  questioning decisions   401, 403–5
  ratifiability as basis of   571–2
Fraudulent character   568–70
Fraudulent trading liability   701–5
  carrying on of business   704–5
  meaning of fraud   702–4
  nature of liability   705
Fraudulent transfer   237–8
Freezing orders   241, 252–4
  voting rights and   397
Fully paid shares   171

Gazette notification   121–2
  alteration of articles   111
  directors   454, 456
    change   122
  dissolutions   121, 122, 718
  issue of certificate of incorporation   38, 52, 53
    alteration   80–1, 86
General meetings   376
  auditor's report to   265
  inspection of minutes   125–6
  laying accounts before   262, 264–5
  reversion of powers to   478–9
  sending accounts before meeting   265–6
  substantial property transactions   511, 514, 517–19
  see also Meetings
Gierke's theory   163
Going concern concept   269
  general power of management   471
Governance of company   14–17
Group accounts   268
  actual dominant influence   279
  control contract   278, 279

Group accounts – *continued*
  individual accounts   280
  parent company   278
  parent and subsidiary company   278–80
  participating interest   279
  related undertakings information   282–3
  small and medium-sized groups exemption
    281
  subgroup exemption   280–1
  subsidiaries excluded   281–2
  see also Accounts
Groups *see* Group accounts: Holding
  companies: Subsidiaries
Guarantee company   41, 42, 44, 53
  re-registration
    from private company   53
    from public company   52
    as unlimited company   53
Guarantees for borrowing   321, 521
  for directors' loans   520

Harmonisation   26–7, 30
Holding companies
  directors   422
  holding shares in   313–14
  shareholders   421–2
  voting rights   422
  see also Group accounts
Honorary members   172
Hybrid companies   45, 49
  change of status   52–4

Identification theory   643–60
  actions against company   658
  attribution of knowledge   646
  corporate conspiracy   647
  corporate manslaughter   648
  criminal liability   646–52, 658–9
  directing mind and will   652, 656–8
  double counting   652–3
  enemy character   645–6
  ethnicity   660
  persons identified   652, 653–8
  religious belief   659–60
Implied powers
  for incidental purposes   71–3
  outside main objects   72–3
  to borrow money   71, 76
  to issue negotiable instruments   72
  to pay for defence   71–2
  to pay gratuities   71, 73–4
Incorporation   1–11
  by Act of Parliament   4
  by ministerial act   5
  by prescription   6
  by registration *see* Registration
  by Royal Charter   4
  certificate *see* Certificate of incorporation
  concession theory   9–10, 13

Incorporation – *continued*
  as corporation sole   3–4
  nature of   1–3
  partnerships   6–7
  quasi-corporations   7–9
  separate personality   3
  sole proprietorship   10
  unincorporated associations   7
  veil of *see* Veil of incorporation
Indebtedness
  in annual return   131
  see also Debts
Individualism   161–2
Indoor management rule *see* Internal
  management principle
Insider dealing
  civil liability   366–9
  confidential fiduciary relationship   358
  definition of offence   359–65
  disqualification order   611–12
  EC Directive   358–9
  inside information
    definition   359–60
    disclosure   363
    see also price sensitive information
  insider   360–1
    having information as   360–1
    primary   361
    professional intermediary   361–2
    restrictions *see* restrictions on insiders
    secondary   361
  investigations   365, 605
  Listing Rules   364
  market information use   364
  options   366
  penalties   365
  price sensitive information   359–60
    release to Stock Exchange   364–5
  professional intermediary   361–2
  reasons for prohibition   358–9
  register of directors' interests   369–71
  regulated market   360, 361, 365
  restrictions on insiders
    acting within price stabilisation rules   363
    dealing   361–2
    disclosing inside information   363
    encouraging others to deal   362
    general defences   363
    market makers' exemption   363
  Stock Exchange model code   365–6
  tippees   361
  Unlisted Securities Market   365
  unpublished information   358
  USA   359
Insolvency
  disclosure   129–30
  legislation   665
  nature of   664
  prohibited use of name   67–8

Insolvency – *continued*
  see also Administration: Administrative
    receiver: Liquidation
Inspection
  companies charges register 346
  company information 123–6
  register of members 374
  registry information 121
Institute of Chartered Accountants in England
  and Wales 541
Institute of Chartered Accountants in Ireland
  541
Institute of Chartered Accountants of Scotland
  541
Insurance companies 268, 275, 276
  limited liability 46
Interest
  participating 279
  post-liquidation 714–15
Intermediaries 203–4, 361–2
Intermediaries offer 210
Internal management principle 103–4, 106,
  458, 558, 574–6, 614, 622–5
  'proper plaintiff' principle 557–8
International bonds 356–7
International Monetary Fund 208
International organisations, legal personality 9
International Stock Exchange of the United
  Kingdom and the Republic of Ireland Ltd
  see Stock Exchange
Introduction, listing by 210
Investigation by Secretary of State 601
  consequences 608–12
  evidence collection 605–7
  expenses recovery 612
  insider dealing 605
  inspection of documents 601–2
  inspectors 602–8
  interruption 607
  into company's affairs 603
  ownership or control 603–4
  regulatory authorities 609
    overseas 607–8
  related companies 605
  share dealings 604
Investment advertisements 214–15, 224–5
  application for listing 214–15
  definition of issuing 215
  statutory controls 214–15
  unauthorised 226
  unlisted securities *see* Unlisted securities
Investment business
  FSA definition 206, 207
  misleading statements and practices 226–7
Investment companies 306
Investment exchanges 204
  FSA recognised 208
Investment Management Regulatory
  Organisation 207

Investments
  by director when board decided against
    529–30
  FSA definition 206
Ireland 28
Irregularity principle 558, 583–6
Issue of shares *see* Allotment of shares

Jobbers *see* Market makers
Jurisdiction 23–4
  change 81–2

Knowing assistance 555, 557
Knowing receipt or dealing 555, 556, 557

Land Charges Registry 323, 353
Landlords, distress 331
Legal charges 324–5, 327–8
Legal personality
  appointment of receiver 328
  artificial entities with 2–3
  artificial separate legal personality 11
  international organisations 9
  nature of 1–3
  partners 6–7
  'person' terminology 10–11
  quasi-corporations 7–9
  see also Corporate personality: Separate legal
    personality
Lender's rights
  action for performance 328–9
  foreclosure 328
  possession 327–8
  sale 326
Liability
  of company
    for director 533–4
    relief from 547–8
  criminal state of mind 649–50
  of director
    for company's wrongs 481
    relief by company 533–4
    relief by court 534–5
  limited *see* Limited liability
  in memorandum 79
    change 83
  strict 650, 651
  vicarious 650–1
Liens 189, 190
  on books 682, 699
Limited liability 2
  accounts of partnerships composed of entities
    with 288–9
  alterations 83
  by guarantee 41, 42, 44, 52, 53
    re-registration as unlimited company 53
  collateral liability 45
  history 45–8
  insurance companies 46

Limited liability– *continued*
 justification for liability   47
 in memorandum   79
 no liability companies   49
 reduction in members   48–9
 in USA   48
'Limited' omission   62, 81, 82
Liquidation   664–5
 application of assets   712–15
  order of priority   713–14
  post-liquidation interest   714–15
  principles of   712–14
  provision for employees   715
 commencement of winding-up   694
 compulsory   687–94
  circumstances for ordering   688–90
  dissolution after   719
  effect on directors   692–4
  first meetings   690–1
  liquidation committee   691–2
  liquidator on making order   690
  petition   687
  petitioners   688
  provisional liquidator appointment   694
  public examination of officers   700–1
  statutory demand   689–90
  staying of proceedings   693–4
 criminal offences suspected   700
 dissolution *see* Dissolution
 fraudulent trading liability   701–5
  carrying on of business, parties to   704–5
  meaning of fraud   702–4
  nature of liability   705
 investigation of affairs   694–701
  court orders to deliver property   695
  duty to cooperate   695
  private examination   695–9
 legislation   665
 liens on books   699
 liquidation committee   686–7, 691–2
 misfeasance proceedings
  creditors' interests   706–7
  examples   706
  nature of   705–6
  ratification by members   707–8
 nature of   664
 Official receiver's investigation and report
   699
 public examination of officers   700–1
 statement of affairs   699–700
 voluntary
  creditors   684
   liquidation committee   686–7
   resolution   684–5, 686
  declaration of solvency   685
  dissolution after   719
  members'   684
   appointment of liquidator   685–6
   resolution   684–5, 686

Liquidation – *continued*
 wrongful trading   708–12
 see also Administration: Administrative
    receiver: Winding-up
Liquidators
 appointment of members'   685–6
 avoidance of charge securing debt incurred
    before charge created   339–41
 liquidation order and   690
 powers, to institute litigation   564
 provisional   694
 resources available to *see* Floating charges:
    Misfeasance proceedings
 see also Official receiver: Winding-up
Listed Companies, articles of association   92
Listed Market   204–5, 308
Listing *see* Official listing
Listing particulars   551
 content   213–14
 disclosure   228
 liability for misrepresentations or omissions
    220–1
 misleading statements and omissions   220–4
 misrepresentation in
  expert's statement   222
  official statements and documents   222
  plaintiff's knowledge   223
  reasonable belief   221–2
  steps to correct defect   222
 omissions   214, 220
 persons responsible   220–1
 supplementary   214
 when required   212–13
Listing Rules   205, 209, 228, 251, 310, 311,
    364
Litigation   474–6
 jurisdiction of courts   23–4
 practice in courts   660–3
Lloyds, FSA exempted   208
Loans *see* Borrowing *and* Marketable loans
London Gazette see Gazette
Losses
 accumulation   305
 realised and unrealised   305

Majority rule
 Foss v Harbottle rule   560–1
 ratifiability principle   558, 560–1, 562
 special majorities   578, 581
Maladministration remedies
 action by company
  against company officers   554–5
  against constructive trustees   555–7
  majority rule   560–1
  rule in *Foss v Harbottle see Foss v
     Harbottle* rule
  ultra vires transactions   571, 577, 578–9,
     581
 company investigations   601–12

Maladministration remedies – *continued*
  consequences 608–12
  investigation by inspectors 602–8
  company's decision not to sue 566–7
  fraud 571–2
  internal management principle 575–6
  irregularity principle 583–6
  liability of administrative receiver 676
  proper plaintiff principle *see* Proper plaintiff
    principle
  suing for loss of value of shares 572–3
  unfair prejudice 586–97
  winding-up, just and equitable 597–600
Management power of directors
  conferred by articles, other than general 476
  division between members and 469–70
  general power of management 470–4
    going concern 471
    members' supervisory power 471–4
    subject to articles 471
  litigation power 474–6
  powers of members only 476–8
    large-scale transaction approval 478
  reversion of powers to members 478–9
  see also Authority: Borrowing
Managers (company)
  duties 536–7
  position 536
Managing director 459–61
Mareva injunction 406
Market information use 364
Market makers 203, 204
  jobbers 204
Market purchases, authority 308–9
Marketable loans
  convertibles *see* Convertibles
  debenture holders, information 356
  debt securities, allotment 355–6
  international bonds 356–7
  stock certificates 355
  stocks 354
  trustees 354–5
  underwriting 356
Matching broker 203, 204
Medium-sized company, abbreviated accounts
  276–7
Meeting, annual general meetings 377–8
Meetings 375–409
  adjournment 400, 407–8
  annual general meetings
    business of 378
    members' own resolutions 378
  audio-video links 376
  authority to call 381–2
  by telephone 376
  chairman 391–2, 459
  circulars accompanying notice 385–8
    members' resolutions etc 388–9
  class 376, 418–20

Meetings – *continued*
  creditors meetings
    administrative receiver and 669–70
    administrator's proposals and 678–9
  decision-making without meeting
    acquiescence 415
    unanimous assent 409–14
    written resolutions 415–16
  extraordinary general meetings 378–80
    courts power to call 380–1
    quorum 381
    requisitioned 379
    serious loss of capital 297
  general meetings 376
    auditor's report to 265
    inspection of minutes 125–6
    laying accounts before 262, 264–5
    reversion of powers to 478–9
    sending accounts before meeting 265–6
    substantial property transactions 511,
      514, 517–19
  irregularity principle 583–6
  membership after notice of 389–90
  minutes 408–9
    of board of directors 458
  notice
    auditor entitled to 382
    authority to call 381–2
    contents 385–8
    failure to give 384–5
    length 383–4
    membership after 389–90
    methods of giving 382–3
      outside UK 383
    persons given notice 382–3
    special 388
    waiver 385
  quorum 390
    board of directors 457–8
    extraordinary general meeting 381
    prohibited director not part of 512–13
    single member meetings 390–1
  resolutions
    acquiescence 415
    elective 394–5
    extraordinary 392–4
    ordinary 392
    requisitioned 389
    special 375, 392–4
    unanimous assent 409–15
    written, of private companies 415–16
  single-member companies 390–1, 416–17
  voting *see* Voting: Voting rights
Members *see* Shareholders
Memorandum of association
  alteration
    jurisdiction change 81–2
    liability 83
    name 80–1

Memorandum of association – *continued*
    notification   86–7, 122
    objects   82–3
    share capital   83
    see also power to alter
articles conflicting with   60
authorised share capital   43, 49–50
constructive notice   59
content
    limited liability   79
    name   61–8
    registered office   68–9
    share capital   79
copies to members   87
deemed notice   624
form of   60–1
objects *see* Objects
power to alter   79–80, 83–4
    restrictions
        imposed by company or members   85
        imposed by court   85
        statutory   84
    registration   37–8, 59
    see also Contractual effect of memorandum
Memorandum of satisfaction   345
Mergers *see* Takeovers
Methodological individualism   162
Minimum share capital   49–50, 195–6
    reduction below   297
Ministerial act, incorporation by   5
Minority shareholders
    cancellation of resolution   375
    compulsory share purchase   243–7, 312
    exit rights in articles   597
    objections to articles change   110
    objections to memorandum change   83–4,
        85
    questioning decisions   403–5
    status change of company   52
    voting and   401
    see also Fraud on the minority; Shareholders
Minutes of meetings   408–9
    board of directors   458
Misfeasance proceedings   705–8
    creditors' interests   706–7
    examples   706
    ratification by members   707–8
Misrepresentation
    attribution to company   197–8
    criminal liability   201–2
    damages   200–1
    limitations on statement   198–9
    listing particulars or prospectuses   220–4
        defences   221–3
        expert's statement   222
        official statements and documents   222
        plaintiff's knowledge   223
        reasonable belief   221–2
        steps to correct defect   222

Misrepresentation – *continued*
    loss of rescission remedy   199–200
    rescission for   197
Money lending companies   521
'Moral person' terminology   10
Morality   32
Moratorium, administration   681
Mortgage, legal charge   324–5

Name of company   36
    abbreviation   126–7
    alteration   80–1
    on bill of exchange   127
    business name other than   65–6
    change   80–1
    charitable companies   130–1
    on cheque   127–8
    credit union   62
    disclosure   126–9
    existing corporations   63
    illegal use of words   62–3
    index of names   63, 80
    limited partnerships   63
    Ltd and plc   61–2
        omission of Ltd   62, 81, 82
    in memorandum   61–8
    misnamed in document   128–9
    other than corporate name   65–6
    passing off   64–5
    patent companies   63
    phoenix companies   67
    pre-registration check   38
    publication   66
    scandalous or obscene words   63
    unregistered   128–9
    use of insolvent company's name   67–8
    words requiring permission   63–4
'Natural person' terminology   10
Negative pledges   330, 344
Negligence of director   483–6
    see also Directors, care, duty of: Directors,
        fiduciary duty
Negotiable instruments
    implied powers to issue   72
    for payment of book debt   350
Net worth of company   185
Nominal share capital *see* Authorised share
    capital
Nominal value   170, 171
Nominee directors   449, 503–4
Nominee shareholder   239
Non-cash assets
    book value   305
    shares in return for   193–4, 196
    valuation of   193–4
Non-voting ordinary shares   175
Novation, pre-incorporation contracts   642

Objects   69–77

Objects – *continued*
  change 82–3
  express powers 76–7
  implied powers
    acts not for company's benefit 73–4
    incidental or conducive 72–3, 77
    for incidental purposes 71–3
  main objects 75
  repudiation of transactions 70
  separate-objects provisions 76–7
  statutory requirements 69
  subjective clauses 78
  substratum 70
  to act as general commercial company 77–8
  ultra vires 69–70, 71, 74
    illegal acts 78–9
    unrestricted 77–8
Off-market purchases 308, 309–10
Off-the-shelf companies 39–40
Offeree companies 241
Offering shares to the public 203–28
  criminal liability
    false and misleading statements 225–6
    false statements by directors 226
    offences by companies 225
    unauthorised advertising 226
  FSA *see* Financial Services Act 1986
  inadequate response 228
  market places for shares 203–6
    intermediaries 203–4
    investment exchanges 204
    Listed Market 204–5
    reasons for going public 205–6
    see also Stock Exchange
  official listing *see* Official listing
  reasons for 205–6
  underwriting 227–8
  unlisted securities *see* Unlisted securities
  see also Financial Services Act 1986
Offeror companies 241
Official listing 49
  advertising *see* investment advertisements
  application circumstances 210–11
  application procedure 209–11
  continuing obligations 211
  discontinuance and suspension of listing 211–12
  failure to obtain 219
  intermediaries offer 210
  introduction 210
  investment advertisements 214–15, 224–5
    statutory controls 214–15
    unauthorised 226
  legal framework 208–9
  listing particulars
    content 213–14
    disclosure 228
    liability for misrepresentations or omissions 220–1

Official listing – *continued*
  misleading statements and omissions 220–4
  misrepresentation in
    expert's statement 222
    official statements and documents 222
    plaintiff's knowledge 223
    reasonable belief 221–2
    steps to correct defect 222
  omissions 214, 220
  persons responsible 220–1
  supplementary 214
  when required 212–13
  listing rules 205, 209, 228, 251, 310, 311, 364
  offer for sale 211
  open offer 210
  public offer 210
  rights issue 210
  secondary offer 211
  selective marketing or placing 210, 211
  vendor consideration placing 210, 211
Official receiver 690
  early dissolution application 719
  investigation and report 699
  misfeasance proceedings 705
  statement of affairs 699–700
Old public companies 50–1
Options 181
  holder of 181
  insider dealing 366
Oral agreement 591
Organic theory 163
Outsider rights 98–100, 104
Over-the-counter purchases 309–10
Owners' equity 185
Ownership
  equitable and beneficial 351
  retention of title agreements 350–2
    operation of law rights 352

Paid up share capital 171
  as stock 178–9
Panel on Takeovers and Mergers 242
Participating interest 279
Particulars *see* Listing particulars
Partly paid up shares 171, 188–91
  calls on 188–9
  transfer of 232
Partnership companies 56, 89
Partnerships 6–7
  prohibition on large 57
  quasi-partnerships 54–6, 75–6, 98, 594–5
  register of names of limited 63
Passing off 64–5
Patent companies, names of 63
Payment out of capital 298–301
  approval 299–300
  resolution to make 299, 300

Pensions
 directors' 468
 directors' widows 74
Perpetual debentures 322
Personal Investment Authority 207, 208
Personal representatives, voting rights 397
Personality *see* Corporate, Legal *and* Separate
  legal personality
Phoenix companies 67
Placing, selective marketing 210, 211
 vendor consideration 210, 211
Pledges 323
 negative 330, 344
Political donations 285
Polls 173, 395, 398–400
 date of resolution 400
Possession right 327–8
 wilful default rule 327
Post-liquidation interest 714–15
Powers *see* Authority *and* Management powers
  of directors
Practitioners' books 31
Pre-emption rights 183–4, 235–6
Pre-incorporation contracts
 agreement to the contrary 642
 personal liability 640–1
 ratification and novation 642
Preference shares 174, 181
 redeemable 297–301
 reduction of capital and 294
Preferential creditors 675–6
Prescription, incorporation by 6
Price sensitive information 359–60
 release to Stock Exchange 364–5
Primary insider 361
Private companies 49–51
 abbreviated accounts 275–7
 appointment of auditor 540
 change of status
  from private to public 196
   from private limited by guarantee 53
  from public company to 52–3
  re-registered as public, from private
    limited by shares 53
 definitions 49–50
 history of distinction between public and
   50–1
 numbers of members 50
 numbers of 56–7
 payments out of capital 298–301
 purchase of own shares 312, 316
 single-member companies 390–1, 416–17
 written resolutions 415–16
Private examination 682, 695–9
 Serious Fraud Office records 696
Producers' cooperatives 101–2
Professional intermediary 361–2
Profit and loss account
 accounting method 187

Profit and loss account – *continued*
 annual requirement 261
 format 269
 true and fair view 271–4
 see also Accounts
Profits
 accumulated unrealised 305
 available for distribution 304
 promoters'
  disclosure 550–2
  legitimate and wrongful 553
 realised and unrealised 304–5
 see also Distribution
Promissory notes authentication 618–19
Promoter 548–53
 definition 548–9
 duties
  disclosure and approval 550–2
  fiduciary 549–50
  statutory 552–3
 profits
  disclosure 550–2
  legitimate and wrongful 553
 rescission 550, 553
Proper plaintiff principle 557–8
 causes 567–70
  fraudulent character 568–70
 company to enforce rights 562–3
 company's decision not to sue 566–7
 derivative actions 563–6
 fraudulent character 568–70
 internal management 575–6
 leave to continue action 573–4
 personal rights 576–8, 580–3
 ratifiability 571–2
 special majorities 578, 581–2
 ultra vires transactions 571, 577, 578–9,
   581
 see also Foss v Harbottle rule
Property of company, control 150–1
Property registers 353
Prospectus 551
 content 213–14, 217
 exemptions 216–17
 investment advertising 224–5
 minimum subscription for first offer 219
 misleading statements and omissions 220–4
 misrepresentation in
  expert's statement 222
  plaintiff's knowledge 223
  reasonable belief 221–2
  steps to correct defect 222
 need for 215–16
 omission of information from 214
 persons responsible for 220–1
 Stock Exchange approval 217–18
 supplementary 214, 217
  failure to issue 223
 time for consideration 218–19

Prospectus – *continued*
  when required 212–13
Provision 185, 186, 304
  for employees 715
Proxies 395–7, 398
Prudence concept 270
Public companies 49–51
  appointment of auditor 539
  certificate to commence business 50, 53,
    195–6
  change of status
    from private to public 196
      limited by guarantee 53
      limited by shares 53
    from public to private 52–3, 196
  definitions 49–50
  distributions 306
  history of distinction between private and
    50–1
  minimum share capital 195–6
  numbers 56–7
  old public companies 50–1
  summary financial statement 266–7
Public examination 700–1
Public limited company 61
Purchase of own shares 190
  authority 308
    market purchase 308–9
    off-market purchase 308, 309–10
  contracts 125, 126, 310
  financial assistance for
    authorisation by private company
      318–19
    authorisation by subsidiary 319
    illegal 314–15
    permissible forms 312
    prohibition on other acquisitions 312–13
    transfer of assets 315–16
  holding shares in holding company 313–14
  inspection of report 125
  off-market
    authority 308, 309–10
    inspection of contract 125, 126
  penalties 316–17
  publicity 310
  restrictions and disclosures 317
  share capital account 310–11

Quantum meruit 109, 465
Quasi-corporations 7–9
Quasi-partnerships 54–6, 75–6, 98
  corporate, exclusion from 594–5
  just and equitable winding-up 597–600
Quorum 390
  board of directors 457–8
  extraordinary general meeting 381
  prohibited director not part of 512–13
  single member meetings 390–1
Quotations 204

Ratification 502–3, 531–3
  acquiescence of members 415
  acts outside actual authority 636–7
  as fraud on the minority 571–2
  of misfeasance 707–8
  pre-incorporation contracts 642
  principle 558, 560–1, 562
  proper plaintiff principle and 571–2
Re-registration
  alteration of memorandum 83, 86
  change of liability 83
  from private to public
    limited by guarantee 53
    limited by shares 53
  from public to private 52–3
  from unlimited to limited 54
Ready-made company 39–40
Realisation of security 322–3
Realist theory 162–3
Receivership *see* Administrative receiver:
    Official receiver
Recognised clearing houses 208
Recognised investment exchanges 208
Reconstructions *see* Voluntary arrangements
Redeemable shares 297–301
  disclosure requirement 301
  issued before 15 June 1982 299
  payment out of capital 298–301
  restrictions on issue 298
Redemption, equity of 322
Redemption premium 298, 354
Reduction of capital
  creditors' interests 294–5
  power to reduce 292–3
  preference shareholder and 294
  procedure 296–7
  role of court 293–4
  serious loss of capital 297
  treatment of different classes 293, 295–6
Register of charges 341–53
  certificate of registration 345
  companies charges register 342
  errors and omissions 346
  failure to register 342–3
  inspection 346
  memorandum of satisfaction 345
  negative pledge 344
  not required 347–52
  procedure for registration 343–4
  property registers 353
  rectification 346
  Scotland and Northern Ireland 344
  terms of charge 344–5
  time limits 343
    extension 346
  to be kept by company 353
    inspection 124
  see also Charges
Register of company secretaries 538

Register of company secretaries – *continued*
  inspection 124
Register of debenture holders 123–4
Register of directors 455
  inspection 124
  notification 456
Register of directors' interests 284, 369–71
  inspection 124
  interests to be notified 370–1
  investigations 371
  obligation to report 369, 513–15
Register of members
  effect of 374–5
  inspection 124, 374
  rectification 374–5
  requirement 373–4
Register of substantial shareholdings 249–54
  company's notice requiring information
    251–2
  details to be notified 250–1
  freezing orders 252–4
  members' requisition of investigation 252
  need to identify interests 248–9
  obligation to notify 249–50
  register 251
Registered company, popularity of form
    11–12
Registered land 323–4
Registered number 38
Registered office 36, 38
  disclosure 131
  in memorandum 68
Registrar of Companies
  annual account filing 274
  articles, notification of alteration 111
  certificate of incorporation
    altered 80–1, 86
    evidence of compliance with CA 1985
      38, 39, 52, 53, 133
    notification in *Gazette* 52, 53, 86–7, 121
  certificate to commence business 50, 53,
    195–6
  charges 323–6, 353
  class rights variation 420
  decision subject to judicial review 38–9
  inspection 121
  memorandum to be registered 37–9, 59
    changes 86
  names 61–8
  power to refuse registration 38–9
  registry information 119–21
  return of allotment 184
  trust deed registration with 355
  see also Registration
Registration
  classification of companies 41–56
  Companies Act 1985 36–9
  companies formed 'for lawful purpose' 38
  documentation required 36–7

Registration – *continued*
  existing companies 57–8
  former Companies Acts 40–1
  incorporation by 4–5
  off-the-shelf companies 39–40
  procedure 36–9
  refusal to register 38–9
  statutory declaration 38
  trade union not registrable 38
  see also Registrar of Companies
Regulated market 360, 361, 365
Religious belief 659–60
Remuneration, directors 462–9, 537
  committee 461–2
  compensation for loss of office 465–6
  disclosure 466–8
  employment status 464–5
  expenses 463
  net of tax agreement prohibition 465
  no entitlement 462
  other services 463–4
  provision in articles for fees 462–3
Renunciation of allotment 180–1, 235
Repudiation of transactions 70
Rescission
  for misrepresentation 197
    limitations 198–9
    loss of remedy 199–200
  promoters 550, 553
Research and development activities 285
Reserves
  for own shares 190, 317
  liability 188
  revaluation 305, 306
  undistributable 306
  see also Capital redemption reserves
Resolutions
  acquiescence 415
  elective 394–5
  extraordinary 392–4
  ordinary 392
  requisitioned 389
  special 375, 392–4
  unanimous assent 409–15
  written, of private companies 415–16
Retention of title agreements 350–2
Revaluation 186–7
Revaluation reserve 187, 305, 306
Revenue recognition 304
Rights issue 210
Romalpa clause 352
  see also Retention of title agreements
Royal Charter, incorporation by 4

Scheme of arrangements *see* Voluntary
    arrangements
Scotland 27–8, 36, 38
Sealing 126, 615–16
  contracts of security 321, 328

Sealing – *continued*
  security contracts given under seal 321
  share certificates 230, 231, 232
Secondary insider 361
Secretary *see* Company secretary: Secretary of
    State
Secretary of State
  actions for maladministration
    consequences 608–12
    inspection of documents 601–2
    unfairly prejudicial conduct 587
  investigations 601–12
    consequences 608–12
    evidence collection 605–7
    expenses recovery 612
    insider dealing 605
    inspection of documents 601–2
    inspectors 602–8
    interruption 607
    into company's affairs 603
    ownership or control 603–4
    regulatory authorities 609
      overseas 607–8
    related companies 605
    share dealings 604
Securities and Futures Authority 207, 208
Securities and Investments Board 207
Security for financial obligations 320–3
  collateral 321, 520, 521
  consensual 321
  discharged 322
  given under seal 321, 328
  realisation 322–3
  redemption 322
  surety 321
  see also Borrowing, security for: Debt
      securities: Guarantees for borrowing
Selective marketing 210, 211
Self-creating theory 164
Self-dealing rule 532–3
Separate legal personality 3, 133–61
  advantages 139
  agency and 144–6
  cases 159–61
  challenging arrangements of affairs 158–9
  characterisation of status or acts 151–2
  control of company property 150–1
  criticism of 161–6
    aggregate theory 162
    autopoietic (self-creating) theory 164
    fiction theory 164–5, 168
    Gierke's theory 163
    individualistic view 161–2
    organic doctrine 163
    realist theory 162–3
    symbolist or bracket theory 162
  deaths of all members 137–8
  enterprise entity 157–8
  exercise of judicial discretion 152–4

Separate legal personality – *continued*
  groups of companies 154–7
  ignoring corporate personality 138–61
  lifting veil 138–61
  Mareva injunctions 149–50
  'puppets' 142
  recognition of 133–8
  sham or pretence 147–50
  statutory provisions 143–4
  taxation 146–7
  see also Corporate *and* Legal personality:
      Identification theory
Serious Fraud Office, private examination
    records 696
Service contract, directors' 125, 469
Settlement systems, Crest 230, 236, 238
Severance payments 73–4
Shadow director 429–30, 493, 515, 520, 523,
    709
  in annual returns 131
Sham or pretence 147–50
Share capital 42, 43–4
  in annual return 131
  authorised 43, 44, 49–50, 171
    alteration 177–8
    increase 178
  authorised minimum 49–50, 195–6
    reduction below 297
  call on partly paid shares 188–9
  called-up 171, 185
  capitalisation 301–2
  distributions *see Distributions*
  erroneous accounts, takeovers and 254–7
  form of contribution 191–4
  maximum see authorised
  measurement of 171
  in memorandum 79
    changes 83
  minimum *see* authorised minimum
  paid up 171
    disclosure 131
    as stock 178–9
  partly paid 171, 188–91
  payment in instalments 191
  payment out of 298
    approval 299–300
    permissible capital payment 299
    purchase of own shares and 310–11
  reduction
    creditors' interests 294–5
    power to reduce 292–3
    preference shareholder and 294
    procedure 296–7
    role of court 293–4
    serious loss of capital 297
    treatment of different classes 293,
        295–6
  serious loss 297
  see also Capital

Share certificates
  balance ticket   233
  dating   230
  description   229–30
  errors on   230–1
  estoppel   230–2
  forged   231–2
  issue   184
  numbering   230
  replacement and duplicate   232
  sealing   230, 231, 232
  signature on   231
Share premium   43, 170, 191
  account   185, 292, 298, 301
    undistributed reserves   306
  debentures and   191
Share transfer   176, 229–57
  balance ticket   233
  directors' approval required   234–6
    refused   234–5, 236
  evidence of title
    bearer form   239
    computers   230
    nominative form   239
    warrants   239
  forged transfers   237–8
  forms   232
  fraudulent transfer   237–8
  freezing orders   241
  instruments of   232–3
  partly paid shares   233
  pre-emption rights   183–4, 235–6
  procedures   232–7
  reforms   254
  renunciation of allotment   235
  restriction on   600
  right to transfer   236
  stamp duty   232, 234
  stamp duty reserve tax   237
  Stock Exchange
    not on   233
    on   236–7
  stop notices and orders   240–1
  title evidence   230–1
  transmission of shares   238–9
  unfairly prejudicial conduct   586–8
Shareholders   2, 3
  access to accounting records   261
  acquiescence *see* Ratification
  agents of, directors are not   480–1
  in annual returns   131, 132
  buying-out requirement   246
  class rights   83, 417–20
  'concert parties'   248, 250
  definition   372–3
  dismissal of directors by   470
  dissentient minority
    cancellation of resolution   375
    compulsory share purchase   243–7, 312

Shareholders – *continued*
    objections to articles change   110
    objections to memorandum change   83–4,
      85
      questioning decisions   403–5
      status change of company   52
      voting and   401
  forgiveness of negligence by directors   486
  general supervisory power   471–4
  honorary members   172
  inter socios agreements   104–7
  investigations   252
  meetings *see* Meetings
  methods of becoming   176
  minimum numbers   50
  names and addresses   124
  nationality   179
  nominee   239
  personal action   576–8, 580–3
  powers   476–8
    large-scale transaction approval   478
    reversion of powers to   478–9
  pre-emption rights   183–4, 235–6
  primacy   14–15
  priority of claims   293, 295–6
  ratification *see* Ratification
  reduction in members   48–9
  register *see* Register of members
  rights   172–3
    dividends   172, 173
    specification of   173–4
  voting *see* Voting *and* Voting rights
Shareholdings register *see* Register of
    substantial shareholdings
Shares
  acceptance   180
  allotment *see* Allotment of shares
  bonus   301–2, 312
  call option   310
  cancellation   177, 178
  classes   172–3
    see also Class rights
  compulsory purchase   243–7, 312
  dealings, investigation of   604
  deferred   175
  dematerialisation   230
  devolution   176
  equity   175
  erroneous accounts and purchase of   254–7
  forfeiture   189–90
  freezing orders   241, 252–4, 397
  future undertakings in return for   194, 196
  in holding company   314
  inspection of interests   124
  'interested in'   251
  issue *see* Allotment of shares
  listing *see* Official listing
  loss of value actions   572–3
  nature of   170–80

Shares – *continued*
  no par value 179–80
  nominal value 43, 44, 50, 170, 171
  non-cash assets, in return for 193–4, 196
  non-voting 175
  offers to public *see* Offering shares to the
    public
  ownership, *see also* title evidence
  partly paid up 171, 188–91
    calls on 188–9
    transfer of 233
  past services paid for in 194, 196
  pre-emption rights 183–4, 235–6
  preference 174, 181
    redeemable 298–301
    reduction of capital and 294
  promises of services in return for 194, 196
  purchase of own *see* Purchase of own shares
  redeemable 297–301
    disclosure requirement 301
    issued before 15 June 1982 299
    payment out of capital 298–301
    restrictions on issue 298
  redemption 121, 125, 126
  rights issue 210
  stop notices 240–1
  stop orders 241
  subscribers 202
  subscription *see* Subscription for shares
  substantial interest register *see* Register of
    substantial shareholdings
  surrender 189, 190
  things in action 175–6
  third party interests 239–41
  title evidence 230–1
    bearer form 239
    computers 230
    nominative form 239
    warrants 239
  transfer *see* Share transfer
  transmission 176, 238–9
  unissued, cancellation of 177, 178
  vendor consideration issue 192
  vesting 176
  warrants 239
Show of hands 173, 395, 398
Signature 614–15
Single-member companies 12, 47, 390–1
  decision-making 416–17
  see also Corporation sole
Small companies 12
  abbreviated accounts 270–1, 275–7, 468
  accounts exemption 263, 468
  auditor exemption 540, 545
  auditor's report 277
  corporate quasi-partnership, exclusion from
    594–5
Societas europa (SE) 27
Sole proprietorship 10, 50

Solvency declaration 685
Sources
  case law 22–6
  Community law 26–31
  legislation 17–22
  practitioners' books 31
Stamp duty
  bearer debentures exempt 355
  share transfers 232, 234
  share warrants 239
  transfer of debentures and convertibles 356
Stamp duty reserve tax 237
Statement of affairs
  administration 681
  administrative receiver 668
  liquidation 699–700
  official receiver 699–700
Statutory demand, compulsory liquidation
    689–90
Stock
  certificates 355
  convertibles *see* Convertibles
  nominal value 354
  paid up share capital as 178–9
  redemption premium 354
  see also Debt securities
Stock Exchange 204–5
  articles of association 92
  Company Announcements Office 310
  Listed Market 204–5, 308
  model code 365–6
  organisation and history 204–5
  prospectus approval 217–18
  release of price sensitive information to
    364–5
  trading outside 233, 548
  transfers not on 233
  transfers on 236–7
Stockholders, equality of 355
Subordination of debt 714
Subscribers 37, 202
Subscription for shares
  defined 192–3
  invitation to subscribe *see* Prospectus
  memorandum signed by subscriber 60
  number of shares taken 60
Subsidiaries
  accounts 278–80
  actual dominant influence 279
  authorisation of assistance to be given by
    319
  directors 422
  EC competition law 158
  excluded from group accounts 281–2
  owning company 421
  participating interest 279
  piercing veil between 143, 154–7
  related undertakings information 282–3
  shareholders 421–2

Subsidiaries – *continued*
  voting rights 422
  see also Group accounts
Substantial property transactions 511, 514,
  517–19
Substantial shareholdings register *see* Register
  of substantial shareholdings
Summary financial statement 266–7
Surety 321
Surrender of shares 189, 190
Symbolist theory 162

Table A, articles of association 88–9, 90–1
Table B and F, memorandum form 60–1
Table G, articles of association 90
Takeovers 241–8
  associates of the offeror 247
  by share exchange 247–8
  choice of consideration 246–7
  City Code 242–3, 248
  compulsory acquisition of minority holdings
    243–7
  convertible securities 247
  directors' fiduciary duty and bids 500–1
  erroneous accounts, liability 254–7
  joint offers 247
  mandatory offer 243
  ninety per cent limit 244, 245, 246
  Panel on Takeovers and Mergers 242
  shareholder requirement to be bought out
    246
  'takeover offer' meaning 243–4
Target company 241
Taxation
  ownership of business and 146–7
  see also Stamp duty
Tippees 361
Trade unions
  quasi-corporations 7–8
  registration as company 38
Trading
  certificate to commence business 50, 53,
    195–6
  see also Fraudulent *and* Wrongful trading
Trading floors 204
Transactions, repudiation 70
Transmission of shares 176, 238–9
'True and fair view' 271–4
Trustee
  in bankruptcy 397
  bare or custodian 371
  equality of stockholders preserved 355
  marketable loans 354–5
  under seal 354
  voting rights 397
Trusts, constructive 509, 555–7
Turquand's case rule 614, 622–5

Ultra vires rule 69–70, 71, 74, 619–20

Ultra vires rule – *continued*
  illegal acts 78–9
  ratification of acts 636–7
  remedies 571, 577, 578–9, 581
  repudiation of transactions 70
  voting 403–5
  see also Objects
Uncertificated securities
  description 230
  estoppel 230–2
Underwriting
  commission 188
    company's power to pay 227
    limits 227
    methods of payment 227–8
  definition 227
  disclosure 228
  marketable loans 356
  underwritten firm 228
Undistributable reserves 306
Unfair prejudice 586–97
  court orders 595–7
  exclusion from corporate quasi-partnership
    594–5
  exit rights in articles 597
  'interests' meaning 588–9
  investigation 611
  meaning 589–91
  petition for relief 586–8
    conduct grounds 591–4
  reform 597
Unincorporated associations 7
United States of America
  incorporation 28–9
  insider dealing 359
  limited liability 48
Unlimited company, change of status 54
Unlisted Securities Market, insider dealing
  365
Unlisted securities, prospectus 551
  content 213–14, 217
  exemptions 215–17
  failure to obtain listing 219
  investment advertising 224–5
  minimum subscription for first offer 219
  misleading statements and omissions 220–4
  misrepresentation in
    expert's statement 222
    plaintiff's knowledge 223
    reasonable belief 221–2
    steps to correct defect 222
  need for 215–16
  omission of information from 214
  persons responsible for 220–1
  restriction on public offers by private
    companies 218
  Stock Exchange approval 217–18
  supplementary 214, 217
    failure to issue 223

Unlisted securities, prospectus – *continued*
time for consideration 218–19
when required 212–13
Unregistered land 323
Unsecured loan stock 181, 355
see also Convertibles

Valuation
assets 306
non-cash 193–4, 306
Veil of incorporation, lifting and piercing
138–61
agency and 144–6
cases 159–61
challenging arrangements of affairs 158–9
characterisation of company's status or acts
151–2
control of company property 150–1
enterprise entity 157–8
exercise of judicial discretion 152–4
sham or pretence 147–50
statutory provisions 143–4
subsidiary companies 143, 154–7
Vendor consideration issue 192
Vendor consideration placing 210, 211
Vesting of shares 176
Vicarious liability 650–1
Voluntary arrangements
approval of proposal 683–4
description 682
proposal 682–3
Voluntary winding up
creditors 684
liquidation committee 686–7
resolution 684–5, 686
declaration of solvency 685
dissolution after 719
members' 684
appointment of liquidator 685–6
resolution 684–5, 686
Voting
bona fide for benefit of company 402–3
casting vote 398, 459
conflict of interest and duty 400–2
director prohibition 512–13
dissentient minorities 401
fraud on minority 403–5
fraudulent 403–5
freezing orders 397

Voting – *continued*
illegal 403–5
Mareva injunction 406
oppressive 403–5
polls 173, 395, 398–400
proper purpose 402–3
rights *see* Voting rights
self-interested 400–2
show of hands 173, 395, 398, 399
ultra vires 403–5
see also Majority rule
Voting rights 173, 395–8
conflict of interest and duty 400–2
corporate shareholders 397
holding or subsidiary companies 422
non-members 397–8
personal representatives 397
proxies 395–7, 398
restrictions on, agreement 406–7
shareholders' 112–13, 392–4
trustees 397
weighted 451

Warrants, share 239
Widows, pensions for directors' widows 74
Wilful default rule 327
Winding-up
commencement 694
compulsory 122
disclosure of 130
floating charges 332–3
just and equitable 597–600
consequences of investigation 609–12
management participation loss 599–600
personal relationship failure 599
quasi-partnerships 597–600
just and equitable winding-up, consequences
of investigation 610–11
management participation loss 599–600
share transfer restriction 600
see also Administration: Administrative
receiver: Liquidation: Voluntary
arrangements
Wrongful trading 708–12

Yellow Book (Listing Rules) 205, 209, 228,
251, 310, 311, 364

Zero-coupon bonds 356